SPINOZA

COMPLETE WORKS

SPINOZA

COMPLETE WORKS

with

Translations by
Samuel Shirley

Edited, with
Introduction and Notes, by
Michael L. Morgan

Hackett Publishing Company, Inc.
Indianapolis / Cambridge

Baruch Spinoza: 1632–1677

Copyright © 2002 by Hackett Publishing Company, Inc.

All rights reserved
Printed in the United States of America

12 11 10 09 08   3 4 5 6 7

For further information, please address:

Hackett Publishing Company, Inc.
P.O. Box 44937
Indianapolis, IN 46244-0937

www.hackettpublishing.com

Text design by Abigail Coyle and Meera Dash

Library of Congress Cataloging-in-Publication Data

Spinoza, Benedictus de, 1632–1677.
    [Works. English. 2002]
    Complete works/Spinoza; translated by Samuel Shirley and others;
  edited, with introduction and notes, by Michael L. Morgan.
       p. cm.
    Includes bibliographical references and index.
    ISBN 0-87220-620-3 (cloth)
    1. Philosophy. I. Shirley, Samuel, 1912– II. Morgan, Michael L., 1944–
  III. Title.

B3958 .S5 2002
199'.492—dc21   2002068497

ISBN-13: 978-0-87220-620-5 (cloth)

The paper used in this publication meets the minimum requirements of
American National Standard for Information Sciences—Permanence of Paper
for Printed Library Materials, ANSI Z39.48-1984.

Contents

Translator's Preface vii
Introduction ix
Chronology xvii
Editorial Notes xxi

Treatise on the Emendation of the Intellect 1
Short Treatise on God, Man, and His Well-Being 31
Principles of Cartesian Philosophy *and* Metaphysical Thoughts 108
Ethics 213
Theological-Political Treatise 383
Hebrew Grammar 584
Political Treatise 676
The Letters 755

Index 961

Translator's Preface

In these translations, I have adhered to the Gebhardt Heidelberg text of 1926 except as noted. Leaving the task of annotation and exposition in the hands of more competent scholars, I shall confine myself in this Preface to a personal odyssey, a sort of voyage around Spinoza.

At Oxford I do not remember that I read anything by Spinoza and very little about him. But that little interested me strangely. So I attended the lectures given by H. H. Joachim, without much understanding. These lectures were delivered in the late afternoon, and as the sun streamed through New College windows onto the gray head of that venerable and beloved figure, it was for me an aesthetic experience rather than an intellectual enlightenment.

But the seed was sown. Many years later, being entrusted with the task of lecturing to university extension adult classes, I chose Spinoza's *Ethics*, using the edition translated by Boyle. That edition was prefaced by an inspiring introduction by Santayana. But there were a number of passages in the translation that puzzled me, and when I sought out the original Latin in a library, I found that they were mistranslations. Writing to the publisher, I pointed out four such passages and provided my own translations. In due course I received a courteous reply, confirming my criticisms and promising to incorporate my corrections in the next reprint. A check for £5 was enclosed (it should be remembered that £5 was worth far more in the 1950s than it is now). The next edition appeared with my corrections.

Now I had tasted—just a sip—of the heady wine of authorship. Ambition grew; could I not improve on the Boyle translation? My offer to do so was courteously refused by the publisher as commercially unviable.

In 1972, at the age of 60, I resigned my post as headmaster of a grammar school. Gifted with the abundant leisure of retirement, I turned my mind to a translation of Spinoza's *Ethics*. This I duly offered to some respected publishers in the United Kingdom. They declined, invariably with courteous regrets, but one of them, fortunately, advised me to try Hackett Publishing Company in the United States.

So began my long and happy connection with Hackett. My translation of the *Ethics* came out in 1982. Encouraged by a few laudatory reviews, I turned my attention to the *Theological-Political Treatise*, a work for which I have a fervent admiration. Thereafter, gently cajoled by Lee Rice, to whom I remain vastly indebted, I continued with the rest of Spinoza's works with the exception of the *Hebrew Grammar* and the *Short Treatise on God, Man, and His Well-Being*, which was originally written in Dutch. The results are here before you.

A word on Spinoza's Latinity. This was criticized by some earlier scholars, perhaps because of his modest admission in Letter 13, where he seeks the help of his more accomplished friends in polishing his hastily composed *Principles of Cartesian Philosophy*. Unsure of himself as he may have been, he nevertheless succeeded in forging for himself a powerful linguistic instrument, wonderfully lucid, devoid of all rhetoric, and with a peculiar charm of its own. It was an appropriate medium of expression for one who, in much of the *Ethics*, was nearing the limits of what it is that can be put into words.

I could not have persisted with the task of translation without a steady conviction of its worthwhileness. To my mind, although Spinoza lived and thought long before Darwin, Freud, Einstein, and the startling implications of quantum theory, he had a vision of truth beyond what is normally granted to human beings. He was relentless in pursuit of a goal that was basically ethical and religious, ridding himself of the anthropocentric bias that is inevitably innate in human beings and manifested in their religious beliefs. His conclusions did not dismay him, as they did so many of his contemporaries when they realized the full implications. Even Henry Oldenburg, his correspondent for many years, in his later letters was appalled when he came to see the full implications of Spinoza's radical thinking. But Spinoza boldly looked reality in the face and, far from being discouraged at what he saw, drew from it a spiritual sustenance, an elevation of mind that supported him all his life. It is this aspect of Spinozism that is captured in the title of Errol Harris' book *Salvation from Despair*. Such, then, are the considerations, purely personal, that have induced me to undertake this lengthy task.

Finally, while I have never contributed to the rich field of Spinozan exegesis, I venture to share with readers an idea that continues to occur to me, one that may be capable of elaboration by other scholars. Genuine artistic creativity seems to us a mysterious business. Many writers, poets, painters, and composers have tried to indicate, with varying success, what happens in this process. They say that they do not know what they are doing or are about to do. They are, as it were, possessed. My own favorite illustration is Book IV of the *Aeneid*, where Vergil becomes so absorbed in the creation of his Dido character that the stammering Aeneas cuts a very unheroic figure; yet he should be the flawless hero, the prototype of his alleged descendant Augustus. Can the essence of God be seen as the source of the ill-understood phenomenon that we call artistic creativity? In the "conatus" of human beings, a *conatus* that derives from God's *potentia*, do we see a shadow, an image, of God's creativity, finding expression most markedly in the process of artistic creativity?

I conclude with a tribute to my wife, who heroically endured for many years my preoccupation with Spinoza.

Samuel Shirley

Introduction

Reading the works of Spinoza, one can be overwhelmed by a sense of abstract rigor and detachment. They may seem to some readers the product of an almost mechanical mental life. This appearance notwithstanding, I am inclined to ascribe to Spinoza a romantic set of virtues. He is among thinkers extraordinarily creative and novel; his thinking is marked by a marvelous intensity and focus; and yet his deepest commitments are to the most embracing unity and sense of comprehensiveness that one can find in the tradition of Western philosophy. In short, Spinoza's writings and his thought are marked by a kind of heroism that is rare and beautiful—even breathtaking.

We are tempted to think that the notion of perspective or points of view, so crucial to the world of art, was not of importance to philosophy until Kant and German Idealism made it so. Kant, it is said, taught us what metaphysics could and could not accomplish by confining its investigations to the viewpoint of human experience and then went on to distinguish between the detached point of view of the scientific enquirer and the engaged point of view of the moral agent. From those beginnings, German Idealism and its twentieth-century legacy made the notion of perspective or point of view central to philosophical accounts of human existence and human experience, from Fichte, Schelling, and Kant to Schopenhauer and Nietzsche, to Husserl, Heidegger, and beyond. And with this legacy came a series of struggles, between the natural and the human sciences, between existentialism and scientific philosophy, between relativism and objectivism, and more.

But perspective was at the center of Spinoza's system. His thinking shows a passion for unity and totality, coupled with a scrupulous fidelity to the integrity of the individual particular. There is no parochialism in Spinoza. His commitment to the progress of scientific enquiry into the natural world belied any such limitation in behalf of his cognitive goals. In every way, in every dimension of our lives, Spinoza saw the common; he saw unity and wholeness. At the same time his allegiance to the universality of the ethical life and its virtues did not annul the personal perspective of human experience. For him life was always a struggle against our finite limitations of perspective and particularity. Life was not life without such limitations, but neither could life be what it could be if we were satisfied with them. The world was of necessity filled with particular objects, but they existed within a single order. We are among those objects, and our goal is to do what we can, in knowledge and conduct, to live with our particularity and yet transcend it. Spinoza was fully aware of the necessity and the complexity of human perspective; he knew what it meant to the hopes for scientific knowledge, for the burdens of religious, moral, and political conflict, and for the possibility of a truly blessed life. In a certain sense, perspective is the fulcrum on which all Spinoza's thinking turns.

Spinoza lived in a world distant from our own. No amount of historical detail and reconstruction can adequately place us in the complex world of Western Europe in the seventeenth century. So much was new and yet so much was old. Spinoza was immersed in all of it, in a world that was, by virtue of its economic and geographical situation, at a crossroads. Spinoza knew about religious orthodoxies and about religious reform; he knew about traditional culture and novelties; he knew about old texts and new thinking, about the tensions between conservative political practice and liberal hopes and aspirations; and he knew about the risks—persecution and possibly death. To him, reason in us was akin to reason in nature; one order permeated everything and enabled us, as rational beings, to understand ourselves and the whole and to live peacefully and calmly within it. This was the key to science, to ethics, and to religion. It was the key to all of life. It was his goal to show, clarify, explain, and teach it—to the benefit of all humankind.

If the key that unlocked the secrets of possibility for us as human beings was unity and totality, the wholeness and order of all things, then the reality that grounded the aspiration to this unity and order was the fact that each of us, as natural objects and as human beings, was precisely located in that unity and order; each of our places was determined in every way, and we were thereby endowed with a very particular point of view on the whole. In a letter to Henry Oldenburg of November 1665 (Ep32), as he attempts to clarify the nature of parts and wholes, Spinoza provides us with a famous image. Each of us is, he tells us, like a little worm in the blood. Nature is like the entire circulatory system or like the entire organism; each of us lives within that system or organism, interacting with only a small part of it and experiencing only a very limited region. Even if we grasp the fact that there is a total system and understand its principles to some degree, our experience is so circumscribed and narrow that we are bound to make mistakes about our understanding of the system and our place in it. Myopia confines our understanding, no matter how we seek to overcome it. And we do. We aspire to experience every detail, every event, and every item as part of the whole, to see it from the perspective of the whole rather than from our own narrow point of view. Our success is limited; we can free ourselves from prejudices and blindness but only to a degree. We can see ourselves and act in terms of the whole, but only within limits. Our goal is to free ourselves from the distortions and corruptions of our finitude, to become free, active, and rational. These are all the same, and are aspects of becoming like the whole, which is what the tradition dignifies with the title "God" or "divine" or "the Highest Good."

I do not believe that Spinoza saw this challenge and this sort of life as an escape from the world. History was riddled with strife and conflict, with prejudice and persecution. Life could be better; it could be harmonious with nature rather than a struggle with it. Religious and political institutions could be renovated to serve human purposes, and human life could be refashioned as well. The ancient Stoics had understood that life in harmony with nature was the best human life, and that in order to achieve such harmony, one had to understand nature. Natural philosophy or science was both the highest achievement of human rationality and the key to living the best human life. Spinoza, I believe, fully sympathized with the broad strokes of this program. Like the Stoics, he revered reason and our rational capacities. Like them, he saw our reason and the reason in nature as intimately linked. Like them, he saw natural philosophy as the key to opening the door of the highest good and the way through that door as leading to tranquility of spirit, harmony with nature, and peace. To be sure, Spinoza was a modern. Natural philosophy meant the developments and achievements of the new science, conducted in the spirit of Descartes and others, grounded in mathematics and a priori reasoning about natural events and causal relations. But if the science was modern and mathematical and the metaphysics constructed as a foundation for that science, the overall role for it and its goals were very similar to those of the ancient Stoics: union with the whole of nature through knowledge of the natural order.

Moreover, Spinoza would call the goal of this project—the human project—"blessedness." He did not shy away from religious terminology, the vocabulary of the Judaism and the Christianity with which he was so familiar. Indeed, it is a remarkable feature of his temperament that his thinking never totally rejected religious themes, beliefs, and vocabulary as much as it sought to refine and refashion them. One might say this about virtually all of the great seventeenth-century philosophers, that they did not decisively reject the religious world out of which they emerged and in which they lived. They sought to retool that world, to come to a new understanding of religious life and to revise religious concepts and terminology. Even those, like Hobbes and Spinoza, who were censored and vilified as atheists, did not reject religion. More correctly, we, from our perspective, can appreciate their philosophical goals as epistemological, ethical, and religious all at once. Spinoza, in these terms, was a religious visionary, a moral innovator, and a philosopher–scientist, not one but all. His passion for unity and wholeness made any fragmentation of this conglomerate undesirable, but the reality was that in his day, given the way that these and other domains of life were lived and experienced, any such fragmentation was quite impossible.

Hence, Spinoza's scientific philosophy and ethics aimed at tranquility in a conflicted and turbulent world; they did not seek escape from that world but rather a renovation of it. His was a worldview for life, not for escape from life. It recommended changes in one's behavior and one's beliefs, practices, and institutions. What it did not recommend was escape from life. It was, as he put it in the *Ethics*, a meditation on life and not on death.

One could seek the perspective of eternity in order to redeem the unavoidable perspective of finitude, but, as living and natural beings, we could not escape the latter and, as human beings, we should not avoid the former. This is the gist of Spinoza's philosophy, his ethics, and his religion. The key to grasping this picture of our hopes and our realities is reason, that ability within us that enables us to understand and make sense of our world and ourselves.

*

Spinoza presents us with the totality of his system in one work: the *Ethics*. He also left us with a preliminary version of that work, as well as two treatises that constitute introductions to his philosophy, and writings that are examples of applications of that work—to politics and religion. Because these do not completely agree with each other, all of this makes it hard to grasp his philosophical system.

To me Spinoza is remarkable for his creativity. He was an heir of a philosophical terminology that came down to the seventeenth century from antiquity, the recovery of ancient philosophies and texts, and its presence in the medieval philosophical tradition. He did not invent terms like "substance," "attribute," "mode," "affect," "essence," "necessity," and "eternity." He was taught the terms, how they were used, what they meant, and more. And he was taught how they figured in the thinking of Descartes, who was, for Spinoza, the bridge between the philosophical tradition and the new philosophy and new science. What Spinoza did was to take the tradition, Descartes' accomplishment, and his own passionate commitments and blend them into a new whole, a new worldview. At one level, it is an extension and modification of Cartesian metaphysics; at another, it has its own character and demands a view of the natural order very different from that of Descartes.

Spinoza has a relentless mind. His commitment to reason involves a commitment to consistency and rigor. This is not to say that he does not allow his reason to leap to conclusions that seem strange and even recalcitrant to us, and it is not to say that he never makes mistakes. What I mean is that he can be understood as starting with certain concepts whose meanings are clear and correct to him and pushing the consequences of accepting those concepts. He can also be understood as observing what Descartes had achieved and yet as believing that Descartes had failed to follow reason to its relentless conclusions because of prejudices, biases to which Descartes had clung and which Spinoza saw as distortions. In the case of the concept of substance, for example, Spinoza thought that he and Descartes largely agreed about what substance means, but he thought too that if so, there was no justification for treating minds and bodies as substances. Moreover, if the principle of sufficient reason was foundational for scientific enquiry and if the natural world and even eternal truths were created by God, then a deep contingency would lie at the heart of nature and human knowledge. And even if one were to treat the physical world as a collection of bodies that causally interact and are capable of being understood by scientific enquiry, why exclude the mind and mental occurrences from similar understanding? Is it not only a prejudice grounded in traditional theological commitments to isolate the mind or the soul, allow it special privileges, and grant it special features? Is it not more consistent with our understanding of nature, science, and the human good to treat the mind and mental phenomena just as one would treat physical ones and yet to do so in a nonreductivist way—that is, without simply treating mental events as identical in some sense with physiological ones?

While it may be a bit of a caricature, it is helpful to see Spinoza as seeking a middle ground regarding the treatment of mind, soul, and mental phenomena in a world where the physical sciences are beginning to take shape in new and exciting ways. On the one hand, the Cartesian strategy could be seen as having isolated the mind in order to save the integrity of certain theological commitments, such as the belief in free will and in the immortality of the soul. Science could not study the mind and mental phenomena in the same way it could study the physical world, using mathematical reasoning and applying it to causality, motion, and so forth. The strategy of materialists like Hobbes, on the other hand, could be seen as reducing mental phenomena to physical ones—that is, basically to motions of various kinds—and defining mental processes and experiences in terms of motions of physical bodies. What Spinoza achieves, its problems notwithstanding, is a middle road. He constructs a view of nature as a whole in which physical events and mental events are both understandable, in which they are related but separate, and in which the sciences of the physical world and of the mental world are related but distinct. It may be that Kant, Dilthey, and Neo-Kantian developments and later debates about the distinction between the natural sciences and the human sciences look like they are built on Cartesian foundations; there is also a sense in which they build on Spinozist ones as well. To the degree that the social sciences and psychology are conceived as requiring a scientific treatment of mental phenomena, they are Spinoza's heirs, whether or not that scientific treatment is conceived of as similar to or different from the methodology of the natural sciences. Indeed, there are post-Kantian attempts by Wilfrid Sellars, John McDowell, and others to distinguish the domain of the mental and the "space of reasons" from the physical or the "space of causes." These can even be treated as a development of Spinoza and his commitment to demystifying the mind and the body and to making both accessible to rational understanding and thereby, in a sense, to human control.

There are two keys to this Spinozist achievement. The first is to conceive of the totality of the natural world as both the sum of all facts—that is, all things in all of their determinations—and the ordering force that determines all those facts to be just the ways they are. To conceive of nature as God and as substance gives the natural world the unity and orderliness that Spinoza believes science aspires to understand and makes it the case that everything we do and are finds its rational place within the totality of nature. The second key to Spinoza's system concerns the "channels" whereby the single ordering force or principle ("God") is the single active causal determining force of all there is, and actually determines things and their states in the world. At the highest level, where these "channels" are virtually identical to God or the one and only substance but are nonetheless wholly distinct from each other, Spinoza calls these "attributes" of substance, and while he thinks that in principle the one and only one substance has all the attributes that there are, there are but two that determine the world in which we live: thought and extension. In short, all the modes—things and their states—that make up the natural world are modes of thought and extension, and while scholars have debated exactly how the distinction between these attributes should be understood, I believe that what Spinoza means is that we understand the single array of facts in the world by using both the physical sciences and the psychological sciences. In the famous Proposition 7 of Part II of the *Ethics* and in the scholium to that proposition, Spinoza indicates just this: that the order and connection of ideas or mental phenomena is one and the same as the order and connection of physical ones. This is a proposition with countless important implications throughout the remainder of the *Ethics* and Spinoza's system.

As far as our attempts to understand the world go, then, for Spinoza these attempts are self-contained and comprehensive. All worldly facts should be examined and studied in the same way; there is a uniformity to all of nature. Mental modes interact causally with mental modes, and physical modes interact causally with physical modes. But since, strictly speaking, there is just one set of facts in nature, what this means is that these two types of scientific understanding are self-contained. We do not use physical causes to help us understand mental phenomena, nor do we use mental causes to help us understand physical phenomena. Moreover, in a sense the sciences of both physical and mental phenomena apply to all things in the world, and this means that Spinoza must show in what sense even inanimate things have mental or ideational correlates and what distinguishes animals and most preeminently human beings among worldly things—that is, what we mean when we say they have minds or souls.

I do not mean to suggest that on all these matters Spinoza was clear and lucid throughout his career and never changed his mind. A careful study of the early *Treatise on the Emendation of the Intellect* and *Short Treatise on God, Man, and His Well-Being*, for example, shows how his thinking developed into the shape we find in the *Ethics*, and we are helped to some degree in understanding how Spinoza's ideas developed by some of the letters in his correspondence. But the basic character of his thinking, I believe, did not change from the time around his excommunication in 1656 until his death in 1677. Throughout his life Spinoza was always committed to finding a way to unite science, ethics, and religion and to articulating a metaphysical system that would make the whole of nature, human life, and religious themes comprehensible. His system was an attempt to work out what made nature unified and an ordered whole and then to see what that picture implied.

*

Between the covers of this collection you will find the totality of Spinoza's writings, all that we now have come to think that he left us. If this is a big book, it is also a small one, particularly when compared to the total written corpus of other philosophers, such as Aristotle, Aquinas, Locke, Kant, Hegel, and Nietzsche. Given Spinoza's impact on subsequent Western philosophy and Western intellectual culture in general, so brilliantly surveyed for example in the recent work of Jonathan Israel (*Radical Enlightenment* [Oxford: Oxford University Press, 2001]), his written legacy is surprisingly spare. Nonetheless, its richness is evident everywhere.

Furthermore, the corpus of Spinoza's works contains a fascinating diversity. There is at its center, of course, the presentation of his system, the *Ethics*. Begun in the early 1660s, this work was probably completed about 1674. It is his lifework, the centerpiece of what came to be known as Spinozism, and one of the great accomplishments of world philosophy and Western intellectual culture.

In addition to the *Ethics* and his philosophical system, Spinoza left us what we might call four different introductions to that work and that system. The first is his handbook on Cartesian philosophy, first composed as a guide to tutoring a student in Descartes' *Principles of Philosophy* and useful for what it shows us about Spinoza's early appreciation of Descartes. The second is his youthful, unfinished work, the *Treatise on the Emendation of the Intellect*. Largely a work on method and definition, this short essay places Spinoza's project within an ethical context. The third introduction is the unfinished *Short Treatise on God, Man, and His Well-Being*, which is a preliminary attempt to begin the system and which Spinoza set aside when he decided to turn to the early parts of the *Ethics*. And finally we can treat the anonymous treatise on biblical interpretation and politics, the *Theological-Political Treatise*, as an introductory work, insofar as it seeks to persuade those with an affinity for philosophy and science how to read Scripture and understand its central ethical teaching; revise traditional interpretations of notions such as prophecy, law, and miracles; and appreciate the relation between church and state. What we have, then, is a mansion with four entrances, any one of which enables us to enter the vast complex of Spinoza's world.

Furthermore, Spinoza has given us, in the *Theological-Political Treatise* and in the unfinished *Political Treatise*, two examples of how his system might be applied more fully to areas dealt with in only a cursory way in the *Ethics*, religion and politics. To be sure, in both cases, there are already indications in the *Ethics* of how Spinoza thinks we should understand religious concepts and institutions and also political life. Especially in various scholia and in the appendix to Part I, he notes how traditional ideas such as creation, miracles, teleology, and free will must be either revised or jettisoned altogether. In Part IV of the *Ethics*, Spinoza sets out the rudiments of his contract theory and of his views on the foundations and purposes of the state. Finally, in Part V, in the famous final propositions of the work, Spinoza defends and reinterprets what he takes to be the eternity of the mind and the goal of the ethical life, an "intellectual love of God" that is blessedness itself, a goal, he says, that is as difficult as it is rare. These indications notwithstanding, the treatises on politics and religion add significantly to our understanding of how Spinoza's naturalism applies to these domains of human experience.

In Chapter 7 of the *Theological-Political Treatise* Spinoza describes his "historical" method for interpreting Scripture. The first requirement for any responsible reader is a study of the Hebrew language. Among Spinoza's writings we have an unfinished treatise on *Hebrew Grammar*, a work that he probably began to write shortly after finishing the *Theological-Political Treatise* at the request of friends. The *Hebrew Grammar* gives us a valuable insight into what he thought that study of Hebrew should involve, Spinoza's understanding of Latin grammar and biblical Hebrew, and his general approach to intellectual activity—in this case a philological and linguistic inquiry.

Lastly, among the writings of Spinoza we are grateful to possess are a sampling of his correspondence—letters to him and many by him. Here we are helped to understand better his philosophical and religious views, but we are also given valuable information about the chronology of his works, about his friends and associates, and about his life. Without these letters, we would know less about Spinoza the person than we currently do and less too about his thinking.

*

I would like to thank Deborah Wilkes, Jay Hullett, and Frances Hackett for the invitation to edit the first English collection of Spinoza's works, for their friendship over many years, and for the wonderful contribution to the study of philosophy that Hackett Publishing Company has made. Needless to say, we are all in the debt of Samuel Shirley, whose commitment to Spinoza and his writings has provided us with splendid translations and made this volume possible. At Hackett, Meera Dash orchestrated the production of the collection with patience and skill. I would also like to thank Abigail Coyle for helping with the design of the volume. Rondo Keele, Inge Van Der Cruysse, Bieneke Heitjama, and Michal Levy assisted with matters Latin, Dutch, and Hebrew. Lee Rice generously provided an extensive chronology, which we modified for this volume. Joshua Shaw assisted with the proofs; he and Lilian Yahng compiled the bulk of the Index.

There is something inspiring and noble about Spinoza's philosophical thinking and his moral vision. An important feature of his *Ethics* is its emphasis on rationality and self-control; we all face the challenges of coping with the worries and the fears that fill our lives, and yet we go on. We can learn this lesson from Spinoza's works; we can also learn it from life. As this project comes to completion, I am thankful for those special people who have helped me to learn it—my wife, Audrey, and my daughters, Debbie and Sara.

Michael L. Morgan

Chronology

1536	Calvin publishes the *Institution of the Christian Religion*.
1565	Beginning of the war of independence of the Spanish-Dutch region against Spain.
1579	The "Union of Utrecht" establishes the United Provinces.
1594	Publication of Socinus' *De Christo Servatore*.
1600?	The Espinosa family emigrates from Portugal to Nantes and thence to Amsterdam.
1603	Arminius and Gomar debate at Leiden on the questions of tolerance and freedom of the will.
1610	Uytenbogaert, a disciple of Arminius and teacher of Oldenbarneveldt, publishes the *Remonstrant Manifesto*.
1618	The Thirty Years War begins.
1619	The Synod of Dordrecht condemns Arminianism and puts Oldenbarnevelt to death. The Collegiant sect is formed. Descartes is a soldier in the army of Maurice of Nassau.
1628	Descartes is living in Holland.
1629	**18 October:** Lodewijk Meyer is baptized at the Old Church in Amsterdam.
1630	**4 November:** Johan Bouwmeester is born in Amsterdam.
1632	**24 November:** Birth of Baruch d'Espinosa at Amsterdam.
1633	Papal condemnation of Galileo, who is placed under house arrest. Descartes decides not to publish *Le Monde*.
1638	The founding of the great Portuguese Synagogue of Amsterdam. Spinoza is registered as a student in the Hebrew school.
1640	Beginning of the English civil war.
1641	Descartes' *Meditationes de Prima Philosophia* is published.
1642	Hobbes publishes *De Cive*.

1644	Descartes published *Principia Philosophiae*.
1647	Descartes' *Méditations Metaphysiques* is published in French translation.
1648	The Peace of Munster. Definitive establishment of the United Provinces.
1649	Charles I of England is executed.
1650	**11 February:** Death of Descartes. **6 November:** A failed coup d'état by William II of Orange. Jan de Witt becomes the Grand Pensioner of the Netherlands.
1651	Beginning of the Anglo-Dutch War. Hobbes publishes *Leviathan*. **30 March:** Bouwmeester is enrolled in philosophy courses at the University of Leiden.
1653	A decree by the States General prohibits the publication and diffusion of Socinian works and ideas.
1654	End of the Anglo-Dutch War. Spinoza begins to meet with a group of "churchless Christians" (Pieter Balling, Jarig Jelles, Jan Rieuwertsz, Franciscus Van den Enden) in Amsterdam. **19 September:** Meyer is enrolled as a student in philosophy at the University of Leiden.
1656	**27 July:** Spinoza is banished from the Jewish community in Amsterdam. He begins the study of humanities, Latin, philosophy, and theater at the school of the ex-Jesuit Van den Enden. **6 October:** Decree of the States of Holland and of Frisia prohibiting the teaching of Cartesianism.
1657	The play *Philedonius* of Van den Enden is produced in Amsterdam. Spinoza is still studying with Van den Enden and may also be enrolled at the University of Leiden.
1658	**27 May:** Bouwmeester receives a doctorate in medicine from the University of Leiden. **25 September:** Meyer is enrolled in courses in medicine at Leiden. Spinoza begins work on the *Treatise on the Emendation of the Intellect* (unfinished).
1659	Adriaan Koerbagh receives a doctorate in medicine from the University of Leiden.
1660	Restoration of the Stuarts in England. Spinoza leaves Amsterdam and moves to Rijnsburg, where he is a familiar visitor among Collegiant circles. He begins work on the *Short Treatise on God, Man, and His Well-Being*. **19 March:** Meyer receives a doctorate in philosophy from the University of Leiden. **20 March:** Meyer receives a doctorate in medicine.
1662	Founding of the Royal Society. Oldenburg is its joint secretary, and Boyle and Newton are charter members. Spinoza completes the first part of the

	(tripartite) *Ethics*. He begins work on the *Principles of Cartesian Philosophy* and *Metaphysical Thoughts*.
1663	Simon de Vries meets with Spinoza at a meeting of the "Spinozistic Circle" in Amsterdam (Ep8). Letters 12 and 12a from Spinoza to Meyer, the latter concerning the publication of the *Principles of Cartesian Philosophy*. Spinoza is installed at Voorburg. He there publishes the *Principles of Cartesian Philosophy* with *Metaphysical Thoughts* as appendix. **31 July:** Spinoza writes to Oldenburg and introduces Petrus Serrarius. **3 August:** Spinoza writes to Meyer concerning Meyer's editorship and preface to the *Principles of Cartesian Philosophy*, which is published several months later.
1664	Beginning of the (second) Anglo-Dutch War.
1665	**28 January:** Spinoza's Letter 21 to Blyenbergh on the interpretation of Scripture. Spinoza makes several visits to Amsterdam, where he probably visits with Meyer during March and April. **26 May:** The new Amsterdam Theater opens with Meyer as its director. **June:** Having completed the first drafts of Parts II and III of the (tripartite) *Ethics*, Spinoza writes to Bouwmeester (Ep28).
1666	**10 June:** Spinoza's Letter 37 to Bouwmeester.
1667	End of the Anglo-Dutch War. Spinoza's Letter 40 to Jelles mentions Isaac Vossius as a friend.
1668	Adriaan Koerbagh's *Een Bloemhof* is published. The author is condemned by ecclesiastical authorities, and imprisoned on 19 July.
1669	**15 October:** Adriaan Koerbagh dies in prison.
1670	Spinoza publishes (anonymously and in Latin) the *Theological-Political Treatise*: ecclesiastical condemnations follow. Posthumous publication of the *Pensées* of Pascal.
1671	Spinoza is installed at The Hague, where he prevents (possibly at the suggestion of Jan de Witt) the appearance of the vernacular edition of the *Theological-Political Treatise* (Ep44).
1672	Louis XIV invades Holland. The French army occupies Utrecht (May). William II of Orange becomes *stadtholder* (July). **20 August:** Jan de Witt and his brother are massacred by a mob probably inspired by Calvinist clergy.
1673	Spinoza declines the chair of philosophy at Heidelberg (Ep47, Ep48). Spinoza visits the military camp of the Prince de Condé. **13 November:** The French occupation of Utrecht ends. **19 July:** The States of Holland publish a formal condemnation of the *Theological-Political Treatise* and "other heretical and atheistic writings," including

the works of Hobbes and the Socinians. Malebranche publishes the *Recherche de la Vérité*, which is accused of being of Spinozist inspiration.

1675 Spinoza completes and circulates the *Ethics* but declines to publish it. He begins work on the *Political Treatise*. Spinoza writes to G. H. Schuller (Ep72) expressing his distrust of Leibniz.

1676 **16 January:** The curator of the University of Leiden issues a new promulgation against Cartesianism. The Synod of The Hague orders an inquiry into the authorship of the *Theological-Political Treatise*.

1677 **21 February:** Death of Spinoza. His friends edit and publish the *Opera Posthuma* and *Nagelate Schriften*, all of whose contents are condemned by the political authorities and Calvinists the following year.

1680 **22 October:** Death of Bouwmeester.

1687 Newton publishes the first edition of the *Mathematical Principles of Natural Philosophy*.

1688 The "Glorious Revolution": William III becomes King of England.

1689 Locke publishes his *Letter on Tolerance* and his *Essay on Civil Government*.

1697 In his *Dictionnaire Historique et Critique*, Bayle characterizes Spinoza as "un athée de système, étrangement vertueux."

1710 Leibniz publishes his *Theodicy*.

Editorial Notes

A Note on the Translations

Of the translations included here, all but those of the *Short Treatise* and the *Hebrew Grammar* are by Samuel Shirley. Shirley's *Theological-Political Treatise* was originally published in 1989 by Brill and then republished by Hackett Publishing first in 1998 and then recently, in a corrected version, in 2001. Shirley's translations of the *Ethics*, the *Principles of Cartesian Philosophy* with *Metaphysical Thoughts*, the *Treatise on the Emendation of the Intellect*, the *Political Treatise*, and *The Letters* were published by Hackett during the past decade. For this volume, the editor has revised and edited the notes and made minor changes in the translations, but the bulk of the writing remains as Shirley translated it. For the *Short Treatise* we have used the translation of A. Wolf first published in 1910; it has been carefully examined by Bieneke Heitjama and Inge Van Der Cruysse and edited by the editor; Wolf used the older A manuscript of the *Short Treatise* and presented alternative readings from the B manuscript in notes. We follow his decisions except in a few cases and provide Spinoza's notes as well as, on some occasions, when important for the reader, alternative versions. In the case of the *Hebrew Grammar*, we have used the translation of Maurice J. Bloom first published by the Philosophical Library in 1964. Rondo Keele checked the Bloom translation against the Gebhardt text, and some modifications have been made. The Hebrew texts have been completely revised and corrected using the Gebhardt and the French translation of the *Hebrew Grammar*. In addition, in several cases, the English has been modified and the translation corrected. An explanation of the system of annotation appears before the first footnote of each work. The Chronology of Spinoza's life and times is based on the chronology prepared by Lee Rice for *The Letters*.

For complete information about Shirley's translations, we direct the reader to the editions of his translations published by Hackett, which also have complete notes and full introductions by the editors of the separate texts. Of special assistance are the introductions and notes of Steven Barbone and Lee Rice to *The Letters* and the *Political Treatise* and those of Seymour Feldman to the *Ethics* and the *Theological-Political Treatise*. The best and most comprehensive recent biography of Spinoza is that of Steven Nadler, *Spinoza: A Life* (Cambridge: Cambridge University Press, 1999).

A complete list of the translations used for this volume is as follows:

xxii   *Editorial Notes*

Treatise on the Emendation of the Intellect* and *Ethics Spinoza, Baruch. *Ethics, Treatise on the Emendation of the Intellect,* and *Selected Letters.* Translated by Samuel Shirley. Edited and introduced by Seymour Feldman. Indianapolis: Hackett Publishing Company, 1992.

Short Treatise Spinoza, Baruch. *Spinoza's Short Treatise on God, Man, and His Well-Being.* Translated and edited, with an introduction and commentary, by A. Wolf. London: Adam and Charles Black, 1910.

Principles of Cartesian Philosophy* and *Metaphysical Thoughts Spinoza, Baruch. *Principles of Cartesian Philosophy* with *Metaphysical Thoughts* and *Lodewijk Meyer's Inaugural Dissertation.* Translated by Samuel Shirley with introduction and notes by Steven Barbone and Lee Rice. Indianapolis: Hackett Publishing Company, 1998.

Theological-Political Treatise Spinoza, Baruch. *Theological-Political Treatise,* second edition. Translated by Samuel Shirley. Introduction by Seymour Feldman. Indianapolis: Hackett Publishing Company, 2001.

Hebrew Grammar Spinoza, Baruch. *Hebrew Grammar [Compendium Grammatices Linguae-Hebraeae].* Edited and translated, with an introduction, by Maurice J. Bloom. New York: Philosophical Library, 1964.

Political Treatise Spinoza, Baruch. *Political Treatise.* Translated by Samuel Shirley. Introduction and notes by Steven Barbone and Lee Rice. Indianapolis: Hackett Publishing Company, 2000.

The Letters Spinoza, Baruch. *The Letters.* Translated by Samuel Shirley. Introduction and notes by Steven Barbone, Lee Rice, and Jacob Adler. Indianapolis: Hackett Publishing Company, 1995.

ABBREVIATIONS

Works of Spinoza

CM	*Metaphysical Thoughts (Cogitata Metaphysica)* (CM1/2 is Part 1, Chapter 2)
E	*Ethics (Ethica)* (followed by arabic numeral for part and internal references)
Ep	*Letters (Epistolae)* (followed by arabic numeral)
KV	*Short Treatise (Korte Verhandeling)* (KV1/2/3 is Part 1, Chapter 2, Paragraph 3)

Editorial Notes xxiii

PPC	*Principles of Cartesian Philosophy (Principia Philosophiae Cartesianae)* (followed by arabic numeral for part and internal references)
TIE	*Treatise on the Emendation of the Intellect (Tractatus de Intellectus Emendatione)* (followed by arabic numeral for paragraph)
TP	*Political Treatise (Tractatus Politicus)* (TP1/2 is Chapter 1, Paragraph 2)
TTP	*Theological-Political Treatise (Tractatus Theologico-Politicus)* (followed by chapter and page number)

Works of Descartes

Med	*Meditations* (followed by arabic numeral)
PPH	*Principles of Philosophy*
Rep	*Replies to Objections*

Internal References

A	Article
App	Appendix
Ax	Axiom
Cor	Corollary
Def	Definition
Dem	Demonstration
Exp	Explication
GenSchol	General Scholium
Lem	Lemma
P	Proposition
Post	Postulate
Pref	Preface
Prol	Prologue
Schol	Scholium

Page numbers, where given for Descartes' *Meditations,* are from Descartes, *Meditations on First Philosophy,* third edition, translated by Donald Cress (Indianapolis: Hackett, 1993) and the Adam-Tannery (AT) edition: Descartes, *Oeuvres de Descartes,* 11 volumes, revised edition, edited by Charles Adam and Paul Tannery (Paris: Vrin 1964–76: reprinted 1996).

Treatise on the Emendation of the Intellect

Scholars agree that the brief Treatise on the Emendation of the Intellect (TIE) is the earliest piece of philosophical writing that we have from Spinoza. It probably dates from the period immediately after his excommunication, between 1657 and 1660. The treatise is unfinished, and it is likely that Spinoza set it aside as his work on the more substantial Short Treatise on God, Man, and His Well-Being progressed. The latter too was left unifinished. Still, these two works exhibit Spinoza's first attempts at a philosophical sytem, and while later books, especially the Ethics, correct and extend these early efforts, the two are valuable glimpses of his mature thought.

    The TIE is often compared with Descartes' Discourse on Method, first published in 1636, and the comparison is apt. Indeed, Spinoza was most likely influenced by Descartes' short introduction to his system. Like the latter, the TIE is an autobiographical work, more personal than most of Spinoza's writings. It sets questions of goals and methods in an ethical context and is largely epistemological in content. Descrates' Discourse is itself indebted to Augustine, and he in turn to Plato and Aristotle. In a sense, then, Spinoza's little work is his protrepticus, *his introduction to and apology for the new scientific philosophy, for reason and for the life of reason. It is a sketch for a justification of the philosophical life, reminiscent of the Plato of* Phaedo *and* Republic *and the Aristotle of* Nicomachean Ethics X, *drawn through the lens of Latin Stoicism.*

    The immediate autobiographical context for the TIE includes Spinoza's excommunication in 1656, his subsequent disengagement from his family's mercantile business and from the Jewish community in Amsterdam, and his more intense involvement with his rationalist, radical friends. By 1661 Spinoza was well known as a Cartesian and as a lens grinder skilled at producing optical lenses. He was associated with rational critics of Scripture like Juan de Prado, Isaac La Peyrère, and Uriel da Costa. Spinoza was a member of the circle around Franciscus Van den Enden, a frequent participant in Collegiant meetings, and an expert in Cartesian philosophy. There is reason to believe that Spinoza's critical spirit and attraction to the revolutionary science of his day were not new. They had been cultivated since his teenage years and came to a head with his public expulsion from the Jewish community. By that time, 27 July 1656, Spinoza had been a student and disciple of Van den Enden for some time and an advocate of tolerance, rational critique, and religious freedom. His traditional Jewish education, thorough as it was, had turned, when he was 14 or 15 years old, into this new set of commitments. The result was a view of God, nature, and the human good more rational and more universal than the traditional establishment could bear.

By 1657 Spinoza's exile was at least sufficient to cut him off from his teachers R. Saul Morteira and R. Manasseh ben Israel and to intensify his radical intellectual friendships with thinkers such as Van den Enden, Lodewijk Meyer, Adriaan Koerbagh, Pieter Balling, Simon de Vries, and Jarig Jelles. He probably lived with Van den Enden for a time, for he was the latter's prize student, and it was at his school that he had first become acquainted with the philosophy of Descartes and much else. He turned to lens grinding to earn a living, increased his scholarly associations by spending time at the university in Leiden, and frequently attended the meetings of the religiously radical Protestant group, the Collegiants.

The TIE, one might speculate, is the first literary product of this intense activity, hence its rather personal and programmatic qualities. It is a work marked by three significant features. First, in it Spinoza valorizes the life of reason and in particular scientific reason and the attainment of a knowledge of nature. Second, Spinoza distinguishes four modes of cognition, two of which, associated with imagination and sensation, are inadequate and defective, and the remaining two of which, involving deductive reasoning and intuitive reason, are the height of human achievement. Finally, Spinoza discusses the requirements of definition, distinguishing the definition of eternal essences from those of dependent and contingent ones. At this point, the text breaks off. It is a beginning, but only that. Some believe Spinoza abandoned the work when other tasks became more compelling; others, however, believe he left the TIE when he came to doubt the fruitfulness of its method. In years to come, the Ethics would mark a new beginning—working from new principles and in a new way.

M.L.M.

Notice to the Reader
(by the Editors of the *Opera Posthuma*)

This "Treatise on the Emendation of the Intellect, etc.," which in its unfinished state we here present to you, dear reader, was written by our author many years ago. He always intended to finish it, but, distracted by his other occupations and taken from us by death, he did not succeed in bringing it to the desired conclusion. But since it contains many excellent and useful things which we are convinced will be of considerable interest to an earnest seeker after truth, we did not wish to deprive you of them. That you may the more readily excuse occasional obscurities and lack of polish that appear in places in the text, we have thought it proper that you, too, should be made aware of these circumstances.

TREATISE ON THE EMENDATION OF THE INTELLECT
AND ON THE WAY BY WHICH IT IS BEST DIRECTED TO THE TRUE KNOWLEDGE OF THINGS

After experience had taught me the hollowness and futility of everything that is ordinarily encountered in daily life, and I realised that all the things which were the source and object of my anxiety held nothing of good or evil in themselves save insofar as the mind was influenced by them, I resolved at length to enquire whether there existed a true good, one which was capable of communicating itself and could alone affect the mind to the exclusion of all else, whether, in fact, there was something whose discovery and acquisition would afford me a continuous and supreme joy to all eternity.

I say 'I resolved at length,' for at first sight it seemed ill-advised to risk the loss of what was certain in the hope of something at that time uncertain. I could well see the advantages that derive from honour and wealth, and that I would be forced to abandon their quest if I were to devote myself to some new and different objective. And if in fact supreme happiness were to be found in the former, I must inevitably fail to attain it, whereas if it did not lie in these objectives and I devoted myself entirely to them, then once again I would lose that highest happiness.

I therefore debated whether it might be possible to arrive at a new guiding principle—or at least the sure hope of its attainment—without changing the manner and normal routine of my life. This I frequently attempted, but in vain. For the things which for the most part offer themselves in life, and which, to judge from their actions, men regard as the highest good, can be reduced to these three headings: riches, honour, and sensual pleasure. With these three the mind is so distracted that it is quite incapable of thinking of any other good. With regard to sensual pleasure, the mind is so utterly obsessed by it that it seems as if it were absorbed in some good, and so is quite prevented from thinking of anything else. But after the enjoyment of this pleasure there ensues a profound depression which, if it does not completely inhibit the mind, leads to its confusion and enervation. The pursuit of honour and wealth, too, engrosses the mind to no small degree, especially when the latter is sought exclusively for its own sake,[a] for it is then regarded as the highest good. Even more so is the mind obsessed with honour, for this is always regarded as a good in itself and the ultimate end to which everything is directed. Then again, in both these cases, there is no repentance as in the case of sensual pleasure. The more each of them is possessed, the more our joy is enhanced, and we are therefore more and more induced to increase them both. But if it should come about that our hopes are disappointed, there ensues a profound depression. And finally, honour has this great drawback, that to attain it we must conduct our lives to suit other men, avoiding what the masses avoid and seeking what the masses seek.

So when I saw that all these things stood in the way of my embarking on a new course, and were indeed so opposed to it that I must necessarily choose between the one alternative and the other, I was forced to ask what was to my greater advantage; for, as I have said, I seemed set on losing a certain good for the sake of an uncertain good. But after a little reflection, I first of all realised that if I abandoned the old ways and embarked on a new way of life, I should be abandoning a good that was by its very nature uncertain—as we can clearly gather from what has been said—in favour of one that was uncertain not of its own nature (for I was seeking a permanent good) but only in respect of its attainment. Then persistent meditation enabled me to see that, if only I could be thoroughly resolute, I should be abandoning certain evils for the sake of a certain good. For I saw that my situation was one of great peril and that I was obliged to seek a remedy with all my might, however uncertain it might be, like a sick man suffering from a fatal malady who, foreseeing certain death unless a remedy is forthcoming, is forced to seek it, however uncertain it be, with all his might, for therein lies all his hope. Now all those objectives that are commonly pursued not only contribute nothing to the preservation of our being but even hinder it, being frequently the cause of the destruction of those who gain possession of them, and invariably the cause of the de-

---

All notes are Spinoza's.

[a] This could be explained more fully and clearly by making a distinction between wealth that is sought for its own sake, for the sake of honour, for sensual pleasure, for health, or for the advancement of the sciences and the arts. But this is reserved for its proper place, such a detailed investigation being inappropriate here.

struction of those who are possessed by them.[b] For there are numerous examples of men who have suffered persecution unto death because of their wealth, and also of men who have exposed themselves to so many dangers to acquire riches that they have finally paid for their folly with their lives. Nor are there less numerous examples of men who, to gain or preserve honour, have suffered a most wretched fate. Finally, there are innumerable examples of men who have hastened their death by reason of excessive sensual pleasure.

These evils, moreover, seemed to arise from this, that all happiness or unhappiness depends solely on the quality of the object to which we are bound by love. For strife will never arise on account of that which is not loved; there will be no sorrow if it is lost, no envy if it is possessed by another, no fear, no hatred—in a word, no emotional agitation, all of which, however, occur in the case of the love of perishable things, such as all those of which we have been speaking. But love towards a thing eternal and infinite feeds the mind with joy alone, unmixed with any sadness. This is greatly to be desired, and to be sought with all our might. However, it was not without reason that I used these words, 'If only I could be earnestly resolute,' for although I perceived these things quite clearly in my mind, I could not on that account put aside all greed, sensual pleasure, and desire for esteem.

This one thing I could see, that as long as my mind was occupied with these thoughts, it turned away from those other objectives and earnestly applied itself to the quest for a new guiding principle. This was a great comfort to me, for I saw that those evils were not so persistent as to refuse to yield to remedies. And although at first these intermissions were rare and of very brief duration, nevertheless, as the true good became more and more discernible to me, these intermissions became more frequent and longer, especially when I realised that the acquisition of money, sensual pleasure, and esteem is a hindrance only as long as they are sought on their own account, and not as a means to other things. If they are sought as means, they will then be under some restriction, and far from being hindrances, they will do much to further the end for which they are sought, as I shall demonstrate in its proper place.

At this point I shall only state briefly what I understand by the true good, and at the same time what is the supreme good. In order that this may be rightly understood, it must be borne in mind that good and bad are only relative terms, so that one and the same thing may be said to be good or bad in different respects, just like the terms perfect and imperfect. Nothing, when regarded in its own nature, can be called perfect or imperfect, especially when we realise that all things that come into being do so in accordance with an eternal order and Nature's fixed laws.

But human weakness fails to comprehend that order in its thought, and meanwhile man conceives a human nature much stronger than his own, and sees no reason why he cannot acquire such a nature. Thus he is urged to seek the means that will bring him to such a perfection, and all that can be the means of his attaining this objective is called a true good, while the supreme good is to arrive at

---

[b] This is to be demonstrated at greater length.

the enjoyment of such a nature, together with other individuals, if possible. What that nature is we shall show in its proper place; namely, the knowledge of the union which the mind has with the whole of Nature.[c]

14 This, then, is the end for which I strive, to acquire the nature I have described and to endeavour that many should acquire it along with me. That is to say, my own happiness involves my making an effort to persuade many others to think as I do, so that their understanding and their desire should entirely accord with my understanding and my desire. To bring this about, it is necessary[d] (1) to understand as much about Nature as suffices for acquiring such a nature, and (2) to establish such a social order as will enable as many as possible to reach this goal

15 with the greatest possible ease and assurance. Furthermore, (3) attention must be paid to moral philosophy and likewise the theory of the education of children; and since health is of no little importance in attaining this end, (4) the whole science of medicine must be elaborated. And since many difficult tasks are rendered easy by contrivance, and we can thereby gain much time and convenience in our daily lives, (5) the science of mechanics is in no way to be despised.

16 But our first consideration must be to devise a method of emending the intellect and of purifying it, as far as is feasible at the outset, so that it may succeed in understanding things without error and as well as possible. So now it will be evident to everyone that my purpose is to direct all the sciences to one end and goal,[e] to wit (as we have said), the achievement of the highest human perfection. Thus everything in the sciences which does nothing to advance us towards our goal must be rejected as pointless—in short, all our activities and likewise our thoughts must be directed to this end.

17 But since we have to continue with our lives while pursuing this end and endeavouring to bring down the intellect into the right path, our first priority must be to lay down certain rules for living, as being good rules. They are as follows:

1. To speak to the understanding of the multitude and to engage in all those activities that do not hinder the attainment of our aim. For we can gain no little advantage from the multitude, provided that we accommodate ourselves as far as possible to their level of understanding. Furthermore, in this way they will give a more favourable hearing to the truth.
2. To enjoy pleasures just so far as suffices to preserve health.
3. Finally, to seek as much money or any other goods as are sufficient for sustaining life and health and for conforming with those social customs that do not conflict with our aim.

18 Having laid down these rules, I shall embark upon the first and most important task, emending the intellect and rendering it apt for the understanding of things

---

[c] This is explained more fully in its proper place.

[d] Note that here I am only concerned to enumerate the sciences necessary to our purpose, without regard to their order.

[e] In the sciences there is only one end, to which all must be directed.

in a manner appropriate to the achievement of our purpose. To this end our natural order of exposition requires that I should here recapitulate all the modes of perceiving which I have hitherto employed in confidently affirming or denying something, so that I may select the best of all, and at the same time begin to know my powers and the nature which I desire to perfect.

If I examine them carefully, they can all be classified under four headings.

1. There is the perception we have from hearsay, or from some sign conventionally agreed upon.
2. There is the perception we have from casual experience; that is, experience that is not determined by intellect, but is so called because it chances thus to occur, and we have experienced nothing else that contradicts it, so that it remains in our minds unchallenged.
3. There is the perception we have when the essence of a thing is inferred from another thing, but not adequately. This happens either when we infer a cause from some effect[f] or when an inference is made from some universal which is always accompanied by some property.
4. Finally, there is the perception we have when a thing is perceived through its essence alone, or through knowledge of its proximate cause.

All these I shall illustrate with examples. By hearsay alone I know the date of my birth, who my parents were, and things of that sort, which I have never doubted. By casual experience I know that I shall die; this I affirm because I have seen that others like me have died, although they have not all lived to the same age nor have they died from the same disease. Again, by casual experience I know that oil has the property of feeding fire, and water of extinguishing it. I know too that a dog is a barking animal and man a rational animal. And it is in this way that I know almost everything that is of practical use in life.

We deduce one thing from another as follows. When we clearly perceive that we sense such-and-such a body and no other, then from this, I say, we clearly infer that the soul is united to the body,[g] a union which is the cause of such-and-such a sensation. But from this[h] we cannot positively understand what is that sensation and union. Or, after I have come to know the nature of vision and realise that it has the property of making us see one and the same thing as smaller at a

---

[f] In such a case, we understand nothing about the cause except what we consider in the effect. This is sufficiently evident from the fact that the cause is then explained only in very general terms: e.g., 'Therefore there is something; therefore there is some power,' etc. Or again from the fact that the cause is expressed negatively: 'Therefore there is not this, or that,' etc. In the second case something clearly conceived is ascribed to the cause by reason of the effect, as we shall show by an example. But it is only the properties, not the particular essence of the thing.

[g] From this example one can clearly see what I have just noted. For by this union we understand nothing beyond the sensation itself; that is, the effect from which we inferred a cause of which we have no understanding.

[h] Such a conclusion, although it be certain, is not to be relied on without great caution; for unless we take great care, we shall immediately fall into error. When things are conceived in this abstract way

distance than if we were to see it near at hand, we infer that the sun is bigger than it appears, and other similar instances.

22   Finally, a thing is perceived through its essence alone when, from the fact that I know something, I know what it is to know something; or, from the fact that I know the essence of the soul, I know that it is united to the body. By the same kind of knowledge we know that two and three are five, and that if two lines are parallel to a third line, they are parallel to one another, and so on. But the things that I have hitherto been able to know by this kind of knowledge have been very few.

23   For the better understanding of all this, I shall make use of a single example, as follows. Three numbers are given; a fourth number is required, which is to the third as the second to the first. Here tradesmen generally tell us that they know what to do to find the fourth number, for they have not forgotten the procedure which they merely learned without proof from their teachers. Others formulate a universal axiom from their experience with simple numbers when the fourth number is self-evident, as in the case of the numbers 2, 4, 3, 6. Here they find that when the second is multiplied by the third and the product is divided by the first, the answer is 6. Seeing that the same number is produced which they knew to be the proportional number without going through the procedure, they conclude that this procedure is always a good way to find the fourth proportional. But math-

24 ematicians, because of the force of the demonstration of Proposition 19 of Book 7 of Euclid, know what numbers are proportional to one another from the nature and property of proportion, which tells us that the product of the first and fourth numbers is equal to the product of the second and third. However, they do not see the adequate proportionality of the given numbers, and if they do see it, they see it not by the force of that proposition but intuitively, without going through any procedure.

25   To choose from these the best mode of perceiving, we should briefly enumerate the means necessary to attain our end, as follows:

1. To have an exact knowledge of our nature which we wish to perfect, and at the same time to know as much of the nature of things as is necessary.
2. Therefrom to infer correctly the differences, agreements and oppositions of things.
3. To conceive aright the extent to which things can, and cannot, be acted upon.
4. To compare this result with the nature and power of man.

From this the highest degree of perfection that man can attain will readily be made manifest.

---

and not through their true essence, they are at once confused by the imagination. For to the things that they conceive abstractly, separately, and confusedly, men apply terms which they use to signify other more familiar things. Consequently, they imagine the former things in the same way as they are wont to imagine the things to which they originally applied these terms.

With these considerations in mind, let us see which mode of perceiving we ought to choose.

As to the first mode, it is self-evident that from hearsay, besides the considerable degree of uncertainty therein, we perceive nothing of the essence of the thing, as our example makes clear. And since a thing's individual existence is not known unless its essence is known (as will later be seen), we can clearly infer from this that any degree of certainty that we have from hearsay must be excluded from the sciences. For no one can ever be affected by mere hearsay unless his own understanding has already preceded it.

As to the second mode, again[i] it cannot be said to contain the idea of the proportion which it seeks. Besides its considerable uncertainty and indefiniteness, no one will in this way perceive anything in natural things except their accidents, which are never clearly understood unless their essences are first known. Hence this mode, too, must be excluded.

As for the third mode, we can in some sense say that we have the idea of the thing, and also that we can make inferences without danger of error. Yet it is not in itself the means of our acquiring our perfection.

Only the fourth mode comprehends the adequate essence of the thing, and is without danger of error. So this is the one we must chiefly adopt. Therefore we shall proceed to explain how it is to be employed, so that we may understand by this kind of knowledge what is unknown, and also may do this as directly as possible. That is, now that we know what kind of knowledge is necessary for us, we must describe the way and method by which we may come to know by this kind of knowledge the things that are needful to be known.

To this end, the first point to consider is that this is not a case of an enquiry extending to infinity. That is, to find the best method of seeking the truth, there is no need of another method for seeking the method of seeking the truth, and there is no need of a third method to seek the second method, and so on to infinity. For in that way we should never arrive at knowledge of the truth, or indeed at any knowledge. The case is analogous to that of material tools, where the same kind of argument could be employed. To work iron, a hammer is needed, and to have a hammer, it must be made. For this purpose there is need of another hammer and other tools, and again to get these there is need of other tools, and so on to infinity. In this way one might try to prove, in vain, that men have no power to work iron.

But the fact is that at first, with the tools they were born with, men succeeded, however laboriously and imperfectly, in making some very simple things; and when these were made they made other more complex things with less labour and greater perfection; and thus advancing gradually from the simplest works to the making of tools, and from tools to other works and other tools, they have reached a point where they can make very many complex things with little labour. In just

---

[i] Here I shall discuss experience at some greater length, and examine the method of proceeding of Empiricists and the new philosophers.

the same way the intellect by its inborn power[j] makes intellectual tools for itself by which it acquires other powers for other intellectual works,[k] and from these works still other tools—or capacity for further investigation—and thus makes steady progress until it reaches the summit of wisdom.

32 That this is the case with the intellect will readily be seen, provided we understand what is the method of seeking truth, and what are those innate tools which are all the intellect needs for making other tools from them so as to progress further. To demonstrate this I proceed as follows.

33 A true idea[l] (for we do have a true idea) is something different from its object (ideatum). A circle is one thing, the idea of a circle another. For the idea of a circle is not something having a circumference and a centre, as is a circle, nor is the idea of a body itself a body. And since it is something different from its object, it will also be something intelligible through itself. That is, in respect of its formal essence the idea can be the object of another objective essence, which in turn, regarded in itself, will also be something real and intelligible, and so on indefinitely.

34 For example, Peter is something real. Now the true idea of Peter is the objective essence of Peter and is in itself something real, something entirely different from Peter. So since the idea of Peter is something real, having its own individual essence, it will also be something intelligible, that is, the object of another idea which has in itself objectively everything that the idea of Peter has formally. And in turn the idea of the idea of Peter again has its own essence, which can also be the object of another idea, and so on without end. This anyone can experience for himself when he realises that he knows what Peter is, and also that he knows that he knows, and again that he knows that he knows that he knows, and so on. From this it is evident that, to understand the essence of Peter, it is not necessary to understand the idea of Peter, and far less the idea of Peter. This is no more than to say that, in order to know, I need not know that I know, and far less do I need to know that I know that I know. It is no more necessary than, in order to understand the essence of a triangle, one needs to understand the essence of a triangle, one needs to understand the essence[m] of a circle. Indeed, in the case of these ideas it is the other way round; for in order to know that I know, it is necessary that I must first know.

35 Hence it is evident that certainty is nothing else than the objective essence itself; that is to say, the way in which we become aware of the formal essence is certainty itself. And from this again it is evident that for the certainty of truth no other

---

[j] By inborn power I mean that which is not caused in us by external causes, as I shall later explain in my Philosophy.

[k] Here they are called works. In my Philosophy, I shall explain what they are.

[l] Note that here we shall endeavour to demonstrate not only what has just been said, but also the correctness of our procedure so far, and likewise other points of primary importance.

[m] Note that we are not here inquiring as to how the first objective essence is innate in us. For that topic belongs to the investigation of Nature, where these matters are dealt with more fully and where we also demonstrate that there is no affirmation or negation or act of will apart from the idea.

sign is needed but to have a true idea. For, as we have shown, in order to know, there is no need for me to know that I know. From this, again, it is clear that no one can know what the highest certainty is unless he has an adequate idea or the objective essence of some thing. For certainty and objective essence are the same.

Since truth, then, needs no sign, and to have the objective essences of things, or—which is the same thing—their ideas, is enough to remove all doubt, it follows that the true method does not consist in seeking a sign of truth after acquiring ideas; the true method is the path whereby truth itself, or the objective essences of things, or ideas (all these mean the same) is to be sought[n] in proper order.

Again, method must necessarily be discourse about reasoning or intellection. That is, method is not reasoning itself which leads to the understanding of the causes of things, and far less is it the understanding of the causes of things. It is the understanding of what is a true idea, distinguishing it from other kinds of perception and examining its nature, so that we may thereby come to know our power of understanding and may so train the mind that it will understand according to that standard all that needs to be understood, laying down definite rules as aids, and also ensuring that the mind does not waste its energy on useless pursuits.

From this we may conclude that method is nothing but reflexive knowledge, or the idea of an idea; and because there is no idea of an idea unless there is first an idea, there will be no method unless there is first an idea. So a good method will be one which shows how the mind is to be directed according to the standard of a given true idea. Again, since the relation between two ideas is the same as the relation between the formal essences of those ideas, it follows that the reflexive knowledge of the idea of the most perfect Being will be more excellent than the reflexive knowledge of other ideas. That is, the most perfect method will be one which shows how the mind should be directed according to the standard of a given idea of the most perfect Being.

From this one can readily understand how the mind, as it understands more things, at the same time acquires other tools which facilitate its further understanding. For, as may be gathered from what has been said, there must first of all exist in us a true idea as an innate tool, and together with the understanding of this idea there would likewise be an understanding of the difference between this perception and all other perceptions. Herein consists one part of our method. And since it is self-evident that the more the mind understands of Nature, the better it understands itself, it clearly follows that this part of our method will become that much more perfect as the mind understands more things, and will become then most perfect when the mind attends to, or reflects upon, the knowledge of the most perfect Being.

Then again, the more things the mind knows, the better it understands both its own powers and the order of Nature. Now the better it understands its own powers, the more easily it can direct itself and lay down rules for its own guidance; and the better it understands the order of Nature, the more easily it can restrain

---

[n] The nature of this seeking in the soul is explained in my Philosophy.

itself from useless pursuits. And it is in this, as we have said, that the whole of our method consists.

41 Moreover, an idea is situated in the context of thought exactly as is its object in the context of reality. Therefore, if there were something in Nature having no interrelation with other things, and if there were also granted its objective essence (which must agree entirely with its formal essence), then this idea likewise would have no interrelation° with other ideas; that is, we could make no inference regarding it. On the other hand, those things that do have interrelation with other things—as is the case with everything that exists in Nature—will be intelligible, and their objective essences will also have that same interrelation; that is, other ideas will be deduced from them, and these in turn will be interrelated with other ideas, and so the tools for further progress will increase. This is what we were endeavouring to demonstrate.

42 Furthermore, from the point just mentioned—that the idea must entirely agree with its formal essence—it is again evident that, for the human mind to reproduce a faithful image of Nature, it must draw all its ideas from that idea which represents the source and origin of the whole of Nature, so that this may likewise become the source of other ideas.

43 Here it may seem surprising that, having said that the good method is one which demonstrates how the mind is to be directed according to the standard of a given true idea, I resort to reasoning to prove this point, which appears to indicate that it is not self-evident. So the question can be raised as to whether our reasoning is sound. If our reasoning is sound, we have to begin from a given idea, and since to begin from a given idea is something that needs proving, we ought again to prove the validity of our reasoning, and then again the validity of that reasoning, and so on ad infinitum.

44 To this I reply that if anyone in his investigation of Nature had by some chance advanced in this way—that is, by acquiring other ideas in proper order according to the standard of a given true idea—he would never have doubted^p his own truth (inasmuch as truth, as we have said, reveals its own self), and all would have progressed smoothly for him. But since this rarely or never happens, I have been constrained to posit those guidelines, so that what we cannot acquire by chance, we may yet acquire by deliberate planning, and also in order to make it clear that, for the validation of truth and sound reasoning, we need no other instruments than truth and sound reasoning. For it is by sound reasoning that I have validated sound

45 reasoning, and still continue so to do. Furthermore, it is this way of thinking that men usually adopt in their own internal meditations.

That the proper order is rarely employed in the investigation of Nature is due to prejudices whose causes I shall later explain in my Philosophy. A further reason, as I shall later show, is the need for a considerable capacity to make accurate distinctions, a very laborious task. And finally, there is the matter of the human

---

° To be interrelated with other things is to produce, or be produced by, other things.

^p Just as here, too, we do not doubt our truth.

condition, which, as has already been shown, is highly unstable. There are yet other reasons, which we shall not pursue.

If anyone perchance should ask why at the very outset I adopted that arrangement in demonstrating the truths of Nature—for does not truth reveal its own self?—I reply by urging him not to reject these things as false because of paradoxes which will occasionally occur here and there. Let him first please to consider the arrangement of our demonstration, and he will then be convinced that we have arrived at the truth. This explains the reason why I began as I did.

But if after this there is some sceptic who still entertains doubt both as to the first truth itself and all the deductions we shall make according to the standard of the first truth, then surely either he is speaking contrary to his own consciousness or else we shall have to declare that there are men whose minds are also blinded either from birth or by reason of their prejudices, that is, through some accident that has befallen them. For they are not even aware of their own selves. If they affirm or doubt something, they do not know that they are doubting or affirming. They say that they know nothing, and they say that they are ignorant of this very fact of knowing nothing. And they do not even say this without qualification; for they are afraid that, in saying they know nothing, they are declaring that they exist, so that in the end they have to maintain silence lest they should perchance say something that has the savour of truth.

Finally, although in matters relating to the usages of life and society necessity has compelled them to suppose their existence, to seek their own good and frequently to affirm and deny things on oath, it is quite impossible to discuss the sciences with them. If a proof is presented to them, they do not know whether the argumentation is valid or not. If they deny, grant or oppose, they do not know that they deny, grant or oppose. So they must be regarded as automata, completely lacking in mind.

Let us now return to our theme. Up to the present, we have in the first place established the end to which we strive to direct all our thoughts. Second, we have learned which is the best mode of perception that will help us to attain our perfection. Third, we have learned which is the path our mind should first take in order to make a good beginning, and that is, to proceed to its enquiry by fixed rules, taking as its standard some given true idea. To do this correctly, our method must enable us, first, to distinguish a true idea from all other perceptions and to restrain the mind from those other perceptions; second, to lay down rules for perceiving things unknown according to the aforementioned standard; third, to establish an orderly procedure which will enable us to avoid useless toil. Having discovered this method, we realised, fourthly, that this method would be most perfect when we possessed the idea of a most perfect Being. So at the outset this must be our chief objective, to arrive at the knowledge of such a Being as speedily as possible.

Let us then make a beginning with the first part of the method, which is, as we have said, to distinguish and separate the true idea from other perceptions, and to keep the mind from confusing false, fictitious, and doubtful ideas with true ideas. Here I intend to dwell on this subject at some length so as to engage my readers in the study of so important a topic, and also because there are many who, failing to attend to the distinction between a true perception and all other perceptions, have come to doubt even their true perceptions. Their condition is like that of men who, when they were awake, did not doubt that they were awake, but having once in their dreams—as is often the case—felt certain that they were wide awake and later found this to be untrue, doubted even their waking experiences. This comes about because they have never distinguished between dreaming and being awake.

51 But I must first warn the reader that I shall not here be discussing the essence of every perception, explaining it through its proximate cause, for this pertains to Philosophy. I shall confine myself to discussing what the method demands; that is, what are the circumstances with which the fictitious, the false, and the doubtful perception are concerned, and how we may be delivered from each of them. Let our first inquiry, then, deal with the fictitious idea.

52 Every perception has for its object either a thing considered as existing or solely the essence of a thing. Now since in most cases fictions are concerned with things considered as existing, I shall deal first with that situation—that is, where the existence of some action is the sole object of the fiction, and the thing which is supposed to be so acting is comprehensible by intellect, or is posited as such. For example, I make up the idea that Peter, whom I well know, is on his way home, is coming to visit me, or the like.[q] Here I ask, with what is such an idea concerned? I see that it is concerned only with what is possible, not with what is necessary, nor with what is impossible.

53 I call a thing impossible if its nature implies that it would be a contradiction for it to exist; necessary, if its nature implies that it would be a contradiction for it not to exist; and possible, if, by its very nature, neither its existence nor its nonexistence implies a contradiction, the necessity or impossibility of its existence being dependent on causes which are unknown to us while we are assuming its existence. So if its necessity or impossibility, which are dependent on external causes, were known to us, it could not then be for us the subject of any fiction.

54 Hence it follows that if there is a God, or some omniscient being, such a being cannot engage in any fiction. For in our own case, knowing as I do that I exist,[r] my existence or nonexistence cannot be a matter of fiction for me; nor again can I engage in the fiction of an elephant that can pass through the eye of a needle; nor, knowing the nature of God,[s] can his existence or nonexistence be a mat-

---

[q] See later on what we shall have to say about hypotheses. These are clearly understood by us, but the fiction consists in our saying that the hypotheses are actually true of the heavenly bodies.

[r] Since a thing, when once it is understood, manifests itself, we need only an example without further proof. The same is true of its contradictory, which needs only to be examined to expose its falsity, as will later become clear when we shall be discussing the fiction that concerns essence.

[s] Note that, although many may say that they doubt the existence of God, they have in mind nothing but a word, or some fictitious idea they call God. This does not accord with the nature of God, as I shall later demonstrate in its proper place.

ter of fiction for me. The same applies to the Chimera, whose nature implies its nonexistence. From this it is evident, as I have said, that eternal truths do not allow of the fiction of which we are here speaking.[†]

But before proceeding further, I must first observe in passing that the difference between the essence of one thing and the essence of another thing is the same as that which holds between the actuality or existence of the one thing and the actuality or existence of the other. So if we were to conceive the existence of Adam, for example, under the general category of existence, this would be the same as if, to conceive his essence, we were to focus our attention on the nature of being, so that we end up by defining Adam as a being. Thus the more generally existence is conceived, the more confusedly it is conceived and the more readily it can be ascribed to any one thing. Conversely, the more singularly existence is conceived, the more clearly it is then understood, and the less likely we are to ascribe it (when we are not attending to the order of Nature) to anything other than the thing itself. This is worth noting.

We must now proceed to consider those cases which are loosely called fictions in common parlance even though we clearly understand that the reality is not as we feign it to be. For example, although I know that the earth is round, nothing prevents my saying to somebody that the earth is a hemisphere, like half an orange on a plate, or saying that the sun moves round the earth, and the like. If we consider these cases, we shall find nothing that is not consistent with what we have already said, provided that we note that, first, we have occasionally fallen into errors of which we are now conscious; and second, that we can entertain the fictitious idea, or at least the thought, that others have fallen into the same error, or may so do, as we once did. This fiction, I say, is feasible for us as long as we see no impossibility and no necessity therein. So when I say to somebody that the earth is not round, and the like, I do no more than to recall to mind an error which I perchance have made, or into which I might have fallen, and thereafter I feign, or think, that the person to whom I tell this is as yet a victim of this same error or is capable of falling into it. As I have said, I can engage in this fiction only as long as I see that no impossibility and no necessity lies therein. For had I understood this to be so, there would have been no room whatsoever for fiction, and it would have to be said that I had done no more than utter words.

It remains for us now furthermore to consider the kind of suppositions that are made in connection with problems: for these, too, not infrequently involve impossibilities. For example, we may say, "Let us suppose that this burning candle is not now burning," or "Let us suppose that it is burning in some imaginary space where there are no bodies." Such suppositions are quite commonly made, although the latter example is obviously understood to be impossible. But in such

---

[†] I shall also presently demonstrate that eternal truths do not admit of fiction of any kind. By an eternal truth I mean one which, if it is affirmative, will never be able to be negative. Thus it is a first and eternal truth that 'God is,' but that 'Adam thinks' is not an eternal truth. That 'there is no Chimera' is an eternal truth, but not that 'Adam does not think.'

cases there is no question of fiction. In the first case I have done no more than recall to memory[u] another candle which was not burning (or I have conceived this candle without a flame), and my thoughts of the latter candle I now transfer to the former, dismissing the flame from my mind. In the second case I merely withdraw my thoughts from the surrounding bodies so that the mind concentrates its attention on the candle alone, regarded in itself. This leads to the conclusion that the candle contains in itself no cause for its own destruction, so that, if there were no surrounding bodies, this candle and likewise its flame would remain immutable, or some such conclusion. Here, then, there is no question of fiction; there are really mere assertions,[v] and no more.

58   Let us now pass on to those fictions which are concerned either with essences alone or with essences combined with some actuality or existence. With regard to these it must especially be noted that, the less the mind understands while yet perceiving more things, the greater its capacity to form fictions; and the more it understands, the less its capacity to form fictions. For example, just as we saw above that while we are actually thinking, it cannot be for us a fictional idea that we are thinking or not thinking, so too, when we have come to know the nature of body, we cannot entertain the idea of an infinite fly; or when we have come to know the nature of the soul,[w] we cannot entertain the idea that it is square — though anything can be put into words. But as we have said, the less men know of Nature, the more easily they can fashion numerous fictitious ideas, as that trees speak, that men can change instantaneously into stones or springs, that ghosts appear in mirrors, that something can come from nothing, even that gods can change into beasts or men, and any number of such fantasies.

59   Someone may perhaps think that the limits of fiction are set by fiction, not by intellection. That is, when I have formed a fictitious idea and then, by some sort of freedom, assented to its existence in reality, this has the consequence that I cannot thereafter think it in any other way. For instance, when I have engaged in the fiction (to speak as they do) that body has a certain nature, and of my own free

---

[u] Later, when we shall be speaking of fictions concerning essences, it will be manifest that fiction never invents or presents to the mind anything new; it recalls to mind only things that are in the brain or the imagination, and the mind attends to all these together in a confused way. For example, the uttering of words and a tree are recalled to memory, and when the mind attends to them in a confused way without distinction, it forms the notion of a tree speaking. The same applies to existence, especially when, as we have said, it is conceived in a very general way as entity, for it is then liable to be attached to all things that occur together in memory. This is a very important point.

[v] This is also the case with hypotheses which are formed to explain the regular movements which accord with celestial phenomena, except that, if the hypotheses are actually applied to the celestial movement, an inference is drawn as to the nature of the heavens, which may nevertheless be quite different. For one may conceive many other causes to explain these movements.

[w] It often happens that a man recalls to mind this term 'soul' and at the same time forms some material image. Now when these two things are presented together in his mind, he is prone to think that he imagines and forms the idea of a material soul, failing to distinguish between word and reality. Here I ask my readers not to be too hasty to refute what I have said, which I hope they will refrain from doing provided that they pay close attention to the examples, and also to what follows.

will I convince myself that this is so in reality, I can no longer entertain the idea, say, of an infinite fly; and when I have formed an idea of the essence of the soul, I can no longer conceive it as square, and so forth.

But this view must be examined. First, either they deny or they grant that we have the capacity to understand something. If they grant this, then it must follow that what they say about fiction also applies to intellection. If they deny it, then let us, who know that we know something, consider what they are saying. They are in fact saying that the soul can be conscious of and perceive, in a variety of ways, not its own self nor things that exist, but only things that are neither in themselves nor anywhere at all; that is, the soul can by its unaided power create sensations or ideas which are not ideas of things. So to some extent they are likening the soul to God. Further, they are saying that we, or our soul, possess a freedom of such a kind that it can constrain our own selves, or the soul's self—nay, it can constrain its own freedom. For after it has formed some fictitious idea and given assent thereto, it cannot think it or fashion it in any other way, and is even compelled by that fictitious idea to form all its other thoughts so as not to conflict with the original fiction—just as here, too, their own fictitious idea compels them to allow the absurdities which I am here reviewing. We shall waste no time on demonstrations to refute this nonsense.

But leaving them to their delusions, we shall endeavour to draw from our discussion with them something true and to our purpose, namely, that when the mind attends to a thing that is both fictitious and false by its very nature, so as to ponder over it and achieve understanding, and then deduces from it in proper order what is to be deduced, it will easily detect its falsity;[x] and if the fictitious idea is by its own nature true, when the mind attends to it so as to understand it, and begins to deduce from it in proper order the conclusions that follow from it, it will proceed smoothly without any interruption—just as we have seen that, in the case of the false fiction just mentioned, the intellect immediately applied itself to exposing its absurdity and the absurdities that follow from it.

We need therefore be in no way apprehensive about engaging in fiction provided that we clearly and distinctly perceive what is really the case. If we were perchance to say that men are suddenly changed into beasts, this is a statement of a very general kind, such that there would be in the mind no conception, that is, no idea or connection of subject with predicate. For if there were such, the mind would at that time see the means and causes, the 'how' and the 'why' such a thing took place. Then again, no attention is given to the nature of the subject and predicate.

Furthermore, provided that the first idea is not fictitious and all the other ideas are deduced from it, the hasty tendency to form fictitious ideas will gradually dis-

---

[x] Although I seem to infer this from experience, and someone may deny its cogency because no proof is attached, he may take this if he wants one. Since there can be nothing in Nature contrary to her laws and all things happen in accordance with her fixed laws, so that definite effects are produced by definite laws in unalterable sequence, it follows that when the soul conceives a thing truly, it will proceed to produce in thought those same effects. See below, where I discuss the false idea.

appear. Then again, since a fictitious idea cannot be clear and distinct but only confused, and since all confusion arises from mind's having only partial knowledge of a complete whole or a unity composed of many constituents—failing to distinguish between the known and the unknown, and also attending at the same time without any distinction to the many constituents contained in a single thing—it follows, first, that if the idea is of a thing completely simple, it can only be clear and distinct. For such a thing would have to be known not in part, but either wholly or not at all. Secondly, it follows that if a thing composed of many constituents is divided in thought into all its simplest parts, and attention is given to each part separately, then all confusion will disappear. Thirdly, it follows that a fictitious idea cannot be simple, but is formed by the blending of various confused ideas of various things and actions existing in Nature; or, as better expressed, fiction results from attending at the same time, without assent, to various ideas of this kind.[y] For if fiction were simple, it would be clear and distinct, and consequently true. And if it were formed from the blending of distinct ideas, their composition would also be clear and distinct, and therefore true. For example, once we know the nature of a circle and also that of a square, we cannot compound the two and make a square circle, or a square soul and the like.

65   Let us then once more sum up briefly and see why we need in no way fear that fiction may be confused with true ideas. For as to the first case we mentioned earlier, i.e., when a thing is clearly conceived, we saw that if the thing which is clearly conceived, and also its existence, is in itself an eternal truth, we cannot engage in any fiction regarding such a thing. But if the existence of the thing conceived is not an eternal truth, we need only to ensure that the existence of the thing is compared with its essence, while at the same time attending to the order of Nature. As to the second case of fiction, which we said to consist in attending simultaneously, without assenting, to various confused ideas of various things and actions existing in Nature, we again saw that a completely simple thing cannot be the object of fiction, but only of intellect. And the same is true of a composite thing provided we attend to its simplest component parts. Indeed, these things cannot be the subject of fiction involving any actions that are not true, for at the same time we shall be compelled to consider how and why such a thing came about.

66   With these matters thus understood, let us now pass on to the investigation of the false idea so as to see with what it is concerned, and how we may guard ourselves against falling into false perceptions. Neither of these objectives will now afford us any difficulty after our investigation of the fictitious idea. For between these ideas there is no difference except that the false idea implies assent; that is (as we have already noted), while the ideas are presented to the mind, there are no causes presented from which it can infer (as in the case of fiction) that they do not arise from things extraneous. It is practically the same as dreaming with one's

---

[y] Fiction, considered in itself, does not much differ from dreaming, except that those causes which their senses present to the waking, from which they infer that those presentations are not presented at that time by things external to them, are not presented in dreaming. Now error, as will soon be manifest, is dreaming while awake, and if it reaches a certain pitch, it is called madness.

eyes open or while wide awake. Therefore the false idea is like the fictitious idea in that it is concerned with, or (as better expressed) has reference to, the existence of a thing whose essence is known, or it is concerned with an essence.

The false idea that has reference to existence is emended in the same way as the fictitious idea. For if the nature of the known thing implies necessary existence, we cannot possibly be deceived regarding the existence of that thing. If the existence of the thing is not an eternal truth (as is its essence) and the necessity or impossibility of its existence depends on external causes, then follow the same course which we indicated in our discussion of fiction, for it can be emended in the same way.

As for the kind of false idea that is related to essences, and also to actions, such perceptions are necessarily always confused, being compounded of various confused perceptions of things existing in Nature, as when men are convinced that divinities are present in woods, in images, in animals and other things, that there are bodies whose mere composition gives rise to intelligence, that corpses can reason, walk and speak, that God can be deceived, and the like. But ideas which are clear and distinct can never be false; for ideas of things which are clearly and distinctly conceived either are absolutely simple or are compounded of absolutely simple ideas—that is, deduced from absolutely simple ideas. But that an absolutely simple idea cannot be false is obvious to everyone, provided that he knows what is truth or understanding, and likewise what is falsity.

As to what constitutes the specific character of truth, it is certain that a true thought is distinguishable from a false thought not merely by its extrinsic relation but more particularly by an intrinsic characteristic. If an architect conceives a building in proper fashion, although such a building has never existed nor is ever likely to exist, his thought is nevertheless a true thought, and the thought is the same whether the building exists or not. On the other hand, if someone says, for example, that Peter exists, while yet not knowing that Peter exists, that thought in respect to the speaker is false, or, if you prefer, not true, although Peter really exists. The statement 'Peter exists' is true only in respect of one who knows for certain that Peter exists.

Hence it follows that there is something real in ideas through which the true are distinguished from the false, and this must now be the subject of our inquiry so that we may possess the best standard of truth (for we have said that we ought to determine our thoughts according to the standard of a given true idea, and method consists in reflexive knowledge) and may get to know the properties of the intellect. Nor must we say that the difference between true and false ideas derives from the fact that a true thought is to know things through their first causes—wherein it would indeed be very different from a false thought as we have explained it above. For a thought is also said to be true when it involves as its object the essence of some basic principle which is uncaused and is known through itself and in itself.

Therefore the specific character of a true thought must be intrinsic to the thought itself without reference to other thoughts. Nor does it acknowledge its object as cause, but must depend on the very power and nature of the intellect. For let us suppose that the intellect has perceived some new entity which has never existed, as some conceive the intellect of God before he created things (a perception which obviously could not have arisen from any object), and that from such a perception it deduces other perceptions in logical order. All those thoughts would be true and would not be determined by any external object, but would depend entirely on the power and nature of the intellect. Therefore that which constitutes the specific character of a true thought must be sought in that very same thought and deduced from the nature of intellect.

72 So to investigate this question, let us set before us a true idea whose object we are absolutely certain depends on our power of thought, there being no object to it in Nature; for such an idea, as is clear from what has been said, will more easily enable us to pursue the enquiry we have in view. For example, to form the concept of a sphere, I invent a cause at will, namely, that a semicircle rotates about its centre, and a sphere, as it were, is produced by this rotation. Now this is, of course, a true idea, and although we know that in Nature no sphere has ever been produced in this way, this is nevertheless a true perception and a very convenient way of forming the concept of a sphere. Now, we should observe that this perception affirms that a semicircle rotates, an affirmation that would be false were it not conjoined with the concept of a sphere, or else with a cause determining such motion; that is, in short, if this were a completely isolated affirmation. For in that case the mind would not be extending its affirmation to anything beyond the motion of the semicircle, and neither is this contained in the concept of a semicircle nor does it originate from the conception of a cause determining the motion. Therefore the falsity consists solely in this, that something is affirmed of a thing when it is not contained in the conception we have formed of the thing, as in this case motion or rest is affirmed of the semicircle. Hence it follows that simple thoughts are bound to be true, such as the simple idea of a semicircle, of motion, of quantity, and so on. Whatever of affirmation is contained in these thoughts is coextensive with their concept, and extends no further. Therefore we may form simple ideas at will without any danger of error.

73 It remains, then, only to inquire by what power the mind can form these simple ideas, and what is the extent of this power; for once this is discovered we shall easily see what is the highest knowledge we can attain. It is certain that this power of the mind does not extend to infinity; for when we affirm of a thing something that is not contained in the concept we form of the thing, this indicates that our perception is defective, or in other words that we have thoughts or ideas that are, as it were, mutilated and fragmentary. For we saw that the motion of the semicircle is false when taken in isolation, but true if it is conjoined with the concept of a sphere, or the concept of some cause determining such motion. Now if it is in the nature of a thinking being, as seems apparently to be the case, to form true or adequate thoughts, it is certain that inadequate ideas arise in us from this, that we are part of some thinking being, some of whose thoughts constitute our mind in their entirety, and some only in part.

74 But we have yet to consider another case, which was not worth raising when dealing with fiction, and wherein one can go far astray. This happens when certain things presented in the imagination are also in the intellect; that is, are clearly

and distinctly conceived. For then, when the distinct is not differentiated from the confused, the result is that certainty, i.e., a true idea, is mixed up with the nondistinct. For example, certain Stoics perhaps heard the word 'soul,' and also that it is immortal, which things they imagined only confusedly. They also imagined, and at the same time understood, that the most subtle bodies penetrate all other bodies and are penetrated by none. Since all these things were presented together in the imagination and were accompanied by the certainty of this axiom, they forthwith became convinced that the mind consists of those most subtle bodies, that those most subtle bodies cannot be divided, and so on.

But we are delivered from this error, too, as long as we make an effort to examine all our perceptions according to the standard of a given true idea, being on our guard, as we initially said, against those perceptions that we have from hearsay or from casual experience. In addition, this kind of mistake arises from their conceiving things in too abstract a way; for it is sufficiently clear in itself that what I conceive in its true object I cannot apply to any other object. Finally, this mistake also arises from their failure to understand the primary elements of Nature as a whole, so that, proceeding without due order and confusing Nature with abstractions (although these are true axioms), they fall into confusion and distort the order of Nature. However, if we proceed with the least possible abstraction and begin at the earliest stage from the primary elements—that is, from the source and origin of Nature—we need in no way fear this kind of mistake. 75

As for our knowledge of the origin of Nature, we need have no fear of confusing it with abstractions. For when things are conceived in an abstract way (as is the case with all universals), they always have a wider extension in the intellect than is really possessed by their particular exemplifications existing in Nature. Again, since there are many things in Nature whose difference is so slight as to be hardly perceptible to the intellect, it can easily come about that they are confused if they are conceived in an abstract way. But since, as we shall later see, the origin of Nature can neither be conceived in an abstract or universal way, nor can it have a wider extension in the intellect than in reality, nor has it any resemblance to things mutable, we need fear no confusion as to its idea, provided we possess the standard of truth as before shown. For this entity is unique and infinite;[z] that is, it is total being, beyond which there is no being.[a] 76

So much for the false idea. It remains for us to enquire into the doubtful idea, that is, to consider what are the things that can lead us to doubt, and also how that doubt may be removed. I am speaking of genuine doubt in the mind, not the sort of doubt that we frequently encounter when somebody verbally asserts that he doubts, although he mentally does not doubt. The correction of the latter is not the province of our method; rather does it pertain to an enquiry into obstinacy and its emendation. 77

---

[z] These are not attributes of God, displaying his essence, as I shall make clear in my Philosophy.

[a] This has already been demonstrated above. For is such a being did not exist, it could never be produced, and so the mind could understand more than Nature could furnish, which has been shown above to be false.

78   Doubt, then, never arises in the soul through the thing itself which is the object of doubt. That is, if there should be only one idea in our consciousness, whether true or false, there will be neither doubt nor certainty, but only a certain kind of awareness. For an idea in itself is nothing but a certain awareness. Doubt arises through another idea, which is not so clear and distinct that we can infer from it any certainty as to the thing which is doubted. That is, the idea which causes us to doubt is not clear and distinct. For example, if someone has never been led, whether by experience or in any other way, to reflect upon the deceptiveness of the senses, he will never entertain doubt as to whether the sun is greater or smaller than it appears. Hence country folk are frequently surprised when they hear that the sun is much greater than the earth's sphere. But reflection on the deceptiveness of the senses induces doubt.[b] If, after being in doubt, a man acquires true knowledge of the senses and of the manner whereby through their means distant things are represented, then the doubt is in turn removed.

79   Hence it follows that it is only when we do not have a clear and distinct idea of God that we can cast doubt on our true ideas on the grounds of the possible existence of some deceiving God who misleads us even in things most certain. That is, this can happen only if, attending to the knowledge we have of the origin of all things, we find nothing there to convince us that he is not a deceiver, with the same conviction that we have when, attending to the nature of a triangle, we find that its three angles are equal to two right angles. But if we do possess such knowledge of God as we have of a triangle, all doubt is removed. And just as we can attain such knowledge of a triangle although not knowing for sure whether some arch-deceiver is misleading us, so too can we attain such knowledge of God although not knowing for sure whether there is some arch-deceiver. Provided we have that knowledge, it will suffice, as I have said, to remove all doubt that we may have concerning clear and distinct ideas.

80   Furthermore, if anyone follows the correct procedure, investigating first what should be first investigated without any interruption in the interconnection of things, and if he knows how to define problems precisely before seeking to solve them, he will never have anything but the most certain ideas, that is, clear and distinct ideas. For doubt is nothing but the suspension of judgment in respect of some affirmation or denial which would be made but that something comes to mind which, being outside our understanding, must render imperfect our knowledge of the thing in question. We may therefore conclude that doubt always arises from want of order in the investigation.

81   These are the matters which I promised to set forth in this first part of our Method. But to omit nothing that can advance our knowledge of the intellect and its powers, I shall add a few words on memory and forgetting. Here the most important point to be considered is that memory is strengthened both by the aid of the intellect and also without its aid. As to the first case, the more intelligible a thing is, the more easily it is retained; the less intelligible, the more easily it is for-

---

[b] That is to say, a man knows that the senses have sometimes deceived him, but he knows this only confusedly, for he does not know in what way the senses deceive him.

gotten. For example, if I give someone a list of unconnected words, he will find it much more difficult to retain them than if I were to give him the same words in the form of a story.

It is also strengthened without the aid of the intellect, namely, through the force wherewith the imagination, or what is termed the common sense, is affected by some singular corporeal thing. I say 'singular,' for the imagination is affected by singular things only. For example, if someone reads just one love story, he will retain it very well as long as he does not read many others of the same kind, for then it flourishes alone in his imagination. But if he reads several of the same kind, he will imagine them all together, and they will easily be confused. I say 'corporeal,' for the imagination is affected only by bodies. Since, then, the memory is strengthened not only by the intellect but also independently of the intellect, we may conclude that it is something different from the intellect, and that the intellect considered in itself does not involve either memory or forgetting.

What, then, is memory? It is nothing but the sensation of impressions in the brain together with the thought of the determinate duration[c] of the sensation. This is further demonstrated by recollection, for in this the soul thinks of that sensation, but without the notion of a continuous duration; and thus the idea of that sensation is not identical with the duration of the sensation, that is, with memory itself. The question as to whether the ideas themselves undergo some corruption will be discussed in my Philosophy.

If this seems quite absurd to anyone, it will be enough for our purpose that he should reflect that, the more singular a thing is, the more easily it is retained, as is evident from the example of the comedy just mentioned. And again, the more intelligible a thing is, the more easily it is retained. Hence we cannot fail to retain a thing that is most singular and sufficiently intelligible.

Thus we have distinguished between the true idea and other perceptions, and we have established that the fictitious, the false, and other ideas have their origin in the imagination, that is, in certain sensations that are (so to speak) fortuitous and unconnected, arising not from the power of the mind but from external causes, in accordance as the body, dreaming or waking, receives various motions. Or if you wish, you may here understand by imagination whatever you please, as long as it is something different from the intellect, and the soul has a passive relation to it. It matters not how you understand it, now that we know that it is something random, and that the soul is passive to it, while we also know how we may be delivered from it with the aid of the intellect. And so let no one be surprised that, without as yet having proved that there is such a thing as body and other important matters, I speak of the imagination, the body, and its constitution. For, as

---

[c] But if the duration is indeterminate, the memory of the thing is imperfect, as each of us seems also to have learned naturally. For it often happens that, to confirm our belief in what someone is telling us, we ask when and where it occurred. And although ideas, too, have their own duration in the mind, since we are accustomed to determine duration with the help of some measure of motion which also involves the imagination, we still do not see in memory anything which appertains solely to the mind.

I have said, it matters not how I understand it, now that I know that it is something random, and so on.

85 But we have demonstrated that a true idea is simple or compounded of simple ideas, and that it shows how and why something is the case, or has been so, and that its ideal effects in the soul correspond to the specific reality of its object. This is identical with the saying of the ancients that true science proceeds from cause to effect, except that, as far as I know, they never conceived the soul, as we are here doing, as acting according to fixed laws, a sort of spiritual automaton.

86 From these demonstrations, as far as was possible in the initial stages of our enquiry, we have acquired knowledge of our intellect, and such a standard of the true idea that we no longer fear we may confuse true ideas with false or fictitious ideas. Nor again will we wonder why we understand some things that do not in any way fall within the scope of the imagination, and why there are in the imagination some things that are completely opposed to the intellect, while there are other things which agree with the intellect. For we know that the operations by which imaginings are produced are subject to other laws which are quite different from the laws of the intellect, and that in relation to imagining, the soul has only a passive rôle.

87 From this we may also see how easily those who have not made a careful distinction between imagination and intellection may fall into grave errors, such as, for instance, that extension must be localised, that it must be finite, that its parts are really distinct from one another, that it is the first and only foundation of all things, that it occupies more space at one time than at another, and many other beliefs of this kind, all of which are completely opposed to truth, as we shall demonstrate in its proper place.

88 Then again, since words are a part of the imagination—that is, since many of our concepts are formed according to the haphazard composition of words in memory from some disposition of the body—there can be no doubt that words no less than imagination can bring about many grave errors unless we exercise great caution in that respect. Add to this that words owe their formation to the

89 whim and understanding of the common people, so that they are merely symbols of things as they are in the imagination, not in the intellect. This is evident from the fact that men have often devised negative terms for all those things that are only in the intellect and not in the imagination (e.g., incorporeal, infinite, etc.), and they also express negatively many things that are really affirmative, and conversely (e.g., uncreated, independent, infinite, immortal, etc.).[d] The reason for this is that the contraries of these words are much more easily imagined, and so they occurred first to the early generations, and they used them as positive terms.

90 Furthermore, we avoid another frequent cause of confusion, one that prevents the intellect from reflecting on itself; viz., by failing to distinguish between imag-

---

[d] We affirm and deny many things because the nature of words, not the nature of things, suffers us to do so; and in our ignorance of the latter, we may easily take the false to be true.

ination and intellection, we think that the things we more easily imagine are clearer to us, and we think that we understand what we imagine. Thus we put first what should be put later, and so the true order of procedure is reversed and there can be no legitimate conclusion drawn.

To move on in turn to the second part[e] of this Method, I shall first set forth our aim in this Method, and then the means of attaining it. Our aim, then, is to have clear and distinct ideas, that is, such as originate from pure mind and not from fortuitous motions of the body. Next, so that all ideas may be subsumed under one, we shall endeavour to connect and arrange them in such a manner that our mind, as far as possible, may reproduce in thought the reality of Nature, both as to the whole and as to its parts.

As to the first point, our ultimate aim, as we have already said, requires that a thing be conceived either through its essence alone or through its proximate cause. That is, if the thing is in itself, or, as is commonly said, self-caused, then it will have to be understood solely through its essence; if the thing is not in itself and needs a cause for its existence, then it must be understood through its proximate cause. For in fact knowledge of the effect is nothing other than to acquire a more perfect knowledge of the cause.[f]

Therefore, as long as we are engaged in an enquiry into real things, it will never be permissible for us to draw a conclusion from what is abstract, and we shall take great care not to mix the things that are merely in the intellect with those things that are in reality. The most secure conclusion is to be drawn from some particular affirmative essence, i.e., from a true and legitimate definition. For, starting from universal axioms alone, the intellect cannot descend to particulars, since axioms are of infinite extension and do not determine the intellect to contemplate one particular thing rather than another. So the correct path to discovery is to develop our thinking from the basis of some given definition, and progress will be more successful and easier as a thing is better defined. Therefore the whole of this second part of our method hinges on this alone: getting to know the conditions of a good definition, and then devising a way to discover them. I shall therefore first discuss the conditions of definition.

For a definition to be regarded as complete, it must explain the inmost essence of the thing, and must take care not to substitute for this any of its properties. To explicate this, passing over other examples so as not to appear bent on exposing the errors of others, I shall choose only the example of an abstract thing where the manner of definition is unimportant, a circle, say. If this is defined as a figure in which the lines drawn from the centre to the circumference are equal, it is obvi-

---

[e] The principal rule of this part, as follows from the first part, is to review all the ideas which we discover in us as originating from pure intellect, so that they may be distinguished from those we imagine. This distinction will have to be elicited from the properties of each, that is, imagination and intellection.

[f] Note that this leads to the conclusion that we cannot properly understand anything of Nature without at the same time extending our knowledge of the first cause, or God.

ous that such a definition by no means explains the essence of a circle, but only one of its properties. And although, as I have said, this is a matter of little importance when it is a question of figures and other mental constructs, it is nevertheless a matter of prime importance when it is a question of physical and real beings. For the properties of things are not understood as long as their essences are not known; and if the latter are neglected, this is bound to distort the interconnections made by our intellect which ought to reproduce the interconnections of Nature, and we shall go far astray from our goal.

96 So if we are to be delivered from this fault, the following requirements must be satisfied in definition.

1. If the thing be a created thing, the definition, as we have said, must include its proximate cause. For example, according to this rule a circle would have to be defined as follows: a figure described by any line of which one end is fixed and the other movable. This definition clearly includes the proximate cause.
2. The conception or definition of the thing must be such that all the properties of the thing, when regarded by itself and not in conjunction with other things, can be deduced from it, as can be seen in the case of this definition of a circle. For from it we clearly deduce that all the lines drawn from the centre to the circumference are equal.

That this is a necessary requirement of a definition is so self-evident to one who pays attention that it does not seem worthwhile spending time in demonstrating it, nor again in showing that according to this second requirement every definition must be affirmative. I am speaking of intellectual affirmation, disregarding verbal affirmation, which, because of poverty of language, may sometimes be expressed negatively, although understood affirmatively.

97 The requirements for the definition of an uncreated thing are as follows:

1. That it should exclude every cause; that is, that the thing should need nothing else for its explanation besides its own being.
2. That, given the definition of the thing, there should remain no room for the question: Does it exist?
3. That, as far as the mind is concerned, it should contain no substantives that can be put in adjectival form; that is, it should not be explicated through any abstractions.
4. And finally (although it is not really necessary to make this observation), it is required that all its properties can be deduced from its definition.

All these points are evident if careful attention is paid.

98 I have also stated that the best basis for drawing a conclusion will be a particular affirmative essence. For the more individualised an idea is, the more distinct

it is, and therefore the clearer it is. Hence our most important task is to seek knowledge of particular things.

As to the ordering of all our perceptions and their proper arrangement and unification, it is required that, as soon as is possible and reason demands, we should ask whether there is a being—and also what kind of being—which is the cause of all things so that its essence represented in thought is also the cause of all our ideas. Then our mind, as we have said, will reproduce Nature as closely as possible; for it will possess in the form of thought the essence, order, and unity of Nature. Hence we can see that it is above all necessary for us always to deduce our ideas from physical things, i.e., from real beings, advancing, as far as we can, in accordance with the chain of causes from one real being to another real being, and in such a manner as never to get involved with abstractions and universals, neither inferring something real from them nor inferring them from something real. For in either case the true progress of the intellect is interrupted. 99

But it should be noted that by the series of causes and real beings I do not here mean the series of mutable particular things, but only the series of fixed and eternal things. It would be impossible for human limitation to grasp the series of mutable particular things, not only because they are innumerable but also because of the infinite number of factors affecting one and the same thing, each of which can be the cause of the existence or nonexistence of the thing. For the existence of mutable particular things has no connection with their essence; that is (as we have said), their existence is not an eternal truth. 100

But neither is there any need for us to understand their series. For the essences of particular mutable things are not to be elicited from their series or order of existing, which would furnish us with nothing but their extrinsic characteristics, their relations, or, at the most, their circumstances. All these are far from the inmost essence of things. This essence is to be sought only from the fixed and eternal things, and at the same time from the laws inscribed in these things as in their true codes, which govern the coming into existence and the ordering of all particular things. Indeed, these mutable particular things depend so intimately and essentially (so to phrase it) on the fixed things that they can neither be nor be conceived without them. Hence, although these fixed and eternal things are singular, by reason of their omnipresence and wide-ranging power they will be to us like universals, i.e., the genera of the definitions of particular mutable things, and the proximate causes of all things. 101

But this being so, there appears to be no small difficulty to surmount before we can arrive at the knowledge of these particular things. For to conceive them all at once is a task far beyond the powers of the human intellect. And, as we have said, the order wherein one thing may be understood before another is not to be sought from their position in the series of existing, nor again from eternal things. For in the latter case all these things are by nature simultaneous. Therefore we must resort to other aids apart from those employed in understanding the eternal things and their laws. However, this is not the appropriate place to give an account of those aids, nor do we need to do so until we have acquired a sufficient knowledge 102

103   of the eternal things and their infallible laws, and have gained an understanding of the nature of our senses.

103   Before we embark upon an enquiry into our knowledge of particular things, it will be timely for us to treat of those aids, all of which will serve to assist us in knowing how to use our senses and to conduct experiments under fixed rules and proper arrangement, such as will suffice to determine the thing which is the object of our enquiry. From these we may finally infer what are the laws of eternal things that govern the thing's production, and may gain an insight into its inmost nature, as I shall duly show. Here, to return to our theme, I shall confine my efforts to setting forth what seems necessary to enable us to attain to knowledge of eternal things, and to frame their definitions on the terms previously explained.

104   To achieve this, we must recall what we said earlier, namely, that when the mind attends to some thought so as to examine it and to deduce from it in proper order what can legitimately be deduced, if it is false, the mind will detect its falsity; but if it is true, the mind will proceed fruitfully without interruption to deduce truths from it. This, I say, is what our purpose requires. For our thoughts cannot be determined on any other foundation.

105   If, therefore, we wish to investigate the first of all things, there has to be some foundation which may direct our thoughts there. Next, since method is reflexive knowledge itself, the foundation which is to give direction to our thoughts can be nothing other than knowledge of what constitutes the specific reality of truth, and knowledge of the intellect, its properties and powers. For when this is acquired, we shall have a foundation from which we shall deduce our thoughts, and a path by which the intellect, according to its capacity, may attain knowledge of eternal things, taking into account, of course, the powers of the intellect.

106   But if, as has been demonstrated in the first part, it pertains to the nature of thought to form true ideas, we must here enquire what we understand by the faculties and power of the intellect. Now since the chief part of our Method is to achieve a good understanding of the powers of the intellect and its nature, we are necessarily constrained (through considerations set out in this second part of our

107 Method) to deduce these simply from the definition of thought and intellect. But so far we have not had any rules for finding definitions; and since we cannot treat of these rules without knowing the nature or definition of the intellect and its power, it follows that either the definition of the intellect must be self-evident or we cannot understand anything. But that definition is not absolutely self-evident. Nevertheless, since its properties—like everything we have from the intellect—can be clearly and distinctly perceived only if their nature is known, the definition of intellect will become self-evident if we attend to its properties that we do understand clearly and distinctly. So let us here enumerate the properties of the intellect, consider them, and begin a discussion of our innate tools.[g]

108   The properties of the intellect which I have chiefly noted and clearly understand are as follows:

---

[g] See above, section 31.

1. That it involves certainty; that is, it knows that things are in reality as they are contained in the intellect in the form of thought.
2. That it perceives some things, or forms some ideas, independently, and some ideas it forms from other ideas. To wit, it forms the idea of quantity independently without attending to other thoughts, but it forms ideas of motion only by attending to the idea of quantity.
3. The ideas that it forms independently express infinity, but determinate ideas are formed from other ideas. For if it perceives the idea of a quantity through a cause, then it determines that idea through the idea of a quantity, as when it perceives that a body is formed from the motion of a plane, a plane from the motion of a line, and a line from the motion of a point. These perceptions do not serve for the understanding of quantity, but only to determine it. This is evident from the fact that we conceive these quantities as formed, as it were, from motion, whereas motion is not perceived unless quantity is perceived; and again we can prolong the motion to form a line of infinite extent, which we could not do if we did not possess the idea of infinite quantity.
4. It forms positive ideas before negative ones.
5. It perceives things not so much under duration as under some form of eternity, and as being of infinite number. Or rather, in its perception of things, it attends neither to number nor duration. But when it imagines things, it perceives them as being of fixed number, with determinate duration and quantity.
6. The clear and distinct ideas that we form seem to follow solely from the necessity of our nature in such a way as to seem to depend absolutely on our power alone. But with confused ideas the contrary is the case; they are often formed without our consent.
7. There are many ways in which the mind can determine the ideas that the intellect forms from other ideas. For example, to determine the plane of an ellipse, the mind supposes that a pencil attached to a string moves about two centres, or alternatively it conceives an infinite number of points always maintaining the same fixed relation to a given straight line, or a cone cut in an oblique plane so that the angle of inclination is greater than the angle at the vertex of the cone. There are innumerable other ways.
8. Ideas are the more perfect as they express a greater degree of perfection of an object. For we do not admire the architect who has designed a chapel as much as one who has designed a splendid temple.

Other things that are referred to thought, such as love, joy, and so on, I shall not pause to consider; for they are neither relevant to our purpose, nor again can they be conceived unless the intellect is perceived. For if perception is entirely removed, all these are removed.

False and fictitious ideas have nothing positive (as we have abundantly shown) through which they are called false or fictitious; they are considered as such only from the defectiveness of our knowledge. Therefore false and fictitious ideas, as such, can teach us nothing concerning the essence of thought; this is to be sought from those positive properties just reviewed. That is, we must now establish some common basis from which these properties necessarily follow; a basis which, when given, necessarily entails these properties, and which, when removed, removes them all.

The rest is lacking.

Short Treatise on God, Man, and His Well-Being

The Short Treatise on God, Man, and His Well-Being *is the second work of Spinoza's early period. It was probably in hand by 1662. At the end of a long letter to Henry Oldenburg, largely taken up with Spinoza's comments on scientific points in a recent book by Robert Boyle, Spinoza refers to a "short work" that he has written on the question of the origin of things and a first cause; the letter (Ep6) was written in early 1662. In addition, there is a reference to a "certain Dutch writing" that speaks of God as the whole universe, written by a Cartesian associated with Van den Enden, among others, in the journal of a Danish visitor to the Low Countries, Olaus Borch; the journal entry is for 3 April 1662. It is tempting to take this Dutch work to be the* Short Treatise, *the only work of Spinoza's written in Dutch. Some scholars also conjecture that the two Dutch versions of the* Short Treatise *are translations of an original Latin text by Spinoza, now lost.*

By 1662, then, Spinoza had sketched the main lines of the new view — his "philosophy" — about God, the human mind, and nature that he had referred to in the TIE. By this time, he had moved from Amsterdam to Rijnsburg, a small village just outside of Leiden, and enjoyed its relative solitude. Rijnsburg was known for its tolerance, and it was close to the university, where he had met friends and folk of common spirit, Adriaan Koerbagh among them. The Short Treatise, *begun in Amsterdam, was continued in this new environment. It is the work of a devoted student of the Cartesian philosophy who was, at the same time, striking out on his own paths.*

The structure of Spinoza's Ethics *is already suggested in the* Short Treatise. *It begins with metaphysics and theology, turns to epistemology and psychology, and ends with ethics and religion. More precisely, Spinoza begins by proving God's existence, eventually discusses the roles of the senses, reason, and the passions in human conduct, and concludes with a eulogy to the life devoted to the love of God, to knowing God and achieving a comprehensive scientific-philosophical understanding of Nature. Like the earlier TIE, the core of the* Short Treatise *is an ancient commitment to the life of* eudaimonia, *an intellectual life that satisfied the scriptural mandate to* imitatio dei *and the philosophical-Stoic desire for harmonious, natural living. But if the structure is traditionally classical, the core that unites Spinoza's classicism with his biblical affinities is the commitment to the identity of God and Nature. Virtually all that is novel in the* Short Treatise *flows from or at least circulates around this deep belief.*

Still the treatise leaves this commitment insufficiently grounded, and Spinoza came to realize this deficiency. Central to his naturalism, to his denial of free will, to his account of human emotions and action, the identity of God with Nature is a strong and determinative principle. It demanded justification and clarification beyond what it received, as did other claims, like the account of the difference between thought and extension and hence of the relation between mind and body. The overall character of Spinoza's understanding of religion, metaphysics, nature, and ethics had taken shape, but its fine lineaments needed elaboration. The project occupied him in the quiet of Rijnsburg and the company of friends and colleagues.

M.L.M.

[Title-page in A]

Short Treatise on God, Man, and His Well-Being

Previously written in the Latin tongue by B.D.S. for the use of his disciples who wanted to devote themselves to the study of Ethics and true Philosophy. And now translated into the Dutch language for the use of the Lovers of Truth and Virtue: so that they who spout so much about it, and put their dirt and filth into the hands of simpletons as though it were ambergris, may just have their mouths stopped, and cease to profane what they do not understand: *God, themselves, and how to help people to have regard for each other's well-being,* and how to heal those whose mind is sick, in a spirit of tenderness and tolerance, after the example of the Lord Christ, our best Teacher

[Title-page in B]

Ethica or Moral Science
Composed in Two Parts
Which Treat

I. Of God's Existence, and Attributes

II. Of Man, with reference to the character and origin of his Passions, the use of his reason in this respect, and the means whereby he is educated to his Happiness and supreme freedom

   Also an Appendix, containing a brief account of the nature of Substance—as well as that of the human Soul, and its union with the Body

Composed by
Benedictus de Spinoza

CONTENTS
OF THE FOLLOWING TWO BOOKS, NAMELY:

THE FIRST BOOK
Treating of God and What Pertains to Him, Contains the Following Chapters

    I. That God Exists
   II. What God Is
       [First Dialogue]
       [Second Dialogue]
  III. That God Is a Cause of All Things
  IV. On God's Necessary Activity
   V. On Divine Providence
  VI. On Divine Predestination
 VII. On the Attributes Which Do Not Pertain to God
VIII. On *Natura Naturans*
  IX. On *Natura Naturata*
   X. What Good and Evil Are

THE SECOND BOOK
Treating of the Perfection of Man So That He May Be in a Position to Become United with God

      [Preface]
   I. On Opinion, Belief, and Knowledge
  II. What Opinion, Belief, and Clear Knowledge Are
 III. The Origin of Passion. Passion Arising from Opinion
 IV. What Comes from Belief, and on the Good and Evil of Man
   V. On Love
  VI. On Hatred
 VII. On Joy and Sorrow

VIII. Esteem and Contempt
IX. Hope and Fear
X. On Remorse and Repentance
XI. On Derision and Jesting
XII. On Glory, Shame, and Shamelessness
XIII. On Favour, Gratitude, and Ingratitude
XIV. On Grief
XV. On the True and the False
XVI. On the Will
XVII. On the Distinction between Will and Desire
XVIII. On the Uses of the Foregoing
XIX. On Our Happiness
XX. Confirmation of the Foregoing
XXI. On Reason
XXII. On True Knowledge, Regeneration, Etc.
XXIII. On the Immortality of the Soul
XXIV. On God's Love of Man
XXV. On Devils
XXVI. On True Freedom

[Appendix I.]   On God
[Appendix II.] On the Human Soul

FIRST PART
On God

Chapter I
That God Exists

As regards the first, namely, whether there is a God, this, we say, can be proved.

  I. In the first place, a priori thus:
    1. Whatever we clearly and distinctly know to belong to the nature[1] of a thing, we can also truly affirm of that thing. Now we can know clearly and distinctly that existence belongs to the nature of God;
    Therefore . . .
    Otherwise also thus:
    2. The essence of things are from all eternity, and unto all eternity shall remain immutable;
    The existence of God is essence;
    Therefore . . .
  II. A posteriori, thus:
    If man has an idea of God, then God[2] must exist *formaliter*;
    Now, man has an idea of God;
    Therefore . . .

Spinoza's notes are indicated by numerals. Notes indicated by letters and enclosed in brackets are those of translator A. Wolf (main annotator for this work) and Michael L. Morgan.

[1] Understand the definite nature through which a thing is what it is, and which can by no means be removed from it without at the same time destroying that thing: thus, for instance, it belongs to the essence of a mountain that it should have a valley, or the essence of a mountain is that it has a valley; this is truly eternal and immutable, and must always be included in the concept of a mountain, even if it never existed, or did not exist now.

[2] From the definition which follows in chapter 2, namely, that God has infinite attributes, we can prove his existence thus: Whatever we clearly and distinctly see to belong to the nature of a thing, that we can also with truth affirm of that thing; now to the nature of a being that has infinite attributes belongs existence, which is an attribute; therefore . . . To assert that this may well be affirmed of the idea, but not of the thing itself, is false: for the Idea does not really consist of the attribute which belongs to this being, so that that which is affirmed is [affirmed] neither of the thing, nor of that which is affirmed of the thing; so that there is a great difference between the Idea and the *Ideatum*: therefore what is affirmed of the thing is not affirmed of the Idea, and vice versa.

The first we prove thus:

> If there is an idea of God, then the cause thereof must exist *formaliter*, and contain in itself all that the idea has *objective*;
> Now there is an idea of God;
> Therefore . . .

In order to prove the first part of this argument we state the following principles, namely:

1. That the number of knowable things is infinite;
2. That a finite understanding cannot apprehend the infinite;
3. That a finite understanding, unless it is determined by something external, cannot through itself know anything; because, just as it has no power to know all things equally, so little also has it the power to begin or to commence to know this, for instance, sooner than that, or that sooner than this. Since, then, it can do neither the one nor the other it can know nothing.

The first (or the major premiss) is proved thus:

> If the imagination of man were the sole cause of his ideas, then it would be impossible that he should be able to apprehend anything, but he can apprehend something;
> Therefore . . .

The first[a] is proved by the first principle, namely, *that the knowable things are infinitely numerous*. Also, following the second principle, man cannot know all, because the human understanding is finite, and if not determined by external things to know this sooner than that, and that sooner than this, then according to the third principle it should be impossible for it to know anything.[3]

---

[a] [Instead of this paragraph B has the following: "Again, since according to the first principle the knowable things are infinite, and according to the second principle the finite understanding cannot comprehend everything, and according to the third principle it has not the power to know this sooner than that, and that sooner than this, it would be impossible for it to know anything, if it were not determined thereto by external things.—A.W.]

[3] Further, to say that this idea is a fiction, this also is false: for it is impossible to have this [idea] if it [the *ideatum*] does not exist; this is shown on pages 37–8, and we also add the following:

It is quite true that when an idea has first come to us from a particular thing, and we have generalised it *in abstracto*, then our understanding may fancy various things about it, and we can add to it many other attributes abstracted from other things. But it is impossible to do this without a prior knowledge of the things themselves from which these abstractions have been made. Once, however, it is assumed that this idea [of God] is a fiction, then all *other ideas* that we have must be fictions no less. If this is so, *whence* comes it that we find such a great difference among them? For as regards *some* we see that it is impossible they should exist; e.g., all monsters supposed to be composed of two natures, such as an animal that should be both a bird and a horse, and the like, for which it is impossible to have a place in Nature, which we find differently constituted; *other ideas* may, but need not, exist; whether, however, they exist or do not exist, their essence is always necessary; such is the idea of a triangle, and that of the love in the soul apart from the body, etc.; so that even if I at first thought that I had imagined these, I am nevertheless compelled afterwards to say

From all this the second point is proved, namely, *that the cause of a man's ideas is not his imagination but some external cause, which compels him to apprehend one thing sooner than another*, and it is no other than this, that the things whose *essentia objectiva* is in his understanding exist *formaliter*, and are nearer to him than other things. If, then, man has the idea of God, it is clear that God must exist *formaliter*, though not *eminenter*, as there is nothing more real or more excellent beside or outside him. Now, that man has the idea of God, this is clear, because he knows his attributes,[4] which attributes cannot be derived from [man] himself, because he is imperfect. And that he knows these attributes is evident from this, namely, that he knows that the infinite cannot be obtained by putting together divers finite parts; that there cannot be two infinites, but *only one*; that it is perfect and immutable, for we know that nothing seeks, of itself, its own annihilation, and also that it cannot change into anything better,[5] because it is per-

---

that they are, and would be, the same no less even if neither I nor anybody had ever thought about them. They are, consequently, not merely imagined by me, and must also have outside me a *subjectum* other than myself, without which *subjectum* they cannot be. In addition to these there is yet *a third idea*, and it is an only one; this one carries with it necessary existence, and not, like the foregoing, the mere possibility of existence: for, in the case of those, their essence was indeed necessary, but not their existence, while in its case, both its existence and its essence are necessary, and it is nothing without them. I therefore see now that the truth, essence, or existence of anything never depends on me: for, as was shown with reference to the second kind of ideas, they are what they are independently of me, whether as regards their essence alone, or as regards both essence and existence. I find this to be true also, indeed much more so, of this third unique idea; not only does it not depend on me, but on the contrary, he alone must be the *subjectum* of that which I affirm of him. Consequently, if he did not exist, I should not be able to assert anything at all about him; although this can be done in the case of other things, even when they do not exist. He must also be, indeed, the *subjectum* of all other things.

From what has been said so far it is clearly manifest that the idea of infinite attributes in the perfect being is no fiction; we shall, however, still add the following:

According to the foregoing consideration of Nature, we have so far not been able to discover more than two attributes only which belong to this all-perfect being. And these give us nothing adequate to satisfy us that this is all of which this perfect being consists, quite the contrary, we find in us *a something* which openly tells us not only of more, but of infinite perfect attributes, which must belong to this perfect being before he can be said to be perfect. And whence comes this idea of perfection? This *something* cannot be the outcome of these two [attributes]: for two can only yield two, and not an infinity. Whence then? From myself, never; else I must be able to give what I did not possess. Whence, then, but from the infinite attributes themselves which tell us *that* they are, without however telling us, at the same time, *what* they are: for only of two do we know what they are.

[4] *His attributes*; it is better [to say], because he knows what is proper to God; for these things [infinity, perfection, etc.] are no attributes of God. Without these, indeed, God could not be God, but it is not through them [that he is God], since they show nothing substantial, but are only like adjectives which require substantives or their explanation.

[5] The cause of this change would have to be either outside, or in it. It cannot be outside, because no substance which, like this, exists through itself depends on anything outside it; therefore it is not *subject to change through it.* Nor can it be in it: because no thing, much less this, desires its own undoing; all undoing comes from outside.[b]

[b] [Again, that there can be no finite substance is clear from this, because in that case it would necessarily have to have something which it had from nothing: which is impossible; for whence has it that wherein it differs from God? Certainly not from God; for he has nothing imperfect or finite, etc.: whence, therefore, but from nothing? (in B)]

fect, which it would not be in that case, or also that such a being cannot be subjected to anything outside it, since it is omnipotent, and so forth.

From all this, then, it follows clearly that we can prove both a priori and a posteriori that God exists. Better, indeed, a priori. For things which are proved in the latter way [a posteriori] must be proved through their external causes, which is a manifest imperfection in them, inasmuch as they cannot make themselves known through themselves, but only through external causes. God, however, who is the first cause of all things, and also the cause of himself [*causa sui*], makes himself known through himself. Hence one need not attach much importance to the saying of Thomas Aquinas, namely, that God could not be proved a priori because he, forsooth, has no cause.

Chapter II
What God Is

Now that we have proved above *that* God is, it is time to show *what* he is. Namely, we say that he is *a being of whom all or infinite attributes are predicated*,[6] *of which attributes every one is infinitely perfect in its kind*. Now, in order to express our views clearly, we shall premise the four following propositions:

1. That there is no finite substance,[7] but that every substance must be infinitely perfect in its kind, that is to say, that in the infinite understanding of God no substance can be more perfect than that which already exists in Nature.

2. That there are not two like substances.

3. That one substance cannot produce another.

4. That in the infinite understanding of God there is no other substance than that which is *formaliter* in Nature.

---

[6] The reason is this, since *Nothing* can have no attributes, the *All* must have all attributes; and just as *Nothing* has no attribute because it is *Nothing*, so that which is *Something* has attributes because it is *Something*. Hence, the more it is *Something*, the more attributes it must have, and consequently God being the most perfect, and all that is Anything, he must also have infinite, perfect, and all attributes.

[7] Once we can prove that there can be no *Finite Substance*, then all *substance* must without limitation belong to the divine being. We do it thus: 1. It must either have limited itself or *some other* must have limited it. It could not have done so itself, because having been infinite it would have had to change its whole essence. Nor can it be limited by another: for this again must be either finite or infinite; the former is impossible, therefore the latter; therefore it [i.e., the other thing] is God. He must, then, have made it finite because he lacked either the power or the will [to make it infinite]: but the first [supposition] is contrary to his omnipotence, the second is contrary to his goodness. 2. That *there can be no finite substance* is clear from this, namely, that, if so, it would necessarily have something which it would have from Nothing, which is impossible. For whence can it derive that wherein it differs from God? Certainly not from God, for he has nothing imperfect or finite, etc. So, whence then but from Nothing? Therefore there is no substance other than infinite. Whence it follows, *that there cannot be two like infinite substances*; for to posit such necessitates limitation. And from this, again, it follows *that one substance cannot produce another;* thus: The cause that we might

As regards the first, namely, that there is no finite substance, etc., should any one want to maintain the opposite, we would ask the following question, namely, whether this substance is finite through itself, whether it has made itself thus finite and did not want to make itself less finite; or whether it is thus finite through its cause, which cause either could not or would not give more? The first [alternative] is not true, because it is impossible that a substance should have wanted to make itself finite, especially a substance which had come into existence through itself. Therefore, I say, it is made finite by its cause, which is necessarily God. Further, if it is finite through its cause, this must be so either because its cause could not give more, or because it would not give more. That he should not have been able to give more would contradict his omnipotence;[8] that he should not have been willing to give more, when he could well do so, savours of ill-will, which is nowise in God, who is all goodness and perfection.

As regards the second, *that there are not two like substances*, we prove this on the ground that each substance is perfect in its kind; for if there were two alike they would necessarily limit one another, and would consequently not be infinite, as we have already shown before.

As to the third, namely, *that one substance cannot produce another*: should any one again maintain the opposite, we ask whether the cause, which is supposed to produce this substance, has or has not the same attributes as the produced [substance]. The latter is impossible, because something cannot come from nothing; therefore the former. And then we ask whether in the attribute which is presumed to be the cause of this produced [substance], there is just as much perfection as in the produced substance, or less, or more. Less, we say, there cannot be, for the

---

suppose to produce this substance must have the same attribute[c] as the one produced, and also either just as much perfection or more or less. The first supposition is not possible, because there would then be two like [substances]. The second also not, because in that case there would be a finite [substance]. Nor the third, because something cannot come from nothing.—Moreover, if the finite[d] came from the infinite, then the infinite[e] would also be finite, etc. Therefore one substance can not produce another. And from this, again, it follows *that all substance must exist "formaliter,"* for if it did not exist, there would be no possibility for it to come into existence.

[c] [B: attributes.]

[d] [B: infinite.]

[e] [B: the cause.]

[8] To say to this *that the nature of the thing required such [limitation] and that it could not therefore be otherwise*, that is no reply: for the nature of a thing can require nothing while it does not exist. Should you say that one may, nevertheless, see what belongs to the nature of a thing which does not exist: that is true as regards its existence, but by no means as regards its essence. And herein lies the difference between *creating* and *generating*. To create is to posit a thing *quo ad essentiam et existentiam simul* [i.e., to give a thing both essence and existence]; while in the case of generation a thing comes forth *quo ad existentiam solam* [i.e., it only receives existence]. And therefore there is now in Nature no creation but only generation. So that when God creates he creates at once the nature of the thing with the thing itself. He would therefore show ill-will if (from lack of will, and not of power) he created the thing in such a way that it should not agree with its cause in essence and existence. However, what we here call creation can really not be said ever to have taken place, and it is only mentioned to indicate what we can say about it, if we distinguish between *creating* and *generating*.

reasons given above. More, also not, we say, because in that case this second one would be finite, which is opposed to what has already been proved by us. Just as much, then; they are therefore alike, and are two like substances, which clearly conflicts with our previous demonstration. Further, that which is created is by no means produced from Nothing, but must necessarily have been produced from something existing. But that something should have come forth from this, and that it should nonetheless have this something even after it has issued from it, that we cannot grasp with our understanding. Lastly, if we would seek the cause of the substance which is the origin of the things which issue from its attribute, then it behoves us to seek also the cause of that cause, and then again the cause of that cause, *et sic in infinitum*; so that if we must necessarily stop and halt somewhere, as indeed we must, it is necessary to stop at this only substance.

As regards the fourth, *that there is no substance or attribute in the infinite understanding of God other than what exists "formaliter" in Nature*, this can be, and is, proved by us: (1) from the infinite power of God, since in him there can be no cause by which he might have been induced to create one sooner or more than another; (2) from the simplicity of his will; (3) because he cannot omit to do what is good, as we shall show afterwards; (4) because it would be impossible for that which does not now exist to come into existence, since one substance cannot produce another. And, what is more, in that case there would be more infinite substances not in existence than there are in existence, which is absurd. From all this it follows then: that of Nature all in all is predicated, and that consequently Nature consists of infinite attributes, each of which is perfect in its kind. And this is just equivalent to the definition usually given of God.

Against what we have just said, namely, that there is no thing in the infinite understanding of God but what exists *formaliter* in Nature, some want to argue in this way: If God has created all, then he can create nothing more; but that he should be able to create nothing more conflicts with his omnipotence; therefore . . .

Concerning the first, we admit that God can create nothing more. And with regard to the second, we say that we own, if God were not able to create all that could be created, then it would conflict with his omnipotence; but that is by no means the case if he cannot create what is self-contradictory; as it is, to say that he has created all, and also that he should be able to create still more. Assuredly it is a far greater perfection in God that he has created all that was in his infinite understanding than if he had not created it, or, as they say, if he had never been able to create it. But why say so much about it? Do they not themselves argue thus,[9] or must they not argue thus from God's omniscience: If God is omniscient then he can know nothing more; but that God can know nothing more is incompatible with his perfection; therefore . . . ? But if God has all in his understanding, and, owing to his infinite perfection, can know nothing more, well then, why can we not say that he has also created all that he had in his understanding, and has made it so that it exists or should exist *formaliter* in Nature?

---

[9] That is, whenever we make them argue from this admission, namely, *that God is omniscient*, then they cannot but argue thus.

Since, then, we know that all alike is in the infinite understanding of God, and that there is no cause why he should have created this sooner and more than that, and that he could have produced all things in a moment, so let us see, for once, whether we cannot use against them the same weapons which they take up against us; namely, thus:

If God can never create so much that he cannot create more, then he can never create what he can create; but that he cannot create what he can create is self-contradictory. Therefore . . .

Now the reasons why we said that all these attributes, which are in Nature, are but one single being, and by no means different things (although we can know them clearly and distinctly the one without the other, and the other without another), are these:

1. Because we have found already before that there must be an infinite and perfect being, by which nothing else can be meant than such a being of which all in all must be predicated. Why? [Because] to a being which has any essence attributes must be referred, and the more essence one ascribes to it, the more attributes also must one ascribe to it, and consequently if a being is infinite then its attributes also must be infinite, and this is just what we call a perfect[f] being.

2. Because of the unity which we see everywhere in Nature. If there were different beings in it[10] then it would be impossible for them to unite with one another.

3. Because although, as we have already seen, one substance cannot produce another, and if a substance does not exist it is impossible for it to begin to exist, we see, nevertheless, that in no substance (which we nonetheless know to exist in Nature), when considered separately, is there any necessity to be real, since existence does not pertain to its separate essence.[11] So it must necessarily follow that Nature, which results from no causes, and which we nevertheless know to exist, must necessarily be a perfect being to which existence belongs.

From all that we have so far said it is evident, then, that we posit extension as an attribute of God; and this seems not at all appropriate to a perfect being: for

---

[f] [B: an infinite.]

[10] That is, if there were different substances which were not connected in one only being, then their union would be impossible, because we see clearly that they have nothing at all in common, it is so with thought and extension of which we nevertheless consist.

[11] That is, if no substance can be other than real, and yet existence does not follow from its essence, when it is considered by itself, it follows that it is not something independent, but must be something, that is, an attribute, of another thing, namely, the one, only, and universal being. Or thus: All substance is real, and when a substance is considered by itself its existence does not follow from its essence; therefore, no existing substance can be known through itself, but it must belong to something else. That is, when with our understanding we consider "substantial" Thought and ["substantial"] Extension, then we consider them only in their essence and not as existing, that is [we do not consider] that their existence necessarily pertains to their essence. When, however, we prove [of each] that it is an attribute of God, we thereby prove a priori that it exists, and a posteriori (as regards extension alone) [we prove its existence] from the modes which must necessarily have it for their *subjectum*.

since extension is divisible, the perfect being would have to consist of parts, and this is altogether inapplicable to God, because he is a simple being. Moreover, when extension is divided it is passive, and with God (who is never passive, and cannot be affected by any other being, because he is the first efficient cause of all) this can by no means be the case.

To this we reply: (1) that "part" and "whole" are not true or real entities, but only "things of reason," and consequently there are in Nature[12] neither whole nor parts. (2) A thing composed of different parts must be such that the parts thereof, taken separately, can be conceived and understood one without another. Take, for instance, a clock which is composed of many different wheels, cords, and other things; in it, I say, each wheel, cord, etc., can be conceived and understood separately, without the composite whole being necessary thereto. Similarly also in the case of water, which consists of straight oblong particles, each part thereof can be conceived and understood, and can exist without the whole; but extension, being a substance, one cannot say of it that it has parts, since it can neither diminish nor increase, and no parts thereof can be understood apart, because by its nature it must be infinite. And that it must be such, follows from this, namely, because if it were not such, but consisted of parts, then it would not be infinite by its nature, as it is said to be; and it is impossible to conceive parts in an infinite nature, since by their nature all parts are finite.[j] Add to this still: if it consisted of different parts then it should be intelligible that supposing some parts thereof to be annihilated, extention might remain all the same, and not be annihilated together with the annihilation of some of its parts; this is clearly contradictory in what is infinite by its own nature and can never be, or be conceived, as limited or finite. Further, as regards the parts in Nature, we maintain that division, as has also been said already before, never takes place in substance, but always and only in the mode of sub-

---

[12] In Nature, that is, in "substantial" Extension; for if this were divided its nature and being would be at once annihilated, as it exists only as infinite extension, or, which comes to the same, it exists only as a whole.

But should you say: is there, in extension, no part prior to all its modes? I say, certainly not. But you may say, since there is motion in matter, it must be in some part of matter, for it cannot be in the whole, because this is infinite; and whither shall it be moved, when there is nothing outside it? Therefore it must be in a part. My answer is: Motion alone does not exist, but only motion and rest together; and this is in the whole, and must be in it, because there is no part in extension. Should you, however, say that there is, then tell me: if you divide the whole of extension then, as regards any part which you cut off from it in thought, can you also separate it in nature from all [other] parts; and supposing this has been done, I ask, what is there between the part cut off[g] and the rest? You must say, a vacuum, or another body, or something of extension itself; there is no fourth possibility. The first will not do, because there is no vacuum, something positive and yet no body; nor the second, because then there would exist a mode, which cannot be, since[h] extension as extension is without and prior to all modes. Therefore the third; and then there is no part but only the whole of extension.[i]

[g] [B: separated.]

[h] [B: therefore.]

[i] [B: but extension one and indivisible.]

[j] [B: because all the parts would have to be infinite by their nature.]

stance. Thus, if I want to divide water, I only divide the mode of substance, and not substance itself. And whether this mode is that of water or something else it is always the same.[k]

Division, then, or passivity, always takes place in the mode; thus when we say that man passes away or is annihilated, then this is understood to apply to man only insofar as he is such a composite being, and a mode of substance, and not the substance on which he depends.

Moreover, we have already stated, and we shall repeat it later, that outside God there is nothing at all, and that he is an *Immanent Cause*. Now, passivity, whenever the agent and the patient are different entities, is a palpable imperfection, because the patient must necessarily be dependent on that which has caused the passivity from outside; it has, therefore, no place in God, who is perfect. Furthermore, of such an agent who acts in himself it can never be said that he has the imperfection of a patient, because he is not affected by another; such, for instance, is the case with the understanding, which, as the philosophers also assert, is the cause of its ideas, since, however, it is an immanent cause, what right has one to say that it is imperfect, howsoever frequently it is affected by itself?[l] Lastly, since substance is [the cause] and the origin of all its modes, it may with far greater right be called an agent than a patient. And with these remarks we consider all adequately answered.

It is further objected, that there must necessarily be a first cause which sets body in motion, because when at rest it is impossible for it to set itself in motion. And since it is clearly manifest that rest and motion exist in Nature, these must, they think, necessarily result from an external cause. But it is easy for us to reply to this; for we concede that, if body were a thing existing through itself, and had no other attributes than length, breadth, and depth, then, if it really rested there would be in it no cause whereby to begin to move itself; but we have already stated before *that Nature is a being of which all attributes are predicated*, and this being so, it can be lacking in nothing wherewith to produce all that there is to be produced.

Having so far discussed what God is, we shall say but a word, as it were, about his attributes: that those which are known to us consist of two only, namely, *Thought* and *Extension*; for here we speak only of attributes which might be called the *proper attributes* of God, through which we come to know him [as he is] in himself, and not [merely] as he acts [towards things] outside himself. All else, then, that men ascribe to God beyond these two attributes, all that (if it otherwise pertains to him) must be either an "extraneous denomination," such as *that he exists through himself*, is *Eternal, One, Immutable*, etc., or, I say, has reference to his activity, such as that he is a *cause, predestines,* and *rules* all things: all which are properties of God, but give us no information as to what he is. But how and in what manner these attributes can nevertheless have a place in God we shall ex-

---

[k] [B: When, therefore, I divide water I do not divide the substance, but only that mode of the substance, which substance, however, variously modified, is always the same.]

[l] [B: And although the understanding, as the philosophers say, is a cause of its ideas, yet, since it is an immanent cause, etc.]

plain in the following chapters. But, for the better understanding of this and in further exposition thereof, we have thought it well and have decided to add the following arguments consisting of a [Dialogue].

[First] Dialogue
Between the Understanding, Love, Reason, and Desire

LOVE: I see, Brother, that both my essence and perfection depend on your perfection; and since the perfection of the object which you have conceived is your perfection, while from yours again mine proceeds, so tell me now, I pray you, whether you have conceived such a being as is supremely perfect, not capable of being limited by any other, and in which I also am comprehended.

UNDERSTANDING: I for my part consider Nature only in its totality as infinite, and supremely perfect, but you, if you have any doubts about it, ask Reason, she will tell you.

REASON: To me the truth of the matter is indubitable, for if we would limit Nature then we should, absurdly enough, have to limit it with a mere Nothing;[m] we avoid this absurdity by stating that it is *One Eternal Unity, infinite, omnipotent*, etc., that is, that Nature is infinite and that all is contained therein; and the negative of this we call Nothing.

DESIRE: Ah indeed! It is wondrously congruous to suppose that *Unity* is in keeping with the *Difference* which I observe everywhere in Nature. But how? I see that thinking substance has nothing in common with *extended substance*, and that the one limits [not] the other; and if, in addition to these substances, you want to posit yet a third one which is perfect in all respects, then look how you involve yourself in manifest contradictions; for if this third one is placed outside the first two, then it is wanting in all the attributes which belong to those two, but this can never be the case with a whole outside of which there is nothing. Moreover if this being is omnipotent and perfect, then it must be such because it has made itself, and not because another has made it; that, however, which could produce both itself and yet another besides would be even more omnipotent. And lastly, if you call it omniscient then it is necessary that it should know itself; and, at the same time, you must know that the knowledge of oneself alone is less than the knowledge of oneself together with the knowledge of other substances. All these are manifest contradictions. I would, therefore, have advised Love to rest content with what I show her, and to look about for no other things.

LOVE: What now, O dishonourable one, have you shown me but what would result in my immediate ruin. For, if I had ever united myself with what you have shown me, then from that moment I should have been persecuted by the two archenemies of the human race, namely, *Hatred* and *Remorse*, and sometimes also by

---

[m] [A and B continue: moreover under the following attributes, namely, that it is *One, Eternal, infinite through itself;* we avoid . . .]

Oblivion; and therefore I turn again to Reason only to proceed and stop the mouths of these foes.

Reason: What you say, O Desire, that there are different substances, that, I tell you, is false; for I see clearly that there is but *One, which exists through itself, and is a support to all other attributes*. And if you will refer to the material and the mental as substances, in relation to the modes which are dependent on them, why then, you must also call them modes in relation to the substance on which they depend: for they are not conceived by you as existing through themselves. And in the same way that willing, feeling, understanding, loving, etc., are different modes of that which you call a thinking substance, in which you bring together and unite all these in one,[n] so I also conclude, from your own proofs, that *Both Infinite Extension and Thought together with all other infinite attributes* (or, according to your usage, other *substances*) are only modes of the *One, Eternal, Infinite Being, who exists through himself*; and from all these we posit, as stated, *An Only One* or a *Unity* outside which nothing can be imagined to be.[o]

Desire: Methinks I see a very great confusion in this argument of yours; for, it seems you will have it that *the whole must be something outside of or apart from its parts*, which is truly absurd. For all philosophers are unanimous in saying that "whole" *is a second notion, and that it is nothing in Nature apart from human thought*. Moreover, as I gather from your example, you confuse *whole* with *cause*: for, as I say, the whole only consists of and [exists] through its parts, and so it comes that you represent the *thinking power* as a thing on which the Understanding, Love, etc., depend. But you cannot call it a *Whole*, only a *Cause of the Effects* just named by you.

Reason: I see decidedly how you muster all your friends against me, and that, after the method usually adopted by those who oppose the truth, you are designing to achieve by quibbling what you have not been able to accomplish with your fallacious reasoning. But you will not succeed in winning Love to your side by such means. Your assertion, then, is, *that the cause (since it is the Originator of the effects) must therefore be outside these*. But you say this because you only know of the *transeunt* and not of the *immanent cause*, which by no means produces anything outside itself, as is exemplified by the Understanding, which is the cause of its ideas. And that is why I called the understanding (insofar as, or because, its ideas depend on it[p]) a *cause*; and on the other hand, since it consists of its ideas, a *whole*: so also *God is both an Immanent Cause with reference to his works or creatures, and also a whole, considered from the second point of view*.

---

n [A: All which you bring to one, and make one from all these; B: to which you bring all and make them into one.]

o [B: . . . One, Eternal, self-subsisting Being in which all is one and united, and outside which unity nothing can be imagined to be.]

p [A: It depends on its ideas.]

Second Dialogue
Between
Erasmus and Theophilus
Relating Partly to the Preceding, Partly to the Following Second Part

ERASMUS: I have heard you say, Theophilus, that God is a *cause of all things*, and, at the same time, that he can be *no other* than an *Immanent* cause. Now, if he is an *immanent cause* of *all things*, how then can you call him a *remote*[q] *cause*? For, that is impossible in the case of an Immanent cause.

THEOPHILUS: When I said that God is a remote[q] cause, I only said it with reference to the things [which God has produced mediately, and not with reference to those] which God (without any other conditions beyond his mere existence) has produced immediately; but on no account did I mean to call him a remote[q] cause absolutely: as you might also have clearly gathered from my remarks. For, I also said that in some respects we can call him a remote cause.

ERASMUS: I understand now adequately what you want to say; but I note also that you have said, *that the effect of the immanent cause remains united with its cause in such a way that together they constitute a whole.* Now, if this is so, then, methinks, God cannot be an immanent cause. For, if he and that which is produced by him together form a whole, then you ascribe to God at one time more essence than at another time. I pray you, remove these doubts for me.

THEOPHILUS: If, Erasmus, you want to extricate yourself from this confusion, then mark well what I am going to tell you now. The essence of a thing does not increase through its union with another thing with which it constitutes a whole; on the contrary, the first remains unchanged. I will give you an illustration, so that you may understand me the better. An image-carver has made from wood various forms after the likeness of the parts of the human body; he takes one of these, which has the form of a human breast, joins it to another, which has the form of a human head, and of these two he makes a whole, which represents the upper part of a human body; would you therefore say that the essence of the head has increased because it has been joined to the breast? That would be erroneous, because it is the same that it was before. For the sake of greater clearness let me give you another illustration, namely, an idea that I have of a triangle, and another resulting from an extension of one of the angles, which extended or extending angle is necessarily equal to the two interior opposite angles, and so forth. These, I say, have produced a new idea, namely, that the three angles of the triangle are equal to two right angles. This idea is so connected with the first, that it can neither be, nor be conceived without the same.[r] Mark well now that although the

---

q [B: prior.]

r [A continues: And of all ideas which any one has we make a whole, or (which is the same) a thing of reason, which we call *Understanding*.]

new idea is joined to the preceding one, the essence of the preceding idea does not undergo any change in consequence; on the contrary, it remains without the slightest change. The same you may also observe in every idea which produces love in itself: this love in no way adds to the essence of the idea. But why multiply illustrations? since you can see it clearly in the subject which I have been illustrating and which we are discussing now. I have distinctly stated that all attributes, which depend on no other cause, and whose definition requires no genus pertain to the essence of God; and since the created things are not competent to establish an attribute, they do not increase the essence of God, however intimately they become united to him. Add to this, that "whole" is but a thing of Reason, and does not differ from the general except in this alone that the general results from various Disconnected individuals, the Whole, from various United individuals; also in this, that the General only comprises parts of the same kind, but the Whole, parts both the same and different in kind.[s]

ERASMUS: So far as this is concerned you have satisfied me. But, in addition to this, you have also said, that *the effect of the inner cause cannot perish so long as its cause lasts*; this, I well see, is certainly true, but if this is so, then how can God be an inner cause of all things, seeing that many things perish? After your previous distinction you will say, that *God is really a cause of the effects which he has produced immediately, without any other conditions except his attributes alone; and that these cannot perish so long as their cause endures; but that you do not call God an inner cause of the effects whose existence does not depend on him immediately, but which have come into being through some other thing, except insofar as their causes do not operate, and cannot operate, without God, nor also outside him,* and that for this reason also, since they are not produced immediately by God, they can perish. But this does not satisfy me. For I see that you conclude, that the human understanding is immortal, because it is a product which God has produced in himself. Now it is impossible that more than the attributes of God should have been necessary in order to produce such an understanding; for, in order to be a being of such supreme perfection, it must have been created from eternity, just like all other things which depend immediately on God. And I have heard you say so, if I am not mistaken. And this being so, how will you reconcile this without leaving over any difficulties?

THEOPHILUS: It is true, Erasmus, that the things (for the existence of which no other thing is required, except the attributes of God) which have been created immediately by him have been created from eternity. It is to be remarked, however, that although in order that a thing may exist there is required a special modification and a thing beside the attributes of God, for all that, God does not cease to be able to produce a thing immediately. For, of the necessary things which are required to bring things into existence, some are there in order that they should produce the thing, and others in order that the thing should be capable of being produced. For example, I want to have light in a certain room; I kindle a light,

---

[s] [B: . . . the general results from various unconnected individuals of the same kind; but the whole from various connected individuals different as well as the same in kind.]

and this lights up the room through itself; or I open a window [shutter], now this act of opening does not itself give light, but still it brings it about that the light can enter the room. Likewise in order to set a body in motion another body is required that shall have all the motion that is to pass from it to the other. But in order to produce in us an idea of God there is no need for another special thing that shall have what is to be produced in us, but only such a body in *Nature* whose idea is necessary in order to represent God immediately. This you could also have gathered from my remarks: for I said that God is only known through himself, and not through something else. However, I tell you this, that so long as we have not such a clear idea of God as shall unite us with him in such a way that it will not let us love anything beside him, we cannot truly say that we are united with God, so as to depend immediately on him. If there is still anything that you may have to ask, leave it for another time; just now circumstances require me to attend to other matters. Farewell.

ERASMUS: Nothing at present, but I shall ponder what you have just told me till the next opportunity. God be with you.

CHAPTER III
That God Is a Cause of All Things

We shall now begin to consider those attributes [of God] which we called *Propria*.[13] And, first of all, how God *is a cause of all things*.

Now, we have already said above *that one substance cannot produce another*; and *that God is a being of whom all attributes are predicated*; whence it clearly follows that all other things can by no means be, or be understood, apart from or outside him. Wherefore we may say with all reason *that God is a cause of all things*.

As it is usual to divide the efficient cause in eight divisions, let me, then, inquire how and in what sense *God* is a cause.

First, then, we say that he is an *emanative* or *productive cause of his works*; and, insofar as there is activity, *an active or operating cause*, which we regard as one and the same, because they involve each other.

Secondly, he is an *immanent*, and not a *transeunt cause*, since all that he produces is within himself, and not outside him, because there is nothing outside him.

Thirdly, God is a *free cause*, and not a *natural* cause, as we shall make clear and manifest when we come to consider *whether God can omit to do what he does*, and then it will also be explained wherein *true freedom* consists.

---

[13] The [attributes] following are called *Propria*, because they are only Adjectives, which cannot be understood without their Substantives. That is to say, without them God would indeed be no God, but still it is not they that constitute God; for they reveal nothing of the character of a Substance, through which alone God exists.

Fourthly, God is a cause *through himself*, and not *by accident*; this will become more evident from the discussion on Predestination.

Fifthly, God is a *principal cause of his works which he has created immediately*, such as movement in matter, etc.; in which there is no place for a subsidiary [instrumental] cause, since this is confined to particular things; as when he dries the sea by means of a strong wind, and so forth in the case of all particular things in Nature.

The subsidiary provoking cause is not [found] *in God*, because there is nothing outside him to incite him. The *predisposing cause*, on the other hand, is his perfection itself; through it he is a cause of himself, and, consequently, of all other things.

Sixthly, God alone is *the first or Initial cause*, as is evident from our foregoing proof.

Seventhly, God is also *a Universal cause*, but only insofar as he produces various things; otherwise this can never be predicated of him, as he needs no one in order to produce any results.

Eighthly, God is the *proximate cause* of the things that are infinite, and immutable, and which we assert to have been created immediately by him, but, in one sense, he is the remote cause of all particular things.

Chapter IV
On God's Necessary Activity

We deny that God can omit to do what he does, and we shall also prove it when we treat of Predestination; when we will show that all things necessarily depend on their causes. But, in the second place, this conclusion also follows from the perfection of God; for it is true, beyond a doubt, *that God can make everything just as perfect as it is conceived in his Idea*; and just as things that are conceived by him cannot be conceived by him more perfectly than he conceives them, so all things can be made by him so perfect that they cannot come from him in a more perfect condition. Again, when we conclude that God could not have omitted to do what he has done, we deduce this from his perfection; because, in God, it would be an imperfection to be able to omit to do what he does; we do not, however, suppose that there is a subsidiary provoking cause in God that might have moved him to action, for then he were no God.

But now, again, there is the controversy whether, namely, of all that is in his Idea, and which he can realise so perfectly, whether, I say, he could omit to realise anything, and whether such an omission would be a perfection in him. Now, we maintain that, since all that happens is done by God, it must therefore necessarily be predetermined by him, otherwise he would be mutable, which would be a great imperfection in him. And as this predetermination by him must be from eternity, in which eternity there is no before or after, it follows irresistibly that God could never have predetermined things in any other way than that in which they are determined now, and have been from eternity, and that God could not have been either before or without these determinations. Further, if God should omit to do anything, then he must either have some cause for it, or not; if he has, then it is necessary that he should omit doing it; if he has not, then it is necessary that he should not omit to do it; this is self-evident. Moreover, in a created thing it is a perfection to exist and to have been produced by God, for, of all imperfection, nonexistence is the greatest imperfection; and since God desires the welfare and perfection of all things, it would follow that if God desired that a certain thing should not exist, then the welfare and perfection of this thing must be supposed to consist in its nonexistence, which is self-contradictory. That is why we deny *that God can omit to do what he does.* Some regard this as blasphemy, and as a belittling of God; but such an assertion results from a misapprehension of what constitutes *true freedom*; this is by no means what they think it is, namely, the ability to do or to omit to do something good or evil; but *true freedom is only, or no other than* [the status of being] *the first cause*, which is in no way constrained or coerced by anything else, and which through its perfection alone is the cause of all perfection; consequently, if God could omit to do this, he would not be perfect: for the ability to omit doing some good, or accomplishing some perfection in what he does, can have no place in him, except through defect.

That God alone is the only free cause is, therefore, clear not only from what has just been said, but also from this, namely, that there is no external cause outside him to force or constrain him; all this is not the case with created things.

Against this it is argued thus: The good is only good because God wills it, and this being so, he can always bring it about that evil should be good. But such reasoning is about as conclusive as if I said: It is because God wills to be God that he is God; therefore it is in his power not to be God, which is absurdity itself. Furthermore, when people do anything, and they are asked why they do it, their answer is, because it is what justice demands. If the question is then put, why justice, or rather the first cause of all that is just, makes such a demand, then the answer must be, because justice wills it so. But, dear me, I think to myself, could Justice really be other than just? By no means, for then it could not be Justice. Those, however, who say that God does all that he does because it is good in itself, these, I say, may possibly think that they do not differ from us. But that is far from being the case, since they suppose that there is something before God to which he has duties or obligations, namely, a cause [through] which [God] desires that this shall be good, and, again, that that shall be just.

Then comes the further controversy, namely, whether God, supposing all things had been created by him in some other way from eternity, or had been ordered and predetermined to be otherwise than they now are, whether, I say, he would then be just as perfect as he is now. To this it may serve as an answer, that if Nature had, from all eternity, been made different from what it is now, then, from the standpoint of those who ascribe to God will and understanding, it would necessarily follow that God had a different will and a different understanding then, in consequence of which he would have made it different; and so we should be compelled to think that God has a different character now from what he had then, and had a different character then from what he has now; so that, if we assume he is most perfect now, we are compelled to say that he would not have been so had he created all things differently. All these things, involving as they do palpable absurdities, can in no way be attributed to God, who now, in the past, and unto all eternity, is, has been, and will remain immutable. We prove this also from the definition that we have given of a free cause, which is not one that can do or omit to do anything, but is only such as is not dependent on anything else, so that whatever God does is done and carried into effect by him as the freest cause. If, therefore, he had formerly made things different from what they are now, it would needs follow that he was at one time imperfect, which is false. For, since God is the first cause of all things, there must be something in him, through which he does what he does, and omits not to do it. Since we say that *Freedom* does not consist in [having the choice of] doing or not doing something, and since we have also shown that that which makes him [God] do anything can be nothing else than his own perfection, we conclude *that, had it not been that his perfection made him do all this, then the things would not exist, and could not come into existence, in order to be what they are now.* This is just like saying: *if God were imperfect then things would be different from what they are now.*

So much as regards the first [attribute]; we shall now pass on to the second attribute, which we call a *proprium* of God, and see what we have to say about it, and so on to the end.

Chapter V
On Divine Providence

The second attribute, which we call a *proprium* [of God] is his Providence, which to us is nothing else than the *striving* which we find in the whole of Nature and in individual things to maintain and preserve their own existence. For it is manifest that no thing could, through its own nature, seek its own annihilation, but, on the contrary, that every thing has in itself a striving to preserve its condition, and to improve itself. Following these definitions of ours we, therefore, posit a *general* and a *special providence. The general* [*providence*] is that through which all things are produced and sustained insofar as they are parts of the whole of Nature. The *special providence* is the striving of each thing separately to preserve its existence [each thing, that is to say], considered not as a part of Nature, but as a whole [by itself]. This is explained by the following example: All the limbs of man are provided for, and cared for, insofar as they are parts of man, this is *general* providence; while *special* [*providence*] is the striving of each separate limb (as a whole in itself, and not as a part of man) to preserve and maintain its own well-being.

Chapter VI
On Divine Predestination

The third attribute, we say, is divine predestination.

1. We proved before that God cannot omit to do what he does; that he has, namely, made everything so perfect that it cannot be more perfect.

2. And, at the same time, that without him nothing can be, or be conceived.

It remains to be seen now whether there are in Nature any accidental things, that is to say, whether there are any things which may happen and may also not happen. Secondly, whether there is any thing concerning which we cannot ask why it is.

Now that there are no accidental things we prove thus: That which has no cause to exist cannot possibly exist; that which is accidental has no cause: therefore . . .

The first is beyond all dispute; the second we prove thus: If any thing that is accidental has a definite and certain cause why it should exist, then it must necessarily exist; but that it should be both accidental and necessary at the same time, is self-contradictory; Therefore . . .

Perhaps some one will say, that *an accidental thing* has indeed no definite and certain cause, but an accidental one. If this should be so, it must be so either *in sensu diviso* or *in sensu composito*, that is to say, either the existence of the cause is accidental, and not its being a cause; or it is accidental that a certain thing (which indeed must necessarily exist in Nature) should be the cause of the occurrence of that accidental thing. However, both the one and the other are false.

For, as regards the first, if the accidental something is accidental because [the existence of] its cause is accidental, then that cause must also be accidental, because the cause which has produced it is also accidental, *et sic in infinitum*.

And since it has already been proved, *that all things depend on one single cause*, this cause would therefore also have to be accidental: which is manifestly false.

As regards the second: if the cause were no more compelled to produce one thing than another, that is, [if the cause were no more compelled] to produce this something than not to produce it, then it would be impossible at once both that it should produce it and that it should not produce it, which is quite contradictory.

Concerning the second [question raised] above, *whether there is no thing in Nature about which one cannot ask why it is*, this remark of ours shows that we have to inquire through what cause a thing is real; for if this [cause] did not exist it were impossible that the thing should exist. Now, we must look for this cause either in the thing or outside the thing. If, however, any one should ask for a rule whereby to conduct this inquiry, we say that none whatever seems necessary. For if existence pertains to the nature of a thing, then it is certain that we must not look outside it for its cause; but if such is not the case, then we must always look outside the thing for its cause. Since, however, the first pertains to God alone, it is thereby proved (as we have already also proved before) that God alone is the first cause of all things. From this it is also evident that this or that will of man (since the existence of the will does not pertain to its essence) must also have an external cause, by which it is necessarily caused; that this is so is also evident from all that we have said in this chapter; and it will be still more evident when, in the second part, we come to consider and discuss the freedom of man.

Against all this others object: how is it possible that God, who is said to be supremely perfect, and the sole cause, disposer, and provider of all, nevertheless permits such *confusion* to be seen everywhere in Nature? Also, *why has he not made man so as not to be able to sin?*

Now, in the first place, it cannot be rightly said that there is *confusion in Nature*, since nobody knows all the causes of things so as to be able to judge accordingly. This objection, however, originates in this kind of ignorance, namely, that they have set up general Ideas, with which, they think, particular things must agree if they are to be perfect. These *Ideas*, they state, are in the understanding of God, as many of *Plato's* followers have said, namely, that these *general Ideas* (such as Rational, Animal, and the like) *have been created by God*; and although those who follow *Aristotle* say, indeed, that these things are not *real* things, only things of Reason, they nevertheless regard them frequently as [real] things, since they have clearly said that his providence does not extend to particular things, but only to kinds; for example, God has never exercised his providence over Bucephalus, etc., but only over the whole genus Horse. They say also that God has no knowledge of particular and transient things, but only of the general, which, in their opinion, are imperishable. We have, however, rightly considered this to be due to their ignorance. For it is precisely the particular things, and they alone, that have a cause, and not the general, because they are nothing.

God then is the cause of, and providence over, particular things only. If particular things had to conform to some other Nature, then they could not conform to their own, and consequently could not be what they truly are. For example, if God had made all human beings like Adam before the fall, then indeed he would only have created Adam, and no Paul nor Peter; but no, it is just perfection in God, that he gives to all things, from the greatest to the least, their essence, or, to express it better, that he has all things perfectly in himself.

As regards the other [objection], *why God has not made mankind so that they should not sin*, to this it may serve [as an answer], that whatever is said about sin is only said with reference to us, that is, as when we compare two things with each other, or [consider one thing] from different points of view. For instance, if someone has made a clock precisely in order to strike and to show the hours, and the mechanism quite fulfils the aims of its maker, then we say that it is good, but if it does not do so, then we say that it is bad, notwithstanding that even then it might still be good if only it had been his intention to make it irregular and to strike at wrong times.

We say then, in conclusion, that Peter must, as is necessary, conform to the Idea of Peter, and not to the Idea of *Man*; good and evil, or sin, these are only modes of thought, and by no means things, or anything that has reality, as we shall very likely show yet more fully in what follows. For all things and works which are in Nature are perfect.

Chapter VII
On the Attributes Which Do Not Pertain to God

Here we shall take up the consideration of those attributes[14] which are commonly attributed to God, but which, nevertheless, do not pertain to him; as also of those through which it is sought to prove the existence of God, though in vain; and also of the rules of accurate definition.

For this purpose, we shall not trouble ourselves very much about the ideas that people commonly have of God, but we shall only inquire briefly into what the Philosophers can tell us about it. Now these have defined God as *a being existing through or of himself, cause of all things, Omniscient, Almighty, eternal, simple, infinite, the highest good, of infinite compassion,* etc. But before we approach this inquiry, let us just see what admissions they make to us.

In the first place, they say that it is impossible to give a true or right definition of God, because, according to their opinion, there can be no definition except *per genus et differentiam*, and as God is not a species of any genus, he cannot be defined rightly, or according to the rules.

In the second place, they say that God cannot be defined, because the definition must describe the thing itself and also positively; while, according to their standpoint, our knowledge of God cannot be of a positive, but only of a negative kind; therefore no proper definition can be given of God.

They also say, besides, that God can never be proved a priori, because he has no cause, but only by way of probability, or from his effects.

Since by these assertions of theirs they admit sufficiently that their knowledge of God is very little and slight, let us now proceed to examine their definition.

In the first place, we do not see that they give us in it any *attribute* or attributes through which it can be known what the thing (God) is, but only some *propria* or

---

[14] As regards the attributes of which God consists, they are only infinite substances, each of which must of itself be infinitely perfect. That this must necessarily be so, we are convinced by clear and distinct reasons. It is true, however, that up to the present only two of all these infinites are known to us through their own essence; and these are thought and extension. All else that is commonly ascribed to God is not any attribute of his, but only certain modes which may be attributed to him either in consideration of all, that is, *all* his attributes, or in consideration of *one* attribute. In consideration of *all* [it is said], for instance, that he is eternal, self-subsisting, infinite, cause of all things, immutable. In consideration of *one* [it is said], for instance, that he is omniscient, wise, etc., which pertains to thought, and, again, that he is omnipresent, fills all, etc., which pertains to extension.

properties which do, indeed, belong to a thing, but never explain what the thing is. For although *self-subsisting, being the cause of all things, highest good, eternal and immutable*, etc., are peculiar to God alone, nevertheless, from those properties we cannot know what that being, to whom these properties pertain, is, and what attributes he has.

It is now also time for us to consider the things which they ascribe to God, and which do not, however, pertain to him,[15] such as *omniscient, merciful, wise*, and so forth, which things, since they are only certain modes of the thinking thing, and can by no means be, or be understood without the substances whose modes they are, can, consequently, also not be attributed to him, who *is a Being subsisting without the aid of anything, and solely through himself.*

Lastly, they call him *the highest good;* but if they understand by it something different from what they have already said, namely, that God *is immutable, and a cause of all things*, then they have become entangled in their own thought, or are unable to understand themselves. This is the outcome of their misconception of good and evil, for they believe that man himself, and not God, is the cause of his sins and wickedness—which, according to what we have already proved, cannot be the case, else we should be compelled to assert that man is also the cause of himself. However, this will appear yet more evident when we come to consider the will of man.

It is necessary that we should now unravel their specious arguments wherewith they seek to excuse their ignorance in Theology.

First of all, then, they say *that a correct definition must consist of a "genus" and "differentia."* Now, although all the Logicians admit this, I do not know where they get it from. And, to be sure, if this must be true, then we can know nothing whatever. For if it is through a definition consisting of *genus* and *differentia* that we can first get to know a thing perfectly, then we can never know perfectly the highest *genus*, which has no *genus* above it. Now then: If the highest *genus*, which is the cause of our knowledge of all other things, is not known, much less, then, can the other things be understood or known which are explained by that *genus*. However, since we are free, and do not consider ourselves in any way tied to their assertions, we shall, in accordance with true logic, propose other rules of definition, namely, on the lines of our division of Nature.

Now we have already seen that the attributes (or, as others call them, substances) are things, or, to express ourselves better and more aptly, [constitute] a being which subsists through itself, and therefore makes itself known and reveals itself through itself.

As to the other things, we see that they are but modes of the attributes, without which also they can neither be, nor be understood. Consequently definitions must be of two kinds (or sorts):

1. The first, namely, are those of attributes, which pertain to a self-subsisting being, these need no genus, or anything, through which they might be better un-

---

[15] That is to say, when he is considered as all that he is, or with regard to all his attributes; *see* on this point page 56 *n.* 14.

derstood or explained: for, since they exist as attributes of a self-subsisting being, they also become known through themselves.

2. The second [kind of definitions] are those [of things] which do not exist through themselves, but only through the attributes whose modes they are, and through which, as their *genus*, they must be understood.

And this is [all that need be said] concerning their statement about definitions. As regards the other [assertion], namely, that God can [not] be known by us adequately, this has been sufficiently answered by D. des Cartes in his answers to the objections relating to these things, page 39.

And the third [assertion], namely, that God cannot be proved a priori, has also already been answered by us. Since God is the cause of himself, it is enough that we prove him through himself, and such a proof is also much more conclusive than the a posteriori proof, which generally rests only on external causes.

Chapter VIII
On *Natura Naturans*

Here, before we proceed to something else, we shall briefly divide the whole of Nature—namely, into *Natura naturans* and *Natura naturata*. By *Natura naturans* we understand a being that we conceive clearly and distinctly through itself, and without needing anything beside itself (like all the attributes which we have so far described), that is, God. The Thomists likewise understand God by it, but their *Natura naturans* was a being (so they called it) beyond all substances.

The *Natura naturata* we shall divide into two, a general, and a particular. The *general* consists of all the modes which depend immediately on God, of which we shall treat in the following chapter; the *particular* consists of all the particular things which are produced by the general mode. So that the *Natura naturata* requires some substance in order to be well understood.

Chapter IX
On *Natura Naturata*

Now, as regards the *general Natura naturata*, or the modes, or creations which depend on, or have been created by, God immediately, of these we know no more than two, namely, *motion* in matter,[16] and the *understanding* in the thinking thing.

---

[16] *Note.*—What is here said about motion in matter is not said seriously. For the Author still intends to discover the cause thereof, as he has already done to some extent a posteriori. But it can stand just as it is, because nothing is based upon it, or dependent thereon. [B omits this note.]

These, then, we say, have been from all eternity, and to all eternity will remain immutable. A work truly as great as becomes the greatness of the work-master.

All that specially concerns *Motion*, such as that it *has been from all eternity, and to all eternity will remain immutable; that it is infinite in its kind; that it can neither be, nor be understood through itself,* but only by means of Extension,—all this, I say, since it [Motion] more properly belongs to a treatise on Natural Science rather than here, we shall not consider in this place, but we shall only say this about it, that it is *a Son, Product, or Effect* created immediately by God.

As regards the *Understanding* in the thinking thing, this, like the first, is also a *Son, Product, or immediate Creation* of God, also created by him from all eternity, and remaining immutable to all eternity. It has but one function, namely, to understand clearly and distinctly all things at all times; which produces invariably an infinite or most perfect satisfaction, which cannot omit to do what it does. Although what we have just said is sufficiently self-evident, still, we shall prove it more clearly afterwards in our account of the Affects of the Soul, and shall therefore say no more about it here.

Chapter X
What Good and Evil Are

In order to explain briefly what good and evil are in themselves, we shall begin thus:

Some things are in our understanding and not in Nature, and so they are also only our own creation, and their purpose is to understand things distinctly: among these we include all relations, which have reference to different things, and these we call *Entia Rationis* [things of reason]. Now the question is, whether good and evil belong to the *Entia Rationis* or to the *Entia Realia* [real things]. But since good and evil are only relations, it is beyond doubt that they must be placed among the *Entia Rationis*; for we never say that something is good except with reference to something else which is not so good, or is not so useful to us as some other thing. Thus we say that a man is bad, only in comparison with one who is better, or also that an apple is bad, in comparison with another which is good or better.

All this could not possibly be said, if that which is better or good, in comparison with which it [the bad] is so called, did not exist.

Therefore, when we say that something is good, we only mean that it conforms well to the general Idea which we have of such things. But, as we have already said before, the things must agree with their particular Ideas, whose essence must be a perfect essence, and not with the general [Ideas], since in that case they would not exist.

As to confirming what we have just said, the thing is clear to us; but still, to conclude our remarks, we will add yet the following proofs:

All things which are in Nature, are either things or actions. Now good and evil are neither things nor actions. Therefore good and evil do not exist in Nature.

For, if good and evil are things or actions, then they must have their definitions. But good and evil (as, for example, the goodness of Peter and the wickedness of Judas) have no definitions apart from the essence of Judas or Peter, because this alone exists in Nature, and they cannot be defined without their essence. Therefore, as above—it follows that good and evil are not things or actions which exist in Nature.

SECOND PART
On Man
And What Pertains to Him

Preface

Having, in the first part, discoursed on God, and on the universal and infinite things, we shall proceed now, in the second part, to the treatment of particular and finite things; though not of all, since they are innumerable, but we shall only treat of those which concern man; and, in the first place, we shall consider here what man is, insofar as he consists of certain modes (contained in the two attributes which we have remarked in God). I say of certain *modes*, for I by no means think that man, insofar as he consists of spirit, soul,[1] or body, is a *substance*. Because, already at the beginning of this book, we proved (1) that no substance can

---

[1] 1. Our soul is either a *substance* or a mode; it is not a substance, because we have already shown that there can be no finite substance; it is therefore a *mode*.

2. Being a mode, then, it must be such either of "substantial" *extension* or of "substantial" *thought*; not of *extension*, because, etc.; therefore of *thought*.

3. "Substantial" *thought*, since it cannot be finite, is infinitely perfect in its kind, and an attribute of God.

4. *Perfect thought* must have a *Knowledge*, Idea, or mode of thought of all and everything *that is real*, of substances as well as of modes, without exception.

5. We say, *that is real*, because we are not speaking here of a Knowledge, Idea, etc., which completely knows the nature of all things as involved in their essence, apart from their individual existence, but only of the Knowledge, Idea, etc., of the particular things which are constantly coming into existence.

6. This Knowledge, Idea, etc., of each particular thing which happens to be real is, we say, the *soul* of this particular thing.

7. All and sundry particular things that are real, have become such through motion and rest, and this is true of all them does of "substantial" extension which we call *bodies*.

8. The differences among these result solely from the varying proportions of motion and rest, through which this is *so*, and not *so*—this is *this*, and not *that*.

9. From such proportion of motion and rest comes also the existence of *our body*; of which,

have a beginning; (2) that one substance cannot produce another; and lastly (3), that there cannot be two like substances.

As man has not been in existence from eternity, is finite, and is like many men, he can be no substance; so that all that he has of thought are only *modes of the attribute thought* which we have attributed to God. And, again, all that he has of form, motion, and other things, are likewise [modes] of *the other attribute which is attributed by us to God.*

And although from this, [namely,] that the nature of man can neither be, nor be understood without the attributes which we ourselves admit to constitute substance, some try to prove that man is a substance, yet this has no other ground than false suppositions. For, since the nature of matter or body existed before the form of this human body existed, that nature cannot be peculiar to the human body, because it is clear that during the time when man was not, it could never belong to the nature of man.

And what they set up as a fundamental principle, [namely,] *that that pertains to the nature of a thing, without which the thing can neither be, nor be understood,* we deny. For we have already shown *that without God no thing can be or be understood.* That is, God must first be and be understood before these particular things can be and be understood. We have also shown that *genera* do not belong to the nature of definition, but that only such things as cannot exist without others, can also not be understood without these. This being so, what kind of a rule shall we, then, state, whereby it shall be known what belongs to the nature of a thing?

---

consequently, no less than of all other things there must be a Knowledge, an Idea, etc., in the thinking thing, and hence at once also *our soul.*

10. This body of ours, however, had a different proportion of motion and rest when it was an unborn embryo; and in due course, when we are dead, it will have a different proportion again; nonetheless there was at that time [before our birth], and there will be then [after death] an idea, knowledge, etc., of our body in the thinking thing, just as there is now; but by no means the same [idea, etc.], since it is now differently proportioned as regards motion and rest.

11. To produce, in "substantial" thought, such an idea, knowledge, mode of thought as ours now is, what is required is, not anybody you please (then it would have to be known differently from what is it), but just such a body having this proportion of motion and rest, and no other: for as the body is, so is the Soul, Idea, Knowledge, etc.

12. As soon, then, as a body has and retains this proportion [which our body has], say e.g., of 1 to 3, then that soul and that body will be like ours now are, being indeed constantly subject to change, but to none so great that it will exceed the limits of 1 to 3; though as much as it changes, so much also does the soul always change.

13. And this change in us, resulting from other bodies acting upon us, cannot take place without the soul, which always changes correspondingly, becoming aware of the change. And [the consciousness of] this change is really what we call feeling.

14. But when other bodies act so violently upon ours that the proportion of motion [to rest] cannot remain 1 to 3, that means death, and the annihilation of the Soul, since this is only an Idea, Knowledge, etc., of this body having this proportion of motion and rest.

15. Still, since it [the soul] is a mode in the thinking substance it could also know, and love this [substance] as well as that of extension, and by uniting with substances (which remain always the same) it could make itself eternal.

Well, the rule is this: That belongs to the nature of a thing, without which the thing can neither be, nor be understood; not merely so, however, but in such wise that the judgment must be convertible, that is, that the predicate can neither be, nor be understood without the thing. Of these modes, then, of which man consists, we shall begin to treat at the commencement of the following first chapter.

Chapter I
On Opinion, Belief, and Knowledge

To begin our consideration of the modes[2] of which man consists, we shall state, (1) what they are, (2) their effects, and (3) their cause.

As regards the first, let us begin with those that are first known to us: namely, *certain ideas* or *the consciousness of the knowledge of ourselves, and of the things which are outside us.*

Now we get these ideas[3] (1) either merely through belief (which belief arises either from experience, or from hearsay), (2) or, in the second place, we acquire them by way of a true belief, (3) or, thirdly, we have them as the result of clear and distinct conception.

The first is commonly subject to error.

The second and third, however, although they differ from one another, cannot err.

To make all this somewhat clearer and more intelligible, we shall give the following illustration taken from the Rule of Three.

Some one[4] has just heard it said that if, in the Rule of Three, the second number is multiplied by the third, and then divided by the first, a fourth number will then be obtained which has the same relation to the third as the second has to the first. And notwithstanding the possibility that he who put this before him might have been lying, he still made his calculations accordingly, and he did so without having acquired any more knowledge of the Rule of Three than a blind man has of colour, so that whatever he may have said about it, he simply repeated as a parrot repeats what it has been taught.

Another,[5] having a more active intelligence, is not so easily satisfied with mere hearsay, but tests it by some actual calculations, and when he finds that they agree

---

[2] The modes of which Man consists are ideas, differentiated as Opinion, true Belief, and clear and distinct Knowledge, produced by objects, each in its own way.

[3] These ideas of this Belief are put first on page 63; here and there they are also called opinion, which they really are.

[4] This one merely forms an opinion, or, as is commonly said, believes through hearsay only. [B omits this note.]

[5] This one thinks or believes not simply through hearsay, but from experience: and these are the two kinds of people who have [mere] opinions. [B omits this note.]

with it, then he gives credence to it. But we have rightly said that this one also is subject to error; for how can he possibly be sure that his experience of a few particulars can serve him as a rule for all?

A third,[6] who is not satisfied with hearsay, because it may deceive, nor with experience of a few particulars, because this cannot possibly serve as a rule, examines it in the light of true Reason, which, when properly applied, has never deceived. This then tells him that on account of the nature of the proportion in these numbers it had to be so, and could not happen otherwise.

A fourth,[7] however, having the clearest knowledge of all, has no need of hearsay, or experience, or the art of reasoning, because by his penetration he sees the proportion in all such calculations immediately.

Chapter II
What Opinion, Belief, and Clear Knowledge Are

We come now to the consideration of the effects of the different grades of knowledge, of which we spoke in the preceding chapter, and, in passing as it were, we shall explain what Opinion, Belief, and clear Knowledge are.

The first [kind of knowledge], then, we call *Opinion*, the second *Belief*, but the third is what we call *clear Knowledge*.

We call it *Opinion* because it is subject to error, and has no place when we are sure of anything, but only in those cases when we are said to guess and to surmise. The second we call *Belief*, because the things we apprehend only with our reason are not seen by us, but are only known to us through the conviction of our understanding that it must be so and not otherwise. But we call that *clear Knowledge* which comes, not from our being convinced by reasons, but from our feeling and enjoying the thing itself, and it surpasses the others by far.

After these preliminary remarks let us now turn to their effects. Of these we say this, namely, that from the first proceed all the "passions" which are opposed to good reason; from the second, the good desires; and from the third, true and sincere Love, with all its offshoots.

We thus maintain that Knowledge is the proximate cause of all the "passions" in the soul. For we consider it once for all impossible that any one, who neither thinks nor knows in any of the preceding ways and modes, should be capable of being incited to Love or Desire or any other mode of Will.

---

[6] This one is certain through true belief, which can never deceive him, and he is properly called a believer.

[7] But this last one is never [merely] of opinion, nor a [mere] believer, but sees the things themselves, not through something else, but through the things themselves.

Chapter III
The Origin of Passion. Passion Due to Opinion

Here, then, let us see how, as we have said, the passions derive their origin from opinion. To do this well and intelligently we shall take some special ones, and prove what we say by using these as illustrations.

Let *Surprise*, then, be the first. This is found in one who knows a thing after the first manner [of Knowledge]; for, since from a few particulars he draws a conclusion which is general, he stands surprised whenever he sees anything that goes against his conclusion;[8] like one who, having never seen any sheep except with short tails, is surprised at the sheep from Morocco which have long ones. So it is related of a peasant that he had persuaded himself that beyond his fields there were no others, but when he happened to miss a cow, and was compelled to go and look for her far away, he was surprised at the great number of fields that there were beyond his few acres. And, to be sure, this must also be the case with many Philosophers who have persuaded themselves that beyond this field or little globe, on which they are, there are no more [worlds] (because they have seen no others). But surprise is never felt by him who draws true inferences. This is the first.

The second is *Love*.[a] Since this arises either from true ideas, or from opinion, or, lastly, from hearsay only, we shall see first how [it arises] from opinion, then

---

[8] This should on no account be taken to mean that a formal inference must always precede astonishment; on the contrary, it exists also without that, namely, when we tacitly believe that a thing is [always] so, and not different from what we are accustomed to see it, hear or think about it, etc. For example, Aristotle says, *a dog is a barking animal*, therefore he concludes, whatever barks is a dog; but when a peasant says *a dog*, he means tacitly just the same that Aristotle did with his definition. So that when the peasant hears the barking he says, *a dog*; and so, if they had heard some other kind of animal bark, the peasant, who had drawn no [explicit] inference, would stand just as astonished as Aristotle, who had drawn an inference. Furthermore, when we become aware of something about which we had never thought before, it is not really such the like of which, whether as a whole or in part, we have not known before, only it is not so constituted in all respects, or we have never been affected by it in the same way, etc.

[a] [The substance of the next three paragraphs is given in the following simpler order in B:
The second is Love. This arises either, 1, from hearsay, or 2, from opinion, or 3, from true ideas.
As regards the first, we generally observe it in the attitude of children to their father; because their father tells them this or that is good they incline towards it, without knowing anything more about it. We see it also in those who, from Love, give their lives for the Fatherland, and also in those who from hearsay about something fall in love with it.
As regards the second, it is certain that whenever any one sees, or thinks he sees, something good, he is always inclined to unite himself with it, and, for the sake of the good which he discerns therein, he chooses it as the best, outside which he then knows nothing better or more agreeable. Yet if ever it happens (as it mostly does happen in these things) that he gets to know something bet-

how [it arises] from [true] ideas; for the first tends to our ruin, and the second to our supreme happiness; and then [we shall see how it arises] from the last.

As regards the first, it is certain that whenever any one sees, or thinks he sees, something good, he is always inclined to unite himself with it, and, for the sake of the good which he discerns therein, he chooses it as the best, outside which he then knows nothing better or more agreeable. Yet if ever it happens (as it mostly does happen in these things) that he gets to know something better than this good at present known to him, then his love changes immediately from the one (first) to the other (second). All this we shall show more clearly when we treat of the freedom of man.

As to love from true ideas,[9] since this is not the place to speak of it, we shall pass it over now, and speak of the third, and last, namely, the Love that comes from hearsay only. This we generally observe in the attitude of children to their father: because their father tells them that this or that is good they incline towards it, without knowing anything more about it. We see it also in those who from Love give their lives for the Fatherland, and also in those who from hearsay about something fall in love with it.

Next, Hatred, the exact opposite of love, arises from error which is the outcome of opinion. For when some one has come to the conclusion that a certain thing is good, and another happens to do something to the detriment of the same thing, then there arises in him a hatred against the one who did it, and this, as we shall explain afterwards, could never happen if the true good were known. For, in comparison with the true good, all indeed that is, or is conceived, is naught but wretchedness itself; and is not such a lover of what is wretched much more deserving of pity than of hatred?

Hatred, lastly, comes also from mere hearsay, as we see it in the Turks against Jews and Christians, in the Jews against the Turks and Christians, in the Christians against the Jews and Turks, etc. For, among all these, how ignorant is the one multitude of the religion and morals of the others!

Desire. Whether (as some will have it) it consists only in a longing or inclination to obtain what is wanting, or (as others will have it[10]) to retain the things which we already enjoy, it is certain that it cannot be found to have come upon any one except for an apparent good [*sub specie boni*]. It is therefore clear that Desire, as also Love which we have already discussed, is the outcome of the first kind of knowledge. For if any one has heard that a certain thing is good, he feels a longing and inclination for the same, as may be seen in the case of an invalid who,

---

ter than this good at present known to him, then his love changes immediately from the one (first) to the other (second). All this we shall show more clearly when we treat of the freedom of man.

    As to love from true ideas, as this is not the place to speak of it, we shall pass it over for the present. [See note 9 below.]

[9] Love that comes from true ideas or clear knowledge is not considered here, as it is not the outcome of opinion; *see*, however, chapter xxii about it.

[10] The first definition is the best, because when the thing is enjoyed the desire ceases; the form [of consciousness] which then prompts us to retain the thing is not desire, but a fear of losing the thing loved.

through hearing the doctor say that such or such a remedy is good for his ailment, at once longs for the same, and feels a desire for it.

Desire arises also from experience, as may be seen in the practice of doctors, who when they have found a certain remedy good several times are wont to regard it as something unfailing.

All that we have just said of these, the same we can say of all other passions, as is clear to everyone. And as, in what follows, we shall begin to inquire which of them are rational, and which of them are irrational, we shall leave the subject now, and say no more about it.

What has now been said of these few though most important [passions] can also be said of all others; and with this we conclude the subject of the Passions which arise from Opinion.

Chapter IV
What Comes from Belief; and on the Good and Evil of Man

Since we have shown in the preceding chapter how the Passions arise from the error of Opinion, let us now see here the effects of the two other modes of Knowing. And first of all, [the effect] of what we have called True Belief.[11]

This shows us, indeed, what a thing ought to be, but not what it really is. And this is the reason why it can never unite us with the object of our belief. I say, then, that it only teaches us what the thing ought to be, and not what it is; between these two there is a great difference. For, as we remarked *à propos* of the example taken from the rule of three, when any one can, by the aid of proportion, find a fourth number that shall be related to the third as the second is to the first, then (having used division and multiplication) he can say that the four numbers must be proportional; and although that is so, he speaks of it nonetheless as of a thing that is beyond him. But when he comes to see the proportion in the way which we have shown in the fourth example, then he says with truth that the thing is so, because then it is in him and not beyond him. Let this suffice as regards the first [effect].

---

[11] Belief is a strong proof based on Reasons, whereby I am convinced in my mind that the thing is really, and just such, outside my understanding, as I am convinced in my mind that it is. I say, *a strong proof based on Reasons*, in order thereby to distinguish it both from Opinion, which is always doubtful and liable to error, and from Knowledge which does not consist in being convinced by Reasons, but in an immediate union with the thing itself. I say, *that the thing is really and just such outside my understanding—really*, because reasons cannot deceive me in this, for otherwise they would not be different from opinion. *Just such*, for it can only tell me what the thing ought to be, and not what it really is, otherwise it would not be different from Knowing. *Outside*, for it makes us enjoy intellectually not what is in us, but what is outside us.

The second effect of true belief is that it brings us to a clearer understanding, through which we love God, and thus it makes us intellectually aware of the things which are not in us, but outside us.

The third effect is, that it gives us the knowledge of good and evil, and shows us all the passions which should be suppressed. And as we have already said that the passions which come from opinion are liable to great evil, it is worth the pains to see how these also are sifted out by this second kind of knowledge, so that we may see what is good and what is bad in them.

To do so conveniently, let us, using the same method as before, look at them closely, so that we may know through it which of them should be chosen and which rejected. But, before proceeding to this, let us first state briefly what is the good and evil of man.

We have already said before that all things are necessarily what they are, and that *in Nature there is no good and no evil.* So that whatever we want man to be [in this respect] must refer to his kind, which is nothing else than a *thing of Reason.* And when we have conceived in our mind an Idea of a perfect man, it should make us look (when we examine ourselves) to see whether we have any means of attaining to such perfection.

Hence, then, whatever advances us towards perfection, we call good, and, on the contrary, what hinders, or also what does not advance us towards it, bad.

I must therefore, I say, conceive a perfect man, if I want to assert anything concerning the good and evil of man, because if I were to consider the good and evil of some individual man, say, e.g., of Adam, I should be confusing a real thing (*ens reale*) with a thing of Reason (*ens Rationis*), which must be most scrupulously avoided by an upright *Philosopher,* for reasons which we shall state in the sequel, or on another occasion. Furthermore, since the destiny of Adam, or of any other individual creature, is not known to us except through the result, so it follows that what we can say even of the destiny of man must be based on the idea which our understanding forms of a perfect man,[12] which destiny, since it is a thing of Reason, we may well know; so also, as already remarked, are good and evil, which are only modes of thinking.

To come gradually to the point: We have already pointed out before how the movement, passions, and activities of the soul arise from ideas, and these ideas we have divided into four kinds, namely, [according as they are based on] mere hearsay, experience, belief, clear knowledge. And from what we have now seen of the effects of all these, it is evident that the fourth, namely, clear knowledge, is the most perfect of all. For opinion often leads us into error. True belief is good only because it is the way to true knowledge, and awakens us to things which are really lovable. So that the final end that we seek, and the highest that we know, is true knowledge. But even this true knowledge varies with the objects that come before it: the better the object is with which it happens to unite itself, so much the bet-

---

[12] For from no individual creature can one derive an Idea that is perfect; for the perfection of this object itself, [that is,] whether it is really perfect or not, cannot be deduced except from a general perfect Idea, or *Ens Rationis.*

ter also is this knowledge. And, for this reason, he is the most perfect man who is united with God (who is the most perfect being of all), and so enjoys him.

Now, in order to find out what is good and bad in the affects or passions, let us, as suggested, take them one by one. And first of all, *Surprise*. This, since it arises either from ignorance or prejudice, is an imperfection in the man who is subject to this perturbance. I say an imperfection, because, through itself, surprise does not lead to any evil.

Chapter V
On Love

Love, which is nothing else than the enjoyment of a thing and union therewith, we shall divide according to the qualities of its object; the object, that is, which man seeks to enjoy, and to unite himself with.

Now some objects are in themselves transient; others, indeed, are not transient by virtue of their cause. There is yet a third that is eternal and imperishable through its own power and might.

The transient are all the particular things which did not exist from all time, or have had a beginning.

The others are all those modes[b] which we have stated to be the cause of the particular modes.

But the third is God, or, what we regard as one and the same, *Truth*.

Love, then, arises from the idea and knowledge that we have of a thing; and according as the thing shows itself greater and more glorious, so also is our love greater.

In two ways it is possible to free ourselves from love: either by getting to know something better, or by discovering that the loved object, which is held by us to be something great and glorious, brings in its train much woe and disaster.

It is also characteristic of love that we never think of emancipating ourselves from it (as from surprise and other passions); and this for the following two reasons: (1) because it is impossible, (2) because it is necessary that we should not be released from the same.

It is *impossible* because it does not depend on us, but only on the good and useful which we discern in the object; it is necessary that these should never have become known to us, if we would not or should not love it; and this is not a matter of our free choice, or dependent on us, for if we knew nothing, it is certain that we should also be nothing.

It is *necessary* that we should not be released from it, because, owing to the weakness of our nature, we could not exist without enjoying something with which we become united, and from which we draw strength.

---

[b] [B: the general modes.]

Now which of these three kinds of objects are we to choose or to reject?

As regards the *transient* (since, as remarked, we must, owing to the weakness of our nature, necessarily love something and become united with it in order to exist), it is certain that our nature becomes nowise strengthened through our loving, and becoming united with, these, for they are weak themselves, and the one cripple cannot carry the other. And not only do they not advance us, but they are even harmful to us. For we have said *that love is a union with the object which our understanding judges to be good and glorious*; and by this we mean such a union whereby both the lover and what is loved become one and the same thing, or together constitute one whole. He, therefore, is indeed always wretched who is united to transient things. For, since these are beyond his power, and subject to many accidents, it is impossible that, when they are affected, he should be free from these affects. And, consequently, we conclude: If those who love transient things that have some measure of reality are so wretched, how wretched must they be who love honour, riches, and pleasures, which have no reality whatever!

Let this suffice to show us how Reason teaches us to keep away from things so fleeting. For what we have just said shows us clearly the poison and the evil which lurk concealed in the love of these things. But we see this yet incomparably clearer when we observe from what glorious and excellent a good we are kept away through the enjoyment of this.

We said before that the things which are transient are beyond our power. But let us be well understood; we do not mean to say that we are a free cause depending upon nothing else; only when we say that some things are in, others beyond our power, we mean by those that are in our power such as we can produce through the order of or together with Nature, of which we are a part; by those which are not in our power, such as, being outside us, are not liable to suffer any change through us, because they are very far removed from our real essence as thus fashioned by Nature.

To proceed, we come now to the second kind of objects, which though eternal and imperishable, are not such through their own power. However, if we institute a brief inquiry here, we become immediately aware that these are only mere modes which depend immediately on God. And since the nature of these is such, they cannot be conceived by us unless we, at the same time, have a conception of God. In this, since he is perfect, our Love must necessarily rest. And, to express it in a word, if we use our understanding aright it will be impossible for us not to love God.

The Reasons why, are clear. *First of all*, because we find that God alone has essence only, and all other things are not essences but modes. And since the modes cannot be rightly understood without the entity on which they immediately depend; and [as] we have already shown before that if, when loving something, we get to know a better thing than that which we then love, we always prefer it immediately, and forsake the first; it follows, therefore, incontrovertibly that when we get to know God, who has all perfection in himself, we must necessarily love him.

Secondly, if we use our understanding well in acquiring a knowledge of things, then we must know them in [relation to] their causes. Now then, since God is a first cause of all other things, therefore, from the nature of the case (*ex rerum natura*), the knowledge of God is, and remains, before the knowledge of all other things: because the knowledge of all other things must follow from the knowledge of the first cause. And true love results always from the knowledge that the thing is glorious and good. What else, then, can follow but that it can be lavished upon no one more ardently than upon the Lord our God? For he alone is glorious, and a perfect good.

So we see now, how we can make love strong, and also how it must rest only in God.

What more we had still to say about love, we shall bear in mind to say it when we consider the last kind of knowledge. In what follows here we shall inquire, as we promised before, as to which of the passions we are to entertain, which we are to reject.

Chapter VI
On Hatred

Hatred is an inclination to ward off from us that which has caused us some harm. Now it is to be remarked that we perform our actions in two ways, namely, either with or without passion. With passion, as is commonly seen in the [conduct of] masters towards their servants who have done something amiss. Without passion, as is related of Socrates, who, when he was compelled to chastise his slave for [the latter's own] good, never did so when he felt that he was enraged against his slave.

Now that we see that our actions are performed by us either with, or without passion, we think that it is clear that those things which hinder or have hindered us can be removed, when necessary, without any perturbation on our part. And so, which is better: that we should flee from the things with aversion and hatred, or that, with the strength of reason, we should (for we think it possible) endure them without loss of temper? First of all, it is certain that when we do what we have to do without passion, then no evil can result therefrom. And, since there is no mean between good and evil, we see that, as it is bad to do anything in a passion, so it must be good to act without it.

But let us examine whether there is any harm in fleeing from things with hatred and aversion.

As regards the hatred which comes from opinion, it is certain that it should have no place in us, because we know that one and the same thing is good for us at one time, bad for us at another time, as is always the case with medicinal herbs.

It therefore depends, in the end, on whether the hatred arises in us only through opinion, and not also through true reasoning. But to ascertain this properly we deem it right to explain distinctly what hatred is, and to distinguish it from aversion.

Now I say that *Hatred* is a perturbation of the soul against some one who has done some ill to us willingly and knowingly. But *aversion* is the perturbation which arises in us against a thing on account of some infirmity or injury which we either know or think is in it by nature. I say, by nature; for when we do not suppose or think that it is so, then, even if we have suffered some hindrance or injury from it, we have no aversion for it, because we may, on the contrary, expect something useful from it. Thus, when someone is hurt by a stone or a knife, he does not on that account feel any aversion for the same.

After these observations let us now briefly consider the consequences of both of them. From hatred there ensues sorrow; and when the hatred is great, it produces anger, which not only, like hatred, seeks to flee from what is hated, but also to annihilate it, when that is practicable: from this great hatred comes also envy. But from aversion there comes a certain sorrow, because we consider ourselves to be deprived of something which, since it is real, must always have its essence and perfection.

From what has just been said it may be easily understood that, if we use our Reason aright, we can feel no hatred or aversion for anything, because, if we do, we deprive ourselves of that perfection which is to be found in everything. We see likewise with our Reason that we can never [reasonably] feel any hatred whatever against anybody, because whatsoever exists in Nature, if we entertain any wish about it, then we must always improve it, whether for our sake or for the sake of the thing itself. And since a perfect man is the best thing for us that we know of all that we have around us or before our eyes, it is by far the best both for us and for all people individually that we should at all times seek to educate them to this perfect state. For only then can we reap the greatest benefit from them, and they from us. The means thereto is, to give regard to them always in the manner in which we are constantly taught and exhorted to do by our good Conscience; for this never prompts us to our undoing, but always to our happiness and well-being.

In conclusion, we say that Hatred and Aversion have in them as many imperfections as Love, on the contrary, has perfections. For this always produces improvement, invigoration, and enlargement, which constitute perfection; while Hatred, on the contrary, always makes for desolation, enervation, and annihilation, which constitute imperfection itself.

Chapter VII
On Joy and Sorrow[c]

Having seen that Hatred and Surprise[d] are such that we may freely say, that they can have no place in those who use their understanding as they should, we shall

---

[c] [B: On Desire and Joy.]

[d] [B: Hatred and Aversion.]

now proceed in the same manner to speak of the other passions. To begin with, Desire and Joy shall come first. Since these arise from the same causes from which love ensues, we shall only say concerning them that we must remember and call to mind what we then said; and with this we leave the subject.

We turn next to Sorrow, of which we may say that it arises only from opinion and imagination which follows therefrom: for it comes from the loss of some good.

Now we have already remarked above, that whatsoever we do should tend towards progress and amelioration. But it is certain that so long as we are sorrowing we render ourselves unfit to act thus; on this account it is necessary that we should free ourselves from it. This we can do by thinking of the means whereby we may recover what we have lost, if it is in our power to do so. If not, [we must reflect] that it is just as necessary to make an end of it, lest we fall a prey to all the miseries and disasters which sorrow necessarily brings in its train. And either course must be adopted with joy; for it is foolish to try to restore and make good a lost good by means of a self-sought and provoked evil.

Lastly, he who uses his understanding aright must necessarily know God first. Now God, as we have shown, is the highest good and all that is good. Hence it follows incontrovertibly, that one who uses his understanding aright can fall a prey to no sorrow. How should he? Since he finds repose in that good which is all that is good, and in which there is the fulness of all joy and contentment.[e]

Sorrow, then, comes from opinion or want of understanding, as explained.

Chapter VIII
On Esteem and Contempt, Etc.

We shall now proceed to speak of Esteem and Contempt, of Self-respect and Humility, of Conceit and Culpable Humility. We shall take them in the above order, and try to distinguish accurately what is good and what is bad in them.

Esteem and Contempt are felt insofar as we know a thing to be something great or small, be this great or little thing in us or outside us.

Self-respect does not extend [to anything] outside us, and is only attributed to one who knows the real worth of his perfection, dispassionately and without seeking esteem for himself.

Humility is felt when anyone knows his own imperfection, without regard to the contempt [of others] for himself; so that Humility does not refer to anything outside the humble man.

Conceit is this, when someone attributes to himself a perfection which is not to be found in him.

---

[e] [B abridges the paragraph as follows: Lastly, he who uses his understanding aright must necessarily know that God is the first and the highest; and rest in him as this supreme good: whence it follows that, since he finds therein all joy and full contentment, no sorrow can befall him.]

Culpable humility is this, when some one attributes to himself an imperfection which he has not. I am not speaking of those hypocrites who, without meaning it, humble themselves in order to deceive others; but only of those who really think they have the imperfections which they attribute to themselves.

From these observations it is sufficiently evident what good and evil there is in each of these passions. For, as regards Self-respect and Humility, these show their excellence through themselves. For we say that the possessor thereof knows his perfection and imperfection for what it is. And this, according to what Reason teaches us, is the most important thing for the attainment of our perfection. Because if we know exactly our powers and perfection, we see thereby clearly what it is we have to do in order to attain our good end. And, on the other hand, if we know our fault and frailty, then we know what we have to avoid.

As regards Conceit and Culpable Humility, the definition of them already shows sufficiently that they arise from a certain opinion; for we said that it [conceit] is attributed to one who ascribes to himself a certain perfection, although he does not possess it, and culpable humility is the precise opposite.

From what has just been said it is evident, then, that just as Self-respect and True Humility are good and salutary, so, on the contrary, Conceit and Culpable Humility are bad and pernicious. For those [Self-respect and True Humility] not only put their possessor into a very good attitude, but are also, besides, the right ladder by which we may rise to supreme bliss. But these [Conceit and Culpable Humility] not only prevent us from attaining to our perfection, but also lead us to utter ruin. Culpable Humility is what prevents us from doing that which we should otherwise have to do in order to become perfect; we see this, for instance, in the case of the Sceptics, who, just because they deny that man can attain to any truth, deprive themselves thereof through this very denial. Conceit on the other hand is what makes us undertake things which tend straight to our ruin; as is seen in the case of all those who had the conceit, and have the conceit, that they stood, and stand, wondrously well in the opinion of God, and consequently brave fire and water, and thus, avoiding no danger, and facing every risk, they die most miserably.

As regards Esteem and Contempt, there is no more to be said about them, we have only to recall to memory what we said before about Love.

Chapter IX
On Hope and Fear, Etc.

We shall now begin to speak of Hope and Fear, of Confidence, Despair, and Vacillation, of Courage, Boldness and Emulation, of Pusillanimity and Timidity, and lastly of Jealousy, and, as is our wont, we shall take them one by one, and then indicate which of these can hinder us, and which can profit us. We shall be able to do all this very easily, if only we attend closely to the thoughts that we can have about a thing that is yet to come, be it good, be it bad.

The ideas which we have about things have reference either

1. To the things themselves; or,
2. To the person who has the ideas.

The ideas that we have as regards the thing itself are these, either the thing is regarded by us as accidental, that is as something which may come or may not come, or [we think] that it necessarily must come. So much as regards the thing itself.

Next, as regards him who thinks about the thing, the case is this: he must do something either in order to advance the thing, or in order to prevent it. Now from these thoughts all these passions result as follows: when we think that a certain thing which is yet to come is good and that it can happen, the soul assumes, in consequence of this, that form which we call *hope*, which is nothing else than a certain kind of joy, though mingled with some sorrow.

And, on the other hand, if we judge that that which may be coming is bad, then that form enters into our soul which we call *fear*.

If, however, the thing is regarded by us as good, and, at the same time, as something that necessarily must come, then there comes into the soul that repose which we call *confidence*; which is a certain joy not mingled with sorrow, as hope is.

But when we think that the thing is bad, and that it necessarily must come, then *despair* enters into the soul; which is nothing else than a certain kind of sorrow.

So far we have spoken of the passions considered in this chapter, and given positive definitions of the same, and have thus stated what each of them is; we may now proceed in a converse manner, and define them negatively. We *hope* that the evil may not come, we *fear* lest the good should not come, we are *confident* that the evil will not come, we *despair* because the good will not come.

Having said this much about the passions insofar as they arise from our thoughts concerning the thing itself, we have now to speak of those which arise from the thoughts relating to him who thinks about the thing; namely:

If something must be done in order to bring the thing about, and we come to no decision concerning it, then the soul receives that form which we call *vacillation*. But when it makes a manly resolve to produce the thing, and this can be brought about, then that is called *courage*; and if the thing is difficult to effect, then that is called *intrepidity* or *bravery*.

When, however, some one decides to do a thing because another (who had done it first) has met with success, then we call it *emulation*. Lastly, if any one knows what he must decide to do in order to advance a good thing, and to hinder a bad one, and yet does not do so, then we call it *pusillanimity*; and when the same is very great, we call it *timidity*. Lastly, *jealousness* or *jalousie* is the anxiety which we feel that we may have the sole enjoyment and possession of something already acquired.

Since we know now whence these passions originate, it will be very easy for us to show which of them are good, and which are bad.

As regards Hope, Fear, Confidence, Despair, and Jealousy, it is certain that they arise from a wrong opinion. For, as we have already shown above, all things have their necessary causes, and must necessarily happen just as they do happen. And although Confidence and Despair seem to have a place in the inviolable order and sequence of causes or to confirm the same, yet (when the truth of the matter is rightly looked into) that is far from being the case. For Confidence and Despair never arise, unless Hope and Fear (from which they derive their being) have preceded them. For example, if any one thinks that something, for which he still has to wait, is good, then he receives that form in his soul which we call Hope; and when he is confident about the acquisition of the supposed good, his soul gains that repose which we call Confidence. What we are now saying about Confidence, the same must also be said about Despair. But, according to that which we have said about Love, this also can have no place in a perfect man: because they presuppose things which, owing to the mutability to which they are subject (as remarked in our account of Love), we must not become attached to; nor (as shown in our account of Hatred) may we even have an aversion to them. The man, however, who persists in these passions is at all times subject to such attachment and aversion.

As regards Vacillation, Pusillanimity, and Timidity, these betray their imperfection through their very character and nature: for whatsoever they do to our advantage comes only negatively from the effects of their nature. For example, some one hopes for something which he thinks is good, although it is not good, yet, owing to his Vacillation or Pusillanimity, he happens to lack the courage necessary for its realisation, and so it comes about that he is negatively or by accident saved from the evil which he thought was good. These Passions, therefore, can also have no place whatever in the man who is guided by true Reason.

Lastly, as regards Courage, Boldness, and Emulation, about these there is nothing else to be said than that which we have already said about Love and Hatred.

Chapter X
On Remorse and Repentance

On the present occasion we shall speak, though briefly, about *remorse* and *repentance*. These never arise except as the result of rashness; because *remorse* comes only from this, that we do something about which we are then in doubt whether it is good, or whether it is bad; and *repentance*, from this, that we have done something which is bad.

And since many people (who use their understanding aright) sometimes (because they lack that habitual readiness which is required in order that the understanding may at all times be used aright) go astray, it might perchance be thought that such Remorse and Repentance might soon set them right again, and thence it might be inferred, as the whole world does infer, that they are good. If, however, we will get a proper insight into them, we shall find that they are not only not good, but that they are, on the contrary, pernicious, and that they are consequently bad. For it is obvious that we always succeed better through Reason and the love of truth than through remorse and sorrow. They are, therefore, pernicious and bad, because they are a certain kind of sorrow, which [sorrow] we have already shown above to be injurious, and which, for that reason, we must try to avert as an evil, and consequently we must likewise shun and flee from these also, which are like it.

Chapter XI
On Derision and Jesting

Derision and jesting rest on a false opinion, and betray an imperfection in him who derides and jests.

The opinion on which they rest is false, because it is supposed that he who is derided is the first cause of the effects which he produces, and that they do not necessarily (like the other things in Nature) depend on God. They betray an imperfection in the Derider; because either that which is derided is such that it is derisible, or it is not such. If it is not such, then it shows bad manners, to deride that which is not to be derided; if it is such, then they [who deride it] show thereby that they recognise some imperfection in that which they deride, which they ought to remedy, not by derision, but much rather by good reasoning.

Laughter does not refer to another, but only to the man who observes some good in himself; and since it is a certain kind of Joy, there is nothing else to be said about it than what has already been said about Joy. I speak of such laughter as is caused by a certain Idea which provokes one to it, and not at all of such laughter as is caused by the movement of the [vital] spirits; as to this (since it has no reference to good or to evil) we had no intention to speak of it here.

As to Envy, Anger, Indignation, we shall say nothing about them here, but only just refer back to what we have already said above concerning hatred.

Chapter XII
On Glory, Shame, and Shamelessness

We shall now also briefly consider *glory*, *shame*, and *shamelessness*. The first is a certain kind of Joy which every one feels in himself whenever he becomes aware that his conduct is esteemed and praised by others, without regard to any other advantage or profit which they may have in view.

Shame is a certain kind of sorrow which arises in one when he happens to see that his conduct is despised by others, without regard to any other disadvantage or injury that they may have in view.

Shamelessness is nothing else than a want, or shaking off, of shame, not through Reason, but either from innocence of shame, as is the case with children, savage people, etc., or because, having been held in great contempt, one goes now to any length without regard for anything.

Now that we know these passions, we also know, at the same time, the vanity and imperfection which they have in them. For Glory and Shame are not only of no advantage, because of what we have observed in their definitions, but also (inasmuch as they are based on self-love, and on the opinion that man is the first cause of his action, and therefore deserving of praise and blame) they are pernicious and must be rejected.

I will not, however, say that one ought to live among men in the same way that one would live away from them, where Glory and Shame have no place; quite the contrary, I admit that we are not only free to utilise them, when we apply them in the service of mankind and for their amelioration, but that we may even do so at the price of curtailing our own (otherwise perfect and legitimate) freedom. For example: if any one wears costly clothes in order to be respected, he seeks a Glory which results from his self-love without any consideration for his fellow-men; but when some one observes that his wisdom (wherewith he can be of service to his neighbours) is despised and trampled under foot simply because he is dressed in shabby clothes, then he will do well if (from the motive to help them) he provides himself with clothes to which they cannot take exception, thereby becoming like his fellow-man in order that he may win over his fellow-man.

Further, as regards Shamelessness, this shows itself to be such that in order to see its deformity all that we need is merely its definition, and that will be enough for us.

Chapter XIII
On Favour, Gratitude, and Ingratitude

Now follows [the consideration] of *favour, gratitude,* and *ingratitude.* As regards the first two, they are the inclinations which the soul has to wish and to do some good to one's neighbour. I say, to wish, [this happens] when good is returned to one who has done some good; I say, to do, [this is the case] when we ourselves have obtained or received some good.

I am well aware that almost all people consider these affects to be good; but, notwithstanding this, I venture to say that they can have no place in a perfect man. For a perfect man is moved to help his fellow-man by sheer necessity only, and by no other cause, and therefore he feels it all the more to be his duty to help the most godless, seeing that his misery and need are so much greater.

Ingratitude is a disregard or shaking off of Gratitude, as Shamelessness is of Shame, and that without any rational ground, but solely as the result either of greed or of immoderate self-love; and that is why it can have no place in a perfect man.

Chapter XIV
On Grief

Grief shall be the last of which we shall speak in our treatment of the passions, and with it we will conclude. Now grief is a certain kind of sorrow arising from the contemplation of some good which we have lost, and [lost] in such a way that there is no hope of recovering the same. It makes its imperfection so manifest that as soon as we only examine it we think it bad. For we have already shown above that it is bad to bind and link ourselves to things which may easily, or at some time, fail us, and which we cannot have when we want them. And since it is a certain kind of sorrow, we have to shun it, as we have already remarked above, when we were treating of sorrow.

I think, now, that I have already shown and proved sufficiently that it is only True Belief or Reason that leads us to the knowledge of good and evil. And so when we come to prove that Knowledge is the first and principal cause[f] of all these passions, it will be clearly manifest that if we use our understanding and Reason aright, it should be impossible for us ever to fall a prey to one of these passions which we ought to reject. I say our *Understanding*, because I do not think that Reason alone is competent to free us from all these: as we shall afterwards show in its proper place.

We must, however, note here as an excellent thing about the passions, that we see and find that all the passions which are good are of such kind and nature that we cannot be or exist without them, and that they belong, as it were, to our essence; such is the case with Love, Desire, and all that pertains to love.

But the case is altogether different with those which are bad and must be rejected by us; seeing that we cannot only exist very well without these, but even that only then, when we have freed ourselves from them, are we really what we ought to be.

To give still greater clearness to all this, it is useful to note that the foundation of all good and evil is *Love bestowed on a certain object*: for if we do not love that object which (*nota bene*) alone is worthy of being loved, namely, God, as we have said before, but things which through their very character and nature are transient, then (since the object is liable to so many accidents, ay, even to annihilation) there necessarily results hatred, sorrow, etc., according to the changes in the object loved. Hatred, when any one deprives him of what he loves. Sorrow, when he happens to lose it. Glory, when he leans on self-love. Favour and Gratitude, when he does not love his fellow-man for the sake of God.

But, in contrast with all these, when man comes to love God who always

---

[f] [B omitted "cause," but the word seems to have been inserted recently—perhaps by Van Vloten, as a marginal pencil note suggests.]

is and remains immutable, then it is impossible for him to fall into this welter of passions. And for this reason we state it as a fixed and immovable principle that God is the first and only cause of all our good and delivers us from all our evil.

Hence it is also to be noted lastly, that only Love, etc., are limitless: namely, that as it increases more and more, so also it grows more excellent, because it is bestowed on an object which is infinite, and can therefore always go on increasing, which can happen in the case of no other thing except this alone. And, maybe, this will afterwards give us the material from which we shall prove the immortality of the soul, and how or in what way this is possible.[g]

Having so far considered all that the third kind of effect of true belief makes known we shall now proceed to speak, in what follows, of the fourth, and last, effect which was not stated by us on page 67.

Chapter XV
On the True and the False

Let us now examine the *true* and the *false*, which indicate to us the fourth, and last, consequence of true belief. Now, in order to do this, we shall first state the definitions of Truth and Falsity. Truth is an affirmation (or a denial) made about a certain thing, which agrees with that same thing; and Falsity is an affirmation (or a denial) about a thing, which does not agree with the thing itself. But this being so, it may appear that there is no difference between the false and the true Idea, or, since the [affirmation or] denial of this or that are mere modes of thought, and [the true and the false Idea] differ in no other way except that the one agrees with the thing, and the other does not, that they are therefore, not really, but only logically different; and if this should be so, one may justly ask, what advantage has the one from his Truth, and what harm does the other incur through his falsity? And how shall the one know that his conception or Idea agrees with the thing more than the other does? Lastly, whence does it come that the one errs, and the other does not?

To this it may, in the first place, serve as an answer that the clearest things of all make known both themselves and also what is false, in such a manner that it would be a great folly to ask how we are to become aware of them: for, since they are said to be the clearest of all, there can never be any other clearness through which they might be made clear; it follows, therefore, that truth at once reveals itself and also what is false, because truth is made clear through truth, that is through itself, and through it also is falsity made clear; but falsity is never revealed

---

[g] [B: And this will give us the material from which we shall, in the twenty-third chapter, make out a case for, and prove, the immortality of the Soul.]

and made manifest through itself. So that any one who is in possession of the truth cannot doubt that he possesses it, while one who is sunk in falsity or in error can well suppose that he has got at the truth; just as someone who is dreaming can well think that he is awake, but one who is actually awake can never think that he is dreaming.

These remarks also explain to some extent what we said about God being the Truth, or that *the Truth is God himself.*

Now the reason why the one is more conscious of his truth than the other is, is because the Idea of [his] affirmation (or denial) entirely agrees with the nature of the thing, and consequently has more essence. It may help some to grasp this better if it be observed that Understanding (although the word does not sound like it) is a mere or pure passivity; that is, that our soul is changed in such a way that it receives other modes of thought, which it did not have before. Now when someone, in consequence of the whole object having acted upon him, receives corresponding forms or modes of thought, then it is clear that he receives a totally different feeling of the form or character of the object than does another who has not had so many causes [acting upon him], and is therefore moved to make an affirmation or denial about that thing by a different and slighter action (because he becomes aware of it only through a few, or the less important, of its attributes). From this, then, we see the perfection of one who takes his stand upon Truth, as contrasted with one who does not take his stand upon it. Since the one changes easily, while the other does not change easily, it follows therefrom that the one has more stability and essence than the other has: likewise, since the modes of thought which agree with the thing have had more causes [to produce them] they have also more stability and essence in them: and, since they entirely agree with the thing, it is impossible that they should after a time be made different or undergo some change, all the less so because we have already seen before that the essence of a thing is unchangeable. Such is not the case with falsity. And with these remarks all the above questions will be sufficiently answered.

Chapter XVI
On the Will

Now that we know the nature of Good and Evil, Truth and Falsity, and also wherein the well-being of a perfect man consists, it is time to begin to examine ourselves, and to see whether we attain to such well-being voluntarily or of necessity.

To this end it is necessary to inquire what the Will is, according to those who posit a Will, and wherein it is different from Desire. Desire, we have said, is the inclination which the soul has towards something which it chooses as a good; whence it follows that before our desire inclines towards something outside, we have already inwardly decided that such a thing is good, and this affirmation, or, stated more generally, the power to affirm and to deny, is called the Will.[13]

It thus turns on the question whether our Affirmations are made voluntarily or necessarily, that is, whether we can make any affirmation or denial about a thing without some external cause compelling us to do so. Now we have already shown that a thing which is not explained[h] through itself, or whose *existence* does not pertain to its *essence*, must necessarily have an external cause; and that a cause which is to produce something must produce it necessarily; it must therefore also follow that each separate act of willing[14] this or that, each separate act of affirm-

---

[13] Now the Will, regarded as Affirmation or Decision is different from true Belief and from Opinion. It differs from True Belief in this, that it extends also to that which is not truly good; and this is so because it lacks that conviction whereby it is clearly seen that it cannot be otherwise; in the case of true belief there is, and must be, this conviction, because from it none but good desires emanate.

But it also differs from Opinion in this, that it can sometimes be quite infallible and certain; this is not the case with Opinion, which consists in guessing and supposing.

So that we can call it Belief insofar as it can proceed with certainty, and Opinion insofar as it is subject to error.

[h] [B: which does not exist.]

[14] It is certain that each separate volition must have an external cause through which it comes into being; for, seeing that existence does not pertain to its essence, its existence must necessarily be due to the existence of something else.

As to the view that the efficient cause thereof is not an Idea but the human Will itself, and that the Understanding is a cause without which the will can do nothing, so that the *Will* in its undetermined form, and also the *Understanding*, are not things of Reason, but real entities—so far as I am concerned, whenever I consider them attentively they appear to be universals, and I can attribute no reality to them. Even if it be so, however, still it must be admitted that Willing is a modification of the Will, and that the Ideas are a mode of the Understanding; the Understanding and the Will are therefore necessarily distinct, and really distinct substances, because [only] substance is modified, and not the mode itself. As the soul is said to direct these two substances, it must be a third substance. All these things are so confused that it is impossible to have a clear and distinct conception about them. For, since the Idea is not in the Will, but in the Understanding, and in consequence of the rule that the mode of one substance cannot pass over into the other substance, love cannot arise in the will: because *to will something when there is no idea of that thing in the willing power* involves self-contradiction. If you say that the Will, owing to its union with the Understanding, also becomes aware of that which the Understanding understands, and thus also loves it, one may retort to this: but since awareness is also an apprehension, it is therefore also a mode of understanding; following the above, however, this cannot be in the Will, even if its union [with the Will] were like that of the soul and body. For suppose that the body is united with the soul, as the philosophers generally maintain, even so the body never feels, nor does the soul become extended.[i] When they say that the Soul directs both the Understanding and the Will, this is not only inconceivable, but even self-contradictory, because by saying so they seem to deny that the will is free, which is opposed to their view. But, to conclude, I have no inclination to adduce all my objections against positing a created finite substance. I shall only show briefly that the Freedom of the Will does not in any way accord with such an enduring creation; namely, that the same activity is required of God in order to maintain a thing in existence as to create it, and that otherwise the thing could not last for a moment; as this is so, nothing can be attributed to it. But we must say that God has created it just as it is; for as it has no power to maintain itself in existence while it exists, much

[i] [A continues: For then a Chimera, in which we conceive two substances, might become one; this is false.]

ing or denying this or that of a thing, these, I say, must also result from some external cause: so also the definition which we have given of a cause is, that it cannot be free.

Possibly this will not satisfy some who are accustomed to keep their understanding busy with things of Reason more than with Particular things which really exist in Nature; and, through doing so, they come to regard a thing of Reason not as such, but as a real thing. For, because man has now this, now that volition, he forms in his soul a general mode which he calls Will, just as from this man and that man he also forms the Idea of man; and because he does not adequately distinguish the real things from the things of Reason, he comes to regard the things of Reason as things which really exist in Nature, and so he regards himself as a cause of some things. This happens not infrequently in the treatment of the subject about which we are speaking. For if any one is asked why people want this or that, the answer usually given is, because they have a will. But, since the Will, as we have said, is only an Idea of our willing this or that, and therefore only a mode of thought, a thing of Reason, and not a real thing, nothing can be caused by it; for out of nothing, nothing comes. And so, as we have shown that the will is not a thing in Nature, but only in fancy, I also think it unnecessary to ask whether the will is free or not free.

I say this not [only] of will in general, which we have shown to be a mode of thought, but also of the particular act of willing this or that, which act of willing some have identified with affirmation and denial. Now this should be clearly evident to every one who only attends to what we have already said. For we have said that the understanding is purely passive; it is an awareness, in the soul, of the essence and existence of things; so that it is never we who affirm or deny something of a thing, but it is the thing itself that affirms or denies, in us, something of itself.

Possibly some will not admit this, because it seems to them that they are well able to affirm or to deny of the thing something different from what they know about the thing. But this is only because they have no idea of the conception which the soul has of the thing apart from or without the words [in which it is expressed]. It is quite true that (when there are reasons which prompt us to do so) we can, in words or by some other means, represent the thing to others differently from what we know it to be; but we can never bring it so far, either by words or by any other means, that we should feel about the things differently from what we feel about them; that is impossible, and clearly so to all who have for once attended to their understanding itself apart from the use of words or other significant signs.

Against this, however, some perchance may say: If it is not we, but the thing itself, that makes the affirmation and denial about itself in us, then nothing can be

---

less, then, can it produce something by itself. If, therefore, any one should say that the soul produces the volition from itself, then I ask, by what power? Not by that which has been, for it is no more; also not by that which it has now, for it has none at all whereby it might exist or last for a single moment, because it is continuously created anew. Thus, then, as there is nothing that has any power to maintain itself, or to produce anything, there remains nothing but to conclude that God alone, therefore, is and must be the efficient cause of all things, and that all acts of Volition are determined by him alone.

affirmed or denied except what is in agreement with the thing; and consequently there is no falsity. For we have said that falsity consists in affirming (or denying) aught of a thing which does not accord with that thing; that is, what the thing does not affirm or deny about itself. I think, however, that if only we consider well what we have already said about Truth and Falsity, then we shall see at once that these objections have already been sufficiently answered. For we have said that the object is the cause of what is affirmed or denied thereof, be it true or false: falsity arising thus, namely, because, when we happen to know something or a part of an object, we imagine that the object (although we only know very little of it) nevertheless affirms or denies that of itself as a whole; this takes place mostly in feeble souls, which receive very easily a mode or an idea through a slight action of the object, and make no further affirmation or denial apart from this.

Lastly, it might also be objected that there are many things which we sometimes want and [sometimes also] do not want, as, for example, to assert something about a thing or not to assert it, to speak the truth, and not to speak it, and so forth. But this results from the fact that Desire is not adequately distinguished from Will. For the Will, according to those who maintain that there is a Will, is only the activity of the understanding whereby we affirm or deny something about a thing, with regard to good or evil. Desire, however, is the disposition of the soul to obtain or to do something for the sake of the good or evil that is discerned therein; so that even after we have made an affirmation or denial about the thing, Desire still remains, namely, when we have ascertained or affirmed that the thing is good; such is the Will, according to their statements, while desire is the inclination, which we only subsequently feel, to advance it—so that, even according to their own statements, the Will may well exist without the Desire, but not the Desire without the Will, which must have preceded it.

All the activities, therefore, which we have discussed above (since they are carried out through Reason under the appearance of good, or are hindered by Reason under the appearance of evil) can only be subsumed under that inclination which is called Desire, and by no means under the designation of Will, which is altogether inappropriate.

Chapter XVII
On the Distinction between Will and Desire

Now that it is known that we have no free will to make an affirmation or a denial, let us just see what is the correct and true distinction between *will* and *desire*, or what may the Will be which was called by the Latins *voluntas*.

According to Aristotle's definition, Desire appears to be a genus containing two species. For he says that the Will is the longing or inclination which one feels towards that which is or seems good. Whence it appears to me that by Desire (or *cupiditas*) he means any inclination, be it towards good, be it towards evil; but when the inclination is only towards what is or appears to be good, or when the man who has such inclination, has it under the appearance of good, then he calls it *voluntas* or good will; while, if it is bad, that is, when we observe in another an inclination towards something which is bad, he calls that *voluptas* or bad will. So that the inclination of the soul is not something whereby affirmations or denials are made, but only an inclination to obtain something which appears to be good, and[j] to flee from what appears to be bad.

It, therefore, remains to inquire now whether the Desire is free or not free. In addition to what we have already said, namely, *that Desire depends on the idea of its objects, and that this understanding must have an external cause*, and in addition also to what we have said about the will, it still remains to prove that Desire is not free. Many people, although they see quite well that the knowledge which man has of various things is a medium through which his longing or inclination passes over from one thing to another, yet fail to observe what that may be which thus lures the inclination from the one to the other.

However, to show that this inclination of ours is not of our own free will (and in order to present vividly before our eyes what it is to pass over, and to be drawn, from one thing to another), we shall imagine a child becoming aware of something for the first time. For example, I hold before him a little Bell, which produces a pleasant sound for his ears, so that he conceives a longing for it; consider now whether he could really help feeling this longing or desire. If you say, Yes, then I ask, how, through what cause is this to happen? Certainly not through something which he knows to be better, because this is all that he knows; nor, again, through its appearing to be bad to him, for he knows nothing else, and this pleasure is the very best that has ever come to him. But perchance he has the freedom to banish from him the longing which he feels; whence it would follow that this longing may well arise in us without our free will, but that all the same we have in us the freedom to banish it from us. This freedom, however, will not bear examination; for what, indeed, might it be that shall be able to annihilate the longing? The longing itself? Surely no, for there is nothing that through its own nature seeks its own undoing. What then might it ultimately be that shall be able to wean him from his longing? Nothing else, forsooth, except that in the natural order and course of things he is affected by something which he finds more pleasant than the first. And, therefore, just as, when we were considering the Will, we said that the human Will is nothing but *this and that* Volition, so also man has no other than *this and that* Desire which is caused by this and that idea;[k] Desire [in the abstract] is not anything actually existing in Nature, but is only an abstraction from the particular acts of desiring this or that. *Desire*, then, as it is not really any-

---

[j] [B: or.]

[k] [B concludes this chapter as follows: If then we say that Desire is free, it is just as if we had said that this or that Desire is the cause of itself, and, already before it existed, had brought it about that it should exist: which is absurdity itself and is impossible. And Desire, regarded as a universal, being nothing but an abstraction from the particular acts of desiring this or that, and, beyond this, not actually existing in Nature, can, as such, also cause nothing.]

thing, can also not really cause anything. So that when we say that *Desire* is free, it is just as much as if we said that *this or that* Desire is its own cause—that is, that before it existed it had already arranged that it should exist; which is absurdity itself, and cannot be.

Chapter XVIII
On the Uses of the Foregoing

Thus we see now that man, being *a part of the whole of Nature,* on which he depends, and by which also he is governed, cannot of himself do anything for his happiness and well-being; let us, then, just see what Uses we can derive from these propositions of ours. And this [is] all the more [necessary] because we have no doubt that they will appear not a little offensive to some.

In the first place, it follows therefrom that we are truly servants, aye, slaves, of God, and that it is our greatest perfection to be such necessarily. For, if we were thrown back upon ourselves, and thus not dependent on God, we should be able to accomplish very little, or nothing, and that would justly give us cause to lament our lot; especially so in contrast with what we now see, namely, that we are dependent on that which is the most perfect of all, in such a way that we exist also as a part of the whole, that is, of him; and we contribute, so to say, also our share to the realisation of so many skilfully ordered and perfect works, which depend on him.

Secondly, this knowledge brings it about that we do not grow proud when we have accomplished something excellent (which pride causes us to come to a standstill, because we think that we are already great, and that we need do nothing further; thereby militating precisely against our own perfection, which consists in this—that we must at all times endeavour to advance further and further); but that, on the contrary, we attribute all that we do to God, who is the first and only cause of all that we accomplish and succeed in effecting.

Thirdly, in addition to the fact that this knowledge inspires us with a real love of our neighbour, it shapes us so that we never hate him, nor are we angry with him, but love to help him, and to improve his condition. All these are the actions of such men as have great perfection or essence.

Fourthly, this knowledge also serves to promote the greatest Common Good, because through it a judge can never side with one party more than with the other, and when compelled to punish the one, and to reward the other, he will do it with a view to help and to improve the one as much as the other.

Fifthly, this knowledge frees us from Sorrow, from Despair, from Envy, from Terror, and other evil passions, which, as we shall presently say, constitute the real hell itself.

Sixthly, this knowledge brings us so far that we cease to stand in awe of God, as others do of the Devil (whom they imagine), lest he should do them harm. For why indeed should we fear God, who is the highest good itself, through whom all things are what they are, and also we who live in him?

Seventhly, this knowledge also brings us so far that we attribute all to God, love him alone because he is the most glorious and the most perfect, and thus offer ourselves up entirely to him; for these really constitute both the true service of God and our own eternal happiness and bliss. For the sole perfection and the final end of a slave and of a tool is this, that they duly fulfil the task imposed on them. For example, if a carpenter, while doing some work, finds his Hatchet of excellent service, then this Hatchet has thereby attained its end and perfection; but if he should think: this Hatchet has rendered me such good service now, therefore I shall let it rest, and exact no further service from it, then precisely this Hatchet would fail of its end, and be a Hatchet no more. Thus also is it with man, so long as he is a part of Nature he must follow the laws of Nature, and this is divine service; and so long as he does this, it is well with him. But if God should (so to say) will that man should serve him no more, that would be equivalent to depriving him of his well-being and annihilating him; because all that he is consists in this, that he serves God.

Chapter XIX
On Our Happiness

Now that we have seen the advantages of this True Belief, we shall endeavour to fulfil the promise we have made, namely, to inquire whether through the knowledge which we already have (as to what is good, what is evil, what truth is, and what falsity is, and what, in general, the uses of all these are), whether, I say, we can thereby attain to our well-being, namely, the LOVE of God (which we have remarked to be our supreme happiness), and also in what way we can free ourselves from the passions which we have judged to be bad.

To begin with the consideration of the last, namely, of the liberation from the passions,[15] I say that, if we suppose that they have no other causes than those which we have assigned to them, then, provided only we use our understanding aright, as we can do very easily[16] (now that we have a criterion of truth and falsity), we shall never fall into them.

---

[15] All passions which come in conflict with good Reason (as is shown above) arise from Opinion. All that is good or bad in them, is shown to us by True Belief; these, however—both, or either of the two—are not able to free us from them. It is only the third kind, namely, True Knowledge, that emancipates from them. And without this it is impossible that we should ever be set free from them, as will be shown subsequently (page 93). Might not this well be that about which, though under different designation, others say and write so much? For who does not see how conveniently we can interpret opinion as sin; belief, as the law which makes sin known; and true knowledge, as grace which redeems us from sin?

[16] Can do very easily; that is to say, when we have a thorough knowledge of good and evil: for then it

But what we have now to prove is that they have no other causes; for this, methinks, it is required that we should study ourselves in our entirety, having regard to the body as well as to the spirit.

And first [we have] to show that in Nature there is a body through whose form and activities we are affected, and thus become aware of it. And the reason why we do this is, because when we get an insight into the activities of the body and the effects which they produce, then we shall also discover the first and foremost cause of all those passions; and, at the same time, also that through which all those passions might be annihilated. From this we shall then also be able to see whether it is possible to do such a thing by the aid of Reason. And then we shall also proceed to speak about our Love of God.

Now to prove that there is a body in Nature, can be no difficult task for us, now that we already know *that* God is, and *what* God is; whom we have defined as a being of infinite attributes, each of which is infinite and perfect. And since extension is an attribute which we have shown to be infinite in its kind, it must therefore also necessarily be an attribute of that infinite being. And as we have also already demonstrated that this infinite being exists, it follows at once that this attribute also exists.

Moreover, since we have also proved that outside Nature, which is infinite, there is, and can be, no being, it is clearly manifest that this effect of body through which we become aware [of it] can proceed from nothing else than from extension itself, and by no means from something else which (as some will have it) has extension in an eminent degree [*eminenter*]: for (as we have already shown in the first chapter) there is no such thing.

We have to remark, therefore, that all the effects which are seen to depend necessarily on extension must be attributed to this attribute; such as Motion and Rest. For if the power to produce these did not exist in Nature, then (even though it [Nature] might have many other attributes) it would be impossible that these should exist. For if a thing is to produce something then there must be that in it through which it, rather than another, can produce that something.

What we have just said here about extension, the same we also wish to be regarded as though it had been said about thought, and further about all that is.

It is to be observed further, that there is nothing whatever in us, but we have the power to become aware of it: so that if we find that there is nothing else in us except the effects of the thinking thing and those of extension, then we may say with certainty that there is nothing else in us.

In order that the workings of both these may be clearly understood, we shall take them up first each by itself only, and afterwards both together; as also the effects of both the one and the other.

Now when we consider extension alone, then we become aware of nothing else in it except Motion and Rest, from which we then discover all the effects that result therefrom. And these two[17] modes of body are such that it is impossible for

---

is impossible to be subject to that from which the passions arise: because when we know and enjoy what is best, that which is worst has no power over us.

[17] Two modes: because Rest is not *Nothing*.

any other thing to change them, except only themselves. Thus, for example, when a stone lies still, then it is impossible that it should be moved by the power of thought or anything else, but [it may] well [be moved] by motion,[1] as when another stone, having greater motion than this has rest, makes it move. Likewise also the moving stone will not be made to rest except through something else which has less motion. It follows, accordingly, that no mode of thought can bring motion or rest into a body. In accordance, however, with what we observe in ourselves, it may well happen that a body which is moving now in one direction may nevertheless turn aside in another direction; as when I stretch out my arm and thereby bring it about that the [vital] spirits which were already moving in a different direction, nevertheless move now in this direction, though not always, but according to the disposition of the [vital] spirits, as will be stated presently.

The cause of this can be none other than that the soul, being an Idea of this body, is united with it in such a way that it and this body, thus constituted, together form a whole.

The most important effect of the other or thinking attribute is an Idea of things, which is such that, according to the manner in which it apprehends them, there arises either Love or Hatred, etc. This effect, then, as it implies no extension, can also not be attributed to the same, but only to thought; so that, whatever the changes which happen to arise in this mode, their cause must on no account be sought for in extension, but only in the thinking thing. We can see this, for instance, in the case of Love, which, whether it is to be suppressed or whether it is to be awakened, can only be thus affected through the idea itself, and this happens, as we have already remarked, either because something bad is perceived to be in the object, or because something better comes to be known.[m] Now whenever these attributes happen to act the one on the other, there results a passivity which one suffers from the other; namely [in the case of extension], through the determination of movements which we have the power to direct in whatever direction we please. The process, then, whereby the one comes to be passively affected by the other, is this: namely, the soul in the body, as has already been remarked, can well bring it about that the [vital] spirits, which would otherwise move in the one direction, should nevertheless move in the other direction; and since these [vital] spirits can also be made to move, and therefore directed, by the body, it may frequently happen that, when the body directs their movements towards one place, while the soul directs them towards another place, they bring about and occasion in us those peculiar fits of depression which we sometimes feel without knowing the reasons why we have them. For otherwise the reasons are generally well known to us.

Furthermore, the power which the soul has to move the [vital] spirits may well be hindered also either because the motion of the [vital] spirits is much diminished, or because it is much increased. Diminished, as when, having run much,

---

[1] [B: by the motion of something else.]

[m] [B: either because something good is perceived in the loved object, or because something bad is perceived in the hated object.]

we bring it about that the [vital] spirits, owing to this running, impart to the body much more than the usual amount of motion,[n] and by losing this [motion] they are necessarily that much weakened; this may also happen through taking all too little food. Increased, as when, by drinking too much wine or other strong drink, we thereby become either merry or drunk, and bring it about that the soul has no power to control the body.

Having said thus much about the influences which the soul exercises on the body, let us now consider the influences of the body on the soul. The most important of these, we maintain, is that it causes the soul to become aware of it, and through it also of other bodies. This is effected by Motion and Rest conjointly, and by nothing else: for the body has nothing else than these wherewith to operate; so that whatever else comes to the soul, besides this awareness, cannot be caused through the body. And as the first thing which the soul gets to know is the body, the result is that the soul loves it so, and becomes united with it. But since, as we have already said before, the cause of Love, Hatred, and Sorrow must not be sought for in the body but only in the soul (because all the activities of the body must proceed from motion and rest), and since we see clearly and distinctly that one love comes to an end as soon as we come to know something else that is better, it follows clearly from all this that, *If once we get to know God, at least with a knowledge as clear as that with which we also know our body, then we must become united with him even more closely than we are with our body, and be, as it were, released from the body.* I say *more closely*, because we have already proved before that without him we can neither be, nor be known; and this is so because we know and must know him, not through something else, as is the case with all other things, but only through himself, as we have already said before. Indeed, we know him better even than we know ourselves, because without him we could not know ourselves at all.

From what we have said so far it is easily gathered which are the chief causes of the passions. For, as regards the Body with its effects, Motion and Rest,[o] these cannot affect the soul otherwise except so as to make themselves known to it as objects; and according to the appearances which they present to it, that is according as they appear good or bad,[18] so also is the soul affected by them, and that [happens] not inasmuch as it is a body (for then the body would be the principal cause of the pas-

---

[n] [B continues thus: in which they had a strong in—and through—flow which weakened them.]
[o] [B adds: or their effects.]
[18] But if it be asked whence comes it that we know that the one is good, the other bad? Answer: Since it is the objects which cause us to become aware of them, we are affected by the one differently, in proportion than by the other. Now these by which we are affected most harmoniously (as regards the proportion of motion and rest, of which they consist) are most agreeable to us, and as they depart more and more from this [harmonious proportion, they tend to be] most disagreeable. And hence arises every kind of feeling of which we become aware, and which, when it acts on our body, as it often does, through material objects, we call impulses; for instance, a man who is sorrowing can be made to laugh, or be made merry, by being tickled, or by drinking wine, etc., which [impulses] the soul becomes indeed aware of, but does not produce. For, when it operates, the merriments are real and of another kind; because then it is no body that operates, but the intelligent soul uses the body as a tool, and, consequently, as the soul is more active in this case, so is the feeling more perfect.

sions), but inasmuch as it is an object like all other things, which would also act in the same way if they happened to reveal themselves to the soul in the same way. (By this, however, I do not mean to say that the Love, Hatred, and Sorrow which proceed from the contemplation of incorporeal things produce the same effects as those which arise from the contemplation of corporeal things; for, as we shall presently say, these have yet other effects according to the nature of the thing through the apprehension of which Love, Hatred, and Sorrow, etc., are awakened in the soul which contemplates the incorporeal things.) So that, to return to our previous subject, if something else should appear to the soul to be more glorious than the body really is, it is certain that the body would then have no power to produce such effects as it certainly does now. Whence it follows,[p] not alone that the body is not the principal cause of the passions, but also that even if there were in us something else besides what we have just stated to be capable, in our opinion, of producing the passions, such a thing, even if there were such, could likewise affect the soul neither more nor differently than the body does in fact now. For it could never be anything else than such an object as would once for all be different from the soul, and would consequently show itself to be such and no other, as we have likewise stated also of the body. So that we may, with truth, conclude that Love, Hatred, Sorrow, and other passions are produced in the soul in various forms according to the kind of knowledge which, from time to time, it happens to have of the thing; and consequently, if once it can come to know the most glorious of all, it should be impossible for any of these passions to succeed in causing it the least perturbation.

Chapter XX
Confirmation of the Foregoing

Now, as regards what we have said in the preceding chapter, the following difficulties might be raised by way of objection.

First, if motion is not the cause of the passions then why is it possible, nevertheless, to banish sorrow by the aid of certain means, as is often done by means of wine? To this it serves [as an answer] that a distinction must be made between the soul's awareness, when it first becomes aware of the body, and the judgment which it presently comes to form as to whether it is good or bad for it.[19]

Now the soul, being such as just stated, has, as we have already shown before, the power to move the [vital] spirits whithersoever it pleases; but this power may, nevertheless, be taken away from it, as when, owing to other causes [arising out] of the body generally, their form, constituted by certain proportions [of motion

---

[p] [A continues thus: not that the body alone is the principal cause of the passions . . .; B: that the body alone is not the principal cause of passions . . .]

[19] That is, between understanding considered generally, and understanding having special regard to the good or evil of the thing.

and rest], disappears or is changed; and when it becomes aware of this [change] in it, there arises sorrow, which varies with the change which the [vital] spirits undergo. This sorrow results from its love for, and union with, the body.[20]

That this is so may be easily deduced from the fact that this sorrow can be alleviated in one of these two ways; either by restoring the [vital] spirits to their original form that is by relieving him of the pain, or by being persuaded by good reasons to make no ado about this body. The first is temporary, and [the sorrow] is liable to return; but the second is eternal, permanent, and unchangeable.

The second objection may be this: as we see that the soul, although it has nothing in common with the body, can yet bring it about that the [vital] spirits, although they were about to move in one direction, nevertheless move now in the other direction, why should it not also be able to effect that a body which is perfectly still and at rest should begin to move itself?[21] Likewise, why should it not

---

[20] Man's sorrow is caused by the thought that some evil is befalling him, namely, through the loss of some good; when such a thought is entertained, the result is, that the [vital] spirits gather about the heart, and, with the help of other parts, press it together and enclose it, just the reverse of what happens in the case of joy. Then the soul becomes aware of this pressure, and is pained. Now what is it that medicines or wine effect? This, namely, that by their action they drive away the [vital] spirits from the heart, and make room again, and when the soul becomes aware of this, it receives new animation, which consists in this, that the thought of evil is diverted by the change in the proportion of motion and rest, which the wine has caused, and it turns to something else in which the understanding finds more satisfaction. But this cannot be the immediate effect of the wine on the soul, but only of the wine on the [vital] spirits.

[21] Now, there is no difficulty here as to how the one mode, which is infinitely different from the other, yet acts on the other; for it is a part of the whole, since the soul never existed without the body, nor the body without the soul. We arrive at this [conclusion] as follows [no page numbers given]:

1. There is a perfect being, page —. 2. There cannot be two substances, page —. 3. No substance can have a beginning, page—. 4. Each is infinite in its kind, page —. 5. There must also be an attribute of thought, page —. 6. There is nothing in Nature, but there is an Idea of it in the thinking thing, resulting from its essence and existence in conjunction, page —. 7. Consequently, now: 8. Since their essence, without their existence, is implied in the designations of things, therefore the Idea of the essence cannot be regarded as something separate; this can only be done when there is both *existence* and *essence*, because then there is an object, which before was not. For example, when the whole wall is white, there is no this or that in, etc. 9. Now, this Idea, considered by itself, and apart from all other Ideas, can be no more than a mere Idea of such a thing, and it cannot be that it has an Idea of such a thing; [add] moreover, that such an Idea, thus regarded, since it is only a part, can have no very clear and very distinct conception of itself and its object, but only the thinking thing, which is the whole of Nature, can have this; for, a part considered without its whole, cannot, etc. 10. Between the Idea and the object there must necessarily be a union, because the one cannot exist without the other: for there is no thing whose Idea is not in the thinking thing, and no Idea can exist unless the thing also exists. Furthermore the object cannot change without the Idea changing also, and vice versa, so that there is here no need for a third thing that should bring about the union of soul and body. It is to be remarked, however, that we are speaking here of such Ideas which necessarily arise from the existence of the things together with their essence in God; but not of the Ideas which the things now actually present to us, [or] produce in us. There is a great difference between these; for the Ideas in God do not arise as they do in us by way of one or more of the senses, which are therefore almost always only imperfectly affected by them; but from their existence and their essence, just as they are. My idea, however, is not yours, although one and the same thing produces them in us.

also be able to move in whatever direction it pleases all other bodies which are already in motion?

But if we recall what we have already said before concerning the thinking thing, it can remove this difficulty for us quite easily. Namely, we then said that although Nature has various attributes, it is, all the same, but one only Being, of which all these attributes are predicated. Besides this we have also said that the thinking thing, too, was but one only thing in Nature, and is expressed in infinite Ideas, in accordance with the infinite things which exist in Nature; for if the body receives such a mode as, for example, the body of Peter, and again another such as is the body of Paul, the result of this is that there are in the thinking thing two different Ideas: namely, one idea of the body of Peter, which constitutes the Soul of Peter, and another of [the body of] Paul, which constitutes the Soul of Paul. Now the thinking thing can well move the body of Peter by means of the Idea of the body of Peter, but not by means of the Idea of the body of Paul; so that the soul of Paul can well move its own body, but by no means that of another, such as that of Peter.[22] And for this reason also it cannot move a stone which rests or lies still: because the stone, again, makes another Idea in the Soul. Hence also it is no less clear that it is impossible that a stone, which is perfectly at rest and still, should be made to move by any mode of thought, for the same reasons as above.

The third objection may be this: We seem to be able to see clearly that we can, nevertheless, produce a certain stillness in the body. For, after we have kept moving our [vital] spirits for a long time, we find that we are tired; which, assuredly, is nothing else than a certain stillness in the [vital] spirits brought about by ourselves. We answer, however, that it is quite true that the soul is a cause of this stillness, but only indirectly; for it puts a stop to the movement not directly, but only through other bodies which it has moved, and which must then necessarily have lost as much as they had imparted to the [vital] spirits. It is therefore clear on all sides that in Nature there is only one and the same kind of motion.

Chapter XXI
On Reason

At present we have to inquire why it happens that sometimes, although we see that a certain thing is good or bad, we nevertheless do not find in us the power either to do the good or to abstain from the bad, and sometimes, however, we do indeed [find this power in us]. This we can easily understand if we consider the

---

[22] It is clear that in man, because he had a beginning, there is to be found no other attribute than such as existed in Nature already before. —And since he consists of such a body of which there must necessarily be an Idea in the thinking thing, and the Idea must necessarily be united with the body, therefore we assert without fear that his Soul is nothing else than this Idea of his body in the

causes that we assigned to opinions, which we stated to be the causes of all affects. These, we then said, [arise] either from hearsay, or from experience. And since all that we find in ourselves has greater power over us than that which comes to us from outside, it certainly follows that Reason can be the cause of the extinction of opinions[23] which we have got from hearsay only (and this is so because reason has not like these come to us from outside), but by no means of those which we have got from experience. For the power which the thing itself gives us is always greater than that which we obtain by way of consequence through a second thing; we noted this difference when speaking of reasoning and of clear understanding, page 62, and we did so with the rule of three as an illustration. For more power comes to us from the understanding of proportion itself, than from the understanding of the rule of proportion. And it is for this reason that we have said so often that one love may be extinguished by another which is greater, because in saying this we did not, by any means, intend to refer to desire which does not, like love, come from true knowledge, but comes from reasoning.

Chapter XXII
On True Knowledge, Regeneration, Etc.

Since, then, Reason has no power to lead us to the attainment of our well-being, it remains for us to inquire whether we can attain it through the fourth, and last, kind of knowledge. Now we have said that this kind of knowledge does not result from something else, but from a direct revelation of the object itself to the understanding. And if that object is glorious and good, then the soul becomes necessarily united with it, as we have also remarked with reference to our body. Hence

---

thinking thing. And as this body has a[q] motion and rest (which has its proportion determined, and is usually altered, through external objects), and as no alteration can take place in the object without occurring also immediately in the Idea, the result is that people feel (*idea reflexiva*).[r] Now I say, *as it has a certain measure or proportion of motion and rest*, because no process can take place in the body without these two concurring.

[q] [B: has a certain measure of . . .]

[r] [B: that people have "reflexive" ideas.]

[23] It is all the same whether we use here the word opinion or passion; and so it is clear why we cannot conquer by means of Reason those that have come to us through experience; for these are nothing else than an enjoyment of, or immediate union with, something that we judge to be good, and Reason, though it teaches us what is better, does not make us enjoy it. Now that which we enjoy in us cannot be conquered by that which we do not enjoy, and is outside us, as that is which Reason suggests. But if these are to be overcome then there must be something that is more powerful; in this way there will be an enjoyment or immediate union with something that is better known and enjoyed than this first; and when this exists victory is always assured; or, indeed, this victory comes also through tasting an evil which is recognised to be greater than the good that was enjoyed, and upon which it follows immediately. Still, experience teaches us that this evil does not necessarily always follow thus, for, etc. *See* pages 68, 86.

it follows incontrovertibly that it is this knowledge which evokes love. So that when we get to know God after this manner then (as he cannot reveal himself, nor become known to us otherwise than as the most glorious and best of all) we must necessarily become united with him. And only in this union, as we have already remarked, does our blessedness consist.

I do not say that we must know him just as he is, or adequately, for it is sufficient for us to know him to some extent, in order to be united with him. For even the knowledge that we have of the body is not such that we know it just as it is, or perfectly; and yet, what a union! What a love!

That this fourth [kind of] knowledge, which is the knowledge of God, is not the consequence of something else, but immediate, is evident from what we have proved before, [namely,] that he is the cause of all knowledge that is acquired through itself alone, and through no other thing; moreover, also from this, that we are so united with him by nature that without him we can neither be, nor be known. And for this reason, since there is such a close union between God and us, it is evident that we cannot know him except directly.

We shall endeavour to explain, next, this union of ours with him through nature and love.

We said before that in Nature there can be nothing of which there should not be an Idea in the soul of that same thing.[24] And according as the thing is either more or less perfect, so also is the union and the influence of the Idea with the thing, or with God himself, less or more perfect. For as the whole of Nature is but one only substance, and one whose essence is infinite, all things are united through Nature, and they are united into one [being], namely, God. And now, as the body is the very first thing of which our soul becomes aware (because as already remarked, nothing can exist in Nature, the Idea of which is not in the thinking thing, this Idea being the soul of that thing) so that thing must necessarily be the first cause of the Idea.[25]

But, as this Idea can by no means find rest in the knowledge of the body without passing on to the knowledge of that without which the body and Idea could neither be, nor be understood, so (after knowing it first) it becomes united with it immediately through love. This union is better understood, and one may gather what it must be like, from its action with the body, in which we see how through knowledge of, and feelings towards corporeal things, there arise in us all the effects which we are constantly becoming aware of in the body, through the movements of the [vital] spirits; and therefore (if once our knowledge and love come to embrace that without which we can neither be, nor be understood, and which

---

[24] This also explains what we said in the first part, namely, that the infinite understanding must exist in Nature from all eternity, and why we called it the son of God. For, as God existed from eternity, his Idea must also be in the thinking thing, that is, in himself from eternity, *objective* this Idea coincides with himself; *see* page 59.

[25] That is our soul being an Idea of the body derives its first being from the body, but it is only a representation of the body, both as a whole and in its parts, in the thinking thing.

is in no way corporeal) how incomparably greater and more glorious will and must be the kind of effects resulting from this union; for these must necessarily be commensurate with the thing with which it is united. And when we become aware of these excellent effects, then we may say with truth, *that we have been born again.* For our first birth took place when we were united with the body, through which the activities and movements of the [vital] spirits have arisen; but this our other or second birth will take place when we become aware in us of entirely different effects of love, commensurate with the knowledge of this incorporeal object, and as different from the first as the corporeal is different from the incorporeal, spirit from flesh. And this may, therefore, all the more justly and truly be called Regeneration, inasmuch as only from this love and union does Eternal and unchangeable existence ensue, as we shall prove.

Chapter XXIII
On the Immortality of the Soul

If only we consider attentively what the Soul is, and whence its change and duration originate, then we shall easily see whether it is mortal or immortal.

Now we have said that the Soul is an Idea which is in the thinking thing, arising from the reality of a thing which exists in Nature. Whence it follows that according to the duration and change of the thing, so must also be the duration and change of the Soul. We remarked, at the same time, that the Soul can become united either *with the body* of which it is the Idea, or *with God*, without whom it can neither be, nor be known.

From this, then, it can easily be seen, (1) that, if it is united with the body alone, and that body happens to perish, then it must perish also; for when it is deprived of the body, which is the foundation of its love, it must perish with it. But (2) if it becomes united with some other thing which is and remains unchangeable, then, on the contrary, it must also remain unchangeable and lasting. For, in that case, through what shall it be possible for it to perish?[s] Not through itself; for as little as it could begin to exist through itself when it did not yet exist, so little also can it change or perish through itself, now that it does exist.

Consequently, that thing which alone is the cause of its *existence*, must also (when it is about to perish) be the cause of its *nonexistence*, because it happens to change itself or to perish.

---

[s] [B concludes this chapter as follows: For that which alone is the cause of the existence of a thing, must also, when it is about to pass away, be the cause of its nonexistence, simply because itself is changing or passing away; or that whereof it is the cause must be able to annihilate itself; but as little as a thing can begin to exist through itself when it does not yet exist, so little also can it change or perish through itself, now that it does exist.]

Chapter XXIV
On God's Love of Man

Thus far we have shown sufficiently, we think, what our love of God is, also its consequences, namely, our eternal duration. So we do not think it necessary here to say anything about other things, such as joy in God, peace of mind, etc., as from what has been said it may easily be seen what there is to or should be said about them. Thus (as we have, so far, only considered our love of God) it still remains to be seen whether there is also a divine love of us, that is, whether God also loves mankind, namely, when they love him. Now, in the first place, we have said that to God no modes of thought can be ascribed except those which are in his creatures; therefore, it cannot be said that God loves mankind, much less [can it be said] that he should love them because they love him, or hate them because they hate him. For in that case we should have to suppose that people do so of their own free will, and that they do not depend on a first cause; which we have already before proved to be false. Besides, this would necessarily involve nothing less than a great mutability on the part of God, who, though he neither loved nor hated before, would now have to begin to love and to hate, and would be induced or made to do so by something supposed to be outside him; but this is absurdity itself.

Still, when we say that God does not love man, this must not be taken to mean that he (so to say) leaves man to pursue his course all alone, but only that because man together with all that is, are in God in such a way, and God consists of all these in such a way, therefore, properly speaking, there can be in him no love for something else: since all form only one thing, which is God himself.

From this it follows also that God gives no laws to mankind so as to reward them when they fulfil them [and to punish them when they transgress them,] or, to state it more clearly, that God's laws are not of such a nature that they could be transgressed. For the regulations imposed by God on Nature, according to which all things come into existence and continue to exist, these, if we will call them laws, are such that they can never be transgressed; such, for instance, is [the law] that the weakest must yield to the strongest, that no cause can produce more than it contains in itself, and the like, which are of such a kind that they never change, and never had a beginning, but all things are subjected and subordinated to them. And, to say briefly something about them: all laws that cannot be transgressed, are divine laws; the reason [is this], because whatsoever happens, is not contrary to, but in accordance with, his own decision. All laws that can be transgressed are human laws; the reason [is this], because all that people decide upon for their own well-being does not necessarily, on that account, tend also to the well-being of the whole of Nature, but may, on the contrary, tend to the annihilation of many other things.

When the laws of Nature are stronger, the laws of men are made null; the divine laws are the final end for the sake of which they exist, and not subordinate;

human [laws] are not.²⁶ Still, notwithstanding the fact that men make laws for their own well-being, and have no other end in view except to promote their own well-being by them, this end of theirs may yet (insofar as it is subordinate to other ends which another has in view, who is above them, and lets them act thus as parts of Nature) serve that end [which] coincides with the eternal laws established by God from eternity, and so, together with all others, help to accomplish everything. For example, although the Bees, in all their work and the orderly discipline which they maintain among themselves, have no other end in view than to make certain provisions for themselves for the winter, still, man who is above them, has an entirely different end in view when he maintains and tends them, namely, to obtain honey for himself. So also [is it with] man, insofar as he is an individual thing and looks no further than his finite character can reach; but, insofar as he is also a part and tool of the whole of Nature, this end of man cannot be the final end of Nature, because she is infinite, and must make use of him, together also with all other things, as an instrument.

Thus far [we have been speaking] of the law imposed by God; it is now to be remarked also that man is aware of two kinds of law even in himself;ᵗ I mean such a man who uses his understanding aright, and attains to the knowledge of God; and these [two kinds of law] result from his fellowship with God, and from his fellowship with the modes of Nature. Of these the one is necessary, and the other is not. For, as regards the law which results from his fellowship with God, since he can never be otherwise but must always necessarily be united with him, therefore he has, and always must have before his eyes the laws by which he must live for and with God. But as regards the law which results from his fellowship with the modes, since he can separate himself from men, this is not so necessary.

Now, since we posit such a fellowship between God and men, it might justly be asked, how God can make himself known to men, and whether this happens, or could have happened, by means of spoken words, or directly through himself, without using any other thing to do it with.

We answer, not by means of words, in any case; for in that case man must have known the signification of the words before they were spoken to him. For example, if God had said to the Israelites, *I am Jehovah your God*, then they would have had to know first, apart from these words, that God existed,ᵘ before they could be assured thereby that it was he [who was speaking to them]. For they already knew quite well then that the voice, thunder and lightning were not God, although the voice proclaimed that it was God. And the same that we say here about words, we also mean to hold good of all external signs.

---

²⁶ [B: The Divine Laws are the final end for which they exist, and are not subordinate: but not so the Human Laws; for when the Laws of Nature are stronger than these they are annihilated.]

ᵗ [B continues: 1. In him who uses his understanding aright and attains to the knowledge of God; these result from his fellowship with God. 2. Those which result from his fellowship with the modes of Nature.]

ᵘ [A: *dat hy God was* [that he was God]; B: *dat God was* [that God existed].]

We consider it, therefore, impossible that God should make himself known to men by means of external signs.

And we consider it to be unnecessary that it should happen through any other thing than the mere essence of God and the understanding of man; for, as the Understanding is that in us which must know God, and as it stands in such immediate union with him that it can neither be, nor be understood without him, it is incontrovertibly evident from this that nothing can ever come into such close touch with the Understanding as God himself can. It is also impossible to get to know God through something else. 1. Because, in that case, such a thing would have to be better known to us than God himself, which is in open conflict with all that we have hitherto clearly shown, namely, that God is a cause both of our knowledge and of all essence, and that without him all individual things not only cannot exist, but cannot even be understood. 2. Because we can never attain to the knowledge of God through any other thing, the nature of which is necessarily finite, even if it were far better known to us; for how is it possible that we should infer an infinite and limitless thing from a finite and limited thing? For even if we did observe some effects or work in Nature the cause of which was unknown to us, still it would be impossible for us to conclude from this that there must be in Nature an infinite and limitless thing in order to produce this result. For how can we know whether many causes have concurred in order to produce this, or whether there was only one? Who is to tell us?

We therefore conclude, finally, that, in order to make himself known to men, God can and need use neither words, nor miracles, nor any other created thing, but only himself.

Chapter XXV
On Devils

We shall now briefly say something about devils, whether they exist or do not exist, and it is this:

If the Devil is a thing that is once for all opposed to God, and has absolutely nothing from God, then he is precisely identical with Nothing, which we have already discussed before.

If, with some, we represent him as a thinking thing that absolutely neither wills nor does any good, and so sets himself, once for all, in opposition to God, then surely he is very wretched, and, if prayers could help, then one ought to pray for his conversion.

But let us just see whether such a wretched thing could even exist for a single moment. And, if we do so, we shall immediately find out that it cannot; for whatever duration a thing has results entirely from the perfection of the thing, and the more essence and godliness things possess, the more lasting are they: therefore, as the Devil has not the least perfection in him, how should he then, I think to myself, be able to exist? Add to this, that the persistence or duration of a mode of the thinking thing only results from the union in which such a mode is, through love, joined to God. As the precise opposite of this union is supposed in the case of the Devils, they cannot possibly exist.

As, however, there is no necessity whatever why we should posit the existence of Devils, why then should they be posited? For we need not, like others, posit Devils in order to find [in them] the cause of Hatred, Envy, Wrath, and such-like passions, since we have found this sufficiently, without such fictions.

Chapter XXVI
On True Freedom

By the assertion of what precedes we not only wanted to make known that there are no Devils, but also, indeed, that the causes (or, to express it better, what we call *Sins*) which hinder us in the attainment of our perfection are in ourselves. We have also shown already, in what precedes, how and in what manner, through reason as also through the fourth kind of knowledge, we must attain to our blessedness, and how the passions which are bad and should be banished must be done away with: not as is commonly urged, namely, that these [passions] must first be subdued before we can attain to the knowledge, and consequently to the love, of God. That would be just like insisting that some one who is ignorant must first forsake his ignorance before he can attain to knowledge. But [the truth is] this, that only knowledge can cause the disappearance thereof—as is evident from all that we have said. Similarly, it may also be clearly gathered from the above that without Virtue, or (to express it better) without the guidance of the Understanding, all tends to ruin, so that we can enjoy no rest, and we live, as it were, outside our element. So that even if from the power of knowledge and divine love there accrued to the understanding not an eternal rest, such as we have shown, but only a temporary one, it is our duty to seek even this, since this also is such that if once we taste it we would exchange it for nothing else in the world.

This being so, we may, with reason, regard as a great absurdity what many, who are otherwise esteemed as great theologians, assert, namely, that if no eternal life resulted from the love of God, then[v] they would seek what is best for themselves: as though they could discover anything better than God! This is just as silly as if a fish (for which, of course, it is impossible to live out of the water) were to say: if no eternal life is to follow this life in the water, then I will leave the water for the land; what else, indeed, can they say to us who do not know God?

Thus we see, therefore, that in order to arrive at the truth of what we assert for sure concerning our happiness and repose, we require no other principles except

---

[v] [B continues thus: people would seek and consider pleasures of sense, merriment, and worldly enjoyments: as though . . .]

only this, namely, to take to heart our own interest, which is very natural in all things. And since we find that, when we pursue sensuousness, pleasures, and worldly things, we do not find our happiness in them, but, on the contrary, our ruin, we therefore choose the guidance of our understanding. As, however, this can make no progress, unless it has first attained to the knowledge and love of God, therefore it was highly necessary to seek this (God); and as (after the foregoing reflections and considerations) we have discovered that he is the best good of all that is good, we are compelled to stop and to rest here. For we have seen that, outside him, there is nothing that can give us any happiness. And it is a true freedom to be, and to remain, bound with the loving chains of his love.

Lastly, we see also that reasoning is not the principal thing in us, but only like a staircase by which we can climb up to the desired place, or like a good genius which, without any falsity or deception, brings us tidings of the highest good in order thereby to stimulate us to pursue it, and to become united with it; which union is our supreme happiness and bliss.

So, to bring this work to a conclusion, it remains to indicate briefly what human freedom is, and wherein it consists. For this purpose I shall make use of these following propositions, as things which are certain and demonstrated.

1. The more essence a thing has, so much more has it also of activity, and so much less of passivity. For it is certain that what is active acts through what it has, and that the thing which is passive is affected through what it has not.

2. All passivity that passes from non-being to being, or from being to non-being, must result from some external agent, and not from an inner one: because nothing, considered by itself, contains in itself the conditions that will enable it to annihilate itself when it exists, or to create itself when it does not exist.

3. Whatever is not produced by external causes can have nothing in common with them, and can, consequently, be neither changed nor transformed by them.

And from these last two [propositions] I infer the following fourth proposition:

4. The effect of an immanent or inner cause (which is all one to me) cannot possibly pass away or change so long as this cause of it remains. For such an effect, just as it is not produced by external causes, so also it cannot be changed [by them]; following the third proposition. And since nothing whatever can come to naught except through external causes, it is not possible that this effect should be liable to perish so long as its cause endures; following the second proposition.

5. The freest cause of all, and that which is most appropriate to God, is the immanent: for the effect of this cause depends on it in such a way that it can neither be, nor be understood without it, nor is it subjected to any other cause; it is, moreover, united with it in such a way that together they form one whole.

Now let us just see what we must conclude from the above propositions. In the first place, then:

1. Since the essence of God is infinite, therefore it has an infinite activity, and an infinite negation of passivity, following the first proposition; and, in consequence of this, the more that, through their greater essence, things are united with God, so much the more also do they have of activity, and the less of passivity: and so much the more also are they free from change and corruption.

2. The true Understanding can never perish; for in itself it can have no cause to destroy itself, following the second proposition. And as it did not emanate from external causes, but from God, so it is not susceptible to any change through them, following the third proposition. And since God has produced it immediately and he is only an inner cause, it follows necessarily that it cannot perish so long as this cause of it remains, following the fourth proposition. Now this cause of it is eternal, therefore it is too.

3. All the effects of the true understanding, which are united with it, are the most excellent, and must be valued above all the others; for as they are inner effects, they must be the most excellent; following the fifth proposition; and, besides this, they are also necessarily eternal, because their cause is such.

4. All the effects which we produce outside ourselves are the more perfect, the more they are capable of becoming united with us, so as to constitute one and the same nature with us; for in this way they come nearest to inner effects. For example, if I teach my neighbours to love pleasure, glory, avarice, then whether I myself also love these or do not love them, whatever the case may be, I deserve to be punished, this is clear. Not so, however, when the only end that I endeavour to attain is, to be able to taste of union with God, and to bring forth true ideas, and to make these things known also to my neighbours; for we can all participate equally in this happiness, as happens when it creates in them the same desire that I have, thus causing their will and mine to be one and the same, constituting one and the same nature, agreeing always in all things.[w]

From all that has been said it may now be very easily conceived what is human freedom,[27] which I define to be this: it is, namely, a firm reality which our understanding acquires through direct union with God, so that it can bring forth ideas in itself, and effects outside itself, in complete harmony with its nature; without, however, its effects being subjected to any external causes, so as to be capable of being changed or transformed by them. Thus it is, at the same time, evident

---

[w] [Instead of the three preceding paragraphs, B has the following:

2. As (according to Proposition II) nothing can be a cause of its own annihilation, nor, if it is not the effect of any external cause, can it (according to Proposition III) be changed by such, but (according to Proposition IV) the effect of an inner cause can neither pass away, nor change so long as this cause thereof endures; it follows that the true understanding, since it is produced by no external cause, but immediately by God, is, through this cause, eternal and immutable, can neither perish nor change, but, with it, necessarily remains eternal and lasting.

3. Since the inner effects of an immanent cause (according to Proposition V) are the most excellent of all, all the effects of the true understanding which are united therewith, must also be valued above all others, and [must] necessarily be eternal with their cause. Whence it follows that

4. The more perfect the effects are which we produce outside us, the more capable are they of becoming united with us so as to constitute one and the same nature with us. It is thus when, through my union with God, I conceive true ideas, and make them known to my neighbours, so that they may likewise participate with me in this happiness, and so that there arises in them a desire like mine, making their will one and the same with mine, so that we thus constitute one and the same nature, agreeing in all things.]

[27] The servitude of a thing consists in being subjected to external causes, freedom, on the contrary, in not being subjected to them, but freed from them.

from what has been said, what things there are that are in our power, and are not subjected to any external causes; we have likewise also proved here, and that in a different way from before, the eternal and lasting duration of our understanding; and, lastly, which effects it is that we have to value above all others.

So, to make an end of all this, it only remains for me still to say to my friends to whom I write this: Be not astonished at these novelties; for it is very well known to you that a thing does not therefore cease to be true because it is not accepted by many. And also, as the character of the age in which we live is not unknown to you, I would beg of you most earnestly to be very careful about the communication of these things to others. I do not want to say that you should absolutely keep them to yourselves, but only that if ever you begin to communicate them to anybody, then let no other aim prompt you except only the happiness of your neighbour, being at the same time clearly assured by him that the reward will not disappoint your labour. Lastly, if, on reading this through, you should meet with some difficulty about what I state as certain, I beseech you that you should not therefore hasten at once to refute it, before you have pondered it long enough and thoughtfully enough, and if you do this I feel sure that you will attain to the[28] enjoyment of the fruits of this tree which you promise yourselves.

ΤΕΛΟΣ
[the end]

APPENDICES

[Appendix 1]
On God

Axioms

1. Substance is, by its nature, prior to all its modifications.
2. Things which are different are distinguished either *realiter* or *modaliter*.
3. Things which are distinguished *realiter* either have different attributes, such as Thought and Extension, or are referred to different attributes, as in the case of Understanding and Motion; one of which belongs to Thought, and the other to Extension.
4. Things which have different attributes, as also the things which belong to different attributes, do not have anything the one of the other.

---

[28] [B concludes: desired END.]

5. That which has not in itself something of another thing, can also not be a cause of the existence of such another thing.

6. It is impossible that that which is a cause of itself should have limited itself.

7. That by which the things are sustained is by its nature prior to such things.

PROPOSITION I
To no substance that exists can one and the same attribute be ascribed that is ascribed to another substance; or (which is the same) in Nature there cannot be two substances, unless they are distinguished *realiter*.[a]

Proof If there are two substances, then they are distinct; and consequently (Axiom 2) they are distinguished either *realiter* or *modaliter*; not *modaliter*, for in that case the modes would by their nature be prior to the substance, which is contrary to the first axiom; therefore, *realiter*; and consequently, what is predicated of the one cannot be predicated of the other, which is what we intended to prove.

PROPOSITION II
One substance cannot be the cause of the existence of another substance.

Proof Such a cause cannot contain in itself anything of such an effect (Prop. 1); because the difference between them is real, and therefore it cannot (Axiom 5) produce it.

PROPOSITION III
Every attribute or substance is by nature infinite, and supremely perfect in its kind.

Proof No substance is produced by another (Prop. 2) and consequently, if it exists, it is either an attribute of God, or it has been its own cause outside God. If the first, then it is necessarily infinite, and supremely perfect in its kind, such as are all other attributes of God. If the second, then it is also necessarily such because (Axiom 6) it could not have limited itself.

PROPOSITION IV
To such an extent does existence pertain by nature to the essence of every substance, that it is impossible to posit in an infinite understanding the Idea of the essence of a substance that does not exist in Nature.

Proof The true essence of an object is something which is *realiter* different from the Idea of the same object; and this something exists (Axiom 3) either *realiter*, or is contained in some other thing which exists *realiter*; from which other thing this essence cannot be distinguished *realiter*, but only *modaliter*; such are all the essences of the things which we see, which before they yet existed were already contained in extension, motion, and rest, and when they do exist are not distin-

---

[a] [B: . . . in Nature there cannot be posited two substances of one and the same nature.]

guished from extension *realiter*, but only *modaliter*. Moreover, it would involve self-contradiction to suppose that the essence of a substance is contained thus in some other thing; because in that case it could not be distinguished from this *realiter*, contrary to the first proposition; also, it could in that case be produced by the subject which contains it, contrary to the second proposition; and lastly, it could not by its nature be infinite and supremely perfect in its kind, contrary to the third proposition. Therefore, as its essence is not contained in any other thing, it must be a thing that exists through itself.

Corollary Nature is known through itself, and not through any other thing. It consists of infinite attributes every one of them infinite and perfect in its kind; to its essence pertains existence, so that outside it there is no other essence or existence, and it thus coincides exactly with the essence of God who alone is glorious and blessed.

[Appendix II]
On the Human Soul

As man is a created finite thing, etc., it necessarily follows that what he has of Thought, and what we call the Soul, is a mode of the attribute which we call Thought, and that nothing else except this mode belongs to his essence: so much so that when this mode comes to naught, the soul perishes also, although the above attribute remains unchanged. Similarly as regards what he has of Extension; what we call Body is nothing else than a mode of the other attribute which we call Extension; when this is destroyed, the human body also ceases to be, although the attribute Extension remains unchanged.

Now in order to understand what this mode is, which we call Soul, and how it derives its origin from the body, and also how its change (only) depends on the body (which to me constitutes the union of soul and body), it must be observed:

1. That the most immediate mode of the attribute which we call thought contains *objective* the formal essence of all things; so much so, that if one could posit a real thing whose essence was not *objective* in the above-named attribute, then this would not be infinite, nor supremely perfect in its kind; contrary to what has already been proved in the third proposition. And since, as a matter of fact, Nature or God is one being of which infinite attributes are predicated, and which contains in itself all the essences of created things, it necessarily follows that of all this there is produced in Thought an infinite Idea, which comprehends *objective* the whole of Nature just as it is *realiter*.

2. It is to be observed that all the remaining modes, such as Love, Desire, Joy, etc., derive their origin from this first immediate mode; and that, too, in such wise, that if it did not precede, then there could be no love, desire, nor joy, etc. Whence it clearly follows that the natural love which prompts everything to preserve its body (I mean the mode) cannot have any other origin than in the Idea or the "ob-

jective" essence of such body which is in the thinking attribute. Further, since for the real existence of an Idea (or "objective" essence) no other thing is required than the thinking attribute and the object (or "formal" essence), it is certain, as we have said, that the Idea, or the "objective" essence, is the most immediate[1] mode of the thinking attribute. And, consequently, there can be in the thinking attribute no other mode, that should belong to the essence of the soul of every thing, except only the Idea, which must be in the thinking attribute when its object exists: for such an idea brings with it the remaining modes of Love, Desire, Joy, etc. Now as the Idea comes from the existence of the object, therefore according as the object changes or perishes, so its Idea must change or perish, and such being the case, it is that which is united with the object.[a]

Lastly, if we should want to proceed and ascribe to the essence of the soul that through which it can be real, we shall be able to find nothing else than the attribute [Thought] and the object of which we have just been speaking; and neither of these can belong to the essence of the Soul, as the object has nothing of Thought, and is *realiter* different from the Soul. And with regard to the attribute, we have also proved already that it cannot pertain to the above-mentioned essence, as appears even more clearly from what we said subsequently; for the attribute as attribute is not united with the object, since it neither changes nor perishes, although the object changes or perishes.

Therefore the essence of the soul consists in this alone, namely, in the existence of an Idea or "objective" essence in the thinking attribute, arising from the essence of an object which in fact exists in Nature. I say, *of an object which in fact exists, etc.*, without more particulars, so as to include under this not only the modes of extension, but also the modes of all the infinite attributes, which have also each its soul, just as in the case of extension. And in order that this definition may be somewhat more fully understood, it should be borne in mind what I have already said when speaking about the attributes, which, I said, are not different as regards their existence, for they are themselves the "subjects" of their essences; also that the essence of every one of the modes is contained in the above-named attributes, and, lastly, that all the attributes are attributes of One infinite Being. Wherefore also, in the ninth chapter of the First Part, I called this Idea *a creation created immediately by God*; since it contains *objective* the "formal" essence of all things,[b] without omission or addition. And this is necessarily but one, considering that all the essences of the attributes, and the essences of the modes comprehended in these attributes, are the essence of one only infinite being. But it has still to be remarked that these modes, now under consideration, [even when] none of them exists, are nevertheless equally comprehended in their attributes; and as

---

[1] I call that mode the most immediate mode, which, in order to exist, requires no other mode in the same attribute.

[a] [B: . . . so this idea of it must change or perish in the same degree or measure of change or annihilation, because it is thus united with the object.]

[b] [B: . . . I called the thinking attribute, or the understanding in the thinking thing, a son, product, or creation created immediately by God, since it contains the "objective" essence of all things . . .]

there is no inequality whatever in the attributes, nor yet in the essences of the modes, there can be no particularity in the idea when there is none in Nature. But as soon as ever some of these modes take on their particular existence, and thereby become in some way different from their attributes (because then their particular existence, which they have in the attribute, as the "subject" of their essence), then there shows itself a particularity in the essences of the modes, and consequently in the "objective" essences of these which are necessarily comprehended in the Idea.[c] And this is the reason why we said, in the definition, that the Idea[d] *arises from an object, which really exists in Nature.* And with this we think we have sufficiently explained what kind of a thing the soul is in general, understanding by this expression not only the Ideas which arise from the existence of corporeal modes, but also those which arise from the existence of every mode of the remaining attributes.

But, since we have no such knowledge of the remaining attributes as we have of extension, let us just see whether, having regard to the modes of extension, we can discover a more special definition, and one that shall be more appropriate to express the essence of our souls, for this is the real task before us. Now we shall presuppose here, as something already demonstrated, that extension contains no other modes than motion and rest, and that every particular material thing is nothing else than a certain proportion of motion and rest, so much so indeed that, even if extension contained nothing else except motion only or rest only, then no particular thing could be shown or exist in the whole of extension; the human body, therefore, is nothing else than a certain proportion of motion and rest. Now the "objective essence" of this actual ratio of motion and rest which is in the thinking attribute, this (we say) is the soul of the body; so that whenever one of these two modes changes into more or less (motion or rest) the Idea or the soul also changes accordingly. For example, when the [amount of] rest happens to increase, while the [quantity of] motion is diminished, then there is produced thereby that pain or sorrow which we call *cold*; but if, on the contrary, this [increase] takes place in the [amount of] motion, then there is produced thereby that pain which we call *heat.*[e] And so when it happens that the degrees of motion and rest are not equal in all the parts of our body, but that some have more motion and rest than others, there arises therefrom a difference of feeling (and thence arises the different kind of pain which we feel when we are struck in the eyes or on the hands with a cane). And when it happens that the external causes, which bring about these changes,

---

[c] [B: in the Thinking Attribute.]

[d] [B: the soul, the idea, or objective essence in the thinking attribute (which is all one to me) arises . . .]

[e] [B continues as follows: But if the proportion of motion and rest is not the same in all the parts of our body, but some of them are provided with more motion or rest than the others, there arises thence a difference of feeling: such as we experience when we are struck with a cane in the eyes or on the hands. Moreover, when the external causes happen to be different, and have not all the same effect, there results therefrom a difference of feeling in one and the same part: such as we experience when the same hand is struck with a piece of wood or of iron. But when the change which occurs in some part restores it to its previous proportion of motion and rest, there arises . . .]

are different from one another, and have not all the same effect, then there results from this a difference of feeling in one and the same part (and from this results the difference of feeling according as one and the same hand is struck with a piece of wood or of iron). And, again, if the change which occurs in a part restores it to its first proportion of motion and rest, there arises from this that joy which we call repose, pleasurable activity, and cheerfulness. Lastly, now that we have explained what feeling is, we can easily see how this gives rise to an *Idea reflexiva*, or the knowledge of oneself, Experience and Reasoning. And from all this (as also because our soul is united with God, and is a part of the infinite Idea, arising immediately from God) there can also be clearly seen the origin of clear knowledge, and the immortality of the soul. But, for the present, what we have said must be enough.

Principles of Cartesian Philosophy and Metaphysical Thoughts

Spinoza is often depicted as a solitary rebel. This is a caricature. In fact, he was one of a group of radical thinkers, deeply involved in the new science and in Cartesian philosophy, who gathered around Franciscus Van den Enden. Others included Lodewijk Meyer, Johan Bouwmeester, Pieter Balling, Simon de Vries, and Jarig Jelles. Spinoza participated with others in what was notorious as a Cartesian revolution, the mechanical philosophy. He, like his friends, was committed to determinism, the condition of human passivity, the intellectual love of God, and more.

The Principles of Cartesian Philosophy *is the most explicit evidence of Spinoza's interest and expertise in Descartes. One of two works published by Spinoza during his lifetime, it appeared in 1663. While living in Rijnsburg, Spinoza acted as a professional tutor, and one of his pupils in Cartesian philosophy was a nineteen-year-old Leiden University student, Johannes Caesarius. According to Spinoza's friend Lodewijk Meyer in his introduction to the 1663 edition, Spinoza's Amsterdam friends had encouraged him to publish the materials on Descartes that he had dictated to Caesarius. In them, Spinoza had recast Descartes' philosophical thinking into a synthetic or demonstrative form both to clarify Descartes' intentions and to secure the details of the system. The result is a work that reveals as much about Spinoza's own thinking as it does about Cartesian philosophy. It was, after all, written on the heels of the TIE and during a period in which Spinoza was still at work on the* Short Treatise, *fully in the spirit of the rest of his philosophical and scientific enquiries.*

Clearly Spinoza is convinced that mathematics is the exemplary science and that presenting philosophical results in a mathematical or geometrical form best reflects their certitude. Descartes' Principles of Philosophy, *published in 1644, was Descartes' attempt to present in this form (that is, synthetically) the views he had come to in the 1630s—in the* Meditations, Discourse, *and essays on optics, astronomy, and geometry—in a more discursive or analytic way. Spinoza's own presentation advances Descartes' achievement. Originally it dealt with Part 2 of Descartes'* Principles *and the beginning of Part 3. At his friends' request, Spinoza added a presentation of Part 1. He did it rather quickly, however, and apologized for its haste.*

Spinoza was explicit about Caesarius' shortcomings, at least at this early stage in his education; he was after all only nineteen. For this reason, Spinoza studiously avoided discussion of his own views which he thought too advanced and for which Caesarius was not yet prepared. His comments on Part 1 and indeed the finished product were, in the end, prepared for his friends and associates and others attuned to the new philosophy. Ostensibly a work of pure exposition and clarification, the published book reveals some differences between Spinoza and Descartes as well as Spinoza's way of clarifying the point of Cartesian philosophy and science. Like John Rawls' account of Kantian moral philosophy, Principles of Cartesian Philosophy is about both its subject and its author.

When the work was published, Spinoza had already moved from Rijnsburg, near Leiden, to the village of Voorburg, outside The Hague. Shortly after the move, he visited Amsterdam for several weeks in order to prepare the lessons on Descartes for publication. Having spent two weeks writing his account of Part 1, he arranged Lodewijk Meyer's assistance in editing the book and writing its preface. Eventually Spinoza appended some comments on the metaphysics of Part 1 and his own thoughts on these matters; these were published in an appendix, the "Cogitata Metaphysica," or "Metaphysical Thoughts." Meyer was careful in his preface to point out where Spinoza differed from Descartes—for example, on mind as a substance and on the freedom of the will. But Meyer was selective; there were many differences of organization and presentation as well as these central differences in substance.

The Principles of Cartesian Philosophy is an important document for a number of reasons. Spinoza's exposition of Cartesian philosophy reflects his interest in the details of science as well as in its foundations. Second, his own "Cogitata Metaphysica," when compared with his exposition of Part 1 and with his later work, expresses the primary role of God in his thinking and the importance of the modal notions of necessity and contingency and the concepts of eternity and duration. Finally, the work confirms Spinoza's role as an expert in and advocate of Cartesianism and its special character as a model of the new philosophy.

M.L.M.

CONTENTS

Principles of Cartesian Philosophy

Preface by Lodewijk Meyer

Part 1

    Prolegomenon
    Definitions
    Axioms
    Prop. 1: We cannot be absolutely certain of anything as long as we do not know that we exist.
    Prop. 2: 'I am' must be self-evident.
    Prop. 3: 'I am', insofar as the 'I' is a thing consisting of body, is not a first principle and is not known through itself.
    Prop. 4: 'I am' cannot be the first known principle except insofar as we think.
    Axioms Taken from Descartes
    Prop. 5: The existence of God is known solely from the consideration of his nature.
    Prop. 6: The existence of God is proved a posteriori from the mere fact that the idea of him is in us.
    Prop. 7: The existence of God is also proved from the fact that we ourselves exist while having the idea of him.
    Prop. 8: Mind and body are distinct in reality.
    Prop. 9: God is a supremely understanding being.
    Prop. 10: Whatever perfection is found in God, is from God.
    Prop. 11: There cannot be more than one God.
    Prop. 12: All things that exist are preserved solely by the power of God.
    Prop. 13: God is supremely truthful, and not at all a deceiver.
    Prop. 14: Whatever we clearly and distinctly perceive is true.
    Prop. 15: Error is not anything positive.
    Prop. 16: God is incorporeal.
    Prop. 17: God is a completely simple being.
    Prop. 18: God is immutable.
    Prop. 19: God is eternal.
    Prop. 20: God has preordained all things from eternity.

Prop. 21: Substance extended in length, breadth, and depth exists in reality, and we are united to one part of it.

PART 2

Postulate
Definitions
Axioms
Prop. 1: Although hardness, weight and the other sensible qualities may be separated from a body, the nature of the body will nevertheless remain unimpaired.
Prop. 2: The nature of body or matter consists only in extension.
Prop. 3: That there should be a vacuum is a contradiction.
Prop. 4: One part of a body does not occupy more space at one time than at another; and, conversely, the same space does not contain more body at one time than at another.
Prop. 5: There are no atoms.
Prop. 6: Matter is indefinitely extended, and the matter of the heavens and the earth is one and the same.
Prop. 7: No body moves into the place of another body unless at the same time that other body moves into the place of another body.
Prop. 8: When a body moves into the place of another body, at the same moment of time the place quitted by it is occupied by another body immediately contiguous to it.
Prop. 9: If a circular tube ABC is full of water and is four times as wide at A as at B, then at the time that the water (or any other fluid body) at A begins to move toward B, the water at B will move at four times that speed.
Prop. 10: The fluid body that moves through the tube ABC (of Prop. 9) receives an indefinite number of degrees of speed.
Prop. 11: The matter that flows through the tube ABC (of Prop. 9) is divided into an indefinite number of particles.
Prop. 12: God is the principal cause of motion.
Prop. 13: God still preserves by his concurrence the same quantity of motion and rest that he originally gave to matter.
Prop. 14: Each single thing, insofar as it is simple and undivided and is considered only in itself, always perseveres in the same state, as far as in it lies.
Prop. 15: Every body in motion tends of itself to continue to move in a straight line, not in a curved line.
Prop. 16: Every body that moves in a circle (e.g., a stone in a sling) is continuously determined to continue in motion at a tangent to that circle.
Prop. 17: Every body that moves in a circle endeavors to move away from the center of the circle that it describes.

Prop. 18: If a body A moves toward a body B, which is at rest, and B loses nothing of its state of rest in spite of the impetus of body A, then neither will A lose anything of its motion, but will retain entirely the same quantity of motion that it had before.

Prop. 19: Motion, regarded in itself, is different from its determination toward a certain direction; and there is no need for a moving body to be for any time at rest in order that it may travel or be repelled in an opposite direction.

Prop. 20: If a body A collides with a body B and takes it along with it, A will lose as much of its motion as B acquires from A because of its collision with A.

Prop. 21: If a body A is twice as large as B and moves with equal speed, A will also have twice as much motion as B, or twice as much force for retaining a speed equal to B's.

Prop. 22: If a body A is equal to a body B, and A is moving at twice the speed of B, the force or motion in A will be twice that in B.

Prop. 23: When the modes of a body are compelled to undergo variation, that variation will always be the least that can be.

Prop. 24, Rule 1: If two bodies, A and B, should be completely equal and should move in a straight line toward each other with equal velocity, on colliding with each other they will both be reflected in the opposite direction with no loss of speed.

Prop. 25, Rule 2: If A and B are unequal in mass, B being greater than A, other conditions being as previously stated, then A alone will be reflected, and each will continue to move at the same speed.

Prop. 26: If A and B are unequal in mass and speed, B being twice the size of A and the motion in A being twice the speed of that in B, other conditions being as before stated, they will both be reflected in the opposite direction, each retaining the speed that it possessed.

Prop. 27, Rule 3: If A and B are equal in mass but B moves a little faster than A, not only will A be reflected in the opposite direction, but also B will transfer to A half the difference of their speeds, and both will proceed to move in the same direction at the same speed.

Prop. 28, Rule 4: If a body A is completely at rest and is a little larger than B, with whatever speed B moves toward A it will never move A, but will be repelled by A in the opposite direction, retaining its original motion.

Prop. 29, Rule 5: If a body A at rest is smaller than B, then however slowly B moves toward A, it will move it along with it, transferring to it such a part of its motion that both bodies thereafter move at the same speed.

Prop. 30, Rule 6: If a body A at rest were exactly equal to a body B, which is moving toward it, to some degree A would be impelled by B, and to some degree B would be repelled by A in the opposite direction.

Prop. 31, Rule 7: If B and A are moving in the same direction, A more slowly and B following it more quickly so that it finally overtakes A, and if A is bigger than B, but B's excess of speed is greater than A's excess of magnitude, then B will transfer to A so much of its motion that both will thereafter move at the same speed in the same direction. But if, on the other hand, A's excess of magnitude should be greater than B's excess of speed, B would be reflected by it in the opposite direction, retaining all its motion.

Prop. 32: If a body B is surrounded on all sides by particles in motion, which at the same time are impelling it with equal force in all directions, as long as no other cause occurs it will remain unmoved in the same place.

Prop. 33: Body B, under the conditions stated previously, can be moved in any direction by any additional force, however small.

Prop. 34: Body B, under the same conditions as previously, cannot move more quickly than it is impelled by the external force, even though the particles by which it is surrounded are in much swifter motion.

Prop. 35: When body B is thus moved by an external impulse, it receives the greatest part of its motion from the bodies by which it is constantly surrounded, and not from the external force.

Prop. 36: If any body (e.g., our hand) can move in any direction whatsoever with equal motion without offering any resistance to any bodies or meeting with any resistance from any other bodies, then in that space through which it would thus move there must necessarily be as many bodies moving in one direction as there are bodies moving in any other direction, their force of speed being equal to one another's and to that of the hand.

Prop. 37: If a body A can be moved in any direction whatsoever by any force, however small, it must necessarily be surrounded by bodies that are moving at the same speed as one another.

PART 3

Postulate
Definitions
Axioms
Prop. 1: The parts into which matter was first divided were not round but angular.
Prop. 2: The force that brought it about that the particles of matter should move about their own centers, at the same time brought

it about that the angles of the particles should be worn away by collision with one another.

Metaphysical Thoughts

Part 1

    Chap. 1: Of Real Being, Fictitious Being, and Being of Reason
    Chap. 2: What Essence Is, What Existence Is, What Idea Is, and What Potency Is
    Chap. 3: Concerning the Necessary, the Impossible, the Possible, and the Contingent
    Chap. 4: Of Duration and Time
    Chap. 5: Of Opposition, Order, Etc.
    Chap. 6: Of the One, the True, and the Good

Part 2

    Chap. 1: Of God's Eternity
    Chap. 2: Of the Unity of God
    Chap. 3: Of the Immeasurableness of God
    Chap. 4: Of the Immutability of God
    Chap. 5: Of the Simplicity of God
    Chap. 6: Of the Life of God
    Chap. 7: Of God's Intellect
    Chap. 8: Of God's Will
    Chap. 9: Of God's Power
    Chap. 10: Of Creation
    Chap. 11: Of God's Concurrence
    Chap. 12: Of the Human Mind

Parts I and II[1] of
René Descartes's

THE PRINCIPLES OF PHILOSOPHY

demonstrated in the geometric manner

by

Benedict de Spinoza of Amsterdam.

To which are added his
Metaphysical Thoughts,

in which are briefly explained the more
difficult problems that arise in both the
general and the special part of Metaphysics.

Amsterdam.
Published by Johannes Rieuwertsz,
in the quarter commonly called
The Dirk van Assen-Steeg,
under the sign Martyrologium. 1663.

Notes without brackets are Spinoza's. Bracketed notes are those of Steven Barbone and Lee Rice (main annotators for this work), translator Samuel Shirley, Spinoza's friend Pieter Balling, and Michael L. Morgan.

[1] [The frontispiece announces only Parts I and II of the PPC; Part III is not mentioned here. —S.B./L.R.]

Preface
To the honest reader, Lodewijk Meyer gives greetings

It is the unanimous opinion of all who seek wisdom beyond the common lot that the best and surest way to discover and to teach truth is the method used by mathematicians in their study and exposition of the sciences, namely, that whereby conclusions are demonstrated from definitions, postulates, and axioms. And indeed rightly so. Because all sure and sound knowledge of what is unknown can be elicited and derived only from what is already known with certainty, this latter must first be built up from the ground as a solid foundation on which thereafter to construct the entire edifice of human knowledge, if that is not to collapse of its own accord or give way at the slightest blow. That the things familiar to mathematicians under the title of definitions, postulates, and axioms are of this kind cannot be doubted by anyone who has even the slightest acquaintance with that noble discipline. For definitions are merely the perspicuous explanations of the terms and names by which matters under discussion are designated, whereas postulates and axioms—that is, the common notions of the mind—are statements so clear and lucid that no one who has simply understood the words aright can possibly refuse assent.

But although this is so, you will find that with the exception of mathematics hardly any branch of learning is treated by this method. Instead, a totally different method is adopted, whereby the entire work is executed by means of definitions and logical divisions interlinked in a chain, with problems and explanations interspersed here and there. For almost all who have applied themselves to establishing and setting out the sciences have believed, and many still do believe, that the mathematical method is peculiar to mathematics and is to be rejected as inapplicable to all other branches of learning.

In consequence, nothing of what they produce is demonstrated with conclusive reasoning. They try to advance arguments that depend merely on likelihood and probability, and in this way they thrust before the public a great medley of great books in which you may look in vain for solidity and certainty. Disputes and strife abound, and what one somehow establishes with trivial arguments of no real weight is soon refuted by another, demolished and shattered with the same weapons. So where the mind, eager for unshakable truth, had thought to find for its labors a placid stretch of water that it could navigate with safety and success, thereafter attaining the haven of knowledge for which it yearned, it finds itself tossed on a stormy sea of opinion, beset on all sides with tempests of dispute, hurled about and carried away on waves of uncertainty, endlessly, with no hope of ever emerging therefrom.

Yet there have not been lacking some who have thought differently and, taking pity on the wretched plight of Philosophy, have distanced themselves from this universally adopted and habitual way of treating the sciences and have entered upon a new and indeed an arduous path bristling with difficulties, so as to leave to posterity the other parts of Philosophy, besides mathematics, demonstrated with mathematical method and with mathematical certainty. Of these, some have arranged in mathematical order and passed on to the world of letters a philosophy already accepted and customarily taught in the schools, whereas others have thus treated a new philosophy, discovered by their own exertions. For a long time, the many who undertook this task met with no success, but at last there arose that brightest star of our age, René Descartes. After bringing forth by a new method from darkness to light whatever had been inaccessible to the ancients, and in addition whatever could be wanting in his own age, he laid the unshakable foundations of philosophy on which numerous truths could be built with mathematical order and certainty, as he himself effectively proved, and as is clearer than the midday sun to all who have paid careful attention to his writings, for which no praise is too great.

Although the philosophical writings of this most noble and incomparable man exhibit the mathematical manner and order of demonstration, yet they are not composed in the style commonly used in Euclid's *Elements* and other geometrical works, the style wherein Definitions, Postulates, and Axioms are first enunciated, followed by Propositions and their demonstrations. They are arranged in a very different way, which he calls the true and best way of teaching, the Analytic way. For at the end of his "Reply to Second Objections,"[2] he acknowledges two modes of conclusive proof. One is by analysis, "which shows the true way by which a thing is discovered methodically and, as it were, a priori"; the other is by synthesis, "which employs a long series of definitions, postulates, axioms, theorems and problems, so that if any of the conclusions be denied, it can be shown immediately that this is involved in what has preceded, and thus the reader, however reluctant and obstinate, is forced to agree."

However, although both kinds of demonstration afford a certainty that lies beyond any risk of doubt, not everyone finds them equally useful and convenient. There are many who, being quite unacquainted with the mathematical sciences and therefore completely ignorant of the synthetic method in which they are arranged and of the analytic method by which they were discovered, are neither able themselves to understand nor to expound to others the things that are discussed and logically demonstrated in these books. Consequently, many who, either carried away by blind enthusiasm or influenced by the authority of others, have become followers of Descartes have done no more than commit to memory his opinions and doctrines. When the subject arises in conversation, they can only prate and chatter without offering any proof, as was once and still is the case with the followers of the Peripatetic philosophy. Therefore, to provide them with some assistance, I have often wished that someone, skilled both in the analytic and synthetic arrangement and thoroughly versed in Descartes's writings and expert in his philosophy, should set his hand to this task, and undertake to arrange in syn-

---

[2] [See AT7, 155–156; cf. the slight variation in the French version at AT9, 121–122.]

thetic order what Descartes wrote in analytic order, demonstrating it in the way familiar to geometricians. Indeed, though fully conscious of my incompetence and unfitness for such a task, I have frequently thought of undertaking it myself and have even made a start. But other distractions, which so often claim my attention, have prevented its completion.

I was therefore delighted to hear from our Author that, while teaching Descartes's philosophy to a certain pupil of his, he had dictated to him the whole of Part II of the *Principia* and some of Part III, demonstrated in that geometric style, and also the principal and more difficult questions that arise in metaphysics and remain unresolved by Descartes, and that, at the urgent entreaties and pleadings of his friends, he has permitted these to be published as a single work, corrected and amplified by himself. So I also commended this same project, at the same time gladly offering my services, if needed, to get this published. Furthermore I urged him—indeed, besought him—to set out Part I of the *Principia* as well in like order to precede the rest, so that the work, as thus arranged from its very beginning, might be better understood and give greater satisfaction. When he saw how reasonable was this proposal, he could not refuse the pleas of a friend and likewise the good of the reader. He further entrusted to my care the entire business both of printing and of publishing because he lives in the country far from the city and so cannot give it his personal attention.[3]

Such then, honest reader, are the contents of this little book, namely, Parts I and II of Descartes's *Principia Philosophiae* together with a fragment of Part III, to which we have added, as an appendix, our Author's *Cogitata Metaphysica*. But when we here say Part I of the *Principia*, and the book's title so announces, we do not intend it to be understood that everything Descartes says there is here set forth as demonstrated in geometric order. The title derives only from its main contents, and so the chief metaphysical themes that were treated by Descartes in his *Meditations* are taken from that book (omitting all other matters that concern Logic and are related and reviewed only in a historical way). To do this more effectively, the Author has transposed word for word almost the entire passage at the end of the "Reply to the Second Set of Objections," which Descartes arranged in geometric order.[4] He first sets out all Descartes's definitions and inserts Descartes's propositions among his own, but he does not place the axioms immediately after the definitions; he brings them in only after Proposition 4, changing their order so as to make it easier to prove them, and omitting some that he did not require.

Although our Author is well aware that these axioms (as Descartes himself says in Postulate 7) can be proved as theorems and can even more neatly be classed as propositions, and although we also asked him to do this, being engaged in more important affairs he had only the space of two weeks to complete this work, and that is why he could not satisfy his own wishes and ours. He does at any rate add a brief explanation that can serve as a demonstration, postponing for another oc-

---

[3] [It appears from Ep12, however, that Spinoza was able to make corrections to the page proofs.]
[4] [AT7, 160–170.]

casion a lengthier proof, complete in all respects, with view to a new edition to follow this hurried one. To augment this, we shall also try to persuade him to complete Part III in its entirety, "Concerning the Visible World" (of which we give here only a fragment, since the Author ended his instruction at this point and we did not wish to deprive the reader of it, little as it is). For this to be properly executed, some propositions concerning the nature and property of Fluids will need to be inserted at various places in Part II, and I shall then do my best to persuade the Author to do this at the time.[5]

It is not only in setting forth and explaining the Axioms that our Author frequently diverges from Descartes but also in proving the Propositions themselves and the other conclusions, and he employs a logical proof far different from that of Descartes. But let no one take this to mean that he intended to correct the illustrious Descartes in these matters, but that our Author's sole purpose in so doing is to enable him the better to retain his already established order and to avoid increasing unduly the number of Axioms. For the same reason, he has also been compelled to prove many things that Descartes propounded without proof, and to add others that he completely omitted.

However, I should like it to be particularly noted that in all these writings, in Parts I and II and the fragment of Part III of the *Principia* and also in the *Cogitata Metaphysica*, our Author has simply given Descartes's opinions and their demonstrations just as they are found in his writings, or such as should validly be deduced from the foundations laid by him. For having undertaken to teach his pupil Descartes's philosophy, his scruples forbade him to depart in the slightest degree from Descartes's views or to dictate anything that did not correspond with, or was contrary to, his doctrines. Therefore no one should conclude that he here teaches either his own views or only those of which he approves. For although he holds some of the doctrines to be true, and admits that some are his own additions, there are many he rejects as false, holding a very different opinion.[6]

Of this sort, to single out one of many, are statements concerning the Will in the Scholium to Proposition 15 of Part I of the *Principia* and in Chapter 12, Part II of the Appendix, although they appear to be laboriously and meticulously proved. For he does not consider the Will to be distinct from the Intellect, far less endowed with freedom of that kind. Indeed, in making these assertions, as is clear from Part 4 of the *Discourse on Method*, the "Second Meditation," and other passages, Descartes merely assumes, and does not prove, that the human mind is an absolutely thinking substance. Although our Author does indeed admit that there is in Nature a thinking substance, he denies that this constitutes the essence of the human mind.[7] He maintains that, just as Extension is not determined by any limits, so Thought, too, is not determined by any limits. And therefore, just as the

---

[5] [For evidence that Spinoza was developing his own theory of fluids, see Ep6, 78–81.]

[6] [Meyer notes three main differences: the substantiality of the human soul, the distinction between the will and intellect, and the freedom to suspend judgment. Spinoza notes his differences with Descartes; see Ep2, 62–63; Ep21, 154–158.]

[7] [Cf. E2P11.]

human body is not Extension absolutely, but only as determined in a particular way in accordance with the laws of extended Nature through motion and rest, so too the human mind or soul is not Thought absolutely, but only as determined in a particular way in accordance with the laws of thinking Nature through ideas, and one concludes that this must come into existence when the human body begins to exist. From this definition, he thinks it is not difficult to prove that Will is not distinct from Intellect, far less is it endowed with the freedom that Descartes ascribes to it.[8] Indeed, he holds that a faculty of affirming and denying is quite fictitious, that affirming and denying are nothing but ideas, and that other faculties such as Intellect, Desire, etc., must be accounted as figments, or at least among those notions that men have formed through conceiving things in an abstract way, such as humanity, stoniness, and other things of that kind.

Here, too, we must not omit to mention that assertions found in some passages, that this or that surpasses human understanding, must be taken in the same sense (i.e., as giving only Descartes's opinion). This must not be regarded as expressing our Author's own view. All such things, he holds, and many others even more sublime and subtle, can not only be conceived by us clearly and distinctly but can also be explained quite satisfactorily, provided that the human intellect can be guided to the search for truth and the knowledge of things along a path different from that which was opened up and leveled by Descartes. And so he holds that the foundations of the sciences laid by Descartes and the superstructure that he built thereon do not suffice to elucidate and resolve all the most difficult problems that arise in metaphysics. Other foundations are required if we seek to raise our intellect to that pinnacle of knowledge.

Finally, to bring my preface to a close, we should like our readers to realize that all that is here treated is given to the public for the sole purpose of searching out and disseminating truth and to urge men to the pursuit of a true and genuine philosophy. And so in order that all may reap therefrom as rich a profit as we sincerely desire for them, before they begin reading we earnestly beg them to insert omitted passages in their proper place and carefully to correct printing errors that have crept in. Some of these are such as may be an obstacle in the way of perceiving the force of the demonstration and the Author's meaning, as anyone will readily gather from looking at them.

---

[8] [Cf. E2P48; E2P49 Cor and Schol.]

THE PRINCIPLES OF PHILOSOPHY
Demonstrated in the Geometric Manner

Part 1

Prolegomenon

Before coming to the Propositions and their Demonstrations, I have thought it helpful to give a concise account as to why Descartes doubted everything, the way in which he laid the solid foundations of the sciences, and finally the means by which he freed himself from all doubts. I should indeed have arranged all this in mathematical order had I not considered that the prolixity involved in this form of presentation would be an obstacle to the proper understanding of all those things that ought to be beheld at a single glance, as in the case of a picture.

Descartes, then, so as to proceed with the greatest caution in his enquiry, attempted:

1. to put aside all prejudice,
2. to discover the foundations on which everything should be built,
3. to uncover the cause of error,
4. to understand everything clearly and distinctly.

To achieve his first, second, and third aims, he proceeded to call everything into doubt, not indeed like a Skeptic whose sole aim is to doubt, but to free his mind from all prejudice so that he might finally discover the firm and unshakable foundations of the sciences, which, if they existed, could thus not escape him. For the true principles of the sciences ought to be so clear and certain that they need no proof, are placed beyond all hazard of doubt, and without them nothing can be demonstrated. These principles, after a lengthy period of doubting, he discovered. Now when he had found them, it was not difficult for him to distinguish true from false, to uncover the cause of error, and so to take precautions against assuming as true and certain what was false and doubtful.

To achieve his fourth and final aim, that of understanding everything clearly and distinctly, his chief rule was to enumerate the simple ideas out of which all others are compounded and to scrutinize each one separately. For when he could perceive simple ideas clearly and distinctly, he would doubtless understand with the same clarity and distinctness all the other ideas compounded from those simple ideas. Having thus outlined my program, I shall briefly explain in what manner he called everything into doubt, discovered the true principles of the sciences, and extricated himself from the difficulties of doubt.

Doubt Concerning All Things

First, then, he reviewed all those things he had gathered from his senses—the sky, the earth, and the like, and even his own body—all of which he had hitherto regarded as belonging to reality. And he doubted their certainty because he had found that the senses occasionally deceived him, and in dreams he had often been convinced that many things truly existed externally to himself, discovering afterward that he had been deluded. And finally there was the fact that he had heard others, even when awake, declare that they felt pain in limbs they had lost long before.[9] Therefore he was able to doubt, not without reason, even the existence of his own body. From all these considerations he could truly conclude that the senses are not a very strong foundation on which to build all science, for they can be called into doubt; certainty depends on other principles of which we can be more sure. Continuing his enquiry, in the second place he turned to the consideration of all universals, such as corporeal nature in general, its extension, likewise its figure, quantity, etc., and also all mathematical truths. Although these seemed to him more certain than any of the things he had gathered from his senses, yet he discovered a reason for doubting them.[10] For others had erred even concerning these. And there was a particularly strong reason, an ancient belief, fixed in his mind, that there was an all-powerful God who had created him as he was, and so may have caused him to be deceived even regarding those things that seemed very clear to him.[11] This, then, is the manner in which he called everything into doubt.

The Discovery of the Foundation of All Science

Now in order to discover the true principles of the sciences, he proceeded to enquire whether he had called into doubt everything that could come within the scope of his thought; thus he might find out whether there was not perchance still something left that he had not yet doubted. For if in the course of thus doubting he should find something that could not be called into doubt either for any of the previous reasons or for any other reason, he quite rightly considered that this must be established as a foundation on which he could build all his knowledge.[12] And although he had already, as it seemed, doubted everything—for he had doubted

---

[9] [The first two arguments are given in Med1, 13–15 (AT7, 18–20) and PPH1A4, whereas the third is not given until Med6, 50 (AT7, 76–77).]
[10] [Med1, 15 (AT7, 20).]
[11] [Med1, 15–16 (AT7, 21–22).]
[12] [Med2, 17 (AT7, 24).]

not only what he had gathered from his senses but also what he had perceived by intellect alone—yet there was still something left to be examined, namely, himself who was doing the doubting, not insofar as he consisted of head, hands, and other bodily parts (since he had doubted these) but only insofar as he was doubting, thinking, etc. Examining this carefully, he realized that he could not doubt it for any of the foregoing reasons. For whether he is dreaming or awake as he thinks, nevertheless he thinks, and is.[13] And although others, or even he himself, had erred with regard to other matters; nevertheless, because they were erring, they were. He could imagine no author of his being so cunning as to deceive him on that score; for it must be granted that he himself exists as long as it is supposed that he is being deceived. In short, whatever other reason for doubting be devised, there could be adduced none of such a kind as not at the same time to make him most certain of his existence. Indeed, the more reasons are adduced for doubting, the more arguments are simultaneously adduced to convince him of his own existence. So, in whatever direction he turns in order to doubt, he is nevertheless compelled to utter these words: "I doubt, I think, therefore I am."[14]

Thus, in laying bare this truth, at the same time he also discovered the foundation of all the sciences, and also the measure and rule for all other truths—that whatever is perceived as clearly and distinctly as this, is true.[15]

It is abundantly clear from the preceding that there can be no other foundation for the sciences than this; everything else can quite easily be called into doubt, but this can by no means be doubted. However, with regard to this foundation, it should be particularly noted that the statement, "I doubt, I think, therefore I am," is not a syllogism with the major premise omitted. If it were a syllogism, the premises should be clearer and better known than the conclusion 'Therefore I am', and so 'I am' would not be the prime basis of all knowledge. Furthermore, it would not be a certain conclusion, for its truth would depend on universal premises which the Author had already called into doubt. So 'I think, therefore I am' is a single independent proposition, equivalent to the following—'I am, while thinking'.

To avoid confusion in what follows (for this is a matter that must be perceived clearly and distinctly), we must next know what we are. For when this has been clearly and distinctly understood, we shall not confuse our essence with others. In order to deduce this from what has gone before, our Author proceeds as follows.

He recalls to mind all thoughts that he once had about himself, that his soul is something tenuous like the wind or fire or the ether, infused among the denser parts of his body; that his body is better known to him than his soul; and that he perceives the former more clearly and distinctly.[16] And he realizes that all this is clearly inconsistent with what he has so far understood. For he was able to doubt

---

[13] [Med2, 17–18 (AT7, 24–25).]
[14] [Med2, 18 (AT7, 25); *Discourse on Method* 4 (AT6, 32–33).]
[15] [Spinoza follows the *Discourse on Method*, rather than the *Meditations* or PPH, in deriving this principle directly from the *cogito*.]
[16] [Med2, 18 (AT7, 25–26).]

his body, but not his own essence insofar as he was thinking. Furthermore, he perceived these things neither clearly nor distinctly, and so, in accordance with the requirements of his method, he ought to reject them as false. Therefore, understanding that such things could not pertain to him insofar as he was as yet known to himself, he went on to ask what was that, pertaining peculiarly to his essence, which he had not been able to call into doubt and which had compelled him to conclude his own existence. Of this kind there were—that he wanted to take precautions against being deceived, that he desired to understand many things, that he doubted everything that he could not understand, that up to this point he affirmed one thing only and everything else he denied and rejected as false, that he imagined many things even against his will, and, finally, that he was conscious of many things as proceeding from his senses. Because he could infer his existence with equal certainty from each of these points and could list none of them as belonging to the things that he had called into doubt, and finally, because all these things can be conceived under the same attribute, it follows that all these things are true and pertain to his nature. And so whenever he said, "I think," all the following modes of thinking were understood—doubting, understanding, affirming, denying, willing, non-willing, imagining, and sensing.[17]

Here it is important to note the following points, which will prove to be very useful later on when the distinction between mind and body is discussed. First, these modes of thinking are clearly and distinctly understood independently of other matters that are still in doubt. Second, the clear and distinct conception we have of them would be rendered obscure and confused if we were to intermingle with them any of the matters of which we are still in doubt.

Liberation from All Doubts

Finally, to achieve certainty about what he had called into doubt and to remove all doubt, he proceeds to enquire into the nature of the most perfect Being, and whether such exists. For when he realizes that there exists a most perfect Being by whose power all things are produced and preserved and to whose nature it is contrary that he should be a deceiver, then this will remove the reason for doubting that resulted from his not knowing the cause of himself. For he will know that the faculty of distinguishing true from false was not given to him by a supremely good and truthful God in order that he might be deceived. And so mathematical truths, or all things that seem to him most evident, cannot be in the least suspect.[18] Then, to remove the other causes for doubting, he goes on to enquire how it comes about that we sometimes err. When he discovered that this arises from our using our free will to assent even to what we have perceived only confusedly, he was immediately able to conclude that he can guard against error in the future provided that

---

[17] [This enumeration is taken from Med2, 20 (AT7, 28).]
[18] [Med3, 34–35 (AT7, 51–52); Med5, 46–47 (AT7, 70–71).]

he gives assent only to what he clearly and distinctly perceives. This is something that each individual can easily obtain of himself because he has the power to control the will and thereby bring it about that it is restrained within the limits of the intellect.[19] But since in our earliest days we have been imbued with many prejudices from which we are not easily freed, in order that we may be freed from them and accept nothing but what we clearly and distinctly perceive, he goes on to enumerate all the simple notions and ideas from which all our thoughts are compounded and to examine them one by one, so that he can observe in each of them what is clear and what is obscure. For thus he will easily be able to distinguish the clear from the obscure and to form clear and distinct thoughts. So he will easily discover the real distinction between soul and body, and what is clear and what is obscure in the deliverance of our senses, and lastly wherein dreaming differs from waking.[20] Thereafter he could no longer doubt that he was awake nor could he be deceived by his senses. Thus he freed himself from all doubts listed previously.

However, before I here make an end, I think I ought to satisfy those who argue as follows: "Because the existence of God is not self-evident to us, it seems that we can never be certain of anything, nor can it ever be known to us that God exists. For from premises that are uncertain (and we have said that, as long as we do not know our own origin), nothing certain can be concluded."

To remove this difficulty, Descartes replies in the following manner. From the fact that we do not as yet know whether the author of our origin may have created us such as to be deceived even in those matters that appear to us most certain, it by no means follows that we can doubt those things that we understand clearly and distinctly through themselves or through a process of reasoning, that is, as long as we are paying attention to it. We can doubt only those things previously demonstrated to be true, which we may remember when we are no longer attending to the reasoning from which we deduced them, and which we have thus forgotten. Therefore, although the existence of God can be known not through itself but only through something else, we can nevertheless attain certain knowledge of God's existence provided that we carefully attend to all the premises from which we conclude it. See *Principia* Part 1 Article 13, and "Reply to Second Objections," No. 3, and at the end of the "Fifth Meditation."

However, because some do not find this reply satisfactory, I shall give another. When we were speaking previously of the certainty and sureness of our existence, we saw that we concluded it from the fact that, in whatever direction we turned the mind's eye, we did not find any reason for doubting that did not by that very fact convince us of our existence. This was so whether we were considering our own nature, whether we were imagining the author of our nature to be a cunning deceiver—in short, whatever reason for doubting we invoked, external to ourselves. Hitherto we had not found this to be so in the case of any other matter. For example, while attending to the nature of a triangle, although we are compelled

---

[19] [Med4, 35–42 (AT7, 52–62).]
[20] [Med6, 47–59 (AT7, 71–90).]

to conclude that its three angles are equal to two right angles, we cannot reach this same conclusion if we suppose that we may be deceived by the author of our nature. Yet this very supposition assured us of our existence with the utmost certainty. So it is not the case that, wherever we turn the mind's eye, we are compelled to conclude that the three angles of a triangle are equal to two right angles; on the contrary, we find a reason for doubting it in that we do not possess an idea of God such as to render it impossible for us to think that God is a deceiver. For one who does not possess the true idea of God—which at the moment we suppose we do not possess—may quite as easily think that his author is a deceiver as think that he is not a deceiver, just as one who does not have the idea of a triangle may indifferently think its angles are equal or not equal to two right angles.

Therefore we concede that, except for our existence, we cannot be absolutely certain of anything, however earnestly we attend to its demonstration, as long as we do not have the clear and distinct conception of God that makes us affirm that God is supremely truthful, just as the idea we have of a triangle makes us conclude that its three angles are equal to two right angles. But we deny that, for this reason, we cannot attain knowledge of anything. For, as is evident from all that has already been said, the whole matter hinges on this alone, that we are able to form such a conception of God as so disposes us that it is not as easy for us to think that God is a deceiver as to think that he is not a deceiver, a conception that compels us to affirm that he is supremely truthful. When we have formed such an idea, the reason for doubting mathematical truths will be removed. For in whatever direction we now turn the mind's eye with the purpose of doubting one of these truths, we shall not find anything that itself does not make us conclude that this truth is most certain, just as was the case with regard to our existence.

For example, if after discovering the idea of God we attend to the nature of a triangle, its idea will compel us to affirm that its three angles are equal to two right angles, whereas if we attend to the idea of God, this too will compel us to affirm that he is supremely truthful, the author and continuous preserver of our nature, and therefore that he is not deceiving us with regard to this truth. And attending to the idea of God (which we now suppose we have discovered), it will be just as impossible for us to think that he is a deceiver as to think, when attending to the idea of a triangle, that its three angles are not equal to two right angles. And just as we can form such an idea of a triangle in spite of not knowing whether the author of our nature is deceiving us, so too we can achieve a clear idea of God and set it before us even though also doubting whether the author of our nature is deceiving us in all things. And provided we possess this idea, in whatever way we may have acquired it, it will be enough to remove all doubts, as has just now been shown.

So having made these points, I reply as follows to the difficulty that has been raised. It is not as long as we do not know of God's existence (for I have not spoken of that) but as long as we do not have a clear and distinct idea of God, that we cannot be certain of anything. Therefore, if anyone wishes to argue against me, his argument will have to be as follows: "We cannot be certain of anything until we have a clear and distinct idea of God. But we cannot have a clear and distinct idea of God as long as we do not know whether the author of our nature is deceiving us. Therefore, we cannot be certain of anything as long as we do not know whether the author of our nature is deceiving us, etc." To this I reply by conceding the major premise and denying the minor. For we do have a clear and distinct idea of a triangle, although we do not know whether the author of our nature is deceiving us; and granted that we have such an idea of God, as I have just shown at some length, we cannot doubt his existence or any mathematical truth.

With this as preface, I now enter upon the work itself.

Definitions

1. Under the word *Thought*, I include all that is in us and of which we are immediately conscious. Thus all operations of the will, intellect, imagination, and senses are thoughts. But I have added 'immediately' so as to exclude those things that are their consequences. For example, voluntary motion has thought for its starting point, but in itself it is still not thought.

2. By the word *Idea*, I understand the specific form (*forma*) of a thought, through the immediate perception of which I am conscious of that same thought.

So whenever I express something in words while understanding what I am saying, this very fact makes it certain that there is in me the idea of that which is meant by those words. And so I do not apply the term 'ideas' simply to images depicted in the fantasy; indeed I do not here term these 'ideas' at all, insofar as they are depicted in the corporeal fantasy (i.e., in some part of the brain) but only insofar as they communicate their form to the mind itself when this is directed toward that part of the brain.

3. By the *objective reality of an idea*, I understand the being of that which is presented through the idea, insofar as it is in the idea.[21]

In the same way one can speak of 'objective perfection' or 'objective art', etc. For whatever we perceive as being in the objects of ideas is objectively in the ideas themselves.

4. When things are, in themselves, such as we perceive them to be, they are said to be *formally* in the objects of ideas, and *eminently* when they are not just such in themselves as we perceive them to be but are more than sufficient to account fully for our perception.

Note that when I say that the cause contains eminently the perfections of its effect, I mean that the cause contains the perfections of the effect with a higher degree of excellence than does the effect itself. See also Axiom 8.

5. Everything in which there is something that we perceive as immediately inhering in a subject, or through which there exists something that we perceive (i.e., some property, quality or attribute whose real idea is in us), is called *substance*. For of substance itself, taken precisely, we have no other idea than that it is a thing

---

[21] [Cf. Med3, 27–28 (AT7, 40–41).]

in which there exists formally or eminently that something which we perceive (i.e., that something which is objectively in one of our ideas).

6. Substance in which thought immediately inheres is called *Mind* (*Mens*).

I here speak of 'Mind' rather than 'Soul' (*anima*) because the word 'soul' is equivocal, and is often used to mean a corporeal thing.

7. Substance that is the immediate subject of extension and of accidents that presuppose extension, such as figure, position, and local motion, is called *Body*.

Whether what is called Mind and what is called Body is one and the same substance, or two different substances, is something to be enquired into later.

8. Substance that we understand through itself to be supremely perfect, and in which we conceive nothing at all that involves any defect or limitation of perfection, is called *God*.

9. When we say that something is contained in the nature or conception of some thing, that is the same as saying that it is true of that thing or can be truly affirmed of it.[22]

10. Two substances are said to be distinct in reality when each one can exist without the other.

We have here omitted the Postulates of Descartes because in what follows we do not draw any conclusions from them. But we earnestly ask readers to read them through and to think them over carefully.[23]

Axioms[24]

1. We arrive at the knowledge and certainty of some unknown thing only through the knowledge and certainty of another thing that is prior to it in certainty and knowledge.

2. There are reasons that make us doubt the existence of our bodies.

This has in fact been shown in the Prolegomenon, and so is here posited as an axiom.

3. If we have anything besides mind and body, this is less known to us than mind and body.

---

[22] [In each of the preceding eight definitions a word or phrase has been italicized to indicate the *definiendum*, but in this definition and the next there is no text italicized. It appears reasonable to assume that Def9 has as *definiendum contained in the nature or conception of some thing* and Def10 *distinct in reality*.]

[23] [The seven postulates (AT7, 162–164) or *demandes* in the French version (AT9, 125–127) are not postulates in the Euclidean sense but are requests from Descartes to his readers to ponder carefully what can be doubted, the preceding definitions, and especially the distinction between clear, distinct perception and obscure, confused perception.]

[24] [The first three axioms are not taken from Descartes; but Meyer, in his preface, has mentioned that Spinoza would expound Descartes's opinions and demonstrations "just as they are found in his writings, or such as should validly be deduced from the foundations laid by him."]

It should be noted that these axioms do not affirm anything about things external to us, but only such things as we find within ourselves insofar as we are thinking things.

Proposition 1
We cannot be absolutely certain of anything as long as we do not know that we exist.

Proof This proposition is self-evident; for he who absolutely does not know that he is likewise does not know that he is a being affirming or denying, that is, that he certainly affirms or denies.

Here it should be noted that although we may affirm or deny many things with great certainty while not attending to the fact that we exist, unless this is presupposed as indubitable, everything could be called into doubt.

Proposition 2
'I am' must be self-evident.

Proof If this be denied, it will therefore be known only through something else, the knowledge and certainty of which will be prior in us to the statement 'I am' (Ax. 1). But this is absurd (Prop. 1). Therefore it must be self-evident. Q.E.D.

Proposition 3
'I am', insofar as the 'I' is a thing consisting of body, is not a first principle and is not known through itself.

Proof There are certain things that make us doubt the existence of our body (Ax. 2). Therefore (Ax. 1) we shall not attain certainty of this except through the knowledge and certainty of something else that is prior to it in knowledge and certainty. Therefore the statement 'I am', insofar as 'I' am a thing consisting of body, is not a first principle and is not known through itself. Q.E.D.

Proposition 4
'I am' cannot be the first known principle except insofar as we think.

Proof The statement 'I am a corporeal thing, or a thing consisting of body' is not a first-known principle (Prop. 3), nor again am I certain of my existence insofar as I consist of anything other than mind and body. For if we consist of anything different from mind and body, this is less well known to us than body (Ax. 3). Therefore 'I am' cannot be the first known thing except insofar as we think. Q.E.D.

Corollary From this it is obvious that mind, or a thinking thing, is better known than body.

But for a fuller explanation read Part 1 of the *Principia* Arts. 11 and 12.

Scholium Everyone perceives with the utmost certainty that he affirms, denies, doubts, understands, imagines, etc., or that he exists as doubting, understanding, affirming, etc.—in short, as thinking. Nor can this be called into doubt. Therefore the statement 'I think' or 'I am, as thinking' is the unique (Prop. 1) and most certain basis of all philosophy. Now in order to achieve the greatest certainty in the sciences, our aim and purpose can be no other than this, to deduce everything from the strongest first principles and to make the inferences as clear and distinct as the first principles from which they are deduced. It therefore clearly follows that we must consider as most certainly true everything that is equally evident to us and that we perceive with the same clearness and distinctness as the already discovered first principle, and also everything that so agrees with this first principle and so depends on it that we cannot doubt it without also having to doubt this first principle.

But to proceed with the utmost caution in reviewing these matters, at the first stage I shall admit as equally evident and equally clearly and distinctly perceived by us only those things that each of us observes in himself insofar as he is engaged in thinking. Such are, for example, that he wills this or that, that he has definite ideas of such-and-such a kind, and that one idea contains in itself more reality and perfection than another—namely, that the one that contains objectively the being and perfection of substance is far more perfect than one that contains only the objective perfection of some accident, and, finally, that the idea of a supremely perfect being is the most perfect of all. These things, I say, we perceive not merely with equal sureness and clarity but perhaps even more distinctly; for they affirm not only that we think but also how we think.

Further, we shall also say that those things that cannot be doubted without at the same time casting doubt on this unshakable foundation of ours are also in agreement with this first principle. For example, if anyone should doubt whether something can come from nothing, he will be able at the same time to doubt whether we, as long as we are thinking, are. For if I can affirm something of nothing—in effect, that nothing can be the cause of something—I can at the same time and with the same right affirm thought of nothing, and say that I, as long as I am thinking, am nothing. Because I find this impossible, it will also be impossible for me to think that something may come from nothing.

With these considerations in mind, I have decided at this point to list here in order those things that at present seem to us necessary for future progress, and to add to the number of axioms. For these are indeed set forth by Descartes as axioms at the end of his "Reply to the Second Set of Objections," and I do not aim at greater accuracy than he. However, not to depart from the order we have been pursuing, I shall try to make them somewhat clearer, and to show how one depends on another and all on this one first principle, 'I am, while thinking', or how their certainty and reasonableness is of the same degree as that of the first principle.

Axioms Taken from Descartes

4. There are different degrees of reality or being; for substance has more reality than accident or mode, and infinite substance, more than finite substance.

Therefore there is more objective reality in the idea of substance than in the idea of accident, and in the idea of infinite substance than in the idea of finite substance.[25]

This axiom is known simply from contemplating our ideas, of whose existence we are certain because they are modes of thinking. For we know how much reality or perfection the idea of substance affirms of substance, and how much the idea of mode affirms of mode. This being so, we also necessarily realize that the idea of substance contains more objective reality than the idea of some accident, etc. See Scholium Prop. 4.

5. A thinking thing, if it knows of any perfections that it lacks, will immediately give these to itself, if they are within its power.[26]

This everyone observes in himself insofar as he is a thinking thing. Therefore (Scholium Prop. 4) we are most certain of it. And for the same reason, we are just as certain of the following:

6. In the idea or concept of every thing, there is contained either possible or necessary existence. (See Axiom 10, Descartes.)

Necessary existence is contained in the concept of God, or a supremely perfect being; for otherwise he would be conceived as imperfect, which is contrary to what is supposed to be conceived. Contingent or possible existence is contained in the concept of a limited thing.

7. No thing, nor any perfection of a thing actually existing, can have nothing, or a nonexisting thing, as the cause of its existence.

I have demonstrated in the Scholium Prop. 4 that this axiom is as clear to us as is 'I am, when thinking'.

8. Whatever there is of reality or perfection in any thing exists formally or eminently in its first and adequate cause.[27]

By 'eminently' I understand: when the cause contains all the reality of the effect more perfectly than the effect itself. By 'formally': when the cause contains all the reality of the effect equally perfectly.

This axiom depends on the preceding one. For if it were supposed that there is nothing in the cause, or less in the cause than in the effect, then nothing in the cause would be the cause of the effect. But this is absurd (Ax. 7). Therefore it is not the case that anything whatsoever can be the cause of a certain effect; it must be precisely a thing in which there is eminently or at least formally all the perfection that is in the effect.

9. The objective reality of our ideas requires a cause in which that same reality is contained not only objectively but also formally or eminently.[28]

This axiom, although misused by many, is universally admitted, for when somebody conceives something new, everyone wants to know the cause of this

---

[25] [Cf. Med3, 27–28 (AT7, 40–42).]
[26] [Cf. Med3, 32–33 (AT7, 48).]
[27] [Cf. Med3, 28 (AT7, 40–41).]
[28] [Cf. Med3, 28 (AT7, 41–42).]

concept or idea. Now when they can assign a cause in which is contained formally or eminently as much reality as is contained objectively in that concept, they are satisfied. This is made quite clear by the example of a machine, which Descartes adduces in Art. 17 Part 1 *Principia*.[29] Similarly, if anyone were to ask whence it is that a man has the ideas of his thought and of his body, no one can fail to see that he has them from himself, as containing formally everything that his ideas contain objectively. Therefore if a man were to have some idea that contained more of objective reality than he himself contained of formal reality, then of necessity we should be driven by the natural light to seek another cause outside the man himself, a cause that contained all that perfection formally or eminently. And apart from that cause no one has ever assigned any other cause that he has conceived so clearly and distinctly.

Furthermore, as for the truth of this axiom, it depends on the previous ones. By Axiom 4 there are different degrees of reality or being in ideas. Therefore (Ax. 8) they need a more perfect cause in accordance with their degree of perfection. But because the degrees of reality that we observe in ideas are not in the ideas insofar as they are considered as modes of thinking but insofar as one presents substance and another merely a mode of substance — or, in brief, insofar as they are considered as images of things — hence it clearly follows that there can be granted no other first cause of ideas than that which, as we have just shown, all men understand clearly and distinctly by the natural light, namely, one in which is contained formally or eminently the same reality that the ideas have objectively.[30]

To make this conclusion more clearly understood, I shall illustrate it with one or two examples. If anyone sees some books (imagine one to be that of a distinguished philosopher and the other to be that of some trifler) written in one and the same hand, and if he pays no attention to the meaning of the words (i.e., insofar as they are symbols) but only to the shape of the writing and the order of the letters, he will find no distinction between them such as to compel him to seek different causes for them. They will appear to him to have proceeded from the same cause and in the same manner. But if he pays attention to the meaning of the words and of the language, he will find a considerable distinction between them. He will therefore conclude that the first cause of the one book was very different from the first cause of the other, and that the one cause was in fact more perfect than the other to the extent that the meaning of the language of the two books, or their words considered as symbols, are found to differ from one another.

I am speaking of the first cause of books, and there must necessarily be one although I admit — indeed, I take for granted — that one book can be transcribed from another, as is self-evident.

The same point can also be clearly illustrated by the example of a portrait, let us say, of some prince. If we pay attention only to the materials of which it is made, we shall not find any distinction between it and other portraits such as to compel

---

[29] [Cf. Rep1, AT7, 104–106.]

[30] We are also certain of this because we experience it ourselves insofar as we are thinking. See preceding Scholium.

us to look for different causes. Indeed, there will be nothing to prevent us from thinking that it was copied from another likeness, and that one again from another, and so ad infinitum. For we shall be quite satisfied that there need be no other cause for its production. But if we attend to the image insofar as it is the image of something, we shall immediately be compelled to seek a first cause such as formally or eminently contains what that image contains representatively. I do not see what more need be said to confirm and elucidate this axiom.

10. To preserve a thing, no lesser cause is required than to produce it in the first place.

From the fact that at this moment we are thinking, it does not necessarily follow that we shall hereafter be thinking. For the concept that we have of our thought does not involve, or does not contain, the necessary existence of the thought. I can clearly and distinctly conceive the thought even though I suppose it not to exist.[31] Now the nature of every cause must contain in itself or involve the perfection of its effect (Ax. 8). Hence it clearly follows that there must be something in us or external to us that we have not yet understood, whose concept or nature involves existence, and that is the reason why our thought began to exist and also continues to exist. For although our thought began to exist, its nature and essence does not on that account involve necessary existence any the more than before it existed, and so in order to persevere in existing it stands in need of the same force that it needs to begin existing. And what we here say about thought must be said about every thing whose essence does not involve necessary existence.

11. Of every thing that exists, it can be asked what is the cause or reason why it exists. See Descartes, Axiom 1.

Because to exist is something positive, we cannot say that it has nothing for its cause (Ax. 7). Therefore we must assign some positive cause or reason why it exists. And this must be either external (i.e., outside the thing itself) or else internal (i.e., included in the nature and definition of the existing thing itself).

The four propositions that follow are taken from Descartes.

Proposition 5

The existence of God is known solely from the consideration of his nature.

Proof To say that something is contained in the nature or concept of a thing is the same as to say that it is true of that thing (Def. 9). But necessary existence is contained in the concept of God (Ax. 6). Therefore it is true to say of God that there is necessary existence in him, or that he exists.[32]

Scholium From this proposition there follow many important consequences. Indeed, on this fact alone—that existence pertains to the nature of God, or that the concept of God involves necessary existence just as the concept of a triangle involves its three angles being equal to two right angles, or that his existence, just

---

[31] This is something everyone discovers in himself, insofar as he is a thinking thing.
[32] [Cf. Med5, 43–46 (AT7, 65–69); E1P11Dem1; KV1/1/1–2.]

like his essence, is an eternal truth—depends almost all knowledge of the attributes of God through which we are brought to love of him and to the highest blessedness. Therefore it is much to be desired that mankind should come round to our opinion on this subject.

I do indeed admit that there are some prejudices that prevent this from being so easily understood by everyone.[33] If anyone, moved by goodwill and by the simple love of truth and his own true advantage, comes to look at the matter closely and to reflect on what is contained in the "Fifth Meditation" and the end of "Replies to the First Set of Objections," and also on what we say about Eternity in Chapter 1 Part 2 of our Appendix, he will undoubtedly understand the matter quite clearly and will in no way be able to doubt whether he has an idea of God (which is, of course, the first foundation of human blessedness). For when he realizes that God is completely different in kind from other things in respect of essence and existence, he will at once see clearly that the idea of God is far different from the ideas of other things. Therefore there is no need to detain the reader any longer on this subject.

PROPOSITION 6
The existence of God is proved a posteriori from the mere fact that the idea of him is in us.

Proof The objective reality of any of our ideas requires a cause in which that same reality is contained not just objectively but formally or eminently (Ax. 9). Now we do have the idea of God (Defs. 2 and 8), and the objective reality of this idea is not contained in us either formally or eminently (Ax. 4), nor can it be contained in anything other than God himself (Def. 8). Therefore this idea of God, which is in us, requires God for its cause, and therefore God exists (Ax. 7).[34]

Scholium There are some who deny that they have any idea of God, and yet, as they declare, they worship and love him. And though you were to set before them the definition of God and the attributes of God, you will meet with no more success than if you were to labor to teach a man blind from birth the differences of colors as we see them. However, except to consider them as a strange type of creature halfway between man and beast, we should pay small heed to their words. How else, I ask, can we show the idea of some thing than by giving its definition and explaining its attributes? Because this is what we are doing in the case of the idea of God, there is no reason for us to be concerned over the words of men who deny the idea of God simply on the grounds that they cannot form an image of him in their brain.

Furthermore, we should note that when Descartes quotes Axiom 4 to show that the objective reality of the idea of God is not contained in us either formally or eminently, he takes for granted that everyone knows that he is not an infinite substance, that is, supremely intelligent, supremely powerful, etc., and this he is en-

---
[33] Read *Principia* Part 1 Art. 16.
[34] [Cf. Med3, 28–31 (AT7, 40–45).]

titled to do. For he who knows that he thinks, also knows that he doubts many things and that he does not understand everything clearly and distinctly.

Finally, we should note that it also follows clearly from Definition 8 that there cannot be a number of Gods, but only one God, as we clearly demonstrate in Proposition 11 of this Part, and in Part 2 of our Appendix, Chapter 2.

Proposition 7
The existence of God is also proved from the fact that we ourselves exist while having the idea of him.

Proof   If I had the force to preserve myself, I would be of such a nature that I would involve necessary existence (Lemma 2). Therefore (Corollary Lemma 1) my nature would contain all perfections. But I find in myself, insofar as I am a thinking thing, many imperfections—as that I doubt, desire, etc.—and of this I am certain (Scholium Prop. 4). Therefore I have no force to preserve myself. Nor can I say that the reason I now lack those perfections is that I now will to deny them to myself, for this would be clearly inconsistent with Lemma 1, and with what I clearly find in myself (Ax. 5).

Further, I cannot now exist, while I am existing, without being preserved either by myself—if indeed I have that force—or by something else that does have that force (Axioms 10 and 11). But I do exist (Scholium Prop. 4), and yet I do not have the force to preserve myself, as has just now been proved. Therefore I am preserved by something else. But not by something else that does not have the force to preserve itself (by the same reasoning whereby I have just demonstrated that I am not able to preserve myself). Therefore it must be by something else that has the force to preserve itself; that is (Lemma 2), something whose nature involves necessary existence; that is (Corollary Lemma 1), something that contains all the perfections that I clearly understand to pertain to a supremely perfect being. Therefore a supremely perfect being exists; that is (Def. 8), God exists. Q.E.D.

Scholium   To demonstrate this proposition Descartes assumes the following two axioms:

1. That which can effect what is greater or more difficult can also effect what is less.
2. It is a greater thing to create or (Ax. 10) to preserve substance than the attributes or properties of substance.

What he means by these axioms I do not know. For what does he call easy, and what difficult? Nothing is said to be easy or difficult in an absolute sense, but only with respect to its cause. So one and the same thing can be said at the same time to be easy and difficult in respect of different causes.[35] Now if, of things that can

---
[35] Take as only one example the spider, which easily weaves a web that men would find very difficult to weave. On the other hand, men find it quite easy to do many things that are perhaps impossible for angels.

be effected by the same cause, he calls those difficult that need great effort and those easy that need less (e.g., the force that can raise fifty pounds can raise twenty-five pounds twice as easily) then surely the axiom is not absolutely true, nor can he prove from it what he aims to prove. For when he says, "If I had the force to preserve myself, I should also have the force to give myself all the perfections that I lack" (because this latter does not require as much power), I would grant him that the strength that I expend on preserving myself could effect many other things far more easily had I not needed it to preserve myself, but I deny that, as long as I am using it to preserve myself,[36] I can direct it to effecting other things however much easier, as can clearly be seen in our example.

And the difficulty is not removed by saying that, because I am a thinking thing, I must necessarily know whether I am expending all my strength in preserving myself, and whether this is also the reason why I do not give myself the other perfections. For—apart from the fact that this point is not at issue, but only how the necessity of this proposition follows from this axiom—if I knew this, I should be a greater being and perhaps require greater strength than I have so as to preserve myself in that greater perfection. Again, I do not know whether it is a greater task to create or preserve substance than to create or preserve its attributes. That is, to speak more clearly and in more philosophic terms, I do not know whether a substance, so as to preserve its attributes, does not need the whole of its virtue and essence with which it may be preserving itself.

But let us leave this and examine further what our noble Author here intends; that is, what he understands by 'easy' and what by 'difficult'. I do not think, nor can I in any way be convinced, that by 'difficult' he understands that which is impossible (and therefore cannot be conceived in any way as coming into being), and by 'easy', that which does not imply any contradiction (and therefore can readily be conceived as coming into being)—although in the "Third Meditation" he seems at first glance to mean this when he says: "Nor ought I to think that perhaps those things that I lack are more difficult to acquire than those that are already in me. For on the contrary it is obvious that it was far more difficult for me, a thinking thing or substance, to emerge from nothing than . . .", etc.[37] This would not be consistent with the Author's words nor would it smack of his genius. For, passing over the first point, there is no relationship between the possible and the impossible, or between the intelligible and the nonintelligible, just as there is no relationship between something and nothing, and power has no more to do with impossible things than creation and generation, with nonentities; so there can be no comparison between them. Besides, I can compare things and understand their relationship only when I have a clear and distinct conception of them all. So I deny that it follows that he who can do the impossible can also do the possible. What sort of conclusion, I ask, would this be? That if someone can make a square circle, he will also be able to make a circle wherein all the lines drawn from

---

[36] [I have diverged from the punctuation of Gebhardt.—S.S.]
[37] [Cf. Med3, 32–33 (AT7, 48).]

the center to the circumference are equal. Or if someone can bring it about that 'nothing' can be acted upon, and can use it as material to produce something, he will also have the power to make something from something. For, as I have said, there is no agreement, or analogy, or comparison or any relationship whatsoever between these things and things like these. Anyone can see this, if only he gives a little attention to the matter. Therefore I think this quite irreconcilable with Descartes's genius.

But if I attend to the second of the two axioms just now stated, it appears that what he means by 'greater' and 'more difficult' is 'more perfect', and by 'lesser' and 'easier', 'less perfect'. Yet this, again, seems very obscure, for there is here the same difficulty as before. As before, I deny that he who can do the greater can, at the same time and with the same effort (as must be supposed in the proposition), do the lesser.

Again, when he says: "It is a greater thing to create or preserve substance than its attributes," surely he cannot understand by attributes that which is formally contained in substance and differs from substance itself only by conceptual abstraction. For then it would be the same thing to create substance as to create attributes. Nor again, by the same reasoning, can he mean the properties of substance which necessarily follow from its essence and definition.

Far less can he mean—and yet he appears to—the properties and attributes of another substance. For instance, if I say that I have the power to preserve myself, a finite thinking substance, I cannot for that reason say that I also have the power to give myself the perfections of infinite substance, which differs totally in essence from my essence. For the force or essence whereby I preserve myself in my being is quite different in kind from the force or essence whereby absolutely infinite substance preserves itself, and from which its powers and properties are distinguishable only by abstract reason.[38] So even though I were to suppose that I preserve myself, if I wanted to conceive that I could give myself the perfections of absolutely infinite substance, I should be supposing nothing other than this, that I could reduce my entire essence to nothing and create an infinite substance anew. This would be much more, surely, than merely to suppose that I can preserve myself, a finite substance.

Therefore, because by the terms 'attributes' or 'properties' he can mean none of these things, there remain only the qualities that substance itself contains eminently (as this or that thought in the mind, which I clearly perceive to be lacking in me), but not the qualities that another substance contains eminently (as this or that motion in extension; for such perfections are not perfections for me, a thinking thing, and therefore they are not lacking to me). But then what Descartes wants to prove—that if I am preserving myself, I also have the power to give myself all the perfections that I clearly see as pertaining to a most perfect being—can in no way be concluded from this axiom, as is quite clear from what I have said

---

[38] Note that the force by which substance preserves itself is nothing but its essence, differing from it only in name. This will be a particular feature of our discussion in the Appendix, concerning the power of God.

previously. However, not to leave the matter unproved, and to avoid all confusion, I have thought it advisable first of all to demonstrate the following Lemmas, and thereafter to construct on them the proof of Proposition 7.

Lemma 1 The more perfect a thing is by its own nature, the greater the existence it involves, and the more necessary is the existence. Conversely, the more a thing by its own nature involves necessary existence, the more perfect it is.

Proof Existence is contained in the idea or concept of everything (Ax.6). Then let it be supposed that A is a thing that has ten degrees of perfection. I say that its concept involves more existence than if it were supposed to contain only five degrees of perfection. Because we cannot affirm any existence of nothing (see Scholium Prop. 4), in proportion as we in thought subtract from its perfection and therefore conceive it as participating more and more in nothing, to that extent we also deny the possibility of its existence. So if we conceive its degrees of perfection to be reduced indefinitely to nought or zero, it will contain no existence, or absolutely impossible existence. But, on the other hand, if we increase its degrees of perfection indefinitely, we shall conceive it as involving the utmost existence, and therefore the most necessary existence. That was the first thing to be proved. Now since these two things can in no way be separated (as is quite clear from Axiom 6 and the whole of Part 1 of this work), what we proposed to prove in the second place clearly follows.

Note 1. Although many things are said to exist necessarily solely on the grounds that there is given a cause determined to produce them, it is not of this that we are here speaking; we are speaking only of that necessity and possibility that follows solely from consideration of the nature or essence of a thing, without taking any account of its cause.

Note 2. We are not here speaking of beauty and other 'perfections', which, out of superstition and ignorance, men have thought fit to call perfections; by perfection I understand only reality or being. For example, I perceive that more reality is contained in substance than in modes or accidents. So I understand clearly that substance contains more necessary and more perfect existence than is contained in accidents, as is well established from Axioms 4 and 6.

Corollary Hence it follows that whatever involves necessary existence is a supremely perfect being, or God.

Lemma 2 The nature of one who has the power to preserve himself involves necessary existence.

Proof He who has the force to preserve himself has also the force to create himself (Ax. 10); that is (as everyone will readily admit), he needs no external cause to exist, but his own nature alone will be a sufficient cause of his existence, either possibly (Ax. 10) or necessarily. But not possibly; for then (through what I have demonstrated with regard to Axiom 10) from the fact that he now existed it would not follow that he would thereafter exist (which is contrary to the hypothesis). Therefore necessarily; that is, his nature involves necessary existence. Q.E.D.

Corollary God can bring about every thing that we clearly perceive, just as we perceive it.

Proof All this follows clearly from the preceding proposition. For there God's existence was proved from the fact that there must exist someone in whom are all the perfections of which there is an idea in us. Now there is in us the idea of a power so great that by him alone in whom it resides there can be made the sky, the earth, and all the other things that are understood by me as possible. Therefore, along with God's existence, all these things, too, are proved of him.

PROPOSITION 8
Mind and body are distinct in reality.

Proof Whatever we clearly perceive can be brought about by God just as we perceive it (Corollary Prop. 7). But we clearly perceive mind, that is (Def. 6), a thinking substance, without body, that is (Def. 7), without any extended substance (Props. 3 and 4); and conversely we clearly perceive body without mind, as everyone readily admits. Therefore, at least through divine power, mind can be without body and body without mind.[39]

Now substances that can be without one another are distinct in reality (Def. 10). But mind and body are substances (Defs. 5, 6, and 7) that can exist without one another, as has just been proved. Therefore mind and body are distinct in reality.

See Proposition 4 at the end of Descartes's "Replies to the Second Set of Objections," and the passages in *Principia* Part 1 from Arts. 22–29. For I do not think it worthwhile to transcribe them here.

PROPOSITION 9
God is a supremely understanding being.

Proof If you deny this, then God will understand either nothing or not everything, that is, only some things. But to understand only some things and to be ignorant of the rest supposes a limited and imperfect intellect, which it is absurd to ascribe to God (Def. 8). And that God should understand nothing either indicates a lack of intellection in God—as it does with men who understand nothing—and involves imperfection (which, by the same definition, cannot be the case with God), or else it indicates that it is incompatible with God's perfection that he should understand something. But because intellection is thus completely denied of God, he will not be able to create any intellect (Ax. 8). Now because intellect is clearly and distinctly perceived by us, God can be its cause (Cor. Prop. 7). Therefore it is far from true that it is incompatible with God's perfection for him to understand something. Therefore he is a supremely understanding being. Q.E.D.

Scholium Although it must be granted that God is incorporeal, as is demonstrated in Prop. 16, this must not be taken to mean that all the perfections of ex-

---
[39] [Cf. Med6, 51 (AT7, 78).]

tension are to be withdrawn from him. They are to be withdrawn from him only to the extent that the nature and properties of extension involve some imperfection. The same point is to be made concerning God's intellection, as is admitted by all who seek wisdom beyond the common run of philosophers, and as will be fully explained in our Appendix Part 2 Chapter 7.

PROPOSITION 10
Whatever perfection is found in God, is from God.

Proof If you deny this, suppose that there is in God some perfection that is not from God. It will be in God either from itself, or from something different from God. If from itself, it will therefore have necessary existence, not merely possible existence (Lemma 2 Prop. 7), and so (Corollary Lemma 1 Prop. 7) it will be something supremely perfect, and therefore (Def. 8) it will be God. So if it be said that there is in God something that is from itself, at the same time it is said that this is from God. Q.E.D. But if it be from something different from God, then God cannot be conceived through himself as supremely perfect, contrary to Definition 8. Therefore whatever perfection is found in God, is from God. Q.E.D.

PROPOSITION 11
There cannot be more than one God.

Proof If you deny this, conceive, if you can, more than one God (e.g., A and B). Then of necessity (Prop. 9) both A and B will have the highest degree of understanding; that is, A will understand everything, himself and B, and in turn B will understand himself and A. But because A and B necessarily exist (Prop. 5), therefore the cause of the truth and the necessity of the idea of B, which is in A, is B; and conversely the cause of the truth and the necessity of the idea of A, which is in B, is A. Therefore there will be in A a perfection that is not from A, and in B a perfection that is not from B. Therefore (Prop. 10) neither A nor B will be a God, and so there cannot be more than one God. Q.E.D.

Here it should be noted that, from the mere fact that something of itself involves necessary existence—as is the case with God—it necessarily follows that it is unique. This is something that everyone can see for himself with careful thought, and I could have demonstrated it here, but not in a manner as comprehensible to all as is done in this proposition.

PROPOSITION 12
All things that exist are preserved solely by the power of God.

Proof If you deny this, suppose that something preserves itself. Therefore (Lemma 2 Prop. 7) its nature involves necessary existence. Thus (Corollary Lemma 1 Prop. 7) it would be God, and there would be more than one God, which is absurd (Prop. 11). Therefore everything that exists is preserved solely by the power of God. Q.E.D.

Corollary 1 God is the creator of all things.

Proof God preserves all things (Prop. 12); that is (Ax. 10), he has created, and still continuously creates, everything that exists.

Corollary 2 Things of themselves do not have any essence that is the cause of God's knowledge. On the contrary, God is also the cause of things with respect to their essence.

Proof Because there is not to be found in God anything of perfection that is not from God (Prop. 10), things of themselves will not have any essence that can be the cause of God's knowledge. On the contrary, because God has created all things wholly, not generating them from something else (Prop. 12 with Cor. 1), and because the act of creation acknowledges no other cause but the efficient cause (for this is how I define 'creation'), which is God, it follows that before their creation things were nothing at all, and therefore God was also the cause of their essence. Q.E.D.

It should be noted that this corollary is also evident from the fact that God is the cause or creator of all things (Cor. 1) and that the cause must contain in itself all the perfections of the effect (Ax. 8), as everyone can readily see.

Corollary 3 Hence it clearly follows that God does not sense, nor, properly speaking, does he perceive. For his intellect is not determined by anything external to himself; all things derive from him.

Corollary 4 God is prior in causality to the essence and existence of things, as clearly follows from Corollaries 1 and 2 of this Proposition.

Proposition 13
God is supremely truthful, and not at all a deceiver.[40]

Proof We cannot attribute to God anything in which we find any imperfection (Def. 8); and because (as is self-evident) all deception or will to deceive proceeds only from malice or fear, and fear supposes diminished power while malice supposes privation of goodness, no deception or will to deceive is to be ascribed to God, a being supremely powerful and supremely good. On the contrary, he must be said to be supremely truthful and not at all a deceiver. Q.E.D. See "Replies to the Second Set of Objections," No. 4.[41]

Proposition 14
Whatever we clearly and distinctly perceive is true.

---

[40] I have not included this axiom among the axioms because it was not at all necessary. I had no need of it except for the proof of this proposition alone, and furthermore, as long as I did not know God's existence, I did not wish to assume as true anything more than what I could deduce from the first known thing, 'I am', as I said in the Scholium to Proposition 4. Again, I have not included among my definitions the definitions of fear and malice because everyone knows them, and I have no need of them except for this one proposition.

[41] [AT7, 142–147.]

Proof The faculty of distinguishing true from false, which is in us (as everyone can discover in himself, and as is obvious from all that has already been proved) has been created and is continuously preserved by God (Prop. 12 with Cor.), that is, by a being supremely truthful and not at all a deceiver (Prop. 13), and he has not bestowed on us (as everyone can discover in himself) any faculty for holding aloof from, or refusing assent to, those things that we clearly and distinctly perceive. Therefore if we were to be deceived in regard to them, we should be deceived entirely by God, and he would be a deceiver, which is absurd (Prop. 13). So whatever we clearly and distinctly perceive is true. Q.E.D.

Scholium Because those things to which we must necessarily assent when they are clearly and distinctly perceived by us are necessarily true, and because we have a faculty for withholding assent from those things that are obscure or doubtful or are not deduced from the most certain principles—as everyone can see in himself—it clearly follows that we can always take precautions against falling into error and against ever being deceived (a point that will be understood even more clearly from what follows), provided that we make an earnest resolution to affirm nothing that we do not clearly and distinctly perceive or that is not deduced from first principles clear and certain in themselves.

Proposition 15
Error is not anything positive.

Proof If error were something positive, it would have as its cause only God, by whom it must be continuously created (Prop. 12). But this is absurd (Prop. 13). Therefore error is not anything positive. Q.E.D.

Scholium Because error is not anything positive in man, it can be nothing else than the privation of the right use of freedom (Schol. Prop. 14). Therefore God must not be said to be the cause of error, except in the sense in which we say that the absence of the sun is the cause of darkness, or that God, in making a child similar to others except for sight, is the cause of blindness. He is not to be said to be the cause of error in giving us an intellect that extends to only a few things. To understand this clearly, and also how error depends solely on the misuse of the will, and, finally, to understand how we may guard against error, let us recall to mind the modes of thinking that we possess, namely, all modes of perceiving (sensing, imagining, and pure understanding) and modes of willing (desiring, misliking, affirming, denying, and doubting); for they can all be subsumed under these two headings.

Now with regard to these modes we should note, first, that insofar as the mind understands things clearly and distinctly and assents to them, it cannot be deceived (Prop. 14); nor again can it be deceived insofar as it merely perceives things and does not assent to them. For although I may now perceive a winged horse, it is certain that this perception contains nothing false as long as I do not assent to the truth that there is a winged horse, nor again as long as I doubt whether there is a winged horse. And because to assent is nothing but to determine the will, it follows that error depends only on the use of the will.

To make this even clearer, we should note, secondly, that we have the power to assent not only to those things that we clearly and distinctly perceive but also to those things that we perceive in any other way. For our will is not determined by any limits. Everyone can clearly see this if only he attends to the following point, that if God had wished to make infinite our faculty of understanding, he would not have needed to give us a more extensive faculty of willing than that which we already possess in order to enable us to assent to all that we understand. That which we already possess would be sufficient for assenting to an infinite number of things.[42] And in fact experience tells us, too, that we assent to many things that we have not deduced from sure first principles. Furthermore, these considerations make it clear that if the intellect extended as widely as the faculty of willing, or if the faculty of willing could not extend more widely than the intellect, or if, finally, we could restrict the faculty of willing within the limits of the intellect, we would never fall into error (Prop. 14).

But the first two possibilities lie beyond our power, for they would involve that the will should not be infinite and the intellect created finite. So it remains for us to consider the third possibility, namely, whether we have the power to restrict our faculty of willing within the limits of the intellect. Now because the will is free to determine itself, it follows that we do have the power to restrict the faculty of assenting within the limits of the intellect, therefore bringing it about that we do not fall into error. Hence it is quite manifest that our never being deceived depends entirely on the use of the freedom of the will. That our will is free is demonstrated in Art. 39 Part 1 of the *Principia* and in the "Fourth Meditation," and is also shown at some length by me in the last chapter of my Appendix. And although, when we perceive a thing clearly and distinctly, we cannot refrain from assenting to it, that necessary assent depends not on the weakness but simply on the freedom and perfection of the will. For to assent to the truth is a perfection in us (as is self-evident), and the will is never more perfect and more free than when it completely determines itself. Because this can occur when the mind understands something clearly and distinctly, it will necessarily give itself this perfection at once (Ax. 3). Therefore we by no means understand ourselves to be less free because we are not at all indifferent in embracing truth. On the contrary, we take it as certain that the more indifferent we are, the less free we are.

So now it remains only to be explained how error is nothing but privation with respect to man, whereas with respect to God it is mere negation. This will easily be seen if we first observe that our perceiving many things besides those that we clearly understand makes us more perfect than if we did not perceive them. This

---

[42] [Cf. Med4, 38 (AT7, 56–57).]

is clearly established from the fact that, if it were supposed that we could perceive nothing clearly and distinctly but only confusedly, we should possess nothing more perfect than this perceiving things confusedly, nor would anything else be expected of our nature. Furthermore, to assent to things, however confused, insofar as it is also a kind of action, is a perfection. This will also be obvious to everyone if he supposes, as previously, that it is contrary to man's nature to perceive things clearly and distinctly. For then it will become quite clear that it is far better for a man to assent to things, however confused, and to exercise his freedom, than to remain always indifferent, that is (as we have just shown), at the lowest grade of freedom. And if we also turn our attention to the needs and convenience of human life, we shall find this absolutely necessary, as experience teaches each of us every day.

Therefore, because all the modes of thinking that we possess are perfect insofar as they are regarded in themselves alone, to that extent that which constitutes the form of error cannot be in them. But if we attend to the way in which modes of willing differ from one another, we shall find that some are more perfect than others in that some render the will less indifferent (i.e., more free) than others. Again, we shall also see that, as long as we assent to confused things, we make our minds less apt to distinguish true from false, thereby depriving ourselves of the highest freedom. Therefore to assent to confused things, insofar as this is something positive, does not contain any imperfection or the form of error; it does so only insofar as we thus deprive our own selves of the highest freedom that is within reach of our nature and is within our power. So the imperfection of error will consist entirely merely in the privation of the highest freedom, a privation that is called error. Now it is called privation because we are deprived of a perfection that is compatible with our nature, and it is called error because it is our own fault that we lack this perfection, in that we fail to restrict the will within the limits of the intellect, as we are able to do. Therefore, because error is nothing else with respect to man but the privation of the perfect or correct use of freedom, it follows that it does not lie in any faculty that he has from God, nor again in any operation of his faculties insofar as this depends on God.[43] Nor can we say that God has deprived us of the greater intellect that he might have given us and has thereby brought it about that we could fall into error. For no thing's nature can demand anything from God, and nothing belongs to a thing except what the will of God has willed to bestow on it. For nothing existed, or can even be conceived, prior to God's will (as is fully explained in our Appendix Part 2 Chapters 7 and 8). Therefore God has not deprived us of a greater intellect or a more perfect faculty of understanding any more than he has deprived a circle of the properties of a sphere, and a circumference of the properties of a spherical surface.

So because none of our faculties, in whatever way it be considered, can point to any imperfection in God, it clearly follows that the imperfection in which the

---

[43] [Med4, 36–39 (AT7, 54–58).]

form of error consists is privation only with respect to man. When related to God as its cause, it can be termed not privation, but only negation.

Proposition 16
God is incorporeal.

Proof Body is the immediate subject of local motion (Def. 7). Therefore if God were corporeal, he would be divided into parts; and this, since it clearly involves imperfection, it is absurd to affirm of God (Def. 8).

Another Proof If God were corporeal, he could be divided into parts (Def. 7). Now either each single part could subsist of itself, or it could not. If the latter, it would be like the other things created by God, and thus, like every created thing, it would be continuously created by the same force by God (Prop. 10 and Ax. 11), and would not pertain to God's nature any more than other created things, which is absurd (Prop. 5). But if each single part exists through itself, each single part must also involve necessary existence (Lemma 2 Prop. 7), and consequently each single part would be a supremely perfect being (Cor. Lemma 2 Prop. 7). But this, too, is absurd (Prop. 11). Therefore God is incorporeal. Q.E.D.

Proposition 17
God is a completely simple being.

Proof If God were composed of parts, the parts (as all will readily grant) would have to be at least prior in nature to God, which is absurd (Cor. 4 Prop. 12). Therefore he is a completely simple being. Q.E.D.

Corollary Hence it follows that God's intelligence, his will or decree, and his power are not distinguished from his essence, except by abstract reasoning.

Proposition 18
God is immutable.

Proof If God were mutable, he could not change in part, but would have to change with respect to his whole essence (Prop. 17). But the essence of God exists necessarily (Props. 5, 6, and 7). Therefore God is immutable. Q.E.D.

Proposition 19
God is eternal.

Proof God is a supremely perfect being (Def. 8), from which it follows that he exists necessarily (Prop. 5). If now we attribute to him limited existence, the limits of his existence must necessarily be understood, if not by us, at any rate by God himself (Prop. 9), because he has understanding in the highest degree. Therefore God will understand himself (i.e. [Def. 8], a supremely perfect being) as not existing beyond these limits, which is absurd (Prop. 5). Therefore God has not a limited but an infinite existence, which we call eternity. See Chapter 1 Part 2 of our Appendix. Therefore God is eternal. Q.E.D.

Proposition 20
God has preordained all things from eternity.

Proof Because God is eternal (Prop. 19), his understanding is eternal, because it pertains to his eternal essence (Cor. Prop. 17). But his intellect is not different in reality from his will or decree (Cor. Prop. 17). Therefore when we say that God has understood things from eternity, we are also saying that he has willed or decreed things thus from eternity. Q.E.D.

Corollary From this proposition it follows that God is in the highest degree constant in his works.

Proposition 21
Substance extended in length, breadth, and depth exists in reality, and we are united to one part of it.

Proof That which is extended, as it is clearly and distinctly perceived by us, does not pertain to God's nature (Prop. 16), but it can be created by God (Cor. Prop. 7 and Prop. 8). Furthermore, we clearly and distinctly perceive (as everyone can discover in himself, insofar as he thinks) that extended substance is a sufficient cause for producing in us pleasure, pain, and similar ideas or sensations, which are continually produced in us even against our will. But if we wish to suppose some other cause for our sensations apart from extended substance—say, God or an angel—we immediately destroy the clear and distinct concept that we have. Therefore,[44] as long as we correctly attend to our perceptions so as to allow nothing but what we clearly and distinctly perceive, we shall be altogether inclined, or by no means uninclined, to accept that extended substance is the only cause of our sensations, and therefore to affirm that the extended thing exists, created by God. And in this we surely cannot be deceived (Prop. 14 with Schol.). Therefore it is truly affirmed that substance extended in length, breadth, and depth exists. This was the first point.[45]

Furthermore, among our sensations, which must be produced in us (as we have already proved) by extended substance, we observe a considerable difference, as when I say that I sense or see a tree or when I say that I am thirsty, or in pain, etc. But I clearly see that I cannot perceive the cause of this difference unless I first understand that I am closely united to one part of matter, and not so to other parts. Because I clearly and distinctly understand this, and I cannot perceive it in any other way, it is true (Prop. 14 with Schol.) that I am united to one part of matter. This was the second point. We have therefore proved what was to be proved.[46]

---

[44] See the proof to Proposition 14 and the Scholium to Proposition 15.
[45] [Cf. Med6, 51–52 (AT7, 78–80).]
[46] [See Med6, 52–53 (AT7, 80–81).]

Note: Unless the reader here considers himself only as a thinking thing, lacking body, and unless he puts aside as prejudices all the reasons that he previously entertained for believing that body exists, his attempts to understand this proof will be in vain.

End of Part 1

THE PRINCIPLES OF PHILOSOPHY

Demonstrated in the Geometric Manner

Part 2

Postulate

Here the only requirement is that everyone should attend to his perceptions as accurately as possible, so that he may distinguish what is clear from what is obscure.

Definitions

1. *Extension* is that which consists of three dimensions. But by extension we do not understand the act of extending, or anything distinct from quantity.
2. By *Substance* we understand that which, in order to exist, needs only the concurrence of God.
3. An *atom* is a part of matter indivisible by its own nature.
4. The *indefinite* is that whose bounds, if it has any, cannot be discovered by human intellect.
5. A *vacuum* is extension without corporeal substance.
6. *Space* is to be distinguished from extension only in thought; there is no difference in reality. Read Art. 10 Part 2 of the *Principia*.
7. That which in our thinking we understand to be divided is *divisible*, at least potentially.
8. *Local motion* is the transfer of one part of matter, or of one body, from the vicinity of those bodies that are immediately contiguous and are regarded as at rest, to the vicinity of other bodies.

This is the definition used by Descartes to explain local motion. To understand this definition correctly, we should consider:

8.1. That by a part of matter he understands all that which is transferred together, although it may in turn consist of many parts.

8.2. That, to avoid confusion, in this definition he refers only to that which is constantly in the moving thing in motion, that is, its being transferred. So this should not be confused, as is commonly done by others, with the force or action that effects the transfer. This force or action is commonly thought to be required only for motion and not for rest, an opinion that is plainly wrong. For, as is self-evident, the same force that is required to impart fixed degrees of motion to a body that is at rest is again required for the withdrawal of those fixed degrees of motion from the same body, and for bringing it entirely to rest. Indeed, this can also be proved by experience, for we use about the same force to propel a boat that is at rest in still water as to halt it suddenly when it is moving. In fact, it would be exactly the same, were we not helped in halting the boat by the weight and resistance of the water displaced by it.

8.3. That he says that the transfer takes place from the vicinity of contiguous bodies to the vicinity of others, and not from one place to another. For place (as he himself has explained in Art. 13 Part 2) is not something real, but depends only on our thought, so that the same body may be said at the same time to change, and not to change, its place. But it cannot be said at the same time to be transferred, and not to be transferred, from the vicinity of a contiguous body. For only certain definite bodies can, at the same moment of time, be contiguous to the same movable body.

8.4. That he does not say, without qualification, that the transfer takes place from the vicinity of contiguous bodies, but only from the vicinity of contiguous bodies that are regarded as at rest. For in order that a body A may be moved away from a body B, which is at rest, the same force and action are required on the one side as on the other. This is evident in the example of a boat that is sticking to the mud or sand at the bottom of the water. To push it forward, an equal force must be applied to the bottom as to the boat. Therefore the force by which bodies are to be moved is expended equally on the moved body and the body at rest. The transfer is indeed reciprocal; if the boat is separated from the sand, the sand is also separated from the boat. Therefore, when bodies separate from one another, if we were to attribute to them without qualification equal motions in opposite directions, refusing to regard one of them as at rest simply on the grounds that there is the same action in the one case as in the other, then we should also be compelled to attribute to bodies that are universally regarded as at rest (e.g., the sand from which the boat is separated) the same amount of motion as to the moving bodies. For, as we have shown, the same action is required on the one side as on the other, and the transfer is reciprocal. But this would be too remote from the normal usages of language. However, although those bodies from which other bodies are separated are regarded as at rest and are also spoken of in this way, we shall remember that everything in the moving body on account of which it is said to move is also in the body at rest.

8.5. Finally, that it is also clear from the definition that each body possesses only one motion peculiar to itself because it is understood to move away only from one set of bodies contiguous to it and at rest. However, if the moving body forms part of other bodies having other motions, we clearly understand that it can also participate in innumerable other motions. But because it is not easy to understand so many motions at the same time, or even to recognize them all, it will be sufficient to consider in each body that unique motion, which is peculiar to it. See Art. 31 Part 2 *Principia*.

9. By a circle of moving bodies we understand only a formation where the last body, in motion because of the impulse of another body, immediately touches the first of the moving bodies, even though the figure formed by all the bodies together through the impulse of a single motion may be very contorted.

Axioms

1. To nothing there belong no properties.
2. Whatever can be taken away from a thing without impairing its integrity does not constitute the thing's essence. But that whose removal destroys a thing constitutes its essence.
3. In the case of hardness, our sense indicates to us nothing else, and we clearly and distinctly understand of it nothing else, than that the parts of hard bodies resist the movement of our hands.
4. If two bodies approach each other, or move away from each other, they will not thereby occupy more or less space.
5. A part of matter, whether it gives way or resists, does not thereby lose the nature of body.
6. Motion, rest, figure, and the like cannot be conceived without extension.
7. Apart from its sensible qualities, nothing remains in body but extension and its affections enumerated in Part 1 of *Principia*.
8. Any one space or extension cannot be greater at one time than at another.
9. All extension can be divided, at least in thought.

No one who has learned even the elements of mathematics doubts the truth of this axiom. For the space between a tangent and a circle can always be divided by an infinite number of larger circles. The same point is also made obvious by the asymptotes of the hyperbola.

10. No one can conceive the boundaries of an extension or space without at the same time conceiving other spaces beyond those boundaries, immediately following on that space.
11. If matter is manifold, and one piece is not in immediate contact with another, each piece is necessarily comprehended within boundaries beyond which there is no matter.
12. The most minute bodies readily give way to the movement of our hands.
13. One space does not penetrate another space, nor is it greater at one time than at another.

14. If a hollow pipe A is of the same length as C, and C is twice as wide as A, and if a liquid passes through pipe A at twice the speed at which a liquid passes through pipe C, the same amount of matter will pass through both pipes in the same space of time. And if in the same time the same amount of matter passes through pipe A as through C, the former will move at twice the speed.

15. Things that agree with a third thing agree with one another; and things that are double a third thing are equal to one another.

16. Matter that moves in diverse ways has at least as many parts, divided in actuality, as there are different degrees of speed to be observed in it at the same time.

17. The shortest line between two points is a straight line.

18. If a body A moving from C toward B is repelled by an opposite impulse, it will move along the same line toward C.

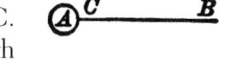

19. When bodies having opposite motions collide with each other, they are both—or at least one of them—compelled to undergo some change.

20. A change in any thing proceeds from a stronger force.

21. When body 1 moves toward body 2 and pushes it, if as a result of this impulse body 8 moves toward body 1, then bodies 1, 2, 3, etc., cannot be in a straight line, and all eight bodies form a complete circle. See Def. 9.

Lemma 1 Where there is extension or space, there is necessarily substance.

Proof Extension or space (Ax. 1) cannot be pure nothing. It is therefore an attribute that must be attributed to some thing, but not to God (Prop. 16 Part 1); therefore it must be attributed to a thing that needs only the concurrence of God to exist (Prop. 12 Part 1), that is (Def. 2 Part 2), to substance. Q.E.D.

Lemma 2 Rarefaction and condensation are clearly and distinctly conceived by us, although we do not grant that bodies occupy more space in rarefaction than in condensation.

Proof Rarefaction and condensation can be clearly and distinctly conceived from the mere fact that parts of a body may move away from, or toward, one another. Therefore (Ax. 4) they will not occupy either more or less space. For if the parts of a body—say, a sponge—by moving toward one another expel the bodies with which its interstices are filled, this in itself will make that body more dense, and its parts will not thereby occupy less space than before (Ax. 4). And if again the parts move away from one another and the gaps are filled by other bodies, there will be rarefaction, but the parts will not occupy more space. And this, which we clearly perceive with the aid of our senses in the case of a sponge, we can conceive with the unaided intellect in the case of all bodies, although their interstices completely escape human sense-perception. Therefore rarefaction and condensation are clearly and distinctly conceived by us, etc. Q.E.D.

I have thought it advisable to set out these Lemmas first, so that the intellect may rid itself of prejudices concerning space, rarefaction, etc., and be rendered apt to understand what is to follow.

Proposition 1
Although hardness, weight, and the other sensible qualities may be separated from a body, the nature of the body will nevertheless remain unimpaired.

Proof In the case of hardness—say, of this stone—our sense-perception indicates to us nothing else, and we clearly and distinctly understand nothing else, than that the parts of hard bodies resist the movement of our hands (Ax. 3). Therefore (Prop. 14 Part 1) hardness also will be nothing else but this. Indeed, if the said body is reduced to the finest powder, its parts will readily give way (Ax. 12); yet it will not lose the nature of body (Ax. 5). Q.E.D.

In the case of weight and the other sensible qualities, the proof proceeds in the same way.

Proposition 2
The nature of body or matter consists only in extension.

Proof The nature of body is not lost as a result of the loss of sensible qualities (Prop. 1 Part 2). Therefore these do not constitute its essence (Ax. 2). Therefore nothing is left but extension and its affections (Ax. 7). So if extension be taken away, nothing will remain pertaining to the nature of body, and it will be completely annulled. Therefore (Ax. 2) the nature of body consists only in extension. Q.E.D.

Corollary Space and body do not differ in reality.

Proof Body and extension do not differ in reality (previous Prop.), and also space and extension do not differ in reality (Def. 6). Therefore (Ax. 15) space and body do not differ in reality. Q.E.D.

Scholium Although we say that God is everywhere,[1] it is not thereby admitted that God is extended (i.e. [previous Prop.], that God is corporeal). For his ubiquity refers only to God's power and his concurrence whereby he preserves all things, so that God's ubiquity does not refer to body or extension any more than to angels and human souls. But it should be noted that when we say that his power is everywhere, we do not exclude his essence; for where his power is, there too is his essence (Cor. Prop. 17 Part 1). We intend to exclude only bodily nature; that is, we mean that God is everywhere not by a corporeal power but by his divine power or essence, which serves alike to preserve extension and thinking things (Prop. 17 Part 1). The latter he certainly could not have preserved if his power, that is, his essence, were corporeal.

---

[1] On this, see a fuller explanation in Appendix, Part 2, Chapters 3 and 9.

Proposition 3
That there should be a vacuum is a contradiction.

Proof   By a vacuum is understood extension without corporeal substance (Def. 3); that is (Prop. 2 Part 2), body without body, which is absurd.

For a fuller explanation, and to correct prejudice concerning the vacuum, read Articles 17 and 18 Part 2 of the *Principia*, where it should be particularly noted that bodies between which nothing lies must necessarily touch one another, and also that to nothing there belong no properties.

Proposition 4
One part of a body does not occupy more space at one time than at another; and, conversely, the same space does not contain more body at one time than at another.

Proof   Space and body do not differ in reality (Cor. Prop. 2 Part 2). Therefore when we say that a space is not greater at one time than at another (Ax. 13), we are also saying that a body cannot be greater (i.e., occupy more space) at one time than at another, which was our first point. Furthermore, from the fact that space and body do not differ in reality, it follows that when we say that body cannot occupy more space at one time than at another, we are also saying that the same space cannot contain more body at one time than at another. Q.E.D.

Corollary   Bodies that occupy equal space, say, gold and air, have the same amount of matter or corporeal substance.

Proof   Corporeal substance consists not in hardness (e.g., of gold) nor in softness (e.g., of air) nor in any of the sensible qualities (Prop. 1 Part 2), but only in extension (Prop. 2 Part 2). Now because, by hypothesis, there is the same amount of space or (Def. 6) extension in the one as in the other; therefore there will also be the same amount of corporeal substance. Q.E.D.

Proposition 5
There are no atoms.

Proof   Atoms are parts of matter that are, by their own nature, indivisible (Def. 3). But because the nature of matter consists in extension (Prop. 2 Part 2), which by its own nature is divisible, however small it be (Ax. 9 and Def. 7); therefore however small a part of matter may be, it is by its own nature divisible. That is, there are no atoms, or parts of matter that are by their own nature indivisible. Q.E.D.

Scholium   The question of atoms has always been a difficult and complicated one. Some assert that there must be atoms, arguing from the impossibility of an infinite being greater than another infinite; and if two quantities—say A and its double—are infinitely divisible, they can also be divided in actuality into an infinite number of parts by the power of God, who understands their infinitely many parts with a single intuition. Therefore, because one infinite cannot be greater than another infinite, as has been said, quantity A will be equal to its double, which is absurd. Then again, they ask whether half an infinite number is also infinite, and whether it is even or odd, and other such questions. To all this Descartes replied that we must not reject what comes within the scope of our intellect, and is therefore clearly and distinctly conceived, because of other things that exceed our intellect or grasp, and that are therefore only perceived very inadequately by us. Now the infinite and its properties exceed the human intellect because that is by nature finite. And so it would be foolish to reject as false, or to doubt, what we clearly and distinctly conceive concerning space, on the grounds that we do not comprehend the infinite. And for this reason Descartes considers as indefinite those things in which we can see no boundaries, such as the extension of the world, the divisibility of the parts of matter, etc. Read Art. 26 Part 1 of the *Principia*.

PROPOSITION 6
Matter is indefinitely extended, and the matter of the heavens and the earth is one and the same.

Proof 1. We cannot imagine the boundaries of extension, that is (Prop. 2 Part 2), of matter, without conceiving other spaces immediately following or beyond them (Ax. 10), that is, without conceiving extension or matter (Def. 6) beyond them, and so on indefinitely. This was the first point.

2. The essence of matter consists in extension (Prop. 2 Part 2), and this is indefinite (first part of this proof); that is, it cannot be conceived by the human intellect as having any boundaries. Therefore (Ax. 11) it is not a manifold but everywhere one and the same. That was the second point.

Scholium So far we have been dealing with the nature or essence of extension. The fact that it exists such as we conceive it, created by God, we have proved in the last Proposition of Part 1, and from Prop. 12 Part 1, it follows that it is now preserved by the same power by which it was created. Then again, in that same last Proposition of Part 1, we proved that, insofar as we are thinking things, we are united to some part of matter, by whose help we perceive that there are in actuality all those variations whereof, by merely contemplating matter, we know it to be capable. Such are divisibility and local motion or movement of one part from one place to another, which we clearly and distinctly perceive provided that we understand that other parts of matter take the place of those that move. And this division and motion are conceived by us in infinite ways, and therefore infinite variations of matter can also be conceived. I say that they are clearly and distinctly conceived by us as long as we conceive them as modes of extension, not as things distinct in reality from extension, as is fully explained in *Principia* Part 1. And although philosophers have fabricated any number of other motions, because we admit nothing but what we clearly and distinctly conceive, and because we do not clearly and distinctly understand extension to be capable of any motion except local motion, nor does any other motion even come within the scope of our imagination, we must not admit any other motion but local motion.

But Zeno, so it is said, denied local motion and did so for various reasons that

Diogenes the Cynic refuted in his own way, by walking about the school where Zeno was teaching these doctrines and disturbing his listeners with his perambulations. When he saw that he was being held by one of the audience so as to prevent his wanderings, he rebuked him, saying: Why have you thus dared to refute your master's arguments? However, it may be that someone could be deceived by Zeno's arguments into thinking that the senses reveal to us something—in this case, motion—entirely opposed to the intellect, with the result that the mind may be deceived even concerning those things that it perceives clearly and distinctly with the aid of the intellect. To prevent this, I shall here set forth Zeno's principal arguments, showing that they rest only on false prejudices because he had no true conception of matter.

In the first place, then, he is reported to have said that, if local motion were granted, the motion of a body moving with a circular motion at the highest speed would be no different from a state of rest. But the latter is absurd; therefore so is the former. He proves the consequence as follows: A body whose every point remains constantly in the same place is at rest. But all the points of a body moving with a circular motion at the highest speed remain constantly in the same place; therefore, etc. He is said to have explained this by the example of a wheel, say, ABC. If the wheel were to move about its center at a certain speed, point A would complete a circle through B and C more quickly than if it were to move at a slower speed. So suppose, for example, that it begins to move slowly, and that after an hour it is in the same place from which it began. Now if it be supposed that it moves at twice that speed, it will be in the same place from which it began after half an hour; and if at four times the speed, after quarter of an hour. And if we conceive the speed to be infinitely increased and the time to be reduced to moments, then the point A at its highest speed will be at all moments, or constantly, in the place from which it began to move, and so it always remains in the same place. And what we understand about point A must also be understood about every point of the wheel. Therefore at the highest speed, all points remain constantly in the same place.

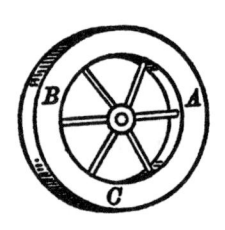

Now, in reply, it should be noted that this is an argument directed against motion's highest speed rather than against motion itself. But we shall not here examine the validity of Zeno's argument; we shall rather disclose the prejudices whereon all this argument depends insofar as it claims to attack motion. In the first place, he supposes that bodies can be conceived to move so quickly that they cannot move more quickly. Secondly, he supposes time to be made up of moments, just as others have conceived quantity to be made up of indivisible points. Both of these suppositions are false. For we can never conceive a motion so fast that we cannot at the same time conceive a faster. It is contrary to our intellect to conceive a motion so fast, however short be its course, that there can be no faster motion.

And the same holds true in the case of slowness. To conceive a motion so slow that there cannot be a slower, involves a contradiction. And regarding time, too, which is the measure of motion, we make the same assertion, that it is clearly contrary to our intellect to conceive a time other than which there can be none shorter.

To prove all this, let us follow in Zeno's footsteps. Let us suppose, with him, that a wheel ABC moves about its center at such a speed that the point A is at every moment in the position A from which it moves. I say that I clearly conceive a speed indefinitely greater than this, and consequently moments that are infinitely less. For let it be supposed that while the wheel ABC moves about its center, with the help of a belt H it causes another wheel, DEF, half its size, to move about its center. Now because the wheel DEF is supposed to be half the size of the wheel ABC, it is plain that the wheel DEF moves at twice the speed of the wheel ABC, and consequently the point D is at every half-moment again in the same place from which it began to move. Then if we assign the motion of the wheel DEF to the wheel ABC, DEF will move four times faster than the original speed, and if we again assign this last speed of the wheel DEF to the wheel ABC, then DEF will move eight times as fast, and so ad infinitum.

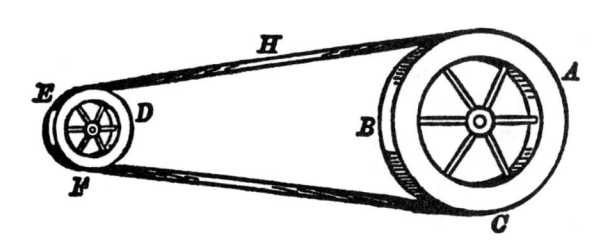

But this is quite clear merely from the concept of matter. For the essence of matter consists in extension, or ever-divisible space, as we have proved, and there is no motion without space. We have also demonstrated that one part of matter cannot occupy two spaces at the same time; for that would be the same as saying that one part of matter is equal to its double, as is evident from what has already been demonstrated. Therefore if a part of matter moves, it moves through some space, a space that, however small it is imagined to be, is nevertheless divisible, and consequently so is the time through which the motion is measured. Consequently the duration of that motion, or its time, is divisible, and is so to infinity. Q.E.D.

Let us now proceed to another fallacious problem, said to have been propounded by Zeno, which is as follows: If a body moves, it moves either in the place in which it is, or in a place in which it is not. But not in a place in which it is; for if it is in any place, it must be at rest. Nor again in a place in which it is not. Therefore the body does not move. But this line of argument is just like the previous one, for it also supposes that there is a time other than which there is no shorter. If we reply that a body moves not in, but from, the place in which it is to a place in which it is not, he will ask whether it has not been in any intermediate places. We may reply by making a distinction: if by 'has been' he means 'has rested', we deny that it has been in any place while it was moving; but if by 'has been' is understood 'has existed', we say that it has necessarily existed while it was moving. He will again ask where it has existed while it was moving. We may once more reply that if by 'where it has existed' he means 'what place it has stayed in' while it was moving, we say that it did not stay in any place; but if he means 'what place it has changed', we say that it has changed all those places that he may wish to assign as belonging to the space through which it was moving. He will go on to ask whether at the same moment of time it could occupy and change its place. To this we finally reply by making the following distinction: If by a moment of time he means a time other than which there can be none shorter, he is asking an unintelligible question, as we have adequately shown, and thus one that does not deserve a reply. But if he takes time in the sense that I have explained previously (i.e., its true sense), he can never assign a time so short that in it a body cannot occupy and change place, even though the time is supposed to be able to be shortened indefinitely; and this is obvious to one who pays sufficient attention. Hence it is quite evident, as we said previously, that he is supposing a time so short that there cannot be a shorter, and so he proves nothing.

Besides these two arguments, there is yet another argument of Zeno's in circulation, which can be read, together with its refutation, in Descartes's *Letters* Vol. 1, penultimate letter.[2]

I should like my readers here to observe that I have opposed Zeno's reasonings with my own reasonings, and so I have refuted him by reason, not by the senses, as did Diogenes. For the senses cannot produce for the seeker after truth anything other than the phenomena of Nature, by which he is determined to investigate their causes; they can never show to be false what the intellect clearly and distinctly grasps as true. This is the view we take, and so this is our method, to demonstrate our propositions with reasons clearly and distinctly perceived by the intellect, disregarding whatever the senses assert when that seems contrary to reason. The senses, as we have said, can do no more than determine the intellect to enquire into one thing rather than another; they cannot convict the intellect of falsity when it has clearly and distinctly perceived something.

PROPOSITION 7

No body moves into the place of another body unless at the same time that other body moves into the place of another body.

Proof (See Diagram of Next Proposition) If you deny this, suppose, if it is possible, that a body A moves into the place of a body B, which I suppose to be equal to A and which does not give way from its own place. Therefore the space that contained only B, by hypothesis, now contains A and B, and so contains twice the amount of corporeal substance as it contained before, which is absurd (Prop. 4 Part 2). Therefore no body moves into the place of another, . . . etc. Q.E.D.

PROPOSITION 8

When a body moves into the place of another body, at the same moment of time the place quitted by it is occupied by another body immediately contiguous to it.

---

[2] [Spinoza probably refers to the Dutch translation of Descartes's letters: *Brieven*, tr. J. H. Glazemaker, Amsterdam, 1661. The letter mentioned is probably to Clerselier, June/July 1646, AT4, 445–447.]

Proof If a body B moves toward D, bodies A and C at the same moment of time will either move toward each other and touch each other, or they will not. If they move toward each other and touch each other, what we have proposed is granted. If they do not move toward each other and the entire space quitted by B lies between A and C, then a body equal to B (Cor. Prop. 2 Part 2 and Cor. Prop. 4 Part 2) lies between. But, by hypothesis, this is not B. Therefore it is another body, which at the same moment of time moves into B's place. And because it moves into B's place at the same moment of time, it can be none other than that which is immediately contiguous, according to Scholium Prop. 6 Part 2. For there we demonstrated that there can be no motion from one place to another such that it does not require a time other than which there is always a shorter time. From this it follows that the space of body B cannot be occupied at the same moment of time by another body that would have to move through some space before it moved into B's place. Therefore only a body immediately contiguous to B moves into its place at the same moment of time. Q.E.D.

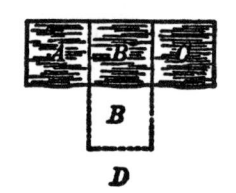

Scholium Because the parts of matter are in reality distinct from one another (Art. 61 *Principia* Part 1), one can exist without another (Cor. Prop. 7 Part 1), and they do not depend on one another. So all those fictions about Sympathy and Antipathy must be rejected as false. Furthermore, because the cause of an effect must always be positive (Ax. 8 Part 1), it must never be said that a body moves to avoid there being a vacuum. It moves only through the impulse of another body.

Corollary In every motion, a complete circle of bodies moves at the same time.

Proof At the time when body 1 moves into the place of body 2, body 2 must move into the place of another body, say, body 3, and so on (Prop. 7 Part 2). Again, at the same moment of time as body 1 moves into the place of body 2, the place quitted by body 1 must be occupied by another body (Prop. 8 Part 2), let us say body 8 or another body immediately contiguous to body 1. Because this occurs only through the impulse of another body (Schol. to this Prop.), which is here supposed to be body 1, all these moving bodies cannot be in the same straight line (Ax. 21) but (Def. 9) form a complete circle. Q.E.D.

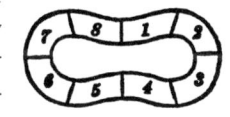

Proposition 9

If a circular tube ABC is full of water and is four times as wide at A as at B, then at the time that the water (or any other fluid body) at A begins to move toward B, the water at B will move at four times that speed.

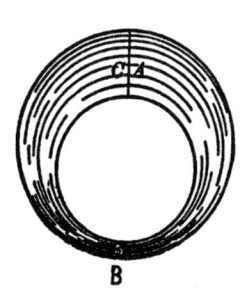

Proof When all the water at A moves toward B, the same amount of water must at the same time move into its place from C, which is immediately contiguous to A (Prop. 8 Part 2). And from B the same amount of water will have to move into the place of C (same Prop.). Therefore (Ax. 14) it will move at four times that speed. Q.E.D.

What we say about the circular tube must also apply to all unequal spaces through which bodies moving at the same time are compelled to pass; for the proof will be the same in the other cases.

Lemma If two semicircles A and B are described about the same center, the space between their circumferences will be everywhere the same. But if two semicircles C and D are described about different centers, the space between their circumferences will be everywhere unequal.

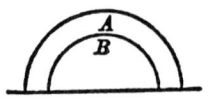

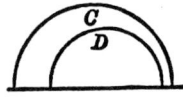

The proof is evident merely from the definition of a circle.

Proposition 10

The fluid body that moves through the tube ABC (of Prop. 9) receives an indefinite number of degrees of speed.

Proof The space between A and B is everywhere unequal (previous Lemma). Therefore (Prop. 9 Part 2) the speed at which the fluid body passes through the tube ABC will be unequal at all points. Furthermore, because we conceive in thought an indefinite number of spaces ever smaller and smaller between A and B (Prop. 5 Part 2), we shall also conceive its inequalities of speed, which are at all points, as indefinite. Therefore (Prop. 9 Part 2) the degrees of speed will be indefinite in number. Q.E.D.

Proposition 11

The matter that flows through the tube ABC (of Prop. 9) is divided into an indefinite number of particles.

Proof The matter that flows through the tube ABC acquires at the same time an indefinite number of degrees of speed (Prop. 10 Part 2). Therefore (Ax. 16) it has an indefinite number of parts into which it is in reality divided. Q.E.D. Read Arts. 34 and 35 Part 2 of the *Principia*.

Scholium So far we have been dealing with the nature of motion. We should now enquire into its cause, which is twofold: (1) the primary or general cause, which is the cause of all the motions in the world, and (2) the particular cause, whereby it comes about that individual parts of matter acquire motions that they did not have before. As to the general cause, because we must admit nothing (Prop. 14 Part 1 and Schol. Prop. 15 Part 1)[3] but what we clearly and distinctly perceive, and because we clearly and distinctly understand no other cause than God, the creator of matter, it is obvious that no other general cause but God must be admitted. And what we here say about motion must also be understood about rest.

---

[3] [Here I deviate from Gebhardt to follow Hubbeling's emendation. — S.S.]

Proposition 12
God is the principal cause of motion.

Proof See the immediately preceding Scholium.

Proposition 13
God still preserves by his concurrence the same quantity of motion and rest that he originally gave to matter.

Proof Because God is the cause of motion and rest (Prop. 12 Part 2), he continues to preserve them by that same power by which he created them (Ax. 10 Part 1), the quantity also remaining the same as when he first created them (Cor. Prop. 20 Part 1). Q.E.D.

Scholium 1. Although in theology it is said that God does many things at his own good pleasure and with the purpose of displaying his power to men, nevertheless, because those things that depend merely on his good pleasure are known by no other means than divine revelation, to prevent philosophy from being confused with theology, they are not to be admitted in philosophy, where enquiry is restricted to what reason tells us.

2. Although motion is nothing but a mode of moving matter, it nevertheless has a fixed and determinate quantity. How this is to be understood will become evident from what follows. Read Art. 36 Part 2 of the *Principia*.

Proposition 14
Each single thing, insofar as it is simple and undivided and is considered only in itself, always perseveres in the same state, as far as in it lies.

Many take this proposition as an axiom, but we shall demonstrate it.

Proof Because everything is in a certain state only by the concurrence of God (Prop. 12 Part 1) and God is in the highest degree constant in his works (Cor. Prop. 20 Part 1), if we pay no attention to any external causes (i.e., particular causes) but consider the thing only in itself, we must affirm that as far as in it lies, it always perseveres in the state in which it is. Q.E.D.

Corollary A body that is once in motion always continues to move unless it is checked by external causes.

Proof This is obvious from the preceding proposition. But to correct prejudice concerning motion, read Arts. 37 and 38 Part 2 of the *Principia*.

Proposition 15
Every body in motion tends of itself to continue to move in a straight line, not in a curved line.

This proposition could well be considered as an axiom, but I shall demonstrate it from the preceding, as follows.

Proof Motion, having only God for its cause (Prop. 12 Part 2), never has of itself any force to exist (Ax. 10 Part 1), but at every moment continues, as it were, to be created by God (by what is demonstrated in connection with the Axiom just cited). Therefore, although we attend only to the nature of the motion, we can never attribute to it, as pertaining to its nature, a duration that can be conceived as greater than another duration. But if it is said that it pertains to the nature of a moving body to describe by its movement a curve, we should be attributing to the nature of motion a longer duration than when it is supposed to be in the nature of a moving body to tend to continue to move in a straight line (Ax. 17). Now because (as we have just proved) we cannot attribute such duration to the nature of motion, then neither can we posit that it is of the nature of a moving body to continue to move in a curve; it must continue to move only in a straight line. Q.E.D.

Scholium Perhaps many will think that this proof is equally effective in showing that it does not pertain to the nature of motion to describe a straight line as in showing that it does not pertain to the nature of motion to describe a curved line, and that this is so because there cannot be posited a straight line other than which there is no shorter, whether straight or curved, nor any curved line other than which there is no shorter curve. However, although I have this in mind, I nevertheless hold that the proof proceeds correctly, because it concludes what was required to be proved solely from the universal essence of lines, that is, their essential specific difference, and not from the length of individual lines, that is, their accidental specific difference. But to avoid making more obscure, by my proof, a thing that is through itself quite clear, I refer my readers to the simple definition of motion, which affirms of motion nothing other than its being the transfer of one part of matter from the vicinity . . . , etc., to the vicinity of other . . . , etc. So unless we conceive this transfer in its simplest form—that is, as proceeding in a straight line—we are attaching to motion something not contained in its essence or definition, and so not pertaining to its nature.

Corollary From this Proposition it follows that every body that moves in a curve is continuously deviating from the line along which it would continue to move of itself, and this is through the force of an external cause (Prop. 14 Part 2).

PROPOSITION 16
Every body that moves in a circle (e.g., a stone in a sling) is continuously determined to continue in motion at a tangent to that circle.

Proof A body that moves in a circle is continuously prevented by an external force from continuing to move in a straight line (Cor. previous Prop.). If this force ceases, the body will of itself proceed to move in a straight line (Prop. 15). Furthermore, I say that a body that moves in a circle is determined by an external cause to proceed to move at a tangent to the circle. If you deny this, suppose that a stone at B is determined (e.g., by a sling) to move not along the tangent BD but along another line conceived as drawn without or within the circle from the same point. When the sling is supposed to be coming from L toward B, let this line be BF. If on the other hand the sling is supposed to be coming from C toward B, let this line be BG. If BH is the line drawn from the center through the circumference, which it cuts at B, I understand the angle GBH to be equal to the angle FBH. But if the stone at B is determined to proceed to move toward F by the sling moving in a circle from L toward B, then it necessarily follows (Ax. 18) that when the sling moves with a contrary determination from C toward B, the stone will be determined to proceed to move in line with BF with a contrary determination and will therefore tend not toward G but toward K. This is contrary to our hypothesis. And because no line except a tangent can be drawn through point B making equal adjacent angles, DBH, ABH, with the line BH,[4] there can be no line but a tangent that can preserve the same hypothesis, whether the sling moves from L to B or from C to B. And so the stone can tend to move along no line but the tangent. Q.E.D.

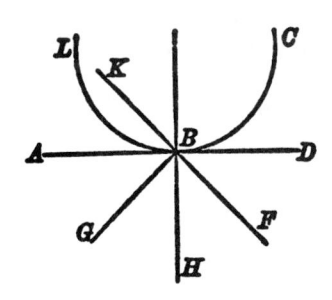

Another Proof Instead of a circle,[5] conceive a hexagon ABH inscribed in a circle, and a body C at rest on one side, AB. Then conceive that a ruler DBE, whose one end I suppose to be fixed at the center D while the other end is free, moves about the center D, continuously cutting the line AB. It is evident that if the ruler DBE, conceived to move in this way, meets the body C just when the ruler cuts the line AB at right angles, by its impact the ruler will determine the body C to proceed to move along the line FBAG toward G, that is, along the side AB produced indefinitely. But because we have chosen a hexagon at random, the same must be affirmed of any other figure that we conceive can be inscribed in a circle, namely, that when a body C, at rest on one side of the figure, is struck by the ruler DBE just when the ruler cuts that side at right angles, it will be determined by that ruler to proceed to move along that side produced indefinitely. Let us conceive, then, instead of a hexagon, a rectilinear figure having an infinite number of sides — that is, by Archimedes's definition, a circle. It is evident that, whenever the ruler DBE meets the body C, it always meets it just when it cuts some side of such a figure at right angles, and thus will never meet the body C without at the same time determining it to proceed to move along that side produced indefinitely. And because any side produced in either direction must always fall outside the figure, that side produced indefinitely will be the tangent to a figure of an infinite number of sides, that is, a circle. If, then, instead of a ruler

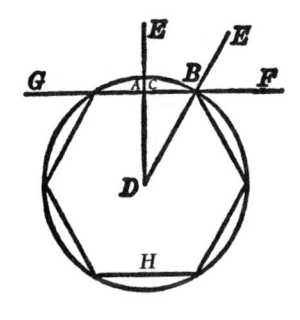

---

[4] This is evident from Propositions 18 and 19 of Book 3 of the *Elements*.
[5] [Spinoza's diagram is mislabeled. A must be at the corner of the hexagon between B and G. In this alternative proof Spinoza substitutes the Archimedean concept of a circle for the Euclidean and provides a direct proof rather than a *reductio* argument.]

we conceive a sling moving in a circle, this will continuously determine the stone to proceed to move at a tangent. Q.E.D.

It should here be noted that both of these proofs can be adapted to any curvilinear figure.

Proposition 17

Every body that moves in a circle endeavors to move away from the center of the circle that it describes.

Proof As long as a body moves in a circle, it is being compelled by some external cause; and if this ceases, it at once proceeds to move at a tangent to the circle (previous Prop.). All the points of this tangent, except that which touches the circle, fall outside the circle (Prop. 16 Book 3 *Elements*) and are therefore further distant from the center. Therefore when a stone moving in a circle in a sling EA is at a point A, it endeavors to continue in a line, all of whose points are farther distant from the center E than any points on the circumference LAB. And this is nothing other than to endeavor to move away from the center of the circle that it describes. Q.E.D.

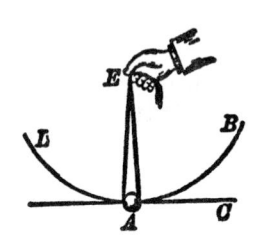

Proposition 18

If a body A moves toward a body B, which is at rest, and B loses nothing of its state of rest in spite of the impetus of body A, then neither will A lose anything of its motion, but will retain entirely the same quantity of motion that it had before.

Proof If you deny this, suppose that body A loses some of its motion without transferring the lost motion to something else, say, to B. When this happens, there will be in Nature a smaller quantity of motion than before, which is absurd (Prop. 13 Part 2). The proof proceeds in the same way with respect to the state of rest of body B, therefore if the one body does not transfer anything to the other body, B will retain all its rest, and A, all its motion. Q.E.D.

Proposition 19

Motion, regarded in itself, is different from its determination toward a certain direction; and there is no need for a moving body to be for any time at rest in order that it may travel or be repelled in an opposite direction.

Proof Suppose, as in the preceding proposition, that a body A moves in a straight line toward a body B and is prevented by body B from continuing further. Therefore (preceding Prop.) A will retain its motion undiminished, and it will not be at rest for even the smallest space of time. However, because it continues to move, it does not move in the same direction as before, for it is supposed to be prevented by B. Therefore, with its motion remaining undiminished and its previous determination lost, it will move in the opposite direction, and not any other (see what is said in Chapter 2 *Dioptrics*). Therefore (Ax. 2) determination does not pertain to the essence of motion but is different from it, and a moving body that is repelled is not at rest for any time. Q.E.D.

Corollary Hence it follows that motion is not contrary to motion.

Proposition 20
If a body A collides with a body B and takes it along with it, A will lose as much of its motion as B acquires from A because of its collision with A.

Proof If you deny this, suppose that B acquires more or less motion from A than A loses. All this difference must be added to or subtracted from the quantity of motion in the whole of Nature, which is absurd (Prop. 13 Part 2). Therefore, because body B can acquire neither more nor less motion, it will acquire just as much motion as A loses. Q.E.D.

Proposition 21 (See Preceding Diagram)
If a body A is twice as large as B and moves with equal speed, A will also have twice as much motion as B, or twice as much force for retaining a speed equal to B's.

Proof
Suppose that instead of A there are two Bs; that is, by hypothesis, one A divided into two equal parts. Each B has a force for remaining in the state in which it is (Prop. 14 Part 2), and this force is equal in both Bs (by hypothesis). If now these two Bs are joined together, their speed remaining the same, they will become one A, whose force and quantity will be equal to two Bs, or twice that of one B. Q.E.D.

Note that this follows simply from the definition of motion. For the greater the moving body, the more the matter that is being separated from other matter. Therefore there is more separation, that is (Def. 8), more motion. See Note 4 regarding the definition of motion.

Proposition 22 (See Diagram Prop. 20)
If a body A is equal to a body B, and A is moving at twice the speed of B, the force or motion in A will be twice that in B.

Proof Suppose that B, when it first acquired a certain force of motion has acquired four degrees of speed. If now nothing is added to this, it will continue to move (Prop. 14 Part 2) and persevere in its state. Suppose that it now acquires an additional force from a further impulse equal to the former. As a result, it will acquire another four degrees of speed in addition to the previous four degrees, which it will also preserve (same Prop.), that is, it will move twice as fast (i.e., as fast as A), and at the same time it will have twice the force (i.e., a force equal to A's). Therefore the motion in A is twice that of B. Q.E.D.

Note that by force in moving bodies we here understand quantity of motion. This quantity must be greater in equal bodies in proportion to their speed of motion, insofar as by that speed equal bodies become more separated in the same time from immediately contiguous bodies than if they were to move more slowly. Thus they also have more motion (Def. 8). But in bodies at rest, we understand by force of resistance the quantity of rest. Hence it follows:

Corollary 1   The more slowly bodies move, the more they participate in rest.

For they offer more resistance to more swiftly moving bodies that collide with them and have less force than they, and they also are less separated from immediately contiguous bodies.

Corollary 2   If a body A moves twice as fast as a body B, and B is twice as great as A, there is the same amount of motion in the greater body B as in the smaller body A, and therefore there is also an equal force.

Proof   Let B be twice the size of A, and let A move with twice the speed of B; then let C be half the size of B and move with half the speed of A. Therefore B (Prop. 21 Part 2) will have a motion twice that of C, and A (Prop. 22 Part 2) will have a motion twice that of C. Therefore (Ax. 15) B and A will have equal motion; for the motion of each is twice that of the third body C. Q.E.D.

Corollary 3   Hence it follows that motion is distinct from speed. For we conceive that, of bodies possessing equal speed, one can have more motion than another (Prop. 21 Part 2), and on the other hand, bodies possessing unequal speed can have equal motion (previous Cor.). This can also be deduced merely from the definition of motion, for it is nothing but the transfer of one body from the vicinity . . . , etc.

But here it should be noted that this third corollary is not inconsistent with the first. For we conceive speed in two ways: either insofar as a body is more or less separated in the same time from immediately contiguous bodies (and to that extent it participates to a greater or lesser degree in motion or rest), or insofar as it describes in the same time a longer or shorter line (and to that extent is distinct from motion).

I could here have added other propositions for a fuller explanation of Prop. 14 Part 2 and could have explained the forces of things in any state whatsoever, as we have here done with regard to motion. But it will suffice to read through Art. 43 Part 2 of the *Principia* and to add only one more proposition, which is necessary for the understanding of what is to follow.

PROPOSITION 23
When the modes of a body are compelled to undergo variation, that variation will always be the least that can be.

Proof   This proposition follows quite clearly from Prop. 14 Part 2.

Proposition 24, Rule 1 (See Diagram Prop. 20)

If two bodies, A and B, should be completely equal and should move in a straight line toward each other with equal velocity, on colliding with each other they will both be reflected in the opposite direction with no loss of speed.

In this hypothesis it is evident that, in order that the contrariety of these two bodies should be removed, either both must be reflected in the opposite direction or the one must take the other along with it. For they are contrary to each other only in respect of their determination, not in respect of motion.

Proof When A and B collide, they must undergo some variation (Ax. 19). But because motion is not contrary to motion (Cor. Prop. 19 Part 2), they will not be compelled to lose any of their motion (Ax. 19). Therefore there will be change only in determination. But we cannot conceive that only the determination of the one, say B, is changed, unless we suppose that A, by which it would have to be changed, is the stronger (Ax. 20). But this would be contrary to the hypothesis. Therefore because there cannot be a change of determination in only the one, there will be a change in both, with A's and B's changing course in the opposite direction—but not in any other direction (see what is said in Chap. 2 *Dioptrics*)— and preserving their own motion undiminished. Q.E.D.

Proposition 25, Rule 2 (See Diagram Prop. 20)

If A and B are unequal in mass, B being greater than A, other conditions being as previously stated, then A alone will be reflected, and each will continue to move at the same speed.

Proof Because A is supposed to be smaller than B, it will also have less force than B (Prop. 21 Part 2). But because in this hypothesis, as in the previous one, there is contrariety only in the determination, and so, as we have demonstrated in the previous proposition, variation must occur only in the determination, it will occur only in A and not in B (Ax. 20). Therefore only A will be reflected in the opposite direction by the stronger B, while retaining its speed undiminished. Q.E.D.

Proposition 26 (See Diagram Prop. 20)

If A and B are unequal in mass and speed, B being twice the size of A and the motion in A being twice the speed of that in B, other conditions being as before stated, they will both be reflected in the opposite direction, each retaining the speed that it possessed.

Proof When A and B move toward each other, according to the hypothesis, there is the same amount of motion in the one as in the other (Cor. 2 Prop. 22 Part 2). Therefore the motion of the one is not contrary to the motion of the other (Cor. Prop. 19 Part 2), and the forces are equal in both (Cor. 2 Prop. 22 Part 2). Therefore this hypothesis is exactly similar to the hypothesis of Proposition 24 Part 2 and so, according to the same proof, A and B will be reflected in opposite directions, retaining their own motion undiminished. Q.E.D.

Corollary From these three preceding propositions it is clear that to change the determination of one body requires equal force as to change its motion. Hence it follows that a body that loses more than half its determination and more than half its motion undergoes more change than one that loses all its determination.

Proposition 27, Rule 3
If A and B are equal in mass but B moves a little faster than A, not only will A be reflected in the opposite direction, but also B will transfer to A half the difference of their speeds, and both will proceed to move in the same direction at the same speed.

Proof By hypothesis, A is opposed to B not only by its determination but also by its slowness, insofar as it participates in rest (Cor. 1 Prop. 22 Part 2). Therefore, even though it is reflected in the opposite direction and only its determination is changed, not all the contrariety of these two bodies is thereby removed. Hence (Ax. 19) there must be a variation both in determination and in motion. But because B, by hypothesis, moves faster than A, B will be stronger than A (Prop. 22 Part 2). Therefore a change (Ax. 20) will be produced in A by B, by which it will be reflected in the opposite direction. That was the first point.

Secondly, as long as it moves more slowly than B, A is opposed to B (Cor. 1 Prop. 22 Part 2). Therefore a variation must occur (Ax. 19) until it does not move more slowly than B. Now in this hypothesis there is no cause strong enough to compel it to move faster than B. So because it can move neither more slowly nor faster than B when it is impelled by B, it will proceed to move at the same speed as B. Again, if B transfers less than half its excess of speed to A, then A will proceed to move more slowly than B. If it transfers more than half, then A will proceed to move more quickly than B. But both these possibilities are absurd, as we have just demonstrated. Therefore a variation will occur until a point is reached when B has transferred to A half its excess of speed, which B must lose (Prop. 20 Part 2). And so both will proceed to move with equal speed in the same direction without any contrariety. Q.E.D.

Corollary Hence it follows that, the greater the speed of a body, the more it is determined to move in the same straight line, and conversely, the more slowly it moves, the less its determination.

Scholium Lest my readers should here confuse the force of determination with the force of motion, I think it advisable to add a few words wherein the force of determination is explained as distinct from the force of motion. If bodies A and C are conceived as equal and moving in a straight line toward each other at equal speed, these two bodies (Prop. 24 Part 2) will be reflected in opposite directions, each preserving its own motion undiminished. But if body C is at B, and moving at an oblique angle toward A, it is clear that it is now less determined to move along the line BD or CA. So although it possesses motion equal to A's, yet the force of C's determination when it moves from directly opposite toward A—a force that is equal to body A's force of determination—is greater than C's force of determination when it moves from B toward A; and it is greater in proportion as the line BA is greater than the line CA. For in proportion as BA is greater than CA, so much more time does B require (with B and A moving at the same speed, as is here supposed) to be able to move along the line BD or CA, along which it opposes the determination of body A. So when C moves from B to meet A at an oblique angle, it will be determined as if it were to proceed to move along the line AB′ toward B′ (which I suppose, it being at a point where the line AB′ cuts BC produced, to be the same distance from C as C is from B). But A, retaining its original motion and determination, will proceed to move toward C, and will push body B along with it, because B, as long as it is determined to motion along the diagonal AB′ and moves with the same speed as A, requires more time than A to describe by its motion any part of the line AC. And to that extent it is opposed to the determination of body A, which is the stronger. But in order for C's force of determination in moving from B to A, insofar as it participates in the direction CA, to be equal to C's force of determination in moving directly toward A (or, by hypothesis, equal to A's force of determination), B will have to have degrees of motion in excess of A in proportion as the line BA is greater than the line CA. And then, when it meets body A at an oblique angle, A will be reflected in the opposite direction toward A′ and B toward B′, both retaining their original motion. But if the excess of B over A is more than the excess of the line BA over the line CA, then B will repel A toward A′, and will impart to it as much of its motion as will make the ratio of the motions of B to A the same as the ratio of the line BA to the line CA, and, losing as much motion as it has transferred to A, it will proceed to move in its original direction. For example, if the line AC is to the line AB as 1 to 2, and the motion of body A is to that of body B as 1 to 5, then B will transfer to A one degree of its motion and will repel it in the opposite direction, and B with four remaining degrees of motion will continue to move in its original direction.

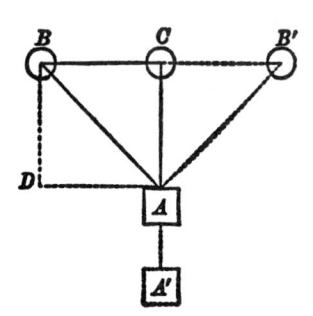

PROPOSITION 28, RULE 4 (See Diagram Prop. 20)[6]

If a body A is completely at rest and is a little larger than B, with whatever speed B moves toward A it will never move A, but will be repelled by A in the opposite direction, retaining its original motion.

Note[7] that the contrariety of these bodies is removed in three ways. (1) When one takes the other along with it, and they thereafter proceed to move at the same speed in the same direction. (2) When one is reflected in the opposite direction and the other retains its original rest. (3) When one is reflected in the opposite direction and transfers some of its motion to the other, which was at rest. There can

---

[6] [Corrected from Prop. 27.]

[7] [This note and the note immediately following P29 were set in smaller type in the first edition, indicating that they were additions that Spinoza made in proof (see Ep15).]

be no fourth possibility (from Prop. 13 Part 2). So we must now demonstrate (by Prop. 23 Part 2) that according to our hypothesis the least change occurs in these bodies.

Proof If B were to move A until they both proceeded to move at the same speed, it would have to transfer to A as much of its motion as A acquires (Prop. 20 Part 2) and would have to lose more than half of its motion (Prop. 21 Part 2), and consequently (Cor. Prop. 27 Part 2) more than half of its determination as well. And so (Cor. Prop. 26 Part 2) it would undergo more change than if it were merely to lose its determination. And if A were to lose some of its rest, but not so much that it finally proceeded to move with equal speed with B, then the opposition of these two bodies would not be removed. For A by its slowness, insofar as that participates in rest, will be opposed to B's speed (Cor. 1 Prop. 22 Part 2). And so B will still have to be reflected in the opposite direction and will lose all its determination and part of its motion, which it has transferred to A. This, too, is a greater change than if it were merely to lose its determination. Therefore, because the change is only in the determination, in accordance with our hypothesis, it will be the least that there can be in these bodies, and therefore (Prop. 23 Part 2) no other change will occur. Q.E.D.

It should be noted that, in the proof of this proposition and also in the case of other proofs, we have not quoted Prop. 19 Part 2, in which it is demonstrated that the whole determination can be changed while yet the motion remains unaltered. Yet attention should be paid to this proposition, so that the force of the proof may be rightly perceived. For in Prop. 23 Part 2 we did not say that the variation will always be the least absolutely, but the least that there can be. But that there can be such a change as we have supposed in this proof, one consisting solely in determination, is evident from Props. 18 and 19 with Cor. Part 2.

PROPOSITION 29, RULE 5 (See Diagram Prop. 30)
If a body A at rest is smaller than B, then however slowly B moves toward A, it will move it along with it, transferring to it such a part of its motion that both bodies thereafter move at the same speed. (Read Art. 50 Part 2 of the Principia.)

In this rule as in the previous one, only three cases could be conceived in which this opposition would be removed. But we shall demonstrate that, according to our hypothesis, the least change occurs in these bodies. And so (Prop. 23 Part 2) their variation, too, must occur in this way.

Proof According to our hypothesis B transfers to A (Prop. 21 Part 2) less than half of its motion and (Cor. Prop. 27 Part 2)[8] less than half of its determination. Now if B were not to take A along with it but were to be reflected in the opposite direction, it would lose all its determination, and a greater variation would occur (Cor. Prop. 26 Part 2). And even greater would be the variation if it lost all its determination and at the same time a part of its motion, as is supposed in the third

---

[8] [I accept Hubbeling's emendation of 17 to 27. —S.S.]

case. Therefore the variation, in accordance with our hypothesis, is the least. Q.E.D.

PROPOSITION 30, RULE 6
If a body A at rest were exactly equal to a body B, which is moving toward it, to some degree A would be impelled by B, and to some degree B would be repelled by A in the opposite direction.

Here again, as in the preceding Prop., only three cases could be conceived. And so it must be demonstrated that we are here positing the least variation that there can be.

Proof If body B takes body A along with it until both are proceeding to move at the same speed, then there will be the same amount of motion in the one as in the other (Prop. 22 Part 2), and (Cor. Prop. 27 Part 2) B will have to lose half its determination and also (Prop. 20 Part 2) half its motion. But if it is repelled by A in the opposite direction, then it will lose all its determination and will retain all its motion (Prop. 18 Part 2). This variation is equal to the former (Cor. Prop. 26 Part 2). But neither of these possibilities can occur. For if A were to retain its own state and could change the determination of B, it would necessarily be stronger than B (Ax. 20), which would be contrary to the hypothesis. And if B were to take A along with it until they were both moving at the same speed, B would be stronger than A, which is also contrary to the hypothesis. Because both of these cases are ruled out, the third case will occur; B will give a slight impulse to A and will be repelled by A. Q.E.D. Read Art. 51 Part 2 of the *Principia*.

PROPOSITION 31, RULE 7 (See Diagram Prop. 30)
If B and A are moving in the same direction, A more slowly and B following it more quickly so that it finally overtakes A, and if A is bigger than B, but B's excess of speed is greater than A's excess of magnitude, then B will transfer to A so much of its motion that both will thereafter move at the same speed in the same direction. But if, on the other hand, A's excess of magnitude should be greater than B's excess of speed, B would be reflected by it in the opposite direction, retaining all its motion.

Read Art. 52 Part 2 of the *Principia*. Here again, as in the preceding propositions, only three cases can be conceived.

Proof Part 1. B being supposed to be stronger than A (Props. 21 and 22 Part 2) cannot be reflected in the opposite direction by A (Ax. 20). Therefore, because B is stronger, it will take A along with it, and in such a way that they proceed to move at the same speed. For then the least change will occur, as can easily be seen from the preceding propositions.

Part 2. B being supposed to be less strong than A (Props. 21 and 22 Part 2) cannot impel A (Ax. 20), nor give it any of its own motion. Thus (Cor. Prop. 14 Part 2) it will retain all its motion, but not in the same direction, for it is supposed to be impeded by A. Therefore (according to Chap. 2 *Dioptrics*) it will be reflected in the opposite direction, not in any other direction, retaining its original motion (Prop. 18 Part 2). Q.E.D.

Note that here and in the preceding propositions we have taken as proved that any body meeting from the opposite direction another body by which it is absolutely impeded from advancing further in the same direction, must be reflected in the opposite direction, not in any other direction. For the understanding of this, read Chap. 2 *Dioptrics*.

Scholium Up to this point, to explain the changes of bodies resulting from their impact on each other, we have considered the two bodies as though isolated from all other bodies, that is, without taking into account bodies that surround them on all sides. But now we shall consider their state and their changes while taking into account bodies that surround them on all sides.

Proposition 32

If a body B is surrounded on all sides by particles in motion, which at the same time are impelling it with equal force in all directions, as long as no other cause occurs it will remain unmoved in the same place.

Proof This proposition is self-evident. For if it were to move in any direction through the impulse of particles coming from one direction, the particles that move it would be impelling it with greater force than other particles that at the same time are impelling it in the opposite direction, with no effect (Ax. 20).[9] This would be contrary to the hypothesis.

Proposition 33

Body B, under the conditions stated previously, can be moved in any direction by any additional force, however small.

Proof Because all bodies immediately contiguous to B are in motion (by hypothesis), and B (Prop. 32) remains unmoved, as soon as they touch B they will be reflected in another direction while retaining their original motion (Prop. 28 Part 2). Thus body B is all the time automatically being left by immediately contiguous bodies. And so, whatever magnitude is assigned to B, no action is required to separate it from immediately contiguous bodies (Note 4 of Def. 8). So any external force striking against it, however small it is imagined to be, is bound to be greater than the force that B possesses for remaining in the same place (for we have just demonstrated that B possesses no force for adhering to its immediately contiguous bodies), and, when added to the impulse of those particles that together with it are impelling B by external force in the same direction, it is also bound to be greater than the force of other particles impelling B in the opposite direction (for, disregarding this external force, the one force was supposed to be equal to the other). Therefore (Ax. 20) body B will be moved in any direction by this external force, however small it be imagined. Q.E.D.

---

[9] [Here I follow the generally accepted emendation of 29 to 20. —S.S.]

Proposition 34
Body B, under the same conditions as previously, cannot move more quickly than it is impelled by the external force, even though the particles by which it is surrounded are in much swifter motion.

Proof Although the particles that, together with the external force, are impelling B in the same direction are in much swifter motion than the external force can move B, yet because (by hypothesis) they have no more force than the bodies that are repelling B in the opposite direction, they will use up all the power of their determination merely in resisting these, without imparting any speed to B (Prop. 32 Part 2). Therefore, because no other circumstances or causes are supposed, B will not receive any amount of speed from any cause other than the external force, and therefore (Ax. 8 Part 1) it cannot move more quickly than it is impelled by the external force. Q.E.D.

Proposition 35
When body B is thus moved by an external impulse, it receives the greatest part of its motion from the bodies by which it is constantly surrounded, and not from the external force.

Proof Even though body B is imagined to be very large, it must be moved by even the smallest impulse (Prop. 33 Part 2). Let us then conceive B as four times as large as the external body by whose force it is impelled. Therefore, because both must move at the same speed (preceding Prop.), there will be four times as much motion in B as in the external body by which it is impelled (Prop. 21 Part 2). Therefore (Ax. 8 Part 1) it does not have the principal part of its motion from the external cause. And because, apart from this cause, no causes are supposed other than the bodies by which it is constantly surrounded (for B is supposed to be not moving of itself), then it is only from the bodies by which it is surrounded (Ax. 7 Part 1) that it receives the principal part of its motion, and not from the external cause. Q.E.D.

Note that here we cannot say, as previously, that the motion of particles coming from one direction is required in order to resist the motion of particles coming from the opposite direction. For bodies moving toward each other with equal motion (as these are supposed) are contrary only by determination,[10] and not by motion (Cor. Prop. 19 Part 2). And so in resisting one another they use up only their determination, and not their motion. Therefore body B can receive no determination, and consequently (Cor. Prop. 27 Part 2) no speed insofar as that is distinct from motion — from adjacent bodies. But it can receive motion; indeed, when the extra force is added, it must necessarily be moved by them, as we have demonstrated in this proposition and as can be clearly seen from the manner of the proof of Proposition 33.

---

[10] See Prop. 24 Part 2, where it is demonstrated that two bodies, in resisting one another, expend their determination, not their motion.

Proposition 36

If any body (e.g., our hand) can move in any direction whatsoever with equal motion without offering any resistance to any bodies or meeting with any resistance from any other bodies, then in that space through which it would thus move there must necessarily be as many bodies moving in one direction as there are bodies moving in any other direction, their force of speed being equal to one another's and to that of the hand.

Proof Any space through which a body can move is bound to be full of bodies (Prop. 3 Part 2). I therefore say that the space through which our hand can thus move is filled with bodies which will move in the manner I have already described. For if you deny this, let them be supposed to be at rest, or to move in a different way. If they are at rest, they will necessarily resist the motion of the hand until its motion is communicated to them (Prop. 14 Part 2), so that finally they will move together with it in the same direction at the same speed (Prop. 20 Part 2). But in the hypothesis they are supposed not to resist; therefore these bodies are in motion. This was the first point to be proved.

Furthermore, they must be moving in all directions. If you deny this, suppose that there is some direction in which they are not moving, say from A toward B. Therefore if the hand is moving from A toward B, it will necessarily meet moving bodies (by the first part of this proof), bodies, by your hypothesis, with a determination different from that of the hand. Therefore they will resist it (Prop. 14 Part 2) until they move along with the hand in the same direction (Prop. 24 and Schol. Prop. 27 Part 2). But, by hypothesis, they do not resist the hand. Therefore they will be moving in all directions. That was the second point.

Again, these bodies will be moving in all directions equaling one another in force of speed. For if they were supposed not to be moving with equal force of speed, suppose that those that are moving from A toward B are not moving with as much force of speed as those that are moving from A toward C. Therefore if the hand (for it is supposed to be able to move with equal motion in all directions without resistance) were to move from A toward B with the same speed with which bodies are moving from A toward C, the bodies moving from A toward B will resist the hand (Prop. 14 Part 2) until they move with a force of speed equal to that of the hand (Prop. 31 Part 2). But this is contrary to the hypothesis. Therefore they will move with equal force of speed in all directions. That was the third point.

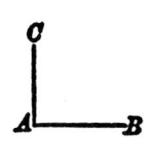

Finally, if the bodies are not moving with the same force of speed as the hand, then the hand will either move more slowly, with less force of speed, or more quickly, with greater force of speed, than the bodies. If the former, the hand will resist the bodies that are following it in the same direction (Prop. 31 Part 2). If the latter, the bodies that the hand is following and with which it is moving in the same direction will resist it (same Prop.). Each of these is contrary to the hypothesis. Therefore, because the hand can move neither more slowly nor more quickly than the bodies, it will move with the same force of speed as the bodies. Q.E.D.

If you ask why I say 'with equal force of speed' and not simply 'with equal speed', read Scholium Cor. Prop. 27 Part 2. If you then ask whether the hand, while moving (e.g., from A toward B), does not resist bodies that are moving at the same time with equal force from B toward A, read Prop. 33 Part 2, from which you will understand that their force is balanced by the force of the bodies moving together with the hand at the same time from A toward B (for, by the third part of this Prop., these two forces are equal).

Proposition 37

If a body A can be moved in any direction whatsoever by any force, however small, it must necessarily be surrounded by bodies that are moving at the same speed as one another.

Proof Body A must be surrounded on all sides by bodies (Prop. 6 Part 2), bodies that are moving equally in all directions. For if they were at rest, body A could not be moved, as is supposed, in any direction whatsoever by any force, however small, but only by such force as could at least be able to move along with itself the bodies immediately contiguous to A Ax. 20 Part 2). Again, if the bodies by which A is surrounded were moving with greater force in one direction than in another—say, with greater force from B toward C than from C toward B—then because it is surrounded on all sides by moving bodies (as we have just now demonstrated), the bodies moving from B toward C would necessarily take A along with them in the same direction (by what we have demonstrated in Prop. 33). So it is not any force, however small, that will suffice to move A toward B; it must be exactly such as would counterbalance the excess of motion of the bodies coming from B toward C (Ax. 20). Therefore they must be moving with equal force in all directions. Q.E.D.

Scholium Because this is the case with bodies called fluid, it follows that fluid bodies are those that are divided into many tiny particles moving with equal force in all directions. And although those particles cannot be seen by any eye, even a lynx's, one must not deny what we have now clearly demonstrated. For from our previously stated Props. 10 and 11, a minuteness of nature such as cannot be determined or attained by any thought, not to say the senses, is sufficiently proved. Furthermore, because it is also well established from what has preceded that bodies resist other bodies merely by their rest, and that we, as our senses indicate, perceive of hardness nothing more than that the parts of hard bodies resist the motion of our hands, we clearly infer that those bodies are hard, all of whose particles are at rest in close proximity to one another. Read Arts. 54, 55, 56 Part 2 of the *Principia*.

End of Part 2

THE PRINCIPLES OF PHILOSOPHY

Demonstrated in the Geometric Manner

Part 3

Having thus set forth the most universal principles of natural things, we must now go on to explain what follows from them. However, because the things that follow from these principles exceed all that our mind can ever survey in thought, and because we are not determined by them to consider some in particular rather than others, we should first of all present a brief account of the most important phenomena whose causes we shall here be investigating. But this you have in Arts. 5–15 Part 3 of the *Principia*. And in Arts. 20–43 is set out the hypothesis that Descartes judges most suitable not only for understanding the phenomena of the heavens but also for seeking out their natural causes.

Then again, because the best way to understand the nature of Plants or Man is to consider in what way they gradually come into existence and are generated from their seeds, we must devise such principles as are the simplest and easiest to know, from which we may demonstrate that the stars, the earth, in short, everything we observe in this visible world, could have arisen as from certain seeds—although we may well know that they never did thus arise. For in this way we shall explain their nature far better than if we were to describe them only as they are now.

I say that we seek principles that are simple and easy to know; for unless they are such, we shall not be in need of them. The only reason why we assign seeds to things is to get to know their nature more easily and, like mathematicians, to ascend from the clearest to the more obscure and from the simplest to the more complex.

Next, we say that the principles we seek are such that we may demonstrate that from them the stars, the earth, etc., could have arisen. For we do not seek causes that suffice only to explain the phenomena of the heavens, as is the common practice of astronomers, but such as may also lead us to knowledge of the things on earth. For we hold that everything we observe to happen above the earth should be counted as phenomena of nature. Now to discover these causes, the following are the requirements of a good hypothesis.

1. Considered only in itself, it must not imply any contradiction.
2. It must be the simplest that can be.

3. Following from (2), it must be very easy to know.
4. Everything that is observed in the whole of nature must be able to be deduced from it.

We have said, finally, that it is allowable for us to assume a hypothesis from which we can deduce, as from a cause, the phenomena of nature, even though we well know that they did not arise in that way. For this to be understood, I shall make use of the following example. If someone were to find drawn on a sheet of paper the curved line we call a parabola and wished to enquire into its nature, it would make no difference whether he were to suppose that the line was first cut from a cone and then imprinted on the paper, or that the line was described as a result of the motion of two straight lines, or that it arose in some other way, provided that his supposition enabled him to demonstrate all the properties of a parabola. Indeed, even though he may know that it originated from the imprinting of a conic section on the paper, he can nevertheless assume any other cause he pleases that seems to him most convenient for explaining all the properties of a parabola. So too, in order to explain the features of nature, we are permitted to assume any hypothesis we please, provided we deduce from it by mathematical inference all the phenomena of nature. And a more important point to note is this, that there is hardly any assumption we can make from which the same effects cannot be deduced—although perhaps with more trouble—from the laws of nature explained previously. For because, by the operation of those laws, matter assumes successively all the forms of which it is capable, if we consider those forms in due order, we shall finally be able to arrive at the form that is the form of this world. So one need fear no error from a false hypothesis.

Postulate

It is requested that the following be taken for granted. All the matter of which this visible world is composed was in the beginning divided by God into particles as near as possible equal to one another. These were not spherical because a number of tiny spheres joined together do not fill a continuous space. These parts were of different shapes and medium size; that is, of a size intermediate between all those of which the heavens and the stars are now composed. The parts possessed in themselves the same amount of motion as is now found in the world and moved with equal speed. Individually, they moved about their own centers, each independently of the others, so as to compose a fluid body such as we think the heavens to be. Many also moved in unison around certain other points, equidistant from one another and arranged in the same way as are now the centers of the fixed stars. Others, again, moved about a somewhat greater number of other points that are equal to the number of the planets, thus forming as many different vortices as there now are stars in the world. See the diagram in Art. 47 Part 3 of the *Principia*.

This hypothesis, regarded in itself, implies no contradiction, for it ascribes to matter nothing except divisibility and motion, modifications that we have already shown to exist in reality in matter; and because we have shown that matter is boundless, and one and the same in the heavens and on earth, we can suppose these modifications to have been in the whole of matter without any danger of contradiction.

Again, this hypothesis is the simplest because it supposes no inequality or dissimilarity in the particles into which matter was divided in the beginning, nor yet in their motion. From this it follows that this hypothesis is also very easy to know. This is also evident from the fact that by this hypothesis nothing is supposed to have been in matter except what everyone immediately knows from the mere concept of matter, divisibility, and local motion.

That everything observed in nature can be deduced from this hypothesis, we shall try to show as far as possible in actual fact, adopting the following order. First, we shall deduce from it the fluidity of the heavens, explaining how this is the cause of light. Then we shall proceed to the nature of the sun, and at the same time to what is observed in the fixed stars. After that we shall speak of comets, and lastly of the planets and their phenomena.

Definitions

1. By *ecliptic* we understand that part of a vortex that, in rotating about its axis, describes the greatest circle.

2. By *poles* we understand the parts of a vortex that are farthest away from the ecliptic or that describe the smallest circles.

3. By *conatus to motion* we understand, not some thought, but that a part of matter is so situated and stirred to motion that it would in fact be going in some direction if it were not impeded by any cause.

4. By *angle* we understand whatever in any body projects beyond a spherical shape.

Axioms

1. A number of small spherical bodies joined together cannot occupy a continuous space.

2. A portion of matter divided into angular parts, if its parts are moving about their own centers, requires more space than if its parts were all at rest and all their sides were immediately contiguous to one another.

3. The smaller a part of matter is, the more easily it is divided by the same force.

4. Parts of matter that are moving in the same direction and in that motion do not withdraw from one another are not in actuality divided.

Proposition 1
The parts into which matter was first divided were not round but angular.

Proof   All matter was in the beginning divided into equal and similar parts (Postulate). Therefore (Ax. 1 and Prop. 2 Part 2) they were not round; and so (Def. 4) they were angular. Q.E.D.

Proposition 2
The force that brought it about that the particles of matter should move about their own centers, at the same time brought it about that the angles of the particles should be worn away by collision with one another.

Proof   In the beginning, all matter was divided into equal (Postulate) and angular (Prop. 1 Part 3) parts. Therefore, if their angles had not been worn away as soon as they began to move about their own centers, then of necessity (Ax. 2) the whole of matter would have had to occupy more space than when it was at rest. But this is absurd (Prop. 4 Part 2). Therefore their angles were worn away as soon as they began to move. Q.E.D.

The rest is lacking.

APPENDIX CONTAINING METAPHYSICAL THOUGHTS

Part 1

In which are briefly explained the principal questions that commonly arise in the general part of Metaphysics, with regard to Being and its modifications.[1]

Chapter 1
Of Real Being, Fictitious Being, and Being of Reason

I shall say nothing about the definition of this Science, nor about its subject matter. My intention here is only to explain matters that are rather obscure and are commonly treated by writers on metaphysics.

---

[1] [The end and purpose of this Part is to show that ordinary Logic and Philosophy serve only to exercise and strengthen the memory, enabling us to keep in mind things that are presented to us through

[*Definition of Being.*] Let us begin, then, with Being, by which I understand 'Everything which, when it is clearly and distinctly perceived, we find to exist necessarily or at least possibly.'

[*The Chimera, the Fictitious Being and the Being of Reason are not beings.*] From this definition, or, if you prefer, description, it follows that a Chimera, a Fictitious Being and a Being of Reason can in no way be classed as beings. For a Chimera, of its own nature, cannot exist. (N.B. By the term 'Chimera', here and in what follows, is to be understood that whose nature involves open contradiction, as is more fully explained in Chapter 3.) A Fictitious Being excludes clear and distinct perception, because a man merely according to his fancy—and not unknowingly, as in the case of the false, but knowingly and wittingly—joins together what he wants to join and separates what he wants to separate. Finally, a Being of Reason is nothing but a mode of thinking, which serves the more easily to retain, explain, and imagine things that are understood. Here it should be noted that by a mode of thinking we understand, as we explained in Schol. Prop. 15 Part 1, all modifications of thought, such as intellect, joy, imagination, etc.

[*By what modes of thinking we retain things.*] That there are certain modes of thinking that serve to retain things more firmly and more easily, and, when we wish, to recall them to mind or to set them before the mind, is an accepted fact for all those who make use of that well-known rule of memory. By this rule, in order to retain something that is quite new and impress it on the memory, we have recourse to another thing, familiar to us, that has something in common with it either in name or in actuality. Similarly, philosophers have arranged all natural things in fixed classes, to which they have recourse when they encounter something new. These classes they call genus, species, etc.

[*By what modes of thinking we explicate things.*] Again, we have modes of thinking for explicating a thing by determining it in comparison with another thing. The modes of thinking by which we do this are called time, number, measure, and such others as there are. Of these, time serves to explicate duration, number (discrete quantity), and measure (continuous quantity).

[*By what modes of thinking we imagine things.*] Finally, because we are also accustomed to depict in our fantasy images of all the things that we understand, it comes about that we imagine nonbeings positively as beings. For the mind, considered only in itself, because it is a thinking thing, has no greater power to affirm than to deny. But because to imagine is nothing other than to sense those traces found in the brain from the motion of the spirits, which is excited in the senses by objects, such a sensing can only be a confused affirmation. Hence it comes about that we imagine as beings all the modes that the mind uses to negate, such as blindness, extremity or limit, boundary, and darkness.

[*Why beings of reason are not ideas of things, and yet are taken to be such.*] Hence it is evident that these modes of thinking are not ideas of things and can

---

the senses at random, without order or connection, and insofar as we can be affected by them only through the senses; but they do not serve to exercise the intellect.—P.B.]

in no way be classed as ideas. So they also have no object (*ideatum*) that exists of necessity or that can exist. The reason why these modes of thinking are taken for ideas of things is that they originate and arise so immediately from real beings that they are easily confused with them by those who do not pay careful attention. Hence they have even given them names as if to signify beings existing outside our mind; and these beings, or rather nonbeings, they have called beings of reason.

[*Being is wrongly divided into Real Being and Being of Reason.*] And so it is easy to see how absurd is that division whereby being is divided into real being and being of reason, for they are dividing being into being and nonbeing, or into being and a mode of thinking. Still, I am not surprised that verbal or grammatical philosophers fall into errors like these, for they judge things from words, not words from things.

[*In what way a Being of Reason can be termed a mere nothing, and in what way it may be termed Real Being.*] No less absurdly does he speak who says that a being of reason is not a mere nothing. For if he seeks outside the intellect what is meant by those words, he will find it is mere nothing, whereas if he understands them as modes of thinking, they are true real beings. For when I ask what is species, I am only enquiring into the nature of that mode of thinking that is in fact a being and is distinct from another mode of thinking. However, these modes of thinking cannot be termed ideas nor can they be said to be true or false, just as love cannot be called true or false, but only good or bad. So when Plato said that man is a featherless biped creature,[2] he erred no more than those who said that man is a rational creature. For Plato knew no less than others that man is a rational creature, but he referred man to a certain class so that, when he wanted to think about man, by having recourse to the class that was easy for him to remember, he could immediately come to think of man. Indeed, it was Aristotle who was gravely at fault if he thought that by that definition of his he had adequately explained human essence. As to whether Plato was right, that is another question; but this is not the place for these matters.

[*In the investigation of things Real Beings should not be confused with Beings of Reason.*] From all that has been said already, it is obvious that there is no agreement between real being and the objects (*ideata*) of a being of reason. Hence it is also easy to see how carefully, in our investigation of things, we must beware of confusing real beings with beings of reason. For it is one thing to enquire into the nature of things, and quite another to enquire into the modes by which we perceive things. If these are confused, we shall not be able to understand either modes of perceiving or nature itself. Indeed—and this is a point of greatest importance—it will be the cause of our falling into grave errors, as has happened to many before us.

[*How a Being of Reason and Fictitious Being are to be distinguished.*] It should also be noted that many people confuse a being of reason with a fictitious being, for they think that a fictitious being is also a being of reason because it has no existence

---

[2] [See Plato, *Statesman*, 266e.]

outside the mind. But if attention is correctly paid to the definitions just given of being of reason and fictitious being, a considerable difference will be found between them both from consideration of their cause and also from their own nature without regard to cause. For we defined fictitious being as the connecting of two terms by mere act of will without any guidance of reason, and therefore a fictitious being can chance to be true. But a being of reason neither depends solely on the will nor does it consist of any terms joined together, as is quite obvious from the definition. So if someone asks whether a fictitious being is a real being or a being of reason, we should reply by repeating what we have just said, namely, that to divide being into real being and being of reason is a mistake, and so the question as to whether fictitious being is real being or being of reason is based on error. For it presupposes that all being is divided into real being and being of reason.

[*The division of Being.*] But let us return to our theme, from which we now seem to have digressed somewhat. From the definition, or, if you prefer, the description of being already given, it is easy to see that being should be divided into being that exists necessarily of its own nature (i.e., whose essence involves existence) and being whose essence involves only possible existence. This last is divided into Substance and Mode, whose definitions are given in Arts. 51, 52, and 56 of Part 1 *Princ. Philosoph.*; so it is not necessary to repeat them here. But concerning this division I want only this to be noted, that we expressly say that being is divided into Substance and Mode, not Substance and Accident. For Accident is nothing more than a mode of thinking, inasmuch as it denotes only a relation [*respectum*]. For example, when I say that a triangle moves, motion is not a mode of the triangle, but of the body that moves. So motion is called accident in relation to the triangle, whereas in relation to body it is a real being or mode. For motion cannot be conceived without body, though it can without a triangle.

Furthermore, for the better understanding of what has already been said and also of what is to come, we shall try to explain what it is that should be understood by the terms 'essence', 'existence', 'idea', and 'potency'. In so doing we are also motivated by the ignorance of some people who do not recognize any distinction between essence and existence, or, if they do recognize it, they confuse what essence is with what idea is or what potency is. So for their sake and the sake of truth, we shall explain the matter as distinctly as possible in what follows.

Chapter 2
What Essence Is, What Existence Is, What Idea Is, and What Potency Is

So that one may clearly grasp what should be understood by these four terms, it is only necessary to reflect upon what we have said about uncreated substance or God, to wit:

[*Creatures are in God eminently.*] 1. God contains eminently what is to be found formally in created things; that is, God possesses attributes of such a kind that in them are contained in a more eminent way all created things. See Part 1 Ax. 8 and Cor. 1 Prop. 12. For example, we clearly conceive extension without any existence, and so, because it has of itself no force to exist, we have demonstrated that it is created by God (last Prop. of Part 1.) And because there must be at least as much perfection in the cause as in the effect, it follows that all the perfections of extension are in God. But because we then saw that an extended thing is of its own nature divisible, that is, it contains imperfection, we therefore could not attribute extension to God (Prop. 16 Part 1), and so we were compelled to take the view that there is an attribute in God that contains in a more excellent way all the perfections of matter (Schol. Prop. 9 Part 1) and that can fulfil the role of matter.

2. God understands himself and all other things, too; that is, he also has in himself all things in the form of thought (Prop. 9 Part 1).

3. God is the cause of all things, and he acts from absolute freedom of will.

[*What Essence is, what Existence is, what Idea is, what Potency is.*] From this, therefore, it can clearly be seen what must be understood by those four things. First, that which is essence is nothing other than the way in which created things are comprehended in the attributes of God. That which is idea refers to the manner in which all things are contained in the idea of God in the form of thought. That which is potency has reference only to the potency of God, whereby from absolute freedom of will he could have created all things not already existing. Finally, that which is existence is the essence of things outside God when considered in itself and is attributed to things after they have been created by God.

[*These four are distinguished from one another only in creatures.*] From this it is evident that these four are distinguished from one another only in created things, but not at all in God. For we do not conceive God to have been in potency in another thing, and his existence and his intellect are not distinguished from his essence.

[A *reply to certain questions concerning Essence.*] From this we can readily reply to the questions that are commonly raised regarding essence. These questions are as follows: whether essence is distinct from existence; if so, whether it is something different from idea, and if that is the case, whether it has any being outside the intellect. To this last question we must surely give assent. Now to the first question we reply by making this distinction, that in God essence is not distinct from existence, because the former cannot be conceived without the latter, but that in other things essence differs from existence, seeing that it can be conceived without existence. To the second question we say that a thing that is clearly and distinctly (i.e., truly) conceived outside the intellect is something different from an idea. But then there is the further question as to whether this being outside the intellect is self-generated or whether it is created by God. To this we reply that formal essence is not self-generated nor again is it created — for both of these would presuppose that it is a thing existing in actuality — but it depends on the divine essence alone, in which all things are contained. And so in this sense we agree with those who say that the essences of things are eternal. It could still be asked how we, not yet understanding the nature of God, understand the essences of things, because they depend on the nature of God alone, as we have just said. In reply I say that this arises from the fact that things are already created. If they had not been created, I would entirely agree that it would be impossible to understand them except after an adequate knowledge of the nature of God, just as it is impossible—indeed, even less possible—to know the nature of the coordinates of a parabola without yet knowing the nature of a parabola.

[*Why in his definition of essence the Author has recourse to the attributes of God.*] Furthermore, it should be noted that although the essences of nonexisting modes are comprehended in their substances, and that which is their essence is in their substances, we have nevertheless chosen to have recourse to God so as to give a general explanation of the essence of modes and substances. Another reason for this procedure is that the essence of modes has been in their substances only since the creation of the substances, and what we were seeking was the eternal being of essences.

[*Why the Author has not reviewed the definitions of others.*] In this connection I do not think it worthwhile to refute those writers whose views differ from ours, nor again to examine their definitions or descriptions of essence and existence; for we would thus be obscuring what is clear. What can be clearer than our understanding of what essence is and what existence is, seeing that we cannot give the definition of anything without at the same time explaining its essence?

[*How the distinction between essence and existence is easily learned.*] Finally, if any philosopher still doubts whether essence is distinguished from existence in created things, he need not toil away over definitions of essence and existence in order to remove that doubt. For if he merely approaches a sculptor or a woodcarver, they will show him how they conceive in set order a nonexistent statue and thereafter bring it into existence for him.

Chapter 3

Concerning the Necessary, the Impossible, the Possible, and the Contingent

[*What is here to be understood by affections.*] Now that the nature of being, insofar as it is being, has been explained, we pass on to the explanation of some of its affections. It should be noted that by affections we here understand what elsewhere, in Art. 52 Part 1 *Princ. Philosoph.*, Descartes has termed attributes. For being, insofar as it is being, does not affect us through itself alone, as substance, and has therefore to be explained through some attribute, from which, however, it is distinguished only by reason. Hence I cannot sufficiently wonder at the subtlety of mind of those who have sought, not without great harm to truth, something that is between being and nothing. But I shall waste no time in refuting their error, because they themselves, in struggling to provide definitions of such affections, disappear from sight in their own vain subtlety.

[*Definition of affections.*] We shall therefore continue on our way, and we say that the affections of being are certain attributes under which we understand the essence or existence of each individual thing, although these attributes are distinguished from the thing only by reason. I shall here attempt to explain some of these affections (for I do not undertake to deal with them all) and to set them apart from those designations that are not affections of any being. And in the first place I shall deal with the Necessary and the Impossible.

[*In how many ways a thing is said to be necessary or impossible.*] There are two ways in which a thing is said to be necessary or impossible, either with respect to its essence or with respect to its cause. With respect to essence we know that God necessarily exists, for his essence cannot be conceived without existence; whereas, with respect to the contradiction involved in its essence, a chimera is incapable of existence. With respect to cause, things (e.g., material things) are said to be either impossible or necessary. For if we have regard only to their essence, we can conceive that clearly and distinctly without existence; therefore they can never exist through the force and necessity of their essence, but only through the force of their cause, God, the creator of all things. So if it is in the divine decree that a thing should exist, it will necessarily exist; if not, it will be impossible for it to exist. For it is self-evident that if a thing has no cause for existence—either an internal or an external cause—it is impossible for it to exist. Now in this second hypothesis a thing is supposed to be such that it cannot exist either by force of its own essence—which I understand to be an internal cause—or by force of the divine decree, the unique external cause of all things. Hence it follows that it is impossible for things, as we suppose them to be in the second hypothesis, to exist.

[*A Chimera is properly called a verbal being.*] Here it should be noted that: 1. Because a chimera is neither in the intellect nor in the imagination, we may properly call it a verbal being, for it can be expressed only in words. For example, we can express a square circle in words, but we cannot in any way imagine it, far less understand it. Therefore a chimera is nothing but a word; and so impossibility cannot be counted among the affections of being, for it is mere negation.

[*Created things depend on God for their essence and existence.*] 2. Not only the existence of created things but also, as we shall later on demonstrate with the greatest certainty in Part 2, their essence and their nature depend solely on God's decree. Hence it clearly follows that created things have no necessity of themselves; for they have no essence of themselves, nor do they exist of themselves.

[*The necessity that is in created things from their cause is either of essence or of existence; but these two are not distinguished in God.*] 3. Finally, the necessity such as is in created things by virtue of their cause is so called either with respect to their essence or with respect to their existence; for these two are distinct in created things, the former depending on the eternal laws of nature, the latter on the series and order of causes. But in God, whose essence is not distinguished from his existence, the necessity of essence is likewise not distinguished from the necessity of existence. Hence it follows that if we were to conceive the entire order of nature, we should find that many things whose nature we clearly and distinctly perceive—that is, whose essence is necessarily such as it is—could in no way exist. For we should find that the existence of such things in nature is just as much impossible as we now see it to be impossible that a huge elephant should pass through the eye of a needle, although we clearly perceive the nature of both. Hence the existence of those things would be only a chimera, which we could neither imagine nor understand.

[*The Possible and the Contingent are not affections of things.*] So much for necessity and impossibility, to which I have thought it advisable to add a few remarks concerning the possible and the contingent. For these two are regarded by some as affections of things, whereas they are in fact nothing but a failure of our intellect, as I shall clearly show when I explain what is to be understood by these two terms.

[*What is the Possible, and what the Contingent.*] A thing is said to be possible when we understand its efficient cause but do not know whether the cause is determined. Hence we can also consider it as possible, but not as either necessary or impossible. But if we attend simply to the essence of the thing and not to its cause, we shall call the thing contingent; that is, we shall consider it as midway between God and a chimera, so to speak, because on the side of essence we find in it no necessity to exist, as in the case of the divine essence, nor again any inconsistency or impossibility, as in the case of a chimera. Now if anyone wishes to call contingent what I call possible, or possible what I call contingent, I shall not oppose him, for it is not my custom to argue about words. It will be enough if he grants us that these two are only the defect of our perception, and not anything real.

[*The Possible and the Contingent are only the defect of our intellect.*] If anyone wishes to deny this, his error can be demonstrated to him with no trouble. For if he attends to nature and the way it depends on God, he will find nothing contingent in things, that is, nothing that can either exist or not exist on the part of the thing, or is a real contingency, as it is commonly called. This is readily apparent from our teaching in Axiom 10 Part 1, to wit, that the same force is required in creating a thing as in preserving it. So no created thing affects anything by its own force, just as no created thing began to exist by its own force. From this it follows that nothing happens except by the power of the all-creating cause—that is, God—who by his concurrence at every moment continues to create all things. Now because nothing happens except by the divine power alone, it is easy to see that those things that happen do so by the force of God's decree and will. But because there is in God no inconstancy or variability (by Prop. 18 and Cor. Prop. 20 Part 1), he must have resolved from eternity to produce those things that he is now producing. And because nothing has a more necessary existence than that which God has decreed should exist, it follows that the necessity to exist has been from eternity in all created things. Nor can we say that those things are contingent because God could have decreed otherwise. For because in eternity there is no when or before or after or any affection of time, it follows that God never existed prior to those decrees so as to be able to decree otherwise.[3]

---

[3] [In order that this proof may be well understood, attention should be given to what is indicated in the second part of the Appendix concerning the will of God, to wit, that God's will or constant

[To reconcile the freedom of our will with God's predestination surpasses human understanding.] As to the freedom of the human will, which we asserted to be free in Schol. Prop. 15 Part 1, this too is preserved by the concurrence of God, nor does any man will or perform anything except what God has decreed from eternity that he should will or perform. How this can be while saving human freedom is beyond our capacity to understand. Yet we must not reject what we clearly perceive because of what we do not know, for if we attend to our nature, we clearly and distinctly understand that we are free in our actions, and that we reach decisions on many things simply on account of our will to do so. Again, if we attend to the nature of God, as we have just shown, we clearly and distinctly perceive that all things depend on him, and that nothing exists except that whose existence God has decreed from eternity. But how the human will continues to be created by God at every moment in such a way as to remain free, we do not know. For there are many things that exceed our grasp and that nevertheless we know to have been brought about by God—for example, the real division of matter into indefinite particles, clearly demonstrated by us in Prop. 11 Part 2, although we do not know how that division comes about.

Note that we here take for granted that those two notions, the possible and the contingent, signify merely the defectiveness of our knowledge regarding the existence of a thing.

Chapter 4
Of Duration and Time

[What is Eternity, Duration, and Time.] From our previous division of being into being whose essence involves existence and being whose essence involves only possible existence, there arises the distinction between eternity and duration. Of eternity we shall speak later at greater length. Here we say only that it is the attribute under which we conceive the infinite existence of God. Duration is the attribute under which we conceive the existence of created things, insofar as they persevere in their actuality. From this it clearly follows that duration is distinguished only by reason from the total existence of a thing. For as much as you take away from the duration of a thing, so much you necessarily take away from its existence. Now in order that duration may be determined, we compare it with the

---

decree is understood only when we conceive the thing clearly and distinctly. For the essence of the thing, considered in itself, is nothing other than God's decree, or his determinate will. But we are also saying that the necessity of existence is no different from the necessity of essence (Chapter 9 of Part 2); that is, when we say that God has decreed that the triangle should exist, we are saying nothing other than that God has so arranged the order of nature and of causes that the triangle should necessarily exist at a particular time. So if we were to understand the order of causes as established by God, we should find that the triangle must exist at a particular time with the same necessity as we now find, when we attend to the triangle's nature, that its three angles are equal to two right angles.—P.B.]

duration of other things that have a fixed and determinate motion, and this comparison is called time. Therefore time is not an affection of things, but a mere mode of thinking, or, as we have previously called it, a being of reason; for it is a mode of thinking serving to explicate duration. Here with regard to duration we should note something that will be useful to us later when we speak about eternity, to wit, that it is conceived as longer and shorter and as if composed of parts, and, secondly, that it is an attribute of existence only, not of essence.

Chapter 5
Of Opposition, Order, Etc.

[*What are Opposition, Order, Agreement, Difference, Subject, Adjunct, etc.*] From our comparing things with one another there arise certain notions that are nevertheless nothing outside things themselves but modes of thinking. This is shown by the fact that if we wish to consider them as things having a place outside thought, we immediately render confused the otherwise clear conception we have of them. Such notions are opposition, order, agreement, difference, subject, adjunct, and any others like these. These notions, I say, are quite clearly perceived by us insofar as we conceive them not as something different from the essences of the things that are opposed, ordered, etc., but merely as modes of thinking whereby we more easily retain or imagine the things themselves. I therefore do not consider it necessary to speak of them at greater length, but pass on to the terms commonly called transcendental.

Chapter 6
Of the One, the True, and the Good

These terms are considered by almost all metaphysicians as the most general affections of being; for they say that every being is one, true and good even though this may not be in anyone's thought. But we shall see what is to be understood regarding these terms when we examine each of them separately.

[*What Unity is.*] Let us begin, then, with the first, to wit, the one. They say that this term signifies something real outside the intellect. But they cannot explain what this adds to being, and this is a clear indication that they are confusing beings of reason with real being and are thereby rendering confused that which they clearly understand. But we on our part say that unity is in no way distinct from the thing itself or additional to being and is merely a mode of thinking whereby we separate a thing from other things that are similar to it or agree with it in some respect.

[*What plurality is, and in what respect God can be called one, and in what respect unique.*] The opposite of unity is plurality, which likewise obviously adds nothing to things, nor is it anything but a mode of thinking, just as we clearly and distinctly understand. Nor do I see what more remains to be said regarding a thing so clear, except that here it should be noted that, insofar as we separate God from other beings, he can be said to be one; but insofar as we conceive that there cannot be more than one of the same nature, he is called unique. In truth, if we wished to look into the matter more rigorously, we might perhaps show that God is only improperly called one and unique. But this question is of little importance—indeed, it is of no importance—to those who are concerned with things rather than words. Therefore we leave this and pass on to the second term, at the same time explaining what the false is.

[*What is the true and what the false, both in the common acceptance and according to philosophers.*] In order that these two, the true and the false, may be correctly perceived, we shall begin with the meaning of words, from which it will be evident that these are only the extrinsic marks of things, and it is only figuratively that they are attributed to things. But because it is the common people who first invent words that are then used by philosophers, it seems relevant for one who seeks the original meaning of a word to enquire what it first denoted among common people, especially when other causes, which might have been derived from the nature of language, are not available for the investigation. The first meaning of true and false seems to have had its origin in storytelling, and the tale was said to be true if it was of something that had occurred in actuality, and false if it was of something that had nowhere occurred. Later, philosophers made use of this signification to denote the agreement or disagreement of an idea with its object (*ideatum*). Therefore an idea is said to be true if it shows us the thing as it is in itself, false if it shows us the thing otherwise than as it really is. For ideas are merely mental narrations or accounts of nature. And hence these terms came to be applied metaphorically to lifeless things, as when we talk about true or false gold, as if the gold presented before us were telling us something about itself that either is in itself or not.

[*The true is not a transcendental term.*] Therefore those who have held that 'the true' is a transcendental term or an affection of being are quite wrong. For this term can be applied to things themselves only improperly, or if you prefer, figuratively.

[*The difference between truth and a true idea.*] If you go on to ask what is truth other than a true idea, ask also what is whiteness other than a white body. For the relationship is the same in both cases.

We have already discussed the cause of the true and the cause of the false. So now there remains nothing to be noted, nor would it have been worthwhile noting even what we have said if writers had not so tied themselves up in trifles like these that they could not then extricate themselves, always looking for a difficulty where there is none.

[*What are the properties of truth? Certainty is not in things.*] The properties of truth, or a true idea, are (1) that it is clear and distinct, (2) that it removes all doubt, or, in a word, that it is certain. Those who look for certainty in things themselves are making the same mistake as when they look for truth in things themselves. And although we may say that a thing is uncertain, we are figuratively taking the *ideatum* for the idea. In the same way we also call a thing doubtful, unless perchance in this case by uncertainty we mean contingency, or a thing that causes us uncertainty or doubt. There is no need to spend more time on these matters, and so we shall proceed to the third term, at the same time explaining what is to be understood by its contrary.

[*Good and Bad are only relative terms.*] A thing is not said to be either good or bad when considered in isolation, but only in relation to another thing for which it is useful in gaining what that thing loves, or contrariwise. Thus each single thing can be called good or bad at the same time in different respects. For example, the counsel that Achitophel gave to Absalom is called good in Holy Scripture, but it was very bad for David, being contrived for his death.[4] And many other things are good, which are not good for all. Thus salvation is good for men, but neither good nor bad for animals or plants, for which it has no relevance. God indeed is said to be supremely good because he benefits all, by his concurrence preserving the being of each individual, than which nothing is more desirable. But no absolute evil exists, as is self-evident.

[*Why some have maintained that there is a metaphysical good.*] But those who keep seeking some metaphysical good not qualified by any relation are laboring under a misapprehension, in that they are confusing a distinction of reason with a real or modal distinction. For they are making a distinction between the thing itself and the conatus [striving] to preserve its own being, which every thing possesses, although they do not know what they mean by *conatus*. For although the thing and its *conatus* are distinguished by reason, or rather, by words (and this is the main cause of their error), the two are in no way distinct from one another in reality.

[*The distinction between things and the* conatus *by which they endeavor to persevere in their state.*] That this may be clearly understood, we shall take an example of a very simple kind. Motion has force to persevere in its own state. This force is surely nothing else than motion itself, the fact that the nature of motion is such as it is. For if I say that in this body A there is nothing else than a certain quantity of motion, from this it clearly follows that, as long as I am attending to the body A, I must always say that the body is moving. For if I were to say that it is losing its force of motion, I am necessarily ascribing to it something else beyond what we supposed in the hypothesis, something that is causing it to lose its nature. Now if this reasoning seems rather obscure, then let us grant that this *conatus* to motion is something other than the very laws and nature of motion. Because, then, you suppose this *conatus* to be a metaphysical good, this *conatus* will also necessarily have a *conatus* to persevere in its own being, and this again another *conatus*, and so ad infinitum. I cannot imagine anything more absurd than this. Now the reason why they make a distinction between the *conatus* of a thing and the thing itself is that they feel in themselves a wanting to preserve themselves, and they imagine a similar wanting in each individual thing.

[*Whether God can be called good before things were created.*] However, the question is raised as to whether God could be called good before he created things; and it seems to follow from our definition that God did not possess any

---

[4] [2 Samuel 17:14.]

such attribute because we say that a thing considered in itself alone cannot be called either good or bad. Many will think this absurd, but why I do not know. We attribute to God many attributes of this kind that did not belong to him, except potentially, before things were created, as when he is called creator, judge, merciful, etc. Therefore arguments like this ought not to be a hindrance to us.

[*How perfection may be ascribed in a relative way, and how it may be ascribed absolutely.*] Furthermore, just as good and bad are only relative terms, so too is perfection, except when we take perfection to mean the very essence of a thing. It is in this sense that we previously said that God possesses infinite perfection, that is, infinite essence or infinite being.

It is not my intention to go farther into these matters. The rest of what concerns the general part of Metaphysics I believe to be sufficiently well known, and therefore not worthwhile pursuing any farther.

APPENDIX CONTAINING METAPHYSICAL THOUGHTS

PART 2

In which are briefly explained the main topics that commonly occur in the special part of Metaphysics, concerning God, his attributes, and the human mind.[1]

Chapter 1
Of God's Eternity

[*The division of Substance.*] We have already shown that in Nature there is nothing but substances and their modes. So one should not here expect us to say anything about substantial forms and real accidents, for these and things of this type are plainly absurd. We then divided substances into two general kinds, extension and thought, and we divided thought into created thought (i.e., the human mind) and uncreated thought (i.e., God). The existence of God we have demonstrated

---

[1] [In this section God's existence is explained in a way quite different from that in which men commonly understand it; for they confuse God's existence with their own, with the result that they imagine God to be something like a man, and they fail to note the true idea of God that they possess, or are quite unconscious of possessing it. And so it comes about that they can neither prove nor conceive God's existence either a priori (i.e., from his true definition or essence) or a posteriori, from the idea of him insofar as it is in us. Therefore in this section we shall try to show as clearly as we can that God's existence is completely different from the existence of created things. —P.B.]

more than adequately both a posteriori, from the idea we have of him, and a priori, from his essence as being the cause of his existence. But because we have treated certain of his attributes more briefly than the importance of the subject requires, we have decided to return to them here, to explain them more fully and also to provide answers to some problems.

[*Duration does not pertain to God.*] The principal attribute that must be considered before all others is God's eternity, whereby we explicate his duration; or rather, to avoid attributing any duration to God, we say that he is eternal. For, as we noted in the first Part, duration is an affection of the existence of things, not of their essence; but we cannot attribute any duration to God, whose existence is of his essence. For whoever attributes duration to God is distinguishing his existence from his essence. There are some, however, who ask whether at this moment God has not been in existence longer than when he created Adam; and it seems to them quite clear that this is so, and thus they hold that duration must in no way be denied to God. But they are guilty of *petitio principii*, in assuming that God's essence is distinct from his existence. They ask whether God, who existed up to the time of Adam, has not existed over more time between the creation of Adam and our time. Thus they are attributing a longer duration to God as each day passes, and they assume that he is, as it were, continuously created by himself. If they did not distinguish God's existence from his essence, they could not possibly attribute duration to God, because duration can in no way pertain to the essences of things. For no one will ever say that the essence of a circle or a triangle, insofar as it is an eternal truth, has lasted longer at this moment than at the time of Adam. Furthermore, because duration is conceived as longer or shorter, or as consisting of parts, it clearly follows that no duration can be attributed to God. For because his being is eternal, that is, there cannot be in it any before or after, we can never attribute duration to God without at the same time destroying the true conception we have of him. That is to say, by attributing duration to him we would be dividing into parts that which of its own nature is infinite and can never be conceived except as infinite.[2]

[*The reasons why writers have attributed duration to God.*] Now the reasons why writers have thus erred are: (1) They have attempted to explain eternity without giving their attention to God, as if eternity could be understood without consideration of the divine essence, or were something other than the divine essence. And this again has arisen because, through poverty of language, we are in the habit of attributing eternity even to things whose essence is distinct from their existence, as when we say that no contradiction is implied in the world having been in existence from eternity; and again when we attribute eternity to the essences of things while we conceive the things as not existing; for we then call the essences eternal. (2) They have been attributing duration to things only insofar as they held them to be subject to continuous variation, and not, as is our practice, in accordance as their essence is distinguished from their existence. (3) Finally, they have distinguished God's essence from his existence, as is the case with created things.

---

[2] [We are dividing his existence into parts, or conceiving it as divisible, when we attempt to explicate it through duration. See Part 1, 4. — P.B.]

These errors, I say, have led them astray. By reason of the first error they have failed to understand what eternity is, taking it rather to be some kind of duration. The second error made it difficult for them to see the difference between the duration of created things and God's eternity. Finally, because duration is only an affection of existence and they have made a distinction between God's existence and his essence, the third error has led to their attributing duration to God, as we have already said.

[*What is Eternity.*] But for the better understanding of what eternity is, and how it cannot be conceived without the divine essence, attention must be given to what we have said already, namely, that created things—that is, all things besides God—always exist solely by the force or essence of God, and not by their own force. Hence it follows that the present existence of things is not the cause of their future existence. Only God's immutability is the cause, which compels us to say that when God has created a thing in the first place, he will thereafter continuously preserve it, that is, he will continue the same action of creating it. From this we conclude:

1. That a created thing can be said to enjoy existence, on the grounds that existence is not of its essence. But God cannot be said to enjoy existence, for God's existence is God himself, just as is his essence. Hence it follows that created things enjoy existence, but this is not so with God.
2. That all created things, while enjoying present duration and existence, are entirely lacking in future duration and existence, because this has to be continuously attributed to them, whereas nothing of the sort can be said of their essence. But because God's existence is of his essence, we cannot attribute future existence to him. For the same existence that he would then have must even now be attributed to him in actuality; or, to speak more properly, infinite actual existence pertains to God in the same way as infinite actual intellect pertains to him. Now this infinite existence I call eternity, which is to be attributed to God alone and not to any created thing, even though, I say, its duration is without beginning or end.

So much for eternity. Of God's necessity I say nothing, there being no need now that we have demonstrated his existence from his essence. Let us proceed, therefore, to his unity.

Chapter 2
Of the Unity of God

We have often wondered at the futile arguments with which writers attempt to prove the unity of God, arguments such as: If one could have created the world, others would have been superfluous; if all things work together to the same end, they have been produced by one maker, and other arguments like these, drawn from the relationship of things or their extrinsic characteristics. So, dismissing all these arguments, we shall here set out our proof as clearly and as briefly as possible, as follows.

[*God is unique.*] Among God's attributes we have also listed the highest degree of understanding, adding that he possesses all his perfection from himself and not from any other source. If you now say that there are more than one God, or supremely perfect beings, these must all necessarily possess understanding in the highest degree. That this may be so, it is not enough that each should understand only himself; for because each must understand all things, he must understand both himself and the others. From this it would follow that the perfection of the intellect of each one would depend partly on himself and partly on another. Therefore no one of them can be a supremely perfect being, that is, as we have just noted, a being that possesses all its perfection from itself, and not from any other source. Yet we have already demonstrated that God is a most perfect being, and that he exists. So we can now conclude that he exists as one alone; for if more than one God existed, it would follow that a most perfect being has imperfection, which is absurd.[3] So much for the unity of God.

Chapter 3
Of the Immeasurableness of God

[*How God is called infinite, and how immeasurable.*] We have previously shown that no being can be conceived as finite and imperfect (i.e., as participating in nothingness) unless we first have regard to the perfect and infinite being, that is, God. So only God must be said to be absolutely infinite, in that we find him to consist in actual fact of infinite perfection. But he can also be said to be immeasurable or boundless insofar as we have regard to this point, that there is no being by which God's perfection can be limited. From this it follows that the infinity of God, in spite of the form of the word, is something most positive; for it is insofar as we have regard to his essence or consummate perfection that we say that he is infinite. But measurelessness is attributed to God only in a relational way; for it does not pertain to God insofar as he is considered absolutely as a most perfect being, but only insofar as he is considered as a first cause that, even though it were most perfect only in relation to secondary beings, would nevertheless be measureless. For there would be no being, and consequently no being could be conceived, more perfect than he by which he might be limited or measured. (For a fuller discussion, see Axiom 9 Part 1.)

[*What is commonly understood by the immeasurableness of God.*] Yet writers on all sides, in treating of the immeasurableness of God, appear to attribute

---

[3] [Even though this proof is quite convincing, nevertheless it does not explain God's unity. I therefore suggest to the reader that we conclude the unity of God more correctly from the nature of his existence, which is not distinguished from God's essence, or which necessarily follows from his essence. — P.B.]

quantity to God. For from this attribute they wish to conclude that God must necessarily be present everywhere, as if they meant that if there were any place where God was not, his quantity would be limited. This same point is even more clearly apparent from another argument they produce to show that God is infinite or measureless (for they confuse these two terms) and also that he is everywhere. If God, they say, is pure activity, as indeed he is, he is bound to be everywhere and infinite. For if he were not everywhere, then either he cannot be wherever he wants to be, or else (note this) he must necessarily move about. This clearly shows that they attribute immeasurableness to God insofar as they consider him to be quantitative; for it is from the properties of extension that they derive these arguments for asserting the immeasurableness of God. Nothing could be more absurd.

[*Proof that God is everywhere.*] If you now ask how, then, shall we prove that God is everywhere, I reply that we have abundantly demonstrated this when we showed that nothing can exist even for a moment without being continuously created by God at every single moment.

[*God's omnipresence cannot be explained.*] Now, for God's ubiquity or his presence in individual things to be properly understood, we should necessarily have to have a clear insight into the inmost nature of the divine will whereby he created things and continuously goes on creating them. Because this exceeds human capacity, it is impossible to explain how God is everywhere.[4]

[*Some hold, wrongly, that God's immeasurableness is threefold.*] Some claim that God's immeasurableness is threefold—that of his essence, his power, and his presence. But this is nonsense, for they seem to distinguish between God's essence and his power.

[*God's power is not distinct from his essence.*] Others, too, have said the same thing more openly, asserting that God is everywhere through power, but not through essence, as if God's power were distinct from all his attributes or his infinite essence. But in fact it can be nothing else; for if it were something else, it would either be some creature or something accidental to the divine essence without which the divine essence could be conceived. Both of these alternatives are absurd; for if it were a creature, it would need God's power for its preservation, and this would give rise to an infinite progression. And if it were something accidental, God would not be a most simple being, contrary to what we have demonstrated previously.

[*Nor is his omnipotence.*] Finally, by the immeasurableness of his presence they again seem to mean something besides the essence of God, through which things have been created and are continuously preserved. This is surely a great absurdity, into which they have fallen through confusing God's intellect with human intellect, and frequently comparing his power with the power of kings.

---

[4] [Here it should be noted that when ordinary folk say that God is over all, they are depicting him as the spectator of a play. From this it is evident, as we say at the end of this chapter, that men are constantly confusing the divine nature with human nature.—P.B.]

Chapter 4
Of the Immutability of God

[*What change is, and what transformation.*] By 'change' we here understand all the variation that can occur in a subject while the essence of the subject remains as it was. But this term is also commonly taken in a broader sense to mean the corruption of things—not an absolute corruption, but such as also includes generation following on the corruption, as when we say that peat is changed into ashes, or men into beasts. But to denote this latter meaning philosophers use yet another word—transformation. Here we are speaking only of that change in which there is no transformation of the subject as when we say that Peter has changed his color, or his character, etc.

[*In God there can be no transformation.*] We must now see whether such changes are applicable to God, for there is no need to say anything about transformation, now that we have shown that God exists necessarily, that is, that God cannot cease to be, or be transformed into another God. For then he would both cease to be, and also there could be more than one God at the same time. Both of these possibilities we have shown to be absurd.

[*What are the causes of change.*] However, for a clearer understanding of what here remains to be said, we must take into consideration that all change proceeds either from external causes, with or without the subject's consent, or from an internal cause and the subject's free choice. For example, that a man becomes darker, falls ill, grows, and the like, all proceed from external causes, the first two against the subject's will, the last in accordance with it. But that he wills, walks, displays anger, etc., proceed from internal causes.

[*God is not changed by something else.*] Now the first-named changes, those that proceed from external causes, cannot possibly apply to God; for he alone is the cause of all things and is not acted on by anyone. Moreover, nothing created has in itself any force to exist, and so far less can it have any force to act on anything outside itself or on its own cause. And although there are many places in Holy Scripture where God has been angry, or sad, etc., because of the sins of men, in these passages the effect is taken as the cause, just as we also say that the sun is stronger and higher in summer than in winter, although it has not changed its position or renewed its strength. And that such is often the teaching even of Holy Scripture is to be seen in Isaiah; for he says in chapter 59, verse 2, when he is rebuking the people: "Your iniquities separate you from your God."

[*Nor again by himself.*] Let us therefore proceed and ask whether any change can come about in God from God himself. We do not grant that there can be such a change in God; indeed, we deny it completely. For every change that depends on the will is designed to change its subject to a better state, and this cannot apply to a most perfect being. Then again, there can be no such change except for the purpose of avoiding something disadvantageous or of acquiring some good that is lacking. In the case of God there can be no place for either of these purposes. Hence we conclude that God is an immutable being.[5] Note that I have here deliberately omitted the commonly accepted divisions of change, although we have also in a sense covered them. For there was no need to deny them individually of God because in Prop. 16 Part 1 we have demonstrated that God is incorporeal, and those commonly accepted divisions refer only to changes in matter.

Chapter 5
Of the Simplicity of God

[*The threefold distinction between things: real, modal, and a distinction of reason.*] Let us proceed to the simplicity of God. In order that this attribute of God may be rightly understood, we must recall what Descartes said in *Princip. Philosophiae* Part 1 Arts. 48 and 49, to wit, that in Nature there is nothing but substances and their modes, whence in Arts. 60, 61, and 62 he deduces a threefold distinction between things—real, modal, and a distinction of reason. What is called a real distinction is that whereby two substances, whether of different or of the same attribute, are distinguished from one another; for example, thought and extension, or the parts of matter. This distinction is recognized from the fact that each of the two can be conceived, and consequently can exist, without the help of the other. Modal distinction is of two kinds, that between a mode of substance and the substance itself, and that between two modes of one and the same substance. The latter we recognize from the fact that, although either mode can be conceived without the help of the other, neither can be conceived without the help of the substance of which they are modes. The former distinction we recognize from the fact that, although the substance can be conceived without its mode, the mode cannot be conceived without the substance. Finally, what is termed a distinction of reason is that which arises between a substance and its attribute, as when duration is distinguished from extension. And this is also recognized from the fact that such a substance cannot be understood without that attribute.

[*How all composition arises, and how many kinds there are.*] All composition arises from these three kinds of distinction. The first composition is that of two or more substances either of the same attribute, as is the case with all composition

---

[5] [Note that this can be much more clearly seen if we attend to the nature of God's will and his decrees. For, as I shall show in due course, God's will, through which he has created things, is not distinct from his intellect, through which he understands them. So to say that God understands that the three angles of a triangle are equal to two right angles is the same as to say that God has willed or decreed that the three angles of a triangle should be equal to two right angles. Therefore, for us to conceive that God can change his decrees is just as impossible as to think that the three angles of a triangle are not equal to two right angles. Furthermore, the fact that there can be no change in God can also be proved in other ways; but, because we aim at brevity, we prefer not to pursue this further.—P.B.]

of two or more bodies, or of different attributes, as is the case with man. The second composition results from the union of different modes. The third composition is not a composition, but is only conceived by reason as if it were so, in order that a thing may thereby be more easily understood. Whatever is not a composition of the first two kinds must be said to be simple.

[*God is a most simple Being.*] It must therefore be shown that God is not a composite thing, from which we can conclude that he is a most simple being; and this we shall easily accomplish. Because it is self-evident that component parts are prior at least by nature to the composite whole, then of necessity those substances from whose coalescence and union God is composed will be prior to God by nature, and each can be conceived through itself without being attributed to God. Again, because they are necessarily distinct from one another in reality, then necessarily each of them can also exist through itself without the help of the others. And thus, as we have just said, there could be as many Gods as there are substances from which it was supposed that God is composed. For because each can exist through itself, it must exist of itself, and therefore it will also have the force to give itself all the perfections that we have shown to be in God, as we have already explained fully in Prop. 7 Part 1, where we demonstrated the existence of God. Now because nothing more absurd than this can be said, we conclude that God is not composed of a coalescence and union of substances. That there is also no composition of different modes in God is convincingly proved from there being no modes in God. For modes arise from an alteration of substance—see *Princ.* Part 1 Art. 56. Finally, if someone wishes to imagine another kind of composition, from the essence of things and their existence, we by no means oppose him. But let him remember that we have already sufficiently demonstrated that these two are not distinct in God.

[*God's Attributes are distinguished only by Reason.*] Hence we can clearly conclude that all the distinctions we make between God's attributes are nothing other than distinctions of reason, and that they are not distinct from one another in reality. Understand these distinctions of reason to be such as I have just referred to, namely, distinctions that are recognized from the fact that such-and-such a substance cannot be without that particular attribute. Hence we conclude that God is a most simple being. So now, disregarding the medley of distinctions made by the Peripatetics, we pass on to the life of God.

Chapter 6
Of the Life of God

[*What philosophers commonly understand by Life.*] For the correct understanding of this attribute, the life of God, it is necessary to explain in general terms what in the case of each individual thing is meant by its life. We shall first examine the opinion of the Peripatetics. By life they understand 'the continuance of the nutritive soul, accompanied by heat'—see Aristotle *De Respirat.* Book 1 Chapter 8.[6] And be-

---

[6] [The reference may be to *De respiratione* 474a25, but see also *De anima* 415a23–25.]

cause they imagined there to be three souls, the vegetative, the sensitive, and the intellective, which they attribute exclusively to plants, animals, and men, it follows, as they themselves acknowledge, that all else is devoid of life. Even so, they did not venture to say that minds and God are without life. Perhaps they were afraid of falling into the contrary view, that if these were without life, they were dead. So Aristotle in his *Metaphysics* Book 11 Chapter 7 gives yet another definition of life, applicable only to minds, namely, that life is the operation of the intellect, and in this sense he attributes life to God, as one who understands and is pure activity.[7]

However, we shall not spend much effort in refuting these views. For as regards the three souls that they attribute to plants, animals, and men, we have already sufficiently demonstrated that these are nothing but fictions, having shown that in matter there is nothing but mechanical structures and their operations. As to the life of God, I do not know why in Aristotle it should be called activity of intellect rather than activity of will, and the like. However, expecting no reply to this, I pass on to explain, as promised, what life is.

[*To what things life can be attributed.*] Although this term is often taken in a figurative sense to mean the character of a man, we shall briefly explain only what it denotes in a philosophical sense. It should be noted that if life is also to be attributed to corporeal things, nothing will be devoid of life; but if only to those things wherein soul is united to body, then it must be attributed only to men, and perhaps also to animals, but not to minds or to God. However, because the word 'life' is commonly used in a wider sense, there is no doubt that it should also be attributed to corporeal things not united to minds and to minds separated from body.

[*What life is, and what it is in God.*] Therefore by life we for our part understand the force through which things persevere in their own being. And because that force is different from the things themselves, we quite properly say that things themselves have life. But the force whereby God perseveres in his own being is nothing but his essence, so that those speak best who call God 'life.' There are some theologians who hold the opinion that it is for this reason—that God is life and is not distinct from life—that the Jews when they swore an oath used to say "by the living Jehovah," and not "by the life of Jehovah," as Joseph, when swearing by Pharaoh's life, said "by the life of Pharaoh."[8]

Chapter 7
Of God's Intellect[9]

[*God is omniscient.*] We previously listed among the attributes of God omniscience, which quite obviously pertains to God because knowledge implies perfection, and God, as a most perfect being, must not lack any perfection. Therefore

---

[7] [This is probably a reference to *Metaphysics* XII, vii (1072b27–29).]

[8] [The reference is to Genesis 42:15–16.]

[9] [From what is demonstrated in the next three chapters in which we treat of God's intellect, his will

knowledge must be attributed to God in the highest degree, that is, a knowledge that does not presume or posit any ignorance or privation of knowledge; for then there would be some imperfection in the attribute itself, that is, in God. From this it follows that God's intellect has never been merely potential, nor does he reach a conclusion by reasoning.

[*The objects of God's knowledge are not things external to God.*] Furthermore, from God's perfection it also follows that his ideas are not defined, as ours are, by objects that are external to God. On the contrary, the things created by God external to God are determined by God's intellect. (N.B.: From this it clearly follows that God's intellect, by which he understands created things, and his will and power, by which he has determined them, are one and the same thing.) For otherwise these objects would have their own nature and essence through themselves and would be prior, at least by nature, to the divine intellect—which is absurd. And because some people have failed to take careful note of this, they have fallen into gross errors. Some have maintained that external to God there is matter, coeternal with him and existing of itself, and that God, understanding this matter, has, according to some, merely reduced it to order, and according to others, has in addition impressed forms on it. Others again have maintained that things of their own nature are either necessary or impossible or contingent, and so God knows the latter also as contingent and is quite ignorant as to whether they exist or not. Finally, others have said that God knows contingent things from their relation to other things, perhaps because of his long experience. Besides these errors I could here mention others of this kind, did I not consider it to be superfluous, because from what has already been said their falsity makes itself apparent.

[*The object of God's knowledge is God himself.*] Let us therefore return to our theme, that outside God there is no object of his knowledge, but he is himself the object of his knowledge, or rather, he is his own knowledge. Those who think that the world is also the object of God's knowledge are much less discerning than those who would maintain that a building constructed by some distinguished architect is the object of the architect's knowledge. For the builder is forced to seek suitable material outside himself as well, whereas God has not sought any material outside himself. Things have been constructed by his intellect or will, both with regard to their essence and their existence.

[*How God knows sin, entities of reason, etc.*] The question now arises as to whether God knows evil or sin, entities of reason, and things of that kind. We re-

---

and his power, it follows quite clearly that the essences of things and the necessity of their existing from a given cause is nothing other than God's determinate will or decree. Therefore God's will is most apparent to us when we conceive things clearly and distinctly. So it is ridiculous that philosophers, when they are ignorant of the causes of things, take refuge in the will of God. We constantly see this happening when they say that the things whose causes are unknown to them have come about only from God's good pleasure and absolute decree. The common people, too, have found no stronger proof of God's providence and guidance than that which they draw from their ignorance of causes. This clearly shows that they have no knowledge whatever of the nature of God's will, attributing to him a human will that is truly quite distinct from our intellect. This I consider to have been the basic cause of superstition, and perhaps of much roguery.—P.B.]

ply that God must necessarily know those things of which he is the cause, especially so because they cannot exist even for a moment except with the divine concurrence. Therefore, because evil and sin have no being in things but only in the human mind when it compares things with one another, it follows that God does not know them as separate from human minds. Entities of reason we have said to be modes of thinking, and it is in this way that they must be understood by God, that is, insofar as we perceive him as preserving and continuing to create the human mind, in whatever way that is constituted. But we are not saying that God has such modes of thinking in himself in order that he may more easily retain what he understands. And if only proper attention is given to these few points we have made, no problem can arise concerning God's intellect that cannot quite easily be solved.

[*How God knows particular things, and how universals.*] But meanwhile we must not pass over the error made by certain people who maintain that God knows nothing but eternal things such as angels and the heavens, which they suppose to be by their own nature not subject to generation and corruption, but that of this world he knows nothing but species, these being likewise not subject to generation and corruption. Such people do indeed seem set on going astray, contriving utter absurdities. For what can be more absurd than to cut off God's knowledge from particular things, which cannot even for a moment be without God's concurrence? Again, they are maintaining that God is ignorant of really existing things, while ascribing to God knowledge of universals, which have no being nor any essence apart from that of particular things. We, on the other hand, attribute to God knowledge of particular things and deny him knowledge of universals except insofar as he understands human minds.

[*In God there is only one simple idea.*] Finally, before bringing this discussion to a close, we ought to deal with the question as to whether there is in God more than one idea or only one most simple idea. To this I reply that God's idea through which he is called omniscient is unique and completely simple. For in actual fact God is called omniscient for no other reason than that he has the idea of himself, an idea or knowledge that has always existed together with God. For it is nothing but his essence and could have had no other way of being.

[*What is God's knowledge concerning created things.*] But God's acquaintance with created things cannot be referred to God's knowledge without some impropriety; for, if God had so willed, created things would have had a quite different essence, and this could have no place in the knowledge that God has of himself. Still, the question will arise as to whether that knowledge of created things, properly or improperly so termed, is manifold or only single. However, in reply, this question differs in no way from those that ask whether God's decrees and volitions are several or not, and whether God's omnipresence, or the concurrence whereby he preserves particular things, is the same in all things. Concerning these matters, we have already said that we can have no distinct knowledge. However, we know with certainty that, just as God's concurrence, if it is referred to God's omnipotence, must be no more than one although manifested in various ways in its effects, so too God's volitions and decrees (for thus we may term his knowledge concerning created things) considered in God are not a plurality, even though they are expressed in various ways through created things, or rather, in created things. Finally, if we look to the whole of Nature by analogy, we can consider it as a single entity, and consequently the idea of God, or his decree concerning *Natura naturata*, will be only one.

Chapter 8
Of God's Will

[*We do not know how God's essence, his intellect by which he understands himself, and his will by which he loves himself, are distinguished.*] God's will, by which he wills to love himself, follows necessarily from his infinite intellect, by which he understands himself, but how these three are distinguished from one another— his essence, his intellect by which he understands himself, and his will by which he wills to love himself—this we fail to comprehend. We are acquainted with the word 'personality', which theologians commonly use to explain this matter. But although we know the word, we do not know its meaning, nor can we form any clear and distinct conception of it, although we firmly believe that in the most blessed vision of God, which is promised to the faithful, God will reveal this to his own.

[*God's will and power, as externally manifested, are not distinguished from his intellect.*] Will and power, as externally manifested, are not distinguished from God's intellect, as is now well established from what has preceded. For we have shown that God has decreed not only that things should exist, but also that they should exist with a certain nature; that is to say, both their essence and existence must have depended on God's will and power. From this we clearly and distinctly perceive that God's intellect and his power and will, whereby he has created, understood, and preserves or loves created things, are in no way distinct from one another save only in respect of our thought.

[*It is improper to say that God hates some things and loves other things.*] Now when we say that God hates some things and loves other things, this is said in the same sense as when Scripture tells us that the earth will vomit forth men, and other things of that kind. But from Scripture itself it can be sufficiently inferred that God is not angry with anyone, and that he does not love things in the way that is commonly believed. For this is in Isaiah, and more clearly in Paul's Epistle to the Romans, Chapter 9: "For the children being not yet born (that is, the sons of Isaac), neither having done any good or evil, that the purpose of God according to election might stand, not of works but of him that calleth, it was said unto her, the elder shall serve the younger, etc."[10] And a little farther on, "Therefore hath he mercy on whom he will, and whom he will he hardeneth. Thou wilt

---
[10] [Romans 9:11–12.]

then say unto me, 'Why doth he yet find fault? For who hath resisted his will?' Nay but, O man, who art thou that replieth against God? Shall the thing formed say unto him who formed it, 'Why has thou made me thus?' Hath not the potter power over the clay, of the same lump to make one vessel unto honor, and another unto dishonor? etc."[11]

[*Why God admonishes men, why he does not save without admonition, and why the impious are punished.*] If you now ask why, then, does God admonish men, to this there is a ready answer: The reason why God has decreed from eternity that he would warn men at a particular time is this, that those whom he has willed to be saved might turn from their ways. If you go on to ask whether God could not have saved them without that warning, we reply that he could have done so. "Why then does he not so save them?" you will perhaps again ask. To this I shall reply when you have told me why God did not make the Red Sea passable without a strong east wind, and why he does not bring about all particular motions without other motions, and innumerable other things that God does through mediating causes. You will again ask, why then are the impious punished, since they act by their own nature and in accordance with the divine decree. But I reply, it is also as a result of the divine decree that they are punished. And if only those ought to be punished whom we suppose to be sinning from free will alone, why do men try to destroy poisonous snakes? For they sin only from their own nature, and can do no other.

[*Scripture teaches nothing that is opposed to the natural light.*] Finally, whatever other passages there are in Holy Scripture that cause uneasiness, this is not the place to explain them. For here the object of our enquiry is confined to what can be attained most certainly by natural reason, and to demonstrate these things clearly is sufficient to convince us that the Holy Book must be teaching the same. For truth is not opposed to truth, nor can Scripture be teaching the nonsense that is commonly supposed. If we were to find in it anything contrary to the natural light, we could refute it with the same freedom with which we refute the Koran and the Talmud. But far be it from us to think that something can be found in Holy Scripture opposed to the light of Nature.

Chapter 9
Of God's Power

[*How God's omnipotence should be understood.*] That God is omnipotent has already been sufficiently demonstrated. Here we shall attempt only to explain in brief how this attribute is to be understood; for many speak of it without proper piety and not according to truth. They say that, by their own nature and not from God's decree, some things are possible, some things impossible, and some things necessary, and that God's omnipotence is concerned only with the possible. We,

---

[11] [Romans 9:18–21.]

however, who have already shown that all things depend absolutely on God's decree, say that God is omnipotent. But having understood that he has decreed some things from the mere freedom of his will, and then that he is immutable, we say now that he cannot act against his own decrees, and that this is impossible simply because it is at variance with God's perfection.

[*All things are necessary with respect to God's decree. It is wrong to say that some things are necessary in themselves, and other things with respect to his decree.*] But perhaps someone will argue that some things we find necessary only while having regard for God's decree, while on the other hand some things we find necessary without regard for God's decree. Take, for example, that Josiah burned the bones of the idolaters on the altar of Jeroboam.[12] If we attend only to Josiah's will, we shall regard the event as a possible one, and in no way having necessarily to happen except from the prophet's having predicted it from God's decree. But that the three angles of a triangle must be equal to two right angles is something that manifests itself.

But surely these people are inventing distinctions in things from their own ignorance. For if men clearly understood the whole order of Nature, they would find all things to be equally as necessary as are the things treated in mathematics. But because this is beyond the reach of human knowledge, certain things are judged by us as possible and not as necessary. Therefore we must say either that God is powerless—because all things are in actual fact necessary—or that God is all-powerful, and that the necessity we find in things has resulted solely from God's decree.

[*If God had made the nature of things other than it is, he would also have had to give us a different intellect.*] Suppose the question is now raised: What if God had decreed things otherwise and had rendered false those things that are now true? Would we still not accept them as quite true? I answer, yes indeed, if God had left us with the nature that he has given us. But he might then, had he so wished, have also given us a nature—as is now the case—such as to enable us to understand Nature and its laws, as they would have been laid down by God. Indeed, if we have regard to his faithfulness, he would have had to do so. This is also evident from the fact, as we have previously stated, that the whole of *Natura naturata* is nothing but a unique entity, from which it follows that man is a part of Nature that must cohere with the rest. Therefore from the simplicity of God's decree it would also follow that if God had created things in a different way, he would likewise have also so constituted our nature that we could understand things as they had been created by God. So although we want to retain the same distinction in God's power as is commonly adopted by philosophers, we are nevertheless constrained to expound it in a different way.

[*The divisions of God's power—absolute, ordered, ordinary, and extraordinary.*] We therefore divide God's power into Ordered and Absolute. We speak of God's absolute power when we consider his omnipotence without regard to his decrees. We speak of his ordered power when we have regard to his decrees.

---

[12] [1 Kings 13:2; 2 Kings 23:16, 20.]

Then there is a further division into the Ordinary and Extraordinary power of God. His ordinary power is that by which he preserves the world in a fixed order. We mean his extraordinary power when he acts beyond Nature's orders—for example, all miracles, such as the ass speaking, the appearance of angels, and the like.[13] Yet concerning this latter power we may not unreasonably entertain serious doubts, because for God to govern the world with one and the same fixed and immutable order seems a greater miracle than if, because of the folly of mankind, he were to abrogate laws that he himself has sanctioned in Nature in the best way and from pure freedom—as nobody can deny unless he is quite blinded. But we shall leave this for the theologians to decide.

Finally, we pass over other questions commonly raised concerning God's power: Does God's power extend to the past? Can he improve on the things that he does? Can he do many other things than he has done? Answers to these questions can readily be supplied from what has already been said.

Chapter 10
Of Creation

That God is the creator of all things we have already established; here we shall now try to explain what is to be understood by creation. Then we shall provide solutions as best we can to those questions that are commonly raised regarding creation. Let us then begin with the first subject.

[*What creation is.*] We say that creation is an operation in which no causes concur beyond the efficient cause; or that a created thing is that which presupposes nothing except God for its existence.

[*The common definition of creation is rejected.*] Here we should note that: 1. We omit the words 'from nothing', which are commonly used by philosophers as if 'nothing' were the matter from which things were produced. This usage of theirs arises from the fact that, being accustomed in the case of generated things to suppose something prior to them from which they are made, in the case of creation they were unable to omit the preposition 'from'. The same confusion has befallen them in the case of matter. Seeing that all bodies are in a place and surrounded by other bodies, when they asked themselves where matter as a whole might be, they replied, "In some imaginary space." So there is no doubt that they have not considered 'nothing' as the negation of all reality but have imagined or pictured it as something real.

[*Our own definition is explained.*] 2. I say that in creation no other causes concur beyond the efficient cause. I might indeed have said that creation denies or excludes all causes beyond the efficient cause. However, I have preferred to say 'concur' so as to avoid having to reply to those who ask whether God in creation did not set before himself an end on account of which he created things. Fur-

---

[13] [Numbers 22:28–31.]

thermore, for better explanation, I have added this second definition, that a created thing presupposes nothing but God; because if God did set before himself some end, then obviously that end was not external to God. For there is nothing external to God by which he may be urged to act.

[*Accidents and Modes are not created.*] 3. From this definition it clearly follows that there is no creation of accidents and modes. For these presuppose a created substance besides God.

[*There was no time or duration before creation.*] 4. Finally, neither time nor duration can be imagined before creation; these began along with things. For time is the measure of duration; or rather, it is nothing but a mode of thinking. Therefore it presupposes not just some created thing, but, in particular, thinking men. As for duration, it ceases when created things cease to be and begins when created things begin to exist—created things, I say, because we have already shown beyond doubt that to God there pertains not duration but eternity. Therefore duration presupposes, or at least posits, created things. Those who imagine duration and time prior to created things labor under the same misconception as those who suppose a space outside matter, as is self-evident. So much for the definition of creation.

[*God's action is the same in creating the world and in preserving it.*] Again, there is no need for us to repeat here what we have demonstrated in Axiom 10 Part 1, namely, that the same amount of force is required for the creation of a thing as for its preservation; that is, God's action in creating the world is the same as in its preservation.

Having noted these points, let us proceed to what we promised in the second place. First, we must ask what is created and what is uncreated; and second, whether what is created could have been created from eternity.

[*What created things are.*] To the first question we reply, in brief, that the created is every thing whose essence is clearly conceived without any existence, and which is nevertheless conceived through itself: for example, matter, of which we have a clear and distinct conception when we conceive it under the attribute of extension, and which we conceive just as clearly and distinctly whether it exists or not.

[*How God's thought differs from ours.*] But perhaps someone will say that we perceive thought clearly and distinctly without existence, and that we nevertheless attribute it to God. To this we reply that we do not attribute to God such thought as is ours, subject to being acted on and confined by the nature of things, but such as is pure activity and thus involving existence, as we have already demonstrated at sufficient length. For we showed that God's intellect and will are not distinct from his power and his essence, which involves existence.

[*There is not something external to God and coeternal with him.*] So because every thing whose essence does not involve existence must, in order to exist, necessarily be created by God and be continuously preserved by the creator as we have already abundantly explained, we shall spend no time in refuting the opinion of those who have maintained that the world, or chaos, or matter stripped of all form, is coeternal with God and thus independent of him. Therefore we must pass on to the second question and enquire whether what has been created could have been created from eternity.

[*What is here denoted by the phrase 'from eternity'.*] For this to be rightly understood, we must examine this phrase 'from eternity', for by this we here mean something entirely different from that which we explained previously when we spoke of God's eternity. Here we mean nothing other than duration without any beginning, or such duration as, even if we were to multiply it by many years or tens of thousands of years, and this product again by tens of thousands, we could still never express by any number, however great.

[*Proof that there could not have been something created from eternity.*] But that there can be no such duration is clearly demonstrated. For if the world were to go backward again from this point of time, it could never have such a duration; therefore neither could the world have reached this point of time from such a beginning. You will perhaps say that for God nothing is impossible; for he is omnipotent, and so can bring about a duration other than which there could be no greater. We reply that God, being omnipotent, will never create a duration other than which a greater cannot be created by him. For the nature of duration is such that a greater or lesser than a given duration can always be conceived, as is the case with number. You will perhaps insist that God has been from eternity and so has endured until the present, and thus there is a duration other than which a greater cannot be conceived. But in this way there is attributed to God a duration consisting of parts, which we have abundantly refuted when we demonstrated that there pertains to God not duration, but eternity. Would that men had thoroughly considered this truth, for then they might very easily have extricated themselves from many arguments and absurdities, and have given themselves up with the greatest delight to the blessed contemplation of this being.

But let us proceed to answer the arguments put forward by certain people, whereby they try to show the possibility of such an infinite duration stretching from the past.

[*From the fact that God is eternal, it does not follow that his effects can also be from eternity.*] First, then, they assert that the thing produced can be contemporaneous with its cause; but because God has been from eternity then his effects could also have been produced from eternity. And then they further confirm this by the example of the son of God, who was produced by the father from eternity. But from what has already been said, one can clearly see that they are confusing duration with eternity, and they are attributing to God merely a duration from eternity, as is also clear from the example they cite. For they hold that the same eternity that they ascribe to the son of God is possible for creatures. Again, they imagine time and duration as prior to the foundation of the world, and they seek to establish a duration without created things, just as others seek to establish an eternity outside God. Both these assertions are already shown to be quite remote from the truth. Therefore we reply that it is quite false that God can communicate his eternity to his creatures, nor is the son of God a creature, but he is, like his father, eternal. So when we say that the father has begotten the son from eternity, we mean simply this, that the father has always communicated his eternity to the son.

[*If God acted necessarily, he would not be of infinite potency.*] Secondly, they argue that, when God acts freely, he is no less powerful than when he acts necessarily; but if God acts necessarily, being of infinite potency he must have created the world from eternity. But this argument, too, can be readily met if we examine its basis. These good people suppose that they can entertain quite different ideas of a being of infinite potency. For they conceive God as of infinite potency both when he acts from the necessity of nature and when he acts freely. We, however, deny that God would be of infinite potency if he were to act from the necessity of nature; and this we may well deny—and indeed they have also necessarily to concede it—now that we have demonstrated that the most perfect being acts freely and can be conceived only as unique. Now if they retort that, even if it is impossible it can nevertheless be posited that God, in acting from the necessity of nature, is of infinite potency, we reply that it is no more permissible to suppose this than to suppose a square circle so as to conclude that all the lines from the center to the circumference are not equal. Not to repeat what we said at an earlier stage, this is well established from what we have just said. For we have just demonstrated that there can be no duration whose double, or whose greater or lesser, cannot be conceived, and therefore a greater or lesser than a given duration can always be created by God, who acts freely with infinite potency. But if God were to act from the necessity of nature, this would in no way follow, for only that duration, which resulted from his nature, could be produced by him, not an infinite number of other durations greater than the given.

Therefore we thus argue in brief; if God were to create the greatest duration, one so great that he could not create one greater, he would necessarily be diminishing his own power. But this latter statement is false, for his power does not differ from his essence; therefore, etc. Again, if God were to act from the necessity of nature, he would have to create a duration such that he himself cannot create a greater. But God, in creating such a duration, is not of infinite potency, for we can always conceive a duration greater than the given. Therefore if God acted from the necessity of nature, he would not be of infinite potency.

[*Whence we have the concept of a duration greater than that which belongs to this world.*] At this point someone may find some difficulty in seeing how, since the world was created five thousand years ago (or more, if the calculations of chronologers are correct), we can nevertheless conceive a greater duration, which we have asserted is not intelligible without created things. This difficulty will be easily removed if he takes note that we understand that duration not simply from the contemplation of created things but from the contemplation of the infinite power of God for creation. For creatures cannot be conceived as existing and having duration through themselves, but only through the infinite power of God, from which alone they have all their duration. See Prop. 12 Part 1 and its Corollary.

Finally, to waste no time here in answering trivial arguments, these points only are to be noted: the distinction between duration and eternity, and that duration is in no way intelligible without created things, nor eternity without God. When these points have been properly perceived, all arguments can very readily be answered; so we think it unnecessary to spend any more time on these matters.

Chapter 11
Of God's Concurrence

Little or nothing remains to be said about this attribute, now that we have shown that God continuously creates a thing as if anew at every moment. From this we have demonstrated that things never have any power from themselves to affect anything or to determine themselves to any action, and that this is the case not only with things outside man but also with the human will. Again, we have also replied to certain arguments concerning this matter; and although many other arguments are frequently produced, I here intend to ignore them, as they principally belong to theology.

However, there are many who, accepting God's concurrence, interpret it in a sense quite at variance with what we have expounded. To expose their fallacy in the simplest way, it should here be noted, as has previously been demonstrated, that present time has no connection with future time (see Ax. 10 Part 1), and that this is clearly and distinctly perceived by us. If only proper attention is paid to this, all their arguments, which may be drawn from philosophy, can be answered without any difficulty.

[*How God's preservation is related to his determining things to act.*] Still, so as not to have touched on this problem without profit, we shall in passing reply to the question as to whether something is added to God's preservation when he determines a thing to act. Now when we spoke about motion, we already hinted at the answer to this question. For we said that God preserves the same quantity of motion in Nature; therefore if we consider the nature of matter in its entirety, nothing new is added to it. But with respect to particular things, in a sense it can be said that something new is added to it. Whether this is also the case with spiritual things is unclear, for it is not obvious that they have such mutual interdependence. Finally, because the parts of duration have no interconnection, we can say that God does not so much preserve things as continue to create them. Therefore, if a man has now a determinate freedom to perform an action, it must be said that God has created him thus at that particular time. Nor can it be objected that the human will is often determined by things external to itself, and that all things in Nature are in turn determined to action by one another; for they are also thus determined by God. No thing can determine the will, nor again can the will be determined, except by the power of God alone. But how this is compatible with human freedom, or how God can bring this about while preserving human freedom, we confess we do not know, as we have already remarked on many occasions.

[*The common division of God's attributes is nominal rather than real.*] This, then, I was resolved to say about the attributes of God, having as yet made no division of them. The division generally given by writers, whereby they divide God's attributes into the incommunicable and the communicable, to speak the truth, seems a nominal rather than a real division. For God's knowledge is no more like human knowledge than the Dog, the constellation in the sky, is like the dog, the barking animal, and perhaps even less so.

[*The Author's own division.*] Our division, however, is as follows. There are some of God's attributes that explicate his essence in action, whereas others, unconcerned with action, set forth the manner of his existing. Of the latter kind are unity, eternity, necessity, etc.: of the former kind are understanding, will, life, omnipotence, etc. This division is quite clear and straightforward and includes all God's attributes.

Chapter 12
Of the Human Mind

We must now pass on to created substance, which we have divided into extended and thinking substance. By extended substance we understood matter or corporeal substance; by thinking substance we understood only human minds.

[*Angels are a subject for theology, not metaphysics.*] Although Angels have also been created, yet, because they are not known by the natural light, they are not the concern of metaphysics. For their essence and existence are known only through revelation, and so pertain solely to theology; and because theological knowledge is completely other than, or entirely different in kind from, natural knowledge, it should in no way be confused with it. So let nobody expect us to say anything about angels.

[*The human mind does not derive from something else, but is created by God. Yet we do not know when it is created.*] Let us then return to human minds, concerning which few things now remain to be said. Only I must remind you that we have said nothing about the time of the creation of the human mind because it is not sufficiently established at what time God creates it, because it can exist without body. This much is clear, that it does not derive from something else, for this applies only to things that are generated, namely, the modes of some substance. Substance itself cannot be generated, but can be created only by the Omnipotent, as we have sufficiently demonstrated in what has gone before.

[*In what sense the human soul is mortal.*] But to add something about its immortality, it is quite evident that we cannot say of any created thing that its nature implies that it cannot be destroyed by God's power; for he who has the power to create a thing has also the power to destroy it. Furthermore, as we have sufficiently demonstrated, no created thing can exist even for a moment by its own nature, but is continuously created by God.

[*In what sense the human soul is immortal.*] Yet, although the matter stands so, we clearly and distinctly see that we have no idea by which we may conceive that substance is destroyed, in the way that we do have ideas of the corruption and generation of modes. For when we contemplate the structure of the human body, we clearly conceive that such a structure can be destroyed; but when we contemplate corporeal substance, we do not equally conceive that it can be reduced to nothing.

Finally, a philosopher does not ask what God can do from the full extent of his power; he judges the nature of things from those laws that God has imparted to them. So he judges to be fixed and sure what is inferred from those laws to be fixed and sure, while not denying that God can change those laws and all other things. Therefore we too do not enquire, when speaking of the soul, what God can do, but only what follows from the laws of Nature.

[*Its immortality is demonstrated.*] Now because it clearly follows from these laws that substance can be destroyed neither through itself nor through some other created substance—as we have abundantly demonstrated over and over again, unless I am mistaken—we are constrained to maintain from the laws of Nature that the mind is immortal. And if we look into the matter even more closely, we can demonstrate with the greatest certainty that it is immortal. For, as we have just demonstrated, the immortality of the soul clearly follows from the laws of Nature. Now those laws of Nature are God's decrees revealed by the natural light, as is also clearly established from the preceding. Then again, we have also demonstrated that God's decrees are immutable. From all this we clearly conclude that God has made known to men his immutable will concerning the duration of souls not only by revelation but also by the natural light.

[*God acts not against Nature but above Nature. How the Author interprets this.*] Nor does it matter if someone objects that God sometimes destroys those natural laws in order to perform miracles. For most of the wiser theologians concede that God never acts contrary to Nature, but above Nature. That is, as I understand it, God has also many laws of operating that he has not communicated to the human intellect; and if they had been communicated to the human intellect, they would be as natural as the rest.

Hence it is quite clearly established that minds are immortal, nor do I see what remains to be said at this point about the human soul in general. Nor yet would anything remain to be said about its specific functioning, if the arguments of certain writers, trying to make out that they do not see and sense what in fact they do see and sense, did not call upon me to reply to them.

[*Why some think the will is not free.*] Some think they can show that the will is not free but is always determined by something else. And this they think because they understand by will something distinct from soul, something they look on as a substance whose nature consists solely in being indifferent. To remove all confusion, we shall first explicate the matter, and when this is done we shall easily expose the fallacies in their arguments.

[*What the will is.*] We have said that the human mind is a thinking thing. From this it follows that, merely from its own nature and considered only in itself, it can do something, to wit, think, that is, affirm and deny. Now these thoughts are either determined by things external to the mind or by the mind alone, because it is itself a substance from whose thinking essence many acts of thought can and must follow. Those acts of thought that acknowledge no other cause of themselves than the human mind are called volitions. The human mind, insofar as it is conceived as a sufficient cause for producing such acts, is called the will.

[*There is will.*] That the soul possesses such a power, although not determined by any external things, can most conveniently be explicated by the example of Buridan's ass. For if we suppose that a man instead of an ass is placed in such a state of equilibrium, he would have to be considered a most shameful ass, and not a thinking thing, if he were to perish of hunger and thirst. Again, the same conclusion is evident from the fact that, as we previously said, we even willed to doubt all things, and not merely to regard as doubtful but to reject as false those things that can be called into doubt. See Descartes's *Princip.* Part 1 Art. 39.

[*The will is free.*] It should further be noted that although the soul is determined by external things to affirm or deny something, it is nevertheless not so determined as if it were constrained by the external things, but always remains free. For no thing has the power to destroy its essence, and therefore what it affirms or denies, it always affirms or denies freely, as is well explained in the "Fourth Meditation." So if anyone asks why the soul wills or does not will this or that, we reply that it is because the soul is a thinking thing, that is, a thing that of its own nature has the power to will and not will, to affirm and deny. For that is what it is to be a thinking thing.

[*The will should not be confused with appetite.*] Now that these matters have been thus explained, let us look at our opponents' arguments.

1. The first argument is as follows. "If the will can will what is contrary to the final pronouncement of the intellect, if it can want what is contrary to its good as prescribed by the final pronouncement of the intellect, then it will be able to want what is bad for it as such. But this latter is absurd; therefore so is the former." From this argument one can clearly see that they do not understand what the will is. For they are confusing it with the appetite that the soul has when it has affirmed or denied something; and this they have learned from their Master, who defined the will as appetite for what is presented as good.[14] But we say that the will is the affirming that such-and-such is good, or the contrary, as we have already abundantly explained in our previous discussion concerning the cause of error, which we have shown to arise from the fact that the will extends more widely than the intellect. Now if the mind had not affirmed from its very freedom that such-and-such is good, it would not want anything. Therefore we reply to the argument by granting that the mind cannot will anything contrary to the final pronouncement of the intellect; that is, the mind cannot will anything insofar as it is supposed not to will it—for that is what is here supposed when the mind is said to have judged something to be bad for it, that is, not to have willed it. But we deny that it absolutely cannot have willed that which is bad for it, that is, cannot have judged it to be good; for that would be contrary to experience. We judge many things that are bad to be good, and on the other hand many things that are good to be bad.

[*The will is nothing other than the mind.*] 2. The second argument—or, if you prefer, the first, for so far there has been none—is as follows: "If the will is not determined to will by the final judgment of the practical intellect, it therefore will determine itself. But the will does not determine itself, because of itself and by its own nature it is undetermined." From this they go on to argue as follows: "If the will is of itself and by its own nature uncommitted to willing and not willing, it

---

[14] [Their "Master" is, of course, Aristotle: see *Rhetoric* 1369a1–4; *De Anima* 433a21–433b5.]

cannot be determined by itself to will. For that which determines must be as much determined as that which it determines is undetermined. But the will considered as determining itself is as much undetermined as is the same will considered as that which is to be determined. For our opponents suppose nothing in the determining will that is not likewise in the will that is either to be determined or that has been determined; nor indeed is it possible for anything to be here supposed. Therefore the will cannot be determined by itself to will. And if it cannot be determined by itself, it must be determined by something else."

These are the very words of Heereboord, Professor of Leiden, by which he clearly shows that by will he understands not the mind itself but something else outside the mind or in the mind, like a blank tablet, lacking any thought and capable of receiving any picture, or rather like a balance in a state of equilibrium, which can be pushed in either direction by any weight whatsoever, according to the determination of the additional weight. Or, finally, like something that neither he nor any other mortal can possibly grasp. Now we have just said—indeed, we clearly showed—that the will is nothing but the mind itself, which we call a thinking thing, that is, an affirming and denying thing. And so, when we look only to the nature of mind, we clearly infer that it has an equal power to affirm and to deny; for that, I say, is what it is to think. If therefore, from the fact that the mind thinks, we infer that it has the power to affirm and deny, why do we seek extraneous causes for the doing of that which follows solely from the nature of the thing?

But, you will say, the mind is not more determined to affirm than to deny, and so you will conclude that we must necessarily seek a cause by which it is determined. Against this, I argue that if the mind of itself and by its own nature were determined only to affirm (although it is impossible to conceive this as long as we conceive it to be a thinking thing), then of its own nature alone it could only affirm and never deny, however many causes may concur. But if it be determined neither to affirm nor deny, it will be able to do neither. And finally, if it has the power to do either, as we have just shown it to have, it will be able to do either from its own nature alone, unassisted by any other cause. This will be obvious to all those who consider a thinking thing as a thinking thing, that is, who do not separate the attribute of thought from the thinking thing. This is just what our opponents do, stripping the thinking thing of all thought and making it out to be like the prime matter of the Peripatetics.

Therefore I reply to their argument as follows, addressing their major premise. If by the will they mean a thing deprived of all thought, we grant that the will is from its own nature undetermined. But we deny that the will is something deprived of all thought; on the contrary, we maintain that it is thought, that is, the power both to affirm and to deny; and surely this can mean nothing else than the sufficient cause for both operations. Furthermore, we also deny that if the will were undetermined (i.e., deprived of all thought), it could be determined by any extraneous cause other than God, through his infinite power of creation. For to seek to conceive a thinking thing that is without any thought is the same as to seek to conceive an extended thing that is without extension.

[*Why philosophers have confused mind with corporeal things.*] Finally, to avoid having to review more arguments here, I merely point out that our opponents, in failing to understand the will and in having no clear and distinct conception of mind, have confused mind with corporeal things. This has arisen for this reason, that the words that they are accustomed to use in referring to corporeal things they have used to denote spiritual things, which they did not understand. For they have been accustomed to apply the word 'undetermined' to those bodies that are in equilibrium because they are impelled in opposite directions by equivalent and directly opposed external causes. So when they call the will undetermined, they appear to conceive it also as a body in a state of equilibrium. And because those bodies have nothing but what they have received from external causes (from which it follows that they must always be determined by an external cause), they think that the same thing follows in the case of the will. But we have already sufficiently explained how the matter stands, and so we here make an end.

With regard to extended substance, too, we have already said enough, and besides these two substances we acknowledge no others. As for real accidents and other qualities, they have been disposed of, and there is no need to spend time refuting them. So here we lay down our pen.

The End

Ethics

Spinoza prepared to publish the Ethics, the comprehensive account of his philosophical system, in 1674. The work and its five parts had been completed after over a decade's labor, and after the turmoil of the years since the Short Treatise *and the publication of the* Principles of Cartesian Philosophy. *The time had come but at the advice of friends, Spinoza felt the danger and the risks too deeply. As he reported to Henry Oldenburg in the fall of 1675, he was attacked both by theologians and by Cartesians and felt compelled to halt publication (Ep68; see Jonathan Israel,* Radical Enlightenment*, 286–7). Indeed, the work—one of the classics of Western philosophy—was only finally published in 1677 after Spinoza's death, in the* Opera Posthuma, *edited by his friends and published by Jan Rieuwertsz. Within a year, on 25 June 1678, it was censored by the States of Holland and West-Friesland as a "profane, atheistic, and blasphemous book."*

Some scholars believe that the appendix to the Short Treatise, *probably composed in 1661 or early 1662, including seven axioms about substance, its attributes, and causality, together with four demonstrations about substance, was already an early version of the mathematically, geometrically organized content of the first book of the* Ethics. *By late 1662 or early 1663, with Spinoza in Rijnsburg, his Amsterdam friends had a copy of an early chapter of Part I "On God." Pieter Balling had delivered it to Simon de Vries, and it soon became the topic of meetings in Amsterdam where it was read and discussed. On and off, then, from 1661 to 1674, Spinoza worked on the* Ethics, *his magnum opus, paying the promissory note made in the TIE and setting out the details of his philosophical account of nature, mind, and the good life.*

By June 1665, Spinoza seems to have had a complete draft in hand, a work of three parts, most likely following the design of the Short Treatise—*"on God, man, and his well-being." Eventually, by 1675, of course, the* Ethics *had been revised and expanded, taking on its now famous five-part structure—on God, humankind and human epistemology, the passions, human bondage to the passions, and rational freedom. A June 1665 letter to Johan Bouwmeester, an Amsterdam friend and associate of Lodewijk Meyer, suggests that the original Part III was nearly complete and ready to be translated from Latin into Dutch, perhaps by Bouwmeester himself (Ep28). This third part contained much of what is found in Parts IV and V of the version we now have. Hence, by the time Spinoza turned, that autumn of 1665, to the* Theological-Political Treatise, *his system was complete.*

A remarkable work it was. The Ethics's five parts famously lay out a system in the style of Euclid's geometry—starting from definitions and axioms and working through theorems or propositions with corollaries, notes or scholia, appendices, and more. The axiomatic style mirrors the system's rationality and exemplifies the way knowledge should be grasped. As the system proceeds from metaphysics through its account of human nature, knowledge, and emotion, to its understanding of human flaws and aspirations, and finally to the ethical goal of human life (a life of freedom and understanding), the work both grounds itself and motivates its readers to conduct their lives according to the best conception of what human life can and should be. In short, Spinoza's magnum opus earns its title.

The book's contents are, in broad terms, well known. Spinoza's is an early modern naturalism, a set of principles underlying a rational, scientific view of religion, nature, psychology, and ethics. In Part I he defines crucial terms such as substance, attribute, mode, eternity, and God. He demonstrates that only one substance, with infinite attributes, exists; it does so necessarily, and every mode that follows from it occurs with precise and necessary determination. This one eternal, necessary, determinate substance is God, and hence nature or the natural world is either identical to it or to certain ways of understanding it. Modes of substance are not properties of substance, as in classical philosophy, but rather things in the world existing in precise states or ways. Modes are manifestations of substance and its attributes, which might be thought of as regulative natural forces.

In Part II, Spinoza introduces the two attributes by which we understand substance and in terms of which substance is manifest to our experience—thought and extension—and builds an account of the mental and physical dimensions of nature. This account leads to a set of propositions about human experience and cognition and, in Part III, of human emotions, feelings, and more, all as the psychological correlates of physical states of the human body. The causal structure of physical bodies, determined by their proportion of motion and rest, and influenced by the lawful interactions of bodies, is correlated with mental states, some cognitive, others affective, in all of nature and in particular in the minds of human beings. Spinoza's psychology is grounded in his physics and in the conception of conatus, the striving of each being to persevere and to manifest its essence; here is the dynamic element in Spinoza's vitalistic conception of nature. In human beings, the conatus takes on certain predictable psychological features. Ultimately, people seek to satisfy desires, feel joy and pleasure, and enhance their well-being, and these goals require increasing harmonious activity within nature and the diminishing of the passions, which mark a person's subordination to beings external to it and failure to satisfy its own preservation. This goal requires as complete and perfect a knowledge of nature as one can attain, a knowledge that corresponds in the mind to the maximizing of life-enhancing physical states on the body's part. Later in the Ethics, Spinoza calls this cognitive goal the "intellectual love of God" or "blessedness," and, in the notorious concluding section of Part V, he associates it with the mind's eternity and thereby with the traditional notion of the immortality of the soul.

Within the confines of this naturalistic system, Spinoza installs some claims that, even in his own day, became famous and even notorious. He also took some steps that have remained perplexing, if not confusing. Spinoza's natural world, for example, is not created, nor does it permit contingency or the existence of miracles. Furthermore, insofar as extension is an attribute of substance, Spinoza's God is physically extended; Spinoza could be and was charged with a kind of atheistic materialism. His natural world is also wholly determined and without goals or purposes. While Spinoza's God is material, human beings—unities of the physical and psychological—are as necessary and determined as God or nature. For this reason, Spinoza denies the existence of free will but not the existence of freedom, which he regards as a feature of actions which are active and rational, performed with a minimum of constraint and external coercion. In this sense, moreover, God is the only perfect being and human life an effort of imitatio dei. People are free, to the degree that they love God, understand God, and indeed emulate God, but for Spinoza these activities and aspirations are no different from seeking to understand nature and to live in harmony with natural law.

There are many obvious outcomes of this ethic of rational self-discipline and peace of mind. One is a life of democratic republicanism in which all citizens equally collaborate in a lawful society aimed at enhancing the well-being of all rational citizens and restraining harmful self-interest in behalf of this goal. In his last years Spinoza would turn, out of a sense of urgency, to an elaboration of these political implications.

M.L.M.

CONTENTS

I. Concerning God

II. Of the Nature and Origin of the Mind

III. Concerning the Origin and Nature of the Emotions

IV. Of Human Bondage, or the Nature of the Emotions

V. Of the Power of the Intellect, or of Human Freedom

PART I
Concerning God

Definitions

1. By that which is self-caused I mean that whose essence involves existence; or that whose nature can be conceived only as existing.
2. A thing is said to be finite in its own kind [*in suo genere finita*] when it can be limited by another thing of the same nature. For example, a body is said to be finite because we can always conceive of another body greater than it. So, too, a thought is limited by another thought. But body is not limited by thought, nor thought by body.
3. By substance I mean that which is in itself and is conceived through itself; that is, that the conception of which does not require the conception of another thing from which it has to be formed.
4. By attribute I mean that which the intellect perceives of substance as constituting its essence.
5. By mode I mean the affections of substance, that is, that which is in something else and is conceived through something else.
6. By God I mean an absolutely infinite being, that is, substance consisting of infinite attributes, each of which expresses eternal and infinite essence.

Explication I say "absolutely infinite," not "infinite in its kind." For if a thing is only infinite in its kind, one may deny that it has infinite attributes. But if a thing is absolutely infinite, whatever expresses essence and does not involve any negation belongs to its essence.

7. That thing is said to be free [*liber*] which exists solely from the necessity of its own nature, and is determined to action by itself alone. A thing is said to be necessary [*necessarius*] or rather, constrained [*coactus*], if it is determined by another thing to exist and to act in a definite and determinate way.
8. By eternity I mean existence itself insofar as it is conceived as necessarily following solely from the definition of an eternal thing.

Explication For such existence is conceived as an eternal truth, just as is the essence of the thing, and therefore cannot be explicated through duration or time, even if duration be conceived as without beginning and end.

Axioms

1. All things that are, are either in themselves or in something else.
2. That which cannot be conceived through another thing must be conceived through itself.

3. From a given determinate cause there necessarily follows an effect; on the other hand, if there be no determinate cause, it is impossible that an effect should follow.

4. The knowledge of an effect depends on, and involves, the knowledge of the cause.

5. Things which have nothing in common with each other cannot be understood through each other; that is, the conception of the one does not involve the conception of the other.

6. A true idea must agree with that of which it is the idea [*ideatum*].

7. If a thing can be conceived as not existing, its essence does not involve existence.

Proposition 1
Substance is by nature prior to its affections.

Proof This is evident from Defs. 3 and 5.

Proposition 2
Two substances having different attributes have nothing in common.

Proof This too is evident from Def. 3; for each substance must be in itself and be conceived through itself; that is, the conception of the one does not involve the conception of the other.

Proposition 3
When things have nothing in common, one cannot be the cause of the other.

Proof If things have nothing in common, then (Ax. 5) they cannot be understood through one another, and so (Ax. 4) one cannot be the cause of the other.

Proposition 4
Two or more distinct things are distinguished from one another either by the difference of the attributes of the substances or by the difference of the affections of the substances.

Proof All things that are, are either in themselves or in something else (Ax. 1); that is (Defs. 3 and 5), nothing exists external to the intellect except substances and their affections. Therefore, there can be nothing external to the intellect through which several things can be distinguished from one another except substances or (which is the same thing) (Def. 4) the attributes and the affections of substances.

Proposition 5
In the universe there cannot be two or more substances of the same nature or attribute.

Proof If there were several such distinct substances, they would have to be distinguished from one another either by a difference of attributes or by a difference of affections (Pr. 4). If they are distinguished only by a difference of attributes, then it will be granted that there cannot be more than one substance of the same attribute. But if they are distinguished by a difference of affections, then, since substance is by nature prior to its affections (Pr. 1), disregarding therefore its affections and considering substance in itself, that is (Def. 3 and Ax. 6), considering it truly, it cannot be conceived as distinguishable from another substance. That is (Pr. 4), there cannot be several such substances but only one.

Proposition 6
One substance cannot be produced by another substance.

Proof In the universe there cannot be two substances of the same attribute (Pr. 5), that is (Pr. 2), two substances having something in common. And so (Pr. 3) one cannot be the cause of the other; that is, one cannot be produced by the other.

Corollary Hence it follows that substance cannot be produced by anything else. For in the universe there exists nothing but substances and their affections, as is evident from Ax. 1 and Defs. 3 and 5. But, by Pr. 6, it cannot be produced by another substance. Therefore, substance cannot be produced by anything else whatsoever.

Another Proof This can be proved even more readily by the absurdity of the contradictory. For if substance could be produced by something else, the knowledge of substance would have to depend on the knowledge of its cause (Ax. 4), and so (Def. 3) it would not be substance.

Proposition 7
Existence belongs to the nature of substance.

Proof Substance cannot be produced by anything else (Cor. Pr. 6) and is therefore self-caused [*causa sui*]; that is (Def. 1), its essence necessarily involves existence; that is, existence belongs to its nature.

Proposition 8
Every substance is necessarily infinite.

Proof There cannot be more than one substance having the same attribute (Pr. 5), and existence belongs to the nature of substance (Pr. 7). It must therefore exist either as finite or as infinite. But it cannot exist as finite, for (Def. 2) it would have to be limited by another substance of the same nature, and that substance also would have to exist (Pr. 7). And so there would exist two substances of the same attribute, which is absurd (Pr. 5). Therefore, it exists as infinite.

Scholium 1 Since in fact to be finite is in part a negation and to be infinite is the unqualified affirmation of the existence of some nature, it follows from Proposition 7 alone that every substance must be infinite.

Scholium 2 I do not doubt that for those who judge things confusedly and are not accustomed to know things through their primary causes it is difficult to grasp the proof of Proposition 7. Surely, this is because they neither distinguish between the modification of substances and substances themselves, nor do they know how things are produced. And so it comes about that they ascribe to substances a beginning which they see natural things as having; for those who do not know the true causes of things confuse everything. Without any hesitation they imagine trees as well as men talking and stones as well as men being formed from seeds; indeed, any forms whatsoever are imagined to change into any other forms. So too, those who confuse the divine nature with human nature easily ascribe to God human emotions, especially so long as they are ignorant of how the latter are produced in the mind. But if men were to attend to the nature of substance, they would not doubt at all the truth of Proposition 7; indeed, this Proposition would be an axiom to all and would be ranked among universally accepted truisms. For by substance they would understand that which is in itself and is conceived through itself; that is, that the knowledge of which does not require the knowledge of any other thing. By modifications they would understand that which is in another thing, and whose conception is formed from the thing in which they are. Therefore, in the case of nonexistent modifications we can have true ideas of them since their essence is included in something else, with the result that they can be conceived through that something else, although they do not exist in actuality externally to the intellect. However, in the case of substances, because they are conceived only through themselves, their truth external to the intellect is only in themselves. So if someone were to say that he has a clear and distinct—that is, a true—idea of substance and that he nevertheless doubts whether such a substance exists, this would surely be just the same as if he were to declare that he has a true idea but nevertheless suspects that it may be false (as is obvious to anyone who gives his mind to it). Or if anyone asserts that substance is created, he at the same time asserts that a false idea has become true, than which nothing more absurd can be conceived. So it must necessarily be admitted that the existence of substance is as much an eternal truth as is its essence.

From here we can derive in another way that there cannot be but one [substance] of the same nature, and I think it worthwhile to set out the proof here. Now to do this in an orderly fashion I ask you to note:

1. The true definition of each thing involves and expresses nothing beyond the nature of the thing defined. Hence it follows that—

2. No definition involves or expresses a fixed number of individuals, since it expresses nothing but the nature of the thing defined. For example, the definition of a triangle expresses nothing other than simply the nature of a triangle, and not a fixed number of triangles.

3. For each individual existent thing there must necessarily be a definite cause for its existence.

4. The cause for the existence of a thing must either be contained in the very nature and definition of the existent thing (in effect, existence belongs to its nature) or must have its being independently of the thing itself.

From these premises it follows that if a fixed number of individuals exist in Nature, there must necessarily be a cause why those individuals and not more or fewer exist. If, for example, in Nature twenty men were to exist (for the sake of greater clarity I suppose that they exist simultaneously and that no others existed in Nature before them), in order to account for the existence of these twenty men, it will not be enough for us to demonstrate the cause of human nature in general; it will furthermore be necessary to demonstrate the cause why not more or fewer than twenty men exist, since (Note 3) there must necessarily be a cause for the existence of each one. But this cause (Notes 2 and 3) cannot be contained in the nature of man, since the true definition of man does not involve the number twenty. So (Note 4) the cause of the existence of these twenty men, and consequently of each one, must necessarily be external to each one, and therefore we can reach the unqualified conclusion that whenever several individuals of a kind exist, there must necessarily be an external cause for their existence. Now since existence belongs to the nature of substance (as has already been shown in this Scholium) the definition of substance must involve necessary existence, and consequently the existence of substance must be concluded solely from its definition. But the existence of several substances cannot follow from the definition of substance (as I have already shown in Notes 2 and 3). Therefore, from the definition of substance it follows necessarily that there exists only one substance of the same nature, as was proposed.

Proposition 9
The more reality or being a thing has, the more attributes it has.

Proof This is evident from Definition 4.

Proposition 10
Each attribute of one substance must be conceived through itself.

Proof For an attribute is that which intellect perceives of substance as constituting its essence (Def. 4), and so (Def. 3) it must be conceived through itself.

Scholium From this it is clear that although two attributes be conceived as really distinct, that is, one without the help of the other, still we cannot deduce therefrom that they constitute two entities, or two different substances. For it is in the nature of substance that each of its attributes be conceived through itself, since all the attributes it possesses have always been in it simultaneously, and one could not have been produced by another; but each expresses the reality or being of substance. So it is by no means absurd to ascribe more than one attribute to one substance. Indeed, nothing in Nature is clearer than that each entity must be conceived under some attribute, and the more reality or being it has, the more are its attributes which express necessity, or eternity, and infinity. Consequently, nothing can be clearer than this, too, that an absolutely infinite entity must necessarily be defined (Def. 6) as an entity consisting of infinite attributes, each of which expresses a definite essence, eternal and infinite. Now if anyone asks by what mark can we distinguish between different substances, let him read the following Propositions, which show that in Nature there exists only one substance, absolutely infinite. So this distinguishing mark would be sought in vain.

Proposition 11
God, or substance consisting of infinite attributes, each of which expresses eternal and infinite essence, necessarily exists.

Proof If you deny this, conceive, if you can, that God does not exist. Therefore (Ax. 7), his essence does not involve existence. But this is absurd (Pr. 7). Therefore, God necessarily exists.

Second Proof For every thing a cause or reason must be assigned either for its existence or for its nonexistence. For example, if a triangle exists, there must be a reason, or cause, for its existence. If it does not exist, there must be a reason or cause which prevents it from existing, or which annuls its existence. Now this reason or cause must either be contained in the nature of the thing or be external to it. For example, the reason why a square circle does not exist is indicated by its very nature, in that it involves a contradiction. On the other hand, the reason for the existence of substance also follows from its nature alone, in that it involves existence (Pr. 7). But the reason for the existence or nonexistence of a circle or a triangle does not follow from their nature, but from the order of universal corporeal Nature. For it is from this latter that it necessarily follows that either the triangle necessarily exists at this moment or that its present existence is impossible. This is self-evident, and therefrom it follows that a thing necessarily exists if there is no reason or cause which prevents its existence. Therefore, if there can be no reason or cause which prevents God from existing or which annuls his existence, we are bound to conclude that he necessarily exists. But if there were such a reason or cause, it would have to be either within God's nature or external to it; that is, it would have to be in another substance of another nature. For if it were of the same nature, by that very fact it would be granted that God exists. But a substance of another nature would have nothing in common with God (Pr. 2), and so could neither posit nor annul his existence. Since, therefore, there cannot be external to God's nature a reason or cause that would annul God's existence, then if indeed he does not exist, the reason or cause must necessarily be in God's nature, which would therefore involve a contradiction. But to affirm this of a Being absolutely infinite and in the highest degree perfect is absurd. Therefore, neither in God nor external to God is there any cause or reason which would annul his existence. Therefore, God necessarily exists.

A Third Proof To be able to not exist is weakness; on the other hand, to be able to exist is power, as is self-evident. So if what now necessarily exists is nothing but finite entities, then finite entities are more potent than an absolutely infinite Entity—which is absurd. Therefore, either nothing exists, or an absolutely infinite Entity necessarily exists, too. But we do exist, either in ourselves or in something else which necessarily exists (Ax. 1 and Pr. 7). Therefore, an absolutely infinite Entity—that is (Def. 6), God—necessarily exists.

Scholium In this last proof I decided to prove God's existence a posteriori so that the proof may be more easily perceived, and not because God's existence does not follow a priori from this same basis. For since the ability to exist is power, it follows that the greater the degree of reality that belongs to the nature of a thing, the greater amount of energy it has for existence. So an absolutely infinite Entity or God will have from himself absolutely infinite power to exist, and therefore exists absolutely.

But perhaps many will not readily find this proof convincing because they are used to considering only such things as derive from external causes. Of these things they observe that those which come quickly into being—that is, which readily exist—likewise readily perish, while things which they conceive as more complex they regard as more difficult to bring into being—that is, not so ready to exist. However, to free them from these misconceptions I do not need at this point to show what measure of truth there is in the saying, "Quickly come, quickly go," neither need I raise the question whether or not everything is equally easy in respect of Nature as a whole. It is enough to note simply this, that I am not here speaking of things that come into being through external causes, but only of substances, which (Pr. 6) cannot be produced by any external cause. For whether they consist of many parts or few, things that are brought about by external causes owe whatever degree of perfection or reality they possess entirely to the power of the external cause, and so their existence has its origin solely in the perfection of the external cause, and not in their own perfection. On the other hand, whatever perfection substance possesses is due to no external cause; therefore its existence, too, must follow solely from its own nature, and is therefore nothing else but its essence. So perfection does not annul a thing's existence: on the contrary, it posits it; whereas imperfection annuls a thing's existence. So there is nothing of which we can be more certain than the existence of an absolutely infinite or perfect Entity; that is, God. For since his essence excludes all imperfection and involves absolute perfection, it thereby removes all reason for doubting his existence and affords the utmost certainty of it. This, I think, must be quite clear to all who give a modicum of attention to the matter.

Proposition 12

No attribute of substance can be truly conceived from which it would follow that substance can be divided.

Proof The parts into which substance thus conceived would be divided will either retain the nature of substance or they will not. In the first case each part will have to be infinite (Pr. 8) and self-caused (Pr. 6) and consist of a different attribute (Pr. 5); and so several substances could be formed from one substance, which is absurd (Pr. 6). Furthermore, the parts would have nothing in common with the whole (Pr. 2), and the whole could exist and be conceived without its parts (Def. 4 and Pr. 10), the absurdity of which none can doubt. But in the latter case in which the parts will not retain the nature of substance—then when the whole substance would have been divided into equal parts it would lose the nature of substance and would cease to be. This is absurd (Pr. 7).

Proposition 13
Absolutely infinite substance is indivisible.

Proof If it were divisible, the parts into which it would be divided will either retain the nature of absolutely infinite substance, or not. In the first case, there would therefore be several substances of the same nature, which is absurd (Pr. 5). In the second case, absolutely infinite substance can cease to be, which is also absurd (Pr. 11).

Corollary From this it follows that no substance, and consequently no corporeal substance, insofar as it is substance, is divisible.

Scholium The indivisibility of substance can be more easily understood merely from the fact that the nature of substance can be conceived only as infinite, and that a part of substance can mean only finite substance, which involves an obvious contradiction (Pr. 8).

Proposition 14
There can be, or be conceived, no other substance but God.

Proof Since God is an absolutely infinite being of whom no attribute expressing the essence of substance can be denied (Def. 6), and since he necessarily exists (Pr. 11), if there were any other substance but God, it would have to be explicated through some attribute of God, and so there would exist two substances with the same attribute, which is absurd (Pr. 5). So there can be no substance external to God, and consequently no such substance can be conceived. For if it could be conceived, it would have to be conceived necessarily as existing; but this is absurd (by the first part of this proof). Therefore, no substance can be or be conceived external to God.

Corollary 1 Hence it follows quite clearly that God is one: that is (Def. 6), in the universe there is only one substance, and this is absolutely infinite, as I have already indicated in Scholium Pr. 10.

Corollary 2 It follows that the thing extended and the thing thinking are either attributes of God or (Ax. 1) affections of the attributes of God.

Proposition 15
Whatever is, is in God, and nothing can be or be conceived without God.

Proof Apart from God no substance can be or be conceived (Pr. 14), that is (Def. 3), something which is in itself and is conceived through itself. Now modes (Def. 5) cannot be or be conceived without substance; therefore, they can be only in the divine nature and can be conceived only through the divine nature. But nothing exists except substance and modes (Ax. 1). Therefore, nothing can be or be conceived without God.

Scholium Some imagine God in the likeness of man, consisting of mind and body, and subject to passions. But it is clear from what has already been proved how far they stray from the true knowledge of God. These I dismiss, for all who have given any consideration to the divine nature deny that God is corporeal. They find convincing proof of this in the fact that by body we understand some quantity having length, breadth, and depth, bounded by a definite shape; and nothing more absurd than this can be attributed to God, a being absolutely infinite.

At the same time, however, by other arguments which they try to prove their point, they show clearly that in their thinking corporeal or extended substance is set completely apart from the divine nature, and they assert that it is created by God. But they have no idea from what divine power it could have been created, which clearly shows that they don't know what they are saying. Now I have clearly proved—at any rate, in my judgment (Cor. Pr. 6 and Sch. 2 Pr. 8)—that no substance can be produced or created by anything else. Furthermore, in Proposition 14 we showed that apart from God no substance can be or be conceived, and hence we deduced that extended substance is one of God's infinite attributes.

However, for a fuller explanation I will refute my opponents' arguments, which all seem to come down to this. Firstly, they think that corporeal substance, insofar as it is substance, is made up of parts, and so they deny that it can be infinite, and consequently that it can pertain to God. This they illustrate with many examples, of which I will take one or two. They say that if corporeal substance is infinite, suppose it to be divided into two parts. Each of these parts will be either finite or infinite. If the former, then the infinite is made up of two finite parts, which is absurd. If the latter, then there is an infinite which is twice as great as another infinite, which is also absurd.

Again, if an infinite length is measured in feet, it will have to consist of an infinite number of feet; and if it is measured in inches, it will consist of an infinite number of inches. So one infinite number will be twelve times greater than another infinite number.

Lastly, if from one point in an infinite quantity two lines, AB and AC, be drawn of fixed and determinate length, and thereafter be produced to infinity, it is clear that the distance between B and C continues to increase and finally changes from a determinate distance to an indeterminate distance.

As these absurdities follow, they think, from supposing quantity to be infinite, they conclude that corporeal substance must be finite and consequently cannot pertain to God's essence.

The second argument is also drawn from God's consummate perfection. Since God, they say, is a supremely perfect being, he cannot be that which is acted upon. But corporeal substance, being divisible, can be acted upon. It therefore follows that corporeal substance does not pertain to God's essence.

These are the arguments I find put forward by writers who thereby seek to prove that corporeal substance is unworthy of the divine essence and cannot pertain to it. However, the student who looks carefully into these arguments will find that I have already replied to them, since they are all founded on the same supposition that material substance is composed of parts, and this I have already shown to be absurd (Pr. 12 and Cor. Pr. 13). Again, careful reflection will show that all those alleged absurdities (if indeed they are absurdities, which is not now under discussion) from which they seek to prove that extended substance is finite do not at all follow from the supposition that quantity is infinite, but that infinite quantity is measurable and is made up of finite parts. Therefore, from the resultant absurdities no other conclusion can be reached but that infinite quantity is not measurable and cannot be made up of finite parts. And this is exactly what we have already proved (Pr. 12). So the weapon they aimed at us is in fact turned against themselves. If therefore from this "reductio ad absurdum" argument of theirs they still seek to deduce that extended substance must be finite, they are surely just like one who, having made the supposition that a circle has the properties of a square, deduces therefrom that a circle does not have a center from which all lines drawn to the circumference are equal. For corporeal substance, which can be conceived only as infinite, one, and indivisible (Prs. 8, 5, and 12) they conceive as made up of finite parts, multiplex, and divisible, so as to deduce that it is finite. In the same way others, too, having supposed that a line is composed of points, can find many arguments to prove that a line cannot be infinitely divided. Indeed, it is just as absurd to assert that corporeal substance is composed of bodies or parts as that a body is composed of surfaces, surfaces of lines, and lines of points. This must be admitted by all who know clear reason to be infallible, and particularly those who say that a vacuum cannot exist. For if corporeal substance could be so divided that its parts were distinct in reality, why could one part not be annihilated while the others remain joined together as before? And why should all the parts be so fitted together as to leave no vacuum? Surely, in the case of things which are in reality distinct from one another, one can exist without the other and remain in its original state. Since therefore there is no vacuum in Nature (of which [more] elsewhere[1]) and all its parts must so harmonize that there is no vacuum, it also follows that the parts cannot be distinct in reality; that is, corporeal substance, insofar as it is substance, cannot be divided.

If I am now asked why we have this natural inclination to divide quantity, I reply that we conceive quantity in two ways, to wit, abstractly, or superficially—in other words, as represented in the imagination—or as substance, which we do only through the intellect. If therefore we consider quantity insofar as we represent it in the imagination—and this is what we more frequently and readily do—we find it to be finite, divisible, and made up of parts. But if we consider it intellectually and conceive it insofar as it is substance—and this is very difficult—then it will be found to be infinite, one, and indivisible, as we have already sufficiently proved. This will be quite clear to those who can distinguish between the imagination and the intellect, especially if this point also is stressed, that matter is everywhere the same, and there are no distinct parts in it except insofar as we conceive matter as modified in various ways. Then its parts are distinct, not really but

---

Notes without brackets are Spinoza's. Bracketed notes are those of Seymour Feldman (main annotator for this work), translator Samuel Shirley, and Michael L. Morgan.

[1] [If this refers to anything in Spinoza's extant works, it must be to his early *Descartes's Principles of Philosophy* II.2–3. —S.F.]

only modally. For example, we conceive water to be divisible and to have separate parts insofar as it is water, but not insofar as it is material substance. In this latter respect it is not capable of separation or division. Furthermore, water, qua water, comes into existence and goes out of existence; but qua substance it does not come into existence nor go out of existence [*corrumpitur*].

I consider that in the above I have also replied to the second argument, since this too is based on the supposition that matter, insofar as it is substance, is divisible and made up of parts. And even though this were not so, I do not know why matter should be unworthy of the divine nature, since (Pr. 14) there can be no substance external to God by which it can be acted upon. All things, I repeat, are in God, and all things that come to pass do so only through the laws of God's infinite nature and follow through the necessity of his essence (as I shall later show). Therefore, by no manner of reasoning can it be said that God is acted upon by anything else or that extended substance is unworthy of the divine nature, even though it be supposed divisible, as long as it is granted to be eternal and infinite.

But enough of this subject for the present.

Proposition 16

From the necessity of the divine nature there must follow infinite things in infinite ways [modis] (that is, everything that can come within the scope of infinite intellect).

Proof This proposition should be obvious to everyone who will but consider this point, that from the given definition of any one thing the intellect infers a number of properties which necessarily follow in fact from the definition (that is, from the very essence of the thing), and the more reality the definition of the thing expresses (that is, the more reality the essence of the thing defined involves), the greater the number of its properties. Now since divine nature possesses absolutely infinite attributes (Def. 6), of which each one also expresses infinite essence in its own kind, then there must necessarily follow from the necessity of the divine nature an infinity of things in infinite ways (that is, everything that can come within the scope of the infinite intellect).

Corollary 1 Hence it follows that God is the efficient cause of all things that can come within the scope of the infinite intellect.

Corollary 2 Secondly, it follows that God is the cause through himself, not *per accidens*.

Corollary 3 Thirdly, it follows that God is absolutely the first cause.

Proposition 17

God acts solely from the laws of his own nature, constrained by none.

Proof We have just shown that an infinity of things follow, absolutely, solely from the necessity of divine nature, or—which is the same thing—solely from the laws of that same nature (Pr. 16); and we have proved (Pr. 15) that nothing can be or be conceived without God, but that everything is in God. Therefore, there can be nothing external to God by which he can be determined or constrained to act. Thus, God acts solely from the laws of his own nature and is constrained by none.

Corollary 1 Hence it follows, firstly, that there is no cause, except the perfection of his nature, which either extrinsically or intrinsically moves God to act.

Corollary 2 It follows, secondly, that God alone is a free cause. For God alone exists solely from the necessity of his own nature (Pr. 11 and Cor. 1 Pr. 14) and acts solely from the necessity of his own nature (Pr. 17). So he alone is a free cause (Def. 7).

Scholium Others take the view that God is a free cause because—so they think—he can bring it about that those things which we have said follow from his nature—that is, which are within his power—should not come about; that is, they should not be produced by him. But this is as much as to say that God can bring it about that it should not follow from the nature of a triangle that its three angles are equal to two right angles, or that from a given cause the effect should not follow, which is absurd.

Furthermore, I shall show later on without the help of this proposition that neither intellect nor will pertain to the nature of God. I know indeed that there are many who think they can prove that intellect in the highest degree and free will belong to the nature of God; for they say they know of nothing more perfect which they may attribute to God than that which is the highest perfection in us. Again, although they conceive of God as having in actuality intellect in the highest degree, they yet do not believe he can bring about the existence of everything which in actuality he understands, for they think they would thereby be nullifying God's power. If, they say, he had created everything that is within his intellect, then he would not have been able to create anything more; and this they regard as inconsistent with God's omnipotence. So they have preferred to regard God as indifferent to everything and as creating nothing but what he has decided, by some absolute exercise of will, to create. However, I think I have shown quite clearly (Pr. 16) that from God's supreme power or infinite nature an infinity of things in infinite ways—that is, everything—has necessarily flowed or is always following from that same necessity, just as from the nature of a triangle it follows from eternity to eternity that its three angles are equal to two right angles. Therefore, God's omnipotence has from eternity been actual and will remain for eternity in the same actuality. In this way, I submit, God's omnipotence is established as being far more perfect. Indeed my opponents—let us speak frankly—seem to be denying God's omnipotence. For they are obliged to admit that God understands an infinite number of creatable things which nevertheless he can never create. If this were not so, that is, if he were to create all the things that he understands, he would exhaust his omnipotence, according to them, and render himself imperfect. Thus, to affirm God as perfect they are reduced to having to affirm at the same time that he cannot bring about everything that is within the bounds of his power. I cannot imagine anything more absurd than this, or more inconsistent with God's omnipotence.

Furthermore, I have something here to say about the intellect and will that is usually attributed to God. If intellect and will do indeed pertain to the eternal essence of God, one must understand in the case of both these attributes something very different from the meaning widely entertained. For the intellect and will that would constitute the essence of God would have to be vastly different from human intellect and will, and would have no point of agreement except the name. They could be no more alike than the celestial constellation of the Dog and the dog that barks. This I will prove as follows. If intellect does pertain to the divine nature, it cannot, like man's intellect, be posterior to (as most thinkers hold) or simultaneous with the objects of understanding, since God is prior in causality to all things (Cor. 1 Pr. 16). On the contrary, the truth and formal essence of things is what it is because it exists as such in the intellect of God as an object of thought. Therefore, God's intellect, insofar as it is conceived as constituting God's essence, is in actual fact the cause of things, in respect both of their essence and their existence. This seems to have been recognized also by those who have asserted that God's intellect, will, and power are one and the same. Since therefore God's intellect is the one and only cause of things, both of their essence and their existence, as we have shown, it must necessarily be different from them both in respect of essence and existence. For that which is caused differs from its cause precisely in what it has from its cause. For example, a man is the cause of the existence of another man, but not of the other's essence; for the essence is an eternal truth. So with regard to their essence the two men can be in full agreement, but they must differ with regard to existence; and for that reason if the existence of the one should cease, the existence of the other would not thereby cease. But if the essence of the one could be destroyed and rendered false, so too would the essence of the other. Therefore, a thing which is the cause of the essence and existence of some effect must differ from that effect both in respect of essence and existence. But God's intellect is the cause of the essence and existence of man's intellect. Therefore, God's intellect, insofar as it is conceived as constituting the divine essence, differs from man's intellect both in respect of essence and existence, and cannot agree with it in any respect other than name—which is what I sought to prove. In the matter of will, the proof is the same, as anyone can readily see.

Proposition 18
God is the immanent, not the transitive, cause of all things.

Proof All things that are, are in God, and must be conceived through God (Pr. 15), and so (Cor. 1 Pr. 16) God is the cause of the things that are in him, which is the first point. Further, there can be no substance external to God (Pr. 14); that is (Def. 3), a thing which is in itself external to God—which is the second point. Therefore, God is the immanent, not the transitive, cause of all things.

Proposition 19
God [is eternal], that is, all the attributes of God are eternal.

Proof God is substance (Def. 6) which necessarily exists (Pr. 11); that is (Pr. 7), a thing to whose nature it pertains to exist, or—and this is the same thing—a thing from whose definition existence follows; and so (Def. 8) God is eternal. Further, by the attributes of God must be understood that which expresses the essence of the Divine substance (Def. 4), that is, that which pertains to substance. It is this, I say, which the attributes themselves must involve. But eternity pertains to the nature of substance (as I have shown in Pr. 7). Therefore, each of the attributes must involve eternity, and so they are all eternal.

Scholium This proposition is also perfectly clear from the manner in which I proved the existence of God (Pr. 11). From this proof, I repeat, it is obvious that God's existence is, like his essence, an eternal truth. Again, I have also proved God's eternity in another way in Proposition 19 of my *Descartes's Principles of Philosophy*, and there is no need here to go over that ground again.

Proposition 20
God's existence and his essence are one and the same.

Proof God and all his attributes are eternal (Pr. 19); that is, each one of his attributes expresses existence (Def. 8). Therefore, the same attributes of God that explicate his eternal essence (Def. 4) at the same time explicate his eternal existence; that is, that which constitutes the essence of God at the same time constitutes his existence, and so his existence and his essence are one and the same.

Corollary 1 From this it follows, firstly, that God's existence, like his essence, is an eternal truth.

Corollary 2 It follows, secondly, that God is immutable; that is, all the attributes of God are immutable. For if they were to change in respect of existence, they would also have to change in respect of essence (Pr. 10); that is—and this is self-evident—they would have to become false instead of true, which is absurd.

Proposition 21
All things that follow from the absolute nature of any attribute of God must have existed always, and as infinite; that is, through the said attribute they are eternal and infinite.

Proof Suppose this proposition be denied and conceive, if you can, that something in some attribute of God, following from its absolute nature, is finite and has a determinate existence or duration; for example, the idea of God in Thought. Now Thought, being assumed to be an attribute of God, is necessarily infinite by its own nature (Pr. 11). However, insofar as it has the idea of God, it is being supposed as finite. Now (Def. 2) it cannot be conceived as finite unless it is determined through Thought itself. But it cannot be determined through Thought itself insofar as Thought constitutes the idea of God, for it is in that respect that

Thought is supposed to be finite. Therefore, it is determined through Thought insofar as Thought does not constitute the idea of God, which Thought must nevertheless necessarily exist (Pr. 11). Therefore, there must be Thought which does not constitute the idea of God, and so the idea of God does not follow necessarily from its nature insofar as it is absolute Thought. (For it is conceived as constituting and as not constituting the idea of God.) This is contrary to our hypothesis. Therefore, if the idea of God in Thought, or anything in some attribute of God (it does not matter what is selected, since the proof is universal), follows from the necessity of the absolute nature of the attribute, it must necessarily be infinite. That was our first point.

Furthermore, that which thus follows from the necessity of the nature of some attribute cannot have a determinate existence, or duration. If this be denied, suppose that there is in some attribute of God a thing following from the necessity of the nature of the attribute, for example, the idea of God in Thought, and suppose that this thing either did not exist at some time, or will cease to exist in the future. Now since Thought is assumed as an attribute of God, it must necessarily exist, and as immutable (Pr. 11 and Cor. 2 Pr. 20). Therefore, outside the bounds of the duration of the idea of God (for this idea is supposed at some time not to have existed, or will at some point cease to exist), Thought will have to exist without the idea of God. But this is contrary to the hypothesis, for it is supposed that when Thought is granted the idea of God necessarily follows. Therefore, the idea of God in Thought, or anything that necessarily follows from the absolute nature of some attribute of God, cannot have a determinate existence, but is eternal through that same attribute. That was our second point. Note that the same holds for anything in an attribute of God which necessarily follows from the absolute nature of God.

PROPOSITION 22
Whatever follows from some attribute of God, insofar as the attribute is modified by a modification that exists necessarily and as infinite through that same attribute, must also exist both necessarily and as infinite.

Proof This proposition is proved in the same way as the preceding one.

PROPOSITION 23
Every mode which exists necessarily and as infinite must have necessarily followed either from the absolute nature of some attribute of God or from some attribute modified by a modification which exists necessarily and as infinite.

Proof A mode is in something else through which it must be conceived (Def. 5); that is (Pr. 15), it is in God alone and can be conceived only through God. Therefore, if a mode is conceived to exist necessarily and to be infinite, both these characteristics must necessarily be inferred or perceived through some attribute of God insofar as that attribute is conceived to express infinity and necessity of existence, or (and by Def. 8 this is the same) eternity; that is (Def. 6 and Pr. 19), insofar as it is considered absolutely. Therefore, a mode which exists necessarily and as infinite must have followed from the absolute nature of some attribute of God, either directly (Pr. 21) or through the mediation of some modification which follows from the absolute nature of the attribute; that is (Pr. 22), which exists necessarily and as infinite.

Proposition 24
The essence of things produced by God does not involve existence.

Proof This is evident from Def. 1. For only that whose nature (considered in itself) involves existence is self-caused and exists solely from the necessity of its own nature.

Corollary Hence it follows that God is the cause not only of the coming into existence of things but also of their continuing in existence, or, to use a scholastic term, God is the cause of the being of things [*essendi rerum*]. For whether things exist or do not exist, in reflecting on their essence we realize that this essence involves neither existence nor duration. So it is not their essence which can be the cause of either their existence or their duration, but only God, to whose nature alone existence pertains (Cor. 1 Pr. 14).

Proposition 25
God is the efficient cause not only of the existence of things but also of their essence.

Proof If this is denied, then God is not the cause of the essence of things, and so (Ax. 4) the essence of things can be conceived without God. But this is absurd (Pr. 15). Therefore, God is also the cause of the essence of things.

Scholium This proposition follows more clearly from Pr. 16; for from that proposition it follows that from the given divine nature both the essence and the existence of things must be inferred. In a word, in the same sense that God is said to be self-caused he must also be said to be the cause of all things. This will be even clearer from the following Corollary.

Corollary Particular things are nothing but affections of the attributes of God, that is, modes wherein the attributes of God find expression in a definite and determinate way. The proof is obvious from Pr. 15 and Def. 5.

Proposition 26
A thing which has been determined to act in a particular way has necessarily been so determined by God; and a thing which has not been determined by God cannot determine itself to act.

Proof That by which things are said to be determined to act in a particular way must necessarily be something positive (as is obvious). So God, from the necessity of his nature, is the efficient cause both of its essence and its existence (Prs. 25 and 16)—which was the first point. From this the second point quite clearly follows as well. For if a thing which has not been determined by God could determine itself, the first part of this proposition would be false, which, as I have shown, is absurd.

Proposition 27
A thing which has been determined by God to act in a particular way cannot render itself undetermined.

Proof This proposition is evident from Axiom 3.

Proposition 28
Every individual thing, i.e., anything whatever which is finite and has a determinate existence, cannot exist or be determined to act unless it be determined to exist and to act by another cause which is also finite and has a determinate existence, and this cause again cannot exist or be determined to act unless it be determined to exist and to act by another cause which is also finite and has a determinate existence, and so ad infinitum.

Proof Whatever is determined to exist and to act has been so determined by God (Pr. 26 and Cor. Pr. 24). But that which is finite and has a determinate existence cannot have been produced by the absolute nature of one of God's attributes, for whatever follows from the absolute nature of one of God's attributes is infinite and eternal (Pr. 21). It must therefore have followed from God or one of his attributes insofar as that is considered as affected by some mode; for nothing exists but substance and its modes (Ax. 1 and Defs. 3 and 5), and modes (Cor. Pr. 25) are nothing but affections of God's attributes. But neither could a finite and determined thing have followed from God or one of his attributes insofar as that is affected by a modification which is eternal and infinite (Pr. 22). Therefore, it must have followed, or been determined to exist and to act, by God or one of his attributes insofar as it was modified by a modification which is finite and has a determinate existence. That was the first point. Then again this cause or this mode (the reasoning is the same as in the first part of this proof) must also have been determined by another cause, which is also finite and has a determinate existence, and again this last (the reasoning is the same) by another, and so ad infinitum.

Scholium Since some things must have been produced directly by God (those things, in fact, which necessarily follow from his absolute nature) and others through the medium of these primary things (which other things nevertheless cannot be or be conceived without God), it follows, firstly, that God is absolutely the proximate cause of things directly produced by him. I say "absolutely" [*absolute*], and not "within their own kind" [*suo genere*], as some say. For the effects of God can neither be nor be conceived without their cause (Pr. 15 and Cor. Pr. 24). It follows, secondly, that God cannot properly be said to be the remote cause of individual things, unless perchance for the purpose of distinguishing these things from things which he has produced directly, or rather, things which follow from his absolute nature. For by "remote cause" we understand a cause which is in no way conjoined with its effect. But all things that are, are in God, and depend on God in such a way that they can neither be nor be conceived without him.

Proposition 29
Nothing in nature is contingent, but all things are from the necessity of the divine nature determined to exist and to act in a definite way.

Proof Whatever is, is in God (Pr. 15). But God cannot be termed a contingent thing, for (Pr. 11) he exists necessarily, not contingently. Again, the modes of the divine nature have also followed from it necessarily, not contingently (Pr. 16), and that, too, whether insofar as the divine nature is considered absolutely (Pr. 21) or insofar as it is considered as determined to act in a definite way (Pr. 27). Furthermore, God is the cause of these modes not only insofar as they simply exist (Cor. Pr. 26), but also insofar as they are considered as determined to a particular action (Pr. 26). Now if they are not determined by God (Pr. 26), it is an impossibility, not a contingency, that they should determine themselves. On the other hand (Pr. 27), if they are determined by God, it is an impossibility, not a contingency, that they should render themselves undetermined. Therefore, all things are determined from the necessity of the divine nature not only to exist but also to exist and to act in a definite way. Thus, there is no contingency.

Scholium Before I go any further, I wish to explain at this point what we must understand by "*Natura naturans*" and "*Natura naturata.*" I should perhaps say not "explain," but "remind the reader," for I consider that it is already clear from what has gone before that by "*Natura naturans*" we must understand that which is in itself and is conceived through itself; that is, the attributes of substance that express eternal and infinite essence; or (Cor. 1 Pr. 14 and Cor. 2 Pr. 17), God insofar as he is considered a free cause. By "*Natura naturata*" I understand all that follows from the necessity of God's nature, that is, from the necessity of each one of God's attributes; or all the modes of God's attributes insofar as they are considered as things which are in God and can neither be nor be conceived without God.

Proposition 30
The finite intellect in act or the infinite intellect in act must comprehend the attributes of God and the affections of God, and nothing else.

Proof A true idea must agree with its object [*ideatum*] (Ax. 6); that is (as is self-evident), that which is contained in the intellect as an object of thought must necessarily exist in Nature. But in Nature (Cor. 1 Pr. 14) there is but one substance—God—and no other affections (Pr. 15) than those which are in God and that can neither be nor be conceived (Pr. 15) without God. Therefore, the finite intellect in act or the infinite intellect in act must comprehend the attributes of God and the affections of God, and nothing else.

Proposition 31
The intellect in act, whether it be finite or infinite, as also will, desire, love, etc., must be related to Natura naturata, *not to* Natura naturans.

Proof By intellect (as is self-evident) we do not understand absolute thought, but only a definite mode of thinking which differs from other modes such as desire, love, etc., and so (Def. 5) must be conceived through absolute thought—that is (Pr. 15 and Def. 6), an attribute of God which expresses the eternal and infinite essence of thought—in such a way that without this attribute it can neither be nor be conceived; and therefore (Sch. Pr. 29) it must be related to *Natura naturata*, not to *Natura naturans*, just like the other modes of thinking.

Scholium The reason for my here speaking of the intellect in act is not that I grant there can be any intellect in potentiality, but that, wishing to avoid any confusion, I want to confine myself to what we perceive with the utmost clarity, to wit, the very act of understanding, than which nothing is more clearly apprehended by us. For we can understand nothing that does not lead to a more perfect cognition of the understanding.

Proposition 32
Will cannot be called a free cause, but only a necessary cause.

Proof Will, like intellect, is only a definite mode of thinking, and so (Pr. 28) no single volition can exist or be determined to act unless it is determined by another cause, and this cause again by another, and so ad infinitum. Now if will be supposed infinite, it must also be determined to exist and to act by God, not insofar as he is absolutely infinite substance, but insofar as he possesses an attribute which expresses the infinite and eternal essence of Thought (Pr. 23). Therefore, in whatever way will is conceived, whether finite or infinite, it requires a cause by which it is determined to exist and to act; and so (Def. 7) it cannot be said to be a free cause, but only a necessary or constrained cause.

Corollary 1 Hence it follows, firstly, that God does not act from freedom of will.

Corollary 2 It follows, secondly, that will and intellect bear the same relationship to God's nature as motion-and-rest and, absolutely, as all natural phenomena that must be determined by God (Pr. 29) to exist and to act in a definite way. For will, like all the rest, stands in need of a cause by which it may be determined to exist and to act in a definite manner. And although from a given will or intellect infinite things may follow, God cannot on that account be said to act from freedom of will any more than he can be said to act from freedom of motion-and-rest because of what follows from motion-and-rest (for from this, too, infinite things follow). Therefore, will pertains to God's nature no more than do other natural phenomena. It bears the same relationship to God's nature as does motion-and-rest and everything else that we have shown to follow from the necessity of the divine nature and to be determined by that divine nature to exist and to act in a definite way.

Proposition 33
Things could not have been produced by God in any other way or in any other order than is the case.

Proof All things have necessarily followed from the nature of God (Pr. 16) and have been determined to exist and to act in a definite way from the necessity of God's nature (Pr. 29). Therefore, if things could have been of a different nature or been determined to act in a different way so that the order of Nature would have been different, then God's nature, too, could have been other than it now is, and therefore (Pr. 11) this different nature, too, would have had to exist, and consequently there would have been two or more Gods, which (Cor. 1 Pr. 14) is absurd. Therefore, things could not have been produced by God in any other way or in any other order than is the case.

Scholium 1 Since I have here shown more clearly than the midday sun that in things there is absolutely nothing by virtue of which they can be said to be "contingent," I now wish to explain briefly what we should understand by "contingent"; but I must first deal with "necessary" and "impossible." A thing is termed "necessary" either by reason of its essence or by reason of its cause. For a thing's existence necessarily follows either from its essence and definition or from a given efficient cause. Again, it is for these same reasons that a thing is termed "impossible"—that is, either because its essence or definition involves a contradiction or because there is no external cause determined to bring it into existence. But a thing is termed "contingent" for no other reason than the deficiency of our knowledge. For if we do not know whether the essence of a thing involves a contradiction, or if, knowing full well that its essence does not involve a contradiction, we still cannot make any certain judgment as to its existence because the chain of causes is hidden from us, then that thing cannot appear to us either as necessary or as impossible. So we term it either "contingent" or "possible."

Scholium 2 It clearly follows from the above that things have been brought into being by God with supreme perfection, since they have necessarily followed from a most perfect nature. Nor does this imply any imperfection in God, for it is his perfection that has constrained us to make this affirmation. Indeed, from its contrary it would clearly follow (as I have just shown) that God is not supremely perfect, because if things had been brought into being in a different way by God, we should have to attribute to God another nature different from that which consideration of a most perfect Being has made us attribute to him.

However, I doubt not that many will ridicule this view as absurd and will not give their minds to its examination, and for this reason alone, that they are in the habit of attributing to God another kind of freedom very different from that which we (Def. 7) have assigned to him, that is, an absolute will. Yet I do not doubt that if they were willing to think the matter over and carefully reflect on our chain of proofs they would in the end reject the kind of freedom which they now attribute to God not only as nonsensical but as a serious obstacle to science. It is needless for me here to repeat what was said in the Scholium to Proposition 17. Yet for their sake I shall proceed to show that, even if it were to be granted that will pertains to the essence of God, it would nevertheless follow from his perfection that things could not have been created by God in any other way or in any other order. This will readily be shown if we first consider—as they themselves grant—

that on God's decree and will alone does it depend that each thing is what it is. For otherwise God would not be the cause of all things. Further, there is the fact that all God's decrees have been sanctioned by God from eternity, for otherwise he could be accused of imperfection and inconstancy. But since the eternal does not admit of "when" or "before" or "after," it follows merely from God's perfection that God can never decree otherwise nor ever could have decreed otherwise; in other words, God could not have been prior to his decrees nor can he be without them. "But," they will say, "granted the supposition that God had made a different universe, or that from eternity he had made a different decree concerning Nature and her order, no imperfection in God would follow therefrom." But if they say this, they will be granting at the same time that God can change his decrees. For if God's decrees had been different from what in fact he has decreed regarding Nature and her order—that is, if he had willed and conceived differently concerning Nature—he would necessarily have had a different intellect and a different will from that which he now has. And if it is permissible to attribute to God a different intellect and a different will without any change in his essence and perfection, why should he not now be able to change his decrees concerning created things, and nevertheless remain equally perfect? For his intellect and will regarding created things and their order have the same relation to his essence and perfection, in whatever manner it be conceived.

Then again, all philosophers whom I have read grant that in God there is no intellect in potentiality but only intellect in act. Now since all of them also grant that his intellect and will are not distinct from his essence, it therefore follows from this, too, that if God had had a different intellect in act and a different will, his essence too would necessarily have been different. Therefore—as I deduced from the beginning—if things had been brought into being by God so as to be different from what they now are, God's intellect and will—that is (as is granted), God's essence—must have been different, which is absurd. Therefore, since things could not have been brought into being by God in any other way or order—and it follows from God's supreme perfection that this is true—surely we can have no sound reason for believing that God did not wish to create all the things that are in his intellect through that very same perfection whereby he understands them.

"But," they will say, "there is in things no perfection or imperfection; that which is in them whereby they are perfect or imperfect, and are called good or bad, depends only on the will of God. Accordingly, if God had so willed it he could have brought it about that that which is now perfection should be utmost imperfection, and vice versa." But what else is this but an open assertion that God, who necessarily understands that which he wills, can by his will bring it about that he should understand things in a way different from the way he understands them—and this, as I have just shown, is utterly absurd. So I can turn their own argument against them, as follows. All things depend on the power of God. For things to be able to be otherwise than as they are, God's will, too, would necessarily have to be different. But God's will cannot be different (as we have just shown most clearly from the consideration of God's perfection). Therefore, neither can things be different.

I admit that this view which subjects everything to some kind of indifferent will of God and asserts that everything depends on his pleasure diverges less from the truth than the view of those who hold that God does everything with the good in mind. For these people seem to posit something external to God that does not depend upon him, to which in acting God looks as if it were a model, or to which he aims, as if it were a fixed target. This is surely to subject God to fate; and no more absurd assertion can be made about God, whom we have shown to be the first and the only free cause of both the essence and the existence of things. So I need not spend any more time in refuting this absurdity.

Proposition 34
God's power is his very essence.

Proof From the sole necessity of God's essence it follows that God is self-caused (Pr. 11) and the cause of all things (Pr. 16 and Cor.). Therefore, God's power, whereby he and all things are and act, is his very essence.

Proposition 35
Whatever we conceive to be within God's power necessarily exists.

Proof Whatever is within God's power must be so comprehended in his essence (Pr. 34) that it follows necessarily from it, and thus necessarily exists.

Proposition 36
Nothing exists from whose nature an effect does not follow.

Proof Whatever exists expresses God's nature or essence in a definite and determinate way (Cor. Pr. 25); that is (Pr. 34), whatever exists expresses God's power, which is the cause of all things, in a definite and determinate way, and so (Pr. 16) some effect must follow from it.

Appendix

I have now explained the nature and properties of God: that he necessarily exists, that he is one alone, that he is and acts solely from the necessity of his own nature, that he is the free cause of all things and how so, that all things are in God and are so dependent on him that they can neither be nor be conceived without him, and lastly, that all things have been predetermined by God, not from his free will or absolute pleasure, but from the absolute nature of God, his infinite power. Furthermore, whenever the opportunity arose I have striven to remove prejudices that might hinder the apprehension of my proofs. But since there still remain a considerable number of prejudices, which have been, and still are, an obstacle—indeed, a very great obstacle—to the acceptance of the concatenation of things in the manner which I have expounded, I have thought it proper at this point to bring these prejudices before the bar of reason.

Now all the prejudices which I intend to mention here turn on this one point, the widespread belief among men that all things in Nature are like themselves in acting with an end in view. Indeed, they hold it as certain that God himself directs everything to a fixed end; for they say that God has made everything for man's sake and has made man so that he should worship God. So this is the first point I shall consider, seeking the reason why most people are victims of this prejudice and why all are so naturally disposed to accept it. Secondly, I shall demonstrate its falsity; and lastly I shall show how it has been the source of misconceptions about good and bad, right and wrong, praise and blame, order and confusion, beauty and ugliness, and the like.

However, it is not appropriate here to demonstrate the origin of these misconceptions from the nature of the human mind. It will suffice at this point if I take as my basis what must be universally admitted, that all men are born ignorant of the causes of things, that they all have a desire to seek their own advantage, a desire of which they are conscious. From this it follows, firstly, that men believe that they are free, precisely because they are conscious of their volitions and desires; yet concerning the causes that have determined them to desire and will they do not think, not even dream about, because they are ignorant of them. Secondly, men act always with an end in view, to wit, the advantage that they seek. Hence it happens that they are always looking only for the final causes of things done, and are satisfied when they find them, having, of course, no reason for further doubt. But if they fail to discover them from some external source, they have no recourse but to turn to themselves, and to reflect on what ends would normally determine them to similar actions, and so they necessarily judge other minds by their own. Further, since they find within themselves and outside themselves a considerable number of means very convenient for the pursuit of their own advantage—as, for instance, eyes for seeing, teeth for chewing, cereals and living creatures for food, the sun for giving light, the sea for breeding fish—the result is that they look on all the things of Nature as means to their own advantage. And realizing that these were found, not produced by them, they come to believe that there is someone else who produced these means for their use. For looking on things as means, they could not believe them to be self-created, but on the analogy of the means which they are accustomed to produce for themselves, they were bound to conclude that there was some governor or governors of Nature, endowed with human freedom, who have attended to all their needs and made everything for their use. And having no information on the subject, they also had to estimate the character of these rulers by their own, and so they asserted that the gods direct everything for man's use so that they may bind men to them and be held in the highest honor by them. So it came about that every individual devised different methods of worshipping God as he thought fit in order that God should love him beyond others and direct the whole of Nature so as to serve his blind cupidity and insatiable greed. Thus it was that this misconception developed into superstition and became deep-rooted in the minds of men, and it was for this reason that every man strove most earnestly to understand and to explain the final causes of all things. But in seeking to show that Nature does nothing in vain—that is, nothing that is not to man's advantage—they seem to have shown only this, that Nature and the gods are as crazy as mankind.

Consider, I pray, what has been the upshot. Among so many of Nature's blessings they were bound to discover quite a number of disasters, such as storms, earthquakes, diseases and so forth, and they maintained that these occurred because the gods were angry at the wrongs done to them by men, or the faults committed in the course of their worship. And although daily experience cried out against this and showed by any number of examples that blessings and disasters befall the godly and the ungodly alike without discrimination, they did not on that account abandon their ingrained prejudice. For they found it easier to regard this fact as one among other mysteries they could not understand and thus maintain their innate condition of ignorance rather than to demolish in its entirety the theory they had constructed and devise a new one. Hence they made it axiomatic that the judgment of the gods is far beyond man's understanding. Indeed, it is for this reason, and this reason only, that truth might have evaded mankind forever had not Mathematics, which is concerned not with ends but only with the essences and properties of figures, revealed to men a different standard of truth. And there are other causes too—there is no need to mention them here—which could have made men aware of these widespread misconceptions and brought them to a true knowledge of things.

I have thus sufficiently dealt with my first point. There is no need to spend time in going on to show that Nature has no fixed goal and that all final causes are but figments of the human imagination. For I think that this is now quite evident, both from the basic causes from which I have traced the origin of this misconception and from Proposition 16 and the Corollaries to Proposition 32, and in addition from the whole set or proofs I have adduced to show that all things in Nature proceed from all eternal necessity and with supreme perfection. But I will make this additional point, that this doctrine of Final Causes turns Nature completely upside down, for it regards as an effect that which is in fact a cause, and vice versa. Again, it makes that which is by nature first to be last; and finally, that which is highest and most perfect is held to be the most imperfect. Omitting the first two points as self-evident, Propositions 21, 22, and 23 make it clear that that effect is most perfect which is directly produced by God, and an effect is the less perfect in proportion to the number of intermediary causes required for its production. But if the things produced directly by God were brought about to enable him to attain an end, then of necessity the last things for the sake of which the earlier things were brought about would excel all others. Again, this doctrine negates God's perfection; for if God acts with an end in view, he must necessarily be seeking something that he lacks. And although theologians and metaphysicians may draw a distinction between a purpose arising from want and an assimilative purpose,[2] they still admit that God has acted in all things for the sake of himself, and

---

[2] [Spinoza alludes here to a late scholastic distinction between two kinds of purposes, or goals: (1) a purpose that satisfies some internal need or lack (*fines indigentiae*); and (2) a purpose that aims to share what one already has with others who lack it (*fines assimilationis*). In the present case, this

not for the sake of the things to be created. For prior to creation they are not able to point to anything but God as a purpose for God's action. Thus they have to admit that God lacked and desired those things for the procurement of which he willed to create the means—as is self-evident.

I must not fail to mention here that the advocates of this doctrine, eager to display their talent in assigning purpose to things, have introduced a new style of argument to prove their doctrine, i.e., a reduction, not to the impossible, but to ignorance, thus revealing the lack of any other argument in its favor. For example, if a stone falls from the roof on somebody's head and kills him, by this method of arguing they will prove that the stone fell in order to kill the man; for if it had not fallen for this purpose by the will of God, how could so many circumstances (and there are often many coinciding circumstances) have chanced to concur? Perhaps you will reply that the event occurred because the wind was blowing and the man was walking that way. But they will persist in asking why the wind blew at that time and why the man was walking that way at that very time. If you again reply that the wind sprang up at that time because on the previous day the sea had begun to toss after a period of calm and that the man had been invited by a friend, they will again persist—for there is no end to questions—"But why did the sea toss, and why was the man invited for that time?" And so they will go on and on asking the causes of causes, until you take refuge in the will of God—that is, the sanctuary of ignorance. Similarly, when they consider the structure of the human body, they are astonished, and being ignorant of the causes of such skillful work they conclude that it is fashioned not by mechanical art but by divine or supernatural art, and is so arranged that no one part shall injure another.

As a result, he who seeks the true causes of miracles and is eager to understand the works of Nature as a scholar, and not just to gape at them like a fool, is universally considered an impious heretic and denounced by those to whom the common people bow down as interpreters of Nature and the gods. For these people know that the dispelling of ignorance would entail the disappearance of that astonishment, which is the one and only support for their argument and for safeguarding their authority. But I will leave this subject and proceed to the third point that I proposed to deal with.

When men become convinced that everything that is created is created on their behalf, they were bound to consider as the most important quality in every individual thing that which was most useful to them, and to regard as of the highest excellence all those things by which they were most benefited. Hence they came to form these abstract notions to explain the natures of things: Good, Bad,

---

distinction implies that when God does something purposively, he acts not to fulfill a need he has, but to benefit creatures. In their commentaries on the *Ethics*, both Lewis Robinson and Harry Wolfson refer to the seventeenth-century Dutch theologian A. Heereboord as Spinoza's source for this distinction (L. Robinson, *Kommentar zu Spinozas Ethik* (Leipzig, 1928), pp. 234–235; H. Wolfson, *The Philosophy of Spinoza* (New York, 1969), vol. 1, p. 432).

The theologians derided by Spinoza hoped to avoid by means of this distinction the suggestion that if God acts purposively, he does so because of a need on his part.]

Order, Confusion, Hot, Cold, Beauty, Ugliness; and since they believed that they are free, the following abstract notions came into being: Praise, Blame, Right, Wrong. The latter I shall deal with later on after I have treated of human nature; at this point I shall briefly explain the former.

All that conduces to well-being and to the worship of God they call Good, and the contrary, Bad. And since those who do not understand the nature of things, but only imagine things, make no affirmative judgments about things themselves and mistake their imagination for intellect, they are firmly convinced that there is order in things, ignorant as they are of things and of their own nature. For when things are in such arrangement that, being presented to us through our senses, we can readily picture them and thus readily remember them, we say that they are well arranged; if the contrary, we say that they are ill arranged, or confused. And since those things we can readily picture we find pleasing compared with other things, men prefer order to confusion, as though order were something in Nature other than what is relative to our imagination. And they say that God has created all things in an orderly way, without realizing that they are thus attributing human imagination to God—unless perchance they mean that God, out of consideration for the human imagination, arranged all things in the way that men could most easily imagine. And perhaps they will find no obstacle in the fact that there are any number of things that far surpass our imagination, and a considerable number that confuse the imagination because of its weakness.

But I have devoted enough time to this. Other notions, too, are nothing but modes of imagining whereby the imagination is affected in various ways, and yet the ignorant consider them as important attributes of things because they believe—as I have said—that all things were made on their behalf, and they call a thing's nature good or bad, healthy or rotten and corrupt, according to its effect on them. For instance, if the motion communicated to our nervous system by objects presented through our eyes is conducive to our feeling of well-being, the objects which are its cause are said to be beautiful, while the objects which provoke a contrary motion are called ugly. Those things that we sense through the nose are called fragrant or fetid; through the tongue, sweet or bitter, tasty or tasteless; those that we sense by touch are called hard or soft, rough or smooth, and so on. Finally, those that we sense through our ears are said to give forth noise, sound, or harmony, the last of which has driven men to such madness that they used to believe that even God delights in harmony. There are philosophers who have convinced themselves that the motions of the heavens give rise to harmony. All this goes to show that everyone's judgment is a function of the disposition of his brain, or rather, that he mistakes for reality the way his imagination is affected. Hence it is no wonder—as we should note in passing—that we find so many controversies arising among men, resulting finally in skepticism. For although human bodies agree in many respects, there are very many differences, and so one man thinks good what another thinks bad; what to one man is well ordered, to another is confused; what to one is pleasing, to another is displeasing, and so forth. I say no more here because this is not the place to treat at length of this subject, and also because all are well acquainted with it from experience. Everybody knows those sayings: "So many heads, so many opinions," "everyone is wise in his own sight," "brains differ as much as palates," all of which show clearly that men's judgment is a function of the disposition of the brain, and they are guided by imagination rather than intellect. For if men understood things, all that I have put forward would be found, if not attractive, at any rate convincing, as Mathematics attests.

We see therefore that all the notions whereby the common people are wont to explain Nature are merely modes of imagining, and denote not the nature of anything but only the constitution of the imagination. And because these notions have names as if they were the names of entities existing independently of the imagination I call them "entities of imagination" [*entia imaginationis*] rather than "entities of reason" [*entia rationis*]. So all arguments drawn from such notions against me can be easily refuted. For many are wont to argue on the following lines: If everything has followed from the necessity of God's most perfect nature, why does Nature display so many imperfections, such as rottenness to the point of putridity, nauseating ugliness, confusion, evil, sin, and so on? But, as I have just pointed out, they are easily refuted. For the perfection of things should be measured solely from their own nature and power; nor are things more or less perfect to the extent that they please or offend human senses, serve or oppose human interests. As to those who ask why God did not create men in such a way that they should be governed solely by reason, I make only this reply, that he lacked not material for creating all things from the highest to the lowest degree of perfection; or, to speak more accurately, the laws of his nature were so comprehensive as to suffice for the production of everything that can be conceived by an infinite intellect, as I proved in Proposition 16.

These are the misconceptions which I undertook to deal with at this point. Any other misconception of this kind can be corrected by everyone with a little reflection.

PART II

OF THE NATURE AND ORIGIN OF THE MIND

I now pass on to the explication of those things that must necessarily have followed from the essence of God, the eternal and infinite Being; not indeed all of them — for we proved in Proposition 16, Part I that from his essence there must follow infinite things in infinite ways — but only those things that can lead us as it were by the hand to the knowledge of the human mind and its utmost blessedness.

Definitions

1. By "body" I understand a mode that expresses in a definite and determinate way God's essence insofar as he is considered as an extended thing. (See Cor. Pr. 25, I.)
2. I say that there pertains to the essence of a thing that which, when granted, the thing is necessarily posited, and by the annulling of which the thing is necessarily annulled; or that without which the thing can neither be nor be conceived, and, vice versa, that which cannot be or be conceived without the thing.
3. By idea I understand a conception of the Mind which the Mind forms because it is a thinking thing.

Explication I say "conception" rather than "perception" because the term perception seems to indicate that the Mind is passive to its object whereas conception seems to express an activity of the Mind.

4. By an adequate idea I mean an idea which, insofar as it is considered in itself without relation to its object, has all the properties, that is, intrinsic characteristics, of a true idea [*ideatum*].

Explication I say "intrinsic" so as to exclude the extrinsic characteristic—to wit the agreement of the idea with that of which it is an idea.

5. Duration is the indefinite continuance of existing.

Explication I say "indefinite" because it can in no wise be determined through the nature of the existing thing, nor again by the thing's efficient cause which necessarily posits, but does not annul, the existence of the thing.

6. By reality and perfection I mean the same thing.
7. By individual things [*res singulares*] I mean things that are finite and have a determinate existence. If several individual things concur in one act in such a way as to be all together the simultaneous cause of one effect, I consider them all, in that respect, as one individual.

Axioms

1. The essence of man does not involve necessary existence; that is, from the order of Nature it is equally possible that a certain man exists or does not exist.
2. Man thinks.
3. Modes of thinking such as love, desire, or whatever emotions are designated by name, do not occur unless there is in the same individual the idea of the thing loved, desired, etc. But the idea can be without any other mode of thinking.
4. We feel a certain body to be affected in many ways.
5. We do not feel or perceive any individual things except bodies and modes of thinking. [N.B.: For Postulates, see after Proposition 13.]

Proposition 1
Thought is an attribute of God; i.e., God is a thinking thing.

Proof Individual thoughts, or this and that thought, are modes expressing the nature of God in a definite and determinate way (Cor. Pr. 25, I). Therefore, there belongs to God (Def. 5, I) an attribute the conception of which is involved in all individual thoughts, and through which they are conceived. Thought, therefore, is one of God's infinite attributes, expressing the eternal and infinite essence of God (Def. 6, I); that is, God is a thinking thing.

Scholium This Proposition is also evident from the fact that we can conceive of an infinite thinking being. For the more things a thinking being can think, the more reality or perfection we conceive it to have. Therefore, a being that can think infinite things in infinite ways is by virtue of its thinking necessarily infinite. Since therefore by merely considering Thought we conceive an infinite being, Thought is necessarily one of the infinite attributes of God (Defs. 4 and 6, I), as we set out to prove.

Proposition 2
Extension is an attribute of God; i.e., God is an extended thing.

Proof This Proposition is proved in the same way as the preceding proposition.

Proposition 3
In God there is necessarily the idea both of his essence and of everything that necessarily follows from his essence.

Proof For God can (Pr. 1, II) think infinite things in infinite ways, or (what is the same thing, by Pr. 16, I) can form the idea of his own essence and of everything that necessarily follows from it. But all that is in God's power necessarily exists (Pr. 35, I). Therefore, such an idea necessarily exists, and only in God (Pr. 15, I).

Scholium By God's power the common people understand free will and God's right over all things that are, which things are therefore commonly considered as contingent. They say that God has power to destroy everything and bring it to nothing. Furthermore, they frequently compare God's power with that of kings. But this doctrine we have refuted in Cors. 1 and 2, Pr. 32, I; and in Pr. 16, I, we proved that God acts by the same necessity whereby he understands himself; that is, just as it follows from the necessity of the divine Nature (as is universally agreed) that God understands himself, by that same necessity it also follows that God acts infinitely in infinite ways. Again, we showed in Pr. 34, I that God's power is nothing but God's essence in action, and so it is as impossible for us to conceive that God does not act as that God does not exist. Furthermore if one wished to pursue the matter, I could easily show here that the power that common people assign to God is not only a human power (which shows that they conceive God as a man or like a man) but also involves negation of power. But I am reluctant to hold forth so often on the same subject. I merely request the reader most earnestly to reflect again and again on what we said on this subject in Part I from Proposition 16 to the end. For nobody will rightly apprehend what I am trying to say unless he takes great care not to confuse God's power with a king's human power or right.

Proposition 4
The idea of God, from which infinite things follow in infinite ways, must be one, and one only.

Proof Infinite intellect comprehends nothing but the attributes of God and his affections (Pr. 30, I). But God is one, and one only (Cor. 1, Pr. 14, I). Therefore, the idea of God, from which infinite things follow in infinite ways, must be one, and one only.

Proposition 5
The formal being[1] of ideas recognizes God as its cause only insofar as he is considered as a thinking thing, and not insofar as he is explicated by any other attribute; that is, the ideas both of God's attributes and of individual things recognize as their efficient cause not the things of which they are ideas, that is, the things perceived, but God himself insofar as he is a thinking thing.

Proof This is evident from Pr. 3, II. For there our conclusion that God can form the idea of his own essence and of everything that necessarily follows therefrom was inferred solely from God's being a thinking thing, and not from his being the object of his own idea. Therefore, the formal being of ideas recognizes God as its cause insofar as he is a thinking thing. But there is another proof, as follows. The formal being of ideas is a mode of thinking (as is self-evident); that is (Cor. Pr. 25, I), a mode which expresses in a definite manner the nature of God insofar as he is a thinking thing, and so does not involve (Pr. 10, I) the conception of any other attribute of God. Consequently (Ax. 4, I), it is the effect of no other attribute but thought; and so the formal being of ideas recognizes God as its cause only insofar as he is considered as a thinking thing.

Proposition 6
The modes of any attribute have God for their cause only insofar as he is considered under that attribute, and not insofar as he is considered under any other attribute.

Proof Each attribute is conceived through itself independently of any other (Pr. 10, I). Therefore, the modes of any attribute involve the conception of their own attribute, and not that of any other. Therefore, they have God for their cause only insofar as he is considered under the attribute of which they are modes, and not insofar as he is considered under any other attribute (Ax. 4, I).

Corollary Hence it follows that the formal being of things that are not modes of thinking does not follow from the nature of God by reason of his first having

---

[1] [I.e., their existence as ideas.—M.L.M.]

known them; rather, the objects of ideas follow and are inferred from their own attributes in the same way and by the same necessity as we have shown ideas to follow from the attribute of Thought.

Proposition 7
The order and connection of ideas is the same as the order and connection of things.

Proof   This is evident from Ax. 4, I; for the idea of what is caused depends on the knowledge of the cause of which it is the effect.

Corollary   Hence it follows that God's power of thinking is on par with his power of acting. That is, whatever follows formally from the infinite nature of God, all this follows from the idea of God as an object of thought in God according to the same order and connection.

Scholium   At this point, before proceeding further, we should recall to mind what I have demonstrated above—that whatever can be perceived by infinite intellect as constituting the essence of substance pertains entirely to the one sole substance. Consequently, thinking substance and extended substance are one and the same substance, comprehended now under this attribute, now under that. So, too, a mode of Extension and the idea of that mode are one and the same thing, expressed in two ways. This truth seems to have been glimpsed by some of the Hebrews,[2] who hold that God, God's intellect, and the things understood by God are one and the same. For example, a circle existing in Nature and the idea of the existing circle—which is also in God—are one and the same thing, explicated through different attributes. And so, whether we conceive Nature under the attribute of Extension or under the attribute of Thought or under any other attribute, we find one and the same order, or one and the same connection of causes—that is, the same things following one another. When I said that God is the cause, e.g., of the idea of a circle only insofar as he is a thinking thing, and of a circle only insofar as he is an extended thing, my reason was simply this, that the formal being of the idea of a circle can be perceived only through another mode of thinking as its proximate cause, and that mode through another, and so ad infinitum, with the result that as long as things are considered as modes of thought, we must explicate the order of the whole of Nature, or the connection of causes, through the attribute of Thought alone; and insofar as things are considered as modes of Extension, again the order of the whole of Nature must be explicated through the attribute of Extension only. The same applies to other attributes. Therefore God, insofar as he consists of infinite attributes, is in fact the cause of things as they are in themselves. For the present, I cannot give a clearer explanation.

---

[2] [The reference is most likely to Moses Maimonides, *The Guide of the Perplexed*, Part 1, Chapter 68.—S.F.]

PROPOSITION 8

The ideas of nonexisting individual things or modes must be comprehended in the infinite idea of God in the same way as the formal essences of individual things or modes are contained in the attributes of God.

Proof This proposition is obvious from the preceding one, but may be understood more clearly from the preceding Scholium.

Corollary Hence it follows that as long as individual things do not exist except insofar as they are comprehended in the attributes of God, their being as objects of thought—that is, their ideas—do not exist except insofar as the infinite idea of God exists; and when individual things are said to exist not only insofar as they are comprehended in the attributes of God but also insofar as they are said to have duration, their ideas also will involve the existence through which they are said to have duration.

Scholium Should anyone want an example for a clearer understanding of this matter, I can think of none at all that would adequately explicate the point with which I am here dealing, for it has no parallel. Still, I shall try to illustrate it as best I can. The nature of a circle is such that the rectangles formed from the segments of its intersecting chords are equal. Hence an infinite number of equal rectangles are contained in a circle, but none of them can be said to exist except insofar as the circle exists, nor again can the idea of any one of these rectangles be said to exist except insofar as it is comprehended in the idea of the circle. Now of this infinite number of intersecting chords let two, E and D, exist. Now indeed their ideas also exist not only insofar as they are merely comprehended in the idea of the circle but also insofar as they involve the existence of those rectangles, with the result that they are distinguished from the other ideas of the other rectangles.

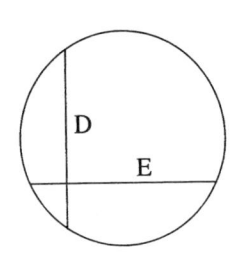

PROPOSITION 9

The idea of an individual thing existing in actuality has God for its cause not insofar as he is infinite but insofar as he is considered as affected by another idea of a thing existing in actuality, of which God is the cause insofar as he is affected by a third idea, and so ad infinitum.

Proof The idea of an individual actually existing thing is an individual mode of thinking distinct from other modes (Cor. and Sch. Pr. 8, II), and so (Pr. 6, II) it has God as its cause only insofar as he is a thinking thing. But not (Pr. 28, I) insofar as he is a thinking thing absolutely, but insofar as he is considered as affected by another definite mode of thinking. And of this latter God is also the cause insofar as he is affected by another definite mode of thinking, and so ad infinitum. But the order and connection of ideas is the same as the order and connection of causes (Pr. 7, II). Therefore, an individual idea is caused by another idea; i.e., God insofar as he is considered as affected by another idea. And this last idea is caused by God, insofar as he is affected by yet another idea, and so ad infinitum.

Corollary Whatsoever happens in the individual object of any idea, knowledge of it is in God only insofar as he has the idea of that object.

Proof Whatsoever happens in the object of any idea, the idea of it is in God (Pr. 3, II) not insofar as he is infinite, but insofar as he is considered as affected by another idea of an individual thing (preceding Pr.). But the order and connection of ideas is the same as the order and connection of things (Pr. 7, II). Therefore, the knowledge of what happens in an individual object is in God only insofar as he has the idea of that object.

Proposition 10
The being of substance does not pertain to the essence of man; i.e., substance does not constitute the form [forma] of man.

Proof The being of substance involves necessary existence (Pr. 7, I). So if the being of substance pertained to the essence of man, man would necessarily be granted together with the granting of substance (Def. 2, II) and consequently man would necessarily exist, which is absurd (Ax. 1, II). Therefore . . . etc.

Scholium This Proposition is also proved from Pr. 5, I, which states that there cannot be two substances of the same nature. Now since many men can exist, that which constitutes the form of man is not the being of substance. This Proposition is furthermore evident from the other properties of substance—that substance is by its own nature infinite, immutable, indivisible, etc., as everyone can easily see.

Corollary Hence it follows that the essence of man is constituted by definite modifications of the attributes of God.

Proof For the being of substance does not pertain to the essence of man (preceding Pr.), which must therefore be something that is in God, and which can neither be nor be conceived without God; i.e., an affection or mode (Cor. Pr. 25, I) which expresses the nature of God in a definite and determinate way.

Scholium All must surely admit that nothing can be or be conceived without God. For all are agreed that God is the sole cause of all things, both of their essence and of their existence; that is, God is the cause of things not only in respect of their coming into being [*secundum fieri*], as they say, but also in respect of their being. But at the same time many assert that that without which a thing can neither be nor be conceived pertains to the essence of the thing, and so they believe that either the nature of God pertains to the essence of created things or that created things can either be or be conceived without God; or else, more probably, they hold no consistent opinion. I think that the reason for this is their failure to observe the proper order of philosophical inquiry. For the divine nature, which they should have considered before all else—it being prior both in cognition and in

Nature—they have taken to be last in the order of cognition, and the things that are called objects of sense they have taken as prior to everything. Hence it has come about that in considering natural phenomena, they have completely disregarded the divine nature. And when thereafter they turned to the contemplation of the divine nature, they could find no place in their thinking for those fictions on which they had built their natural science, since these fictions were of no avail in attaining knowledge of the divine nature. So it is little wonder that they have contradicted themselves on all sides.

But I pass over these points, for my present purpose is restricted to explaining why I have not said that that without which a thing can neither be nor be perceived pertains to the essence of the thing. My reason is that individual things can neither be nor be conceived without God, and yet God does not pertain to their essence. But I did say that that necessarily constitutes the essence of a thing which, when posited, posits the thing, and by the annulling of which the thing is annulled; i.e., that without which the thing can neither be nor be conceived, and vice versa, that which can neither be nor be conceived without the thing.

Proposition 11
That which constitutes the actual being of the human mind is basically nothing else but the idea of an individual actually existing thing.

Proof The essence of man (Cor. Pr. 10, II) is constituted by definite modes of the attributes of God, to wit (Ax. 2, II), modes of thinking. Of all these modes the idea is prior in nature (Ax. 3, II), and when the idea is granted, the other modes—modes to which the idea is prior by nature—must be in the same individual (Ax. 3, II). And so the idea is that which basically constitutes the being of the human mind. But not the idea of a nonexisting thing; for then (Cor. Pr. 8, II) the idea itself could not be said to exist. Therefore, it is the idea of an actually existing thing. But not the idea of an infinite thing, for an infinite thing (Prs. 21 and 22, I) must always necessarily exist, and this is absurd (Ax. 1, II). Therefore, that which first constitutes the actual being of the human mind is the idea of an individual actually existing thing.

Corollary Hence it follows that the human mind is part of the infinite intellect of God; and therefore when we say that the human mind perceives this or that, we are saying nothing else but this: that God—not insofar as he is infinite but insofar as he is explicated through the nature of the human mind, that is, insofar as he constitutes the essence of the human mind—has this or that idea. And when we say that God has this or that idea not only insofar as he constitutes the essence of the human mind but also insofar as he has the idea of another thing simultaneously with the human mind, then we are saying that the human mind perceives a thing partially or inadequately.

Scholium At this point our readers will no doubt find themselves in some difficulty and will think of many things that will give them pause. So I ask them to proceed slowly step by step with me, and to postpone judgment until they have read to the end.

Proposition 12
Whatever happens in the object of the idea constituting the human mind is bound to be perceived by the human mind; i.e., the idea of that thing will necessarily be in the human mind. That is to say, if the object of the idea constituting the human mind is a body, nothing can happen in that body without its being perceived by the mind.

Proof Whatever happens in the object of any idea, knowledge thereof is necessarily in God (Cor. Pr. 9, II) insofar as he is considered as affected by the idea of that object; that is (Pr. 11, II), insofar as he constitutes the mind of something. So whatever happens in the object of the idea constituting the human mind, knowledge thereof is necessarily in God insofar as he constitutes the nature of the human mind; that is (Cor. Pr. 11, II), knowledge of that thing is necessarily in the mind; i.e., the mind perceives it.

Scholium This Proposition is also obvious, and is more clearly understood from Sch. Pr. 7, II, above.

Proposition 13
The object of the idea constituting the human mind is the body—i.e., a definite mode of extension actually existing, and nothing else.

Proof If the body were not the object of the human mind, the ideas of the affections of the body would not be in God (Cor. Pr. 9, II) insofar as he constitutes our mind, but insofar as he constitutes the mind of another thing; that is (Cor. Pr. 11, II), the ideas of the affections of the body would not be in our mind. But (Ax. 4, II) we do have ideas of the affections of a body. Therefore, the object of the idea constituting the human mind is a body, a body actually existing (Pr. 11, II). Again, if there were another object of the mind apart from the body, since nothing exists from which some effect does not follow (Pr. 36, I), there would necessarily have to be in our mind the idea of some effect of it (Pr. 12, II). But (Ax. 5, II) there is no such idea. Therefore, the object of our mind is an existing body, and nothing else.

Corollary Hence it follows that man consists of mind and body, and the human body exists according as we sense it.

Scholium From the above we understand not only that the human Mind is united to the Body but also what is to be understood by the union of Mind and Body. But nobody can understand this union adequately or distinctly unless he first gains adequate knowledge of the nature of our body. For what we have so far demonstrated is of quite general application, and applies to men no more than to other individuals, which are all animate, albeit in different degrees. For there is necessarily in God an idea of each thing whatever, of which idea God is the cause in the same way as he is the cause of the idea of the human body. And so whatever we have asserted of the idea of the human body must necessarily be asserted of the idea of each thing. Yet we cannot deny, too, that ideas differ among themselves as do their objects, and that one is more excellent and contains more reality than another, just as the object of one idea is more excellent than that of another and contains more reality. Therefore, in order to determine the difference between the human mind and others and in what way it surpasses them, we have to know the nature of its object (as we have said), that is, the nature of the human body. Now I cannot here explain this nature, nor is it essential for the points that I intend to demonstrate. But I will make this general assertion, that in proportion as a body is more apt than other bodies to act or be acted upon simultaneously in many ways, so is its mind more apt than other minds to perceive many things simultaneously; and in proportion as the actions of one body depend on itself alone and the less that other bodies concur with it in its actions, the more apt is its mind to understand distinctly. From this we can realize the superiority of one mind over others, and we can furthermore see why we have only a very confused knowledge of our body, and many other facts which I shall deduce from this basis in what follows. Therefore, I have thought it worthwhile to explicate and demonstrate these things more carefully. To this end there must be a brief preface concerning the nature of bodies.

Axiom 1   All bodies are either in motion or at rest.

Axiom 2   Each single body can move at varying speeds.

Lemma 1   Bodies are distinguished from one another in respect of motion-and-rest, quickness and slowness, and not in respect of substance.

Proof   The first part of this Lemma I take to be self-evident. As to bodies not being distinguished in respect of substance, this is evident from both Pr. 5 and Pr. 8, Part I, and still more clearly from Sch. Pr. 15, Part I.

Lemma 2   All bodies agree in certain respects.

Proof   All bodies agree in this, that they involve the conception of one and the same attribute (Def. 1, II), and also in that they may move at varying speeds, and may be absolutely in motion or absolutely at rest.

Lemma 3   A body in motion or at rest must have been determined to motion or rest by another body, which likewise has been determined to motion or rest by another body, and that body by another, and so ad infinitum.

Proof   Bodies are individual things (Def. 1, II) which are distinguished from one another in respect of motion-and-rest (Lemma 1), and so (Pr. 28, I) each body must have been determined to motion or rest by another individual thing, namely, another body (Pr. 6, II), which is also in motion or at rest (Ax. 1). But this body again—by the same reasoning—could not have been in motion or at rest unless it had been determined to motion or rest by another body, and this body again—by the same reasoning—by another body, and so on, ad infinitum.

Corollary   Hence it follows that a body in motion will continue to move until it is determined to rest by another body, and a body at rest continues to be at rest until it is determined to move by another body. This, too, is self-evident; for when I suppose, for example, that a body A is at rest and I give no consideration to other moving bodies, I can assert nothing about body A but that it is at rest. Now if it should thereafter happen that body A is in motion, this surely could not have resulted from the fact that it was at rest; for from that fact nothing else could have followed than that body A should be at rest. If on the other hand A were supposed to be in motion, as long as we consider only A, we can affirm nothing of it but that it is in motion. If it should thereafter happen that A should be at rest, this surely could not have resulted from its previous motion; for from its motion nothing else could have followed but that A was in motion. So this comes about from a thing that was not in A, namely, an external cause by which the moving body A was determined to rest.

Axiom 1   All the ways in which a body is affected by another body follow from the nature of the affected body together with the nature of the body affecting it, so that one and the same body may move in various ways in accordance with the various natures of the bodies causing its motion; and, on the other hand, different bodies may be caused to move in different ways by one and the same body.

Axiom 2   When a moving body collides with a body at rest and is unable to cause it to move, it is reflected so as to continue its motion, and the angle between the line of motion of the reflection and the plane of the body at rest with which it has collided is equal to the angle between the line of incidence of motion and the said plane.

So far we have been discussing the simplest bodies, those which are distinguished from one another solely by motion-and-rest, quickness and slowness. Now let us advance to composite bodies.

Definition   When a number of bodies of the same or different magnitude form close contact with one another through the pressure of other bodies upon them, or if they are moving at the same or different rates of speed so as to preserve an unvarying relation of movement among themselves, these bodies are said to be united with one another and all together to form one body or individual thing, which is distinguished from other things through this union of bodies.

Axiom 3   The degree of difficulty with which the parts of an individual thing or composite body can be made to change their position and consequently the degree of difficulty with which the individual takes on different shapes is proportional to the extent of the surface areas along which they are in close contact. Hence bodies whose parts maintain close contact along large areas of their surfaces I term hard; those whose parts maintain contact along small surface areas I term soft; while those whose parts are in a state of motion among themselves I term liquid.

Lemma 4 If from a body, or an individual thing composed of a number of bodies, certain bodies are separated, and at the same time a like number of other bodies of the same nature take their place, the individual thing will retain its nature as before, without any change in its form [*forma*].

Proof Bodies are not distinguished in respect of substance (Lemma 1). That which constitutes the form of the individual thing consists in a union of bodies (preceding definition). But this union, by hypothesis, is retained in spite of the continuous change of component bodies. Therefore, the individual thing will retain its own nature as before, both in respect of substance and of mode.

Lemma 5 If the parts of an individual thing become greater or smaller, but so proportionately that they all preserve the same mutual relation of motion-and-rest as before, the individual thing will likewise retain its own nature as before without any change in its form.

Proof The reasoning is the same as in the preceding Lemma.

Lemma 6 If certain bodies composing an individual thing are made to change the existing direction of their motion, but in such a way that they can continue their motion and keep the same mutual relation as before, the individual thing will likewise preserve its own nature without any change of form.

Proof This is evident; for, by hypothesis, the individual thing retains all that we, in defining it, asserted as constituting its form.

Lemma 7 Furthermore, the individual thing so composed retains its own nature, whether as a whole it is moving or at rest, and in whatever direction it moves, provided that each constituent part retains its own motion and continues to communicate this motion to the other parts.

Proof This is evident from its definition, which you will find preceding Lemma 4.

Scholium We thus see how a composite individual can be affected in many ways and yet preserve its nature. Now previously we have conceived an individual thing composed solely of bodies distinguished from one another only by motion-and-rest and speed of movement; that is, an individual thing composed of the simplest bodies. If we now conceive another individual thing composed of several individual things of different natures, we shall find that this can be affected in many other ways while still preserving its nature. For since each one of its parts is composed of several bodies, each single part can therefore (preceding Lemma), without any change in its nature, move with varying degrees of speed and consequently communicate its own motion to other parts with varying degrees of speed. Now if we go on to conceive a third kind of individual things composed of this second kind, we shall find that it can be affected in many other ways without any change in its form. If we thus continue to infinity, we shall readily conceive the whole of Nature as one individual whose parts—that is, all the constituent bodies—vary in infinite ways without any change in the individual as a whole.

If my intention had been to write a full treatise on body, I should have had to expand my explications and demonstrations. But I have already declared a different intention, and the only reason for my dealing with this subject is that I may readily deduce therefrom what I have set out to prove.

Postulates

1. The human body is composed of very many individual parts of different natures, each of which is extremely complex.
2. Of the individual components of the human body, some are liquid, some are soft, and some are hard.
3. The individual components of the human body, and consequently the human body itself, are affected by external bodies in a great many ways.
4. The human body needs for its preservation a great many other bodies, by which, as it were [*quasi*], it is continually regenerated.
5. When a liquid part of the human body is determined by an external body to impinge frequently on another part which is soft, it changes the surface of that part and impresses on it certain traces of the external body acting upon it.
6. The human body can move external bodies and dispose them in a great many ways.

PROPOSITION 14
The human mind is capable of perceiving a great many things, and this capacity will vary in proportion to the variety of states which its body can assume.

Proof The human body (Posts. 3 and 6) is affected by external bodies in a great many ways and is so structured that it can affect external bodies in a great many ways. But the human mind must perceive all that happens in the human body (Pr. 12, II). Therefore, the human mind is capable of perceiving very many things, and . . . etc.

PROPOSITION 15
The idea which constitutes the formal being of the human mind is not simple, but composed of very many ideas.

Proof The idea which constitutes the formal being of the human mind is the idea of the body (Pr. 13, II), which is composed of a great number of very composite individual parts (Postulate 1). But in God there is necessarily the idea of every individual component part (Cor. Pr. 8, II). Therefore (Pr. 7, II), the idea of the human body is composed of these many ideas of the component parts.

PROPOSITION 16

The idea of any mode wherein the human body is affected by external bodies must involve the nature of the human body together with the nature of the external body.

Proof All the modes wherein a body is affected follow from the nature of the body affected together with the nature of the affecting body (Ax. 1 after Cor. Lemma 3). Therefore, the idea of these modes will necessarily involve the nature of both bodies (Ax. 4, I). So the idea of any mode wherein the human body is affected by an external body involves the nature of the human body and the external body.

Corollary 1 Hence it follows that the human mind perceives the nature of very many bodies along with the nature of its own body.

Corollary 2 Secondly, the ideas that we have of external bodies indicate the constitution of our own body more than the nature of external bodies. This I have explained with many examples in Appendix, Part I.

PROPOSITION 17

If the human body is affected in a way [modo] *that involves the nature of some external body, the human mind will regard that same external body as actually existing, or as present to itself, until the human body undergoes a further modification which excludes the existence or presence of the said body.*

Proof This is evident; for as long as the human body is thus affected, so long will the human mind (Pr. 12, II) regard this affection of the body; that is (by the preceding Proposition), so long will it have the idea of a mode existing in actuality, an idea involving the nature of an external body; that is, an idea which does not exclude but posits the existence or presence of the nature of the external body. So the mind (Cor. 1 of the preceding proposition) will regard the external body as actually existing, or as present, until . . . etc.

Corollary The mind is able to regard as present external bodies by which the human body has been once affected, even if they do not exist and are not present.

Proof When external bodies so determine the fluid parts of the human body that these frequently impinge on the softer parts, they change the surfaces of these softer parts (Post. 5). Hence it comes about (Ax. 2 after Cor. Lemma 3) that the fluid parts are reflected therefrom in a manner different from what was previously the case; and thereafter, again coming into contact with the said changed surfaces in the course of their own spontaneous motion, they are reflected in the same way as when they were impelled toward those surfaces by external bodies. Consequently, in continuing this reflected motion they affect the human body in the same manner, which manner will again be the object of thought in the mind (Pr. 12, II); that is (Pr. 17, II), the mind will again regard the external body as present. This will be repeated whenever the fluid parts of the human body come into contact with those same surfaces in the course of their own spontaneous motion. Therefore, although the external bodies by which the human body has once been affected may no longer exist, the mind will regard them as present whenever this activity of the body is repeated.

Scholium   So we see how it comes about that we regard as present things which are not so, as often happens. Now it is possible that there are other causes for this fact, but it is enough for me at this point to have indicated one cause through which I can explicate the matter just as if I had demonstrated it through its true cause. Yet I do not think that I am far from the truth, since all the postulates that I have assumed contain scarcely anything inconsistent with experience; and after demonstrating that the human body exists just as we sense it (Cor. Pr. 13, II), we may not doubt experience.

In addition (preceding Cor. and Cor. 2 Pr. 16, II), this gives a clear understanding of the difference between the idea, e.g., of Peter which constitutes the essence of Peter's mind, and on the other hand the idea of Peter which is in another man, say Paul. The former directly explicates the essence of Peter's body, and does not involve existence except as long as Peter exists. The latter indicates the constitution of Paul's body rather than the nature of Peter; and so, while that constitution of Paul's body continues to be, Paul's mind will regard Peter as present to him although Peter may not be in existence. Further, to retain the usual terminology, we will assign the word "images" [*imagines*] to those affections of the human body the ideas of which set forth external bodies as if they were present to us, although they do not represent shapes. And when the mind regards bodies in this way, we shall say that it "imagines" [*imaginari*].

At this point, to begin my analysis of error, I should like you to note that the imaginations of the mind, looked at in themselves, contain no error; i.e., the mind does not err from the fact that it imagines, but only insofar as it is considered to lack the idea which excludes the existence of those things which it imagines to be present to itself. For if the mind, in imagining nonexisting things to be present to it, knew at the same time that those things did not exist in fact, it would surely impute this power of imagining not to the defect but to the strength of its own nature, especially if this faculty of imagining were to depend solely on its own nature; that is (Def. 7, I), if this faculty of imagining were free.

Proposition 18

If the human body has once been affected by two or more bodies at the same time, when the mind afterward imagines one of them, it will straightway remember the others too.

Proof   The mind imagines (preceding Cor.) any given body for the following reason, that the human body is affected and conditioned by the impressions of an external body in the same way as it was affected when certain of its parts were acted upon by the external body. But, by hypothesis, the human mind was at that time conditioned in such a way that the mind imagined two bodies at the same time. Therefore, it will now also imagine two bodies at the same time, and the mind, in imagining one of them, will straightway remember the other as well.

Scholium Hence we clearly understand what memory is. It is simply a linking of ideas involving the nature of things outside the human body, a linking which occurs in the mind parallel to the order and linking of the affections of the human body. I say, firstly, that it is only the linking of those ideas that involve the nature of things outside the human body, not of those ideas that explicate the nature of the said things. For they are in fact (Pr. 16, II) ideas of the affections of the human body which involve the nature both of the human body and of external bodies. Secondly, my purpose in saying that this linking occurs in accordance with the order and linking of the affections of the human body is to distinguish it from the linking of ideas in accordance with the order of the intellect whereby the mind perceives things through their first causes, and which is the same in all men.

Furthermore, from this we clearly understand why the mind, from thinking of one thing, should straightway pass on to thinking of another thing which has no likeness to the first. For example, from thinking of the word "pomum" [apple] a Roman will straightway fall to thinking of the fruit, which has no likeness to that articulated sound nor anything in common with it other than that the man's body has often been affected by them both; that is, the man has often heard the word "pomum" while seeing the fruit. So everyone will pass on from one thought to another according as habit in each case has arranged the images in his body. A soldier, for example, seeing the tracks of a horse in the sand will straightway pass on from thinking of the horse to thinking of the rider, and then thinking of war, and so on. But a peasant, from thinking of a horse, will pass on to thinking of a plough, and of a field, and so on. So every person will pass on from thinking of one thing to thinking of another according as he is in the habit of joining together and linking the images of things in various ways.

Proposition 19

The human mind has no knowledge of the body, nor does it know it to exist, except through ideas of the affections by which the body is affected.

Proof The human mind is the very idea or knowledge of the human body (Pr. 13, II), and this idea is in God (Pr. 9, II) insofar as he is considered as affected by another idea of a particular thing; or, since (Post. 4) the human body needs very many other bodies by which it is continually regenerated, and the order and connection of ideas is the same (Pr. 7, II) as the order and connection of causes, this idea is in God insofar as he is considered as affected by the ideas of numerous particular things. Therefore, God has the idea of the human body, or knows the human body, insofar as he is affected by numerous other ideas, and not insofar as he constitutes the nature of the human mind; that is (Cor. Pr. 11, II), the human mind does not know the human body. But the ideas of the affections of the body are in God insofar as he does constitute the nature of human mind; i.e., the human mind perceives these affections (Pr. 12, II) and consequently perceives the human body (Pr. 16, II), and perceives it as actually existing (Pr. 17, II). Therefore, it is only to that extent that the human mind perceives the human body.

Proposition 20

There is also in God the idea or knowledge of the human mind, and this follows in God and is related to God in the same way as the idea or knowledge of the human body.

Proof Thought is an attribute of God (Pr. 1, II), and so (Pr. 3, II) the idea of both Thought and its affections—and consequently of the human mind as well—must necessarily be in God. Now this idea or knowledge of the mind does not follow in God insofar as he is infinite, but insofar as he is affected by another idea of a particular thing (Pr. 9, II). But the order and connection of ideas is the same as the order and connection of causes (Pr. 7, II). Therefore, the idea or knowledge of the mind follows in God and is related to God in the same way as the idea or knowledge of the body.

Proposition 21

This idea of the mind is united to the mind in the same way as the mind is united to the body.

Proof That the mind is united to the body we have shown from the fact that the body is the object of the mind (Prs. 12 and 13, II), and so by the same reasoning the idea of the mind must be united to its object—that is, to the mind itself—in the same way as the mind is united to the body.

Scholium This proposition is understood far more clearly from Sch. Pr. 7, II. There we showed that the idea of the body and the body itself—that is (Pr. 13, II), mind and body—are one and the same individual thing, conceived now under the attribute of Thought and now under the attribute of Extension. Therefore, the idea of the mind and the mind itself are one and the same thing, conceived under one and the same attribute, namely, Thought. The idea of the mind, I repeat, and the mind itself follow in God by the same necessity and from the same power of thought. For in fact the idea of the mind—that is, the idea of an idea—is nothing other than the form [*forma*] of the idea insofar as the idea is considered as a mode of thinking without relation to its object. For as soon as anyone knows something, by that very fact he knows that he knows, and at the same time he knows that he knows that he knows, and so on ad infinitum. But I will deal with this subject later.

Proposition 22

The human mind perceives not only the affections of the body but also the ideas of these affections.

Proof The ideas of ideas of affections follow in God and are related to God in the same way as ideas of affections, which can be proved in the same manner as Pr. 20, II. But the ideas of affections of the body are in the human mind (Pr. 12, II); that is (Cor. Pr. 11, II), in God insofar as he constitutes the essence of the human mind. Therefore, the ideas of these ideas will be in God insofar as he has knowledge or the idea of the human mind; that is (Pr. 21, II), they will be in the human mind itself, which therefore perceives not only the affections of the body but also the ideas of these affections.

Proposition 23
The mind does not know itself except insofar as it perceives ideas of affections of the body.

Proof The idea or knowledge of the mind (Pr. 20, II) follows in God and is related to God in the same way as the idea or knowledge of the body. But since (Pr. 19, II) the human mind does not know the human body—that is (Cor. Pr. 11, II), since the knowledge of the human body is not related to God insofar as he constitutes the nature of the human mind—therefore, neither is knowledge of the mind related to God insofar as he constitutes the essence of the human mind. And so (Cor. Pr. 11, II) the human mind to that extent does not know itself. Again, the ideas of the affections by which the body is affected involve the nature of the human body (Pr. 16, II); that is (Pr. 13, II), they are in agreement [*conveniunt*] with the nature of the mind. Therefore, the knowledge of these ideas will necessarily involve knowledge of the mind. But (preceding Pr.) the knowledge of these ideas is in the human mind. Therefore, the human mind knows itself but only to that extent.

Proposition 24
The human mind does not involve an adequate knowledge of the component parts of the human body.

Proof The component parts of the human body do not pertain to the essence of the body itself save insofar as they preserve an unvarying relation of motion with one another (Def. after Cor. Lemma 3), and not insofar as they can be considered as individual things apart from their relation to the human body. For the parts of the human body (Post. 1) are very composite individual things, whose parts can be separated from the human body (Lemma 4) without impairing in any way its nature and specific reality [*forma*], and can establish a quite different relation of motion with other bodies (Ax. 1 after Lemma 3). Therefore (Pr. 3, II), the idea or knowledge of any component part will be in God, and will be so (Pr. 9, II) insofar as he is considered as affected by another idea of a particular thing, a particular thing which is prior in Nature's order to the part itself (Pr. 7, II). Further, the same holds good of any part of an individual component part of the human body, and so of any component part of the human body there is knowledge in God insofar as he is affected by very many ideas of things, and not insofar as he has the idea only of the human body, that is (Pr. 13, II), the idea that constitutes the nature of the human mind. So (Cor. Pr. 11, II) the human mind does not involve adequate knowledge of the component parts of the human body.

Proposition 25
The idea of any affection of the human body does not involve an adequate knowledge of an external body.

Proof We have shown that the idea of an affection of the human body involves the nature of an external body insofar as the external body determines the human body in some definite way (Pr. 16, II). But insofar as the external body is an individual thing that is not related to the human body, the idea or knowledge of it is in God (Pr. 9, II) insofar as God is considered as affected by the idea of another thing which is (Pr. 7, II) prior in nature to the said external body. Therefore, an adequate knowledge of the external body is not in God insofar as he has the idea of an affection of the human body; i.e., the idea of an affection of the human body does not involve an adequate knowledge of an external body.

Proposition 26
The human mind does not perceive any external body as actually existing except through the ideas of affections of its own body.

Proof If the human body is not affected in any way by an external body, then (Pr. 7, II) neither is the idea of the human body—that is (Pr. 13, II), the human mind—affected in any way by the idea of the existence of that body; i.e., it does not in any way perceive the existence of that external body. But insofar as the human body is affected in some way by an external body, to that extent it perceives the external body (Pr. 16, II, with Cor. 1).

Corollary Insofar as the human mind imagines [*imaginatur*] an external body, to that extent it does not have an adequate knowledge of it.

Proof When the human mind regards external bodies through the ideas of affections of its own body, we say that it imagines [*imaginatur*] (see Sch. Pr. 17, II), and in no other way can the mind imagine external bodies as actually existing (preceding Pr.). Therefore, insofar as the mind imagines external bodies (Pr. 25, II), it does not have adequate knowledge of them.

Proposition 27
The idea of any affection of the human body does not involve adequate knowledge of the human body.

Proof Any idea whatsoever of any affection of the human body involves the nature of the human body only to the extent that the human body is considered to be affected in some definite way (Pr. 16, II). But insofar as the human body is an individual thing that can be affected in many other ways, the idea . . . etc. (see Proof Pr. 25, II).

Proposition 28
The ideas of the affections of the human body, insofar as they are related only to the human mind, are not clear and distinct, but confused.

Proof The ideas of the affections of the human body involve the nature both of external bodies and of the human body itself (Pr. 16, II), and must involve the nature not only of the human body but also of its parts. For affections are modes in which parts of the human body (Post. 3), and consequently the body as a whole, are affected. But (Prs. 24 and 25, II) an adequate knowledge of external bodies, as also of the component parts of the human body, is not in God insofar as he is considered as affected by the human mind, but insofar as he is considered as affected by other ideas. Therefore, these ideas of affections, insofar as they are related only to the human mind, are like conclusions without premises; that is, as is self-evident, confused ideas.

Scholium The idea that constitutes the nature of the human mind is likewise shown, when considered solely in itself, not to be clear and distinct, as is also the idea of the human mind and the ideas of affections of the human body insofar as they are related only to the human mind, as everyone can easily see.

PROPOSITION 29
The idea of the idea of any affection of the human body does not involve adequate knowledge of the human mind.

Proof The idea of an affection of the human body (Pr. 27, II) does not involve adequate knowledge of the body itself; in other words, it does not adequately express the nature of the body; that is (Pr. 13, II), it does not adequately agree [*convenit*] with the nature of the mind. So (Ax. 6, I) the idea of this idea does not adequately express the nature of the human mind; i.e., it does not involve an adequate knowledge of it.

Corollary Hence it follows that whenever the human mind perceives things after the common order of nature, it does not have an adequate knowledge of itself, nor of its body, nor of external bodies, but only a confused and fragmentary knowledge. For the mind does not know itself save insofar as it perceives ideas of the affections of the body (Pr. 23, II). Now it does not perceive its own body (Pr. 19, II) except through ideas of affections of the body, and also it is only through these affections that it perceives external bodies (Pr. 26, II). So insofar as it has these ideas, it has adequate knowledge neither of itself (Pr. 29, II) nor of its own body (Pr. 27, II) nor of external bodies (Pr. 25, II), but only a fragmentary [*mutilatam*] and confused knowledge (Pr. 28, II and Sch.).

Scholium I say expressly that the mind does not have an adequate knowledge, but only a confused and fragmentary knowledge, of itself, its own body, and external bodies whenever it perceives things from the common order of nature, that is, whenever it is determined externally—namely, by the fortuitous run of circumstance—to regard this or that, and not when it is determined internally, through its regarding several things at the same time, to understand their agreement, their differences, and their opposition. For whenever it is conditioned internally in this or in another way, then it sees things clearly and distinctly, as I shall later show.

PROPOSITION 30
We can have only a very inadequate knowledge of the duration of our body.

Proof The duration of our body does not depend on its essence (Ax. 1, II), nor again on the absolute nature of God (Pr. 21, I), but (Pr. 28, I) it is determined to exist and to act by causes which are also determined by other causes to exist and to act in a definite and determinate way, and these again by other causes, and so ad infinitum. Therefore, the duration of our body depends on the common order of nature and the structure of the universe. Now there is in God adequate knowledge of the structure of the universe insofar as he has ideas of all the things in the universe, and not insofar as he has only the idea of the human body (Cor. Pr. 9, II). Therefore, knowledge of the duration of our body is very inadequate in God insofar as he is considered only to constitute the nature of the human mind. That is (Cor. Pr. 11, II), this knowledge is very inadequate in the human mind.

PROPOSITION 31
We can have only a very inadequate knowledge of the duration of particular things external to us.

Proof Each particular thing, just like the human body, must be determined by another particular thing to exist and to act in a definite and determinate way, and this latter thing again by another, and so on ad infinitum (Pr. 28, I). Now since we have shown in the preceding Proposition that from this common property of particular things we can have only a very inadequate knowledge of the duration of the human body, in the case of the duration of particular things we have to come to the same conclusion: that we can have only a very inadequate knowledge thereof.

Corollary Hence it follows that all particular things are contingent and perishable. For we can have no adequate knowledge of their duration (preceding Pr.), and that is what is to be understood by contingency and perishability (Sch. 1, Pr. 33, I). For apart from this there is no other kind of contingency (Pr. 29, I).

PROPOSITION 32
All ideas are true insofar as they are related to God.

Proof All ideas, which are in God, agree completely with the objects of which they are ideas (Cor. Pr. 7, II), and so they are all true (Ax. 6, I).

PROPOSITION 33
There is nothing positive in ideas whereby they can be said to be false.

Proof If this be denied, conceive, if possible, a positive mode of thinking which constitutes the form [*forma*] of error or falsity. This mode of thinking cannot be in God (preceding Pr.), but neither can it be or be conceived externally to God (Pr. 15, I). Thus there can be nothing positive in ideas whereby they can be called false.

PROPOSITION 34
Every idea which in us is absolute, that is, adequate and perfect, is true.

Proof When we say that there is in us an adequate and perfect idea, we are saying only this (Cor. Pr. 11, II), that there is adequate and perfect idea in God insofar as he constitutes the essence of our mind. Consequently, we are saying only this, that such an idea is true (Pr. 32, II).

Proposition 35

Falsity consists in the privation of knowledge which inadequate ideas, that is, fragmentary and confused ideas, involve.

Proof There is nothing positive in ideas which constitutes the form [*forma*] of falsity (Pr. 33, II). But falsity cannot consist in absolute privation (for minds, not bodies, are said to err and be deceived), nor again in absolute ignorance, for to be ignorant and to err are different. Therefore, it consists in that privation of knowledge which inadequate knowledge, that is, inadequate and confused ideas, involves.

Scholium In Sch. Pr. 17, II I explained how error consists in the privation of knowledge, but I will give an example to enlarge on this explanation. Men are deceived in thinking themselves free, a belief that consists only in this, that they are conscious of their actions and ignorant of the causes by which they are determined. Therefore, the idea of their freedom is simply the ignorance of the cause of their actions. As to their saying that human actions depend on the will, these are mere words without any corresponding idea. For none of them knows what the will is and how it moves the body, and those who boast otherwise and make up stories of dwelling places and habitations of the soul provoke either ridicule or disgust.

As another example, when we gaze at the sun, we see it as some two hundred feet distant from us. The error does not consist in simply seeing the sun in this way but in the fact that while we do so we are not aware of the true distance and the cause of our seeing it so. For although we may later become aware that the sun is more than six hundred times the diameter of the earth distant from us, we shall nevertheless continue to see it as close at hand. For it is not our ignorance of its true distance that causes us to see the sun to be so near; it is that the affection of our body involves the essence of the sun only to the extent that the body is affected by it.

Proposition 36

Inadequate and confused ideas follow by the same necessity as adequate, or clear and distinct, ideas.

Proof All ideas are in God (Pr. 15, I), and insofar as they are related to God, they are true (Pr. 32, II) and adequate (Cor. Pr. 7, II). So there are no inadequate or confused ideas except insofar as they are related to the particular mind of someone (see Prs. 24 and 28, II). So all ideas, both adequate and inadequate, follow by the same necessity (Cor. Pr. 6, II).

Proposition 37

That which is common to all things (see Lemma 2 above) and is equally in the part as in the whole does not constitute the essence of any one particular thing.

Proof If this is denied, conceive, if possible, that it does constitute the essence of one particular thing, B. Therefore, it can neither be nor be conceived without B (Def. 2, II). But this is contrary to our hypothesis. Therefore, it does not pertain to B's essence, nor does it constitute the essence of any other particular thing.

Proposition 38

Those things that are common to all things and are equally in the part as in the whole can be conceived only adequately.

Proof Let A be something common to all bodies, and equally in the part of any body as in the whole. I say that A can be conceived only adequately. For its idea (Cor. Pr. 7, II) will necessarily be in God both insofar as he has the idea of the human body and insofar as he has the ideas of affections of the human body, affections which partly involve the natures of both the human body and external bodies (Prs. 16, 25, and 27, II). That is (Prs. 12 and 13, II), this idea will necessarily be adequate in God insofar as he constitutes the human mind; that is, insofar as he has the ideas which are in the human mind. Therefore, the mind (Cor. Pr. 11, II) necessarily perceives A adequately, and does so both insofar as it perceives itself and insofar as it perceives its own body or any external body; nor can A be perceived in any other way.

Corollary Hence it follows that there are certain ideas or notions common to all men. For (by Lemma 2) all bodies agree in certain respects, which must be (preceding Pr.) conceived by all adequately, or clearly and distinctly.

Proposition 39

Of that which is common and proper to the human body and to any external bodies by which the human body is customarily affected, and which is equally in the part as well as in the whole of any of these bodies, the idea also in the mind will be adequate.

Proof Let A be that which is common and proper to the human body and to any external bodies and which is equally in the human body as in those same external bodies, and which is finally equally in the part of any external body as in the whole. There will be in God an adequate idea of A (Cor. Pr. 7, II) both insofar as he has the idea of the human body and insofar as he has ideas of those posited external bodies. Let it now be supposed that the human body is affected by an external body through that which is common to them both, that is, A. The idea of this affection will involve the property A (Pr. 16, II), and so (Cor. Pr. 7, II) the idea of this affection, insofar as it involves the property A, will be adequate in God insofar as he is affected by the idea of the human body; that is (Pr. 13, II), insofar as he constitutes the nature of the human mind. So this idea will also be adequate in the human mind (Cor. Pr. 11, II).

Corollary Hence it follows that the mind is more capable of perceiving more things adequately in proportion as its body has more things in common with other bodies.

PROPOSITION 40

Whatever ideas follow in the mind from ideas that are adequate in it are also adequate.

Proof This is evident. For when we say that an idea follows in the human mind from ideas that are adequate in it, we are saying no more than that there is in the divine intellect an idea of which God is the cause, not insofar as he is infinite nor insofar as he is affected by ideas of numerous particular things, but only insofar as he constitutes the essence of the human mind.

Scholium 1 I have here set forth the causes of those notions that are called "common," and which are the basis of our reasoning processes. Now certain axioms or notions have other causes which it would be relevant to set forth by this method of ours; for thus we could establish which notions are useful compared with others, and which are of scarcely any value. And again, we could establish which notions are common to all, which ones are clear and distinct only to those not laboring under prejudices [*praejudiciis*] and which ones are ill-founded. Furthermore, this would clarify the origin of those notions called "secondary"—and consequently the axioms which are based on them—as well as other related questions to which I have for some time given thought. But I have decided not to embark on these questions at this point because I have set them aside for another treatise,[3] and also to avoid wearying the reader with too lengthy a discussion of this subject. Nevertheless, to omit nothing that it is essential to know, I shall briefly deal with the question of the origin of the so-called "transcendental terms," such as "entity," "thing," "something" [*ens, res, aliquid*].

These terms originate in the following way. The human body, being limited, is capable of forming simultaneously in itself only a certain number of distinct images. (I have explained in Sch. Pr. 17, II what an image is.) If this number be exceeded, these images begin to be confused, and if the number of distinct images which the body is capable of forming simultaneously in itself be far exceeded, all the images will be utterly confused with one another. This being so, it is evident from Cor. Pr. 17 and Pr. 18, II that the human mind is able to imagine simultaneously and distinctly as many bodies as there are images that can be formed simultaneously in its body. But when the images in the body are utterly confused, the mind will also imagine all the bodies confusedly without any distinction, and will comprehend them, as it were, under one attribute, namely, that of entity, thing, etc. This conclusion can also be reached from the fact that images are not always equally vivid, and also from other causes analogous to these, which I need not here explicate. For it all comes down to this, that these terms signify ideas confused in the highest degree.

---

[3] [This is Spinoza's incomplete essay, *On the Improvement of the Understanding.*]

Again, from similar causes have arisen those notions called "universal," such as "man," "horse," "dog," etc.; that is to say, so many images are formed in the human body simultaneously (e.g., of man) that our capacity to imagine them is surpassed, not indeed completely, but to the extent that the mind is unable to imagine the unimportant differences of individuals (such as the complexion and stature of each, and their exact number) and imagines distinctly only their common characteristic insofar as the body is affected by them. For it was by this that the body was affected most repeatedly, by each single individual. The mind expresses this by the word "man," and predicates this word of an infinite number of individuals. For, as we said, it is unable to imagine the determinate number of individuals.

But it should be noted that not all men form these notions in the same way; in the case of each person the notions vary according as that thing varies whereby the body has more frequently been affected, and which the mind more readily imagines or calls to mind. For example, those who have more often regarded with admiration the stature of men will understand by the word "man" an animal of upright stature, while those who are wont to regard a different aspect will form a different common image of man, such as that man is a laughing animal, a featherless biped, or a rational animal. Similarly, with regard to other aspects, each will form universal images according to the conditioning of his body. Therefore, it is not surprising that so many controversies have arisen among philosophers who have sought to explain natural phenomena through merely the images of these phenomena.

Scholium 2   From all that has already been said it is quite clear that we perceive many things and form universal notions:

1. From individual objects presented to us through the senses in a fragmentary [*mutilate*] and confused manner without any intellectual order (see Cor. Pr. 29, II); and therefore I call such perceptions "knowledge from casual experience."

2. From symbols. For example, from having heard or read certain words we call things to mind and we form certain ideas of them similar to those through which we imagine things (Sch. Pr. 18, II).

Both these ways of regarding things I shall in future refer to as "knowledge of the first kind," "opinion," or "imagination."

3. From the fact that we have common notions and adequate ideas of the properties of things (see Cor. Pr. 38 and 39 with its Cor., and Pr. 40, II). I shall refer to this as "reason" and "knowledge of the second kind."

Apart from these two kinds of knowledge there is, as I shall later show, a third kind of knowledge, which I shall refer to as "intuition." This kind of knowledge proceeds from an adequate idea of the formal essence of certain attributes of God to an adequate knowledge of the essence of things. I shall illustrate all these kinds of knowledge by one single example. Three numbers are given; it is required to find a fourth which is related to the third as the second to the first. Tradesmen have no hesitation in multiplying the second by the third and dividing the product by the first, either because they have not yet forgotten the rule they learned without proof from their teachers, or because they have in fact found this correct in the case of very simple numbers, or else from the force of the proof of Proposition 19 of the Seventh Book of Euclid, to wit, the common property of proportionals. But in the case of very simple numbers, none of this is necessary. For example, in the case of the given numbers 1, 2, 3, everybody can see that the fourth proportional is 6, and all the more clearly because we infer in one single intuition the fourth number from the ratio we see the first number bears to the second.

Proposition 41
Knowledge of the first kind is the only cause of falsity; knowledge of the second and third kind is necessarily true.

Proof In the preceding Scholium we asserted that all those ideas which are inadequate and confused belong to the first kind of knowledge; and thus (Pr. 35, II) this knowledge is the only cause of falsity. Further, we asserted that to knowledge of the second and third kind there belong those ideas which are adequate. Therefore (Pr. 34, II), this knowledge is necessarily true.

Proposition 42
Knowledge of the second and third kind, and not knowledge of the first kind, teaches us to distinguish true from false.

Proof This Proposition is self-evident. For he who can distinguish the true from the false must have an adequate idea of the true and the false; that is (Sch. 2 Pr. 40, II), he must know the true and the false by the second or third kind of knowledge.

Proposition 43
He who has a true idea knows at the same time that he has a true idea, and cannot doubt its truth.

Proof A true idea in us is one which is adequate in God insofar as he is explicated through the nature of the human mind (Cor. Pr. 11, II). Let us suppose, then, that there is in God, insofar as he is explicated through the nature of the human mind, an adequate idea, A. The idea of this idea must also necessarily be in God, and is related to God in the same way as the idea A (Pr. 20, II, the proof being of general application). But by our supposition the idea A is related to God insofar as he is explicated through the nature of the human mind. Therefore, the idea of the idea A must be related to God in the same way; that is (Cor. Pr. 11, II), this adequate idea of the idea A will be in the mind which has the adequate idea A. So he who has an adequate idea, that is, he who knows a thing truly (Pr. 34, II), must at the same time have an adequate idea, that is, a true knowledge of his knowledge; that is (as is self-evident), he is bound at the same time to be certain.

Scholium I have explained in the Scholium to Pr. 21, II what is an idea of an idea; but it should be noted that the preceding proposition is sufficiently self-evident. For nobody who has a true idea is unaware that a true idea involves absolute certainty. To have a true idea means only to know a thing perfectly, that is, to the utmost degree. Indeed, nobody can doubt this, unless he thinks that an idea is some dumb thing like a picture on a tablet, and not a mode of thinking, to wit, the very act of understanding. And who, pray, can know that he understands something unless he first understands it? That is, who can know that he is certain of something unless he is first certain of it? Again, what standard of truth can there be that is clearer and more certain than a true idea? Indeed, just as light makes manifest both itself and darkness, so truth is the standard both of itself and falsity.

I think I have thus given an answer to those questions which can be stated as follows: If a true idea is distinguished from a false one only inasmuch as it is said to correspond with that of which it is an idea, then a true idea has no more reality or perfection than a false one (since they are distinguished only by an extrinsic characteristic) and consequently neither is a man who has true ideas superior to one who has only false ideas. Secondly, how do we come to have false ideas? And finally, how can one know for certain that one has ideas which correspond with that of which they are ideas? I have now given an answer, I repeat, to these problems. As regards the difference between a true and a false idea, it is clear from Pr. 35, II that the former is to the latter as being to non-being. The causes of falsity I have quite clearly shown from Propositions 19 to 35 with the latter's Scholium, from which it is likewise obvious what is the difference between a man who has true ideas and one who has only false ideas. As to the last question, how can a man know that he has an idea which corresponds to that of which it is an idea, I have just shown, with abundant clarity, that this arises from the fact that he does have an idea that corresponds to that of which it is an idea; that is, truth is its own standard. Furthermore, the human mind, insofar as it perceives things truly, is part of the infinite intellect of God (Cor. Pr. 11, II), and thus it is as inevitable that the clear and distinct ideas of the mind are true as that God's ideas are true.

Proposition 44
It is not in the nature of reason to regard things as contingent, but as necessary.

Proof It is in the nature of reason to perceive things truly (Pr. 41, II), to wit (Ax. 6, I), as they are in themselves; that is (Pr. 29, I), not as contingent, but as necessary.

Corollary 1 Hence it follows that it solely results from imagination [*imaginatio*] that we regard things, both in respect of the past and of the future, as contingent.

Scholium I shall explain briefly how this comes about. We have shown above (Pr. 17, II and Cor.) that although things may not exist, the mind nevertheless always imagines them as present unless causes arise which exclude their present existence. Further, we have shown (Pr. 18, II) that if the human body has once been affected by two external bodies at the same time, when the mind later imagines one of them, it will straightway call the other to mind as well; that is, it will regard both as present to it unless other causes arise which exclude their present existence. Furthermore, nobody doubts that time, too, is a product of the imagination, and arises from the fact that we see some bodies move more slowly than others, or more quickly, or with equal speed. Let us therefore suppose that yesterday a boy saw Peter first of all in the morning, Paul at noon, and Simon in the evening, and that today he again sees Peter in the morning. From Pr. 18, II it is clear that as soon as he sees the morning light, forthwith he will imagine the sun as traversing the same tract of sky as on the previous day, that is, he will imagine a whole day, and he will imagine Peter together with morning, Paul with midday, and Simon with evening; that is, he will imagine the existence of Paul and Simon with reference to future time. On the other hand, on seeing Simon in the evening he will refer Paul and Peter to time past by imagining them along with time past. This train of events will be the more consistent the more frequently he sees them in that order. If it should at some time occur that on another evening he sees James instead of Simon, then the following morning he will imagine along with evening now Simon, now James, but not both together. For we are supposing that he has seen only one of them in the evening, not both at the same time. Therefore, his imagination will waver, and he will imagine, along with a future evening, now one, now the other; that is, he will regard neither of them as going to be there for certain, but both of them contingently. This wavering of the imagination occurs in the same way if the imagination be of things which we regard with relation to past or present time, and consequently we shall imagine things, as related both to present and past or future time, as contingent.

Corollary 2   It is in the nature of reason to perceive things in the light of eternity [*sub quadam specie aeternitatis*].

Proof   It is in the nature of reason to regard things as necessary, not as contingent (previous Pr.). Now it perceives this necessity truly (Pr. 41, II); that is, as it is in itself (Ax. 6, I). But (Pr. 16, I) this necessity is the very necessity of God's eternal nature. Therefore, it is in the nature of reason to regard things in this light of eternity. Furthermore, the basic principles of reason are those notions (Pr. 38, II) which explicate what is common to all things, and do not explicate (Pr. 37, II) the essence of any particular thing, and therefore must be conceived without any relation to time, but in the light of eternity.

Proposition 45
Every idea of any body or particular thing existing in actuality necessarily involves the eternal and infinite essence of God.

Proof   The idea of a particular thing actually existing necessarily involves both the essence and the existence of the thing (Cor. Pr. 8, II). But particular things cannot be conceived without God (Pr. 15, I). Now since they have God for their cause (Pr. 6, II) insofar as he is considered under that attribute of which the things themselves are modes, their ideas (Ax. 4, I) must necessarily involve the conception of their attribute; that is (Def. 6, I), the eternal and infinite essence of God.

Scholium   Here by existence I do not mean duration, that is, existence insofar as it is considered in the abstract as a kind of quantity. I am speaking of the very nature of existence, which is attributed to particular things because they follow in infinite numbers in infinite ways from the eternal necessity of God's nature (Pr. 16, I). I am speaking, I repeat, of the very existence of particular things insofar as they are in God. For although each particular thing is determined by another particular thing to exist in a certain manner, the force by which each perseveres in existing follows from the eternal necessity of God's nature. See Cor. Pr. 24, I.

Proposition 46
The knowledge of the eternal and infinite essence of God which each idea involves is adequate and perfect.

Proof The proof of the preceding proposition is universally valid, and whether a thing be considered as a part or a whole, its idea, whether of whole or part, involves the eternal and infinite essence of God (preceding Pr.). Therefore, that which gives knowledge of the eternal and infinite essence of God is common to all things, and equally in the part as in the whole. And so this knowledge will be adequate (Pr. 38, II).

Proposition 47
The human mind has an adequate knowledge of the eternal and infinite essence of God.

Proof The human mind has ideas (Pr. 22, II) from which (Pr. 23, II) it perceives itself, its own body (Pr. 19, II), and external bodies (Cor. 1, Pr. 16 and Pr. 17, II) as actually existing, and so it has an adequate knowledge of the eternal and infinite essence of God (Prs. 45 and 46, II).

Scholium Hence we see that God's infinite essence and his eternity are known to all. Now since all things are in God and are conceived through God, it follows that from this knowledge we can deduce a great many things so as to know them adequately and thus to form that third kind of knowledge I mentioned in Sch. 2 Pr. 40, II, of the superiority and usefulness of which we shall have occasion to speak in Part V. That men do not have as clear a knowledge of God as they do of common notions arises from the fact that they are unable to imagine God as they do bodies, and that they have connected the word "God" with the images of things which they commonly see; and this they can scarcely avoid, being affected continually by external bodies. Indeed, most errors result solely from the incorrect application of words to things. When somebody says that the lines joining the center of a circle to its circumference are unequal, he surely understands by circle, at least at that time, something different from what mathematicians understand. Likewise, when men make mistakes in arithmetic, they have different figures in mind from those on paper. So if you look only to their minds, they indeed are not mistaken; but they seem to be wrong because we think that they have in mind the figures on the page. If this were not the case, we would not think them to be wrong, just as I did not think that person to be wrong whom I recently heard shouting that his hall had flown into his neighbor's hen, for I could see clearly what he had in mind. Most controversies arise from this, that men do not correctly express what is in their mind, or they misunderstand another's mind. For, in reality, while they are hotly contradicting one another, they are either in agreement or have different things in mind, so that the apparent errors and absurdities of their opponents are not really so.

Proposition 48
In the mind there is no absolute, or free, will. The mind is determined to this or that volition by a cause, which is likewise determined by another cause, and this again by another, and so ad infinitum.

Proof The mind is a definite and determinate mode of thinking (Pr. 11, II), and thus (Cor. 2, Pr. 17, I) it cannot be the free cause of its actions: that is, it cannot possess an absolute faculty of willing and nonwilling. It must be determined to will this or that (Pr. 28, I) by a cause, which likewise is determined by another cause, and this again by another, etc.

Scholium In the same way it is proved that in the mind there is no absolute faculty of understanding, desiring, loving, etc. Hence it follows that these and similar faculties are either entirely fictitious or nothing more than metaphysical entities or universals which we are wont to form from particulars. So intellect and will bear the same relation to this or that idea, this or that volition, as stoniness to this or that stone, or man to Peter and Paul. As to the reason why men think they are free, we explained that in the Appendix to Part I.

But before proceeding further, it should here be noted that by the will I mean the faculty of affirming and denying, and not desire. I mean, I repeat, the faculty whereby the mind affirms or denies what is true or what is false, not the desire whereby the mind seeks things or shuns them. But now that we have proved that these faculties are universal notions which are not distinct from the particulars from which we form them, we must inquire whether volitions themselves are anything more than ideas of things. We must inquire, I say, whether there is in the mind any other affirmation and denial apart from that which the idea, insofar as it is an idea, involves. On this subject see the following proposition and also Def. 3, II, lest thought becomes confused with pictures. For by ideas I do not mean images such as are formed at the back of the eye—or if you like, in the middle of the brain—but conceptions of thought.

Proposition 49
There is in the mind no volition, that is, affirmation and negation, except that which an idea, insofar as it is an idea, involves.

Proof There is in the mind (preceding Pr.) no absolute faculty of willing and non-willing, but only particular volitions, namely, this or that affirmation, and this or that negation. Let us therefore conceive a particular volition, namely, a mode of thinking whereby the mind affirms that the three angles of a triangle are equal to two right angles. This affirmation involves the conception, or idea, of a triangle; that is, it cannot be conceived without the idea of a triangle. For to say that A must involve the conception of B is the same as to say that A cannot be conceived without B. Again, this affirmation (Ax. 3, II) cannot even be without the idea of a triangle. Therefore, this idea can neither be nor be conceived without the idea of a triangle. Furthermore, this idea of a triangle must involve this same affirmation, namely, that its three angles are equal to two right angles. Therefore, vice versa, this idea of a triangle can neither be nor be conceived without this affirmation, and so (Def. 2, II) this affirmation belongs to the essence of the idea of a triangle, and is nothing more than the essence itself. And what I have said of this volition (for it was arbitrarily selected) must also be said of every volition, namely, that it is nothing but an idea.

Corollary Will and intellect are one and the same thing.

Proof Will and intellect are nothing but the particular volitions and ideas (Pr. 48, II and Sch.). But a particular volition and idea are one and the same thing (preceding Pr.). Therefore, will and intellect are one and the same thing.

Scholium By this means we have removed the cause to which error is commonly attributed. We have previously shown that falsity consists only in the privation that fragmentary and confused ideas involve. Therefore, a false idea, insofar as it is false, does not involve certainty. So when we say that a man acquiesces in what is false and has no doubt thereof, we are not thereby saying that he is certain, but only that he does not doubt, or that he acquiesces in what is false because there is nothing to cause his imagination to waver. On this point see Sch. Pr. 44, II. So however much we suppose a man to adhere to what is false, we shall never say that he is certain. For by certainty we mean something positive (Pr. 43, II and Sch.), not privation of doubt. But by privation of certainty we mean falsity.
    But for a fuller explanation of the preceding proposition some things remain to be said. Then, again, there is the further task of replying to objections that may be raised against this doctrine of ours. Finally, to remove every shred of doubt, I have thought it worthwhile to point out certain advantages of this doctrine. I say certain advantages, for the most important of them will be better understood from what we have to say in Part V.
    I begin, then, with the first point, and I urge my readers to make a careful distinction between an idea—i.e., a conception of the mind—and the images of things that we imagine. Again, it is essential to distinguish between ideas and the words we use to signify things. For since these three—images, words, and ideas— have been utterly confused by many, or else they fail to distinguish between them through lack of accuracy, or, finally, through lack of caution, our doctrine of the will, which it is essential to know both for theory and for the wise ordering of life, has never entered their minds. For those who think that ideas consist in images formed in us from the contact of external bodies are convinced that those ideas of things whereof we can form no like image are not ideas, but mere fictions fashioned arbitrarily at will. So they look on ideas as dumb pictures on a tablet, and misled by this preconception they fail to see that an idea, insofar as it is an idea,

involves affirmation or negation. Again, those who confuse words with idea, or with the affirmation which an idea involves, think that when they affirm or deny something merely by words contrary to what they feel, they are able to will contrary to what they feel. Now one can easily dispel these misconceptions if one attends to the nature of thought, which is quite removed from the concept of extension. Then one will clearly understand that an idea, being a mode of thinking, consists neither in the image of a thing nor in words. For the essence of words and images is constituted solely by corporeal motions far removed from the concept of thought. With these few words of warning, I turn to the aforementioned objections.

The first of these rests on the confident claim that the will extends more widely than the intellect, and therefore is different from it. The reason for their belief that the will extends more widely than the intellect is that they find—so they say—that they do not need a greater faculty of assent, that is, of affirming and denying, than they already possess, in order to assent to an infinite number of other things that we do not perceive, but that we do need an increased faculty of understanding. Therefore, will is distinct from intellect, the latter being finite and the former infinite.

Second, it may be objected against us that experience appears to tell us most indisputably that we are able to suspend judgment so as not to assent to things that we perceive, and this is also confirmed by the fact that nobody is said to be deceived insofar as he perceives something, but only insofar as he assents or dissents. For instance, he who imagines a winged horse does not thereby grant that there is a winged horse; that is, he is not thereby deceived unless at the same time he grants that there is a winged horse. So experience appears to tell us most indisputably that the will, that is, the faculty of assenting, is free, and different from the faculty of understanding.

Third, it may be objected that one affirmation does not seem to contain more reality than another; that is, we do not seem to need greater power in order to affirm that what is true is true than to affirm that what is false is true. On the other hand, we do perceive that one idea has more reality or perfection than another. For some ideas are more perfect than others in proportion as some objects are superior to others. This, again, is a clear indication that there is a difference between will and intellect.

Fourth, it may be objected that if man does not act from freedom of will, what would happen if he should be in a state of equilibrium like Buridan's ass? Will he perish of hunger and thirst? If I were to grant this, I would appear to be thinking of an ass or a statue, not of a man. If I deny it, then the man will be determining himself, and consequently will possess the faculty of going and doing whatever he wants.

Besides these objections there may possibly be others. But since I am not obliged to quash every objection that can be dreamed up, I shall make it my task to reply to these objections only, and as briefly as possible.

To the first objection I reply that, if by the intellect is meant clear and distinct ideas only, I grant that the will extends more widely than the intellect, but I deny that the will extends more widely than perceptions, that is, the faculty of conceiving. Nor indeed do I see why the faculty of willing should be termed infinite any more than the faculty of sensing. For just as by the same faculty of willing we can affirm an infinite number of things (but in succession, for we cannot affirm an infinite number of things simultaneously), so also we can sense or perceive an infinite number of bodies (in succession) by the same faculty of sensing. If my objectors should say that there are an infinite number of things that we cannot sense, I retort that we cannot grasp them by any amount of thought, and consequently by any amount of willing. But, they say, if God wanted to bring it about that we should perceive these too, he would have had to give us a greater faculty of perceiving, but not a greater faculty of willing than he has already given us. This is the same as saying that if God wishes to bring it about that we should understand an infinite number of other entities, he would have to give us a greater intellect than he already has, so as to encompass these same infinite entities, but not a more universal idea of entity. For we have shown that the will is a universal entity, or the idea whereby we explicate all particular volitions; that is, that which is common to all particular volitions. So if they believe that this common or universal idea of volitions is a faculty, it is not at all surprising that they declare this faculty to extend beyond the limits of the intellect to infinity. For the term "universal" is applied equally to one, to many, and to an infinite number of individuals.

To the second objection I reply by denying that we have free power to suspend judgment. For when we say that someone suspends judgment, we are saying only that he sees that he is not adequately perceiving the thing. So suspension of judgment is really a perception, not free will. To understand this more clearly, let us conceive a boy imagining a winged horse and having no other perception. Since this imagining involves the existence of a horse (Cor. Pr. 17, II), and the boy perceives nothing to annul the existence of the horse, he will regard the horse as present and he will not be able to doubt its existence, although he is not certain of it. We experience this quite commonly in dreams, nor do I believe there is anyone who thinks that while dreaming he has free power to suspend judgment regarding the contents of his dream, and of bringing it about that he should not dream what he dreams that he sees. Nevertheless, it does happen that even in dreams we suspend judgment, to wit, when we dream that we are dreaming. Furthermore, I grant that nobody is deceived insofar as he has a perception; that is, I grant that the imaginings of the mind, considered in themselves, involve no error (see Sch. Pr. 17, II). But I deny that a man makes no affirmation insofar as he has a perception. For what else is perceiving a winged horse than affirming wings of a horse? For if the mind should perceive nothing apart from the winged horse, it would regard the horse as present to it, and would have no cause to doubt its existence nor any faculty of dissenting, unless the imagining of the winged horse were to be connected to an idea which annuls the existence of the said horse, or he perceives that the idea which he has of the winged horse is inadequate. Then he will either necessarily deny the existence of the horse or he will necessarily doubt it.

In the above I think I have also answered the third objection by my assertion that the will is a universal term predicated of all ideas and signifying only what is common to all ideas, namely, affirmation, the adequate essence of which, insofar as it is thus conceived as an abstract term, must be in every single idea, and the same in all in this respect only. But not insofar as it is considered as constituting the essence of the idea, for in that respect particular affirmations differ among themselves as much as do ideas. For example, the affirmation which the idea of a circle involves differs from the affirmation which the idea of a triangle involves as much as the idea of a circle differs from the idea of a triangle. Again, I absolutely deny that we need an equal power of thinking to affirm that what is true is true as to affirm that what is false is true. For these two affirmations, if you look to their meaning and not to the words alone, are related to one another as being to nonbeing. For there is nothing in ideas that constitutes the form of falsity (see Pr. 35, II with Sch. and Sch. Pr. 47, II). Therefore, it is important to note here how easily we are deceived when we confuse universals with particulars, and mental constructs [*entia rationis*] and abstract terms with the real.

As to the fourth objection, I readily grant that a man placed in such a state of equilibrium (namely, where he feels nothing else but hunger and thirst and perceives nothing but such-and-such food and drink at equal distances from him) will die of hunger and thirst. If they ask me whether such a man is not to be reckoned an ass rather than a man, I reply that I do not know, just as I do not know how one should reckon a man who hangs himself, or how one should reckon babies, fools, and madmen.

My final task is to show what practical advantages accrue from knowledge of this doctrine, and this we shall readily gather from the following points:

1. It teaches that we act only by God's will, and that we share in the divine nature, and all the more as our actions become more perfect and as we understand God more and more. Therefore, this doctrine, apart from giving us complete tranquillity of mind, has the further advantage of teaching us wherein lies our greatest happiness or blessedness, namely, in the knowledge of God alone, as a result of which we are induced only to such actions as are urged on us by love and piety. Hence we clearly understand how far astray from the true estimation of virtue are those who, failing to understand that virtue itself and the service of God are happiness itself and utmost freedom, expect God to bestow on them the highest rewards in return for their virtue and meritorious actions as if in return for the basest slavery.

2. It teaches us what attitude we should adopt regarding fortune, or the things that are not in our power, that is, the things that do not follow from our nature; namely, to expect and to endure with patience both faces of fortune. For all things follow from God's eternal decree by the same necessity as it follows from the essence of a triangle that its three angles are equal to two right angles.

3. This doctrine assists us in our social relations, in that it teaches us to hate no one, despise no one, ridicule no one, be angry with no one, envy no one. Then again, it teaches us that each should be content with what he has and should help his neighbor, not from womanish pity, or favor, or superstition, but from the guid-

ance of reason as occasion and circumstance require. This I shall demonstrate in Part IV.

4. Finally, this doctrine is also of no small advantage to the commonwealth, in that it teaches the manner in which citizens should be governed and led; namely, not so as to be slaves, but so as to do freely what is best.

And thus I have completed the task I undertook in this Scholium, and thereby I bring to an end Part II, in which I think I have explained the nature of the human mind and its properties at sufficient length and as clearly as the difficult subject matter permits, and that from my account can be drawn many excellent lessons, most useful and necessary to know, as will partly be disclosed in what is to follow.

PART III

Concerning the Origin and Nature of the Emotions

Preface

Most of those who have written about the emotions [*affectibus*] and human conduct seem to be dealing not with natural phenomena that follow the common laws of Nature but with phenomena outside Nature. They appear to go so far as to conceive man in Nature as a kingdom within a kingdom. They believe that he disturbs rather than follows Nature's order, and has absolute power over his actions, and is determined by no other source than himself. Again, they assign the cause of human weakness and frailty not to the power of Nature in general, but to some defect in human nature, which they therefore bemoan, ridicule, despise, or, as is most frequently the case, abuse. He who can criticize the weakness of the human mind more eloquently or more shrilly is regarded as almost divinely inspired. Yet there have not been lacking outstanding figures who have written much that is excellent regarding the right conduct of life and have given to mankind very sage counsel; and we confess we owe much to their toil and industry. However, as far as I know, no one has defined the nature and strength of the emotions, and the power of the mind in controlling them. I know, indeed, that the renowned Descartes, though he too believed that the mind has absolute power over its actions, does explain human emotions through their first causes, and has also zealously striven to show how the mind can have absolute control over the emotions. But in my opinion he has shown nothing else but the brilliance of his own genius, as I shall demonstrate in due course; for I want now to return to those who prefer to abuse or deride the emotions and actions of men rather than to understand them. They will doubtless find it surprising that I should attempt to treat of the faults and follies of mankind in the geometric manner, and that I should propose to bring logical reasoning to bear on what they proclaim is opposed to reason, and is vain, absurd, and horrifying. But my argument is this: in Nature nothing happens which can be attributed to its defectiveness, for Nature is always the same, and its force and power of acting is everywhere one and the same; that is, the laws and rules of Nature according to which all things happen and change from one form to another are everywhere and always the same. So our approach to the understanding of the nature of things of every kind should likewise be one and the same; namely, through the universal laws and rules of Nature. Therefore the emotions of hatred, anger, envy, etc., considered in themselves, follow from the same necessity and force of Nature as all other particular things. So these emotions are assignable to definite causes through which they can be understood, and have definite properties, equally deserving of our investigation as the properties of any other thing, whose mere contemplation affords us pleasure. I shall, then, treat of the nature and strength of the emotions, and the mind's power over them, by the same method as I have used in treating of God and the mind, and I shall consider human actions and appetites just as if it were an investigation into lines, planes, or bodies.

Definitions

1. I call that an adequate cause whose effect can be clearly and distinctly perceived through the said cause. I call that an inadequate or partial cause whose effect cannot be understood through the said cause alone.

2. I say that we are active when something takes place, in us or externally to us, of which we are the adequate cause; that is, (by preceding Def.), when from our nature there follows in us or externally to us something which can be clearly and distinctly understood through our nature alone. On the other hand, I say that we are passive when something takes place in us, or follows from our nature, of which we are only the partial cause.

3. By emotion [*affectus*] I understand the affections of the body by which the body's power of activity is increased or diminished, assisted or checked, together with the ideas of these affections.

Thus, if we can be the adequate cause of one of these affections, then by emotion I understand activity, otherwise passivity.

Postulates

1. The human body can be affected in many ways by which its power of activity is increased or diminished; and also in many other ways which neither increase nor diminish its power of activity.

This postulate or axiom rests on Postulate 1 and Lemmata 5 and 7, following Pr. 13, II.

2. The human body can undergo many changes and nevertheless retain impressions or traces of objects (see Post. 5, II) and consequently the same images of things for the definition of which see Sch. Pr. 17, II.

Proposition 1
Our mind is in some instances active and in other instances passive. Insofar as it has adequate ideas, it is necessarily active; and insofar as it has inadequate ideas, it is necessarily passive.

Proof In every human mind, some of its ideas are adequate, others are fragmentary and confused (Sch. Pr. 40, II). Now ideas that are adequate in someone's mind are adequate in God insofar as he constitutes the essence of that mind (Cor. Pr. 11, II); and furthermore those ideas that are inadequate in the mind are also adequate in God (same Cor.), not insofar as he contains in himself the essence of that mind only, but insofar as he contains the minds of other things as well. Again, from any given idea some effect must necessarily follow (Pr. 36, I), of which God is the adequate cause (Def. 1, III) not insofar as he is infinite but insofar as he is considered as affected by the given idea (Pr. 9, II). But in the case of an effect of which God is the cause insofar as he is affected by an idea which is adequate in someone's mind, that same mind is its adequate cause (Cor. Pr. 11, II). Therefore our mind (Def. 2, III), insofar as it has adequate ideas, is necessarily active—which is the first point. Again, whatever necessarily follows from an idea that is adequate in God not insofar as he has in himself the mind of one man only, but insofar as he has the minds of other things simultaneously with the mind of the said man, the mind of that man is not the adequate cause of it, but the partial cause (Cor. Pr. 11, II), and therefore (Def. 2, III) insofar as the mind has inadequate ideas, it is necessarily passive—which was the second point. Therefore our mind etc.

Corollary Hence it follows that the more the mind has inadequate ideas, the more it is subject to passive states [*passionibus*]; and, on the other hand, it is the more active in proportion as it has a greater number of adequate ideas.

Proposition 2
The body cannot determine the mind to think, nor can the mind determine the body to motion or rest, or to anything else (if there is anything else).

Proof All modes of thinking have God for their cause insofar as he is a thinking thing, and not insofar as he is explicated by any other attribute (Pr. 6, II). So that which determines the mind to think is a mode of Thinking, and not of Extension; that is (Def. 1, II), it is not the body. That was our first point. Now the motion-and-rest of a body must arise from another body, which again has been determined to motion or rest by another body, and without exception whatever arises in a body must have arisen from God insofar as he is considered as affected by a mode of Extension, and not insofar as he is considered as affected by a mode of Thinking (Pr. 6, II); that is, it cannot arise from mind, which (Pr. 11, II) is a mode of Thinking. That was our second point. Therefore the body cannot . . . etc.

Scholium This is more clearly understood from Sch. Pr. 7, II, which tells us that mind and body are one and the same thing, conceived now under the attribute of Thought, now under the attribute of Extension. Hence it comes about that the order or linking of things is one, whether Nature be conceived under this or that attribute, and consequently the order of the active and passive states of our body is simultaneous in Nature with the order of active and passive states of the mind. This is also evident from the manner of our proof of Pr. 12, II.

Yet, although the matter admits of no shadow of doubt, I can scarcely believe, without the confirmation of experience, that men can be induced to examine this view without prejudice, so strongly are they convinced that at the mere bidding of the mind the body can now be set in motion, now be brought to rest, and can perform any number of actions which depend solely on the will of the mind and the exercise of thought. However, nobody as yet has determined the limits of the body's capabilities: that is, nobody as yet has learned from experience what the body can and cannot do, without being determined by mind, solely from the laws of its nature insofar as it is considered as corporeal. For nobody as yet knows the structure of the body so accurately as to explain all its functions, not to mention that in the animal world we find much that far surpasses human sagacity, and that sleepwalkers do many things in their sleep that they would not dare when awake — clear evidence that the body, solely from the laws of its own nature, can do many things at which its mind is amazed.

Again, no one knows in what way and by what means mind can move body, or how many degrees of motion it can impart to body and with what speed it can cause it to move. Hence it follows that when men say that this or that action of the body arises from the mind which has command over the body, they do not know what they are saying, and are merely admitting, under a plausible cover of words, that they are ignorant of the true cause of that action and are not concerned to discover it.

"But," they will say, "whether or not we know by what means the mind moves the body, experience tells us that unless the mind is in a fit state to exercise thought, the body remains inert. And again, experience tells us that it is solely within the power of the mind both to speak and to keep silent, and to do many other things which we therefore believe to depend on mental decision." Now as to the first point, I ask, does not experience also tell them that if, on the other hand, the body is inert, the mind likewise is not capable of thinking? When the body is at rest in sleep, the mind remains asleep with it and does not have that power of entertaining thoughts which it has when awake. Again, I think that all have experienced the fact that the mind is not always equally apt for concentrating on the same object; the mind is more apt to regard this or that object according as the body is more apt to have arising in it the image of this or that object.

"But," they will say, "it is impossible that the causes of buildings, pictures, and other things of this kind, which are made by human skill alone, should be deduced solely from the laws of Nature considered only as corporeal, nor is the human body capable of building a temple unless it be determined and guided by mind." However, I have already pointed out that they do not know what the body can do, or what can be deduced solely from a consideration of its nature, and that experience abundantly shows that solely from the laws of its nature many things occur which they would never have believed possible except from the direction of mind—for instance, the actions of sleepwalkers, which they wonder at when they are awake. A further consideration is the very structure of the human body, which far surpasses in ingenuity all the constructions of human skill; not to mention the point I made earlier, that from Nature, considered under any attribute whatsoever, infinite things follow.

As to the second point, the human condition would indeed be far happier if it were equally in the power of men to keep silent as to talk. But experience teaches us with abundant examples that nothing is less within men's power than to hold their tongues or control their appetites. From this derives the commonly held view that we act freely only in cases where our desires are moderate, because our appetites can then be easily held in check by the remembrance of another thing that frequently comes to mind; but when we seek something with a strong emotion that cannot be allayed by the remembrance of some other thing, we cannot check our desires. But indeed, had they not found by experience that we do many things of which we later repent, and that frequently, when we are at the mercy of conflicting emotions, we "see the better and do the worse," there would be nothing to prevent them from believing that all our actions are free. A baby thinks that it freely seeks milk, an angry child that it freely seeks revenge, and a timid man that he freely seeks flight. Again, the drunken man believes that it is from the free decision of the mind that he says what he later, when sober, wishes he had not said. So, too, the delirious man, the gossiping woman, the child, and many more of this sort think that they speak from free mental decision, when in fact they are unable to restrain their torrent of words. So experience tells us no less clearly than reason that it is on this account only that men believe themselves to be free, that they are conscious of their actions and ignorant of the causes by which they are determined; and it tells us too that mental decisions are nothing more than the appetites themselves, varying therefore according to the varying disposition of the body. For each man's actions are shaped by his emotion; and those who furthermore are a prey to conflicting emotions know not what they want, while those who are free from emotion are driven on to this or that course by a slight impulse.

Now surely all these considerations go to show clearly that mental decision on the one hand, and the appetite and physical state of the body on the other hand, are simultaneous in nature; or rather, they are one and the same thing which, when considered under the attribute of Thought and explicated through Thought, we call decision, and when considered under the attribute of Extension and deduced from the laws of motion-and-rest, we call a physical state. This will become clearer from later discussion, for there is now another point which I should like you to note as very important. We can take no action from mental decision unless the memory comes into play; for example, we cannot utter a word unless we call the word to mind. Now it is not within the free power of the mind to remember or to forget anything. Hence comes the belief that the power of the mind whereby we can keep silent or speak solely from mental decision is restricted to the case of a remembered thing. However, when we dream that we are speaking, we think that we do so from free mental decision; yet we are not speaking, or if we are, it is the result of spontaneous movement of the body. Again, we dream that we are keeping something secret, and that we are doing so by the same mental decision that comes into play in our waking hours when we keep silent about what we know. Finally, we dream that from a mental decision we act as we dare not act when awake. So I would very much like to know whether in the mind there are two sorts of decisions, dreamland decisions and free decisions. If we don't want to carry madness so far, we must necessarily grant that the mental decision that is believed to be free is not distinct from imagination and memory, and is nothing but the affirmation which an idea, insofar as it is an idea, necessarily involves (Pr. 49, II). So these mental decisions arise in the mind from the same necessity as the ideas of things existing in actuality, and those who believe that they speak, or keep silent, or do anything from free mental decision are dreaming with their eyes open.

Proposition 3

The active states [actiones] of the mind arise only from adequate ideas; its passive states depend solely on inadequate ideas.

Proof The first thing that constitutes the essence of the mind is nothing else but the idea of a body actually existing (Prs. 11 and 13, II), which idea is composed of many other ideas (Pr. 15, II), of which some are adequate (Cor. Pr. 38, II) while others are inadequate (Cor. Pr. 29, II). Therefore, whatever follows from the nature of the mind and must be understood through the mind as its proximate cause must necessarily follow from an adequate idea or an inadequate idea. But insofar as the mind has inadequate ideas, it is necessarily passive (Prop. 1, III). Therefore, the active states of mind follow solely from adequate ideas, and thus the mind is passive only by reason of having inadequate ideas.

Scholium We therefore see that passive states are related to the mind only insofar as the mind has something involving negation: that is, insofar as the mind is considered as part of Nature, which cannot be clearly and distinctly perceived through itself independently of other parts. By the same reasoning I could demonstrate that passive states are a characteristic of particular things just as they are of the mind, and cannot be perceived in any other way; but my purpose is to deal only with the human mind.

Proposition 4

No thing can be destroyed except by an external cause.

Proof This proposition is self-evident, for the definition of anything affirms, and does not negate, the thing's essence: that is, it posits, and does not annul, the thing's essence. So as long as we are attending only to the thing itself, and not to external causes, we can find nothing in it which can destroy it.

Proposition 5

Things are of a contrary nature, that is, unable to subsist in the same subject, to the extent that one can destroy the other.

Proof If they were able to be in agreement with one other, or to coexist in the same subject, there could be something in the said subject which could destroy it, which is absurd (preceding Pr.). Therefore . . . etc.

Proposition 6

Each thing, insofar as it is in itself, endeavors to persist in its own being.

Proof Particular things are modes whereby the attributes of God are expressed in a definite and determinate way (Cor. Pr. 25, I), that is (Pr. 34, I), they are things which express in a definite and determinate way the power of God whereby he is and acts, and no thing can have in itself anything by which it can be destroyed, that is, which can annul its existence (Pr. 4, III). On the contrary, it opposes everything that can annul its existence (preceding Pr.); and thus, as far as it can and as far as it is in itself, it endeavors to persist in its own being.

Proposition 7

The conatus[1] with which each thing endeavors to persist in its own being is nothing but the actual essence of the thing itself.

Proof From the given essence of a thing certain things necessarily follow (Pr. 36, I), nor do things effect anything other than that which necessarily follows from their determinate nature (Pr. 29, I). Therefore, the power of any thing, or the conatus with which it acts or endeavors to act, alone or in conjunction with other things, that is (Pr. 6, III), the power or conatus by which it endeavors to persist in its own being, is nothing but the given, or actual, essence of the thing.

Proposition 8

The conatus with which each single thing endeavors to persist in its own being does not involve finite time, but indefinite time.

Proof If it involved a limited period of time which would determine the duration of the thing, then solely from the power by which the thing exists it would follow that it could not exist after that limited period of time, but is bound to be destroyed. But (Pr. 4, III), this is absurd. Therefore, the conatus with which a thing exists does not involve any definite period of time. On the contrary (by the same Pr. 4, III), if it is not destroyed by an external cause, it will always continue to ex-

---

[1] [The term "conatus" plays an important role in Spinoza's psychology. It expresses Spinoza's view that each thing exemplifies an inherent tendency toward self-preservation and activity. This term has a long history, going back to Cicero, who used it to express Aristotle's and the Stoics' notion of impulse (*horme*). It was later used by medieval and early modern philosophers, such as Hobbes, to connote the natural tendency of an organism to preserve itself.]

ist by that same power by which it now exists. Therefore, this conatus involves an indefinite time.

PROPOSITION 9
The mind, both insofar as it has clear and distinct ideas and insofar as it has confused ideas, endeavors to persist in its own being over an indefinite period of time, and is conscious of this conatus.

Proof The essence of the mind is constituted by adequate and inadequate ideas (as we showed in Pr. 3, III), and so (Pr. 7, III) it endeavors to persist in its own being insofar as it has both these kinds of ideas, and does so (Pr. 8, III) over an indefinite period of time. Now since the mind (Pr. 23, II) is necessarily conscious of itself through the ideas of the affections of the body, therefore the mind is conscious of its conatus (Pr. 7, III).

Scholium When this conatus is related to the mind alone, it is called Will [*voluntas*]; when it is related to mind and body together, it is called Appetite [*appetitus*], which is therefore nothing else but man's essence, from the nature of which there necessarily follow those things that tend to his preservation, and which man is thus determined to perform. Further, there is no difference between appetite and Desire [*cupiditas*] except that desire is usually related to men insofar as they are conscious of their appetite. Therefore, it can be defined as follows: desire is "appetite accompanied by the consciousness thereof."

It is clear from the above considerations that we do not endeavor, will, seek after or desire because we judge a thing to be good. On the contrary, we judge a thing to be good because we endeavor, will, seek after and desire it.

PROPOSITION 10
An idea that excludes the existence of our body cannot be in our mind, but is contrary to it.

Proof Whatsoever can destroy our body cannot be therein (Pr. 5, III), and so neither can its idea be in God insofar as he has the idea of our body (Cor. Pr. 9, II); that is (Prs. 11 and 13, II), the idea of such a thing cannot be in our mind. On the contrary, since (Prs. 11 and 13, II) the first thing that constitutes the essence of the mind is the idea of an actually existing body, the basic and most important element of our mind is the conatus (Pr. 7, III) to affirm the existence of our body. Therefore, the idea that negates the existence of our body is contrary to our mind.

PROPOSITION 11
Whatsoever increases or diminishes, assists or checks, the power of activity of our body, the idea of the said thing increases or diminishes, assists or checks the power of thought of our mind.

Proof This proposition is evident from Pr. 7, II, or again from Pr. 14, II.

Scholium We see then that the mind can undergo considerable changes, and can pass now to a state of greater perfection, now to one of less perfection, and it is these passive transitions [*passiones*] that explicate for us the emotions of Pleasure [*laetitia*] and Pain [*tristitia*]. So in what follows I shall understand by pleasure "the passive transition of the mind to a state of greater perfection," and by pain "the passive transition of the mind to state of less perfection." The emotion of pleasure when it is simultaneously related to mind and body I call Titillation [*titillatio*] or Cheerfulness [*hilaritas*]; the emotion of pain when it is similarly related I call Anguish [*dolor*] or Melancholy [*melancholia*]. But be it noted that titillation and anguish are related to man when one part of him is affected more than others, cheerfulness and melancholy when all parts are equally affected. As to Desire [*cupiditas*], I have explained what it is in Sch. Pr. 9, III, and I acknowledge no primary emotion other than these three [i.e. pleasure, pain, and desire]; for I shall subsequently show that the others arise from these three. But before going further, I should like to explain Pr. 10, III at greater length, so that there may be a clearer understanding of the way in which an idea may be contrary to an idea.

In Sch. Pr. 17, II we demonstrated that the idea which constitutes the essence of the mind involves the existence of the body for as long as the body exists. Then from what we proved in Cor. Pr. 8, II and its Sch., it follows that the present existence of our mind depends solely on this, that the mind involves the actual existence of the body. Finally we proved that the power of the mind whereby it imagines [*imaginatur*] and remembers things depends also on this (Prs. 17 and 18, II, and Sch.), that it involves the actual existence of the body. From this it follows that the present existence of the mind and its capacity to perceive through the senses are annulled as soon as the mind ceases to affirm the present existence of the body. But the cause of the mind's ceasing to affirm this existence of the body cannot be the mind itself (Pr. 4, III), nor again that the body ceases to be. For (Pr. 6, II) the cause of the mind's affirming the existence of the body is not that the body began to exist; therefore, by the same reasoning, it does not cease to affirm the existence of the body on account of the body's ceasing to be. This results from another idea, which excludes the present existence of our body and consequently that of our mind, and which is therefore contrary to the idea that constitutes the essence of our mind (Pr. 8, II).

PROPOSITION 12
The mind, as far as it can, endeavors to think of those things that increase or assist the body's power of activity.

Proof As long as the human body is affected in a manner that involves the nature of an external body, so long will the human mind regard that latter body as present (Pr. 17, II). Consequently (Pr. 7, II), as long as the human mind regards some external body as present, that is (Sch. Pr. 17, II), thinks of it, so long is the human body affected in a manner that involves the nature of that external body. Accordingly, as long as the mind thinks of those things that increase or assist our body's power of activity, so long is the body affected in ways that increase or assist its power of activity (Post. 1, III); and, consequently, so long is the mind's power of thinking increased or assisted (Pr. 11, III). Therefore (Pr. 6 or 9, III), the mind, as far as it can, endeavors to think of those things.

Proposition 13

When the mind thinks of those things that diminish or check the body's power of activity, it endeavors, as far as it can, to call to mind those things that exclude the existence of the former.

Proof As long as the mind thinks of something of this kind, so long is the power of mind and body diminished or checked (as we have proved in the preceding proposition). Nevertheless the mind will continue to think of it until it thinks of another thing that excludes the present existence of the former (Pr. 17, II); that is, (as we have just demonstrated), the power of mind and body is diminished or checked until the mind thinks of something else that excludes the thing's existence, something which the mind therefore (Pr. 9, III) endeavors, as far as it can, to think of or call to mind.

Corollary Hence it follows that the mind is averse to thinking of things that diminish or check its power and the body's power.

Scholium From what has been said we clearly understand what are Love [*amor*] and Hatred [*odium*]. Love is merely "pleasure accompanied by the idea of an external cause," and hatred is merely "pain accompanied by the idea of an external cause." Again, we see that he who loves necessarily endeavors to have present and to preserve the thing that he loves; on the other hand, he who hates endeavors to remove and destroy the thing that he hates. But we shall deal with these matters more fully in due course.

Proposition 14

If the mind has once been affected by two emotions at the same time, when it is later affected by the one it will also be affected by the other.

Proof If the human body has once been affected by two bodies at the same time, when the mind later thinks of the one it will straightway recall the other too (Pr. 18, II). Now the images formed by the mind reflect the affective states of our body more than the nature of external bodies (Cor. 2, Pr. 16, II). Therefore if the body, and consequently the mind (Def. 3, III), has once been affected by two emotions, when it is later affected by the one, it will also be affected by the other.

Proposition 15

Anything can indirectly [per accidens] be the cause of Pleasure, Pain, or Desire.

Proof Let it be supposed that the mind is affected by two emotions simultaneously, of which one neither increases nor diminishes its power of activity, and the other either increases it or diminishes it (Post. 1, III). From the preceding proposition it is clear that when the mind is later affected by the former as its true cause—which, by hypothesis, of itself neither increases nor diminishes the mind's power of thinking—it will straightway be affected by the other, which does increase or diminish its power of thinking; that is (Sch. Pr. 11, III), it will be affected by pleasure or pain. So the former will be the cause of pleasure or pain, not through itself, but indirectly. In this same way it can readily be demonstrated that the former thing can indirectly be the cause of desire.

Corollary From the mere fact that we have regarded a thing with the emotion of pleasure or pain of which it is not itself the efficient cause, we may love or hate that thing.

Proof From this mere fact it comes about (Pr. 14, III) that the mind, when later thinking of this thing, is affected by the emotion of pleasure or pain; that is (Sch. Pr. 11, III), the power of the mind and body is increased or diminished, etc. Consequently (Pr. 12, III), the mind desires to think of the said thing, or is averse to it (Cor. Pr. 13, III); that is (Sch. Pr. 13, III), it loves or hates the said thing.

Scholium Hence we understand how it can come about that we love or hate some things without any cause known to us, but merely from Sympathy and Antipathy, as they are called. We should also classify in this category those objects that affect us with pleasure or pain from the mere fact that they have some resemblance to objects that are wont to affect us with the same emotions, as I shall demonstrate in the next Proposition.

I realize that the writers who first introduced the terms "sympathy" and "antipathy" intended them to mean certain occult qualities. Nevertheless, I think it is permissible for us to denote by them qualities that are also familiar or manifest.

Proposition 16

From the mere fact that we imagine a thing to have something similar to an object that is wont to affect the mind with pleasure or pain, we shall love it or hate it, although the point of similarity is not the efficient cause of these emotions.

Proof By hypothesis, the point of similarity has been regarded by us in the object with the emotion of pleasure or pain; and so (Pr. 14, III) when the mind is affected by its image, it will also straightway be affected by the one or other emotion. Consequently, the thing which we perceive to have this said point of similarity will indirectly be the cause of pleasure or pain (Pr. 15, III); and thus (preceding Corollary), we shall love or hate the thing even though the point of similarity is not the efficient cause of these emotions.

Proposition 17

If we imagine that a thing which is wont to affect us with an emotion of pain, has something similar to another thing which is wont to affect us with an equally great emotion of pleasure, we shall hate it and love it at the same time.

Proof By hypothesis, this thing is in itself a cause of pain, and (Sch. Pr. 13, III) insofar as we imagine it with this emotion, we hate it. But, in addition, insofar as we imagine it to have something similar to another thing which is wont to affect us with an equally great emotion of pleasure, we shall love it with an equally strong emotion of pleasure (preceding Pr.). So we shall hate it and love it at the same time.

Scholium This condition of the mind arising from two conflicting emotions is called "vacillation," which is therefore related to emotion as doubt is related to imagination (Sch. Pr. 44, II), and there is no difference between vacillation and doubt except in respect of intensity. But it should be observed that in the preceding Proposition I deduced these vacillations from causes which are, in the case of one emotion, a direct cause, and in the case of the other an indirect cause. This I did because they could in this way be more readily deduced from what had preceded, and not because I deny that vacillations generally arise from an object which is the efficient cause of both emotions. For the human body is composed (Post. 1, II) of very many individual bodies of different nature, and so (Ax. 1 after Lemma 3, q.v. after Pr. 13, II) it can be affected by one and the same body in many different ways; on the other hand, since one and the same thing can be affected in many ways, it can likewise affect one and the same part of the body in different ways. From this we can readily conceive that one and the same object can be the cause of many conflicting emotions.

PROPOSITION 18
From the image of things past or future man is affected by the same emotion of pleasure or pain as from the image of a thing present.

Proof As long as a man is affected by the image of a thing, he will regard the thing as present even though it may not exist (Pr. 17, II and Cor.), and he does not think of it as past or future except insofar as its image is joined to the image of past or future time (Sch. Pr. 44, II). Therefore the image of a thing, considered solely in itself, is the same whether it be related to future, past, or present; that is (Cor. 2, Pr. 16, II), the state of the body, or the emotion, is the same whether the image be of a thing past or future or present. So the emotion of pleasure, and of pain, is the same whether the image be of a thing past or future or present.

Scholium 1 Here I call a thing past or future insofar as we have been, or shall be, affected by it; for example, insofar as we have seen or shall see it, it has refreshed or will refresh us, it has injured or will injure us, etc. For insofar as we imagine it in this way, to that extent we affirm its existence; that is, the body is not affected by any emotion that excludes the existence of the thing, and so (Pr. 17, II) the body is affected by the image of the thing in the same way as if the thing itself were present. However, since it is generally the case that those who have had much experience vacillate when they are regarding a thing as future or past and are generally in doubt as to its outcome (Sch. Pr. 44, II), the result is that emotions that arise from similar images of things are not so constant, but are generally disturbed by images of other things until men become more assured of the outcome.

Scholium 2 From what has just been said we understand what is Hope [*spes*], Fear [*metus*], Confidence [*securitas*], Despair [*desperatio*], Joy [*gaudium*], and Disappointment [*conscientiae morsus*]. Hope is "inconstant pleasure, arising from the image of a thing future or past, of whose outcome we are in doubt." Fear is "inconstant pain, likewise arising from the image of a thing in doubt." Now if the element of doubt be removed from these emotions, hope becomes confidence and fear becomes despair, that is "pleasure or pain arising from a thing which we have feared or have hoped." Joy is "pleasure arising from the image of a past thing of whose outcome we have been in doubt." Finally, disappointment is "the pain opposite to joy."

Proposition 19
He who imagines that what he loves is being destroyed will feel pain. If, however, he imagines that it is being preserved, he will feel pleasure.

Proof The mind, as far as it can, endeavors to imagine whatever increases or assists the body's power of activity (Pr. 12, III), that is (Sch. Pr. 13, III), those things it loves. But the imagination is assisted by whatever posits the existence of the thing, and, on the other hand, is checked by whatever excludes the existence of the thing (Pr. 17, II). Therefore, the images of things that posit the existence of the loved object assist the mind's conatus wherewith it endeavors to imagine the loved object, that is (Sch. Pr. 11, III), they affect the mind with pleasure. On the other hand, those things that exclude the existence of the loved object check that same conatus of the mind, that is (by the same Scholium), they affect the mind with pain. Therefore, he who imagines that what he loves is being destroyed will feel pain, . . . etc.

Proposition 20
He who imagines that a thing that he hates is being destroyed will feel pleasure.

Proof The mind (Pr. 13, III) endeavors to imagine whatever excludes the existence of things whereby the body's power of activity is diminished or checked; that is (Sch. Pr. 13, III), it endeavors to imagine whatever excludes the existence of things that it hates. So the image of a thing that excludes the existence of what the mind hates assists this conatus of the mind; that is (Sch. Pr. 11, III), it affects the mind with pleasure. Therefore, he who thinks that that which he hates is being destroyed will feel pleasure.

Proposition 21
He who imagines that what he loves is affected with pleasure or pain will likewise be affected with pleasure or pain, the intensity of which will vary with the intensity of the emotion in the object loved.

Proof As we have shown in Proposition 19, III, the images of things which posit the existence of the object loved assist the mind's conatus whereby it endeavors to think of the object loved. But pleasure posits the existence of that which feels pleasure, and the more so as the emotion of pleasure is stronger; for pleasure (Sch. Pr. 11, III) is a transition to a state of greater perfection. Therefore the image, which is in the lover, of the pleasure of the object loved, assists his mind's conatus; that is (Sch. Pr. 11, III), it affects the lover with pleasure, and all the more to the extent that this emotion is in the object loved. That was the first point. Again, insofar as a thing is affected with some pain, to that extent it is being destroyed, and the more so according to the extent to which it is affected with pain (same Sch. Pr. 11, III). Thus (Pr. 19, III), he who imagines that what he loves is affected with pain will likewise be affected with pain, the intensity of which will vary with the intensity of this emotion in the object loved.

Proposition 22

If we imagine that someone is affecting with pleasure the object of our love, we shall be affected with love toward him. If on the other hand we think that he is affecting with pain the object of our love, we shall likewise be affected with hatred toward him.

Proof He who affects with pleasure or pain the object of our love affects us also with pleasure or pain, assuming that we think of the object of our love as affected with that pleasure or pain (preceding Pr.). But it is supposed that this pleasure or pain is in us accompanied by the idea of an external cause. Therefore (Sch. Pr. 13, III), if we think that someone is affecting with pleasure or pain the object of our love, we shall be affected with love or hatred toward him.

Scholium Proposition 21 explains to us what is Pity [*commiseratio*], which we may define as "pain arising from another's hurt." As for pleasure arising from another's good, I know not what to call it. Furthermore, love toward one who has benefited another we shall call Approval [*favor*], and on the other hand hatred toward one who has injured another we shall call Indignation [*indignatio*]. Finally, it should be observed that we pity not only the thing which we have loved (as we have demonstrated in Pr. 21), but also a thing for which we have previously felt no emotion, provided that we judge it similar to ourselves (as I shall show in due course). Likewise, we approve of one who has benefited someone like ourselves; and on the other hand, we are indignant with one who has injured someone like ourselves.

Proposition 23

He who imagines that what he hates is affected with pain will feel pleasure; if, on the other hand, he thinks of it as affected with pleasure, he will feel pain. Both of these emotions will vary in intensity inversely with the variation of the contrary emotion in that which he hates.

Proof Insofar as the thing hated is affected with pain, it is being destroyed, and the more so according to the degree of pain (Sch. Pr. 11, III). So (Pr. 20, III) he who imagines the object hated to be affected with pain will, on the contrary, be affected with pleasure, and the more so as he imagines the object hated to be affected with more pain. That was the first point. Again, pleasure posits the existence of that which feels pleasure (same Sch. Pr. 11, III), and the more so as the pleasure is conceived to be greater. If anyone imagines him whom he hates to be affected with pleasure, this thought will check his conatus (Pr. 13, III): that is (Sch. Pr. 11, III), he who hates will be affected with pain, etc.

Scholium This pleasure can scarcely be unalloyed and devoid of conflict of feeling. For (as I shall forthwith demonstrate in Proposition 27) insofar as he imagines a thing similar to himself to be affected with an emotion of pain, to that extent he is bound to feel pain, and contrariwise if he imagines it to be affected with pleasure. But here it is only his hate that we are considering.

Proposition 24

If we imagine someone to be affecting with pleasure a thing that we hate, we shall be affected with hate toward him too. If on the other hand we think of him as affecting with pain the said thing, we shall be affected with love toward him.

Proof The proof follows the same lines as Pr. 22, III.

Scholium These and similar emotions of hatred are related to Envy [*invidia*], which can therefore be defined as "hatred insofar as it is considered to dispose a man to rejoice in another's hurt and to feel pain at another's good."

Proposition 25

We endeavor to affirm of ourselves and of an object loved whatever we imagine affects us or the loved object with pleasure, and, on the other hand, to negate whatever we imagine affects us or the loved object with pain.

Proof What we imagine affects the object loved with pleasure or pain affects us with pleasure or pain (Pr. 21, III). Now the mind (Pr. 12, III) endeavors, as far as it can, to think of things that affect us with pleasure; that is (Pr. 17, II and Cor.), to regard them as present; and, on the other hand (Pr. 13, III), to exclude the existence of things that affect us with pain. Therefore, we endeavor to affirm of ourselves and the loved object whatever we imagine affects us or the object loved with pleasure, and vice versa.

Proposition 26

We endeavor to affirm of that which we hate whatever we imagine affects it with pain, and on the other hand to deny what we imagine affects it with pleasure.

Proof This proposition follows from Proposition 23, III, as does the preceding proposition from Proposition 21, III.

Scholium Thus we see that it easily happens that a man may have too high an opinion of himself and of the object loved, and on the other hand too mean an opinion of the object of his hatred. This way of thinking, when it concerns the man who has too high an opinion of himself, is called Pride [*superbia*], and is a kind of madness, in that a man dreams with his eyes open that he can do all those things that his imagination encompasses, which he therefore regards as real, exulting in them, as long as he is incapable of thinking of those things that exclude their existence and limit his power of activity. Therefore, pride is "pleasure arising from the fact that a man has too high an opinion of himself." Again, "pleasure that arises from the fact that a man has too high an opinion of another" is called Over-esteem [*existimatio*]. Finally, "pleasure arising from the fact that a man has too mean an opinion of another" is called Disparagement [*despectus*].

Proposition 27
From the fact that we imagine a thing like ourselves, toward which we have felt no emotion, to be affected by an emotion, we are thereby affected by a similar emotion.

Proof Images of things are affections of the human body, the ideas of which set before us external bodies as present (Sch. Pr. 17, II); that is (Pr. 16, II), the ideas of these affections involve the nature of our own body and simultaneously the nature of the external body as present. If therefore the nature of the external body is similar to the nature of our own body, then the idea of the external body in our thinking will involve an affection of our own body similar to the affection of the external body. Consequently, if we imagine someone like ourselves to be affected by an emotion, this thought will express an affection of our own body similar to that emotion. So from the fact that we imagine a thing like ourselves to be affected by an emotion, we are affected by a similar emotion along with it. But if we hate a thing similar to ourselves, to that extent (Pr. 23, III) we shall be affected by a contrary, not similar, emotion along with it.

Scholium This imitation of emotions, when it is related to pain, is called Pity (see Sch. Pr. 22, III), but when it is related to desire it is called Emulation [*aemulatio*], which is therefore "nothing else but the desire of some thing which has been engendered in us from the belief that others similar to ourselves have this same desire."

Corollary 1 If we believe that someone, for whom we have felt no emotion, affects with pleasure a thing similar to ourselves, we shall be affected by love toward him. If, on the other hand, we believe that he affects the said object with pain, we shall be affected with hatred toward him.

Proof This is proved from the preceding Proposition in the same way as Proposition 22 from Proposition 21, III.

Corollary 2 The fact that its distress affects us with pain cannot cause us to hate a thing that we pity.

Proof If we could hate it on that account, then (Pr. 23, III) we should be pleased at its pain, which is contrary to our hypothesis.

Corollary 3 As far as we can, we endeavor to free from distress the thing that we pity.

Proof That which affects with pain a thing that we pity affects us too with similar pain (preceding Pr.), and so we shall endeavor to devise whatever annuls the existence of the former or destroys it (Pr. 13, III): that is (Sch. Pr. 9, III), we shall seek to destroy it; i.e. we shall be determined to destroy it. So we shall endeavor to free from its distress the thing we pity.

Scholium This will or appetite to do good which arises from our pitying the thing to which we wish to do good is called Benevolence [*benevolentia*], which is therefore "nothing else but desire arising from pity." As to love and hatred toward one who has done good or ill to a thing that we think to be like ourselves, see Sch. Pr. 22, III.

PROPOSITION 28
We endeavor to bring about whatever we imagine to be conducive to pleasure; but we endeavor to remove or destroy whatever we imagine to be opposed to pleasure and conducive to pain.

Proof As far as we can, we endeavor to imagine whatever we think to be conducive to pleasure (Pr. 12, III): that is (Pr. 17, II), we endeavor, as far as we can, to regard it as present, that is, existing in actuality. But the conatus of the mind, that is, its power to think, is equal to and simultaneous in nature with the conatus of the body, that is, its power to act (as clearly follows from Cor. Pr. 7 and Cor. Pr. 11, II). Therefore in an absolute sense we endeavor, that is, we seek and purpose (which is the same thing by Sch. Pr. 9, III), to bring about its existence. That was our first point. Further, if we imagine that which we believe to be the cause of pain, that is (Sch. Pr. 13, III), that which we hate, as being destroyed, we shall feel pleasure (Pr. 20, III), and so (by the first part of this proposition) we shall endeavor to destroy it, or (Pr. 13, III) to remove it from us so as not to regard it as present. That was our second point. Therefore we endeavor to bring about . . . etc.

PROPOSITION 29
We also endeavor to do whatever we imagine men[2] to regard with pleasure, and on the other hand we shun doing whatever we imagine men to regard with aversion.

Proof From the fact that we imagine men love or hate something, we shall love or hate the same thing (Pr. 27, III); that is (Sch. Pr. 13, III), from that very fact we shall feel pleasure or pain at the presence of the thing. So (preceding Pr.) we shall endeavor to do whatever we imagine men love or regard with pleasure . . . etc.

Scholium This conatus to do, and also to avoid doing, something simply in order to please men is called Ambition [*ambitio*], especially when we endeavor so earnestly to please the multitude that we do, or avoid doing, things to our own hurt or another's hurt; otherwise, it is called Kindliness [*humanitas*]. Again, the pleasure with which we think of another's action whereby he has endeavored to please us I call Praise [*laus*], and the pain with which, on the other hand, we dislike his action I call Blame [*vituperium*].

---

[2] Here, and in what follows, by "men" I understand men for whom we have felt no emotion.

Proposition 30

If anyone has done something which he imagines affects others with pleasure, he will be affected with pleasure accompanied by the idea of himself as cause; that is, he will regard himself with pleasure. If, on the other hand, he imagines he has done something which affects others with pain, he will regard himself with pain.

Proof He who imagines he affects others with pleasure or pain will by that very fact be affected with pleasure or pain (Pr. 27, III). Now since man (Prs. 19 and 23, II) is conscious of himself through the affections by which he is determined to act, he who has done something which he thinks affects others with pleasure will be affected with pleasure along with the consciousness of himself as cause; that is, he will regard himself with pleasure. The contrary likewise follows.

Scholium Since love (Sch. Pr. 13, III) is pleasure accompanied by the idea of an external cause, and hate is pain also accompanied by the idea of an external cause, this pleasure and this pain are species of love and hatred. But as love and hatred have reference to external objects, we shall assign different names to these emotions. The pleasure that is accompanied by an external cause we shall call Honor [*gloria*], and the pain that is its opposite we shall call Shame [*pudor*]; but be it understood that this is when the pleasure or pain arises from a man's belief that he is praised or blamed. Otherwise, the pleasure that is accompanied by the idea of an internal cause I shall call Self-contentment [*Acquiescentia in se ipso*], and the pain that is its opposite I shall call Repentance [*paenitentia*]. Again, since it is possible (Cor. Pr. 17, II) that the pleasure with which a man imagines he affects others is only imaginary, and (Pr. 25, III) everyone endeavors to imagine of himself whatever he thinks affects himself with pleasure, it can easily happen that a vain man may be proud and imagine that he is popular with everybody, when he in fact is obnoxious.

Proposition 31

If we think that someone loves, desires, or hates something that we love, desire, or hate, that very fact will cause us to love, desire, or hate the thing more steadfastly. But if we think he dislikes what we love, or vice versa, then our feelings will fluctuate.

Proof From the mere fact that we imagine someone loves something, we shall love that same thing (Pr. 27, III). But even apart from this consideration we are supposing that we love that same thing. Therefore, to the existing love there is added a further cause whereby it is nurtured, and by that very fact we shall love more steadfastly the object of our love. Again, from the fact that we think someone dislikes something, we shall dislike the same thing (by the same proposition). But if we suppose that at the same time we love the thing, we shall therefore at the same time love and dislike that thing; that is (see Sch. Pr. 17, III), our feelings will fluctuate.

Corollary From this and from Pr. 28, III it follows that everyone endeavors, as far as he can, that what he loves should be loved by everyone, and what he hates should be hated by everyone. Hence that saying of the poet:

> As lovers, let our hopes and fears be alike,
> Insensitive is he who loves what another leaves.[3]

Scholium This conatus to bring it about that everyone should approve of one's loves and hates is in reality ambition (see Sch. Pr. 29, III). So we see that it is in everyone's nature to strive to bring it about that others should adopt his attitude to life; and while all strive equally to this end they equally hinder one another, and in all seeking the praise or love of all, they provoke mutual dislike.

Proposition 32

If we think that someone enjoys something that only one person can possess, we shall endeavor to bring it about that he should not possess that thing.

Proof From the mere fact that we imagine somebody to enjoy something (Pr. 27, III and Cor. 1) we shall love that thing and desire to enjoy it. But by hypothesis we think that this pleasure is impeded by the fact that that person is enjoying the thing in question. Therefore (Pr. 28, III), we shall endeavor to bring it about that he should not possess it.

Scholium We therefore see that human nature is in general so constituted that men pity the unfortunate and envy the fortunate, in the latter case with a hatred proportionate to their love of what they think another possesses (by the preceding Proposition). Furthermore, we see that from the same property of human nature from which it follows that men are compassionate, it likewise follows that they are prone to envy and ambition. Finally, we shall find that common experience confirms all these points, especially if we turn our attention to childhood. For we find that children, their bodies being, as it were, continually in a state of equilibrium, laugh or weep merely from seeing others laugh or weep, and whatever else they see others do they immediately want to imitate. In short, they want for themselves whatever they see others take pleasure in because, as we have said, the images of things are the very affections of the human body, that is, the ways in which the human body is affected by external causes and disposed to this or that action.

Proposition 33

If we love something similar to ourselves, we endeavor, as far as we can, to bring it about that it should love us in return.

Proof We endeavor, as far as we can, to think of something we love in preference to other things (Pr. 12, III). So if the thing be like ourselves, we shall endeavor to affect it with pleasure in preference to other things (Pr. 29, III); that is, we shall endeavor, as far as we can, to bring it about that the object of our love should be affected with pleasure accompanied by the idea of ourselves, that is (Sch. Pr. 13, III), that it should love us in return.

---

[3] [Ovid, *Amores*, 11, 19.—S.S.]

Proposition 34

The greater the emotion with which we imagine the object of our love is affected toward us, the greater will be our vanity.

Proof By the preceding proposition, we endeavor to bring it about, as far as we can, that the object of our love should love us in return; that is (Sch. Pr. 13, III), that the object of our love should be affected with pleasure accompanied by the idea of ourselves. So the greater the pleasure with which we think that the object of our love is affected because of us, the more is this endeavor assisted; that is (Pr. 11, III and Sch.), the greater the pleasure with which we are affected. Now since our pleasure is due to our having affected with pleasure another person like ourselves, we regard ourselves with pleasure (Pr. 30, III). Therefore, the greater the emotion which we think the object loved is affected toward us, with that much greater pleasure shall we regard ourselves; that is (Sch. Pr. 30, III), the greater will be our vanity.

Proposition 35

If anyone thinks that there is between the object of his love and another person the same or a more intimate bond of friendship than there was between them when he alone used to possess the object loved, he will be affected with hatred toward the object loved and will envy his rival.

Proof The greater the love wherewith one thinks the object of his love is affected toward him, the greater will be his vanity (by the preceding proposition); that is (Sch. Pr. 30, III), the more he will be pleased. So (Pr. 28, III) he will endeavor, as far as he can, to imagine the object loved as bound to him as intimately as possible, and this conatus, or appetite, is fostered if he imagines someone else desires the same thing for himself (Pr. 31, III). But we are supposing that this conatus, or appetite, is checked by the image of the object loved accompanied by the image of him with whom the object loved is associating. Therefore (Sch. Pr. 11, III), this will cause him to be affected with pain accompanied by the idea of the object loved as cause and simultaneously by the image of his rival; that is (Sch. Pr. 13, III), he will be affected with hatred toward the object loved and at the same time toward his rival (Cor. Pr. 15, III), whom he will envy because (Pr. 23, III) he enjoys the object loved.

Scholium This hatred toward the object of one's love, joined with envy, is called Jealousy [*zelotypia*], which is therefore nothing else but "vacillation arising from simultaneous love and hatred accompanied by the idea of a rival who is envied." Furthermore, this hatred toward the object of his love will be greater in proportion to the pleasure wherewith the jealous man was wont to be affected as a result of the returning of his love by the object of his love, and also in proportion to the emotion wherewith he was affected toward him whom he thinks of as being intimately associated with the object of his love. For if he used to hate him, that very fact will make him hate the object of his love (Pr. 24, III) because he thinks of it as affecting with pleasure that which he hates, and also (Cor. Pr. 15, III) because he is compelled to associate the image of the object of his love with the image of one whom he hates. This is generally the case with love toward a woman; for he who thinks of a woman whom he loves as giving herself to another will not only feel pain by reason of his own appetite being checked but also, being compelled to associate the image of the object of his love with the sexual parts of his rival, he feels disgust for her. Then there is in addition the fact that the jealous man will not receive the same warm welcome as he was wont to receive from the object of his love, and this is a further reason for the lover's pain, as I shall now demonstrate.

Proposition 36

He who recalls a thing which once afforded him pleasure desires to possess the same thing in the same circumstances as when he first took pleasure therein.

Proof Whatever a man has seen together with the object that has afforded him pleasure will be indirectly a cause of pleasure (Pr. 15, III), and so (Pr. 28, III) he will desire to possess all this together with the object that afforded him pleasure, that is, he will desire to possess the object along with all the same attendant circumstances as when he first took pleasure in the object.

Corollary If therefore he finds one of those attendant circumstances missing, the lover will feel pain.

Proof Insofar as he finds some attendant circumstance missing, to that extent he imagines something that excludes its existence. Now since he desires that thing or circumstance (preceding proposition) by reason of his love, then (Pr. 19, III) insofar as he thinks it to be lacking he will feel pain.

Scholium This pain, insofar as it regards the absence of that which we love, is called Longing [*desiderium*].

Proposition 37

The desire arising from pain or pleasure, hatred or love, is proportionately greater as the emotion is greater.

Proof Pain diminishes or checks man's power of activity (Sch. Pr. 11, III), that is (Pr. 7, III), it diminishes or checks the conatus wherewith a man endeavors to persist in his own being; and therefore it is contrary to this conatus (Pr. 5, III), and the conatus of a man affected by pain is entirely directed to removing the pain. But, by the definition of pain, the greater the pain, the greater the extent to which it must be opposed to man's power of activity. Therefore the greater the pain, with that much greater power of activity will a man endeavor to remove the pain; that is (Sch. Pr. 9, III), with that much greater desire, or appetite, will he endeavor to remove the pain. Again, since pleasure (Sch. Pr. 11, III) increases or assists man's power of activity, it can readily be demonstrated in the same way that a man affected with pleasure desires nothing other than to preserve it, and with all the greater desire as the pleasure is greater. Finally, since hatred and love are emotions of pain or pleasure, it follows in the same way that the conatus, appetite, or desire arising through hatred or love is greater in proportion to the hatred and love.

Proposition 38

If anyone has begun to hate the object of his love to the extent that his love is completely extinguished, he will, other things being equal, bear greater hatred toward it than if he had never loved it, and his hatred will be proportionate to the strength of his former love.

Proof If anyone begins to hate the object of his love, more of his appetites are checked than if he had never loved it. For love is pleasure (Sch. Pr. 13, III), which a man endeavors to preserve as far as he can (Pr. 28, III), and this he does (same Sch.) by regarding the object loved as present and affecting it with pleasure (Pr. 21, III), as far as he can. This conatus (preceding Pr.) is the greater as the love is greater, as also is the conatus that the object loved should return his love (Pr. 33, III). But these conatus are checked by hatred toward the object loved (Cor. Pr. 13 and Pr. 23, III). Therefore, for this reason, too, the lover will be affected with pain (Sch. Pr. 11, III) which will be proportionate to his previous love; that is, in addition to the pain that was the cause of his hatred, a further pain arises from the fact that he has loved the object. Consequently, he will regard the loved object with a greater emotion of pain, that is (Sch. Pr. 13, III), he will bear greater hatred toward it than if he had not loved it, and his hatred will be proportionate to the strength of his former love.

Proposition 39

He who hates someone will endeavor to injure him unless he fears that he will suffer a greater injury in return. On the other hand, he who loves someone will by that same law endeavor to benefit him.

Proof To hate someone is (Sch. Pr. 13, III) to imagine someone to be the cause of one's pain. So (Pr. 28, III) he who hates someone will endeavor to remove or destroy him. But if he fears from him something more painful, or (which is the same thing), a greater injury, which he thinks he can avoid by not inflicting the harm he was intending on him whom he hates, he will desire to refrain from so doing (same Pr. 28, III), and this conatus (Pr. 37, III) will be greater than that which was directed toward inflicting harm. This latter conatus will therefore prevail, as we have said. The second part of this proof proceeds on the same lines. Therefore, he who hates someone . . . etc.

Scholium By "good" I understand here every kind of pleasure and furthermore whatever is conducive thereto, and especially whatever satisfies a longing of any sort. By "bad" I understand every kind of pain, and especially that which frustrates a longing. For I have demonstrated above (Sch. Pr. 9, III) that we do not desire a thing because we judge it to be good; on the contrary, we call the object of our desire good, and consequently the object of our aversion bad. Therefore, it is according to his emotion that everyone judges or deems what is good, bad, better, worse, best, or worst. Thus the miser judges wealth the best thing, and its lack the worst thing. The ambitious man desires nothing so much as public acclaim, and dreads nothing so much as disgrace. To the envious man nothing is more pleasant than another's unhappiness, and nothing more obnoxious than another's happiness. Thus, every man judges a thing good or bad, advantageous or disadvantageous, according to his own emotion.

Now the emotion whereby a man is so disposed as to refrain from what he wants to do or to choose to do what he does not want is called Timidity [*timor*], which is merely fear insofar as a man is thereby disposed to avoid by a lesser evil what he judges to be a future evil (see Pr. 28, III). But if the evil that he fears is disgrace, then timidity is called Bashfulness [*verecundia*]. Finally, if the desire to avoid a future evil is checked by the apprehension of another evil, so that he does not know what preference to make, then fear is called Consternation [*consternatio*], especially if both the feared evils are of the greatest.

Proposition 40
He who imagines he is hated by someone to whom he believes he has given no cause for hatred will hate him in return.

Proof He who imagines someone to be affected with hatred will by that very fact himself be affected with hatred (Pr. 27, III), that is (Sch. Pr. 13, III), pain accompanied by the idea of an external cause. But, by hypothesis, he himself thinks that there is no other cause of this pain than he who hates him. Therefore, from the fact that he imagines that he is hated by someone, he will be affected by pain accompanied by the idea of him who hates him; that is (by the same Sch.), he will hate that person.

Scholium But if he thinks that he has provided just cause for hatred, then (Pr. 30, III and Sch.) he will be affected with shame. But this (Pr. 25, III) is rarely the case. Furthermore, this reciprocation of hatred can also arise from the fact that hatred is followed by a conatus to injure him who is hated (Pr. 39, III). So he who imagines he is hated by someone will imagine him to be the cause of some evil or pain, and so he will be affected with pain, or fear, accompanied by the idea of him who hates him as being the cause; that is, he will be affected with hatred in return, as we said above.

Corollary 1 He who imagines that one he loves is affected with hatred toward him, will suffer the conflicting emotions of hatred and love. For insofar as he imagines he is hated by him, he is determined to hate him in return (preceding Pr.). But, by hypothesis, he nevertheless loves him. Therefore, he will suffer the conflicting emotions of hatred and love.

Corollary 2 If anyone imagines that he has suffered some injury through hatred at the hands of one toward whom he has previously felt no emotion, he will immediately endeavor to return the said injury.

Proof He who imagines that someone is affected with hatred toward him will hate him in return (preceding Pr.), and he will endeavor to devise anything that can affect that person with pain (Pr. 26, III), and will seek to inflict it on him (Pr. 39, III). But, by hypothesis, the first thing of that kind that comes to his mind is the injury that has been inflicted on himself. Therefore, he will immediately endeavor to inflict that same injury on that person.

Scholium The conatus to inflict injury on one whom we hate is called Anger [*ira*]. The conatus to return an injury which we have suffered is called Revenge [*vindicta*].

Proposition 41
If anyone thinks that he is loved by someone and believes that he has given no cause for this (which is possible through Cor. Pr. 15 and Pr. 16, III), he will love him in return.

Proof This is proved in the same way as the preceding proposition. See also its Scholium.

Scholium If he believes that he has given just cause for this love, he will exult in it (Pr. 30, III and Sch.), which is more often the case (Pr. 25, III); and we have said that the contrary occurs when someone thinks that he is hated by someone (see Sch. preceding Pr.). Now this reciprocal love, and consequently (Pr. 39, III) the conatus to benefit one who loves us and who (same Pr. 39, III) endeavors to benefit us, is called Gratitude [*gratia seu gratitudo*]. So it is evident that men are far more inclined to revenge than to repay a benefit.

Corollary He who imagines that he is loved by one whom he hates will feel conflicting emotions of hate and love. This is proved in the same way as the first corollary of the preceding proposition.

Scholium If hatred prevails, he will endeavor to injure him by whom he is loved, and this emotion is called Cruelty [*crudelitas*], especially if it is believed that he who loves has not given any cause for hatred between them.

Proposition 42
He who, moved by love or hope of honor, has conferred a benefit on someone, will feel pain if he sees that the benefit is ungratefully received.

Proof He who loves a thing similar to himself endeavors, as far as he can, to bring it about that he is loved in return (Pr. 33, III). So he who through love confers a benefit upon someone does so through his longing to be loved in return; that is (Pr. 34, III), through hope of honor, or (Sch. Pr. 30, III) pleasure. Thus (Pr. 12, III), he will endeavor as far as he can to imagine this cause of honor, i.e. to regard it as actually existing. But, by hypothesis, he thinks of something else that excludes the existence of the said cause. Therefore (Pr. 19, III), by that very fact he will feel pain.

Proposition 43
Hatred is increased by reciprocal hatred, and may on the other hand be destroyed by love.

Proof If someone thinks that one whom he hates is affected with hatred toward him, a new source of hatred thereby arises (Pr. 40, III), while the old hatred, by hypothesis, still continues. But if, on the other hand, he thinks that the said person is affected with love toward him, insofar as he thinks this, he regards himself with pleasure (Pr. 30, III), and to that extent (Pr. 29, III) he will endeavor to please him; that is (Pr. 41, III), to that extent he endeavors not to hate him nor affect him with any pain. This conatus (Pr. 37, III) will vary proportionately to the strength of the emotion from which it arises, and so if it should be greater than the emotion which arises from hatred whereby he endeavors to affect the object of his hatred with pain (Pr. 26, III), it will prevail over it and will eradicate the feeling of hatred.

Proposition 44
Hatred that is fully overcome by love passes into love, and the love will therefore be greater than if it had not been preceded by hatred.

Proof The proof proceeds along the same lines as that of Pr. 38, III. For he who begins to love the object that he hated, that is, used to regard with pain, will feel pleasure by the very fact that he loves, and to this pleasure which love involves (see its Def. in Sch. Pr. 13, III) is added the further pleasure arising from the fact that the conatus to remove the pain which hatred involves (as we demonstrated in Pr. 37, III) is very much assisted, accompanied by the idea of the one whom he hated as being the cause.

Scholium Although this is so, nobody will endeavor to hate an object or be affected with pain in order to enjoy this greater feeling of pleasure; that is, nobody will desire to suffer hurt in the hope of recovering his health. For everyone will endeavor always to preserve his own being and to remove pain, as far as he can. If it were possible to conceive the contrary, that a man should want to hate someone so that he might later feel greater love for him, he will always want to be hating him. For the greater was the hatred, the greater will be the love; so he will always want his hatred to go on growing. And for the same reason a man will endeavor to be more and more ill so as later to enjoy greater pleasure from the restoration of health. So he will always endeavor to be ill, which is absurd (Pr. 6, III).

Proposition 45
If anyone imagines that someone similar to himself is affected with hatred toward a thing similar to himself, which he loves, he will hate him.

Proof The object loved returns the hatred of him who hates it (Pr. 40, III), and so the lover who thinks that someone hates the object loved is thereby made to think of the object of his love as affected by hatred, that is (Sch. Pr. 13, III), as affected by pain. Consequently he feels pain (Pr. 21, III), a pain that is accompanied by the idea of him who hates the object of his love as being the cause; that is (Sch. Pr. 13, III), he will hate him.

Proposition 46

If anyone is affected with pleasure or pain by someone of a class or nation different from his own and the pleasure or pain is accompanied by the idea of that person as its cause, under the general category of that class or nation, he will love or hate not only him but all of that same class or nation.

Proof This is evident from Pr. 16, III.

Proposition 47

The pleasure that arises from our imagining that the object of our hatred is being destroyed or is suffering some other harm is not devoid of some feeling of pain.

Proof This is evident from Pr. 27, III. For insofar as we imagine a thing similar to ourselves to be affected with pain, to that extent we feel pain.

Scholium This Proposition can also be proved from Cor. Pr. 17, II. For whenever we call a thing to mind, although it may not actually exist, we regard it as present, and the body is affected in the same way. Therefore insofar as his remembrance of the thing is strong, to that extent the man is determined to regard it with pain. And whereas this determination, the image of the thing still persisting, is checked by the remembrance of those things that exclude its existence, it is not completely annulled, and so the man feels pleasure only insofar as this determination is checked. Hence it comes about that the pleasure that arises from the harm suffered by the object of our hatred is revived whenever we call to mind the said thing. For, as we have said, when the image of the said thing is activated, since it involves the existence of the thing it determines one to regard the thing with the same pain as when one was wont to regard it when it did exist. But since one has associated with the image of the said thing other images which exclude its existence, this determination to pain is immediately checked, and one feels a renewed pleasure, and this is so whenever the series of events is repeated.

It is this same cause that makes men feel pleasure whenever they recall some past ill and makes them enjoy talking about perils from which they have been saved. For when they imagine some peril they regard it as though it were still to come and are determined to fear it, a determination which is again checked by the idea of their escape which they associated with the idea of this peril when they did in fact escape it. This idea makes them feel safe once more, and so their pleasure is renewed.

Proposition 48

Love and hatred toward, say, Peter are destroyed if the pain involved in the latter and the pleasure involved in the former are associated with the idea of a different cause; and both emotions are diminished to the extent that we think Peter not to have been the only cause of either emotion.

Proof This is evident merely from the definitions of love and hatred, for which see Sch. Pr. 13, III. For pleasure is called love for Peter, and pain, hatred for Peter, for this reason alone, that Peter is considered the cause of the one or other emotion. When this consideration is completely or partly removed, the emotion toward Peter disappears or is diminished.

Proposition 49
Love and hatred toward a thing that we think of as free must both be greater, other conditions being equal, than toward a thing subject to necessity.

Proof A thing that we think of as free has to be perceived through itself independently of other things (Def. 7, I). If therefore we think it to be the cause of pleasure or pain, by that very fact we shall love or hate it (Sch. Pr. 13, III), and with the utmost love or hatred that can arise from the postulated emotion (preceding Pr.). But if we think of the thing which is the cause of the said emotion as subject to necessity, then we shall think of it not as the sole cause of the said emotion but together with other causes (same Def. 7, I), and so (preceding Pr.) love and hatred toward it will be less.

Scholium Hence it follows that, deeming themselves to be free, men feel more love and hatred toward one another than toward other things. Then there is the additional factor of imitation of emotions, for which see Prs. 27, 34, 40, and 43, III.

Proposition 50
Anything can be the indirect cause of hope or fear.

Proof This proposition is proved in the same way as Pr. 15, III, q.v., together with Sch. 2, Pr. 18, III.

Scholium Things that are indirectly causes of hope or fear are called good or bad omens. Again, insofar as these same omens are the cause of hope or fear, to that extent they are the cause of pleasure or pain (by Defs. of hope and fear, q.v., Sch. 2, Pr. 18, III), and consequently (Cor. Pr. 15, III) to that extent we love or hate them and (Pr. 28, III) we endeavor to procure them as means to fulfil our hopes or to remove them as obstacles or causes of fear. Furthermore, it follows from Pr. 25, III that we are so constituted by nature that we are ready to believe what we hope and reluctant to believe what we fear, and that we overestimate and underestimate in such cases. This is the origin of Superstition [*superstitiones*], to which men are everywhere a prey.

I do not think it worthwhile to demonstrate here the vacillations that arise from hope and fear, since it follows merely from the definition of these emotions that there is no hope without fear and no fear without hope (as I shall explain at greater length in due course). Furthermore, insofar as we hope or fear something, to that extent we love or hate it, and so everyone can easily apply to hope and fear what we have said concerning love and hatred.

Proposition 51
Different men can be affected in different ways by one and the same object, and one and the same man can be affected by one and the same object in different ways at different times.

Proof   The human body (Post. 3, II) is affected by external bodies in a great many ways. So two men may be affected at the same time in different ways, and so (Ax. 1 after Lemma 3, q.v., after Pr. 13, II) they can be affected by one and the same object in different ways. Again (same Post.), the human body can be affected now in one way, now in another, and consequently (same Ax.) it can be affected in different ways at different times by one and the same object.

Scholium   We therefore see that it is possible that what one man loves, another hates, what one man fears, another fears not, and that one and the same man may now love what he previously hated and may now dare what he previously feared, and so on. Again, since everyone according to his emotions judges what is good, what is bad, what is better and what is worse (Sch. Pr. 39, III), it follows that men vary as much in judgment as in emotion.[4] So it comes about that in comparing different men we distinguish between them solely by difference of emotion, and call some fearless, others timid, and others by other epithets. For example, I shall call fearless one who despises an evil that I am wont to fear, and if furthermore I have regard to the fact that his desire to inflict injury on one he hates and to benefit one whom he loves is not checked by apprehension of an evil which is wont to restrain me, I shall call him daring. Again, he who fears an evil which I am wont to despise will appear to me timid, and if furthermore I have regard to the fact that his desire is checked by apprehension of an evil which cannot restrain me, I shall say he is cowardly. And this is how everyone judges. Finally, as a result of this characteristic of man and the variability of his judgment—such as the fact that man's judgment is often governed solely by emotion, and that things which he believes to make for pleasure or pain and which he therefore (Pr. 28, III) endeavors to promote or remove are often merely imaginary, not to mention other points mentioned in Part II concerning the uncertainty of things—we readily conceive that a man may often be responsible for the pain and pleasure that he feels; that is, for being affected both with pain and pleasure, accompanied by the idea of himself as its cause. Thus, we readily understand what repentance [*paenitentia*] and self-contentment are. Repentance is pain accompanied by the idea of oneself as its cause, and self-contentment is pleasure accompanied by the idea of oneself as its cause, and these emotions are extremely intense since men believe themselves to be free (see Pr. 49, III).

PROPOSITION 52
To an object that we have previously seen in conjunction with others or that we imagine to have nothing but what is common to many other objects, we shall not give as much regard as to that which we imagine to have something singular.

Proof   As soon as we think of an object that we have seen in conjunction with others, we immediately recall the others as well (Pr. 18, II and Sch.) and thus from

---

[4] We have shown in Sch. Pr. 13, II that this can be so although the human mind is part of the divine intellect.

regarding the one we immediately pass on to regarding another. The same holds good of an object which we think to have nothing but what is common to many others. For by that very fact we suppose that we are regarding in it nothing that we have not previously seen in other objects. But in supposing that we perceive in some object something special that we have never seen before we are saying only this, that the mind, while regarding that object, contains nothing in itself to the contemplation of which it can pass on from contemplation of that object. Therefore, the mind is determined to regard only that object. Therefore ... etc.

Scholium This affection of the mind, or thought of a special thing, insofar as it alone engages the mind is called Wonder [*admiratio*], which, if evoked by an object that we fear, is called Consternation, because wonder at an evil keeps a man so paralyzed in regarding it alone that he is incapable of thinking of other things whereby he might avoid the evil. But if that which we wonder at be a man's prudence, industry, or something of that sort, since by that very fact we regard the man as far surpassing us, then wonder is called Veneration [*veneratio*]; otherwise, if we are wondering at a man's anger, envy, and so on, we call it Horror [*horror*]. Again, if we wonder at the prudence, industry, etc. of a person we love, our love will thereby be the greater (Pr. 12, III), and this love joined with wonder or veneration we call Devotion [*devotio*]. We may also in the same manner conceive hatred, hope, confidence, and other emotions as joined with wonder, and thus we can deduce more emotions than can be signified by accepted terms. Hence it is clear that the names for emotions have been taken from common usage rather than from detailed knowledge of them.

The opposite of wonder is Contempt [*contemptus*], whose cause, however, is generally as follows. From seeing someone wondering at loving, fearing, etc. something, or because something at first sight seems similar to things that we wonder at, love, fear, etc. (by Pr. 15 and Cor. and Pr. 27, III), we are determined to wonder at, love, fear, etc. the same thing. But if from the presence of the thing or from closer contemplation we are compelled to deny of it all that can be the cause of wonder, love, fear, etc., then the mind from the very presence of the thing remains determined to reflect on what is lacking in the object rather than what is in it, whereas from the presence of an object it is customary for the mind to reflect especially on what is in the object. Further, just as devotion arises from wonder at a thing that we love, so does Derision [*irrisio*] from contempt for a thing we hate or have feared, and Scorn [*dedignatio*] from contempt of folly, just as veneration from wonder at prudence. Finally, we can conceive of love, hope, honor, and other emotions as joined with contempt, and therefrom we can deduce yet other emotions, which again we are not wont to distinguish from others by special names.

PROPOSITION 53
When the mind regards its own self and its power of activity, it feels pleasure, and the more so the more distinctly it imagines itself and its power of activity.

Proof Man knows himself only through the affections of his body and their ideas (Prs. 19 and 23, II). When therefore it happens that the mind can regard its own self, by that very fact it is assumed to pass to a state of greater perfection, that is (Sch. Pr. 11, III), to be affected with pleasure, and the more so the more distinctly it is able to imagine itself and its power of activity.

Corollary The more a man imagines he is praised by others, the more this pleasure is fostered. For the more he thinks he is praised by others, the more he thinks that others are affected with pleasure by him, and this accompanied by the idea of himself (Sch. Pr. 29, III). So (Pr. 27, III) he is affected with greater pleasure, accompanied by the idea of himself.

Proposition 54
The mind endeavors to think only of the things that affirm its power of activity.

Proof The mind's conatus, or power, is the very essence of the mind (Pr. 7, III). But the essence of the mind affirms only what the mind is and can do (as is self-evident), and not what the mind is not and cannot do. So the mind endeavors to think only of what affirms, or posits, its power of activity.

Proposition 55
When the mind thinks of its own impotence, by that very fact it feels pain.

Proof The essence of the mind affirms only what the mind is and can do; that is, it is of the nature of the mind to think only of those things that affirm its power of activity (preceding Pr.). Therefore, when we say that the mind, in regarding itself, thinks of its own impotence, we are simply saying that while the mind is endeavoring to think of something that affirms its power of activity, this conatus is checked; that is, it feels pain (Sch. Pr. 11, III).

Corollary This pain is fostered all the more if one thinks he is blamed by others. The proof is on the same lines as Cor. Pr. 53, III.

Scholium This pain, accompanied by the idea of our own impotence, is called Humility [*humilitas*]. The pleasure that arises from regarding ourselves is called Self-love [*philautia*] or Self-contentment [*acquiescentia in se ipso*]. And since this pleasure is repeated whenever a man regards his own capabilities, that is, his power of activity, the result is again that everyone is eager to tell of his exploits and to boast of his strength both of body and mind, and for this reason men bore one another. From this it again follows that men are by nature envious (see Sch. Pr. 24, and Sch. Pr. 32, III), that is, they rejoice at the weakness of their fellows and are pained at their accomplishments. For whenever a man imagines his own actions he is affected with pleasure (Pr. 53, III), and the more so as his actions express greater perfection and he imagines them more distinctly; that is (by what was said in Sch.1, Pr. 40, II), the more he can distinguish them from the actions of others and regard them as something special. Therefore, everybody will most enjoy regarding himself when he regards in himself something that he denies of others. But if what he affirms of himself belongs to the universal idea of man or animal, he will derive no such great joy therefrom, and he will on the other hand feel pain if he thinks of his actions as inferior, compared with the actions of others. This pain (Pr. 28, III) he will endeavor to remove by wrongly interpreting the actions of his fellows or by embellishing his own as much as he can. It is therefore clear that men are prone to hatred and envy, and this is accentuated by their upbringing. For parents are wont to incite their children to excellence solely by the spur of honor and envy. But perhaps there remains a shadow of doubt on the grounds that we not infrequently admire the virtues of men and venerate them. To remove this shadow of doubt I shall add the following Corollary.

Corollary Nobody envies another's virtue unless he is his peer.

Proof Envy is hatred itself (Sch. Pr. 24, III) or pain (Sch. Pr. 13, III); that is (Sch. Pr. 11, III), an affection whereby a man's power of activity, that is, his conatus, is checked. Now man (Sch. Pr. 9, III) endeavors or desires to do nothing save what can follow from his given nature. Therefore, a man will not desire to be attributed to himself any power of activity, or (which is the same thing) virtue, which is proper to the nature of another and foreign to his own. So his desire cannot be checked, that is (Sch. Pr. 11, III), he cannot be pained, by reason of his regarding some virtue in somebody unlike himself; consequently he cannot envy him. But he would envy his peer, who is assumed to be of the same nature as himself.

Scholium So when we said in Sch. Pr. 52, III that we venerate a man as a result of wondering at his prudence, strength of mind, and so on, this comes about (as is obvious from the proposition) because we think these virtues are special to him and not common to our nature, and so we do not envy him them any more than we envy trees their height, lions their strength, etc.

PROPOSITION 56
There are as many kinds of pleasure, pain, desire and consequently of every emotion that is compounded of these (such as vacillation) or of every emotion that is derived from these (love, hatred, hope, fear, etc), as there are kinds of objects by which we are affected.

Proof Pleasure, pain, and consequently the emotions that are compounded of these or derived from them are passive emotions (Sch. Pr. 11, III). Now we are necessarily passive (Pr. 1, III) insofar as we have inadequate ideas, and only insofar as we have inadequate ideas are we passive (Pr. 3, III). That is to say (Sch. Pr. 40, II), we are necessarily passive only to the extent that we form mental images [*imaginamur*], i.e. (Pr. 17, II and Sch.) to the extent that we are affected in a way that involves both the nature of our own body and the nature of an external body. Therefore the explication of the nature of every passive emotion must necessarily include an expression of the nature of the object by which we are affected. The pleasure arising from object A involves the nature of object A and the pleasure arising from object B involves the nature of object B, and so these two emotions of pleasure are different in nature because they arise from causes of different natures. So too the emotion of pain that arises from one object is different in nature from the pain that arises from a different cause, and this must also be understood of love, hatred, hope, fear, and vacillation. Therefore, there are necessarily as many kinds of pleasure, pain, love, hatred, etc. as there are kinds of objects by which we are affected. Now desire is the very essence, or nature, of each individual insofar as that is conceived as determined by some given state of its constitution to do something (Sch. Pr. 9, III). Therefore, according as each individual is affected from external causes with various kinds of pleasure, pain, love, hate, etc., that is, according as his nature is conditioned in various ways, so must his desire be of different kinds; and the nature of one desire must differ from the nature of another to the same extent as the emotions, from which each single desire arises, differ amongst themselves. Therefore, there are as many kinds of desire as there are kinds of pleasure, pain, love, etc., and consequently (by what has been proved) as there are kinds of objects by which we are affected.

Scholium Among the kinds of emotional states which (by the preceding proposition) must be very numerous, most noteworthy are Dissipation [*luxuria*], Drunkenness [*ebrietas*], Lust [*libido*], Avarice [*avaritia*], and Ambition [*ambitio*], which are only concepts springing from love or desire, and which explicate the nature of both these emotions through the objects to which they are related. For by dissipation, drunkenness, lust, avarice, and ambition we mean quite simply uncontrolled love or desire for feasting, drinking, sex, riches, and popular acclaim. Furthermore, these emotions have no opposites insofar as we distinguish them from other emotions solely through the objects to which they are related. For Self-control [*temperantia*], Sobriety [*sobrietas*], and Chastity [*castitas*], which we are wont to oppose to dissipation, drunkenness, and lust, are not emotions or passive states, but indicate the power of the mind that controls these emotions.

However, I cannot here give an account of the remaining kinds of emotion, for they are as many as there are kinds of objects; nor, if I could, is it necessary. For it suffices for our purpose, which is to determine the strength of the emotions and the power of the mind over them, to have a general definition of all the individual emotions. It is sufficient, I repeat, to understand the common properties of the emotions and the mind so as to determine the nature and the extent of the mind's power in controlling and checking the emotions. So although there is a great difference between this and that emotion of love, hatred, or desire, e.g. between the love toward one's children and love toward one's wife, there is no need for us to investigate these differences and to trace any further the nature and origin of the emotions.

Proposition 57

Any emotion of one individual differs from the emotion of another to the extent that the essence of the one individual differs from the essence of the other.

Proof This proposition is obvious from Ax. 1, q.v., after Lemma 3 Sch. Pr. 13, II. But we shall nevertheless prove it from the definitions of the three primary emotions.

All emotions are related to desire, pleasure or pain, as is made clear by the definitions we have given of them. Now desire is the very nature or essence of every single individual (see its definition in Sch. Pr. 9, III). Therefore, the desire of each individual differs from the desire of another to the extent that the nature or essence of the one differs from the essence of the other. Again, pleasure and pain are passive emotions whereby each individual's power, that is, his conatus to persist in his own being, is increased or diminished, assisted or checked (Pr. 11, III and Sch.). But by the conatus to persist in one's own being, insofar as it is related to mind and body together, we understand appetite and desire (Sch. Pr. 9, III). Therefore, pleasure and pain is desire or appetite, insofar as it is increased or diminished, assisted or checked, by external causes; that is, (by the same Sch.), it is each individual's very nature. So each individual's pleasure or pain differs from the pleasure or pain of another to the extent that the nature or essence of the one also differs from that of the other. Consequently, any emotion . . . etc.

Scholium Hence it follows that the emotions of animals that are called irrational (for now that we know the origin of mind we can by no means doubt that beasts have feelings) differ from the emotions of men as much as their nature differs from human nature. Horse and man are indeed carried away by lust to procreate, but the former by equine lust, the latter by human lust. So too the lusts and appetites of insects, fishes, and birds are bound to be of various different kinds. So although each individual lives content with the nature wherewith he is endowed and rejoices in it, that life wherewith each is content and that joy are nothing other than the idea or soul [*anima*] of the said individual, and so the joy of the one differs from the joy of another as much as the essence of the one differs from the essence of the other. Finally, it follows from the preceding proposition that there is also no small difference between the joy which guides the drunkard and the joy possessed by the philosopher, a point to which I wish to draw attention in passing.

So much for emotions that are related to man insofar as he is passive. It remains for me to add a few words concerning emotions that are related to man insofar as he is active.

Proposition 58
Besides the pleasure and desire that are passive emotions, there are other emotions of pleasure and desire that are related to us insofar as we are active.

Proof When the mind conceives itself and its power to act, it feels pleasure (Pr. 53, III). Now the mind necessarily regards itself when it conceives a true, that is, adequate, idea (Pr. 43, II). But the mind does conceive adequate ideas (Sch.2, Pr. 40, II). Therefore it feels pleasure, too, insofar as it conceives adequate ideas, that is (Pr. 1, III), insofar as it is active. Again, it is both insofar as it has clear and distinct ideas and insofar as it has confused ideas that the mind endeavors to persist in its own being (Pr. 9, III). But by conatus we understand desire (Sch. Pr. 9, III). Therefore, desire is also related to us insofar as we understand, i.e., insofar as we act (Pr. 1, III).

Proposition 59

Among all the emotions that are related to the mind insofar as it is active, there are none that are not related to pleasure or desire.

Proof All emotions are related to desire, pleasure or pain, as is shown by the definitions we have given of them. Now by pain we understand that which diminishes or checks the mind's power of thinking (Pr. 11, III, and Sch.). So insofar as the mind feels pain, to that extent its power of understanding, that is, its power of activity, is diminished or checked (Pr. 1, III). So no emotions of pain can be related to the mind insofar as it is active, but only emotions of pleasure and desire, which (preceding Pr.) are to that extent also related to the mind.

Scholium All the activities which follow from emotions that are related to the mind insofar as it exercises understanding I refer to Strength of mind [*fortitudo*], which I subdivide into Courage [*animositas*] and Nobility [*generositas*]. By courage I understand "the desire whereby every individual endeavors to preserve his own being according to the dictates of reason alone." By nobility I understand "the desire whereby every individual, according to the dictates of reason alone, endeavors to assist others and make friends of them." So I classify under courage those activities that are directed solely to the advantage of the agent, and those that are directed to the advantage of another I classify under nobility. So self-control, sobriety, and resourcefulness in danger, etc. are kinds of courage; Courtesy [*modestia*] and Mercy [*clementia*] are kinds of nobility.

And now I think I have explained the principal emotions and vacillations that arise from the combination of the three basic emotions—desire, pleasure, and pain—and have clarified them through their first causes. From this it is clear that we are in many respects at the mercy of external causes and are tossed about like the waves of the sea when driven by contrary winds, unsure of the outcome and of our fate. But I have said that I have clarified only the principal conflicts of feeling, not all that can be. For by proceeding in the same manner as above we can readily demonstrate that love is joined with repentance, scorn, shame, and so on. Indeed, from what has been said I think everyone is quite convinced that emotions can be combined with one another in so many ways and give rise to so many variations that they cannot be numbered. But it suffices for my purpose to have enumerated only the principal emotions; for those I have passed over would be a matter of curiosity rather than utility.

However, one further point should be observed concerning love. It frequently happens, while we are enjoying what we were seeking, that from that very enjoyment the body changes to a new condition, as a result of which it is differently determined and different images are activated in it, and at the same time the mind begins to think of and desire other things. For example, when we think of something that is wont to delight us with its taste, we desire to enjoy it, to eat it. But while we are thus enjoying it the stomach is being filled and the body is changing its condition. If therefore, with the body now in a different condition, the image of the said food is fostered by its being set before us, and consequently also the conatus or desire to eat the food, this conatus, or desire, will be opposed by the new condition of the body, and consequently the presence of the food which we used to want will be hateful, and this is what we call Satiety [*fastidium*] and Weariness [*taedium*].

I have passed by those external affections of the body which can be observed in the case of emotions, such as trembling, pallor, sobbing, laughter, and so on, because they are related to the body without any relation to the mind. Finally, with regard to the definitions of emotions there are certain points to be noted, and I shall therefore repeat those definitions here in proper order, accompanied by such observations as I think necessary in each case.

DEFINITIONS OF THE EMOTIONS

1. Desire is the very essence of man insofar as his essence is conceived as determined to any action from any given affection of itself.

Explication   We said above in Sch. Pr. 9, III that desire is appetite accompanied by consciousness of itself, and that appetite is the very essence of man insofar as his essence is determined to such actions as contribute to his preservation. But in the same Scholium I also noted that in fact I acknowledge no difference between human appetite and desire. For whether or not a man is conscious of his appetite, the appetite remains one and the same. So to avoid appearing to be guilty of tautology, I declined to explicate desire through appetite; my object was so to define it as to include all the endeavors of human nature that we term appetite, will, desire, or urge. I could merely have said: "Desire is the very essence of man insofar as his essence is conceived as determined to some action"; but then it would not follow from this definition (Pr. 23, II) that the mind can be conscious of its own desire or appetite. Thus, in order to involve the cause of this consciousness it was necessary (by the same Pr.) to add "from any given affection of itself." For by "any affection of the human essence" we understand "any condition [*constitutio*] of the said essence," whether it be innate, whether it be conceived solely through the attribute of Thought or solely through the attribute of Extension, or whether it be related to both attributes together. So here I mean by the word "desire" any of man's endeavors, urges, appetites, and volitions, which vary with man's various states, and are not infrequently so opposed to one another that a man may be drawn in different directions and know not where to turn.

2. Pleasure is man's transition from a state of less perfection to a state of greater perfection.

3. Pain is man's transition from a state of greater perfection to a state of less perfection.

Explication   I say "transition," for pleasure is not perfection itself. If a man were to be born with the perfection to which he passes, he would be in possession of it without the emotion of pleasure. This is clearer in the case of pain, the contrary emotion. For nobody can deny that pain consists in the transition to a state of less perfection, not in the less perfection itself, since man cannot feel pain insofar as he participates in any degree of perfection. Nor can we say that pain consists in the privation of greater perfection, for privation is nothing, whereas the emotion of pain is an actuality, which therefore can be nothing other than the actuality of the transition to a state of less perfection; that is, the actuality whereby a man's power of activity is diminished or checked (Sch. Pr. 11, III).

As to the definitions of Cheerfulness, Titillation, Melancholy, and Anguish, I omit them because they are related chiefly to the body, and are only species of pleasure and pain.

4. Wonder is the thought of any thing on which the mind stays fixed because this particular thought has no connection with any others. See Proposition 52 and its Scholium.

Explications In Sch. Pr. 18, II we demonstrated the reason why the mind, from thinking of one thing, passes immediately on to the thought of another, and that is that in such cases the images are bound together and so ordered that one follows another. This concept cannot cover the case when the image is a strange one. The mind will be kept in contemplation of the said thing until it is determined by other causes to think of other things. So the thought of an unusual thing, considered in itself, is of the same nature as other thoughts, and for this reason I do not count wonder among the emotions; nor do I see why I should do so, since this distraction of the mind arises from no positive cause that distracts it from other things, but only from the lack of a cause for determining the mind, from the contemplation of one thing, to think of other things.

Therefore, as I noted in Sch. Pr. 11, III, I acknowledge only three basic or primary emotions, pleasure, pain, and desire; and I have made mention of wonder only because it is customary for certain emotions derived from the three basic emotions to be signified by different terms when they are related to objects that evoke our wonder. There is an equally valid reason for my adding here a definition of contempt.

5. Contempt is the imagining [*imaginatio*] of some thing that makes so little impact on the mind that the presence of the thing motivates the mind to think of what is not in the thing rather than of what is in the thing. See Sch. Pr. 52, III.

I here pass over the definitions of Veneration and Scorn because, as far as I know, there are no emotions that take their name from them.

6. Love is pleasure accompanied by the idea of an external cause.

Explication This definition explains quite clearly the essence of love. The definition given by writers who define love as "the lover's wish to be united with the object of his love" expresses not the essence of love, but a property of it; and since these writers have not sufficiently grasped the essence of love, neither have they succeeded in forming any clear conception of its property. This has led to the universal verdict that their definition is very obscure. However, be it noted that when I say that in the case of a lover it is a property to wish to be united with the object of his love, by "wish" I do not mean consent or deliberate intention, that is, free decision (for in Pr. 48, II we proved this to be fictitious), nor again desire to be united with the loved object when it is absent or to continue in its presence when it is there; for love can be conceived without any one particular desire. By "wish" I mean the contentment that is in the lover by reason of the presence of the object of his love, by which the lover's pleasure is strengthened, or at least fostered.

7. Hatred is pain accompanied by the idea of an external cause.

Explication The points here to be noted can be easily perceived from the Explication of the preceding Proposition. See also Sch. Pr. 13, III.

8. Inclination [*propensio*] is pleasure accompanied by the idea of a thing which is indirectly the cause of the pleasure.

9. Aversion [*aversio*] is pain accompanied by the idea of a thing which is indirectly the cause of the pain. (For these see Sch. Pr. 15, III.)

10. Devotion is love toward one at whom we wonder.

Explication We demonstrated in Pr. 52, III that Wonder [*admiratio*] arises from the strangeness of a thing. So if it happens that we often think about the object of our wonder, we shall cease to wonder at it. So we see that the emotion of devotion can easily degenerate into mere love.

11. Derision is pleasure arising from our imagining that there is in the object of our hate something that we despise.

Explication Insofar as we despise a thing that we hate, to that extent we deny existence regarding it (Sch. Pr. 52, III) and to that extent we feel pleasure (Pr. 20, III). But since we are supposing that what a man derides he nevertheless hates, it follows that this pleasure is not unalloyed (Sch. Pr. 47, III).

12. Hope is inconstant pleasure arising from the idea of a thing future or past, of whose outcome we are in some doubt.

13. Fear is inconstant pain arising from the idea of a thing future or past, of whose outcome we are in some doubt.

For these see Sch. 2, Pr. 18, III.

Explication From these definitions it follows that there is no hope without fear and no fear without hope. For he who is in hopeful suspense and has doubts as to the outcome of a thing is assumed to be imagining something that excludes the existence of the hoped-for thing, and so to that extent he feels pain (Pr. 19, III). Consequently, as long as he is in hopeful suspense, he fears as to the outcome. On the other hand, he who is in a state of fear, that is, is unsure of the occurrence of a thing that he hates, is also imagining something that excludes the existence of the said thing, and so (Pr. 20, III) he feels pleasure, and to that extent he entertains hope of its not happening.

14. Confidence is pleasure arising from the idea of a thing future or past, concerning which reason for doubt has been removed.

15. Despair is pain arising from the idea of a thing future or past concerning which reason for doubt has been removed.

Explication Therefore confidence arises from hope and despair from fear when reason for uncertainty as to the outcome of a thing has been removed. This comes about either because man imagines a thing past or future as being at hand and regards it as present, or because he thinks of other things that exclude the existence of those things that were causing his uncertainty. For although we can never be certain as to the outcome of particular things (Cor. Pr. 31, II), it is possible for us not to be doubtful as to their outcome. For we have demonstrated (Sch. Pr. 49, II) that not having doubts concerning a thing is different from being certain of the thing. So it is possible for us to be affected by the same emotion of pleasure or pain from the image of a thing past or future as from the image of a thing present, as we proved in Proposition 18, III, q.v., with Sch.

16. Joy is pleasure accompanied by the idea of a past thing whose outcome was contrary to our fear.

17. Disappointment [*conscientiae morsus*] is pain accompanied by the idea of a past thing whose outcome was contrary to our hope.

18. Pity is pain accompanied by the idea of ill that has happened to another whom we think of as like ourselves. See Sch. Pr. 22 and Sch. Pr. 27, III.

Explication There seems to be no difference between pity and compassion [*misericordia*], unless perhaps pity has reference to a particular occurrence of emotion, while compassion has regard to a set disposition to that emotion.

19. Approbation is love toward one who has benefited another.

20. Indignation is hatred toward one who has injured another.

Explication I know that these words are commonly used with a different meaning. But my purpose is to explain not the meaning of words but the nature of things, and to assign to things terms whose common meaning is not very far away from the meaning I decide to give them. Let this one reminder suffice. As to the cause of these emotions, see Cor. 1, Pr. 27 and Sch. Pr. 22, III.

21. Over-esteem is to think too highly of someone by reason of love.

22. Disparagement [*despectus*] is to think too meanly of someone by reason of hatred.

Explication Over-esteem is therefore a result, or a property, of love, and disparagement of hatred. So over-esteem can also be defined as "love, insofar as it so affects a man that he thinks too highly of the object of his love"; and disparagement as "hatred, insofar as it so affects a man that he thinks too meanly of the object of his hatred." For these see Sch. Pr. 26, III.

23. Envy is hatred, insofar as it so affects a man that he is pained at another's good fortune and rejoices at another's ill-fortune.

Explication The opposite of envy is commonly said to be compassion which therefore, with some distortion of its usual meaning, can be defined thus:

24. Compassion is love, insofar as it so affects a man that he rejoices at another's good and feels pain at another's hurt.

Explication As to envy, see Sch. Pr. 24, III and Sch. Pr. 32, III.

Such are the emotions of pleasure and pain which are accompanied by the idea of an external thing as direct [*per se*] or indirect [*per accidens*] cause. From these I pass on to other emotions which are accompanied by the idea of an internal thing as cause.

25. Self-contentment is pleasure arising from a man's contemplation of himself and his power of activity.

26. Humility is pain arising from a man's contemplation of his own impotence, or weakness.

Explication Self-contentment is the opposite of humility insofar as by the former we understand pleasure that arises from our regarding our power of activity. But insofar as we also understand by it pleasure accompanied by the idea of some deed which we think we have done from free decision of the mind, then its opposite is repentance, which we define thus:

27. Repentance is pain accompanied by the idea of some deed which we believe we have done from free decision of the mind.

Explication We have demonstrated the causes of these emotions in Sch. Pr. 51, III and Prs. 53,54,55, III and its Sch. As for free decision of the mind, see Sch. Pr. 35, II. But here we should also note that it is not surprising that all our actions that are customarily called wrong are followed by pain, and those which are said to be right, by pleasure. For we readily understand from what has been said that our upbringing is chiefly responsible for this. By disapproving of wrong actions and frequently rebuking their children when they commit them, and contrariwise by approving and praising right actions, parents have caused the former to be associated with painful feelings and the latter with pleasurable feelings. This is further confirmed by experience. For not all people have the same customs and religion. What some hold as sacred, others regard as profane; what some hold as honorable, others regard as disgraceful. So each individual repents of a deed or exults in it according to his upbringing.

28. Pride is thinking too highly of oneself by reason of self-love.

Explication So pride differs from over-esteem, for the latter is related to an external object, while pride is related to a subject who thinks too highly of himself. However, as over-esteem is an effect or property of love, so is pride of self-love, and so it can also be defined as "love of self, or self-contentment, insofar as it so affects a man that he thinks too highly of himself" (see Sch. Pr. 26, III). This emotion has no opposite, for nobody thinks too meanly of himself by reason of self-hatred. Indeed, nobody thinks too meanly of himself insofar as he thinks this or that is beyond his capability. For whenever a man thinks something is beyond his capability, he necessarily thinks so, and by this belief he is so conditioned that he really cannot do what he thinks he cannot do. For while thinking that he cannot do this or that, he is not determined to do it, and consequently it is impossible that he should do it.

However, if we direct our attention solely to the way that others see him, we can conceive it as possible that a man may think too meanly of himself. For it can happen that a man, regarding with pain his own weakness, should think that everyone despises him, and this while the rest of the world is very far from despising him. Furthermore, a man may think too meanly of himself if he denies of himself in present time something related to future time of which he is not sure, as that he may say that he cannot achieve any certainty, or that he can desire or do nothing that is not wrong or disgraceful, and so on. Again, we can say that a man thinks too meanly of himself when we see that from excessive fear of disgrace he does not dare what others who are his peers dare. So we can take this emotion, which I shall call Self-abasement [*abjectio*], to be the opposite of pride. For as pride arises from self-contentment, so self-abasement arises from humility. Therefore we shall define it as follows:

29. Self-abasement is thinking too meanly of oneself by reason of pain.

Explication We usually oppose humility to pride, but then we are having regard to the effects of the two emotions rather than their nature. For we usually apply the term "proud" to one who exults overmuch [Sch. Pr. 30, III], who talks only of his own virtues and the faults of others, who expects to take precedence over all, and who goes about with the pomp and style usually affected by those far above him in station. On the other hand, we apply the term "humble" to one who blushes frequently, who confesses his faults and talks of the virtues of others, who gives way to all, and who goes about downcast and careless of his appearance.

Now these emotions, humility and self-abasement, are very rare; for human nature, considered in itself, strives against them as far as it can (Prs. 13 and 54, III). So those who are believed to be most self-abased and humble are generally the most ambitious and envious.

30. Honor is pleasure accompanied by the idea of some action of ours which we think that others praise.

31. Shame is pain accompanied by the idea of some action of ours that we think that others censure.

Explication For these, see Sch. Pr. 30, III. But one should here observe the difference between shame and bashfulness. Shame is the pain that follows on a deed of which we are ashamed. Bashfulness is the fear or apprehension of shame, whereby a man is restrained from some disgraceful act. The opposite of bashfulness is usually Impudence [*impudentia*], which is not really an emotion, as I shall demonstrate in due course. But the names of emotions, as I have noted, have regard more to usage than to their nature.

Herewith I have completed my proposed task of explicating the emotions of pleasure and pain. I now pass on to those emotions that are related to desire.

32. Longing is desire or appetite for possessing something, a desire fostered by remembrance of the said thing and at the same time checked by remembrance of other things that exclude the existence of the said object of appetite.

Explication As I have often said, when we recall something we are thereby conditioned to regard it with the same emotion as if the thing were actually present. But in our waking hours, this disposition or conatus is generally restrained by the images of things that exclude the existence of that which we recall. So when we remember a thing that affected us with some kind of pleasure, by that very fact we endeavor to regard it as present along with that same emotion of pleasure; but this conatus is straightway checked by the remembrance of things that exclude the existence of the said thing. Therefore longing is really the opposite pain to the pleasure that arises from the absence of a thing that we hate, concerning which see Sch. Pr. 47, III. But as the word "longing" seems to have regard to desire, I classify this emotion under emotions of desire.

33. Emulation is the desire for something, engendered in us from the fact that we think others to have the same desire.

Explication When someone flees because he sees others fleeing, or fears because he sees others fearing, or again, on seeing that someone has burnt his hand, draws his hand back and makes a movement of the body as if his own hand were burnt, we say that he is imitating another's emotion, not that he is emulating him. This is not because we realize that the causes of imitation and emulation are different, but because it is the usual practice to call only him emulous who imitates what we judge to be honorable, useful, or pleasant. As to the cause of emulation, see Pr. 27, III and Sch. As to the reason why envy is generally associated with this emotion, see Pr. 32, III and Sch.

34. Gratitude is the desire, or eagerness of love [*amoris studium*], whereby we endeavor to benefit one who, from a like emotion of love, has bestowed a benefit on us. See Pr. 39, and Sch. Pr. 41, III.

35. Benevolence is the desire to benefit one whom we pity. See Sch. Pr. 27, III.

36. Anger is the desire whereby we are urged from hatred to inflict injury on one whom we hate. See Pr. 39, III.

37. Revenge is the desire whereby we are urged from mutual hatred to inflict injury on one who, from like emotion, has injured us. See Cor. 2, Pr. 40, III and Sch.

38. Cruelty, or savageness [*saevitia*], is the desire whereby someone is urged to inflict injury on one whom we love or whom we pity.

Explication The opposite of cruelty is mercy, which is not a passive emotion but the power of the mind whereby a man controls anger and revenge.

39. Timidity is the desire to avoid a greater evil, which we fear, by a lesser evil. See Sch. Pr. 39, III.

40. Boldness is the desire whereby someone is urged to some dangerous action which his fellows fear to undertake.

41. Cowardice is a term applied to one whose desire is checked by apprehension of a danger which his fellows dare to face.

Explication So cowardice is simply the fear of some evil which most people are not wont to fear. So I do not classify it as an emotion of desire. Still, I have decided to explain it here because it is the opposite of boldness insofar as we attend to desire.

42. Consternation is a term applied to one whose desire to avoid evil is checked by a feeling of wonder at the evil that he fears.

Explication So consternation is a kind of cowardice. But since consternation arises from a twofold timorousness, it can therefore more fittingly be defined as "fear that holds a man in such a state of stupefaction and hesitation that he is not able to remove the evil." I say "stupefaction" inasmuch as we mean that his desire to remove the evil is checked by a feeling of wonder. I say "hesitation" insofar as we conceive the said desire to be checked by apprehension of another evil by which he is equally tormented, with the result that he knows not which of the two to avert. For this see Sch. Pr. 39 and Sch. Pr. 52, III. With regard to cowardice and boldness, see Sch. Pr. 51, III.

43. Courtesy [*humanitas*] or Politeness [*modestia*] is desire to do things that please men and avoid things that displease them.

44. Ambition is the immoderate desire for honor.

Explication Ambition is the desire whereby all emotions (Prs. 27 and 31, III) are encouraged and strengthened; and thus this emotion can scarcely be overcome. For as long as a man is subject to any desire, he is necessarily subject to this one. "The best men," said Cicero, "are particularly led by the hope of renown. Even philosophers, in the books that they write in condemnation of fame, add their names thereto . . ." and so on.[5]

45. Dissipation is the immoderate desire, or also love, of sumptuous living.
46. Drunkenness is the immoderate desire and love of drinking.
47. Avarice is the immoderate desire and love of riches.
48. Lust is also the desire and love of sexual intercourse.

Explication Whether this desire for sex is moderate or not, it is usually called lust.

These five emotions (as I noted in Sch. Pr. 56, III) have no opposites. For politeness is a species of ambition (concerning which see Sch. Pr. 29, III); and self-control, sobriety, and chastity, too, I have already noted as indicating the power of the mind, not its passivity. And although it is possible that a miser, an ambitious or a timid man may abstain from excessive food, drinking and sex, yet avarice, ambition, and timidity are not the opposites of dissipation, drunkenness, and lust. For the miser generally longs to gorge himself on other people's food and drink. The ambitious man will not exercise any kind of self-control if secrecy is assured; and if he should live in the company of drunkards and libertines, he will be more prone to these vices because he is ambitious. The timid man does what he wants not to do. Although the miser may cast his riches into the sea to avoid death, he nevertheless remains a miser. If a libertine is pained at not being able to indulge himself, he does not on that account cease to be a libertine. Fundamentally, these emotions do not have regard so much to the activities of sumptuous living, drinking, and so on, as to appetite and love. Therefore, these emotions have no opposites except for courage and nobility, with which I shall deal hereafter.

---

[5] [Cicero, *Pro Archia*, II.—S.S.]

I pass over the definitions of jealousy and other vacillations, both because they arise from the combination of emotions which we have already defined and because the majority have no names, which shows that for practical purposes it suffices to know them in a general way. Now it is clear from the definitions of the emotions we have dealt with that they all spring from desire, pleasure, or pain, or rather that they are nothing apart from these three emotions, each of which is wont to appear under various names according to their various contexts and extrinsic characteristics. If now we direct our attention to these basic emotions and to the explanation we have already given of the nature of the mind, we can define emotions, insofar as they are related only to the mind, as follows:

General Definition of Emotions

The emotion called a passive experience is a confused idea whereby the mind affirms a greater or less force of existence of its body, or part of its body, than was previously the case, and by the occurrence of which the mind is determined to think of one thing rather than another.

Explication I say in the first place that an emotion, or passivity of the mind, is a "confused idea." For we have demonstrated (Pr. 3, III) that the mind is passive only to the extent that it has inadequate or confused ideas. Next, I say "whereby the mind affirms a greater or less force of existence of its body or part of its body than was previously the case." For all ideas that we have of bodies indicate the actual physical state of our own body rather than the nature of the external body (Cor. 2, Pr. 16, II). Now the idea that constitutes the specific reality of emotion must indicate or express the state of the body or some part of it, which the body or some part of it possesses from the fact that its power of activity or force of existence [*vis existendi*] is increased or diminished, assisted or checked. But it should be noted that when I say "a greater or less force of existence than was previously the case," I do not mean that the mind compares the body's present state with its past state, but that the idea that constitutes the specific reality of emotion affirms of the body something that in fact involves more or less reality than was previously the case. And since the essence of the mind consists in this (Prs. 11 and 13, II), that it affirms the actual existence of its body, and by perfection we mean the very essence of a thing, it therefore follows that the mind passes to a state of greater or less perfection when it comes about that it affirms of its body, or some part of it, something that involves more or less reality than was previously the case. So when I said above that the mind's power of thinking increases or diminishes, I meant merely this, that the mind has formed an idea of its body or some part of it that expresses more or less reality than it had been affirming of it. For the excellence of ideas and the actual power of thinking are measured by the excellence of the object. Lastly, I added "by the occurrence of which the mind is determined to think of one thing rather than another" in order to express the nature of desire in addition to the nature of pleasure and pain as explicated in the first part of the definition.

PART IV

Of Human Bondage, or the Strength of the Emotions

Preface

I assign the term "bondage" to man's lack of power to control and check the emotions. For a man at the mercy of his emotions is not his own master but is subject to fortune, in whose power he so lies that he is often compelled, although he sees the better course, to pursue the worse. In this Part I have set myself the task of demonstrating why this is so, and also what is good and what is bad in emotions. But before I begin, I should like to make a few preliminary observations on perfection and imperfection, and on good and bad.

He who has undertaken something and has brought it to completion[1] will say that the thing is completed; and not only he but everyone who rightly knew, or thought he knew, the intention and aim of the author of that work. For example, if anyone sees a work (which I assume is not yet finished) and knows that the aim of the author is to build a house, he will say that the house is imperfect. On the other hand, as soon as he sees that the work has been brought to the conclusion that its author had intended to give it, he will say that it is perfect. But if anyone sees a work whose like he had never seen before, and he does not know the artificer's intention, he cannot possibly know whether the work is perfect or imperfect.

This appears to have been the original meaning of these terms. But when men began to form general ideas and to devise ideal types of houses, buildings, towers, and so on, and to prefer some models to others, it came about that each called "perfect" what he saw to be in agreement with the general idea he had formed of the said thing, and "imperfect" that which he saw at variance with his own preconceived ideal, although in the artificer's opinion it had been fully completed. There seems to be no other reason why even natural phenomena (those not made by human hand) should commonly be called perfect or imperfect. For men are wont to form general ideas both of natural phenomena and of artifacts, and these ideas they regard as models, and they believe that Nature (which they consider does nothing without an end in view) looks to these ideas and holds them before

---

[1] [The Latin term *perfectus*, which is crucial in this Preface, can mean both "perfect" and "completed." For Spinoza the emphasis here is upon completion: that which has been finished or accomplished is perfect; contrarily, that which is not yet completed is imperfect. Spinoza will go on to say that we eventually learn to make evaluative judgments on the basis of what we have come to take as completed specimens of things. The latter now become normative models for further comparison and valuation.]

herself as models. So when they see something occurring in Nature at variance with their preconceived ideal of the thing in question, they believe that Nature has then failed or blundered and has left that thing imperfect. So we see that men are in the habit of calling natural phenomena perfect or imperfect from their own preconceptions rather than from true knowledge. For we have demonstrated in Appendix, Part I that Nature does not act with an end in view; that the eternal and infinite being, whom we call God, or Nature, acts by the same necessity whereby it exists. That the necessity of his nature whereby he acts is the same as that whereby he exists has been demonstrated (Prop. 16, I). So the reason or cause why God, or nature, acts, and the reason or cause why he exists, are one and the same. Therefore, just as he does not exist for an end, so he does not act for an end; just as there is no beginning or end to his existing, so there is no beginning or end to his acting. What is termed a "final cause" is nothing but human appetite insofar as it is considered as the starting point or primary cause of some thing. For example, when we say that being a place of habitation was the final cause of this or that house, we surely mean no more than this, that a man, from thinking of the advantages of domestic life, had an urge to build a house. Therefore, the need for a habitation insofar as it is considered as a final cause is nothing but this particular urge, which is in reality an efficient cause, and is considered as the prime cause because men are commonly ignorant of the causes of their own urges; for, as I have repeatedly said, they are conscious of their actions and appetites but unaware of the causes by which they are determined to seek something. As to the common saying that Nature sometimes fails or blunders and produces imperfect things, I count this among the fictions with which I dealt in Appendix I.

So perfection and imperfection are in reality only modes of thinking, notions which we are wont to invent from comparing individuals of the same species or kind; and it is for this reason that I previously said (Def. 6, II) that by reality and perfection I mean the same thing. For we are wont to classify all the individuals in Nature under one genus which is called the highest genus, namely, the notion of Entity, which pertains to all the individuals in Nature without exception. Therefore insofar as we classify individuals in Nature under this genus and compare them with one another and find that some have more being or reality than others, to that extent we say some are more perfect than others. And insofar as we attribute to them something involving negation, such as limit, end, impotence and so on, to that extent we call them imperfect because they do not affect our minds as much as those we call perfect, and not because they lack something of their own or because Nature has blundered. For nothing belongs to the nature of anything except that which follows from the necessity of nature of its efficient cause; and whatever follows from the necessity of the nature of its efficient cause must necessarily be so.

As for the terms "good" and "bad," they likewise indicate nothing positive in things considered in themselves, and are nothing but modes of thinking, or notions which we form from comparing things with one another. For one and the same thing can at the same time be good and bad, and also indifferent. For example, music is good for one who is melancholy, bad for one in mourning, and neither good nor bad for the deaf. However, although this is so, these terms ought to be retained. For since we desire to form the idea of a man which we may look to as a model of human nature, we shall find it useful to keep these terms in the sense I have indicated. So in what follows I shall mean by "good" that which we certainly know to be the means for our approaching nearer to the model of human nature that we set before ourselves, and by "bad" that which we certainly know prevents us from reproducing the said model. Again, we shall say that men are more perfect or less perfect insofar as they are nearer to or farther from this model. For it is important to note that when I say that somebody passes from a state of less perfection to a state of greater perfection, and vice versa, I do not mean that he changes from one essence or form to another (for example, a horse is as completely destroyed if it changes into a man as it would be if it were to change into an insect), but that we conceive his power of activity, insofar as this is understood through his nature, to be increased or diminished.

Finally, by perfection in general I shall understand reality, as I have said; that is, the essence of anything whatsoever in as far as it exists and acts in a definite manner, without taking duration into account. For no individual thing can be said to be more perfect on the grounds that it has continued in existence over a greater period of time. The duration of things cannot be determined from their essence, for the essence of things involves no fixed and determinate period of time. But any thing whatsoever, whether it be more perfect or less perfect, will always be able to persist in existing with that same force whereby it begins to exist, so that in this respect all things are equal.

Definitions

1. By *good* I understand that which we certainly know to be useful to us.
2. By *bad* I understand that which we certainly know to be an obstacle to our attainment of some good.

For these, see the foregoing preface, toward the end.

3. I call individual things *contingent* insofar as, in attending only to their essence, we find nothing that necessarily posits their existence or necessarily excludes it.
4. I call individual things *possible* insofar as, in attending to the causes by which they should be brought about, we do not know whether these causes are determined to bring them about.

In Sch. 1, Pr. 33, I, I did not differentiate between possible and contingent because at that point it was unnecessary to distinguish carefully between them.

5. In what follows, by *conflicting emotions* I shall understand those that draw a man in different directions, although they belong to the same genus, such as dissipation and avarice, which are species of love, and contrary not by nature, but indirectly [*per accidens*].
6. In Schs. 1 and 2, Pr. 18, III I have explained what I mean by emotion toward a thing future, present, and past.

But it should be further noted that just as we cannot distinctly imagine spatial distance beyond a certain limit, the same is true of time. That is, just as we are wont to imagine that all those objects more than 200 feet away from us, or whose distance from our position exceeds what we can distinctly imagine, are the same distance from us and appear to be in the same plane, so too in the case of objects whose time of existence is farther away from the present by a longer distance than we are wont to distinctly imagine, we think of them all as equally far from the present, and we refer them to one point of time, as it were.

7. By the *end* for the sake of which we do something, I mean appetite.

8. By *virtue* and *power* I mean the same thing; that is (Pr. 7, III), virtue, insofar as it is related to man, is man's very essence, or nature, insofar as he has power to bring about that which can be understood solely through the laws of his own nature.

Axiom

There is in Nature no individual thing that is not surpassed in strength and power by some other thing. Whatsoever thing there is, there is another more powerful by which the said thing can be destroyed.

Proposition 1

Nothing positive contained in a false idea can be annulled by the presence of what is true, insofar as it is true.

Proof Falsity consists solely in the privation of knowledge, a privation which is involved in inadequate ideas (Pr. 35, II), and it is not by possessing something positive that they are called false (Pr. 33, II). On the contrary, insofar as they are related to God, they are true (Pr. 32, II). If therefore what is positive in a false idea were to be annulled by the presence of what is true, insofar as it is true, a true idea would be annulled by itself, which is absurd (Pr. 4, III). Therefore . . . etc.

Scholium This proposition is more clearly understood from Cor. 2, Pr. 16, II. For imagination [*imaginatio*] is an idea that indicates the present disposition of the human body more than the nature of an external body, not indeed distinctly, but confusedly, whence it comes about that the mind is said to err. For example, when we gaze at the sun, it seems to us to be about 200 feet away; and in this we are deceived as long as we are unaware of its true distance. With knowledge of its distance the error is removed, but not the imagining [*imaginatio*], that is, the idea of the sun that explicates its nature only insofar as the body is affected by it. Thus although we know its true distance, we shall nevertheless see it as being close to us. For as we said in Sch. Pr. 35, II, it is not by reason of our ignorance of its true distance that we see it as being so near, but because the mind conceives the magnitude of the sun insofar as the body is affected by it. In the same way, when the rays of the sun falling on the surface of water are reflected back to our eyes, we see it as if it were in the water although we know its true position. Similarly other imaginings whereby the mind is deceived, whether they indicate the natural disposition of the body or the increase or diminution of its power of activity, are not contrary to what is true and do not disappear at the presence of truth. It does indeed happen that when we mistakenly fear some evil, the fear disappears when we hear the truth. But the contrary also happens; when we fear an evil that is assuredly going to overtake us, the fear likewise disappears on our hearing false tidings. So imaginings do not disappear at the presence of what is true insofar as it is true, but because other imaginings that are stronger supervene to exclude the present existence of the things we imagine, as we demonstrated in Pr. 17, II.

Proposition 2

We are passive insofar as we are a part of Nature which cannot be conceived independently of other parts.

Proof We are said to be passive when something arises in us of which we are only the partial cause (Def. 2, III); that is (Def. 1, III), something that cannot be deduced solely from the laws of our own nature. So we are passive insofar as we are a part of Nature which cannot be conceived independently of other parts.

Proposition 3

The force [vis] whereby a man persists in existing is limited, and infinitely surpassed by the power of external causes.

Proof This is clear from the Axiom of this Part. In the case of every man there is something else, say A, more powerful than he, and then there is another thing, say B, more powerful than A, and so ad infinitum. Therefore, the power of a man is limited in comparison with something else, and is infinitely surpassed by the power of external causes.

Proposition 4

It is impossible for a man not to be part of Nature and not to undergo changes other than those which can be understood solely through his own nature and of which he is the adequate cause.

Proof The power whereby each single thing, and consequently man, preserves its own being is the very power of God, or Nature (Cor. Pr. 24, I), not insofar as it is infinite but insofar as it can be explicated through actual human essence (Pr. 7, III). Therefore, the power of man insofar as it is explicated through his actual essence is part of the infinite power of God, or Nature, that is, of God's essence (Pr. 34, I). This is the first point. Again, if it were possible for man to undergo no changes except those which can be understood solely through his own nature, it would follow (Prs. 4 and 6, III) that he cannot perish but would always necessarily exist; and this would have to follow from a cause whose power is either finite or infinite, namely, either from the power of man alone, in that he would be capable of removing from himself all changes which might arise from external causes, or else from the infinite power of Nature, by which all particular things would be so governed that man could undergo no changes other than those that serve for his preservation. But of these alternatives the first is absurd (by the preceding proposition, whose proof is universal and can be applied to all particular things). Therefore, if it were possible that man could undergo no changes except such as could be understood through man's nature alone, and consequently (as I have already demonstrated) that he should always necessarily exist, this would have to follow from the infinite power of God. Consequently (Pr. 16, I), the entire order of Nature as conceived under the attributes of Extension and Thought would have to be deducible from the necessity of the divine nature insofar as it is considered as affected by the idea of some man. And so it would follow (Pr. 21, I) that man would be infinite, which is absurd (by the first part of this proof). Therefore, it is impossible that man should not undergo any changes except those of which he is the adequate cause.

Corollary Hence it follows that man is necessarily always subject to passive emotions, and that he follows the common order of Nature, and obeys it, and accommodates himself to it as far as the nature of things demands.

PROPOSITION 5
The force and increase of any passive emotion and its persistence in existing is defined not by the power whereby we ourselves endeavor to persist in existing, but by the power of external causes compared with our own power.

Proof The essence of a passive emotion cannot be explicated through our own essence alone (Defs.1 and 2, III); that is (Pr. 7, III), the power of a passive emotion cannot be defined by the power whereby we endeavor to persist in our own being, but (as we have demonstrated in Pr. 16, II) must necessarily be defined by the power of an external cause compared with our own power.

PROPOSITION 6
The force of any passive emotion can surpass the rest of man's activities or power so that the emotion stays firmly fixed in him.

Proof The force and increase of any passive emotion and its persistence in existing is defined by the power of an external cause compared with our own power (by the preceding proposition) and so (Pr. 3, IV) can surpass man's power.

PROPOSITION 7
An emotion cannot be checked or destroyed except by a contrary emotion which is stronger than the emotion which is to be checked.

Proof An emotion, insofar as it is related to the mind, is an idea whereby the mind affirms a greater or less force of existence in its body than was previously the case (General Definition of Emotions, near the end of Part III). So when the mind is assailed by an emotion, the body at the same time is affected by an affection whereby its power of acting is increased or diminished. Furthermore, this affection of the body (Pr. 5, IV) receives from its own cause its force for persisting in its own being, and therefore this force cannot be checked or destroyed except by a corporeal cause (Pr. 6, II) which affects the body with an affection contrary to the other (Pr. 5, III) and stronger than it (Ax. IV). So (Pr. 12, II) the mind will be affected by the idea of an affection stronger than and contrary to the earlier one; that is (by the General Definition of Emotions), the mind will be affected by an emotion stronger than and contrary to the previous one, an emotion which will exclude or destroy the existence of the previous one. So an emotion cannot be either destroyed or checked except by a contrary and stronger emotion.

Corollary An emotion, insofar as it is related to the mind, can neither be checked nor destroyed except through the idea of an affection of the body contrary to and stronger than the affection which we are experiencing. For the emotion we are experiencing can neither be checked nor destroyed except by an emotion stronger than and contrary to it (preceding Pr.), that is, except through the idea of an affection of the body stronger than and contrary to the affection we are experiencing (General Definition of Emotions).

Proposition 8
Knowledge of good and evil is nothing other than the emotion of pleasure or pain insofar as we are conscious of it.

Proof We call good or bad that which is advantageous, or an obstacle, to the preservation of our being (Defs. 1 and 2, IV); that is (Pr. 7, III), that which increases or diminishes, helps or checks, our power of activity. Therefore insofar as we perceive some thing to affect us with pleasure or pain (by the definitions of pleasure and pain, q.v., in Sch. Pr. 11, III), we call it good or bad; and so knowledge of good and evil is nothing other than the idea of pleasure or pain which necessarily follows from the emotion of pleasure or pain (Pr. 22, II). But this idea is united to the emotion in the same way as the mind is united to the body (Pr. 21, II); that is (as has been demonstrated in the Scholium to the same Proposition), this idea is not distinct in reality from the emotion, or, in other words (by the General Definition of the Emotions), from the idea of an affection of the body, save only in conception. Therefore, this knowledge of good and evil is nothing other than the emotion itself, insofar as we are conscious of it.

Proposition 9
An emotion whose cause we think to be with us in the present is stronger than it would be if we did not think the said cause to be with us.

Proof An imagining [*imaginatio*] is an idea whereby the mind regards a thing as present (see its definition in Sch. Pr. 17, II), but which indicates the disposition of the human body rather than the nature of the external thing (Cor. 2, Pr. 16, II). Therefore, an emotion (by the General Definition of Emotions) is an imagining insofar as it indicates the disposition of the body. Now an imagining (Pr. 17, II) is more intense as long as we think of nothing that excludes the present existence of the external thing. Therefore that emotion, too, whose cause we think to be with us in the present, is more intense or stronger than it would be if we did not think the said cause to be with us.

Scholium When I asserted above in Proposition 18, III that from the image of a thing future or past we are affected by the same emotion as if the thing we are thinking of were present, I deliberately gave warning that this is true only insofar as we attend to the image of the thing; for an image is of the same nature whether or not we picture things as present. But I did not deny that the image becomes feebler when we regard as present to us other things which exclude the present existence of a future thing. I omitted to emphasize this at the time because I had decided to treat of the strength of the emotions in this Part.

Corollary The image of a thing future or past, that is, a thing which we regard as related to our future or past time to the exclusion of present time, is feebler, other things being equal, than the image of a present thing. Consequently, the emotion toward a thing future or past, other things being equal, is weaker than an emotion toward a present thing.

Proposition 10
We are affected toward a future thing which we imagine to be imminent more intensely than if we were to imagine its time of existence to be farther away from the present. We are also affected by remembrance of a thing we imagine to belong to the near past more intensely than if we were to imagine it to belong to the distant past.

Proof Insofar as we imagine a thing to be imminent or to belong to the near past, by that very fact we are imagining something that excludes the thing's presence to a less degree than if we were to imagine that its future time of existence was farther from the present or that it happened long ago (as is self-evident). So to that extent (preceding proposition) we are more intensely affected toward it.

Scholium From our note to Definition 6, IV, it follows that with regard to objects that are distant from the present by a longer interval of time than comes within the scope of our imagination, although we know that they are far distant in time from one another, we are affected toward them with the same degree of faintness.

Proposition 11
An emotion toward a thing which we think of as inevitable [necessarius] is more intense, other things being equal, than emotion toward a thing possible, or contingent, that is, not inevitable.

Proof Insofar as we imagine a thing to be inevitable, to that extent we affirm its existence. On the other hand, insofar as we imagine a thing not to be inevitable, we deny its existence (Sch. 1, Pr. 33, I), and therefore (Pr. 9, IV) emotion toward an inevitable thing, other things being equal, is more intense than emotion toward something not inevitable.

Proposition 12

Emotion toward a thing which we know not to exist in the present, and which we imagine to be possible, is, other things being equal, more intense than emotion toward a contingent thing.

Proof Insofar as we imagine a thing to be contingent, we are not affected by any image of another thing that posits the existence of the former (Def. 3, IV). On the contrary, by hypothesis, we are thinking of things that exclude its present existence. But insofar as we think of a thing as possible in the future, we are thinking of things that posit its existence (Def. 4, IV); that is (Pr. 18, III), things that encourage hope or fear. Therefore, emotion toward a possible thing is more intense.

Corollary Emotion toward a thing which we know not to exist in the present and which we think of as contingent is much feebler than if we were to think of the thing as with us in the present.

Proof Emotion toward a thing that we imagine to exist in the present is more intense than if we were to imagine it to belong to the future (Cor. Pr. 9, IV), and much stronger than it would be if we were to think of that future time as far distant from the present (Pr. 10, IV). Therefore, emotion toward a thing whose time of existence we imagine to be far distant from the present is much weaker than it would be if we were to imagine the said thing to be present, but is nevertheless (preceding Pr.) more intense than it would be if we were to imagine the said thing to be contingent. So emotion toward a contingent thing is much feebler than it would be if we were to imagine the thing to be with us in the present.

Proposition 13

Emotion toward a contingent thing which we know not to exist in the present is, other things being equal, feebler than emotion toward a thing past.

Proof Insofar as we imagine a thing to be contingent, we are not affected by the image of any other thing that posits the existence of the former (Def. 3, IV). On the contrary, by hypothesis, we are imagining things that exclude its present existence. But insofar as we think of the said thing as belonging to the past, to that extent it is assumed that we are thinking of something that brings it back to memory, that is, which activates the image of the thing (Pr. 18, II and Sch.), and therefore to that extent causes us to regard the thing as present (Cor. Pr. 17, II). So (Pr. 9, IV) emotion toward a contingent thing which we know not to exist in the present is, other things being equal, feebler than emotion toward a thing past.

Proposition 14

No emotion can be checked by the true knowledge of good and evil insofar as it is true, but only insofar as it is considered as an emotion.

Proof An emotion is an idea whereby the mind affirms a greater or less force of existence of its body than was previously the case (by the General Definition of Emotions), and so (Pr. 1, IV) it contains nothing positive that can be annulled by the presence of what is true. Consequently, true knowledge of good and evil cannot check an emotion by virtue of being true. But insofar as it is an emotion (Pr. 8, IV), if it be stronger than the emotion which is to be checked, to that extent only (Pr. 7, IV) it can check an emotion.

Proposition 15
Desire that arises from the true knowledge of good and evil can be extinguished or checked by many other desires that arise from the emotions by which we are assailed.

Proof From the true knowledge of good and evil, insofar as this is an emotion (Pr. 8, IV), there necessarily arises desire (Definition of Emotions 1), whose strength is proportionate to the strength of the emotion from which it arises (Pr. 37, III). But since this desire, by hypothesis, arises from our truly understanding something, it therefore follows in us insofar as we are active (Pr. 3, III), and so must be understood solely through our essence (Def. 2, III). Consequently (Pr. 7, III), its force and increase must be defined solely in terms of human power. Now desires that arise from emotions by which we are assailed are also greater in proportion to the strength of the emotions, and so their force and increase (Pr. 5, IV) must be defined in terms of the power of external causes which indefinitely surpasses our power when compared with it (Pr. 3, IV). So desires that arise from emotions of this kind may be stronger than that desire which arises from the true knowledge of good and evil, and therefore (Pr. 7, IV) are able to check or extinguish it.

Proposition 16
The desire that arises from a knowledge of good and evil insofar as this knowledge has regard to the future can be the more easily checked or extinguished by desire of things that are attractive in the present.

Proof Emotion toward a thing that we imagine to be future is feebler than emotion toward something present (Cor. Pr. 9, IV). But desire that arises from the true knowledge of good and evil, even when this knowledge is concerned with things that are good in the present, can be extinguished or checked by any chance desire (by the preceding proposition, whose proof is universally valid). Therefore, desire that arises from the said knowledge insofar as it has regard to the future can be the more easily checked or extinguished . . . etc.

Proposition 17
Desire that arises from the true knowledge of good and evil insofar as this knowledge is concerned with contingent things can be even more easily checked by desire for things which are present.

Proof This proposition is proved in the same way as the preceding proposition, from Cor. Pr. 12, IV.

Scholium I think I have thus demonstrated why men are motivated by uncritical belief [*opinio*] more than by true reasoning, and why the true knowledge of good and evil stirs up conflict in the mind and often yields to every kind of passion. Hence the saying of the poet, "I see the better course and approve it, but I pursue the worse course."[2] Ecclesiastes seems to have had the same point in mind when he said: "He who increaseth knowledge increaseth sorrow."[3] My purpose in saying this is not to conclude that ignorance is preferable to knowledge, or that there is no difference between a fool and a wise man in the matter of controlling the emotions. I say this because it is necessary to know both the power of our nature and its lack of power, so that we can determine what reason can and cannot do in controlling the emotions, and in this Part I have said that I shall treat only of human weakness. As for the power of reason over the emotions, it is my intention to treat of that in a separate Part.

PROPOSITION 18
Desire arising from pleasure is, other things being equal, stronger than desire arising from pain.

Proof Desire is the very essence of man (Definition of Emotions 1); that is (Pr. 7, III), the conatus whereby man endeavors to persist in his own being. Therefore the desire that arises from pleasure is assisted or increased by the very emotion of pleasure (by Definition of Pleasure, q.v., in Sch. Pr. 11, III); whereas the desire that arises from pain is diminished or checked by the very emotion of pain (same Sch.). So the force of the desire that arises from pleasure must be defined by human power together with the power of an external cause, whereas the desire that arises from pain must be defined by human power alone. Therefore, the former is stronger than the latter.

Scholium I have thus briefly explained the causes of human weakness and inconstancy, and why men do not abide by the precepts of reason. It now remains for me to demonstrate what it is that reason prescribes for us, and which emotions are in harmony with the rules of human reason, and which are contrary to them. But before I embark on the task of proving these things in our detailed geometrical order, it would be well first of all to make a brief survey of the dictates of reason, so that my meaning may be more readily grasped by everyone.

Since reason demands nothing contrary to nature, it therefore demands that every man should love himself, should seek his own advantage (I mean his real advantage), should aim at whatever really leads a man toward greater perfection, and, to sum it all up, that each man, as far as in him lies, should endeavor to preserve his own being. This is as necessarily true as that the whole is greater than its part (Pr. 4, III).

Again, since virtue (Def. 8, IV) is nothing other than to act from the laws of one's own nature, and since nobody endeavors to preserve his own being (Pr. 7, III) except from the laws of his own nature, it follows firstly that the basis of virtue is the very conatus to preserve one's own being, and that happiness consists in a

---

[2] [Ovid, *Metamorphoses* VII, 20. —S.S.]
[3] [*Ecclesiastes* 1:18. —S.S.]

man's being able to preserve his own being. Secondly, it follows that virtue should be sought for its own sake, and that there is nothing preferable to it or more to our advantage, for the sake of which it should be sought. Thirdly, it follows that those who commit suicide are of weak spirit and are completely overcome by external causes opposed to their own nature. Further, it follows from Post. 4, II that we can never bring it about that we should need nothing outside ourselves to preserve our own being and that we should live a life quite unrelated to things outside ourselves. Besides, if we consider the mind, surely our intellect would be less perfect if the mind were in solitude and understood nothing beyond itself. Therefore, there are many things outside ourselves which are advantageous to us and ought therefore to be sought. Of these none more excellent can be discovered than those which are in complete harmony with our own nature. For example, if two individuals of completely the same nature are combined, they compose an individual twice as powerful as each one singly.

Therefore, nothing is more advantageous to man than man. Men, I repeat, can wish for nothing more excellent for preserving their own being than that they should all be in such harmony in all respects that their minds and bodies should compose, as it were, one mind and one body, and that all together should endeavor as best they can to preserve their own being, and that all together they should aim at the common advantage of all. From this it follows that men who are governed by reason, that is, men who aim at their own advantage under the guidance of reason, seek nothing for themselves that they would not desire for the rest of mankind; and so are just, faithful, and honorable.

These are the dictates of reason, which I have decided to set forth in brief at this point before embarking upon their more detailed demonstration. This I have done so that I may, if possible, gain the attention of those who believe that the principle that every man is bound to seek his own advantage is the basis, not of virtue and piety, but of impiety. Now that I have briefly shown that the contrary is the case, I proceed to its proof, using the same method as hitherto.

Proposition 19
Every man, from the laws of his own nature, necessarily seeks or avoids what he judges to be good or evil.

Proof Knowledge of good and evil is (Pr. 8, IV) the emotion of pleasure or pain insofar as we are conscious of it, and therefore every man (Pr. 28, III) necessarily seeks what he judges to be good and avoids what he judges to be evil. But this appetite is nothing other than man's very essence or nature (Definition of Appetites, q.v. in Sch. Pr. 9, III and Definition of Emotions 1). Therefore every man, solely from the laws of his own nature, necessarily seeks or avoids . . . etc.

Proposition 20
The more every man endeavors and is able to seek his own advantage, that is, to preserve his own being, the more he is endowed with virtue. On the other hand, insofar as he neglects to preserve what is to his advantage, that is, his own being, to that extent he is weak.

Proof Virtue is human power, which is defined solely by man's essence (Def. 8, IV); that is, it is defined solely by the conatus whereby man endeavors to persist in his own being (Pr. 7, III). Therefore, the more every man endeavors and is able to preserve his own being, the more he is endowed with virtue, and consequently (Prs. 4 and 6, III) insofar as he neglects to preserve his own being, to that extent he is weak.

Scholium Therefore nobody, unless he is overcome by external causes contrary to his own nature, neglects to seek his own advantage, that is, to preserve his own being. Nobody, I repeat, refuses food or kills himself from the necessity of his own nature, but from the constraint of external causes. This can take place in many ways. A man kills himself when he is compelled by another who twists the hand in which he happens to hold a sword and makes him turn the blade against his heart; or when, in obedience to a tyrant's command, he, like Seneca,[4] is compelled to open his veins, that is, he chooses a lesser evil to avoid a greater. Or it may come about when unobservable external causes condition a man's imagination and affect his body in such a way that the latter assumes a different nature contrary to the previously existing one, a nature whereof there can be no idea in mind (Pr. 10, III). But that a man from the necessity of his own nature should endeavor to cease to exist or to be changed into another form, is as impossible as that something should come from nothing, as anyone can see with a little thought.

PROPOSITION 21
Nobody can desire to be happy, to do well and to live well without at the same time desiring to be, to do, and to live; that is, actually to exist.

Proof The proof of this proposition, or rather, the fact itself, is self-evident, and also follows from the definition of desire. For the desire (Definition of Emotions 1) to live happily, to do well and so on is the very essence of man; that is (Pr. 7, III), the conatus whereby every man endeavors to preserve his own being. Therefore nobody can desire . . . etc.

PROPOSITION 22
No virtue can be conceived as prior to this one, namely, the conatus to preserve oneself.

Proof The conatus to preserve itself is the very essence of a thing (Pr. 7, III). Thus, if any virtue could be conceived as prior to this one — namely, this conatus — then (Def. 8, IV) the essence of a thing would be conceived as prior to itself, which is obviously absurd. Therefore no virtue . . . etc.

---

[4] [Seneca (4 B.C.–A.D. 66), the Roman writer and statesman, committed suicide under political pressure rather than suffer public disgrace. In many of his essays and letters he praised and justified suicide under certain conditions.]

Corollary The conatus to preserve oneself is the primary and sole basis of virtue. For no other principle can be conceived as prior to this one (preceding Pr.), and no virtue can be conceived independently of it (Pr. 21, IV).

Proposition 23
Insofar as a man is determined to some action from the fact that he has inadequate ideas, he cannot be said, without qualification, to be acting from virtue; he can be said to do so only insofar as he is determined from the fact that he understands.

Proof Insofar as a man is determined to action from the fact that he has inadequate ideas, to that extent (Pr. 1, III) he is passive; that is (Defs. 1 and 2, III), he does something that cannot be perceived solely in terms of his own essence, that is (Def. 8, IV), something that does not follow from his own virtue. But insofar as he is determined to an action from the fact that he understands, to that extent he is active (Pr. 1, III); that is (Def. 2, III), he does something that is perceived solely in terms of his own essence, that is (Def. 8, IV), which follows adequately from his own virtue.

Proposition 24
To act in absolute conformity with virtue is nothing else in us but to act, to live, to preserve one's own being (these three mean the same) under the guidance of reason, on the basis of seeking one's own advantage.

Proof To act in absolute conformity with virtue is nothing else (Def. 8, IV) but to act according to the laws of one's own nature. But we are active only insofar as we understand (Pr. 3, III). Therefore, to act from virtue is nothing else in us but to act, to live, and to preserve one's own being under the guidance of reason, on the basis (Cor. Pr. 22, IV) of seeking one's own advantage.

Proposition 25
Nobody endeavors to preserve his being for the sake of some other thing.

Proof The conatus whereby each thing endeavors to preserve its own being is defined solely by the essence of the thing itself (Pr. 7, III); given this essence alone, and not from the essence of any other thing, it necessarily follows (Pr. 6, III) that every one endeavors to preserve his own being. Moreover, this proposition is obvious from Cor. Pr. 22, IV. For if a man were to endeavor to preserve his own being for the sake of another thing, then that thing would be the primary basis of his virtue (as is self-evident), which is absurd (by the aforementioned corollary). Therefore nobody . . . etc.

Proposition 26
Whatever we endeavor according to reason is nothing else but to understand; and the mind, insofar as it exercises reason, judges nothing else to be to its advantage except what conduces to understanding.

Proof The conatus to preserve itself is nothing but the essence of a thing (Pr. 7, III), which, insofar as it exists as such, is conceived as having a force to persist in existing (Pr. 6, III) and to do those things that necessarily follow from its given nature (see Definition of Appetite in Sch. Pr. 9, III). But the essence of reason is nothing other than our mind insofar as it clearly and distinctly understands (see its Definition in Sch. 2, Pr. 40, II). Therefore (Pr. 40, II), whatever we endeavor according to reason is nothing else but to understand. Again, since this conatus of the mind wherewith the mind, insofar as it exercises reason, endeavors to preserve its own being is nothing else but a conatus to understand (by the first part of this proof), this conatus to understand (Cor. Pr. 22, IV) is therefore the primary and only basis of virtue, and it is not for some further purpose that we endeavor to understand things (Pr. 25, IV). On the contrary, the mind, insofar as it exercises reason, cannot conceive any good for itself except what is conducive to understanding (Def. 1, IV).

Proposition 27

We know nothing to be certainly good or evil except what is really conducive to understanding or what can hinder understanding.

Proof The mind, insofar as it exercises reason, seeks nothing else but to understand, and judges nothing else to be to its advantage except what is conducive to understanding (preceding Pr.). But the mind (Prs. 41 and 43, II, and Sch.) possesses no certainty save insofar as it has adequate ideas, or (which is the same thing by Sch. Pr. 40, II) insofar as it exercises reason. Therefore, we do not know anything to be certainly good except what is truly conducive to understanding, or certainly evil except what can hinder understanding.

Proposition 28

The mind's highest good is the knowledge of God, and the mind's highest virtue is to know God.

Proof The highest object that the mind can understand is God, that is (Def. 6, I), an absolutely infinite being, and one without whom (Pr. 15, I) nothing can be or be conceived. Thus (Prs. 26 and 27, IV) the mind's utmost advantage or (Def. 1, IV) its highest good is knowledge of God. Again, the mind is active only to the extent that it understands (Prs. 1 and 3, III), and to that extent only (Pr. 23, IV) can it be said without qualification to act from virtue. So the absolute virtue of the mind is to understand. But the highest thing the mind can understand is God (as we have just proved). Therefore, the highest virtue of the mind is to understand or to know God.

Proposition 29

No individual thing whose nature is quite different from ours can either assist or check our power to act, and nothing whatsoever can be either good or evil for us unless it has something in common with us.

Proof The power of each individual thing (and consequently of man (Cor. Pr. 10, II), whereby he exists and acts is determined only by another particular thing (Pr. 28, I) whose nature (Pr. 6, II) must be understood through the same attribute as that through which human nature is conceived. So our power to act, in whatever way it be conceived, can be determined, and consequently assisted or checked, by the power of another individual thing which has something in common with us, and not by the power of a thing whose nature is entirely different from our own. And since we call good or evil that which is the cause of pleasure or pain (Pr. 8, IV), that is (Sch. Pr. 11, III), which increases or diminishes, assists or checks our power of activity, a thing whose nature is entirely different from our own can be neither good nor evil for us.

Proposition 30
No thing can be evil for us through what it possesses in common with our nature, but insofar as it is evil for us, it is contrary to us.

Proof We call bad that which is the cause of pain (Pr. 8, IV), that is (through Definition of Pain, q.v. in Sch. Pr. 11, III), that which diminishes or checks our power of activity. So if something were bad for us through that which it has in common with us, that thing would be able to diminish or check the very thing that it has in common with us, which is absurd (Pr. 4, III). So nothing can be bad for us through that which it has in common with us. On the contrary, insofar as it is bad—that is (as we have just demonstrated), insofar as it can diminish or check our power of activity—to that extent (Pr. 5, III) it is contrary to us.

Proposition 31
Insofar as a thing is in agreement with our nature, to that extent it is necessarily good.

Proof Insofar as a thing is in agreement with our nature, it cannot be bad (preceding Pr.). Therefore, it is necessarily either good or indifferent. If we make the latter assumption, namely, that it is neither good nor bad, then nothing will follow from its nature (Ax. 3, IV)[5] which serves to preserve our nature; that is (by hypothesis), which serves to preserve the nature of the thing itself. But this is absurd (Pr. 6, III). Therefore, insofar as it is in agreement with our nature, it is necessarily good.

Corollary Hence it follows that the more a thing is in agreement with our nature, the more advantageous it is to us, that is, the more it is good; and, conversely, the more advantageous a thing is to us, to that extent it is in more agreement with

---

[5] [The standard Latin text of Gebhardt has a reference to Axiom 3 of Part IV. However, in our current text there is only *one* axiom for Part IV. Translators have suggested various corrections; but Gebhardt notes in his critical apparatus that in Spinoza's original draft of the *Ethics* there were probably several axioms for Part IV. In the final version all but one of these axioms were deleted, although in Proposition 31 Spinoza still has Axiom 3 in mind.—S.S.]

our nature. For insofar as it is not in agreement with our nature, it is necessarily either different from our nature or contrary to it. If it is different (Pr. 29, IV), it can be neither good nor bad; but if contrary, it will therefore be contrary also to that which is in agreement with our nature, that is (preceding Pr.), contrary to our good; that is, it will be evil. So nothing can be good save insofar as it is in agreement with our nature. So the more a thing is in agreement with our nature, the more advantageous it is to us, and vice versa.

Proposition 32
Insofar as men are subject to passive emotions, to that extent they cannot be said to agree in nature.

Proof Things which are said to agree in nature are understood to agree in respect of their power (Pr. 7, III), not in respect of their weakness or negation, and consequently (Sch. Pr. 3, III) not in respect of passive emotions. Therefore men, insofar as they are subject to passive emotions, cannot be said to agree in nature.

Scholium This is also self-evident. For he who says that white and black agree only in the fact that neither is red is making an absolute assertion that white and black agree in no respect. So, too, if someone says that stone and man agree only in this respect, that they are both finite, or weak, or that they do not exist from the necessity of their own natures, or that they are indefinitely surpassed by the power of external causes, he is making the general assertion that stone and man agree in no respect. For things that agree only negatively, that is, in what they do not possess, in reality agree in nothing.

Proposition 33
Men can differ in nature insofar as they are assailed by emotions that are passive, and to that extent one and the same man, too, is variable and inconstant.

Proof The nature or essence of emotions cannot be explicated solely through our own essence or nature (Defs. 1 and 2, III), but must be defined by the potency, that is (Pr. 7, III), the nature, of external causes as compared with our own power. Hence there are as many kinds of each emotion as there are kinds of objects by which we are affected (Pr. 56, III), and men are affected in different ways by one and the same object (Pr. 51, III), and to that extent they differ in nature. Finally, one and the same man (Pr. 51, III) is affected in different ways toward the same object, and to that extent he is variable . . . etc.

Proposition 34
Insofar as men are assailed by emotions that are passive, they can be contrary to one another.

Proof A man, Peter, for example, can be the cause of Paul's feeling pain because Peter has something similar to a thing that Paul hates (Pr. 16, III), or because Peter has sole possession of a thing that Paul also loves (Pr. 32, III and Sch.), or for other reasons (for the principal reasons, see Sch. Pr. 55, III). Thus it will come about (Def. of Emotions 7) that Paul will hate Peter. Consequently, it will easily happen (Pr. 40, III, and Sch.) that Peter will hate Paul in return; thus (Pr. 39, III), they will endeavor to injure each other, that is (Pr. 30, IV), they will be contrary to each other. But the emotion of pain is always a passive emotion (Pr. 59, III). Therefore men, insofar as they are assailed by passive emotions, can be contrary to one another.

Scholium I said that Paul hates Peter because he thinks that Peter possesses something that Paul also loves, from which at first sight it seems to follow that these two are injurious to each other as a result of loving the same thing, and consequently of their agreeing in nature. So if this is true, Propositions 30 and 31, IV would be false. But if we examine this question with scrupulous fairness, we find that there is no contradiction at any point. These two do not dislike each other insofar as they agree in nature, that is, insofar as they both love the same thing, but insofar as they differ from each other. For insofar as they both love the same thing, each one's love is thereby fostered (Pr. 31, III); that is (Def. of Emotions 6), each one's pleasure is fostered. Therefore, it is by no means true that insofar as they both love the same thing and agree in nature, they dislike each other. As I have said, the reason for their dislike is none other than that they are assumed to differ in nature. For we are supposing that Peter has an idea of the loved thing as now in his possession, while Paul has an idea of the loved thing lost to him. Hence the latter is affected with pain, while the former is affected with pleasure, and to that extent they are contrary to each other. In this way we can readily demonstrate that all other causes of hatred depend on men being different in nature, and not on a point wherein they agree.

PROPOSITION 35

Insofar as men live under the guidance of reason, to that extent only do they always necessarily agree in nature.

Proof Insofar as men are assailed by passive emotions, they can be different in nature (Pr. 33, IV) and contrary to one another (preceding Pr.). But we say that men are active only insofar as they live under the guidance of reason (Pr. 3, III). Thus, whatever follows from human nature, insofar as it is defined by reason, must be understood (Def. 2, III) through human nature alone as its proximate cause. But since everyone, in accordance with the laws of his own nature, aims at what he judges to be good and endeavors to remove what he judges to be evil (Pr. 19, IV), and since furthermore what he judges from the dictates of reason to be good or evil is necessarily good or evil (Pr. 41, II), it follows that insofar as men live under the guidance of reason, to that extent only do they necessarily do the things which are necessarily good for human nature and consequently for every single man; that is (Cor. Pr. 31, IV), which agree with the nature of every single man. So men also are necessarily in agreement insofar as they live under the guidance of reason.

Corollary 1 There is no individual thing in the universe more advantageous to man than a man who lives by the guidance of reason. For the most advantageous thing to man is that which agrees most closely with his nature (Cor. Pr. 31, IV); that is (as is self-evident), man. But man acts absolutely according to the laws of his own nature when he lives under the guidance of reason (Def. 2, III), and only to that extent is he always necessarily in agreement with the nature of another man (preceding Pr.). Therefore, among individual things there is nothing more advantageous to man than a man who . . . etc.

Corollary 2 It is when every man is most devoted to seeking his own advantage that men are of most advantage to one another. For the more every man seeks his own advantage and endeavors to preserve himself, the more he is endowed with virtue (Pr. 20, IV), or (and this is the same thing (Def. 8, IV)) the greater the power with which he is endowed for acting according to the laws of his own nature; that is (Pr. 3, III), for living by the guidance of reason. But it is when men live by the guidance of reason that they agree most in nature (preceding Pr.). Therefore (preceding Cor.), it is when each is most devoted to seeking his own advantage that men are of most advantage to one another.

Scholium What we have just demonstrated is also confirmed by daily experience with so many convincing examples as to give rise to the common saying: "Man is a God to man." Yet it is rarely the case that men live by the guidance of reason; their condition is such that they are generally disposed to envy and mutual dislike. Nevertheless they find solitary life scarcely endurable, so that for most people the definition "man is a social animal" meets with strong approval. And the fact of the matter is that the social organization of man shows a balance of much more profit than loss. So let satirists deride as much as they like the doings of mankind, let theologians revile them, and let the misanthropists [*melancholici*] heap praise on the life of rude rusticity, despising men and admiring beasts. Men will still discover from experience that they can much more easily meet their needs by mutual help and can ward off ever-threatening perils only by joining forces, not to mention that it is a much more excellent thing and worthy of our knowledge to study the deeds of men than the deeds of beasts. But I shall say more on this subject later on.

PROPOSITION 36
The highest good of those who pursue virtue is common to all, and all can equally enjoy it.

Proof To act from virtue is to act by the guidance of reason (Pr. 24, IV), and whatever we endeavor to do in accordance with reason is to understand (Pr. 26, IV). So (Pr. 28, IV) the highest good of those who pursue virtue is to know God; that is (Pr. 47, II and Sch.) a good that is common to all men and can be possessed equally by all men insofar as they are of the same nature.

Scholium Somebody may ask: "What if the highest good of those who pursue virtue were not common to all? Would it not then follow, as above (Pr. 34, IV), that men who live by the guidance of reason, that is (Pr. 35, IV), men insofar as they agree in nature, would be contrary to one another?" Let him take this reply, that it arises not by accident but from the very nature of reason that men's highest good is common to all, because this is deduced from the very essence of man insofar as that is defined by reason, and because man could neither be nor be conceived if he did not have the ability to enjoy this highest good. For it belongs to the essence of the human mind (Pr. 47, II) to have an adequate knowledge of the eternal and infinite essence of God.

Proposition 37
The good which every man who pursues virtue aims at for himself he will also desire for the rest of mankind, and all the more as he acquires a greater knowledge of God.

Proof Insofar as men live by the guidance of reason, they are most useful to man (Cor. 1, Pr. 35, IV), and so (Pr. 19, IV) by the guidance of reason we shall necessarily endeavor to bring it about that men should live by the guidance of reason. But the good that every man who lives according to the dictates of reason, that is (Pr. 24, IV), who pursues virtue, seeks for himself is to understand (Pr. 26, IV). Therefore the good which every man who pursues virtue seeks for himself he will also desire for the rest of mankind. Again, desire, insofar as it is related to mind, is the very essence of mind (Def. of Emotions 1). Now the essence of mind consists in knowledge (Pr. 11, II) which involves the knowledge of God (Pr. 47, II), without which (Pr. 15, I) it can neither be nor be conceived. So the more the essence of the mind involves knowledge of God, the greater the desire with which he who pursues virtue desires for another the good which he seeks for himself.

Another Proof The good which a man seeks for himself, and loves, he will love with greater constancy if he sees others loving the same thing (Pr. 31, III). Thus (Cor. Pr. 31, III) he will endeavor that others should love the same thing. And because this good (preceding Pr.) is common to all, and all can enjoy it, he will therefore endeavor (by the same reasoning) that all should enjoy it, and the more so (Pr. 37, III) the more he enjoys this good.

Scholium 1 He who from emotion alone endeavors that others love what he himself loves and live according to his way of thinking acts only by impulse, and therefore incurs dislike, especially from those who have different preferences and who therefore strive and endeavor by that same impulse that others should live according to their way of thinking. Again, since the highest good sought by men under the sway of emotion is often such that only one man can possess it, the result is that men who love it are at odds with themselves; and, while they rejoice to sing the praises of the object of their love, they are afraid of being believed. But he who endeavors to guide others by reason acts not from impulse but from kindly concern, and is entirely consistent with himself.

Whatever we desire and do, whereof we are the cause insofar as we have the idea of God, that is, insofar as we know God, I refer to Religion [*religio*]. The desire to do good which derives from our living by the guidance of reason, I call Piety [*pietas*]. Again, the desire to establish friendship with others, a desire that characterizes the man who lives by the guidance of reason, I call Sense of Honor [*honestas*]; and I use the term "honorable" for what is praised by men who live by the guidance of reason, and "base" for what is opposed to the establishing of friendship. Moreover, I have demonstrated what are the foundations of the state. Again, the difference between true virtue and weakness can readily be apprehended from what has been said above; namely, true virtue is nothing other than to live by the guidance of reason, and so weakness consists solely in this, that a man suffers himself to be led by things external to himself and is determined by them to act in a way required by the general state of external circumstances, not by his own nature considered only in itself.

These are the proofs which I undertook in Sch. Pr. 18, IV to establish. From this it is clear that the requirement to refrain from slaughtering beasts is founded on groundless superstition and womanish compassion rather than on sound reason. The principle of seeking our own advantage teaches us to be in close relationship with men, not with beasts or things whose nature is different from human nature, and that we have the same right over them as they over us. Indeed, since every individual's right is defined by his virtue or power, man's right over beasts is far greater than their rights over man. I do not deny that beasts feel; I am denying that they are on that account debarred from paying heed to our own advantages and from making use of them as we please and dealing with them as best suits us, seeing that they do not agree with us in nature and these emotions are different in nature from human emotions (Sch. Pr. 57, III).

It remains for me to explain what is just, what is unjust, what is sin and what is merit. On these matters, see the following Scholium.

Scholium 2 In Appendix Part I I undertook to explain what is praise, what is blame, what is merit, what is sin, what is just and what is unjust. With regard to praise and blame, I have explained them in Sch. Pr. 29, III. The occasion has now arrived for me to speak of the others. But I must first speak briefly of man in a state of nature and of man in society.

Every man exists by the sovereign natural right, and consequently by the sovereign natural right every man does what follows from the necessity of his nature. So it is by the sovereign natural right that every man judges what is good and what is bad, and has regard for his own advantage according to his own way of thinking (Prs. 19 and 20, IV), and seeks revenge (Cor. 2, Pr. 40, III), and endeavors to preserve what he loves and to destroy what he hates (Pr. 28, III). Now if men lived by the guidance of reason, every man would possess this right of his (Cor. 1, Pr. 35, IV) without any harm to another. But since men are subject to emotions (Cor. Pr. 4, IV) which far surpass the power or virtue of men (Pr. 6, IV), they are therefore often pulled in different directions (Pr. 33, IV) and are contrary to one another (Pr. 34, IV), while needing each other's help (Sch. Pr. 35, IV).

Therefore, in order that men may live in harmony and help one another, it is necessary for them to give up their natural right and to create a feeling of mutual confidence that they will refrain from any action that may be harmful to another. The way to bring this about (that men who are necessarily subject to passive emotions (Cor. Pr. 4, IV) and are inconstant and variable (Pr. 33, IV) should establish a mutual confidence and should trust one another) is obvious from Pr. 7, IV and Pr. 39, III. There it was demonstrated that no emotion can be checked except by a stronger emotion contrary to the emotion which is to be checked, and that every man refrains from inflicting injury through fear of greater injury. On these terms, then, society can be established, provided that it claims for itself the right that every man has of avenging himself and deciding what is good and what is evil; and furthermore if it has the power to prescribe common rules of behavior and to pass laws to enforce them, not by reason, which is incapable of checking the emotions (Sch. Pr. 17, IV), but by threats.

Now such a society, strengthened by law and by the capacity to preserve itself, is called a State [*civitas*]: and those who are protected by its rights are called Citizens [*cives*]. From this it can readily be understood that in a state of nature there is nothing that is universally agreed upon as good or evil, since every man in a state of nature has regard only to his own advantage and decides what is good and what is bad according to his own way of thinking and only insofar as he has regard to his own advantage, and is not bound by any law to obey anyone but himself. Thus in a state of nature wrongdoing cannot be conceived, but it can be in a civil state where good and bad are decided by common agreement and everyone is bound to obey the state. Wrongdoing is therefore nothing other than disobedience, which is therefore punishable only by the right of the State, and on the other hand obedience is held to be merit in a citizen because he is thereby deemed to deserve to enjoy the advantages of the state.

Again, in a state of nature nobody is by common agreement the owner [*dominus*] of any thing, and in nature there is nothing that can be said to belong to this man rather than that man. Everything belongs to everybody, and accordingly in a state of nature there cannot be conceived any intention to render to each what is his own or to rob someone of what is his. That is, in a state of nature nothing can be said to be just or unjust; this is so only in a civil state, where it is decided by common agreement what belongs to this or that man. From this it is clear that justice and injustice, wrongdoing and merit, are extrinsic notions, not attributes that explicate the nature of the mind. But I have said enough on this subject.

Proposition 38
That which so disposes the human body that it can be affected in more ways, or which renders it capable of affecting external bodies in more ways, is advantageous to man, and proportionately more advantageous as the body is thereby rendered more capable of being affected in more ways and of affecting other bodies in more ways. On the other hand, that which renders the body less capable in these respects is harmful.

Proof In proportion as the body is rendered more capable in these respects, so is the mind rendered more capable of apprehension (Pr. 14, II); so that which disposes the body in this way and renders it more capable in these respects is necessarily good or advantageous (Prs. 26 and 27, IV), and the more so as it renders the body more capable in these respects. On the other hand (by inversion of the same

Pr. 14, II, and Prs. 26 and 27, IV), that which renders it less capable in these respects is harmful.

Proposition 39

Whatever is conducive to the preservation of the proportion of motion-and-rest, which the parts of the human body maintain toward one another, is good; and those things that effect a change in the proportion of motion-and-rest of the parts of the human body to one another are bad.

Proof The human body needs many other bodies for its preservation (Post.4, II). But that which constitutes the form [*forma*] of the human body consists in this, that its parts communicate their motions to one another in a certain fixed proportion (Def. before Lemma 4, q.v. after Pr. 13, II). Therefore, whatever is conducive to the preservation of the proportion of motion-and-rest, which the parts of the human body maintain toward one another, preserves the form of the human body and, consequently (Posts.3 and 6, II), brings it about that the human body can be affected in many ways and can affect external bodies in many ways, and is, therefore (by preceding Pr.), good. Again, whatever effects a change in the proportion of motion-and-rest of the parts of the human body (by the same Def. II) causes the human body to assume a different form; that is (as is self-evident, and as we noted at the end of the Preface to Part IV), it causes it to be destroyed, and consequently quite incapable of being affected in many ways, and is, therefore, bad (preceding Pr.).

Scholium In Part V I shall explain to what extent these things can hinder or be of service to the mind. But here it should be noted that I understand a body to die when its parts are so disposed as to maintain a different proportion of motion-and-rest to one another. For I do not venture to deny that the human body, while retaining blood circulation and whatever else is regarded as essential to life, can nevertheless assume another nature quite different from its own. I have no reason to hold that a body does not die unless it turns into a corpse; indeed, experience seems to teach otherwise. It sometimes happens that a man undergoes such changes that I would not be prepared to say that he is the same person. I have heard tell of a certain Spanish poet who was seized with sickness, and although he recovered, he remained so unconscious of his past life that he did not believe that the stories and tragedies he had written were his own. Indeed, he might have been taken for a child in adult form if he had also forgotten his native tongue. And if this seems incredible, what are we to say about babies? A man of advanced years believes their nature to be so different from his own that he could not be persuaded that he had ever been a baby if he did not draw a parallel from other cases. But I prefer to leave these matters unresolved, so as not to afford material for the superstitious to raise new problems.

Proposition 40

Whatever is conducive to man's social organization, or causes men to live in harmony, is advantageous, while those things that introduce discord into the state are bad.

Proof Whatever things cause men to live in harmony cause them also to live by the guidance of reason (Pr. 35, IV), and so are good (Prs. 26 and 27, IV), while those things that introduce discord are bad (by the same reasoning).

Proposition 41
Pleasure is not in itself bad, but good. On the other hand, pain is in itself bad.

Proof Pleasure (Pr. 11, III and Sch.) is an emotion whereby the body's power of activity is increased or assisted. Pain, on the other hand, is an emotion whereby the body's power of activity is diminished or checked. Therefore (Pr. 38, IV) pleasure in itself is good . . . etc.

Proposition 42
Cheerfulness [hilaritas] cannot be excessive; it is always good. On the other hand, melancholy is always bad.

Proof Cheerfulness (see its definition in Sch. Pr. 11, III) is pleasure which, insofar as it is related to the body, consists in this, that all parts of the body are affected equally; that is (Pr. 11, III), the body's power of activity is increased or assisted in such a way that all its parts maintain the same proportion of motion-and-rest toward one another. Thus (Pr. 39, IV) cheerfulness is always good, and cannot be excessive. But melancholy (see again its definition in same Sch. Pr. 11, III) is pain, which, insofar as it is related to the body, consists in this, that the body's power of activity is absolutely diminished or checked, and therefore (Pr. 38, IV) it is always bad.

Proposition 43
Titillation [titillatio] can be excessive and bad. But anguish [dolor] can be good to the extent that titillation or pleasure is bad.

Proof Titillation is pleasure which, insofar as it is related to the body, consists in one or more of the body's parts being affected more than the rest. (See its definition in Sch. Pr. 11, III.) The power of this emotion can be so great as to surpass the other activities of the body (Pr. 6, IV) and to stay firmly fixed therein, and thus hinder the body's ability to be affected in numerous other ways. So (Pr. 38, IV) it can be bad. Again, anguish [*dolor*] on the other hand, which is pain, cannot be good considered solely in itself (Pr. 41, IV). However, because its force and increase is defined by the power of an external cause compared with our own power (Pr. 5, IV), we can therefore conceive this emotion as having infinite degrees of strength and infinite modes (Pr. 3, IV). Thus, we can conceive it as being able to check titillation so that it does not become excessive, and to that extent (by the first part of this proposition) it would prevent the body from being rendered less capable. Therefore, to that extent it is good.

Proposition 44
Love and desire can be excessive.

Proof Love is pleasure (Def. of Emotions 6) accompanied by the idea of an external cause. Therefore, titillation (Sch. Pr. 11, III) accompanied by the idea of an external cause is love, and thus love (by the preceding Pr.) can be excessive. Again, the strength of a desire is in proportion to that of the emotion from which it arises (Pr. 37, III). Therefore, just as an emotion (Pr. 6, IV) can surpass the other activities of man, so too a desire arising from that same emotion can surpass the other desires, and can therefore be excessive in the same way as was the case with titillation in the previous proposition.

Scholium Cheerfulness, which I have asserted to be good, is more easily conceived than observed. For the emotions by which we are daily assailed are generally related to some part of the body which is affected more than the rest. Therefore, emotions are as a general rule excessive and keep the mind obsessed with one single object to such an extent that it cannot think of anything else. And although men are subject to numerous emotions, and so few are found who are always assailed by one and the same emotion, yet there are some in whom one and the same emotion stays firmly fixed. For sometimes we see men so affected by one object that they think they have it before them even though it is not present. When this happens to a man who is not asleep, we say he is delirious or mad, and no less mad are those thought to be who are fired with love, dreaming night and day only of their sweetheart or mistress, for they usually provoke ridicule. But when the miser thinks of nothing but gain or money, and the ambitious man of honor, they are not reckoned as mad, for they are usually unpopular and arouse disgust. But in reality avarice, ambition, lust, etc. are kinds of madness, although they are not accounted as diseases.

PROPOSITION 45
Hatred can never be good.

Proof We endeavor to destroy the man we hate (Pr. 39, III); that is (Pr. 37, IV), we endeavor to do something that is bad. Therefore . . . etc.

Scholium Note that here and in what follows, by hatred I mean only hatred toward men.

Corollary 1 Envy, derision, contempt, anger, revenge, and the other emotions related to hatred or arising from hatred are bad. This is also clear from Pr. 39, III and Pr. 37, IV.

Corollary 2 Whatever we desire as a result of being affected by hatred is base, and, in a state, unjust. This is also clear from Pr. 39, III and from the definitions of base and unjust, q.v. in Sch. Pr. 37, IV.

Scholium I make a definite distinction between derision (which in Cor. 1 I said is bad) and laughter. For laughter, and likewise merriment, are pure pleasure, and so, provided that they are not excessive, they are good in themselves (Pr. 41, IV). Certainly nothing but grim and gloomy superstition forbids enjoyment. Why is it less fitting to drive away melancholy than to dispel hunger and thirst? The principle that guides me and shapes my attitude to life is this: no deity, nor anyone else but the envious, takes pleasure in my weakness and my misfortune, nor does he take to be a virtue our tears, sobs, fearfulness, and other such things that are a mark of a weak spirit. On the contrary, the more we are affected with pleasure, the more we pass to state of greater perfection; that is, the more we necessarily participate in the divine nature. Therefore, it is the part of a wise man to make use of things and to take pleasure in them as far as he can (but not to the point of satiety, for that is not taking pleasure). It is, I repeat, the part of a wise man to refresh and invigorate himself in moderation with good food and drink, as also with perfumes, with the beauty of blossoming plants, with dress, music, sporting activities, theaters, and the like, in which every man can indulge without harm to another. For the human body is composed of many parts of various kinds which are continually in need of fresh and varied nourishment so that the entire body may be equally capable of all the functions that follow from its own nature, and consequently that the mind may be equally capable of simultaneously understanding many things. So this manner of life is in closest agreement both with our principles and with common practice. Therefore, of all ways of life, this is the best and is to be commended on all accounts. There is no need for me to deal more clearly or at greater length with this subject.

PROPOSITION 46

He who lives by the guidance of reason endeavors as far as he can to repay with love or nobility another's hatred, anger, contempt, etc. toward himself.

Proof All emotions of hatred are bad (Cor. 1 preceding Pr.), and thus he who lives by the guidance of reason will endeavor as far as he can not to be assailed by emotions of hatred (Pr. 19, IV), and consequently (Pr. 37, IV) he will also endeavor that another should not suffer these same emotions. But hatred is increased by reciprocal hatred, and can on the other hand be extinguished by love (Pr. 43, III), so that hatred is transformed into love (Pr. 44, III). Therefore, he who lives by the guidance of reason will endeavor to render back love, that is, nobility (for whose definition see Sch. Pr. 59, III), in return for another's hatred, etc.

Scholium He who wishes to avenge injuries through reciprocal hatred lives a miserable life indeed. But he who strives to overcome hatred with love is surely fighting a happy and carefree battle. He resists several opponents as easily as one, and stands in least need of fortune's help. Those whom he conquers yield gladly, not through failure of strength but through its increase. All this follows so clearly solely from the definitions of love and intellect that there is no need of detailed proof.

PROPOSITION 47

The emotions of hope and fear cannot be good in themselves.

Proof The emotions of hope and fear cannot be without pain. For fear is pain (Def. of Emotions 13), and there cannot be hope without fear (see Def. of Emotions 12 and 13, Explications). Therefore (Pr. 41, IV), these emotions cannot be good in themselves, but only insofar as they can check excessive pleasure (Pr. 43, IV).

Scholium We should add that these emotions indicate a lack of knowledge and a weakness of mind, and for this reason, too, confidence, despair, joy, and disappointment are also indications of our weakness. For although confidence and joy are emotions of pleasure, they imply a preceding pain, namely, hope and fear. Therefore, the more we endeavor to live by the guidance of reason, the more we endeavor to be independent of hope, to free ourselves from fear, and to command fortune as far as we can, and to direct our actions by the sure counsel of reason.

PROPOSITION 48
The emotions of over-esteem [existimatio] and disparagement [despectus] are always bad.

Proof These emotions (Def. of Emotions 21 and 22) are opposed to reason, and so (Prs. 26 and 27, IV) are bad.

PROPOSITION 49
Over-esteem is apt to render its recipient proud.

Proof If we see that someone by reason of love has too high an opinion of us, we are inclined to exult (Sch. Pr. 41, III), that is, to be affected with pleasure (Def. of Emotions 30), and we readily believe whatever good we hear said of us (Pr. 25, III). Thus, we shall think too highly of ourselves through self-love; that is (Def. of Emotions 28), we shall be inclined to pride.

PROPOSITION 50
In the man who lives by the guidance of reason, pity is in itself bad and disadvantageous.

Proof Pity is pain (Def. of Emotions 18) and therefore in itself it is bad (Pr. 41, IV). Now the good that follows from it (that we endeavor to free from distress one whom we pity (Cor. 3, Pr. 27, III)) we desire to do solely from the dictates of reason (Pr. 37, IV), and it is only from the dictates of reason that we desire to do something that we certainly know to be good (Pr. 27, IV). So in the man who lives by the guidance of reason pity in itself is bad and disadvantageous.

Corollary Hence it follows that the man who lives by the dictates of reason endeavors, as far as he can, not to be touched by pity.

Scholium He who rightly knows that all things follow from the necessity of the divine nature and happen in accordance with the eternal laws and rules of Nature will surely find nothing deserving of hatred, derision, or contempt nor will he pity anyone. Rather, as far as the virtue of man extends, he will endeavor to do well, as the saying goes, and be glad. Furthermore, he who is easily touched by the emotion of pity and is moved by another's distress or tears often does something which he later regrets, both because from emotion we do nothing that we certainly know to be good and because we are easily deceived by false tears. Now I emphasize that I am here speaking of the man who lives by the guidance of reason. For he who is moved neither by reason nor by pity to render help to others is rightly called inhuman. For (Pr. 27, III) he seems to be unlike a man.

Proposition 51

Approbation [favor] is not opposed to reason; it can agree with reason and arise from it.

Proof Approbation is love toward one who has benefited another (Def. of Emotions 19); thus it can be related to the mind insofar as the mind is said to be active (Pr. 59, III), that is (Pr. 3, III), insofar as it understands. Therefore it is in agreement with reason . . . etc.

Another Proof He who lives by the guidance of reason desires for another, too, the good that he seeks for himself (Pr. 37, IV). Therefore, as a result of seeing someone do good to another, his own conatus to do good is assisted; that is (Sch. Pr. 11, III), he will feel pleasure accompanied (by hypothesis) by the idea of him who has benefited another and so he feels well-disposed toward him (Def. of Emotions 19).

Scholium Indignation, as we have defined it (Def. of Emotions 20), is necessarily evil (Pr. 45, IV). But it should be noted that when the sovereign power, through its duty to safeguard peace, punishes a citizen who has injured another, I am not saying that it is indignant with citizen. It punishes him not because it is stirred by hatred to destroy the citizen, but from a sense of duty [*pietate*].

Proposition 52

Self-contentment [acquiescentia in se ipso] can arise from reason, and only that self-contentment which arises from reason is the highest there can be.

Proof Self-contentment is the pleasure arising from a man's contemplation of himself and his power of activity (Def. of Emotions 25). Now man's true power of activity, or his virtue, is reason itself (Pr. 3, III), which man regards clearly and distinctly (Prs. 40 and 43, II). Therefore self-contentment arises from reason. Again, in contemplating himself a man perceives clearly and distinctly, that is, adequately, only what follows from his power of activity (Def. 2, III), that is (Pr. 3, III), what follows from his power of understanding. So the greatest self-contentment there can be arises only from this contemplation.

Scholium In fact self-contentment is the highest good we can hope for. For (as we proved in Pr. 25, IV) nobody endeavors to preserve his own being for the sake of something else. And because this self-contentment is increasingly fostered and strengthened by praise (Cor. Pr. 53, III), and on the other hand is increasingly disturbed by blame (Cor. Pr. 55, III), honor [*gloria*] is the greatest incentive, and we can scarcely endure life in disgrace.

PROPOSITION 53
Humility is not a virtue; that is, it does not arise from reason.

Proof   Humility is the pain arising from a man's contemplation of his own weakness (Def. of Emotions 26). Now insofar as a man knows himself by true reason, to that extent he is assumed to understand his own essence, that is (Pr. 7, III), his own power. Therefore if a man, in contemplating himself, perceives some weakness in himself, this does not arise from his understanding himself but (Pr. 55, III) from the checking of his power of activity. Now if we suppose that a man conceives his own weakness from understanding something more powerful than himself, by the knowledge of which he measures his own power of activity, we are conceiving only that the man understands himself distinctly; that is (Pr. 26, IV), that his power of activity is assisted. Therefore the humility, or the pain, that arises from a man's contemplation of his own weakness, does not arise from true contemplation or reason, and is not a virtue but a passive emotion.

PROPOSITION 54
Repentance is not a virtue, i.e. it does not arise from reason; he who repents of his action is doubly unhappy or weak.

Proof   The first part of this Proposition is proved in the same way as the preceding proposition. The second part is evident simply from the definition of this emotion (Def. of Emotions 27). For the subject suffers himself to be overcome first by a wicked desire [*cupiditas*], and then by pain.

Scholium   As men seldom live according to the dictates of reason, these two emotions, humility and repentance, and also hope and fear, bring more advantage than harm; and thus, if sin we must, it is better to sin in their direction. For if men of weak spirit should all equally be subject to pride, and should be ashamed of nothing and afraid of nothing, by what bonds could they be held together and bound? The mob is fearsome, if it does not fear. So it is not surprising that the prophets, who had regard for the good of the whole community, and not of the few, have been so zealous in commending humility, repentance, and reverence. And in fact those who are subject to these emotions can be far more readily induced than others to live by the guidance of reason in the end, that is, to become free men and enjoy the life of the blessed.

PROPOSITION 55
Extreme pride, or self-abasement, is extreme ignorance of oneself.

Proof   This is clear from Definition of Emotions 28 and 29.

PROPOSITION 56
Extreme pride, or self-abasement, indicates extreme weakness of spirit.

Proof   The primary basis of virtue is to preserve one's own being (Cor. Pr. 22, IV), and this by the guidance of reason (Pr. 24, IV). So he who is ignorant of himself is ignorant of the basis of all the virtues, and consequently of all the virtues. Again, to act from virtue is nothing else but to act from the guidance of reason (Pr. 24, IV), and he who acts from the guidance of reason must necessarily know that he acts from the guidance of reason (Pr. 43, II). Therefore, he whose ignorance of himself (and consequently as I have just demonstrated, of all the virtues) is extreme, acts least of all from virtue; that is (as is evident from Def. 8, IV), he is most impotent in spirit. And so (by the preceding Pr.) extreme pride or self-abasement indicates extreme weakness of spirit.

Corollary   Hence it clearly follows that the proud and the self-abased are most subject to emotions.

Scholium   But self-abasement can be more easily corrected than pride, since the latter is an emotion of pleasure, while the former is an emotion of pain. So the latter is stronger than the former (Pr. 18, IV).

Proposition 57
The proud man loves the company of parasites or flatterers, and hates the company of those of noble spirit.

Proof   Pride is the pleasure arising from a man's thinking too highly of himself (Def. of Emotions 28 and 6), a belief which the proud man will endeavor to foster as much as he can (Sch. Pr. 13, III). So the proud love the company of parasites and flatterers (I omit their definitions as being too well-known) and shun the company of those of noble spirit, who value them according to their deserts.

Scholium   It would be tedious to recount here all the ills that spring from pride, for the proud are subject to all the emotions, though to love and pity least of all. But I must not omit here to mention that the term "proud" is also applied to a man who thinks too meanly of others, and so in this sense pride should be defined as the pleasure arising from false belief, in that a man thinks himself above others. And the self-abasement which is the opposite of this pride should be defined as the pain arising from false belief, in that a man thinks himself beneath others. Now on this basis we readily conceive that the proud man is necessarily envious (Sch. Pr. 55, III) and hates most those who are praised for their virtues—a hatred that cannot easily be conquered by their love and kindness (Sch. Pr. 41, III)—and finds pleasure only in the company of those who humor his weakness of spirit and turn his folly to madness.

Although self-abasement is the opposite of pride, the self-abased man is very close to the proud man. For since his pain arises from judging his own weakness by the power or virtue of others, his pain will be assuaged, that is, he will feel pleasure, if his thoughts are engaged in contemplating other people's faults. This is the origin of the proverb: "The consolation of the wretched is to have fellows in misfortune." On the other hand, he will be more pained in proportion as he thinks himself lower than others. Hence it comes about that the self-abased are more prone to envy than all others, and that they, more than any, endeavor to keep watch on men's deeds with a view to criticizing rather than correcting them, and they end up by praising only self-abasement and exulting in it even while still preserving the appearance of self-abasement.

Now these results follow from this emotion with the same necessity as it follows from the nature of a triangle that its angles are equal to two right angles, and I have already stated that it is only in respect of the good of man that I call these and similar emotions evil. But the laws of Nature have regard to the universal order of Nature, of which man is a part. I have thought first to note this in passing lest anyone should think that my intention here has been to recount the faults and absurdities of mankind rather than to demonstrate the nature and properties of things. As I said in the Preface to Part III, I consider human emotions and their properties on the same footing with other natural phenomena. And surely human emotions indicate, if not human power, at any rate the power and intricacy of Nature to no less a degree than many other things that evoke our wonder and whose contemplation gives pleasure. But I am going on to point out what features in our emotions bring advantage or harm to men.

Proposition 58
Honor is not opposed to reason, but can arise from it.

Proof This is evident from Def. of Emotions 30, and from the definition of honorable, for which see Sch. 1, Pr. 37, IV.

Scholium Vainglory, as it is called, is the self-contentment that is fostered only by popular esteem and ceases with it; that is (Sch. Pr. 52, IV), the highest good which everyone loves, ceases. So it happens that he who exults in popular esteem has the daily burden of anxiously striving, acting and contriving to preserve his reputation. For the populace is fickle and inconstant, and unless a reputation is preserved it soon withers away. Indeed, since all are eager to capture the applause of the populace, each is ready to decry another's reputation. As a result, since the prize at stake is what is esteemed the highest good, there arises a fierce desire to put down one's rivals in whatever way one can, and he who finally emerges victorious prides himself more on having hindered another than on having gained an advantage for himself. So this kind of glory, or self-contentment, is really vain because it is nothing.

As to what is to be remarked about Shame [*pudor*], this can readily be gathered from our account of compassion and repentance. I shall merely add this, that shame, like pity, although not a virtue, can be good insofar as it is an indication that the man who feels ashamed has a desire to live honorably, just as is the case with anguish, which is said to be good insofar as it indicates that the injured part has not yet putrefied. Therefore, although the man who is ashamed of some deed is in fact pained, he is nearer perfection than the shameless man who has no desire to live honorably.

I have now completed my undertaking to deal with the emotions of pleasure and pain. As for desires, they are, of course, good or evil insofar as they arise from good or evil emotions. But in truth all desires insofar as they are engendered in us from passive emotions, are blind (as can easily be gathered from a reading of

Sch. Pr. 44, IV) and would be ineffective if men could readily be induced to live only according to the dictates of reason, as I shall now demonstrate in brief.

Proposition 59
In the case of all actions to which we are determined by a passive emotion, we can be determined thereto by reason without that emotion.

Proof To act from reason is nothing else but to do what follows from the necessity of our own nature considered solely in itself (Pr. 3 and Def. 2, III). Now pain is bad to the extent that it diminishes or checks this power of action (Pr. 41, IV). Therefore, we cannot be determined from this emotion to any action that we could not do if we were guided by reason. Moreover, pleasure is bad to the extent that it hinders a man's capacity for action (Prs. 41 and 43, IV), and to that extent also we cannot be determined to any action that we could not do if we were guided by reason. Finally, insofar as pleasure is good, it is in agreement with reason (for it consists in this, that a man's power of activity is increased or assisted), and it is a passive emotion only insofar as a man's power of activity is not increased to such a degree that he adequately conceives himself and his actions (Pr. 3, III and Sch.) Therefore, if a man affected with pleasure were brought to such a degree of perfection that he were adequately to conceive himself and his actions, he would be capable, indeed, more capable, of those same actions to which he is now determined by passive emotions. Now all emotions are related to pleasure, pain, or desire (see Explication of Def. of Emotions 4), and desire is merely the endeavor to act (Def. of Emotions 1). Therefore, in the case of all actions to which we are determined by a passive emotion, we can be guided thereto by reason alone, without the emotion.

Another Proof Any action is said to be bad insofar as it arises from our having been affected with hatred or some evil emotion (Cor. 1, Pr. 45, IV). But no action, considered solely in itself, is good or evil (as we demonstrated in the Preface, Part IV), but one and the same action can be now good, now evil. Therefore, we can be guided by reason to that same action which is now bad, that is, which arises from an evil emotion (Pr. 19, IV).

Scholium An example will make this clearer. The act of striking a blow, insofar as it is considered physically and insofar as we look only to the fact that a man raises an arm, clenches his fist and violently brings his arm down, is a virtue, conceived as resulting from the structure of the human body. So if a man, stirred by anger or hatred, is determined to clench his fist or move his arm, this happens because (as we demonstrated in Part II), one and the same action can be associated with any images whatsoever. And so we can be determined to one and the same action both from images of things which we conceive confusedly and from those we conceive clearly and distinctly. It is therefore clear that if men could be guided by reason, all desire that arises from passive emotion would be ineffective [*nullius esset usus*].

Now let us see why desire that arises from an emotion, that is, a passive emotion, is called blind.

Proposition 60

Desire that arises from the pleasure or pain that is related to one or more, but not to all, parts of the body takes no account of the advantage of the whole man.

Proof Let it be supposed that part A of the body is so strengthened by the force of some external cause that it prevails over the other parts (Pr. 6, IV). This part will not endeavor to abate its own strength in order that other parts of the body may perform their function, for then it would have to possess the force or power to abate its own strength, which is absurd (Pr. 6, III). Therefore that part of the body, and consequently the mind too (Prs. 7 and 12, III), will endeavor to preserve the existing condition. Therefore, the desire that arises from such an emotion of pleasure takes no account of the whole. Now if we suppose on the other hand that part A is checked so that the other parts prevail over it, it can be proved in the same way that desire arising from pain likewise takes no account of the whole.

Scholium Therefore, since pleasure is usually related to one part of the body (Sch. Pr. 44, IV), we usually desire to preserve our being without taking account of our entire well-being. There is also the fact that the desires by which we are most enslaved (Cor. Pr. 9, IV) take into account only the present, not the future.

Proposition 61

Desire that arises from reason cannot be excessive.

Proof Desire (Def. of Emotions 1), considered absolutely, is man's very essence insofar as he is conceived as determined in any manner to some action. Therefore desire that arises from reason, that is (Pr. 3, III), desire that is engendered in us insofar as we are active, is man's very essence of nature insofar as it is conceived as determined to such actions as are adequately conceived through man's essence alone (Def. 2, III). So if this desire could be excessive, human nature, considered absolutely, could exceed itself, that is, it could do more than it can do, which is a manifest contradiction. Therefore, this desire cannot be excessive.

Proposition 62

Insofar as the mind conceives things in accordance with the dictates of reason, it is equally affected whether the idea be of the future, in the past, or the present.

Proof Whatsoever the mind conceives under the guidance of reason, it conceives under the same form of eternity or necessity (Cor. 2, Pr. 44, II), and is affected with the same certainty (Pr. 43, II and Sch.). Therefore, whether the idea be of the future, the past, or the present, the mind conceives the thing with the same necessity and is affected with the same certainty; and whether the idea be of the future, the past, or the present, it will nevertheless be equally true (Pr. 41, II); that is (Def. 4, II), it will nevertheless always have the same properties of an adequate idea. Therefore, insofar as the mind conceives things according to the dictates of reason, it is affected in the same way, whether the idea be of a thing future, past, or present.

Scholium If we could have an adequate knowledge of the duration of things and could determine by reason the periods of their existence, we should regard things future with the same emotion as things present, and the mind would seek the good that it conceives as future just as much as present good. Consequently, it would necessarily prefer a future greater good to a lesser present good, and would by no means seek that which is good in the present but the cause of future evil, as we shall later demonstrate. But we can have only a very inadequate knowledge of the duration of things (Pr. 31, II), and we determine the periods of existence of things by imagination alone (Sch. Pr. 44, II), which is more strongly affected by the image of a thing present than of a thing future. Thus it comes about that the true knowledge we have of good and evil is only abstract or universal, and the judgment that we make concerning the order of things and the connection of causes so that we may determine what is good or bad for us in the present pertains more to the imagination than to reality. So it is not surprising that desire that arises from a knowledge of good and evil, insofar as this knowledge has reference to the future, can be more readily checked by desire of things that are attractive in the present. See Pr. 16, IV.

Proposition 63
He who is guided by fear, and does good so as to avoid evil, is not guided by reason.

Proof All emotions that are related to the mind insofar as it is active, that is (Pr. 3, III), emotions that are related to reason, are emotions of pleasure and desire only (Pr. 59, III). Therefore (Def. of Emotions 13), he who is guided by fear and does good through fear of evil is not guided by reason.

Scholium The superstitious, who know how to censure vice rather than to teach virtue, and who are eager not to guide men by reason but to restrain them by fear so that they may shun evil rather than love virtue, have no other object than to make others as wretched as themselves. So it is not surprising that they are generally resented and hated.

Corollary Through the desire that arises from reason we pursue good directly and shun evil indirectly.

Proof The desire that arises from reason can arise only from an emotion of pleasure that is not passive (Pr. 59, III), that is, from a pleasure that cannot be excessive (Pr. 61, IV), and not from pain; and therefore this pleasure (Pr. 8, IV) arises from knowledge of good, not of evil. So by the guidance of reason we directly aim at the good, and only to that extent do we shun evil.

Scholium This corollary can be illustrated by the example of the sick man and the healthy man. The sick man eats what he dislikes through fear of death. The healthy man takes pleasure in his food and thus enjoys a better life than if he were to fear death and directly seek to avoid it. Likewise the judge who condemns a man to death not through hatred or anger but solely through love of public welfare is guided only by reason.

Proposition 64
Knowledge of evil is inadequate knowledge.

Proof Knowledge of evil is pain itself (Pr. 8, IV) insofar as we are conscious of it. Now pain is a transition to a state of less perfection (Def. of Emotions 3), which therefore cannot be understood through man's essence itself (Prs. 6 and 7, III) and so is a passive emotion (Def. 2, III) which depends on inadequate ideas (Pr. 3, III). Consequently knowledge of it (Pr. 29, II)—that is, knowledge of evil—is inadequate knowledge.

Corollary Hence it follows that if the human mind had only adequate ideas, it could not form any notion of evil.

Proposition 65
By the guidance of reason we pursue the greater of two goods and the lesser of two evils.

Proof The good that prevents us from enjoying a greater good is in reality an evil; for evil and good are terms used (as I have demonstrated in the Preface to Part IV) insofar as we compare things with one another, and by the same reasoning a lesser evil is in reality a good. Therefore (Cor. Pr. 63, IV), by the guidance of reason we aim at or pursue only the greater good and the lesser evil.

Corollary Under the guidance of reason we pursue a lesser evil for a greater good, and we reject a lesser good which is the cause of a greater evil. For what is here called the lesser evil is in reality a good, and the good on the other hand an evil. Therefore, we choose the former and reject the latter (Cor. Pr. 63, IV).

Proposition 66
Under the guidance of reason we seek a future greater good in preference to a lesser present good, and a lesser present evil in preference to a greater future evil.

Proof If the mind could have an adequate knowledge of what is to come, it would be affected by the same emotion toward a future thing as toward a present thing (Pr. 62, IV). Thus insofar as we have regard to reason itself, as we assume we are doing in this proposition, a thing is the same whether it is supposed to be a greater good or evil in the future or in the present. Therefore (Pr. 65, IV), we seek a future greater good in preference to a lesser present good . . . etc.

Corollary Under the guidance of reason we choose a present lesser evil which is the cause of a future greater good, and we reject a present lesser good which is the cause of a future greater evil. This corollary is related to the preceding proposition, just as Cor. Pr. 65 to Pr. 65.

Scholium If these statements be compared with what we have demonstrated in this Part up to Pr. 18 with reference to the strength of the emotions, we shall readily see the difference between the man who is guided only by emotion or belief and the man who is guided by reason. The former, whether he will or not, performs actions of which he is completely ignorant. The latter does no one's will but his own, and does only what he knows to be of greatest importance in life, which he therefore desires above all. So I call the former a slave and the latter a free man, of whose character and manner of life I have yet a few things to say.

Proposition 67
A free man thinks of death least of all things, and his wisdom is a meditation of life, not of death.

Proof A free man, that is, he who lives solely according to the dictates of reason, is not guided by fear of death (Pr. 63, IV), but directly desires the good (Cor. Pr. 63, IV); that is (Pr. 24, IV), to act, to live, to preserve his own being in accordance with the principle of seeking his own advantage. So he thinks of death least of all things, and his wisdom is a meditation upon life.

Proposition 68
If men were born free, they would form no conception of good and evil so long as they were free.

Proof I have said that a free man is he who is guided solely by reason. Therefore, he who is born free and remains free has only adequate ideas and thus has no conception of evil (Cor. 64, IV), and consequently no conception of good (for good and evil are correlative).

Scholium It is clear from Pr. 4, IV that the hypothesis in this proposition is false and cannot be conceived except insofar as we have regard solely to the nature of man, or rather, to God not insofar as he is infinite but only insofar as he is the cause of man's existence. This and other truths that we have already demonstrated seem to be what Moses intended by his history of the first man. For in that narrative no other power of God is conceived save that whereby he created man; that is, the power whereby he had regard only for man's advantage. And this is the point of the story that God forbade the free man to eat of the tree of the knowledge of good and evil, saying that as soon as he should eat of it he would straightway fear death instead of desiring to live. Again, the story goes that when man had found woman, who agreed entirely with his own nature, he realized that there could be nothing in Nature more to his advantage than woman. But when he came to believe that the beasts were like himself, he straightway began to imitate their emotions (Pr. 27, III) and to lose his freedom, which the Patriarchs later regained under the guidance of the spirit of Christ, that is, the idea of God, on which alone it depends that a man should be free and should desire for mankind the good that he desires for himself, as I have demonstrated above (Pr. 37, IV).

Proposition 69
The virtue of a free man is seen to be as great in avoiding dangers as in overcoming them.

Proof An emotion cannot be checked or removed except by a contrary emotion stronger than the emotion which is to be checked (Pr. 7, IV). But blind daring [*caeca audacia*] and fear are emotions that can be conceived as equally strong (Prs. 5 and 3, IV). Therefore the virtue or strength of mind (for its definition see Sch. Pr. 59, III) needed to check daring must be equally as great as that needed to check fear; that is (Def. of Emotions 40 and 41), the free man avoids dangers by that same virtue as that whereby he attempts to overcome them.

Corollary Therefore, for a free man timely retreat is as much a mark of courage as is fighting; that is, the free man chooses flight by the same courage or spiritedness as he chooses battle.

Scholium I have explained in Sch. Pr. 59, III what courage is, or what I understand by it. By danger I mean everything that can be the cause of some evil, such as pain, hatred, discord, etc.

Proposition 70

The free man who lives among ignorant people tries as far as he can to avoid receiving favors from them.

Proof Every man judges what is good according to his own way of thinking (Sch. Pr. 39, III). Thus the ignorant man who has conferred a favor on someone will value it according to his own way of thinking, and if he sees that the recipient values it less, he will feel pain (Pr. 42, III). Now the free man tries to establish friendship with others (Pr. 37, IV) and not to repay men with favors that are equivalent in their eyes. Rather he tries to guide himself and others by the free judgment of reason and to do only those things that he himself knows to be of primary importance. Therefore, to avoid both the hatred of the ignorant and the need to comply with their expectations, and so as to make reason his sole ruler, he will endeavor as far as he can to avoid their favors.

Scholium I say, "as far as he can"; for men, however ignorant, are still men, who in time of need can bring human help, than which nothing is more valuable. So it often happens that it is necessary to accept a favor from them, and consequently to return it so as to give them satisfaction. Furthermore, we should exercise caution even in avoiding their favors so as to avoid appearing to despise them or to be reluctant through avarice to repay them, thus giving offense by the very attempt to escape their hatred. Thus in avoiding favors one should take account of what is advantageous and honorable.

Proposition 71

Only free men are truly grateful to one another.

Proof Only free men are truly advantageous to one another and united by the closest bond of friendship (Pr. 35, IV and Cor. 1), and are equally motivated by love in endeavoring to benefit one another (Pr. 37, IV). And thus (Def. of Emotions 34) only free men are truly grateful to one another.

Scholium The gratitude mutually exhibited by men who are governed by blind desire is more in the nature of a bargain or inducement than gratitude. Moreover, ingratitude is not an emotional state. Nevertheless, ingratitude is base, because it generally is a sign that a man is affected with excessive hatred, anger, pride, or avarice, etc. For if out of stupidity a man knows not how to repay benefits, he is not an ungrateful man; and far less so is he who is not won over by the gifts of a loose woman to serve her lust, nor by the gifts of a thief to conceal his thefts, nor by the gifts of anyone of like character. On the contrary, he shows a steadfast spirit, in that he refuses to be corrupted by gifts to his own hurt or that of society.

Proposition 72
The free man never acts deceitfully, but always with good faith.

Proof If the free man, insofar as he is free, were to act deceitfully, he would be doing so in accordance with the dictates of reason (for it is in this respect only that we term him free), and thus to act deceitfully would be a virtue (Pr. 24, IV), and consequently (by the same proposition), in order to preserve his own being, it would be better for every man to act deceitfully, that is (as is self-evident), it would be better for men to agree in words only, but to be contrary to one another in reality, which is absurd (Cor. Pr. 31, IV). Therefore the free man . . . etc.

Scholium The question may be asked: "What if a man could by deception free himself from imminent danger of death? Would not consideration for the preservation of his own being be decisive in persuading him to deceive?" I reply in the same way, that if reason urges this, it does so for all men; and thus reason urges men in general to join forces and to have common laws only with deceitful intention; that is, in effect, to have no laws in common at all, which is absurd.

Proposition 73
The man who is guided by reason is more free in a state where he lives under a system of law than in solitude where [he] obeys only himself.

Proof The man who is guided by reason is not guided to obey out of fear (Pr. 63, IV), but insofar as he endeavors to preserve his own being according to the dictates of reason—that is (Sch. Pr. 66, IV), insofar as he endeavors to live freely—he desires to take account of the life and the good of the community (Pr. 37, IV), and consequently (as I have pointed out in Sch. 2, Pr. 37, IV) to live according to the laws of the state. Therefore, the man who is guided by reason desires to adhere to the laws of the state so that he may live more freely.

Scholium These and similar observations that we have made concerning the true freedom of man are related to strength of mind, that is (Pr. 59, III), courage and nobility. I do not think it worthwhile at this point to give separate proof of all the properties of strength of mind, and far less to show that the strong-minded man hates nobody, is angry with nobody, envies nobody, is indignant with nobody, despises nobody, and is in no way prone to pride. For these points and all that concern the true way of life and religion are readily proved from Prs. 37 and 46, IV, to wit, that hatred is to be conquered by returning love, and that every man who is guided by reason aims at procuring for others, too, the good that he seeks for himself. Furthermore, as we have noted in Sch. Pr. 50, IV and elsewhere, the strong-minded man has this foremost in his mind, that everything follows from the necessity of the divine nature, and therefore whatever he thinks of as injurious or bad, and also whatever seems impious, horrible, unjust, and base arises from his conceiving things in a disturbed, fragmented, and confused way. For this reason his prime endeavor is to conceive things as they are in themselves and to remove obstacles to true knowledge, such as hatred, anger, envy, derision, pride, and similar emotions that we have noted. And so he endeavors, as far as he can, to do well and to be glad, as we have said.

In the next Part, I shall pass on to demonstrate the extent to which human virtue can achieve these objectives, and the nature of its power.

Appendix

In this Part my exposition of the right way of living is not arranged so that it can be seen at one view. The proofs are scattered so as to meet the convenience of logical deduction one from another. So I propose to gather them together here, and arrange them under their main headings.

1. All our endeavors or desires follow from the necessity of our nature in such a way that they can be understood either through it alone as their approximate cause, or insofar as we are a part of Nature, a part that cannot be adequately conceived through itself independently of the other individual parts.

2. Desires that follow from our nature in such a way that they can be understood through it alone are those that are related to the mind insofar as the mind is conceived as consisting of adequate ideas. The other desires are related to the mind only insofar as it conceives things inadequately; and their force and increase must be defined not by human power but by the power of things external to us. So the former are rightly called active emotions, the latter passive emotions. For the former always indicate our power, the latter our weakness and fragmentary knowledge.

3. Our active emotions, that is, those desires that are defined by man's power, that is, by reason, are always good; the other desires can be either good or evil.

4. Therefore it is of the first importance in life to perfect the intellect, or reason, as far as we can, and the highest happiness or blessedness for mankind consists in this alone. For blessedness is nothing other than that self-contentment that arises from the intuitive knowledge of God. Now to perfect the intellect is also nothing other than to understand God and the attributes and actions of God that follow from the necessity of his nature. Therefore for the man who is guided by reason, the final goal, that is, the highest Desire whereby he strives to control all the others, is that by which he is brought to an adequate conception of himself and of all things that can fall within the scope of his understanding.

5. So there is no rational life without understanding, and things are good only insofar as they assist a man to enjoy the life of the mind, which is defined by un-

derstanding. Those things only do we call evil which hinder a man's capacity to perfect reason and to enjoy a rational life.

6. But since all those things of which man is the efficient cause are necessarily good, nothing evil can befall a man except from external causes, namely, insofar as he is a part of the whole of Nature, whose laws human nature is constrained to obey, and to which it must conform in almost an infinite number of ways.

7. A man is bound to be a part of Nature and to follow its universal order; but if he dwells among individuals who are in harmony with man's nature, by that very fact his power of activity will be assisted and fostered. But if he be among individuals who are by no means in harmony with his nature, he will scarcely be able to conform to them without a great change in himself.

8. Whatsoever in nature we deem evil, that is, capable of hindering us from being able to exist and to enjoy a rational life, it is permissible for us to remove in whatever seems the safer way. On the other hand, whatever we deem good, that is, advantageous for preserving our being and for enjoying a rational life, it is permissible for us to take for our use and to use it as we please. And as an absolute rule, it is permissible by the highest natural right for everyone to do what he judges to be to his own advantage.

9. Nothing can be more in harmony with the nature of anything than other individuals of the same species, and so (see No. 7) there is nothing more advantageous to man for preserving his own being and enjoying a rational life than a man who is guided by reason. Again, since among particular things we know of nothing more excellent than a man who is guided by reason, nowhere can each individual display the extent of his skill and genius more than in so educating men that they come at last to live under the sway of their own reason.

10. Insofar as men feel envy or some other emotion of hatred toward one another, they are contrary to one another; consequently, the more powerful they are, the more they are to be feared than other individuals of Nature.

11. Nevertheless men's hearts are conquered not by arms but by love and nobility.

12. It is of the first importance to men to establish close relationships and to bind themselves together with such ties as may most effectively unite them into one body, and, as an absolute rule, to act in such a way as serves to strengthen friendship.

13. But to this end skill and watchfulness are needed. For men are changeable (few there are who live under the direction of reason) and yet for the most part envious, and more inclined to revenge than to compassion. So it needs an unusually powerful spirit to bear with each according to his disposition and to restrain oneself from imitating their emotions. On the other hand, those whose skill is to criticize mankind and to censure vice rather than to teach virtue, and to shatter men's spirit rather than strengthen it, are a stumbling block both to themselves and to others. Hence many men, over-impatient and with false religious zeal, have chosen to live among beasts rather than among men, just as boys or young men, unable patiently to endure the upbraidings of their parents, run away to join the

army, and prefer the hardships of war and tyrannical discipline to the comfort of home and parental admonition, and suffer any burdens to be imposed on them so long as they can spite their parents.

14. So although men for the most part allow lust to govern all their actions, the advantages that follow from living in their society far exceed the disadvantages. Therefore it is better to endure their injuries with patience, and to apply oneself to such measures as promote harmony and friendship.

15. Conduct that brings about harmony is that which is related to justice, equity, and honorable dealing. For apart from resenting injustice and unfairness, men also resent what is held to be base, or contempt for the accepted customs of the state. But for winning their love the most important factors are those that are concerned with religion and piety, for which see Schs.1 and 2, Pr. 37, and Sch. Pr. 46 and Sch. Pr. 73, IV.

16. Harmony is also commonly produced by fear, but then it is untrustworthy. Furthermore, fear arises from weakness of spirit, and therefore does not belong to the use of reason. Neither does pity, although it bears the appearance of piety.

17. Again, men are won over by generosity, especially those who do not have the wherewithal to produce what is necessary to support life. Yet it is far beyond the power and resources of a private person to come to the assistance of everyone in need. For the wealth of a private person is quite unequal to such a demand. It is also a practical impossibility for one man to establish friendship with all. Therefore the care of the poor devolves upon society as a whole, and looks only to the common good.

18. The care to be taken in accepting favors and in returning them must be of quite a different kind, for which see Sch. Pr. 70 and Sch. Pr. 71, IV.

19. Furthermore, love of a mistress, that is, sexual lust that arises from physical beauty, and in general all love that acknowledges any other cause than freedom of the spirit, easily passes in hatred unless (and this is worse) it be a kind of madness, and then it is fostered by discord rather than harmony.

20. As for marriage, it is certain that this is in agreement with reason if the desire for intercourse be engendered not simply by physical beauty but also by love of begetting children and rearing them wisely, and if, in addition, the love of both man and woman has for its cause not merely physical beauty but especially freedom of the spirit.

21. Flattery, too, produces harmony, but at the cost of base servility, or through perfidy. None are more taken in by flattery than the proud, who want to be foremost, but are not.

22. In self-abasement there is a false appearance of piety and religion. And although self-abasement is opposed to pride, the self-abased man is closest to the proud man. See Sch. Pr. 57, IV.

23. Shame, too, contributes to harmony, but only in matters that cannot be concealed. Again, since shame is species of pain, it does not concern the use of reason.

24. The other painful emotions toward men are directly opposed to justice, equity, honor, piety, and religion; and although indignation seems to bear an out-

ward show of equity, it is a lawless state of society where each is permitted to pass judgment on another's deeds and assert his own or another's right.

25. Courtesy, that is, the desire to please men as determined by reason, is related to piety (as we have said in Sch. 1, Pr. 37, IV). But if it arises from emotion, it is ambition, or the desire whereby under a false cover of piety men generally stir up discord and quarrelling. For he who desires to help others by word or deed to enjoy the highest good along with him, will strive above all to win their love, but not to evoke their admiration so that some system of philosophy may be named after him, nor to afford any cause whatsoever for envy. Again, in ordinary conversation he will beware of talking about the vices of mankind and will take care to speak only sparingly of human weakness, but will dwell on human virtue, or power, and the means to perfect it, so that men may thus endeavor as far as they can to live in accordance with reason's behest, not from fear or dislike, but motivated only by the emotion of pleasure.

26. Except for mankind, we know of no individual thing in Nature in whose mind we can rejoice, and with which we can unite in friendship or some kind of close tie. So whatever there is in Nature external to man, regard for our own advantage does not require us to preserve it, but teaches us to preserve or destroy it according to its varying usefulness, or to adapt it to our own use in whatever way we please.

27. The advantage that we get from things external to us, apart from the experience and knowledge we gain from observing them and changing them from one form to another, is especially the preservation of the body, and in this respect those things above all are advantageous which can so feed and nourish the body that all its parts can efficiently perform their function. For as the body is more capable of being affected in many ways and of affecting external bodies in many ways, so the mind is more capable of thinking (see Prs. 38 and 39, IV). But there appear to be few things of this kind in Nature; wherefore to nourish the body as it should be one must use many foods of different kinds. For the human body is composed of numerous parts of different natures, which need a continual supply of food of various sorts so that the whole body is equally capable of all that can follow from its nature, and consequently that the mind too is equally capable of conceiving many things.

28. Now to provide all this the strength of each single person would scarcely suffice if men did not lend mutual aid to one another. However, money has supplied a token for all things, with the result that its image is wont to obsess the minds of the populace, because they can scarcely think of any kind of pleasure that is not accompanied by the idea of money as its cause.

29. But this vice is characteristic only of those who seek money not through poverty nor to meet their necessities, but because they have acquired the art of money-making, whereby they raise themselves to a splendid estate. They feed the body from habit, but thriftily, because they believe that what they spend on preserving the body is lost to their goods. But those who know the true use of money set the limit of their wealth solely according to their needs, and live content with little.

30. Since those things are good which assist the parts of the body to perform their function, and pleasure consists in this, that a man's power is assisted or increased insofar as he is composed of mind and body, all those things that bring pleasure are good. On the other hand, since things do not act with the object of affecting us with pleasure, and their power of acting is not adjusted to suit our needs, and, lastly, since pleasure is usually related to one part of the body in particular, the emotions of pleasure (unless one exercises reason and care), and consequently the desires that are generated from them, can be excessive. There is this further point, that from emotion we place prime importance on what is attractive in the present, and we cannot feel as strongly about the future. See Sch. Pr. 44 and Sch. Pr. 60, IV.

31. But superstition on the other hand seems to assert that what brings pain is good and what brings pleasure is bad. But, as we have already said (Sch. Pr. 45, IV), nobody but the envious takes pleasure in my weakness and my misfortune. For the more we are affected with pleasure, the more we pass to a state of greater perfection, and consequently the more we participate in the divine nature. Nor can pleasure ever be evil when it is controlled by true regard for our advantage. Now he who on the other hand is guided by fear and does good in order to avoid evil is not guided by reason.

32. But human power is very limited and is infinitely surpassed by the power of external causes, and so we do not have absolute power to adapt to our purposes things external to us. However, we shall patiently bear whatever happens to us that is contrary to what is required by consideration of our own advantage, if we are conscious that we have done our duty and that our power was not extensive enough for us to have avoided the said things, and that we are a part of the whole of Nature whose order we follow. If we clearly and distinctly understand this, that part of us which is defined by the understanding, that is, the better part of us, will be fully resigned and will endeavor to persevere in that resignation. For insofar as we understand, we can desire nothing but that which must be, nor, in an absolute sense, can we find contentment in anything but truth. And so insofar as we rightly understand these matters, the endeavor of the better part of us is in harmony with the order of the whole of Nature.

PART V

OF THE POWER OF THE INTELLECT, OR OF HUMAN FREEDOM

PREFACE

I pass on finally to that part of the *Ethics* which concerns the method or way leading to freedom. In this part, then, I shall be dealing with the power of reason, pointing out the degree of control reason has over the emotions, and then what is freedom of mind, or blessedness, from which we shall see how much to be preferred is the life of the wise man to the life of the ignorant man. Now we are not concerned here with the manner or way in which the intellect should be perfected, nor yet with the science of tending the body so that it may correctly perform its functions. The latter is the province of medicine, the former of logic. Here then, as I have said, I shall be dealing only with the power of the mind or reason. Above all I shall be showing the degree and nature of its command over the emotions in checking and controlling them. For I have already demonstrated that we do not have absolute command over them.

Now the Stoics thought that the emotions depend absolutely on our will, and that we can have absolute command over them. However, with experience crying out against them they were obliged against their principles to admit that no little practice and zeal are required in order to check and control emotions. One of them tried to illustrate this point with the example of two dogs, if I remember correctly, one a house dog, and the other a hunting dog; in the end he succeeded in training the house dog to hunt and the hunting dog to refrain from chasing hares.

This view is much favored by Descartes. He maintained that the soul or mind is united in a special way with a certain part of the brain called the pineal gland, by means of which the mind senses all movements that occur in the body, as well as external objects, and by the mere act of willing it can move the gland in various ways. He maintained that this gland is suspended in the middle of the brain in such a way that it can be moved by the slightest motion of the animal spirits. He further maintained that the number of different ways in which the gland can be suspended in the middle of the brain corresponds with the number of different ways in which the animal spirits can impinge upon it, and that, furthermore, as many different marks can be imprinted on the gland as there are external objects impelling the animal spirits toward it. As a result, if by the will of the soul, which can move it in various ways, the gland is later suspended in that particular way in which it had previously been suspended by a particular mode of agitation of the spirits, then the gland will impel and determine the animal spirits in the same way as they had previously been acted upon by a similar mode of suspension of the gland. He furthermore maintained that every single act of willing is by nature united to a particular motion of the gland. For example, if anyone wills to gaze at a distant object, this act of willing will bring about the dilation of the pupil. But if he thinks only of dilating the pupil, it will be useless for him to will this, because the motion of the gland which serves to impel the spirits toward the optic nerve in a manner that will bring about dilation or contraction of the pupil has not been joined by nature to the act of willing its contraction or dilation, but only to the act of willing to gaze at distant or near objects. Finally, he maintained that although each motion of this gland seems to have been connected through nature from the beginning of our lives to particular thoughts, these motions can be joined to other thoughts through training, and this he endeavors to prove in Article 50, Part I of *On the Passions of the Soul*. From this he concludes that there is no soul so weak that it cannot, through good guidance, acquire absolute power over its passions. For these passions are defined by him as "perceptions, or feelings, or disturbances of the soul, which are related to the soul as species, and which are produced (note well!), preserved and strengthened through some motion of the spirits." (See Article 27, Part 1, *On the Passions of the Soul*.) But as we are able to join any motion of the gland, and consequently of the spirits, to any act of willing, and as the determination of the will depends only on our own power, if therefore we determine our will by the sure and firm decisions in accordance with which we want to direct the actions of our lives, and if to these decisions we join the movements of the passions which we want to have, we shall acquire absolute command over our passions.

Such is the view of this illustrious person (as far as I can gather from his own words), a view which I could scarcely have believed to have been put forward by such a great man, had it been less ingenious. Indeed, I am lost in wonder that a philosopher who had strictly resolved to deduce nothing except from self-evident bases and to affirm nothing that he did not clearly and distinctly perceive, who had so often censured the Scholastics for seeking to explain obscurities through occult qualities, should adopt a theory more occult than any occult quality. What, I ask, does he understand by the union of mind and body? What clear and distinct conception does he have of thought closely united to a certain particle of matter? I should have liked him, indeed, to explain this union through its proximate cause. But he had conceived mind as so distinct from body that he could assign no one cause either of this union or of mind itself, and found it necessary to have recourse to the cause of the entire universe, that is, God. Again, I should like to know how many degrees of motion mind can impart to that pineal gland of his, and by what force it can hold it suspended. For I know not whether this gland can be moved about more slowly or more quickly by the mind than by animal spirits, and whether the movements of the passions which we have joined in a close union with firm decisions cannot again be separated from those decisions by corporeal causes, from which it would follow that, although the mind firmly decides to face danger and joins to that decision the motions of boldness, when the danger appears, the gland may assume such a form of suspension that the mind can think only of flight. And surely, since will and motion have no common standard, there cannot be any comparison between the power or strength of the mind and body, and consequently the strength of the latter cannot possibly be determined by the strength of the former. There is the additional fact that this gland is not to be found located in the middle of the brain in such a way that it can be driven about so easily and in so many ways, nor do all nerves extend as far as the cavities of the brain.

Finally, I omit all Descartes's assertions about the will and its freedom, since I have already abundantly demonstrated that they are false. Therefore, since the power of the mind is defined solely by the understanding, as I have demonstrated above, we shall determine solely by the knowledge of the mind the remedies for the emotions—remedies which I believe all men experience but do not accurately observe nor distinctly see—and from this knowledge we shall deduce all that concerns the blessedness of the mind.

Axioms

1. If two contrary actions are instigated in the same subject, a change must necessarily take place in both or in the one of them until they cease to be contrary.
2. The power of an effect is defined by the power of the cause insofar as its essence is explicated or defined through the essence of its cause.

This Axiom is evident from Pr. 7, III.

Proposition 1
The affections of the body, that is the images of things, are arranged and connected in the body in exactly the same way as thoughts and the ideas of things are arranged and connected in the mind.

Proof The order and connection of ideas is the same (Pr. 7, II) as the order and connection of things, and, vice versa, the order and connection of things is the same (Cor. Pr. 6 and Pr. 7, II) as the order and connection of ideas. Therefore, just as the order and connection of ideas in the mind occurs in accordance with the order and connection of the affections of the body (Pr. 18, II), so, vice versa (Pr. 2, III), the order and connection of the affections of the body occurs in just the way that thoughts and the ideas of things are arranged and connected in the mind.

Proposition 2
If we remove an agitation of the mind, or emotion, from the thought of its external cause, and join it to other thoughts, then love or hatred toward the external cause, and also vacillations, that arise from these emotions will be destroyed.

Proof That which constitutes the form of love or hatred is pleasure or pain accompanied by the idea of an external cause (Def. of Emotions 6 and 7). So when the latter is removed, the form of love or hatred is removed with it; and thus these emotions, and those that arise from them, are destroyed.

PROPOSITION 3

A passive emotion ceases to be a passive emotion as soon as we form a clear and distinct idea of it.

Proof A passive emotion is a confused idea (Gen. Def. of Emotions). So if we form a clear and distinct idea of the emotion, this idea is distinguishable only in concept from the emotion insofar as the latter is related only to mind (Pr. 21, II and Sch.); and so the emotion will cease to be passive (Pr. 3, III).

Corollary So the more an emotion is known to us, the more it is within our control, and the mind is the less passive in respect of it.

PROPOSITION 4

There is no affection of the body of which we cannot form a clear and distinct conception.

Proof What is common to all things can only be conceived adequately (Pr. 38, II), and thus (Pr. 12 and Lemma 2 which comes after Sch. Pr. 13, II) there is no affection of the body of which we cannot form a clear and distinct conception.

Corollary Hence it follows that there is no emotion of which we cannot form a clear and distinct conception. For an emotion is the idea of an affection of the body (Gen. Def. of Emotions), which must therefore involve some clear and distinct conception (preceding Pr.).

Scholium Since there exists nothing from which some effect does not follow (Pr. 36, I), and all that follows from an idea that is adequate in us is understood by us clearly and distinctly (Pr. 40, II), it therefore follows that everyone has the power of clearly and distinctly understanding himself and his emotions, if not absolutely, at least in part, and consequently of bringing it about that he should be less passive in respect of them. So we should pay particular attention to getting to know each emotion, as far as possible, clearly and distinctly, so that the mind may thus be determined from the emotion to think those things that it clearly and distinctly perceives, and in which it finds full contentment. Thus the emotion may be detached from the thought of an external cause and joined to true thoughts. The result will be that not only are love, hatred, etc. destroyed (Pr. 2, V) but also that the appetites or desires that are wont to arise from such an emotion cannot be excessive (Pr. 61, IV). For it is very important to note that it is one and the same appetite through which a man is said both to be active and to be passive. For example, we have shown that human nature is so constituted that everyone wants others to live according to his way of thinking (Cor. Pr. 31, III). Now this appetite in a man who is not guided by reason is a passive emotion which is called ambition, and differs to no great extent from pride. But in a man who lives according to the dictates of reason it is an active emotion, or virtue, which is called piety (Sch. 1, Pr. 37, IV and second proof of that same Proposition). In this way all appetites or desires are passive emotions only insofar as they arise from inadequate ideas, and they are accredited to virtue when they are aroused or generated by adequate ideas. For all desires whereby we are determined to some action can arise both from adequate and from inadequate ideas (Pr. 59, IV). To return to the point from which I digressed, there is available to us no more excellent remedy for the emotions than that which consists in a true knowledge of them, since there is no other power of the mind than the power of thought and of forming adequate ideas, as I have shown above (Pr. 3, III).

Proposition 5
An emotion toward a thing which we imagine merely in itself, and not as necessary, possible, or contingent, is the greatest of all emotions, other things being equal.

Proof   An emotion toward a thing that we imagine to be free is greater than an emotion toward a necessary thing (Pr. 49, III), and consequently still greater than an emotion toward a thing that we imagine to be possible or contingent (Pr. 11, IV). But to imagine something as free can be nothing else than to imagine it merely in itself, while we are ignorant of the causes by which it has been determined to act (Sch. Pr. 35, II). Therefore, an emotion toward a thing that we imagine merely in itself is greater, other things being equal, than an emotion toward a necessary, possible, or contingent thing, and consequently it is the greatest of all emotions.

Proposition 6
Insofar as the mind understands all things as governed by necessity, to that extent it has greater power over emotions, i.e. it is less passive in respect of them.

Proof   The mind understands all things to be governed by necessity (Pr. 29, I) and to be determined to exist and to act by an infinite chain of causes (Pr. 28, I). And so (preceding Pr.) to that extent the mind succeeds in becoming less passive to the emotions that arise from things, and (Pr. 48, III) less affected toward the things themselves.

Scholium   The more this knowledge (namely, that things are governed by necessity) is applied to particular things which we imagine more distinctly and more vividly, the greater is this power of the mind over the emotions, as is testified by experience. For we see that pain over the loss of some good is assuaged as soon as the man who has lost it realizes that that good could not have been saved in any way. Similarly, we see that nobody pities a baby because it cannot talk or walk or reason, and because it spends many years in a kind of ignorance of self. But if most people were born adults and only a few were born babies, then everybody would feel sorry for babies because they would then look on infancy not as a natural and necessary thing but as a fault or flaw in Nature. There are many other examples of this kind that we might note.

Proposition 7
Emotions which arise or originate from reason are, if we take account of time, more powerful than those that are related to particular things which we regard as absent.

Proof We do not look on a thing as absent by reason of the emotion with which we think of it, but by reason of the body being affected by another emotion which excludes the existence of the said thing (Pr. 17, II). Therefore, the emotion that is related to a thing that we regard as absent is not of a kind to overcome the rest of man's activities and power (see Pr. 6, IV). On the contrary, its nature is such that it can be checked in some way by those affections which exclude the existence of its external cause (Pr. 9, IV). But an emotion that arises from reason is necessarily related to the common properties of things (see Def. of Reason in Sch. 2, Pr. 40, II) which we regard as being always present (for there can be nothing that excludes their present existence) and which we always think of in the same way (Pr. 38, II). Therefore, such an emotion always remains the same. Consequently (Ax. 1, V), emotions which are contrary to it and are not fostered by their external causes must adapt themselves to it more and more until they are no longer contrary; and to that extent an emotion that arises from reason is more powerful.

Proposition 8
The greater the number of causes that simultaneously concur in arousing an emotion, the greater the emotion.

Proof Several causes acting together are more effective than if they were fewer (Pr. 7, III). So (Pr. 5, IV) the more simultaneous causes there are in arousing an emotion, the stronger will be the emotion.

Scholium This Proposition is also obvious from Ax. 2, V.

Proposition 9
An emotion that is related to several different causes, which the mind regards together with the emotion itself, is less harmful, and we suffer less from it and are less affected toward each individual cause, than if we were affected by another equally great emotion which is related to only one or to a few causes.

Proof An emotion is bad or harmful only insofar as the mind is thereby hindered from being able to think (Pr. 26 and 27, IV). Thus, an emotion whereby the mind is determined to regard several objects simultaneously is less harmful than another equally great emotion which so keeps the mind in the contemplation of only one or few objects that it cannot think of anything else. This is the first point. Again, because the essence of the mind, that is (Pr. 7, III), its power, consists only in thought (Pr. 11, II), it follows that the mind is less passive through an emotion by which it is determined to regard several things all together than through an equally great emotion which keeps the mind engrossed in the contemplation of only one or few objects. This is the second point. Finally, this emotion (Pr. 48, III), insofar as it is related to several external causes, is also less toward each cause.

Proposition 10
As long as we are not assailed by emotions that are contrary to our nature, we have the power to arrange and associate affections of the body according to the order of the intellect.

Proof Emotions that are contrary to our nature, that is (Pr. 30, IV), which are bad, are bad to the extent that they hinder the mind from understanding (Pr. 27, IV). Therefore, as long as we are not assailed by emotions contrary to our nature, the power of the mind whereby it endeavors to understand things (Pr. 26, IV) is not hindered, and thus it has the ability to form clear and distinct ideas, deducing them from one another (Sch. 2, Pr. 40 and Sch. Pr. 47, II). Consequently (Pr. 1, V), in this case we have the ability to arrange and associate affections of the body according to the order of the intellect.

Scholium Through the ability to arrange and associate rightly the affections of the body we can bring it about that we are not easily affected by bad emotions. For (Pr. 7, V) greater force is required to check emotions arranged and associated according to intellectual order than emotions that are uncertain and random. Therefore the best course we can adopt, as long as we do not have perfect knowledge of our emotions, is to conceive a right method of living, or fixed rules of life, and to commit them to memory and continually apply them to particular situations that are frequently encountered in life, so that our casual thinking is thoroughly permeated by them and they are always ready to hand. For example, among our practical rules, we laid down (Pr. 46, IV and Sch.) that hatred should be conquered by love or nobility, and not repaid with reciprocal hatred. Now in order that we may have this precept of reason always ready to hand we should think about and frequently reflect on the wrongs that are commonly committed among mankind, and the best way and method of warding them off by nobility of character. For thus we shall associate the image of a wrong with the presentation of this rule of conduct, and it will always be at hand for us (Pr. 18, II) when we suffer a wrong. Again, if we always have in readiness consideration of our true advantage and also of the good that follows from mutual friendship and social relations, and also remember that supreme contentment of spirit follows from the right way of life (Pr. 52, IV), and that men, like everything else, act from the necessity of their nature, then the wrong, or the hatred that is wont to arise from it, will occupy just a small part of our imagination and will easily be overcome. Or if the anger that is wont to arise from grievous wrongs be not easily overcome, it will nevertheless be overcome, though not without vacillation, in a far shorter space of time than if we had not previously reflected on these things in the way I have described, as is evident from Prs. 6, 7, and 8, V. We ought, in the same way, to reflect on courage to banish fear; we should enumerate and often picture the everyday dangers of life, and how they can best be avoided and overcome by resourcefulness and strength of mind.

But it should be noted that in arranging our thoughts and images we should always concentrate on that which is good in every single thing (Cor. Pr. 63, IV and Pr. 59, III) so that in so doing we may be determined to act always from the emotion of pleasure. For example, if anyone sees that he is devoted overmuch to the pursuit of honor, let him reflect on its proper function, and the purpose for which it ought to be pursued, and the means by which it can be attained, and not on its abuse and hollowness and the fickleness of mankind and the like, on which nobody reflects except from a morbid disposition. It is by thoughts like these that the most ambitious especially torment themselves when they despair of attaining the honor that they covet, and in vomiting forth their anger they try to make some show of wisdom. It is therefore certain that those who raise the loudest outcry about the abuse of honor and about worldly vanity are most eager for honor. Nor is this trait confined to the ambitious: it is shared by all who meet with adverse fortune and are weak in spirit. For the miser, too, who is in poverty, does not cease to talk of the abuse of money and the vices of the rich, with the result that he merely torments himself and makes it clear that he resents not only his own poverty but also the wealth of others. So, too, those who have been ill-received by a sweetheart are obsessed by thoughts of the fickleness and deceitfulness of women and the other faults commonly attributed to them, but immediately forget about all this as soon as they again find favor with their sweetheart. Therefore, he who aims solely from love of freedom to control his emotions and appetites will strive his best to familiarize himself with virtues and their causes and to fill his mind with the joy that arises from the true knowledge of them, while refraining from dwelling on men's faults and abusing mankind and deriving pleasure from a false show of freedom. He who diligently follows these precepts and practices them (for they are not difficult) will surely within a short space of time be able to direct his actions for the most part according to reason's behest.

Proposition 11
In proportion as a mental image is related to more things, the more frequently does it occur—i.e. the more often it springs to life—and the more it engages the mind.

Proof In proportion as an image or emotion is related to more things, the more causes there are by which it can be aroused and fostered, all of which the mind, by hypothesis, regards simultaneously as a result of the emotion. And so the emotion thereby occurs more frequently—i.e. springs to life more often—and engages the mind the more (Pr. 8, V).

Proposition 12
Images are more readily associated with those images that are related to things which we clearly and distinctly understand than they are to others.

Proof Things that are clearly and distinctly understood are either the common properties of things or deductions made from them (see Def. of Reason in Sch. 2, Pr. 40, II) and consequently they are more often before the mind (preceding Pr.). So it is more likely that we should regard other things in conjunction with these than in conjunction with different things, and consequently (Pr. 18, II) that they should more readily be associated with these than with others.

Proposition 13
The greater the number of other images with which an image is associated, the more often it springs to life.

Proof The greater the number of images with which an image is associated, the more causes there are by which it can be aroused (Pr. 18, II).

Proposition 14
The mind can bring it about that all the affections of the body—i.e. images of things—be related to the idea of God.

Proof There is no affection of the body of which the mind cannot form a clear and distinct conception (Pr. 4, V), and so the mind can bring it about (Pr. 15, I) that they should all be related to the idea of God.

Proposition 15
He who clearly and distinctly understands himself and his emotions loves God, and the more so the more he understands himself and his emotions.

Proof He who clearly and distinctly understands himself and his emotions feels pleasure (Pr. 53, III) accompanied by the idea of God (preceding Pr.). So (Def. of Emotions 6) he loves God, and, by the same reasoning, the more so the more he understands himself and his emotions.

Proposition 16
This love toward God is bound to hold chief place in the mind.

Proof This love is associated with all the affections of the body (Pr. 14, V), and is fostered by them all (Pr. 15, V), and so (Pr. 11, V) it is bound to hold chief place in the mind.

Proposition 17
God is without passive emotions, and he is not affected with any emotion of pleasure or pain.

Proof All ideas, insofar as they are related to God, are true (Pr. 32, III), that is (Def. 4, II), they are adequate. Thus (Gen. Def. of Emotions), God is without passive emotions. Again, God cannot pass to a state of greater or less perfection (Cor. 2, Pr. 20, I), and so (Def. of Emotions 2 and 3) he is not affected with any emotion of pleasure or pain.

Corollary Strictly speaking, God does not love or hate anyone. For God (preceding Pr.) is not affected with any emotion of pleasure or pain, and consequently (Def. of Emotions 6 and 7) he neither loves nor hates anyone.

Proposition 18
Nobody can hate God.

Proof The idea of God which is in us is adequate and perfect (Prs. 46 and 47, II). Therefore, insofar as we contemplate God, we are active (Pr. 3, III). Consequently (Pr. 59, III), there can be no pain accompanied by the idea of God; that is (Def. of Emotions 7), nobody can hate God.

Corollary Love toward God cannot turn to hatred.

Scholium It may be objected that in understanding God to be the cause of all things we thereby consider God to be the cause of pain. To this I reply that insofar as we understand the causes of pain, it ceases to be a passive emotion (Pr. 3, V); that is (Pr. 59, III), to that extent it ceases to be pain. So insofar as we understand God to be the cause of pain, to that extent we feel pleasure.

Proposition 19
He who loves God cannot endeavor that God should love him in return.

Proof If a man were so to endeavor, he would therefore desire (Cor. Pr. 17, V) that God whom he loves should not be God, and consequently (Pr. 19, III) he would desire to feel pain, which is absurd (Pr. 28, III). Therefore he who loves God . . . etc.

Proposition 20
This love toward God cannot be tainted with emotions of envy or jealousy, but is the more fostered as we think more men to be joined to God by this same bond of love.

Proof This love toward God is the highest good that we can aim at according to the dictates of reason (Pr. 28, IV) and is available to all men (Pr. 36, IV), and we desire that all men should enjoy it (Pr. 37, IV). Therefore (Def. of Emotions 23), it cannot be stained by the emotion of envy, nor again by the emotion of jealousy (Pr. 18, V and Def. of Jealousy, q.v. in Sch. Pr. 36, III). On the contrary (Pr. 31, III), it is the more fostered as we think more men to be enjoying it.

Scholium We can in the same way demonstrate that there is no emotion directly contrary to this love by which this love can be destroyed; and so we may conclude that this love toward God is the most constant of all emotions, and insofar as it is related to the body it cannot be destroyed except together with the body. As to its nature insofar as it is related solely to the mind, this we shall examine later on.

With this I have completed the account of all the remedies for the emotions: that is, all that the mind, considered solely in itself, can do against the emotions. From this it is clear that the power of the mind over the emotions consists:

1. In the very knowledge of the emotions (Sch. Pr. 4, V).
2. In detaching the emotions from the thought of their external cause, which we imagine confusedly. (See Pr. 2 together with Sch. Pr. 4, V.)
3. In the matter of time, in respect of which the affections that are related to things we understand are superior to those which are related to things that we conceive in a confused or fragmentary way (Pr. 7, V).
4. In the number of causes whereby those affections are fostered which are related to the common properties of things, or to God (Prs. 9 and 11, V).
5. Lastly, in the order wherein the mind can arrange its emotions and associate them one with another (Sch. Pr. 10 and also Prs. 12, 13, 14, V).

But in order that this power of the mind over the emotions may be better understood, it is important to note that we call emotions strong when we compare the emotion of one man with that of another, and when we see one man more than another assailed by the same emotion, or when we compare with one another the emotions of the same man and find that the same man is affected or moved by one emotion more than by another. For (Pr. 5, IV) the strength of every emotion is defined by the power of an external cause as compared with our own power. Now the power of the mind is defined solely by knowledge, its weakness or passivity solely by the privation of knowledge; that is, it is measured by the extent to which its ideas are said to be inadequate. Hence it follows that that mind is most passive whose greatest part is constituted by inadequate ideas, so that it is characterized more by passivity than by activity. On the other hand, that mind is most active whose greatest part is constituted by adequate ideas, so that even if the latter mind contains as many inadequate ideas as the former, it is characterized by those ideas which are attributed to human virtue rather than by those that point to human weakness.

Again, it should be noted that emotional distress and unhappiness have their origin especially in excessive love toward a thing subject to considerable instability, a thing which we can never completely possess. For nobody is disturbed or anxious about any thing unless he loves it, nor do wrongs, suspicions, enmities, etc. arise except from love toward things which nobody can truly possess.

So from this we readily conceive how effective against the emotions is clear and distinct knowledge, and especially the third kind of knowledge (for which see Sch. Pr. 47, II) whose basis is the knowledge of God. Insofar as they are passive emotions, if it does not completely destroy them (Pr. 3, and Sch. Pr. 4, V), at least it brings it about that they constitute the least part of the mind (Pr. 14, V). Again, it begets love toward something immutable and eternal (Pr. 15, V) which we can truly possess (Pr. 45, II), and which therefore cannot be defiled by any of the faults that are to be found in the common sort of love, but can continue to grow more and more (Pr. 15, V) and engage the greatest part of the mind (Pr. 16, V) and pervade it.

And now I have completed all that concerns this present life; for, as I said at the beginning of this Scholium, in this brief account I have covered all the remedies against the emotions. This everyone can see who gives his mind to the contents of this Scholium, and likewise to the definitions of the mind and its emotions, and lastly to Props. 1 and 3, III. So it is now time to pass on to those matters that concern the duration of the mind without respect to the body.

Proposition 21

The mind can exercise neither imagination nor memory save while the body endures.

Proof It is only while the body endures that the mind expresses the actual existence of its body and conceives the affections of the body as actual (Cor. Pr. 8, II). Consequently (Pr. 26, II), it does not conceive any body as actually existing save while its own body endures. Therefore (see Def. of Imagination in Sch. Pr. 17, II), it cannot exercise either imagination or memory save while the body endures (see Def. of Memory in Sch. Pr. 18, II).

Proposition 22

Nevertheless, there is necessarily in God an idea which expresses the essence of this or that human body under a form of eternity [sub specie aeternitatis].

Proof God is the cause not only of the existence of this or that human body but also of its essence (Pr. 25, I), which must therefore necessarily be received through God's essence (Ax. 4, I) by a certain eternal necessity (Pr. 16, I), and this conception must necessarily be in God (Pr. 3, II).

Proposition 23

The human mind cannot be absolutely destroyed along with body, but something of it remains, which is eternal.

Proof In God there is necessarily a conception, or idea, which expresses the essence of the human body (preceding Pr.) and which therefore is necessarily something that pertains to the essence of the human mind (Pr. 13, II). But we assign to the human mind the kind of duration that can be defined by time only insofar as the mind expresses the actual existence of the body, an existence that is explicated through duration and can be defined by time. That is, we do not assign duration to the mind except while the body endures (Cor. Pr. 8, II). However, since that which is conceived by a certain eternal necessity through God's essence is nevertheless a something (preceding Pr.), this something, which pertains to the essence of mind, will necessarily be eternal.

Scholium As we have said, this idea, which expresses the essence of the body under a form of eternity, is a definite mode of thinking which pertains to the essence of mind, and which is necessarily eternal. Yet it is impossible that we should remember that we existed before the body, since neither can there be any traces of this in the body nor can eternity be defined by time, or be in any way related to time. Nevertheless, we feel and experience that we are eternal. For the mind senses those things that it conceives by its understanding just as much as those which it has in its memory. Logical proofs are the eyes of the mind, whereby it sees and observes things. So although we have no recollection of having existed before the body, we nevertheless sense that our mind, insofar as it involves the essence of the body under a form of eternity, is eternal, and that this aspect of its existence cannot be defined by time, that is, cannot be explicated through duration. Therefore, our mind can be said to endure, and its existence to be defined by a definite period of time, only to the extent that it involves the actual existence of the body, and it is only to that extent that it has the power to determine the existence of things by time and to conceive them from the point of view of duration.

Proposition 24

The more we understand particular things, the more we understand God.

Proof This is evident from Cor. Pr. 25, I.

Proposition 25
The highest conatus of the mind and its highest virtue is to understand things by the third kind of knowledge.

Proof The third kind of knowledge proceeds from the adequate idea of certain of God's attributes to the adequate knowledge of the essence of things (see its definition in Sch. 2, Pr. 40, II), and the more we understand things in this way, the more we understand God (preceding Pr.). Therefore (Pr. 28, IV), the highest virtue of the mind, that is (Def. 8, IV), its power or nature, or its highest conatus (Pr. 7, III), is to understand things by this third kind of knowledge.

Proposition 26
The more capable the mind is of understanding things by the third kind of knowledge, the more it desires to understand things by this same kind of knowledge.

Proof This is evident; for insofar as we conceive the mind to be capable of understanding things by the third kind of knowledge, to that extent we conceive it as determined to understand things by that same kind of knowledge. Consequently (Def. of Emotions 1), the more the mind is capable of this, the more it desires it.

Proposition 27
From this third kind of knowledge there arises the highest possible contentment of mind.

Proof The highest virtue of the mind is to know God (Pr. 28, IV), that is, to understand things by the third kind of knowledge (Pr. 25, V), and this virtue is all the greater the more the mind knows things by the third kind of knowledge (Pr. 24, V). So he who knows things by this third kind of knowledge passes to the highest state of human perfection, and consequently (Def. of Emotions 2) is affected by the highest pleasure, this pleasure being accompanied (Pr. 43, II) by the idea of himself and his own virtue. Therefore (Def. of Emotions 25), from this kind of knowledge there arises the highest possible contentment.

Proposition 28
The conatus, or desire, to know things by the third kind of knowledge cannot arise from the first kind of knowledge, but from the second.

Proof This proposition is self-evident. For whatever we understand clearly and distinctly, we understand either through itself or through something else which is conceived through itself. That is, ideas which are clear and distinct in us or which are related to the third kind of knowledge (Sch. 2, Pr. 40, II) cannot follow from fragmentary or confused ideas which (same Sch.) are related to the first kind of knowledge, but from adequate ideas, that is (same Sch.), from the second or third kind of knowledge. Therefore (Def. of Emotions 1), the desire to know things by the third kind of knowledge cannot arise from the first kind of knowledge, but from the second.

Proposition 29

Whatever the mind understands under a form of eternity it does not understand from the fact that it conceives the present actual existence of the body, but from the fact that it conceives the essence of the body under a form of eternity.

Proof Insofar as the mind conceives the present existence of its body, to that extent it conceives a duration that can be determined by time, and only to that extent does it have the power to conceive things in relation to time (Pr. 21, V and Pr. 26, II). But eternity cannot be explicated through duration (Def. 8, I and its explication). Therefore, to that extent the mind does not have the power to conceive things under a form of eternity. But since it is the nature of reason to conceive things under a form of eternity (Cor. 2, Pr. 44, II), and since it belongs to the nature of mind, too, to conceive the essence of the body under a form of eternity (Pr. 23, V), and since there belongs to the essence of mind nothing but these two ways of conceiving (Pr. 13, II), it follows that this power to conceive things under a form of eternity pertains to the mind only insofar as it conceives the essence of the body under a form of eternity.

Scholium We conceive things as actual in two ways: either insofar as we conceive them as related to a fixed time and place, or insofar as we conceive them to be contained in God and to follow from the necessity of the divine nature. Now the things that are conceived as true or real in this second way, we conceive under a form of eternity, and their ideas involve the eternal and infinite essence of God, as we demonstrated in Pr. 45, II. See also its Scholium.

Proposition 30

Our mind, insofar as it knows both itself and the body under a form of eternity, necessarily has a knowledge of God, and knows that it is in God and is conceived through God.

Proof Eternity is the very essence of God insofar as this essence involves necessary existence (Def. 8, I). Therefore, to conceive things under a form of eternity is to conceive things insofar as they are conceived through God's essence as real entities; that is, insofar as they involve existence through God's essence. Therefore, our mind, insofar as it knows itself and the body under a form of eternity, necessarily has knowledge of God, and knows . . . etc.

Proposition 31

The third kind of knowledge depends on the mind as its formal cause insofar as the mind is eternal.

Proof The mind conceives nothing under a form of eternity except insofar as it conceives the essence of its body under a form of eternity (Pr. 29, V), that is (Prs. 21 and 23, V), except insofar as the mind is eternal. Therefore (preceding Pr.), insofar as it is eternal, it has knowledge of God, knowledge which is necessarily adequate (Pr. 46, II). Therefore, the mind, insofar as it is eternal, is capable of knowing all the things that can follow from this given knowledge of God (Pr. 40, II): that is, of knowing things by the third kind of knowledge (see its definition in Sch. 2, Pr. 40, II), of which the mind is therefore (Def. 1, III) the adequate or formal cause insofar as it is eternal.

Scholium So the more each man is advanced in this kind of knowledge, the more clearly conscious he is of himself and of God, that is, the more perfect and blessed he is, as will become even more evident from what is to follow. But here it should be noted that although we are at this point certain that the mind is eternal insofar as it conceives things under a form of eternity, yet, to facilitate the explanation and render more readily intelligible what I intend to demonstrate, we shall consider the mind as if it were now beginning to be and were now beginning to understand things under a form of eternity, as we have been doing up to now. This we may do without any danger of error, provided we are careful to reach no conclusion except from premises that are quite clear.

Proposition 32
We take pleasure in whatever we understand by the third kind of knowledge, and this is accompanied by the idea of God as cause.

Proof From this kind of knowledge there arises the highest possible contentment of mind (Pr. 27, V), that is (Def. of Emotions 25), the highest possible pleasure, and this is accompanied by the idea of oneself, and consequently (Pr. 30, V) also by the idea of God, as cause.

Corollary From the third kind of knowledge there necessarily arises the intellectual love of God [*amor Dei intellectualis*]. For from this kind of knowledge there arises (preceding Pr.) pleasure accompanied by the idea of God as cause, that is (Def. of Emotions 6), the love of God not insofar as we imagine him as present (Pr. 29, V) but insofar as we understand God to be eternal. And this is what I call the intellectual love of God.

Proposition 33
The intellectual love of God which arises from the third kind of knowledge is eternal.

Proof The third kind of knowledge is eternal (Pr. 31, V and Ax. 3, I), and therefore (by the same Ax. 3, I) the love that arises from it is also necessarily eternal.

Scholium Although this love toward God has had no beginning (preceding Pr.), it yet has all the perfections of love just as if it had originated in the manner we supposed in the Corollary to the preceding Proposition. There is no difference, except that the mind has possessed from eternity those perfections which we then supposed to be accruing to it, accompanied by the idea of God as eternal cause. If pleasure consists in the transition to a state of greater perfection, blessedness must surely consist in this, that the mind is endowed with perfection itself.

Proposition 34
It is only while the body endures that the mind is subject to passive emotions.

Proof Imagining is the idea whereby the mind regards some thing as present (see its definition in Sch. Pr. 17, II), an idea which, however, indicates the present state of the body rather than the nature of an external thing (Cor. 2, Pr. 16, II). Therefore, an emotion (Gen. Def. of Emotions) is an imagining insofar as it indicates the present state of the body. So (Pr. 21, V) it is only while the body endures that the mind is subject to passive emotions.

Corollary Hence it follows that no love is eternal except for intellectual love [*amor intellectualis*].

Scholium If we turn our attention to the common belief entertained by men, we shall see that they are indeed conscious of the eternity of the mind, but they confuse it with duration and assign it to imagination or to memory, which they believe to continue after death.

Proposition 35
God loves himself with an infinite intellectual love.

Proof God is absolutely infinite (Def. 6, I); that is (Def. 6, II), God's nature enjoys infinite perfection, accompanied (Pr. 3, II) by the idea of itself, that is (Pr. 11 and Def. 1, I), by the idea of its own cause; and that is what, in Cor. Pr. 32. V, we declared to be intellectual love.

Proposition 36
The mind's intellectual love toward God is the love of God wherewith God loves himself not insofar as he is infinite, but insofar as he can be explicated through the essence of the human mind considered under a form of eternity. That is, the mind's intellectual love toward God is part of the infinite love wherewith God loves himself.

Proof This, the mind's love, must be related to the active nature of the mind (Cor. Pr. 32, V and Pr. 3, III), and is therefore an activity whereby the mind regards itself, accompanied by the idea of God as cause (Pr. 32, V and Cor.); that is (Cor. Pr. 25, I and Cor. Pr. 11, II), an activity whereby God, insofar as he can be explicated through the human mind, regards himself, accompanied by the idea of himself. And therefore (preceding Pr.) this love of God is part of the infinite love wherewith God loves himself.

Corollary Hence it follows that God, insofar as he loves himself, loves mankind, and, consequently, that the love of God toward men and the mind's intellectual love toward God are one and the same.

Scholium From this we clearly understand in what our salvation or blessedness or freedom consists, namely, in the constant and eternal love toward God, that is, in God's love toward men. This love or blessedness is called glory in the Holy Scriptures, and rightly so. For whether this love be related to God or to the mind, it can properly be called spiritual contentment, which in reality cannot be distinguished from glory (Def. of Emotions 25 and 30). For insofar as it is related to God, it is (Pr. 35, V) pleasure (if we may still use this term) accompanied by the idea of himself, and this is also the case insofar as it is related to the mind (Pr. 27, V). Again, since the essence of our mind consists solely in knowledge, whose principle and basis is God (Pr. 15, I and Sch. Pr. 47, II), it follows that we see quite clearly how and in what way our mind, in respect of essence and existence, follows from the divine nature and is continuously dependent on God.

I have thought this worth noting here in order to show by this example the superiority of that knowledge of particular things which I have called "intuitive" or "of the third kind," and its preferability to that abstract knowledge which I have called "knowledge of the second kind."

For although I demonstrated in a general way in Part I that everything (and consequently the human mind, too) is dependent on God in respect of its essence and of its existence, that proof, although legitimate and exempt from any shadow of doubt, does not so strike the mind as when it is inferred from the essence of each particular thing which we assert to be dependent on God.

PROPOSITION 37

There is nothing in Nature which is contrary to this intellectual love, or which can destroy it.

Proof This intellectual love follows necessarily from the nature of the mind insofar as that is considered as an eternal truth through God's nature (Prs. 33 and 29, V). Therefore, if there were anything that was contrary to this love, it would be contrary to truth, and consequently that which could destroy this love could cause truth to be false, which, as is self-evident, is absurd. Therefore, there is nothing in Nature ... etc.

Scholium The Axiom in Part IV is concerned with particular things insofar as they are considered in relation to a definite time and place, of which I think no one can be in doubt.

PROPOSITION 38

The greater the number of things the mind understands by the second and third kinds of knowledge, the less subject it is to emotions that are bad, and the less it fears death.

Proof The essence of the mind consists in knowledge (Pr. 11, II). Therefore, the greater the number of things the mind knows by the second and third kinds of knowledge, the greater is the part of it that survives (Prs. 23 and 29, V), and consequently (preceding Pr.) the greater is that part of it that is not touched by emotions contrary to our nature; that is (Pr. 30, IV), by emotions that are bad. Therefore, the greater the number of things the mind understands by the second and third kinds of knowledge, the greater is that part of it that remains unimpaired, and consequently the less subject it is to emotions ... etc.

Scholium Hence we understand that point which I touched upon in Sch. Pr. 39, IV and which I promised to explain in this part, namely that death is less hurtful in proportion as the mind's clear and distinct knowledge is greater, and consequently the more the mind loves God. Again, since (Pr. 27, V) from the third kind of knowledge there arises the highest possible contentment, hence it follows that the human mind can be of such a nature that that part of it that we have shown to perish with the body (Pr. 21, V) is of no account compared with that part of it that survives. But I shall be dealing with this at greater length in due course.

Proposition 39
He whose body is capable of the greatest amount of activity has a mind whose greatest part is eternal.

Proof He whose body is capable of the greatest amount of activity is least assailed by emotions that are evil (Pr. 38, IV), that is (Pr. 30, IV), by emotions that are contrary to our nature. Thus (Pr. 10, V) he has the capacity to arrange and associate the affections of the body according to intellectual order and consequently to bring it about (Pr. 14, V) that all the affections of the body are related to God. This will result (Pr. 15, V) in his being affected with love toward God, a love (Pr. 16, V) that must occupy or constitute the greatest part of the mind. Therefore (Pr. 33, V), he has a mind whose greatest part is eternal.

Scholium Since human bodies are capable of a great many activities, there is no doubt that they can be of such a nature as to be related to minds which have great knowledge of themselves and of God, and whose greatest and principal part is eternal, with the result that they scarcely fear death. But in order that this may be more clearly understood, it should here be remarked that our lives are subject to continual variation, and as the change is for the better or worse, so we are said to be fortunate or unfortunate. For he who passes from being a baby or child into being a corpse is said to be unfortunate; while, on the other hand, to have been able to pass the whole of one's life with a healthy mind in a healthy body is regarded as a mark of good fortune. And in fact he who, like a baby or a child, has a body capable of very little activity and is most dependent on external causes, has a mind which, considered solely in itself, has practically no consciousness of itself, of God, or of things, while he whose body is capable of very considerable activity has a mind which, considered solely in itself, is highly conscious of itself and of God and of things. In this life, therefore, we mainly endeavor that the body of childhood, as far as its nature allows and is conducive thereto, should develop into a body that is capable of a great many activities and is related to a mind that is highly conscious of itself, of God, and of things, and in such a way that everything relating to its memory or imagination should be of scarcely any importance in comparison with its intellect, as I have already stated in the Scholium to the preceding Proposition.

Proposition 40
The more perfection a thing has, the more active and the less passive it is. Conversely, the more active it is, the more perfect it is.

Proof The more perfect a thing is, the more reality it has (Def. 6, II); consequently (Pr. 3, III and Sch.), the more active it is and the less passive. This proof proceeds in the same manner in inverse order, from which it follows that a thing is the more perfect as it is more active.

Corollary Hence it follows that the part of the mind that survives, of whatever extent it may be, is more perfect than the rest. For the eternal part of the mind (Prs. 23 and 29, V) is the intellect, through which alone we are said to be active (Pr. 3, III), whereas that part which we have shown to perish is the imagination (Pr. 21, V), through which alone we are said to be passive (Pr. 3, III and Gen. Def. of Emotions). Therefore, the former (preceding Pr.), of whatever extent it be, is more perfect than the latter.

Scholium This is what I had resolved to demonstrate concerning the mind insofar as it is considered without reference to the existence of the body. It is clear from this, and also from Pr. 21, I and other propositions, that our mind, insofar as it understands, is an eternal mode of thinking which is determined by another eternal mode of thinking, and this again by another, and so on ad infinitum, with the result that they all together constitute the eternal and infinite intellect of God.

PROPOSITION 41
Even if we did not know that our mind is eternal, we should still regard as being of prime importance piety and religion and, to sum up completely, everything which in Part IV we showed to be related to courage and nobility.

Proof The first and only basis of virtue, that is, of the right way of life (Cor. Pr. 22 and Pr. 24, IV), is to seek one's own advantage. Now in order to determine what reason prescribes as advantageous we took no account of the mind's eternity, a topic which we did not consider until Part V. So although at that point we were unaware that the mind is eternal, we regarded as being of prime importance whatever is related to courage and nobleness. So even if now we were unaware of the mind's eternity, we should still regard the said precepts of reason as being of prime importance.

Scholium The common belief of the multitude seems to be quite different. For the majority appear to think that they are free to the extent that they can indulge their lusts, and that they are giving up their rights to the extent that they are required to live under the commandments of the divine law. So they believe that piety and religion, in fact everything related to strength of mind, are burdens which they hope to lay aside after death, when they will receive the reward of their servitude, that is, of piety and religion. And it is not by this hope alone, but also and especially by fear of incurring dreadful punishment after death, that they are induced to live according to the commandments of the divine law as far as their feebleness and impotent spirit allows. And if men did not have this hope and this fear, and if they believed on the contrary that minds perish with bodies and that they, miserable creatures, worn out by the burden of piety, had no prospect of further existence, they would return to their own inclinations and decide to shape their lives according to their lusts, and to be ruled by fortune rather than by themselves. This seems to me no less absurd than if a man, not believing that he can sustain his body on good food forever, were to decide to glut himself on poisons and deadly fare; or, on realizing that the mind is not eternal or immortal, he preferred to be mad and to live without reason. Such attitudes are so absurd that they are scarcely worth recounting.

Proposition 42
Blessedness is not the reward of virtue, but virtue itself. We do not enjoy blessedness because we keep our lusts in check. On the contrary, it is because we enjoy blessedness that we are able to keep our lusts in check.

Proof   Blessedness consists in love toward God (Pr. 36, V and Sch.), a love that arises from the third kind of knowledge (Cor. Pr. 32. V), and so this love (Prs. 59 and 3, III) must be related to the mind insofar as the mind is active; and therefore it is virtue itself (Def. 8, IV). That is the first point. Again, the more the mind enjoys this divine love or blessedness, the more it understands (Pr. 32, V); that is (Cor. Pr. 3, V), the more power it has over the emotions and (Pr. 38, V) the less subject it is to emotions that are bad. So the mind's enjoyment of this divine love or blessedness gives it the power to check lusts. And since human power to keep lusts in check consists solely in the intellect, nobody enjoys blessedness because he has kept his emotions in check. On the contrary, the power to keep lusts in check arises from blessedness itself.

Scholium   I have now completed all that I intended to demonstrate concerning the power of the mind over the emotions and concerning the freedom of the mind. This makes clear how strong the wise man is and how much he surpasses the ignorant man whose motive force is only lust. The ignorant man, besides being driven hither and thither by external causes, never possessing true contentment of spirit, lives as if he were unconscious of himself, God, and things, and as soon as he ceases to be passive, he at once ceases to be at all. On the other hand, the wise man, insofar as he is considered as such, suffers scarcely any disturbance of spirit, but being conscious, by virtue of a certain eternal necessity, of himself, of God and of things, never ceases to be, but always possesses true spiritual contentment.

If the road I have pointed out as leading to this goal seems very difficult, yet it can be found. Indeed, what is so rarely discovered is bound to be hard. For if salvation were ready to hand and could be discovered without great toil, how could it be that it is almost universally neglected? All things excellent are as difficult as they are rare.

End

THEOLOGICAL-POLITICAL TREATISE

Spinoza's Theological-Political Treatise (TTP) *has recently become a subject of great interest. There are many reasons for this fascination. One is its political and religious role in the Low Countries and throughout Europe, in its own day, as a document of radical religious critique and the subject of intense debate. Another concerns its role as a hermeneutical work and an early contribution to biblical criticism. A third reason for recent interest is its treatment of scriptural faith and Judaism within a defense of liberal democracy, toleration, and freedom of expression. A fourth concerns the role of Spinoza and the TTP in a tradition of liberalism that extends to Adam Smith and has provided western European thinkers, in the wake of the collapse of Marxism, with an appealing political perspective.*

Furthermore, unlike Spinoza's system, which was his lifelong philosophical preoccupation, the TTP was one outcome of a very personal struggle at a very particular historical moment. In it Spinoza confronted his Judaism, the Bible and interpretations of it, religious beliefs and practices, and the urgencies of political and religious debate in the Dutch provinces around 1665. Rather than a response to general intellectual developments, the TTP was a response to very particular historical events, and its audience was not philosophical colleagues in a narrow sense but rather a wider public, albeit one with precise skills, interests, and sympathies.

Like his friends Lodewijk Meyer and Adriaan Koerbagh, Spinoza was the object of severe accusations and attack by theologians and the Reformed Church. In 1666, in reaction to the publication of his Philosophica sacrae scripturae interpres (Philosophy the Interpreter of Scripture), *with its starkly philosophical, rational reading of Scripture, Meyer was publicly charged with atheism. Perhaps in part in response to the furor over Meyer's book and in part as an act of self-defense, Spinoza interrupted work on the* Ethics *and turned to the Bible, religion, science, and politics. In a famous letter of October 1665 to Henry Oldenburg, he described his new project: to expose the prejudices of the theologians, to defend himself against the charge of atheism, and to defend science and freedom of speech. Moreover, his work was further encouraged by the deeply disturbing plight of his friend Adriaan Koerbagh. The Koerbagh brothers, Adriaan and Jan, had known Spinoza since his days in Rijnsburg and his visits to the university in Leiden. Over the years, they had become adherents of Spinoza's naturalism and* in 1668 published an explicit and controversial defense of it, with an attack on Christianity, entitled "A Light Shining in Dark Places." Arrested, tried, and convicted, Adriaan died in prison in 1669; it is likely that Spinoza, especially in his advocacy of liberal democracy and his defense of tolerance and free speech, was thinking of his martyred friend (Steven Nadler, Spinoza: A Life [Cambridge University Press, 1999], 266–7).

Published anonymously in 1670 under a false imprint, the TTP unleashed a flood of criticisms and recriminations, from Reformed theologians and Cartesians alike. Spinoza was charged with atheism, sacrilege, and idolatry. Such impassioned furor warned Spinoza against a Dutch translation, the popularity of the book notwithstanding, and in 1671, in a letter to his friend Jarig Jelles, he pleaded for him to prevent the translation. If the intensity of public attacks was new, the material in the TTP was not, at least not wholly so. In a sense, at least in the first fifteen of its twenty chapters, devoted to the Bible and religion, Spinoza was returning to themes and ideas that probably originated for him in the years before his excommunication in 1656.

The TTP can be read as a work of biblical interpretation or hermeneutics and also as a work of political theory. In its first fifteen chapters, Spinoza presents a method for reading the Bible; a treatment of several large themes—prophecy, miracles, and law: an account of the Bible's authorship, structure, and history; and an interpretation of the Bible's goals and purposes. In Chapters 16 to 20, Spinoza explains the nature of the state and argues for toleration and freedom of expression. The work is filled with controversial, provocative ideas and views. Spinoza analyzes prophecy in terms of the abilities of the prophets, the context for their teaching, and the attitudes of their audiences. He denies the existence of miracles as traditionally understood, as divine interruptions of the causal order of nature, and reinterprets them as events for which no explanation is currently available. The Bible, he argues, is a human book that teaches a moral faith—charity and benevolence—and that does not contain scientific or metaphysical truths. Moreover, Spinoza defends liberal democracy and the toleration of scientific-philosophical thinking in a way that entails a moral life of reason, justice, mutual concern, and virtue. It is a life free from passion, a life of reason, of cooperation and justice for all citizens. In a world of monarchs, absolute rulers, and aristocratic privilege and a world rife with religious influence and hegemony over the affairs of private life and of government, Spinoza's scientific, naturalistic account of religion, ethics, and politics is radical. It was inflammatory and very quickly became notorious.

M.L.M.

CONTENTS

Preface

1. Of Prophecy
2. Of the Prophets
3. Of the vocation of the Hebrews, and whether the gift of prophecy was peculiar to them
4. Of the Divine Law
5. Of the reason for the institution of ceremonial observances. Belief in the Biblical narratives: in what way and for whom it is necessary
6. Of Miracles
7. Of the Interpretation of Scripture
8. In which it is shown that the Pentateuch and the Books of Joshua, Judges, Ruth, Samuel and Kings were not written by themselves. The question of their authorship is considered. Was there one author, or several, and who were they?
9. An enquiry into further matters relating to these same books, namely, whether Ezra gave them a final revision, and whether the marginal notes found in the Hebrew codices were variant readings
10. An examination of the remaining books of the Old Testament by the same method as was used with the previous books
11. An enquiry as to whether the Apostles wrote their Epistles as Apostles and prophets, or as teachers. The function of the Apostles is explained
12. Of the true original of the Divine Law. In what respect Scripture is called holy and the Word of God. It is shown that Scripture, insofar as it contains the Word of God, has come down to us uncorrupted
13. It is shown that Scripture teaches only very simple doctrines and inculcates nothing but obedience, and that concerning the nature of God it teaches only what men can imitate by a definite code of conduct
14. An analysis of faith, the faithful and the fundamental principles of faith. Faith is finally set apart from philosophy
15. It is demonstrated that neither is theology ancillary to reason nor reason to theology. The reason why we are convinced of the authority of Holy Scripture
16. The basis of the state; the natural and civil right of the individual, and the right of sovereign powers

17. It is demonstrated that nobody can, or need, transfer all his rights to the sovereign power. An account of the Hebrew state as it was in the time of Moses, and after his death before the institution of monarchy, and its success. Finally, the reasons why it came about that the theocratic state fell, and could scarcely have continued without civil strife
18. From the commonwealth of the Hebrews and their history some political principles are deduced
19. It is shown that the right over matters of religion is vested entirely in the sovereign, and that the external forms of worship should be such as accord with the peace of the commonwealth, if we would serve God aright
20. It is shown that in a free commonwealth every man may think as he pleases, and say what he thinks

Spinoza's Supplementary Notes to the *Tractatus Theologico-Politicus*

The Theological-Political Tractate

Containing

Various Disquisitions,

By means of which it is shown not only that Freedom of Philosophising can be allowed in Preserving Piety and the Peace of the Republic: but also that it is not possible for such Freedom to be upheld except when accompanied by the Peace of the Republic and Piety Themselves.

The First Epistle of John, Chapter 4, Verse 13.
Through this means we recognise that we remain in God, and God remains in us—that He gave to us from His own Spirit.

Hamburg,
from Heinrich Künraht.
1670

PREFACE

If men were able to exercise complete control over all their circumstances, or if continuous good fortune were always their lot, they would never be prey to superstition. But since they are often reduced to such straits as to be without any resource, and their immoderate greed for fortune's fickle favours often makes them the wretched victims of alternating hopes and fears, the result is that, for the most part, their credulity knows no bounds. In critical times they are swayed this way or that by the slightest impulse, especially so when they are wavering between the emotions of hope and fear; yet at other times they are overconfident, boastful and arrogant.

No one can be unaware of these truths, even though I believe that men generally know not their own selves. For no one can have lived in this world without realising that, when fortune smiles at them, the majority of men, even if quite unversed in affairs, are so abounding in wisdom that any advice offered to them is regarded as an affront, whereas in adversity they know not where to turn, begging for advice from any quarter; and then there is no counsel so foolish, absurd or vain which they will not follow. Again, even the most trivial of causes are enough to raise their hopes or dash them to the ground. For if, while possessed by fear, they see something happen that calls to mind something good or bad in the past, they believe that this portends a happy or unhappy issue, and this they therefore call a lucky or unlucky omen, even though it may fail them a hundred times. Then again, if they are struck with wonder at some unusual phenomenon, they believe this to be a portent signifying the anger of the gods or of a supreme deity, and they therefore regard it as a pious duty to avert the evil by sacrifice and vows, susceptible as they are to superstition and opposed to religion. Thus there is no end to the kind of omens that they imagine, and they read extraordinary things into Nature as if the whole of Nature were a partner in their madness.

This being the case, we see that it is particularly those who greedily covet fortune's favours who are the readiest victims of superstition of every kind, and it is especially when they are helpless in danger that they all implore God's help with prayers and womanish tears. Reason they call blind, because it cannot reveal a sure way to the vanities that they covet, and human wisdom they call vain, while the delusions of the imagination, dreams and other childish absurdities are taken to be the oracles of God. Indeed, they think that God, spurning the wise, has written his decrees not in man's mind but in the entrails of beasts, or that by divine inspiration and instigation these decrees are foretold by fools, madmen or birds. To such madness are men driven by their fears.

It is fear, then, that engenders, preserves and fosters superstition. If anyone seeks particular examples to confirm what I have said, let him consider Alexander. It was only when he first learnt to fear fortune at Pylae Susidis (Curtius, Book

5, ch. 4) that superstition drove him to employ seers.¹ After his victory over Darius he ceased to consult prophets and seers until he was once more dismayed by his plight. With the Bacrians having deserted and Scyths taking the offensive while he himself lay wounded on his sickbed, he again (Curtius, Book 7, ch. 7) "having recourse once more to superstition, that mockery of human wisdom, bade Aristander, in whom he had instilled his own credulity, enquire the issue by sacrifices." Numerous examples of this kind can be cited, illustrating quite clearly the fact that only while fear persists do men fall prey to superstition, that all the objects of spurious religious reverence have been no more than phantoms, the delusions springing from despondency and timidity, and that, finally, it is in the times of the state's gravest perils that seers have held the strongest sway over the people and have been most formidable to their own rulers. But since I consider that this is quite common knowledge, I will say no more.

This being the origin of superstition—in spite of the view of some who assign it to a confused idea of deity possessed by all mortals—it clearly follows that all men are by nature liable to superstition. It follows that superstition, like all other instances of hallucination and frenzy, is bound to assume very varied and unstable forms, and that, finally, it is sustained only by hope, hatred, anger and deceit. For it arises not from reason but from emotion, and emotion of the most powerful kind. So men's readiness to fall victim to any kind of superstition makes it correspondingly difficult to persuade them to adhere to one and the same kind. Indeed, as the multitude remains ever at the same level of wretchedness, so it is never long contented, and is best pleased only with what is new and has not yet proved delusory. This inconstancy has been the cause of many terrible uprisings and wars, for—as is clear from the above, and as Curtius, too, says so well in Book 4, ch. 10—"the multitude has no ruler more potent than superstition." So it is readily induced, under the guise of religion, now to worship its rulers as gods, and then again to curse and condemn them as mankind's common bane. To counteract this unfortunate tendency, immense efforts have been made to invest religion, true or false, with such pomp and ceremony that it can sustain any shock and constantly evoke the deepest reverence in all its worshippers. In this the Turks have achieved the greatest measure of success. They hold even discussion of religion to be sinful, and with their mass of dogma they gain such a thorough hold on the individual's judgment that they leave no room in the mind for the exercise of reason, or even the capacity to doubt.

Granted, then, that the supreme mystery of despotism, its prop and stay, is to keep men in a state of deception, and with the specious title of religion to cloak the fear by which they must be held in check, so that they will fight for their servi-

---

Spinoza's notes are indicated by asterisks; most of these are Supplementary Notes, which appear at the end of the work (page 573). Notes by Seymour Feldman (main annotator for this work), translator Samuel Shirley, and Michael L. Morgan are indicated by numerals and appear in brackets.

¹ [Spinoza makes ample use here and in Chapter 17 of the first-century (A.D.) Roman historian Quintus Curtius Rufus, the author of a biography of Alexander the Great, *Historiae Alexandri Magni*. —S.F.]

tude as if for salvation, and count it no shame, but the highest honour, to spend their blood and their lives for the glorification of one man. Yet no more disastrous policy can be devised or attempted in a free commonwealth. To invest with prejudice or in any way coerce the citizen's free judgment is altogether incompatible with the freedom of the people. As for those persecutions that are incited under the cloak of religion, they surely have their only source in this, that law intrudes into the realm of speculative thought, and that beliefs are put on trial and condemned as crimes. The adherents and followers of these beliefs are sacrificed, not to the public weal, but to the hatred and savagery of their opponents. If under civil law 'only deeds were arraigned, and words were not punished',[2] persecutions of this kind would be divested of any appearance of legality, and disagreement would not turn into persecution.

Now since we have the rare good fortune to live in a commonwealth where freedom of judgment is fully granted to the individual citizen and he may worship God as he pleases, and where nothing is esteemed dearer and more precious than freedom, I think I am undertaking no ungrateful or unprofitable task in demonstrating that not only can this freedom be granted without endangering piety and the peace of the commonwealth, but also the peace of the commonwealth and piety depend on this freedom.

This, then, is the main point which I have sought to establish in this treatise. For this purpose my most urgent task has been to indicate the main false assumptions that prevail regarding religion—that is, the relics of man's ancient bondage—and then again the false assumptions regarding the right of civil authorities. There are many who, with an impudence quite shameless, seek to usurp much of this right and, under the guise of religion, to alienate from the government the loyalty of the masses, still prone to heathenish superstition, so that slavery may return once more. But before going on to discuss briefly my arrangement of this exposition, I shall first set forth the causes that have induced me to write.

I have often wondered that men who make a boast of professing the Christian religion, which is a religion of love, joy, peace, temperance and honest dealing with all men, should quarrel so fiercely and display the bitterest hatred towards one another day by day, so that these latter characteristics make known a man's creed more readily than the former. Matters have long reached such a pass that a Christian, Turk, Jew or heathen can generally be recognised as such only by his physical appearance or dress, or by his attendance at a particular place of worship, or by his profession of a particular belief and his allegiance to some leader. But as for their way of life, it is the same for all. In seeking the causes of this unhappy state of affairs, I am quite certain that it stems from a wide-spread popular attitude of mind which looks on the ministries of the Church as dignities, its offices as posts of emolument and its pastors as eminent personages. For as soon as the Church's true function began to be thus distorted, every worthless fellow felt an intense desire to enter holy orders, and eagerness to spread abroad God's religion degener-

---

[2] [Tacitus, *Annals*, I, 12.—S.S.]

ated into base avarice and ambition. The very temple became a theatre where, instead of Church teachers, orators held forth, none of them actuated by desire to instruct the people, but keen to attract admiration, to criticise their adversaries before the public, and to preach only such novel and striking doctrine as might gain the applause of the crowd. This inevitably gave rise to great quarrels, envy and hatred, which no passage of time could assuage. Little wonder, then, that of the old religion nothing is left but the outward form—wherein the common people seem to engage in base flattery of God rather than his worship—and that faith has become identical with credulity and biased dogma. But what dogma!—degrading rational man to beast, completely inhibiting man's free judgment and his capacity to distinguish true from false, and apparently devised with the set purpose of utterly extinguishing the light of reason. Piety and religion—O everlasting God—take the form of ridiculous mysteries, and men who utterly despise reason, who reject and turn away from the intellect as naturally corrupt—these are the men (and this is of all things the most iniquitous) who are believed to possess the divine light! Surely, if they possessed but a spark of the divine light, they would not indulge in such arrogant ravings, but would study to worship God more wisely and to surpass their fellows in love, as they now do in hate. They would not persecute so bitterly those who do not share their views: rather would they show compassion, if their concern was for men's salvation, and not for their own standing.

Furthermore, if they did indeed possess some divine light, this would surely be manifested in their teaching. I grant that they have expressed boundless wonder at Scripture's profound mysteries, yet I do not see that they have taught anything more than the speculations of Aristotelians or Platonists, and they have made Scripture conform to these so as to avoid appearing to be the followers of heathens. It was not enough for them to share in the delusions of the Greeks: they have sought to represent the prophets as sharing in these same delusions. This surely shows quite clearly that they do not even glimpse the divine nature of Scripture, and the more enthusiastic their admiration of these mysteries, the more clearly they reveal that their attitude to Scripture is one of abject servility rather than belief. And this is further evident from the fact that most of them assume as a basic principle for the understanding of Scripture and for extracting its true meaning that it is throughout truthful and divine—a conclusion which ought to be the end result of study and strict examination; and they lay down at the outset as a principle of interpretation that which would be far more properly derived from Scripture itself, which stands in no need of human fabrications.

When I pondered over these facts, that the light of reason is not only despised but is condemned by many as a source of impiety, that merely human suppositions are regarded as divine doctrine and that credulity is looked upon as faith; and when I saw that the disputes of philosophers are raging with violent passion in Church and Court and are breeding bitter hatred and faction which readily turn men to sedition, together with other ills too numerous to recount here, I deliberately resolved to examine Scripture afresh, conscientiously and freely, and to admit nothing as its teaching which I did not most clearly derive from it. With this precaution I formulated a method of interpreting the Bible, and thus equipped I began first of all to seek answers to these questions: What is prophecy? In what way did God reveal himself to the prophets? Why were these men acceptable to God? Was it because they attained rare heights in their understanding of God and Nature? Or was it only because of their piety? With the answers to these questions I had no difficulty in deciding that the authority of the prophets carries weight only in matters concerning morality and true virtue, and that in other matters their beliefs are irrelevant to us.

I then went on to enquire why the Hebrews were called God's chosen people. When I realised that this was for no other reason than that God chose for them a certain territory where they might live in security and wellbeing, I was led to understand that the Law revealed by God to Moses was simply the laws of the Hebrew state alone, and was therefore binding on none but the Hebrews, and not even on them except while their state still stood. Furthermore, to ascertain whether Scripture taught that the human intellect is naturally corrupt, I resolved to enquire whether universal religion—i.e. the divine law revealed to all mankind through the Prophets and the Apostles—differed from the teachings of the natural light of reason; and, again, whether miracles contravene the order of Nature, and whether they demonstrate God's existence and providence with greater clarity and certainty than events which we understand clearly and distinctly through their prime causes.

Now I found nothing expressly taught in Scripture that was not in agreement with the intellect or that contradicted it, and I also came to see that the prophets taught only very simple doctrines easily comprehensible by all, setting them forth in such a style and confirming them by such reasoning as would most likely induce the people's devotion to God. So I was completely convinced that Scripture does not in any way inhibit reason and has nothing to do with philosophy, each standing on its own footing. To demonstrate this in logical order and to settle the whole question conclusively, I show in what way Scripture must be interpreted, and how all our understanding of Scripture and of matters spiritual must be sought from Scripture alone, and not from the sort of knowledge that derives from the natural light of reason. I then pass on to indicate the prejudiced beliefs that originate from the fact that the common people, prone to superstition and prizing the legacy of time above eternity itself, worship the books of Scripture rather than the Word of God. Thereafter I show that the revealed Word of God is not to be identified with a certain number of books, but is a simple conception of the divine mind as revealed to the prophets; and that is—to obey God with all one's heart by practising justice and charity. I point out how this teaching in Scripture is adapted to the understanding and beliefs of those to whom the Prophets and Apostles were wont to proclaim the Word of God, with the purpose that men might embrace it willingly and with all their heart. Then, the fundamental principles of faith being now made clear, I reach the conclusion that the object of knowledge by revelation is nothing other than obedience, and so it is completely distinct from natural knowledge in its purpose, its basis and its method, that these two have nothing in common, that they each have a separate province that does not intrude on the other, and that neither should be regarded as ancillary to the other.

Furthermore, as men's ways of thinking vary considerably and different beliefs are better suited to different men, and what moves one to reverence provokes ridicule in another, I repeat the conclusion already stated, that everyone should be allowed freedom of judgment and the right to interpret the basic tenets of his faith as he thinks fit, and that the moral value of a man's creed should be judged only from his works. In this way all men would be able to obey God wholeheartedly and freely, and only justice and charity would be held in universal esteem.

After thus making clear the freedom granted to every man by the revelation of the Divine Law, I pass on to the second part of our subject, namely, the claim that this freedom can be granted without detriment to public peace or to the right of civil authorities, and should be so granted, and cannot be withheld without great danger to peace and grave harm to the entire commonwealth. To establish these points, I begin with the natural right of the individual; this is co-extensive with the individual's desire and power. Nobody is bound by natural right to live as another pleases, each man being the guardian of his own freedom. I go on to prove that nobody can really part with this right except by transferring his power of self-defence to another, and he to whom each man has transferred his right to live as he pleases together with his power of self-defence must necessarily retain absolute control over this natural right. Hence I show that those who hold the sovereignty possess the right over everything that is within their power and are the sole guardians of law and freedom, and that subjects should act in all matters solely in accordance with the sovereign's decree. However, since nobody can so deprive himself of the power of self-defence as to cease to be a human being, I conclude that nobody can be absolutely deprived of his natural rights, and that by a quasi-natural right subjects do retain some rights which cannot be taken from them without imperilling the state, and which therefore are either tacitly conceded or explicitly agreed by the rulers.

From these considerations I pass on to the Hebrew commonwealth, which I describe at some length so as to show in what way and by whose decision religion began to acquire the force of law, together with numerous other incidental matters of interest. Thereafter I prove that governments are the guardians and interpreters of religious law as well as civil law, and they alone have the right to decide what is just and unjust, what is pious and impious. I finally conclude that they can best retain this right and preserve the state in safety only by granting to the individual citizen the right to have his own opinions and to say what he thinks.

Such, learned reader, are the topics which I here submit for your consideration, topics which I am sure you will find interesting by reason of the great importance of the issues discussed in the entire work and in each separate chapter. I would say more, but I do not want my Preface to expand to a volume, especially since I believe its main points are quite familiar to philosophers. To others I seek not to commend this treatise, for I have no reason to expect them to approve it in any way. I know how deeply rooted in the mind are the prejudices embraced under the guise of piety. I know, too, that the masses can no more be freed from their superstition than from their fears. Finally, I know that they are unchanging in their obstinacy, that they are not guided by reason, and that their praise and blame is at the mercy of impulse. Therefore I do not invite the common people to read this work, nor all those who are victims of the same emotional attitudes. Indeed, I would prefer that they disregard this book completely rather than make themselves a nuisance by misinterpreting it after their wont. For without any advantage to themselves they would stand in the way of others for whom a more liberal approach to philosophical questions is prevented by this one obstacle, that they believe that reason must be the handmaiden of theology. These latter, I am confident, will derive great profit from this work.

However, as there are many who will not have the leisure, or perhaps the inclination, to peruse the whole of this work, I feel obliged to state at this point, as also at the conclusion of the treatise, that I have written nothing that I would not willingly submit to the scrutiny and judgment of my country's government. If anything of what I say is deemed by them to contravene the laws of our country or to be injurious to the common good, I am ready to withdraw it. I realise that I am human and may have erred. But I have taken great pains to avoid error and to ensure that my writing should be in complete agreement with our country's laws, with piety, and with morality.

CHAPTER 1

Of Prophecy[1]

Prophecy, or revelation, is the sure knowledge of some matter revealed by God to man. A prophet is one who interprets God's revelations to those who cannot attain to certain knowledge of the matters revealed, and can therefore be convinced of them only by simple faith. For the Hebrew word for prophet is '*nabi*',[*] that is, speaker and interpreter; but it is always used in Scripture in the sense of interpreter of God, as we gather from Exodus chapter 7 v. 1, where God says to Moses, "See, I have made thee a God to Pharaoh, and Aaron thy brother shall be thy prophet." This implies that because Aaron was acting the part of prophet in interpreting Moses' words to Pharaoh, Moses would be to Pharaoh as God, or one acting in God's place.

Prophets will be the subject of my next chapter; here I shall treat of prophecy. From the definition given above, it follows that natural knowledge can be called prophecy, for the knowledge that we acquire by the natural light of reason depends solely on knowledge of God and of his eternal decrees. However, since this natural knowledge is common to all men—for it rests on foundations common to all men—it is not so highly prized by the multitude who are ever eager for what is

---

[1] [Throughout Chapters 1 and 2 Spinoza has Maimonides' *Guide of the Perplexed* before him. The reader should consult Part 2, chapters 32–45 of the *Guide*.]

[*] See Supplementary Note 1.

strange and foreign to their own nature, despising their natural gifts. Therefore prophetic knowledge is usually taken to exclude natural knowledge. Nevertheless, the latter has as much right as any other kind of knowledge to be called divine, since it is dictated to us, as it were, by God's nature insofar as we participate therein, and by God's decrees. It is no different from what is generally termed divine knowledge except that the latter transcends the bounds of the former and cannot be accounted for by the laws of human nature considered in themselves. Yet in respect of the certainty involved in natural knowledge and the source from which it derives, i.e. God, it is in no way inferior to prophetic knowledge. I discount the fantastic view that the prophets had human bodies but nonhuman minds, so that their sensations and consciousness were of an entirely different order from our own.

But although natural knowledge is divine, its professors cannot be called prophets;* for the rest of mankind can apprehend and be convinced of what they teach with an assurance in no way inferior to theirs, and it is not through mere faith that they do so.

Since, then, the human mind contains the nature of God within itself in concept, and partakes thereof, and is thereby enabled to form certain basic ideas that explain natural phenomena and inculcate morality, we are justified in asserting that the nature of mind, insofar as it is thus conceived, is the primary cause of divine revelation. For, as I have just pointed out, all that we clearly and distinctly understand is dictated to us by the idea and nature of God—not indeed in words, but in a far superior way and one that agrees excellently with the nature of mind, as everyone who has tasted intellectual certainty has doubtless experienced in his own case.[2] However, my main purpose being to treat only of what concerns Scripture alone, these few words on the natural light will suffice. So I pass on to treat more fully of other sources of knowledge, and other means by which God reveals to man that which transcends the bounds of natural knowledge—and also that which is within its scope, for there is nothing to prevent God from communicating by other means to man that which we can know by the natural light.

However, our discussion must be confined to what is drawn only from Scripture. For what can we say of things transcending the bounds of our intellect except what is transmitted to us by the prophets by word or writing? And since there are no prophets among us today, as far as I know, our only recourse is to peruse the sacred books left to us by the prophets of old, taking care, however, not to make metaphorical interpretations or to attribute anything to the prophets which they themselves did not clearly declare. Now it is important to note here that the Jews never make mention of intermediate or particular causes nor pay any heed to them, but to serve religion and piety or, as it is commonly called, devoutness, they refer everything to God. For example, if they make money by some transaction,

---

* See Supplementary Note 2.
[2] [Spinoza, *Ethics*, 2.34, 49 Scholium, 4.30; Letter 32.]

they say it has come to them from God; if it happens that they desire something, they say that God has so disposed their hearts; and if some thought enters their heads, they say that God has told them this. Hence we must not accept as prophecy and supernatural knowledge whatever Scripture says God told someone, but only what Scripture expressly declares, or can be deduced from the particular context, to have been prophecy or revelation.

An examination of the Bible will show us that everything that God revealed to the prophets was revealed either by words, or by appearances, or by a combination of both. The words and appearances were either real and independent of the imagination of the prophet who heard or saw, or they were imaginary, the prophet's imagination being so disposed, even in waking hours, as to convince him that he heard something or saw something.

With a real voice God revealed to Moses the laws which he willed to be enjoined on the Hebrews, as is clear from Exodus ch. 25 v. 22 where God says, "And there I will meet with thee and commune with thee from that part of the cover which is between the two Cherubim." This clearly shows that God employed a real voice, since Moses found God there ready to speak with him whenever he wished. This voice, whereby the Law was proclaimed, was the only instance of a real voice, as I shall presently show.

There may be a case for believing that the voice with which God called Samuel was real, for in 1 Sam. ch. 3 v. 21 we read, "And the Lord appeared to Samuel again in Shiloh, for the Lord revealed himself to Samuel in Shiloh by the word of the Lord," implying that the appearing of the Lord to Samuel consisted in God's manifesting himself to him by word; that is to say, Samuel heard God speaking. However, since we are required to make a distinction between the prophesying of Moses and that of other prophets, we are bound to take the view that this voice heard by Samuel was imaginary. This view is supported by the fact that the voice resembled the voice of Eli, which was quite familiar to Samuel, and so might be the more readily imagined. When thrice called by God, he thought it was Eli calling.

The voice heard by Abimelech was imaginary, for in Gen. ch. 20 v. 6 we read, "And God said unto him in a dream. . . ." So the will of God was conveyed to him not in waking hours but in sleep, a time when the imagination is not naturally apt to depict what is most existent.

Some Jews take the view that the words of the Decalogue were not pronounced by God, but that the Israelites heard only a noise without distinct words, and during its continuance they apprehended the Ten Commandments by direct intuition. I was at one time inclined to this view, seeing that the words of the Decalogue in Exodus differ from the words of the Decalogue in Deuteronomy. Since God spoke only once, it would seem to follow that the Decalogue is intended to convey the meaning, and not the actual words, of God. However, unless we would do violence to Scripture, it must undoubtedly be conceded that what the Israelites heard was a real voice; for in Deut. ch. 5 v. 4 it expressly says, "The Lord talked with you face to face," that is, just as two men ordinarily exchange thoughts through the medium of their two bodies. So it would be more in conformity with Scripture that God did really create a voice by which he revealed the Decalogue.

As for the reason for the discrepancy in the wording and reasoning of the two versions, I refer you to Chapter 8.

Yet even so, the difficulty is not entirely removed. It seems quite alien to reason to assert that a created thing, dependent on God in the same way as other created things, should be able to express or display, factually or verbally, through its own individuality, God's essence or existence, declaring in the first person, "I am the Lord your God, etc." Granted, when someone utters the words "I understand," we all realise that it is the speaker's mind, not his mouth, that understands. But it is because the mouth is identified with the person of the speaker, and also because the hearer knows what it is to understand, that he readily grasps the speaker's meaning through comparison with himself. Now in the case of people who previously knew nothing of God but his name, and desired to speak with him so as to be assured of his existence, I fail to see how their need was met through a created thing (which is no more related to God than are other created things, and does not pertain to God's nature) which declared, "I am the Lord." What if God had manipulated the lips of Moses—but why Moses? the lips of some beast—so as to pronounce the words "I am the Lord"? Would the people thereby have understood God's existence?

Again, it is the indisputable meaning of Scripture that God himself spoke (for which purpose he descended from Heaven to Mount Sinai) and that not only did the Jews hear him speaking but their chief men even beheld him (Exodus ch. 24). Nor did the Law revealed to Moses—to which nothing might be added and from which nothing might be taken away, and which was established as the nation's statutes—ever require us to believe that God is incorporeal or that he has no form or figure, but only that he is God, in whom the Jews must believe and whom alone they must worship. And to dissuade them from forsaking his worship, it forbade them to assign any image to him or to make any; for, as they had not seen God's image, any image they could make would not resemble God but must necessarily resemble some created thing which they had seen. So when they worshipped God through that image, their thoughts would not be of God but of that which the image resembled, and so in the end they would attach to that thing the glory and worship of God. But indeed, Scripture does clearly indicate that God has a form, and that when Moses heard God speaking, it befell him to see God, but to behold only his back parts. So I have no doubt that here lies some mystery, which I shall discuss more fully later on. For the present I shall go on to point out those passages in Scripture which indicate the means whereby God has revealed his decrees to man.

That revelation has occurred through images alone is clear from 1 Chron. ch. 21, where God displays his anger to David through an angel grasping a sword. So, too, in the case of Balaam. Maimonides and some others take the view that this and all other instances of an apparition of an angel—as to Manoah and to Abraham when he was about to sacrifice his son—occurred in dreams, on the grounds that nobody could have seen an angel with his eyes open. But this is mere rubbish. They are concerned only to extort from Scripture some Aristotelian nonsense and some fabrications of their own; and this I regard as the height of absurdity.

It was by images, unreal and dependent only on the prophet's imagination, that God revealed to Joseph his future dominion.

It was through images and words that God revealed to Joshua that he himself would fight on their behalf. He caused to appear to him an angel with a sword as if to lead his army, and he had also revealed this in words, which Joshua had heard from an angel. In the case of Isaiah, too (ch. 6), it was conveyed to him through a vision that God's providence was forsaking the people: he saw God, the thrice Holy, sitting on his throne on high, and the Israelites stained with the filth of their sins, sunk in foulness, and thus far removed from God. Thereby he understood the present miserable plight of the people, while its future calamities were revealed to him by words that seemed to issue from God. I could quote many similar examples from the Bible, but I think they are sufficiently familiar to all.

But the position here outlined receives even clearer confirmations in Numbers ch. 12 v. 6, 7, "If there be a prophet among you, I the Lord will make myself known unto him in a vision (that is, through figures and symbols, for in the case of Moses' prophecy God declared that there was vision without symbols) and I will speak unto him in a dream (that is, not in actual words and a real voice). But not thus (will I reveal myself) to Moses. With him will I speak mouth to mouth, by seeing and not by dark speeches, and the similitude of the Lord shall he behold"; that is to say, beholding me as a friend might do, and not in terror, shall he speak with me—Exodus ch. 33 v. 11. Therefore there can be no doubt that other prophets did not hear a real voice, and this is further confirmed by Deut. ch. 34 v. 10, "And there stood (meaning 'arose') not a prophet since in Israel like unto Moses, whom the Lord knew face to face," which must be taken to mean 'through voice alone', for not even Moses ever saw the Lord's face (Exodus ch. 33).

These are the only means of communication between God and man that I find in the Bible, and so, as I have previously shown, no other means should be alleged or admitted. We may quite clearly understand that God can communicate with man without mediation, for he communicates his essence to our minds without employing corporeal means. Nevertheless, a man who can perceive by pure intuition that which is not contained in the basic principles of our cognition and cannot be deduced therefrom must needs possess a mind whose excellence far surpasses the human mind. Therefore I do not believe that anyone has attained such a degree of perfection surpassing all others, except Christ. To him God's ordinances leading men to salvation were revealed not by words or by visions, but directly, so that God manifested himself to the Apostles through the mind of Christ as he once did to Moses through an audible voice. The Voice of Christ can thus be called the Voice of God in the same way as that which Moses heard. In that sense it can also be said that the Wisdom of God—that is, wisdom that is more than human—took on human nature in Christ, and that Christ was the way of salvation.

But I must here ask it to be noted that I am certainly not alluding to the doctrines held by some Churches about Christ, nor am I denying them; for I freely confess that I do not understand them. What I have just stated I gather from Scripture itself. Nowhere have I read that God appeared to Christ or spoke with him, but that God was revealed to the Apostles through Christ, that Christ is the way of salvation, that the ancient Law was transmitted through an angel, not directly by God and so on. Therefore, if Moses spoke with God face to face as a man may do with his fellow (that is, through the medium of their two bodies), then Christ communed with God mind to mind.

Therefore we may conclude that, with the exception of Christ, God's revelations were received only with the aid of the imaginative faculty, to wit, with the aid of words or images. Hence it was not a more perfect mind that was needed for the gift of prophecy, but a more lively imaginative faculty, as I shall demonstrate more clearly in the next chapter. At this point we must ask what is meant in the Bible by the prophets' being filled with the Spirit of God, or the prophets speaking with the Spirit of God. To this end we must first ask the meaning of the Hebrew word 'ru'ah', which is commonly translated as Spirit.[3]

The basic meaning of the word 'ru'ah' is wind, as is well known, but it is often used in many other senses, which nevertheless derive from this source. It is used to mean:

1. Breath. Psalm 135 v. 17, "Neither is there any Spirit in their mouths."
2. Life, or breathing. 1 Samuel ch. 30 v. 12, "His Spirit came again to him," that is, he started breathing.
3. Hence, courage and strength, as in Joshua ch. 2 v. 11, "Neither did there remain any more spirit in any man." Likewise Ezekiel ch. 2 v. 2, "And the Spirit (i.e. strength) entered into me and set me on my feet."
4. Hence—virtue or capacity, as in Job ch. 32 v. 8, "But there is a Spirit in man," that is, wisdom is not to be sought exclusively among the old, for I now see that it depends on the virtue and capacity of the individual person. So also Numbers ch. 27 v. 18, ". . . a man in whom there is the Spirit."
5. Disposition of mind. Numbers ch. 14 v. 24, ". . . because he had another Spirit in him," that is, a different disposition or attitude of mind. Likewise Proverbs ch. 1 v. 23, "I will pour out my Spirit unto you," that is, my mind. In this sense, too, it is used to mean will, or decision, desire, and urge, as in Ezekiel ch. 1 v. 12, "Whither the Spirit was to go, they went." Likewise Isaiah ch. 30 v. 1, ". . . for weaving schemes, but not of my Spirit." Also ch. 29 v. 10, ". . . for the Lord hath poured out on you the Spirit (i.e. the desire) of deep sleep." Also Judges ch. 8 v. 3, ". . . then their Spirit (i.e. urge) was abated." Likewise Proverbs ch. 16 v. 32, "He that ruleth his Spirit (i.e. desire) is better than he who taketh a city." Again, ch. 25 v. 28, "He that hath no rule over his own Spirit." Also Isaiah ch. 33 v. 11, "Your Spirit as fire shall devour you." Moreover, the word "ru'ah," insofar as it means the mind, serves to express all the passions, and also the gifts, of the mind. Lofty spirit means pride, lowly spirit humility, evil spirit hatred and melancholy, good spirit kindliness. There is the spirit of jealousy, the spirit (i.e. desire) of fornication, the spirit of wisdom, of counsel, of bravery, that is to say (Hebrew tends to use nouns rather than adjectives), a wise, prudent, courageous mind, or the virtue of wisdom, prudence, courage. Then there is the spirit of kindness, and so on.

---

[3] [Maimonides, *Guide of the Perplexed*, 1.40.]

6. Mind itself, or Soul, as in Eccles. ch. 3 v. 19, "They all have the one Spirit (or Soul)"; ". . . and the Spirit shall return to God."[4]

7. Finally, it can mean the quarters of the world (because of the winds that blow thence), and also the sides of any thing facing towards those quarters. See Ezekiel ch. 37 v. 9, and ch. 42 v. 16, 17, 18, 19 etc.

We should now note that a thing is referred to God and said to be of God in the following ways:

1. As belonging to God's nature, being, so to speak, a part of God, in such phrases as 'the power of God,' 'the eyes of God.'

2. Because it is in God's power and acts at God's behest, as in the Bible the heavens are called 'the heavens of God,' as being God's chariot and habitation, Assyria is called 'the scourge of God,' Nebuchadnezzar, 'the servant of God' and so on.

3. As being dedicated to God; e.g. 'the temple of God,' 'a Nazarene of God,' 'the bread of God' and so on.

4. As being told us by the prophets, not revealed through the natural light of reason. Thus the Law of Moses is called the Law of God.

5. As an expression of the superlative degree, as 'the mountains of God,' that is, very high mountains; 'the sleep of God,' that is, very deep sleep. In this sense we should explain Amos ch. 4 v. 11, where God himself says, "I have overthrown you as the overthrow of the Lord came upon Sodom and Gomorrah," meaning that memorable overthrow; for since God is speaking in the first person, the passage cannot properly be explained in any other way. The natural wisdom of Solomon, too, is called 'the wisdom of God'; that is, divine, or above normal. In the Psalms, too, cedars are called 'the cedars of God' to express their extraordinary size. And in 1 Samuel ch. 11 v. 7, ". . . and the fear of God fell upon the people," very great fear is meant.

In this same sense, whatever the Jews did not understand, being at that time ignorant of its natural causes, was referred to God.[5] Thus a storm was called the chiding of God, thunder and lightning were called the arrows of God; for they thought that God kept the winds shut up in caves, which they called the treasuries of God. In this belief they differed from the Gentiles, in that they believed the ruler of the winds to be God, not Aeolus. For the same reason miracles are called the works of God, that is, wonderful works. For surely all natural phenomena are the works of God, existing and acting through the divine power alone. So in this sense the Psalmist calls the Egyptian miracles 'the powers of God,' because, to the surprise of the Hebrews, they opened the way to salvation in the midst of perils, thus evoking their extreme wonder.

Since unusual works of Nature are called works of God, and trees of unusual size are called trees of God, it should occasion us no surprise that in Genesis men of extraordinary strength and great stature are called sons of God, although impi-

---

[4] [Eccles. ch. 12 v. 7. The reference is omitted in the text.]

[5] [Maimonides, *Guide of the Perplexed*, 2.48.]

ous robbers and whoremongers. So any quality whatsoever whereby one surpassed all others used to be referred to God in olden days, and not only by Jews but by Gentiles too. When Pharaoh heard the interpretation of his dream, he said that Joseph possessed the mind of the gods; and Nebuchadnezzar, too, told Daniel that he possessed the mind of the holy gods. Indeed, this is quite common in Latin literature. Works of art are said to have been 'wrought by a divine hand,' which, translated into Hebrew, would be 'wrought by the hand of God,' as any Hebrew scholar would know.

So those passages of Scripture that make mention of the Spirit of God can now be readily understood and explained. In certain passages 'the Spirit of God' and 'the Spirit of Jehovah' mean simply a very fierce, dry, deadly wind, as in Isaiah ch. 40 v. 7, "the wind of Jehovah blew upon it," that is, a very dry, deadly wind. Also Genesis ch. 1 v. 2, ". . . and the wind of God moved upon the water," i.e. a very strong wind. Then again, it is used to mean high courage. The courage of Gideon and of Samson is called in the Bible 'the Spirit of God,' that is, a bold disposition, ready for anything. So, too, any virtue or power above the normal is called the Spirit (i.e. Virtue) of God, as in Exodus ch. 31 v. 3, ". . . and I will fill him (Bezaleel) with the Spirit of God," that is, as Scripture explains, with talent and skill above the common lot of mankind. Similarly, Isaiah ch. 11 v. 2, "and the Spirit of the Lord shall rest upon him," that is, as the prophet goes on to explain in more detail in the manner customary to biblical writing, the virtue of wisdom, of counsel, of might and so on. So, too, the melancholy of Saul is called 'the evil Spirit of God,' that is, a very profound melancholy; for Saul's servants who called his melancholy 'the melancholy of God' suggested to him that he should send for a musician to divert him by playing the harp, which indicates that by the melancholy of God they understood a natural melancholy.

Again, the Spirit of God can mean man's mind, as in Job ch. 27 v. 3, ". . . and the Spirit of God in my nostrils," the allusion being to Genesis "And God breathed into man's nostrils the breath of life." So, too, Ezekiel, prophesying to the dead (ch. 37 v. 14), ". . . and I shall put my Spirit into you and ye shall live," that is, I shall restore you to life. The same meaning occurs in Job ch. 34 v. 14, "if he will (meaning God), he will gather unto himself his Spirit (that is, the mind he has given us) and his breath." In the same way we should understand Genesis ch. 6 v. 3, "my Spirit shall not always reason (or strive) in man, for that he is flesh"; that is, man hereafter will act from the dictates of his flesh, and not of the mind which I gave him so that he might discern the good. So, too, Psalm 51 v. 10, 11, "Create in me a clean heart, O God, and renew a seemly (or orderly) Spirit (that is, desire) in me. Cast me not away from Thy presence, and take not the Spirit of Thy holiness from me." Since sin was believed to arise from the flesh alone and the mind was the cause of only good impulses, he invokes God's help against fleshly desire, but he prays that the mind which God, the Holy One, gave him, should be preserved merely.

Again, since Scripture, in concession to the frailty of the multitude, is wont to depict God in the likeness of man and to attribute to him mind, heart, emotions, and even body and breath, the Spirit of God is often used in the Bible to mean the mind, disposition, emotion, strength and breath of God. Thus Isaiah ch. 40 v. 13, "Who hath directed the Spirit (i.e. mind) of God?" that is, who but God himself has determined God's mind to will anything; and ch. 63 v. 10, ". . . and with bitterness and pain they vexed his Holy Spirit." Hence it comes to be used for the Law of Moses, which displays God's mind, as it were; as in Isaiah ch. 63 v. 11, "Where is he that put his Holy Spirit within him?"—to wit, the Law of Moses, as can be gathered from the context. Also Nehemiah ch. 9 v. 20, "Thou gavest also Thy good Spirit (i.e. mind) to instruct them," for he is speaking of the occasion of the giving of the Law. And the same allusion is made in Deut. ch. 4 v. 6 where Moses says, "for this (namely, the Law) is your wisdom and your understanding." So, too, Psalm 143 v. 10 "Thy good Spirit will lead me unto the level land," that is, your mind revealed to me will lead me to the right way.

The Spirit of God may also mean, as we have seen, the breath of God; for breath, too, just like mind, heart and body, is incorrectly attributed to God in Scripture, as in Psalm 33 v. 6. Again, it can mean the power, force, or virtue of God, as in Job ch. 33 v. 4, "The Spirit of God hath made me," that is, the virtue or power, or, if you prefer, the decree of God. For the Psalmist, in the language of poetry, also says, "By the command of God were the heavens made, and all the host of them by the spirit (or breath) of his mouth," that is, by his decree, uttered, as it were, in one breath. Likewise, in Psalm 139 v. 7, "Whither shall I go from thy Spirit, or whither shall I flee from thy sight?" That is, as the Psalmist goes on to amplify his words, Whither can I go as to beyond thy power and thy presence?

Finally, the Spirit of God is used in the Bible to express the emotions of God, namely, his kindness and his mercy, as in Micah ch. 2 v. 7, "Is the Spirit of the Lord (that is, his mercy) straitened? Are these (cruelties) his works?" Likewise Zechariah ch. 4 v. 6, "Not by my might, nor by power, but by my Spirit alone," that is, by my mercy. It is also in this sense, I think, that we should understand ch. 7. v. 12 of the same prophet, "They made their hearts of adamant stone, lest they should obey the Law and the commands that God hath sent from his Spirit (that is, his mercy) by the prophets of old." In the same sense, again, Haggai says, "My Spirit (i.e. my grace) remains among you. Fear ye not" (ch. 2 v. 5).

As for Isaiah ch. 48 v. 16, "And now the Lord God, and his Spirit, hath sent me," this can be taken as referring either to God's merciful heart or to his mind as revealed in the Law. For he says, "From the beginning (that is, from the time when I first came to you to preach God's anger and his sentence pronounced against you) I spoke not in secret. From the time when sentence was pronounced, there was I (as he himself has testified in ch. 7); but now I am a messenger of joy, sent by God's mercy to prophesy your restoration." But he can also, as I said, be understood as referring to God's mind as revealed in the Law, meaning that he had come to warn them again by command of the Law, namely, Leviticus ch. 19 v. 17; and therefore he warns them in the same circumstances and the same manner as Moses was wont to warn them, and like Moses, he ends by preaching the restoration. However, the first explanation seems to me more likely.

To return now to the main purpose of this chapter, the following Scriptural expressions are now quite clear: the Spirit of the Lord was upon a prophet, the Lord poured his Spirit into men, men were filled with the Spirit of God and with the Holy Spirit and so on. They mean merely this, that the prophets were endowed with an extraordinary virtue exceeding the normal,* and that they devoted themselves to piety with especial constancy. Furthermore, they perceived the mind and thought of God; for we have seen that in Hebrew 'Spirit' means both the mind and the mind's thoughts, and it was for this reason that the Law, since it displays the mind of God, is called the Spirit or the mind of God. Therefore the imaginative faculty of the prophets, insofar as it was the instrument for the revelation of God's decrees, could equally well be called the mind of God, and the prophets could be said to have possessed the mind of God. Now the mind of God and his eternal thoughts are inscribed in our minds, too, and therefore we also, in Scriptural language, perceive the mind of God. But since natural knowledge is common to all men, it is not so highly prized, as I have already said, and particularly in the case of the Hebrews, who vaunted themselves above all men—indeed, despising all men, and consequently the sort of knowledge that is common to all men.

Finally, the prophets were said to possess the Spirit of God because men did not know the causes of prophetic knowledge, which evoked their wonder. They therefore referred it like all other portents to God, and were wont to call it divine knowledge.

We can now have no hesitation in affirming that the prophets perceived God's revelations with the aid of the imaginative faculty alone, that is, through the medium of words or images, either real or imaginary. Since we find no mention in Scripture of any other means than these, it is not permissible for us to invent any, as I have already made clear. As to the particular laws of Nature involved in revelation, I confess my ignorance. I might, indeed, have followed others in saying that it happened through the power of God, but this would be mere quibbling: it would be the same as trying to explain the specific reality of a particular thing by means of some transcendental term. For everything takes place through the power of God. Indeed, since Nature's power is nothing but the power of God, it is beyond doubt that ignorance of natural causes is the measure of our ignorance of the power of God. So it is folly to have recourse to the power of God when we do not know the natural cause of some phenomenon—that is, when we do not know the power of God.[6] However, there is no need anyway for us now to have an understanding of the cause of prophetic knowledge. As I have already indicated, our enquiry is here confined to the teachings of Scripture, with view to drawing our own conclusions from these, as from data presented by Nature. The causes of these Scriptural teachings are not our concern.

Since, then, the prophets perceived the revelations of God with the aid of the imaginative faculty, they may doubtless have perceived much that is beyond the limits of intellect. For many more ideas can be constructed from words and images than merely from the principles and axioms on which our entire natural knowledge is based.

---

* See Supplementary Note 3.
[6] [Spinoza, *Ethics*, 1.25, 34–35.]

Now we see why the perceptions and the teachings of the prophets were nearly all in the form of parables and allegories, and why all spiritual matters were expressed in corporeal form; for this is more appropriate to the imaginative faculty. We shall no longer wonder why Scripture, or the prophets, speak so strangely or obscurely of the Spirit, or mind, of God, as in Numbers ch. 11 v. 17 and in 1 Kings ch. 22 v. 2 etc., and again why God was seen by Micaiah as seated, by Daniel as an old man clothed in white garments, by Ezekiel as fire; why the Holy Spirit was seen by those with Christ as a dove descending, by the Apostles as tongues of flame, and by Paul at his conversion as a great light. All this is in full agreement with the common imagination of Gods and Spirits.

Finally, the imaginative faculty being fleeting and inconstant, the gift of prophecy did not remain with the prophets for long, nor did it often occur; it was very rare, manifesting itself in very few men, and infrequently even in them. This being so, we must now enquire whence the prophets derived their certainty of what they perceived merely through their imagination rather than through assured rational principles. However, on this point it is to Scripture that we must once again have recourse, since on this subject, as I have said, we possess no scientific knowledge, which is to say that we cannot explain it through its first causes. What Scripture has to say on the certainty of the prophets will be the subject of the next chapter, which will be about the prophets.

CHAPTER 2

Of the Prophets

It follows from the last chapter, as I have already stated, that the prophets were not endowed with a more perfect mind, but with a more vivid power of imagination. Scripture, too, provides ample material to confirm this. In the case of Solomon, it is clear that he surpassed others in wisdom, but not in the gift of prophecy. Heman, Darda and Kalkol were also men of outstanding wisdom, but not prophets;[1] on the other hand, countrymen who had no learning whatsoever—indeed, even women of humble station, like Hagar, the handmaiden of Abraham—were endowed with the gift of prophecy. This fact is in no way at variance with experience and reason. Those with a more powerful imagination are less fitted for purely intellectual activity, while those who devote themselves to the cultivation of their more powerful intellect, keep their imagination under greater control and restraint, and they hold it in rein, as it were, so that it should not invade the province of intellect.

Therefore those who look to find understanding and knowledge of things natural and spiritual in the books of the Prophets go far astray. In response to the de-

---

[1] [See 1 Kings 5:11.—M.L.M.]

mands of our age, of philosophy, and of truth itself, I have resolved to demonstrate this point at some length, disregarding the rantings of superstition, the bitter enemy of those who are devoted to true knowledge and true morality. Alas, things have now come to such a pass that those who openly declare that they do not possess the idea of God and that they know God only through created things (of whose causes they are ignorant) do not blush to accuse philosophers of atheism.

To treat the subject methodically, I shall show that prophecy varied not only with the imagination and the temperament of each prophet but also with the beliefs in which they had been brought up, and that their prophesying never made the prophets more learned, as I shall go on to explain in more detail. But I must first discuss the question of the certainty of the prophets, for two reasons: because it is relevant to the subject of this chapter, and also because it has some bearing on the general thesis I am seeking to prove.

Imagination by itself, unlike every clear and distinct idea, does not of its own nature carry certainty with it.[2] In order that we may attain certainty of what we imagine, there has to be something in addition to imagination, namely, reasoning. Hence it follows that prophecy cannot of itself carry certainty, because, as I have shown, it depended solely on the imagination. So the prophets were not assured of God's revelation through the revelation itself, but through a sign. This is clear in the case of Abraham (Gen. ch. 15 v. 8) who, when he heard God's promise, asked for a sign. He did indeed believe in God, and he did not seek a sign so as to have faith in God, but to know that this was God's promise to him. This is even clearer in the case of Gideon, who says to God, "Show me a sign (that I may know) that it is Thou who talkest to me." See Judges ch. 6 v. 17. To Moses, too, God says, "And let this be a sign that I have sent thee." Hezekiah, who had long known Isaiah to be a prophet, asked for a sign of the prophecy predicting his recovery from sickness. This makes it clear that the prophets always received some sign to assure them of the certainty of their prophetic imaginings. It is for this reason that Moses warns the Jews (Deut. ch. 18, last verse) to seek a sign from the prophet, namely, the issue of some future event. In this respect, then, prophecy is inferior to natural knowledge, which needs no sign, but of its own nature carries certainty.

Moreover, the certainty afforded by prophecy was not a mathematical certainty, but only a moral certainty. This, again, is made clear in Scripture, for in Deut. ch. 13 Moses gives warning that if any prophet should seek to introduce new gods, even if he should confirm his teaching by signs and wonders, he must nevertheless be condemned to death. For, as Moses goes on to say, "The Lord also worketh signs and miracles to try his people." Christ, too, gives his disciples a similar warning in Matthew ch. 24 v. 24. Indeed, Ezekiel clearly tells us (ch. 14 v. 9) that God sometimes deceives men by false revelations, "And when a prophet (that is, a false prophet) is deceived and hath spoken a thing, I, the Lord, have deceived that prophet." Micaiah (1 Kings ch. 22 v. 23) bears a similar witness in the case of Ahab's prophets.

---

[2] [Spinoza, *Ethics*, 2.40, Scholium 2.]

Although this seems to prove that prophetic revelation is a matter open to much doubt, it nevertheless did possess a considerable degree of certainty, as I have said. For God never deceives the good and his chosen ones: in accordance with the ancient proverb (1 Samuel ch. 24 v. 13), and as is clearly shown by the story of Abigail and her speech, God uses the good as the instruments of his goodness and the wicked as the executors and tools of his wrath. This is also quite clear from the case of Micaiah quoted above: although God had resolved to deceive Ahab through prophets, he employed only false prophets, whereas to the good prophet he revealed what was true and did not forbid him to proclaim the truth. Still, the prophet's certainty was only of a moral kind, as I have said; for nobody can justify himself before God, or boast that he is the instrument of God's goodness. This is what Scripture tells us, and shows in actuality; for God's anger misled David to number the people, although Scripture bears ample witness to David's piety.

Therefore the certainty of the prophets was based entirely on these three considerations:

1. That the things revealed were most vividly imagined, just as we are wont to be affected by objects in our waking hours.

2. The occurrence of a sign.

3. Lastly and most important, that the minds of the prophets were directed exclusively towards what was right and good.

Although Scripture does not invariably make mention of a sign, it should nevertheless be assumed that the prophets always received a sign. Scripture does not always relate in full every detail and circumstance, as many scholars have remarked, but tends rather to take such things for granted. Furthermore, we can allow that, when their prophecy revealed nothing beyond what was contained in the Law of Moses, the prophets stood in no need of a sign, for the Law was their assurance. For example, Jeremiah's prophecy concerning the destruction of Jerusalem was supported by the prophecies of other prophets and by the threats of retribution contained in the Law, and so needed no sign; but Hananiah, who in the face of all the prophets prophesied the speedy restoration of the state, necessarily needed a sign, in the absence of which he ought to have doubted his prophecy until it might be confirmed by the event he had prophesied. See Jeremiah ch. 28 v. 9.

Therefore the certainty acquired by the prophets from signs was not a mathematical certainty—that is, the certainty that necessarily derives from the apprehension of what is apprehended or seen—but only of a moral kind, and the signs were vouchsafed only to convince the prophet. It therefore follows that the signs vouchsafed were suited to the beliefs and capacity of the prophet. A sign that would validate his prophecy for one prophet might fail to convince another who held different beliefs, and so the signs varied in the case of each prophet. Similarly, revelation also varied, as we have said, in the case of each prophet according to his temperament, the nature of his imagination, and the beliefs he had previously held. It varied with temperament in this way, that if the prophet was of a cheerful disposition, then victories, peace and other joyful events were revealed to him; for it is on things of this kind that the imagination of such people dwells. If he was of a gloomy disposition, then wars, massacres, and all kinds of calamities were revealed to him. And just as a prophet might be merciful, gentle, wrathful, stern and so forth, so he was more fitted for a particular kind of revelation. In the same way, too, revelation varied with the type of imagination. If the prophet was a man of culture, it was also in a cultivated way that he perceived God's mind; if he lacked an orderly mind, in a disorderly way. The same applies to revelations that took the form of images; the visions were of oxen and cows and the like if the prophet was a countryman, of captains and armies in the case of a soldier, of a royal throne and suchlike if he was a courtier. Finally, prophecy varied with the different beliefs of the prophets. To the Magi (see Matth. ch. 2) who believed in the follies of astrology, Christ's birth was revealed through imagining a star rising in the East. To the augurs of Nebuchadnezzar (see Ezekiel ch. 21 v. 26) the destruction of Jerusalem was revealed in entrails, whereas the king himself understood it from oracles and from the flight of arrows which he shot into the air. To those prophets who believed that men act from free choice and from their own power, God was revealed as one who is aloof and unaware of future human actions. All this we shall illustrate by individual cases taken from Scripture.

The first point is evident from the case of Elisha (2 Kings ch. 3 v. 15) who, in order to prophesy to Jehoram, called for a harp, and could apprehend the mind of God only when he had been beguiled by its music. Only then did he prophesy glad tidings to Jehoram and his company; until then this could not come about because of his anger against the king, and those who are angered against a man are apt to imagine evil, not good, concerning him. As to the view advanced by some[3] that God does not reveal himself to the angry and the gloomy, this has no substance whatsoever. When Moses was angered against Pharaoh, God revealed to him the terrible slaughter of the firstborn (see Exodus ch. 11 v. 8), and this without the assistance of a harp. To Cain, too, in his rage, God was revealed. To Ezekiel, impatient with anger, was revealed the wretched plight and obstinacy of the Jews (see Ezekiel ch. 3 v. 14). Jeremiah, when deeply saddened and utterly weary of life, prophesied the calamities of the Jews, with the result that Josiah refused to consult him, but instead consulted a woman of his time, she being more fitted from her feminine character to receive a revelation of God's mercy (2 Chron. ch. 34). Micaiah, too, never prophesied any good to Ahab, though other true prophets did so (as is clear from 1 Kings ch. 20); throughout his life he prophesied evil (see 1 Kings ch. 22 v. 8) and, more clearly, 2 Chron. ch. 18 v. 7). So the prophets were temperamentally more fitted for one kind of revelation rather than another.

Again, the style of prophecy varied according to the manner of speaking of each prophet. The prophecies of Ezekiel and Amos were lacking in refinement, unlike those of Isaiah and Nahum, which were composed in a cultured style. Any Hebrew scholar who cares to look into this matter more closely, if he compares cer-

---

[3] [Here Spinoza alludes to a rabbinic notion quoted by Maimonides in *Guide* 2.36.]

tain chapters in the different prophets dealing with the same subject-matter, will find a considerable stylistic difference. Let him compare the courtly Isaiah's chapter 1 v. 11–20 with the rustic Amos' chapter 5 v. 21–24. Then let him compare the arrangement and logical argument of Jeremiah's prophecy concerning Edom (ch. 49) with the arrangement and logical argument of Obadiah. Let him again compare Isaiah chapter 40 v. 19, 20 and chapter 44 from v. 8 with Hosea chapter 8 v. 6 and chapter 13 v. 2. These and other passages, when rightly examined, will readily show that God has no particular style of speech, but in accordance with the learning and capacity of the prophet the style was cultured, compressed, stern, unrefined, prolix or obscure.

Prophetic visions and symbolism, even when conveying the same meaning, varied considerably. For Isaiah and Ezekiel, the glory of the Lord leaving the temple was represented in different ways. Now the Rabbis maintain that both visions were exactly the same, but that Ezekiel, being a countryman, was struck with a boundless wonder, and so he related the vision in every detail.[4] However, unless they have received a trustworthy tradition—which I do not believe—this is plainly an invention. Isaiah saw seraphim with six wings, Ezekiel beasts with four wings; Isaiah saw God clothed and sitting on a royal throne, Ezekiel saw him in the likeness of fire. Doubtless they both saw God as they were wont to imagine him.

Furthermore, there were differences not only in the form taken by revelations but in their clarity. The revelations of Zechariah were too obscure to be understood by him without explanation, as is clear from the narrative. The revelations of Daniel could not be understood by the prophet even when they were explained. This obscurity did not arise from any difficulty in the matter to be revealed (for this was concerned with only human affairs, and these do not exceed human capacity except as relating to the future) but solely from the nature of Daniel's imagination, which was not equally capable of prophecy in waking hours as in sleep. This is evident from the fact that at the very beginning of the revelation he was so terrified that he almost despaired of his strength. So the obscurity of things revealed to him and his failure to understand them even when explained was caused by the inadequacy of his imagination and his strength. And here it should be noted that the words heard by Daniel, as we have pointed out, were only imaginary; so it is not surprising that in his state of terror he imagined these words so confusedly and obscurely that afterwards he could understand nothing of them. Those who say that God did not wish to make a clear revelation to Daniel appear not to have read the words of the angel, who expressly said (ch. 10 v. 14), "Now I am come to make thee understand what shall befall thy people in the latter days." So those matters remained obscure because no one was found at that time with sufficient power of imagination to receive a clearer revelation. Lastly, the prophets to whom it was revealed that God would take away Elijah tried to convince Elisha that he had been taken to another place where they might still find him; which clearly proves that they had not understood God's revelation.

---

[4] [This is another rabbinic doctrine quoted by Maimonides, in *Guide* 3.6.]

There is no need to deal with this subject in greater detail. Scripture makes it absolutely clear that God bestowed a far greater gift of prophecy on one prophet than on another. But I shall show in more detail and at greater length that prophecies or revelations also varied in accordance with the ingrained beliefs of the prophets, and that the prophets held various, even contrary beliefs, and various prejudices. (The matters I refer to concern purely philosophic speculation, for with regard to uprightness and morality the case is quite different.) This I consider to be a point of some importance, for I shall eventually conclude from it that the gift of prophecy did not render the prophets more learned, but left them with the beliefs they had previously held, and therefore we are in no way bound to believe them in matters of purely philosophic speculation.

All commentators have displayed an extraordinary eagerness to convince themselves that the prophets knew everything attainable by human intellect; and although certain passages in Scripture make it absolutely clear that there were some things the prophets did not know, rather than admit that there was anything the prophets did not know, they prefer to declare that they do not understand those passages, or alternatively they strive to twist the words of Scripture to mean what they plainly do not mean. If either of these options is permissible, we can bid Scripture farewell. If that which is absolutely clear can be accounted obscure and incomprehensible or else interpreted at will, it will be vain for us to try to prove anything from Scripture. For example, nothing in Scripture could be clearer than that Joshua, and perhaps the writer who composed his history, thought that the sun goes round the earth and the earth does not move, and that the sun stood still for a time. Yet there are many who, refusing to admit that there can be any mutability in the heavens, explain this passage so that it means something quite different. Others, who have adopted a more scientific attitude and understand that the earth moves and the sun is motionless or does not revolve around the earth, make every effort to extort this meaning in the teeth of the Scriptural text. Indeed, I wonder at them. Do we have to believe that the soldier Joshua was a skilled astronomer, that a miracle could not be revealed to him, or that the sun's light could not remain above the horizon for longer than usual without Joshua's understanding the cause? Both alternatives seem to me ridiculous. I prefer the simple view that Joshua did not know the cause of that extension of daylight, and that he and all the host along with him believed that the sun revolves around the earth with a diurnal motion and on that day it stood still for a while, this being the cause of the prolonged daylight. They did not take account of the fact that, as a result of the excessive coldness of the atmosphere at that time (see Joshua ch. 10 v. 11), there may have been an unusually great refraction of light, or something of the sort, which is not our present concern.

Similarly, the sign of the shadow going back was revealed to Isaiah according to his understanding, namely, through the retrogression of the sun. For he, too, thought that the sun moves and the earth is still. He probably had not the faintest notion of parhelia. We need have no hesitation in maintaining this view, for the sign could really have occurred and Isaiah could have predicted it to the king without knowing its true cause.

As to the building of the Temple by Solomon, if indeed that was revealed to him by God, we must take the same view, namely, that all its measurements were revealed to Solomon in accordance with his understanding and beliefs. As we are not required to believe that Solomon was a mathematician, we may assume that Solomon did not know the ratio between the circumference and diameter of a circle, and that, in common with ordinary workmen, he thought it was three to one. If it is permissible to declare that we do not understand the text of 1 Kings ch. 7 v. 23 I do not know what in Scripture we can understand. The narrative of the building of the Temple is there straightforwardly set forth, and as a mere matter of history. Indeed, if it is permissible to pretend that the writer meant something different, but for reasons unknown to us decided to write in that way, this is nothing else but the utter ruination of the whole of Scripture. Everyone will have equal right to adopt the same attitude to every Scriptural passage, and thus whatever human malice can devise in the way of absurdity and iniquity can be both defended and perpetrated without impairing the authority of Scripture. But the view we are maintaining implies no impiety. Solomon, Isaiah, Joshua and the others were indeed prophets: but they were also men, subject to human limitations.

The revelation to Noah that God was destroying the human race was also made in accordance with his understanding, for he thought that the world beyond Palestine was uninhabited. And not only matters of this kind but other more important matters could have been, and in fact were, beyond the knowledge of the prophets without prejudice to their piety. Their teaching concerning the attributes of God was in no way singular. Their beliefs about God were shared by the vast majority of their time, and their revelations were accommodated to these beliefs, as I shall show by ample Scriptural testimony. Thus one may easily see that they won such praise and repute not so much for sublimity and pre-eminence of intellect as for piety and faithfulness.

Adam, to whom God was first revealed, did not know that God is omnipresent and omniscient, for he hid from God and attempted to excuse his sin before God as if he had to do with a man. So in his case, too, God was revealed in accordance with his understanding, that is, as one who is not everywhere, and as not knowing where Adam was, or Adam's sin. For Adam heard, or thought he heard, God walking in the garden, calling him and seeking him out, and then, seeing his guilty bearing, asking him whether he had eaten of the forbidden tree. Therefore Adam knew none of God's attributes except that God was the maker of all things. To Cain, too, God was revealed in accordance with his understanding, that is, as having no knowledge of human affairs; nor did Cain need to have any higher conception of God before he could repent of his sin.

To Laban God revealed himself as the God of Abraham, because Laban believed that every nation had its own special God. See Gen. ch. 31 v. 29. Abraham, too, did not know that God is everywhere and has foreknowledge of all things; for when he heard the sentence against the people of Sodom, he prayed God not to execute the sentence until he knew whether they all deserved that punishment, saying, "Peradventure there be fifty righteous within the city" (Gen. ch. 18 v. 24). Nor did God appear to him differently in revelation, for in Abraham's imagination God speaks thus, "I will go down now, and see whether they have done altogether according to the cry of it which is come unto me, and if not, I will know." Again, God's testimony concerning Abraham implies only that he was obedient and commanded his household to ways of justice and goodness (see Gen. ch. 18 v. 19); it does not imply that Abraham's conception of God was more sublime than others.

Moses, too, did not completely comprehend that God is omniscient, and that all human actions are governed solely by God's decree. Although God had told him (Exodus ch. 3 v. 18) that the Israelites would hearken to him, he still doubted, and answered (Exodus ch. 4 v. 1), "But if they will not believe me and hearken unto my voice. . . ." So for Moses, too, God was revealed as not determining future human actions and unaware of them; for God gave him two signs, and said (Exodus ch. 4 v. 8), "And it shall come to pass that if they will not believe the first sign, they will believe the latter sign; and if they believe not the latter sign, take some waters of the river. . . ." Indeed, if anyone will examine without prejudice what Moses says, he will clearly find that Moses' belief about God was this, that he is a Being who has always existed, exists, and will always exist. That is why he gives God the name Jehovah, which in Hebrew expresses these three tenses of the verb 'to be'. As for God's nature, Moses taught no more than that God is merciful, gracious etc. and extremely jealous, as is evident from many passages in the Pentateuch. Further, he believed and taught that this Being was so different from all other beings that he could not be expressed by any image of a visible thing, nor even beheld, not so much because this was intrinsically impossible as because of human inadequacy; and furthermore he was one alone, or unique, in respect of his power. Moses did indeed concede that there were beings who (doubtless in accordance with God's arrangement and behest) acted in God's place; that is, beings to whom God gave the authority, right and power to guide nations, to look after them and care for them. But he taught that this Being whom it was their duty to worship was the highest and supreme God, or (to use the Hebrew phrase), the God of Gods. Thus, in the canticle of Exodus (ch. 15 v. 11) he said, "Who is like unto thee, O Lord, among the Gods?" And Jethro says (ch. 18 v. 11), "Now I know that the Lord is greater than all the Gods," as much as to say, "At last I am forced to admit to Moses that Jehovah is greater than all the gods and his power is without equal." There is some doubt as to whether Moses believed those beings who acted in God's place were created by God; for he said nothing, as far as we know, about their creation and origin.

He furthermore taught that this Being had reduced our visible world from chaos to order (Gen. ch. 1 v. 2) and had given Nature its seeds. He therefore possesses supreme right and power over things, and (Deut. ch. 10 v. 14, 15) in virtue of this supreme right and power he had chosen the Hebrew nation for himself alone, together with a certain territory (Deut. ch. 4 v. 19 and ch. 32 v. 8, 9), leaving other nations and lands to the care of other Gods standing in his place. For this reason he was called the God of Israel and the God of Jerusalem (2 Chron. ch. 32 v. 19), while other Gods were called the Gods of other nations. For this same reason the Jews believed that the land which God had chosen for himself demanded a special form of worship, quite different from that of other lands; indeed, it could not suffer the worship of other Gods, a worship belonging to other lands. It was believed that those peoples whom the king of Assyria brought into the land of the Jews were torn to pieces by lions because they knew not the form of worship for the Deity of that land (2 Kings ch. 17 v. 25, 26). And according to ibn Ezra,[5] when Jacob resolved to seek his native land, it was for this reason that he told his sons to prepare themselves for a new form of worship and to put away strange Gods, that is, the worship of the Gods of the land where they were then dwelling (Gen. ch. 35 v. 2, 3). And David, too, complaining to Saul that because of his persecution he was forced to live away from his native land, said that he was driven out of the heritage of the Lord and sent to worship other Gods (1 Sam. ch. 26 v. 19). And finally, Moses believed that this Being, or God, had his dwelling in the heavens (see Deut. ch. 33 v. 27), a belief wide-spread among the Gentiles.

If we now examine Moses' revelations, we shall find that they were adapted to these beliefs. Since he believed that it was in God's nature to experience those feelings that I have mentioned—mercy, graciousness and so on—God was revealed to him in conformity with this belief and under these attributes (see Exodus ch. 34 v. 6, 7, where we are told in what manner God appeared to Moses; also the Decalogue v. 4, 5). Again, it is related (Exodus ch. 33 v. 18) that Moses asked of God that he might behold him; but since Moses, as we have said, had formed no image of God in his brain, and (as I have already shown) God is revealed to the prophets only in accordance with the nature of their imagination, God did not appear to Moses in the form of an image. This came about, I repeat, because Moses' imagination was not receptive to such an image; for other prophets—Isaiah, Ezekiel, Daniel and the rest—testify that they saw God. For this reason God answered Moses, "Thou canst not see my face"; and since Moses believed that God was visible, that is, visibility was not in contradiction with the divine nature (for otherwise he would not have made such a request), God added, "For no one shall look on me and live." So God gives a reason in conformity with Moses' beliefs; God does not say that to see him is in contradiction with the divine nature—as in fact it is—but that it is impossible because of human inadequacy.

Again, in order to reveal to Moses that through worshipping the calf the Israelites had now become no different from other nations, God said (Exodus ch. 33 v. 2, 3), that he would send an angel, that is, a being, to take care of the Israelites in place of the Supreme Being, but that he himself would withdraw from them. In this way Moses was left with no grounds for supposing that the Israelites were more beloved of God than the rest of the nations whom God had also entrusted to the care of other beings or angels, as is clear from verse 16, same chapter. Finally, since it was thought that God dwelt in the heavens, he was revealed

---

[5] [Abraham ibn Ezra (1092–1167) was one of the leading figures in the Spanish-Jewish "Golden Age." He was an outstanding biblical exegete, noted for his rigorous philological approach to the text. He was also a good astronomer and mathematician and wrote several philosophical treatises.]

as descending from heaven onto a mountain, and Moses even climbed the mountain to speak with God, which he certainly need not have done if he could just as well have imagined God as being everywhere.

The Israelites knew scarcely anything of God, although he was revealed to them. This they made abundantly clear when a few days later they transferred to a calf the honour and worship due to him, believing the calf to be the Deity who had led them out of Egypt. Indeed, it would be hardly likely that men addicted to Egyptian superstition, uncultured and sunk in degrading slavery, should have had any sound understanding of God, or that Moses could have taught them anything more than a moral code—not, indeed, as a philosopher might inculcate the morality that is engendered by freedom of spirit, but as a lawgiver, compelling people to live good lives by command of law. Therefore the right way of life, or true living, and the worship and love of God was for them bondage rather than true freedom, the grace and gift of God. For Moses commanded them to love God and keep his Law, to regard their past blessings—such as the escape from Egyptian bondage—as bestowed by God; and he further made terrifying threats if they should transgress these commandments, while promising many blessings if they observed them. So he taught them in the same way as parents teach children who have not reached the age of reason. It is therefore certain that they had no understanding of the excellence of virtue and true blessedness.

Jonah thought to flee from the sight of God, which goes to show that he, too, believed that God had entrusted the care of lands outside Judea to other powers, who were nevertheless installed by him. There is no one in the Old Testament who speaks more rationally of God than Solomon, who possessed the natural light of reason beyond all men of his time. And so he also considered himself above the Law (for that was given only for men not well endowed with reason and the instruction of the natural intellect) and paid little heed to all the laws regarding the king, consisting of three main articles (see Deut. ch. 17 v. 16, 17). Indeed, he plainly violated these laws (in which, however, he did wrong, and by indulgence in pleasures behaved in a way unworthy of a philosopher), and taught that all fortune's gifts to mankind are vanity (see Eccl.), that men possess nothing more excellent than understanding, and can suffer no greater punishment than their folly (see Proverbs ch. 16 v. 22).

But let us return to the prophets, whose different beliefs we have also undertaken to note. The Rabbis who have bequeathed to us the only extant books of the prophets regarding the sayings of Ezekiel as so irreconcilable with those of Moses (as is narrated in the Treatise of Sabbatus[6] ch. 1 fol. 13 p. 2) that they had some thoughts of rejecting his book from the canon, and would doubtless have put it aside if a certain Hananiah had not undertaken to explain it. This he is said to have accomplished with much labour and zeal (as is there narrated), though it is by no means clear how he did so, whether by writing a commentary which has

---

[6] [The Treatise of Sabbatus—a reference to the Tractate Shabbat of the Babylonian Talmud, mentioned again in Chapter 10.]

perchance perished, or by having the audacity to alter Ezekiel's words and expressions, embellishing them as he pleased. However that may be, chapter 18 certainly seems to be at variance with Exodus ch. 34 v. 7, with Jeremiah ch. 32 v. 18, and other texts.

Samuel believed that God never repents of any decision he has made (see 1 Sam. ch. 15 v. 29); for when Saul repented of his sin and wished to worship God and seek forgiveness, Samuel said that God would not alter his decree against him. But to Jeremiah, on the other hand, it was revealed (see ch. 18 v. 8, 10) that, whether God has decreed good or whether he has decreed evil for any nation, he turns back the decree provided that men also change for the better or worse from the time of his sentence. Now Joel taught that God repents only of having decreed evil (see Joel ch. 2 v. 13). Finally, it is quite clear from Gen. ch. 4 v. 7 that men can overcome the temptations of sin and act righteously; for this is what was told to Cain—who nevertheless did not overcome those temptations, as is clear from Scripture and from Josephus.[7] This is obviously in agreement with the chapter of Jeremiah just quoted, for it is there said that God repents of his decree pronounced for the good or hurt of men in accordance with their willingness to change their ways and manner of life. But Paul, on the other hand, is quite clear that men have no dominion over the temptations of the flesh save by the special vocation and grace of God. See Epistle to the Romans chapter 9 from verse 10 on. As for his attributing righteousness to God (ch. 3 v. 5 and ch. 6 v. 19), he corrects himself for thus speaking in a merely human fashion and through the frailty of the flesh.

So now the point we set out to prove has been made abundantly clear, namely, that God adapted his revelations to the understanding and beliefs of the prophets, who may well have been ignorant of matters that have no bearing on charity and moral conduct but concern philosophic speculation, and were in fact ignorant of them, holding conflicting beliefs. Therefore knowledge of science and of matters spiritual should by no means be expected of them. So we conclude that we must believe the prophets only with regard to the purpose and substance of the revelation; in all else one is free to believe as one will. For example, the revelation of Cain teaches us only that God admonished him to live the true life, for that alone is the object and substance of the revelation, which does not teach free will or philosophic doctrines.[8] Therefore, although the wording and the reasoning of admonition seem clearly to imply freedom of the will, we are entitled to hold a contrary opinion, since the wording and reasoning were adapted to Cain's understanding alone. Similarly, the meaning of the revelation to Micaiah is no more than this, that God revealed to Micaiah the true issue of the battle between Ahab and Aram, and so this alone we are bound to believe. Whatever else is contained in that revelation, concerning the true and false Spirit of God, the heavenly host standing on either side of God, and all the other details of that revelation—all this

---

[7] [Josephus A.D. 37–100. Took part in the revolt of A.D. 66, but surrendered, came over to the Roman side, and took up residence at Rome. His main historical works are the *History of the Jewish War* and *Antiquities of the Jews*.]

[8] [Spinoza, *Ethics*, 2.48–49; Letters 2 and 21.]

has no relevance for us, and everyone may believe of them as much as is in consonance with his reason.

With regard to the reasonings whereby God showed to Job his power over all things—if indeed it is true that this was revealed to Job and that the author's purpose was to compose a historical narrative and not, as some believe, to display his own ideas—the same point must be made, namely, that these arguments were accommodated to Job's understanding and propounded to convince him alone. They are not arguments of universal validity to convince all men. The same conclusions must be reached regarding the reasonings of Christ whereby he convicts the Pharisees' obstinacy and ignorance and exhorts his disciples to the true life; that is, he adapted his reasonings to the beliefs and principles of each individual. For example, when he said to the Pharisees (see Matth. ch. 12 v. 26), "And if Satan cast out Satan, he is divided against himself; how shall then his kingdom stand?" his only purpose was to refute the Pharisees according to their own principles, not to teach that there are devils, or any kingdom of devils. Similarly, when he said to his disciples (Matth. ch. 18 v. 10), "Take heed that ye despise not one of these little ones; for I say unto you that in heaven their angels. . . ." and so on, the point of his teaching is merely a warning against pride and contempt, and not those other details which he brings into his argument only for the better persuasion of his disciples.

Finally, the same point must be made to cover all the sayings and signs of the Apostles, and there is no need for me to deal with these matters at greater length. If I had to enumerate all the passages of Scripture composed 'ad hominem'—i.e. according to the individual's understanding—and which cannot be upheld as divine doctrine without great prejudice to philosophy, I should depart far from the brevity which is my aim. Let it suffice, then, to have touched on a few instances of general application, and let the zealous reader examine the rest for himself. However, although it is only those points we have made concerning prophets and prophecy that are especially relevant to my main purpose—namely, the differentiation of philosophy from theology—still, as I have touched on this question in a general way, we may well go on to enquire whether the gift of prophecy was peculiar to the Hebrews or whether it was shared by other nations; and then what conclusion should be reached regarding the vocation of the Hebrews. This will be the subject of our next chapter.

CHAPTER 3

Of the vocation of the Hebrews, and whether the gift of prophecy was peculiar to them

Everyone's true happiness and blessedness consists solely in the enjoyment of good, not in priding himself that he alone is enjoying that good to the exclusion of others. He who counts himself more blessed because he alone enjoys wellbeing not shared by others, or because he is more blessed and fortunate than others, knows not what is true happiness and blessedness, and the joy he derives therefrom, if it be not mere childishness, has its only source in spite and malice. For example, a man's true happiness and blessedness consists solely in wisdom and knowledge of truth, and not in that he is wiser than others, or that others are without true knowledge. This adds nothing at all to his wisdom, that is, his true happiness. So he who rejoices for this reason rejoices at another's misfortune, and is therefore spiteful and malicious, knowing neither true wisdom nor the peace of the true life.[1]

So when Scripture, in exhorting the Hebrews to obey the Law, says that God has chosen them for himself above all other nations (Deut. ch. 10 v. 15), "that he is nigh unto them as he is not unto others" (Deut. ch. 4 v. 4, 7), that for them alone he has ordained just laws (same ch. v. 8), that he has made himself known only to them before all others (same ch. v. 32) and so forth, it is speaking merely according to the understanding of those who, as was shown in the previous chapter and as Moses also testifies (Deut. ch. 9 v. 6, 7), knew not true blessedness. For surely they would have been no less blessed if God had called all men equally to salvation, nor would God have been less close to them for being equally close to others, nor would their laws have been less just or they themselves less wise if those laws had been ordained for all men. Miracles would have displayed God's power no less if they had been wrought for other nations as well, and the Hebrews would have been no less in duty bound to worship God if God had bestowed all these gifts equally upon all men. When God tells Solomon (1 Kings ch. 3 v. 12) that no one shall be as wise as he in time to come, this seems to be just a figure of speech, intending to signify exceptional wisdom. Be that as it may, it is quite incredible that God should have promised Solomon, for his greater happiness, that he would never bestow such wisdom on anyone thereafter. This would in no way have increased Solomon's understanding, nor would the wise king have been any the less grateful for such a gift even if God had said that he would bestow the same wisdom on all men.

However, although we assert that Moses was speaking to the understanding of the Hebrews in the passages of the Pentateuch just quoted, we do not mean to deny that God ordained those laws in the Pentateuch for them alone, nor that he spoke only to them, nor that the Hebrews witnessed marvels such have never befallen any other nation. Our point is merely this, that Moses wished to admonish the Hebrews in a particular way, using such reasoning as would bind them more firmly to the worship of God, having regard to the immaturity of their understanding. Further, we wished to show that the Hebrews surpassed other nations not in knowledge nor in piety, but in quite a different respect; or (to adopt the language of Scripture directed to their understanding) that the Hebrews were chosen by God above all others not for the true life nor for any higher under-

---

[1] [Spinoza, *Ethics*, 4.36–37, 5.42.]

standing—though often admonished thereto—but for a quite different purpose. What that purpose was, I shall now proceed to demonstrate.

But before I begin, I wish to explain briefly what I shall hereafter mean by God's direction, by God's help, external and internal, by God's calling, and, finally, by fortune. By God's direction I mean the fixed and immutable order of Nature, or chain of natural events; for I have said above, and have already shown elsewhere, that the universal laws of Nature according to which all things happen and are determined are nothing but God's eternal decrees, which always involve eternal truth and necessity. So it is the same thing whether we say that all things happen according to Nature's laws or that they are regulated by God's decree and direction.[2] Again, since the power of Nature in its entirety is nothing other than the power of God through which alone all things happen and are determined, it follows that whatever man—who is also a part of Nature—acquires for himself to help to preserve his own being, or whatever Nature provides for him without any effort on his part, all this is provided for him solely by the divine power, acting either through human nature or externally to human nature. Therefore whatever human nature can effect solely by its own power to preserve its own being can rightly be called God's internal help, and whatever falls to a man's advantage from the power of external causes can rightly be called God's external help. And from this, too, can readily be deduced what must be meant by God's choosing, for since no one acts except by the predetermined order of Nature—that is, from God's eternal direction and decree—it follows that no one chooses a way of life for himself or accomplishes anything except by the special vocation of God, who has chosen one man before others for a particular work or a particular way of life. Finally, by fortune I mean simply God's direction insofar as he directs human affairs through causes that are external and unforeseen.

With these preliminary remarks, let us return to our purpose, which is to see why it was that the Hebrew nation was said to have been chosen by God before all others. To demonstrate this, I proceed as follows.

All worthy objects of desire can be classified under one of these three general headings:

1. To know things through their primary causes.
2. To subjugate the passions; i.e. to acquire the habit of virtue.
3. To live in security and good health.

The means that directly serve for the attainment of the first and second objectives, and can be considered as the proximate and efficient causes, lie within the bounds of human nature itself, so that their acquisition chiefly depends on human power alone; i.e. solely on the laws of human nature. For this reason it is obvious that these gifts are not peculiar to any nation but have always been common to all mankind—unless we entertain the delusion that Nature at some time cre-

---

[2] [Spinoza, *Ethics*, 1.16, 29, 33, especially Scholium 2.]

ated different species of men. But the means that serve for the attainment of security and physical wellbeing lie principally in external circumstances, and are called the gifts of fortune because they mainly depend on the operation of external causes of which we are in ignorance. So in this matter the fool and the wise man have about an equal chance of happiness or unhappiness. Nevertheless, much can be effected by human contrivance and vigilance to achieve security and to avoid injuries from other men and from beasts. To this end, reason and experience have taught us no surer means than to organise a society under fixed laws, to occupy a fixed territory, and to concentrate the strength of all its members into one body, as it were, a social body.[3] However, a quite considerable degree of ability and vigilance is needed to organise and preserve a society, and therefore that society will be more secure, more stable and less exposed to fortune, which is founded and governed mainly by men of wisdom and vigilance, while a society composed of men who lack these qualities is largely dependent on fortune and is less stable. If the latter nevertheless endures for some considerable time, this is to be attributed to some other guidance, not its own. Indeed, if it overcomes great perils and enjoys prosperity, it cannot fail to marvel at and worship God's guidance (that is to say, insofar as God acts through hidden external causes, and not through the nature and mind of man); for what it has experienced is far beyond its expectation and belief, and can truly be regarded even as a miracle.

Through this alone, then, do nations differ from one another, namely, in respect of the kind of society and laws under which they live and are governed. Thus the Hebrew nation was chosen by God before all others not by reason of its understanding nor of its spiritual qualities, but by reason of its social organisation and the good fortune whereby it achieved supremacy and retained it for so many years. This is quite evident from Scripture itself. A merely casual perusal clearly reveals that the Hebrews surpassed other nations in this alone, that they were successful in achieving security for themselves and overcame great dangers, and this chiefly by God's external help alone. In other respects they were no different from other nations, and God was equally gracious to all. For in respect of their understanding (as we have shown in the preceding chapter) it is clear that the Hebrews' ideas of God and Nature were quite commonplace, and so it was not in respect of their understanding that they were chosen by God before others. Nor yet in respect of virtue and the true life, for in this matter again they were on the same footing as other nations, very few of them being chosen. Therefore their election and vocation consisted only in the material success and prosperity of their state; nor do we see that God promised anything other than this to the Patriarchs* or their successors. Indeed, in return for their obedience the Law promises them nothing other than the continuing prosperity of their state and material advantages, whereas disobedience and the breaking of the Covenant would bring about the downfall of their state and the severest hardships. This is not surprising, for the

---

[3] [Spinoza, *Ethics*, 4.37, especially Scholium 2.]

* See Supplementary Note 4.

purpose of an organised society and state (as is clear from what has just been said, and as I shall show at greater length hereafter) is to achieve security and ease. Now a state can subsist only if the laws are binding on all individuals. If all the members of one society choose to disregard the laws, by that very fact they will dissolve that society and destroy the state. Therefore, in return for their consistent observance of the laws, the only promise that could be made to the society of the Hebrews was their security** with its attendant advantages; whereas for disobedience no surer punishment could be foretold than the downfall of their state, accompanied not only by the usual unhappy consequences but by additional troubles, peculiar to them, entailed by the special constitution of their state. This latter point I need not labour at present, but this I will add, that the laws contained in the Old Testament were revealed and ordained for the Jews alone; for as God chose them only for the establishing of a special kind of society and state, they must also have had laws of a special kind. As to whether God ordained special laws for other nations as well and revealed himself through prophecy for their lawgivers—that is, under those attributes by which they were accustomed to imagine God—I cannot be sure. But this at least is evident from Scripture, that other nations also had their own state and their special laws by God's external guidance. To prove this I shall cite two Scriptural passages only.

In Genesis ch. 14 v. 18, 19, 20 it is related that Melchizedek was king of Jerusalem and priest of the Most High God, and in his capacity of priest (Num. ch. 6 v. 23) he blessed Abraham, and Abraham, the beloved of God, gave a tenth part of all his spoils to this priest of God. All this shows well enough that before God founded the nation of Israel he had established kings and priests in Jerusalem and had appointed rites and laws for them. Whether he did so through prophecy is, as I have said, unclear. But of this, at least, I am sure, that while Abraham lived there he lived religiously according to those laws. For Abraham had not received from God any special rites, and yet it states in Gen. ch. 26 v. 5 that he observed the worship, precepts, statutes and laws of God. This must undoubtedly refer to the worship, precepts, statutes and laws of king Melchizedek. Malachi, in ch. 1 v. 10, 11 rebukes the Jews with these words: "Who is there among you that would shut the doors (of the temple) lest fire be kindled on mine altars for nought? I have no pleasure in you . . . etc. From the rising of the sun even unto the going down of the same my name is great among the nations, and everywhere incense is offered unto me, and a pure offering. For my name is great among nations, saith the Lord of hosts." Surely by these words, which can be interpreted as referring only to his present time unless we do violence to the text, he abundantly testifies that the Jews at that time were no more beloved of God than were other nations. Indeed, he indicates that by his miracles God made himself known to other nations more so than to the Jews of that time—who had then partly regained their independence without miraculous intervention—and that the Gentiles possessed rites and ceremonies by which they were acceptable to God.

** See Supplementary Note 5.

But I leave these considerations, for it is sufficient for my purpose to have demonstrated that the choosing of the Jews referred only to the following facts: their temporal material prosperity and freedom—i.e. their political independence—and to the manner and means whereby they achieved it, and consequently to their laws as well, insofar as these were necessary for the preservation of their special kind of state, and, finally, to the way in which these laws were revealed. But in other matters, wherein consists the true happiness of man, they were on the same footing as other nations. So when Scripture says (Deut. ch. 4 v. 7) that no other nation has its Gods so nigh unto them as the Jews have their God, this must be understood in respect of independence of their state, and as referring only to the time when so many miracles befell them, and so forth. For in respect of understanding and virtue, that is, in respect of blessedness, God is equally gracious to all, as we have already stated and proved by reason. This is also well established from Scripture, for the Psalmist says (Psalm 145 v. 18), "The Lord is nigh to all them that call upon him, to all that call upon him in truth." Likewise in the same Psalm, v. 9, "The Lord is good to all, and his tender mercies are over all his works." In Psalm 33 v. 15 it is clearly stated that God has given the same understanding to all, in these words, "He fashioneth our hearts alike." The Hebrews considered the heart to be the seat of the soul and the understanding, as I think everybody knows. Again, from Job ch. 28 v. 28 it is clear that God ordained this law for the whole human race: to revere God and to abstain from evildoing, i.e. to act righteously; and so Job, although a Gentile, was to God the most acceptable of all men, for he surpassed all men in piety and religion. Finally, it is quite evident from Jonah ch. 4 v. 2 that not only to the Jews but to all mankind God is gracious, merciful, long-suffering and abundant in kindness, and loath to punish. For Jonah says, "Therefore I resolved to flee before to Tarshish, for I knew (namely, from the words of Moses, Exodus ch. 34 v. 6) that Thou art a gracious God, merciful . . . etc." and therefore likely to pardon the Ninevites.

We therefore conclude (since God is equally gracious to all and the Hebrews were chosen only with respect to their social organisation and their government) that the individual Jew, considered alone apart from his social organisation and his government, possesses no gift of God above other men, and there is no difference between him and a Gentile. Since, then, it is true that God is equally gracious, merciful etc. to all men, and since the function of the prophet was to teach not the special laws of his country but true virtue, and to admonish men thereto, there is no doubt that all nations possessed prophets and that the gift of prophecy was not peculiar to the Jews. In actual fact, this is borne out by history, both secular and sacred; and although the sacred history of the Old Testament does not specify that other nations had as many prophets as the Hebrews, or indeed that any Gentile prophet was expressly sent by God to the nations, this has no significance; for the Hebrews were concerned to record their own history, not that of other nations. It is therefore sufficient that in the Old Testament we find that Gentiles and the uncircumcised, such as Noah, Enoch, Abimelech, Balaam etc., did in fact prophesy, and furthermore that Hebrew prophets were sent by God not only to their own nation but to many others. Ezekiel prophesied for all nations that were then known. Indeed, as far as we know, Obadiah prophesied only to the Idumaeans, and Jonah was chiefly a prophet to the Ninevites. Isaiah bewails and foretells the calamities, and prophesies the restoration, not only of the Jews but of other nations. In chapter 16 v. 9 he says, "Therefore will I bewail Jazer with weeping," and in chapter 19 he foretells first the calamities of the Egyptians and then their restoration (see same chapter v. 19, 20, 21, 25), saying that God will send a saviour to free them, that God will make himself known to them, and that the Egyptians will worship God with sacrifices and gifts; and finally he calls that nation the blessed Egyptians, the people of God. All this is certainly worthy of special note. Lastly, Jeremiah is called the prophet not only of the Hebrew nation but of all nations absolutely (Jer. ch. 1 v. 5). He, too, bemoans the coming calamities of nations and foretells their restoration, for in chapter 48 v. 31 he says of the Moabites, "Therefore will I howl for Moab, I will cry out for all Moab," and in verse 36, "Therefore mine heart will sound for Moab like timbrels"; and he prophesies their eventual restoration, as also the restoration of the Egyptians, the Ammonites and the Elamites.

Therefore there is no doubt that other nations, like the Jews, also had their prophets, who prophesied to them and to the Jews. Although Scripture makes mention of only one man, Balaam, to whom was revealed the future of the Jews and of other nations, we should not suppose that Balaam's prophesying was confined to that one occasion; the narrative makes it quite clear that he had long been renowned for his prophecy and other divine gifts. Balak, ordering him to be summoned, said (Num. ch. 22 v. 6), "For I know that he whom thou blessest is blessed, and he whom thou cursest is cursed." So we see that he possessed the same power that God bestowed on Abraham (Gen. ch. 12 v. 3). Then Balaam, as was his custom in prophesying, told the messengers to await him until God's will should be revealed to him. When he was prophesying, that is, when he was interpreting the true mind of God, he was wont to say of himself, "The word of him who hears the words of God, who knows the knowledge (or mind, or foreknowledge) of the Most High, who sees the vision of the Almighty, falling into a trance, but having his eyes open." Finally, after blessing the Hebrews by God's command, he began, as was his custom, to prophesy to other nations and to foretell their future.[4]

All this abundantly shows that he had always been a prophet, or that he had frequently prophesied, and (another point to be here noted) that he possessed that which especially afforded prophets certainty of truth of their prophecy, namely, a mind bent only on that which is good and right. For he neither blessed nor cursed whomsoever he pleased, as Balak thought, but only those whom God willed to be blessed or cursed. That is why he answered Balak, "If Balak should give me his house full of silver and gold, I cannot go beyond the commandment of the Lord to do good or ill as I will. What the Lord saith, that shall I speak." As for the Lord being angry with him while he was on the way, the same thing befell Moses when

---

[4] [The issue of Balaam, especially the question of his prophetic status, was debated in rabbinic literature. Maimonides believed that Balaam was a legitimate prophet (*Guide*, 2.42, 45).]

he was setting out for Egypt at God's command (Exodus ch. 4 v. 24); as to his receiving money for prophesying, Samuel did the same (1 Sam. ch. 9 v. 7, 8); and if he sinned in any way (see 2 Ep. Peter ch. 2 v. 15, 16 and Jude v. 11), "there is not a just man on earth who always doeth good and sinneth not" (Eccl. ch. 7 v. 20). Indeed, his prayers must have always had much influence with God and his power of cursing must have been very considerable, since it is often found in Scripture, as testimony of God's great mercy towards the Israelites, that God would not hearken to Balaam and changed his cursing to blessing (Deut. ch. 23 v. 6, Josh. ch. 24 v. 10, Nehem. ch. 13 v. 2). He must therefore have been most acceptable to God, for the prayers and cursings of the wicked move God not at all. So since he was a true prophet, and yet Joshua (ch. 13 v. 22) referred to him as a soothsayer or augur, it is clear that this title, too, was an honourable one, and that those whom the Gentiles called augurs and soothsayers were true prophets, while those whom Scripture often accuses and condemns were false soothsayers, deceiving the Gentiles as false prophets deceived the Jews. And this is also quite clearly established from other passages of Scripture. Therefore we conclude that the gift of prophecy was not peculiar to the Jews, but was common to all nations.

The Pharisees,[5] however, vigorously contend that this divine gift was peculiar to their nation, whereas other nations (such is the ingenuity of superstition!) foretold the future with the aid of some diabolical power. The chief evidence they adduce to give authoritative support to this belief is Exodus ch. 33 v. 16, where Moses says to God, "For wherein shall it be known here that I and thy people have found grace in thy sight? Is it not when thou goest with us? So shall we be separated, I and thy people, from all the people that are on the face of the earth." From this, I repeat, they would infer that Moses besought God that he should be present to the Jews and reveal himself to them by prophecy, and, further, that he should grant this grace to no other nation. Surely, it is absurd that Moses should grudge God's presence to the Gentiles, or that he should have ventured to make such a petition to God. The fact is that when Moses realised the character and the obstinate spirit of his nation, he saw clearly that they could not accomplish their undertaking without mighty miracles and the special external help of God, and must assuredly perish without such help; and so he besought this special external help of God so that it should be evident that God willed them to be saved. For he speaks as follows (ch. 34 v. 9), "If now I have found favour in thy sight, O Lord, let my Lord, I pray thee, go among us, for it is a stiff-necked people . . ." and so on. Thus the reason why he sought God's special external help was the obstinacy of the people, and the fact that Moses sought nothing beyond this special external help is made even clearer by God's answer. For God answered at once

---

[5] [Spinoza's use of the term 'Pharisee' here is contentious and prejudicial. Although in Chapter 18 Spinoza correctly applies this term to a particular sect, or party, within the Judaism of the Roman period, here he uses it as a general term for all Jews who follow the Oral Law, codified in the Mishnah and commented upon in the Talmud. To Christians this word connoted a variety of negative attitudes deriving from the New Testament, especially the Gospel of Matthew (see especially chapter 23).]

(same chapter v. 10), "Behold, I make a covenant; before all thy people I will do marvels such as have not been done in all the earth, nor in any nation. . . ." Therefore Moses is here concerned with the choosing of the Hebrews only in the way I have explained, and sought nothing else from God.

However, in Paul's Epistle to the Romans I find another text which carries more weight with me, namely, chapter 3 v. 1, 2, where Paul's teaching appears to differ from that which we have here presented. He says, "What advantage, then, hath the Jew? Or what profit is there of circumcision? Much every way: chiefly because unto them were committed the oracles of God." But if we have regard to the main doctrine that Paul is concerned to teach, we shall find nothing at variance with the view we are here presenting; on the contrary, his doctrine is the same as ours. For in verse 29 of the same chapter he says that God is the God of both Jews and Gentiles, and in chapter 2 v. 25, 26, "If thou be a breaker of the law, thy circumcision is made uncircumcision; on the other hand, if uncircumcision keep the righteousness of the law, his uncircumcision shall be counted for circumcision." Again, in chapter 3 v. 9 and chapter 4 v. 15 he says that all alike, Jews and Gentiles, were under sin, but that there can be no sin without the commandment and the Law. This makes it quite clear (as we have also shown above from Job ch. 28 v. 28) that to all men without exception was revealed the law under which all men lived—namely, the law which has regard only to the true virtue, not that law which is established to suit the requirements of a particular state and is adapted to the character of one nation.

Finally, Paul concludes that, since God is the God of all nations—that is, he is equally gracious to all—and since all mankind were equally under the law and under sin, it was for all nations that God sent his Christ to free all men alike from the bondage of the law, so that no longer would they act righteously from the law's command but from the unwavering resolution of the heart. Thus Paul's teaching coincides exactly with ours. So when he says, "To the Jews alone were entrusted the oracles of God," we should either take it as meaning that only to the Jews were the laws entrusted in writing while to other nations they were communicated by revelation and conception alone, or we must say (since Paul's aim is to refute objections that could be raised only by the Jews) that Paul is answering in accordance with the understanding and beliefs of the Jews of that time. For in order to preach that which he had partly seen and partly heard, he was a Greek with the Greeks and a Jew with the Jews.

It now only remains for us to answer the arguments of those who would convince themselves that the election of the Jews was not a temporal matter, concerned only with their commonwealth, but was eternal; for, they say, we see that the Jews still survive in spite of having lost their commonwealth and being scattered all over the world for so many years, separated from all nations; and that this has befallen no other nation. And again, they say, there are many passages of Holy Scripture that appear to tell us that God has chosen the Jews for himself unto eternity; and so, although they have lost their commonwealth, they nevertheless remain God's chosen ones. The passages which they think most convincing in teaching this eternal election are chiefly the following:

1. Jeremiah chapter 31 v. 36, where the prophet testifies that the seed of Israel shall remain God's people unto eternity, comparing them with the fixed order of the heavens and of Nature.

2. Ezekiel chapter 20 v. 32 and following, where the prophet apparently means that, although the Jews may deliberately turn away from the worship of God, God will nevertheless gather them together again from all the lands where they are scattered and lead them to the wilderness of peoples, as he led their fathers to the wilderness of Egypt; and from there eventually, after separating them from the rebellious and the transgressors, he will bring them to his Holy Mountain, where the whole house of Israel shall worship him.

Other passages are also cited, especially by the Pharisees, but I think I shall satisfy everybody if I reply to these two. This will occasion me no difficulty when I show from Scripture itself that God did not choose the Hebrews unto eternity, but only on the same terms as he had earlier chosen the Canaanites. These also had priests (as I have shown above) who devoutly worshipped God, and yet God rejected them because of their dissolute living, their folly, and their corrupt worship. For Moses (Lev. ch. 18 v. 27, 28) warns the Israelites not to defile themselves with abominations like the Canaanites, lest the land spew them out as it had spewed out those peoples that used to dwell there. And in Deuteronomy ch. 8 v. 19, 20 he threatens them with utter destruction in the plainest possible terms, speaking as follows, "I testify against you this day that ye shall surely perish; as the nations which the Lord destroyed before your face, so shall ye perish." And many other passages to this effect are to be found in the Law, expressly indicating that God did not choose the Hebrew nation absolutely, nor unto eternity. So if the prophets foretold for them a new, eternal covenant involving the knowledge, love and grace of God, it can be easily proved that this promise was made for the godly alone. For in that same chapter of Ezekiel which we have just quoted it is explicitly stated that God will cut off from them the rebellious and the transgressors; and in Zephaniah chapter 3 v. 11, 12 that God will take from their midst the proud, leaving behind the poor. And since this election has regard to true virtue, it is not to be imagined that it was promised only to the godly among the Jews to the exclusion of all others. We must evidently believe that the true Gentile prophets, whom we have shown to be found among all nations, made the same promise to the faithful of their own nations and comforted them thereby. Therefore this eternal covenant involving the knowledge and love of God is universal, as is clearly shown from Zephaniah chapter 3 v. 10, 11, so that in this respect no difference can be granted between Jews and Gentiles, nor therefore any special election of the Jews beyond that which we have already indicated.

As to the fact that the prophets, in speaking of this election which refers only to true virtue, intermingled many sayings regarding sacrifices and other ceremonies and the rebuilding of the Temple and the city, such figurative expressions, after the manner and nature of prophecy, were intended to convey a spiritual message, so that they might also indicate to the Jews, whose prophets they were, the impending restoration of their commonwealth and temple, to be expected at the time of Cyrus. Therefore at the present time there is nothing whatsoever that the Jews can arrogate to themselves above other nations.

As to their continued existence for so many years when scattered and stateless, this is in no way surprising, since they have separated themselves from other nations to such a degree as to incur the hatred of all, and this not only through external rites alien to the rites of other nations but also through the mark of circumcision, which they most religiously observe. That they are preserved largely through the hatred of other nations is demonstrated by historical fact. When the King of Spain formerly compelled the Jews to embrace the religion of his kingdom or else to go into exile, a considerable number of Jews accepted Catholicism. Now since all the privileges of native Spaniards were granted to those who embraced their religion, and they were then considered worthy of full civic rights, they were so speedily assimilated to the Spaniards that after a short while no trace of them was left, nor any remembrance. But just the opposite fate befell those whom the King of Portugal compelled to embrace his country's religion. Although converted to this religion, they lived on their own, because the king declared them unworthy of civic rights.[6]

The mark of circumcision, too, I consider to be such an important factor in this matter that I am convinced that this by itself will preserve their nation forever. Indeed, were it not that the fundamental principles of their religion discourage manliness, I would not hesitate to believe that they will one day, given the opportunity—such is the mutability of human affairs—establish once more their independent state, and that God will again choose them.[7] The Chinese afford us an outstanding example of such a possibility. They, too, religiously observe the custom of the pigtail which sets them apart from all other people, and they have preserved themselves as a separate people for so many thousands of years that they far surpass all other nations in antiquity. They have not always maintained their independence, but they did regain it after losing it, and will no doubt recover it again when the spirit of the Tartars becomes enfeebled by reason of luxurious living and sloth.

In conclusion, should anyone be disposed to argue that the Jews, for this reason or any other, have been chosen by God unto eternity, I shall not oppose him, provided that he holds that this election, be it temporal or eternal, insofar as it is peculiar to the Jews, is concerned only with the nature of their commonwealth

---

[6] [Spinoza tries to make a distinction between the Inquisition in Spain and the one in Portugal. But he overestimates the openness of Spanish society and government to converted Jews. Not too long after the establishment of the Inquisition in Spain, "laws of blood purity" were passed to prevent converted Jews from obtaining important positions in Spanish government and in the church. Many Spanish Jewish converts attempted to preserve secretly some aspects of Jewish belief and practice while they led Christian lives in public.]

[7] [This passage has had an interesting "history." Some of the early Zionist theoreticians and leaders (e.g., David ben Gurion) saw in this passage hints of the revival of an independent Jewish state grounded in a secular ideology. It is highly unlikely, however, that Spinoza himself had any such thoughts.]

and their material welfare (since this is the only distinguishing mark between one nation and another); whereas in respect of understanding and true virtue there is no distinction between one nation and another, and in regard to these matters God has not chosen one nation before another.

CHAPTER 4

Of the Divine Law

The word law, taken in its absolute sense, means that according to which each individual thing—either all in general or those of the same kind—act in one and the same fixed and determinate manner, this manner depending either on Nature's necessity or on human will. A law which depends on Nature's necessity is one which necessarily follows from the very nature of the thing, that is, its definition; a law which depends on human will, and which could more properly be termed a statute [*ius*], is one which men ordain for themselves and for others with view to making life more secure and more convenient, or for other reasons.

For example, the fact that all bodies colliding with smaller bodies lose as much of their own motion as they impart to other bodies is a universal law governing all bodies, and follows from Nature's necessity. Similarly, the fact that a man, in remembering one thing, forthwith calls to mind another like it, or which he has seen along with it, is a law that necessarily follows from the nature of man. But the fact that men give up, or are compelled to give up, their natural right and bind themselves to live under fixed rules, depends on human will. And although I grant that, in an absolute sense, all things are determined by the universal laws of Nature to exist and to act in a definite and determinate way,[1] I still say that these latter laws depend on human will. My reasons are as follows:

1. Man, insofar as he is part of Nature, constitutes a part of the power of Nature. Thus whatever follows from the necessity of man's nature—that is, from Nature as we conceive her to be determinately expressed in man's nature—follows from human power, even though it does so necessarily. Therefore the enacting of these man-made laws may quite legitimately be said to depend on human will, for it depends especially on the power of the human mind in the following respect, that the human mind, insofar as it is concerned with the perception of truth and falsity, can be quite clearly conceived without these man-made laws, whereas it cannot be conceived without Nature's necessary law, as defined above.

2. We ought to define and explain things through their proximate causes. Generalisations about fate and the interconnection of causes can be of no service to

---

[1] [Spinoza, *Ethics*, 1.29, 33.]

us in forming and ordering our thoughts concerning particular things. Furthermore, we plainly have no knowledge as to the actual co-ordination and interconnection of things—that is, the way in which things are in actual fact ordered and connected—so that for practical purposes it is better, indeed, it is essential, to consider things as contingent. So much for law taken in the absolute sense.

Still, it seems to be by analogy that the word law is applied to natural phenomena, and ordinarily 'law' is used to mean simply a command which men can either obey or disobey, inasmuch as it restricts the total range of human power within set limits and demands nothing that is beyond the capacity of that power. So it seems more fitting that law should be defined in its narrower sense, that is, as a rule of life which man prescribes for himself or for others for some purpose. However, since the true purpose of law is usually apparent only to the few and is generally incomprehensible by the great majority in whose lives reason plays little part, in order to constrain all men alike legislators have wisely devised another motive for obedience, far different from that which is necessarily entailed by the nature of law. For those who uphold the law they promised what most appeals to the masses, while threatening transgressors with dire retribution, thus endeavouring to keep the multitude on a curb, as far as is practicable. Thus it came about that law was mainly regarded as rules of conduct imposed on men through the supremacy of others, and consequently those who obey the law are said to live under the law and appear to be in bondage. And in truth he who renders to each his own through fear of the gallows is constrained in his action by another's command and threat of punishment, and cannot be called a just man. But he who renders to each his own through awareness of the true principle of law and its necessity, is acting steadfastly and at his own will, not another's, and so he is rightly termed a just man. This I take to be Paul's intended meaning when he said that those who lived under the law could not be justified through the law; for justice, as commonly defined, is the steadfast and constant will to render to each his own. It is for this reason, too, that Solomon said in Proverbs ch. 21 v. 15, "It is a joy to the just when judgment is done; but the workers of iniquity are in fear."

So since law is simply a rule of conduct which men lay down for themselves or for others to some end, it can be divided into human and divine law. By human law I mean a prescribed rule of conduct whose sole aim is to safeguard life and the commonwealth; by divine law I mean that which is concerned only with the supreme good, that is, the true knowledge and love of God. This law I call divine because of the nature of the supreme good, which I shall now briefly explain as clearly as I can.

Since our intellect forms the better part of us, it is evident that, if we wish to seek what is definitely to our advantage, we should endeavour above all to perfect it as far as we can, for in its perfection must consist our supreme good. Now since all our knowledge, and the certainty that banishes every possible doubt, depend solely on the knowledge of God—because, firstly, without God nothing can be or be conceived, and secondly, everything can be called into doubt as long as we have no clear and distinct idea of God[2]—it follows that our supreme good and

---

[2] [Spinoza, *Ethics*, 1.15; TIE, 39, 49, 79.]

perfection depends solely on the knowledge of God. Again, since nothing can be or be conceived without God, it is clear that everything in Nature involves and expresses the conception of God in proportion to its essence and perfection; and therefore we acquire a greater and more perfect knowledge of God as we gain more knowledge of natural phenomena. To put it another way, since the knowledge of an effect through its cause is nothing other than the knowledge of a property of that cause, the greater our knowledge of natural phenomena, the more perfect is our knowledge of God's essence, which is the cause of all things. So the whole of our knowledge, that is, our supreme good, not merely depends on the knowledge of God but consists entirely therein. This also follows from the principle that man's perfection is the greater, or the reverse, according to the nature and perfection of the thing that he loves above all others. So he who loves above all the intellectual cognition of God, the most perfect Being, and takes especial delight therein, is necessarily most perfect, and partakes most in the highest blessedness.

This, then, is the sum of our supreme good and blessedness,[3] to wit, the knowledge and love of God. So the means required to achieve this end of all human action—that is, God insofar as his idea exists in us—may be termed God's commands, for they are ordained for us by God himself, as it were, insofar as he exists in our minds. So the rules for living a life that has regard to this end can fitly be called the Divine Law. An enquiry as to what these means are, and what are the rules of conduct required for this end, and how there follow therefrom the fundamental principles of the good commonwealth and social organisation, belongs to a general treatise on Ethics. Here my discussion will be confined to a general consideration of the Divine Law.

Since the love of God is man's highest happiness and blessedness, and the final end and aim of all human action, it follows that only he observes the Divine Law who makes it his object to love God not through fear of punishment nor through love of some other thing such as sensual pleasure, fame and so forth, but from the mere fact that he knows God, or knows that the knowledge and love of God is the supreme good. So the sum of the Divine Law and its chief command is to love God as the supreme good; that is, as we have said, not from fear of some punishment or penalty nor from love of some other thing from which we desire to derive pleasure. For this truth is told us by the idea of God, that God is our supreme good, i.e. that the knowledge and love of God is the final end to which all our actions should be directed. But carnal man cannot understand these things; he thinks them foolish because he has too stunted a knowledge of God, and in this supreme good, it does only in philosophic thinking and pure activity of mind, he finds nothing to touch, to eat, or to feed the fleshly appetites which are his chief delight. But those who recognise that they have no more precious gift than intellect and a sound mind are sure to regard these as very substantial blessings.

---

[3] [*Ethics*, 5.24–27, 30–33.]

We have now explained the essential nature of the Divine Law, and have defined human laws as all those which have a different aim. But from the latter category we must except laws that have been sanctioned by revelation, for in this case, too, things are referred to God, as we have already shown. And in this sense the Law of Moses, although it was not of universal application but specially adapted to the character and preservation of one particular people, can nevertheless be termed the Law of God, or Divine Law, since we believe it to have been sanctioned by prophetic insight.

If we now consider the nature of the natural Divine Law as we have just explained it, we shall see:

1. That it is of universal application, or common to all mankind. For we have deduced it from human nature as such.

2. That it does not demand belief in historical narratives of any kind whatsoever. For since it is merely a consideration of human nature that leads us to this natural Divine Law, evidently it applies equally to Adam as to any other man, and equally to a man living in a community as to a hermit. Nor can the belief in historical narratives, however certain, give us knowledge of God, nor, consequently, of the love of God. For the love of God arises from the knowledge of God, a knowledge deriving from general axioms that are certain and self-evident, and so belief in historical narratives is by no means essential to the attainment of our supreme good. However, although belief in historical narratives cannot afford us the knowledge and love of God, I do not deny that their study can be very profitable in the matter of social relations. For the more we observe and the better we are acquainted with the ways and manners of men—and it is their actions that best provide this knowledge—the more prudently we can live among them, and the more effectively we can adapt our actions and conduct to their character, as far as reason allows.

3. We see that the natural Divine Law does not enjoin ceremonial rites, that is, actions which in themselves are of no significance and are termed good merely by tradition, or which symbolise some good necessary for salvation, or, if you prefer, actions whose explanation surpasses human understanding. For the natural light of reason enjoins nothing that is not within the compass of reason, but only what it can show us quite clearly to be a good, or a means to our blessedness. The things whose goodness derives only from authority and tradition, or from their symbolic representation of some good, cannot perfect our intellect; they are mere shadows, and cannot be counted as actions that are, as it were, the offspring and fruit of intellect and sound mind. There is no need for me to go further into this matter.

4. Finally, we see that the supreme reward of the Divine Law is the law itself, namely, to know God and to love him in true freedom with all our heart and mind. The penalty it imposes is the deprivation of these things and bondage to the flesh, that is, an inconstant and irresolute spirit.

Having made these points, we must now enquire:

1. Whether by the natural light of reason we can conceive God as a lawgiver or ruler, ordaining laws for men.

2. What is the teaching of Holy Scripture concerning this natural light and law.
3. For what purpose were ceremonial rites originally instituted.
4. What good is served by knowing the sacred historical narratives, and by believing them.

The first two questions I shall discuss in this chapter, reserving the last two for the next chapter.

Our conclusion as to the first question is easily deduced from the nature of God's will, which is not distinct from his intellect except from the perspective of human reason. That is to say, God's will and God's intellect[4] in themselves are in reality one and the same thing; they are distinct only in relation to the thoughts we form when we think of God's intellect. For example, when we have regard only to the fact that the nature of a triangle is eternally contained in the divine nature as an eternal truth, then we say that God has the idea of a triangle, or that he understands the nature of a triangle. But when thereafter we consider the fact that it is solely from the necessity of the divine nature, and not from the necessity of the essence and nature of a triangle, that the nature of a triangle is thus contained in the divine nature—or rather, the necessity of the essence and properties of a triangle, insofar as they are also conceived as eternal truths, depends not on the nature of a triangle but solely on the necessity of the divine nature and intellect—then that which we termed God's intellect we call God's will or decree. Therefore in respect of God our affirmation is one and the same, whether we say that God has eternally willed and decreed that the three angles of a triangle should be equal to two right angles, or that God has understood this fact.

Hence it follows that God's affirmations and negations always involve eternal necessity or truth. So if, for example, God said to Adam that he willed that Adam should not eat of the tree of knowledge of good and evil, it would have been a contradiction in terms for Adam to be able to eat of that tree. And so it would have been impossible for Adam to eat of it, because that divine decree must have involved eternal necessity and truth. However, since Scripture tells us that God did so command Adam, and that Adam did nevertheless eat of the tree, it must be accepted that God revealed to Adam only the punishment he must incur if he should eat of that tree; the necessary entailment of that punishment was not revealed. Consequently, Adam perceived this revelation not as an eternal and necessary truth but as a law, that is to say, an enactment from which good or ill consequence would ensue not from the intrinsic nature of deed performed but only from the will and absolute power of some ruler. Therefore that revelation, solely in relation to Adam and solely because of the limitations of his knowledge, was a law, and God was a kind of lawgiver or ruler. For this same reason, namely, their lack of knowledge, in relation to the Hebrews alone the Decalogue was a law; for,

---

[4] [*Ethics*, 1.32.]

not knowing God's existence as an eternal truth, it was inevitable that they should have perceived as a law what was revealed to them in the Decalogue, namely, that God existed, and that God alone must be worshipped. But if God had spoken to them directly, employing no physical means, they would have perceived this not as a law, but as an eternal truth.

What we are here saying about the Israelites and Adam also applies to all the prophets who laid down laws in God's name; they did not perceive God's decrees adequately, as eternal truths. For example, in the case of Moses, too, we have to say that, as a result of revelation or basic principles revealed to him, he perceived a way by which the people of Israel could well be united in a particular territory to form a political union or state, and also a way by which that people could well be constrained to obedience. But he did not perceive, nor was it revealed to him, that this way was the best of all ways, nor that the end for which they were striving would be a consequence necessarily entailed by the general obedience of the people in such a territory. Therefore he perceived all these things not as eternal truths, but as instructions and precepts, and he ordained them as laws of God. Hence it came about that he imagined God as a ruler, lawgiver, king, merciful, just and so forth; whereas these are all merely attributes of human nature, and not at all applicable to the divine nature.

Now what I have said applies only to the prophets who laid down laws in God's name, but not to Christ. With regard to Christ, although he also appears to have laid down laws in God's name, we must maintain that he perceived things truly and adequately; for Christ was not so much a prophet as the mouthpiece of God. It was through the mind of Christ (as we showed in Chapter 1) that God made revelations to mankind just as he once did through angels, i.e. through a created voice, visions etc. Therefore to maintain that God adapted his revelation to Christ's beliefs would be equally irrational as to maintain that God formerly adapted his revelations to the beliefs of angels in communication, that is, to the beliefs of a created voice and visions, so as to communicate to the prophets what was to be revealed. This would be the height of absurdity, especially so since Christ was sent to teach not only the Jews but the entire human race. Thus it was not enough for him to have a mind adapted to the beliefs of the Jews alone; his mind had to be adapted to the beliefs and doctrines held in common by all mankind, that is, to those axioms that are universally true. And surely this fact, that God revealed himself to Christ, or to Christ's mind, directly, and not through words and images as in the case of the prophets, can have only this meaning, that Christ perceived truly, or understood, what was revealed. For it is when a thing is perceived by pure thought, without words or images, that it is understood.[5]

Christ, then, perceived truly and adequately the things revealed to him; so if ever he proclaimed these things as law, he did so because of the people's ignorance and obstinacy. Therefore in this matter he acted in God's place, adapting

---

[5] [*Ethics*, 2.40, Scholium 2.]

himself to the character of the people. So although his sayings were somewhat clearer than those of other prophets, his teaching of things revealed was still obscure and quite often took the form of parables, especially when he was addressing those to whom it had not yet been granted to understand the kingdom of Heaven (see Matth. ch. 13 v. 10, and ff.). But doubtless, to those to whom it was granted to know the mysteries of Heaven, his teaching took the form of eternal truths, not of prescribed laws. In this way he freed them from bondage to the law, while nevertheless giving further strength and stability to the law, inscribing it deep in their hearts.

Paul, too, appears to be making the same point in certain passages, namely, in his Epistle to the Romans, chapter 7 v. 6 and chapter 3 v. 28. Yet he, too, is unwilling to speak openly, but, as he says in the same Epistle chapter 3 v. 5 and in chapter 6 v. 19 he speaks only after the manner of men. This he expressly states when he calls God just, and it was undoubtedly in concession to the frailty of the flesh that he also ascribes to God mercy, grace, anger, and so forth, adapting his words to the character of the common people, or (as he also says in the First Epistle to the Corinthians, chapter 3 v. 1, 2) to the character of carnal man. For in the Epistle to the Romans chapter 9 v. 18 he tells us outright that God's anger and mercy depend not on man's works but on God's vocation, that is, his will; and further, that no one is justified from the works of the law, but only from faith (see Epistle to the Romans chapter 3 v. 28), by which he surely means nothing other than the full consent of the mind. Lastly, he says that no one becomes blessed unless he has in himself the mind of Christ (Rom. ch. 8 v. 9), meaning that he would thereby perceive the laws of God as eternal truths.

We therefore conclude that it is only in concession to the understanding of the multitude and the defectiveness of their thought that God is described as a lawgiver or ruler, and is called just, merciful and so on, and that in reality God acts and governs all things solely from the necessity of his own nature and perfection, and his decrees and volitions are eternal truths, always involving necessity.[6] So much for the first point I had proposed to explain and demonstrate.

Let us, then, pass on to the second point, and perusing the Holy Writ, let us see what it tells us concerning the natural light of reason and this Divine Law. The first thing we encounter is the narrative of the first man, where we are told that God forbade Adam to eat of the tree of knowledge of good and evil. This seems to mean that God commanded Adam to do good and to seek it for its goodness, not insofar as it is contrary to evil; that is, to seek good from love of good, and not from fear of evil. For, as we have shown, he who does good from true knowledge and love of good acts freely and with a steadfast mind, whereas he who does good from fear of evil acts under constraint of evil, in bondage, and lives under another's sway. This single command given by God to Adam comprehends the natural Divine Law in its entirety, and is in absolute agreement with the dictates

---

[6] [*Ethics*, 1.16.]

of the natural light of reason. It would not be difficult to explain on this basis the whole narrative or parable of the first man, but I refrain from so doing for two reasons. First, I cannot be absolutely sure that my explanation would be in agreement with the author's intention; secondly, there are many who do not grant that this narrative is a parable, firmly maintaining that it is a straightforward account of fact.

It will therefore be better to adduce other passages of Scripture, especially the words of one who speaks from the power of the natural light wherein he surpassed all the sages of his time, one whose sayings have been accepted by the people as having the same sanctity as those of the prophets. I refer to Solomon, who is commended in the Scriptures not so much for prophecy and piety as for prudence and wisdom. In his Proverbs he calls man's intellect the fount of true life, and regards misfortune as consisting only in folly. Thus, he says in chapter 16 v. 22, "Understanding (is) a wellspring of life to him that hath it,* and the punishment of fools is their folly." Here it should be noted that in Hebrew the word 'life' without qualification signifies 'true life', as is clear from Deuteronomy chapter 30 v. 19. He thus identifies the fruit of intellect with true life alone, its privation being itself a punishment, in complete agreement with our remarks on the fourth point concerning the Divine Law. That this fountain of life, i.e. the intellect alone, prescribes laws for the wise—as we have also shown—is plainly taught by this same sage. For he says in chapter 13 v. 14, "The law of the wise is a fountain of life," that is, as is clear from the text just quoted, the intellect. Again, in chapter 3 v. 13 he tells us most explicitly that the intellect makes a man blessed and happy and affords true peace of mind. For he says, "Happy is the man that findeth wisdom, and the son of man that getteth understanding." This is because, as he goes on to say in v. 16, 17, "Length of days** is in her right hand, and in her left hand riches and honour. Her ways" (that is, the ways pointed out by knowledge) "are ways of pleasantness, and all her paths are peace." So Solomon, too, holds the opinion that only the wise live with tranquil and steadfast mind, unlike the wicked, whose minds are agitated by conflicting emotions; and so (as Isaiah, too, says in chapter 57 v. 20) they have neither peace nor rest.

Finally, we should particularly note the passages in the second chapter of the Proverbs of Solomon, which most clearly confirm our view. For in verse 3 of that chapter he begins thus, "If thou criest after knowledge and liftest up thy voice for understanding . . . then shalt thou understand the fear of the Lord and find knowledge of the Lord." ('Knowledge' may perhaps be 'love', for the Hebrew word 'Jadah' can have both meanings.) "For the Lord" (note well) "giveth wisdom. Out of his mouth cometh knowledge and understanding." By these words he is surely indicating as clearly as can be, first, that only wisdom or intellect teaches us to fear

---

* Latin—*domini*. A Hebrew idiom. That which possesses something, or contains it in its nature, is called lord of that thing. Thus a bird is called lord of wings in Hebrew, because it possesses wings; an intelligent being is called lord of intellect, because it possesses intellect.

** A Hebrew idiom, meaning simply 'life.'

God wisely, that is, to worship him with true devotion; and secondly, that wisdom and knowledge flow from the mouth of God and God bestows this upon us. This is the point we have also demonstrated above, namely, that our intellect and knowledge depend solely on the idea or our understanding of God, and spring from it and are perfected by it. Then Solomon goes on to say most explicitly, in verse 9, that this knowledge includes the true principles of Ethics and Politics, which can be deduced therefrom. "Then shalt thou understand righteousness and judgment and equity, yea, every good path." Not content with this, he continues, "When wisdom entereth into thy heart and knowledge is pleasant unto thy soul, discretion* shall preserve thee, and understanding shall keep thee." All this is plainly in accord with natural knowledge, for it is natural knowledge that teaches us ethics and true virtue, once we have arrived at the knowledge of things and have tasted the excellence of understanding.

Thus Solomon, too, takes the view that the happiness and peace of the man who cultivates his natural understanding depends mainly not on the sway of fortune (that is, on God's external help) but on his own internal virtue (or God's internal help), because he owes his self-preservation mainly to his own vigilance, conduct and wise counsel.

Finally, we must here by no means omit the passage in Paul's Epistle to the Romans chapter 1 v. 20, where he speaks thus (as Tremellius translates from the Syriac text), "For the invisible things of God from the creation of the world are clearly seen through the intellect in the things that are made, even his power and his Godhead which is unto eternity, so that they are without excuse." Here he quite clearly indicates that, by the natural light of reason, all can clearly understand the power and eternal divinity of God, from which they can know and infer what they should seek and what they should avoid. So he concludes that all are without excuse and cannot plead ignorance, which they could assuredly do if he were speaking of a supernatural light, and of the passion and resurrection of Christ in the flesh, and so forth. And he therefore continues a little later at verse 24 as follows, "Therefore God gave them up to the unclean lusts of their hearts..." through the rest of the chapter, describing the vices of ignorance and setting them forth as the punishment of ignorance. This is plainly in accord with the Proverbs of Solomon, chapter 16 v. 22, which we have already quoted, "The punishment of fools is their folly." It is not surprising, then, that Paul says that the wicked are without excuse. For as each sows, so shall he reap; out of evil, unless it be wisely corrected, evil inevitably follows, and out of good, good, if hearts be steadfast.

Therefore Scripture unreservedly commends the natural light and the natural Divine Law. And with this I have completed the task undertaken in this chapter.

---

* The Hebrew word 'mezima' properly means thought, deliberation and vigilance.

CHAPTER 5

*Of the reason for the institution of ceremonial observances.
Belief in the Biblical narratives: in what way
and for whom it is necessary*

In the previous chapter we showed that the Divine Law, which makes men truly blessed and teaches the true life, is of universal application to all men. Indeed, our method of deducing it from human nature shows that it must be considered as innate in the human mind and inscribed therein, as it were. Now ceremonial observances—those, at least, that are laid down in the Old Testament—were instituted for the Hebrews alone, and were so adapted to the nature of their government that they could not be practised by the individual but involved the community as a whole. So it is evident that they do not pertain to the Divine Law, and therefore do not contribute to blessedness and virtue. They have regard only to the election of the Hebrews, that is (as we demonstrated in Chapter 3), to their temporal and material prosperity and peaceful government, and therefore could have been of practical value only while their state existed. If in the Old Testament we find them included in God's law, this can only be because they owed their institution to revelation, or to principles revealed therein. However, since reason, be it of the soundest, carries little weight with the common run of theologians, I now intend to confirm by Scriptural authority what we have just demonstrated; and then, for greater clarity, I shall go on to show how and why ceremonial observances served to strengthen and preserve the Jewish state.

Of all Isaiah's teachings nothing is clearer than this, that the Divine Law, taken in a strict sense, signifies not ceremonial observance, but the universal law that consists in the true way of life. In chapter 1 v. 10, where the prophet calls upon his countrymen to hear from him the Divine Law, he first excludes from it sacrifices of every kind and all festivals, and then goes on to teach the law itself (see verses 16, 17) which he summarises under these few headings: cleanliness of heart, the habit or practice of virtue, or good actions, and succouring the helpless. Testimony no less striking is given by the passage in Psalm 40 v. 6, 8, where the Psalmist addresses God, "Sacrifice and offering thou didst not desire, mine ears hast thou opened;* burnt offering and sin-offering hast thou not required; I delight to do thy will, O my God; yea, thy law is within my heart." So it is only what is inscribed in the heart, or mind, that the Psalmist calls God's law, and he excludes from it ceremonial observances; for the latter are good not by nature but by convention, and so are not inscribed in the heart. Besides these passages, Scripture contains others giving the same testimony, but it is enough to have cited these two.

---

* A Hebrew expression signifying understanding.

The fact that the observance of ceremonies has regard only to the temporal prosperity of the state and in no way contributes to blessedness is also evident from Scripture, which for ceremonial observance promises nothing but material advantages and pleasures, while blessedness is promised only for observance of the universal Divine Law. In the five books commonly attributed to Moses the only promise made, as I have already said, is worldly success—honours or fame, victory, riches, life's pleasures and health. And although these five books contain much about moral teaching as well as ceremonial observance, these passages are not set forth as moral teachings of universal application to all men, but as commands particularly adapted to the understanding and character of only their state. For example, it is not as a teacher or prophet that Moses forbids the Jews to kill or to steal; it is as a lawgiver or ruler that he issues these commands. He does not justify his precepts by reasoning, but attaches to his commands a penalty, a penalty which can vary, and must vary, to suit the character of each single nation, as we well know from experience. So, too, his command not to commit adultery has regard only to the good of the commonwealth and state. If he had intended this to be a moral precept that had regard not merely to the good of the commonwealth but to the peace of mind and the true blessedness of the individual, he would have condemned not merely the external act but the very wish, as did Christ, who taught only universal moral precepts (see Matth. ch. 5 v. 28). It is for this reason that Christ promises a spiritual reward, not, like Moses, a material reward. For Christ, as I have said, was sent not to preserve the state and to institute laws, but only to teach the universal law. Hence, we can readily understand that Christ by no means abrogated the law of Moses, for it was not Christ's purpose to introduce new laws into the commonwealth. His chief concern was to teach moral doctrines, keeping them distinct from the laws of the commonwealth. This was mainly on account of the ignorance of the Pharisees, who thought that the blessed life was his who observed the laws of the commonwealth, i.e. the law of Moses; whereas, in fact, this law concerned only public good, and its aim was to coerce the Hebrews rather than instruct them.

But let us return to our theme, and cite other passages of Scripture which promise for ceremonial observance nothing but material benefits, reserving blessedness solely for the universal Divine Law. None of the prophets spoke more clearly on this subject than Isaiah. In chapter 58, after his condemnation of hypocrisy he commends the freeing of the oppressed and charity towards oneself and one's neighbour, promising in return, "Then shall thy light break forth as the morning, and thine health shall spring forth speedily, and thy righteousness shall go before thee; the glory of the Lord shall gather thee in."* Then he goes on to commend the Sabbath, too, and for its diligent observance he promises, "Then shalt thou delight thyself in the Lord,** and I shall cause thee to ride upon the high places of the earth,*** and feed thee with the heritage of Jacob, thy father; for the mouth of the

---

* A Hebrew expression referring to death. 'To be gathered unto one's people' means to die. See Genesis chapter 49 v. 29, 33.

** Means 'to take honourable pleasure,' as in the Dutch saying, 'Met Godt en met eere.'

*** Means 'to hold sway,' like holding a horse on the rein.

Lord hath spoken it." So we see that, in return for the freeing of the oppressed and for charity, the prophet promises a healthy mind in a healthy body, and the glory of the Lord even after death; but in return for the observance of ceremonies he promises only the security of the state, prosperity, and material success.

In Psalms 15 and 24 no mention is made of ceremonies but only of moral doctrine, obviously because their only theme is blessedness, and this alone is set before us, although by way of parable. For it is evident that by 'the hill of God' and 'his tabernacle' and the abiding therein is meant blessedness and peace of mind, not the mount of Jerusalem nor the tent of Moses; for nobody dwelt in these places, and they were looked after by those of the tribe of Levi. Then again, all those sayings of Solomon which I quoted in the previous chapter also promise true blessedness simply in return for the cultivation of intellect and wisdom, for from wisdom will the fear of God come to be understood, and the knowledge of God be found.

That the Hebrews are not bound to practise their ceremonial rites since the destruction of their state is clear from Jeremiah, who, when he saw and proclaimed the imminent ruin of the city, said that God delights only in those who know and understand that he exercises lovingkindness, judgment and righteousness in the earth, and so thereafter only those who know these things are to be deemed worthy of praise (see chapter 9 v. 23). This is as much as to say that after the destruction of the city, God demanded no special service of the Jews and sought nothing of them thereafter except the natural law by which all men are bound.

The New Testament, too, plainly supports this view; for, as I have said, it teaches only moral doctrine and the promised reward is the Kingdom of Heaven, while the Apostles made no mention of ceremonial rites once they had extended the preaching of the Gospel to other nations who were bound by the laws of a different commonwealth. The Pharisees did indeed retain these rites, or a great part of them, after the loss of their independent state; but their object in so doing was to oppose the Christians rather than to please God. For when they were led away in captivity to Babylon after the first destruction of the city, they straightway abandoned their observance of ceremonies. Indeed, they turned their backs on the entire Mosaic Law, consigned to oblivion the laws of their native land as being obviously pointless, and began to be assimilated to other nations, as Ezra and Nehemiah make abundantly clear. Therefore there is no doubt that, since the fall of their independent state, Jews are no more bound by the Mosaic Law than they were before their political state came into being. For while they were living among other nations before the exodus from Egypt, they had no special laws to themselves; they were bound by no law other than the natural law, and doubtless the law of the state in which they dwelt, insofar as that was not opposed to the natural Divine Law.

As to the fact that the Patriarchs offered sacrifice to God, I think they did this in order to stimulate a feeling of reverence in their minds, which were accustomed from childhood to seeing sacrifice offered. For all men from the time of Enoch were quite familiar with the offering of sacrifice, and consequently this was the principle means of inducing reverence. Thus the Patriarchs sacrificed to God not through some command imposed on them by God, nor because they were instructed by the universal principles of the Divine Law, but only from contemporary custom. And if they did so by anyone's command, that command was simply the existing law of the commonwealth in which they were dwelling, by which they, too, were bound, as we have remarked both in this chapter and in Chapter 3 when speaking of Melchizedek.

With these quotations I think I have confirmed my view by Scriptural authority. It now remains for me to show how and why ceremonial rites served to preserve and strengthen the Hebrew state. This I shall demonstrate as briefly as possible, arguing from universally valid principles.

The formation of a society is advantageous, even absolutely essential, not merely for security against enemies but for the efficient organisation of an economy. If men did not afford one another mutual aid, they would lack both the skill and the time to support and preserve themselves to the greatest possible extent. All men are not equally suited to all activities, and no single person would be capable of supplying all his own needs. Each would find strength and time fail him if he alone had to plough, sow, reap, grind, cook, weave, stitch and perform all the other numerous tasks to support life, not to mention the arts and sciences which are also indispensable for the perfection of human nature and its blessedness. We see that those who live in a barbarous way with no civilising influences lead a wretched and almost brutish existence, and even so their few poor and crude resources are not acquired without some degree of mutual help.

Now if men were so constituted by nature as to desire nothing but what is prescribed by true reason, society would stand in no need of any laws. Nothing would be required but to teach men true moral doctrine, and they would then act to their true advantage of their own accord, whole-heartedly and freely. But human nature is far differently constituted. All men do, indeed, seek their own advantage, but by no means from the dictates of sound reason. For the most part the objectives they seek and judge to be beneficial are determined only by fleshly desire, and they are carried away by their emotions, which take no account of the future or of other considerations. Hence no society can subsist without government and coercion, and consequently without laws to control and restrain men's lusts and their unbridled urges. Yet human nature will not submit to unlimited repression, and, as Seneca[1] says in his tragedy, rule that depends on violence has never long continued; moderate rule endures. For as long as men act only from fear, they are doing what they are most opposed to doing, taking no account of the usefulness and the necessity of the action to be done, concerned only not to incur capital or other punishment. Indeed, they inevitably rejoice at misfortune or injury to their ruler even when this involves their own considerable misfortune, and they wish every ill on him, and bring this about when they can. Again, men are impatient above all at being subject to their equals and under their rule. Finally, there is nothing more difficult than to take away freedom from men to whom it has once been granted.

---

[1] [In the *Troades*. The same quotation occurs in Chapter 16.—S.S.]

From this it follows, first, that either the entire community, if possible, should hold the reins of government as a single body, so that all are thus required to render obedience to themselves and no one to his equal; or, alternatively, if sovereignty is invested in a few men or in one alone, he should be endowed with some extraordinary quality, or must at least make every effort to convince the masses of this. Secondly, in every state laws should be so devised that men may be influenced not so much by fear as by hope of some good that they urgently desire; for in this way each will be eager to do his duty. Finally, since obedience consists in carrying out orders simply by reason of the authority of a ruler, it follows that this has no place in a community where sovereignty is vested in all the citizens, and laws are sanctioned by common consent. In such a community the people would remain equally free whether laws were multiplied or diminished, since it would act not from another's bidding but from its own consent. But the opposite is the case when sovereignty is vested absolutely in one man alone; for all do the state's bidding on the authority of only one man. So unless they have been brought up from the beginning to give unquestioning obedience to a ruler, he will find it difficult to institute new laws when they are needed and to deprive the people of a freedom that has once been granted.

From these general considerations let us pass on to the particular case of the commonwealth of the Hebrews. When they first went out from Egypt, being no longer bound by the laws of any nation, they were at liberty to sanction any new laws they pleased or to establish new ordinances, to maintain a state wherever they wished and to occupy any lands they wished. However, the task of establishing a wise system of laws and of keeping the government in the hands of the whole community was quite beyond them; for they were in general inexperienced in such matters and exhausted by the wretched conditions of slavery. Therefore government had to remain in the hands of one man who would issue commands and enforce them on others; who would, in short, ordain laws and thereafter interpret them. Such sovereignty Moses easily succeeded in keeping in his hands, because he surpassed all others in divine power which he convinced the people that he possessed, providing many proofs thereof (see Exodus chapter 14 last verse and chapter 19 v. 9). He, then, by the divine power with which he was gifted, established a system of law and ordained it for the people. But in so doing he made every effort to see that the people should do their duty willingly rather than through fear. To this he was urged by two considerations, the obstinate nature of a people who cannot be coerced merely by force, and the imminence of war. To achieve military success soldiers have to be encouraged rather than terrorised by threats of punishment, for in this way each will seek to distinguish himself by valorous deeds and courage, and not merely try to avoid punishment. This, then, was the reason why Moses, by his divine power and authority, introduced a state religion: it was to make the people do their duty from devotion rather than fear. Furthermore, he bound them by consideration of benefits received, while promising many more benefits from God in the future. And the laws he established were not unduly harsh, as anyone who studies them will readily grant, especially if he considers the number of circumstantial details required for the conviction of the accused.[2]

Finally, in order that a people incapable of self-rule should be utterly subservient to its ruler, he did not allow these men, habituated as they were to slavery, to perform any action at their own discretion. The people could do nothing without being required at the same time to remember the law and to follow its commands, which were dependent solely on the ruler's will. Ploughing, sowing, reaping were not permitted at their discretion, but had to accord with the fixed and determinate command of the law. They could not even eat, dress, cut their hair, shave, make merry or do anything whatsoever except in accordance with commands and instructions laid down by the law. And this was not all; they had to have certain signs on their doorposts, on their hands and between the eyes, to give them constant reminder of the duty of obedience.

This, then, was the object of ceremonial observance, that men should never act of their own volition but always at another's behest, and that in their actions and inward thoughts they should at all times acknowledge that they were not their own masters but completely subordinate to another. From all these considerations it is quite indisputable that ceremonial observances contribute nothing to blessedness, and that those specified in the Old Testament, and indeed the whole Mosaic Law, were relevant only to the Hebrew state, and consequently to no more than temporal prosperity.

With regard to Christian ceremonies, namely, baptism, the Lord's Supper, festivals, public prayers and all the other ceremonies that are, and always have been, common to all Christendom, if they were ever instituted by Christ or the Apostles (of which I am not yet convinced), they were instituted only as external symbols of a universal Church, not as conducing to blessedness or as containing an intrinsic holiness. Therefore, although it was not to support a sovereign state that these ceremonies were instituted, yet their only purpose was the unification of a particular society, and thus he who lives in solitude is by no means bound by them. Indeed, he who lives under a government where the Christian religion is forbidden is required to abstain from these ceremonies, and can nevertheless live a blessed life. There is an instance of this in Japan, where the Christian religion is forbidden. The Dutch who live there are required by the East India Company to refrain from practising any external rites. I do not think it necessary to support this view by other authority; and although it would not be difficult to deduce it also from the fundamental principles of the New Testament and perhaps to demonstrate it by further convincing testimony, I leave this topic the more willingly as I am anxious to move on to other points. I therefore proceed to the second topic I

---

[2] [Spinoza is alluding here to the requirements of Jewish criminal law that prescribe in a case involving capital punishment—for example, murder—that the murderer had to be forewarned by two witnesses. These witnesses must have informed the perpetrator of the gravity of the act and the specific punishment for it. If any of these conditions is absent, the killer cannot be punished with death.]

proposed to discuss in this chapter: for whom, and in what way, belief in the narratives of Holy Scripture is requisite. To examine this question by the natural light of reason, I think it proper to proceed as follows.

If anyone, in arguing for or against a proposition which is not self-evident, seeks to persuade others to accept his view, he must prove his point from premises that are granted, and he must convince his audience on empirical grounds or by force of reason; that is, either from what sense-perception tells them occurs in Nature, or through self-evident intellectual axioms. Now unless experience is such as to be clearly and distinctly understood, it cannot have so decisive an effect on a man's understanding and dispel the mists of doubt as when the desired conclusion is deduced solely from intellectual axioms, that is, from the mere force of the intellect and its orderly apprehensions. This is especially so if the point at issue is a spiritual matter and does not come within the scope of the senses.

Now the process of deduction solely from intellectual axioms usually demands the apprehension of a long series of connected propositions, as well as the greatest caution, acuteness of intelligence, and restraint, all of which qualities are rarely to be found among men. So men prefer to be taught by experience rather than engage in the logical process of deduction from a few axioms. Hence it follows that if anyone sets out to teach some doctrine to an entire nation—not to say the whole of mankind—and wants it to be intelligible to all in every detail, he must rely entirely on an appeal to experience, and he must above all adapt his arguments and the definitions relevant to his doctrine to the understanding of the common people, who form the greatest part of mankind. He must not set before them a logical chain of reasoning nor frame the kind of definitions that are best suited to logical thinking. Otherwise he will be writing only for the learned; that is, he will be comprehensible only to a small minority.

Therefore, since the whole of Scripture was revealed in the first place for an entire nation, and eventually for all mankind, its contents had to be adapted particularly to the understanding of the common people, and it had to appeal only to experience. Let us explain more clearly. The teachings of Scripture that are concerned only with philosophic matters can be summed up as follows: that there is a God or Being who made all things and who directs and sustains the world with supreme wisdom; that he takes the utmost care of men, that is, those of them who live moral and righteous lives; and that he severely punishes the others and cuts them off from the good. Now Scripture establishes this simply by appealing to experience, that is, by its historical narratives; it does not provide any definitions of the terms it employs, but its language and reasoning is adapted to the understanding of the common people. And although experience can give no clear knowledge of these matters, and cannot teach what God is and in what way he sustains and directs all things and cares for men, it can still teach and enlighten men as far as suffices to impress on their minds obedience and devotion.

I think we have now shown quite clearly for whom, and in what way, belief in the narratives of Holy Scripture is requisite. From what we have already demonstrated it undoubtedly follows that knowledge of these writings and belief in them is in the highest degree necessary for the common people who lack the ability to perceive things clearly and distinctly. It further follows that he who rejects these writings because he does not believe in God, or does not believe that God cares for the world and mankind, is an impious person. But he who, while unacquainted with these writings, nevertheless knows by the natural light that there is a God having the attributes we have recounted, and who also pursues a true way of life, is altogether blessed—indeed, more blessed than the multitude, because in addition to true beliefs he also has a clear and distinct conception of God. Finally, it follows that he who is neither acquainted with these Biblical narratives nor has any knowledge from the natural light, if he be not impious or obstinate, is yet hardly human and close to being a beast, possessing none of God's gifts.

However, it should here be noted that when we say that it is in the highest degree requisite for the multitude to be acquainted with the Biblical narratives, we do not mean that they need to know absolutely all the narratives of Holy Scripture, but only those narratives that are of the first importance, and which, taken alone, display quite clearly the teachings we have just recounted, and make a striking impression on men's minds. For if all the Scriptural narratives were essential for demonstrating its teachings, and no conclusion could be drawn except by taking complete account of them all without exception, then surely the conclusive demonstration of its doctrine would be beyond the understanding and powers not only of the common people but of any human being. For who could pay attention all at once to such a vast number of narratives, to all the accompanying detail and the partial accounts of a doctrine that would have to be drawn from so many diverse narratives? For my part, I cannot believe that those who bequeathed to us the Scriptures in their present form were men of such outstanding ability as to be capable of following in detail a demonstration of that kind. Still less am I convinced that the doctrine of Scripture cannot be understood without our hearing of the quarrels of Isaac, Achitophel's advice to Absalom, the civil war between the men of Judah and the men of Israel, and other chronicles of this kind. Nor can I believe that historical narratives could not have demonstrated this doctrine to the earlier Jews of the time of Moses quite as well as to the contemporaries of Ezra. The common people, then, need to be acquainted only with those narratives that are most effective in instilling obedience and devotion. But the common people are not themselves qualified to judge of these narratives, being more disposed to take pleasure in the stories and in strange and unexpected happenings than in the doctrine implicit in the narratives; and, therefore, besides reading the narratives they also stand in need of pastors or ministers of the Church to instruct them in a way suited to their limited intelligence.

However, let us not stray from our theme, but proceed to the conclusion which it was our main purpose to prove, namely, that belief in historical narratives of any kind whatsoever has nothing to do with the Divine Law, that it does not in itself make men blessed, that its only value lies in the lesson conveyed, in which respect alone some narratives can be superior to others. So the narratives of the Old and New Testament differ in excellence from non-sacred writings and from one another to the extent that they inspire salutary beliefs. Therefore if a man reads the narratives of Holy Scripture and has complete faith in them, and yet pays no heed to the lesson that Scripture thereby aims to convey, and leads no better life, he might just as well have read the Koran or a poetic drama or at any rate ordinary history, giving the same attention as common people do to such writings. On the other hand, as we have said, he who is totally unacquainted with the Biblical narratives, but nevertheless holds salutary beliefs and pursues the true way of life, is absolutely blessed and has within him the spirit of Christ.

Now the Jews take a completely contrary view. They maintain that true beliefs and a true way of life contribute nothing to blessedness as long as men embrace them only from the natural light of reason, and not as teachings revealed to Moses by prophetic inspiration. This is what Maimonides ventures openly to affirm in chapter 8 of Kings, Law 11, "Every man who takes to heart the seven commandments* and diligently follows them belongs to the pious of nations and is heir to the world to come; that is to say, if he takes them to heart and follows them because God has ordained them in his Law, and has revealed to us through Moses that they were formerly ordained for the sons of Noah. But if he follows them through the guidance of reason, he is not a dweller among the pious nor among the wise of nations."[3] Such are the words of Maimonides, to which Rabbi Joseph,[4] son of Shem Tob, in his book called *Kebod Elohim*, or *Glory of God*, adds this, that although Aristotle (whom he considers to have written the finest work on Ethics, esteeming him above all others) may have neglected none of the precepts of true morality—which he also advocated in his own Ethics—and may have diligently followed all these teachings, this could not have furthered his own salvation, because he embraced these doctrines not as divine teachings prophetically revealed, but solely through the dictates of reason.

However, I think that any attentive reader will be convinced that these are mere figments of imagination, unsupported by rational argument or Scriptural authority. To state this view is sufficient to refute it. Nor do I here intend to refute the view of those who maintain that the natural light of reason can give no sound instruction in matters concerning true salvation. Those who deny to themselves a faculty

---

* N.B. The Jews believe that God gave Noah seven commandments, which alone are binding on all peoples; but to the Jews alone he gave many other commandments, making them more blessed than the rest.

[3] [Spinoza's reference to Maimonides is elliptical; the full citation should be Maimonides' Code of Law (*Mishneh Torah*), *Book of Kings*, chapter 8, law 11. As some modern scholars have noted, Spinoza's text of Maimonides' Code is not accurate. Whereas in the *TTP*, Spinoza reads "... nor among the wise of nations," the correct reading is "but only of the wise of nations." That is, according to Maimonides, the non-Jew must accept the moral law as revealed by God in order to merit entry into the World-to-Come, or in Spinoza's language, to be blessed. If not, the non-Jew who observes the moral commandments from rational argument and considerations is just wise, not pious or blessed. Maimonides' position was not universally accepted by Jews. Spinoza, however, uses it as a weapon against Judaism and also by implication any religion that makes dogmatic belief and ritual observances necessary conditions for blessedness.]

[4] [Joseph ben Shem Tov, a fifteenth-century Spanish Jewish scholar, was a critical Maimonidean, who had reservations concerning the extent to which Aristotelian philosophy could be made consistent with Judaism and conversely. In addition to the treatise cited by Spinoza, he wrote a commentary on Aristotle's *Nicomachean Ethics*.]

for sound reasoning cannot claim to prove their assertion by reasoning. And if they claim for themselves some suprarational faculty, this is the merest fiction, and far inferior to reason. This has been shown clearly enough by the manner of life they usually adopt. But there is no need to speak more openly about such people. This only will I add: we cannot know anyone except by his works. He who abounds in these fruits—charity, joy, peace, patience, kindness, goodness, faithfulness, gentleness and self-control, against which (as Paul says in Galatians chapter 5 v. 22) the law is not laid down, he, whether he be taught by reason alone or by Scripture alone, is in truth taught by God, and is altogether blessed.

Thus I have completed all that I undertook to discuss regarding the Divine Law.

CHAPTER 6

Of Miracles

Just as men are accustomed to call divine the kind of knowledge that surpasses human understanding, so they call divine, or the work of God, any work whose cause is generally unknown. For the common people suppose that God's power and providence are most clearly displayed when some unusual event occurs in Nature contrary to their habitual beliefs concerning Nature, particularly if such an event is to their profit or advantage. They consider that the clearest possible evidence of God's existence is provided when Nature deviates—as they think—from her proper order. Therefore they believe that all those who explain phenomena and miracles through natural causes, or who strive to understand them so, are doing away with God, or at least God's providence. They consider that God is inactive all the while that Nature pursues her normal course, and, conversely, that Nature's power and natural causes are suspended as long as God is acting. Thus they imagine that there are two powers quite distinct from each other, the power of God and the power of Nature, though the latter is determined in a definite way by God, or—as is the prevailing opinion nowadays—created by God. What they mean by the two powers, and what by God and Nature, they have no idea, except that they imagine God's power to be like the rule of some royal potentate, and Nature's power to be a kind of force and energy.

Therefore unusual works of Nature are termed miracles, or works of God, by the common people; and partly from piety, partly for the sake of opposing those who cultivate the natural sciences, they prefer to remain in ignorance of natural causes, and are eager to hear only of what is least comprehensible to them and consequently evokes their greatest wonder. Naturally so, since it is only by abolishing natural causes and imagining supernatural events that they are able to worship God and refer all things to God's governance and God's will; and it is when they imagine Nature's power subdued, as it were, by God that they most admire God's power.

This idea seems to have originated with the early Jews. In order to refute the beliefs of the Gentiles of their time who worshipped visible gods—the Sun, the Moon, the Earth, Water, Sky and so on—and to prove to them that these gods were weak and inconstant, or changeable and under the command of an invisible God, they boasted of their miracles, from which they further sought to prove that the whole of Nature was directed for their sole benefit by command of God whom they worshipped. This idea has found such favour with mankind that they have not ceased to this day to invent miracles with view to convincing people that they are more beloved of God than others, and are the final cause of God's creation and continuous direction of the world.

To what lengths will the folly of the multitude not carry them? They have no sound conception either of God or of Nature, they confuse God's decisions with human decisions, and they imagine Nature to be so limited that they believe man to be its chief part.

I have now devoted enough space to setting forth the beliefs and prejudices of the multitude concerning Nature. However, for the sake of orderly exposition, I shall demonstrate:

1. That no event can occur to contravene Nature, which preserves an eternal fixed and immutable order. At the same time I shall explain what is to be understood by a miracle.

2. That neither God's essence nor God's existence—nor, consequently, God's providence—can be known from miracles. All these can be far better apprehended from Nature's fixed and immutable order.

3. I shall cite a number of passages in Scripture to prove that, by God's decrees and volitions, and consequently God's providence, Scripture itself means nothing other than Nature's order, which necessarily follows from her eternal laws.

4. Finally, I shall discuss the method of interpreting Scriptural miracles, and the chief points to be noted regarding the narratives of miracles.

These are the principal topics which form the subject-matter of this chapter, and which I furthermore consider to be of no small profit in furthering the purpose of this entire work.

As to the first point, this is easily demonstrated from what I have set forth in Chapter 4 concerning the Divine Law; namely, that all that God wills or determines involves eternal necessity and truth; for by establishing the identity of God's intellect with God's will we showed that we make the same affirmation in saying that God wills something as in saying that God understands that thing. Therefore the necessity whereby it follows from the divine nature and perfection that God understands some thing as it is, is the same necessity from which it follows that God wills that thing as it is. Now since nothing is necessarily true save by the divine decree, it quite clearly follows that the universal laws of Nature are merely God's decrees, following from the necessity and perfection of the divine nature. So if anything were to happen in Nature contrary to her universal laws, it would also be necessarily contrary to the decree, intellect and nature of God. Or if anyone were to maintain that God performs some act contrary to the laws of Nature, he would at the same time have to maintain that God acts contrary to his own nature—of which nothing could be more absurd. The same could also be easily proved from the fact that the power of Nature is the divine power and virtue, and the divine power is the very essence of God. But I prefer to pass this by for the present.

Nothing, then, can happen in Nature* to contravene her own universal laws, nor yet anything that is not in agreement with these laws or that does not follow from them. For whatever occurs does so through God's will and eternal decree; that is, as we have already shown, all that happens does so in accordance with laws and rules which involve eternal necessity and truth. Nature, then, always observes laws and rules involving eternal necessity and truth although these are not all known to us, and thus it also observes a fixed and immutable order. Nor can any sound reasoning persuade us to attribute to Nature a limited power and virtue, and to regard her laws as having only a restricted application. For since the virtue and power of Nature is the very virtue and power of God, and the laws and rules of Nature are God's very decrees, there can be no doubt that Nature's power is infinite, and her laws sufficiently wide to extend to everything that is conceived even by the divine intellect. Otherwise it would surely have to be maintained that God created Nature so ineffective and prescribed for her laws and rules so barren that he is often constrained to come once more to her rescue if he wants her to be preserved, and the course of events to be as he desires. This I consider to be utterly divorced from reason.

So from these considerations—that nothing happens in Nature that does not follow from her laws, that her laws cover everything that is conceived even by the divine intellect, and that Nature observes a fixed and immutable order—it follows most clearly that the word miracle can be understood only with respect to men's beliefs, and means simply an event whose natural cause we—or at any rate the writer or narrator of the miracle—cannot explain by comparison with any other normal event. I might indeed have said that a miracle is that whose cause cannot be explained on scientific principles known to us by the natural light of reason. However, since miracles were wrought according to the understanding of the common people who were quite ignorant of the principles of science, men of old doubtless regarded as a miracle whatever they could not explain in the way in which the common people are accustomed to explain natural phenomena, that is, by resorting to memory so as to call to mind a similar happening which is ordinarily regarded without wonder. For the common people are not satisfied that they understand a thing until they can regard it without wonder. So men of old, and in general all men up to the present day, had no other criterion of a miracle, and therefore there are undoubtedly many alleged miracles in Scripture whose causes can be easily explained from known scientific principles. This is what we indicated in Chapter 2 when we spoke of the sun standing still in the time of Joshua and its retrogression in the time of Ahaz. But we shall presently treat of this matter more fully in discussing the interpretation of miracles, as I have undertaken to do in this chapter.

---

* Here, by Nature, I do not mean simply matter and its modifications, but infinite other things besides matter.

It is now time to pass on to our second point, namely, to show that miracles cannot provide us with any understanding either of God's essence or his existence or his providence, and that on the contrary these are far better apprehended from the fixed and immutable order of Nature. My proof proceeds as follows. Since God's existence is not self-evident,* it must necessarily be inferred from axiomatic truths which are so firm and incontrovertible that there can neither be, nor be conceived, any power that could call them into question. At any rate, once we have inferred from them God's existence, we are bound to regard them as such if we seek to establish beyond all shadow of doubt our inference from them to God's existence. For if we could conceive that these axiomatic truths themselves can be impugned by any power, of whatever kind it be, then we should doubt their truth and consequently the conclusion following therefrom, namely God's existence; nor could we ever be certain of anything. Further, we know that something agrees with or contravenes Nature only when we can prove that it agrees with or contravenes those basic truths. Therefore if we could conceive that in Nature something could be produced by some power, of whatever kind it be, to contravene Nature, it would contravene those primary axioms. So it must be rejected as absurd, or else (as we have just shown) the primary axioms, and consequently God, and all our apprehensions of every kind must be called into doubt. It is therefore far from being the case that miracles—understanding thereby something that contravenes the order of Nature—prove for us God's existence; on the contrary, they cast doubt on it, since but for them we could be absolutely certain of God's existence, in the assurance that all Nature follows a fixed and immutable order.

But let it be supposed that a miracle is that which cannot be explained through natural causes. This can be understood in two ways: either that it does have natural causes which the human intellect cannot ascertain, or that it owns no cause but God, or the will of God. However, since all things that come to pass through natural causes are also attributable solely to the power and will of God, it really comes down to this, that a miracle, whether or not it has natural causes, is an event that cannot be explained through a cause, that is, an event that surpasses human understanding. But from such an event, and from anything at all that surpasses our understanding, we can understand nothing. For whatever we clearly and distinctly understand must become known to us either through itself or through some other thing that is clearly and distinctly understood through itself. Therefore from a miracle, or an event that surpasses our understanding we can understand neither God's essence nor his existence nor anything whatsoever of God or Nature. On the contrary, knowing that all things are determined and ordained by God and that the workings of Nature follow from God's essence, while the laws of Nature are God's eternal decrees and volitions, we must unreservedly conclude that we get to know God and God's will all the better as we gain better knowledge of natural phenomena and understand more clearly how they depend on their first cause, and how they operate in accordance with Nature's eternal laws. There-

---

* See Supplementary Note 6.

fore, as far as concerns our understanding, those events which we understand clearly and distinctly have far better right to be termed works of God, and to be referred to God's will, than those of which we are quite ignorant, even though the latter appeal strongly to the imagination and evoke men's wonder. For it is only those works of Nature which we clearly and distinctly understand that afford us a higher knowledge of God, and indicate with the utmost clarity God's will and decrees. So those who have recourse to the will of God when there is something they do not understand are but trifling; this is no more than a ridiculous way of avowing one's ignorance.

Furthermore, granting that any conclusion could be drawn from miracles, God's existence could not possibly be concluded therefrom. For since a miracle is an event of a limited nature, expressing a power that is never other than fixed and limited, from such an effect we could not possibly conclude the existence of a cause whose power is infinite; the most we could conclude is the existence of a cause whose power is greater than that effect. I say 'the most' because an event can also be the result of several simultaneously concurring causes, the force and power of the result being less than all the causes taken together, but far greater than the power of each separate cause. Now since the laws of Nature (as we have shown) are infinite in their scope and are conceived by us as having an eternal quality, and since Nature operates in accordance with them in a fixed and immutable order, the laws themselves give us some indication of the infinity, eternity and immutability of God.

Therefore we conclude that from miracles we cannot gain knowledge of God, his existence and providence, and that these can be far better inferred from Nature's fixed and immutable order. In arriving at this conclusion I am speaking of miracle insofar as it means only an event that surpasses, or is thought to surpass, man's understanding. For insofar as it were supposed to destroy or interrupt the order of Nature or to contravene her laws, in that sense (as I have just shown) not only could it give us no knowledge of God but it would take from us what knowledge we naturally have, and would cast doubt on God and on all things.

And here I do not acknowledge any difference between an event contrary to Nature and a supernatural event; (that is, according to some, an event that does not contravene Nature but nevertheless cannot be produced or brought about by Nature). For since a miracle occurs not externally to Nature but within Nature, even though it be claimed to be supernatural, yet it must necessarily interrupt Nature's order which otherwise we would conceive as fixed and immutable by God's decrees. So if there were to occur in Nature anything that did not follow from her laws, this would necessarily be opposed to the order which God maintains eternally in Nature through her universal laws. So this would be contrary to Nature and Nature's laws, and consequently such a belief would cast doubt on everything, and would lead to atheism.

I think I have now established my second point on a firm footing, from which we may once more reach the conclusion that a miracle, either contrary to Nature or above Nature, is mere absurdity, and therefore a miracle in Scripture can mean nothing else (as we have said) but a natural event which surpasses, or is believed to surpass, human understanding. But before moving on to my third point, I should like to confirm by Scriptural authority our assertion that we cannot gain knowledge of God through miracles. Although Scripture never states this overtly, this conclusion can readily be inferred from it, especially from the passage where Moses (Deut. ch. 13) commands that a false prophet should be condemned to death even though he should perform miracles. It runs as follows: "(Although) the sign of wonder come to pass, whereof he spoke unto thee . . . thou shalt not hearken to the voice of that prophet . . . for the Lord your God proveth you . . . that prophet shall be put to death. . . ." For this it clearly follows that miracles can be performed by false prophets, too, and that from miracles men may accept false gods quite as readily as the true God, unless they are well fortified by true knowledge and love of God. For he adds, "For the Lord your God proveth you, to know whether ye love him with all your heart and with all your soul."

Again, their many miracles did not enable the Israelites to form any sound conception of God, as the facts bear witness. When they were convinced that Moses had departed from them, they asked Aaron to give them visible deities, and their idea of God, formed after all their many miracles, was—a calf! Asaph, although he had heard of so many miracles, nevertheless doubted God's providence, and might have turned aside from the true path had he not finally achieved an understanding of true blessedness (see Psalm 73). Solomon, too, in whose time the Jews reached the height of their prosperity, suspects that all things happen by chance. See Ecclesiastes chapter 3 v. 19, 20, 21, and chapter 9 v. 2, 3 etc.

Finally, nearly all the prophets found considerable difficulty in reconciling the order of Nature and vicissitudes of men with the conception they had formed of God's providence, whereas this has never afforded difficulty to philosophers, who endeavour to understand things not from miracles but from clear conceptions. For they place true happiness solely in virtue and peace of mind, and they strive to conform with Nature, not to make Nature conform with them; for they are assured that God directs Nature in accordance with the requirements of her universal laws, and not in accordance with the requirements of the particular laws of human nature. Thus God takes account of the whole of Nature, and not of the human race alone.

Therefore even Scripture itself makes it evident that miracles do not afford true knowledge of God, nor do they clearly teach God's providence. As to the many passages in Scripture to the effect that God wrought wonders so as to make himself known to men—as in Exodus chapter 10 v. 2, where God deceived the Egyptians and gave signs of himself so that the Israelites might know that he was God—it does not follow therefrom that miracles really conveyed this; it only follows that the beliefs of the Jews were such that they could be readily convinced by these miracles. For we have already shown clearly in Chapter 2 that deliverances of a prophetic nature—i.e. those that are inspired by revelation—are not derived from universal and fundamental axioms, but from the prior assumptions and beliefs, however absurd, of those to whom the revelation is made, or those whom the Holy Spirit seeks to convince. This is a point I have illustrated with many examples, and also with the testimony of Paul, who was a Greek with the Greeks and a Jew with the Jews. But although these miracles succeeded in carrying conviction with the Egyptians and the Jews on the basis of their prior assumptions, they could not impart the true idea and knowledge of God but could only bring about these peoples' admission that there was a Deity more powerful than anything known to them, and that he cared above all men for the Hebrews, whose affairs at that time had prospered beyond expectation. Miracles did not teach them that God cares equally for all; only philosophy can teach that. So the Jews, and all those for whom God's providence was exemplified solely by differences in the condition of human affairs and by inequalities of fortune, were convinced that the Jews were more beloved of God than other peoples, in spite of the fact that, as we showed in Chapter 3, the Jews did not excel others in true human perfection.

I now proceed to my third point, demonstrating from Scripture that God's decrees and commandments, and consequently God's providence, are in truth nothing but Nature's order; that is to say, when Scripture tells us that this or that was accomplished by God or by God's will, nothing more is intended than that it came about by accordance with Nature's law and order, and not, as the common people believe, that Nature for that time suspended her action, or that her order was temporarily interrupted. But Scripture does not directly teach what is not relevant to its doctrine; for it is not the part of Scripture (as we showed in connection with the Divine Law) to teach things through their natural causes or to engage in pure philosophy. Therefore the point we here seek to establish must be gathered by implication from certain Scriptural narratives which happen to be related more fully and in more detail. I shall therefore cite a number of these passages.

In 1 Samuel chapter 9 v. 15, 16 it is related that God revealed to Samuel that he would send Saul to him. Yet God did not send Saul to Samuel in the way that men ordinarily send someone to someone else; God's sending was merely the ordinary course of Nature. Saul was in search of his lost asses (as related in the previous chapter) and was thinking of returning home without them when, at his servant's suggestion, he went to the prophet Samuel to learn where he might find them. Nowhere in the entire narrative is it stated that, beyond this natural course of events, Saul received any command of God to visit Samuel.

In Psalm 105 v. 24 we are told that God changed the hearts of the Egyptians so as to hate the Israelites. But this, again, was a quite natural change, as is evident from Exodus chapter 1, where a weighty reason is given as to why the Egyptians were moved to reduce the Israelites to slavery.

In Genesis chapter 9 v. 13 God tells Noah that he will set a rainbow in the cloud. This act of God, again, is assuredly nothing other than the refraction and reflection of the sun's rays which they undergo in droplets of water.

In Psalm 147 v. 18 the natural action and warmth of the wind whereby frost and snow are melted is called the word of God; and in v. 15, wind and cold are called the command and word of God.

In Psalm 104 v. 4 wind and fire are called the messengers and ministers of God, and there are many other such passages in Scripture which clearly indicate that God's decree, command, edict and word are nothing other than the action and order of Nature.

Therefore there can be no doubt that all the events narrated in Scripture occurred naturally; yet they are referred to God because, as we have already shown, it is not the part of Scripture to explain events through their natural causes; it only relates to those events that strike the imagination, employing such method and style as best serves to excite wonder, and consequently to instil piety in the minds of the masses. So if we find in Scripture some things for which we can assign no cause and which seems to have happened beyond—indeed, contrary to—Nature's order, this should not perplex us. We need have no hesitation in believing that what truly happened, happened naturally.

This view receives further confirmation from the fact that many circumstantial details were found to accompany miracles, although these are not always recorded, especially where the style is of a poetic character. The circumstances accompanying miracles, I repeat, clearly show that miracles need natural causes. For instance, so that the Egyptians should be infected with boils, Moses had to scatter ashes in the air (Exodus ch. 9 v. 10). The locusts, too, invaded the land of Egypt by God's command through natural means, namely, through an east wind which blew a whole day and night, and it was through a strong west wind that they quitted the land (Exodus ch. 10 v. 14, 19). By that same command of God, too, the sea opened a path for the Jews (Exodus ch. 14 v. 21), that is, through an east wind which blew strongly all night long. Again, in order that Elisha could revive a child who was thought to be dead, he had to lie over him several times until the child first regained warmth and at last opened his eyes (2 Kings ch. 4 v. 34, 35). So, too, in St. John's Gospel chapter 9 we are told of some accompanying actions which Christ employed to heal the blind man, and there are numerous other instances in Scripture, all going to show that miracles need something other than the absolute command of God, as it is called. Therefore we are justified in believing that, although the circumstances attendant on miracles and the natural causes of miracles are not narrated always and in full, the miracles did not occur without them. This is again clear from Exodus chapter 14 v. 27, where we are merely told that the sea returned to its strength once more solely at the bidding of Moses, no mention being made of any wind; yet in the Song of Moses (ch. 15 v. 10) it is said that this came about because God blew with his wind (that is, a very strong wind). So this attendant circumstance is omitted in the narrative, thereby making the miracle appear all the greater.

But perhaps someone will insist that we find numerous events in Scripture which defy explanation through natural causes, as that the sins of men and their prayers can be the cause of rain and the earth's fertility, or that faith could heal the blind, or other incidents of a similar kind narrated in the Bible. But I consider that I have already replied to such objections. For I have shown that Scripture does not explain things through their proximate causes; in its narratives it merely employs such order and such language as is most effective in moving men—and particularly the common people—to devotion. That is why it speaks of God and events in terms far from correct, its aim being not to convince on rational grounds but to appeal to and engage men's fantasy and imagination. If Scripture were to describe the downfall of an empire in the style adopted by political historians, the common people would not be stirred, whereas they are deeply affected when all is described in poetical language and referred to God, as is customary in Scripture. So when Scripture tells us that the earth is barren because of men's sins, or that the blind were healed by their faith, we should accept this in the same way as when it tells us that God is angry because of men's sins, that he is grieved, that he repents of the good he has promised or done, or that he remembers a promise as a result of seeing a sign, and numerous other assertions that are either of a poetical character or are narrated in accordance with the beliefs and preconceptions of the writer.

Therefore we may now conclude with absolute assurance that everything related in Scripture as having truly happened came to pass necessarily according to the laws of Nature, as everything does. If anything be found in Scripture which can be conclusively proved to contravene the laws of Nature, or which could not possibly follow from them, we have to believe that this was inserted into Holy Scripture by sacrilegious men. For whatever is contrary to Nature is contrary to reason, and whatever is contrary to reason is absurd, and should therefore be rejected.

It now remains for us to remark on just a few more points regarding the interpretation of Scripture, or rather, to recall them—for the main points have already been mentioned—and to illustrate them with a few examples, as I proposed to do here in the fourth section. My purpose is that no one, by misinterpreting some miracle, should heedlessly come to think that he has found something in Scripture contrary to the light of Nature.

It very rarely happens that men relate an event exactly as it took place without introducing into it something of their own judgment. Indeed, when they see or hear something strange, they will generally be so much influenced by their own preconceived beliefs—unless they are strictly on their guard against them—that what they perceive is something quite different from what they really see or hear to have happened. This is especially so if the occurrence surpasses the understanding of the narrator or listener, and in particular if it is to his interest that the event should come about in a certain way. In consequence, chronicles and histories reflect the writer's own beliefs rather than the actual facts, and one and the same occurrence is so differently related by two men holding different beliefs that they seem to be speaking of two different events, and there is often little difficulty in elucidating the beliefs of the chronicler and historian simply from their narratives.

In confirmation I could quote many examples both from writers of natural history and from chroniclers, did I not think it superfluous; but I will cite one example from Holy Scripture, leaving the reader to judge of the rest. In the time of Joshua, the Hebrews (as I have previously indicated) shared the common belief that the sun moves with a diurnal motion (as it is termed) and the earth is at rest, and to this preconceived belief they adapted the miracle that befell them in the battle against the five kings. They did not simply relate that the day in question was longer than usual; they said that the sun and moon stood still, ceasing from their motion. At that time this interpretation may have stood them in good stead in refuting the Gentiles who worshipped the sun, and in proving by actual experience that the sun was under the control of another deity, at whose bidding it must alter its natural course. So partly through piety and partly influenced by preconceived beliefs, they conceived and related this event quite differently from the way it could really have come about.

Therefore, to interpret Scriptural miracles and to understand from their accounts how they really took place, one must know the beliefs of those who originally related them and left us written records of them, and one must distinguish between these beliefs and what could have been presented to their senses. Otherwise we shall confuse their beliefs and judgments with the miracle as it really happened. And awareness of their beliefs is of further importance in avoiding confusion between what really happened and what was imagined and was no more than prophetic symbolism. For many things are related in Scripture as real, and were also believed to be real, but were nevertheless merely symbolical and imaginary; as that God, the supreme Being, came down from heaven (Exodus ch. 19 v. 18 and Deut. ch. 5 v. 19) and that Mount Sinai smoked because God descended upon it surrounded by fire, and that Elijah ascended to heaven in a chariot of fire and with horses of fire. All these were merely symbolical representations, adapted to the belief of those who have transmitted them to us as they were represented to them, that is, as actual happenings. All who have any smattering of education know that God does not have a right hand or a left hand, that he neither moves nor is at rest, nor is he in any particular place, but is absolutely infinite, and contains within himself all perfections. These truths, I say, are known by those whose judgment is formed from the perceptions of pure intellect, and not from the way the imagination is affected by their outward senses. This latter is the case with the masses, who therefore imagine God as corporeal, holding royal sway from his throne in the vault of heaven above the stars—which they believe to be at no great distance from the earth. Numerous occurrences in Scripture are adapted to these and similar beliefs, as we have pointed out, and therefore ought not to be accepted as real by philosophers.

Finally, for the proper understanding of the reality of miracles, it is important to be acquainted with the diction and metaphors affected by the Hebrews. He who does not pay sufficient attention to this will ascribe to Scripture many miracles which Scriptural writers never intended as such, thus completely failing to understand not only events and miracles as they really happened but also the meaning of the writers of the Sacred Books. Thus Zechariah (ch. 14 v. 7), speaking about some future war, says, "It shall be one day known only to the Lord, (for it shall be) neither day nor night, but at evening time it shall be light." By these words he seems to be predicting a great miracle; yet his meaning is quite simply that the battle will be in balance throughout the whole day, its issue being known only to God, and that at evening time they will gain victory. For it was with expressions like these that the prophets used to predict and write of the victories and defeats of nations. Similarly, we see Isaiah (ch. 13) describing the destruction of Babylon in the following way, "... since the stars of heaven and the constellations thereof shall not give their light, the sun shall be darkened in his going forth, and the moon shall not cause her light to shine." Surely nobody, I imagine, believes that these things happened at the destruction of that empire, nor, as he goes on to add, ". . . therefore I will make the heavens to tremble, and the earth shall be removed from her place."

Similarly Isaiah, in the penultimate verse of chapter 48, intending to convey to the Jews that they would return from Babylon to Jerusalem in safety and would not suffer from thirst on the journey, says, "And they thirsted not when he led them through the wilderness, he caused water to flow out of the rocks for them, he clave the rock and the waters flowed." By these words, I say, he means no more than that the Jews would find springs in the desert—as is not unusual—from which they would quench their thirst; for when the Jews returned to Jerusalem by Cyrus' consent, there is no record of any such miracles befalling them. In Holy Scripture we find many such passages which are simply modes of speech affected by the Jews. There is no need for me to review them all now in detail, but I should like only to make the general point that the Hebrews used to employ this style of speech not merely for rhetorical effect but also—and most of all—from motives of piety. It is for this reason that in Holy Scripture 'Bless God' is substituted for 'Curse God' (see 1 Kings ch. 21 v. 10 and Job ch. 2 v. 9); and for the same reason they referred everything to God, with the result that Scripture appears to be relating nothing but miracles even when it is speaking of the most natural things, as we have already illustrated with many examples. Therefore we should believe that when Scripture says that God hardened Pharaoh's heart, no more is meant than that Pharaoh was obstinate; when it is said that God opened the windows of heaven, this means no more than there was a heavy rainstorm, and so on. If we bear these points well in mind, and also reflect that many of the narratives are very brief, shorn of all detail and defective in many ways, we shall find practically nothing in Scripture that can be shown to contradict the light of Nature, whereas many passages which seemed very obscure we can understand and readily interpret with a little thought.

I think I have now demonstrated quite clearly what I had proposed to demonstrate. Nevertheless, before I bring this chapter to a close, there remains a further point to which I should like to draw attention, namely, that in here discussing miracles I have adopted a method very different from that employed in dealing with prophecy. In the matter of prophecy I made no assertion that I could not infer from grounds revealed in Holy Scripture, whereas in this chapter I have drawn my main conclusions solely from basic principles known by the natural light of reason. This procedure I have adopted deliberately because in dealing with prophecy, since it surpasses human understanding and is a purely theological question, revelation provided the only basis for making any assertion about it, or even for understanding its essential nature. So in the case of prophecy I had no alternative but to compile a historical account, and from that to formulate certain principles which would give me some degree of insight into the nature and properties of prophecy. But in the matter of miracles, since the object of our inquiry—namely, whether we can admit that something can happen in Nature which is contrary to her laws, or which could not follow therefrom—is plainly of a philosophical character, no such procedure was necessary. On the contrary, I deemed it the wiser course to attempt to solve this problem from basic principles known by the natural light, these being of all things best known to us. I say that I deemed it the wiser course, for I might also have solved this problem quite easily from the pronouncements and basic doctrines of Scripture alone. This I shall here briefly demonstrate, so that it may be clear to all.

In certain passages Scripture asserts of Nature in general that she observes a fixed and immutable order, as in Psalm 138 verse 6 and Jeremiah chapter 31 verses 35, 36. Furthermore, in Ecclesiastes chapter 1 verse 10 the Sage tells us quite clearly that nothing new happens in Nature, and in verses 11, 12 to illustrate this same point he says that although occasionally something may happen that seems new, it is not new, but has happened in ages past beyond recall. For, as he says, there is today no remembrance of things past, nor will there be remembrance of things today among those to come. Again, in chapter 3 verse 11 he says that God has ordered all things well for their time, and in verse 14 he says that he knows that whatever God does will endure forever, neither can anything be added to it nor taken away from it. All these passages clearly convey the teaching that Nature observes a fixed and immutable order, that God has been the same throughout all ages that are known or unknown to us, that the laws of Nature are so perfect and fruitful that nothing can be added or taken away from them, and that miracles seem something strange only because of man's ignorance.

These, then, are the express teachings of Scripture: nowhere does it say that something can happen in Nature that contravenes her laws or that cannot follow from her laws; so neither should we impute such a doctrine to Scripture. Then there is the further fact that miracles stand in need of causes and attendant circumstances (as we have already shown); they do not result from some kind of royal government which the masses attribute to God, but from the divine government and decree; that is (as we have also shown from Scripture), from Nature's laws and order. Finally, miracles can be wrought even by false prophets, as is proved from Deuteronomy chapter 13 and Matthew chapter 24 verse 24.

Hence it follows on the plainest evidence that miracles were natural occurrences, and therefore they should be explained in such a way that they seem to be neither 'new' things (to use Solomon's expression) nor things contrary to Nature, but things approximating as closely to natural occurrences as the facts allowed. To render this interpretation easier for everyone, I have set forth certain rules drawn only from Scripture. Nevertheless, although I say that this is Scripture's teaching, I do not mean to suggest that Scripture enjoins this teaching as something requisite for salvation; I mean only that the prophets take the same view as I. Therefore on these matters everyone is entitled to hold whatever view he feels will better bring him with sincere heart to the worship of God and to religion. This was also the opinion of Josephus, for towards the end of Book 2 of his *Antiquities*, he writes as follows: "Let no one baulk at the word miracle, if men of ancient times, unsophisticated as they were, see the road to safety open up through the sea, whether revealed by God's will or of its own accord. Those men, too, who accompanied Alexander, king of Macedon, men of much more recent times,[1] found the Pamphylian sea divide for them, offering a passage when there was no other way, it being God's will to destroy the Persian empire through him. This is admitted to be true by all who have written of Alexander's deeds. Therefore on these matters let everyone think as he will." Such are the words of Josephus, showing his attitude to belief in miracles.

CHAPTER 7

Of the Interpretation of Scripture

On every side we hear men saying that the Bible is the Word of God, teaching mankind true blessedness, or the path to salvation. But the facts are quite at variance with their words, for people in general seem to make no attempt whatsoever to live according to the Bible's teachings. We see that nearly all men parade their own ideas as God's Word, their chief aim being to compel others to think as they do, while using religion as a pretext. We see, I say, that the chief concern of theologians on the whole has been to extort from Holy Scripture their own arbitrarily invented ideas, for which they claim divine authority. In no other field do they display less scruple and greater temerity than in the interpretation of Scripture, the mind of the Holy Spirit, and if while so doing they feel any misgivings, their fear is not that they may be mistaken in their understanding of the Holy Spirit and may stray from the path to salvation, but that others may convict them of error, thus annihilating their personal prestige and bringing them into contempt.

Now if men were really sincere in what they profess with regard to Holy Scripture, they would conduct themselves quite differently; they would not be racked by so much quarrelling and such bitter feuding, and they would not be gripped by this blind and passionate desire to interpret Scripture and to introduce innovations in religion. On the contrary, they would never venture to accept as Scriptural doctrine what was not most clearly taught by Scripture itself. And finally, those sacrilegious persons who have had the hardihood to alter Scripture in several places would have been horrified at the enormity of the crime and would have stayed their impious hands. But ambition and iniquity have reached such a pitch that religion takes the form not so much of obedience to the teachings of the Holy Spirit as of defending what men have invented. Indeed, religion is manifested not in charity but in spreading contention among men and in fostering the bitterest hatred, under the false guise of zeal in God's cause and a burning enthusiasm. To

---

[1] [Here the Latin *"olim et antiquitus a resistentibus"* is transcribed by Spinoza from Rufinus Aquileiensis (1475), whose translation of Josephus was found in Spinoza's library. As it stands, the passage makes no sense. Either the reading was corrupt, or Rufinus failed to understand the Greek idiom χθὲς καὶ πρώην γεγόνασιν. I have therefore translated this phrase from the Greek of Josephus. — S.S.]

these evils is added superstition, which teaches men to despise reason and Nature, and to admire and venerate only that which is opposed to both. It is therefore not surprising that, to make Scripture appear more wonderful and awe-inspiring, they endeavour to explicate it in such a way that is seems diametrically opposed both to reason and to Nature. So they imagine that the most profound mysteries lie hidden in the Bible, and they exhaust themselves in unravelling these absurdities while ignoring other things of value. They ascribe to the Holy Spirit whatever their wild fancies have invented, and devote their utmost strength and enthusiasm to defending it. For human nature is so constituted that what men conceive by pure intellect, they defend only by intellect and reason, whereas the beliefs that spring from the emotions are emotionally defended.

In order to escape from this scene of confusion, to free our minds from the prejudices of theologians and to avoid the hasty acceptance of human fabrications as divine teachings, we must discuss the true method of Scriptural interpretation and examine it in depth; for unless we understand this we cannot know with any certainty what the Bible or the Holy Spirit intends to teach. Now to put it briefly, I hold that the method of interpreting Scripture is no different from the method of interpreting Nature, and is in fact in complete accord with it. For the method of interpreting Nature consists essentially in composing a detailed study of Nature from which, as being the source of our assured data, we can deduce the definitions of the things of Nature. Now in exactly the same way the task of Scriptural interpretation requires us to make a straightforward study of Scripture, and from this, as the source of our fixed data and principles, to deduce by logical inference the meaning of the authors of Scripture. In this way—that is, by allowing no other principles or data for the interpretation of Scripture and study of its contents except those that can be gathered only from Scripture itself and from a historical study of Scripture—steady progress can be made without any danger of error, and one can deal with matters that surpass our understanding with no less confidence than those matters which are known to us by the natural light of reason.

But to establish clearly that this is not merely a sure way, but the only way open to us, and that it accords with the method of interpreting Nature, it should be observed that Scripture frequently treats of matters that cannot be deduced from principles known by the natural light; for it is chiefly made up of historical narratives and revelation. Now an important feature of the historical narratives is the appearance of miracles; that is, as we showed in the previous chapter, stories of unusual occurrences in Nature, adapted to the beliefs and judgment of the historians who recorded them. The revelations, too, were adapted to the beliefs of the prophets, as we showed in Chapter 2; and these do, indeed, surpass human understanding. Therefore knowledge of all these things—that is, of almost all the contents of Scripture—must be sought from Scripture alone, just as knowledge of Nature must be sought from Nature itself.

As for the moral doctrines that are also contained in the Bible, although these themselves can be demonstrated from accepted axioms, it cannot be proved from such axioms that Scripture teaches these doctrines: this can be established only from Scripture itself. Indeed, if we want to testify, without any prejudgment, to the divinity of Scripture, it must be made evident to us from Scripture alone that it teaches true moral doctrine; for it is on this basis alone that its divinity can be proved. We have shown that the chief characteristic which established the certainty of the prophets was that their minds were directed to what was right and good; hence this must be made evident to us, too, before we can have faith in them. We have already shown that miracles can never give proof of God's divinity, apart from the fact that they could be wrought even by a false prophet. Therefore the divinity of Scripture must be established solely from the fact that it teaches true virtue. Now this can be established only from Scripture. If this could not be done, our acceptance of Scripture and our witness to its divinity would argue great prejudice on our part. Therefore all knowledge of Scripture must be sought from Scripture alone.

Finally, Scripture does not provide us with definitions of the things of which it speaks, any more than Nature does. Therefore, just as definitions of the things of Nature must be inferred from the various operations of Nature, in the same way definitions must be elicited from the various Biblical narratives as they touch on a particular subject. This, then, is the universal rule for the interpretation of Scripture, to ascribe no teaching to Scripture that is not clearly established from studying it closely. What kind of study this should be, and what are the chief topics it should include, must now be explained.

1. It should inform us of the nature and properties of the language in which the Bible was written and which its authors were accustomed to speak. Thus we should be able to investigate, from established linguistic usage, all the possible meanings of any passage. And since all the writers of both the Old and the New Testaments were Hebrews, a study of the Hebrew language must undoubtedly be a prime requisite not only for an understanding of the books of the Old Testament, which were written in that language, but also for the New Testament. For although the latter books were published in other languages, their idiom is Hebraic.

2. The pronouncements made in each book should be assembled and listed under headings, so that we can thus have to hand all the texts that treat of the same subject. Next, we should note all those that are ambiguous or obscure, or that appear to contradict one another. Now here I term a pronouncement obscure or clear according to the degree of difficulty with which the meaning can be elicited from the context, and not according to the degree of difficulty with which its truth can be perceived by reason. For the point at issue is merely the meaning of the texts, not their truth. I would go further: in seeking the meaning of Scripture we should take every precaution against the undue influence, not only of our own prejudices, but of our faculty of reason insofar as that is based on the principles of natural cognition. In order to avoid confusion between true meaning and truth of fact, the former must be sought simply from linguistic usage, or from a process of reasoning that looks to no other basis than Scripture.

For further clarification, I shall give an example to illustrate all that I have here said. The sayings of Moses, "God is fire," and "God is jealous," are perfectly clear as long as we attend only to the meanings of the words; and so, in spite of their obscurity from the perspective of truth and reason, I classify these sayings as clear.

Indeed, even though their literal meaning is opposed to the natural light of reason, this literal meaning must nevertheless be retained unless it is in clear opposition to the basic principles derived from the study of Scripture. On the other hand, if these statements in their literal interpretation were found to be in contradiction with the basic principles derived from Scripture, they would have to be interpreted differently (that is, metaphorically) even though they were in complete agreement with reason. Therefore the question as to whether Moses did or did not believe that God is fire must in no wise be decided by the rationality or irrationality of the belief, but solely from other pronouncements of Moses. In this particular case, since there are several other instances where Moses clearly tells us that God has no resemblance to visible things in heaven or on the earth or in the water, we must hence conclude that either this statement or all those others must be explained metaphorically. Now since one should depart as little as possible from the literal meaning, we should first enquire whether this single pronouncement, 'God is fire,' admits of any other than a literal meaning; that is, whether the word 'fire' can mean anything other than ordinary natural fire. If the word 'fire' is not found from linguistic usage to have any other meaning, then neither should this statement be interpreted in any other way, however much it is opposed to reason, and all other passages should be made to conform with it, however much they accord with reason. If this, too, should prove impossible on the basis of linguistic usage, then these pronouncements would have to be regarded as irreconcilable, and we should therefore suspend judgment regarding them. However, since the word 'fire' is also used in the sense of anger or jealousy (Job ch. 31 v. 12), Moses' pronouncements are easily reconciled, and we can properly conclude that these two statements, 'God is fire' and 'God is jealous' are one and the same statement.

Again, as Moses clearly teaches that God is jealous and nowhere tells us that God is without passions or emotions, we must evidently conclude that Moses believed this, or at least that he intended to teach this, however strongly we may be convinced that this opinion is contrary to reason. For, as we have shown, it is not permissible for us to manipulate Scripture's meaning to accord with our reason's dictates and our preconceived opinions; all knowledge of the Bible is to be sought from the Bible alone.

3. Finally, our historical study should set forth the circumstances relevant to all the extant books of the prophets, giving the life, character and pursuits of the author of every book, detailing who he was, on what occasion and at what time and for whom and in what language he wrote. Again, it should relate what happened to each book, how it was first received, into whose hands it fell, how many variant versions there were, by whose decision it was received into the canon, and, finally, how all the books, now universally regarded as sacred, were united into a single whole. All these details, I repeat, should be available from a historical study of Scripture; for in order to know which pronouncements were set forth as laws and which as moral teaching, it is important to be acquainted with the life, character and interests of the author. Furthermore, as we have a better understanding of a person's character and temperament, so we can more easily explain his words.

Again, to avoid confusing teachings of eternal significance with those which are of only temporary significance or directed only to the benefit of a few, it is also important to know on what occasion, at what period, and for what nation or age all these teachings were written down. Finally, it is important to know the other details we have listed so that, in addition to the authenticity of each book, we may also discover whether or not it may have been contaminated by spurious insertions, whether errors have crept in, and whether these have been corrected by experienced and trustworthy scholars. All this information is needed by us so that we may accept only what is certain and incontrovertible, and not be led by blind impetuosity to take for granted whatever is set before us.

Now when we possess this historical account of Scripture and are firmly resolved not to assert as the indubitable doctrine of the prophets anything that does not follow from this study or cannot be most clearly inferred from it, it will then be time to embark on the task of investigating the meaning of the prophets and the Holy Spirit. But for this task, too, we need a method and order similar to that which we employ in interpreting Nature from the facts presented before us. Now in examining natural phenomena we first of all try to discover those features that are most universal and common to the whole of Nature, to wit, motion-and-rest and the rules and laws governing them which Nature always observes and through which she constantly acts; and then we advance gradually from these to other less universal features. In just the same way we must first seek from our study of Scripture that which is most universal and forms the basis and foundation of all Scripture; in short, that which is commended in Scripture by all the prophets as doctrine eternal and most profitable for all mankind. For example, that God exists, one alone and omnipotent, who alone should be worshipped, who cares for all, who loves above all others those who worship him and love their neighbours as themselves. These and similar doctrines, I repeat, are taught everywhere in Scripture so clearly and explicitly that no one has ever been in any doubt as to its meaning on these points. But what God is, in what way he sees and provides for all things and similar matters, Scripture does not teach formally, and as eternal doctrine. On the contrary, we have clearly shown that the prophets themselves were not in agreement on these matters, and therefore on topics of this kind we should make no assertion that claims to be the doctrine of the Holy Spirit, even though the natural light of reason may be quite decisive on that point.

Having acquired a proper understanding of this universal doctrine of Scripture, we must then proceed to other matters which are of less universal import but affect our ordinary daily life, and which flow from the universal doctrine like rivulets from their source. Such are all the specific external actions of true virtue which need a particular occasion for their exercise. If there be found in Scripture anything ambiguous or obscure regarding such matters, it must be explained and decided on the basis of the universal doctrine of Scripture. If any passages are found to be in contradiction with one another, we should consider on what occasion, at what time, and for whom they were written. For example, when Christ says, "Blessed are they that mourn, for they shall be comforted," we do not know from this text what kind of mourners are meant. But as Christ thereafter teaches that we should take thought for nothing save only the kingdom of God and His righteousness, which he commends as the highest good (Matth. ch. 6 v. 33), it follows that by mourners he means only those who mourn for man's disregard of the kingdom of God and His righteousness; for only this can be the cause of mourning for those who love nothing but the kingdom of God, or justice, and utterly despise whatever else fortune has to offer.

So, too, when Christ says, "But if a man strike you on the right cheek, turn to him the left also" and the words that follow, if he were laying this command on judges in the role of lawgiver, this precept would have violated the law of Moses. But he expressly warns against this (Matth. ch. 5 v. 17). Therefore we should consider who said this, to whom, and at what time. This was said by Christ, who was not ordaining laws as a lawgiver, but was expounding his teachings as a teacher, because (as we have already shown) he was intent on improving men's minds rather than their external actions. Further, he spoke these words to men suffering under oppression, living in a corrupt commonwealth where justice was utterly disregarded, a commonwealth whose ruin he saw to be imminent. Now we see that this very same teaching, which Christ here expounds when the ruin of the city was imminent, was also given by Jeremiah in similar circumstances at the first destruction of the city (Lamentations ch. 3 v. 30). Thus it was only at the time of oppression that the prophets taught this doctrine which was nowhere set forth as law; whereas Moses (who did not write at a time of oppression, but—please note—was concerned to found a good commonwealth), although he likewise condemned revenge and hatred against one's neighbour, yet demanded an eye for an eye. Therefore it clearly follows simply on Scriptural grounds that this teaching of Christ and Jeremiah concerning the toleration of injury and total submission to the wicked applies only in situations where justice is disregarded and at times of oppression, but not in a good commonwealth. Indeed, in a good commonwealth where justice is upheld, everyone who wants to be accounted as just has the duty to go before a judge and demand justice for wrongdoing (Lev. ch. 5 v. 1), not out of revenge (Lev. ch. 19 v. 17, 18), but with the purpose of upholding justice and the laws of his country, and to prevent the wicked from rejoicing in their wickedness. All this is plainly in accord with the natural reason. I could produce many more similar examples, but I think this is sufficient to explain my meaning and the usefulness of this method, which is my only object at present.

Now up to this point we have confined our investigation to those Scriptural pronouncements which are concerned with moral conduct, and which can be the more easily elucidated because on such subjects there has never been any real difference of opinion among the writers of the Bible. But other biblical passages which belong only to the field of philosophical speculation do not yield so easily to investigation. The approach is more difficult, for the prophets differed among themselves in matters of philosophical speculation (as we have already shown) and their narratives conform especially to the prejudices of their particular age. So we are debarred from deducing and explaining the meaning of one prophet from some clearer passages in another, unless it is most plainly established that they were of one and the same mind. I shall therefore briefly explain how in such cases we should elicit the meaning of the prophets from the study of Scripture. Here, again, we must begin from considerations of a most general kind, first of all seeking to establish from the clearest Scriptural pronouncements what is prophecy or revelation and what is its essential nature; then what is a miracle, and so on with other subjects of a most general nature. Thereafter we must move on to the beliefs of individual prophets, and from there finally to the meaning of each particular revelation or prophecy, narrative and miracle. We have already pointed out with many apposite examples what great caution we should exercise in these matters to avoid confusing the minds of the prophets and historians with the mind of the Holy Spirit and with factual truth, and so I do not think it necessary to say any more on this subject. But with regard to the meaning of revelation, it should be observed that this method only teaches us how to discover what the prophets really saw or heard, and not what they intended to signify or represent by the symbols in questions. The latter we can only guess at, not infer with certainty from the basis of Scripture.

We have thus set out our plan for interpreting Scripture, at the same time demonstrating that this is the only sure road to the discovery of its true meaning. I do indeed admit that those are better informed (if there are any) who are in possession of a sure tradition or true explanation transmitted from the prophets themselves, as the Pharisees claim, or those who have a pontiff whose interpretation of Scripture is infallible, as the Roman Catholics boast. However, as we cannot be sure either of the tradition in question or of the authority of the pontiff, we cannot base any certain conclusion on them. The latter is denied by the earliest Christians, the former by the most ancient sects of the Jews; and if, furthermore, we examine the succession of years (to mention nothing else) through which this tradition is traced right back to Moses, which the Pharisees have accepted from their Rabbis, we shall find that it is incorrect, as I prove elsewhere. Therefore such a tradition should be regarded with the utmost suspicion; and although our method requires us to accept as uncorrupted a certain tradition of the Jews — namely, the meaning of the words of the Hebrew language, which we have accepted from them — we can be quite sure of the one while doubting the other. For while it may occasionally have been in someone's interest to alter the meaning of some passage, it could never have been to anyone's interest to change the meaning of a word. Indeed, this is very difficult to accomplish, for whoever would try to change the meaning of a word would also have to explain all the writers who wrote in that language and used that word in its accepted meaning, in each case taking account of the character or intention of the writer; or else he would have to falsify the text, a task requiring much circumspection. Then again, a language is preserved by the learned and unlearned alike, whereas books and the meaning of their contents are preserved only by the learned. Therefore we can readily conceive that the learned may have altered or corrupted the meaning of some passage in a rare book which they had in their possession, but not the meaning of words. Besides which, if anyone should wish to change the customary meaning of a word, he would find it difficult to maintain consistency thereafter both in his writing and in his speaking.

For these and other reasons we may readily assume that it could never have entered anyone's mind to corrupt a language, whereas there may frequently have been an intention to corrupt the meaning of a writer by altering what he wrote or by giving it a wrong interpretation. Therefore, since our method (based on the principle that knowledge of Scripture must be sought only from Scripture) is the only true method, if there is anything that it cannot achieve for us in our pursuit of a complete understanding of Scripture, we must regard this as quite unattainable.

At this point I have to discuss any difficulties and shortcomings in our method which may stand in the way of our acquiring a complete and assured knowledge of the Holy Bible. The first important difficulty in our method is this, that it demands a thorough knowledge of the Hebrew language. Where is this now to be obtained? The men of old who used the Hebrew language have left to posterity no information concerning the basic principles and study of this language. At any rate, we possess nothing at all from them, neither dictionary nor grammar nor textbook on rhetoric. The Hebrew nation has lost all its arts and embellishments (little wonder, in view of the disasters and persecutions it has suffered) and has retained only a few remnants of its language and of its books, few in number. Nearly all the words for fruits, birds, fishes have perished with the passage of time, together with numerous other words. Then again, the meanings of many nouns and verbs occurring in the Bible are either completely unknown or subject to dispute. We are deprived not only of these, but more especially of the knowledge of Hebrew phraseology. The idiom and modes of speech peculiar to the Hebrew nation have almost all been consigned to oblivion by the ravages of time. So we cannot always discover to our satisfaction all the possible meanings which a particular passage can yield from linguistic usage; and there are many passages where the sense is very obscure and quite incomprehensible although the component words have a clearly established meaning.

Besides our inability to present a complete account of the Hebrew language, there is the further problem presented by the composition and nature of that language. This gives rise to so many ambiguities as to render it impossible to devise a method* that can teach us with certainty how to discover the true meaning of all Scriptural passages; for apart from the sources of ambiguity that are common to all languages, there are others peculiar to Hebrew which give rise to many ambiguities. These I think it worth listing here.

First, ambiguity and obscurity in the Bible are often caused by the fact that letters involving the same organ of speech are substituted one for another. The Hebrews divide all letters of the alphabet into five classes in accordance with the five oral instruments employed in their pronunciation, namely, the lips, the tongue, the teeth, the palate and the throat. For example, ה, ע, ח, א *alef, ḥet, ʿayin, hē* are called gutturals, and are used one in place of another without any distinction apparent to us. For instance, אל *el*, which means 'to', is often used for על *ʿal*, which means 'above', and vice-versa. As a result, any parts of a text may often be rendered ambiguous or appear to be meaningless utterances.

---

* See Supplementary Note 7.

A second ambiguity arises from the multiple meanings of conjunctions and adverbs. For example, ו *vav* serves indiscriminately to join and to separate, and can mean 'and', 'but', 'because', 'however' and 'then'. כ *ki* has seven or eight meanings: 'because', 'although', 'if', 'when', 'just as', 'that', 'a burning' and so on. This is the case with almost all particles.

Thirdly—and the source of many ambiguities—verbs in the Indicative mood lack the Present, the Past Imperfect, the Pluperfect and the Future Perfect, and other tenses in common use in other languages. In the Imperative and Infinitive moods verbs lack all the tenses except the Present, and in the Subjunctive there are no tenses at all. And although all the tenses and moods thus lacking could have been supplied, with ease and even with great elegance, by definite rules deduced from the fundamental principles of language, the writers of old showed complete disregard for such rules, and indiscriminately used Future for Present and Past, and contrariwise Past for Future, and furthermore used Indicative for Imperative and Subjunctive, to the great detriment of clarity.

Besides these three sources of ambiguity in Hebrew there remain two more to be noted, both of which are of far greater importance. First, the Hebrews do not have letters for vowels. Secondly, it was not their custom to punctuate their texts, nor to give them force or emphasis; and although vowels and punctuation thus lacking are usually supplied by points and accents, these cannot satisfy us, having been devised and instituted by men of a later age whose authority should carry no weight with us. The ancient writers did not employ points (that is, vowels and accents), as is abundantly testified; men of later ages added both of these in accordance with their own interpretation of the Bible. Therefore the accents and points that we now have are merely contemporary interpretations, and deserve no more credibility and authority than other commentaries. Those who fail to realise this do not understand the justification of the author of the Epistle to the Hebrews (ch. 11 v. 21) in giving an interpretation of the text of Genesis ch. 47 v. 31 very different from that of the pointed Hebrew text—as if the Apostle ought to have been taught the meaning of Scripture by those who inserted points! In my opinion it is the latter who should be regarded as at fault. To make this clear to all, and to show how different interpretations arise simply from the absence of vowels, I shall here set down both interpretations.

Those who inserted the points interpreted the passage as follows: 'and to Israel bent over (or, changing ע *'ayin* into א *alef*, a letter of the same organ, towards) the head of the bed.' The author of the Epistle reads 'and Israel bent over the head of his staff,' reading 'mate' for '*mita*', the only difference being in the vowels. Now since in this part of the story there is only a question of Jacob's age, and not of his illness which is mentioned in the next chapter, it seems more probable that the historian intended to say that Jacob bent over the head of his staff (which men of advanced age employ to support themselves), not of the bed; and this is especially so because this interpretation does not require the substitution of one letter for another. Now my purpose in giving this example is not only to harmonise the passage in the Epistle to the Hebrews with the text of Genesis, but also to show how little confidence is to be placed in modern points and accents. Thus he who would interpret Scripture without any prejudice is in duty bound to hold these in doubt and to examine them afresh.

To return to our theme, such being the structure and nature of the Hebrew language, it is quite understandable that such a number of ambiguities must arise that no method can be devised for deciding them all. For we have no grounds for expecting that this can be completely achieved from a comparison of different passages, which we have shown to be the only way to elicit the true meaning from the many senses which a particular passage can yield with linguistic justification. It is only by chance that a comparison of passages can throw light on any particular passage, since no prophets wrote with the deliberate purpose of explaining another's words, or his own. And furthermore, we can draw no conclusion as to the meaning of one prophet or apostle from the meaning of another except in matters of moral conduct, as we have already convincingly demonstrated; no such conclusions can be drawn when they are dealing with philosophical questions, or are narrating miracles or history. I could bring further examples to prove this point, that there are many inexplicable passages in Scripture; but I prefer to leave this subject for the present, and I shall proceed to a consideration of the points that still remain: the further difficulties we encounter in this true method of Scriptural interpretation, or in what way it falls short.

One further difficulty consequent upon this method is this, that it requires an account of the history of all the biblical books, and this for the most part we cannot provide. As I shall make clear at some length at a later stage, we either have no knowledge at all or but doubtful knowledge of the authors—or if you prefer the expression, the writers—of many of the books. Again, we do not even know on what occasion or at what time these books of unknown authorship were written. Furthermore, we do not know into whose hands all these books fell, or in whose copies so many different readings were found, nor yet again whether there were not many other versions in other hands. When I touched on this topic I did make a brief reference to the importance of knowing all these details, but there I deliberately passed over certain considerations which must now be taken up.

If we read a book relating events which are incredible or incomprehensible, or which is written in a very obscure style, and if we do not know the author or the time or the occasion of its composition, it well be vain for us to try to achieve a greater understanding of its true meaning. Deprived of all these facts we cannot possibly know what was, or could have been, the author's intention. But if we are fully informed of these facts, we are in a position to form an opinion free from all danger of mistaken assumptions; that is to say, we ascribe to the author, or to him for whom he wrote, no more and no less than his just meaning, concentrating our attention on what the author could have had in mind, or what the time and the occasion demanded. I imagine that everyone is agreed on this; for it often happens that we read in different books stories that are much alike, and form very different judgments of them according to our opinions of the writers. I remember once having read a book about a man named Orlando Furioso who used to ride a winged monster in the sky, fly over any regions he chose and singlehanded slay huge numbers of men and giants, together with other similar fantastic happenings which are quite incomprehensible in respect to our intellect. Now I had read a similar story in Ovid about Perseus, and another story in the books of Judges and Kings about Samson, who singlehanded and unarmed slew thousands of men, and of Elijah, who flew through the air and finally went to heaven in a chariot and horses of fire. These stories, I repeat, are obviously similar, yet we form a very different judgment of each. The first writer was concerned only to amuse, the second had a political motive, the third a religious motive, and it is nothing else but our opinion of the writers that brings us to make these judgments. It is therefore evident that in the case of obscure or incomprehensible writings, it is essential for us to have some knowledge of the authors if we seek to interpret their writings. And for the same reasons, to choose the correct reading out of the various readings of unclear narratives, we have to know in whose manuscript these different readings are found, and whether there were ever some other versions supported by men of greater authority.

In the case of certain books of the Bible, our method of interpretation involves the further difficulty that we do not possess them in the language in which they were first written. The Gospel according to Matthew and undoubtedly the Epistle to the Hebrews were written in Hebrew, it is commonly held, but are not extant in that form. There is some doubt as to the language in which the Book of Job was written. Ibn Ezra, in his commentaries, asserts that it was translated into Hebrew from another language, and that this is the reason for its obscurity. I say nothing of the apocryphal books, since their authority is of a very different kind.

Such then, is a full account of the difficulties involved in this method of interpreting Scripture from its own history, such as we possess. These difficulties, which I undertook to recount, I consider so grave that I have no hesitation in affirming that in many instances we either do not know the true meaning of Scripture or we can do no more than make conjecture. But on the other hand I must again emphasise, with regard to all these difficulties, that they can prevent us from grasping the meaning of the prophets only in matters beyond normal comprehension, which can merely be imagined; it is not true of matters open to intellectual perception, whereof we can readily form a clear conception.* For things which of their own nature are readily apprehended can never be so obscurely worded that they are not easily understood; as the proverb says, 'a word to the wise is enough.' Euclid, whose writings are concerned only with things exceedingly simple and perfectly intelligible, is easily made clear by anyone in any language; for in order to grasp his thought and to be assured of his true meaning there is no need to have a thorough knowledge of the language in which he wrote. A superficial and rudimentary knowledge is enough. Nor need we enquire into the author's life, pursuits and character, the language in which he wrote, and for whom and when, nor what happened to his book, nor its different readings, nor how it came to be accepted and by what council. And what we here say of Euclid can be said of all who have written on matters which of their very nature are capable of intellectual apprehension.

---

* See Supplementary Note 8.

Thus we can conclude that, with the help of such a historical study of Scripture as is available to us, we can readily grasp the meanings of its moral doctrines and be certain of their true sense. For the teachings of true piety are expressed in quite ordinary language, and being directed to the generality of people they are therefore straightforward and easy to understand. And since true salvation and blessedness consist in true contentment of mind and we find our true peace only in what we clearly understand, it most evidently follows that we can understand the meaning of Scripture with confidence in matters relating to salvation and necessary to blessedness. Therefore we have no reason to be unduly anxious concerning the other contents of Scripture; for since for the most part they are beyond the grasp of reason and intellect, they belong to the sphere of the curious rather than the profitable.

I consider that I have now displayed the true method of Scriptural interpretation and have sufficiently set forth my opinion on this matter. Furthermore, I have no doubt that it is now obvious to all that this method demands no other light than the natural light of reason. For the nature and virtue of that light consists essentially in this, that by a process of logical deduction that which is hidden is inferred and concluded from what is known, or given as known. This is exactly what our method requires. And although we grant that our method does not suffice to explain with certainty everything that is found in the Bible, this is the consequence not of the defectiveness of the method but of the fact that the path which it tells us is the true and correct one has never been pursued nor trodden by men, and so with the passage of time has become exceedingly difficult and almost impassable. This I imagine is quite clear from the very difficulties I have recounted.

It now remains for me to examine the views of those who disagree with me. The first to be considered is held by those who maintain that the natural light of reason does not have the power to interpret Scripture, and that a supernatural light is absolutely essential for this task. What they mean by this light that is beyond the natural light I leave them to explain. For my own part, I can only surmise that they wish to admit, using rather obscure terminology, that they too are for the most part in doubt as to the true meaning of Scripture; for if we consider their explanations, we find that they contain nothing of the supernatural—indeed, nothing but the merest conjectures. Let them be compared if you please, with the explanations of those who frankly admit that they possess no other light but the natural light. They will be found to be remarkably similar; that is to say, their explanations are human, the fruit of long thought, and elaborately devised. As to their assertions that the natural light is insufficient for this task, that is plainly false, for two reasons. In the first place, we have already proved that the difficulty of interpreting Scripture arises not from the lack of power of the natural light, but from the negligence (not to say malice) of those who failed to compile a historical study of Scripture while that was still possible. Secondly, everyone will admit, I imagine, that this supernatural light is a divine gift granted only to the faithful. Now the prophets and the apostles preached not only to the faithful, but especially to unbelievers and the impious. So their audiences must have been capable of understanding the meaning of the prophets and the apostles; otherwise these latter would have appeared to be preaching to children and babies, not to men endowed with reason. Moses, too, would have ordained his laws in vain if they could have been understood only by the faithful, who stand in no need of law. Therefore those who look to a supernatural light to understand the meaning of the prophets and the apostles are sadly in need of the natural light; and so I can hardly think that such men possess a divine supernatural gift.

Maimonides took a quite different view; for he held that every passage of Scripture admits of various—and even contrary—meanings, and that we cannot be certain of the true meaning of any passage unless we know that, as we interpret it, there is nothing in that passage that is not in agreement with reason, or is contrary to reason. If in its literal sense it is found to be contrary to reason, then however clear the passage may appear, he maintains that it must be interpreted in a different way. This view he sets out most clearly in chapter 25 of part 2 of his book 'More Nebuchim,'[1] where he says: "Know that it is not the Scriptural texts concerning the creation of the world that withholds me from saying that the world has existed from eternity. The texts that teach that the world was created are not more numerous than those that teach that God is corporeal. There are ways, not barred to us, nor even difficult of access, by which we can explain those texts that deal with the question of the world's creation. Our explanation could have followed the same lines as when we denied corporeality of God; and perhaps this might have been much easier to achieve, and we might have explained the texts and established the eternity of the world more plausibly than when we explained Scripture in a way that removed the notion of corporeality from God, blessed be He. Yet there are two reasons that prevent me from so doing and from believing that the world is eternal. First, there is clear proof that God is not corporeal, and it is necessary to explain all those passages whose literal meaning is contrary to that proof; for it is certain that they must then have an explanation other than the literal. But the eternity of the world has not been proved; so it is not necessary to do violence to the Scriptural texts and explain them away merely because of a plausible opinion, when we might incline to a contrary opinion with some degree of reason. Secondly, the belief that God is incorporeal is not contrary to the basic tenets of the Law, whereas the belief that the world is eternal, in the way that Aristotle held, destroys the very foundations of the Law."

Such are the words of Maimonides, and they clearly confirm what we said above. For if he had been convinced on rational grounds that the world is eternal, he would not have hesitated to distort and explain away Scripture until it appeared to teach the same doctrine. Indeed, he would have been quite convinced that Scripture, in spite of its plain denials at every point, intended to teach this same doctrine of the eternity of the world. So he cannot be sure of the true meaning of Scripture, however clearly stated, as long as he can doubt the truth of what it says, or as long as he is not convinced of it. For as long as we are not convinced of the truth of a statement, we cannot know whether it is in conformity with rea-

---

[1] [The title of the book that Spinoza cites is the Hebrew title for Maimonides' *Guide of the Perplexed*.]

son or contrary to it, and consequently neither can we know whether the literal meaning is true or false.

If this view were correct, I would unreservedly concede that we need a light other than the natural light to interpret Scripture; for nearly all the contents of Scripture are such as cannot be deduced from principles known by the natural light, as we have already shown. Thus the natural light does not enable us to reach any decisions as to their truth, nor therefore as to the true sense and meaning of Scripture. For this purpose we should necessarily need another kind of light. Then again, if this view were correct, it would follow that the common people, for the most part knowing nothing of logical reasoning or without leisure for it, would have to rely solely on the authority and testimony of philosophers for their understanding of Scripture, and would therefore have to assume that philosophers are infallible in their interpretations of Scripture. This would indeed be a novel form of ecclesiastical authority, with very strange priests or pontiffs, more likely to excite men's ridicule than veneration. And although our own method demands a knowledge of Hebrew, for which study the common people can likewise have no leisure, it is not open to the same sort of objection. The common people of the Jews and Gentiles for whom the prophets and apostles once preached and wrote, understood the language of the prophets and apostles and thereby they also comprehended the meaning of the prophets, but without understanding the rational justification of the prophets' message. Yet, according to Maimonides, this understanding was also necessary if they were to grasp the meaning of the prophets. There is nothing, then, in our method that requires the common people to abide by the testimony of biblical commentators, for I can point to a people who were familiar with the language of the prophets and apostles. But Maimonides cannot point to a people capable of understanding the causes of things, which would be a necessary basis for understanding the meaning of the prophets. And as to the common people of our own time, we have already shown that whatsoever is necessary for salvation, even though its rational justification be not understood, can be readily grasped in any language, because it is couched in ordinary and familiar terms; and it is this understanding, not the testimony of biblical commentators, that gains acceptance with the common people. And as for the rest of Scripture, the common people are on the same footing as the learned.

But let us return to the view put forward by Maimonides, and examine it more closely. In the first place, he assumes that the prophets were in agreement on all matters, and that they were outstanding philosophers and theologians; for he holds that they based their conclusions on scientific truth. But in Chapter 2 we have shown that this is not so. Then again, he assumes that the meaning of Scripture cannot be established from Scripture itself. For scientific truth is not established from Scripture itself, which does not engage in demonstrations and does not validate its teaching by appealing to definitions and first causes. And therefore, according to Maimonides, neither can Scripture's true meaning be established from itself, and should not be sought from it. But it is evident from this chapter that this point, too, is false. We have demonstrated both by reasoning and by examples that the meaning of Scripture is established from Scripture alone, and should be sought only from Scripture even when it is speaking of matters known by the natural light of reason. Finally, he assumes that it is legitimate for us to explain away and distort the words of Scripture to accord with our preconceived opinions, to deny its literal meaning and change it into something else even when it is perfectly plain and absolutely clear. Such licence, apart from being diametrically opposed to the proofs advanced in this chapter and elsewhere, must strike everyone as excessive and rash.

However, granting him this considerable degree of liberty, what in the end can it effect? Assuredly, nothing whatsoever. Those things that are not subject to proof and which make up the greater part of Scripture cannot yield to an enquiry of this sort, nor be explained or interpreted according to this rule; whereas by pursuing our method we can explain many things of this kind and investigate them with confidence, as we have already shown both by reason and by concrete example. And in the case of things that are by their nature comprehensible, their meaning can easily be elicited merely from their context, as we have also shown. Thus this method of Maimonides is plainly of no value. Furthermore, he clearly deprives the common people of any confidence they can have in the meaning of Scripture derived from simply perusing it; and yet this confidence is available to all by pursuing a different method. Therefore we can dismiss Maimonides' view as harmful, unprofitable and absurd.

As to the tradition of the Pharisees, we have already declared that it lacks consistency, while the authority of the Popes of Rome stands in need of clearer evidence. This is my only reason for impugning the latter, for if they could prove it from Scripture itself with the same degree of certainty as did the Jewish High Priests of long ago, I should not be influenced by the fact that among the Popes there have been found heretics and impious men. Among the Hebrew High Priests, too, in the past were found heretics and impious men, who gained the priesthood by underhanded means; and yet by Scriptural sanction they possessed the supreme power to interpret the Law. See Deut. ch. 17 v. 11, 12 and ch. 33 v. 10, and Malachi ch. 2 v. 8. But since the Popes can produce no such evidence, their authority remains highly suspect. The example of the Jewish High Priest ought not to deceive one into thinking that the Catholic religion also stands in need of a high priest; for it should be noted that the laws of Moses, being his country's civil laws, necessarily stood in need of some public authority to uphold them. If every man were free to interpret the civil laws as he chose, no state could survive; by that very fact it would be instantly dissolved, and public right would become private right.

Now with religion the case is quite different. Since it consists in honesty and sincerity of heart rather than in outward actions, it does not pertain to the sphere of public law and authority. Honesty and sincerity of heart is not imposed on man by legal command or by the state's authority. It is an absolute fact that nobody can be constrained to a state of blessedness by force or law; to this end one needs godly and brotherly exhortation, a good upbringing, and most of all, a judgment that is independent and free.

Therefore, as the sovereign right to free opinion belongs to every man even in matters of religion, and it is inconceivable that any man can surrender this right, there also belongs to every man the sovereign right and supreme authority to judge freely with regard to religion, and consequently to explain it and interpret it for himself. The supreme authority to interpret laws and the supreme judgment on affairs of state is vested in magistrates for this reason only, that these belong to the sphere of public right. Thus for the same reason the supreme authority to explain religion and to make judgment concerning it is vested in each individual, because it belongs to the sphere of individual right.

It is, then, far from true that the authority of the Hebrew High Priest in interpreting his country's laws enables us to infer the Pope's authority to interpret religion; on the contrary, a more obvious inference is that the interpretation of religion is vested above all in each individual. And this again affords further proof that our method of Scriptural interpretation is the best. For since the supreme authority for the interpretation of Scripture is vested in each individual, the rule that governs interpretation must be nothing other than the natural light that is common to all, and not any supernatural light, nor any eternal authority. Nor must this rule be so difficult as not to be available to any but skilled philosophers; it must be suited to the natural and universal ability and capacity of mankind. We have shown that our rule answers to this description; for we have seen that such difficulties as are now to be found in it have arisen from the negligence of men, and are not inherent in our method.

CHAPTER 8

In which it is shown that the Pentateuch and the Books of Joshua, Judges, Ruth, Samuel and Kings were not written by themselves. The question of their authorship is considered. Was there one author, or several, and who were they?

In the preceding chapter we discussed the foundations and principles of Scriptural knowledge, and showed that this consists simply in a thorough historical study of Scripture. In spite of its indispensability, the writers of ancient times failed to compile such a study, or if in fact they did compile or transmit one, it has disappeared through the ravages of time, consequently leaving us to a great extent deprived of the foundations and principles of Scriptural knowledge. This loss would not have been so serious if later generations had kept within the bounds of truth and had faithfully transmitted to their successors the few facts they had received or discovered, without the addition of new ideas of their own devising. As it is, the historical study of Scripture has remained not merely incomplete but prone to error; that is, the foundations of Scriptural knowledge are not only too scanty to form the basis for a complete understanding, but are also unsound. It belongs to my purpose to correct these faults and to remove common theological prejudices. But I fear that I approach this task too late; for matters have almost reached such a pass that men will not endure correction on this subject, and will obstinately defend what they have embraced in the name of religion. It is only with very few, comparatively speaking, that there seems any place left for reason, so pervasively have these prejudices seized upon men's minds. However, I shall make the attempt and persevere in my efforts, since there is no reason for utter despair.

To treat the matter in logical order, I shall first deal with misconceptions regarding the true authorship of the Sacred Books, beginning with the Pentateuch. The author is almost universally believed to be Moses, a view so obstinately defended by the Pharisees that they have regarded any other view as heresy. It was for this reason that ibn Ezra, a man of enlightened mind and considerable learning, who was the first, as far as I know, to call attention to this misconception, did not venture to explain his meaning openly, and expressed himself somewhat obscurely in words which I shall here not hesitate to elucidate, making his meaning quite plain.

The words of ibn Ezra in his commentary on Deuteronomy are as follows: "'Beyond the Jordan, etc.' If you understand the mystery of the twelve, and also 'Moses wrote the Law,' and, 'the Canaanite was then in the land,' 'it shall be revealed on the Mount of God,' and again 'Behold his bed, a bed of iron,' then shall you know the truth." In these few words he gives a clear indication that it was not Moses who wrote the Pentateuch but someone else who lived long after him, and that it was a different book that Moses wrote. To make this clear, he draws attention to the following points:

1. The preface to Deuteronomy could not have been written by Moses, who did not cross the Jordan.

2. The Book of Moses was inscribed in its entirety on no more than the circumference of a single altar (Deut. ch. 27 and Joshua ch. 8 v. 30 etc.), and this altar, according to the Rabbis, consisted of only twelve stones. From this it follows that the Book of Moses must have required far less space than the Pentateuch. This, I say, was what our author meant by his reference to 'the mystery of the twelve,' unless he was referring to the twelve curses in the aforementioned chapter of Deuteronomy. Perhaps he believed that these could not have been contained in Moses' Book of the Law, because Moses bids the Levites read out these curses in addition to the recital of the Law, so as to bind the people by oath to observe the recited laws. Or again he may have wished to draw attention to the last chapter of Deuteronomy concerning the death of Moses, a chapter consisting of twelve verses. But there is no need here to give closer scrutiny to these and other conjectures.

3. Deuteronomy ch. 31 v. 9 says, "And Moses wrote the Law." These words cannot be ascribed to Moses; they must be those of another writer narrating the deeds and writings of Moses.

4. In Genesis ch. 12 v. 6 when the narrative tells of Abraham journeying through the land of Canaan, the historian adds, "the Canaanite was then in the

land," thereby clearly excluding the time at which he was writing. So this passage must have been written after the death of Moses when the Canaanites had been driven out and no longer possessed those lands. In his commentary of this passage ibn Ezra makes the same point in these words: "'And the Canaanite was then in the land.' It appears that Canaan (the grandson of Noah) took the land of Canaan which had been in the possession of another. If this is not the true meaning, some mystery lies here, and let him who understands it keep silent." That is to say, if Canaan invaded that land, then the sense will be that the Canaanite was already in the land, as opposed to some past time when the land was inhabited by another nation. But if Canaan was the first to settle in that region (as follows from Gen. ch. 10), then the words are intended to exclude the present time, that is, the time of the author. This could not be Moses, in whose time the land was still possessed by the Canaanites; and this is the mystery concerning which ibn Ezra urges silence.

5. In Genesis ch. 22 v. 14 Mount Moriah* is called the Mount of God, a name it did not acquire until after it was assigned to the building of the temple. This choice of mountain was not made in the time of Moses, for Moses does not indicate any position as chosen by God. On the contrary, he foretells that God will at some time choose a place to which his name will be given.

6. Lastly, in Deuteronomy ch. 3 v. 11, in the narrative about Og, king of Bashan, these words are inserted, "Only Og, king of Bashan, remained as the sole survivor of the giants.** Behold, his bedstead was a bedstead of iron, the bedstead that is now in Rabbah of the children of Ammon, nine cubits long...." This parenthesis shows most clearly that the writer of these books lived long after the time of Moses, for this manner of speaking can characterise only one who is narrating ancient history and is pointing to relics to prove his assertion. There is no doubt that this bed was first discovered in the time of David, who conquered this city, as related in 2 Sam. ch. 12 v. 30. A further example of words being inserted in Moses' narrative occurs a little further on, where the same historian says, "Jair, the son of Manasseh, took all the region of Argob as far as the Geshurite and Maacathite border, and called them after his own name Bashan Havvoth Jair unto this day." The historian, I say, added these words so as to explain the words of Moses which he had just related, to wit, "And the rest of Gilead and all Bashan, the kingdom of Og, gave I unto the half-tribe of Manasseh, all the region of Argob with all Bashan, which is called the land of giants." There is no doubt that at the time of this writer the Hebrews knew what was Havvoth Jair of the tribe of Judah, but not under the name of the region of Argob, nor the land of giants. So he was forced to explain what these places were that were so called in antiquity, and at the same time give reason why in his time they took the name of Jair, who was of the tribe of Judah, not Manasseh (see 1 Chron. ch. 2 v. 21, 22).

---

* See Supplementary Note 9.

** The Hebrew *'rephaim'* means 'the condemned,' and from 1 Chron. ch. 20 it also appears to be a proper name. For this reason I think it is here a family name.

We have now set forth the view of ibn Ezra, and the passages of the Pentateuch which he cites in support. Yet he did not call attention to all such passages, nor even the principal ones; for there are many other passages in these books, and of greater significance, which have yet to be cited.

1. The writer of these books not only speaks of Moses in the third person, but also bears witness to many details concerning him: for instance, 'God talked with Moses' 'God spake with Moses face to face' 'Moses was the meekest of men' (Num. ch. 12 v. 3), 'Moses was wrath with the captains of the host' (Num. ch. 31 v. 14), 'Moses, the man of God' (Deut. ch. 33 v. 1), 'Moses, the servant of God, died,' 'There has never arisen in Israel a prophet like Moses,' and so on. On the other hand, in Deuteronomy, where the Law, which Moses had expounded to the people and put in written form, is set forth, Moses speaks and narrates his deeds in the first person; for instance, 'God spoke to me' (Deut. ch. 2 v. 1, 17 etc.), 'I prayed to God,' and so on. However, later on towards the end of the book, after the historian has reported the words of Moses, he again continues the narrative in the third person, telling how Moses handed over to the people in written form the Law he had expounded, with his last admonition, and how he came to the end of his life. All these considerations—the manner of speaking, the giving of testimony, the very structure of the entire history—lead us to the plain conclusion that these books were written not by Moses, but by another.

2. It should further be added that this history not only narrates the death of Moses, his burial, and the thirty days mourning of the Hebrews, but also draws a comparison between Moses and all the other prophets who came after him, declaring that he excelled them all. "There has never arisen in Israel a prophet like Moses," he says, "whom God knew face to face." Such testimony could never have been given by Moses of himself, nor by any immediate successor, but by someone who lived many generations later, and particularly so since the historian seems to be speaking of some remote time, as in "there has never arisen a prophet," etc. And he says of his place of burial, "Nobody knows it unto this day."

3. Some places are indicated not by the names they bore in Moses' time, but by other names which they only later acquired. For instance, Abraham "pursued the enemy even unto Dan" (Gen. ch. 14 v. 14), a name not given to that city until long after the death of Joshua (Judges ch. 18 v. 29).

4. The narrative sometimes continues beyond the death of Moses, for in Exodus ch. 16 v. 35 we are told that 'the children of Israel did eat manna forty years until they came to a land inhabited, until they came unto the borders of the land of Canaan'; that is to say, until the time referred to in Joshua ch. 5 v. 12. Again, in Genesis ch. 36 v. 31 we read, 'These are the kings that reigned in Edom before there reigned any king over the children of Israel.' Undoubtedly the historian here lists the kings of Idumaea before David conquered that people* and set up governors in the land (2 Sam. ch. 8 v. 14).

Thus from the foregoing it is clear beyond a shadow of doubt that the Pentateuch was not written by Moses, but by someone who lived many generations af-

---

* See Supplementary Note 10.

ter Moses. But let us now turn our attention, if you please, to the books which Moses did write and which are cited in the Pentateuch; for we shall see from them that they were different from the Pentateuch. In the first place, then, Exodus ch. 17 v. 14 tells us that Moses, by God's command, wrote an account of the war against Amalek. In that chapter we are not told what book this was, but in Numbers ch. 21 v. 12 reference is made to a certain book called the 'Book of the Wars of God,' which undoubtedly included the history of this war against Amalek together with all the stages of their journeyings (which in Numbers ch. 33 v. 2 the author of the Penteteuch testifies were also written by Moses). Again, Exodus ch. 24 v. 4, 7 gives evidence of another book called the 'Book of the Covenant,'* which Moses read before the Israelites when they first entered into a covenant with God. Now this book or document contained very little, namely, the laws or commandments of God which are set out in Exodus from chapter 20 v. 22 to chapter 24, and this no one will deny who reads the aforesaid chapter impartially and with sound judgment. There we read that as soon as Moses realised the feelings of the people with regard to a covenant with God, he immediately wrote down God's utterances and laws, and in the morning, when certain ceremonies had been performed, he read out the terms of the covenant to the whole congregation. When the terms had been read out and no doubt understood by the entire assembly, the people bound themselves with full consent. It therefore follows both from the brief time taken in writing down the book and from the manner of the ratifying of the covenant, that this book contained nothing more than the few items I have mentioned.

Lastly, it is clear that in the fortieth year from the departure out of Egypt Moses explained all the laws that he made (see Deut. ch. 1 v. 5) and bound the people anew to observe them (Deut. ch. 29 v. 14), and finally wrote a book containing these laws as explained and this new covenant (see Deut. ch. 31 v. 9). This book was called the Book of the Law of God, to which Joshua later added an account of the covenant by which the people of his time bound themselves once more, making a covenant with God for the third time (see Josh. ch. 24 v. 25, 26). Now since there is no extant book containing this covenant of Moses together with the covenant of Joshua, we have to grant that this book has perished—or else we must share in the madness of the Chaldaean Paraphrast Jonathan,[1] distorting the words of Scripture just as we please. Confronted by this problem, this commentator preferred to corrupt Scripture rather than admit his ignorance. The passage in the book of Joshua (ch. 24 v. 26) which runs, "And Joshua wrote these words in the book of the Law of God," he translates in Chaldaic, "And Joshua wrote these words and kept them together with the book of the Law of God." What can you do with those who see nothing but what they please? What else is this, I ask, but to reject Scripture itself and fashion a new Scripture of one's own devising?

---

* The Hebrew word 'sepher' often means letter or writing.
[1] [The Chaldaean Paraphrast Jonathan was Jonathan ben Uzziel, first century A.D., who produced an Aramaic (Chaldaean) translation or paraphrase of the Bible, called a Targum. Maimonides held him in high regard.]

We may therefore conclude that the book of the Law of God which Moses wrote was not the Pentateuch, but a quite different book which the author of the Pentateuch inserted in proper order in his own work; and this conclusion follows on the clearest evidence not only from what has just been said but also from what I am about to state. In the passage of Deuteronomy just quoted which tells us that Moses wrote the book of the Law, the historian adds that Moses gave it into the hands of the priests, and that he further ordered them to read it out to the entire people at an appointed time. This indicates that the book in question was much shorter than the Pentateuch, seeing that it could be read through at a single assembly so as to be understood by all. Nor must we here omit to mention that, of all the books that Moses wrote, it was only this one of the second covenant and the Canticle[2] (which he later added so that all the people might learn it) that he commanded to be religiously guarded and preserved. For by the first covenant he had bound only those who were present, whereas by the second covenant he also bound those who should come after them (Deut. ch. 29 v. 14, 15). He therefore commanded that this book of the second covenant be religiously preserved for future generations, and with it, as we have said, the Canticle, which particularly concerns future generations. Since, then, there is no evidence that Moses wrote any other books but these, and he gave no instructions for any other book but this book of the Law together with the Canticle to be preserved religiously for posterity, and finally, since there are many passages in the Pentateuch that could not have been written by Moses, it follows that there are no grounds for holding Moses to be the author of the Pentateuch, and that such an opinion is quite contrary to reason.

Now at this point someone will perhaps ask whether, in addition to the above, Moses did not write down laws when they were first revealed to him; that is, whether over the space of forty years he did not write down any of the laws which he made except those few which I have stated were contained in the book of the first covenant. To this I reply that, although I would grant it to be a reasonable assumption that Moses wrote down the laws at the time and place where he happened to promulgate them, I deny that it is therefore legitimate for us to affirm this. We have previously shown that in matters like this we must assert nothing but what is established from Scripture itself, or what logically proceeds solely from the fundamental principles of Scripture. It is not enough that such an assertion should appear reasonable. Moreover, neither does reason itself compel us to this conclusion. It is possible that the elders communicated Moses' decrees to the people in writing, and that later the historian gathered these together and inserted them in due order in the life of Moses.

So much for the five books of Moses; it is now time for us to examine the other books. The book of Joshua can likewise be shown, by similar arguments, not to be by the hand of Joshua; for it is someone else who testifies of Joshua that his fame was spread throughout the world (ch. 6 v. 27), that he omitted nothing of what

---

[2] [Spinoza is referring to Moses' song in Deuteronomy 33.]

Moses had commanded him (ch. 8 last verse and ch. 11 v. 15), that he grew old and summoned the entire people to an assembly, and that finally he breathed his last. Then again, some events are narrated that happened after Joshua's death, as that after his death the Israelites continued to worship God as long as men who had known him were still alive. And in chapter 16 v. 10 we read that Ephraim and Manasseh 'did not drive out the Canaanites that dwelt in Gezer, but (he adds) the Canaanites have dwelt among the Ephraimites unto this day, and served as tributaries.' This is the same as the narrative in Judges, chapter 1, and the turn of phrase 'even unto this day' indicates that the writer is speaking of ancient times. Similar to this is the text of chapter 15, last verse, concerning the sons of Judah, and the history of Caleb from verse 13 of the same chapter. Again, the events narrated in chapter 22 from verse 10 on, when the two tribes and a half built an altar beyond Jordan, seem to have taken place after the death of Joshua; for throughout the story there is no mention of Joshua, and it is the people alone who hold council as to waging war, send delegates and await the reply they bring, which they finally approve. Lastly, the passage in chapter 10 v. 14 clearly proves that this book was written many generations after Joshua, for it testifies, "There was no day like that, either before it or after it, that the Lord hearkened unto the voice of a man," etc. Therefore if Joshua wrote any book at all, it must be that which is quoted in ch. 10 v. 13 of this same history.

As for the book of Judges, I imagine that nobody of sound judgment can believe that it was written by the judges themselves, for the summary of the whole book in chapter 2 clearly shows that the entire book is the work of a single historian. Then again, since the writer often remarks that in those times there was no king in Israel, there can be no doubt that it was written after the institution of monarchy.

We need spend little time in considering the books of Samuel, inasmuch as the history is continued long after his lifetime. However, I should like it to be noted that this book, too, was written many generations after Samuel. In book 1, chapter 9 v. 9 the historian remarks in parenthesis, "Beforetimes in Israel, when a man went to inquire of God, thus he spoke, 'Come, let us go to a seer'; for he that is now called a prophet was beforetime called a seer."

Lastly, the books of Kings, as is made clear by their contents, are taken from the books of the Acts of Solomon (see 1 Kings ch. 11 v. 41), from the chronicles of the kings of Judah (1 Kings ch. 14 v. 19, 29), and from the chronicles of the kings of Israel.

We may therefore conclude that all the books we have so far considered are the works of other hands, and that their contents are narrated as ancient history.

If we now turn our attention to the interconnection and the main theme of all these books, we shall easily see that they are all the work of a single historian who set out to write the antiquities of the Jews from their first beginnings until the first destruction of the city.[3] These books are so connected with one another that this

---

[3] [This is Jerusalem.]

alone is sufficient to enable us to decide that they form the narrative of a single historian. As soon as he reaches the end of the narrative of the life of Moses, the historian passes on to the life of Joshua with these words: "Now after the death of Moses, the servant of the Lord, it came to pass that the Lord spake unto Joshua . . . ," and when this narrative ends with the death of Joshua, he begins the history of the Judges with exactly the same transitional words, "Now after the death of Joshua it came to pass that the children of Israel asked the Lord. . . ." To this book he joins the story of Ruth as an appendix, with these words: "Now it came to pass in the days when the Judges ruled that there was a famine in the land." Then there is the same sort of transition between Ruth and the first Book of Samuel, at the end of which he proceeds with his customary transitional phrase to the second book. Then, without completing the history of David, he moves on to the first Book of Kings, and, continuing the history of David, he goes on with the same transition to the second Book of Kings.

Again, the construction and order of the narratives also shows that there was only one historian, with a fixed aim in view. He begins by narrating the first origins of the Hebrew nation, and then continues in an orderly way to relate on what occasions and at what times Moses made his laws and his numerous prophecies. He then goes on to tell how the Israelites invaded the promised land in accordance with Moses' prophecies (see Deut. ch. 7), and how, after possessing the land, they forsook their laws (Deut. ch. 31 v. 16) and thereafter met with many misfortunes (same ch. v. 17). Then he relates how the people decided to choose kings (Deut. ch. 17 v. 14), who likewise prospered or failed according to the reverence they paid to the laws, and, finally, how their kingdom was destroyed as Moses had foretold. With regard to other matters that are not relevant to the observance of the Law, our historian either keeps silent or refers the reader to other historians. Thus all these books have but a single theme, to set forth the words and commandments of Moses and to demonstrate their truth by the course of history.

When we consider in unison these three points, namely, the unity of theme of all these books, their interconnections, and the fact that they were written by a later hand many generations after the events, we may conclude, as I have just stated, that they were all the work of a single historian. The identity of this historian is not susceptible to certain proof, but I believe it was Ezra, a conjecture supported by a number of weighty reasons.

The historian (whom we already know to be a single individual) continues his history up to the liberation of Jehoiachin, adding that he sat at the king's table all the days of his life (that is, either Jehoiachin's life or the life of the son of Nebuchadnezzar, for the meaning is by no means clear). Hence it follows that the historian could not have been anyone before Ezra. Now Scripture testifies of Ezra alone of all men of his time (Ezra ch. 7 v. 10) that he devoted himself to seek the Law of God and to set it forth, and that he was a scribe learned in the Law of Moses (Ezra ch. 7 v. 6). Therefore I cannot imagine anyone but Ezra as the writer of these books.

Again, on examining this testimony concerning Ezra, we note that he devoted himself not only to seek the Law of God but also to set it forth, and in Nehemiah ch. 8 v. 8 we are also told that "they read the book of the Law distinctly, and caused them to understand, and they understood the Scripture." Now since Deuteronomy contains not only the book of the Law of Moses, or most of it, but also many passages inserted for its fuller explanation, I conjecture that Deuteronomy is that book of the Law of God, written, set forth and explained by Ezra, which they read at that time. As to the numerous parenthetic insertions in Deuteronomy which serve for fuller explanation, I gave two examples of this in discussing the views of ibn Ezra, and there are many more such passages to be found; for example, chapter 2 v. 12, "The Ḥorites also dwelt in Seir beforetime, but the children of Esau drove them out and destroyed them from before them, and dwelt in their stead, as Israel did unto the land of his possession, which the Lord gave unto him." Here he is explaining verses 3 and 4 of the same chapter, saying that Mount Seir, which had come to the children of Esau for their possession, was not seized by them uninhabited, but that they invaded it and expelled and destroyed the Horites who formerly dwelt there, just as after Moses' death the Israelites expelled the Canaanites.

Other parenthetic insertions in the words of Moses are verses 6, 7, 8, 9 of chapter 10; for it is obvious that verse 8, which begins, "At that time the Lord separated the tribe of Levi" must refer back to verse 5, and not to the death of Aaron, which Ezra seems to have inserted at this point only because Moses, when he recounted the story of the worship of the calf, had said (ch. 9 v. 20), that he had prayed to God on Aaron's behalf. Ezra then goes on to explain that, at the time of which Moses is here speaking, God had chosen for himself the tribe of Levi, thus giving reason for the election and the exclusion of the Levites from a share in the inheritance; and thereafter he continues the thread of the history in the words of Moses. Then there is also the preface to the book, and all those passages where Moses is spoken of in the third person. And there were doubtless many other passages, which we cannot now identify, which were added or given a different expression by the historian, so that they might be more easily comprehended by his contemporaries.

If, I say, we possessed Moses' original book of the Law, I doubt not that we should find considerable differences both in the wording of his commandments and in the order of the text and in the explanations given. If only the Decalogue of Deuteronomy be compared with the Decalogue of Exodus (where its history is explicitly given) the former is found to differ from the latter on all these points. In the former the fourth commandment not only takes a different form but is set out at much greater length, and the reasoning on which it is based is quite different from that given in the Exodus Decalogue. And finally, the order in which the tenth commandment is here set forth is also quite different from that of Exodus.

It is my opinion, as I have already said, that the discrepancies here and elsewhere are due to Ezra because he was explaining the Law of God to the people of his own time, and therefore this is the book of the Law of God as presented and set forth by Ezra. And this book, I believe, was the first of all the books which I have attributed to him. This conjecture is supported by the fact that it contains the laws of his country—which are the most urgent need of a people—and also that this book, unlike all the others, is not joined to the preceding book by a transitional phrase, but begins independently with 'These are the words of Moses. . . .' Now when he had completed this task and had instructed the people in the laws, I believe he applied himself to composing a complete history of the Hebrew nation from the creation of the world to the final destruction of the city, and into this work he inserted the book of Deuteronomy in its appropriate place. Perhaps he called the first five books by the name of Moses because their principal subject is the life of Moses, the name deriving from the main theme. For the same reason he called the sixth book the book of Joshua, the seventh the book of Judges, the eighth Ruth, the ninth and perhaps the tenth the books of Samuel, and the eleventh and twelfth the books of Kings. On the question as to whether Ezra put the final touches to this work and completed it as he intended, see the next chapter.

CHAPTER 9

An enquiry into further matters relating to these same books, namely, whether Ezra gave them a final revision, and whether the marginal notes found in the Hebrew codices were variant readings

In the preceding chapter we discussed the question of the true authorship of the books therein considered. In support of our theory we considered some obscure passages which can be clarified only by this theory, a fact which in itself emphasises how much our theory contributes to a complete understanding of these books. But apart from the question of authorship, we have yet to draw attention to some other points of interest in the books themselves, the comprehension of which is denied to people in general by the prevalence of superstition. Of these the most important is this, that Ezra (whom I shall regard as the author of the aforementioned books until a more likely candidate appears) did not make a final revision of the narratives contained in these books and confined himself to making a collection of the histories from various writers, sometimes simply copying them down as they were and leaving them to posterity without proper scrutiny and arrangement.

The reasons (if it was not his untimely death) which prevented him from completing this work in final detail are beyond my conjecture. But although the ancient Hebrew historians are lost to us, the few remnants that we do possess make the fact indisputable. The history of Hezekiah (2 Kings ch. 18 from v. 17 on) was copied from Isaiah's account just as it appeared in the chronicles of the kings of Judah, for we have it in its entirety in the book of Isaiah—which was included in the chronicles of the kings of Judah (see 2 Chron. ch. 32 v. 32)—in exactly the same words as in the other narrative, with a few exceptions.* Hence we are bound to conclude that there existed various versions of this narrative of Isaiah—unless one should prefer to imagine that here, again, there lurk some mysteries. Moreover, the ending of 2 Kings is repeated in the last chapter of Jeremiah v. 31–34. In addition, we find that 2 Sam. ch. 7 is repeated in 1 Chron. ch. 17; but in a number of places the words are seen to have undergone such a remarkable change** that it is obvious that the two chapters are taken from two different copies of the story of Nathan. Finally, the genealogy of the kings of Idumaea, in Gen. ch. 36 v. 31 on, is also repeated in the same words in 1 Chron. ch. 1, although it is clear that the author of the latter book took his materials from other historians, and not from the twelve books we have ascribed to Ezra. Therefore there can be no doubt that if the historians themselves were available to us, we should have direct proof of our contention. But since they are lost to us, our only resource is to examine the histories that we do possess, considering their order and interconnections, the various repetitions and the discrepancies in the reckoning of years, from which we may judge of the rest.

Let us then consider these histories, or at least the most noteworthy; and in the first place the story of Judah and Tamar (Gen. 38), where the historian begins his narration thus: "And it came to pass at that time that Judah departed from his brethren. . . ." The time here mentioned must refer not to the passage that immediately precedes it in Genesis but to a quite different time*** of which it is the immediate continuation. For from the former time—that is, the time when Joseph was taken away to Egypt—until the time when the patriarch Jacob also set out thither with all his household, we can reckon no more than twenty-two years. Joseph was seventeen years old when he was sold by his brothers, and he was thirty years old when he was summoned by Pharaoh from prison. If we add to this the seven years of plenty and the two years of famine, we arrive at a total of twenty-two years. Now nobody can conceive that in this space of time so many events could have taken place: that Judah begat three children, one after another, from the one wife whom he married at that time, that the eldest of these married Tamar when he was of age, that when he died the second son married her in turn, and also died, that some time after these events Judah unwittingly had intercourse with his own daughter-in-law Tamar, that she bore him twins, of whom one also became a father within the aforesaid period. Thus, since all these events cannot be accommodated within the time specified in Genesis, the reference must be to some immediately preceding time in the narrative of a different book. Therefore Ezra must have simply copied out this story, too, inserting it into the rest of his work without critical examination.

Now it has to be admitted that not only this chapter but the entire story of

---

* See Supplementary Note 11.
** See Supplementary Note 12.
*** See Supplementary Note 13.

Joseph and Jacob was gathered and copied down from different sources, such are the number of inconsistencies to be found in it. Genesis chapter 47 tells us that Jacob was 130 years old when first Joseph brought him to salute Pharaoh. If we subtract the twenty-two years he passed in sorrowing for Joseph's absence, and the seventeen years which was Joseph's age when he was sold, and finally the seven years he served for Rachel, we find that he was old indeed, eighty-four in fact, when he married Leah, while Dinah was scarcely seven years old* when she was violated by Shechem, and Simeon and Levi had scarcely reached the ages of twelve and eleven when they spoiled that entire city and slew all its people with the sword.

There is no need for me here to review the whole of the Pentateuch. If one merely observes that all the contents of these five books, histories and precepts, are set forth with no distinction or order and with no regard to chronology, and that frequently the same story is repeated, with variations, it will readily be recognised that all these materials were collected indiscriminately and stored together with view to examining them and arranging them more conveniently at some later time. And not only the contents of these five books but the other histories in the remaining seven books right down to the destruction of the city were compiled in the same way. Nobody can fail to see that in chapter 2 of Judges at verse 6 there appears on the scene a new historian who had also written of Joshua's deeds, and that his words are simply set down unchanged. For after our historian has related in the last chapter of Joshua how Joshua died and was buried, and in the first chapter of Judges has promised to continue the history after Joshua's death, what logical connection—if he really intended to pursue the thread of his story—could he have claimed between the preceding verses and what he here begins to relate of Joshua?**

In the same way, too, chapters 17, 18 etc. of 1 Samuel are taken from another historian, who held that the reason why David began to frequent Saul's court was very different from that given in chapter 16 of this same book. He did not think that it was by his servants' advice that Saul summoned David to his presence (as is related in chapter 16), but that, happening to be sent by his father to his brothers in camp, David first came to Saul's attention through his victory over the Philistine Goliath, and was detained at his court. I suspect that the same applies to chapter 26 of this same book, where the historian appears to repeat the narrative of chapter 24, but gives a different version. But I pass over this point, and proceed to examine the question of chronology.

In 1 Kings chapter 6 we are told that Solomon built his temple 480 years after the exodus from Egypt, but the narratives themselves require a much greater number of years.

---

* See Supplementary Note 14.
** See Supplementary Note 15.

	Years
Moses governed the people in the desert	40
According to Josephus and other writers, Joshua, who lived to the age of 110, led the people for no more than	26
Cushan Rishathaim held the people in subjection	8
Othniel, son of Kenaz, was judge*	40
Eglon, king of Moab, held rule over the people	18
Ehud and Shamgar were judges	80
Jabin, king of Canaan, again held the people in subjection	20
Thereafter the people were at peace	40
Then they were in subjection to Midian	7
In the time of Gideon they were free	40
They were under the rule of Abimelech	3
Tola, son of Pua, was judge	23
Jair was judge	22
The people were again in subjection to the Philistines and the Ammonites	18
Jephtha was judge	6
Ibzan the Bethlehemite was judge	7
Elon the Zebulunite was judge	10
Abdon the Pirathonite was judge	8
The people were again in subjection to the Philistines	40
Samson was judge**	20
Eli was judge	40
The people were again in subjection to the Philistines until they were freed by Samuel	20
David reigned	40
Solomon reigned before building the temple	4
Total	580

To this total must be added the period after the death of Joshua when the Hebrew state flourished before it was subjugated by Cushan Rishathaim, a period which I believe covered a considerable number of years. For I cannot be persuaded that immediately after the death of Joshua all those who witnessed his marvelous doings perished all at once, and that their successors rejected their laws at a single stroke and plunged from the heights of virtue into the depths of wickedness and indolence, or that Cushan Rishathaim subjugated them at one blow. Since each of these circumstances requires about a generation, there can be no doubt that the book of Judges, chapter 2 v. 7, 9, 10 covers the history of many years which it passes over in silence.

Furthermore, we must add the years when Samuel was judge, the number of which is again not given in Scripture; and then there are the years of Saul's reign,

---

* See Supplementary Note 16.
** See Supplementary Note 17.

which I have omitted in the above calculation because the history of Saul does not make clear the length of his reign. There is indeed the statement in 1 Samuel chapter 13 v. 1 that he reigned two years, but the text there is mutilated, and the narrative itself also postulates a longer period. That the text is mutilated cannot be doubted by anyone who has the slightest acquaintance with the Hebrew language, for it begins thus, "Saul was in his __ year when he began to reign, and he reigned for two years over Israel." Who can fail to see, I repeat, that the number of years of Saul's age when he began to reign has been omitted? And I do not think that anyone can doubt too that the narrative itself requires a greater number for the years of his reign. For chapter 27 v. 7 of the same book tells us that David sojourned among the Philistines, to whom he had fled for refuge from Saul, a year and four months. By this calculation the other events of his reign must have occupied eight months, a conclusion which I imagine no one will accept. Josephus, at least, at the end of his sixth book of *Antiquities*, emends the text thus: "Saul reigned eighteen years during Samuel's lifetime, and two years after his death."

Indeed, this entire narrative in chapter 13 is in complete disagreement with what has gone before. At the end of chapter 7 we are told that the Philistines were so crushed by the Hebrews that they dared not invade their borders during Samuel's lifetime. Yet in chapter 13 we are told that, in Samuel's lifetime, the Hebrews were invaded by the Philistines and reduced to such a state of wretchedness and poverty that they were deprived of weapons wherewith to defend themselves, and even of the means of making them. I should certainly be hard put to it if I were to attempt to reconcile all the narratives of the first book of Samuel so that they might present the appearance of having been written and arranged by a single historian. But I return to my theme. The years of Saul's reign, then, should be added to our previous calculation. And finally, I have not taken into account the years of anarchy of the Hebrews, since their number is not clear from Scripture. I cannot be sure, I say, of the time taken up by those events which are recorded from chapter 17 to the end of the book of Judges.

Thus it clearly follows that neither can a true system of chronology be established from the narratives nor are the narratives consistent with one another in this matter, but differ widely. Therefore it must be admitted that these narratives were compiled from different sources, without any proper arrangement or scrutiny. And there seems to have been just as great a chronological discrepancy between the books of the chronicles of the kings of Judah and those of the kings of Israel. The chronicles of the kings of Israel recorded that Jehoram, the son of Ahab, began his reign in the second year of the reign of Jehoram, the son of Jehoshaphat (2 Kings ch. 1 v. 17); but in the chronicles of the kings of Judah we are told that Jehoram, the son of Jehoshaphat, began his reign in the fifth year of the reign of Jehoram, the son of Ahab (2 Kings ch. 8 v. 16).

Furthermore, anyone who cares to compare the narratives of the book of Chronicles with the narratives of the books of Kings will find many similar discrepancies, which I need not recount here, and far less need I consider the commentaries wherein writers seek to reconcile these narratives. The Rabbis run quite wild, and such commentators as I have read indulge in dreams, fantasies, and in the end corrupt the language altogether. For example, in the second book of Chronicles where we read that "Forty and two years old was Ahaziah when he began to reign," some of them pretend that these years are reckoned from the reign of Omri, not from the birth of Ahaziah. If they could prove this to be the real meaning of the author of the book of Chronicles, I should not hesitate to declare that he did not know how to speak. They indulge in many other fancies of this sort; and if these were true, I should declare outright that the ancient Hebrews knew neither their own language nor how a narrative should be arranged, I should acknowledge no method or rule for the interpretation of Scripture, and there would be no restriction whatsoever on the imagination.

If anyone thinks that my criticism here is of too sweeping a nature and lacking sufficient foundation, I would ask him to undertake to show us in these narratives a definite plan such as might legitimately be imitated by historians in their chronicles. In his attempts to interpret the narratives and to harmonise them, let him adhere with absolute strictness* to the actual diction and to the manner of exposition, arrangement and organisation of the texts, and then provide such an explanation as may furnish us with a model to imitate in our own writing. If he succeeds, I shall at once admit defeat, and he will be my mighty Apollo. For I confess that all my efforts over a long period have resulted in no such discovery. Indeed, I may add that I write nothing here that is not the fruit of lengthy reflection; and although I have been educated from boyhood in the accepted beliefs concerning Scripture, I have felt bound in the end to embrace the views I here express. But there is no point in taking up the reader's time on this subject, presenting him with a hopeless task: it has been necessary to confront this issue in order to make my position clearer, and so I now pass on to the remaining topics which I undertook to discuss, concerning the fate that befell these books.

In addition to our previous remarks, we have to observe that these books were not so preserved by posterity as not to suffer the intrusion of some errors. The scribes of old have noted several doubtful readings and also a number of mutilated passages, but not all that there are. I shall not at this point discuss the question as to whether the errors are of such a kind as to cause serious difficulty to the reader. In my opinion, however, they are of minor importance, at any rate to those who have an enlightened approach to Scripture. This much I can say with certainty, that in the matter of moral doctrine I have never observed a fault of variant reading that could give rise to obscurity or doubt in such teaching. But there are many who deny the possibility of any fault having occurred even in the other texts; they maintain that God by some singular act of providence has preserved all the Sacred Books uncorrupted. They say that the variant readings signal mysteries most profound; they contend that the same is true of the twenty-eight cases of asterisks in mid-paragraph, and that great secrets lurk even in the markings above the letters. I do not know whether these views proceed from folly and a feeble-minded devoutness or from arrogance and malice, to the end that they alone may be cred-

---

* See Supplementary Note 18.

ited with possessing the secrets of God. This much I do know, that I have found in their writings nothing that smacks of divine secrets, but mere childishness. I have also read, and am acquainted with, a number of Cabbalistic[1] triflers whose madness passes the bounds of my understanding.

That some errors have crept in, as we have said, will not be denied, I believe, by anyone of sound judgment who reads the passages concerning Saul (which I have already quoted from 1 Sam. ch. 13 v. 1) and also 2 Sam. ch. 6 v. 2, "And David arose and went with all the people that were with him from Judah to bring up from there the ark of God." Nobody can fail to see that the place to which they went to bring up from there the ark of God, namely, Kirjath Jeharim,* has been omitted. Nor again can we deny that 2 Sam. ch. 13 v. 37 has been corrupted and mutilated: "And Absalom fled and went to Talmai, the son of Ammihud, king of Geshur, and he mourned for his son every day, and Absalom fled and went to Geshur, and was there three years."** There are other instances of this kind which I know I have previously noted, but cannot at present recall.

That the marginal notes which are found in many places in the Hebrew Codices were doubtful readings, nobody again can doubt who notices that most of these have originated from the remarkable similarity between Hebrew letters; the similarity between כ *kaf,* and ב *bet,* י *yad* and ו *vav,* ד *dalet* and ר *resh* and so on. For example, in 2 Sam. ch. 5 v. 24, we have בשמעך 'in the (time) in which thou hearest,' and in the margin כשמעך 'when thou hearest.' And in Judges ch. 21 v. 22 'when their fathers or brothers come to us לרוב in multitude' (that is, 'often'), in the margin is written לריב 'to complain.'

In the same way, many other variant readings have also arisen from the use of letters called mutes, which for the most part are not pronounced, and are used indiscriminately one in place of another. For example, in Leviticus chapter 25 verse 30 we have 'and the house will be established which is in the city without a wall'— אשר לא חומה, but in the margin is written אשר לו חומה, 'which is in the walled city.'

Although this is self-evident, I should like to reply to the arguments of certain Pharisees whereby they try to convince us that the marginal notes were inserted by the writers of the Sacred Books themselves with the purpose of signifying some mystery. The first of these arguments, to which I attach little weight, derives from the practice of reading the Scriptures aloud. If, they say, these notes are added because of a difference of reading on which later generations could not decide, why has the custom prevailed that the marginal readings should everywhere be given preference? Why, they ask, has the preferred reading been written in the margin? They could on the contrary have written the text itself as they wished it to be read, and they should not have relegated to the margin the meaning and reading of which they most approved.

---

[1] [Spinoza alludes here to the Jewish mystical tradition, commonly known as Qabbalah. One of Spinoza's own teachers, Menasseh ben Israel, was a keen Qabbalist. Indeed, Qabbalah was widely disseminated among Spanish Jewish scholars after the Expulsion.]

* See Supplementary Note 19.

** See Supplementary Note 20.

The second argument, which has some plausibility, derives from the nature of the case, namely, that errors find their way into a text by chance, not by design; and that which is the effect of chance occurs at random. Now in the Pentateuch the word נערה 'girl', is always, with one exception, incorrectly written without the ה *hē*, contrary to grammatical rule, whereas in the margin it is correctly written according to the universal grammatical rule. Could this, too, have come about through a scribe's copying error? How could it have happened that the pen always slipped up when this word occurred? Then again, they could easily have supplied what was missing and made the correction with good conscience, according to the rules of grammar. Therefore, since these readings are not due to chance and such obvious faults have remained uncorrected, the argument runs that they were the deliberate work of the original writers, so as to signify something.

However, these arguments are easily answered. The argument from the development of their usage in reading aloud the Scriptures carries no weight with me. Superstition may have played some part, and perhaps the custom developed because they considered both versions equally good or feasible, and so decided that the one should be written and the other read so that neither should be rejected. That is to say, in so important a matter they feared to make a final decision lest they should mistakenly prefer the false to the true. So they resolved to show no preference for the one above the other, as must certainly have been the case if they had ordered only the one to be written and read, especially so when the marginal notes are not written in the Sacred Books. Or perhaps this came about through their deciding that certain things, although correctly written down, should nevertheless be read in the way indicated by a marginal note. Thus came the general rule that the Bible should be read according to the marginal notes.

I shall now discuss the motive that induced the scribes to mark certain words to be read expressly from the margin. For not all marginal notes are doubtful readings; they also occur in the case of expressions that had passed out of common usage, namely, obsolete words, and terms that the approved manners of the time did not permit to be read aloud in a public assembly. Writers of old, in their simple way, called things plainly by their names with no courtly circumlocution. Later on, when vice and intemperance were rife, words which in the mouths of the ancients were free from obscenity began to be regarded as obscene. There was no need to alter Scripture on this account, but in concession to the weak-mindedness of the common people they introduced the custom in public readings of substituting more acceptable words for sexual intercourse and excrement, as are marked in the marginal notes.

Finally, whatever the reason for the development of the practice of reading and interpreting Scripture according to the marginal version, it was certainly not that a true interpretation must thus result. For apart from the fact that the Rabbis themselves in the Talmud are often at variance with the Massoretes,[2] and possessed

---

[2] [Massoretes. A name given to the succession of scholars who labored from about the sixth century to the tenth century to produce an authoritative version of the Hebrew Bible. They introduced vowel signs.]

other readings which they regarded as correct—as I shall show in due course—there are also some marginal notes which seem less in accord with Hebrew linguistic usage. For example, in 2 Samuel ch. 14 v. 22 we read "in that the king hath fulfilled the request of his servant," a quite regular construction, and in agreement with that of verse 15 of the same chapter. But the margin has עבדך 'of thy servant,' which does not agree with the person of the verb. So, too, in the last verse of chapter 16 of the same book, we read 'as when one enquires (ישאל) of the word of God,' while in the margin the word איש (someone) is added as the subject of the verb. This appears to have been done in error, for it is the common practice of the Hebrew language to express the impersonal of a verb by the third person singular active, as grammarians well know. And there are several marginal notes of this kind which cannot be given preference over the written version.

As for the second argument of the Pharisees, this is also easily met by my earlier statement, namely, that besides doubtful readings the scribes also marked obsolete words. For there is no doubt that in the Hebrew language, as in other languages, many words were rendered obsolete and antiquated by later usage; and these were found in the Bible by the latest generation of scribes, who, as we have said, marked them all as having to be read in public according to contemporary usage. It is for this reason that the word נער *na'ar* is always found marked, because in antiquity it was of common gender, and meant the same as the Latin word '*juvenis*' (a young person). So, too, the capital city of the Hebrews used to be called in ancient times Jerusalem, not Jerusalaim. I take a similar view regarding the pronoun הוא meaning 'he' or 'she', that is, that the later scribes changed the ו *vav* into י *yad* (a frequent change in Hebrew) when they intended to signify the feminine gender, whereas the ancients used to distinguish the feminine from the masculine only by a change of vowel. So, too, the irregular forms of certain verbs in earlier times differed from those of later times. Finally, the ancient writers made use of the paragogic[3] letters האמנתיו with an elegance peculiar to their time. All this I could illustrate with many more examples, were I not afraid of wearying the reader.

If I am asked what are my grounds for classifying words as obsolete, I reply that I do so because I often find them in the most ancient writers—that is, the Bible—and yet later writers ceased to use them; and in the case of other languages this is the only justification for classifying words as obsolete, even though they are also dead languages. But perhaps I shall be further pressed with the question why, since I have maintained that most of these marginal notes are doubtful readings, there are never more than two readings of a single passage. Why are there not sometimes three or more? Then again, some passages in Scripture, corrected in a marginal note, are so obviously contrary to grammar that we cannot believe that the scribes could have had any hesitation in deciding which was correct.

But here again there is no difficulty in answering. In reply to the first point, I say that there were in fact more readings than we now find marked in the codices. The

---

[3] [This is a technical grammatical term deriving from Greek grammar. It is the addition of a letter or syllable to the end of a word, especially to give emphasis or to modify the meaning.]

Talmud notes several that were passed over by the Massoretes, differing so markedly from their version in many passages that the superstitious editor of the Bomberg Bible[4] was finally forced to admit in his preface that he could not reconcile them. "Here we can make no reply," he said, "except what we have stated above, namely, that the Talmudic practice is in contradiction with the Massoretes." So we do not have sufficient grounds for maintaining that there never were more than two readings of a single passage. Nevertheless, I do readily grant—indeed, I positively believe—that no more than two readings of a single passage have ever been found, and this for two reasons. First, what we have shown to be the cause of the difference in these readings can admit of no more than two readings. We have shown that the chief source of ambiguity was the similarity of certain letters, and therefore this ambiguity nearly always resolved itself into the question as to which of two letters should be accepted, ב *bet* or כ *kaf,* י *yad* or ו *vav,* ד *dalet* or ר *resh* and so on. These letters are of frequent occurrence, and thus it could often come about that either letter yielded a reasonable meaning. Again, it might be a question of whether a syllable was long or short, its quantity depending on the letters called mutes. There is the further point that not all marginal notes are doubtful readings: we have mentioned that many were inserted for the sake of decency, and others to explain obsolete and antiquated words. The second reason that convinces me that not more than two readings of a single passage are found is this, that I believe that the scribes found very few original manuscripts, perhaps not more than two or three. In the Treatise of the Scribes,[5] סופרים chapter 6, there is mention of only three, which they allege were made by Ezra himself. Be that as it may, if they possessed three manuscripts we can naturally suppose that two would always be in agreement in any one passage. Indeed, it would have been quite extraordinary if in the case of three manuscripts each gave a different reading of one and the same text.

How it came about that after the time of Ezra there existed so few manuscripts will surprise no one who has read either the first book of the Maccabees, chapter 1, or Josephus' *Antiquities,* Book 12, chapter 5. Indeed, it seems miraculous that they could have saved these few after such a fierce and lengthy persecution. Nobody, I imagine, can doubt this if he has read the history of these times with any attention. Thus we can see why nowhere do we find more than two doubtful readings. Therefore this cannot possibly lead to the conclusion that the marked passages in the Bible were deliberately written incorrectly so as to signify some mysteries.

As to the second argument, that certain passages are so incorrectly written that there could be no shadow of doubt that they violated the grammatical rules of all times, and that therefore they should have been unhesitatingly corrected and not merely accompanied by a marginal note, I attach little weight to this. I am not bound to know what religious scruple induced the scribes to refrain from so doing. Perhaps they were prompted by a sincere wish to transmit the Bible to pos-

---

[4] [The Bomberg Bible was printed by D. Bomberg (a Christian) at Venice, 1524–1525, edited by Jacob ben Hayyim.]
[5] [This is a treatise in the Babylonian Talmud.]

terity in the exact condition in which they had found it in the few original manuscripts, while noting in the margin the discrepancies in the manuscripts, not as doubtful readings, but as variant readings. The only reason for my calling them doubtful readings is that in fact I find them nearly all to be of such a kind that I cannot determine which should be preferred to the other.

Finally, apart from these doubtful readings, the scribes have noted a number of cases of mutilated texts by leaving a space in mid-paragraph. The Massoretes have counted them, enumerating twenty-eight cases where a space is left in mid-paragraph. Whether they believe that some mystery also lurks in this number I do not know, but the Pharisees religiously preserve a fixed area of empty space. To take one example, in Genesis chapter 4 v. 8 we read, "And Cain said to his brother . . . and it came to pass while they were in the field that Cain. . . ." A space is left where we might have expected to learn what Cain said to his brother. There are twenty-eight such spaces left by the scribes, apart from passages we have already noted. Yet many of these passages would not be recognised as mutilated, were it not for the space. But I have said enough on this subject.

CHAPTER 10

An examination of the remaining books of the Old Testament by the same method as was used with the previous books

I now pass on to the remaining books of the Old Testament. Of the two books of Chronicles I have nothing particular or important to remark, except that they were written some considerable time after Ezra, and perhaps after the restoration of the temple by Judas Maccabee.* For in chapter 9 of the first book the historian tells us 'what families first of all (that is, in the time of Ezra) dwelt in Jerusalem,' and then in verse 17 he gives the names of the porters, two of whom are also mentioned in Nehemiah ch. 11 v. 19. This shows that these books were written some considerable time after the rebuilding of the city. As to the authorship of these books, their authority, usefulness and doctrine, I can say nothing. Indeed, I find it quite astonishing that they were accepted among the Sacred Books by those who excluded from the canon the book of Wisdom, the book of Tobit, and other books that are called apocryphal. But it is not my purpose to disparage the authority of the Chronicles; since they have been given universal acceptance, I also leave them, for what they are.

The Psalms were also gathered together and divided into five books in the time of the second temple; for on the evidence of Philo Judaeus[1] Psalm 88 was pub-

---

* See Supplementary Note 21.

[1] [The Philo Judaeus mentioned here by Spinoza is *not* the famous Jewish philosopher and biblical exegete of Alexandria, Egypt (first century A.D.). Later in this chapter (page 494) Spinoza refers to

lished while king Jehoiachin was still a prisoner in Babylon, and Psalm 89 when Jehoiachin obtained his freedom. I do not believe that Philo would ever have made this statement unless either it was the accepted belief of his time or he had learned it from trustworthy sources.

The Proverbs of Solomon, I believe, were also collected at that time, or at least in the time of king Josiah, for in chapter 25 v. 1 we read, "These are also the Proverbs of Solomon, which the men of Hezekiah, king of Judah, copied out." At this point I cannot refrain from remarking on the audacity of the Rabbis who wanted this book, and also Ecclesiastes, to be excluded from the canon and to be kept with the others that are now missing. This they would actually have done had they not found some passages where the Law of Moses is commended. It is indeed a matter of deep regret that decisions of high and sacred import rested with these men. However, I am obliged to them for allowing these books, too, to come down to us, though I cannot help doubting their good faith in transmitting them, a matter which I shall not here subject to keen scrutiny.

I pass on, then, to the books of the Prophets. On turning my attention to these, I find that the prophecies they contain were gathered from other books, and were not always set down in these books in the same order in which they were spoken or written by the prophets themselves; nor again are they all contained there, but only those that the compilers could find in various sources. Hence these books are only fragmentary writings of the prophets. For Isaiah began to prophesy in the reign of Uzziah, as the writer himself testifies in the first verse. Now Isaiah not only prophesied at that time but also wrote a full account of Uzziah's acts (see 2 Chron. ch. 26 v. 22), a book that is now lost. We have shown that what we do possess is taken from the chronicles of the kings of Judah and Israel. Furthermore, the Rabbis maintain that Isaiah also prophesied in the reign of Manasseh, by whom he was finally put to death; and although this may be a myth, it does appear that they believed that not all of Isaiah's prophecies are extant.

The prophecies of Jeremiah, which are narrated in the manner of history, were selected and compiled from various chronicles. For not only are they gathered together in a confused mass with no regard to chronological order but, furthermore, there are different versions of the same story. In chapter 21 the writer gives as the reason for Jeremiah's arrest that, on being consulted by Zedekiah, he prophesied the destruction of the city; then, interrupting his narrative, in chapter 22 he passes on to Jeremiah's outcry against Jehoiachin, who reigned before Zedekiah, predicting the king's captivity. Then in chapter 25 the writer describes the prophet's revelations prior to these events, in the fourth year of Jehoiachin's reign. Then he moves on to the events of the first year of this king's reign, continuing to pile up prophecies with no regard of chronological order, until in chapter 38 he resumes

---

a Philo Judaeus again and mentions his work, *The Book of Times*. The philosopher Philo of Alexandria wrote no such book. According to the modern Hebrew translator of the TTP, Chayyim Wirszubski, Spinoza is actually referring to a book attributed to "Philo Judaeus" by the Italian scholar Johannes Annius of Viterbo. Most probably, suggests Wirszubski, Spinoza found this reference in the Renaissance Italian Jewish historian Azariah de Rossi's *Me'or 'Einaiyyim*, Book 3, chapter 32.]

what he began to relate in chapter 21, as if the intervening fifteen chapters were a parenthesis. For the connecting words at the beginning of chapter 38 relate to verses 8, 9 and 10 of chapter 21. He then describes Jeremiah's final arrest in very different terms, and assigns a reason for his long stay in prison which is very different from that related in chapter 37. Thus one may clearly see that all these narratives were taken from different historians, and the incoherence can have no other explanation.

The prophecies contained in the remaining chapters of the book, where Jeremiah speaks in the first person, seem to have been copied from a volume that Baruch wrote at Jeremiah's dictation; for, as chapter 36 v. 2 makes clear, this contained only what was revealed to the prophet from the time of Josiah to the fourth year of Jehoiachin, the point at which this book begins. The narrative from chapter 45 v. 2 to chapter 51 v. 59 also seems to have been copied from the same volume.

The book of Ezekiel, too, is only a fragment, as is clearly indicated by the early verses. Who can fail to see that the transitional words with which the book begins relate to things previously said, making a connection between those things and things yet to come? But it is not only the transition, it is the entire structure of the work that presupposes other writings. That the book begins with the thirtieth year shows that the prophet is continuing a narrative, not beginning one; and this is noted by the writer himself in a parenthesis in verse 3, "And the word of the Lord came often unto Ezekiel, the son of Buzi, a priest in the land of the Chaldeans . . . ," as if to say that the words of Ezekiel which he had thus far written related to other revelations that had come to him before his thirtieth year. Then again, Josephus in his *Antiquities*, Book 10, chapter 7 tells us that Ezekiel foretold that Zedekiah would not see Babylon; but this is not told us in the book of Ezekiel now extant, which on the contrary tells us in chapter 17 that he would be taken to Babylon as captive.*

With regard to Hosea, we cannot say with certainty that he wrote more than is contained in the book of his name. Yet I am surprised that we do not possess more writings of one who, on the testimony of the author, prophesied for eighty-four years. This much we know as a general fact, that the writers of these books did not collect the prophecies of all who prophesied, nor all the prophecies of those prophets whom we do possess. Of the prophets who prophesied in the reign of Manasseh, of whom general mention is made in 2 Chron. ch. 33 v. 10, 18, 19, we possess no prophecies whatsoever, nor do we possess all the prophecies of our twelve prophets. In the case of Jonah, only the prophecies concerning the Ninevites are available, although he also prophesied to the Israelites, for which see 2 Kings ch. 14 v. 25.

With regard to the book of Job, and Job himself, there has been considerable controversy among writers.[2] Some think that Moses wrote the book, and that the

---

* See Supplementary Note 22.

[2] [The authorship of the Book of Job was debated by the Rabbis in the Talmud (Babylonian Talmud, Treatise Bava Batrah, 15a). They also discussed the question of whether Job was a historical figure or only an allegorical type. Maimonides favored the latter view (*Guide of the Perplexed*, 3.22).]

whole story is nothing but a parable. This is the view of certain Rabbis in the Talmud, and is also favoured by Maimonides in his 'More Nebuchim.' Others have believed that the story is true, of whom some have thought that Job lived in the time of Jacob and married his daughter Dinah. But ibn Ezra, as I have previously said, asserts in his commentary on this book that it was translated into Hebrew from another language. I wish he could have demonstrated this more convincingly, for we might therefrom conclude that the Gentiles, too, possessed sacred books. I therefore leave the question unresolved, but I would surmise that Job was a Gentile, a man of great steadfastness who experienced first of all prosperity, then calamity, and finally the utmost good fortune; for he is so named among others by Ezekiel chapter 14 v. 14. I believe that the vicissitudes of Job and his steadfastness gave occasion for much discussion concerning God's providence, or at least induced the author of this book to compose his dialogue. The contents of the book, and likewise its style, seem not to be the work of a man wretchedly ill, lying amid ashes, but of one meditating at ease in a library. I am also inclined to agree with ibn Ezra that this book is a translation from another language, for its poetic style seems to be characteristic of the Gentiles. The Father of the gods twice summons a council; Momus,[3] who is here called Satan, criticises God's words with the utmost freedom and so on. But these are mere conjectures, and not firmly founded.

I pass on to the book of Daniel. From chapter 8 on it undoubtedly contains the writings of Daniel himself, but I do not know whence the first seven chapters were derived. Since they were written in Chaldaic except for the first chapter, we may surmise that they were taken from the chronicles of the Chaldeans. If this could be clearly established, it would afford striking evidence to prove that Scripture is sacred only insofar as we understand through it the matters therein signified, and not insofar as we understand merely the words or the language and sentences whereby these matters are conveyed. It would further prove that books that teach and tell of the highest things are equally sacred, in whatever language and by whatever nation they were written. This much, at least, we can remark, that these chapters were written in Chaldaic, and are nevertheless as sacred as the rest of the Bible.

To this book of Daniel the first book of Ezra is so linked that it is easily recognised to be the work of the same author, who continues the history of the Jews from their first captivity on. And I have no doubt that the book of Esther is linked with this book, for the connective words with which it begins can refer to no other book. It cannot be believed that this is the same book as that which Mordecai wrote, for in chapter 9 v. 20, 21, 22 somebody else tells of Mordecai that he wrote letters, giving their contents; and again in verse 31 of the same chapter he says that Queen Esther established by edict the arrangements pertaining to the feast of Lots (Purim), and that this was written in the book—that is, as the Hebrew idiom indicates, in a

---

[3] [In ancient Greek literature and mythology Momus was a fault-finding personification (Hesiod, *Theogony*, 214). Spinoza's identification of Momus with the biblical Satan suggests that the Bible, too, is a literary document analogous to Greek myths and that we should regard and study the former as we do the latter.]

book well known at the time of writing. This book has perished along with the others, as ibn Ezra admits and must be universally admitted. Finally, for the rest of the acts of Mordecai the historian refers us to the chronicles of the kings of Persia. Therefore there can be no doubt that this book was also written by the same historian who related the history of Daniel and Ezra; and so, too, was the book of Nehemiah,* for it is called the second book of Ezra. We can affirm, then, that these four books—the books of Daniel, Ezra, Esther and Nehemiah—were written by one and the same historian. As to the identity of the writer, I cannot even hazard a guess. But to help us to understand from what sources the historian, whoever he was, may have acquired his knowledge of these histories, perhaps simply transcribing the greatest part of them, it should be observed that the governors or rulers of the Jews in the time of the second temple, like the kings in the time of the first temple, kept a succession of scribes or chroniclers who wrote their annals or chronicles. For the chronicles or annals of the kings are quoted in numerous places in the books of Kings, while those of the rulers and priests of the second temple are first quoted in Nehemiah chapter 12 v. 23, and then again in 1 Maccabees chapter 16 v. 24. This is undoubtedly the book (see Esther ch. 9 v. 31) of which we have just spoken, containing the decree of Esther and the acts of Mordecai, a book which we said, with ibn Ezra, is no longer extant. From this book, then, were derived or copied all the contents of the four books in question, for no other book is quoted by their author, nor do we know of any other book of acknowledged authority.

That these books were not written by Ezra or Nehemiah is obvious from Nehemiah chapter 12 v. 10, 11, where the genealogy of the high priests is traced from Jeshua to Jaddua, the sixth high priest, a man who met Alexander the Great at a time when the Persian Empire was almost completely subjugated (see Josephus' *Antiquities*, Book 11, chapter 8), or who, according to Philo Judaeus in his book of *Times*, was the sixth and last high priest under the Persians. Indeed, in verse 22 of this same chapter of Nehemiah, this is made quite clear. "The Levites," says the historian, "in the days of Eliashab, Joiada, Johanan and Jaddua were recorded above** the reign of Darius the Persian," that is, in the chronicles. Now I cannot imagine that anyone would believe that Ezra*** or Nehemiah lived long enough to survive fourteen Persian kings. For Cyrus was the first to grant the Jews permission to rebuild their temple, and from this time to Darius, the fourteenth and last Persian king, is a period of more than 200 years. Therefore I have no doubt that these books were written some time after Judas Maccabee restored the worship in the temple; and this is supported by the fact that at that time the spurious books of Daniel, Ezra and Esther were published by certain ill-disposed persons who were no doubt of the sect of the Sadducees,[4] for the Pharisees never accepted

---

* See Supplementary Note 23.

** Unless this means 'beyond' it was an error of the scribe who wrote על 'above' instead of עד—'up to'.

*** See Supplementary Note 24.

[4] [A conservative sect, belonging mainly to the upper class and associated with the priestly families. On certain matters of doctrine they differed from the Pharisees, who, according to Josephus, "profess to be more religious than the rest and to explain the laws more precisely."]

these books, to the best of my knowledge. And although we find in the so-called fourth book of Ezra certain stories that also appear in the Talmud, these books should not on that account be attributed to the Pharisees; for, except for the most ignorant, they are all of them convinced that these stories were added by some trifler. In fact, I believe that this was the work of some people whose object was to bring universal ridicule on the traditions of the Pharisees.

Perhaps the reason why these four books were written and published at that particular time was to demonstrate to the people that Daniel's prophecies were fulfilled, thereby strengthening their devotion to religion and giving them, in the midst of such grievous misfortunes, some hope of better things and salvation to come. However, although these books belong to a period so much later and more recent, many errors have crept in as a result, I imagine, of the hastiness of the writers. Marginal notes, which I discussed in the preceding chapter, are to be found in these books as in the others, but in greater number, and there are in addition some passages which can have no other explanation, as I shall proceed to show. But let me first observe with regard to the marginal readings in these books, that if we take the Pharisees' view that these notes go back as far as the writers of these books, then we shall have to say that the writers—if there were more than one—must have marked these marginal notes because they found that the chronicles which were their sources had been incorrectly written, and although there were some glaring faults, they did not venture to correct the writings of their predecessors of long ago. There is no need for me to enlarge once again on this subject; and I shall therefore move on to point out such errors as are not indicated in the margin.

In the first place, there is no way of knowing how many faults have found their way into chapter 2 of Ezra. Verse 64 gives the sum total of all the items separately enumerated in the chapter as 42,360, yet the addition of the items there enumerated gives the figure of 29,818. Thus there must be a mistake either in the sum total or in the separate items. Now the total is probably to be regarded as correct, because everyone would doubtless have remembered it as a noteworthy thing, whereas this does not apply to the separate items. If an error had occurred in the sum total, everyone would have noticed it, and it would easily have been corrected. This view is plainly confirmed by chapter 7 of Nehemiah, where this chapter of Ezra (called the register of genealogy) was copied, as is expressly stated in verse 5 of the same chapter of Nehemiah. The sum total here given agrees exactly with that given in the book of Ezra, whereas the items are very different, some being greater and some less than in Ezra, and totalling 31,089. Therefore there can be no doubt that, both in Ezra and Nehemiah, it is only in the separate items that errors have occurred.

The commentators who attempt to reconcile these obvious discrepancies exercise each one his imagination according to his ingenuity, and while paying homage to every letter and word of Scripture, they merely succeed, as I have previously indicated, in exposing to contempt the writers of the Bible, as if these did not know how to speak or to arrange what they had to say. Indeed, they do no more than obscure the plain meaning of Scripture. If it were legitimate to extend their mode of interpretation to the whole of Scripture, there would not be a sentence whose true meaning could not be called into doubt. But I shall waste no more time on this subject, for I am convinced that if an historian were to allow himself the same liberties that the commentators in their religious fervour grant to the writers of the Bible, he would be laughed to scorn by those very commentators. And if they regard as blasphemous anyone who asserts that Scripture is in some places faulty, by what name, pray, shall I call those who read into Scripture whatever takes their fancy, who expose the sacred historians as stammering in utter confusion, who reject the plainest and most evident meaning of Scripture? What can be clearer in Scripture than that Ezra with his companions, in the register of genealogy written in chapter 2 of the book called by his name, has given the itemised total of all those who set out for Jerusalem? For he included in that total not only those who could give account of their lineage but also those who could not do so. What can be clearer than that Nehemiah (ch. 7 v. 5) simply copied down this register? Those who offer another explanation are just denying the true meaning of Scripture, and consequently Scripture itself. They think it a mark of piety to alter some passages of Scripture to harmonise with others—an absurd piety, in that they adapt clear passages to suit the obscure, the correct to suit the faulty, and they contaminate what is sound with what is corrupt. Yet far be it from me to accuse of blasphemy those who have no malicious intent, for to err is human.

But I return to my theme. Besides the undoubted arithmetical errors in the register of genealogy both in Ezra and in Nehemiah, several others are to be remarked in family names, and many more in the genealogies, in the histories, and even in the prophecies, I fear. The prophecy of Jeremiah, chapter 22, concerning Jeconiah seems in no way to agree with his history (see the end of 2 Kings, and Jeremiah, and 1 Chron. ch. 3 v. 17, 18, 19), and especially the words of the last verse of that chapter. Nor again do I see how he could have said, "Thou shalt die in peace" of Zedekiah, whose eyes were put out after his sons were slain before him (Jer. ch. 34 v. 5). If prophecies are to be interpreted by the event, these names should be interchanged, Jeconiah for Zedekiah and Zedekiah for Jeconiah. But this would be too paradoxical a proceeding, and so I prefer to leave this as an insoluble problem, especially since any mistake here must be attributed to the historian, and not to a fault in the original manuscripts.

As for the other difficulties I have mentioned, I do not intend to deal with them here as I would only weary the reader, and in any case they have already been noticed by others. Faced with the glaring contradictions which he saw in the genealogies I have spoken of, R. Shlomo[5] was driven to give vent to these words (see his commentaries on 1 Chron. ch. 8): "The fact that Ezra (whom he takes to be the author of Chronicles) differs from Genesis in the names he gives to the sons of Benjamin and in the genealogy he establishes, and that again he differs from Joshua in his references to most of the cities of the Levites, is due to differences

---

[5] [R. Shlomo—this is R. Shlomo Yitzhaki 1040–1105, better known by the abbreviation Rashi. A French rabbinical scholar, whose commentary on the Bible won great fame.]

that he found in the original manuscripts." A little further on he says: "The genealogy of Gibeon and others is set down twice in different ways because in the case of each genealogy Ezra found several registers giving different versions. In copying these he followed the version of the majority of manuscripts; but when there were an equal number of differing genealogies, he gave both versions." Thus he unquestionably admits that these books were compiled from original manuscripts of doubtful accuracy and certainty. Indeed, the commentators themselves, in their attempts to reconcile various passages, frequently do nothing more than indicate the causes of errors. Finally, no one of sound judgment, I imagine, can believe that the sacred historians deliberately wrote in such a way as to present the appearance of contradicting one another over and over again.

Perhaps someone will object that in this way I am plainly subverting Scripture, for according to this argument all may suspect it of being faulty at all points. But on the contrary, I have shown that by my approach to the problem I am doing a service to Scripture by preventing its clear and uncontaminated passages from being made to fit with faulty passages, and thus being corrupted. Nor does the corrupt state of certain passages give grounds for bringing them all under suspicion. No book is ever free from faults; has anyone ever suspected books of being faulty through and through on that account? Surely no one would think so, especially if a book is clearly expressed and the author's meaning unmistakable.

Having now completed my task of enquiring into the books of the Old Testament, I find no difficulty in concluding that no canon of the Sacred Books existed before the Maccabees,* that those books which we now possess were chosen from many others by the Pharisees of the second temple—who were also responsible for the set form of prayers—and that these books were accepted solely on their authority. Therefore those who propose to prove the authority of Holy Scripture are required to prove the authority of each separate book. Proving the divine origin of one book does not sufficiently prove the divine origin of all; otherwise one would have to maintain that the council of Pharisees was infallible in making its selection, which is impossible to demonstrate. Now the evidence that compels me to maintain that the Pharisees alone were responsible for selecting the books of the Old Testament and introducing them into the canon is this, that in the last chapter of Daniel, verse 2, the resurrection of the dead is foretold, a doctrine denied by the Sadducees. Secondly, in the Talmud the Pharisees themselves clearly confirm my view: in the Treatise of Sabbatus, chapter 2, folio 30, page 2, we read, "R. Jehuda, entitled Rabi, has said, 'The learned sought to suppress the book of Ecclesiastes because its words are at variance with the words of the Law (i.e. the book of the Law of Moses). Why did they not suppress it? Because its beginning is in accordance with the Law and its ending is in accordance with the Law.'" And a little further on, "They also sought to suppress the book of Proverbs." And finally, in the same treatise, chapter 1, folio 13, page 2, "Verily, name that man for good, he who was called Neḥunya, son of Hezekiah. Had it not been for him, the

---

* See Supplementary Note 25.

book of Ezekiel would have been suppressed because its words were at variance with the words of the Law. . . ." Here is clear evidence that men learned in the Law summoned a council to decide what books should be received as sacred and what books should be excluded. Therefore whoever seeks assurance as to the authority of all the books, let him again call a council and require each book to be justified.

At this point we should proceed to a similar examination of the books of the New Testament. But I gather that this has been done by men highly skilled in the sciences and particularly in languages, and furthermore my knowledge of Greek is insufficient for venturing upon such an undertaking. And finally, we are without the originals of the books, which were written in Hebrew. For these reasons I prefer to leave this task. However, there are certain points particularly relevant to my general theme, and to these I shall draw attention in the following chapter.

CHAPTER 11

An enquiry as to whether the Apostles wrote their Epistles as Apostles and prophets, or as teachers. The function of the Apostles is explained

Nobody who reads the New Testament can doubt that the Apostles were prophets. However, prophets did not speak at all times from revelation, but only on rare occasions, as we showed towards the end of Chapter 1; and so the question may be raised as to whether the Apostles wrote their Epistles as prophets, from revelation and express mandate like Moses, Jeremiah and others, or as private individuals or teachers. This is particularly a matter of some doubt because in 1 Cor. ch. 14 v. 6 Paul speaks of two kinds of preaching, one from revelation and the other from knowledge, so that the question may properly be raised as to whether the Apostles in their Epistles were prophesying or teaching.

Now if we examine the style of the Epistles, we shall find it to be entirely different from that of prophecy. It was the constant practice of the prophets to declare at all points that they were speaking at God's command, as in the phrases, 'Thus saith the Lord,' 'The Lord of hosts saith,' 'The commandment of the Lord' and so on. This seems to have been the case not only when they addressed public assemblies but also in their epistles containing revelations, as is clear from that of Elijah written to Jehoram (2 Chron. ch. 21 v. 12), which likewise begins 'Thus saith the Lord.' But in the Epistles of the Apostles we find nothing like this; on the contrary, in 1 Cor. ch. 7 v. 40 Paul speaks according to his own opinion. Indeed, there are numerous instances of expressions indicating lack of positive certainty, such as 'We therefore think'* (Rom. ch. 3 v. 28) and 'For I think' (Rom. ch. 8 v. 18) and many

---

* See Supplementary Note 26.

others of this kind. There are, furthermore, many expressions far removed from the authoritativeness of prophecy, such as 'But I speak this by way of concession to weakness, not of command' (1 Cor. ch. 7 v. 6), and 'I give my judgment as one that hath obtained the mercy of the Lord to be faithful' (1 Cor. ch. 7 v. 25), and many other instances. We must also remember that when in the aforementioned chapter the Apostle says that he has or has not the instruction or commandment of God, he does not mean an instruction or commandment revealed to him by God, but only the teachings of Christ in the Sermon on the Mount.

Furthermore, if we examine the manner in which the Apostles expound the Gospel in their Epistles, we see that this, too, is markedly different from that of the prophets. For the Apostles everywhere employ argument, so that they seem to be conducting a discussion rather than prophesying. The prophetic writings, on the other hand, contain only dogma and decrees, for they represent God as speaking not like one who reasons, but one who makes decrees issuing from the absolute power of his nature. Then again, the authority of a prophet does not permit of argumentation, for whoever seeks to base his dogmatic assertions on reason thereby submits them to the arbitrary judgment of the individual. This is just what Paul, because he reasons, seems to have done, declaring in 1 Cor. ch. 10 v. 15, "I speak as to wise men; judge ye what I say."

Finally, as we demonstrated in Chapter 1, it was not by virtue of the natural light—that is, by the exercise of reason—that the prophets perceived what was revealed to them. Although the Pentateuch contains some instances where conclusions seem to follow from a process of inference, a closer examination will show that these can in no way be regarded as instances of conclusive argumentation. For example, when Moses said to the Israelites in Deut. ch. 31 v. 27, "If, while I am yet alive with you, ye have been rebellious against the Lord, how much more so after my death," this must not be taken as meaning that Moses intends to prove by rational argument that the Israelites will necessarily turn away from the true worship of God after his death. The argument would have been false, as can be shown from Scripture itself; for the Israelites continued faithful during the lifetime of Joshua and the elders, and again later on during the lifetime of Samuel, David, Solomon and others. Therefore these words of Moses are merely a moral exhortation where, in a rhetorical expression, he predicts the future backsliding of the people as his lively imagination enabled him to picture it. The view that Moses, in seeking to make his prediction credible to the people, spoke not as a prophet from revelation but on his own initiative, I reject for the following reason: in verse 21 of the same chapter we are told that God revealed this very thing to Moses in different words. Now surely Moses stood in no need of plausible reasoning in order to give him greater assurance of God's prediction and decree, but it was necessary that it should be vividly impressed on his imagination, as we showed in Chapter 1. This could be most effectively achieved by his imagining the people's present obstinacy, which he had often experienced, as extending into the future.

All the arguments employed by Moses in the Pentateuch are to be understood in this same way. They are not derived from textbooks of logic, but are merely figures of speech whereby he expressed God's decrees more effectively and imagined them in lively fashion. I do not absolutely deny that the prophets may have argued from the basis of revelation, but this much I will assert, that the more use the prophets make of logical reasoning, the more closely does their revelatory knowledge approach to natural knowledge, and the surest mark of supernatural knowledge in the prophets is their proclamation of pure dogma, or decrees, or judgment. And thus Moses, the greatest of the prophets, never engaged in logical argument, whereas in the case of Paul the lengthy chains of logical argumentation such as we find in the Epistle to the Romans were most certainly not written from supernatural revelation.

Therefore the modes of expression and discussion employed by the Apostles in the Epistles clearly show that these originated not from revelation and God's command but from their own natural faculty of judgment, and contain nothing but brotherly admonitions mingled with courteous expressions (very different, indeed, from prophetic authoritativeness), such as Paul's apology in Rom. ch. 15 v. 15, "I have written to you more boldly in some sort, my brethren." We can also reach the same conclusion from the fact that nowhere do we read that the Apostles were commanded to write, but only to preach whithersoever they went, and to confirm their words by signs. Their personal presence and their signs were essential for the conversion of the Gentiles to religion, and their strengthening therein, as Paul himself expressly indicates in Rom. ch. 1 v. 11, "But I long to see you," he said, "so that I may impart to you the gift of the Spirit, to the end that you may be strengthened."

Here it may be objected that the same line of argument could prove that neither was it as prophets that the Apostles did their preaching; for in journeying to various places to preach they were not acting by the express mandate of God, as were the prophets in time gone by. We read in the Old Testament that Jonah went to Nineveh to preach, and at the same time that he was expressly sent there, and that it was revealed to him what he should there preach. So also it is related of Moses in considerable detail that he set out to Egypt as God's emissary, and at the same time he was told what he must say to the people of Israel and to Pharaoh, and what wonders he must perform to gain their credence. Isaiah, Jeremiah and Ezekiel are expressly ordered to preach to the Israelites. Lastly, the prophets preached only what Scripture tells us they had received from God, whereas the New Testament very rarely tells us anything like this of the Apostles when they travelled about preaching. On the contrary, there are some passages which expressly indicate that the Apostles used their own initiative in deciding where to preach, as illustrated by the argument, amounting to a quarrel, between Paul and Barnabas (Acts ch. 15 v. 37, 38 etc.). And they were often frustrated, too, in their proposed journey, as Paul again testifies in Rom. ch. 1 v. 13, "Oftentimes I proposed to come to ye, and was prevented," and in ch. 15 v. 22, "For which cause I have been oftentimes hindered from coming to you," and in the last chapter of 1 Cor. v. 12, "And touching my brother Apollos, I greatly desired him to come unto you with the brethren, but his will was not at all to come; but when he shall have convenient time. . . ." Therefore, taking into account expressions like these and the disagreements among the Apostles, and also that Scripture does not testify, as in the case of the prophets of old, that it was by God's command that they went about to preach, the conclusion should have been that in their preaching, too, the Apostles acted as teachers, not as prophets.

But this difficulty is easily resolved if we consider the difference between the Apostles and the prophets of the Old Testament, in respect of their calling. The latter were called to preach and prophesy only to certain nations, not to all nations, and they therefore needed a clear specific mandate for each nation. But the Apostles were called to preach to all men without restriction, and to convert all men to religion. So wherever they went they were fulfilling Christ's command. Nor did they need, before their mission, a revelation of what they were to preach; for they were disciples of Christ, who had told them: "But when they deliver you up, take no thought of how or what ye shall speak, for it shall be given you in that same hour what ye shall speak" (see Matth. ch. 10 v. 19, 20). We may conclude, then, that the Apostles were inspired by special revelation only in what they orally preached when confirmed by signs, while that which they taught in writing or orally without the attestation of signs was spoken or written from knowledge, that is, natural knowledge (see 1 Cor. ch. 14 v. 6).

There is no problem for us in the fact that all the Epistles begin by setting forth the credentials of apostleship, because the Apostles, as I shall go on to show, were granted not only the gift of prophecy but also authority to teach. That is why we grant that they wrote the Epistles as Apostles, and it was for this reason that each began by affirming the credentials of his apostleship. Or perhaps it was with view to winning the good will of the reader, and gaining his attention, that they first of all testified that they were those who were well known to all the faithful from their preaching, and had already shown on clear evidence that they were teaching true religion and the way of salvation. For I observe that all the statements made in these Epistles regarding the calling of the Apostles and their possessing the Holy and Divine Spirit refer to their past preaching, except only for those passages where 'the Spirit of God' and 'the Holy Spirit' are used in the sense of a mind, pure, blessed, devoted to God and so on (a point we discussed in our first chapter). For instance, in 1 Cor. ch. 7 v. 40, Paul says, "But she is happy if she so abide after my judgment, and I think that I also have the Spirit of God," where by the Spirit of God he means his very mind, as the context shows. For his meaning is, 'I count as blessed a widow who does not remarry, I, who have resolved to live unmarried, and think myself blessed.' There are other similar passages, which I need not quote here.

Since, then, we must maintain that the Epistles of the Apostles were dictated solely by the natural light, we have now to consider how the Apostles were able, from natural knowledge alone, to teach matters that do not fall within its scope. But if we attend to what we said in Chapter 7 of this treatise regarding Scriptural interpretation, the difficulty will disappear. For although the contents of the Bible for the most part surpass our understanding, they may safely be the subject of discourse provided that we admit no principles of interpretation other than those that Scripture presents. In the same way the Apostles, on the basis of what they had seen and heard and had acquired by revelation, were able to reach many conclusions and make many inferences, and to teach these to men at their own discretion. Furthermore, although religion as preached by the Apostles—who simply related the story of Christ—does not come within the scope of reason, yet its substance, which consists essentially in moral teachings as does the whole of Christ's doctrine,* can be readily grasped by everyone by the natural light of reason.

Finally, the Apostles needed no supernatural light to adapt a religion, which they had previously confirmed with signs, to the common understanding of mankind so as to be readily and sincerely accepted by everyone; nor yet did they need a supernatural light in their task of exhortation. This is the object of the Epistles, to teach and exhort men in whatever way each Apostle judged would best strengthen them in religious faith. And here we should recall a point recently mentioned, namely, that the Apostles had received not only the power to preach the story of Christ as prophets—that is, confirming it with signs—but also the authority to teach and exhort in whatever way each should think best. Both these gifts are clearly indicated by Paul in 2 Timoth. ch. 1 v. 11, "Whereunto I am appointed a preacher, and an Apostle, and a teacher of the Gentiles," and again in 1 Timoth. ch. 2 v. 7, "Whereunto I am ordained a preacher and an Apostle (I speak the truth in Christ, and lie not), a teacher of the Gentiles in faith (note this) and verity." In these passages, I say, he clearly indicates his credentials both as an Apostle and as a teacher, while his authority to exhort whomsoever he would, on all occasions, is indicated in Philem. v. 8, thus, "Although I might be much bold in Christ to enjoin thee that which is fitting, yet. . . ." Here we should observe that if Paul had received from God, in his capacity of prophet, that which it behoved him to enjoin on Philemon, and which it was his duty as a prophet to enjoin on him, surely it would have been wrong for him to change God's command into an entreaty. Therefore he must be understood as referring to his freedom to exhort, which belonged to him as a teacher, not a prophet.

However, it does not as yet clearly follow that the Apostles were empowered to choose the method of teaching which each one judged the best; we have merely shown that by virtue of their apostleship they were not only prophets but teachers. To justify the former assertion we might call on the assistance of reason, which clearly tells us that he who has the authority to teach has also the authority to choose his own way of teaching. But it would be more satisfactory to demonstrate this entirely from Scripture, which makes it perfectly clear that each of the Apostles chose his own particular way, as shown by these words of Paul, Rom. ch. 15 v. 20, "striving to preach the Gospel not where Christ was named, lest I should build upon another man's foundation." Now if all the Apostles employed the same method of teaching and had built the Christian religion on the same foundation, Paul could have had no justification in referring to another Apostle's work as 'another man's foundation,' inasmuch as it was the same as his own. But since he does so refer to it, we have to conclude that each Apostle built religion on a dif-

---

* See Supplementary Note 27.

ferent foundation, and that in their capacity as teachers the Apostles were in just the same position as other teachers; they each have their own method, so that they always prefer to instruct those who are beginners and have never studied under any other master, whether in the case of languages, the sciences, and even mathematics, of whose truth no one can doubt.

Again, if we study the Epistles themselves with some care, we shall see that, while the Apostles were in agreement about religion itself, they differed widely as to its foundations. In order to strengthen men in their religious faith and to show that salvation depends solely on the grace of God, Paul taught that no one can boast by reason of works, but only his faith, and no one can be justified by works (see Rom. ch. 3 v. 27, 28), and he goes on to teach the complete doctrine of predestination. James, on the other hand, in his Epistle teaches that man is justified by works, and not by faith alone (ch. 2 v. 24), and his doctrine of religion is confined within a small compass, leaving out all those discussions we find in Paul.

Finally, there can be no doubt that these differences between the Apostles in the grounding of their religion gave rise to many disputes and schisms to vex the Church continually right from the time of the Apostles, and they will assuredly continue to vex the Church until the day comes when religion shall be separated from philosophic speculation and reduced to the few simple doctrines that Christ taught his people. This was impossible for the Apostles, because the Gospel was then unknown to mankind; so to avoid offending men's ears by the novelty of its doctrine, they adapted it, as far as possible, to the character of their contemporaries (see 1 Cor. ch. 9 v. 19, 20 etc.), building on foundations that were most familiar and accepted at that time. Thus none of the Apostles did more philosophising than Paul, who was called to preach to the Gentiles. The other Apostles, preaching to the Jews who despised philosophy, likewise adapted themselves to the character of their listeners (see Galat. ch. 2 v. 11 etc.), and taught a religious doctrine free from all philosophic speculation. Happy indeed would be our age, if we were to see religion freed again from all superstition.

CHAPTER 12

Of the true original of the Divine Law. In what respect Scripture is called holy and the Word of God. It is shown that Scripture, insofar as it contains the Word of God, has come down to us uncorrupted

Those who look upon the Bible, in its present form, as a message for mankind sent down by God from heaven, will doubtless cry out that I have committed the sin against the Holy Spirit in maintaining that the Word of God is faulty, mutilated, adulterated and inconsistent, that we possess it only in fragmentary form, and that the original of God's covenant with the Jews has perished. However, I am confident that reflection will at once put an end to their outcry; for not only reason itself, but the assertions of the prophets and the Apostles clearly proclaim that God's eternal Word and covenant and true religion are divinely inscribed in men's hearts—that is, in men's minds—and that this is the true handwriting of God which he has sealed with his own seal, this seal being the idea of himself, the image of his own divinity, as it were.

To the early Jews religion was transmitted in the form of written law because at that time they were just like children; but later on Moses (Deut. ch. 30 v. 6) and Jeremiah (ch. 31 v. 33) told them of a time to come when God would inscribe his law in their hearts. So while it was proper only for the Jews of long ago, and especially the Sadducees, to strive in defence of a law written on tablets, this does not apply to those who have the law inscribed in their minds. Whoever reflects on this will find nothing in what I have said that is at variance with God's word or true religion and faith, or can weaken it; on the contrary, he will realise that I am strengthening it, as I have also shown towards the end of Chapter 10. If this were not so, I should have resolved to remain completely silent; indeed, to avoid creating any difficulties, I should gladly have conceded that in Scripture there lie hidden mysteries of the deepest kind. But since this approach has led to gross superstition and other pernicious ills, of which I have spoken in the preface to Chapter 7, I feel I must not abandon my task, and all the more so because religion stands in no need of the trappings of superstition. On the contrary, its glory is diminished when it is embellished with such fancies.

But it will be said that, although God's law is inscribed in our hearts, Scripture is nevertheless the Word of God, and it is no more permissible to say of Scripture that it is mutilated and contaminated than to say this of God's Word. In reply, I have to say that such objectors are carrying their piety too far, and are turning religion into superstition; indeed, instead of God's Word they are beginning to worship likenesses and images, that is, paper and ink. This much I do know, I have said nothing unworthy of God's Word, for I have affirmed nothing that I have not proved to be true by the plainest of arguments, and therefore I also declare with certainty that I have said nothing that is impious or that smacks of impiety. I do admit that some ungodly men who find religion a burden can assume from my views a licence to sin and, without any justification and merely to gratify their desires, can conclude therefrom that Scripture is at all points faulty and contaminated, and therefore has no authority. But such people are beyond help; as the old saying goes, nothing can be so accurately stated as to be incapable of distortion by misrepresentation. Those who wish to give rein to their desires can easily find any reason for so doing. Men were no better in time gone by when they had the original writings, the Ark of the Covenant, and indeed the prophets and the Apostles in person, nor were they any more obedient. All men, Jews and Gentiles alike, have always been the same, and in every age virtue has been exceedingly rare.

However, to remove any remaining doubt, we must now demonstrate in what sense the terms 'sacred' and 'divine' should be applied to Scripture and to any inanimate thing, and then we must show what the Word of God really is, that it is not confined within the compass of a set number of books, and, further, that Scripture could not have been corrupted insofar as it teaches what is necessary for obedience and salvation. From such a demonstration everyone will readily be able to see that we have said nothing against the Word of God or given any occasion for impiety.

A thing is called sacred and divine when its purpose is to foster piety and religion, and it is sacred only for as long as men use it in a religious way. If men cease to be pious, the thing will likewise cease to be sacred; if it is devoted to impious uses, then that which before was sacred will become unclean and profane. For example, Jacob called a certain place Beth El (House of God) because there he worshipped God who was revealed to him. But the prophets called that same place 'house of inquity' (see Amos ch. 5 v. 5 and Hosea ch. 10 v. 5) because the Israelites, at the instigation of Jeroboam, were there wont to sacrifice to idols. Another example will make the point quite clear. Words acquire a fixed meaning solely from their use; if in accordance with this usage they are so arranged that readers are moved to devotion, then these words will be sacred, and likewise the book containing this arrangement of words. But if these words at a later time fall into disuse so as to become meaningless, or if the book falls into utter neglect, whether from malice or because men no longer feel the need of it, then both words and book will be without value and without sanctity. Lastly, if these words are arranged differently, or if by custom they acquire a meaning contrary to their original meaning, then both words and book will become impure and profane instead of sacred. Thus it follows that nothing is sacred or profane or impure in an absolute sense apart from the mind, but only in relation to the mind. This again is made abundantly clear in many passages of Scripture. To take one case at random, Jeremiah says in ch. 7 v. 4 that the Jews of his time were wrong to call Solomon's temple the temple of God; for, as he goes on to say in the same chapter, the temple was entitled to God's name only as long as it was a place of resort for men who worshipped God and upheld righteousness. If it became a place of resort for murderers, thieves, idolaters and other scoundrels, then it was better termed a den of sinners.

I find it strange that Scripture tells us nothing of what became of the Ark of the Covenant; but there can be no doubt that it perished or was burnt along with the temple, in spite of the fact that the Hebrews regarded nothing as more sacred or more worthy of reverence. So Scripture likewise is sacred, and its words divine, only as long as it moves men to devotion towards God; but if it is utterly disregarded by them, as it was once by the Jews, it is nothing more than paper and ink, and their neglect renders it completely profane, leaving it exposed to corruption. So if it then suffers corruption or perishes, it is wrong to say that the Word of God suffers corruption or perishes, just as in the time of Jeremiah it would have been wrong to say that the temple, which at that time was the temple of God, had perished in flames. Jeremiah makes the same point with regard to the Law, for he rebukes the ungodly of his time with these words: "Wherefore say you that we are the learned, and that the Law of God is with us? Surely, it has been composed in vain, in vain has the pen of the scribes (been made)." That is to say, although

Scripture is in your keeping, you are wrong in saying that you have the Law of God, since you have rendered it vain.

So, too, when Moses broke the first tablets, he certainly did not in his anger cast from his hands and shatter the Word of God—this would be inconceivable of Moses and of the Word of God—but merely stones which, although previously sacred because on them was inscribed the Covenant under which the Jews had bound themselves to obey God, were now without any sanctity whatever, the Jews having nullified that Covenant by worshipping the calf. And for the same reason the second tablets could not avoid destruction along with the Ark. It is therefore not surprising that the original of Moses' writing, too, is no longer extant, and that the events we previously described have befallen the books which we do possess, seeing that even the true original of God's Covenant, the most sacred of all things, could have completely perished.

Let them cease, therefore, to bring the charge of impiety against us, who have said nothing contrary to the Word of God, nor corrupted it; let them turn their anger, if they have any just cause for anger, against those men of ages past whose wickedness desecrated the Ark, the temple, the Law and all things sacred, exposing them to corruption. Furthermore, if in accordance with the saying of the Apostle in 2 Cor. ch. 3 v. 3 they have within themselves the Epistle of God, written not with ink but with the Spirit of God, not on tablets of stone but on the fleshly tablets of the heart, let them cease to worship the letter and to show so much concern for it.

I think I have now satisfactorily explained in what sense Scripture should be regarded as sacred and divine. We have next to consider what is to be rightly understood by the phrase '*dabar Jehovah*' (the Word of the Lord). '*Dabar*' means word, speech, command and thing. In Chapter 1 we have already explained the reasons why a thing is said in Hebrew to be of God, and is referred to God, and from this we can readily understand what Scripture means by the word, speech, command, thing of God. We therefore need not go over all that ground again, nor repeat what we said in Chapter 6 in the third section of our exposition concerning miracles. A reference to the points there made will itself be sufficient to afford a better understanding of what I now intend to say: the phrase 'Word of God,' when used in connection with anything other than God himself, properly means the Divine Law which we discussed in Chapter 4; that is, religion universal to the entire human race, or catholic religion. For this, see Isaiah ch. 1 v. 10 etc., where he teaches the true way of life as consisting not in ceremonial observance but in charity and sincerity of heart, calling it God's Law and God's Word without distinction.

The expression is also used metaphorically for Nature's order and destiny (because in reality this is dependent on and follows from the eternal decree of the divine nature), and especially for that part of Nature's order that the prophets had foreseen; for the prophets did not envisage future events as the result of natural causes, but as God's will and decrees. Again, this expression is also used for any edict of any prophet insofar his perception resulted not from the natural light which is common to all, but from his special power or prophetic gift. This use of the expression was natural to the prophets, because in actual fact they were wont to perceive God as a lawgiver, as we showed in Chapter 4. There are, then, three reasons why Scripture is called the Word of God: because it teaches true religion, of which God is the eternal Author; because it relates predictions of the future as God's decrees; and lastly, because the real authors of Scripture taught for the most part not from the natural light common to all but from a light peculiar to themselves, and they represented God as making these utterances. And although, besides these features, Scripture contains a great deal of merely historical narrative such as can be apprehended by the natural light, it takes the name 'Word of God' from its most important aspect.

It can thus be readily seen in what sense God is to be understood as the author of the Bible: it is not because God willed to confer on men a set number of books, but because of the true religion that is taught therein. And this also explains for us why the Bible is divided into the Old and New Testaments. Before the coming of Christ the prophets used to proclaim religion as the law of their own country by virtue of the covenant made in the time of Moses, whereas after the coming of Christ the Apostles preached religion to all men as a universal law solely by virtue of Christ's Passion. The books of the New Testament contained no different doctrine, nor were they written as documents of a covenant, nor was the universal religion—which is entirely in accord with Nature—anything new, except in relation to men who knew it not. "He was in the world," says John the Evangelist, ch. 1 v. 10, "and the world knew Him not."

Therefore, even if we possessed fewer books of the Old Testament, we should not be deprived of the Word of God, whose proper meaning, as we have said, is true religion. After all, we do not regard ourselves at present as deprived of the Word of God in spite of being without many very important writings, such as the book of the Law, which was zealously guarded in the temple as the original of the Covenant, and the books of the Wars, the books of the Chronicles, and numerous others from which our Old Testament books were gathered and compiled. And there are many other arguments to confirm this view.

1. In the case of both Testaments, the books were not written by express command at one and the same time for all ages. They were the fortuitous work of certain men who wrote according to the requirements of their age and of their own particular character, as is clearly shown by the calling of the prophets (who were called to admonish the ungodly of their time) and also by the Epistles of the Apostles.

2. To understand Scripture and the mind of the prophets is by no means the same thing as to understand the mind of God, that is, to understand truth itself. This follows from our discussion of the prophets in Chapter 2, and we showed in Chapter 6 that this also applies to the narratives and the miracles. But this cannot be said of those passages that are concerned with true religion and true virtue.

3. The books of the Old Testament were selected out of many books, and were finally assembled and approved by a council of Pharisees, as we showed in Chapter 10. The books of the New Testament were also admitted to the canon by the decrees of certain Councils, who rejected as spurious several other books held by

many as sacred. But the membership of these councils (both of Pharisees and of Christians) did not consist of prophets, but only of teachers and scholars. Still, it must be granted that they took the Word of God as their standard in making their selection, and so they must have been acquainted with the Word of God before they approved all the books.

4. The Apostles wrote not as prophets but as teachers (as we said in the preceding chapter), and they chose such methods of teaching as they thought best adapted to those whom they wished to instruct at the time. Hence it follows (as we showed at the end of that same chapter) that their writings contain many things that are no longer relevant to religion.

5. Finally, there are four Evangelists in the New Testament; and who can believe that God willed to tell the story of Christ and impart it in writing to mankind four times over? And although one version may contain some details that are omitted in another, and one version is often helpful to the understanding of another, we should not thus conclude that all that was related in the four Gospels was essential for us to know, and that God chose the Evangelists to write so that the life of Christ might be better understood. Each Evangelist preached his message in a different place, and each wrote down in simple style what he had preached with view to telling clearly the story of Christ, and not with view to explaining the other Evangelists. If a comparison of their different versions sometimes produces a readier and clearer understanding, this is a matter of chance, and it occurs only in a few passages whose obscurity would not have rendered the story less clear or mankind less blessed.

We have thus shown that it is only in respect of religion—i.e. in respect of the universal divine law—that Scripture can properly be called the Word of God. It remains for us now to show that Scripture, insofar as it is properly thus called, is neither faulty, nor corrupted, nor mutilated. Now I here apply the terms 'faulty', 'corrupted' and 'mutilated' to that which is so incorrectly written and composed that its meaning cannot be arrived at from linguistic usage, or be derived from Scripture alone. I am not going to say that Scripture, insofar as it contains the Divine Law, has always preserved the same markings, the same letters and the same words (I leave this to be proved by the Massoretes, who zealously worship the letter), but I will say this, that its meaning—and only in respect of meaning can any utterance be called divine—has reached us uncorrupted, even if it be supposed that the words by which it was originally expressed have undergone many changes. Such alterations, as we have seen, take nothing away from the divinity of Scripture; for Scripture would be just as divine even if it had been written in different words or in a different language. Therefore there can be no doubt that the Divine Law has come down to us in this respect uncorrupted. For from Scripture itself we learn that its message, unclouded by any doubt or any ambiguity, is in essence this, to love God above all, and one's neighbour as oneself. There can be no adulteration here, nor can it have been written by a hasty and errant pen; for if doctrine differing from this is to be found anywhere in Scripture, all the rest of its teaching must also have been different. For this is the basis of the whole structure of religion; if it is removed, the entire fabric crashes to the ground, and then such a Scripture would not be the sort of thing we are now discussing, but a quite different book. It is, then, incontestable that this has always been the teaching of Scripture, and therefore no error capable of corrupting this meaning can have entered without its being immediately observed by all, nor could anyone have deliberately corrupted it without his evil intent being at once detected.

Since, then, it must be maintained that this fundamental principle is uncorrupted, the same must be granted of all that indisputably follows therefrom and is likewise fundamental, such as that God exists, that He provides for all things, that He is omnipotent, that by His decrees the good prosper and the wicked are cast down, and that our salvation depends solely on His grace. For all these are doctrines which are plainly taught throughout Scripture, and which it was at all times bound to teach if all the rest of its teachings were not to be vain and without foundation. And we must accept as equally uncorrupted, inasmuch as they quite clearly follow from this universal basis, all its other moral teachings, such as to uphold justice, to help the helpless, to do no murder, to covet no man's goods and so on. None of these, I say, could have been corrupted by human malice or destroyed by time's decay; for if any part of them had disappeared, the underlying universal principle would at once have restored it, especially the doctrine of charity, which is everywhere commended in the highest degree in both Testaments. Furthermore, although there is no crime so abominable as not to have been committed by someone, there is no one who, to excuse his crimes, would attempt to destroy the law or to introduce some impiety as eternal doctrine and the road to salvation. For we see that human nature is so constituted that any man (be he king or subject) who has committed a base action seeks to cloak his deed with such outward show as to give the impression of having done nothing contrary to justice and decency. We may therefore accept without reservation that the universal Divine Law, as taught by Scripture, has reached us uncorrupted.

Besides the above, there are other things which we cannot doubt have been transmitted to us in good faith, such as the chief historical narratives of Scripture, these being well known to all. It was the custom of the Jewish people in ancient times to chant their nation's history in psalms. The chief facts of the life of Christ, too, and his Passion were immediately spread abroad throughout the whole Roman Empire. It is therefore impossible to believe that, without the connivance of a large part of mankind — which is quite inconceivable — later generations handed down a version of the main outlines of these events different from what they had received. So any alterations or faults can have occurred only with respect to minor matters, such as a few details in history or prophecy designed to foster people's devotion, or in a few miracles so as to perplex philosophers, or in speculative matters after schismatics had begun the practice of introducing these into religion in order that each of them might buttress his own fictions by misusing divine authority. But for salvation it matters little whether these are instances of corruption or not, as I shall explain in full in the next chapter; though I believe this is already proved by what I have previously said, especially in Chapter 2.

CHAPTER 13

It is shown that Scripture teaches only very simple doctrines and inculcates nothing but obedience, and that concerning the nature of God it teaches only what men can imitate by a definite code of conduct

In Chapter 2 of this treatise we showed that the prophets possessed only an extraordinary power of imagination, not of intellect; and that God did not reveal to them any philosophic mysteries, but only things of a very simple nature, adapted to their preconceived beliefs. Then in Chapter 5 we showed that Scripture conveys and teaches its message in a way best suited to the comprehension of all men, not resorting to a chain of deductive reasoning from axioms and definitions, but speaking quite simply. And to induce belief, it relies only on past events, such as miracles and histories, to confirm its message, employing such style and mode of expression as is most likely to make a strong impression on men's minds. (On this subject see the third section of Chapter 6.) Finally, in Chapter 7 we showed that the difficulty in understanding Scripture lies only in its language, and not in the high level of its argumentation. We may add furthermore that the prophets preached not to scholars but to all Jews without exception, and the Apostles were wont to teach their Gospel in churches which were places of public assembly. From all these considerations it follows that Scriptural doctrine contains not abstruse speculation or philosophic reasoning, but very simple matters able to be understood by the most sluggish mind.

I am therefore astonished at the ingenuity displayed by those, of whom I have already spoken, who find in Scripture mysteries so profound as not to be open to explanation in any human language, and who have then imported into religion so many matters of a philosophic nature that the Church seems like an academy, and religion like a science, or rather, a subject for debate. Yet why should I be surprised that men who vaunt themselves on possessing a supernatural light refuse to yield precedence in knowledge to men who possess nothing more than the natural light? I should indeed be surprised if they taught any purely philosophic doctrine which was new and not already a commonplace in ages past among Gentile philosophers (whom they nevertheless accuse of blindness); for if you enquire as to the nature of the mysteries which they see lurking in Scripture, you will certainly find nothing but the notions of an Aristotle or a Plato or the like, which often seem to suggest the fantasies of any uneducated person rather than the findings of an accomplished biblical scholar.

However, I do not go so far as to maintain that nothing whatsoever of a purely philosophic nature is to be found in Scripture's teaching, for in the last chapter we set forth certain affirmations of this kind as Scripture's basic principles. But this much I will say, that such affirmations are very few, and of a very simple nature. What they are, and on what grounds they are determined, I now intend to explain; and this we can easily do now that we know that Scripture's aim was not to impart scientific knowledge; for this leads obviously to the conclusion that Scripture demands nothing from men but obedience, and condemns not ignorance, but only obstinacy. Furthermore, since obedience to God consists solely in loving one's neighbour (for he who loves his neighbour in obedience to God's command has fulfilled the Law, as Paul says in Romans chapter 13 v. 8), it follows that Scripture commands no other kind of knowledge than that which is necessary for all men before they can obey God according to this commandment, and without which men are bound to be self-willed, or at least unschooled to obedience. Other philosophic questions which do not directly tend to this end, whether they be concerned with knowledge of God or with knowledge of Nature, have nothing to do with Scripture, and should therefore be dissociated from revealed religion.

Now although, as we have said, this is now quite obvious to all, nevertheless, since this matter is of cardinal importance to the concept of religion, I shall go into the whole question more carefully and explain it more clearly. To this end I must in the first place demonstrate that the intellectual or exact knowledge of God is not a gift shared by all the faithful, as is obedience; secondly, that the knowledge which God through the medium of his prophets has required of all men universally, and which every man is in duty bound to possess, is no other than the knowledge of his divine justice and charity. Both of these points can be readily demonstrated from Scripture.

The first clearly follows from Exodus ch. 6 v. 3, where in order to emphasise the singular grace bestowed on Moses, God says to him, "And I appeared unto Abraham, unto Isaac, and unto Jacob as *El Shaddai*, but by my name Jehovah was I not known to them." For a clearer explanation of this passage it should be observed that *El Shaddai* means in Hebrew 'the God who suffices,' because to each man he gives that which suffices for him; and although '*Shaddai*' is often used by itself to mean God, there can be no doubt that in all cases the word '*El*', God, is to be understood. Again, it should be observed that in Scripture no word but 'Jehovah' is to be found to indicate the absolute essence of God, as unrelated to created things. That is why the Hebrews contend that this is, strictly speaking, God's only name, the other names being forms of address; and it is a fact that the other names of God, whether substantive or adjectival, are attributes belonging to God insofar as he is considered as related to created things, or manifested through them. For example, take אל *El* (or, with the paragogic ה *he*, אלה *Eloha*), which signifies nothing other than 'powerful', as all agree, and belongs to God only through his pre-eminence, in the way that the term 'Apostle' belongs to Paul. The qualities of his potency are explicated by additional adjectives, such as the great, the awful, the just, the merciful *El* (mighty one); or else, to embrace them all in one, this word is used in the plural with a singular meaning, a common practice in Scripture.

Now since God tells Moses that he was not known to the patriarchs by the name 'Jehovah', it follows that they were not acquainted with any attribute of God that expresses his absolute essence, but only with his deeds and promises, that is, his power as manifested through visible things. Yet in saying this to Moses God is not accusing the patriarchs of want of faith; on the contrary, he is extolling their trust and faith which, although they could not attain to Moses' special knowledge of God, led them to believe in the sureness and certainty of God's promises. In this they were unlike Moses who, despite his more exalted conception of God, yet doubted God's promises, and reproached God for bringing the Jews to a worse plight instead of the promised salvation.

The patriarchs, then, did not know God's distinctive name, and God tells Moses this in praise of their singlemindedness and faith, and also to signify the special grace granted to Moses. Hence it clearly follows, as we asserted in the first place, that men are not bound as a command to know God's attributes; this is a special gift granted only to certain of the faithful. It is not worth the effort to demonstrate this by further Scriptural testimony, for who can fail to see that the faithful have not all possessed an equal knowledge of God, and that nobody can be wise by command any more than he can live and exist by command? Men, women, children, all are equally capable of obedience by command, but not of wisdom by command. Now if anyone says that, while there is no need to understand God's attributes, there is a duty to believe them straightforwardly without proof, he is plainly talking nonsense. In the case of things invisible which are objects only of the mind, proofs are the only eyes by which they can be seen; therefore those who do not have such proofs can see nothing at all of these things. So when they merely repeat what they have heard of such matters, this is no more relevant to or indicative of their mind than the words of a parrot or a puppet speaking without meaning or sense.

However, before going any further, I should explain why Genesis often says that the patriarchs invoked God as Jehovah, which seems flatly to contradict what has been said above. Now if we have regard to the demonstration of Chapter 8, we shall find that there is no real contradiction. In that chapter we showed that the writer of the Pentateuch did not apply to things and places the exact names that were in use at the time to which he was referring, but names more familiar to the time of the writer. So in Genesis God as invoked by the patriarchs is signified by the name 'Jehovah', not because he was known to them by this name but because this was the name most revered by the Jews. This, I say, is the view we must take, seeing that our Exodus text expressly states that God was not known to the patriarchs by that name. There is a further reason in Exodus ch. 3 v. 13, where Moses desires to know the name of God: if this name had previously been known, it must surely have been known to Moses. We must therefore hold to the view we put forward, that the faithful patriarchs did not know this name of God, and that knowledge of God is God's gift, not a command.

It is now time to pass on to our second point, which is to show that God through his prophets asks no other knowledge of himself than the knowledge of his divine justice and charity, that is, such attributes of God as men find it possible to imitate by a definite rule of conduct. This is the express teaching of Jeremiah, who in chapter 22 v. 15, 16 says, speaking of king Josiah, "Thy father did eat and drink and do judgment and justice; then it was well with him. He judged the cause of the poor and the needy; then it was well with him. For (note well) this is what it is to know me, said the Lord." The passage in chapter 9 v. 23 is no less clear. "But let him that glorieth glory in this, that he understandeth and knoweth me, that I am the Lord who exerciseth lovingkindness, judgment and righteousness in the earth, for in these things I delight, saith the Lord." The same point is also made in Exodus ch. 34 v. 6, 7, where God reveals to Moses, who desires to see and know him, no other attributes than those which make manifest the divine justice and charity. Finally, we should here call particular attention to that passage in John — of which more hereafter — where he singles out charity as the only means of making God manifest (since nobody has seen God), and concludes that he who has charity truly has God, and knows God.

We see, then, that Jeremiah, Moses and John sum up very briefly the knowledge of God which it is the duty of every man to have, and they hold it to consist simply in what we asserted, that God is supremely just and supremely merciful, that is, the one perfect pattern of the true life. Furthermore, Scripture never expressly gives a definition of God, nor does it enjoin on us the acceptance of any other attributes than those I have just described, nor does it formally commend other attributes as it does these. All this leads us to the conclusion that the intellectual knowledge of God which contemplates his nature as it really is in itself — a nature which men cannot imitate by a set rule of conduct nor take as their example — has no bearing on the practice of a true way of life, on faith, and on revealed religion, and that consequently men can go far astray in this matter without sinning. It is therefore by no means surprising that God adapted himself to the imagination and the preconceived beliefs of the prophets, and that the faithful have entertained very diverse ideas about God, as we demonstrated with many examples in Chapter 2. And it is again not at all surprising that the Sacred Books frequently speak so inexactly about God, attributing to him hands, feet, eyes, ears, mind, movement and even emotions such as jealousy, pity and so forth, and depicting him as a judge sitting on a royal throne in heaven, with Christ on his right hand. For they are speaking in accordance with the understanding of the common people, in whom Scripture seeks to inculcate obedience, not learning.

Yet the common run of theologians have argued that those passages which their natural light has convinced them are not in agreement with the divine nature should be interpreted in a metaphorical way, while whatever is beyond their understanding must be taken literally. But if every passage of the former kind in Scripture was meant to be understood and interpreted metaphorically, Scripture must have been written not for the common people and the uneducated masses, but for the learned alone, and for philosophers in particular. Indeed, if it were a sin to believe with simple piety and faith those ideas about God which we have just recounted, then surely the prophets should have exercised the greatest care to avoid such expressions, having regard to the limited intelligence of the common people; and they should have made it their primary aim to teach the attributes of God explicitly and clearly in the manner that every man is required to accept them. Nowhere has this been done.

Thus we should reject the view that anything of piety or impiety attaches to beliefs taken simply in themselves without respect to works. A man's beliefs should be regarded as pious or impious only insofar as he is thereby induced to obey the moral law, or else assumes from them the licence to sin or rebel. Therefore if anyone by believing what is true becomes self-willed, he has a faith which in reality is impious; and if by believing what is false he becomes obedient to the moral law, he has a faith which is pious. For we have shown that true knowledge of God is not commanded, but is a divine gift, and that God has asked no other knowledge from men but knowledge of his divine justice and charity, this knowledge being necessary not for philosophical understanding, but for obedience to the moral law.

CHAPTER 14

An analysis of faith, the faithful and the fundamental principles of faith. Faith is finally set apart from philosophy

Anyone who gives any thought to this question cannot fail to realise that, for a true comprehension of faith, it is essential to understand that Scripture is adapted to the intellectual level not only of the prophets but of the unstable and fickle Jewish multitude. He who indiscriminately accepts everything in Scripture as being the universal and absolute teaching about God, and does not distinguish precisely what is adapted to the understanding of the masses, is bound to confuse the beliefs of the masses with divine doctrine, to proclaim as God's teaching the figments and arbitrary opinions of men, and to abuse Scriptural authority. Who, I ask, does not see this as the main reason why so many quite contradictory beliefs are taught by different sects as articles of faith, which they confirm with many citations from Scripture, so that in the Netherlands the saying '*Geen ketter sonder letter*'[1] has long become a proverb? The Sacred Books were not the work of a single writer, nor were they written for a people of a single age; they were written by a number of men of different character and different generations over a period of time which, taking them all into account, will be found to extend to about two thousand years, and perhaps much longer.

However, I will not level the charge of impiety against those sectaries simply because they adapt the words of Scripture to their own beliefs. Just as Scripture was once adapted to the understanding of the people of that time, in the same way anyone may now adapt it to his own beliefs if he feels that this will enable him to obey God with heartier will in those matters that pertain to justice and charity. My accusation against them is this, that they refuse to grant this same freedom to others. All those who do not share their opinions, however righteous and truly vir-

---

[1] [No heretic without a text.]

tuous the dissenters may be, they persecute as God's enemies, while those who follow their lead, however dissolute they may be, they cherish as God's elect. Surely nothing more damnable than this, and more fraught with danger to the state, can be devised.

So in order to establish what are the limits of individual freedom of opinion in regard to faith, and who should be seen as belonging to the faithful in spite of their diverse opinions, we must define faith and its basic principles. This I propose to do in this present chapter, at the same time distinguishing between faith and philosophy, this being the main object of this entire treatise.

To demonstrate these matters in good order, let us look again at the chief aim of Scripture in its entirety, for this will furnish us with a true norm for defining faith. In the last chapter we said that the aim of Scripture is simply to teach obedience, a statement which surely no one can deny. For who can fail to see that both the Testaments are simply a training for obedience, that each has as its purpose this alone, that men should sincerely hearken to God? Leaving out of account the demonstrations of the last chapter, I shall say that Moses' aim was not to convince the Israelites by reasoned argument, but to bind them by a covenant, by oaths and by benefits received; he induced the people to obey the Law under threat of punishment, while exhorting them thereto by promise of rewards. These are all means to promote obedience, not to impart knowledge. The message of the Gospel is one of simple faith; that is, belief in God and reverence for God, or—which is the same thing—obedience to God. So in order to prove what is already quite plain, there is no need for me to compile a list of the Scriptural texts that commend obedience, which are to be found in abundance in both Testaments. Then again, Scripture itself tells us quite clearly over and over again what every man should do in order to serve God, declaring that the entire Law consists in this alone, to love one's neighbour. Therefore it is also undeniable that he who by God's commandments loves his neighbour as himself is truly obedient and blessed according to the Law, while he who hates or takes no thought for his neighbour is rebellious and disobedient. Finally, there is universal agreement that Scripture was written and disseminated not just for the learned but for all men of every time and race, and this by itself justifies us in concluding that Scripture does not require us to believe anything beyond what is necessary for the fulfilling of the said commandment.

Therefore this commandment is the one and only guiding principle for the entire common faith of mankind, and through this commandment alone should be determined all the tenets of faith that every man is in duty bound to accept. Since it is abundantly clear that this is so, and that from this fundamental principle alone all else can legitimately be inferred simply by the process of reason, let everyone consider for himself how it can have come about that so many disputes have arisen in the Church. Can this be due to any other causes than those I have recounted at the beginning of Chapter 7? These, then, are the considerations which now induce me to explain in what manner and by what means necessary the tenets of faith are to be derived from the fundamental principle we have discovered. Unless I can achieve this, operating within definite rules, it will rightly be held that I have so far accomplished nothing. For anyone will still be able to foist on religion whatever doctrine he pleases under this same pretext, that it is a means for inculcating obedience. This is especially so when it is the divine attributes that are at issue.

For a complete and methodical demonstration, I shall begin with the definition of faith. According to our fundamental principle, faith must be defined as the holding of certain beliefs about God such that, without these beliefs, there cannot be obedience to God, and if this obedience is posited, these beliefs are necessarily posited. This definition is so clear, and follows so obviously from what has already been proved, that it needs no explanation. I shall now briefly show what consequences it entails. First, faith does not bring salvation through itself, but only by reason of obedience; or, as James says (ch. 2 v. 17), faith in itself without works is dead. For this point, see the whole of chapter 2 of the Epistle of James. Secondly, it follows that he who is truly obedient necessarily possesses a true and saving faith; for, as we have said, obedience being posited, faith is necessarily posited. This is again expressly stated by the same Apostle in chapter 2 v. 18, "Show me thy faith without thy works, and I will show thee my faith by my works." Likewise John, in 1 Ep. ch. 4 v. 7, 8, "Everyone that loveth (his neighbour) is born of God and knoweth God. He that loveth not, knoweth not God; for God is love." From these considerations it again follows that only by works can we judge anyone to be a believer or an unbeliever. If his works are good, he is a believer, however much he may differ in religious dogma from other believers; whereas if his works are evil, he is an unbeliever, however much he may agree with them verbally. For obedience being posited, faith is necessarily posited, and faith without works is dead. The Apostle John again expressly teaches this same doctrine in verse 13 of the same chapter. "Hereby," he says, "we know that we dwell in him and he in us, because he hath given us his Spirit." By 'spirit' he means love, whence he concludes (that is, from premises he has already accepted) that he who has love truly has the spirit of God. Indeed, since nobody has seen God he concludes therefrom that it is only through love of one's neighbour that one can perceive or be conscious of God, and thus no one can discover any other attribute of God except this love, insofar as we participate therein. Even if this argument is not conclusive, it nevertheless shows John's meaning quite clearly; but a far clearer statement is made in chapter 2 v. 3, 4 of the same Epistle, where he most explicitly teaches what I am here maintaining. "And hereby do we know that we know him, if we keep his commandments. He that saith, I know him, and keepeth not his commandments, is a liar, and the truth is not in him." From this we can again conclude that the true enemies of Christ are those who persecute the righteous and the lovers of justice because these disagree with them and do not uphold the same religious dogmas. Those who love justice and charity we know by that very fact to be the faithful, and he who persecutes the faithful is an enemy of Christ.

Finally, it follows that faith requires not so much true dogmas as pious dogmas, that is, such as move the heart to obedience; and this is so even if many of those beliefs contain not a shadow of truth, provided that he who adheres to them knows not that they are false. If he knew that they were false, he would necessarily be a rebel, for how could it be that one who seeks to love justice and obey God should worship as divine what he knows to be alien to the divine nature? Yet men may err from simplicity of mind, and, as we have seen, Scripture condemns only obstinacy, not ignorance. Indeed, this conclusion necessarily follows simply from the definition of faith, whose every part must be derived from that universal basic principle already demonstrated, and from the single purpose underlying the whole of Scripture, unless we allow ourselves to put our own arbitrary constructions on it. Now this definition does not expressly demand true dogmatic belief, but only such beliefs as are necessary for obedience, that is, those that strengthen the will to love one's neighbour. It is only through this love, as John says, that every man is in God, and God in every man.

Each man's faith, then, is to be regarded as pious or impious not in respect of its truth or falsity, but as it is conducive to obedience or obstinacy. Now nobody questions that there is to be found among men a wide variety of temperament, that all men are not equally in agreement in all matters and are influenced by their beliefs in different ways, so that what moves one man to devotion will move another to ridicule and contempt. Hence it follows that a catholic or universal faith must not contain any dogmas that good men may regard as controversial; for such dogmas may be to one man pious, to another impious, since their value lies only in the works they inspire. A catholic faith should therefore contain only those dogmas which obedience to God absolutely demands, and without which such obedience is absolutely impossible. As for other dogmas, every man should embrace those that he, being the best judge of himself, feels will do most to strengthen him in love of justice. Acceptance of this principle would, I suggest, leave no occasion for controversy in the Church.

I can now venture to enumerate the dogmas of the universal faith, the basic teachings which Scripture as a whole intends to convey. These must all be directed (as evidently follows from what we have demonstrated in these two chapters) to this one end: that there is a Supreme Being who loves justice and charity, whom all must obey in order to be saved, and must worship by practising justice and charity to their neighbour. From this, all the tenets of faith can readily be determined, and they are simply as follows:

1. God, that is, a Supreme Being, exists, supremely just and merciful, the exemplar of true life. He who knows not, or does not believe, that God exists, cannot obey him or know him as judge.

2. God is one alone. No one can doubt that this belief is essential for complete devotion, reverence, that is, love towards God; for devotion, reverence and love spring only from the pre-eminence of one above all others.

3. God is omnipresent, and all things are open to him. If it were believed that things could be concealed from God, or if it were not realised that he sees everything, one might doubt, or be unaware of the uniformity of the justice wherewith he directs everything.

4. God has supreme right and dominion over all things. He is under no jurisdiction, but acts by his absolute decree and singular grace. All are required to obey him absolutely, while he obeys none.

5. Worship of God and obedience to him consists solely in justice and charity, or love towards one's neighbour.

6. All who obey God by following this way of life, and only those, are saved; others, who live at pleasure's behest, are lost. If men did not firmly believe this, there is no reason why they should obey God rather than their desires.

7. God forgives repentant sinners. There is no one who does not sin, so that without this belief all would despair of salvation, and there would be no reason to believe that God is merciful. He who firmly believes that God forgives men's sins from the mercy and grace whereby he directs all things, and whose heart is thereby the more inspired by love of God, that man verily knows Christ according to the spirit, and Christ is in him.

No one can fail to realise that all these beliefs are essential if all men, without exception, are to be capable of obeying God as prescribed by the law explained above; for if any one of these beliefs is nullified, obedience is also nullified. But as to the question of what God, the exemplar of true life, really is, whether he is fire, or spirit, or light, or thought, or something else, this is irrelevant to faith. And so likewise is the question as to why he is the exemplar of true life, whether this is because he has a just and merciful disposition, or because all things exist and act through him and consequently we, too, understand through him, and through him we see what is true, just, and good. On these questions it matters not what beliefs a man holds. Nor, again, does it matter for faith whether one believes that God is omnipresent in essence or in potency, whether he directs everything from free will or from the necessity of his nature, whether he lays down laws as a ruler or teaches them as being eternal truths, whether man obeys God from free will or from the necessity of the divine decree, whether the rewarding of the good and the punishing of the wicked is natural or supernatural. The view one takes on these and similar questions has no bearing on faith, provided that such a belief does not lead to the assumption of greater licence to sin, or hinders submission to God. Indeed, as we have already said, every man is in duty bound to adapt these religious dogmas to his own understanding and to interpret them for himself in whatever way makes him feel that he can the more readily accept them with full confidence and conviction. For, as we have already pointed out, just as in olden days faith was revealed and written down in a form which accorded with the understanding and beliefs of the prophets and people of that time, so, too, every man has now the duty to adapt it to his own beliefs, so as thus to accept it without any misgivings or doubts. For we have shown that faith demands piety rather than truth; faith is pious and saving only by reason of the obedience it inspires, and consequently nobody is faithful except by reason of his obedience. Therefore the best faith is not necessarily manifested by him who displays the best arguments, but by him who displays the best works of justice and charity. How salutary this doctrine is, and how necessary in the state if men are to live in peace and harmony, and how many important causes of disturbance and crime are thereby aborted at source, I leave everyone to judge for himself.

Before proceeding further, it should here be observed that, from what has just been demonstrated, we are now in a position to provide a convincing answer to the difficulties we raised in Chapter 1 when we were discussing God's speaking to the Israelites from Mount Sinai. Although the voice which the Israelites heard could not have given those men a philosophical or mathematical certainty of God's existence, it sufficed to strike them with awe of God as they had previously known him, and to induce them to obedience, this being the purpose of that manifestation. For God was not seeking to teach the Israelites the absolute attributes of his essence (he revealed none of these things at the time), but to break down their obstinacy and bring them to obedience. Therefore he assailed them, not with arguments, but with the blare of trumpets, with thunder and with lightnings (see Exodus ch. 20 v. 20).

It now remains for me finally to show that between faith and theology on the one side and philosophy on the other there is no relation and no affinity, a point which must now be apparent to everyone who knows the aims and bases of these two faculties, which are as far apart as can be. The aim of philosophy is, quite simply, truth, while the aim of faith, as we have abundantly shown, is nothing other than obedience and piety. Again, philosophy rests on the basis of universally valid axioms, and must be constructed by studying Nature alone, whereas faith is based on history and language, and must be derived only from Scripture and revelation, as we showed in Chapter 7. So faith allows to every man the utmost freedom to philosophise, and he may hold whatever opinions he pleases on any subjects whatsoever without imputation of evil. It condemns as heretics and schismatics only those who teach such beliefs as promote obstinacy, hatred, strife and anger, while it regards as the faithful only those who promote justice and charity to the best of their intellectual powers and capacity.

Finally, since what I have here demonstrated forms the most important part of the subject of this treatise, before proceeding further I do most earnestly beg the reader to be good enough to read these two chapters with careful attention and to reflect on them repeatedly. Let him accept my assurance that my purpose in writing these chapters has not been to introduce innovations but to correct abuses, such as I hope one day to see corrected.

CHAPTER 15

It is demonstrated that neither is theology ancillary to reason nor reason to theology. The reason why we are convinced of the authority of Holy Scripture

Those who do not understand the distinction between philosophy and theology argue as to whether Scripture should be ancillary to reason, or reason to Scripture; that is, whether the meaning of Scripture should be made to conform with reason, or reason with Scripture. The latter view is upheld by the sceptics who deny the certainty of reason, the former by the dogmatists. But it is clear from our earlier findings that both parties are utterly mistaken, for whichever view we embrace we are forced to do violence either to reason or to Scripture. We have demonstrated that Scripture teaches only piety, not philosophy, and that all its contents were adapted to the understanding and preconceived beliefs of the common people. Therefore he who seeks to make Scripture conform with philosophy is sure to ascribe to the prophets many ideas which they never dreamed of, and will quite distort their meaning. On the other hand, he who makes reason and philosophy ancillary to theology has to accept as divinely inspired utterances the prejudices of a common people of long ago, which will gain a hold on his understanding and darken it. Thus they will both go wildly astray, the one spurning reason, the other siding with reason.

The first among the Pharisees who openly maintained that Scripture must be made to conform with reason was Maimonides, whose opinion we reviewed in Chapter 7 and refuted on many grounds. Although this writer was held in great esteem by the Pharisees, most of them desert him on this issue, favouring the view of a certain R. Jehuda Alpakhar,[1] who, while seeking to avoid the error of Maimonides, fell into the opposite error. He maintained* that reason should be ancillary to Scripture, and completely subservient to it. He held that nothing in Scripture requires a metaphorical explanation merely on the grounds that its literal meaning is contrary to reason, but only if it is contrary to Scripture itself, that is, to the clear pronouncements of Scripture. Hence he formulated the universal rule that whatever Scripture teaches in dogmatic form and quite expressly affirms must be accepted as absolutely true simply on its own authority. No other dogma in the Bible will be found to be in contradiction with this directly, but only by implication, and this comes about because the Scriptural style of expression often

---

[1] [Jehuda Alpakhar (or 'Alfakar') was an important thirteenth-century Spanish Jewish physician residing in Toledo. In the anti-Maimonidean debates in Spain he supported the opponents of Maimonides. Spinoza refers to him also in Letter 43.]

* I remember once reading this in a letter against Maimonides, contained in a collection of letters said to belong to Maimonides.

appears to assume what is contrary to its express doctrine. Therefore it is only such passages that should be explained metaphorically. For example, Scripture clearly tells us that God is one alone (Deut. ch. 6 v. 4), and nowhere will any passage be found directly asserting that there is more than one God. But there are many passages where God speaks of himself, and the prophets speak of him, in the plural. This is merely a figure of speech, and does not really intend to indicate that there are in fact a number of Gods. Therefore all such expressions are to be explained metaphorically, not on the grounds that it is contrary to reason that there should be more than one God, but because Scripture itself directly asserts that God is one alone. Similarly, since Scripture directly asserts (according to Alpakhar) in Deuteronomy ch. 4 v. 15 that God is incorporeal, it is on the authority of this passage alone, not of reason, that we must believe that God has no body, and consequently it is on the authority of Scripture alone that we have to give a metaphorical explanation to all those passages that attribute to God hands, feet and so on. It is only through their figurative mode of expression that they appear to assume that God is corporeal.

Such is the view of Alpakhar. Insofar as he aims to explain Scripture through Scripture, I give him credit, but I am surprised that a man endowed with reason should seek to abolish reason. It is indeed true that, as long as we are simply concerned with the meaning of the text and the prophets' intention, Scripture should be explained through Scripture; but having extracted the true meaning, we must necessarily resort to judgment and reason before we can assent thereto. Now if reason, in spite of her protests, is nevertheless to be made completely subservient to Scripture, must this submission be effected with reason's concurrence, or without it, blindly? If the latter, then surely we are behaving like fools, without judgment. If the former, then it is only at reason's behest that we accept Scripture, which we would therefore not accept if it were repugnant to reason. And again, I ask, who can give mental acceptance to something against which his reason rebels? For what else is mental denial but reason's rebellion? I am utterly astonished that men can bring themselves to make reason, the greatest of all gifts and a light divine, subservient to letters that are dead, and may have been corrupted by human malice; that it should be considered no crime to denigrate the mind, the true handwriting of God's word, declaring it to be corrupt, blind and lost, whereas it is considered to be a heinous crime to entertain such thoughts of the letter, a mere shadow of God's word. They think it pious to put no trust in reason and their own judgment, impious to doubt the trustworthiness of those who have transmitted to us the Sacred Books. This is not piety, but mere folly. But what, I ask, is troubling them? What are they afraid of? Is it that religion and faith cannot be upheld unless men deliberately cultivate ignorance and completely turn their backs on reason? Such an attitude is surely the mark of fear on Scripture's behalf rather than confidence. But let it never be said that religion and piety seek to enslave reason, or reason religion, or that either of them is incapable of maintaining its own sovereignty in complete harmony with the other. This is a theme to which I shall soon return, for in the meantime I should like first of all to consider R. Alpakhar's rule.

As we have said, he holds that we must accept as true or reject as false everything that Scripture affirms or denies, and secondly, that Scripture never expressly affirms or denies anything that contradicts what it elsewhere affirms or denies. The rashness of both these assertions will be apparent to all. I pass by his failure to perceive that Scripture consists of different books written at different times for different men by different authors. And there is the further point that these assertions are made on his own authority without any evidence from either reason or Scripture; for he ought to have shown that those passages that contradict other passages only by implication can have a plausible metaphorical explanation based on the nature of language and a consideration of their context; and furthermore that Scripture has come down to us uncorrupted.

But let us examine the question methodically. With regard to his first assertion, I ask whether, if reason protests, we are nevertheless obliged to accept as true or reject as false whatever Scripture affirms or denies. Perhaps he will reply that there is nothing in Scripture which contradicts reason. But I insist that Scripture expressly affirms and teaches that God is jealous (in the Decalogue itself and in Exod. ch. 34 v. 14, in Deut. ch. 4 v. 24 and in many other places); this is contrary to reason, but must still, by his account, be posited as true. Indeed, if there should be any other passages in Scripture implying that God is not jealous, they would have to be explained metaphorically so that they seem to have no such implication. So, too, Scripture expressly says that God came down to Mount Sinai (Exod. ch. 19 v. 20) and ascribes to him other movements from place to place, nor does it anywhere expressly say that God does not move. So this must be accepted by all as true, and as to Solomon's assertion that God is not contained in any one place (1 Kings ch. 8 v. 27), since it does not maintain but merely implies that God does not move, it must be so explained as not to deprive God of movement. Similarly, the heavens would have to be taken as the dwelling-place and throne of God, because Scripture expressly says so. And there are numerous statements of this kind, made in accordance with the beliefs of the prophets and the multitude, which only reason and philosophy, not Scripture, tells us are false, and which nevertheless are all to be taken as true in our author's view, there being no appeal to reason.

Next, he is wrong in affirming that one passage does not directly contradict another, but only by implication. Moses directly affirms that God is fire (Deut. ch. 4 v. 24) and directly denies that God has any likeness to visible things (Deut. ch. 4 v. 12). If our author replies that the latter statement's denial that God is fire is not direct, but only by implication, and must therefore be made to conform with the former statement so as to avoid the appearance of contradiction, come then, let us grant that God is fire. Or better, lest we seem as crazy as he, let us put this question aside and take another example. Samuel directly denies that God ever repents (1 Sam. ch. 15 v. 29); on the other hand, Jeremiah asserts that God repents of the good and evil that he may have decreed (Jer. ch. 18, v. 8, 10). Well, then, are not these teachings directly opposed to each other? So which of the two is he going to explain metaphorically? Each of these assertions is made as universally valid, and each contradicts the other; what the one directly affirms, the other directly denies. Thus, by his own rule, he is required to accept something as true and at the same time reject it as false.

Then again, what difference does it make if one passage should contradict another not directly but only by implication, if the implication is clear, and if the context and nature of the passage do not permit of a metaphorical interpretation? There are many such instances in the Bible, as we mentioned in Chapter 2 where we showed that the prophets held diverse and contrary opinions, and there are the particularly glaring contradictions in the historical narratives to which we drew attention in Chapters 9 and 10. There is no need for me here to review them all again, for in my earlier remarks I have said enough to expose the absurdities consequent on the acceptance of this rule, its falsity, and the author's rashness in proposing it.

We may therefore dismiss the views of both Alpakhar and Maimonides, and we may maintain as incontrovertible that neither is theology required to be subordinated to reason nor reason to theology, and that each has its own domain. The domain of reason, as we have said, is truth and wisdom, the domain of theology is piety and obedience. For the power of reason, as we have already demonstrated, does not extend so far as to enable us to conclude that men can achieve blessedness simply through obedience without understanding, whereas this alone is the message of theology, which commands only obedience and neither seeks nor is able to oppose reason. As we showed in the last chapter, theology defines its religious dogmas only so far as suffices to secure obedience, and it leaves it to reason to decide exactly how these dogmas are to be understood in respect of truth; for reason is in reality the light of the mind, without which the mind sees nothing but dreams and fantasies.

By theology I here mean, in precise terms, revelation insofar as it manifests Scripture's objective as we have stated it, that is, the way of achieving obedience, or the dogmas of true piety and faith. In other words, by theology I mean the Word of God properly so called, which does not consist in a set number of books (see Chapter 12). Theology thus understood, if you consider its precepts and moral teaching, will be found to agree with reason; and if you look to its purpose and end, it will be found to be in no respect opposed to reason, and is therefore valid for all men.

With regard to Scripture taken in its entirety, we have already shown in Chapter 7 that its meaning is not to be derived from investigation of Nature in general—which is the basis of philosophy only—but simply from studying it in itself; and we should not be deterred if, after thus discovering the true meaning of Scripture, we find that it is at some points opposed to reason. Whatever instances of this kind are to be found in the Bible, or whatever things men may fail to understand without detriment to their love of their fellow men, we can be sure that these have no bearing on theology or the Word of God, and consequently anyone may hold whatever opinions he pleases on such matters without censure. We may therefore conclude without reservation that neither must Scripture be made to conform with reason, nor reason with Scripture.

However, since reason cannot demonstrate the truth or falsity of this fundamental principle of theology, that men may be saved simply by obedience, we may also be asked why it is that we believe it. If we accept this principle without reason, blindly, then we too are acting foolishly without judgment; if on the other hand we assert that this fundamental principle can be proved by reason, then theology becomes a part of philosophy, and inseparable from it. To this I reply that I maintain absolutely that this fundamental dogma of theology cannot be investigated by the natural light of reason, or at least that nobody has been successful in proving it, and that therefore it was essential that there should be revelation. Nevertheless, we can use judgment before we accept with at least moral certainty that which has been revealed. I say 'with moral certainty,' for we have no grounds for expecting to reach greater certainty in this matter than did the prophets to whom it was originally revealed; and yet their certainty was only of a moral kind, as we have shown in Chapter 2 of this treatise.

So those who attempt to prove Scripture's authority by demonstrations of a mathematical order go far astray, for the authority of the Bible is dependent on the authority of the prophets, and can thus have no stronger arguments to support it than those by which the prophets of old were wont to convince the people of their authority. Indeed, our own certainty as to this authority can have no other foundation than that on which the prophets based their certainty and authority. Now we have shown that the certainty of the prophets rested entirely on these three factors—first, a distinct and vivid imagination, second, a sign, third and most important, a heart turned to what is right and good. They based their claims on no other considerations, and so there are no other considerations by which their authority could be proved either to the people to whom they once spoke face to face, or to us to whom they speak in writing.

The first of these factors, their vivid imagination, was a personal quality confined to the prophets, and therefore our certainty regarding revelation can rest, and ought to rest, entirely on the other two, the sign and the doctrine they taught. And this is what Moses too expressly asserts, for in Deuteronomy ch. 18 he bids the people obey the prophet who should give a true sign in the name of the Lord, but to condemn to death that same man if he should prophesy falsely even in the name of the Lord, and likewise him who should seek to turn the people away from the true religion, even if he were to confirm his authority by signs and wonders (see Deut. ch. 13). Hence it follows that a true prophet can be distinguished from a false prophet by his doctrine and his miracles taken together. For it is such a one that Moses declares to be a true prophet, and bids us trust without fear of deceit; while he condemns as false prophets deserving of death those who make false prophecies even in the name of the Lord, or those who preach false gods, even if they have wrought true miracles.

Therefore we too must accept only this one reason for believing in Scripture—that is, in the prophets—namely, their teaching as confirmed by signs. For since we see that the prophets commend above all else justice and charity and have no other objective, we may hence conclude that it was no evil intent but sincere conviction that prompted them to teach that men may achieve blessedness by obedience and faith. And because they furthermore confirmed this teaching with signs, we are convinced that they were not speaking at random nor were they out of their senses while prophesying. This conclusion is further corroborated when we realise that all their moral teaching is in full agreement with reason, for it is no accident that the Word of God proclaimed by the prophets agrees in all respects with the Word of God that speaks in our hearts. The Bible, I say, conveys to us this certainty just as well as did the living voice of the prophets to the Jews of old. For we showed towards the end of Chapter 12 that Scripture has come down to us uncorrupted in respect of its doctrine and its chief historical narratives.

Therefore, although this fundamental principle underlying all theology and Scripture cannot be demonstrated with mathematical exactitude, we may yet accept it without our judgment being called into question. It would be folly to refuse to accept, merely on the grounds that it cannot be proved with mathematical certainty, that which is abundantly confirmed by the testimony of so many prophets, that which is the source of so much comfort to those less gifted with intelligence, and of considerable advantage to the state, and which we can believe without incurring any peril or hurt. Could we live our lives wisely if we were to accept as true nothing that could conceivably be called into doubt on any principle of scepticism? Are not most of our actions in any case fraught with uncertainty and hazard?

I do indeed admit that those who think that philosophy and theology are mutually contradictory and that therefore one or the other must be deprived of its sovereignty and set aside, have good reason for seeking to put theology on a solid foundation and for attempting to prove it with mathematical accuracy. Who but a desperate madman would be so rash as to turn his back on reason, or to hold the arts and sciences in contempt, while denying the certainty of reason? Even so, we cannot entirely absolve them from censure, in that they seek the help of reason in the task of repelling reason, and they try to employ the certainty of reason to disparage reason's certainty. While they are aiming to prove the truth and authority of theology by mathematical demonstrations and to deprive reason and the natural light of its authority, they are simply drawing theology into the domain of reason, and are quite clearly implying that her authority has no brilliance unless it is illuminated by the natural light of reason.

If on the other hand they boast that their own assurance rests entirely on the inward testimony of the Holy Spirit and that they invoke the aid of reason solely for the purpose of convincing unbelievers, we should still give no credit to their words, for we can now readily prove that they are prompted to say this either from emotional bias or from vainglory. From the preceding chapter it quite clearly follows that the testimony of the Holy Spirit is concerned only with good works— which therefore Paul, too, in his Epistle to the Galatians ch. 5 v. 22 calls 'the fruits of the Holy Spirit'—and that the Holy Spirit itself is nothing other than the peace of mind that results from good actions. As for the truth and certainty of those questions which are the subject only of speculative philosophy, no spirit bears testimony other than reason, which alone, as we have shown, has asserted its claim to the realm of truth. So if they contend that they possess some other spirit that gives them certainty of truth, this is an idle boast; they speak from emotional bias; or else, through dread of being worsted by philosophers and exposed to public ridicule, they seek refuge in the sacred. But all in vain; for what altar can he find to shelter him, who is guilty of betraying reason?

But I will say no more of these men, since I think I have satisfactorily made my case by demonstrating on what grounds philosophy must be distinguished from theology, what is the essential nature of each, and that neither of them is subordinate to the other, each of them holding its own domain without contradicting the other. Finally, as opportunity arose, I have also shown the absurdities, the damage and the harm that have resulted from the fact that men have thoroughly confused these two faculties, failing to make an accurate distinction between them and to separate the one from the other.

Before I continue, I wish to emphasise in express terms—though I have said it before—the importance and necessity of the role that I assign to Scripture, or revelation. For since we cannot perceive by the natural light that simple obedience is a way to salvation,* and since only revelation teaches us that this comes about by God's singular grace which we cannot attain by reason, it follows that Scripture has brought very great comfort to mankind. For all men without exception are capable of obedience, while there are only a few—in proportion to the whole of humanity—who acquire a virtuous disposition under the guidance of reason alone. Thus, did we not have this testimony of Scripture, the salvation of nearly all men would be in doubt.

CHAPTER 16

The basis of the state; the natural and civil right of the individual, and the right of sovereign powers

Up to this point our object has been to separate philosophy from theology and to show that the latter allows freedom to philosophise for every individual. It is therefore time to enquire what are the limits of this freedom of thought, and of saying what one thinks, in a well-conducted state. To approach this question in an orderly way, we must discuss the basis of the state, and prior to that, before giving any consideration to the state and to religion, we must discuss the natural right of the individual.[1]

By the right and established order of Nature I mean simply the rules governing the nature of every individual thing, according to which we conceive it as naturally determined to exist and to act in a definite way. For example, fish are

---

* See Supplementary Note 31.

[1] [Throughout this chapter there are echoes of the political philosophy of Thomas Hobbes, whose treatise *De Cive* (On the Citizen) Spinoza had read.]

determined by nature to swim, and the big ones to eat the smaller ones. Thus it is by sovereign natural right that fish inhabit water, and the big ones eat the smaller ones. For it is certain that Nature, taken in the absolute sense, has the sovereign right to do all that she can do; that is, Nature's right is co-extensive with her power. For Nature's power is the very power of God, who has sovereign right over all things.[2] But since the universal power of Nature as a whole is nothing but the power of all individual things taken together,[3] it follows that each individual thing has the sovereign right to do all that it can do; i.e. the right of the individual is co-extensive with its determinate power.

Now since it is the supreme law of Nature that each thing endeavours to persist in its present being, as far as in it lies, taking account of no other thing but itself,[4] it follows that each individual has the sovereign right to do this, that is (as I have said), to exist and to act as it is naturally determined. And here I do not acknowledge any distinction between men and other individuals of Nature, nor between men endowed with reason and others to whom true reason is unknown, nor between fools, madmen and the sane. Whatever an individual thing does by the laws of its own nature, it does with sovereign right, inasmuch as it acts as determined by Nature, and can do no other. Therefore among men, as long as they are considered as living under the rule of Nature alone, he who is not yet acquainted with reason or has not yet acquired a virtuous disposition lives under the sole control of appetite with as much sovereign right as he who conducts his life under the rule of reason. That is to say, just as the wise man has the sovereign right to do all that reason dictates, i.e. to live according to the laws of reason, so, too, a man who is ignorant and weak-willed has the sovereign right to do all that is urged on him by appetite, i.e. to live according to the laws of appetite. This is the same doctrine as that of Paul, who declares that prior to the law—that is, as long as men are considered as living under Nature's rule—there can be no sin.

Thus the natural right of every man is determined not by sound reason, but by his desire and his power. For not all men are naturally determined to act in accordance with the rules and laws of reason. On the contrary, all men are born in a state of complete ignorance, and before they can learn the true way of life and acquire a virtuous disposition, even if they have been well brought up, a great part of their life has gone by. Yet in the meantime they have to live and preserve themselves as far as in them lies, namely, by the urging of appetite alone, for Nature has given them nothing else and has denied them the actualised power to live according to sound reason. Therefore they are no more in duty bound to live according to the laws of a sound mind than a cat to live according to the laws of a lion's nature. Thus whatever every man, when he is considered as solely under the dominion of Nature, believes to be to his advantage, whether under the guidance of sound reason or under passion's sway, he may by sovereign natural right

---

[2] [*Ethics*, 1.17, Scholium 34–35.]
[3] [*Ethics*, 2.13, Lemma 7, Scholium, Letter 32.]
[4] [*Ethics*, 3.6–7.]

seek and get for himself by any means, by force, deceit, entreaty or in any other way he best can, and he may consequently regard as his enemy anyone who tries to hinder him from getting what he wants.

From this it follows that Nature's right and her established order, under which all men are born and for the most part live, forbids only those things that no one desires and no one can do; it does not frown on strife, or hatred, or anger, or deceit, or on anything at all urged by appetite. This is not surprising, for Nature's bounds are not set by the laws of human reason which aim only at man's true interest and his preservation, but by infinite other laws which have regard to the eternal order of the whole of Nature, of which man is but a particle. It is from the necessity of this order alone that all individual things are determined to exist and to act in a definite way. So when something in Nature appears to us as ridiculous, absurd or evil, this is due to the fact that our knowledge is only partial, that we are largely ignorant of the order and coherence of the whole of Nature and want all things to be arranged to suit our reason. Yet that which our reason declares to be evil is not evil in respect of the order and laws of universal Nature, but only in respect of the laws of our own nature.

However, there cannot be any doubt as to how much more it is to men's advantage to live in accordance with the laws and sure dictates of our reason, which, as we have said, aim only at the true good of men.[5] Furthermore, there is nobody who does not desire to live in safety free from fear, as far as is possible. But this cannot come about as long as every individual is permitted to do just as he pleases, and reason can claim no more right than hatred and anger. For there is no one whose life is free from anxiety in the midst of feuds, hatred, anger and deceit, and who will not therefore try to avoid these as far as in him lies. And if we also reflect that the life of men without mutual assistance must necessarily be most wretched and must lack the cultivation of reason, as we showed in Chapter 5, it will become quite clear to us that, in order to achieve a secure and good life, men had necessarily to unite in one body. They therefore arranged that the unrestricted right naturally possessed by each individual should be put into common ownership, and that this right should no longer be determined by the strength and appetite of the individual, but by the power and will of all together. Yet in this they would have failed, had appetite been their only guide (for by the laws of appetite all men are drawn in different directions), and so they had to bind themselves by the most stringent pledges to be guided in all matters only by the dictates of reason (which nobody ventures openly to oppose, lest he should appear to be without capacity to reason) and to keep appetite in check insofar as it tends to another's hurt, to do to no one what they would not want done to themselves, and to uphold another's right as they would their own.

At this point we must consider how this covenant is to be made so as to ensure its stability and validity. Now it is a universal law of human nature that nobody rejects what he judges to be good except through hope of a greater good or fear of

---

[5] [*Ethics*, 4.18, Scholium 35, 37, Scholium 2.]

greater loss, and that no one endures any evil except to avoid a greater evil or to gain a greater good. That is to say, everyone will choose of two goods that which he judges the greater, and of two evils that which seems to him the lesser. I say expressly 'that which in his belief is the greater or lesser'; I do not say that the facts necessarily correspond with his judgment. This law is so deeply inscribed in human nature that it should be counted among the eternal truths universally known. Now from this law it necessarily follows that nobody is going to promise in all good faith* to give up his unrestricted right, and in general nobody is going to keep any promises whatsoever, except through fear of a greater evil or hope of a greater good. To make the point more clearly understood, suppose that a robber forces me to promise to give him my goods at his pleasure. Now since, as I have already shown, my natural right is determined by power alone, it is quite clear that if I can free myself from this robber by deceit, promising him whatever he wants, I have the natural right to do so, that is, to pretend to agree to whatever he wants. Or suppose that in all good faith I have promised somebody that I will not taste food or any other nourishment for twenty days, and that I later realised that I had made a foolish promise which could be kept only with considerable hurt to myself. Since by natural right I am bound to choose the lesser of two evils, I have the sovereign right to break faith and go back on my pledged word. Now this, I say, is justified by natural right, whether it was true and infallible reasoning or whether it was fallible belief that made me realise I was wrong to have made the promise. For whether my conviction is true or false, I shall be in fear of a terrible evil, one which therefore, by Nature's law, I shall do everything to avoid.

We may thus conclude that the validity of an agreement rests on its utility, without which the agreement automatically becomes null and void. It is therefore folly to demand from another that he should keep his word for ever, if at the same time one does not try to ensure that, if he breaks his word, he will meet with more harm than good. This point is particularly relevant in considering the constitution of a state. Now if all men could be readily induced to be guided by reason alone and to recognise the supreme advantage and the necessity of the state's existence, everyone would entirely forswear deceit. In their desire for this highest good, the preservation of the state, all men would in absolute good faith abide entirely by their agreement, and would regard it as the most important thing in the world to keep their word, this being the strongest shield of the state. But it is by no means the case that all men can always be readily induced to be guided by reason; for each is drawn by his own pleasure,[6] and the mind is frequently so beset by greed, ambition, envy, anger and the like that no room is left for reason. Therefore although men may make promises with every mark of sincerity, and pledge themselves to keep their word, nobody can rely on another's good faith unless the promise is backed by something else; for everyone has the natural right to act deceitfully and is not bound to keep his engagements except through hope of greater

---

* See Supplementary Note 32.

[6] [A quotation adapted from Vergil, *Eclogues*, II, 65, "*trahit sua quemque voluptas.*"—S.S.]

good or fear of greater evil. However, since we have already demonstrated that everyone's natural right is determined by his power alone, it follows that to the extent that each transfers his power to another, whether by force or voluntarily, to that extent he also necessarily surrenders his right to him, and the sovereign right over all men is held by him who holds the supreme power whereby he can compel all by force and coerce them by threat of the supreme penalty, universally feared by all. This right he will retain only as long as he has this power of carrying into execution whatever he wills; otherwise his rule will be precarious, and nobody who is stronger than he will need to obey him unless he so wishes.

Therefore, without any infringement of natural right, a community can be formed and a contract be always preserved in its entirety in absolute good faith on these terms, that everyone transfers all the power that he possesses to the community, which will therefore alone retain the sovereign natural right over everything, that is, the supreme rule which everyone will have to obey either of free choice or through fear of the ultimate penalty. Such a community's right is called a democracy, which can therefore be defined as a united body of men which corporately possesses sovereign right over everything within its power. Hence it follows that the sovereign power is bound by no law, and all must obey it in all matters; for this is what all must have covenanted tacitly or expressly when they transferred to it all their power of self-defence, that is, all their right. If they intended that there should be anything reserved to themselves, they should have taken the precaution at the same time to make secure provision to uphold it. Since they did not do so, and could not have done so without the division and consequent destruction of the state, they thereby submitted themselves absolutely to the will of the sovereign power. Since they did this without reservation and (as we have shown) by force of necessity and by the persuasion of reason itself, it follows that, unless we wish to be enemies of the state and to act against reason which urges us to uphold the state with all our might, it is our duty to carry out all the orders of the sovereign power without exception, even if those orders are quite irrational. For reason bids us carry out even such orders, so as to choose the lesser of two evils.

Furthermore, the danger involved in submitting oneself absolutely to the command and will of another was not such as to cause grave misgivings. As we have shown, sovereign powers possess the right of commanding whatever they will only for as long as they do in fact hold supreme power. If they lose this power, with it they also lose the right of complete command, which passes to one man or a number of men who have acquired it and are able to retain it. Therefore it is exceedingly rare for governments to issue quite unreasonable commands; in their own interest and to retain their rule, it especially behoves them to look to the public good and to conduct all affairs under the guidance of reason. For, as Seneca says, 'violenta imperia nemo continuit diu'—tyrannical governments never last long. There is the further fact that in a democracy there is less danger of a government behaving unreasonably, for it is practically impossible for the majority of a single assembly, if it is of some size, to agree on the same piece of folly. Then again, as we have also shown, it is the fundamental purpose of democracy to avoid the follies of appetite and to keep men within the bounds of reason, as far as possible, so that they may live in peace and harmony. If this basic principle is removed, the whole fabric soon collapses. It is for the sovereign power alone, then, to have regard to these considerations, while it is for the subjects, as I have said, to carry out its orders and to acknowledge no other right but that which the sovereign power declares to be a right.

Now perhaps it will be thought that in this way we are turning subjects into slaves, the slave being one who acts under orders and the free man one who does as he pleases. But this is not completely true, for the real slave is one who lives under pleasure's sway and can neither see nor do what is for his own good, and only he is free who lives whole-heartedly under the sole guidance of reason.[7] Action under orders—that is, obedience—is indeed to some extent an infringement of freedom, but it does not automatically make a man a slave; the reason for the action must enter into account. If the purpose of the action is not to the advantage of the doer but of him who commands, then the doer is a slave, and does not serve his own interest. But in a sovereign state where the welfare of the whole people, not the ruler, is the supreme law, he who obeys the sovereign power in all things should be called a subject, not a slave who does not serve his own interest. And so that commonwealth whose laws are based on sound reason is the most free, for there everybody can be free as he wills,* that is, he can live whole-heartedly under the guidance of reason. Similarly, although children are in duty bound to obey all the commands of their parents, they are not slaves; for the parents' commands have as their chief aim the good of the children. We therefore recognise a great difference between a slave, a son, and a subject, who accordingly may be defined as follows. A slave is one who has to obey his master's commands which look only to the interests of him who commands; a son is one who by his father's command does what is to his own good; a subject is one who, by command of the sovereign power, acts for the common good, and therefore for his own good also.

I think I have thus demonstrated quite clearly the basis of the democratic state, which I have elected to discuss before all others because it seemed the most natural form of state, approaching most closely to that freedom which nature grants to every man. For in a democratic state nobody transfers his natural right to another so completely that thereafter he is not to be consulted; he transfers it to the majority of the entire community of which he is part. In this way all men remain equal, as they were before in a state of nature. And there is this further reason why I have chosen to discuss at some length only this form of state: thereby my main purpose is best served, which is to discuss the benefits of freedom in a commonwealth. I therefore omit the discussion of the basic principles of other forms of government. To understand their right we do not now need to know how they have arisen, and frequently continue to arise, for this has been made abundantly clear from what

---

[7] [Parts 4 and 5 of the *Ethics* are concerned with the main topics of Spinoza's philosophy: human bondage and human freedom.]
* See Supplementary Note 33.

we have already proved. Whoever holds sovereign power, be it vested in one person or a few persons or in all the people, it is quite clear that to him belongs the sovereign right of commanding what he will. Furthermore, whoever transfers to another his power of self-defence, whether voluntarily or under compulsion, has fully ceded his natural right and has consequently resolved to obey the other absolutely in all matters; and this he is obliged to do without reservation, as long as the king, or the nobles, or the people retain the sovereign power they have received, which was the basis for the transference of right. I need say no more.

Now that we have demonstrated the basis and right of the state, we can easily determine what is a citizen's civil right, what is a wrong, and what is justice and injustice in a state; and then what is an ally, what is an enemy, and what is treason. By a citizen's civil right we can only mean the freedom of every man to preserve himself in his present condition, a freedom determined by the edicts of the sovereign power and upheld by its authority alone. For when the individual has transferred to another the right to live as he pleases, a right which is limited only by his power—in other words, when he has transferred to another his freedom and power of self-defence—he is then bound to live entirely as the other directs and to trust in him entirely for his defence.

A wrong occurs when a citizen or subject is forced to suffer some injury at the hands of another, contrary to his civil right, i.e. contrary to the edict of the sovereign power. For a wrong cannot be conceived except in a civil condition, nor yet can a wrong be done to subjects by sovereign powers, whose right is not limited. Therefore it can occur only as between private citizens, who are bound by law not to injure one another.

Justice is a set disposition to render to every man what is his by civil right. Injustice is to deprive a man, under the guise of legality, of what belongs to him by true interpretation of the law. These are also called equity and inequity, because those appointed to judge lawsuits are required to hold all men as equal without respect to persons, and to uphold equally everyone's right, neither envying the rich nor despising the poor.

Allies are the men of two states who, to avoid being exposed to the hazards of war or to gain some other advantage, pledge themselves to abstain from mutual aggression and to afford each other aid when occasion demands, each state still retaining its independence. This contract will remain in force for as long as its basis—namely, the consideration of danger or advantage—persists; for nobody makes a contract, or is bound to abide by an agreement, except through hope of some good or apprehension of some evil. If the basis is removed, the agreement becomes void of itself, a fact abundantly illustrated by experience. For although two different states may make a treaty of mutual non-aggression, they nevertheless try as far as they can to prevent the other from becoming too powerful, and they place their trust in words only if they are well assured of the purpose and interest of each party in making the treaty. Without this assurance they fear a breach of faith, and rightly so. For who but a fool who knows nothing of the right of sovereign powers will rest content with the words and promises of someone who maintains the sovereign power and right to do whatever he pleases, one for whom the welfare and advantage of his own state must be his supreme law? And even if piety and religion are taken into account, we shall still see that no one who holds the reins of government can, without doing wrong, abide by his promises to the harm of his country. For he cannot keep whatever promise he sees likely to be detrimental to his country without violating his pledge to his subjects, a pledge by which he is most firmly bound, and whose fulfilment usually involves the most solemn promises.

An enemy is one who lives outside the state on such terms that neither as an ally nor as a subject does he recognise its sovereignty. For it is not hatred but the state's right that makes a man an enemy; and the state's right against one who does not recognise its sovereignty by any kind of treaty is the same as its right against one who has done it an injury, for it can rightly compel him either to submit or to enter into alliance, by any means.

Treason applies only in the case of subjects or citizens who by agreement, whether implicit or explicit, have transferred all their right to the state. A subject is said to have committed this crime if he has attempted for any reason to seize for himself the sovereign power's right or to transfer it to another. I say 'if he has attempted,' for if men were to be condemned only after the deed was done, in most cases it would be too late for the state to try to do this after the seizure of its right or its transference to another. Again, I say without qualification 'he who for any reason attempts to seize for himself the sovereign power's right,' thus making no distinction between cases where either injury or gain to the entire state would have unquestionably resulted. Whatever be the reason for the attempt, he is guilty of treason and is rightly condemned. In war, indeed, there is complete agreement that this is fully justified. If a man leaves his post and approaches the enemy without his commander's knowledge, even though he has ventured on this action with good intention—but nevertheless his own—and has overcome the enemy, he is rightly condemned to death because he has violated his oath and the commander's right. Now it is not universally realised quite so clearly that all citizens without exception are always bound by this right, yet the point at issue is exactly the same. For since the state must be preserved and governed solely by the policy of the sovereign power and it is covenanted that this right belongs absolutely to it alone, if anyone embarks on some undertaking of public concern on his own initiative and without the knowledge of the supreme council, he has violated the right of the sovereign power and is guilty of treason and is rightly and properly condemned, even if, as we have said, the state was sure to gain some advantage from his action.

To remove the last shadow of doubt, it remains for us now to deal with the following objection. Is not our earlier assertion, that everyone who is without the use of reason has the sovereign natural right in a state of nature to live by the laws of appetite, in clear contradiction with the divine law as revealed? For since all men without exception, whether or not they have the use of reason, are equally required by God's command to love their neighbour as themselves, we cannot, without doing wrong, inflict injury on another and live solely by the laws of appetite.

However, we can easily answer this objection if we confine our attention to the state of nature only, for this is prior to religion in nature and in time. For nobody knows by nature* that he has any duty to obey God. Indeed, this knowledge cannot be attained by any process of reasoning; one can gain it only by revelation confirmed by signs. Therefore prior to revelation nobody can be bound by a divine law of which he cannot be aware. So a state of nature must not be confused with a state of religion; we must conceive it as being without religion and without law, and consequently without sin and without wrong, as we have in fact done, quoting Paul in confirmation. And it is not only in respect of men's ignorance that we conceive the state of nature as prior to, and lacking, the revelation of God's law, but also in respect of that freedom with which all men are born. For if men were by nature bound by the divine law, or if the divine law were a law by nature, there would have been no need for God to enter into a contract with men and to bind them by covenant and by oath. Therefore we must concede without qualification that the divine law began from the time when men by express covenant promised to obey God in all things, thereby surrendering, as it were, their natural freedom and transferring their right to God in the manner we described in speaking of the civil state. But I shall later treat of these matters at greater length.

But we still have to meet the objection that sovereign powers are no less bound by this divine law than are their subjects, whereas we have said that they retain their natural right and are not restricted in their right. In order to dispose completely of this difficulty, which originates from consideration of natural right rather than the state of nature, I assert that in a state of nature everyone is bound to live by the revealed law from the same motive as he is bound to live according to the dictates of sound reason, namely, that to do so is to his greater advantage and necessary for his salvation. He may refuse to do so, but at his own peril. He is thus bound to live according as he himself wills, and no other, and to acknowledge no man as judge or as rightful arbitrator over religion. This is the right, I say, that has been retained by the sovereign, who can indeed consult others but is not bound to acknowledge anyone as judge or any person but himself as claiming any right, except a prophet expressly sent by God and proving his mission by indisputable signs. Yet not even then is he forced to acknowledge a human judge, but only God himself. And if the sovereign power refuses to obey God as revealed in his Law, he may do so to his own peril and hurt without any violation of right, civil or natural. For civil right depends only on his decree, while natural right depends on the laws of Nature, which are adapted not to religion (whose sole aim is the good of man) but to the order of Nature as a whole, that is, to God's eternal decree, which is beyond our knowledge. This truth seems to have been glimpsed by those who maintain that man can sin against the revealed will of God, but not against the eternal decree by which he has pre-ordained all things.

We may now be asked, "What if the sovereign's command contravenes religion and the obedience we have promised to God by express covenant? Should we obey the divine command or human command?" As I shall later be dealing with this question in more detail, I shall here make only this brief reply: we must

---

* See Supplementary Note 34.

obey God before all things when we have a sure and indubitable revelation. But in matters of religion men are especially prone to go astray and contentiously advance many ideas of their own devising, as is abundantly testified by experience. It is therefore quite clear that, if nobody were bound by right to obey the sovereign power in those matters which he thinks to pertain to religion, the state's right would then inevitably depend on judgments and feelings that vary with each individual. For nobody would be bound by it if he considered it to be contrary to his own faith and superstitious belief, and so on this pretext everyone could assume unrestricted freedom to do as he pleases. Now since the right of the state is in this way utterly destroyed, it follows that it belongs completely to the sovereign power, on whom alone both divine and natural right impose the duty of preserving and safeguarding the laws of the state, to make what decisions it thinks fit concerning religion, and all are bound by their pledged word, which God bids them keep inviolate, to obey the sovereign power's decrees and commands in this matter.[8]

But if those at the head of government are heathens, we must either make no contract with them, resolving to suffer anything rather than to transfer our right to them; or, if we have made a contract transferring our right to them and thereby deprived ourselves of the right to defend ourselves and our religion, we are bound, or may be compelled, to obey them and keep our pledge. An exception is made in the case of one to whom God, by sure revelation, has promised his special help against the tyrant, or has given specific exemption. Thus we see that three young men alone out of all the Jews in Babylon refused to obey Nebuchadnezzar, being assured of God's help. All the rest—with the exception of Daniel also, whom the king had worshipped—no doubt obeyed, being compelled by right, perhaps with the thought that they were given into the king's hands by God's decree, and that it was by God's design that the king held and preserved his supreme dominion. On the other hand Eleazar[9] while his country still stood, resolved to give his people an example of steadfastness, so that by following him they would be encouraged to endure anything rather than allow their right and power to be transferred to the Greeks, and would go to any lengths to avoid having to swear allegiance to heathens.

What I have said is confirmed by common experience. In the interests of greater security the rulers of Christian countries do not hesitate to make treaties with Turks and heathens, and to order those of their subjects who go to dwell with them not to assume more freedom in secular and religious matters than is specified in the treaty or is granted by the government concerned. This is clear from the treaty made by the Dutch with the Japanese, of which I have already made mention.

---

[8] [Spinoza will qualify somewhat this thesis in Chapter 20.]

[9] [Spinoza is referring here to Eleazar, a brother of Judah Maccabee, whose family, the Hasmoneans, revolted against the Greek king of Syria and Mesopotamia, Antiochus ("Epiphanes") IV in 166 B.C. Although the Israelites were victorious, Eleazar was killed in battle. According to Josephus, he attacked an elephant on which he believed Antiochus was seated, and died when it fell upon him (Josephus, *The Wars*, 1.1.5; *Jewish Antiquities*, 12.6.1, 12.9.5).]

CHAPTER 17

It is demonstrated that nobody can, or need, transfer all his rights to the sovereign power. An account of the Hebrew state as it was in the time of Moses, and after his death before the institution of monarchy, and its success. Finally, the reasons why it came about that the theocratic state fell, and could scarcely have continued without civil strife

The picture presented in the last chapter of the overriding right of sovereign powers and the transference to them of the individual's natural right, though it comes quite close to actual practice and can increasingly be realised in reality, must nevertheless remain in many respects no more than theory. Nobody can so completely transfer to another all his right, and consequently his power, as to cease to be a human being, nor will there ever be a sovereign power that can do all it pleases. It would be vain to command a subject to hate one to whom he is indebted for some service, to love one who has done him harm, to refrain from taking offence at insults, from wanting to be free of fear, or from numerous similar things that necessarily follow from the laws of human nature. This is shown I think, quite clearly by actual experience; for men have never transferred their right and surrendered their power to another so completely that they were not feared by those very persons who received their right and power, and that the government has not been in greater danger from its citizens, though deprived of their right, than from its external enemies. If men could in fact be so completely deprived of their natural right as thereafter to be powerless* to do anything except by the will of those who hold the supreme right, then indeed the subjects of the most violent tyranny would be without resource, a condition which I imagine no one can possibly envisage. It must therefore be granted that the individual reserves to himself a considerable part of his right, which therefore depends on nobody's decision but his own.

However, for a proper understanding of the extent of the government's right and power, it should be observed that the government's power is not strictly confined to its power of coercion by fear, but rests on all the possible means by which it can induce men to obey its commands. It is not the motive for obedience, but the fact of obedience, that constitutes a subject. Whatever be the motives that prompt a man to carry out the commands of the sovereign power, whether it be fear of punishment, hope of reward, love of country or any other emotion, while it is he who makes the decision, he is nevertheless acting under the control of the

---

* See Supplementary Note 35.

sovereign power. From the fact, then, that a man acts from his own decision, we should not forthwith conclude that his action proceeds from his own right, and not from the right of the government. For whether a man is urged by love or driven by fear of a threatened evil, since in both cases his action always proceeds from his own intention and decision, either there can be no such thing as sovereignty and right over subjects or else it must include all the means that contribute to men's willingness to obey. Consequently, whenever a subject acts in accordance with the commands of the sovereign power, whether he is motivated by love, or fear, or (and this is more frequently the case) a mixture of hope and fear, or by reverence—which is an emotion compounded of fear and awe—or whatever be his motive, he acts from the ruler's right, not from his own.

This point is again clearly established from the fact that obedience is not so much a matter of outward act as internal act of mind. Therefore he who wholeheartedly resolves to obey another in all his commands is fully under another's dominion, and consequently he who reigns over his subjects' minds holds the most powerful dominion. If the strongest dominion were held by those who are most feared, then it would assuredly be held by tyrants' subjects, for they are most feared by their tyrants. Then again, although command cannot be exercised over minds in the same way as over tongues, yet minds are to some degree under the control of the sovereign power, who has many means of inducing the great majority to believe, love, hate etc. whatever he wills. Thus, although it is not by direct command of the sovereign power that these results are produced, yet experience abundantly testifies they often proceed from the authoritative nature of his power and from his guidance, that is, from his right. Therefore there is no absurdity in conceiving men whose beliefs, love, hatred, contempt and every single emotion is under the sole control of the governing power.

But although the right and power of government, when conceived in this way, are quite extensive, there can never be any government so mighty that those in command would have unlimited power to do anything they wish. This, I think, I have already clearly shown. As to the question of how, in spite of this, a state can be formed so as to achieve constant stability, I have already said that it is not my intention to discuss this. Still, in pursuing my theme, I shall draw attention to the means of achieving this end which Moses of old learned from divine revelation; then we shall consider the course taken by the history of the Jews, from which we shall eventually see what exactly are the most important concessions that sovereign powers should make to their subjects to ensure the greater security and prosperity of the state.

Reason and experience tell us quite clearly that the preservation of the state depends mainly on the subjects' loyalty and virtue and their steadfastness in carrying out orders, but the means whereby they should be induced to persevere in their loyalty and virtue are not so readily apparent. For all, both rulers and ruled, are but men, and as such prone to forsake duty for pleasure.[1] Indeed, those who

---

[1] [A quotation from Terence, *Andria*, 77–78, "*a labore proclives ad libidenem.*"—S.S.]

have experienced the fickleness of the masses are almost reduced to despair; for the masses are governed solely by their emotions, not by reason; they rush wildly into everything, and are readily corrupted either by avarice or by luxurious living. Every single man thinks he knows everything, and wants to fashion the world to his liking; he considers things to be fair or unfair, right or wrong, according as he judges them to be to his profit or loss. Vanity makes him despise his equals, nor will he be guided by them. Through envy of superior fame or fortune—which is never equal for all men—he desires another's misfortune and takes pleasure therein. There is no need for me to go through the whole catalogue, for everyone knows to what wickedness men are frequently persuaded by dissatisfaction with their lot and desire for change, by hasty anger, by disdain of poverty, and how their minds are engrossed and agitated by these emotions.

To guard against all these dangers, to organise a state in such a way as leaves no place for wrongdoing, or better still, to frame such a constitution that every man, whatever be his character, will set public right before private advantage, this is the task, this the toil.[2] The need to find a solution has driven men to devise many expedients, yet the position has never been attained where the state was not in greater danger from its citizens than from the external enemy, and where its rulers were not in greater fear of the former than the latter. Let Rome be witness, unconquerable by her enemies, yet so often conquered and wretchedly oppressed by her own citizens, and particularly in the civil war between Vespasian and Vitellius. (See Tacitus' *Histories*, at the beginning of Book 4, where he describes the sad plight of the city.) Alexander, as Curtius says towards the end of Book 8, thought it a less exacting task to maintain prestige abroad than at home, believing that his greatness might be destroyed by his own people. Fearing such a fate for himself, he besought his friends with these words: "Do you but keep me safe from internal treachery and domestic plots; I will fearlessly face the hazards of war and fighting. Philip was safer in battle than in the theatre. He often emerged unscathed from the enemy's violence: he could not escape from that of his own people. And if you reflect on the deaths of other kings, you will find more who died at the hands of their own people than at the hands of the enemy." See Q. Curtius, Book 9, chapter 6.

It was for this reason, then, to render themselves secure, that kings who in ancient times seized power, tried to persuade men that they were descended from the immortal gods, thinking that if only their subjects and all men should regard them not as their equals but should believe them to be gods, they would willingly suffer their rule and would readily submit. Thus Augustus persuaded the Romans that he traced his origin to Aeneas, who was thought to be the son of Venus and ranked among the gods. He wanted to be worshipped with temples and godlike statues, with attendant flamens and priests (Tac. *Ann.* 1). Alexander wished to be saluted as the son of Jupiter, a wish that seems to have been motivated by policy rather than pride, as shown by his reply when attacked by Hermolaus. "It was," he

---

[2] [Vergil, *Aeneid*, VI, 129, "*hoc opus, hic labor est.*" —S.S.]

said, "quite absurd for Hermolaus to demand of me that I should take no account of Jupiter, by whose oracle I am recognised. Am I responsible even for the answers of the gods? He offered me the name of son; to accept this" — note well! — "was by no means incongruous with the designs we are pursuing. Would that the Indians, too, might believe me to be a god! In war, prestige is an important factor, and a false belief has often done duty for truth" (Curtius, Book 8, chapter 8). In these few remarks he cleverly contrives to foist a deception on the ignorant, while at the same time hinting at the reason for the pretence. The same is true of Cleon's speech, attempting to persuade the Macedonians to bow to the king's demand. After giving pretence the gloss of truth by extolling Alexander's deeds and reviewing his achievements, he passes on to the question of expedience, as follows: "The Persians show wisdom as well as piety in worshipping their kings as gods, for majesty is the bulwark of the state's security." And he concludes by saying, "For my part, I will prostrate myself to the ground when the king enters the banquet. Others should do likewise, especially those endowed with wisdom" (Curtius, Book 8, chapter 5).

But the Macedonians were too sensible, and only utter barbarians allow themselves to be so blatantly deceived and to become slaves instead of subjects, with no interests of their own. Others, however, have succeeded more easily in convincing men that royalty is sacred and is God's regent on earth, that it is established by God, not by the votes and consent of men, and is preserved and sustained by God's special providence and help. Other ideas of this kind have been devised by monarchs for the security of their rule, but all these I pass over, and in order to reach my intended goal I shall confine myself, as I have said, to noting and examining only the things that Moses of old learned to this end by divine revelation.

We have already said in Chapter 5 that, after their departure from Egypt, the Hebrews were no longer bound by the laws of any other nation, but were free to establish new laws as they pleased, and to occupy whatever lands they wished. For after their liberation from the intolerable oppression of the Egyptians, being bound by no covenant to any mortal man they regained their natural right over everything that lay within their power, and every man could decide afresh whether to retain it or to surrender it and transfer it to another. Finding themselves thus placed in this state of nature, they hearkened to Moses, in whom they all placed the greatest confidence, and resolved to transfer their right not to any mortal man, but to God alone. Without much hesitation they all promised, equally and with one voice, to obey God absolutely in all his commands and to acknowledge no other law but that which he should proclaim as such by prophetic revelation. Now this promise, or transference of right to God, was made in the same way as we have previously conceived it to be made in the case of an ordinary community when men decide to surrender their natural right. For it was by express covenant and oath (Exod. ch. 24 v. 7) that they surrendered their natural right and transferred it to God, which they did freely, not by forcible coercion or fear of threats. Furthermore, to ensure that the covenant should be fixed and binding with no suspicion of deceit, God made no covenant with them until they had experienced his wonderful power which alone had saved them, and which alone might save them in time to come (Exod. ch. 19 v. 4, 5). For it was through this very belief, that God's power alone could save them, that they transferred to God all their natural power of self-preservation—which they probably thought they themselves had hitherto possessed—and consequently all their right.

It was God alone, then, who held sovereignty over the Hebrews, and so this state alone, by virtue of the covenant, was rightly called the kingdom of God, and God was also called the king of the Hebrews. Consequently, the enemies of this state were the enemies of God; citizens who aimed to seize the sovereignty were guilty of treason against God, and the laws of the state were the laws and commands of God. So in this state civil law and religion—which we have shown to consist only in obedience to God—were one and the same thing; the tenets of religion were not just teachings but laws and commands; piety was looked upon as justice, impiety as crime and injustice. He who forsook his religion ceased to be a citizen and by that alone became an enemy, and he who died for his religion was regarded as having died for his country. In short, there was considered to be no difference whatsoever between civil law and religion. Hence this form of government could be called a theocracy, its citizens being bound only by such law as was revealed by God. However, all this was a matter of theory rather than fact, for in reality the Hebrews retained their sovereign right completely, as will become clear when I describe the manner and method of the government of this state, which I now intend to set forth.

Since the Hebrews did not transfer their right to any other man, but, as in a democracy, they all surrendered their right on equal terms, crying with one voice, "Whatever God shall speak, we shall do" (no one being named as mediator), it follows that this covenant left them all completely equal, and they all had an equal right to consult God, to receive and interpret his laws; in short, they all shared equally in the government of the state. It was for this reason, then, that on the first occasion they all approached God on equal terms to hear what he wished to command. But on this first appearance before God they were so terrified and so thunderstruck at hearing God speak that they thought their last hour had come. So, overwhelmed with fear they went to Moses again, saying, "Behold, we have heard God speaking in the midst of the fire; now therefore why should we die? For this great fire will surely consume us; if again we are to hear the voice of God, we shall surely die. Go thou near therefore, and hear all that our God shall say. And speak thou (not God) to us. All that God shall speak unto thee, we shall hear and do (Exod. ch. 20 v. 18)."

By this they clearly abrogated the first covenant, making an absolute transfer to Moses of their right to consult God and to interpret his decrees. For at this point what they promised was not, as before, to obey all that God should speak to them, but what God should speak to Moses. (See Deut. ch. 5 after the Decalogue, and ch. 18 v. 15, 16.) Therefore Moses was left as the sole lawgiver and interpreter of God's laws, and thus also the supreme judge, whom no one could judge, and who alone acted on God's behalf among the Hebrews, that is, held the supreme kingship, since he alone had the right to consult God, to give God's answers to the people, and to compel them to obey. He alone, I say, for if anyone during Moses' lifetime sought to make any proclamation in God's name, even if he were a true prophet he was nevertheless guilty of claiming the supreme sovereignty (Num. ch. 11 v. 28).*

Here we should observe that although the people chose Moses, they had no right to choose his successor. For as soon as they transferred to Moses their right to consult God and promised without reservation to regard him as the divine oracle, they completely lost all their right and were bound to accept as chosen by God whichever successor Moses should choose. Now if Moses had chosen a successor to have, like himself, complete control over the state, that is, the right to consult God alone in his tent, and consequently the authority to make and repeal laws, to make decisions on war and peace, to send envoys, to appoint judges, to choose a successor, in short, to exercise all the functions of a sovereign, the state would have become simply a monarchy. There would have been no difference but this, that ordinarily a monarchy is ruled in accordance with a decree of God which is hidden even from the monarch, whereas the Hebrew state would be, or should have been, ruled in a definite way by God's decree revealed to the monarch alone. This difference does not diminish the monarch's dominion and right over all his subjects; on the contrary, it increases it. As for the people, in both cases they are equally subject and equally ignorant of God's decree, for in both cases they are dependent on what the monarch says, understanding from him alone what is right and what is wrong. And by believing that the monarch issues commands only in accordance with God's decree as revealed to him, the people would in fact be more, not less, under the monarch's dominion. However, Moses appointed no such successor, but left the state to be so governed by those who came after him that it could be called neither a democracy nor an aristocracy nor a monarchy, but a theocracy. While the right to interpret the laws and to promulgate God's answers was vested in one man, the right and power to govern the state in accordance with laws thus expounded and answers thus made known was vested in another. See Num. ch. 27 v. 21.** For a clearer understanding of this situation, I shall explain in an orderly way how the whole state was governed.

First, the people were commanded to build a dwelling to serve as the palace of God, the state's supreme sovereign. This palace was to be built at the expense not of one man but of the entire people, so that the dwelling where God was to be consulted should belong to the nation as a whole. The Levites were chosen to be the courtiers and administrators of this palace of God, while Aaron, the brother of Moses, was chosen to be at their head, in second place, as it were, to God their king, to be succeeded by his sons by hereditary right. Therefore Aaron, as next to God, was the supreme interpreter of God's laws, giving the people the answers of the divine oracle and entreating God on the people's behalf. Now if, along with these functions, he had held the right of issuing commands, his position would

---

* See Supplementary Note 36.
** See Supplementary Note 37.

have been that of an absolute monarch. But this right was denied him, and in general the whole tribe of Levi was so completely divested of civil rights that they did not have even a legal share of territory, like the other tribes, to provide them at least with a livelihood. Moses ordained that they should be maintained by the rest of the people, yet always be held in the highest honour by the common people as the only tribe dedicated to God.

Next, a military force was formed from the remaining twelve tribes, and they were ordered to invade the land of Canaan and to divide it into twelve parts which would be allocated to the tribes by lot. For this task twelve captains were chosen, one from each tribe, who, together with Joshua and the high priest Eleazar, were given the right to divide the territory into twelve equal parts to be allocated by lot. Joshua was chosen as commander-in-chief of the armed forces, and he alone had the right in emergencies to consult God, not, however, like Moses, alone in his tent or in the tabernacle, but through the mediation of the high priest, to whom alone God's answers were given. Furthermore, Joshua alone had the authority to promulgate God's commands as told him by the high priest and to compel the people's obedience, to devise and apply the means of executing these commands, to choose from the armed forces whom he wished and as many as he wished, to send envoys in his own name; in short, the complete control of war was in his hands alone. There was no successor to his position by hereditary right; only at a time of national emergency was one chosen, and then only by God's direct intervention. At all other times all matters concerning war and peace were in the hands of the captains of the tribes, as I shall presently show. Finally, all men between the ages of twenty and sixty were ordered to bear arms and to form armies recruited only from the people, which swore allegiance not to the commander-in-chief nor to the high priest, but to their religion and to God. They were thus called the armies and hosts of God, and correspondingly God was called by the Hebrews the Lord of Hosts. It was for this reason that in great battles on whose issue depended victory or defeat for the whole people the ark of the covenant was borne in the midst of the army, so that on seeing their king in their midst, as it were, the people would fight with all their might.[3]

From these commands left by Moses to his successors we can plainly see that it was ministers, not masters of the state, that Moses appointed. To no one did he give the right to consult God in solitude and wherever he wished, and therefore to no one did he give the authority, which he himself possessed, to make and repeal laws, to decide on war and peace, and to choose men for religious and secular office, all these being the prerogative of a sovereign. The high priest did indeed have the right to interpret the laws and to deliver God's answers, but only when requested by the commander-in-chief or the supreme council or similar authorities, and not whenever he wished, like Moses. On the other hand the commander-in-chief and the councils could consult God whenever they wished but

---

[3] [Like Machiavelli, for whom Spinoza had considerable respect, Spinoza advocates a citizen military, not mercenaries. This was one of the good features of the ancient Israelite state (Machiavelli, *The Prince*, chapters 12–14; Spinoza, *Political Treatise*, 5.7).]

could receive God's answers only from the high priest. Therefore God's words as given by the priest were not decrees, as when given by Moses, but only answers; only when accepted by Joshua and the councils did they have the force of commands and decrees. Moreover, the high priest who received God's answers from God possessed no armed force and held no rightful command, while those who had the right to the possession of land did not have the right to make laws.

Then again, the high priest, in the case both of Aaron and his son Eleazar, was indeed chosen by Moses; but after the death of Moses nobody had the right to choose the high priest; son succeeded father by hereditary right. The commander-in-chief was also appointed by Moses, and assumed his office not by virtue of the high priest's right, but by the right of Moses granted to him. So on the death of Joshua the high priest did not choose anyone in his place, nor did the captains consult God on the question of a new commander. Each captain retained Joshua's command over the military force of his own tribe, and they all collectively took over Joshua's command over the entire military force. There seems to have been no need for a commander-in-chief except when they had to join forces against a common enemy, a circumstance which occurred mainly in Joshua's time when not all the tribes had as yet a fixed territory and everything was held in common. But when all the tribes had divided among themselves those territories which they held by right of conquest and those which it was their mission yet to conquer, and all things were no longer held in common, thereby there ceased to be any reason for a common commander; for as a result of the allocation the different tribes must have been regarded as confederated states rather than as fellow citizens. With respect to God and religion they must indeed have been regarded as fellow citizens, but in respect of the right of one tribe as against another they were only members of a confederation, in much the same position (disregarding the common temple) as the High Confederated Estates of the Netherlands. For the division into shares of property held in common simply implies that each member now owns his share alone, the others having surrendered their right to that particular share. This, then, was Moses' purpose in appointing captains of the tribes, that after the division of the state each captain should assume control over his own part, including the right to consult God through the high priest about the affairs of his own tribe, to command his own military forces, to found and fortify cities, to appoint judges in each city, to attack the enemies of his own particular state, in short, to carry out all the duties of war and peace. He was not required to recognise any other judge than God* or a prophet expressly sent by God. If he rebelled against God, it was the duty of the other tribes to attack him as an enemy who had violated the terms of his agreement, not to pass judgment on him as a subject.

That this was the situation is exemplified in Scripture. After Joshua's death it was the children of Israel who consulted God, not a new commander-in-chief. Now when it was learnt that it fell to the tribe of Judah to be the first to attack its

---

* See Supplementary Note 38.

enemy, this tribe alone made an agreement with the tribe of Simeon to join forces in attacking their common enemies. The other tribes were not included in this agreement (Judges ch. 1 v. 1, 2, 3); each tribe waged war separately (as we are told in the same chapter) against its own enemy, imposing terms of submission and alliance on whom it would, although they had been commanded to spare no one on any terms and to destroy them utterly. For this sin they were no doubt reproved, but nobody was in a position to call them to account. It was not for such reasons that the tribes began to take up arms against one another and to interfere in another's affairs. But the tribe of Benjamin, which had wronged other tribes and had so violated the bond of peace that none of the confederates could lodge safely among them, was attacked as an enemy, and after three battles the victors slaughtered them all indiscriminately, guilty and innocent alike, by right of war, a deed which they later bewailed with a repentance that came too late.

These examples plainly confirm what we have just said regarding the right of each tribe. But perhaps the question will be raised—who appointed the successor to the captains of each tribe? Now on this point I cannot find anything definite in Scripture itself, but I conjecture that, since each tribe was divided into families whose heads were chosen from their more senior members, the senior of these succeeded by right to the office of captain. For it was from the seniors that Moses chose his seventy colleagues to sit with him on the supreme council. Those who had charge of the government after Joshua's death are called 'elders' in Scripture; and, finally, the use of the word 'elders' to mean judges was a common practice among the Hebrews, as I think everyone knows. But for our purpose it matters little if this point remains undecided; it is enough to have shown that after Moses' death no one exercised all the functions of a sovereign. The management of affairs was not entirely in the hands of one man, or one council, or the people; some affairs were managed by one tribe and others by the rest, with equal right in each case. Thus it clearly follows that after Moses' death the state was left neither as a monarchy nor an aristocracy nor a democracy, but, as we have said, a theocracy, and for the following reasons. First, the royal seat of government was the temple, and it was only in respect of the temple that all the tribes were fellow citizens, as we have shown. Secondly, all their citizens had to swear allegiance to God, their supreme judge, to whom alone they had promised absolute obedience in all things. Finally, when a commander-in-chief was needed, he was chosen only by God. This is what Moses explicitly foretold to the people in God's name in Deut. ch. 18 v. 15, and was confirmed in actual fact by the choosing of Gideon, Samson and Samuel. Hence we cannot have any doubt that the other faithful leaders were also chosen in like manner, even though this is not expressly stated in the narrative.

Our survey being now complete, it is time for us to see how far a constitution framed on these lines was able to exercise control over men's minds and to so restrain both rulers and ruled that neither would the latter rebel nor the former become tyrants.

Those who govern the state or hold the reins of power always strive to cloak with a show of legality whatever wrong they commit, persuading the people that this action was right and proper; and this they can easily achieve when the interpretation of the law is entirely in their hands. For this in itself undoubtedly affords them the greatest latitude in doing whatever they want and whatever their appetite suggests, whereas they are largely deprived of this freedom if the right to interpret the laws is vested in somebody else, and likewise if the true interpretation of the laws is so obvious that it is not open to doubt. This makes it clear that the captains of the Hebrews found their scope for transgression severely curtailed by the fact that the entire right to interpret the laws was assigned to the Levites (Deut. ch. 21 v. 5) who had no share either in the administration of the state or in its territory, and who saw their entire welfare and prestige dependent on a true interpretation of the law. Furthermore, the entire populace was required to assemble at an appointed place every seventh year to learn the laws from the priest, and in addition everyone was expected to read and re-read the book of the Law on his own, constantly and with the utmost concentration. See Deut. ch. 31 v. 9 etc. and ch. 6 v. 7. Thus, if only in their own interests, the captains had to take great care to govern entirely in accordance with laws laid down and familiar to all, if they wished to enjoy the highest esteem of a people who would then revere them as ministers of God's kingdom and as God's vice-regents. If they acted otherwise they must have inevitably encountered the bitterest hatred—such as religious hatred is wont to be—on the part of their subjects.

Among other considerations that restrained the unbridled licence of the captains was one of considerable importance, in that the armed forces were recruited from the whole citizen body with no exceptions between the ages of twenty and sixty, and that the captains were not allowed to hire foreign mercenaries. This, I repeat, was of considerable importance, for it is a fact that rulers can subjugate a people simply by means of hired mercenaries, while there is nothing they fear more than the independence of a citizen soldiery who have won freedom and glory for their country by their valour, their toil, and the heavy price of blood. It was for this reason that when Alexander was about to fight his second battle against Darius, he refrained from rebuking Parmenio on hearing his advice, but instead rebuked Polypercon, who was merely supporting Parmenio. For, as Curtius says in Book 4, chapter 13, having recently rebuked Parmenio more severely than he might have wished, he did not venture to castigate him again. Nor was he able to suppress the Macedonians' freedom—of which, as I have already said, he was in great fear—until he had increased the number of troops recruited from prisoners of war far above the level of the Macedonians. Only then could he give rein to the vicious propensities that had long been held in check by the independence of his best countrymen. Now if this independence of a citizen soldiery can restrain the rulers of a secular state who usually claim for themselves all the credit for victories, it must have exercised far greater restraint on the Hebrew captains whose soldiers fought not for their captain's glory, but for the glory of God, and who did not join battle until they had received God's assent.

Another check on the Hebrew captains was the fact that religion was the only tie that bound them all together. Therefore if one of them transgressed against religion and began to violate individual rights given by God, the others could treat him as an enemy and lawfully subdue him.

A third check was afforded by the fear of the appearance of a new prophet. If a man of proven virtue could show by certain acknowledged signs that he was a prophet, he thereby, like Moses, assumed the supreme right to command in the name of God to him alone revealed, not consulted only through the mediation of a priest, as was the case with the captains. And there is no doubt that if the people were oppressed, such prophets could easily gain support, and by signs of no great significance they could convince the people of whatever they wished. On the other hand, if the government were properly conducted, the captain could ensure in good time that the prophet should first stand before him to be examined as to whether he was of proven virtue, whether he possessed sure and indubitable signs of his mission, and whether his message in God's name was consistent with the accepted teachings and common laws of his country. If his signs were less than satisfactory, or his teaching innovatory, he could rightly be condemned to death. In the other event, he was accepted only on the captain's authority and testimony.

Fourthly, there was the fact that the captain had no superiority over others by nobility of descent or right of birth; the government of the state was in his hands only by reason of his age and qualities.

Finally, the captains and the entire armed force did not have any reason to prefer war to peace. The army, as we have said, was entirely a citizen force, and therefore matters of both war and peace were in the same hands. Thus the soldier in the camp was a citizen in the forum, the officer in the camp was a judge in the law-court, and the commander-in-chief in the camp was a ruler in civil life. Therefore nobody could want war for war's sake, but only for the sake of peace and the defence of freedom; and possibly the captain refrained from new ventures as far as he could so as to avoid having to approach the high priest and stand before him to the detriment of his dignity. So much, then, for the reasons that kept the captains within due bounds.

We must now consider what were the restraints on the people, though these are also plainly indicated by the basic principles of the state. Even a cursory examination will at once reveal that these must have kindled such an ardent patriotism in the hearts of the citizens that it could never enter anyone's mind to betray or desert his country; on the contrary, they must all have been of such a mind as to suffer death rather than a foreign yoke. For having transferred their right to God, believing that their kingdom was God's kingdom and that they alone were God's children, while the other nations were God's enemies for whom they therefore felt an implacable hatred (for this, too, they believed to be a mark of piety; see Psalm 139 v. 21, 22), they could think of nothing more abhorrent than to swear allegiance and promise obedience to a foreigner, and they could conceive of nothing more wicked and abominable than to betray their country, that is, the very kingdom of the God whom they worshipped. Indeed, it was regarded as utterly disgraceful even to emigrate, for the religious rites which it was their constant duty to practise could be performed only on their native soil; it alone was held to be holy ground, the rest of the world being unclean and profane. It was for this reason that David, when driven into exile, complained to Saul in these words: "If those who stir thee up against me be men, they are accursed, for they shut me out from walking in the inheritance of the Lord, saying, 'Go and worship other gods.'" For the same reason—and this is here specially noteworthy—no citizen was condemned to exile; for the wrongdoer does indeed deserve to be punished, but not to be outraged.

Therefore the patriotism of the Hebrews was not simply patriotism but piety, and this, together with hatred for other nations, was so fostered and nourished by their daily ritual that it inevitably became part of their nature. For their daily worship was not merely quite different, making them altogether unique and completely distinct from other peoples, but also utterly opposed to others. Hence this daily invective, as it were, was bound to engender a lasting hatred of a most deep-rooted kind, since it was a hatred that had its source in strong devotion or piety and was believed to be a religious duty—for that is the bitterest and most persistent of all kinds of hatred. And this was reinforced by the universal cause of the continuous growth of hatred, to wit, the reciprocation of hatred; for the other nations inevitably held them in bitter hatred in return.

How all these factors—their freedom from human rule, their devotion to their country, their absolute right against all others and a hatred that was not only permissible but a religious duty, the hostility of all around them, their distinctive customs and rites—how all these factors, I say, combined to fortify the hearts of the Hebrews to endure all things for their country with unexampled steadfastness and valour, is confirmed by reason and attested by experience. Never while their city stood could they long endure foreign dominion, and that was why Jerusalem was wont to be called the rebellious city (Ezra ch. 4 v. 12, 15). It was with the greatest difficulty that the Romans succeeded in destroying their second state (a mere shadow of the first, the priests having usurped the right to govern), as Tacitus bears witness in these words in *Histories*, Book 2: "Vespasian had brought to an end the Jewish War except for the siege of Jerusalem, a task rendered more severe and difficult by the character of the people and the obstinacy of their superstitious beliefs rather than by the sufficiency of their resources to endure the hardships of a siege."

But beside these factors, whose influence is a matter of subjective assessment, there was another feature of this state, peculiar to it and of indisputable weight, which must have been most effective in deterring citizens from contemplating defection and from ever wanting to desert their country, to wit, the motive of self-interest, the strength and life of all human action. This, I say, was a feature peculiar to this state. Nowhere else did citizens have stronger right to their possessions than did the subjects of this state, who had an equal share with the captain in lands and fields, and were each the owners of their share in perpetuity. For if any man was compelled by poverty to sell his farm or field, it had to be restored to him when the jubilee came round, and there were other similar enactments to prevent the alienation of real estate. Then again, nowhere could poverty have been lighter to endure than there, where charity to one's neighbour, that is, to one's fellow citizen, was a duty to be practised with the utmost piety so as to gain the favour of God, their king. Thus the Hebrew citizens could enjoy a good life only in their own country; abroad they could expect only hurt and humiliation.

Moreover, the following considerations were particularly effective not only in keeping them in their native land but also in avoiding civil war and in removing the causes of strife, namely, that no man served his equal, but only God, that charity and love towards one's fellow citizen was regarded as a supreme religious duty and was fostered to no small degree by the common hatred they had for other nations, and other nations for them. A further important factor was their training in strict obedience, imposing the duty of following a definite prescribed law in all that they did. A man might not plough when he pleased, but only at fixed times and seasons, and then with only one kind of animal at a time; likewise, he might sow and reap only in a certain way and at a certain time. To sum up, their life was one long schooling in obedience (see Chapter 5 regarding ceremonial practices). Therefore to men so habituated to it obedience must have appeared no longer as bondage, but freedom. From this it must also have followed that nobody desired what was forbidden and all desired what was commanded, an attitude considerably encouraged by the requirement to give themselves up to rest and rejoicing at certain seasons of the year, not for self-indulgence, but to serve God with a cheerful heart. Three times a year they feasted before the Lord (Deut. ch. 16). On the seventh day of every week they had to cease from all work and give themselves over to rest; and in addition to these, other times were appointed when innocent rejoicing and feasting were not merely permitted but enjoined. In my opinion no more effective means can be devised to influence men's minds, for nothing can so captivate the mind as joy springing from devotion, that is, love mingled with awe. Nor was there much likelihood that repetition would bring about boredom; the ceremonial appointed for feast days recurred only at lengthy intervals and was varied in character. Furthermore, there was their deep reverence for their temple because of its special rites and the ceremonies required before one was allowed to enter, a reverence which they most religiously preserved at all times, so that even today Jews cannot read without the deepest horror of Manasseh's crime in daring to introduce an idol into the very temple. No less was the people's reverence for the Law, which was most zealously guarded in the inmost shrine. Hence in this state there was little danger of murmurings and unorthodoxy on the part of the people. No one ventured to pass judgment in matters of religion; they had to obey all that was commanded them on the authority of God's answer received in the temple, or of the Law established by God, without any resort to reason.

I have thus, I think, set forth quite clearly, though briefly, the main features of the Hebrew state. It now remains for me to enquire into the reasons why the Hebrews so frequently forsook the Law, and why they were so many times conquered, and why it came about in the end that their state was utterly destroyed. Perhaps at this point it will be suggested that this resulted from the stubbornness of the race. However, this is a foolish suggestion, for why was this nation more stubborn than others? Was it by nature? But surely nature creates individuals, not nations, and it is only difference of language, of laws, and of established customs that divides individuals into nations. And only the last two, laws and customs, can be the source of the particular character, the particular mode of life, the particular set of attitudes that signalise each nation. So if it had to be allowed that the Hebrews were stubborn beyond other mortals, this would have to be attributed to the defectiveness of their laws or of their established customs. It is, of course, true that if God had willed their state to be of longer duration, he would also have given them laws and ordinances of a different kind and would have established a different mode of government. So we can only say that their God was angry with them, not only, as Jeremiah says in chapter 32 verse 21, from the foundation of their city, but right from the time when their laws were ordained. Ezekiel, too, makes the same point in chapter 20 verse 25, where he says: "I gave them also statutes that were not good and judgments whereby they should not live, in that I polluted them in their gifts by rejecting all that opened the womb (that is, the firstborn) so that I might make them desolate, to the end that they might know that I am the Lord."

In order that we may rightly understand these words and the cause of the destruction of the state, we should observe that it had first been intended to entrust the entire ministry of religion to the firstborn, not to the Levites (Num. ch. 8 v. 17); but when all except the Levites had worshipped the calf, the firstborn were rejected as defiled and the Levites were chosen in their place (Deut. ch. 10 v. 8). The more I consider the change, the more I am forced to exclaim in the words of Tacitus, "At that time, God's concern was not for their security, but for vengeance."[4] I cannot sufficiently marvel that such was the wrath of heaven[5] that God framed their very laws, whose sole end should always be the honour, welfare and security of the people, with the intention of avenging himself and punishing the people, with the result that their laws appeared to them to be not so much laws—that is, the safeguard of the people—as penalties and punishments. All the gifts that they were required to make to the Levites and priests, as likewise the compulsory redemption of their firstborn by a payment to the Levites for each one, and the fact that the Levites alone were privileged to perform the sacred rites—all this was a constant reminder of their defilement and rejection. Then again, the Levites were continually finding occasion to rebuke them, for among so many thousands of people one may well imagine there were many would-be theologians making themselves a nuisance. As a result, the people were keen to keep watch over the Levites—who were no doubt just human—and, as often happens, to accuse them all for the misdeeds of one. Hence there were continual murmurings, culminating in a sense of resentment at having to maintain in idleness men who were unpopular and unrelated to them by blood, especially when food was dear. Little wonder, then, that in times of peace when there were no more striking miracles and no men of unquestionable authority appeared on the scene, the people's morale began to fail through discontent and greed, and eventually they looked for change, forsaking a worship which, although worship of God, nevertheless involved their humiliation and was also the object of suspicion. Little wonder that their rulers—and rulers are always seeking ways to keep for themselves supreme

---

[4] [Tacitus, *Histories*, I, 3. An adaptation of *"non esse curae deis securitatem nostram, esse ultionem."* —S.S.]

[5] [An adaptation of Vergil, *Aeneid*, I, 11, *"tantaene animis caelestibus irae?"* —S.S.]

sovereignty over the state—made every concession to the people and introduced new forms of worship, with the view to securing the people's favour and alienating them from the high priest.

Now if the constitution of the state had been as first intended, all the tribes would have enjoyed equal right and honour, and the whole structure of the state would have been quite sound. For who would have wished to violate the sacred right of their own kinsfolk? What more could they have wanted than to maintain their own kinsfolk, their brothers and fathers, as a religious duty, to be taught by them the interpretation of the laws, and to await God's answers from them. Moreover, if all the tribes had preserved equal right to the sacred offices, they would thus have remained far more closely united. Even so, there would still have been no dangerous consequences if the election of the Levites had been inspired by anything other than anger and revenge. However, as I have said, their God was angry with them, and, to repeat the words of Ezekiel, he polluted them in their gifts by rejecting all that opened the womb, so as to make them desolate.

The historical narratives themselves provide further confirmation of this view. As soon as the people found themselves with abundant leisure in the wilderness, many of them, of no mean standing, began to resent this election, and found in this a reason for believing that Moses was acting not by divine decree, but at his own pleasure, in that he had chosen his own tribe before all others and had bestowed on his own brother the office of high priest in perpetuity. They therefore went to him, raising a tumult and crying that all were equally holy and that it was wrong for him to be exalted above all others.[6] In no way could Moses pacify them, but a miracle intervened as a sign of his faithfulness, and they were all wiped out. Then came a new and widespread revolt of the entire people, who believed that the men had perished not by God's judgment but by the devising of Moses. When a great disaster or plague had at last reduced them to exhaustion, he succeeded in pacifying them, but their condition was such that they all preferred death to life. It would therefore be truer to say of that time that there was a cessation of rebellion rather than a restoration of harmony. This is confirmed by the words of Scripture in Deuteronomy chapter 31 verse 21, where, after foretelling that the people would fall away from the practice of their religion after his death, God says to Moses, "For I know their desire, and what they are about this day, even before I have brought them to the land which I swore." And a little later Moses speaks thus to the people, "For I know thy rebellion and thy stiff neck. If while I have lived among you ye have been rebellious against the Lord, how much more after my death."

And this is what in fact occurred, as we know. There ensued great changes, unbounded licence, self-indulgence and sloth, leading to a general decline until, after being frequently subjugated, they came to open rupture with divine rule and sought a mortal king, making the seat of government a court rather than a temple, with all the tribes no longer retaining a common citizenship on the basis of the divine rule and the priesthood, but by allegiance to a king. But here was ample material for fresh sedition, which led ultimately to the downfall of the entire

---

[6] [Here Spinoza is alluding to the rebellion of Korah, related in Numbers 16.]

state. For what can be more intolerable to kings than to rule by sufferance, and to allow a dominion within their dominion? The first kings to be chosen from private station were content with the rank to which they had been elevated, but when their sons succeeded by hereditary right they gradually began to bring about extensive changes so as to hold the absolute sovereignty in their own hands alone. This they lacked to a considerable extent as long as control over the laws was exercised not by them but by the high priest, who guarded the laws in the sanctuary and interpreted them to the people. Thus the kings were bound by the laws no less than their subjects, and had no right to repeal them or to enact new laws of equal authority. A further contributory factor was that the right of the Levites debarred kings just as much as their subjects from administering the sacred rites: they were equally unholy. Lastly, there was the fact that the security of their rule depended solely on the will of one man, who was seen as a prophet. Of this last they had seen examples, such as the emphatic independence shown by Samuel in giving orders to Saul, and the facility with which he was able to transfer the sovereignty to David because of a single fault. Therefore they saw an empire within their empire, and they ruled on sufferance.

To overcome these restrictions they permitted other temples to be dedicated to the gods to avoid further occasion to consult the Levites, and then they sought out other men to prophesy in God's name, so as to have prophets to counter the true prophets. But their various attempts never succeeded in achieving their aims. For the prophets, always resourceful, awaited their opportunity in the rule of a successor, which is always precarious as long as the memory of his predecessor remains fresh. Then, by their divine authority, they could readily induce someone hostile to the king and of high repute to champion the divine right and claim the sovereignty, or some portion of it, by right. Yet the prophets in their turn met with no great success by these methods; for even though they removed a tyrant, the causes of tyranny remained. Thus they merely succeeded in installing a new tyrant at the cost of much citizen blood. There was no end, then, to discord and civil wars, but the causes which led to the violation of the divine law were always the same, and could be removed only along with the whole constitution.

We have now seen in what manner religion was introduced into the Hebrew commonwealth, and how the state might have lasted indefinitely if the just anger of the lawgiver had allowed it to continue in its original form. But since this was impossible, it was bound eventually to come to an end. I have here been discussing only the first state; the second[7] was a mere shadow of the first, in that people were bound by the right of the Persians to whom they were subject, and after the restoration of independence the priests usurped the right of government, thereby holding absolute power. Hence the priests became inflamed with the desire to combine secular and religious rule. For this reason I have thought it un-

---

[7] [The destruction of the Temple in 586 B.C. by the Babylonians is commonly taken to be the end of the First Commonwealth; the Second Commonwealth is usually understood to have commenced with the restoration of the High Priesthood in Jerusalem in 538 B.C. under the sponsorship of the Persian King Cyrus.]

necessary to say more about the second state. As to whether the first state, regarding only its lasting qualities, is a model to be imitated, or whether it is a pious duty to imitate it as far as possible, this will become clear in the following chapters. Here, in conclusion, I would like merely to emphasise a point already indicated. From the findings of this present chapter it clearly emerges that the divine right, or the right of religion, originates in a contract, without which there is no right but natural right, and so the Hebrews were not required as a religious duty to practise piety towards peoples who were not party to the contract, but only towards their fellow citizens.

CHAPTER 18

From the commonwealth of the Hebrews and their history some political principles are deduced

Although the Hebrew state, as in the previous chapter we have conceived it to be, might have lasted indefinitely, it is not possible to imitate it now, nor would it be advisable. If any people should resolve to transfer their right to God, they would have to make a covenant expressly with God, as did the Hebrews, and so it would be necessary to have not only the consent of those transferring their right but also the consent of God to whom the right was to be transferred. God, however, has revealed through his Apostles that his covenant is no longer written in ink or engraved on tablets of stone, but is inscribed by God's spirit in men's hearts. Then again, this form of state might possibly meet the needs of those who intend to live for themselves alone with no external ties, shutting themselves away within their own boundaries and cutting themselves off from the rest of the world; but it would not suit those who have to have dealings with the outside world. It follows that this form of state would be practicable for only a very few. However, although it cannot be imitated in all respects, it possessed many features which are at least worthy of note, and which it may perhaps be quite profitable to imitate. But since, as I have mentioned, it is not my purpose to compose a full-length treatise on the state, I shall omit most of these features and shall draw attention only to those that are relevant to my goal.

First, it is not inconsistent with God's kingship to elect a supreme ruler who would have complete command over the state. For after the Hebrews had transferred their right to God, they gave the supreme sovereignty to Moses, who thus had sole authority to enact and repeal laws in God's name, to choose ministers of the sacred rites, to judge, to instruct, to punish — in short, to be an absolute ruler in all matters. Secondly, although the ministers of the sacred rites were the interpreters of the laws, it was not for them to judge citizens or to excommunicate anyone: this right belonged only to judges and captains chosen from the people. (See Joshua chapter 6 verse 26; Judges chapter 21 verse 18; and 1 Samuel chapter 14 verse 24.) And if, furthermore, we turn our attention to the course of events in the history of the Hebrews, we shall find other points equally worthy of note.

1. There were no religious divisions among the people until the high priests in the second state acquired the authority to issue decrees and to transact government business—an authority which they sought to render permanent by usurping the government and finally demanding the title of kings. The reason for these sectarian divisions is readily seen. In the first state no decrees could bear the name of a high priest: they had no right to issue decrees, only the right to give God's answers when requested by the captains or the councils. Therefore during that period they could have had no desire to make innovations: they wanted only to administer and uphold what was approved by custom and tradition. For the only way in which they could safely preserve their own independence in the face of the captains was to keep the laws intact. But after they had acquired the power to transact government affairs and had added to the priesthood the right of secular rule, they each began to seek self-glorification both in religious and secular matters. They extended pontifical authority to all areas, and in the field of religious rites, dogma and all else they continually issued new decrees for which they claimed no less sanctity and authority than for the laws of Moses. As a result, religion degenerated into pernicious superstition, and the true meaning and interpretation of the laws was corrupted.

Furthermore, while the priests at the beginning of the restoration were pursuing the path to secular rule, in order to gain the support of the masses they indulged them in every way, approving their deeds, however impious, and adapting Scripture to suit their immorality. Malachi bears witness to their conduct in the most impressive terms. Rebuking the priests of his day, he calls them despisers of God's name, and then goes on to chide them thus: "The priest's lips are the guardians of knowledge and the law is sought from his mouth, because he is the emissary of God. But ye have departed out of the way, ye have made the Law a stumbling-block to many, ye have corrupted the covenant of Levi, saith the Lord of hosts" (Malachi ch. 2 v. 1–9). He then proceeds to accuse them of interpreting the laws at their pleasure, and of having no regard for God, but only for persons. But the priests, however careful they were, must certainly have failed to conceal these actions from the more intelligent citizens, who therefore maintained with increasing boldness that the only laws to be kept were the written laws, while the decrees which the Pharisees (who, as Josephus tells us in his *Antiquities*, were drawn mainly from the common people) mistakenly called 'the traditions of the fathers' should be discarded. Be that as it may, there is no possible doubt that the servile attitude of the high priests, the corruption of religion and the laws, the enormous proliferation of the latter, all gave serious and frequent occasion for arguments and quarrels that could never be appeased. For when men begin to dispute with superstitious fervour, and the civil authority favours one side or the other, they cannot be reconciled and inevitably split into sects.

2. It is worthy of remark that the prophets, men of private station, in exercising their freedom to warn, to rebuke and to censure, succeeded in annoying men rather than reforming them, whereas men who were admonished or castigated by

kings were more apt to turn from their ways. Indeed, even devout kings often found prophets intolerable because of their assumption of authority to decide what action was pious or impious, and even to berate the kings themselves if the latter had the hardihood to transact any business, public or private, against their judgment. King Asa, who according to Scripture was a pious ruler, consigned the prophet Hanani to prison (2 Chron. ch. 16) for venturing to reproach him too freely in the matter of the treaty made with the king of Aramaea. There are other examples to show that such freedom brought religion more harm than good, not to mention that great civil wars also originated from the prophets' retention of so important a right.

3. It is also noteworthy that as long as the people was sovereign there was only one civil war, and even that ended with peace completely restored, the victors showing such compassion to the conquered that they sought every means to restore them to their former dignity and power. But after the people, who were little accustomed to kings, changed the original form of their state to monarchy, there was practically no end to civil wars, and the fighting reached such ferocity as to surpass all previous record. In a single battle—and this is almost incredible—500,000 Israelites were slain by the men of Judah, while in turn in another battle the Israelites slew a great number of the men of Judah (the figure is not given in Scripture), captured their king, almost demolished the walls of Jerusalem and, as proof of an anger that knew no bounds, completely sacked the temple. Laden with the enormous booty of their brethren and glutted with blood, they took hostages and, leaving the king in his almost devastated kingdom, they laid down their arms, relying for their security on the weakness rather than the good faith of the men of Judah. For the men of Judah, recovering their strength a few years later, once more went forth to battle, where the Israelites were again victorious, slaying 120,000 of the men of Judah, taking captive their women and children to the number of 200,000, and again seizing considerable booty. Exhausted by these battles and by others that are narrated in the course of their history, they eventually fell prey to their enemies.

Furthermore, if we reckon up the periods of unbroken peace enjoyed under the two forms of government, we shall again find a considerable difference. Before the monarchy there were several periods of forty years, and one incredible period of eighty years, when peace prevailed both at home and abroad. But after the establishment of monarchy wars were no longer to be fought for peace and freedom, but for glory, and we find that all the kings waged war with the exception of Solomon, whose outstanding quality, wisdom, could find better scope in peace than in war. Add to this the fatal ambition for royal power, which in most cases made the path to the throne a very bloody one.

Finally, as long as the people held the reins of government, the laws remained uncorrupted and were observed with greater constancy. For before the monarchy very few prophets arose to admonish the people, whereas after the election of kings we find an abundance of them at the same time. Obadiah rescued a hundred from death, hiding them so as to save them from execution along with the rest. Nor do we see the people being deceived by false prophets until the rule of kings, whose favour is eagerly sought by most men. Then there is the further fact that the people — in whom there is generally a proud or humble spirit according to changing circumstance — was ready to mend its ways in time of disaster, turning to God, restoring the laws, and thus extricating itself from all peril; whereas kings, who are unvaryingly proud-spirited and who cannot change course without humiliation, adhered obstinately to their faults right up to the final destruction of the city.

From these considerations we can clearly see:

1. How disastrous it is for both religion and state to grant to religious functionaries any right to issue decrees or to concern themselves with state business. Stability is far better assured if these officials are restricted to giving answers only when requested, and at other times to teaching and practising only what is acknowledged as customary and traditional.

2. How dangerous it is to refer to religious jurisdiction matters that are purely philosophical, and to legislate concerning beliefs that are frequently subject to dispute, or can so be. Tyranny is most violent where individual beliefs, which are an inalienable right, are regarded as criminal. Indeed, in such circumstances the anger of the mob is usually the greatest tyrant of all. It was in giving way to the anger of the Pharisees that Pilate ordered the crucifixion of Christ, whom he knew to be innocent. Then again, it was with the purpose of casting down the rich from their privileged position that the Pharisees began to instigate religious inquisitions and to accuse the Sadducees of impiety. Following this example of the Pharisees, the vilest hypocrites, urged on by that same fury which they call zeal for God's law, have everywhere persecuted men whose blameless character and distinguished qualities have excited the hostility of the masses, publicly denouncing their beliefs and inflaming the savage crowd's anger against them. And this shameless licence, sheltering under the cloak of religion, is not easy to suppress. This is especially so where sovereign powers have introduced a religious sect of which they are not themselves the founders; for they are then regarded not as interpreters of religious law but as mere members of the sect, that is, as acknowledging the sectarian teachers to be the interpreters of religious law. So in these matters the common people have little regard for the authority of magistrates, holding in high esteem the authority of sectarian leaders, and they believe that even kings should bow down to interpretations made by the latter. To avoid these evils, then, the safest course for the commonwealth is to define piety and religious observance as consisting only in works, that is, simply in the exercise of charity and just dealing, and to allow individual free judgment in all other matters. But more of this later.

3. How essential it is for both commonwealth and religion that the sovereign power should be given the right to decide what is right and what is wrong. For if the right to pass judgment on actions could not be given even to the prophets of God without great harm to the commonwealth and religion, far less should it be given to those who can neither foretell the future nor work miracles. However, I shall be dealing with this at full-length in the next chapter.

4. Finally, we see how fatal it is for a people unaccustomed to the rule of kings, and already possessing established laws, to set up a monarchy. For neither will the people be able to endure such autocratic rule nor the monarch to tolerate laws

and rights of the people which have been instituted by someone of inferior authority. Still less could the sovereign persuade himself to uphold these laws, since they could not have been designed to take any account of a king, but were instituted for a people, or a council, which regarded itself as sovereign. So in upholding the ancient rights of the people the king would appear to be its servant rather than its master. Therefore a newly established monarch will make every effort to introduce new laws and to reconstitute the state's legal code to his own advantage, reducing the people to a point where it will find it not so easy to abolish monarchy as to set it up.

Here, however, I must not fail to point out that there is also no less danger involved in removing a monarch, even if his tyranny is apparent to all. The people, accustomed to royal rule and constrained by that alone, will despise and mock a lesser authority; and therefore, on removing one king, it will find it necessary to appoint another in his place, as did the prophets of old. And the successor will be a tyrant not by choice, but by necessity; for how will he be able to endure the sight of the citizens' hands reeking with royal blood, of the people rejoicing in regicide as in a glorious deed, a deed perpetrated as a warning for him alone? Surely, if he wants to be a king, if he does not wish to acknowledge the people as judge of kings and master over him, if he does not wish to reign on sufferance, he must avenge the death of his predecessor, and for his own sake make an example that will warn the people against daring to repeat such a crime. But he cannot easily avenge the tyrant's death by the execution of citizens without defending the cause of the tyrant who preceded him, approving his actions, and consequently following in his footsteps.

This, then, is the reason why a people has often succeeded in changing tyrants, but never in abolishing tyranny or substituting another form of government for monarchy. A sad example of this truth is provided by the English people, who under the form of law sought grounds for removing their monarch,[1] but with his disappearance found it quite impossible to change their form of government. After much bloodshed they resorted to hailing a new monarch by a different name[2] (as if the whole question at issue was a name), and he succeeded in maintaining his place only by utterly destroying the royal line, killing the king's friends, or those thought to be so. He went to war, disrupting the peace whose leisure might breed murmurings, so that the populace would turn its thoughts away from the execution of the king to fresh matters that would engage its full attention. Too late, then, did the people come to realise that to save their country they had done nothing other than violate the right of their lawful king and change everything for the worse. Therefore, when the opportunity came, it decided to retrace its steps, and was not satisfied until it saw a complete restoration of the former state of affairs.[3]

Now perhaps the Romans will be produced as an example to prove that a people can easily remove a tyrant; but I hold that this example entirely confirms

---

[1] [Charles I, executed in 1649.]
[2] [Cromwell assumed the title of Protector.]
[3] [The Restoration of 1660.]

my view. It is true that the Romans found it far easier to remove a tyrant and change the form of their state because the right to appoint the king and his successor was vested in the people itself; and furthermore the people, composed as it was of rebels and criminals, had not yet acquired the habit of obedience to kings, having killed three of the previous six. Yet all that they succeeded in doing was to appoint several tyrants in place of one,[4] and these kept them wretchedly embroiled in wars, foreign and civil, until at last the government became once more a monarchy with merely a change of name, as in England.[5]

As for the Estates of Holland, as far as we know they never had kings, but counts, to whom the right of sovereignty was never transferred. As the High Estates of Holland make plain in the document published by them at the time of Count Leicester,[6] they have always reserved to themselves the authority to remind the said counts of their duty, and have retained the power to uphold this authority of theirs and the freedom of the citizens, to assert their rights against the counts if the latter proved tyrannical, and to keep them on such a tight rein that they could do nothing without the permission and approval of the Estates. From this it follows that sovereign right was always vested in the Estates, and it was this sovereignty that the last count[7] attempted to usurp. Therefore it is by no means true that the Estates revolted against him, when in fact they recovered their original sovereignty which had almost been lost.

These examples, then, fully confirm our assertion that every state must necessarily preserve its own form, and cannot be changed without incurring the danger of utter ruin. These are the points which I have here thought worthy of remark.

CHAPTER 19

It is shown that the right over matters of religion is vested entirely in the sovereign, and that the external forms of worship should be such as accord with the peace of the commonwealth, if we would serve God aright

When I said above that only those who hold the sovereign power have an overall right and that all law is dependent on their decision alone, I intended not only civil but religious law; for in the case of the latter, too, they must be both inter-

---

[4] [This seems a very odd account of the period of the Roman Republic.]

[5] [Presumably a reference to Augustus, who was styled '*princeps*'.]

[6] [The Earl of Leicester, sent by Elizabeth with some forces to help the Dutch in 1585, was offered and accepted the title of supreme governor of the United Provinces. Spinoza here refers to the document setting forth the rights of the Provinces, which Leicester swore to uphold. He resigned in 1588.]

[7] [Philip II of Spain.]

preters and guardians. I now wish to draw particular attention to this point and to discuss it at full length in this chapter; for there are many who emphatically deny that this right over religion belongs to sovereign powers, and they refuse to acknowledge them as interpreters of the divine law. Hence they presume to accuse and traduce sovereigns, and even to excommunicate them from the Church, as Ambrose once did to the Emperor Theodosius.[1] But in so doing they are making a division of the sovereignty and actually paving the way to their own supremacy, as I shall demonstrate in the course of this chapter. But first I intend to show that religion acquires the force of law only by decree of those who hold the sovereignty, and that God has no special kingdom over men except through the medium of temporal rulers. Furthermore, the practice of religion and the exercises of piety must accord with the peace and welfare of the commonwealth, and consequently must be determined only by sovereigns, who therefore must also be its interpreters. I speak expressly of acts of piety and the outward forms of religion, not of piety itself and the inward worship of God, or of the means whereby the mind is inwardly led to worship God in sincerity of heart; for inward worship of God and piety itself belong to the sphere of individual right (as we showed at the end of Chapter 7) which cannot be transferred to another. Furthermore, the meaning I here attach to the kingdom of God is, I think, quite clear from Chapter 14. There we showed that he who practises justice and charity in accordance with God's command is fulfilling God's law, from which it follows that the kingdom of God is where justice and charity have the force of law and command. And here I acknowledge no distinction whether it is by the natural light of reason or by revelation that God teaches and commands the true practice of justice and charity, for it matters not how the practice of these virtues is revealed to us as long as it holds the place of supreme authority and is the supreme law for men. So if I now show that justice and charity can acquire the force of law and command only through the right of the state, I can readily draw the conclusion—since the state's right is vested in the sovereign alone—that religion can acquire the force of law only from the decree of those who have the right to command, and that God has no special kingdom over men save through the medium of those who hold the sovereignty.

Now this truth, that the practice of justice and charity does not acquire the force of law save from the right of the state, is clear from our previous discussion. For we showed in Chapter 16 that in a state of nature reason possesses no more right than does appetite, and those who live in accordance with the laws of appetite have just as much right to everything within their power as those who live in accordance with the laws of reason. It was in consequence of this that we could not conceive sin to exist in a state of nature, nor God as a judge who punishes men for their sins: all things came to pass in accordance with laws common to universal Nature, and the same fate—to quote Solomon—befell the righteous and the wicked, the pure and the impure, and there was no place for justice and charity. In order that the precepts of true reason—that is, as we showed in our discussion of the divine law in Chapter 14, the very precepts of God—might have the

---

[1] [In A.D. 390.]

absolute force of law, we saw that every man must surrender his natural right and that they must all transfer that right to the whole community, or to a number of men, or to one man. And not until then did we obtain a clear idea of what is justice and injustice, right and wrong. Therefore justice and, in sum, all the precepts of true reason, including charity towards one's neighbour, acquire the force of law and command only from the right of the state, that is (as we demonstrated in the same chapter), only from the decree of those who possess the right to command. And since (as I have already shown) God's kingdom consists simply in the rule of justice and charity, or true religion, it follows (as we asserted) that God has no kingdom over men save through the medium of those who hold the sovereignty. And this is equally so, I repeat, whether we consider religion to be revealed by the natural light or by prophecy; the proof applies in all cases, since religion is the same and equally revealed by God in whatever way we suppose men have come to know it.

Thus it was that, even in the case of religion revealed through prophecy, before it could have the force of law with the Hebrews it was necessary that every one of them should first surrender his natural right, and that all should by common consent resolve to obey only what was revealed to them by God through prophecy. This is an exact parallel to what we have shown to be the development of a democracy, where all by common consent resolve to live only by the dictates of reason. Now although the Hebrews went further by transferring their right to God, this transference was notional rather than practical; for in reality (as we have seen above) they retained their sovereignty absolutely until they transferred it to Moses, who from then on remained an absolute ruler, and through him alone did God reign over the Hebrews. Moreover, this fact—that religion acquires the force of law solely from the right of the state—also explains why Moses could not punish those who violated the Sabbath before the covenant, and were thus still in possession of their own right (Exod. ch. 16 v. 27); but this he could do after the covenant (Num. ch. 15 v. 36), that is, after every man had surrendered his right and the Sabbath had acquired the force of law from the right of the state.

Finally, this also explains why, with the destruction of the Hebrew state, their revealed religion ceased to have the force of law. We cannot doubt that, as soon as the Hebrews transferred their right to the king of Babylon, the kingdom of God and the divine law came to an abrupt end; for in so doing they completely annulled the covenant whereby they had promised to obey all that God should speak, which had been the basis of God's kingdom. They were no longer able to abide by it, because from that time on they were no longer possessed of their own right (as they had been in the wilderness or in their own country), but were subject to the king of Babylon whom, as we have shown in Chapter 16, they were bound to obey in all things. Jeremiah expressly reminds them of this in chapter 29 verse 7, "Seek the peace of that city whither I have brought you captive; for in the peace thereof shall ye have peace." Now they could not seek the peace of that city as officers of state—for they were captives—but only as slaves, that is, by rendering the absolute obedience that shuns insurrection, by keeping the laws and ordinances of the state, however different they might be from the laws to which they were accustomed in their own land, and so forth.

From all these considerations it follows quite clearly that among the Hebrews religion acquired the force of law solely from the right of the state, and, with the destruction of the state, religion could no longer be regarded as the command of a particular state, but as the universal doctrine of reason. I say 'of reason,' for the universal religion had not yet become known through revelation. We may therefore conclude with finality that religion, whether revealed by the natural light or by prophecy, acquires the force of command solely from the decree of those who have the right to command, and that God has no special kingdom over men save through those who hold the sovereignty. This also follows, and can be more clearly understood, from what we said in Chapter 4; for there we showed that God's decrees all involve eternal truth and necessity, and that God cannot be conceived as a ruler or lawgiver enacting laws for mankind. Therefore the divine teachings revealed by the natural light or by prophecy do not acquire the force of command from God directly; they must acquire it from those, or through the medium of those, who have the right to command and to issue decrees, and consequently it is only by their mediation that we can conceive of God as reigning over men and directing human affairs according to justice and equity. This conclusion is supported by experience; for indications of divine justice are to be found only where just men reign; elsewhere—to quote Solomon once more—we see the same fate befalling the just and the unjust, the pure and the impure. And this it is that has caused many men, who thought that God rules directly over men and orders the whole of Nature to their advantage, to doubt the divine providence. Therefore, since it is established both by reason and experience that the divine law is entirely dependent on the decrees of rulers, it follows that these are also the interpreters of the divine law. How this is so we shall see presently, for it is now time to demonstrate that the external forms of religion and the entire practice of piety must accord with the peace and preservation of the commonwealth, if we would serve God aright. When this has been proved, we shall readily understand in what way sovereigns are the interpreters of religion and piety.

There can be no doubt that devotion to one's country is the highest form of devotion that can be shown; for if the state is destroyed nothing good can survive, everything is endangered, and anger and wickedness reign supreme amidst universal fear. Hence it follows that any act of piety towards one's neighbour must be impious if it results in harm to the commonwealth as a whole, and any impious act committed against him must be accounted pious if it is done for the sake of the preservation of the commonwealth. For example, if someone who is quarrelling with me wants to take my coat, it is an act of piety to give him my cloak as well; but when it is judged that this is detrimental to the preservation of the state, it is then a pious act to bring him to justice, even though he must be condemned to death. That is why Manlius Torquatus[2] gained renown: the people's welfare had more weight with him than devotion to his son.

---

[2] [He executed his son for disobeying orders in a battle against the Latins, 340 B.C. (Livy, VIII).]

This being so, it follows that the welfare of the people is the highest law, to which all other laws, both human and divine, must be made to conform. But since it is the duty of the sovereign alone to decide what is necessary for the welfare of the entire people and the security of the state, and to command what it judges to be thus necessary, it follows that it is also the duty of the sovereign alone to decide what form piety towards one's neighbour should take, that is, in what way every man is required to obey God. From this we clearly understand in what way the sovereign is the interpreter of religion; and, furthermore, we see that no one can rightly obey God unless his practice of piety—which is the duty of every man—conforms with the public good, and consequently, unless he obeys all the decrees of the sovereign. For since we are bound by God's command to practise piety towards all men without exception and to harm no man, it follows that no one is permitted to assist anyone to another's hurt, far less to the detriment of the commonwealth as a whole. So no one can exercise piety towards his neighbour in accordance with God's command unless his piety and religion conform to the public good. But no private citizen can know what is good for the state except from the decrees of the sovereign, to whom alone it belongs to transact public business. Therefore no one can practise piety aright nor obey God unless he obeys the decrees of the sovereign in all things. This is confirmed by actual practice. For whether a man be a citizen or an alien, a person in private station or one holding command over others, if the sovereign condemns him to death or declares him an enemy, no subject is permitted to come to his assistance. Similarly, although the Hebrews were told that everyone should love his neighbour as himself (Lev. ch. 19 v. 17, 18), they were nevertheless required to inform the judge of anyone who had committed an act that contravened the edicts of the law (Lev. ch. 5 v. 1 and Deut. ch. 13 v. 8, 9) and to kill him if he was condemned to death (Deut. ch. 17 v. 7).

Then again, in order to preserve the freedom they had won and keep complete control over the territories they had seized, the Hebrews, as we explained in Chapter 17, found it necessary to adapt religion to the needs of their own state alone and to separate themselves from other nations. It was for this reason that they were told: "Love thy neighbour and hate thine enemy"[3] (Matth. ch. 5 v. 43). But when they had lost their independence and were led captive to Babylon, Jeremiah counselled them to take thought for the safety of that city (as well), to which they had been led captive. And after Christ saw that they would be dispersed throughout the whole world, he taught that they should practise piety to all without exception. All these considerations clearly show that religion has always been adapted to the good of the commonwealth.

If I am now asked by what right were Christ's disciples, men of private station, enabled to preach religion, I reply that they did so by right of the power they had received from Christ against unclean spirits (Matth. ch. 10 v. 1). For I expressly stated above at the end of Chapter 16 that all men are bound to keep faith even

---

[3] [As the editors of the New Oxford Edition of the Bible comment, there is no such commandment in the Hebrew Bible (see on Matthew 5:43).]

with a tyrant except for him to whom God, by sure revelation, has promised his special aid against the tyrant. Therefore no one may take precedent from this unless he also has the power to perform miracles. This point is likewise made manifest by the fact that Christ also bade his disciples not to fear those who kill the body (Matth. ch. 10 v. 28). If this command had been laid on every man, no state could continue in existence, and that saying of Solomon (Prov. ch. 24 v. 21), "My son, fear God and the king," would have been impiety, which is far from true. Thus it must be granted that the authority which Christ gave the disciples was a unique occurrence, and cannot be regarded as an example for others.

As for the arguments by which my opponents seek to separate religious right from civil right, maintaining that only the latter is vested in the sovereign while the former is vested in the universal church, these are of no account, being so trivial as not even to merit refutation. But one thing I cannot pass over in silence, how lamentably deceived they are when, to support this seditious opinion (pardon the bluntness of this expression) they cite the example of the Hebrew high priest who once had control over matters of religion—as if the priests did not receive this right from Moses (who, as I have shown above, alone possessed the sovereignty) and could not also have been deprived of it by his decree. For it was Moses who appointed not only Aaron but his son Eleazar and his grandson Phineas, and gave them the authority to carry out their priestly duties. This authority was held by successive high priests only insofar as they were regarded as representatives of Moses, that is, of the sovereign power. For, as I have already shown, Moses did not choose anyone to succeed to his rule: he divided all its functions in such a way that those who followed him were regarded as his deputies, carrying on the government as if the king were absent, not dead. It is true that in the second Hebrew state the high priests held this right absolutely, but that was after they combined the right of secular rule with the priesthood. Therefore the right of the priesthood has always depended on the edict of the sovereign, and the high priests have never held it except when it was combined with secular power. Indeed, the right over religion was always vested absolutely in the kings (as will become clear from what I have still to say at the end of this chapter) with this one exception: they were not permitted to set their hands to the ministry of sacred rites in the temple, because all who were not descended from Aaron were regarded as unholy. Such a situation, of course, does not obtain in a Christian state.

Thus we cannot doubt that in modern times religion—whose ministry demands outstanding moral qualities, not lineage, and therefore does not exclude as unholy those who hold the sovereignty—belongs solely to the right of the sovereign. No one has the right and power to exercise control over it, to choose its ministers, to determine and establish the foundations of the church and its doctrine, to pass judgment on morality and acts of piety, to excommunicate or to accept into the church, and to provide for the poor, except by the authority and permission of the sovereign. These doctrines are not only shown to be true (which we have just done) but also to be essential both to religion and to the preservation of the state. For everyone knows how much importance the people attach to the right and authority over religion, and how they all revere every single word of him who possesses that authority, so that one might even go so far as to say that he to whom this authority belongs has the most effective control over minds. Therefore anyone who seeks to deprive the sovereign of this authority is attempting to divide the sovereignty; and as a result, as happened long ago in the case of the kings and priests of the Hebrews, there will inevitably arise strife and dissensions that can never be allayed. Indeed, he who seeks to deprive the sovereign of this authority is paving the way to his own ascendancy, as we have already said. For what decisions can be taken by sovereigns if this right is denied them? They can decide nothing whatsoever, whether concerning war or peace or any other matter, if they are to wait on the utterance of another who will tell them whether that which they judge to be beneficial is pious or impious. On the contrary, everything will be done according to the decree of him who has the right to judge and decide what is pious or impious, right or wrong.

Every age has seen such instances, of which I will quote only one, as typical of them all. The Pope of Rome, being granted this right absolutely, began gradually to establish his ascendancy over all the kings until he actually attained the pinnacle of dominion. Whenever attempts were later made by monarchs, in particular by the Emperors of Germany, to diminish his authority in the slightest degree, they met with no success; these very efforts merely increased that authority to a considerable degree. Yet what no monarch could achieve by fire and sword, churchmen succeeded in doing by pen alone;[4] and this in itself provides a clear indication of the strength and power of religious authority, and gives further warning of the necessity for the sovereign to keep it in his own hands. Now if we also reflect on the points made in the previous chapter, we shall see that his retention of this authority is also a strong influence in promoting religion and piety. For there we saw that, although the prophets were endowed with a divine virtue, yet, being men of private station, in exercising their freedom to admonish, to rebuke and to denounce, they had the effect of provoking men rather than reforming them, whereas those who were admonished or castigated by kings were more likely to turn from their ways. Then again, the kings themselves, simply because this right did not fully belong to them, frequently forsook their religion, taking with them nearly all the people. It is a well-established fact that this has frequently occurred even in Christian states for the same reason.

Now perhaps at this point I shall be asked: "Then if those who hold the sovereignty choose to be impious, who will be the rightful champion of piety? Are the rulers still to be regarded as the interpreters of religion?" To this I ask in return: "What if churchmen (who are also but human, and, as private citizens, are entitled to have regard for their own affairs) or any others to whom it is proposed to entrust control over religion, should choose to be impious? Are they even then to be regarded as the interpreters of religion?" It is indeed true that if those who hold

---

[4] [A reference to Luther and Calvin.]

the sovereignty choose to go what way they will, then, whether or not they have control over religion, all things, both religious and secular, will go to ruin: but this will come about far more quickly if private citizens seditiously seek to be the champions of religious law. Therefore nothing whatsoever is gained by denying this right to sovereigns; on the contrary, evil is aggravated. For, as was the case with the Hebrew kings to whom this right was not unconditionally granted, this very fact is likely to drive them to impiety, and in consequence injury and damage to the entire commonwealth become certain and inevitable instead of uncertain and possible. So whether we have regard to the truth of the matter, or the security of the state, or the advancement of piety, we are forced to maintain that divine law, or religious law, also depends absolutely on the decree of sovereigns, who are its interpreters and champions. It follows that the ministers of God's word are those who are authorised by their sovereign to teach piety in the form that, by decree of the sovereign, is adapted to the public good.

It now remains for me, in addition, to indicate the reason why this right has always been the subject of disputes in Christian states, whereas the Hebrews, to the best of my knowledge, never entertained any doubt about it. It would certainly seem extraordinary that a matter so plain and so vitally important should always have been called into question, and that sovereigns have never held this right without controversy—nay, without grave danger of sedition and harm to religion. Indeed, if we could not assign any assured cause for this phenomenon, I might easily be convinced that all the findings of this chapter are merely theoretical, the kind of speculative thinking that can never be of practical importance. But in fact, when we review the origins of the Christian religion, the cause of this phenomenon is completely revealed. It was not kings who were the first teachers of the Christian religion, but men of private station who, despite the will of those who held the sovereignty and were their rulers, were long accustomed to address private religious assemblies, to institute and perform sacred rites, to make all arrangements and decisions on their own responsibility without any regard to the state. Many years later, when their religion began to be adopted by the state, the churchmen were obliged to teach it to the emperors themselves in the form they had given it, from which it was an easy step for them to gain recognition as its teachers and interpreters, and furthermore as the pastors of the church and virtually God's representatives. And to prevent Christian kings from later seizing this authority for themselves, the churchmen devised the very effective precaution of forbidding marriage to the chief ministers of the church and to the supreme interpreter of religion. In addition, they multiplied religious dogmas to such an extent and confused them with so much philosophy that the supreme interpreter of religion had to be a consummate philosopher and theologian and to have time for a host of idle speculations. This effectively ruled out all but men of private station with abundant leisure.

Now with the Hebrews the position was quite different. Their church originated together with their state, and Moses, the absolute ruler of that state, taught the people their religion, arranged the sacred offices and appointed those who were to administer them. Thus a quite different situation developed, where the royal authority carried the greatest weight with the people, and kings most decidedly held the right over religion. For although no one held absolute sovereignty after Moses' death, the right to make decisions both in matters religious and in other matters was vested in the captains, as I have already shown. Then again, for instruction in religion and piety the people were required to attend on the supreme judge no less than the high priest (Deut. ch. 17 v. 9, 11). Finally, although the kings did not possess a right equal to that of Moses, almost all the organisation of religious ministry and appointment thereto depended on their decision. David, for instance, arranged the entire construction of the temple (1 Chron. ch. 28 v. 11, 12 etc.); then out of all the Levites he chose 24,000 for the psalm-singing, 6,000 to supply candidates for appointment as judges and officers, 4,000 doorkeepers and 4,000 to play musical instruments (1 Chron. ch. 23 v. 4, 5). He further divided these into companies (of which he also chose the leaders), so that each company should do duty as its turn came round (same chapter, verse 6). The priests he likewise divided into as many companies. But to avoid having to go into every detail, I refer the reader to 2 Chron. ch. 8 v. 13, where we read that the worship of God, as established by Moses, was conducted in the temple by Solomon's command; and in verse 14 that he (Solomon) appointed companies of priests in their ministries and companies of Levites, etc. in accordance with the command of David, the man of God. And finally, in verse 15, the historian testifies that "they departed not from the commandment of the king unto the priests and Levites in any matter, nor in the administration of the treasuries."

From all these considerations, together with other narratives concerning the kings, it follows quite clearly that the entire practice of religion and its ministry depended solely on the command of the kings. When I stated above that they did not have the same right as Moses to appoint the high priest, to consult God directly and to condemn prophets who should prophesy during their lifetime, this was only because the prophets, from the nature of the authority they possessed, could appoint a new king and pardon regicide. I did not mean that they were permitted to summon to judgment and lawfully impeach* a king if he dared to contravene the laws. Therefore if there had been no prophets who by special revelation could assuredly grant pardon for regicide, the kings would have had absolute right over all matters, both sacred and secular. Hence sovereigns of our times, who neither have prophets nor are bound by right to acknowledge any (not being subject to the laws of the Hebrews), even if they be not celibate, possess this right absolutely; and provided they do not allow religious dogmas to be multiplied or to be confused with philosophy, they will always retain this right.

---

* See Supplementary Note 39.

CHAPTER 20

It is shown that in a free commonwealth every man may think as he pleases, and say what he thinks[1]

If minds could be as easily controlled as tongues, every government would be secure in its rule, and need not resort to force; for every man would conduct himself as his rulers wished, and his views as to what is true or false, good or bad, fair or unfair, would be governed by their decision alone. But we have already explained at the beginning of Chapter 17 that it is impossible for the mind to be completely under another's control; for no one is able to transfer to another his natural right or faculty to reason freely and to form his own judgment on any matters whatsoever, nor can he be compelled to do so. Consequently, a government that attempts to control men's minds is regarded as tyrannical, and a sovereign is thought to wrong his subjects and infringe their right when he seeks to prescribe for every man what he should accept as true and reject as false, and what are the beliefs that will inspire him with devotion to God. All these are matters belonging to individual right, which no man can surrender even if he should so wish.

I admit that judgment can be influenced in numerous ways—some of them almost past belief—and to such an extent that, although it is not directly subject to another's command, it may be so dependent on another's words that it can properly be said in that respect to belong to his right. But in spite of all that ingenuity has been able to devise in this field, it has never attained such success that men did not ever find that the individual citizen has his own ideas in plenty, and that opinions vary as much as tastes. Moses had gained the strongest of holds on the minds of his people not by deception but by his divine virtue, for he was thought to be a man of God whose every word and action was divinely inspired; yet even he was not exempt from their murmurings and criticisms, and far less so were other monarchs. Now if such exemption from criticism were conceivable, it would surely be in the case of a monarchy, not a democracy, where the sovereignty is corporately held by all the people, or a great part of them. The reason for this, I imagine, is obvious to all.

So however much sovereigns are believed to possess unlimited right and to be the interpreters of law and piety, they will never succeed in preventing men from exercising their own particular judgment on any matters whatsoever and from being influenced accordingly by a variety of emotions. It is true that sovereigns can by their right treat as enemies all who do not absolutely agree with them on all matters, but the point at issue is not what is their right, but what is to their interest. I grant that by this right they can govern in the most oppressive way and exe-

---

[1] [Tacitus, *Histories*, I, 1, 4, "*ubi sentire quae velis et quae sentias dicere licet.*"—S.S.]

cute citizens on the most trivial pretexts, but no one can imagine that by so doing they are acting in accordance with the judgment of sound reason. Indeed, since they cannot so act without endangering the whole fabric of the state, we can even argue that they do not have the absolute power to do these and other such things, and consequently that they do not have the absolute right to do so. For we have demonstrated that the right of sovereigns is determined by their power.

If no man, then, can give up his freedom to judge and think as he pleases, and everyone is by absolute natural right the master of his own thoughts, it follows that utter failure will attend any attempt in a commonwealth to force men to speak only as prescribed by the sovereign despite their different and opposing opinions. Not even men well versed in affairs can keep silent, not to say the lower classes. It is the common failing of men to confide what they think to others, even when secrecy is needed. Therefore the most tyrannical government will be one where the individual is denied the freedom to express and to communicate to others what he thinks, and a moderate government is one where this freedom is granted to every man. However, it is also undeniable that words can be treasonable as well as deeds; and so, while it is impossible to deprive subjects completely of this freedom, to grant it unreservedly could have the most disastrous consequences. Therefore it is our present task to enquire to what extent this freedom can and should be granted to all without endangering the peace of the commonwealth and the right of the sovereign. This, as I indicated at the beginning of Chapter 16, was the main purpose of this part of my treatise.

It follows quite clearly from my earlier explanation of the basis of the state that its ultimate purpose is not to exercise dominion nor to restrain men by fear and deprive them of independence, but on the contrary to free every man from fear so that he may live in security as far as is possible, that is, so that he may best preserve his own natural right to exist and to act, without harm to himself and to others. It is not, I repeat, the purpose of the state to transform men from rational beings into beasts or puppets, but rather to enable them to develop their mental and physical faculties in safety, to use their reason without restraint and to refrain from the strife and the vicious mutual abuse that are prompted by hatred, anger or deceit. Thus the purpose of the state is, in reality, freedom.

Furthermore, we have seen that the one essential feature in the formation of a state was that all power to make laws should be vested in the entire citizen body, or in a number of citizens, or in one man. For since there is a considerable diversity in the free judgment of men, each believing that he alone knows best, and since it is impossible that all should think alike and speak with one voice, peaceful existence could not be achieved unless every man surrendered his right to act just as he thought fit. Thus it was only the right to act as he thought fit that each man surrendered, and not his right to reason and judge. So while to act against the sovereign's decree is definitely an infringement of his right, this is not the case with thinking, judging, and consequently with speaking, too, provided one does no more than express or communicate one's opinion, defending it through rational conviction alone, not through deceit, anger, hatred or the will to effect such changes in the state as he himself decides. For example, suppose a man maintains that a certain law is against sound reason, and he therefore advocates its repeal. If he at the same time submits his opinion to the judgment of the sovereign power (which alone is competent to enact and repeal laws), and meanwhile does nothing contrary to what is commanded by that law, he deserves well of the state, acting as a good citizen should do. But if on the contrary the purpose of his action is to accuse the magistrate of injustice and to stir up popular hatred against him, or if he seditiously seeks to repeal that law in spite of the magistrate, he is nothing more than an agitator and a rebel.

Thus we see how the individual citizen can say and communicate to others what he thinks without infringing the right and authority of the sovereign, that is, without violating the peace of the commonwealth. He must leave it to the sovereign to decide what action is to be taken in all circumstances, and must not act contrary to its decision, even if frequently his action has to be in conflict with what he judges and openly proclaims to be good. This entails no violation of justice and piety; indeed, he is bound to act thus if he wants to be a just and pious man. For, as we have shown, justice depends solely on the decree of the sovereign, and nobody save one who lives in accordance with the sovereign's established decrees can be a just man. As for piety, this (by our findings in the previous chapter) is demonstrated in its highest form in the service of the peace and tranquillity of the commonwealth, which, however, cannot be preserved if every man is to live simply as he thinks fit. So it is impious, as well, for the subject to contravene his sovereign's decree just as he pleases; for if this were permitted to everyone, the ruin of the state would inevitably ensue. Indeed, as long as a man is acting in accordance with the sovereign's decrees, he cannot be acting against the decree and dictates of his own reason; for it was with the full approval of reason that he resolved to transfer to the sovereign his right to live by his own judgment. But my argument is further confirmed by actual practice: in the councils of authorities, both sovereign and subordinate, it rarely happens that there is a unanimous vote in favour of some measure; yet everything is done by the common decision of all, whether they have voted for or against. But I must return to my theme.

Our discussion of the basis of the state has revealed how the individual citizen can exercise freedom of judgment without infringing the right of the sovereign. The same considerations enable us just as well to determine what political beliefs are seditious: they are those which, when posited, immediately have the effect of annulling the covenant whereby everyone has surrendered his right to act just as he thinks fit. For example, if anyone holds the opinion that the sovereign is not possessed of full power, or that promises need not be kept, or that it behoves everyone to live as he pleases, or if he holds other such views as are directly opposed to the said covenant, he is guilty of sedition, not so much because of his judgment and belief as because of the action that is implicit therein. For merely to hold such an opinion is to violate the pledge tacitly or expressly given to the sovereign. And therefore other beliefs, those in which there is no implication of action such as the breaking of the covenant, the exaction of revenge, the indulgence of anger and so forth, are not seditious, except perchance in a state which is in some way corrupted, a state where superstitious and ambitious men who cannot tolerate men of integrity have gained such a great reputation that the common people pay more heed to them than to the sovereign. We do not deny, however, that there are in addition certain views, which have the appearance of being concerned merely with questions of truth and falsity, but are nevertheless put forward and popularised with malicious purpose. But these, too, we have already dealt with in Chapter 15, and reached a conclusion that left reason nonetheless free.

Finally, if we also reflect on the fact that every man's loyalty to the state can be known only from his works—just as his devotion to God can be known only from his works, that is, his charity to his neighbour—we are left in no doubt that a good commonwealth grants to every man the same freedom to philosophise as we have seen is granted by religious faith. I do indeed admit that there may sometimes be some disadvantages in allowing such freedom, but what institution was ever so wisely planned that no disadvantage could arise therefrom? He who seeks to regulate everything by law will aggravate vices rather than correct them. What cannot be prohibited must necessarily be allowed, even if harm often ensues. How many are the evils that arise from dissipation, envy, avarice, drunkenness and the like? Yet we tolerate these, because although they are in reality vices they cannot be prohibited by legal enactment. Much more, then, should we allow freedom of judgment, which is assuredly a virtue, and cannot be suppressed. Furthermore, it can produce no untoward results that cannot be contained, as I shall presently show, by the magistrates' authority; not to mention that this freedom is of the first importance in fostering the sciences and the arts, for it is only those whose judgment is free and unbiased who can attain success in these fields.

But let it be supposed that this freedom can be suppressed and that men can be kept under such control that they dare not whisper anything that is not commanded by the sovereign. Still, it will certainly never come to pass that men will think only what they are bidden to think. It would thus inevitably follow that in their daily lives men would be thinking one thing and saying another, with the result that good faith, of first importance in the state, would be undermined and the disgusting arts of sycophancy and treachery would be encouraged. This is the source of false dealing and the corruption of all honest accomplishments. But it is far beyond the bounds of possibility that all men can be made to speak to order. On the contrary, the greater the effort to deprive them of freedom of speech, the more obstinately do they resist: not indeed the greedy, the flatterers and other poor-spirited souls who find their greatest happiness in gloating over their moneybags and cramming their bellies, but those to whom a good upbringing, integrity and a virtuous disposition have given a more liberal outlook. Men in general are so constituted that their resentment is most aroused when beliefs which they think to be true are treated as criminal, and when that which motivates their pious conduct to God and man is accounted as wickedness. In consequence, they are emboldened to denounce the laws and go to all lengths to oppose the magistrate, considering it not a disgrace but honourable to stir up sedition and to resort to any outrageous action in this cause.

Granted, then, that human nature is thus constituted, it follows that laws enacted against men's beliefs are directed not against villains but against men of good character, and their purpose is to provoke honourable men rather than to restrain the wicked. Nor can they be enforced without great danger to the state. Furthermore, such laws are quite ineffective; for those who are convinced of the validity of beliefs that are condemned by law will not be able to obey the law, while those who reject these beliefs as false will regard the law in question as enacted for their special benefit, and their exultation over such laws will make it difficult for the magistrate to repeal them thereafter, even if he should so wish. In addition to these considerations, there are the lessons learnt from the history of the Hebrews, Chapter 18, under the second heading.

Finally, how many divisions in the church have arisen mainly from attempts made by magistrates to settle the disputes of scholars by legislation! If men were not possessed by the hope of enlisting the law and the magistrate on their side, of triumphing over their opponents amid the universal applause of the mob and of gaining office, they would never engage in such malicious strife against one another nor would they be agitated by such frenzy. This is demonstrated not only by reason but by experience with its daily examples. Laws of this kind, prescribing what everyone must believe and prohibiting the saying or writing of anything that opposes this or that opinion, have often been enacted to pander to, or rather to surrender to, the anger of those who cannot endure enlightened minds, men who, by the exercise of a stern authority can easily turn the devotion of the unruly masses into a rage, inciting them against whomsoever they will. Yet how much better it would be to curb the frenzied anger of the mob instead of passing useless laws which can be broken only by those who love the virtues and the arts, and reducing the state to such straits that it cannot endure men of noble character! What greater misfortune can be imagined for a state than that honourable men should be exiled as miscreants because their opinions are at variance with authority and they cannot disguise the fact? What can be more calamitous than that men should be regarded as enemies and put to death, not for any crime or misdeed, but for being of independent mind? That the scaffold, the terror of evildoers, should become the glorious stage where is presented a supreme example of virtuous endurance, to the utter disgrace of the ruling power? Those who are conscious of their own probity do not fear death as criminals do, nor do they beg for mercy, for they are not tormented with remorse for shameful deeds. On the contrary, they think it an honour, not a punishment, to die in a good cause, and a glorious thing to die for freedom. What sort of lesson, then, is learnt from the death of such men, whose cause is beyond the understanding of those of sluggish and feeble spirit, is hated by troublemakers, but is dear to the hearts of all good men? The only lesson to be drawn from their death is to emulate them, or at least to revere them.

Therefore, if honesty is to be prized rather than obsequiousness, and if sovereigns are to retain full control and not be forced to surrender to agitators, it is imperative to grant freedom of judgment and to govern men in such a way that the different and conflicting views they openly proclaim do not debar them from living together in peace. This system of government is undoubtedly the best and its disadvantages are fewer because it is in closest accord with human nature. For we have shown that in a democracy (which comes closest to the natural state) all the citizens undertake to act, but not to reason and to judge, by decision made in common. That is to say, since all men cannot think alike, they agree that a proposal supported by a majority of votes shall have the force of a decree, meanwhile retaining the authority to repeal the same when they see a better alternative. Thus the less freedom of judgment is conceded to men, the further their distance from the most natural state, and consequently the more oppressive the regime.

Moreover, to confirm that any disadvantages consequent on this freedom can be avoided simply by the sovereign's authority, and by this authority alone men can be restrained from harming one another even when their opinions are in open conflict, examples are ready to hand, and I need go no distance to find them. Take the city of Amsterdam, which enjoys the fruits of this freedom, to its own considerable prosperity and the admiration of the world. In this flourishing state, a city of the highest renown, men of every race and sect live in complete harmony; and before entrusting their property to some person they will want to know no more than this, whether he is rich or poor and whether he has been honest or dishonest in his dealings. As for religion or sect, that is of no account, because such considerations are regarded as irrelevant in a court of law; and no sect whatsoever is so hated that its adherents—provided that they injure no one, render to each what is his own, and live upright lives—are denied the protection of the civil authorities. On the other hand, in time past when politicians and the Estates of the Provinces began to intervene in the religious controversy between the Remonstrants and the Counter-Remonstrants,[2] it resulted in a division in the church. Many other instances in that period provide clear evidence that laws enacted to settle religious controversies have the effect of angering men rather than reforming them, that they give some men the opportunity to assume unbounded licence, and that, furthermore, divisions in the church do not arise from zeal for truth (which breeds only courtesy and tolerance) but from lust for supremacy. From this it is clearer than the sun at noon that the real schismatics are those who condemn the writings of others and seditiously incite the quarrelsome mob against the writers, rather than the writers themselves, who usually write only for scholars and appeal to reason alone; and that, finally, the real disturbers of peace are those who, in a free commonwealth, vainly seek to abolish freedom of judgment, which cannot be suppressed.

I have thus shown:

1. That it is impossible to deprive men of the freedom to say what they think.

2. That this freedom can be granted to everyone without infringing the right and authority of the sovereign, and that the individual citizen can preserve this freedom without infringing that right, provided that he does not presume there-

---

[2] [During the seventeenth century the new Dutch Republic was theologically and politically divided between two Protestant groups, the Remonstrants and the Counter-Remonstrants. The former supported the republic and favored a more liberal theology, rejecting for example the Calvinist doctrine of predestination. The Counter-Remonstrants sided with the monarchist faction and adhered to orthodox Calvinist theology.]

from to make any innovation in the constitution or to do anything that contravenes the established laws.

3. That every man can possess this freedom without endangering public peace, and any troubles that may arise from this freedom can easily be held in check.

4. That every man can also possess that freedom without endangering piety.

5. That laws enacted concerning speculative matters are quite useless.

6. Finally, we have shown not only that this freedom can be granted without detriment to public peace, to piety, and to the right of the sovereign, but also that it must be granted if these are to be preserved. For when a contrary course is taken and attempts are made to deprive men of this freedom, and the beliefs of dissenters (but not their minds, which alone are capable of wrongdoing) are brought to trial, the exemplary punishment inflicted on honourable men seems more like martyrdom, and serves not so much to terrorise others as to anger them and move them to compassion, if not to revenge. Upright dealing and good faith are undermined, sycophants and traitors are encouraged, and opponents of freedom exult because their anger has won the day and they have converted the government to their creed, of which they are regarded as the interpreters. As a result, they even venture to usurp the government's authority and right, and they unashamedly boast that they have been chosen directly by God and that their decrees are divinely inspired, whereas those of the sovereign are merely human and should therefore give way before divine decrees—that is, their own. Nobody can fail to see that all this is directly opposed to the welfare of the state. Therefore we have to conclude, as we did in Chapter 18, that the state can pursue no safer course than to regard piety and religion as consisting solely in the exercise of charity and just dealing, and that the right of the sovereign, both in religious and secular spheres, should be restricted to men's actions, with everyone being allowed to think what he will and to say what he thinks.

I have now completed the task I set myself in this treatise. It only remains for me to state expressly that it contains nothing that I would not willingly submit to the scrutiny and judgment of my country's government. If they consider any part of my writing to be contrary to the laws of my country or to be prejudicial to the general good, I retract it. I know that I am human, and may have erred. Yet I have taken great pains not to err, and I have made it my prime object that whatever I have written should be in complete accord with my country's laws, with piety and with morality.

SPINOZA'S SUPPLEMENTARY NOTES TO THE *TRACTATUS THEOLOGICO-POLITICUS*

[Notes numbered 28, 29, 30 in Gebhardt's edition have been omitted. Those notes merely refer the reader to *Philosophia S. Scripturae Interpres*, a tract written by Spinoza's friend Lodewijk Meyer, and bound together with Spinoza's *Tractatus* in one of its editions.]

Chapter 1

Note 1: 'nabi'. If the third radical is one of those termed 'mutes', it is customarily omitted and instead the second letter is doubled. Thus קָלָה by the omission of the mute ה becomes קוֹלֵל and then קוֹל and נָבָא becomes נוֹבֵב whence נִיב שְׂפָתִים—utterance or speech. Similarly בזא becomes בזז or בוז. (שגה משגה שגג שהג : המה המם). (בלה בלל בלעל). Therefore R. Shlomo was quite correct in interpreting this word as נָבָא, and was wrongly criticised by ibn Ezra, whose knowledge of Hebrew was not profound. It should further be noted that the word נבואה—prophecy is of general application, and embraces every kind of prophesying, whereas other nouns are more specific and refer to a particular kind of prophesying. This point, I believe, is familiar to all scholars.

Note 2: 'its professors cannot be called prophets'. That is, interpreters of God. For an interpreter of God is one who has a revelation of God's decrees which he interprets to others who have not had this revelation, and who accept it solely in reliance on the prophet's authority and the confidence he enjoys. Now if those who listen to prophets were themselves to become prophets just as those who listen to philosophers become philosophers, the prophet would not be an interpreter of divine decrees; for his hearers would rely not on the testimony and authority of the prophet but on the divine revelation itself and on their own inward testimony, just as the prophet does. Similarly, sovereign powers are the interpreters of their own sovereign right, since the laws that they enact are upheld only by their own sovereign authority, and are supported only by their own testimony.

Note 3: 'that the prophets were endowed with an extraordinary virtue exceeding the normal'. Although some men possess gifts that nature does not bestow on others, they are not said to surpass human nature unless the gifts that are peculiar to them are such as cannot be understood from the definition of human nature. For example, a giant is of unusual size, but his size is still human. It is granted to few to be able to compose poetry extempore, but this is still a human gift, as also is the gift whereby someone, while wide awake, imagines certain things as vividly as if they were actually present before him. But if someone were to possess a quite different means of perception and quite different grounds of knowledge, he would assuredly surpass the bounds of human nature.

Chapter 3

Note 4: 'Patriarchs'. In chapter 15 of Genesis we are told that God said to Abraham that he would be his protector and would give him an exceedingly great reward; to which Abraham replied that he had nothing very much to look forward to, since he was childless and stricken with years.

Note 5: 'their security'. It is clear from Mark ch. 10 v. 21 that to achieve eternal life it is not enough to keep the commandments of the Old Testament.

Chapter 6

Note 6: 'Since God's existence is not self-evident'. We doubt the existence of God, and consequently everything else, as long as we do not have a clear and distinct idea of God, but only a confused idea. Just as he who does not rightly know the nature of a triangle does not know that its three angles are equal to two right angles, so he who conceives the divine nature in a confused way does not see that existence pertains to the nature of God. Now in order that we may conceive God's nature clearly and distinctly, we have to fix our attention on certain very simple axioms called universal axioms, and connect to them those attributes that belong to the divine nature. Only then does it become clear to us that God necessarily exists and is omnipresent, and only then do we see that all our conceptions involve God's nature and are conceived through God's nature, and, finally, that everything that we adequately conceive is true. But for this see the Preface to my book entitled '*The Principles of Philosophy Demonstrated in a Geometrical Manner.*'

Chapter 7

Note 7: 'impossible to devise a method'. That is, impossible for us who are not used to this language and lack a systematic account of its phraseology.

Note 8: 'conception'. By things comprehensible I mean not only those which can be logically proved but also those which we are wont to accept with moral certainty and to hear without surprise, although they can by no means be proved. Anyone can comprehend Euclid's propositions before they are proved. Similarly, I call comprehensible those narratives, whether of future or past events, that do not exceed human belief, and likewise laws, institutions and customs, although they cannot be proved with mathematical certainty. But mysterious symbols, and narratives that exceed all human belief, I call incomprehensible. Yet even among these there are many that yield to examination by our method, so that we can perceive the author's meaning.

CHAPTER 8

Note 9: 'Mount Moriah'. Thus named not by Abraham, but by the historian, who says that the place which in his day was called 'in the mount of the Lord it shall be revealed' was called by Abraham 'the Lord will provide.'

Note 10: 'before David conquered that people'. From this time until the reign of Jehoram, when they gained independence (2 Kings ch. 8 v. 20), the Idumaeans had no king. Governors, appointed by the Jews, took the place of kings (1 Kings ch. 22 v. 47), and therefore the governor of Edom is called 'king' (2 Kings ch. 3 v. 9). There is some doubt as to whether the last of the Idumaean kings had begun his reign before Saul became king, or whether in this chapter of Genesis, Scripture intended to list only the kings who were unconquered until their death. However, it is plain folly to attempt to include Moses, who by the divine will established a Hebrew state very different from monarchy, in the list of Hebrew kings.

CHAPTER 9

Note 11: 'exceptions'. For example, in 2 Kings ch. 18 v. 20 the text has the second person, 'Thou hast said—but they are no more than words—etc.', whereas in Isaiah ch. 36 v. 5 we have 'I have said—but they are no more than words—that war needs counsel and courage.' Again, in verse 22 the text of Kings reads 'But ye may say unto me', the verb being in the plural, whereas Isaiah has the verb in the singular. Furthermore, the words in Kings, same chapter, verse 32, 'a land of oil olive and of honey, that ye may live and not die: and hearken not to Hezekiah' are missing in Isaiah. There are many other differences of reading of this kind, and no one can determine which is to be preferred.

Note 12: 'remarkable change'. For example, in 2 Sam. ch. 7 v. 6 we have (וָאֶהְיֶה מִתְהַלֵּךְ בְּאֹהֶל וּבְמִשְׁכָּן)—'and I have continually wandered with tent and tabernacle'; but in 1 Chron. ch. 17 v. 5 we have (וָאֶהְיֶה מֵאֹהֶל אֶל־אֹהֶל וּמִמִּשְׁכָּן)—'and I have been from tent to tent and from tabernacle', with a change of מִתְהַלֵּךְ to מֵאֹהֶל, בְּאֹהֶל to אֶל־אֹהֶל and בְּמִשְׁכָּן to מִמִּשְׁכָּן. Again in verse 10 of the same chapter of Samuel we have לְעַנּוֹתוֹ—'to afflict him', while in verse 9 of the quoted chapter of Chronicles we have לְבַלֹּתוֹ—'to wear him down'. For anyone who is not quite blind or completely mad a single reading of these chapters will reveal many discrepancies of this kind, some of considerable importance.

Note 13: 'the time here mentioned must refer . . . to a quite different time'. That this passage refers to the time when Joseph was sold is not only evident from the context itself but can also be inferred from the age of Judah, who was then in his twenty-second year at the most, if one may base one's calculation on his preceding history. From the last verse of Genesis ch. 29 it is clear that Judah was born ten years after the patriarch Jacob began to serve Laban, and Joseph fourteen years. Now since Joseph was seventeen years old at the time he was sold, Judah could not have been more than twenty-one. So those who believe that Judah's long absence from home took place before Joseph was sold are seeking to delude themselves, and are more concerned for the sanctity of Scripture than for accuracy.

Note 14: 'while Dinah was scarcely seven years old'. The opinion advanced by some that Jacob wandered about between Mesopotamia and Bethel for eight or ten years savours of the ridiculous, if I may say so without disrespect to ibn Ezra. Jacob had good reason for haste, not only because he no doubt longed to see his aged parents, but also for a most important purpose, to fulfill the vow he had made when he fled from his brother (Gen. ch. 28 v. 20, ch. 31 v. 13 and ch. 35 v. 1), a vow which God also bade him fulfill, promising to help him to return to his country. However, if these considerations seem mere conjectures rather than cogent reasoning, let us grant that Jacob, driven by a more malignant fate than Ulysses, spent eight or ten or even more years on this short journey. Even so, our objectors cannot deny that Benjamin was born in the last year of this wandering, that is, according to their view and their theory, when Joseph was fifteen or sixteen or thereabouts; for Jacob parted from Laban seven years after Joseph was born. Now the period of time from Joseph's seventeenth year until the patriarch travelled to Egypt does not exceed twenty-two years, as I have shown in this chapter. Thus at that point of time—that is, when he set out to Egypt—Benjamin was twenty-three or twenty-four years old at the most, at which time, in the early flowering of his life, he must have been a grandfather (see Gen. ch. 46 v. 21, and compare with Num. ch. 26 v. 38, 39, 40 and with 1 Chron. ch. 8 v. 1 and the verses that follow); for Belah, his firstborn, had already begotten two sons, Ard and Naaman. This is surely no less absurd than to maintain that Dinah was seven years old when she was violated, not to mention the other absurdities that are entailed by this manner of arranging history. Thus it is clear that unscholarly attempts to solve difficulties produce further difficulties, confusing and clouding the question even more.

Note 15: 'he here begins to relate of Joshua'. That is to say, the terms used and the order of narration differ from those employed in the book of Joshua.

Note 16: 'Othniel, son of Kenaz, was judge 40 years'. Rabbi Levi ben Gerson[1] and some others believe that these 40 years, which Scripture declares to have

---

[1] [Gersonides, of Provence, 1288–1344, the most outstanding scholar of his age. Biblical exegete and philosopher.]

been passed in freedom, should be calculated from the death of Joshua and thus include the preceding 8 years when the people were subject to Cushan Rishathaim, while the following 18 years should be included in the total of the 80 years when Ehud and Shamgar were judges. In the same way, they think that the other years of subjection are always included in the years which Scripture declares to have been passed in freedom. But Scripture expressly computes how many years the Hebrews passed in subjection and how many years in freedom, and in chapter 2 v. 18 it expressly tells us that the Hebrews always enjoyed prosperity in the time of the Judges. So it is perfectly clear that our Rabbi (in other respects a man of great learning) and the others who follow him, when trying to solve such difficulties, are not so much explaining Scripture as emending it.

This is also true of those who maintain that, in the summation of years which Scripture here makes, only the years of a properly administered Jewish state were taken into account, while the periods of anarchy and subjection, being unhappy interludes in the history of the Jewish state, must have been ignored. Now Scripture does indeed pass over in silence the periods of anarchy, but the years of subjection are narrated quite as fully as the years of independence, and are not erased from Jewish history, as is wildly suggested. Ezra—whom we have shown to be the author of these books—in 1 Kings ch. 6 intended to include in that complete total all the years from the exodus from Egypt to the fourth year of Solomon's reign, a fact so clear that no biblical scholar has ever doubted it. For, leaving aside for the present the precise wording of the text, the genealogy of David given at the end of the book of Ruth and in 1 Chron. ch. 2 fails to account in full for such a large figure as 480 years. Nahshon was chief of the tribe of Judah in the second year after the exodus (Num. ch. 7 v. 11, 12), and thus died in the wilderness along with all those who at the age of 20 were capable of military service; and his son Salmon crossed the Jordan with Joshua. Now this Salmon, according to the said genealogy, was David's great-great-grandfather. If we subtract from this grand total of 480 years the 4 years of Solomon's reign, the 70 years of David's life and the 40 years spent in the wilderness, we find that David was born 366 years after the passage of the Jordan, and that his father, grandfather, great-grandfather and great-great-grandfather must each have begotten children when they were 90 years old.

Note 17: 'Samson was judge'. Samson was born after the Philistines had subjugated the Hebrews. There is some doubt as to whether the 20 years here mentioned should be reckoned among the years of independence, or whether they are included in the immediately preceding 40 years when the people were under the yoke of the Philistines. For my part, I am of the opinion that it is more probable and more credible that the Hebrews recovered their freedom at the time when the most eminent of the Philistines perished along with Samson. My only reason for refusing to include Samson's 20 years in the period of subjugation to the Philistines is this, that Samson was born after the Philistines had subjugated the Hebrews. There is a further reason, the mention made in the Tractate Shabbat of a certain book of Jerusalem where it is stated that Samson judged the people for 40 years. However, it is not a question of these years alone.

Note 18: 'with absolute strictness'. Otherwise, they are not explaining the words of Scripture, but emending them.

Note 19: 'Kirjath Jeharim'. Kirjath Jeharim is also called Baal Judah. Hence Kimḥi[2] and some others think that the words 'Baale Judah', which I have here translated as 'from the people of Judah', signify the name of a town. But they are wrong, because בַּעֲלֵי is plural. Moreover, comparing the text of Samuel with the text of 1 Chronicles, we see that David did not arise and go forth from Baal, but that he went thither. If the author of 2 Samuel had intended to indicate the place whence David removed the ark, then the Hebrew would have run as follows: "Then David arose and set forth ... etc. from Baal Judah, and took from there the ark of God."

Note 20: 'and was there three years'. Some commentators have emended the text as follows: "And Absalom fled and went to Talmai, the son of Ammihud, king of Geshur, where he remained for three years, and David wept for his son all the time that he was at Geshur." Now if this is to be called interpretation, and if one can assume such licence in expounding Scripture, transposing entire phrases, adding to them and subtracting from them, then I declare that it is permissible to corrupt Scripture and to treat it as a piece of wax on which one can impose whatever forms one chooses.

Chapter 10

Note 21: 'and perhaps after the restoration of the temple by Judas Maccabee'. This possibility—though it is more akin to certainty—is based on the genealogy from king Jeconiah, given in 1 Chron. ch. 3 and continuing as far as the sons of Elioneai, who were thirteenth in direct line from Jeconiah. It should be observed that Jeconiah had no children when he was imprisoned, but he had two children while in prison, as far as can be conjectured by the names he gave them. Now he seems to have had grandchildren—again making conjecture from their names—after his release from prison; and therefore Pedaiah (which means 'God hath delivered'), who according to this chapter is said to be the father of Zerubbabel, was born in the thirty-seventh or thirty-eighth year of Jeconiah's captivity, that is, thirty-three years before Cyrus gave the Jews permission to return. Therefore Zerubbabel, whom Cyrus put in charge of the Jews, seems to have been thirteen or fourteen years old at the most. But I have preferred to keep silent on these matters for reasons which our difficult times do not allow me to explain. A word to the wise is enough. If they will peruse with some care the list of the descendants of Jeconiah given in 1 Chron. ch. 3 from verse 17 to the end of the chapter, and compare the Hebrew text with the Septuagint version, they will have no difficulty in seeing that these books were published after the second restoration of

---

[2] [David Kimḥi was a thirteenth-century French Jewish biblical exegete and defender of Maimonides.]

the city by Judas Maccabee when the descendants of Jeconiah had lost the throne, and not before then.

Note 22: 'he would be taken to Babylon as captive'. Thus no one could have suspected that Ezekiel's prophecy contradicted Jeremiah's prediction, as everyone suspected according to Josephus' narrative. But the event proved them both right.

Note 23: 'Nehemiah'. The historian himself testifies in chapter 1 verse 1 that the greater part of this book is taken from the book that Nehemiah wrote. But there can be no doubt that the passage from chapter 8 to chapter 12 verse 26, and also the last two verses of chapter 12 inserted as a parenthesis into the words of Nehemiah, were added by the historian who lived after Nehemiah.

Note 24: 'Ezra'. Ezra was the uncle of the first high priest, Joshua (see Ezra ch. 7 v. 1 and 1 Chron. ch. 6 v. 13, 14, 15), and accompanied Zerubbabel from Babylon to Jerusalem (see Nehem. ch. 12 v. 1). But it appears that when he saw the state of confusion among the Jews, he returned to Babylon, as also did some others (Nehem. ch. 1 v. 2), and remained there until the reign of Artaxerxes when, being granted his request, he went for a second time to Jerusalem. Nehemiah, too, went with Zerubbabel to Jerusalem in the time of Cyrus. See Ezra, ch. 2 v. 2 and 63, and compare with ch. 10 v. 2 and ch. 12 v. 1 of Nehemiah. As to the translation of the word '*Atirshata*' by 'ambassador', there is no authority for this, whereas it is quite certain that those Jews whose duty it was to attend the court were given new names. Thus Daniel was Balteshazzar, and Zerubbabel Sheshbazzar (see Dan. ch. 1 v. 7, Ezra ch. 1 v. 8 and ch. 5 v. 14). Nehemiah was called Atirshata, but by virtue of his office he was termed פֶּחָה—procurator or president. See Nehem. ch. 5 v. 14 and ch. 12 v. 26.

Note 25: 'that no canon of the Sacred Books existed before the Maccabees'. The Synagogue termed 'the Great' did not originate until after Asia had been subjugated by the Macedonians. As to the assertion made by Maimonides, R. Abraham ben David[3] and others, that the presidents of the Council were Ezra, Daniel, Nehemiah, Haggai, Zechariah etc., this is an absurd fiction, based only on a rabbinical tradition that the Persian empire lasted no more than 34 years. This is their only way of proving that the decrees of the Great Synagogue or Synod—which was composed of Pharisees only, and whose decrees were rejected by the Sadducees—were transmitted by prophets who had received them from other prophets all the way back to Moses, who had received them from God himself and had transmitted them orally, not in writing. But let the Pharisees cling to their belief with their wonted obstinacy. The wise, being well acquainted with the reasons for councils and Synods and knowing of the quarrels between Pharisees and Sadducees, can easily imagine the reasons for the summoning of that Great Synagogue or Council. This much is certain, that no prophets took part in that council, and that the decrees of the Pharisees, which they call 'traditions', derived their authority from that Council.

---

[3] [Abraham ben David was a twelfth-century Spanish Jewish historian and philosopher. Spinoza seems to be referring to the latter's historical treatise *Sefer Ha-Qabbalah* (*The Book of Tradition*).]

Chapter 11

Note 26: 'we therefore think'. Translators here render λογίζομαι as '*concludo*'—I infer, and they maintain that in Paul's writing the word λογίζομαι is synonymous with συλλογίζομαι, whereas in fact the Greek λογίζομαι has the same force as the Hebrew חשב—to reckon, think, consider. This meaning is in full agreement with the Syriac text. The Syriac translation (if indeed it is a translation, which is a matter of doubt since we know neither the translator nor the time of publication, and the vernacular language of the Apostles was none other than Syriac) renders this text of Paul as 'מתרעינן הכיל', which Tremellius correctly translates as '*arbitramur igitur*'—'we therefore think'. For the word 'רעינא' which derives from this verb means '*arbitratus*'—thinking. In Hebrew 'רעינא' is רְעוּתָא *reutha*—'will'. Therefore the Syriac word means 'we will' or 'we think'.

Note 27: 'the whole of Christ's doctrine'. In effect, the teachings of Jesus in the Sermon on the Mount, related in Matthew, chapter 5.

Chapter 15

Note 31: 'that simple obedience is a way to salvation'. That is, it is not reason but revelation that can teach us that it is enough for blessedness or salvation for us to accept the divine decrees as laws or commandments, and that there is no need to conceive them as eternal truths. This is made clear by what we have demonstrated in Chapter 4.

Chapter 16

Note 32: 'promise in all good faith'. In a civil state, where what is good and what is evil is decided by the right of the whole community, it is correct to make a distinction between deception with good intent (*dolus bonus*) and deception with malicious intent (*dolus malus*). But in a state of nature, where everyone is his own judge and possesses the perfect right to prescribe and interpret laws for himself and even to repeal them if he thinks this is to his advantage, it is impossible to conceive that anyone can act with malicious intent to deceive.

Note 33: 'everybody can be free as he wills'. A man can be free in any kind of state, for a man is free, of course, to the extent that he is guided by reason. Now (although Hobbes[4] thinks otherwise) reason is entirely in favour of peace; but

---

[4] [The only occasion in this work where Hobbes (1588–1679) is mentioned by name, although his influence is clear. Spinoza must have carefully studied his *De Cive*.]

peace cannot be secured unless the general laws of the state are kept inviolate. Therefore the more a man is guided by reason, that is, the more free he is, the more steadfastly he will observe the laws of the state and obey the commands of the sovereign whose subject he is.

Note 34: 'For nobody knows by nature'. When Paul says that men are without means of escape, he is speaking in merely human terms. For in chapter 9 v. 18 of the same Epistle he expressly teaches that God has mercy on whom he will and makes stubborn whom he will, and that men are without excuse not because they have been forewarned but because they are in God's power like clay in the hands of the potter, who from the same lump makes one vessel to honour and another vessel to dishonour. As for the divine natural law whose chief commandment, as we have said, is to love God, I have called it a law in the same sense as philosophers apply the term 'law' to the universal rules of Nature according to which all things come to pass. For love of God is not obedience but a virtue necessarily present in a man who knows God aright, whereas obedience has regard to the will of him who commands, and not to necessity and truth. Now since we do not know the nature of God's will, while we are quite certain that everything that happens comes to pass from God's power alone, it is only from revelation that we can know whether God wishes to receive honour from men like some temporal ruler. Furthermore, we have shown that the divine commandments appear to us as commandments or ordinances only as long as we do not know their cause. Once this is known, they cease to be commandments, and we embrace them as eternal truths, not as commandments; that is, obedience forthwith passes into love, which arises from true knowledge by the same necessity as light arises from the sun. Therefore by the guidance of reason we can love God, but not obey him; for by virtue of reason we can neither accept divine commandments as divine while not knowing their cause, nor can we conceive God as a ruler enacting laws.

Chapter 17

Note 35: 'as thereafter to be powerless'. Two common soldiers undertook to make one man Emperor of Rome in place of another, and they succeeded. Tacitus, *Histories*, Book 1.[5]

Note 36: '(Num. ch. 11 v. 28)'. In this passage two men are accused of prophesying in the camp, and Joshua urges their arrest. This he would not have done if it had been lawful for anyone to deliver God's oracles to the people without Moses' permission. But Moses thought fit to acquit the accused, and he rebuked Joshua for urging him to assert this royal right at a time when he was so weary of ruling that he preferred to die rather than continue to rule alone, as is clear from verses 14 and 15 of the same chapter. For he replied to Joshua thus: "Enviest thou for

---

[5] [A reference to the murder of Caligula and the accession of Claudius.]

my sake? Would God that all the Lord's people were prophets!" That is to say, would that the right to consult God were vested in the entire people, who would thus be sovereign. Therefore Joshua's error lay not in the question of right but in the occasion of its exercise, and he was rebuked by Moses in the same way as Abishai was rebuked by David when he urged David to condemn to death Shimei, who was undoubtedly guilty of treason. See 2 Sam. ch. 19 v. 22, 23.

Note 37: 'See Num. ch. 27 v. 21'. Verses 19 and 23 of this chapter are mistranslated in such versions as I have seen. These verses do not mean that Moses gave Joshua commands or instructions, but that he properly constituted or established him as captain. This turn of phrase is quite common in Scripture, as in Exod. ch. 18 v. 23, 1 Sam. ch. 13 v. 14, Josh. ch. 1 v. 9, 1 Sam. ch. 25 v. 30 and elsewhere.

Note 38: 'to recognise any other judge than God'. The Rabbis imagine that what is known as the Great Sanhedrin was instituted by Moses, and many Christians share in this delusion. Moses did indeed choose seventy colleagues to assist him in the task of government, being unable to bear alone the burden of the whole people. But at no time did he enact a law establishing a college of seventy members. On the contrary, he commanded that each tribe should appoint judges in the cities that God had given them, to decide lawsuits in accordance with the laws that he had laid down. If it should happen that the judges themselves were in doubt as to the law, they were to approach the high priest, as being the supreme interpreter of the laws, or the judge who was at that time their superior (for he had the right to consult the high priest) so as to settle the question according to the high priest's interpretation. If a lower judge should maintain that he was not bound to pass judgment in accordance with the opinion of the high priest as received from the high priest himself or from his own superior, he was to be condemned to death by whatever supreme judge had appointed him a subordinate judge. See Deut. ch. 17 v. 9. This person might be the commander-in-chief of all Israel, like Joshua, or he might be the captain of a single tribe (in whom, after the partition of the land was vested the right of consulting the high priest concerning the affairs of his tribe, of deciding on war or peace, of fortifying cities, of appointing judges and so on), or he might be the king, to whom all or some of the tribes had transferred their right.

In confirmation I could cite many instances from history, but I will confine myself to one of outstanding importance. When the Shilonite prophet appointed Jeroboam king, he thereby gave him the right of consulting the high priest and of appointing judges; in short, Jeroboam held over the ten tribes all the right that Rehoboam held over two tribes. Therefore Jeroboam could set up a supreme council of state at his court by the same right by which Jehoshaphat set up his council at Jerusalem (see 2 Chron. ch. 19 v. 8 on). For it is clear that Jeroboam, insofar as he was king by God's command, and consequently Jeroboam's subjects, were not required by the law of Moses to submit to the jurisdiction of Rehoboam, since they were not his subjects, and far less to the jurisdiction of the court established by Rehoboam at Jerusalem and subordinate to him. Thus a supreme court was established in each of the separate and independent divisions of the Hebrew state. Those who disregard the varied political arrangements of the Hebrews and fail to distinguish between them find themselves involved in many difficulties.

CHAPTER 19

Note 39: 'and lawfully impeach'. Here particular attention should be paid to my discussion of right in Chapter 16.

Hebrew Grammar

In Chapter 7 of the Theological-Political Treatise *Spinoza* indicates that one requirement for interpreting Scripture is a knowledge of its language, and with regard to the Hebrew Bible, that means a knowledge of Hebrew grammar and more. In fact, Spinoza studied Hebrew all his life and was acquainted with traditional Jewish commentaries on biblical Hebrew as well as grammars of biblical Hebrew and classical Latin, including the famous grammar by J. Buxtorf (the Thesaurus Grammaticus Linguae Sanctae Hebraeae of 1620) and those by his teachers R. Saul Morteira and R. Mannaseh ben Israel. Probably about the time Spinoza was completing the TTP (1669–1671), he began work on his own Hebrew grammar, a work that remained unfinished at his death. In their introduction to the Opera Posthuma, Lodewijk Meyer and Johan Bouwmeester explain that Spinoza began the grammar "at the request of some of his friends who very much studied the holy language," among whom was surely Meyer himself, the author of a famous Dutch dictionary and of Philosophia sacrae scripturae interpres (Philosophy the Interpreter of Scripture), a controversial treatise published a few years earlier (in 1666). Like some of his close associates, then, Spinoza deserves to be called a philologist and grammatical scholar as well as a philosopher and a scientist.

In the TTP Spinoza approaches religion and the Bible as a social scientist, and in that work and in the later Political Treatise, his discussion of the state and politics is also from a naturalistic point of view. The Hebrew Grammar reveals the same spirit. The Bible may be Spinoza's only evidence for Hebrew as a spoken, natural language used by Jews in biblical antiquity, but his goal is not to reveal the language's character as a sacred or mysterious system. Rather it is to understand its structure as a living language. His is a work "for those who desire to speak Hebrew, and not just chant it."

Spinoza intended the grammar to have two parts. Part I was to set out the letters of the Hebrew alphabet and to lay out the forms of verbs, nouns, and other parts of speech. Of special interest here were conjugations, declensions, vocalization, and so forth. Part II would then give an account of sentence structure, syntax, and so forth. Spinoza completed thirty-three chapters of Part I and none of Part II.

The grammar, while indebted to the work of medieval commentators like David Kimchi and recent grammarians like Buxtorf, is rather distinctive. Spinoza uses Latin as a model and so forces Hebrew into a Latinate pattern, with *conjugations, declensions, and other structures akin to those found in an inflected language. He also treats Hebrew as a noun-based language, a peculiarity given the standard tendency to focus on Hebrew's verbal character and the centrality of the triliteral root in Hebrew grammar. It is likely that Spinoza's grammatical enquiry, then, mirrors the commitments of his philosophical thinking overall. It is guided, on the one hand, by his scientific naturalism and, on the other, by his commitment to a priori reasoning akin to that found in geometry— or, in this case, in Latin, viewed by him as reflecting a pure, a priori structure.*

M.L.M.

CONTENTS

1. Of the Letters and Vowels in General
2. Of the Letters
3. Of the Vowels
4. Of the Accents
5. Of the Noun
6. Of the Inflection of Nouns
7. Of Masculine and Feminine Gender
8. Of the Construct Case of Nouns
9. Of the Twofold Use of the Noun
10. Of the Preposition and the Adverb
11. Of the Pronouns
12. Of the Infinitive Nouns
13. Of the Conjugation
14. Of Verbs
15. Of Passive Verbs
16. Of Active Verbs
17. Of Passive Intensive Verbs
18. Of the Derivative Active Verb
19. Of the Derivative Passive Verb
20. Of the Active Reflexive Verbs
21. Of the Passive Reflexive Verb
22. Of Verbs of the Second Conjugation
23. Of Verbs of the Third Conjugation
24. Verbs of the Fourth Conjugation
25. Verbs of the Fifth Conjugation
26. Composite Verbs
27. Verbs of the Sixth Conjugation
28. Verbs of the Seventh Conjugation
29. Verbs of the Eighth Conjugation
30. Of Defective Verbs
31. Another Class of Defectives
32. Concerning Deponent Verbs
33. Of the Nominative Participle

Notice to the Reader

The Concise Grammar of the Hebrew Language which is here offered to you, kind reader, the author undertook to write at the request of certain of his friends who were diligently studying the Sacred Tongue, inasmuch as they recognized him rightly as one who had been steeped in it from his earliest youth, was diligently devoted to it for many years afterward, and had achieved a complete understanding of the innermost essence of the language.

All who are acquainted with this great man will cherish and revere this book, although, like many of his other works, it is unfinished because of the untimely death of the author. We present it to you in its incomplete state, kind reader, because we do not doubt that the author's and our effort will be of great benefit to you and quite worthy of study by you.

CHAPTER 1

OF THE LETTERS AND VOWELS IN GENERAL

Since letters and vowels are the bases of all languages, we must first of all determine what among the Hebrews is a letter and what is a vowel. A *letter* is a sign of a sound made by the movement of the mouth that causes a certain sound to be heard. For example, א signifies that the origin of the sound is heard by the opening of the throat; ב shows the origin of the sound to be heard in the opening of the lips; ג by the end of the tongue and the palate, etc.

A *vowel* is a sign indicating a certain and determined sound. From which we learn that vowels among the Hebrews are not letters; and therefore among the Hebrews vowels are called *souls of letters*, and letters without vowels are *bodies without souls*. Indeed, to make the difference between letters and vowels more clearly intelligible, it is possible to explain it suitably by the example of a flute touched by fingers for playing. The vowels are the musical sound of the flute, the letters are the openings touched by the fingers. But enough of this.

CHAPTER 2

OF THE SHAPE, SIGNIFICANCE, NAMES, CLASSIFICATIONS, AND PECULIARITIES OF THE LETTERS

The Hebrews have twenty-two letters whose shape and order as they occur among the most ancient scribes is this:

אבגדהוזחטי, etc.

> א   A letter no other European language can explain. It indicates, as we have said, the opening of the throat. Its name is Aleph.

ב	b	The name is Bet.
ג	g	Gimel; if it is without a dot it is weak.
ד	d	Dalet; without a dot it is weak.
ה	h	called He. It indicates that the originating sound comes from the deepest part of the throat.
ו	v	Vav and also *w*; and I believe that it never was pronounced otherwise by the ancients; and also it is not a vowel but a letter indicating that the originating sound is heard in the lips.
ז	z	Zain.
ח	ch	Chet.
ט	t	Tet.
י		Yod. It indicates that the origin of the sound is heard in the middle of the tongue and the palate and, like the ו *w*, the י *i* is also sometimes without sound.
כ	k	Kaf, if it has a dot in the middle; otherwise it has the force of *ch* or the Greek χ.
ל	l	Lamed.
מ	m	Mem.
נ	n	Nun.
ס	s	Samech.
ע		Ayin.
פ	p	Pe, if it has a dot in the middle; otherwise it has the force of *ph*.
צ	ts	Tsade.
ק	q	Qof.
ר	r	Resh, weak in the middle of a word, harsh in the beginning.
ש	sh	Shin, if the dot is on the right bar; if it is on the left it is the same as Samech.
ת	th	(Thaw) weak; with a dot, however, it has the force of *t*.

Among all these letters there are five which are written differently in the beginning or the middle of a word and differently at the end of a word, namely כמנפצ. So the kaf, when it occurs at the end of a word, its bottom line is elongated thus ך; the mem, however, is closed up at the bottom thus ם; the remaining three, like the כ, are lengthened out thus: ןףץ. Finally also the Hebrews for the sake of brevity usually combine the א and ל thus ﭏ.

This is the Syriac script, which Ezra preferred over the ancient Hebrew letters, and which the Pharisees superstitiously followed in their holy writings. In reality the authors frequently used other scripts. See Buxtorf, Thesaur.[1]

Further, the letters were divided by the grammarians for greater usefulness into five classes, namely into gutturals, labials, dentals, linguals, and palatals. אהחע (ahacha) are called gutturals, בומף (bumaph) labials, גיכק (gichaq) palatals, דטלנת (datlenath) linguals, זסצרש (zastserash) dentals.

Every letter in the middle of a word must have either a long or a short or a very short vowel, except these four אהוי (ehevi), which are therefore called *mutes* or *quiescents*.

Hence it is that when a consonant needs to be doubled between two vowels, it is not actually doubled, but rather the doubling is indicated by a dot which is called דגש *dagesh*, like פקד instead of פקקד *piqqed*.

Gutturals occurring between two vowels are unable to be doubled because they indicate a certain opening of the throat and a form of breathing; thus, like the letter H among the Latins, so among the Hebrews gutturals between two vowels may not be doubled. Also the letter ר *r*, because it is always weak in the middle of a word, may likewise not be doubled, and on that account these five letters אהחער never have the dagesh point in them. Next it must be noted that although a dagesh indicates the doubling of letters between two vowels it is not always true in the reverse that every dagesh means the doubling of a letter. The same punctuation is also used to convert the בגדכפת *begadkephat* letters from weak into aspirate sounds as we have shown in its place. Finally, a dot at times occurs in the letter ה at the end of a word for reasons which I shall explain in its place, but then it is not called a dagesh, but a מפיק *mappiq*.

The letters בגדכפת at the beginning of a word are aspirate, that is, they are "dageshed" unless the last letter of the preceding word is one of the quiescents. For then, generally they are weak, unless the quiescent is a ה with a mappiq, or the preceding word ending in the quiescent letter has a great accent. Finally, letters of the same organ of speech are often substituted one for the other in the Scriptures, and an א for an ע, a ס for a ז, ב for פ, ט for a ת, etc. The reason for this, I think, is that the Scriptures were written by men of various dialects, and that now the dialects are not recognizable, namely from which tribe this or that dialect originated. That this language had this in common with the others is substantiated by Scripture itself. For the Ephraimites everywhere substituted a ס *samech* for a ש, letters which really are from the same organ of speech. Nevertheless, although in Sacred Scripture occasionally one letter is changed for another of the same organ, one may not now follow this example. For if it were otherwise, then the dialects would confuse the language.

Notes by Spinoza are indicated by asterisks. Notes by translator Maurice J. Bloom (main annotator for this work) and Michael L. Morgan are indicated by numerals and appear in brackets.

1. [Johannis Buxtorf, *Thesaurus Grammaticus Linguae Sanctae Hebraeae* . . . Bâle, 1651 (first edition, 1609), p. 2.—M.L.M.]

CHAPTER 3

Of the Vowels; to Wit, of Their Shape, Name, Significance, and Properties

Vowels, as we have said, are not letters among the Hebrews, but, as it were, *"souls of letters."* Therefore, they are either understood or indicated by punctuations adjoining the letters in this manner:

- בַּ If a line is drawn under the letter, this means that the sound heard after the letter is *a*, which is called a *patach* פתח.
- בָּ If the line also has a dot, it denotes the composite sound of *a* and *o* and is called a *kametz* קמץ.
- בֶּ If there are three points, the sound denoted is *e*, or as many believe, the Greek sound η, which is called a *segol* סגול.
- בֵּ If two dots are placed side by side, it denotes a sound composed of *a* and *i*, which is called a *tsere* צרי.
- בְּ If they are, however, placed one on top of the other, the sound denoted is of a short *e* and is called a *sheva* שוא.
- בִּ Next, if one dot is placed under a letter, it denotes that the sound to be heard after the letter is *i*, which is called *chirek* חירק.
- בֹּ But, if the dot is placed above the top of the letter, the sound denoted is like *o* and is called *cholem*.
- בֻּ If three points are under a letter at an oblique angle leaning toward the left, the sound is like upsilon υ and it is called *kibbutz* קבוץ.
- בוּ Finally, if a letter vav is added having a dot in the middle, the sound denoted is composed of *o* and *u*, like the Greek υ, and is called a *shurek* שורק.

The diphthong *ai* is indicated by a patach and a yod after it, like דְּבָרַי *debarai*, unless there is a great accent, of which more in the following chapter. The diphthong *au* is indicated by a kametz ָ followed by a yod and a vav, like דְּבָרָיו *debarau*, and also with a patach, like קַו *kau* (a line); Portuguese Jews,[1] however, usually pronounce it *debarav*. Finally, *eu* is expressed with a vav after a *tsere*, like שָׁלֵו *shaleu*. Whether in addition they had others I am not able to say for certain,

---

1. [Spinoza calls Portuguese Jews Lusitanian Jews after the ancient name of the area. —M.J.B.]

because for the most part we are ignorant of the manner of pronunciation of the ancients.

Every vowel sound is always heard after the letter, except if one of the three gutturals הח״ע occurs at the end of a word after a tsere, a chirek or a cholem, or a shurek. For then it is punctuated with a patach which is sounded before the letter and which is on that account usually called by the grammarians a *furtive patach*, like שֹׁמֵעַ *shomeahg*, גָּבוֹהַּ *gaboah*, פָּתוּחַ *patuach*, etc.

Usage frequently requires that some letters between two vowels should be doubled for certain reasons; and we have already said that this doubling is denoted by inserting a dagesh point into the letter to be doubled; and frequently it happens that the letter which the usage of the language requires to be doubled is one of the gutturals which cannot be doubled, as we have indicated in Chapter 2. Therefore, when that occurs, the preceding vowel is changed in this manner. If the antecedent vowel of the guttural letter to be doubled is a patach ־ , then the dagesh point which should be inserted into a guttural letter is placed under the patach ־ and it becomes a kametz ־ָ , like הָעוֹבֵר, *ha'ober* in place of הַעוֹבֵר; but in nouns before a ה and an ע the patach is changed into a segol ֶ like הֶעָנָן *he 'anan* in placc of הַעָנָן. If it is a chirek, then the dot is added to it and it becomes a tsere ֵ like מֵהֶם *mehem* in place of מִהֶם. Finally, if the vowel kibbutz precedes the guttural letter to be doubled, it is changed into a cholem וֹ or into a shurek וּ. But this is not universal; sometimes it remains unchanged; indeed the letter ו after a kibbutz can be doubled. And hence it is clear why the vowels kametz ־ָ , tsere ֵ , segol ֶ , cholem וֹ, and shurek וּ never occur before a doubled letter between two vowels — that is, before a dagesh point, which serves as double letters.

Vowels are properly divided into long and short; namely, a patach ־ is a short *a*, but a kametz ־ָ is both a long and a short vowel. It has the significance of either a long *a* or a short *o*, like פְּקֵדָה, *pakedah* where each is a long *a*, like גָּרְנִי *gorni*, where the kametz under the gimel is pronounced like a short *o*. A segol ֶ is short, whereas a tsere ֵ is long, and a sheva ְ is the shortest vowel; but a chirek ִ, if it is followed by a quiescent yod, is a long *i*; otherwise, it is short; a cholem וֹ is a long *o* and it generally has with it a quiescent vav and occasionally a ה or an א. A kibbutz ֻ is short and, finally, a shurek וּ is long.

I know that this kind of division displeases Rabbi Abraham de Balmes,[2] but without any reason; for that usage has established it to be so is evident from the following; the first thing that comes to mind is that a letter which is usually supplied by a dagesh may also be compensated by changing the preceding syllable from a short into a long one, even though the letter to be doubled is other than a guttural, like הֵתֵל *hethel* for הִתֵּל *hitthel* or הִתְתֵּל *hiththel*.

The vowel sheva ְ , because it is the shortest, is sometimes hastened over and adheres to the preceding syllable and sometimes is pronounced; the former נָח is called by the Hebrew grammarians Nach *quiescent* (silent sheva), and the latter נָע Na' *mobile* (moving sheva).

---

2. [Abraham Ben Meir de Balmes (1440–1523), author of the well-known grammar "Mikneh Abraham."]

A sheva ְ is pronounced when it occurs at the beginning of a word, or in the middle after a long vowel, like בְּרֵאשִׁית *bereshith*, where the sheva ְ under the בּ is pronounced, because it occurs at the beginning of the word; also like the following, because they occur in the middle of a word after long vowels, namely פָּקְדָה *pakedah*; בָּרְכוּ *berechu*; יִירְאוּ *yireu*; פּוֹקְדִים *pokedim*; הוּבְאוּ *hubeu*. If on the other hand, two shevas follow each other consecutively, the second is pronounced as in the word תִּפְקְדוּ, *tiphkedu*, where the first sheva is silent and the second is pronounced. And hence it is that a sheva noted under a letter punctuated by a dagesh is also to be pronounced, like פִּקְדוּ *pikkedu*. For the point in the קּ denotes that the ק is doubled and the first one is silenced. And for the same reason also a sheva is pronounced when one letter is in the middle of a word, but is not doubled between two vowels, like הִנְנִי *hineni*, where the sheva under the first נ is pronounced. For if it had been silenced, then the נ also would have been silenced and would have to adhere to the preceding syllable, and in place of הִנְנִי *hineni*, it would have been written הִנִּי *hinni*.

For the rest, the remaining shevas are always silenced, and it should be especially noted that we expressly stated that every sheva which is pronounced occurs either at the beginning or in the middle of a word. But at the end it is never pronounced.

That it may be better understood, let this be noted, that every sheva is an absolute vowel which cannot be heard but must always adhere either to the previous or succeeding vowel; and so it is that no monosyllable is punctuated by a sheva. Hence it is apparent that a silent sheva is nothing more than the shortest *e*, adhering to the preceding syllable; however, the pronounced sheva is nothing else than the shortest *e* adhering to the following syllable; that is why when it is found before a syllable it is on that account to be pronounced even more distinctly. Whence it follows that in the beginning of a word it is impossible to adhere to the preceding syllable. At the end, on the other hand, it is impossible to adhere to the following syllable; and what is more, at the end of a word a dagesh is always silenced, whether after a long syllable or after a short one, whether under a dageshed letter or under a weak one, and finally, whether only one or two occur together.

However, when it happens that a sheva occurs in the middle of a word after a long syllable, the rule of pronunciation requires that it adhere to the succeeding; and if there should be two shevas then the first adheres to the preceding and the second to the succeeding syllable. Further, it is also evident why at the beginning of a word there are never two shevas and also not in the middle after a long syllable. For two shevas cannot adhere to a succeeding syllable.

Gutturals do not have a pronounced sheva ְ, and they rarely have a silent sheva; but instead they have three intermediate vowels, between the short and the shortest, which are thus designated ֲ ֱ ֳ, and are called חֲטָפִים *chatefim*. The first denotes a vowel shorter than a patach; the second a vowel shorter than a short kametz or a short *o*; the third, finally, midway between a segol, short *e*, and a shortest sheva; and these are distinguished from shevas in that they never occur before a simple sheva, and that they not only do not follow one after the other in the beginning, but also not in the middle and not at the end of a word; in the rest, however, they agree with all shevas, and also in this, that they do not occur alone, nor do they have an accent under them.

These are the main regulations to be observed with respect to vowels, and we especially reiterate the rule about shevas, namely that two shevas never occur at the beginning of a word, and that gutturals never have a pronounced sheva under them, and rarely a silent one. For their usage is remarkable.

CHAPTER 4

OF THE ACCENTS

The rules which are usually transmitted concerning the accents are more of a hindrance than an aid to students of the Hebrew language. They should be tolerated only if they facilitate a proper understanding of the pronunciation of the language. But if you should consult the experts they would all be forced to admit that they do not know the reason for so great a number of accents. But to me it seems that there is a valid reason for it. At first I was strongly of the opinion that their inventor introduced them not only for the raising and the lowering of the voice and to adorn speech but also to indicate animated expression, which is usually produced by a change of voice, by the expression of the face, the movement of the body, the spreading of the hands, the winking of the eyes, the stamping of the feet, a curve of the mouth, a motion of the eyelids, spreading of the lips, and the various other gestures which aid a speaker to make clear his thoughts to his hearers. One tone of the voice expresses irony while another tone indicates simplicity. There is a tone in which we praise someone, another in which we express admiration, still another for vituperation, and yet another for mockery. Thus we change our voice and expression for every emotion. Nevertheless the originators of the letters in all languages failed to indicate these expressions in the written forms of speech. This is due to the fact that we can express our meaning much better orally than in writing. I suspected that the originator of the accents in the Hebrew language wanted to correct this fault. But when I examined the matter further I was unable to find this to be true. Indeed they succeeded rather to confuse not only these animated emotions but also speech itself. There is no distinction when the Scriptures speak ironically or when with simplicity and the same accent has different meanings in the composition of the parts of speech, and it also has the properties of a punctuation mark, and of a semicolon and of a double punctuation. So that it would seem that there is still a lack of accents with all the great number of them. Therefore I now believe that their introduction came after the Pharisees introduced the custom of reading the Bible in public assemblies every Sabbath in order that it should not be read too rapidly (as is usually done in the repetition of prayers). And for this reason I shall leave the minute regulations about them to the Pharisees and Massorites, and mention here only that which seems to have some purpose.

The accent serves to separate or join language and also to raise or depress a syllable. There is no accent indicating the end of a verse or a clause. These two points: הָאָ֫רֶץ usually indicate a sign which is called a סִילּוּק *siluk*, and generally, not always, as we have already shown, it declares the statement to be completed.[1] But the parts of single sentences are separated by accents; and I understand these "parts of sentences" to consist of not only verbs but also cases of the noun. To be sure, the accent which here and there has the property of a comma is used also to separate the nominative and the verb from the accusative, and from the other cases. Understand, when the accusative follows the nominative; therefore, if the accusative is placed between the verb and the noun, then the verb, the accusative, and the nominative constitute only one part of the verse and are like two verbs which are united *and* joined together, and they have no other noun except the nominative case put between them. And if a verse has only one part to be separated it is separated by an accent which is called טַרְחָא *tarcha*, which is denoted below the letter thus כּ. But if it has two parts to be divided, then the first is denoted by a טַרְחָא *tarcha*, the second also has an accent which is called אֶתְנָח *athnach*, which is denoted under the letter thus הֿ like אֱלֹהִים; and this accent is preeminent among all which separate sentences into parts, as will become clear from what follows. A sentence may have only one athnach, except only rarely it may have two. But if a verse should have three parts to be divided, then the first is denoted by a טרחא *tarcha*, the second by an אתנח *athnach*, and the third again by a טרחא *tarcha*. If it has four, however, the first is generally denoted by two dots above the word, like דֶּ֫שֶׁא *deshe*, which accent is usually called זָקֵף קָטֹן *zakef katon*, the second טרחא, the third אתנח and the fourth again טרחא. Further, if in a sentence five parts are to be separated, then the first generally should be denoted by a dot above the word which is called רְבִ֫יעַ *rabi'a*, like אֱ֗לֹהִים, the second by a זקף קטון, the third by a טרחא, the fourth again by a אתנח, and the fifth by a טרחא. Finally, if there are six, then the first is a רביע, the second זקף קטון, the third טרחא, the fourth אתנח, the fifth again זקף קטון, and finally the sixth טרחא. And in this manner, when still more parts which should be separated occur, many other signs are usually adduced, but the properties of זקף קטון and the רביע are plainly similar; and they therefore often also displace one another; but I will refrain from speaking of these, as also of those which only serve to indicate an accent which is part of a phrase in which there are as a consequence of the divisions, some of these which are for this reason called by the grammarians *serviles*. But it should be pointed out that the טרחא serves not only to divide parts of sentences but also to indicate a סִילּוּק and an אֶתְנָח. For after a טַרְחָא no dividing accent may follow except an אתנח or a סילוק and contrarily

---

1. [We call this *Sof Pasuk*.]

there is no אתנח or סילוק סילוק which is not preceded by a טרחא, the reason for which we will tell presently. A word that has no accent either above or below is usually joined with the succeeding word by a straight line which the grammarians call a מקף *makaf*, like כי־טוֹב *ki-tob*.

Next, the accents serve, as we have said, both to elevate and depress a syllable. As we have already shown in these very examples, they should be placed either above or below the letter of the word whose vowel is to be elevated or depressed. Thus in דֶּשֶׁא the זקף קטון is above the ד because it is pronounced *déshe* and not *deshé*; on the other hand אֱלֹהִים has the רביע above the ה because it is pronounced *elohím* and not *elóhim*. Every word whose accent is below or above its last syllable is called מִלְרַע *millera'*, which means *from below*; if, however, it is above or below the penultimate, it is called מִלְעֵיל *mille'el*, which means *from above*. But when a siluk is denoted neither below nor above but after a word, as also a makaf, then on that account the word before the siluk and makaf is denoted by a small line below it, namely under the syllable in which the accent should have been, like הָאָרֶץ *haaretz*, where, before the siluk, under the א there is a small line indicating that the accent should have been under the kametz. So also עֹשֵׂה־פְרִי *'oseh-peri* has a little line, before the מקף, under the ע, indicating that the cholem should be stressed. This line is usually called a גַּעְיָא *ga'ya*. It is not used, however, if the word before the makaf has only one vowel, like כִּי־טוֹב.

Polysyllables usually have two accents. One is either in the ultimate or penultimate, indicated as we have shown by whether the word is *mille'el* or *millera'*; the other is in the antepenultimate or its antecedent, indicating the syllable to be stressed, like בְּמוֹעֲדֵיכֶם הַגּוֹעָדִים. And this accent is frequently a ga'ya, appearing almost always before a composite sheva. Further, you will observe not rarely that polysyllables have three accents, like וַיְבָרְכֵהוּ.

Moreover, in order to know which syllables should be stressed or lengthened, or where words should be marked by two or three accents, these rules should first be observed, namely: all vowels before a pronounced sheva are marked with a גַּעְיָא *ga'ya* (of which I spoke in the previous chapter), that is, it is lengthened somewhat the better to know that the sheva which follows it belongs to the following syllable whence it follows that every vowel before a compound sheva, be it a short or a long vowel, should be marked with this accent, like נַעֲשֶׂה. For a compound sheva can never be silenced, that is, it belongs not to the preceding but to the succeeding syllable. Next, it follows that a long vowel before a simple sheva should be stressed or it should be marked with this accent, so that it will be clearly understood that the sheva was not lost from it but belongs to the succeeding syllable. Hence, בֵּרְכוּ, פָּקְדָה, הוּבְאוּ, שֹׁמְרִים are marked with the accent גַּעְיָא; and also הִנְנִי, although it is short, yet on account of the succeeding sheva its pronunciation is lengthened. But although a sheva under a dageshed letter should also be pronounced, nevertheless, the vowel preceding it is not marked with a ga'ya unless the letter to be doubled is one of those which do not admit a dagesh point, or may not be doubled, of which see Chapter 2; and I suppose that this is because a dagesh means that the first of the doubled letters (the assumed letter) belongs to the preceding vowel, its sheva having been swallowed up with it; and what is more a vowel before a sheva under a dageshed letter should be considered like a vowel which is followed by two shevas, the first of which, as we have said above, should be silent, and the second pronounced, or the first of which should belong to the preceding, and the second to the succeeding syllable.

Next, if a vowel after any sheva requires to be lengthened then the vowel before the same sheva is lengthened; and this rule is always true, whether the sheva is expressed or assumed; for example, הַכְּנַעֲנִי, since the patach after the simple sheva should be lengthened on account of the composite sheva after it, for the same reason also the patach before the same simple sheva is lengthened. Thus also תִּתְנַחֲלוּ, וַיִּשְׁתַּחֲווּ, etc., for this very same reason have two ga'yas each. And I say the same is true when a sheva is assumed, like מִמָּחֳרַת, where under each מ there is a ga'ya because it should be read מִמְמָחֳרַת the kametz indeed does have a sheva before it, which is compensated by the dagesh point, and, because of the composite sheva following it, it should be lengthened. The vowel before this sheva that is compensated by a dagesh point is also lengthened. So וִיבָרֶכְךָ, הַנַּעֲרָה, בַּמַּחֲנֶה, הַמַּעֲשֶׂה, and many others of this type are denoted by a doubling of the ga'ya.

Two long vowels without an accent or a ga'ya in the same word are not to be found. If indeed the penultimate and antepenultimate syllables should be long, or if an accent should be necessary in the antepenultimate, or if in the ultimate, then the antepenultimate will have a ga'ya, like אָנֹכִי whose kametz is lengthened when the accent is in the ultimate, otherwise, namely when the accent is in the penultimate, it is omitted, like דָּן אָנֹכִי; thus וַהֲקִימֹתִי, נְשִׂיאֵיהֶם, הַכּוֹכָבִים, etc., have a ga'ya in the antepenultimate; but if a word should have many long vowels it will always be observed that no two long vowels occur without either an accent or a ga'ya, like בִּשְׁבוּעֹתֵיכֶם.

And this should be noted, a kibbutz sometimes replaces a shurek, and then it should be considered as long, like מִשְׁבֻּעָתִי where, because the shurek of the noun שְׁבוּעָה has been changed into a kibbutz, the kibbutz is lengthened like a long vowel; otherwise it is always short.

Next, it should be noted that a short vowel to which a sheva adheres is to be considered as a long one, like מוֹלַדְתִּי מְנֻקְתָּהּ, etc., where a long before a short, to which a sheva adheres, is lengthened, like a long before a long, which does not have an accent; thus also the two first vowels in הִתְיַצְּבוּ are long because a sheva adheres to each, the first being expressed and the latter, however, compensated by the dagesh in the צ. Short vowels are excepted when they frequently replace a simple sheva so that no two should occur at the beginning of a word, as we have already pointed out in Chapter 3, for example, the first vowel in תִּפְקְדוּ is short because it is in place of a short sheva, because it usurps the place of a sheva. It happens then that a short vowel before a short vowel is lengthened because the second short is put in place of a compound sheva to which, as we have said, a ga'ya always antecedes, like וַיֶּחֱרְדוּ, because it is written in place of וַיֶּחֶרְדוּ.

Finally, a ו vav before a י yod with a ַ patach is denoted variously, with and without a ga'ya, like וַיְדַבֵּר and וַֽיְדַבֵּר.

And these are the principal rules of this accent as far as it is possible to know them from the vowels alone. There still remains another to be recognized concerning the preposition, which we will explain in its place.

For the rest, I do not have anything to say about the fact that the Jews, because of the musical accent ~, which they call a *zarka*, now bring in a ga'ya into the syllable antecedent to it, because it is not followed by those who either wish to speak Hebrew or to chant it.

This, however, should be noted, that frequently another accent is put in place of a ga'ya; indeed, some words have two accents. And one of their syllables is lengthened, which would otherwise not be lengthened because of the preceding rules.

And this, I say, therefore, is because two different accents which should precede servile accents follow one another alternately only rarely; for example, after an athnach a siluk does not follow immediately, and not a זָקֵף קָטֹן and vice versa after a siluk only most rarely will a zakef katon follow, and not an athnach. But if the word which follows one of these accents has to have one of them, then at that place two accents are denoted, and one usually lengthens its syllable, however, it would otherwise not be lengthened, like Isaiah chap. 7, vs. 18, יֹאמְרֵי מִצְרַיִם וְלִדְבוֹרָה where וְלִדְבוֹרָה, because of the zakef katon, has another accent over the ל, its syllable being lengthened contrary to the general rule, on account of the preceding athnach. Thus also Numbers chap. 28, vs. 20 and 28 וּמִנְחָתָם, because it follows immediately after a siluk, has two accents, and the vowel below the מ, contrary to the general rule, is lengthened; and also Deuteronomy chap. 12, vs. 1 לְרִשְׁתָּהּ כָּל־הַיָּמִים. And for this reason, also, Deuteronomy chap. 13, vs. 12, וְכָל־יִשְׂרָאֵל contrary to the general rule of the makaf, an accent is put above כָּל; and in this manner many examples are found and many more of them where the ga'ya is changed into an accent for one reason or another.

Finally, it should be noted that among the dividing accents there is one which is called קַדְמָא *kadma*, which is always denoted above the end of a word in this manner הָעוֹלִים and in this way is it indeed differentiated from another of the serviles which is called אַזְלָא *azla*, which is always denoted above the syllable in which the accent should be. If then the word accented by this קַדְמָא should be denoted as *mille'el*, it needs another accent which indicates that the accent should be in the penultimate; like יָלִים, in case that this accent should be denoted, over the dalet the accent אַזְלָא should also be denoted so that it will be known that the word is *mille'el* מִלְעֵל.

In addition to this, I have found another reason why a word may be denoted by a dual accent; namely when a *millera'* word, for reasons I shall mention later, reverts to a *mille'el*, like the syllables before being held, the accent remains in the ultimate, and the penultimate where there should also be an accent is denoted by another accent. But this rule is plainly useless for the second accent is of no use whatever.

And now it is time to show which words have an accent in the ultimate and which in the antepenultimate, that is, which should be מִלְעֵיל and which מִלְרַע; but since this cannot be discerned from vowels and letters alone, I shall postpone the matter until I shall come to the verbs. Here I will add only this, namely that the athnach and the siluk often render words which are *millera'* into *mille'el*. That is to say when their syllables, both ultimate and antepenultimate, are long, as when אָנֹכִי is designated by accent athnach or siluk, it can be rendered מִלְעֵיל, like אָנֹכִי דָן. But if the penultimate should be a sheva which, as we have already said, never has an accent, then the verbs change the ׃ into a kametz and nouns into a ֶ. Thus, if פָּקְדוּ is denoted with an athnach the sheva under the ק changes into a ָ and it becomes פָּקָדוּ; but, in place of שְׁמָךְ, if it has an athnach, it is שְׁמֶךְ. In participles of the feminine gender, however, it changes into both a segol and a kametz; and this also happens when the accent should be זָקֵף קָטוֹן.

Next, it should be noted that the accent athnach and the siluk destroy the properties of a dividing accent before them and, as it were, snatch them away. Whence it is that the only dividing accent which may precede these two accents is a tarcha which, therefore, indicates that an athnach or siluk follows and which also, therefore, does not have the properties of a dividing accent; for it does not render the words מִלְעֵיל and it can often be followed by a zakef katon or another dividing accent and it may be followed immediately after itself by an athnach or siluk. Wherefore, with what we have said above, that two dividing accents do not follow themselves immediately, it is understood concerning all except the טַרְחָא which, as we have said, has lost on that account the dividing properties of an athnach and siluk.

CHAPTER 5

OF THE NOUN

Among the Latins speech is divided into eight parts, but it is doubtful if among the Hebrews it is divided into so many parts. For all Hebrew words, except for a few interjections and conjunctions and one or two particles, have the force and properties of nouns. Because the grammarians did not understand this they considered many words to be irregular which according to the usage of the language are most regular, and they were ignorant of many things which are necessary to know for a proper understanding of the language. Whether they resolved that Hebrews had as many parts of speech as the Latins or less, we will, however, refer to all of them, excepting, as we have said, only the interjections and conjunctions, and one or two particles, as nouns. The reason for this and to what extent this makes the language easily understood will become clear from the following.

I shall now explain what I understand by a noun. By a noun I understand a word by which we signify or indicate something that is understood. However, among things that are understood there can be either things and attributes of things, modes and relationships, or actions, and modes and relationships of actions. Hence, we sum up easily the various kinds of nouns. For example, the noun אִישׁ is a *man*; חָכָם *learned*, גָּדוֹל *big*, etc., are attributes of a man; הֹלֵךְ *walking*, יוֹדֵעַ *knowing* are modes; בֵּין *between*, תַּחַת *under*, עַל *above*, etc., are nouns which show the relationship a man has to other things. Thus הָלוֹךְ *walking* is a noun of action which has no relationship to time. This must here be noted: the mode which the Latins call infinitive is among the Hebrews a pure unadulterated noun, and therefore an infinitive knows nothing about present, nor past, nor any time whatever. Next מְהֵרָה *quickly* is a mode of motion; הַיּוֹם *today*, מָחָר *tomorrow*, etc., are relationships of time which also express other modes.

There are then six kinds of nouns: 1. The substantive noun, which is divided into the proper and the common, as noted. 2. The adjective. 3. The relative or preposition. 4. The participle. 5. The infinitive. 6. The adverb. To these the pronoun is added because it takes the place of the substantive noun, like אֲנִי *I*, אַתָּה *thou*, הוּא *he*, etc.

For the rest, however, this should be pointed out: that by means of a proper substantive noun it is possible to indicate only a single individual, for each and every individual has a proper noun for himself only and so every action; and thence it is that the proper substantive noun and that the infinitive and the adverb, because they are like adjectives of action, with which they agree in number, are expressed only in the singular. The rest, however, are expressed both in the singular and plural. I say *"the rest"* for prepositions also have the plural number, of which see Chapter 10. Next, people, and especially the Hebrews, are accustomed to grant all things human attributes, like *the earth hears, is attentive*, etc., and perhaps for this or another reason all names of things are divided into masculines and feminines. But how to recognize this and for what reason a noun is inflected from the single number into the plural we shall speak of in the following chapter.

CHAPTER 6

OF THE INFLECTION OF NOUNS FROM SINGULAR INTO PLURAL

Nouns are inflected from singular into plural in the masculine by adding a long chirek and ם, and in the feminine a long *o* and ת. For example, גַּן *a garden*, because it is in the masculine gender, has the plural גַּנִּים. So from עֵץ *a tree*, אֹח

a brother, it is עֵצִים, אַחִים; but, אוֹת *a sign*, because it is in the feminine gender, has the plural אוֹתוֹת, and so נֵר *a candle*, נֵרוֹת, and עוֹר *a skin*, עוֹרוֹת, etc. Certain things are excepted which, although masculines, are inflected like feminines in the plural and contrarily feminines which are inflected like masculines, and certain things which are inflected in both ways, like אָבוֹת *fathers* from the singular אָב *a father*, which is in the masculine gender. Contrarily, נָשִׁים *women* is a feminine noun which lacks a singular and ends like a masculine; but הֵיכָל *a temple* ends both ways, namely הֵיכָלִים and הֵיכָלוֹת. Further, it is noted of neuter nouns that they are declined like feminines, like גְּדוֹלוֹת.

The second reason why vowels are modified is the presence of three long vowels in a word which, if it is not מִלְעֵיל, must therefore have two accents; moreover, the penultimate syllable that precedes chirek and cholem cannot be punctuated by patach unless the word is *mille'el*, etc. The catalogue of all these nouns is found at the end of the book; I decided that it was not worth the bother to put them here, for they are learned more easily through usage than by rules.

Next, nouns which end in a ה, whether they are masculine or feminine, omit the ה and ת with the last syllable, like עָלֶה *a leaf*, plural עָלִים, and נְקֵבָה *a female* נְקֵבוֹת, אִשָּׁה *a woman* אִשּׁוֹת. It should be noted that the feminine ending in a ה frequently changes the ה into ת and the preceding two syllables into twin segols ֶ ֶ, or, if it is accented athnach or siluk, into a kametz ָ and a segol ֶ. Thus עֲטָרָה *a crown* becomes עֲטֶרֶת, and with the athnach or siluk עֲטָרֶת. Also from פּוֹקְדָה *visiting* it becomes פּוֹקֶדֶת and פּוֹקָדֶת. But if the penultimate letter is ח or ע, then the syllables are changed into patach, like שׁוֹמַעַת *hearing* and בֹּרַחַת *fleeing*, in place of שְׁמָעָה and בְּרָחָה. This also takes place with substantives, like צִפַּחַת. Whence it is that all feminine nouns of this form that end in ת are inflected into plurals in the same manner as those which end in ה.

In addition to this, nouns generally also change vowels in the plural; namely, if the penultimate should be a ָ kametz it is generally changed into a sheva, like דָּבָר *a word* דְּבָרִים *words*, זָקֵן *an elder* זְקֵנִים *elders*, שָׂמֵחַ *a joyful one* שְׂמֵחִים *joyful ones*, נָקִי *a pure one* נְקִיִּים *pure ones*, רָחוֹק *a distant one* רְחוֹקִים *distant ones*, בָּרוּךְ *a blessed one* בְּרוּכִים *blessed ones*. Thus the penultimate kametz ָ (for example: זִכָּרוֹן *a memory* and גִּלָּיוֹן *a volume*) is changed into a sheva and becomes זִכְרוֹנוֹת, and גִּלְיוֹנִים. But if the ultimate should be a kametz or a monosyllabic noun, then the ָ generally remains unchanged or sometimes changes into a patach; like כּוֹכָב *a star* כּוֹכָבִים *stars*, שַׂר *a prince* שָׂרִים *princes*, יָם *a sea* יַמִּים *seas*, שׁוֹשָׁן *a rose* שׁוֹשַׁנִּים *roses*. To these, also, should be referred those which end in a ה because in the plural, as we have already said, they omit the last syllable together with the ה and they should change exactly like monosyllables or like those whose last syllable is a kametz; example: שָׂדֶה *a field*, קָנֶה *a reed*, etc., because they omit the segol ֶ with the ה in the plural follow the rule of monosyllables, and retain the ָ in the plural, namely שָׂדוֹת *fields*, and קָנִים *reeds*; and so also מַמְלָכָה *a kingdom*, because it omits the ultimate ָ with the ה in the plural it retains the penultimate in the plural, like those whose ultimate is a ָ and is inflected מַמְלָכוֹת *kingdoms*. For this reason also those which end in a ת retain in the plural the penultimate ָ, like תּוֹלַעַת *a worm* תּוֹלָעִים *worms*; indeed, although the last syllable is not omitted, the kametz ָ, however, remains, like זָוִית *an angle* זָוִיוֹת *angles,* עָמִית *a companion* עֲמִיתִים *companions,* גָּלוּת *a captivity* גָּלֻיוֹת *captivities.*

The penultimate tsere also changes into a sheva, but before a cholem and a shurek it is retained, as עֵנָב *a grape* עֲנָבִים *grapes* changes the tsere into a sheva; but אֵלוֹן retains the tsere and is inflected אֵלוֹנִים. Further, a noun whose last vowel is a tsere ֵ changes it into a sheva if the vowel antecedent to it is one of those which are always retained in the plural or which are not changed into a ָ, like מַקֵּל *a stick* מַקְלוֹת *sticks,* פּוֹקֵד *a visiting* פּוֹקְדִים *visitings,* עִוֵּר *a blind man* עִוְּרִים *blind men,* but after a sheva or a syllable which is changed into a sheva, the tsere is retained like זָקֵן *an elder* זְקֵנִים *elders,* זְאֵב *a wolf* זְאֵבִים *wolves,* etc.

Monosyllables and disyllables which end in a ה or a ת retain the tsere, like נֵר *a candle* נֵרוֹת *candles,* עֵד *a witness* עֵדִים *witnesses,* רֵעֶה *a friend* רֵעִים *friends,* שְׁאֵלָה *a question* שְׁאֵלוֹת *questions.*

Besides this there are certain monosyllables whose tsere is changed into a chirek, but these we are reserving for the catalogue together with the other special exceptions promised at the end of the book.

A penultimate segol changes into a sheva but an ultimate into a kametz, that is because all nouns in plural are *millera'* and all those whose penultimate is a segol ֶ are *mille'el*. And so, if the second segol were retained in the plural, then the accent would have to be in the penultimate contrary to common usage in the plural. For this reason, then, from מֶלֶךְ *a king* it is מְלָכִים *kings,* אֶבֶן *a stone* אֲבָנִים *stones,* צֶדֶק *justice* צְדָקוֹת *justices,* זֶבַח *a sacrifice* זְבָחִים *sacrifices,* נֶחָמָה *a consolation* נְחָמוֹת *consolations,* חֵטְא *a sin* חֲטָאִים *sins,* בֹּקֶר *a morning* בְּקָרִים *mornings.* And this change of the ultimate segol into a kametz and the penultimate into a sheva is plainly an analogue. We have indeed shown that polysyllables which end in a ה frequently change the ה into a ת and the vowels into double segol, like עֲטָרָה into עֲטֶרֶת; פְּקֻדָּה into פְּקֻדַּת. Next, as in the preceding case, this too, is to be noted, that a noun which ends in a ה or a ת since both the ה and the ת of the ultimate syllable are left out in the plural, the penultimate segol obtains the nature of the ultimate and is changed into a ָ, except for those whose penultimate segol is really used in place of a sheva, as are all participles and the nouns formed from them. E.g., פֹּקֶדֶת in place of פֹּקְדָה and תּוֹלֶדֶת in place of תּוֹלְדָה are used because of the athnach or siluk accent; but in the plural they again receive a sheva, like פֹּקְדוֹת, תּוֹלְדוֹת. Finally, a penultimate segol to which a sheva is joined cannot be changed into a sheva for no two shevas should occur in the beginning of a word; and on that account it is either retained in the plural or changed into a patach, like אֶשְׁנָב *a lattice* אֶשְׁנָבִים[1] *lattices,* מֶרְכָּבָה *a chariot* מֶרְכָּבוֹת *chariots.* When a cholem comes before a segol it changes into a sheva, like בֹּקֶר *a morning* in the plural בְּקָרִים, אֹהֶל *a tent* אֹהָלִים, etc. Certain ones are excepted, of which in the catalogue; and in addition certain ones are monosyllables which occasionally change it into a kametz like יוֹם *a day* יָמִים *days* plural, רֹאשׁ *a head* רָאשִׁים *heads,* but more often the cholem is retained, for גּוֹי *a tribe* has the plural גּוֹיִם and אוֹר *a light*

---

1. [So Spinoza has the plural, but it should be אֲשְׁנַבִּים in the plural.]

אוּרִים, etc.[2] and as in those which end in ת and have a double segol, like פֹּקֶדֶת. A patach nowhere is changed in the plural unless before a י, like יַיִן *wine* יֵינוֹת *wines*, זַיִת *an olive* זֵיתִים *olives*. Also בַּהֶרֶת is in the plural בֶּהָרוֹת.

The chirek always remains unchanged, except for those to which we referred in the preceding rules which omit it in the plural and besides this a very few nouns which are referred to in the catalogue. And I speak here only of the chirek proper but not of the one which is placed at the beginning of a word before a sheva for the reason that two shevas should not occur in the beginning. They are recognized from the fact that they have a paragogic ה at the end, namely אִמְרָה *a saying* used in place of אֹמֶר and so in the plural it is אֲמָרוֹת. So also דִּמְעָה *a tear*, because it is substituted for דֶּמַע, is in the plural דְּמָעוֹת. For, as we have already shown, an ultimate segol ֶ is changed into a kametz ָ and an ultimate ָ kametz in the plural should be retained; but a penultimate cholem and ֶ are changed into a sheva.

The kibbutz and shurek are never changed in the plural; however, the shurek has this to be noted, that words ending in ות do not always drop the shurek in the plural like the remaining nouns ending in a ה and ת, which always, as we have said, drop the ultimate syllable in the plural. For מַלְכוּת *kingdom* is in the plural מַלְכֻיּוֹת and חֲנוּת *a shop* חֲנֻיּוֹת.

Finally, a sheva cannot change for any other reason than that no two shevas should occur at the beginning. For we see in the majority of cases that the changes are from long into short vowels. However, the fact that פְּרִי *fruit* is in the plural פֵּרוֹת and כְּלִי *a vessel* כֵּלִים shows only that the letter י in the singular is paragogic and that is why the tsere which otherwise would be used here has been changed into a sheva; and when the paragogic י drops out in the plural, then the tsere remains in the plural, or, better, it returns again.

By these rules anyone at all may learn easily to inflect nearly all singulars into plurals, and to recognize the singular from the plural. It remains now to add something about the dual number.

In addition to the plural certain nouns are also inflected into the dual number by adding these letters, whether they are masculine or feminine: י and ם and the vowels patach and chirek; like יוֹם *a day* יוֹמַיִם *two days*, whose plural is יָמִים, שָׁנָה *a year* שְׁנָתַיִם *two years*. And in this manner it was possible, observing the rules of the pioneers of the language, to inflect all nouns, had not the latter ones neglected this by using this termination to express in the plural many things which are naturally dual or which consist of two parts, like יָד *a hand*, plural יָדַיִם *yadaim*, instead of יָדוֹת *yadoth*; אֹזֶן *an ear*, plural אָזְנַיִם *ears*, and thus with other things that are dual. Further, because *tongs* constitute two parts, they are called מֶלְקָחַיִם and *shears* מִסְפָּרַיִם.[3]

For this reason, then, it is not now permissible to use this ending to indicate the dual number, except only in those nouns which are found in the Bible thus to reflect the dual number.

---

2. [The first edition here adds wrongly "otherwise it is always retained."]
3. [Thus in the Holy Scriptures, but it should be מִסְפָּרַיִם.]

CHAPTER 7

OF THE MASCULINE AND FEMININE GENDER

Nouns which indicate males or things which pertain to males are masculine; those which indicate females or things which pertain to females are feminine. But those which express other things are common; and, although most of them occur in the Bible either in masculine or feminine, it approaches the neuter case. Some occur as feminine only once and in all others are always found to be masculine and contrarily some are masculine in only one place. E.g.: the word כָּנָף *a wing* is in the feminine gender everywhere except twice (in the second book of Chronicles chapter 3, verses 11 and 12) and for this reason considered common gender by the writers. Were it not for this most beloved book of Chronicles they would without doubt place it among the feminines. If we had more such nouns perhaps all rules would change and those which now number among the exceptions would be regular and contrarily, many regulars would be exceptions. For, as I said in a word, there are many who wrote a grammar of the Scriptures but none who wrote a grammar of the Hebrew language. But to the proposition. We see also how the Scriptures refer in the same sentence one noun to both genders indiscriminately, like Genesis chapter 32, verse 9 אִם יָבוֹא עֵשָׂו אֶל הַמַּחֲנֶה הָאַחַת וְהִכָּהוּ *if Esau should come to the one camp and smite it*; and in this matter I shall entirely agree with Rabbi Shelomo (Rashi), who states כָּל דָּבָר שֶׁאֵין בּוֹ רוּחַ חַיִּים זָכְרֵהוּ וְנָקְבֵהוּ *"everything which doesn't have the spirit of life express it either in masculine or feminine gender."* See his commentary in the place referred to.[1]

Adjectives are changed from masculine to feminine by adding to them a ת or ה, with a kametz ָ , and by changing the syllables in accordance with the preceding rules; e.g., חָכָם *wise* חֲכָמָה *feminine*, גָּדוֹל *great* גְּדוֹלָה *feminine*, בָּרוּךְ *blessed* בְּרוּכָה *feminine*, פֹּקֵד *visiting* פּוֹקְדָה and פּוֹקֶדֶת *feminine*, אִישׁ *a man* אִשָּׁה *a woman*, גְּבִיר *a master* גְּבִירָה *a mistress*.

The exceptions are those which have a double segol ֶ , both of which should be changed into ֵ . But in order that two should not occur at the beginning of a word the first is changed into a patach, like מֶלֶךְ *a king* מַלְכָּה *a queen*, which according to the preceding rules ought to be מֶלְכָה.

Masculine adjectives ending in a ה change the last syllable into a ָ , like יָפֶה *pretty* into יָפָה, רֹאֶה *seeing*, feminine רֹאָה, etc. Further, those ending in י are changed in feminine either like the preceding or simply by adding a ת, like שֵׁנִי *second*, in feminine שְׁנִיָּה or שֵׁנִית; שְׁנַיִם *seconds*, in feminine שְׁנִיּוֹת. And this

---

1. [This comment is not in Rashi's commentary but in Ibn Ezra.]

condition occurs particularly in those adjectives by which it is indicated from which tribe or region someone is, like עִבְרִי *a Hebrew man*, feminine עִבְרִיָּה and עִבְרִית *a Hebrew woman*; it must be noted that all these adjectives are formed in the masculine gender from the proper nouns of their lands of birth or parentage by the addition of a yod with a chirek preceding it, and by changing the syllables according to the rules of the following chapter which deals with the construct of nouns, as from יִשְׂרָאֵל comes יִשְׂרָאֵלִי, from עֵבֶר comes עִבְרִי, from חֶבֶר comes חֶבְרִי, and from כּוּשׁ *Ethiopia* comes כּוּשִׁי and from יְרוּשָׁלֵם comes יְרוּשַׁלְמִי *a Jerusalemite*. To all these nouns in masculine plural only a ם, is added, like עִבְרִים *Hebrews*, כּוּשִׁים *Ethiopians*. If the noun from which this is formed ends in a plural form, then this is left off. For example, מִצְרַיִם *Egypt* becomes מִצְרִי *an Egyptian*, and this, as I have said, is changed into feminine by the addition of a ת or a ה with a kametz ָ preceding it. But in the plural they are always inflected like feminines which end in a ה like מִצְרִיּוֹת, עִבְרִיּוֹת, etc.

And hence it seems to have been a fact that just as the regular ending ה together with the preceding kametz ָ, or the ת, and the plural וֹת almost made adjectives into feminines, so the Hebrews generally were accustomed also to consider substantives, which ended in ה or ת in singular and in וֹת in plural, to be of the feminine gender, unless perhaps it is a fact that they mistook the origin of the gender of adjectives. But of this enough.

CHAPTER 8

OF THE CONSTRUCT CASE OF NOUNS

Things are expressed either absolutely or in relationship to other things, so that they may be indicated more clearly and distinctly. For example: *"The earth is big,"* "the earth" is expressed in an absolute state; but *"God's earth is big,"* here, "earth" is in a relative state because it is expressed more effectively or indicated more clearly, and this is called the construct state. I will now tell in orderly fashion the manner in which this is usually expressed, beginning with the manner of the singular.

Nouns which ended in a ה preceded by a kametz or a cholem, change the ה into a ת and the kametz ָ into a patach ־. Thus תְּפִלָּה becomes in construct case תְּפִלַּת, and means *somebody's prayer*. So עָשָׂה *to do* becomes in construct case עֲשׂוֹת *somebody's doing*, as in יוֹם עֲשׂוֹת יְהוָה אֱלֹהִים *the day of the Lord God's doing*.

Those which have a double or only a single kametz in the absolute, change in the construct case the penultimate into a sheva and the ultimate into a patach, like דְּבַר from דָּבָר *a word*, כִּכַּר זָהָב *a talent of gold* from כִּכָּר *a talent*,

חָכָם from חָכָם *a wise man*, as Job in chapter 9 called God חֲכַם לֵבָב *wise of heart*. So בָּרוּךְ *blessed*, שָׁלוֹם *peace*, פָּקוֹד *visiting*, זָקֵן *old*, etc., change the penultimate kametz to a sheva; so also צְדָקָה *justice*, בְּרָכָה *a blessing*, change the ultimate kametz into a patach, and the penultimate into a sheva, and the ה into a ת as we have already said, thus becoming בִּרְכַת, צִדְקַת. It is only because two shevas cannot occur at the beginning of a word that the first sheva is changed into chirek. This is always the case, I cannot reiterate this too often, with every chirek and patach before a sheva.

A penultimate tsere is sometimes changed into a sheva, and an ultimate sometimes to a patach, like שְׂעַר from שֵׂעָר *hair*, and פְּאַת from פֵּאָה *a corner*, זְקַן from זָקֵן *an elder*, מְקַל from מַקֵּל *a stick*. But most frequently both the ultimate and the penultimate remain unchanged. Indeed, these and many others like them are completely uncertain; at times a noun changes the tsere and at times it retains it, which shows that in the Scriptures the dialects are mixed up. Thus everyone is at liberty either to change or to leave both the tsere and the kametz in the ultimate; except for the tsere before a ּ which always should be retained because of common usage, like הֵיכָל *a temple*, for example. The word אַשְׁמוּרָה occurs everywhere in the Scriptures in the construct case as אַשְׁמֹרֶת, and תַּעֲלוּמָה and תַּלְאוּבָה become תַּלְאוּבַת and תַּעֲלוּמַת. Therefore I say everyone is free to write אַשְׁמוֹרֶת for אַשְׁמוּרַת and תַּלְאוּבַת for תַּלְאוּבֶת, even though neither is found in the Scriptures. And what I have said about the tsere and the kametz should be said about everything that does not follow a fixed rule. But of this I shall treat copiously in another place. Here let me add a word concerning the matter of which I have spoken thus far, and which I regard to be no less essential toward the purpose of this chapter and toward the general knowledge of this language.

In the previous chapter, we have said that the feminine endings ה ָ and ת and the plural ות are characteristic of adjectives and participles, doubtless because the same noun may have an adjective, which sometimes is referred to as masculine and sometimes as feminine, and for that reason, at one time or another requires either of two endings. This is not the case with the substantive nouns and, therefore, it sometimes happens that substantive nouns which express neither masculine nor feminine are referred to as of feminine gender when they end in ה or ת; or perhaps this is (as we have said) because they derive their origin from feminine adjectives. But it is something else that I intend here: namely, that just as the determinations of the substantives originate from adjectives and participles, so the changes, which nouns experience in the construct case, derive their origin from mutations of infinitives and the participles. For all Hebrew nouns (as is known to all experts in this language) are derived from forms of verbs. It should be added that first and foremost the use of substantive nouns is to indicate something absolute and not relative. Indeed the latter is impossible for proper nouns; which thus are never found in construct case. But actions are seldom expressed without either an active or passive relationship, and, therefore, are rarely found in the absolute state. However it may be, the variations of the substantives are easily learned from the ways in which the infinitive and participial nouns vary. Thus there is no doubt that the one derives its origin from the other. I shall now list here a few examples and their variations in the construct case, as a model for the changes of all nouns, so that they may be easily committed to memory.

Forms of Infinitives

	Absolute State	Construct State
to visit*	פָּקוֹד	פְּקוֹד and פְּקָד־
		פָּקְדָה from פְּקוֹדַת and
to be visited	נִפְקוֹד always absolute	
	and תִּפָּקֵד	הִפָּקֵד
to visit frequently	פַּקֵּד and פַּקֵּד	פַּקֵּד
to be visited frequently	פֻּקֹּד	פֻּקֹּד
to cause or make someone to visit	הַפְקֵד	הַפְקִיד
to be caused to visit	הָפְקֵד	הָפְקֵד
to cause oneself to be visited	הִתְפַּקֵּד	הִתְפַּקֵּד
to approach	נָגוֹשׁ	גֶּשֶׁת
to reveal	גָּלֹה / גָּלוֹת	גְּלוֹת / גְּלוֹת
to surround	סוֹב	סָב and סוֹב־
to find	מָצוֹא	מְצוֹא and מְצֹאת / מְצֹאת
to open	פָּקֹחַ	פְּקֹחַ

These are the principal examples of the infinitives. And now I proceed toward the participles.

---

*The infinitive in the absolute state often agrees with the perfect tense: for דבר *to speak* also means *he has spoken*; גָּדֵל *to grow*, בָּשֵׁל *to cook* have the form of the perfect, as I have shown in its place. Therefore, I have no doubt that פָּקָד with a double kametz and פָּקַד with kametz and patach were also forms of the infinitive, from which form comes פְּקָד in the construct, namely from פָּקָד, פְּקָד, and פָּקַד. And let it suffice to note this in passing here because it is more extensively discussed under the subject of conjugations.

Forms of Participles
Active

Construct	Absolute	
פֹּקֵד and פֹּקֶד and פֹּקְדֵי	פֹּקֵד	visiting, masc. gender
פֹּקְדֵי	פֹּקְדִים	m. p.
	פֹּקְדָה	f. s.
	and	
פֹּקֶדֶת	פֹּקֶדֶת	f. s. or פֹּקַדְתְּ or פֹּקַדְתִּי
פֹּקְדוֹת	פֹּקְדוֹת	f. p.
מְפַקֵּד*	מְפַקֵּד	visiting frequently, m. s.
מְפַקְּדֵי	מְפַקְּדִים	m. p.
	מְפַקְּדָה	
	and	} f. s.
מְפַקֶּדֶת	מְפַקֶּדֶת	
מְפַקְּדוֹת	מְפַקְּדוֹת	f. p.
מַפְקִיד	מַפְקִיד	make someone visit, m. s.
מַפְקִידֵי	מַפְקִידִים	
מַפְקִידַת	מַפְקִידָה	f. s., from which also
	and	מַפְקֶדֶת
מַפְקֶדֶת	מַפְקֶדֶת	
מִתְפַּקֵּד	מִתְפַּקֵּד	visiting oneself, or causing oneself to visit, m. s.
מִתְפַּקְּדֵי	מִתְפַּקְּדִים	m. p.
	מִתְפַּקְּדָה	
	and	} f. s.
מִתְפַּקֶּדֶת	מִתְפַּקֶּדֶת	
מִתְפַּקְּדוֹת	מִתְפַּקְּדוֹת	f. p.
גְּדֵל and גָּדֵל	גָּדֵל	growing, m. s.
גְּדֵלֵי	גְּדֵלִים	m. p.
גְּדֵלַת	גְּדֵלָה	f. s.
גְּדֵלוֹת	גְּדֵלוֹת	f. p.
בָּא	בָּא	coming, m. s.
בָּאֵי[1]	בָּאִים	m. p.
בָּאַת	בָּאָה	f. s.
בָּאוֹת	בָּאוֹת	f. p.

---

*In the Bible this participle construct is not found and the meaning does not seem to have been able to be expressed relatively to the extent that it is now always accepted. Nevertheless, since this form is also used occasionally with the same meaning, there is no reason that it should be less able to have a construct.

1. [Actually בָּאֵי.—M.L.M.]

גֹּלֶה	גֹּלֶה		*revealing*, m. s.
גֹּלֵי	גֹּלִים		m. p.
גֹּלַת	גֹּלָה		f. s.
גֹּלוֹת	גֹּלוֹת		

And thus:

מְגַלֶּה	מְגַלֶּה	*one who reveals*, m. s.
מְגַלֵּי	מְגַלִּים	m. p.
מְגַלַּת	מְגַלָּה	f. s.

etc.

שׁוֹמֵעַ	שׁוֹמֵעַ and שׁוֹמֵעַ	*hearing*, m. s.
שׁוֹמְעֵי	שׁוֹמְעִים	m. p.
שׁוֹמַעַת	שׁוֹמְעָה and שׁוֹמַעַת	f. s.
שׁוֹמְעוֹת	שׁוֹמְעוֹת	f. p.

Thus:

שְׂבַע	שָׂבֵעַ	*satisfying*
שְׂבֵעֵי	שְׂבֵעִים	m. p.
שְׂבֵעַת	שְׂבֵעָה	f. s.
שְׂבֵעוֹת	שְׂבֵעוֹת	f. p.

Passive

Construct	Absolute	
נִפְקָד	נִפְקָד	*being visited*, m. s.
נִפְקְדֵי	נִפְקָדִים	m. p.
	נִפְקָדָה	
		f. s.
נִפְקֶדֶת	נִפְקֶדֶת	
נִפְקָדוֹת	נִפְקָדוֹת	f. p.
etc.	מְפוֹקָד and	
		m. s., *being visited frequently*
מְפֻקָּד	מְפֻקָּד	
מְפֻקְּדֵי	מְפֻקָּדִים	m. p.

	מְפֻקָּדָה and מְפֻקֶּדֶת	}	f. s.
מְפֻקֶּדֶת מְפֻקָּדוֹת	מְפֻקָּדוֹת		f. p.
	מָפְקָד		*made to visit*, m. s.
	מָפְקָדִים		m. p.
	מָפְקֶדֶת and מָפְקָדָה	}	f. s.
	מָפְקָדוֹת		f. p.
פְּקוּד	פָּקוּד and פָּקֻד	}	*visited*, verbal adjective, m. s.
פְּקוּדֵי	פְּקוּדִים and פְּקֻדִים		m. p.
פְּקֻדַת פְּקוּדוֹת	פְּקוּדָה and פְּקֻדָה and פְּקֻדַת		f. s.
	פְּקוּדוֹת and פְּקֻדוֹת		f. p.
	פּוּקָד and פֻּקָד	}	*frequently visited*, adjective, m. s.
	פּוּקָדִים and פֻּקָדִים		m. p.
	פּוּקָדָה and פֻּקָדַת and פֻּקֶדֶת	}	f. s.
	פּוּקָדוֹת and פֻּקָדוֹת		f. p.

Besides these, there are the other forms of the participles, but I am of the opinion these will suffice for the present, so that anyone can easily learn to change a noun from the absolute state to the construct. This rule should be observed: vowels which are unchangeable are retained in the construct case, for example monosyllables and also those referred to as disyllables whose first vowel is a sheva, like כְּתָב *writing*, זְאֵב *a wolf*, etc., a double segolate, patach, chirek, and sheva. A cholem is generally retained also but before a makaf we see that it is changed to a short *o*. The shurek very rarely or perhaps never is changed, and if occasionally a kibbutz is used in its place, it does not on that account become a construct, but because one may serve for the other; for a shurek is a vowel composed of a cholem and a kibbutz, and therefore, in place of a shurek we frequently see used either a cholem or a kibbutz.

But the reason that עֲוֶל, אָוֶן, מָוֶת, and others of this type are in construct עֲוֶל, מָוֶת, and אָוֶן, etc., is due to common usage of the language. We have already said above that a kametz before a segol replaces the first segol at the end of a sentence, or in the middle of a sentence to divide one part of it from the other, like עֲטֶרֶת for עֲטֶרֶת and פּוֹקֶדֶת for פּוֹקֶדֶת. Therefore עָוֶל, etc., occurs in the absolute state in place of the construct עֲוֶל.

But it should be noted that in this language it is mostly the custom to render the ו vav quiescent, changing the syllable into a cholem; which is the most frequent usage and it is seen most prevalent in respect to this noun because in the Scriptures it is only once found in the construct, otherwise everywhere from עֹל *fraud* it is עוֹל and from אָוֶן *wickedness* אוֹן; and so in the rest of these forms.

Finally, may I add something also about the ending of the plural. We see that the plural ending וֹת is always retained in the construct; but יִם loses the ם and the chirek changes into a tsere. This pattern also holds true with the construct of dual יִם, which similarly loses the ם with the chirek, and the patach changes to tsere, like from עֵינַיִם *eyes*, it becomes עֵינֵי in the construct state; and this I believe makes it that every patach before י with a chirek follows this form in the construct, making it from בַּיִת *a house* בֵּית and from יַיִן *wine* יֵין, etc.

Now before I pass on to the last, I must first of all note that I understand by the word noun all classes of nouns. Every noun, except the proper noun (as we have already said), can be in genitive or can be changed to genitive; and particularly the relative form, or the preposition which is always indicated as relative, and on that account can almost always become a genitive, and is frequently changed; all of which I shall illustrate here very clearly by examples.

בֵּית אֱלֹהִים	*House of God.* Both are substantives.
לֵב חָכָם	*A heart of a wise one.* First is a substantive. The second adjective.
חֲכַם לֵבָב	*Wise of heart.* ⎫ Opposite of above.
גְּדוֹל הָעֵצָה	*Great of counsel.* ⎭
אוֹהֲבֵי טוֹב	*Lovers of good.* ⎫ The first words are participles.
רוֹאֵי הַשֶּׁמֶשׁ	*Seers of the sun.* ⎭
בְּרֹא אֱלֹהִים	*The creation of God.* First is an infinitive.
יוֹם בְּרֹא אֱלֹהִים	*Day of the creation of God.* Inf. which simultaneously modifies and is modified.
מַשְׁכִּימֵי קוּם	*Early ones to rise,* that is, *those who are quick to rise.*
מַשְׁכִּימֵי בַבֹּקֶר	*Early in the morning,* preposition in the genitive and participle in the construct.

לִפְנֵי יְהוָה   *Before the Lord.* Preposition is construct from לִפָנִים *before,* so from תָּוֶךְ *the midst,* it is תּוֹךְ *in the midst of.*

עֲדֵי עַד   *Until and until,* that is, indefinite time, here the preposition modifies and is modified.

מַכַּת בִּלְתִּי סָרָה   *Plague without ceasing,* that is, *a plague which does not cease.* Adverb is *not* modified.

אֵין חָכְמָה   *Not wise;* here the word אֵין construct from אַיִן is like in absolute state בַּיִן which like בֵּין changes in construct state, as we have said, from the patach and chirek into a tsere.

Finally, I want to remind you again, and again, that you consider carefully in your mind all that has been said in Chapter 5 about the noun. For nobody will be able to cultivate this language profitably, unless he rightly learns what we have said there, namely, that the verbs, the participles, the prepositions, and the adverbs among the Hebrews are all pure unmixed nouns.

CHAPTER 9

OF THE TWOFOLD USE OF THE NOUN AND OF ITS DECLENSION

As an appellative noun we wish to indicate either one individual or many certain indefinite persons, and also one or many certain and known ones; something which among the Latins makes no difference[1] but among the Hebrews and others there is a great difference. To be sure אִישׁ or אִישִׁים may signify any *man* or all *men.* But if any one wants to signify only a man or men of whom he has spoken already or who is supposed to be denoted, he should put in front of the noun a ה with a patach and double the first letter of the noun, that is to dagesh it; and if the first letter should be one of those which are not able to be doubled, then the ה should have a kametz in place of the patach, like וְהָאִישׁ גַּבְרִיאֵל *and the man Gabriel.* But it should be noted that both the dagesh and the kametz may be compensated by a ga'ya, הַמְכַסֶּה, הֶחָוִי, etc. And this ה should be called הַיְדִיעָה, that is, the ה of knowledge, because it indicates a known thing and therefore, I shall call it the indicative.

---

1. [Spinoza here wishes to indicate that in Latin there is no definite or indefinite article before a noun.]

Indeed truly this kind of use of the ה can have a place only in appellatives, adjectives, and participles; but not in proper nouns, in infinitives, nor in adverbs; and because it can signify only a single object, it may also not be in plurals of the same group; and with regard to relative nouns they never appear in the absolute state but only in the construct. But first let it be noted about this ה that it never comes before a genitive noun, for reasons which I shall show in this chapter.

Further, because all nouns among the Hebrews are indeclinable, the case is expressed generally only by a preposition, so called. I said "so called." For with prepositions, as we have already said (indeed they are nouns), the genitive usually prevails; but as among the Greeks, ablative prepositions govern the genitive, and only by their meaning does the genitive take place of the ablative, so it is among the Hebrews everything occurs in the genitive and only by their meaning does the genitive take the place of all the other cases.

These are the prepositions of the cases generally used: לְ, אֶל, בְּ, מִ and מִן, עִם, etc. Of these לְ, בְּ preceding the noun are punctuated with a sheva. The מִ, however, because it is used in place of מִן, is punctuated with a chirek and the ן is compensated by the dagesh point in the succeeding letter; as all may see in the following examples:

Both לְ with sheva, and אֶל indicate the dative; בְּ, מִ, מִן, and עִם the ablative; the accusative, however, has no preposition, but in its place the particle אֵת should be used, which, therefore, never governs a genitive but always an accusative. The remaining cases have no prepositions. Therefore, when we said above that the genitive is used in place of the remaining cases, it is understood, in place of the dative and ablative, because these are expressed only by prepositions. But all these will become clearly intelligible from the following examples.

Example of an Indefinite Appellative Noun

Singular

Nom.	דָּבָר	a word
Gen.	דָּבָר	Recognized by the construct of the preceding noun and its gender.
Dat.	לְדָבָר	Understand the preposition expresses the meaning of the dative and is in the construct state, and the noun is genitive. Further it should be noted that when the לְ indicates *"terminus ad quem"* it is possible to be substituted by a ה at the end of the word, like אַרְצָה for לְאֶרֶץ *to the ground*.
Acc.	דָּבָר	Recognized by the active verb.
Voc.	דָּבָר	
Abl.	מִדָּבָר	Understand this like the above in the dative.

Plural

Nom.	דְּבָרִים
Gen.	דְּבָרִים
Dat.	לִדְבָרִים
Acc.	דְּבָרִים
Voc.	דְּבָרִים
Abl.	מִ or בִּדְבָרִים

Example of a Noun with the Definite Article ה

Singular

Nom. Gen.	הַדָּבָר
Dat.	לְהַדָּבָר for לַדָּבָר
Acc.	אֶת־הַדָּבָר
Voc.	הַדָּבָר
Abl.	בְּהַדָּבָר for בַּדָּבָר

Plural

Nom. Gen.	הַדְּבָרִים
Dat.	לְהַדְּבָרִים for לַדְּבָרִים
Acc.	אֶת הַדְּבָרִים
Voc.	הַדְּבָרִים
Abl.	בְּהַדְּבָרִים for בַּדְּבָרִים

Example of a Masculine Substantive Noun and Adjective

ה with the Definite Article

Great God

Nom. Gen.	אֵל גָּדוֹל
Dat.	לְאֵל גָּדוֹל
	etc.

Nom. Gen.	הָאֵל הַגָּדוֹל
Dat.	לָאֵל הַגָּדוֹל
Acc.	אֶת הָאֵל הַגָּדוֹל

Example of the Feminine Gender

ה with the Definite Article

Nom. Gen.	מְנוֹרָה יָפָה
Dat.	לִמְנוֹרָה יָפָה
	etc.

Nom. Gen.	הַמְּנוֹרָה הַיָּפָה
Dat.	לַמְּנוֹרָה הַיָּפָה
Acc.	אֶת הַמְּנוֹרָה הַיָּפָה
	etc.

Example of a Relative Noun

Nom. ⎫
Gen. ⎭ תּוֹךְ *midst*

Dat. לְתוֹךְ, אֶל תּוֹךְ *to the midst*
Acc. תּוֹךְ
Abl. בְּתוֹךְ, מִתּוֹךְ *in* and *from the midst*, etc.

Note: תּוֹךְ is really in the construct state and it is formed from תָּוֶךְ like from עָוֶל *fraud* comes עוֹל. I took the example of the construct, because as I said, prepositions are hard to conceive in the absolute state, and therefore, they are never declined with the definite article ה, because the ה usually applies to a thing already explained and known; whereas the construct applies to a thing to be explained and determined by the genitive, that is, a thing not yet known. And here I say the ה and construct, *frequently*, but I did not say it *always* applies; for often indeed in the highest eloquence, it is permissible to substitute the definite article for the construct, and the construct for the definite article ה; for example, it is more eloquent to say כָּל־נְבִיאֵי *all prophets* for כָּל־הַנְּבִיאֵי. Because הַנְּבִיאִים signifies prophets already known and נְבִיאֵי in the construct and understood as genitive, signifies prophets of an already known thing, namely of God, of truth, etc. So to say הַשֹּׁתִים בְּמִזְרְקֵי יַיִן *they who drink in bowls of wine* in place of בַּמִּזְרָקִים is more eloquent. But of this at length in the Syntaxes. Here let it suffice to show in general that the construct, like the definite article ה, is able to be understood as a genitive, as a thing known, which cannot take place in the case prepositions.

Another Example of a Relative Noun

Singular

Nom. ⎫
Gen. ⎭ קֶדֶם *aforetime*

Dat. לְקֶדֶם
Acc. קֶדֶם
Abl. מִקֶּדֶם

Plural

Nom. ⎫
Gen. ⎭ קַדְמֵי *much aforetime*

Dat. לְקַדְמֵי
Acc. קַדְמֵי
Abl. מִקַּדְמֵי *from aforetime*
(Prov. 8:23 מִקַּדְמֵי אֶרֶץ really means *from all the aforetimes of the earth*.)

Another Relative Noun

חוּץ   *outside*
מִחוּץ   a particle which means *outside*

Declined like a noun as follows:

Nom. ⎫
Gen. ⎬ מִחוּץ *outside*
Dat.   אֶל מִחוּץ *to the outside*
Acc.   מִחוּץ
Abl.   בְּמִחוּץ; *and so with the rest*

Another Example of an Adverb

Nom. ⎫
Gen. ⎬ מָתַי *when*
Dat.   לְמָתַי *to the when,* that is, *in that time*
Acc.   מָתַי
Abl.   בְּמָתַי, *etc.*

Nom. ⎫
Gen. ⎬ חִנָּם *vainly*
Dat.   אֶל חִנָּם *in vain, etc.*

Nom. ⎫
Gen. ⎬ עוֹד *hitherto*
Dat.   לְעוֹד *to the hitherto*
Acc.   עוֹד
Abl.   בְּעוֹד, מֵעוֹד *from* and *in the hitherto,* that is, *in time, at the time*

Example of an Infinitive

Nom. ⎫
Gen. ⎬ פָּקוֹד
Dat.   לִפְקוֹד
Acc.   פָּקוֹד
Abl.   בִּפְקוֹד
       כִּפְקוֹד
       מִפְּקוֹד

Participles are declined like adverbs.

Examples of Adverbs

Nom. ⎫   Nom. ⎫
Gen. ⎬ לֹא *no* Gen. ⎬ טֶרֶם *before, not yet, scarcely*

Dat.	לְלֹא	to no	Dat.	לְטֶרֶם	to the scarcely, not as yet
Acc.	לֹא		Acc.	טֶרֶם	
Abl.	מִלֹּא	from no	Abl.	מִטֶּרֶם, בְּטֶרֶם	from before, in, or at a time

From these examples, everyone is able easily to see according to what system all nouns which are construct are declined. But it should be noted I have nicely omitted the case of prepositions when from the meaning it is not possible to be in doubt, like Proverbs chapter 22, verse 21 לְהָשִׁיב אֲמָרִים אֱמֶת לְשֹׁלְחֶיךָ *to bring back words with truth to them that send you.* Indeed since אֲמָרִים is in absolute state, the genitive אֱמֶת cannot refer to it, but it should have the prefixed preposition בְּ, which is here omitted. So, 1 Kings chapter 2, verse 7: וְהָיוּ בְּאֹכְלֵי שֻׁלְחָנֶךָ *and they shall be of those that eat at thy table;* where also the preposition אֶל or עַל in the genitive is rightly understood by a construct participle. Much more of this will be said at great length in the section on Syntax.

CHAPTER 10

Of the Preposition and the Adverb

We have said above, in Chapter 5, that prepositions are nouns which indicate the relationship of one individual to another. We have also said that the same relationship may be expressed in both the singular and plural. The first statement, namely that I believe that prepositions are nouns, is based on the two previous chapters. But that prepositions should occur in the plural also might perhaps appear absurd to many; but why should they not, since they are also nouns? But you may say relationships are not species which have many individuals under them, and for that reason they should, in common with proper nouns, not be able to be in the plural. But though it seems that some species do not have many relationships, yet prepositions nevertheless are inflected from singular into plural. How this is able to be done, I intend to explain here briefly.

Although prepositions cannot indicate many relationships simultaneously, nevertheless they are inflected from singular to plural in the absolute state as well as the construct state; but prepositions in the absolute state are only relationships of themselves, abstractly conceived and not expressed; but then they express not so much the relationship as the place or time with relation to some thing. For example from בֵּין *between,* the plural is בֵּינוֹת, which indeed signifies not the relationship of one individual to another but the places between others (about which see Ezek. 10:2); or as I have said, it is the preposition itself whose relation is conceived in the abstract, like from אָחוֹר to the plural אֲחוֹרִים *posteriors*, or better *backward*. In accordance with this pattern many prepositions as well as adverbs can be formed, although in the Scriptures they are never found thus formulated.

Further, prepositions are declined also in the construct state, that is insofar as their relationships are indicated both in singular and in plural; which is either because the relationship is conceived as existing many times, or because the relationship should be expressed intensely. For example אַחַר *after* becomes in the plural אַחֲרֵי, which means *much after*, as the Rabbis have very well pointed out. Thus אֶל *to* becomes in the plural אֱלֵי *much to*, that is, *how much can be done*; so from עַל *above*, it is עֲלֵי, and from עַד *until* עֲדֵי. Hence עֲדֵי עַד means *in eternity*, that is *everything which can be conceived*; thus מִקַּדְמֵי אָרֶץ means *from all before the earth*; and in this manner nearly all prepositions can be declined whether in the singular or the plural.

But לִפְנֵי *before*, a preposition which has no singular, is an exception to this. For it is declined in the plural only because it is formed from the substantive פָּנִים *a face* or *anterior*, which lacks a singular.

Finally, we consider adverbs also as nouns by which an action is determined as to its manner, time, place, activity, order, etc. For example, *well, ill, speedily, tomorrow, yesterday, always, outside, once, firstly, secondly*, etc. Reason indicates that these all lack a plural. And they are not able to be conceived abstractly, like prepositions, as is evident per se. And although the Latins frequently tried to stretch out adverbs, like *very kindly, very early in the morning*, etc., nevertheless, had they been expressed in the plural among the Hebrews as is frequently the case with prepositions, it would seem absurd indeed, to the Hebrews. For prepositions which indicate relationships can, like substantive nouns, have attributes, without being expressed directly; but adverbs, which are modes of action, are like adjectives of verbs; by means of them nothing more is intended than to serve as attributes of attributes, as if to add adjectives to adjectives. Next, adverbs, which, as I have said, are like adjectives of verbs, should agree in number with their substantive, that is with their verb, which occurs only in the singular. Therefore, to express the meaning: *very early in the morning, very kindly*, etc., the Hebrews used the verb itself, and instead of one of the adverbs, they used a verb or a noun. For example, *he rose up very early in the morning* is expressed in Hebrew, *he hastened completely to the arising*, and *he acted very kindly, he acted completely with kindness*, as we shall explain in its place under Syntax.

But it should be noted that adverbs, like adjectives, are frequently formed into substantives. But instead of being inflected in the plural, they are usually repeated, like מַעְלָה מַעְלָה *upward upward*, that is *to the top all the way up*; on the other hand, מַטָּה מַטָּה *lower, lower* means *to the bottom all the way down*. Thus מְאֹד means *very*, and מְאֹד מְאֹד *to the highest grade, very*, and *exceedingly*; likewise מְעַט *little* מְעַט מְעַט *gradually*; and in this manner the others.

CHAPTER 11

Of the Pronouns

Before I go over to the conjugations it is necessary that I give attention to the pronouns. For without the latter the former can scarcely be taught. What a pronoun is and into how many classes it is divided is known to all. I will here relate the manner it is changed in number from singular into plural, and from masculine into feminine, and how they are declined.

Personal Pronouns

Singular *Plural*

I	אֲנִי / אָנֹכִי		אֲנַחְנוּ / נַחְנוּ / אָנוּ	We		*Note:* The gender is common, as everywhere in the first person, because speech itself indicates sufficiently whether it is masculine or feminine.
You	אַתָּה masc. gen.		אַתֶּם	You	masc.	
You	אַתְּ fem. gen.		אַתֶּן	You	f. and with ה added אַתֵּנָה	
He	הוּא		הֵם	They	m. " " ה " הֵמָּה	
She	הִיא		הֵן	They	f. " " ה " הֵנָּה	

The plural ending of these differs greatly from the usual, for the masculine does not end in ים nor the feminine in וֹת. Also the feminine ending here even differs from that of the adjective. Finally, the feminine אַתְּ seems to have been also אַתִּי, and הִיא to have been הוּא differing from the masculine by different vocalization. In the Bible this is found frequently with corrections by the Massorites because the original forms were obsolete.

Indicatives or Demonstratives

this $\begin{cases} \text{זֶה} \\ \text{זוּ} \\ \text{לְז} \end{cases}$ without plurals

this (f.) $\begin{cases} \text{זֹה} \\ \text{זֹאת} \\ \text{זוּ} \end{cases}$

these $\begin{cases} \text{אֵלֶּה} \\ \text{אֵל} \end{cases}$ without singulars

The ה indicative serves as a relative pronoun both in singular and plural, or in its place שׁ, followed by a dagesh in the succeeding letter; but most frequently אֲשֶׁר occurs in the Bible.

Separate possessives are not used, but they are affixed to the construct of a noun in this way:

Example of the Substantive Noun דָּבָר (a Word) from Which the Construct Is דְּבַר

Nominative Singular Suffixes

| דְּבָרִי | my word | |
| דְּבָרְךָ | your word | m. |

(and if the accent is אתנח or סילוק: דְּבָרֶךָ)

דְּבָרֵךְ and דְּבָרֵךְ	your word	f.
דְּבָרוֹ	his word	m.
דְּבָרָהּ	her word	f.

Plural Suffixes

דְּבָרֵנוּ	our word	
דְּבַרְכֶם	your word	m.
דְּבַרְכֶן	your word	f.
דְּבָרָם	their word	m.
דְּבָרָן	their word	f.

From Construct Plural דִּבְרֵי

N.B. A ָ does not occur under the ר, unless the accent is an אַתְנַח or סִילוּק. Otherwise instead of ָ it is punctuated with a patach.	דְּבָרַי	my words	
	דְּבָרֶיךָ	your words	m.
	דְּבָרַיִךְ	your words	f.
	דְּבָרָיו	their words	m.
	דְּבָרֶיהָ	their words	f.

Plural Nouns and Plural Suffixes

N.B. The second and third persons, whose noun is plural, are always added to the construct plurals.	דְּבָרֵינוּ	our word	
	דִּבְרֵיכֶם	your words	m.
	דִּבְרֵיכֶן	your words	f.
	דִּבְרֵיהֶם	their words	m.
	דִּבְרֵיהֶן	their words	f.

Thus from the construct תְּפִילַת *prayer of* we have תְּפִילָתִי, תְּפִילָתְךָ, etc., and in the plural תְּפִילוֹתַי, etc. So from בַּיִת, construct of the substantive noun בַּיִת *house*, it is בֵּיתִי *my house*, and from plural construct בָּתֵּי, it is בָּתֶּיךָ *your house*, etc.

Examples of Nominative Singular Participles and with Suffixes

An Example of Masculine פּוֹקֵד

פּוֹקְדִי and פּוֹקְדֵנִי	my visit	
פּוֹקֶדְךָ	your visit	(m.)
דֵךְ	your visit	(f.)
פּוֹקְדוֹ	his visit	(m.)
פּוֹקְדָהּ	her visit	(f.)

An Example of Feminine פֹּקֶדֶת

פֹּקַדְתִּי	my visit	
פֹּקַדְתְּךָ	your visit	(m.)
תֵּךְ	your visit	(f.)
פֹּקַדְתּוֹ	his visit	(m.)
תָּהּ	her visit	(f.)

An Example of Plural Masculine פְּקֻדַי

פְּקֻדַי	my visits
פְּקֻדֶיךָ	your visits (m.)
דַיִךְ	your visits (f.)
פְּקֻדָיו	his visits

etc., as in the substantive.

An Example of Plural Feminine פְּקֻדוֹת

פְּקֻדוֹתַי	my visits
פְּקֻדוֹתֶיךָ	your visits (m.)
תַיִךְ	your visits (f.)

etc., as in the substantive.

An Example of the Infinitive Construct פְּקֹד

פָּקְדִי	to visit me
פָּקְדְךָ	to visit you (m. s.)
פָּקְדֵךְ	to visit you (f. s.)
פָּקְדוֹ	to visit him (m. s.)
דָהּ	to visit her (f. s.)
פָּקְדֵנוּ	to visit us
פָּקְדְכֶם	to visit you (m. p.)
כֶן	to visit you (f. p.)
פָּקְדָם	to visit them (m. p.)
דָן	to visit them (f. p.)

An Example of the Relative בֵּין Between (Sing.)

בֵּינִי and בֵּינֶנִי	between me
בֵּינְךָ	between you (m. s.)
נֵךְ	between you (f. s.)
בֵּינוֹ	between him (m. s.)
נָהּ	between her (f. s.)
בֵּינֵנוּ	between us
בֵּינְכֶם	between you (m. p.)
etc.	

An Example of the Relative בֵּינִי (Plur.)

בֵּינִי	between me	
בֵּינְךָ	between you	(m. s.)
בֵּינַיִךְ	between you	(f. s.)
בֵּינָיו	between him	
בֵּינֶיהָ	between her	
בֵּינֵינוּ	between us	
בֵּינֵיכֶם	between you	(m. p.)
כֶן	between you	(f. p.)
הֶם	between them	
הֶן	between them	

Thus from the singular and the plural it is:

תַּחְתִּי	תַּחַת
תַּחְתֵּנִי	תַּחְתִּי
תַּחְתֶּיךָ	תַּחְתְּךָ
תֵּךְ etc.	תַּחְתַּיִךְ etc.

But אֶל *to*, עַל *upon*, אַחַר *after*, עַד *until* have no suffixes in the singular; in the plurals, however, they are as follows:

עֲלֵי	אֱלֵי	אַחֲרֵי	עֲדֵי
עָלַי	אֵלַי	אַחֲרַי	עֲדַי
עָלֶיךָ	אֵלֶיךָ	אַחֲרֶיךָ	etc.
עָלַיִךְ	אֵלַיִךְ	אַחֲרַיִךְ	
etc.	אֵלָיו	אַחֲרָיו	
	אֵלֶיהָ	etc.	
	אֵלֵינוּ		
	etc.		

Inseparable prepositions, then, do not have a plural.

בְּ	and	לְ		Ex מִן	from
בִּי	in me and me	לִי	to me	מִמֶּנִּי	and מִנִּי
בְּךָ	in you (m.)	לְךָ? and לָךְ	to you (m.)	מִמְּךָ	
בָּךְ	in you (f.)	לָךְ	to you (f.)	מִמֵּךְ	
בּוֹ	in him (m.)	לוֹ	to him (m.)	מִמֶּנּוּ and מִנְהוּ and מֶנְהוּ	
בָּהּ	in her (f.)	לָהּ	to her (f.)	מִמֶּנָּה	

בָּנוּ	לָנוּ	מִמֶּנּוּ
בָּכֶם	etc.	מִכֶּם and מִמְּכֶם
כֶּן		כֶּן כֶּן
בָּהֶם		מִנְהֶם and מֵהֶם and מִמְּהֶם
הֶן		הֶן הֶן הֶן

Examples of Adverbs

כְּמוֹ like, as		אַיֵּה where		הִנֵּה	behold
כָּמוֹנִי				הִנְּנִי	
כָּמוֹךָ		אֵיךְ and אֵיכָה where are you?		הִנְּךָ	
כָּמוֹנוּ		אֵיךְ f.		הִנּוּ and הִנּוֹ	
etc.		אַיּוֹ where is he?		etc.	
		אַיֶּכֶם where are you? m. p.			
		כֶּן where are you? f. p.			
		אַיָּם where are they? m. p.			
		זְ where are they? f. p.			

From the construct of the adverb אַיִן not, which we have said is אֵין, we have:

אֵינֶנִּי not I		אֵינֶנּוּ not we	
אֵינְךָ not you		אֵינְכֶם not you m. p.	
אֵינֵךְ		כֶּן not you f. p.	
אֵינוֹ and אֵינֶנּוּ not he		אֵינָם and אֵינְהֶם m. p.	
אֵינָה and אֵינֶנָּה		הֶן f. p.	

From עוֹד until it is:

עוֹדִי	until I	עוֹדֵנוּ	until we
עוֹדְךָ	until you m. s.	עוֹדְכֶם	until you m. p.
עוֹדֵךְ	until you f. s.	כֶּן	until you f. p.
עוֹדוֹ and עוֹדֶנּוּ	until he m. s.	עוֹדָם	until they m. p.
עוֹדָה and עוֹדֶנָּה	until she f. s.	דְ	until they f. p.

And the rest are declined in the same manner. The reason that vowels of the construct are not retained but are changed in various ways is that nouns contain at least one syllable and it is lengthened when it requires an accent. This is the special reason why vowels change to shorter ones when they add, in the plural, another long syllable with an accent, for otherwise doubtless דָּבָר would in plural be דְּבָרִים, and also other words like it, and they would necessarily require a doubled accent (as we have shown in Chapter 4), and the first syllable would have to be lengthened, which cannot be done so often without great trouble.

As a result, because of the changes which suffixes bring about in vowels, the rules are followed both in changes in plural and in construct. I submit, however, that in order to add a suffix with an accent they could have changed the rules of the plural construct; nor can I easily explain why this could not be done. For just as from מַלְכֵי construct plural of the noun מֶלֶךְ it is מַלְכִי *my king*, so also from construct plural of the noun דִּבְרֵי it could have become דִּבְרֵי *my word*, instead of from the absolute דְּבָרִים to become דְּבָרַי because a noun with a suffix should truly have the significance of a construct. I know indeed that in this manner not infrequently the kind of ambiguity is avoided which often arises if the rule of the plural construct is followed. For if it had been דִּבְרֵי *my word* (developed from דִּבְרֵי) and it had been זָכָר (developed from זִכְרֵי, plural construct of זָכָר *a male*), these nouns may be easily confused with דֶּבֶר *pestilence*, and זֵכֶר *memorial*, and thus appear like דִּבְרִי *my pestilence*, and זִכְרִי *my memorial*. In the same manner many other nouns would be confused, if nouns to which a suffix is added were to follow the rule of plural constructs. And however much this reason seems to carry weight, still I do not dare to affirm for certain that the Hebrews were unwilling to avoid this confusion. For it appears that the Hebrews were not by any means strongly moved to avoid ambiguity, a thing which I could demonstrate with many examples, except that I judge this superfluous. Therefore I am more inclined to believe that the pronominal suffix is added to the construct case of the noun both in singular and plural, and דְּבָרַי *my word*, etc., זְקָנִי *my beard*, etc., are really formed from דְּבַר and זְקַן, the construct singulars of דָּבָר and זָקֵן; however, the ָ kametz of the absolute state was retained because the penultimate before a chirek and cholem requires a kametz, unless of course the noun is מִלְעֵיל as in the case of זַיִת *an olive*, בַּיִת *a house*, or when the letter punctuated by a chirek or a cholem contains a dagesh point, like סַפִּיר *a sapphire*, רַתּוֹק *a chain*. So also from the construct חֲצַר *a courtyard* it is חֲצֵרוֹ *his courtyard*, retaining the tsere of the absolute חָצֵר because, as we have said, a penultimate before a cholem and chirek, cannot be a patach. And in this way all constructs which have a patach in the ultimate and a sheva in the penultimate retain the vowel of the ultimate in the absolute state with a pronominal suffix. But if the penultimate in the construct is not a sheva but one of the vowels which is retained in the plural, such as a patach, a cholem without the accent, a chirek, etc., then the pronominal suffixes are added according to the rules of the construct plurals of nouns, as from פֹּקְדֵי, the construct plural of the participle פֹּקֵד, it is פֹּקְדֵי *my visiting*, and from מַקְלוֹת, the construct plural of the substantive מַקֵּל, it is מַקְלִי *my staff*, etc.

Further monosyllables too, in adding pronominal suffixes, follow the rules of construct plurals. So then שָׂרֵי, חִצֵּי, עֵדַי, etc., the plural constructs of the nouns שַׂר *a prince*, חֵץ *a dart*, עֵד *a witness*, etc., it is שָׂרַי, חִצַּי, עֵדַי, etc.

Nouns which are מִלְעֵיל whose accent, as we have said, changes by the addition of a suffix, are also obliged to follow the rule of construct plurals. Among these are considered all whose penultimate is a segol or a cholem before a segol.

Hence from צֶדֶק, מֶלֶךְ, plural constructs of the substantives זִבְחֵי, צִדְקֵי, מַלְכֵי, זֶבַח, it is מַלְכִי *my king*, צִדְקִי *my righteousness*, and זִבְחִי *my sacrifice*, and from אָזְנִי, construct plural of the substantive אֹזֶן it is אָזְנִי *my ear*; and in the same way from the construct plural substantive גֹּדֶל, רֹחַב, אֹרֶךְ etc., it is גָּדְלִי *my greatness*, רָחְבִּי *my breadth*, אָרְכִּי *my length*, etc.

Concerning nouns which end in a ה and which usually change it into a ת and the preceding two syllables into segol, they are joined with suffixes only in this latter form, and then both segols are modified in the same way as the preceding. For example, in place of תִּפְאָרָה *glory*, עֲטָרָה *a crown*, גְּבִירָה *a lady*, etc., the more elegant form תִּפְאֶרֶת, עֲטֶרֶת, גְּבֶרֶת is frequently used; they, therefore, take on suffixes only in this second form, namely by changing both segols in the same manner as nouns which have the double segol usually do in the construct plural; that is they change the first syllable into a patach or chirek, the second into a sheva. Consequently from תִּפְאֶרֶת it is תִּפְאַרְתִּי *my glory*, and from עֲטֶרֶת it is עֲטַרְתִּי *my crown*, from גְּבֶרֶת it is גְּבִרְתִּי *my lady*. So because קְטוּרָה is used in place of קְטֹרֶת it takes on the suffix in the same way, like a noun whose penultimate is a cholem which has to be changed into a chatuf kametz, and it becomes קְטָרְתִּי *my incense*.

Whence it happens that participles do not take on suffixes in the form of פּוֹקֵדָה but only in the form of פּוֹקֶדֶת, as we have already shown in the paradigms of the participles. But the remaining nouns which end in ה and do not usually change like the preceding, change only the affixed ה into a ת as usual in the construct, except that the ultimate kametz ָ , for reasons already mentioned, is retained and is not changed into a patach as in the construct. Thus from תְּפִלָּה, whose construct is תְּפִלַּת, it is תְּפִלָּתִי *my prayer*; and from בַּקָּשָׁה, whose construct is בַּקָּשַׁת, it is בַּקָּשָׁתִי *my petition*, and in the same the rest are added to the singular construct.

Next, some ה endings, which are retained in construct are generally left off with the suffixes, like שָׂדֶה *a field*, שָׂדְךָ *your field*, מַעֲשֶׂה *a deed*, מַעֲשַׂי *my deed*; and so the others which do not change the ה into a ת in a construct. I said indeed that the ה generally, but not absolutely, is left off, because in the third person it is usually retained, like שָׂדֵהוּ *his field*, מַעֲשֵׂהוּ *his deed*, etc. Thus far concerning the way the suffixes are added to singular nouns in the accepted way. Now let me say a word about the way the same are added acceptably to the plural.

To the plural nouns which end in וֹת both singular and plural suffixes are added without any changes of the construct in the first, second, and third persons; for example בְּרָכָה *a blessing* is in the plural בְּרָכוֹת, and the construct is בִּרְכוֹת, and hence it is בִּרְכוֹתַי, בִּרְכוֹתֶיךָ, בִּרְכוֹתָיו *my, your, his blessings*, etc. So also אֹרַח *a way* is in the plural אֳרָחוֹת and its construct is אָרְחוֹת and hence אָרְחוֹתַי, אָרְחוֹתֶיךָ *my, your ways*; and in this manner all the others which end in וֹת.

But those that end in ים, all of which follow the construct singular, do the same in the plural when the suffix is the singular, or the first person plural; but the second and third person plural suffixes are added to construct plural without changing it, as we have shown in the first paradigm of the substantive noun דָּבָר.

Finally, those which in singular follow the plural construct like מֶלֶךְ, זֶבַח, שֶׁמֶן, etc., suffixes are added to them in plural in the same way as to those with a double kametz. For מֶלֶךְ in the plural becomes מְלָכִים like דָּבָר, דְּבָרִים. And so it is מְלָכַי, מְלָכֶיךָ, מְלָכָיו, מַלְכֵיהֶם, etc., just as in דָּבָר. So also שֶׁרֶשׁ root is in plural שָׁרָשִׁים from which it is שָׁרָשַׁי, שָׁרָשֶׁיךָ, שָׁרָשָׁיו, everywhere retaining the double kametz and therefore doubling the accent. This is concerning the possessive pronouns.

There remains that I add a few words also about the declension of the personal pronoun. With the exception of the indicative, and the relative אֲשֶׁר which, what, that, in that way, and the prefix שֶׁ, none are declinable. But they are developed in this manner:

The Nominative

אֲנִי I   אַתָּה you   הוּא he

The Dative

לִי to me   לְךָ to you   לוֹ to him

The accusative is added to the particle אֵת in this way:

אֹתִי me   אֹתְךָ you   אֹתוֹ him

The Ablative

בִּי in me   בְּךָ in you   בּוֹ in him

And in the same way the plural is formed.
Indicatives are declined like nouns:

m. Nom.	זֶה	this	Sing.
	and		
m. Gen.	הַזֶּה		
m. Dative	לָזֶה		
m. Acc.	הַזֶּה		
m. Abl.	בָּזֶה, מִזֶּה, etc.		

f. Nom.	⎧ זֹאת ⎫	this	Sing.
f. Gen.	⎩ הַזֹּאת ⎭		
f. Dat.	לְזֹאת and לָזֹאת		
Nom. ⎫	הָאֵלֶּה and אֵלֶּה	these	Plur.
Gen. ⎭			
Dat.	לְאֵלֶּה לָאֵלֶּה		

The Relative

אֲשֶׁר and שֶׁ

Nom. ⎫	אֲשֶׁר	Nom. ⎧	שֶׁהָיָה	who was
Gen. ⎭		Gen. ⎩		
Dat.	לַאֲשֶׁר	Dat.	לְשֶׁהָיָה	
	etc.		etc.	

CHAPTER 12

OF THE INFINITIVE NOUNS, THE VARIATIONS OF THEIR FORMS AND KINDS

Infinitive nouns express an action in either an active or a passive relationship. For example: *to visit someone* is recorded in the active, and *to be visited by someone* in the passive. Next, the nouns express action either simply or intensely, whether related in the active or passive; like *to call upon* and *to visit*, *to break* and *to destroy*. The first of these expresses a simple action of *calling upon* and *breaking*, but the second expresses a stronger or more frequent action of *calling upon* and *breaking*.

The Hebrew forms by which an action recorded in the active mood are most simply expressed are פָּקוֹד, פָּקֵד, פָּקַד, and פָּקַד, whose constructs (as we said in Chapter 8) are פְּקוֹד and פְּקַד. But those which express an action recorded in the passive mood are נִפְקֹד, הִפָּקֵד, and הִפָּקוֹד.[1] These forms פָּקַד, פָּקֵד, and

---

1. [Modern grammarians call these *kal* and *niph'al*.]

פָּקוֹד express an action with relation to the intensity or frequency of the act. These forms are particularly distinguished from the former in that the second letter is doubled, and therefore they always have a dagesh in that letter. Finally, a distinct intensive action recorded in the passive is expressed by a kibbutz and a cholem with a dagesh in the second letter, in the Sacred Scriptures; like גֻּנַּב.[2]

Besides, the Hebrews are accustomed to relate an action toward the first cause which brought it into being, as it were one action arising from another or as something performed by its own function; for example פָּקוֹד means *to visit*, הַפְקֵד, הִפְקִיד, or הַפְקִיד means *to cause someone to visit*. מָלוֹךְ means *to reign*, הַמְלִיךְ, etc., *to cause someone to reign*. So from אָכוֹל *to eat*, it is הַאֲכִיל *to cause another to eat*, and from בּוֹא *to come* it is הָבִיא *to cause to come*, or *to bring*; יָדוֹעַ *to know*, הוֹדִיעַ *make one to know*, or *reveal*. And in the passive form, these are הָפְקֵד *to be caused to visit*, הָמְלַךְ *to be caused to reign*, etc.[3]

Not only names of actions but also names of things which bring it about that a thing fulfill its function, as I have said, are related to the cause in the same manner. Thus from מָטָר *rain* it is הַמְטִיר *to make it rain*, and from אֹזֶן *an ear* it is הַאֲזִין *to make an ear perform its function*, that is, *to listen*, and from שָׁלוֹם *peace* it is הִשְׁלִים *to establish peace* or *to make firm*, and so many more in this manner.

There are, then, six kinds of infinitives, by which both the active and the passive are expressed. First: פָּקוֹד, etc., *to visit*. Second: נִפְקוֹד, הִפָּקֵד, etc., *to be visited*. Third: פַּקֵּד, etc., *to visit frequently*. Fourth: פֻּקַּד *to be visited frequently*. Fifth: הִפְקִיד, etc., *to bring it about that someone visits*, or *to cause someone to visit*. Sixth: (finally) הָפְקֵד *to be made to visit*. And these, as we have said, express the kinds of action whether relating to the active or passive mood.

But because it frequently happens that one and the same person is both the actor and the person acted upon, it was necessary for the Hebrews to form a new and seventh kind of infinitive which should express an action recorded simultaneously in the active and passive, that it, which should have the form of active and passive at the same time. For example in Hebrew it is impossible to say *I visit myself* through any kind of a personal pronoun, because פָּקוֹד אוֹתִי means *another to visit me*, that is, *someone visits me*, and פָּקְדִי or פָּקְדִי means *my visiting someone*, that is, *that I visit someone*. Therefore it was necessary to devise another form of infinitive which would express an action related to the active mood or to the imminent cause; and this is usually expressed by placing before the third kind of infinitive the syllable הִת, with a dagesh, like הִתְפַּקֵּד which as we have said, means *visiting oneself* or *causing oneself to visit*, or something like *serving to visit oneself*, as we shall explain at length in the chapters on Syntax.

---

2. [Modern grammarians call these *pi'el* and *pu'al*.]
3. [Modern grammarians call these *hiph'il* and *hoph'al*.]

CHAPTER 13

OF THE CONJUGATION

Up until now we have shown the mutations of the infinitive noun by which it expresses any relationship other than time which it bears either through the construct, or by the addition of a preposition, or by means of suffixes, or for a variety of reasons which are usually given. It remains for us to explain the other causes for mutations and those in which this type of noun is unusual. That infinitive nouns differ in many ways because of the tense to which they refer and the mode which they express is common to every language; and, because I write largely for those who are versed in other languages, I refrain from explaining what tense is and what mode is, but I will show only that which among the Hebrews is unusual in this respect.

The Hebrews usually refer actions to no other time than to the past and the future. The reason for this seems to be that they acknowledge only these two divisions of time, and that they consider the present tense only as a point, that is as the end of the past and the beginning of the future. I say they viewed time to be like a line consisting of many points each of which they considered the end of one part and the beginning of another. And these tenses are principally differentiated by signs of the person, that is those signs of the person which precede or are added to certain forms of the infinitive. I said, *principally*. For the third person past is differentiated from the rest because it never has the sign of person. For example, פָּקַד, פָּקֹד, פָּקָד, פָּקֵד are forms of the infinitive of the first kind, and they have the power of substantive nouns; but in speech they are generally used as adjectives which agree with their nominatives in gender, number, and case, and they indicate an action as relating to the past. Hence הוּא פָּקַד, הוּא חָפֵץ, הוּא יָכוֹל means *he visited, he was able, he wanted*; but הִיא פָּקְדָה, הִיא חָפְצָה, הִיא יָכְלָה means *she visited, she was able, she wanted*. Thus it is clear that the forms of the infinitive are like substantive adjectives, but when tense and person are determined they become like adjectives which must agree with nominative as well as the substantive, as we have said, in gender, number, and case. This third person masculine past is differentiated only in that it lacks the personal endings; but the others, namely the first and second person singulars, have the endings which are put after these forms like פָּקַדְתָּ *you* (m.) *have visited*, פָּקַדְתְּ *you* (f.) *have visited*, and פָּקַדְתִּי *I have visited*, etc., as will be seen in the following.

Next, the forms of the infinitive construct are פְּקֹד and פְּקָד and by using the signs of the person prefixed to these as with adjectives, and with the perfect, the future is indicated like אֶפְקֹד or אֶפְקָד *I shall visit*, תִּפְקֹד *you will visit*, etc., as will also be seen in the following. This is true of infinitives when they refer to a certain time.

Now let us see what changes occur in these nouns when they express the different modes.[1] Indeed the Hebrews were not very much disturbed by these. For, just as cases were recognized only by prepositions or the construction of a sentence, so also were modes generally recognized from adverbs. And, to be sure, almost all nations neglected to modify nouns in order to determine the case as something superfluous; and distinctions of mode seemed superfluous to all. For no nation that I know of distinguishes the interrogative mode from the indicative mode, and we do not see any confusion of speech from it; and so there can be no confusion of speech from it among the Hebrews as long as their language flourishes, if all modes, except the imperative, agree with the indicative.

The Hebrews then distinguish only the imperative mode from the others, namely, by taking the infinitive construct and inflecting it without any sign of person, and without any relationship as to time, in this manner, פְּקֹד or פְּקָד *you visit* (m. s.) פִּקְדִי *you visit* (f. s.) פִּקְדוּ *you visit* (m. p.). פְּקֹדְנָה *you visit* (f. p.). But this mode is excessively imperious and is therefore not used in the presence of equals, and much less in the presence of superiors, but rather in its place we usually use the future; whence one may affirm that the past and future of the mode we are treating are not any more indicatives than any other modes by which an action with relationship to time can be expressed.

We have shown all the reasons then for which infinitive nouns are changed into various modes. These changes together with the others we shall call *conjugations*, and the infinitive nouns, so far as they are thus conjugated, we shall name *verbs*. We shall say a few words concerning the number of their conjugations, for not all infinitives (which is a common fault of all languages) are conjugated in the same way.

The grammarians usually divide the conjugations into seven, as that many varieties of infinitives are found in each and every action, as we have shown in the previous chapter. But, if this division is valid then the Latins would have only two, namely, an active and a passive, and the Greeks would have three conjugations, namely active, passive, and intermediate, and for this reason, irregular verbs are confused with regular verbs, as indeed common grammarians do by following this rule.

But if they say that these seven classes of infinitives all have the same force and they do not differ naturally but only in the form of conjugation, the Latins, by virtue of their deponent verbs, which are the only ones to differ from active verbs in conjugation, do indeed have only two conjugations.

So that we may teach them more easily we are dividing them into eight, of which the *first* will be those verbs whose infinitive never contains gutturals nor quiescent letters; *second* the verbs whose infinitive ends in א; the *third* whose infinitive ends in ה; the *fourth* whose infinitive ends in ח or ע or ר; the *fifth*

---

1. [Spinoza here refers to the four modes: indicative, interrogative, subjunctive, and imperative.]

whose infinitive begins with a י; *sixth* whose infinitive has quiescent ו, י, or א in the middle; *seventh* whose infinitive has an א, ה, ח, or ע at the beginning; *eighth* whose infinitive has a guttural ח or ע, or a non-quiescent א or ה. I think that this is enough to say in general regarding tense, mode, and conjugation.

But perhaps for many who are accustomed to other languages it will seem absurd that I should declare verbs indicating past and future, or in imperative mode, to be adjectives, and that infinitives are to me nothing but substantive adjectives. And this, I say, might also seem absurd, namely that nouns should require an accusative. In truth the Hebrew language bears testimony that this is not incompatible with the nature of nouns, where indeed nouns, which express action in the abstract, require an accusative, or a case of a verb. For example: *The love of the Lord toward the sons of Israel* is thus expressed in the Scriptures: אהבת יהוה את בני ישראל, lit.: *The Lord's love of the children of Israel*. The noun *love* requires the accusative just like the verb אהב *to love:* and similarly, many others will be found, of which in the Syntaxes.

But this should by no means be passed over, that for this reason nouns can serve for infinitives, לְאַהֲבָה אֶת יְהוָה *to a love of the Lord,* for *to love the Lord,* לְיִרְאָה אֶת יְהוָה *to a fear of the Lord* for *to fear the Lord,* לְאַשְׁמָה בָּהּ *to a guilt by it,* and many more in this manner.

CHAPTER 14

OF VERBS OF THE FIRST CONJUGATION

PARADIGMS
Simple Active Verbs (KAL[1])

The forms of the infinitive in absolute state, as we have already frequently said, are פָּקֹד, פָּקַד, פָּקָד, and פְּקֹד; in the construct they are פְּקֹד and פְּקָד. The past tense is formed from the absolute in this way:

Fem.	Masc.		Fem.	Masc.
פָּקְדָה	פָּקַד	(he) (she) visited	פְּקָדָה	פָּקֹד
פָּקַדְתְּ	פָּקַדְתָּ	you visited	פְּקֹדְתְּ	פְּקֹדְתָּ

---

1. [The term *kal*, used by modern Hebrew historians, does not occur in Spinoza's work.]

פָּקַדְתִּי	I visited (common gender)	פָּקַדְתִּי
פָּקְדוּ	they visited (common gender)	פָּקְדוּ
פְּקַדְתֶּן פְּקַדְתֶּם	you visited	פְּקַדְתֶּן פְּקַדְתֶּם
פָּקַדְנוּ	we visited	פָּקַדְנוּ

פָּקַד and פָּקֹד follow the first formula פָּקַד.

The imperative is formed from the construct in this way:

Feminine		Masculine	
פִּקְדִי and	פְּקִדִי	פְּקֹד or פְּקַד	you visit (s.)
פְּקֹדְןָ or	פְּקֹדְנָה	פִּקְדוּ or פָּקְדוּ	you visit (pl.)

The future is formed from the imperative in this way:

Fem.	Masc.		Fem.	Masc.
	אֶפְקֹד	I shall visit		אֶפְקַד
תִּפְקְדִי	תִּפְקֹד	you shall visit	תִּפְקְדִי	תִּפְקַד
תִּפְקֹד	יִפְקֹד	(he) (she) shall visit	תִּפְקַד	יִפְקַד
	נִפְקֹד	we shall visit		נִפְקַד
תִּפְקֹדְנָה	{ תִּפְקְדוּ יִפְקְדוּ }	you shall visit they shall visit	תִּפְקַדְנָה	{ תִּפְקְדוּ יִפְקְדוּ }

and יִפְקְדֶנָה like מַלְכֻיוֹת יַעֲמֹדְנָה Daniel 8:22, and 1 Samuel 6:12, וַיִּשַּׁרְנָה הַפָּרוֹת, etc.

Notes on the Infinitive

We have shown in the proper place that infinitives are declined like other nouns. I should like to add this, that their cases are indicated not only by the prepositional prefixes ל, ב, כ, מ, but also by other prepositions, like לִפְנֵי שַׁחֵת יְהוָֹה *before the destruction of the Lord*, that is, *before he destroyed*, עַד אֲבוֹד *until the loss*, for *while they were losing*, etc.

Since there are so many infinitive forms in the past tense of every verb it is clear why the same verb uses now this and now that form, like גְּדֹל (Numbers 6:15) and גָּדוֹל (2 Samuel 5:10) *to grow*, דְּבֵר and דַּבֵּר *to speak*, and others similarly. To be sure in Isaiah 47:14 לְחָמָם occurs. Although in the Scriptures there is not found an infinitive with a double kametz ָ , I do not doubt that the Hebrews did have these and all the other forms of the infinitive which I mentioned. For, as I said, among the Hebrews verbs are adjectives which agree with the nominative in gender, number, and case; and these adjectives absolutely point to the infinitive, without using a nominative as if it were a substantive without gender.

And when you take completely any form of the past and the imperative without the nominative you are expressing the infinitive. Nay more, but also the participle itself, as I shall show in its place, can become a substantive, and may be used for an infinitive. N.B. כַּהֲתִימְךָ שֹׁדֵד Isaiah 31:1.

Further, it is customary to supplement the past infinitive with the paragogic letter ה which in the construct is changed to ת. Thus from קְרוֹב it is קָרְבָה *to approach*, whose construct is קָרוֹבַת. To this construct the suffixes are added in this manner קָרְבָתִי, קָרְבָתְךָ, קָרְבָתוֹ, *my, your, his approach*, etc. So from יָכוֹל *to be able* it is יְכָלָה, and in the construct יְכֹלֶת, like מִבִּלְתִּי יְכֹלֶת יְהוָה *because the Lord is not able*, and with suffixes added it is יְכָלְתִּי, יְכָלְתְּךָ, יְכָלְתּוֹ *my, your, his ability*, etc.

Further, instead of a ה, we are able to add a נ to the infinitive, an example of which is found in the book of Esther chapter 9, verse 5, where אֲבָדְן *to persist* is found instead of אֲבֹד.

Next, the construct פְּקֹד, if it lacks an accent, changes the cholem to kametz chatuf, like לִפְנֵי מְלָךְ־מֶלֶךְ *before the reign of the king*.

Finally, the example in Ezra 10:17, where לִדְרִיוֹשׁ occurs instead of לִדְרוֹשׁ *to inquire*, which the grammarians note as an exception, to me seems as something strange and I do not venture to explain it.

Notes on the Past Tense

פָּקַד, פָּקֹד, פָּקֵד, and פָּקַד differ from infinitives, as we have said, in that they are in the past tense, masculine in gender, and singular in number, and in the infinitive they have no gender nor number; and this difference is easily recognized by practice in speech itself.

The feminine פָּקְדָה, when it has the accent אתנח or סִילּוּק, changes the sheva into a kametz, cholem, or tsere, that is into the masculine form, without that change of sound which came from the addition of the ה, so that the feminine form פָּקְדָה is פָּקַד; and from פָּקֹד, פָּקֹדָה; and, finally, from פָּקֵד, פָּקֵדָה.

פָּקַדְתָּ has the letter ת as characteristic of the second person, taken from the pronoun אַתָּה *you*; and sometimes the ה from the pronoun also remains, like בְּגַדְתָּה, but more often it is usual to omit it.

Verbs which end in ת lose it in the second and first persons, and are compensated by a dagesh in the succeeding ת, like כָּרַתָּ, כָּרַתְּ, כָּרַתִּי *he cut, you cut, I cut*.

פָּקַדְתְּ in the second person feminine has the ending taken from the feminine pronoun אַתְּ *you*; and the obsolete אַתִּי, which we noted above is the obsolescent expression פָּקַדְתִּי for פָּקַדְתְּ like Ruth 3:3 וְשָׁכַבְתִּי *you slept* (f.) for שָׁכַבְתְּ; and so many more which have been corrected by the Massorites doubtless because they were obsolete.

פָּקַדְתִּי has the ending from the pronoun אֲנִי *I*. The gender is common as everywhere in the first person.

פָּקְדוּ, the ending in the plural is the same as with the pronoun, which ends in the plural, as we have noted above, in ו and not ם־, like the rest of the adjectives. It occurs also for euphony with the paragogic ן like יָדְעוּן *they knew*. I believe that the ancients were accustomed to distinguish here the masculine from the feminine by the quiescent א and ה, namely, *they visited* (m.) פָּקְדוּא *they visited* (f.) פָּקְדָה. Examples of this sort are found in the Scriptures, like Deut. 21:7 יָדֵינוּ לֹא שָׁפְכָה *our hands did not spill*, and Joshua 10:24 אַנְשֵׁי הַמִּלְחָמָה הֶהָלְכוּא *men of war who went*. But later writers seem to have disregarded these quiescent letters, because in the pronunciation no difference is able to be sensed, and also because they might be confused with paragogic letters.

Moreover, when the accent is אתנח or סילוק the penultimate sheva is changed, as in the singular third person feminine, into a ָ, ֵ, or a cholem, becoming in place of פָּקְדוּ either פָּקֵדוּ, פָּקָדוּ or פָּקֹדוּ.

Finally פְּקַדְתֶּם, פְּקַדְתֶּן and פְּקַדְנוּ take on the endings from the pronouns אַתֶּם, אַתֶּן *you* and אֲנַחְנוּ *we*.

Notes on the Imperative

I have placed the imperative before the future, because the latter is formed from the former, and because the future is very frequently used in place of the imperative, so that it is possible to affirm that the future among the Hebrews agrees both with the indicative and the imperative modes.

We have said that the forms of the imperative are פְּקֹד and פְּקַד, if you please also פְּקֵד; to which the paragogic ה is not rarely added, so that from פְּקֹד it is פָּקְדָה, and from פְּקַד it is פִּקְדָה (m.) *you visit!* From this comes the infinitive form הָאָכָה, יִרְאָה and with the accent athnach or siluk it is פְּקֹדָה; when the accent is eliminated, as in the infinitive, it changes the cholem into a kametz chatuf, like פְּסָל־לְךָ *hew thyself*.

Notes on the Future

אֶפְקֹד and אֶפְקַד, when the paragogic ה is added to them, change the cholem and patach into a sheva, and become אֶפְקְדָה *I shall visit*. But when accented with either an אתנח or a סילוק the cholem remains, and the ־ changes to ָ, becoming אֶפְקֹדָה and אֶפְקָדָה.

And תִּפְקְדִי with the paragogic ן becomes תִּפְקְדִין *you* (f.) *will visit*, and from the form תִּפְקַד it is תִּפְקַדִין, namely changing the ־ to a ַ on account of the following chirek.

נִפְקֹד, when the paragogic ה is added to it, changes the cholem into ְ and becomes נִפְקְדָה, but accented with אתנח and סילוק, like in first person singulars the חֹלֶם is retained and the ־ changes to a ָ.

And תִּפְקְדוּ with paragogic ן becomes תִּפְקְדוּן and תִּפְקְדוּן and תִּפְקֻדוּן. If it has a dividing accent it retains the form of the singular becoming תִּפְקֹדוּ and תִּפְקְדוּ *you* (m. p.) *will visit*. Before a monosyllable, because the accent should be on the penultimate, a shurek is usually used in place of a cholem, like יִשְׁפּוּטוּ הֵם (Exod. 18:26) *they judged themselves*. Finally in the case of Leviticus 21:5 לֹא יִקְרְחָה קָרְחָה I believe it to be a mistake of the copyist who wrote קָרְחָה twice hastily.

תִּפְקֹדְנָה and תִּפְקַדְנָה: the ה can be left off, like תִּלְבָּשְׁ *dressed*; and as from the feminine singular תִּפְקֹד the third person plural can become תִּפְקְדוּ, so that both in singular and in plural, the third person feminine agrees with the second person masculine. Thus Jeremiah 49:1 וְאַלְמְנוֹתֶיךָ עָלַי תִּבְטָחוּ *and let your widows trust in me*, in place of תִּבְטַחְנָה. The reason the letter ט has the ָ in place of the ַ is that the ָ is used on account of the סִילוּק, as we have said it is everywhere.

CHAPTER 15

Of Passive Verbs (Niph'al[1])

The sign of the passive is a נ prefixed to the verb, which requires often to be compensated by a dagesh, because never do two signs (characteristics) attach to a verb. Therefore their forms of infinitive are נִפְקַד, נִפְקוֹד, הִפָּקֵד, and הִפָּקוֹד. The נ in the two which have a ה is compensated by a dagesh. Of the two first the forms are produced in this manner.

The Past

f.	m.	
נִפְקְדָה	נִפְקַד or נִפְקוֹד	*he is visited.*
נִפְקַדְתְּ	נִפְקַדְתָּ	
	נִפְקַדְתִּי	
	נִפְקְדוּ	
נִפְקַדְתֶּן	נִפְקַדְתֶּם	
	נִפְקַדְנוּ	

The Imperative

f.	m.
הִפָּקְדִי	הִפָּקֵד
הִפָּקַדְנָה	הִפָּקְדוּ

---

1. [Here again, the term *niph'al* is not used by Spinoza.]

Another Form of the Imperative

f.	m.
נִפְקְדִי	נִפְקַד
נִפְקַדְנָה	נִפְקְדוּ

The Future

f.	m.
	אֶפָּקֵד and אֶפָּקַד
תִּפָּקְדִי	תִּפָּקֵד
תִּפָּקֵד	יִפָּקֵד
	נִפָּקֵד
תִּפָּקַדְנָה	תִּפָּקְדוּ
and	
תִּפָּקֵדְנָה	יִפָּקְדוּ

Notes

Although in the Scriptures the infinitive נִפְקָד does not occur, nevertheless it is certain from what was said above that the formulas of all modes express the infinitive when they are used as substantives which are of no gender; and truly there is no reason why this form of infinitive should less be able to express the past, than the form נִפְקַד especially when it is possible to use both forms in the past tense, like נַחְתּוֹם and נֶחְתָּם it is sealed.

Verbs which end in ן leave it off in the first and second person, compensating it with a dagesh. This will be observed in what follows: that not only the ן, but also where any other doubled letter occurs, the first should always have a quiescent sheva, like תִּצָּפְנָה in place of תִּצָּפֶנָּה. For if this were not so (as was said in Chapter 3), then the sheva ִ would have to be pronounced, when otherwise it always is silent. It should be observed that when the verb has the accent אתנח or סִילוּק, the last syllable, if it is long, remains and it is not changed to a sheva, as it otherwise should. I said *if it is long*, for were it a patach, it would be changed to a kametz; for example from the future אֶפָּקֵד when the paragogic ה is added it is אֶפָּקְדָה *I am visited*. But if it has a pausal accent, the tsere is retained, becoming אֶפָּקֵדָה. But נִפְקְדָה *she is visited*, with a similar accent does not retain the patach of the masculine נִפְקַד but changes to a ָ , becoming נִפְקָדָה; on the other hand the cholem of the masculine נִפְקֹד, because it is long, remains, becoming נִפְקֹדָה. This rule will be observed wherever verbs have a sheva mobile in the penultimate. I do not need to mention this constantly.

The imperative הִפָּקֵד, because it occurs frequently in the Scriptures, is considered regular; but in the form of נִפְקַד, נִפְקְדִי, etc., because it occurs only once in the Bible (namely, Joel chap. 4, vs. 11), is considered either as irregular, or completely neglected. I do not know whether they believed the purpose of the Scriptures to be the language rather than the teachings.

Finally, the future in this conjugation is augmented for the sake of elegance, as in the active verb, with the paragogic ה, like אֶכָּבְדָה for אֶכָּבֵד *I am honored*; nor is it inelegant in the plural of the same to add a ן after the וּ, like יִכָּרֵתוּן for יִכָּרְתוּ *they were cut off*; which is being used also in the conjugations to follow.

CHAPTER 16

OF THE ACTIVE INTENSIVE VERB WITH A DAGESH (PI'EL[1])

We touched briefly above upon the significance of this verb form only because we wanted to show its origin; but since it has various uses it is necessary that we explain it accurately, because already something of its manner has been discussed. The principal and common use of this form is to intensify the simple verb. This is done in various ways, either by rendering an intransitive verb into a transitive, or by broadening its significance, or by expressing it with feeling, etc. For example שָׂמַח means *to be happy* שִׂמַּח renders the verb from the intransitive into transitive and signifies *to make someone happy*; and these changes apply also to nominal verbs, like דִּבֵּר *to make words* or *speak*, which is from דָּבָר *a word*. שָׁלַח means to *send somebody somewhere* while שִׁלַּח means *to dismiss someone*, namely an *assembly*, a *servant*, etc. Next שָׁבַר (Belgian *schillen*) means *he broke*, שִׁבֵּר means *he broke strongly* or *he destroyed*.

By the way, this verb sometimes has meaning contrary to the simple active verb, like חָטָא *he sinned*, חִטֵּא *he purified*. But since this form of usage seems already to have disappeared from the language, one should not form new forms in this manner except those which are found in Scriptures. The infinitive forms are פַּקֵּד, פַּקֵּד, פָּקוֹד, and פִּקּוֹד.

Past			Imperative		Future		
f.	m.		f.	m.	f.	m.	
פִּקְּדָה	פִּקֵּד	3. sing.	פַּקְּדִי	פַּקֵּד		אֲפַקֵּד	1. sing.
פִּקַּדְתְּ	פִּקַּדְתָּ	2.	פַּקֵּדְנָה	פַּקְּדוּ	תְּפַקְּדִי	תְּפַקֵּד	2.
	פִּקַּדְתִּי	1.				יְפַקֵּד	3.

---

1. [Spinoza does not use this term.]

פָּקְדוּ	3. plur.		נִפְקֹד	1. plur.
פְּקַדְתֶּם פְּקַדְתֶּן	2.		תִּפְקְדוּ ⎱ תִּפְקֹדְנָה	2.
פָּקַדְנוּ	1.		יִפְקְדוּ ⎰	3.

Notes on the Infinitive

To the infinitive form פְּקֹד the paragogic ה is added for elegance, becoming פְּקֹדָה, and with the athnach or siluk פְּקֹדָה *to visit often*, changing the sheva into a tsere.

Incidentally, to this form of the infinitive there is sometimes prefixed the definite article ה, like וְהַקְטֵר אֲשֶׁר יַקְטִירוּן[2] and *that burnt offering that they offered (et illud suffumigare, quod suffumigabant). En dat geduurig Wierooken* (Jer. 44:21). In Belgian, the continuous burnt offering. So הַדַּבֵּר *the speaking (illud loqui), dat hoog spreken, dat kaekelen zal kaekelen zal gedaan zijn.* In Belgian, the lofty speaking/the sounds like cackling. The ה serves here not so much to indicate a definite action, but also to express action with indignation, reproach, aversion, or some other emotion; and for this reason I believe that this definite article ה can be placed only before a *pi'el* form of the verb.

Next if the middle radical is a ר, which cannot have a dagesh, then the previous short syllable changes to long, namely a ִ into a ֵ , and a chirek into a tsere, like בָּרֵךְ instead of בַּרֵּךְ, and בָּרֵךְ instead of בָּרֵךְ *to bless* (see Numbers 23:24).

But grammarians think that the dagesh is also compensated by a cholem, when the middle radical is a ר or any other letter that does usually admit a dagesh. But they are mistaken; because those of this conjugation which have a cholem and a tsere are not intensive verbs but simple verbs whose infinitives, as we have already said, have the form of a participle, namely by taking the participle without any relationship as to gender. Thus זֹעֵם *to detest* is really a simple verb whose infinitive is the participle itself taken without a substantive, and if to this the paragogic ה is added it becomes זֹעֲמָה, which is also used in place of the infinitive, just like the infinitive שָׁמוֹר *observe* and זָכוֹר *keep*, of which in the section on Syntax. But here I speak expressly of verbs of this conjugation. As for conjugations of verbs which have as the middle radical a vav or yod like בִּין *to discern*, קוּם *to arise*, the intensives are without a dagesh, but the third radical is doubled in place of the second, becoming בּוֹנֵן from בִּין, and קוֹמֵם from קוּם. But of this in its place. What deceived the grammarians, I think, is nothing else than that they didn't believe that there exists a simple active verb שָׁרָשׁ *to take root, to root out*; and so they considered its participle, שֹׁרֵשׁ, which occurs in Isaiah 40:24 as the past tense of an intensive verb of the first conjugation, and

---

2. [This seems a misquotation. The proper citation is Jer. 44:21, אֶת־הַקִּטֵּר אֲשֶׁר קִטַּרְתֶּם, "The offering which ye offered." — M.L.M.]

confused it with the passive שָׁרֵשׁ from the intensive verb שֵׁרֵשׁ. The double meaning of this verb helped not a little in this, where one is plainly contrary to the other (if we should have faith in the punctuators of the Bible). In chapter 31 of Job it means *to root out*; in Jer. 12:2 it means *to take root*. Truly I doubt the passage in Jer., or else the punctuators instead of שָׁרְשׁוּ have punctuated שֵׁרְשׁוּ. But of this enough.

Further, in the form פְּקֹד without the accent, the ֵ changes to ֶ like דַּבֶּר־לְךָ *speak to you*.

Finally, of verbs whose second and third radical is the same letter, the intensive usually doubles the first, inserting the duplicate letter between the second and the third radicals, like קִלְקֵל from קָלַל *to be neat*, סִכְסֵךְ *to protect* from סָכַךְ *to cover*, גִּלְגֵּל *to revolve* from גָּלַל *to roll*, and so the others.

Notes on the Past Tense

The past tense often changes the tsere into a patach, like שָׁבַר and שִׁבֵּר *to break in pieces*, or into a segol, like דִּבֶּר *he has spoken*.

Notes on the Imperative

The imperative also often changes the tsere into a patach, and before the makaf into a segol, and from פְּקֹד it becomes either פְּקַד or פְּקֶד, and פְּקַדְנָה, in place of פְּקֹדְנָה. For the rest it agrees in all with the infinitive.

Notes on the Future

From אֶפְקֹד, adding the paragogic ה, it becomes אֶפְקְדָה, and with the accent athnach or siluk אֶפְקֹדָה; from יִפְקְדוּ, תִּפְקְדוּ adding the paragogic ן, it becomes יִפְקְדוּן. So that the paragogic ה renders the penultimate short from long, the ן on the other hand makes it long from short. Finally in place of תִּפְקֹדְנָה it is often, as in the imperative תִּפְקַדְנָה.

CHAPTER 17

Of Passive Intensive Verbs (Pu'al[1])

Infinitive	The Past			The Imperative is lacking	The Future		
	f.	m.		f.		m.	
פֻּקֹד	פֻּקְדָה	פֻּקַּד	3. sing.			אֲפֻקַּד	3. sing.
	פֻּקַדְתְּ	פֻּקַדְתָּ	2.	תְּפֻקְּדִי		תְּפֻקַּד	2.
		פֻּקַדְתִּי	1.			יְפֻקַּד	1.
		פֻּקְּדוּ	3. pl.			נְפֻקַּד	3. pl.
	פֻּקַדְתֶּן	פֻּקַדְתֶּם	2.	תְּפֻקַּדְנָה {		תְּפֻקְּדוּ	2.
		פֻּקַּדְנוּ	1.			יְפֻקְּדוּ	1.

The use of this form of the verb is very rare, nor is there in the Scriptures any other form of it in the infinitive. On the contrary, I remember to have seen it in the Scriptures only a single time;[2] but, I do not doubt that the future אֲפֻקַּד is formed from another form of the formula פֻּקַּד, and consequently, that the Hebrews had, in addition to the infinitive פֻּקֹד also the form פֻּקַּד. For besides that we have shown that the future is everywhere formed from the infinitive, in the rest of the conjugations, as we shall see, the infinitive has a patach which, however, agrees with the others in the rest of the tenses. In addition I do not doubt that they had a third form פֻּקַּד with a kametz chatuf, because this is also used in the other conjugations, and the ֻ and ָ chatuf have the same force as you will see below in Chapter 19.

However, since the middle radical is a ר, which does not admit a dagesh, the ֻ is changed into a cholem, like טוֹרָף *to be torn in pieces*.

Finally, because this passive form is sufficiently distinguished from the active by the vowels, on that account the letter נ, the characteristic of the passive, was most often neglected. Usually, however, it was also added, and in place of פֻּקַּד as a rule נְפֻקַּד was written like "יְדֵיכֶם נְגֹאֲלוּ בַדָּם" *your hands are polluted with*

---

1. [This term is not used by Spinoza.—M.L.M.]
2. [Spinoza is probably referring to Gen. 40:15.—M.L.M.]

blood, the ב being punctuated with הִלֵּם because of the succeeding א, which cannot take a dagesh. The grammarians note this as an exception because it occurs only rarely in the Scriptures, as if composed of a simple passive and intensive verb. To be sure, as we have said, they wrote grammar of the Scriptures, not of the language. I believe, however, that in the future tense this letter נ was always neglected because on account of the characteristic of the person, it had to be pointed with a dagesh; and, since the letters פ and ק also had to be doubled, it could scarcely be pronounced.

CHAPTER 18

OF THE DERIVATIVE (CAUSATIVE) VERB (HIPHʿIL[1])

We have shown above in Chapter 12 that this verb is derived or formed from the names of things or actions, that is from either a substantive noun or a simple verb. When it is formed from a simple verb it requires an active accusative, namely, a person upon whom the action is visited, and it takes a nominative as the remote cause, namely, the person who causes another to be visited. But when it is formed from a noun, it has the force of a simple verb, the reason for which can be easily understood from what was said there. Truly we have said that by this verb is expressed what anyone does in order that a thing should accomplish its own function, that is, that actually it has its own proper use. So that when this verb is formed from a simple verb, then it signifies that someone brings it about that an efficient cause (or that which we understand as a nominative of simple active verb) may actually accomplish its use. But when it is formed from a noun then it signifies nothing else but that someone simply makes use of a thing. And therefore it happens that this verb doesn't always have an active accusative, but they are like the verbs of the first form *(kal)* both active and passive (transitive and intransitive), as we have shown above by many examples. Its forms in the infinitive are הַפְקִיד, הַפְקֵד, הַפְקֵד, and הַפְקֵד, etc.

From those the tenses are formed in this manner:

---

1. [This term is not used by Spinoza.—M.L.M.]

The Past

f.	m.	
הִפְקִידָה	הִפְקִיד	3. sing.
הִפְקַדְתְּ	הִפְקַדְתָּ	2.
	הִפְקַדְתִּי	1.
	הִפְקִידוּ	3. pl.
הִפְקַדְתֶּן	הִפְקַדְתֶּם	2.
	הִפְקַדְנוּ	1.

The Imperative

f.	m.	
הַפְקִידִי	הַפְקֵד	2. sing.
הַפְקֵדְנָה	הַפְקִידוּ	2. pl.

The Future

f.	m.	
	אַפְקִיד	1. sing.
תַּפְקִידִי	תַּפְקִיד	2.
תַּפְקִיד	יַפְקִיד	3.
	נַפְקִיד	1. pl.
תַּפְקֵדְנָה {	תַּפְקִידוּ	2.
	יַפְקִידוּ	3.

or

| | אַפְקֵד | 1. |
| 2. תַּפְקֵד 2. f. תִּפְקְדִי | | |

Notes

It is characteristic of this form that the ה never changes to a ת as many grammarians think, because they are misled by a text in Hosea 11:3. For תִּרְגַּלְתִּי, as Moses Kimchi* rightly states, is a noun, and is the nominative of the succeeding verb קָחָם, the final י, however, is paragogic, often being added to nouns for the sake of elegance. For as from אָהֵבַת it becomes אֲהַבְתִּי, and from אוֹיֶבֶת it becomes אוֹיַבְתִּי so also from תַּרְגֶּלֶת it becomes תִּרְגַּלְתִּי, and it means *a woman who teaches children to walk, to talk*, etc. Those who think otherwise plainly do not understand the text. Also, grammarians think that the characteristic of this

---

* "קָחָם זכר תרגלתי נקבה על דרך תפלצתך השיא אותך." That is, the word קָחָם is masculine, and תרגלתי is feminine gender, in the same way as occurs in Jeremiah 49:16 תִּפְלַצְתְּךָ הִשִּׁיא אֹתָךְ.

verb may change into an א, namely in Isaiah chap. 63, vs. 3. But I think that of this there is no instance given in the Scriptures; but I do not deny that it is permissible. For a verb whose characteristic is הִתְ usually changes ה into א and chirek into ־ִ. About this matter see Chapter 20.

CHAPTER 19

OF THE DERIVATIVE PASSIVE VERB (HOPHʿAL[1])

The infinitive forms are הָפְקֵד and הֻפְקַד and I believe it may also become הָפְקַד. For the passive is distinguished from the active by the kibbutz and kametz chatuf, whence:

	The Past				The Imperative	
f.	m.			f.	m.	
הָפְקְדָה	הָפְקַד }	3. sing.		הָפְקְדִי	הָפְקַד	sing.
... ָה	הֻפְקַד }			הָפְקַדְנָה	הָפְקְדוּ	plur.
הָפְקַדְתְּ	הָפְקַדְתָּ }	2.			The Future	
... ָה	הֻפְקַדְתָּ }			f.	m.	
etc.	הָפְקַדְתִּי	1.		אֻפְקַד and אָפְקַד		1. sing.
	הָפְקְדוּ	3. plur.		תָּפְקְדִי	תָּפְקַד	2.
הֵן .... הָפְקַדְתֶּם		2.		תָּפְקַד	יָפְקַד	3.
	הָפְקַדְנוּ	1.			נָפְקַד	1. plur.
				תָּפְקַדְנָה	{ תָּפְקְדוּ	2.
					{ יָפְקְדוּ	3.

The imperative of the verb is most rare. However, it is found in Ezekiel chap. 32, vs. 19 with the paragogic ה and Job chap. 21, vs. 2[2] and it seems to mean *to make one to be visited*, like the section in Ezekiel רְדָה וְהָשְׁכְּבָה אֶת עֲרֵלִים, *descend, and be thou laid with the uncircumcised*. Its meaning is easily recognized in the past and future from the active meaning, as I have explained sufficiently. However, the reason that many say that this verb form lacks the

---

1. [Term not used by Spinoza. — M.L.M.]
2. [It is not found in the verse cited by Spinoza. Perhaps he refers to verse 5 in the same chapter הָשַׁמּוּ "and be astonished."]

imperative is because it is not possible to command any one to an action which depends on others. This is easy to contradict; the imperative mode means both *to command* and *to wish*. When God said to Moses, *"Die upon the Mount,"* He did not really command that he should die, but rather He expressed His decree and purpose concerning the life of Moses.

CHAPTER 20

OF THE ACTIVE REFLEXIVE VERBS (*HITHPAEL*[1])

We shall call this the reflexive verb, because, as we have already said, by it we express what an object experiences from its own self; or rather, because the accusative is not a different thing from the nominative, like when *a man visits himself, is refreshed*, when *he entreats himself*, when *he guards himself*, etc. Or when *a man causes himself to visit another, applies himself toward walking, toward knowing*, etc.

Thus the significance of this verb is dual, of which one looks toward the verb form פָּקַד and the other toward the verb הִפְקִיד. For inasmuch as פָּקַד means that *someone visits another*, we need another verb form which can mean that *someone is visiting himself*; and inasmuch as הִפְקִיד means that *someone is making (causing) another to visit* there is similarly a need for another verb form which can mean that *someone is making himself to be visited*.

This verb form is recognized by the syllable הִת placed before the form פָּקַד and פַּקֵּד; like הִתְפַּקֵּד, *to visit oneself* or *to cause to visit oneself*, הִתְיַצֵּב *to station oneself* (Spanish *pararse*: to halt oneself), הִתְהַלֵּךְ *to walk about* (Spanish *pasearse, andarse*). This syllable can also, on account of the characteristics of time, be removed and be compensated by a dagesh, as I shall presently show.

Next, if the first radical is one of the dental letters, namely ס or שׁ then the ת is transposed; if however it is a ז or צ then it is not transposed, but rather the ת changes into a ד and the צ into a ט. Thus from שָׁמַר *to guard* it becomes הִשְׁתַּמֵּר *to guard oneself*, or *to make oneself to be guarded*, and from צָדַק *to be just* it becomes הִצְטַדֵּק *to justify oneself* (Belgian *zich ontschuldigen*: to justify oneself), and finally from זָמַן *to prepare* (*something at the right time*) it becomes הִזְדַּמֵּן *to prepare oneself at the right time*.

Finally the ה can change into an א and the accompanying chirek into a segol, like אֶתְחַבֵּר *to join oneself* instead of הִתְחַבֵּר.

---

1. [Term not used by Spinoza.—M.L.M.]

646 Hebrew Grammar

The forms of the infinitive are הִצְטַדֵּק, הִשְׁתַּמֵּר, אֶתְפַּקֵּד, הִתְפַּקֵּד, הִתְפַּקֵּד, and הִוָּדַע, to which no doubt form הִתְפַּקֵד should be added. For the past of this verb form can also end in a chirek. See Lev. 11:44 and 20:7, and Ezekiel 38 last verse. Further, since its first meaning looks to the form פָּקַד or פָּקֵד, then the second which looks to the verb הִפְקִיד ought to be able to end no less in a chirek than in a patach or tsere.

The Past

f.	m.	
הִתְפַּקְדָה	הִתְפַּקֵּד and הִפְקֵד	3. sing.
הִתְפַּקַדְתְּ	הִתְפַּקַדְתָּ	2.
	הִתְפַּקַדְתִּי	1.
	הִתְפַּקְדוּ	3. pl.
תֶּן	הִתְפַּקַדְתֶּם	2.
	הִתְפַּקַדְנוּ	1.

The Imperative

f.	m.	
הִתְפַּקְדִי	הִתְפַּקֵד	sing.
הִתְפַּקֵדְנָה	הִתְפַּקְדוּ	pl.

The Future

f.	m.	
	אֶתְפַּקֵד	1. sing.
תִּתְפַּקְדִי	תִּתְפַּקֵד	2.
תִּתְפַּקֵד	יִתְפַּקֵד	3.
	נִתְפַּקֵד	1. pl.
תִּתְפַּקֵדְנָה	{ תִּתְפַּקְדוּ	2.
	יִתְפַּקְדוּ	3.

Notes

This verb form has in common with the simple and intensive verbs that the ultimate tsere changes into a patach, but the chirek is retained, and is not changed into a patach in the second and first person like הִפְקִיד. So in Ezekiel 38, last verse, is found הִתְגַּדַּלְתִּי *magnify myself,* הִתְקַדַּשְׁתִּי *sanctify myself,* and Lev. chap. 11, vs. 44 and chap. 20, vs. 7, וְהִתְקַדִּשְׁתֶּם *sanctify yourselves.*

Also the patach is everywhere retained, in the past as well as in the imperative and future, except when the accent is athnach or siluk. For then it changes into a ָ.

Next, verbs whose first radical is ת, or ט or ד lose the letter ת, and compensate it by a dagesh, like הִטַּהַר *he purified himself* for הִתְטַהַר.

In the future the ה is disregarded altogether because of the personal pronominal prefixes; but the ת can be compensated by a dagesh, like תִּנָּבֵא in place of תִּתְנַבֵּא, *make yourself a prophet;* which also occurs in the past, like הִנַּבֵּאתִי for הִתְנַבֵּאתִי, *I made myself a prophet* or *I applied myself to prophesy.*

Also, I have neglected to note here about these verbs that the sheva mobile is changed into a ָ on account of an athnach or siluk; and that to the plural ending in וּ frequently a ן is added, and to the infinitives, and all others which end like infinitives, a ה is added for elegance; and finally that the future third person plural feminine gender coincides with the second person plural masculine gender, as it does in the singular, because they have all this in common with simple verbs, where all this is noted.

CHAPTER 21

OF THE PASSIVE REFLEXIVE VERB (HOTHPAAL[1])

This verb form seems ignored by all the grammarians whom I know, and on that account I had chosen to be silent about it, until it became necessary to deal with it. Although the meaning of the active reflexive verb may look toward both the verb פָּקַד and הִפְקִיד the passive does not ever look to נִפְקַד but always to הֻפְקַד. For it never means *to be visited by oneself* but *to expose oneself to be visited,* or *to make it that one is visited by oneself.* The reason for this (as I shall show under Syntax), is that among the Hebrews passive verbs do not have an ablative following them. For the Hebrews use the passive form only for brevity, namely to indicate not an active but a passive activity, like קוֹלִי נִשְׁמַע *my voice is heard;* but when it is necessary for them to indicate in both directions, like *my voice is heard by God,* then the active form of the verb is used, namely יְהוָה שָׁמַע קוֹלִי *the Lord*

---

1. [Term not used by Spinoza.—M.L.M.]

heard my voice. But קוֹלִי נִשְׁמַע מֵיְהוָה is inappropriate in common speech. The verb form הִתְפַּקֵּד, insofar as it means *to visit oneself,* cannot have a passive; but insofar as it means that *someone makes himself to be visiting,* it does have the passive form הָתְפַּקֵּד, which, as we have said, means *to cause oneself to be visited,* or *to effect that he is visited,* like Numbers 2:33 וְהַלְוִיִּם לֹא הָתְפָּקְדוּ *and the Levites were not (caused to be) numbered among the children of Israel.* And Deut. 24:4, אַחֲרֵי אֲשֶׁר הֻטַּמָּאָה *after that she is defiled,* where the ה because of the ט is compensated by a dagesh, as in the active.

Next, this verb form differs from its active form in the same way as the passive reflexive differs from הִפְקִיד. For as from הִפְקִיד the passive is הָפְקַד and הִפְקִיד, so from הִתְפַּקֵּד it is הָתְפַּקֵּד and הָתְפַּקֵּד like the form of the examples we have shown.

Next, the ה may also be supplanted with a dagesh, as in the active form, like אַחֲרֵי הֻכַּבֵּס אֶת הַנֶּגַע *after (he made it that) the plague is washed out (by itself)* (Lev. 3:55), or *(after it happened that the plague washed itself out).* Note that *the plague* is in the accusative case, which will be explained in the Syntax.

Finally, in place of a ה a נ may be substituted (namely the form of the passive of the simple verb and intensive) and the ה may be compensated by a dagesh, like Deut. 21:8, וְנִכַּפֵּר לָהֶם הַדָּם *and the blood shall be forgiven them,* in place of וְנִתְכַּפֵּר. Thus I am persuaded that the letter נ is the universal characteristic form of passive, but in all cases, except in simple passive verbs, it is omitted for the reasons I have mentioned in Chapter 17.

These are the forms of the infinitive of this conjugation הָתְפַּקֵּד, הִתְפַּקֵּד or נִפְקַד or נִתְפַּקֵּד, הֻפְקַד.

The past tense, the imperative, and the future agree with the active in the remaining forms.

CHAPTER 22

OF VERBS OF THE SECOND CONJUGATION (ל"א)

We have said that these verbs of the second conjugation are the verbs which end in an א, namely in a guttural and quiescent letter. Wherein these differ from verbs of the first conjugation will be shown by the paradigm.

Paradigm of the Simple Active Verb (Kal)

The forms of the infinitive are מְצוֹא, מָצֹא, מוֹצֵא, מָצֹא, מָצָא, מָצֹא, or with the paragogic ה מָצֹא, and also מְצֹאת in place of מְצֹאת.

	1. Past			2. Another Form			3. Another Form	
	m.	f.		m.	f.		m.	f.
3. sing.	מָצָא	מָצְאָה or מָצְאת	3.	מָצָא	מָצְאָה	3.	מָצָא	מָצְאָה
2.	מָצָאתָ	מָצָאת	2.	מָצָאתָ	מָצָאת	2.	מָצָאתָ	מָצָאת
1.	מָצָאתִי		1.	מַצָאתִי		1.	מִצֵאתִי	
3. pl.	מָצְאוּ		3.	מָצְאוּ		3.	מָצוּ	
2.	מְצָאתֶם תֵן		2.	מְצָאתֶם תֵן		2.	מְצָאתֶם תֵן	
1.	מָצָאנוּ		1.	מָצָאנוּ		1.	מָצָאנוּ	

The form פָּקַד does not appear here, and on that account the second ָ and tsere are retained in the remaining persons and not changed to patach as in verbs of the first conjugation. Further, the form מָצוֹא is not found in the past and I believe it is not used. Finally, in the second and third forms the א is mainly omitted, like מָלֵתִי in place of מָלֵאתִי *I am full.*

	Imperative			Future		
	m.	f.		m.	f.	
sing.	מְצָא	מִצְאִי		אֶמְצָא		1. sing.
	or			תִּמְצָא	תִּמְצְאִי	2.
	מְצוֹא			יִמְצָא	תִּמְצָא	3.
pl.	מִצְאוּ or מְצֶאנָה			etc.		

The imperative with paragogic ה does not change the sheva into a chirek, as in verbs of the first conjugation, but it remains together with the kametz, making it instead of מְצָא into מָצְאָה *(you) find.* These facts together with what we have noted above about the past, are the peculiarities of this verb form; for the rest it agrees with the verbs of the first conjugation. Let me now go into the paradigm of the passive verb of this conjugation.

Paradigm of a Simple Passive Verb (Niph'al[1])
Infinitives

1.	2.		3.
נִמְצָא	נִמְצוֹא	and	הִמָּצֵא

---

1. [Term not used by Spinoza.—M.L.M.]

The Past

	1.			2.			3. (without the א)	
f.	m.		f.	m.		f.	m.	
נִמְצָאָה	נִמְצָא		נִמְצֵאת	נִמְצָא	3.	נִמְצְתָה	נִמְצָא	3.
	and ⎱ 3. sing.	נִמְצֵאת	נִמְצֵאתָ	2.	נִמְצֵת	נִמְצֵתָ	2.
נִמְצָאָה	נִמְצָא ⎰		נִמְצֵאתִי	1.		נִמְצֵתִי	1.
or				נִמְצְאוּ	3.		נִמְצוּ	3.
נִמְצְאָתָה								
נִמְצֵאת	נִמְצֵאתָ	2.	תֶן	נִמְצֵאתֶם	2.	תֶן	נִמְצֵתֶם	2.
	נִמְצֵאתִי	1.		נִמְצֵאנוּ	1.		נִמְצֵנוּ	1.
	נִמְצְאוּ	3. pl.				or		
תֶן	נִמְצֵאתֶם	2.				נִמְצֵת	נִמְצֵתָ	
	נִמְצֵאנוּ	1.					נִמְצֵתִי	
							etc.	

The imperative and the future agree in everything with the imperative and future of the first conjugation. Further, the remaining verbs of this conjugation differ from the verbs of the first in the same way as we see these two מָצָא and נִמְצָא differ from פָּקַד and נִפְקַד; namely that instead of a patach, a kametz is inserted in every place, but in its place a chirek is substituted in the second and first persons; except in הִמְצִיא where the chirek in the first and second person changes to tsere, like הִמְצֵאתָ, הִמְצֵאתִי, הִמְצִיאוּ, הִמְצֵאתֶם, etc.; and also that the tsere is always retained and not changed into a patach, like פָּקַד פָּקַד and finally that the א may also be omitted.

CHAPTER 23

OF THE VERBS OF THE THIRD CONJUGATION (ל"ע)

This conjugation consisting of verbs ending in ה does not differ much from the preceding one; indeed it conforms with it very often. This is because the א may frequently serve in place of the ה, and contrarily the ה may frequently serve in place of the א. They differ only in that while a verb ending in א most frequently retains it and only rarely does it change the ־ָ into a chirek in the second and first persons, on the other hand, those ending in a ה rarely retain it, and they are frequently wont to change the ־ָ into a long chirek and rarely into a short one. Next, they differ also in another way; the ה may be punctuated with a מַפִּיק and the verb is not punctuated by a double ־ָ but a ־ָ and a ־ַ, like the verbs of the first conjugation. Four verbs of this group have been observed; namely, גָּבַהּ,

תָּמָה‎, נָגָה‎, כָּמָה‎, which are conjugated like verbs of the first conjugation, and for this reason I consider them to be of that group.

Further, certain of these verbs ending in ה‎ have a peculiarity which we will note in its place after the paradigm. Here may I add this in general to be heard by all: first, that a ה‎ after a chirek and tsere and shurek usually changes to י‎ and after a חוֹלֶם‎ into a ו‎; second, that a final ה‎ either because of an additional syllable or on account of the construct changes into a ת‎; and finally, that a quiescent and guttural letter usually interchange one for the other, or one may even omit them. Indeed, we have already shown above that a ה‎ after a sheva frequently disappears. And that this may be observed in verbs, as in nouns, will be evident from the following paradigm.

Paradigm of a Simple Verb (Kal[1])
of the Third Conjugation

The infinitive has the following forms גְּלֹה}א‎, גְּלָא‎, גְּלוֹ‎, גְּלִי‎, גְּלוֹת‎, גָּלֹה‎, and גָּלוֹת‎, or with the paragogic י‎, גָּלוֹתִי‎.

	The Past			The Imperative			The Future	
f.	m.		f.	m.		f.	m.	
גָּלְתָה גָּלְתָ גָּלַתְ	גָּלָה	3. sing.	גְּלִי	גְּלֵה	sing.	תִּגְלִי	אֶגְלֶה	1. sing.
גָּלִית and גָּלִית	גָּלִיתָ	2.	תִּגְלֶינָה	גְּלוּ	pl.	תִּגְלֶה	תִּגְלֶה	2.
	גָּלִיתִי	1.		and		תִּגְלֶה	יִגְלֶה	3.
גָּלָיו or	גָּלוּ	3. pl.		גָּלָיו			נִגְלֶה	1. pl.
גָּלִיתֶן	גָּלִיתֶם	2.				תִּגְלֶינָה { תִּגְלוּ		2.
	גָּלִינוּ	1.				יִגְלוּ		3.
						and		
						יִגְלָיו and יִגְלָיו		

Notes

We have already noted that an ה‎ can come in place of a א‎, or be altogether omitted either in the first and second persons plural of the past and in all the futures, and that a yod is not substituted in its place, but it is conjugated like מָצָא‎. But this should be noted first, that when the ה‎ is removed in the future its accent is moved toward its first syllable, and the sheva changes into a segol, becoming 1. אֶגֶל‎, 2. תִּגֶל‎, 3. יִגֶל‎, etc. But if the middle radical of the root is one of the mutes or quiescent letters, then the sheva remains, like יִשְׁבְּ‎ in place of יִשְׁבֶּה‎ *to take captive*,

---

1. [Term not used by Spinoza.—M.L.M.]

and יָשְׁקְ *to drink*. When a ה is changed into a yod, then the vowels are transposed, and they are 1. אֶגְלִי, 2. תִּגְלִי, 3. יִגְלִי, etc., in place of אֶגְלֶה, תִּגְלֶה, יִגְלֶה.

Next, the ה of the verb usually is changed not into a ה but into a yod when another ת is added. So חָסָה has the feminine חָסְיָה instead of חָסְתָה. So אֶגְלֶה with the added paragogic ה becomes not אֶגְלְתָה but אֶגְלְיָה.

Finally, the second and third persons plural in the future תִּגְלוּ and יִגְלוּ do not usually add the paragogic ן; but their second form, i.e., תִּגְלְיוּ and יִגְלְיוּ, does, like יִשְׁתָּיוּן יִרְבְּיֻן, etc.

Paradigms of the Passive Verb of the Third Conjugation (Niph'al[2])

Infinitive Forms

1. נִגְלָה   2. נִגְלֹה   3. נִגְלוֹת   4. הִגָּלֵה   5. הִגָּלוֹת

The Past

  f.   m.

  1.   2.

נִגְלְתָה and נִגְלֵת   נִגְלָה   or   נִגְלְתָה   נִגְלָה
נִגְלֵיתָ   נִגְלֵית   נִגְלֵית   נִגְלֵיתָ
                              etc.

The Imperative   The Future

                                f.   m.

                                         אֶגָּלֶה   sing.
הִגָּלִי   הִגָּלֶה   תִּגָּלִי   תִּגָּלֶה
הִגָּלֶינָה   הִגָּלוּ   תִּגָּלֶה   יִגָּלֶה
           or
נִגְלִי   נִגְלֶה   נִגָּלֶה   pl.
נִגְלֶינָה   נִגְלוּ   תִּגָּלֶינָה { תִּגָּלוּ
                                            יִגָּלוּ

This verb form has nothing singular which we have not noted in the preceding one, except that by the dropping of the ה of the future neither the accent nor the syllable changes. For with the dropped ה it is conjugated 1. אֶגָּל, 2. תִּגָּל, 3. יִגָּל, etc. I doubt whether the second and third persons of the plural always omit the ה, or, whether as in the active *(kal)*, change it to a י. However, I believe that all the other things which we noted about the preceding ones pertain to this verb form.

---

2. [Term not used by Spinoza.—M.L.M.]

Paradigms of the Intensive Verbs of the Third Conjugation (Pi'el[3])

The forms of the infinitive are:

1. גַּלֵּה   2. גַּלֵּה or גַּלִּי   3. גַּלֹּה   4. גַּלּוֹת and with the ה paragogic גַּלּוֹתִי.

	Past			Imperative			Future		
f.	m.					f.	m.		
גִּלְּתָה	גִּלָּה	3.		גַּלֵּה	2.		אֲגַלֶּה	1. sing.	
גִּלִּית	גִּלִּיתָ	2.	גַּלִּי { or			תְּגַלִּי	תְּגַלֶּה	2.	
etc.				גַּל		תְּגַלֶּה	יְגַלֶּה	3.	
or							נְגַלֶּה	1. pl.	
	גִּלָּה	3.		גַּלּוּ	2.		תְּגַלּוּ		
גִּלִּית	גִּלִּיתָ		גַּלֶּינָה { and			תְּגַלֶּינָה { and		2.	
etc.				גַּלְיוּ			תְּגַלֶּיהָ		
							יְגַלְיוּ & יְגַלּוּ	3.	

This verb form also remains מִלְרַע in the future when the ה is dropped, and the vowels are not changed. For the dropped ה makes it 1. אֲגַל, 2. תְּגַל, 3. יְגַל, etc.

Paradigms of the Passive Intensive Verbs of the Third Conjugation (Pu'al[4])

Infinitives: 1. גֻּלֹּה   2. גֻּלֹּה or גֻּלּוֹת.

	The Past				The Future		
f.	m.			f.	m.		
גֻּלְּתָה	גֻּלָּה	3. or גֻּלָּה			אֲגֻלֶּה	1. sing.	
גֻּלִּית	גֻּלֵּתָ	2. גֻּלֵּתָ		תְּגֻלִּי	תְּגֻלֶּה	2.	
	גֻּלֵּתִי	1. etc.		תְּגֻלֶּה	נְגֻלֶּה	3.	
	גֻּלּוּ	3. pl.					
תֵּן	גֻּלֵּתֶם	2.					
	גֻּלֵּינוּ	1.					

---

3. [Term not used by Spinoza.—M.L.M.]
4. [Term not used by Spinoza.—M.L.M.]

654 Hebrew Grammar

In Chapter 17 we noted that a kametz chatuf can be used in place of a ָ. The verbs of this conjugation provide many examples of this, as in Proverbs chap. 24, vs. 31 כָּסֻּ פָנָיו *its face was covered*, and Psalms chapter 72 last verse כָּלּוּ תְפִילוֹת *the prayers are ended.*

The fact that the ָ changes to a cholem, when the middle letter of the root cannot receive a dagesh, is similar to the verbs of the first conjugation; and I have not undertaken to note anything in this conjugation unless it differs with verbs of the first conjugation.

Paradigms of the Causative Active of the Third Conjugation (Hiph'il[5])

The forms of its infinitive are:

1. הַגְלָה   2. הַגְלָה   3. הַגְלֵה   4. הַגְלוֹת   5. הַגְלוֹת.

	Past		Imperative		Future	
f.	m.		f.	m.	f.	m.
הִגְלְתָה	הִגְלָה 3. sing.		הַגְלִי	הַגְלֵה sing.		אַגְלֶה 1. sing.
and	and				תַּגְלִי	תַּגְלֶה 2.
הִגְלַת	הִגְלָה					etc.
הִגְלַת	הִגְלִיתָ 2.		הַגְלֶינָה	הַגְלוּ pl.		
	etc.					
הִגְלְתָה	הִגְלָה 3.					
הִגְלִית	הִגְלִיתָ 2.					
	etc.					

The future and imperative, when the ה is dropped, are punctuated with double segol, becoming תֶּגֶל, אֶגֶל instead of אַגְלֶה, תַּגְלֶה, etc. But if the middle letter of the root is a mute or quiescent letter, then the - remains, and ָ changes into a ָ like יַשְׁקְ for יַשְׁקֶה *he makes to drink*, that is, *he gives a drink*, יַרְא for יַרְאֶה *he makes to see*, or *he shows*, etc.

As for the causative passive (*hoph'al*) הָגְלָה, הֻגְלָה, or הָגְלוֹת and the reciprocal passive (*hithpael*), הִתְגַּלָּה, הִתְגַּלֶּה, or הִתְגַּלּוֹת, they are marked in the same way as the preceding ones in the present, imperative, and future, and they have nothing singular about them which I have not noted about the simple verbs (*kal*) of this conjugation.

---

5. [Term not used by Spinoza.—M.L.M.]

CHAPTER 24

Verbs of the Fourth Conjugation ל"ע AND ל"ח

What especially distinguishes these verbs, so to speak, is that a ח and an ע never adhere to a long vowel, and that they do not ever have a ׃ after a long vowel or before another silent sheva, and rarely after a short vowel. Whence it is, that if at the end of words, after a tsere, there happens to occur a chirek, cholem, or shurek, there will be a furtive patach, of which we spoke in Chapter 3. Also, the second person of the feminine gender, which usually has a double sheva in the last syllable, has a patach in place of the first sheva.

Therefore the simple active verbs of this conjugation have the infinitive forms: 1. שְׁמוֹעַ 2. שְׁמַע or שָׁמֵעַ 3. שְׁמוֹעַ or שָׁמֵעַ, and, with the paragogic ה, שִׁמְעָה and שָׁמְעָה. There is no infinitive with a double ׃, like שָׁמֵעַ or פָּקֹד because, as we have said, a ח and an ע do not adhere to a long vowel.

Also, the past does not have a furtive patach but a contracted one: שָׁמַע *he heard*, שָׁמַעְתָּ *you heard*, etc. In the feminine, שָׁמְעָה *she heard*, שָׁמַעַתְּ *you* (f.) *heard* instead of שָׁמַעְתְּ. For, as I have said, ע and ח before a resting sheva do not take another sheva. Concerning this matter see Chapter 3 toward the end.

The past form for פָּקֹד should be שָׁמֵעַ and for the form שָׁמוֹעַ פָּקֹד, but this may, as I have said, be shortened into שָׁמַע, and so the imperative שְׁמוֹעַ into שְׁמַע, and the future אֶשְׁמוֹעַ into אֶשְׁמַע.

These rules are observed also in the rest of the verb forms, and there is no need to explain them at length. May I add this, however, that Isaiah chapter 19, verse 6 has הֶאֱזְנִיחוּ instead of הִזְנִחוּ or הֶאֱזְנִיחוּ *they shall be made foul*, or *made to be rejected*. I doubt whether this form of the passive verb is derived properly from these conjugations, or that it is common to all, or that in place of הַפְקֵד one may substitute הֶאֱפְקִיד, as for הִזְנַח and הַשְׁמַע one may write הֶאֱזְנִיחַ and הֶאֱשְׁמִיעַ.

CHAPTER 25

Verbs of the Fifth Conjugation (פ"י)

The verbs, whose first root letter is the quiescent י usually drop it or change it into a ו. And so the simple active verbs *(kal)* in addition to the infinitives

יָשַׁב, יֵשֵׁב, and יָשׁוֹב or יֵשֵׁב, often have שַׁב, שֵׁב, and שֵׁב; and also when a paragogic ה or ת is added the י is always dropped, and it becomes שִׁבְה from יִשְׁבָה and שֶׁבֶת instead of יֶשֶׁבֶת. In the past tense the י always remains, in the imperative it frequently is dropped, and finally in the future it is either quiescent or dropped. For example, from the form יָשַׁב and יֵשֵׁב the imperative becomes שַׁב and שֵׁב. Therefore, they differ also in this respect from verbs of the first conjugation in that their imperatives are not formed from the infinitive יְשֹׁב; which came about perhaps for the reason that they are not to be confused with verbs whose median radical is ו, of which we shall speak in its proper place. These verbs therefore are conjugated in the imperative in this manner:

The Imperative

	f.	m.
		שַׁב
שִׁבִי	{	or
		שֵׁב
		or
		שְׁבָה
שְׁבֶנָה		שְׁבוּ

The Future

f.		m.	
אֵשֵׁב or אֶשַׁב			1.
תֵּשֵׁב or תֵּשַׁב			2.
	etc.		

or with the quiescent:

| אִישֵׁב or אֵישֵׁב |
| תִּישֵׁב תֵּישֵׁב תֵּישְׁבִי |
| etc. |

The pausal accents athnach and siluk, in the imperative, change their sheva into a ֵ , and so שְׁבָה, שְׁבִי, and שְׁבוּ become שֵׁבָה, שֵׁבִי, and שֵׁבוּ.

Next, although in the Bible the imperative יְשֵׁב or יְשַׁב is not found I believe that it was nevertheless in use, and from it was formed the form of the future אִישֵׁב and אֵישַׁב. The verb יָרֵא, being composed from this and the second conjugations, has the imperative יְרָא *fear*. So from יָכֹל *be able*, by changing the י into a ו, the future is formed אוּכַל, תּוּכַל, יוּכַל, etc., which I believe may not be permitted in the others, so as not to be confused with the future of the passive reflexive verb, which the verb יָכֹל lacks.

Next, passive verbs *(niph'al)* change the י into a ו, and are in the infinitive הִוָּשֵׁב in place of הִיָּשֵׁב, and, if I am not mistaken, נוֹשַׁב in place of נִישַׁב, from which the past third person נוֹשַׁב, the second person, נוֹשַׁבְתָּ, etc., and also from the infinitive הִוָּשֵׁב the imperative is formed:

f.	m.	
הִוָּשְׁבִי	הִוָּשֵׁב	2. sing.
הִוָּשַׁבְנָה	הִוָּשְׁבוּ	2. plur.

and the future 1. אִוָּשֵׁב, 2. תִּוָּשֵׁב, etc.

Next, the intensives, both active and passive, (*pi'el* and *pu'al*), agree altogether with verbs of the first conjugation. The י is retained and does not become quiescent unless the passive form should have the character נ (which, as I said in Chapter 17, is usually also prefixed to the passive intensive); but in that case the י also changes into a ו, like נוּלְדוּ for יֻלְדוּ and נוּלַד for יֻלַד. Next, the future of the active verb may also be contracted, and in place of יְיַשֵּׁב it may be written יַשֵּׁב and יַבֵּשׁ in place of יְיַבֵּשׁ. In the causative, however, it (the yod) is either silent or, as happens mostly, changed to a ו. Thus in the infinitive they have הוֹשֵׁב instead of הוֹשִׁיב הַיְשִׁיב or הֵישֵׁב instead of הַיְשִׁיב.

	The past is formed from the first הוֹשִׁיב.		The imperative is formed from the second הוּשַׁב and הֵישֵׁב.
f.	m.	f.	m.
הוֹשִׁיבָה	הוֹשִׁיב 3.	הוֹשִׁיבִי and הֵישִׁיבִי	הוֹשֵׁב, הוֹשֵׁב
הוֹשַׁבְתְּ	הוֹשַׁבְתָּ 2.	הוֹשֵׁבְנָה	הוֹשִׁיבוּ
	etc.		

Where the י is either silent or changed to a ו.

Finally, the future ending of these, as in verbs of the first conjugation, is either a chirek or a tsere; but the י, as in the imperative, is either silenced or changed into a ו; so that is has the following forms: הוֹשֵׁב and הוֹשִׁיב, feminine הוֹשִׁיבִי, etc.

The Future

	1.			2.			3.			4.	
f.	m.		f.	m.		f.	m.		f.	m.	
	אוֹשֵׁב			אוֹשִׁיב 1.			אִישֵׁב 1.			אִישִׁיב	
תּוֹשִׁיבִי	תּוֹשֵׁב		תּוֹשִׁיבִי	תּוֹשִׁיב 2.		תִּישְׁבִי	תִּישֵׁב 2.		תִּישִׁיבִי	תִּישִׁיב	
תּוֹשֵׁב	יוֹשֵׁב			etc.			etc.			etc.	
	etc.										

And here it must above all be noted, that it is not necessary in these to exclude the characteristic letter of the verb form on account of the characteristic letter of the tense; but one is free to either retain or omit it in the first and second forms above, and in the third and fourth to put a yod in its place. Namely; in place of אוֹשֵׁב, תּוֹשֵׁב, יוֹשֵׁב one is able to write אֲהוֹשֵׁב, תְּהוֹשֵׁב, יְהוֹשֵׁב, etc., and in place of יֵישֵׁב, תֵּישֵׁב, אֵישֵׁב to write יַיְשֵׁב, תַּיְשֵׁב, אַיְשֵׁב, etc., changing the characteristic ה into a י. So also for אוֹשִׁיב and אִישִׁיב it is permitted to write אֲהוֹשִׁיב and אַיְשִׁיב.

Next, be it noted that the causative verb form יָשַׁר *to be straight* generally retains the י in the infinitive, imperative, and future; and in this it agrees with verbs of the first conjugation. So that it has the infinitive הִישֵׁר, the imperative f. הִישִׁירִי, m. הִישֵׁר, and the future 1. אִישֵׁר, 2. תִּישֵׁר, 3. יִישֵׁר, etc.

Next, the causative from יָצָא *to go out* also appears to be similar in that it retains the yod since at times the scribes in Genesis chap. 8, vs. 17 allowed the imperatives to be read both הוֹצֵא and הַיְצֵא.* I doubt that in these two there is anything unique. Thus far concerning the active accusative verb.

The passive *(hoph'al)* changes the י into a ו, or omits it. The forms of the infinitives are הוּשַׁב and הֻשַׁב, or הוּשֶׁבֶת and הֻשֶׁבֶת. The past third person m. הוּשַׁב f. הוּשְׁבָה, 2. הוּשַׁבְתָּ, etc.; or 3. הֻשַׁב 2. הֻשַׁבְתָּ, etc. The imperative m. הוּשַׁב f. הוּשְׁבִי. The future 1. אוּשַׁב, 2. m. תּוּשַׁב f. תּוּשְׁבִי, etc.

The reciprocal reflexive active verbs *(hithpael)* of this conjugation either retain the י, and agree entirely with verbs of the first conjugation, or change it to a ו; so that the infinitives are הִתְיַשֵּׁב and הִתְוַשֵּׁב, and, except for this, they do not differ in any other way from verbs of the first conjugation.

Finally, the reciprocal passives, which have the characteristic letter נ, and usually compensate the ת with a dagesh (which form I have shown the reciprocal passive to have in addition to others in Chapter 21), change the י into a ו; like וְנִוַּסְרוּ *and they were made to be disciplined* Ezekiel 23:48. Of the other forms indeed, like הִתְיַשֵּׁב, נִתְיַשֵּׁב, etc., none are extant, as far as I know, but this does not mean they are on that account impossible.

It must be noted here that there are some verbs whose first root letter is י or נ, like יָקַשׁ *to lay a snare*, whose first letter, in place of a י, is frequently נ, and in place of יָקַשׁ it is נָקַשׁ. Since verbs whose primary root letter is נ, are generally defective verbs (as I shall show below) it seems that these verbs imitate other defective verbs. There is another reason for this which must especially be noted here, namely that letters of the same root are not infrequently transposed, like חָתַר and חָרַת *to dig*, and כֶּשֶׂב and כֶּבֶשׂ *a lamb*. This transposition is observed very often in verbs of this conjugation, like יָעֵף and עָיֵף *to be weary*, יָצַר and צָיַר *to give form*; whence it is that these verbs resemble the verbs of the sixth conjugation, whose middle quiescent radical frequently is missing. For by the transposition of the י from יָצַר it becomes, as we have said, צָיַר whose infinitive צִיּוֹר is contracted into צוּר, namely into the form of the infinitive of the sixth conjugation; so יָגוֹר *to fear*, by transposing the י and changing it into a ו, as above, the infinitive becomes גוּר and יָבוֹשׁ *to be ashamed* also has the infinitive בּוֹשׁ. For this same reason יָצַק, יָצַג, and the others whose primary radical is a י at one time follow this mode and at other times follow the sixth conjugation in accordance with linguistic analogy (of which below).

---

* [The *ketib* is הוֹצֵא and the *keri* is הַיְצֵא.]

CHAPTER 26

Composite Verbs from This Fifth and Three Preceding Conjugations

The composite verbs, concerning which I want to deliberate here briefly, are those whose first root letter is י, and the third an א or a ה or even an ע. But because their mode of conjugation can easily be recognized from the preceding I have judged it quite superfluous to treat them in detail and to increase the number of conjugations. I think, however, that it is worthwhile to state a few things about them.

Of those ending in א, we know two only, namely יָצָא *to go out* and יָרֵא *to fear*, which on account of the quiescent א always have a long ultimate syllable, like verbs of the second conjugation. In the remaining forms, however, יָצָא conforms with verbs of the fifth, except that the infinitive, instead of צֵאת, is צֵאת. Also, the verb יָרֵא in the simple active *(kal)* always retains the י, and it does not quiesce except in the future. Thus the infinitive and imperative are יְרֹא and יְרָא, and with the paragogic ה, יִרְאָה, but the future is 1. אִירָא 2. תִּירָא 3. יִירָא.

Those which end in ה, like verbs of the second conjugation, change the ה into either a י or a ו, and are ended in the same way. As to the letter yod which remains, it is either quiescent in the simple active *(kal)* future or is changed into a ו, but never lost. For example, יָפָה, יָפֹה, יְפוֹת *to be beautiful*, becomes in the imperative יְפֵה, and in the future: 1. m. אִיפֶה, 2. תִּיפֶה, f. תִּיפִי, etc. When the ה is eliminated it is 1. אִיף, 2. תִּיף, 3. יִיף, etc. But יָרֹה *to throw* is in the imperative יְרֵה, but the י is changed in the future into ו and it becomes 1. אוֹרֶה, 2. תּוֹרֶה, 3. יוֹרֶה, and eliminating the ה, it is אוֹר, תּוֹר, יוֹר, etc. The rest of the verb forms, namely passive *(niph'al)* causative *(hiph'il)*, and reciprocal *(hithpael)* follow the paradigms of the fifth conjugation.

Finally, those which end in ה or ע follow the paradigms of the fourth and fifth conjugations. For example, יָדַע, יְדֹעַ *to know* is contracted into יָדַע, and eliminating the י it becomes דַּע, דָּע, דֵּעַ. Hence the imperative דַּע *know*, and the future אֵדַע, תֵּדַע, and with the paragogic ה, אֵדְעָה. Next the simple passive *(niph'al)* infinitive is נוֹדַע and הִוָּדֵעַ. The relative active *(hiph'il)* הוֹדִיעַ and הוֹדַע, and the passive *(hoph'al)* הוּדַע. Finally, the reciprocal active *(hithpael)* is הִתְוַדֵּעַ and the passive *(hothpael)* הָתְוַדַּע, נִתְוַדַּע, etc. These are the things I undertook to relate about this matter.

CHAPTER 27

VERBS OF THE SIXTH CONJUGATION (AYIN ALEPH, AYIN VAV, AND AYIN YOD)

Those verbs which have a quiescent א, י, or ו as the middle root letter generally give it up. Understand, when they are truly quiescent, like קָאם *to rise up*, שׁוֹב *to return*, גִּיל *to rejoice*; otherwise they are always retained, like שָׁאוֹל *to ask*, עָוֹת *to pervert*, אָיַב *to be hostile*, etc. Further, since those which have a quiescent א as the middle root letter change it most frequently into ו and, except for three or four times, none are found of which it is certain that they have an א as the middle root letter, therefore the grammarians recognize two classes of verbs having a quiescent middle root letter, namely, one consisting of those which have a middle ו, and the other of those which have a middle י.

Moreover, קָאם *he got up*, and רָאם *to be high*, because they occur only once in Scripture, and like אָדוֹשׁ *to thresh*, whose א (which we have shown to happen often) is transposed, are considered as irregular. As a matter of fact, both those which have a middle א and those which have a middle י usually change them into a ו. For just as קָאם is replaced by קוּם *to get up*, so also שִׂישׂ *to rejoice* is replaced by שׂוֹשׂ, and לִין *to pass the night* by לוּן, etc. Hence I do not doubt the fact that these three quiescent groups belong to one class especially because their mode of conjugation is the same. To wit: the infinitive of the simple active verb is frequently קוֹם and קוּם, or by dropping the ו, קָם and קַם. Indeed it is very rarely found with an א and those which have a י like שִׂישׂ, לִין etc., we have shown that it frequently is changed to a ו. In the past tense however the quiescent is most frequently dropped. Their form generally is:

	f.		m.	
	קָמָה		קָם	3. sing.
	קָמְתְּ		קַמְתָּ	2.
			קַמְתִּי	1.
etc.	קָמוּ	or	קָמוּ	3. pl.

The past may also be punctuated with a ־ֶ, ־ֵ, and a cholem in place of a ־ָ, like בָּז *he despised*, אוֹר *he lights*, בּוֹשׁ *he was ashamed*, מֵת *he died*. Because the middle root letter is missing, the first is punctuated with the same vowel and the third root letter usually adheres to it. And there are many forms of the past tense which, like the verbs of the first conjugation, have a second vowel to which the third root adheres, (as we have shown in Chapter 14), which is either ָ , or ֵ , or ֵ , or וֹ.

Next, just like those of the first conjugation, so also verbs of this conjugation change in the second and first persons the ָ and the ֵ into a ְ , and they retain the cholem. But they have this unique quality, that in the third person singular of the feminine gender and in the third plural they do not change, like verbs of the first conjugation, the cholem, or the ָ , or the ֵ into a sheva, even when the accent is not אתנח, or סִילוּק. For, if it were to change into a sheva, the first root letter in the past would have too short a vowel, contrary to the common practice of the past simple form of the tense.

Further, those which have a yod in the middle usually may retain it also in the past: for example רִיב *to quarrel* has the past 3. רָב, 2. רַבְתָּ, etc., or 3. רִיב, 2. רִיבוֹתָ, f. רִיבוֹת, 1. רִיבוֹתִי, etc. But others believe, and not without reason, that these are forms of the intensive verb *(pi'el)* in place of רוֹבֵב; (of which in a moment), and also others believe them to be reciprocal verbs *(hithpael)* with the ה omitted, for what reason I do not know.

The imperative has all forms of the infinitive, namely:

m.	f.	m.	f.	m.	f.	m.	f.
קָם	קָמִי	קֹם	קֹמִי	קוֹם	קוֹמִי	קוּם	קוּמִי
	etc.		etc.		etc.	קוּמוּ	קוּמְנָה

And these forms of the future אָקוּם and אָקֹם or אָקוֹם and אָקָם.

And to all these forms of the imperative and future the paragogic ה is added for elegance, like קוּמָה *get up*, שֻׁבָה *return*, אָקוּמָה *I shall arise*, etc.

The passive *(niph'al)* keeps the form of the active *(kal)* קוֹם and the הֻפְקַד form becomes הָקוֹם, and the נִפְקַד form becomes, I believe, נָקוֹם; whence:

The Past

m.	f.	
נָקוֹם	נָקוֹמָה	3. sing.
נְקוּמוֹתָ	נְקוּמוֹת	2.
נְקוּמוֹתִי		1.
נָקוֹמוּ		3. pl.
נְקוּמוֹתֶם	הֶן	2.
נְקוּמוֹנוּ		1.

The Imperative

m.	f.	
הָקוֹם	הָקוֹמִי	sing.
הָקוֹמוּ	הָקוֹמְנָה	pl.

The Future

m.	f.	
אָקוֹם		1. sing.
תָּקוֹם	תָּקוֹמִי	2.
יָקוֹם	תָּקוֹם	3.
	etc.	
נָקוֹם		1. pl.
תָּקוֹמוּ		2.

The intensive form of the verb *(pi'el)* is unable to double the middle radical א, seeing that it is a guttural. It may be compensated by a long vowel, but since it is most generally omitted, like the ו and י, on this account verbs of this conjugation are rarely able to double the second root letter, but generally double the third root letter. Accordingly from קוֹם *to get up* it becomes קוֹמֵם *to erect*; whence the pasts 3. m. קוֹמֵם f. קוֹמְמָה, 2. m. קוֹמַמְתָּ, f. קוֹמַמְתְּ, etc., and the imperative m. קוֹמֵם f. קוֹמְמִי, etc., finally the futures 1. אֲקוֹמֵם, 2. תְּקוֹמֵם, f. תְּקוֹמְמִי, etc.

The passive intensive (*pu'al*) is distinguished from the active (*pi'el*) only by the patach. Namely, from the active (*pi'el*) קוֹמֵם, the passive becomes קוֹמַם *to be erected*. Whence the pasts 3. m. קוֹמַם, f. קוֹמְמָה, 2. קוֹמַמְתָּ, and the futures 1. אֲקוֹמַם, 2. תְּקוֹמַם, f. תְּקוֹמְמִי. This mode was common among the ancients in conjugating the verbs of this conjugation. But the later ones made from the verb חוֹב *to owe* or *to be indebted* the intensive (*pi'el*) חִיֵּב (perhaps not to be confused with חוֹבֵב *to love*) and from קוֹם they made קִיֵּם *to establish, to affirm*, and the others in this manner.

Then, not infrequently it is usual to double the first root letter, like כִּלְכֵּל from כּוּל. But of this see Chapter 31.

Beside these forms, some grammarians attribute another form in the intensive (*pi'el*), namely, 3. קָיִם, 2. קִימוֹתָ, f. קִימוֹת, 1. קִימוֹתִי, etc., and it seems that they do not stray from the truth.

Further, the causative verbs (*hiph'il*) lose the quiescent middle radical, and they become in the infinitive הָקֵם, הָקִים, and הָקִים; in the past, however, they imitate the endings of the simple active (*kal*), or (which is more frequently observed in the Bible) the passive (*niph'al*).

Thus it is

The Past Tense

f.		m.			f.	m.	
הֲקִימָה	sing.	הֵקִים	3.	or	הֲקִימָה	הֵקִים	3.
הֲקִימוֹת		הֲקִימוֹתָ	2.		הֲקַמְתְּ	הֲקַמְתָּ	2.
		הֲקִימוֹתִי	1.		etc.	הֲקַמְתִּי	1.
	pl.	הֵקִימוּ	3.				
תֵּן		הֲקִימוֹתֶם	2.				
		הֲקִימוֹנוּ	1.				

The Imperative

	f.	m.			
	הָקִימִי	הָקֵם	or	הָקֵים	sing.
	הָקֵמְנָה	הָקִימוּ			pl.

and hence the future 1:   *and the second future:*

f.	m.		f.	m.	
	אָקִים	1.		אָקֵם	1. sing.
תָּקִימִי	תָּקִים	2.	תָּקִימִי	תָּקֵם	2.
תָּקִים	יָקִים	3.	תָּקֵם	יָקֵם	3.
etc.	etc.			נָקֵם	pl.
				תָּקֵמוּ	

But when the accent is put on the first syllable, the ֵ changes to a ֶ, namely, אָקֶם, תָּקֶם, etc.

The passive *(hoph'al)* also losing the quiescent letter, has the infinitive הוּקֵם and הוּקַם or הָקֵם and הָקַם, and the past 3. הוּקַם, 2. m. הוּקַמְתָּ, f. הוּקַמְתְּ, or 3. הָקַם, 2. m. הָקַמְתָּ, and so forth; with which also the future agrees. For it is either 1. אוּקַם, 2. m. תוּקַם, f. תוּקְמִי, etc., or אָקַם, תָּקַם, etc.

Next the reciprocal *(hithpael)* is formed, like in the other conjugations, from its intensive *(pi'el)* קוֹמֵם, namely by prefixing to it the syllable הִתְ, and although the intensive *(pi'el)* of this conjugation never ends in a ַ but always in a ֵ, the reciprocal *(hithpael)*, however, is ended by both the ַ and the ֵ. Namely: The infinitive הִתְקוֹמֵם and הִתְקוֹמַם. The past 3. m. הִתְקוֹמֵם, f. הִתְקוֹמְמָה, etc. The imperative הִתְקוֹמֵם. The future אֶתְקוֹמֵם, etc.

And there is nothing else to note here which they do not have in common with the verbs of the first conjugation.

Further, composite verbs of this and the third conjugation do not exist. For those which have the middle root letter ו or י, and the third root letter ה their middle root letter does not quiesce, like טָוָה *to spin*, לָוָה *to borrow*, הָיָה *to be*, etc.

Those which have an א as the final root letter are only בּוֹא *to come*, and נוֹא *to restrain*, whose simple active *(kal)* in the past always retains the א on account of the quiescent ָ, as מָצָא, and the imperative retains the cholem, namely m. s. בּוֹא, f. בּוֹאִי and בֹּאִי, m. p. בּוֹאוּ and בֹּאוּ, f. בֹּאנָה and בֹּאנָה.[1]

The future beside 1. אָבוֹא, 2. תָּבוֹא, f. תָּבֹאִי, etc., has also the fem. 1. אָבֹאָה, 2. תָּבֹאתִי, 3. תָּבֹאתָה. Each of these verbs lacks the simple passive *(niph'al)* and the intensive active and passive *(pi'el* and *pu'al)*. The causative is generally terminated like מָצָא; namely the past active *(hiph'il)* 3. m. הֵבִיא, f. הֵבִיאָה, 2. הֵבֵאתָ, f. הֵבֵאת, 1. הֵבֵאתִי, etc. But frequently it also is 3. הֵבִיא, 2. הֲבִיאוֹת, f. הֲבִיאוֹת, like הֲקִימוֹת, הֵקִים, etc. The passive *(hoph'al)* however is, 1. הוּבָא, הוּבֵאתָ etc. The reflexive *(hithpael)* is lacking in each, namely both בּוֹא and נוֹא. And concerning those whose third root letter is a ה or an ע much has already been observed, which was said in Chapter 24.

---

1. [This should be בּוֹאנָה or בֹּאינָה. — M.L.M.]

CHAPTER 28

VERBS OF THE SEVENTH CONJUGATION (PEH GUTTURALS[1])

We have said above, in Chapters 2 and 3, that gutturals are never doubled, but in their place the preceding syllable is changed from a short vowel to a long one. Also, they rarely have a silent sheva and never a pronounced one (moving sheva), but that in place of this one of three composites is used. This should be observed chiefly about the verbs of this and the following conjugation, and in addition also the rule that a simple sheva can never follow a composite sheva, for then both would have to be pronounced, which according to Chapter 3, cannot be done.

The paradigm verb of this conjugation is אָזַר *to gird*. The forms of its infinitive are: 1. אֱזֹר, 2. אֲזֹר, 3. אָזֹר, 4. אֹזֹר.

The Past

f.	m.	
אָזְרָה	אָזַר	3. sing.
אָזַרְתְּ	אָזַרְתָּ	2.

The Imperative

f.	m.	
אִזְרִי	אֱזֹר	sing.
אֱזֹרְנָה	אִזְרוּ	plur.

The Future

f.	m.	
	אֶאֱזֹר	1. sing.
	[with the ה parag.] and אֶאֱזְרָה	
תַּאַזְרִי	תַּאֲזֹר	2.
or	or	
תַּאֲזְרִי	תֶּאֱזֹר	etc.
	נֶאֱזֹר	plur.
תֶּאֱזֹרְנָה	תֶּאֶזְרוּ	
	etc.	

Not infrequently, in the future tense, it is usual also for the א to be silenced and to be omitted in the first person; but then it is punctuated by a -, like אֹמַר *I said*, תֹּאמַר *you said*, f. תֹּאמְרִי, etc.

---

1. [Term not used by Spinoza. — M.L.M.]

Then the ה in the future tense may have a silent ְ , like תַּחְפֹּץ, *you want*. But when this is to avoid two shevas occurring at the beginning of a word, the first is not changed into a chirek, as otherwise it should, but into that vowel from which the ְ was compounded.

The forms of the infinitive in the simple passive (*niph'al*) are הֵאָזוֹר, נֵאָזוֹר, and נֵאָזֹר whence:

	The Past			The Imperative			The Future	
f.	m.		f.	m.		f.	m.	
נֶאֶזְרָא	נֶאֱזֹר	1. sing.	הֵאָזְרִי	הֵאָזֵר	sing.		אֵאָזֵר	1.
נֶאֶזְרְתְּ	נֶאֱזַרְתָּ	2.			etc.	תֵּאָזְרִי	תֵּאָזֵר	2.
						etc.	etc.	

From נֶאֶזְרָה, when the accent is athnach or siluk, it becomes נֶאֱזָרָה, or נֶאֶזְרָה with the quiescent א, and in the same manner for נֶאֶזְרוּ it becomes נֶאֱזָרוּ.

The intensive has nothing unique to note either in the active (*pi'el*) or passive (*pu'al*). The forms of the infinitive of the causative active (*hiph'il*) are הַאֲזִיר, הַאֲזֵר, and הַאֲזִיר.

	The Past			The Imperative			The Future	
f.	m.		f.	m.		f.	m.	
הֶאֱזִירָה	הֶאֱזִיר	3.	הַאֲזִירִי	הַאֲזֵר		תַּאֲזִירִי	אַאֲזִיר	1.
רְתְּ	הֶאֱזַרְתָּ	2.		and הַאֲזֵר			תַּאֲזִיר	2.
	etc.						or	
			הֶאֱזִירְנָה	הַאֲזִירוּ			אַאֲזֵר	1.
							תַּאֲזֵר	2. etc.

Here too the א frequently quiesces in the future, becoming 1. אֹזִיר or אָזִיר or אָזֵר 2. תּוֹזִיר or תָּזִיר, etc.

The infinitive passive (*hoph'al*) is הָאֳזַר; whence:

	The Past			The Imperative			The Future	
f.	m.		f.	m.		f.	m.	
הָאֳזְרָה	הָאֳזַר	3.	הָאֳזְרִי	הָאֳזַר and הָאֳזַר		תָּאֳזְרִי	אָאֳזַר	1.
רְתְּ	הָאֳזַרְתְּ					תָּאֳזַר	תָּאֳזַר	2.
	etc.		הָאֳזַרְנָה	הָאֳזְרוּ			etc.	

There is nothing unique to note either in the active (reflexive) or the passive (reflexive). Finally the manner of conjugating the compound verb (composed of this and the preceding) anyone can easily learn from what has been already taught.

CHAPTER 29

VERBS OF THE EIGHTH CONJUGATION (AYIN GUTTURALS[1])

In respect to these, what we have noted in the preceding chapter should be noted especially, nor is it necessary to illustrate it by examples. However, they differ most strongly in this, that their intensive forms are always without any dagesh punctuation which gutturals cannot have, and in place of the dagesh they do not usually change the preceding vowel from a short to a long one. Other intensive verbs, as we have said, usually double the middle letter of the root, or when this cannot be done, change the preceding vowel into a long one, like בֵּרֵךְ for בְּרֵךְ, and אֲבָרֵךְ for אַבְרֵךְ. But I have said that the verbs of this conjugation cannot double the middle, nor do they usually change the preceding syllable on that account. Thus שָׂחַק *to be merry* has the intensive שִׂחֵק *to make merry (play)*, and בָּעַר *to burn* has בִּעֵר *to kindle*, and טָהַר, טִהֵר *to cleanse*, כִּהֵן *to administer*, or *to perform the sacred service*, נִאֵץ *to stir up*. But in many cases those which have an א do change the syllable into a long vowel like בָּאֵר *to explain*, מֵאֵן *to be unwilling*, תָּאַב *to loathe*, and others likewise. Finally with regard to compound verbs, composed of this and the preceding conjugations, it should be noted this can be learned easily from the preceding.

CHAPTER 30

OF DEFECTIVE VERBS

By defective verbs I mean those of which one of the root letters is deficient, as are the verbs of the second and third conjugations, or those whose first root letter is a י, or a נ, or those whose middle root is an א, or a נ, or a י, or those whose second and third root is the same letter. Concerning the verbs of the first and second conjugations and concerning those whose first root is a י or whose middle root is an א or a ו, we have spoken in Chapters 22, 23, 25, 26, and 27. It remains that I speak concerning the two other defective groups. First concerning those

---

1. [Term not used by Spinoza.—M.L.M.]

whose primary root is a נ. Of these I say that many of them, though not all, in certain cases either omit or retain the נ, but since it is required to be compensated by a dagesh, it is called defective only in writing but not in pronunciation. No, I say, on that account, even though a syllable is occasionally missing. For monosyllabic verbs, provided that no letter of the root is missing, are not usually defective, just as polysyllables like יָדַע should also not be called superfluous.

Their paradigm is a verb of the first conjugation נָגַשׁ to approach, whose form of the simple infinitive (kal) is also גַּשׁ, and with the paragogic ה, גְּשָׁה, and whose construct is גֶּשֶׁת.

	The Imperative			The Future	
	f.	m.		f.	m.
גְּשִׁי and	גְּשִׁי	גַּשׁ and	גַּשׁ sing.		אֶגַּשׁ 1.
גַּשְׁנָה		גְּשׁוּ pl.		תִּגְּשִׁי	תִּגַּשׁ 2.

The past always is analogous (to the first conjugation) and with the paragogic ה, אֶגְּשָׁה, and with the athnach or siluk accent אֶגָּשָׁה.

The verb נָתוֹן *to give, to concede*, instead of תֶּנֶת, has תֵּת, and the imperative תֵּן *give*; whence the future אֶתֵּן, תִּתֵּן, etc.

The second conjugation verb נָשָׂא *to bear, to carry*, imitates the verb נָגַשׁ.

Of these which are of the third conjugation, all the simple active *(kal)* with the exception of future are analogous, like נָטָה or נָטוֹת, etc., *to stretch, to incline*. Its imperative is נְטֵה; but the future is אֶטֶּה, etc., and with the dropping of the ה it is אַט, תֵּט, יֵט, etc.

Next, verbs of the fourth conjugation imitate the paradigm of the first, like נָפַח *to blow* פַּח, and with a paragogic ה, פְּחָה and with a ת פַּחַת.

The verbs of the sixth are always analogous and like verbs of the eighth conjugation, except the Aramaic נְחַת *to descend*, of which I am in doubt.

The simple passive *(niph'al)* is analogous, except that in the past, because of the characteristic נ of the *niph'al*, the root letter נ is omitted and is compensated by a dagesh, like נִגַּשׁ for נִנְגַּשׁ. To be sure, this analogy is one of those of which we spoke in Chapter 15.

Next, the intensive verb, both active *(pi'el)* and passive *(pu'al)*, is always analogous. The causative *(hiph'il)*, instead of הַנְגִּישׁ, הַנְגֵּשׁ, and הַנְגִּישׁ, is הִגִּישׁ, הַגֵּשׁ, and הַגִּישׁ.

	The Past			The Imperative			The Future	
	f.	m.		f.	m.		f.	m.
הִגִּישָׁה	הִגִּישׁ	3.	הַגִּישִׁי	הַגֵּשׁ		אַגִּישׁ and	אַגֵּשׁ	1.
הִגַּשְׁתְּ	שְׁתָּ	2.				תַּגִּישִׁי	תַּגֵּשׁ	2.
	הִגַּשְׁתִּי	1.		הַגֵּשׁ		תַּגִּישׁ	יַגֵּשׁ	3.
			הַגֵּשְׁנָה	הַגִּישׁוּ pl.		etc.		

Thus the verb of the third conjugation נָטָה has the causative (hiph'il) הִטָּה, הַטָּה, and הַטּוֹת. Whence the past הִטָּה, f. הִטְּתָה, 2. הִטֵּיתָ, and the imperative הַטֵּה, and the future אַטֶּה 2. תַּטֶּה, f. תַּטִּי, etc., or with the dropped ה it is אַט, יט, etc. So also the fourth conjugation נָסַע *to move out* has the reflexive הִסִּיעַ, or contracted to הִסַּע, whence the future אַסַּע, אַסִּיעַ, etc.

For the rest, it is noted that the causative form of the verb (hiph'il) very frequently lacks the נ, like the simple (kal); except verbs of the sixth and the eighth conjugations, which, as we have said, are always analogous. The causative passive (hoph'al) infinitive is either הֻגַּשׁ or הֻגַּשׁ.

	The Past			The Imperative			The Future	
	f.	m.		f.	m.		f.	m.
3.	הֻגְּשָׁה	הֻגַּשׁ		הֻגְּשִׁי	הֻגַּשׁ	1.		אֻגַּשׁ
2.	etc.	הֻגַּשְׁתָּ		etc.		2.	תֻּגְּשִׁי	תֻּגַּשׁ

The reflexive, both active (hithpael) and passive (hothpael), is analogous.

Finally the verb לָקַח *to take*. This must be referred to here because it alone follows this paradigm. But the others whose first root letter is a ל are analogous.

CHAPTER 31

ANOTHER CLASS OF DEFECTIVES

Verbs which have the same second and third root letter usually lose one. For example, סָבַב *to encircle* frequently has the infinitive סֹב, or without the accent סָב with a ָ chatuf; in addition it is occasionally סוּב and סַב, like בְּרָן־יַחַד *with a shout (song) together*. Hence the past, instead of סָבַב frequently is:

	The Past			Imperative instead of סְבֹב			Future	
	f.	m.		f.	m.		f.	m.
3.	סַבָּה	סַב		סוֹבִי	סוֹב sing.	1.		אָסוֹב
2.	סַבּוֹת	סַבּוֹתָ		סֻבֶּינָה	סוֹבוּ pl.	2.	תָּסוֹבִי	תָּסוֹב
1.		סַבּוֹתִי		סַבִּי	סַב sing.	3.	תָּסוֹב	יָסוֹב
3.		סַבּוּ		סֻבֶּינָה	סֹבוּ pl.	1.		נָסוֹב
2.	סַבּוֹתֶן	סַבּוֹתֶם		סוּבִי	סוּב sing.	2.	תְּסֻבֶּינָה	תָּסוֹבוּ
1.		סַבּוֹנוּ		סוּבֶינָה	סוּבוּ pl.	3.		יָסוֹבוּ

The third person past, both singular and plural, may have a cholem instead of a patach, like סֹב, plural סֹבוּ; then the וּ is frequently lost altogether, making it סַבְתָ, סֹב, אָסֹב instead of סוֹב, סַבוֹת, and אָסוֹב. The future frequently agrees with the future of those verbs whose first root letter is a נ, that is, instead of אָסוֹב, יָסוֹב, it often is אָסוֹב, תָסוֹב, יָסוֹב, etc., compensating the long syllable by a dagesh. Finally, from the form of the imperative סוּב the future also is formed יָסוּב, תָסוּב, אָסוּב, etc.

The forms of the passive infinitive (niph'al) are נָסַב, and הָסוֹב, and הָסֵב or הָסַב.

	The Past			The Imperative			The Future	
f.	m.		f.	m.		f.	m.	
נָסְבָה נָסְבָה	נָסַב	3.	הֲסָבִּי	הָסֵב	sing.		אָסֵב	1.
וֹת	נְסַבּוֹת	2.	הֲסָבֶּנָה	הָסֵבּוּ	pl.	תְסִבִּי	תָסֵב	2.
	נְסַבּוֹתִי	1.	or			etc.	יָסֵב	3.
	נָסַבּוּ	3.	הֲסֹבִי	הָסוֹב			or	
תֶן	נְסַבּוֹתֶם	2.	הֲסֹבֶינָה	הָסוֹבּוּ			אָסוֹב	1.
	נְסַבּוֹנוּ	1.				תְסוֹב תְסוֹבִי		2.

The past tense agrees also with those (verbs) whose first is a נ and is נָסַב, נְסַבּוֹת instead of נָסַב, נָסַבְתָ, and, the third person, both singular and plural, also has either a ־ or cholem instead of a ־, namely נָסֹב or נֹסַב for נָסַב and נְסֹבִי or נֹסֹבּוּ for נְסַבִּי and נָסַבּוּ.

The intensive (pi'el) is often analogous, like כָּתַת to beat, חָלֵל to profane, כָּהָה to grow dim, but more often the first letter is doubled and interposed between the others (like סִכְסֵךְ to incite for סָכַךְ, and גִלְגֵּל to revolve for גָלַל). This is particularly so if the doubled verbs are of the second, third, and fourth conjugations, like טֵאטֵא the intensive (pi'el) of the second conjugation verb טָאָא to sweep; and לְהַלְהֵ from the third conjugation verb לָהָה to languish and שַעֲשֵׁעַ from the fourth conjugation שָׁעַע to be delighted, to play, and also תִּעְתַּע from תָּעַע to mock, and עִרְעֵר from עָרַר to be alone. Also it seems that a large number of both active (pi'el) and passive (pu'al) agrees with the intensives of the sixth conjugation. So that, as from קוּם the active (pi'el) is קוֹמֵם and the passive (pu'al) קוֹמָם, so from סוּב the intensive (pi'el) is סוֹבֵב and the passive (pu'al) is סוֹבָב.

The causative (hiph'il) hardly ever observes the analogy. The infinitive in most cases is like הָסֵב or הָסָב and הָסַב. Hence:

	The Past		or		The Imperative			The Future	
f.	m.		f.	m.			f.	m.	
הֲסִבָּה	הֵסֵב	3. s.	הָסֵבִּי	הָסֵב	s.		אָסֵב	1.
הֲסִבּוֹת	הֲסִבּוֹת	2.	הֲסִבֶּינָה	הָסֵבּוּ	pl.		תָּסֵבִּי	תָּסֵב	2.
	הֲסִבּוֹתִי	1.					תָּסֵב	יָסֵב	3.
	הֵסֵבּוּ	3. pl.					נָסֵב	1.
הֲסִבּוֹתֶן	הֲסִבּוֹתֶם	2.					תָּסֵבּוּ	2.
	הֲסִבּוֹנוּ	1.		תְּסֻבֶּינָה			יָסֵבּוּ	3.

Here also the kametz is as in the simple form (kal) usually compensated, becoming אָסֵב in place of אָסָב. And, when the accent is transposed to the first syllable the ֵ changes to a ָ , like יָסֶד־לְךָ he will incite you. The passive (pu'al) infinitive is הָסֵב, הוּסֵב, and הֻסַב, and with the paragogic ה הָסַבָּה changing the ו into a ֻ chatuf.

	Past			Imperative			Future	
f.	m.		f.	m.		f.	m.	
הוּסַבָּה	הוּסַב	3.	הוּסַבִּי	הוּסַב	sing.		אוּסַב	1.
וֹת	הוּסַבּוֹת	2.		and		תּוּסַבִּי	תּוּסַב	2.
	הוּסַבּוֹתִי	1.	הֲסִבִּי	הֲסֵב			etc.	
and							or	
הֲסַבָּה	הֲסֵב		הוּסַבֶּינָה הוּסַבּוּ	pl.		אֲסַב	1.
etc.						תָּסֵבִּי	תָּסֵב	2.
							etc.	

The reflexive (hithpael) generally follows the paradigm of the sixth conjugation; but the second, third, and fourth conjugations are generally formed from the intensive form (pi'el), like הִשְׁתַּעֲשֵׁעַ to delight oneself, הִתְלַהְלֵהַּ to tire oneself, הִתְמַהְמֵהַּ to linger. But שָׁחַח to lay waste, and כָּהָה to grow dim follow the paradigm of the sixth.

From this it appears that these defective verbs may easily be confused so that it often occurs with defectives of this kind that you may be doubtful whether their roots are of the second, or third, or fifth, or sixth conjugation; the reason for this I shall show here briefly. For I believe I owe you this clarification that you may understand.

Every kind of defective verb usually compensates the deficient letter by doubling the second or third radical of the root. For example, בָּזָא is a second conjugation verb and means to divide; but very frequently the א is missing and in its place the middle radical is doubled, making it בָּזַז or בּוּז. So also the second conjugation verb זָכָה meaning to be pure; but often in place of the ה the middle letter is doubled, becoming זָכַךְ, whence it is that this verb sometimes follows the third conjugation and sometimes those that have a doubled middle root, like סָלָה and סִלְסֵל, חָרָה and חַרְחֵר; and like doubled middle letter verbs they also follow the infinitive of the third conjugation, like שָׁמוֹת *to be desolate* for שָׁמוֹם or שׁוּם, חָמוֹת *to be warm* for חָמוֹם or חוֹם, and so the others. Also the fifth conjugation verb יָזֵם *to plan*, when the י is lost it is compensated by זָמַם, and also the verb, חָמוֹם or חוֹם for יָחוֹם *to be made warm*, and רוֹק for יָרוֹק *to spit*, etc. Whence it is that these double letter verbs also imitate the fifth conjugation. So with verbs of the sixth conjugation on account of the doubling of the third letter of the root: instead of שׁוּךְ it is שָׂכַךְ *to cover*, and instead of מָס *to melt* it is מָסַס or מוֹס and צָר *he bound* becomes צָרַר. And so it is that they also imitate the sixth conjugation (concerning which see also what we have noted at the end of Chapter 25), and vice versa these doubled ones especially the intensives among them, they also frequently double the first root letter, as these doubled verbs usually do. Thus פּוּר has the pi'el פּוֹרֵר and פִּרְפֵּר. To these belong also the defectives with a נ as first root letter. Thus instead of נָאַר *to abhor* it is אָרַר *to curse*, as from נָקַב *to curse* it is קָבַב, and from נָצַל it is צָלַל; whence the future feminine third person is תִּצְלֶינָה and תִּצְלַנָה *they will ring*, and thus instead of נָשַׁם it is שָׁמַם *to abandon*, and in this manner the others; whence it is that these doubled and all defectives imitate either this or other conjugations.

This is what I have thought worthwhile to admonish students of this language. For having noted this they will be able to investigate with certainty and without hesitation all the roots of the defective verbs.

CHAPTER 32

Concerning Deponent Verbs, and Quadriliteral Verbs, and Incidentally Concerning the Composition of Verbs, Modes, and Tenses

Only two or three simple deponent verbs exist, namely: נִשְׁבּוֹעַ *to swear*, נִלְחַם *to fight*, and perhaps also נִשְׁעַן *to be supported*. I have clearly said *simple* verbs because there are no intensives, causatives, or reciprocals which are passive in form and active in meaning. And therefore נִשְׁבַּע *to swear*, has the causative (hiph'il) הִשְׁבִּיעַ *to cause to swear*, which is active both in meaning and form.

Further, there are, in existence, many verbs consisting of more than three root letters, which I now venture to examine. They are, for example, פֹּרֵשׂ for פּוֹרֵשׂ *to spread* (see Job chapter 26, verse 9) and יְכַרְסְמֶנָּה for יְרַמְסֶנָה *he ravaged it* (see Psalms chap. 80, vs. 14) and מְכֻרְבָּל for מְחֻגָּר *clothed* (see 1 Chron. 15:27). But this last form from the Chaldaic noun כַּרְבַּלְתָּא, which means a *garment, cloak, coverlet, red cap,* or *the comb of a rooster*. But the worst fault of examples is that they persuade me easily. For not only do these occur only once, but also we know nothing of the source from which they are derived, and they seem to refer to a verb which has acquired its meaning in common with others.

But, without conjecturing about this, let us state this in general that there has been no verb observed which, because of the characteristics of the verb form, the tense, or the person, consists of more than three root letters, except the intensives which are formed from some substantive or an adjective (we have said above in Chapter 16, that this verb form is composed either from a simple verb or from a noun). For example: from חֲצֹצְרָה *a trumpet* there is חִצֹּצֵר *to blow a trumpet*; and from חֲמַרְמַר, the diminutive of חָמַר, there is חֳמַרְמַר *he became reddened*. So from יְפֵיפָה, diminutive from יָפָה *to be beautiful*, it is יָפְיָפִיתָ *you have become more beautiful*. Those which are formed from monosyllables follow either the intensives of the double letter verbs or the sixth conjugation; like קַרְקַר *to demolish a wall*, which is formed from קִיר *a wall*, and שֵׁרֵשׁ *to eradicate* is from שֹׁרֶשׁ *a root*. See Chapter 16. But enough of this.

It is now time that I conclude those matters that refer to conjugation of the verbs, and that I add something about the composite verbs. Grammarians call composite verbs those which are composed from two different conjugations, or from two forms of the same root, or from a noun, a participle, and a verb. Concerning them it is usually added that there are some which express two modes or two tenses at the same time. For example, there are two composites of the fifth and sixth conjugations; namely: הוֹשַׁבוֹתִי which is composed of יָשַׁב *to sit* and שׁוּב *to return*, otherwise it would have been either הוֹשַׁבְתִּי from יָשַׁב, or הֲשִׁבוֹתִי from שׁוּב; the other is הֵיטִיבוֹתָ which is composed from יָטַב and טוֹב *to be good*, which would otherwise have been either הֵיטַבְתָּ from יָטַב, or הֲטִיבוֹתָ from טוֹב. In the first place it seems the prophet expresses both meanings simultaneously and he seemed to indicate both; in the second place whichever mode is assumed he expresses the same thing. Therefore I do not doubt but that in this manner one may compose other verbs of the fifth and sixth conjugations.

Further some grammarians have noted, partly out of ignorance and partly having been deceived by a correction of the copy, as in the case of אֶתְּקֶנְךָּ (Jeremiah chap. 22, vs. 24) which they thought to be composed of נָתַק *to tear out*, and תָּקַן *to mend* but the נ often prefixed before the future. But מְקַלְלוֹנִי (Jeremiah 15:10) for מְקַלְלַי seems really to be a fault of a hasty pen (scribal error). And in this way, but mostly out of ignorance, they noted many composites from two verb forms of the same root; for example, נְכַפַּר *he has been forgiven*, נִוַּסְּרוּ *they disciplined themselves*, and נִשְׁתָּוָה *he was made equal*, they believed to be composed from the simple passive *(niphʻal)* and the reflexive *(hithpael)*; because they simply didn't know of the reflexive passive *(nithpael)*, as I have already shown in Chapter 21. So they considered יָלְדְתְּ, שְׁכַנְתְּ, יָשַׁבְתְּ, and מִקְנֻנְתְּ composites from the participle and the past without any real foundation. For who ever taught them that a participle cannot end like a past, and for יוֹשֶׁבֶת it could not be said יוֹשַׁבְתְּ; but מִשְׁתַּחֲוִיתֶם for מִשְׁתַּחֲוִים (Ezekiel 8:16) seems really a fault of hasty pen (scribal error). In addition, they considered as a compound verb תָּבֹאתִי instead of תָּבֹאִי composed from the past and the future, but they did not see that in this future the paragogic ה, because of the addition of a syllable, changed into a ת, as we have already admonished in Chapter 27. But I do not wish to weary the students, but on the contrary only to admonish them that they be not agitated very much by this.

CHAPTER 33

OF THE NOMINATIVE PARTICIPLE

Participles are adjectives which express an action, or all things usually expressed by a verb as it has an effect on a thing or a relationship as to tense. Thus it is that there exist as many kinds of participles as verbs; namely simple *(kal)*, intensives *(pi'el)*, causatives *(hiph'il)*, and reflexives *(hithpael)*, and all of them both in the active and passive.

They are formed from the verbs in this manner. The simple active form *(kal)* פָּקַד also has the form פֹּקֵד and I claim it also to be a participle. And thus the simple masculine *(kal)* participle is פֹּקֵד, and with the paragogic י פֹּקְדִי, feminine פֹּקֵדָה, פֹּקֶדֶת, or פֹּקַדְתְּ, and with the paragogic י it is פֹּקַדְתִּי. Then from the passive *(niph'al)* נִפְקַד the masculine participle is נִפְקָד and, with the paragogic י, it is נִפְקְדִי feminine נִפְקֶדֶת or נִפְקָדָה.

From the intensive *(pi'el)* פִּקֵּד the masculine participle is מְפַקֵּד, feminine מְפַקְּדָה or מְפַקֶּדֶת, and the passive פֻּקַּד *(pu'al)* is in the masculine מְפֻקָּד, etc., or פֻּקָּד feminine פֻּקָּדָה or פֻּקֶּדֶת or פֻּקַּדְתְּ, etc.

So from the causative *(hiph'il)* הִפְקִיד the masculine is מַפְקִיד, feminine מַפְקִידָה; and from the passive *(hoph'al)* הָפְקַד or הֻפְקַד the masculine is מָפְקָד or מֻפְקָד, etc.

And finally, from the reflexive *(hithpael)* הִתְפַּקֵּד the masculine is מִתְפַּקֵּד, etc. Reflexive passive participles do not exist, except מְתֻנָאָץ, or (compensating the ת by a dagesh) מְנֻאָץ; whose characteristic sign מְת is in the active form, but the verb נוּאַץ has the passive form, contrary to the customary usage of this verb form (of which see Chapter 21), and therefore I do not venture to decide anything about it.

Further, the simple participles, which are formed from neuter verbs, usually use the form of the infinitive פָּקֵד, like יָשֵׁן *sleeping*, דָּבֵק *cleaning*, etc.

Next, the passive participle is most frequently formed from its active, becoming from פָּקֹד (by changing the cholem into וּ) פָּקוּד *visited*. But these are very often changed into adjectives.

And I call these participles since they signify a mode by which a thing is considered as in the present. But they themselves are frequently changed into pure adjectives which signify the attributes of things; for example, סוֹפֵר is a participle, which means *a counting man*, that is, *who is now occupied in counting*, but most frequently it is used as an attribute without any relationship as to time, and signifies a man *who has the job of counting*, namely *a scribe*. So שׁוֹפֵט signifies *a man who is occupied in judging* and frequently is attributed to a man who has the office of judging, i.e., it has the same value as among the Latins, the word Judex (Judge). So the passive participle נִבְחָר (*chosen*, that is, *a man* or *a thing which is now actually chosen*) is frequently attributed to a thing *distinguished (excellent)*, namely of things *chosen above all*; and in this manner intensive participles and others change often into attributes, that is into adjectives which have no relationship to time whatever.

Next, I believe that the simple participles whose prefix is מ should be distinct from the rest of participles. They are those like מְשׁוֹפֵט *a litigant*, מַלְשִׁין *one who offends with the tongue*. We do not want to exaggerate, but it seems that the simple and the intensive and the rest, all had the characteristic letter מ, and that the later writers abolished it in the simple form; or perhaps intensive participles are formed from simple ones, and that is why their roots lack an intensive verb. This regarding participles in general, and of those which are formed from verbs of the first conjugation.

From verbs of the second conjugation masculine participles are formed in the same manner as the preceding ones but the feminine participles do not have the double segol. The א is mostly quiescent, and in place of נִמְצָאָה, מוֹצָאָה, etc., it is נִמְצֵאת, מֹצֵאת, etc. The simple participle is also מְצֵאת.

Further, the participles of this conjugation usually drop the א altogether and they follow the same procedure as we have said about their verbs.

Participles of the third conjugation very often have a segol in place of a ֵ, like גָּלֶה; in the feminine either the ה disappears altogether, like גֹּלָה for גֹּלְהָה or it is changed into a י, and the ֶ into a chirek, like פּוֹרִיָּה *fruitful*.

Adjectives of this and the second conjugations, which follow the form פָּקוּד change the א or ה into a י, like מָצוּי *existing* or *inventing* from מָצָא, and גָּלוּי *revealed* from גָּלָה. I do not need to note here all the adjectives of every conjugation in detail since they regularly follow the rules of the verbs from which they were formed.

The participles formed from the verbs whose first root letter is a נ (*peh nun* verbs) follow the form of the verb; that is, if the past lacks the נ of the root, the participle also will lack it, and contrarily, if the past is analogous (to the first conjugation) the participle also will be analogous. For example the simple active נֹגֵשׁ

has the past נָגַשׁ, and the participle נוֹגֵשׁ, namely both analogous; and the causative הִגִּישׁ has the past הִגִּישׁ, and the participle מַגִּישׁ, that is, both are defective.

However, the participles formed from defective double roots regularly have the active simple סוֹבֵב; but the remaining participles follow the past of the verb. Namely from the simple passive נָסַב the masculine is נָסָב the feminine נְסַבָּה and from the intensive סֹבֵב it is מְסוֹבֵב and from סוֹבַב it is מְסוֹבָב, and so from the causative past הֵסֵב it is מֵסֵב, and from הוּסַב it is מוּסָב, and finally from the reflexive הִסְתּוֹבֵב it is מִסְתּוֹבֵב. For the rest, the inflection of the participles from singular to plural follows the rules common to the nouns, of which see Chapter 6.

The rest is missing.

Political Treatise

Spinoza began the Political Treatise *(TP) in 1675 or 1676. In the last letter we have from him, from 1676, he discusses the work and describes its first six chapters. During 1674 and 1675 he had returned to the* Ethics, *making final preparation for its publication, which was in the end delayed. He then turned to the new treatise, which remained incomplete at his death on 21 February 1677. The TP was to be a purely political tract, building on the final five chapters of the* Theological-Political Treatise *(TTP). It was written at the urging of a friend and aggravated by the political urgencies of the 1670s as well as out of his deep concern for stability and peace.*

The early 1670s witnessed a Dutch political upheaval that led to political assassinations and the replacement of the liberal regime with a more repressive one. In 1672, with the invasion of French and German armies and the capture of Utrecht and several other cities, the era of the liberal pensionary Jan de Witt came to an end. De Witt and his brother were murdered by a hysterical, uncontrolled mob in a hideous fashion. Whether Spinoza knew de Witt personally and how he was viewed by the statesman are matters of dispute. We have a report that in a rare show of emotion, Spinoza was ready to denounce publicly the barbarity of the de Witt assassination until restrained by his landlord in The Hague. True or not, the tale reflects something about the desperate situation and the danger that Spinoza confronted in the wake of the publication of the TTP and as he worked to complete his systematic philosophy. His fame extended throughout Europe; he was sought, feared, and doubtless hated. By 1674 the TTP had been censored often and recently by the Court of Holland as a threat to religion and the church. Its printing, distribution, or sale was to be severely punished. Also in 1674 Van den Enden, who was in Paris, was arrested, tried, and hanged. One can imagine the fears that ran through Spinoza's mind in such a climate of repression and violence. Increasingly, he was alone—old friends like Simon de Vries and Pieter Balling having died, others including Koerbagh, de Witt, and Van den Enden executed as the result of persecution and fear. It is not surprising that Spinoza's thoughts turned to politics.

Spinoza set as his task the analysis of various types of constitution and their suitability for producing peace and stability. His world was filled with increasing fear and repression; it provided him personally with fame but forced him to confront the spectacle of public violence. It was a world that seemed to demand the stern but wise hand of reason and science to examine its structure and to identify how peace might best be achieved. To give a rational argument for the preeminent character of a democratic polity: this was the Political Treatise's primary purpose. It was to build on his understanding of human psychology and human nature, the content of Ethics II and III, and to derive an account of the most suitable constitution, a liberal democracy.

What we have of the Political Treatise consists of eleven chapters: two on monarchy, three on aristocracy, an incomplete chapter on democracy, and five introductory chapters dealing with natural right, sovereignty, and the highest aims of the state. Building on the foundation of his psychology and social psychology, Spinoza explores the advantages and disadvantages of the traditional modes of political organization. Like Hobbes, he founds the social compact in the self-interest, natural power, and rights of its participants. Sovereignty is constituted naturally, by the agreement of individuals who, with hopes and fears, seek defense from assault and a stable, tranquil situation, a condition of peace and opportunity for well-being. In Hobbes, individuals leave the state of nature in order to establish the civil state; in Spinoza, on the contrary, individuals are in both the state of nature and the civil state at once, as is the sovereign. The authority of the latter rests precisely on the surplus of its power over that of its citizens.

Spinoza, however, unlike Hobbes, argues that the best form of government is a democracy, in which citizens grant sovereignty to themselves as one mind, who vote on all law and whose will is in fact the will of the people. Spinoza realized that real states can only approximate the democratic ideal, and the Political Treatise *occupies itself with accounts of how real states of the three basic kinds can best serve the purposes of the ideal democratic model. Monarchies, for example, should not be absolute; rather the ruler's power should be qualified through the activity of a strong council. The best actual monarchy, that is, should be a constitutional monarchy, a judgment that Spinoza makes knowing full well the long Dutch history concerning the Prince of Orange and the role of the stadtholder. Similarly, when Spinoza turns to an aristocratic or oligarchic form of government, he describes a state with three bodies—legislative, executive, and judicial—with a system of a division of power, checks and balances, and a sufficiently large class of patricians to act wisely and honestly for the benefit of all. Ultimately, whether an actual government is democratic, aristocratic, or monarchical, the aim is the same; the well-being of all. This means that freedom and toleration are essential, as long as they are compatible with the state's peace and security.*

As one turns to the Political Treatise *and its relation to the* Theological-Political Treatise, *a number of issues surface. Clearly, the TTP is more polemical and is devoted substantially to theological issues, biblical interpretation, and clerical authority. But the* Political Treatise *is still concerned with a natural, rational understanding of human nature, and the ways that actual forms of government serve or do not serve the natural flourishing of human life. In the TTP Spinoza focuses on ecclesiastical power and repression. In the* Political Treatise *he turns to the power of citizens, their passions and their interests, and the way such power can harm or benefit life in the state. There is reason to believe that*

Spinoza's thinking does not change in the two works but rather has a different emphasis and takes a different shape. The TTP was an interruption in the preparation of the Ethics *for publication; the* Political Treatise *is its philosophical and systematic development. Each has its special place in Spinoza's life and philosophical career.*

M.L.M.

CONTENTS

1. [Introduction]
2. [Natural Right]
3. [Sovereign Powers]
4. [Rights of Sovereign Powers]
5. [The Highest Aim of Society]
6. [Monarchy: Its Nature]
7. [Monarchy: Its Organisation]
8. [Aristocracy: The First Model]
9. [Aristocracy: The Second Model]
10. [Aristocracy: Its Organisation]
11. [Democracy: Its Nature (unfinished)]

POLITICAL TREATISE

in which it is shown how a community governed as a Monarchy or as an Aristocracy should be organised if it is not to degenerate into a Tyranny, and if the Peace and Freedom of its citizens is to remain inviolate.

CHAPTER 1
[Introduction][1]

[1] Philosophers look upon the passions by which we are assailed as vices, into which men fall through their own fault. So it is their custom to deride, bewail, berate them, or, if their purpose is to appear more zealous than others, to execrate them. They believe that they are thus performing a sacred duty, and that they are attaining the summit of wisdom when they have learnt how to shower extravagant praise on a human nature that nowhere exists and to revile that which exists in actuality. The fact is that they conceive men not as they are, but as they would like them to be. As a result, for the most part it is not ethics they have written, but satire; and they have never worked out a political theory that can have practical application, only one that borders on fantasy or could be put into effect in Utopia or in that golden age of the poets where there would naturally be no need of such. Therefore, while theory is believed to be at variance with practice in all practical sciences, this is particularly so in the case of political theory, and no men are regarded as less fit for governing a state than theoreticians or philosophers.

[2] Statesmen, on the other hand, are believed to aim at men's undoing rather than their welfare, and they have a reputation for cunning rather than wisdom. No doubt experience has taught them that there will be vices as long as there are men.[2] So while they seek to anticipate human wickedness, employing those arts which they have learnt from long experience and which men habitually practise when guided by fear rather than by reason, they appear to be the enemies of religion, especially so to theologians, who believe that sovereign powers ought to deal with public affairs according to the same moral principles as are binding on the private individual. Yet there can be no doubt that statesmen have written about political matters much more effectively than philosophers. For since ex-

---

Notes are by Steven Barbone and Lee Rice (main annotators for this work) and translator Samuel Shirley.

[1] [Chapter titles in brackets were added by the editors of the TP.—S.B./L.R.]
[2] [Tacitus, *Histories* IV, lxxiv, 2.]

perience has been their guide, there is nothing they have taught that is remote from practice.[3]

[3] Indeed, I am fully convinced that experience has revealed every conceivable form of commonwealth[4] where men may live in harmony, and also the means whereby a people may be governed or restrained within fixed bounds. So I do not believe that our researches in this field can lead us to anything not at variance with experience and practice that has not already been discovered and tried. For human nature is such that men cannot live without some common code of law,[5] and such codes have been instituted and public affairs conducted by men of considerable intelligence, both astute and cunning. So it is hardly credible that we can conceive anything of possible benefit to the community that opportunity or chance has not already suggested and that men engaged in public affairs and concerned for their own security have not already discovered.

[4] Therefore in turning my attention to political theory it was not my purpose to suggest anything that is novel or unheard of, but only to demonstrate by sure and conclusive reasoning such things as are in closest agreement with practice, deducing them from human nature as it really is. And in order to enquire into matters relevant to this branch of knowledge in the same unfettered spirit as is habitually shown in mathematical studies, I have taken great care not to deride, bewail, or execrate human actions, but to understand them. So I have regarded human emotions such as love, hatred, anger, envy, pride, pity, and other agitations of the mind not as vices of human nature but as properties pertaining to it in the same way as heat, cold, storm, thunder, and such pertain to the nature of the atmosphere. These things, though troublesome, are inevitable, and have definite causes through which we try to understand their nature. And the mind derives as much enjoyment in contemplating them aright as from the knowledge of things that are pleasing to the senses.

[5] For this much is quite certain, and proved to be true in our *Ethics*, that men are necessarily subject to passions, and are so constituted that they pity the unfortunate, envy the fortunate, and are more inclined to vengeance than to compassion. Furthermore, each man wants others to live according to his way of thinking, approving what he approves and rejecting what he rejects. Consequently, since all men are equally desirous of preeminence, they fall to quarrelling and strive their utmost to best one another; and he who emerges victorious is more elated at having hindered someone else than at having gained an advantage for himself. And although all are convinced that religion, on the other hand, teaches that each should love his neighbour as himself, that is, that he should uphold another's right just as his own, we have shown that this conviction is of little avail

---

[3] [The allusion is to Machiavelli, who also argued that the principles of public morality are not the same as those of individual ethics.]

[4] [The Latin *civitas* is usually rendered "commonwealth" in what follows.]

[5] [*extra commune aliquod jus*. This is the first time Spinoza uses the term *jus*, a very difficult term to render into the modern idiom. In what follows, *jus* is usually rendered as "law" or "right" depending on the sense and context of the passage in which it is used.]

against the passions. It is effective, no doubt, at death's door, that is, when sickness has subdued the passions and a man lies helpless; or again in places of worship where men have no dealings with one another; but it has no weight in law-court or palace, where it would be needed most of all. We have also shown that reason can indeed do much to control and moderate the passions; but at the same time we have seen that the path taught by reason is a very difficult one, so that those who believe that ordinary people or those who are busily engaged in public business can be persuaded to live solely at reason's behest are dreaming of the poets' golden age or of a fairy tale.

[6] So if the safety of a state[6] is dependent on some man's good faith, and its affairs cannot be properly administered unless those responsible for them are willing to act in good faith, that state will lack all stability. If it is to endure, its government must be so organised that its ministers cannot be induced to betray their trust or to act basely, whether they are guided by reason or by passion. Nor does it matter for the security of the state what motives induce men to administer its affairs properly, provided that its affairs are in fact properly administered. Freedom of spirit or strength of mind is the virtue of a private citizen: the virtue of a state is its security.

[7] Finally, since all men everywhere, whether barbarian or civilised, enter into relationships with one another and set up some kind of civil order, one should not look for the causes and natural foundations of the state in the teachings of reason, but deduce them from the nature and condition of men in general. This I propose to do in the next chapter.

Chapter 2
[Natural Right]

[1] In our *Tractatus theologico-politicus* we dealt with natural right[1] and civil right,[2] and in our *Ethics* we explained what is sin, what is righteousness, what is justice, what is injustice,[3] and what is human freedom.[4] But to save the readers of this treatise the trouble of consulting other works for things that are most closely concerned with this treatise, I have decided to explain them here once more, presenting logical proof.

---

[6] ["State" here translates the Latin *imperium* (from *imperare*, "to command"), which in principle refers to the administration of civil power. In Hobbes it is often translated as "sovereign" or "sovereignty," but the latter is preferable, since for both Hobbes and Spinoza the sovereign power is not a person, though its administration may be vested in one person or many.]

[1] [See TTP16/526–535.]

[2] [See TTP16/535.]

[3] [See E4P37Schol2.]

[4] [This is the general topic of E5.]

[2] Any natural thing can be adequately conceived, whether it actually exists or not. Therefore, just as the coming into existence of natural things cannot be concluded from their definition, so neither can their perseverance in existing; for their essence in the form of idea is the same after they have begun to exist as it was before they existed. Therefore, just as their coming into existence cannot follow from their essence, so neither can their perseverance in existing. The same power[5] that they need in order to begin to exist, they also need in order to continue to exist. Hence it follows that the power of natural things by which they exist, and consequently by which they act, can be no other than the eternal power of God. For if it were some other power, itself created, it would not be able to preserve its own self, and consequently it would not be able to preserve natural things; it would itself stand in need of that same power to persevere in existing as it needed to be created.

[3] So from the fact that the power of natural things by which they exist and act is the very power of God, we can readily understand what is the right of Nature. Since God has right over all things, and God's right is nothing other than God's power insofar as that is considered as absolutely free, it follows that every natural thing has as much right from Nature as it has power to exist and to act. For the power of every natural thing by which it exists and acts is nothing other than the power of God, which is absolutely free.

[4] By the right of Nature, then, I understand the laws or rules of Nature in accordance with which all things come to be; that is, the very power of Nature. So the natural right of Nature as a whole, and consequently the natural right of every individual, is coextensive with its power.[6] Consequently, whatever each man does from the laws of his own nature, he does by the sovereign right of Nature, and he has as much right over Nature as his power extends.

[5] So if human nature were so constituted that men lived only as reason prescribes and attempted nothing other than that, then the right of Nature, insofar as that is considered as specific to man, would be determined solely by the power of reason.[7] But men are led by blind desire more than by reason, and therefore their natural power or right must be defined not by reason but by any appetite by which they may be determined to act and by which they try to preserve themselves. I do indeed admit that in the case of those desires that do not arise from reason, men are not so much active as passive. But since we are here discussing the universal power or right of Nature, we cannot acknowledge any difference between desires that are engendered in us by reason and those arising from other causes. For in both cases they are the effects of Nature, explicating the natural force whereby man strives to persist in his own being.[8] Whether a man be wise or

---

[5] [*potentia.*]

[6] [This is probably a veiled critique of Hobbes, who distinguishes natural right from natural law (*De cive* XIV, 3), and argues that the latter, in contrast to the former, is prescriptive (*De cive* II, 1).]

[7] [Another veiled critique of Hobbes, for whom natural right is defined in terms of 'right reason' (*De cive* I, 7).]

[8] [*in suo esse:* The *conatus*, or drive for self-preservation, is the actual essence of the human individual, according to E3P7, and the source of both action and passion (E5P4Schol).]

ignorant, he is a part of Nature, and everything whereby a man is determined to act should be referred to the power of Nature insofar as this power is expressed through the nature of this or that man. For whether a man is led by reason or solely by desire, he does nothing that is not in accordance with the laws and rules of Nature, that is (Section 4 of this Chapter), he acts by the right of Nature.

[6] Yet most people believe that the ignorant violate the order of Nature rather than conform to it; they think of men in Nature as a state within a state. They hold that the human mind is not produced by natural causes but is directly created by God and is so independent of other things that it has an absolute power[9] to determine itself and to use reason in a correct way. But experience teaches us only too well that it is no more in our power to have a sound mind than to have a sound body. Again, since each thing, as far as in it lies, endeavours to preserve its own being, we cannot have the slightest doubt that, if it were equally in our power to live at reason's behest as to be led by blind desire, all would be led by reason and would order their lives wisely, which is by no means the case. For everyone is drawn by his own pleasure.[10] Nor do theologians remove this difficulty by maintaining that the cause of this weakness in human nature is the vice or sin whose origin was the fall of our first parent. For if the first man, too, had as much power to stand as to fall, and if he was in his right mind and with his nature unimpaired, how could it have come about that knowingly and deliberately he fell? Their answer is that he was deceived by the Devil. But who was it who deceived the Devil?[11] Who, I ask, caused the one who was the most outstanding of all intelligent creatures to become so insane that he willed to be greater than God? Did not he, who had a sound mind, endeavour to preserve himself and his own being, as far as in him lay? Again, how could it have come about that the first man himself, being of sound mind and master of his own will, allowed himself to be led astray and beguiled? If he had the power to use reason aright, he could not have been deceived, for, as far as in him lay he must have endeavoured to preserve his own being and his sound mind. But, by hypothesis, this was in fact within his power; therefore he must have preserved his sound mind and could not have been deceived. His history, however, shows this to be false; and so it must be admitted that it was not in the power of the first man to use reason aright, and that, like us, he was subject to passions.

[7] Now it is undeniable that man, like other individual things, endeavours to preserve his own being as far as in him lies. For if there could here be any possible difference, it would have to arise from man's having a free will. Yet the more free we conceived man to be, the more we were compelled to maintain that he must necessarily preserve himself and be of sound mind, as will readily be granted

---

[9] [*potestatem.*]

[10] [Vergil, *Eclogues* II, 65.]

[11] [On belief in the Devil and Spinoza's rejection of it, see KV2/25. For more on the story of Adam, see E4P68Schol; TTP4/430–433; Ep19.]

by everyone who does not confuse freedom with contingency. Freedom, in fact, is virtue or perfection; so anything that signifies weakness in man cannot be referred to his freedom. Therefore a man can certainly not be called free on the grounds that he is able not to exist, or that he is able not to use his reason; he can be called free only insofar as he has the power[12] to exist and to act in accordance with the laws of human nature. So the more free we consider a man to be, the less we can say that he is able not to use his reason and to choose evil before good; and so God, who exists, understands, and acts with absolute freedom, also exists, understands, and acts necessarily, that is, from the necessity of his own nature. For there is no doubt that God acts with the same freedom with which he exists. Therefore, as he exists from the necessity of his own nature, so he also acts from the necessity of his own nature; that is, he acts from absolute freedom.

[8] We therefore conclude that it is not in every man's power[13] always to use reason and to be at the highest pitch of human freedom, but yet he always endeavours as far as in him lies to preserve his own being and (since every man has right to the extent that he has power), whether he be wise or ignorant, whatever he endeavours and does, he endeavours and does by the sovereign right of Nature. From this it follows that Nature's right and established order, under which all men are born and for the most part live, forbids only those things that no one desires and no one can do; it does not frown on strife, or hatred, or anger, or deceit, or on anything at all urged by appetite. This is not surprising, for Nature's bounds are set not by the laws of human reason whose aim is only man's true interest and preservation, but by infinite other laws which have regard to the eternal order of the whole of Nature, of which man is but a tiny part. It is from the necessity of this order alone that all individual things are determined to exist and to act in a definite way. So if something in Nature appears to us as ridiculous, absurd, or evil, this is due to the fact that our knowledge is only partial, that we are for the most part ignorant of the order and coherence of Nature as a whole, and that we want all things to be directed as our reason prescribes. Yet that which our reason declares to be evil is not evil in respect of the order and laws of universal Nature, but only in respect of our own particular nature.[14]

[9] Furthermore, it follows that every man is subject to another's right for as long as he is in the other's power,[15] and he is in control of his own right to the extent that he can repel all force, take whatever vengeance he pleases for injury done to him, and, in general, live as he chooses to live.

[10] One man has another in his power if he holds him in bonds, or has deprived him of the arms and means of self-defence or escape, or has terrorised him,

---

[12] [*potestatem.*]

[13] [*potestate.* Contrast *potestas* with *potentia* which is the 'power' Spinoza speaks of at the end of this sentence.]

[14] [Perhaps a veiled criticism of Grotius, for whom natural right includes the sense of moral justice.]

[15] [Here and in the next paragraph the phrase is *sub potestate habere*—to have or gain control over something or someone.]

or has so attached the other to himself by benefit conferred that the man would rather please his benefactor than himself and live as the other would wish rather than at his own choosing. He who holds another in his power in the first or second way holds only the other's body, not his mind; in the third or fourth way he has made the other's body and his mind subject to his own right, but only as long as fear or hope endures. When one or the other is removed, the man remains in control of his own right.[16]

[11] The faculty of judgment, too, can be subject to another's right to the extent that one man can be deceived by another. Hence it follows that the mind is fully in control of itself only to the extent that it can use reason aright. Indeed, since human power should be assessed by strength of mind rather than robustness of body, it follows that those in whom reason is most powerful and who are most guided thereby are most fully in control of their own right. So I call a man altogether free insofar as he is guided by reason, because it is to that extent that he is determined to action by causes that can be adequately understood solely through his own nature, even though he is necessarily determined to action by these causes. For freedom (as I have shown in Section 9 of this Chapter) does not remove the necessity of action, but imposes it.

[12] If a man has given his pledge to someone, promising only verbally to do this or that which it was within his right to do or not to do, the pledge remains valid for as long as he who made it has not changed his mind. For he who has the power[17] to break faith has in reality not given up his right; he has given no more than words. Therefore, being by natural right judge of his own case, if he judges rightly or wrongly (for to err is human) that the loss resulting from the pledge he has given outweighs the advantage, his own belief will lead him to conclude that the pledge should be broken, and it is by natural right (Section 9 of this Chapter) that he will break his pledge.[18]

[13] If two men come together and join forces, they have more power over Nature, and consequently more right, than either one alone; and the greater the number who form a union in this way, the more right they will together possess.

[14] Insofar as men are assailed by anger, envy, or any emotion deriving from hatred, they are drawn apart and are contrary to one another and are therefore the more to be feared, as they have more power and are more cunning and astute than other animals. And since men are by nature especially subject to these emotions (as we said in Section 5 of the previous Chapter), men are therefore by nature enemies. For he is my greatest enemy whom I must most fear and against whom I must most guard myself.

---

[16] [The Latin phrase is *sui juris*, one of the most difficult seventeenth-century juridical phrases to translate adequately.]

[17] [*potestatem*.]

[18] [*fidem solvendam*, i.e., a breaking of faith or pledge. Spinoza does not use either *pactum* (contract) or *contractum* (treaty) here because these imply the presence of sanctions. Here he differs markedly from Hobbes, for whom the *civitas* arises by *pactum*.]

[15] Now (by Section 9 of this Chapter) every man in the state of Nature[19] is in control of his own right just as long as he can guard himself from being subjugated by another, and it is vain for one man alone to try to guard himself against all others. Hence it follows that as long as human natural right is determined by the power of each single individual and is possessed by each alone, it is of no account and is notional rather than factual, since there is no assurance that it can be made good. And there is no doubt that the more cause for fear a man has, the less power, and consequently the less right, he possesses. Furthermore, it is scarcely possible for men to support life and cultivate their minds without mutual assistance.[20] We therefore conclude that the natural right specific to human beings can scarcely be conceived except where men have their rights in common and can together successfully defend the territories which they can inhabit and cultivate, protect themselves, repel all force, and live in accordance with the judgment of the entire community. For (by Section 13 of this Chapter) the greater the number of men who thus unite in one body, the more right they will all collectively possess. And if it is on these grounds—that men in a state of Nature can scarcely be in control of their own right—that the Schoolmen want to call man a social animal, I have nothing to say against them.

[16] When men hold their rights in common and are all guided, as it were, by one mind,[21] it is certain (Section 13 of this Chapter) that each of them has that much less right the more he is exceeded in power by the others collectively. That is to say, he has in reality no right over Nature except that which is granted him by the communal right. For the rest, he is bound to carry out any command that is laid on him by communal consensus, or else (Section 4 of this Chapter) he may be rightly compelled to do so.

[17] This right, which is defined by the power of a people,[22] is usually called sovereignty,[23] and is possessed absolutely by whoever has charge of affairs of state, namely, he who makes, interprets, and repeals laws, fortifies cities, makes decisions regarding peace and war, and so forth. If this charge belongs to a council composed of the people in general, then the state is called a democracy; if the council is restricted to certain chosen members, the state is called an aristocracy; and if the management of affairs of state and consequently the sovereignty is in the hands of one man, then the state is called a monarchy.

---

[19] [*in statu naturali*. A more literal rendering would be "in the natural state," but this may suggest to the modern reader a reading of presocietal conditions more close to Rousseau or Locke. The translation "state of Nature" has been used consistently in what follows.]

[20] [So Spinoza conceives the natural state as one of almost total bondage, in contrast to Hobbes, who regards it as a state of human freedom.]

[21] [The Latin—*una veluti mente*—denotes a counterfactual condition, because civil society itself does not have a mind in the theoretical sense of this term deployed by Spinoza in the *Ethica*.]

[22] [*potentia multitudinis*. In what follows, *multitudo* is usually rendered as "people," the English term "multitude" having a somewhat pejorative connotation more akin to Spinoza's term *vulgus*. The phrase is common in seventeenth-century juridical writings.]

[23] [*imperium*.]

[18] From what we have shown in this Chapter, it becomes quite clear that in a state of nature there is no sin; or if a man sins, he sins against himself, not against another. For no one is bound by the law of Nature to pander to another's humour unless he so chooses, nor to regard as good or bad anything other than what he decides is good or bad from his own way of thinking. And the law of Nature forbids nothing at all except that which is not within anyone's power to do. (See Sections 5 and 8 of this Chapter.) But sin is action that cannot lawfully be done. Now if it were the case that men are bound by Nature's ordinance to be guided by reason, then they would all necessarily be guided by reason; for Nature's ordinances are the ordinances of God (Sections 2 and 3 of this Chapter), which God has established by that same freedom by which he exists. These ordinances therefore follow from the necessity of the divine nature (Section 7 of this Chapter) and are thus eternal and inviolable. But the fact is that men are mainly guided by appetite devoid of reason; yet even so they do not violate Nature's order but necessarily conform to it. Therefore the ignorant or weak-willed man is no more bound by the law of Nature to live his life wisely than the sick man is bound to be of sound body.

[19] Therefore sin cannot be conceived except in a state, that is, where what is good and bad is decided by the common law of the entire state and where (Section 16 of this Chapter) no one has the right to do anything other than what is in conformity with the common decree and consent. For (as we said in the previous Section) sin is that which cannot lawfully be done, i.e., is prohibited by law, while obedience is the constant will to do what by law is good and what the common decree requires to be done.

[20] However, the term 'sin' is also commonly used of that which is contrary to the dictates of sound reason, and the term 'obedience' of the constant will to control the appetites as prescribed by reason. Now if human freedom consisted in giving free rein to appetite, and human servitude to the rule of reason, I would entirely agree with this. But since human freedom is the greater as a man is more able to be guided by reason and control his appetites, it would be incorrect to call the life of reason 'obedience', and apply the term 'sin' to that which is in fact a weakness of the mind rather than an instance of the mind's freedom from its own control, something through which a man can be called a slave rather than free. See Sections 7 and 11 of this Chapter.

[21] However, reason teaches men to practise piety[24] and to be calm and kindly in their disposition, which is possible only in a state. Moreover, it is impossible for a people to be guided as if by one mind, as is required in a state, unless its laws are such as are prescribed by reason. Therefore it is not so improper for men who are accustomed to live in a state to apply the term 'sin' to that which is contrary to the dictates of reason. For the laws of a good state (Section 18 of this Chapter) ought to be established in accordance with the dictates of reason. As for my say-

---

[24] [The term *pietas* denotes reverence or respect for law, and does not have an exclusively religious meaning. In classical contexts (Cicero or Vergil) it is often translated as "patriotism," and in Spinoza it is often taken to be the highest form of civil duty.]

ing (Section 18 of this Chapter) that man in a state of Nature, if he sins at all, sins against himself, see Chapter 4, Sections 4 and 5, where it is shown in what sense it can be said that he who holds the sovereign power and is possessed of the right of Nature can be bound by laws and can sin.

[22] As far as religion is concerned, it is also quite certain that the more a man loves God and worships him with all his heart, the more he is free and the more completely obedient to his own self. Still, when we have regard not to Nature's order—of which we are ignorant—but only to the dictates of reason as they concern religion (at the same time realising that these are revealed to us by God as though speaking within us, or that they were also revealed to the prophets in the form of laws) then, speaking in human fashion, we say that he who loves God with all his heart is obedient to God, and he who is guided by blind desire is a sinner.[25] But we must always remember that we are in God's hands as clay in the hands of the potter,[26] who from the same lump makes some vessels unto honour and others unto dishonour.[27] So a man can indeed act contrary to these decrees of God insofar as they have been inscribed as laws upon our minds or the minds of the prophets, but he cannot act against the eternal decree of God, which is inscribed on universal Nature and which takes into account the order of Nature in its entirety.

[23] Therefore, just as sin and obedience, taken in the strict sense, can be conceived only in a state, the same is true of justice and injustice. For there is nothing in Nature that can rightly be said to belong to one man and not another; all things belong to all, that is, to all who have the power[28] to gain possession of them. But in a state, where what belongs to one man and not to another is decided by common laws, a man is called just who has the constant will to render to every man his own; and he is called unjust who endeavours to appropriate to himself what belongs to another.

[24] With regard to praise and blame, we have explained in our *Ethics* that these are feelings of pleasure and pain accompanied by the idea of human virtue or weakness as a cause.[29]

CHAPTER 3
[Sovereign Powers]

[1] The order maintained by any state is called civil; the body of the state in its entirety is called a commonwealth, and the public business of the state, under the

---

[25] [Perhaps a concession to Hobbes, who holds that men can sin against God even in the natural state (*De cive* I, 10).]

[26] [*in Dei potestate sicut lutum in potestate figuli.*]

[27] [Romans 9:21.]

[28] [*potestatem.*]

[29] [These are in fact *not* the definitions which Spinoza gives in the *Ethics:* See, by way of contrast, E3P29Schol.]

control of one who holds the sovereignty, is called affairs of state. We call men citizens insofar as they enjoy all the advantages of the commonwealth by civil right; we call them subjects[1] insofar as they are bound to obey the ordinances or laws of the commonwealth. Finally, as we said in Section 17 of the previous Chapter, there are three kinds of civil order, namely, democracy, aristocracy, and monarchy. But before I start to discuss each of these separately, I shall first point out those features that pertain in general to a civil order. Of these, the foremost to be considered is the supreme right of the commonwealth or of the sovereign.

[2] It is evident from Section 15 of the previous Chapter that the right of the state or of the sovereign is nothing more than the right of Nature itself and is determined by the power not of each individual but of a people which is guided as if by one mind.[2] That is to say, just as each individual in the natural state has as much right as the power he possesses, the same is true of the body and mind of the entire state. So the individual citizen or subject has that much less right as the commonwealth exceeds him in power (see Section 16 of the previous Chapter). Consequently the individual citizen does nothing and possesses nothing by right beyond what he can defend by common decree of the commonwealth.

[3] If a commonwealth grants to anyone the right, and consequently the power[3] (for otherwise, by Section 12 of the previous Chapter, such a grant is of no practical effect), to live just as he pleases, thereby the commonwealth surrenders its own right and transfers it to him to whom it gives such power.[4] If it gives this power[5] to two or more men, allowing each of them to live just as he pleases, thereby it has divided the sovereignty; and if, finally, it gives this power[6] to every one of the citizens, it has thereby destroyed itself, ceasing to be a commonwealth, and everything reverts to the natural state. All this is quite obvious from what has already been said. Thus it follows that it is quite inconceivable that each citizen be permitted by ordinance of the commonwealth to live just as he pleases, and consequently the natural right of every man to be his own judge necessarily ceases in a civil order. I say expressly, "by ordinance of the commonwealth," for every man's natural right (if we consider the matter correctly) does not cease in a civil order; for in a state of Nature and in a civil order alike man acts from the laws of his own nature and has regard for his own advantage. In both these conditions, I repeat, man is led by fear or hope to do or refrain from doing this or that. The main difference between the two conditions is this, that in the civil order all men fear the same things, and all have the same ground of security, the same way of life. But this does not deprive the individual of his faculty of judgment, for he who

---

[1] [order = *status*; civil = *civilis*; commonwealth = *civitas*; state = *respublica* citizens = *cives*; subjects = *subditi*.]
[2] [Again the counterfactual *veluti*.]
[3] [*potestatem*.]
[4] [*potestatem*.]
[5] [*potestatem*.]
[6] [*potestatem*.]

has resolved to obey all the commands of the commonwealth, whether through fear of its power or love of tranquillity, is surely providing for his own security and his own advantage in his own way.

[4] Furthermore, it is also inconceivable that every citizen should be permitted to put his own interpretation on the decrees or laws of the commonwealth. For if this were permitted to every citizen, he would thereby be his own judge, since it would be quite simple for him to excuse or to put a favourable gloss on his own doings with an appearance of legality. Consequently, he would adopt a way of living to suit only himself, and this (by the previous Section) is absurd.

[5] We see, then, that the individual citizen is not in control of his own right, but is subject to the right of the commonwealth, whose every command he is bound to carry out, and he does not have any right to decide what is fair or unfair, what is righteous or unrighteous. On the contrary, since the body of the state must be guided as if by a single mind[7] (and consequently the will of the commonwealth must be regarded as the will of all), what the commonwealth decides to be just and good must be held to be so decided by every citizen. Thus, although a subject may consider the decrees of the commonwealth to be unfair, he is nevertheless bound to carry them out.

[6] But, it may be objected, is it not contrary to the dictates of reason to subject oneself entirely to the judgment of another? And, consequently, is not the civil order contrary to reason? And from this it would follow that the civil order is irrational and could be instituted only by men destitute of reason, not by men who are guided by reason. However, since reason teaches nothing contrary to Nature, as long as men are subject to passions (Section 5, Chapter 1),[8] sound reason cannot require that each man should remain in control of his own right; that is to say (Section 15, previous Chapter) reason declares this to be an impossibility. Again, the teaching of reason is wholly directed to seeking peace, but peace cannot be achieved unless the common laws of the commonwealth are kept inviolate. So the more a man is guided by reason—that is (Section 11 of the previous Chapter), the more he is free—the more steadfast he will be in preserving the laws of the state and in carrying out the commands of the sovereign whose subject he is. Furthermore, a civil order is established in a natural way in order to remove general fear and alleviate general distress, and therefore its chief aim is identical with that pursued by everyone in the natural state who is guided by reason, but pursued in vain (Section 15, previous Chapter). Therefore, if a man who is guided by reason has sometimes to do, by order of the commonwealth, what he knows to be contrary to reason, this penalty is far outweighed by the good he derives from the civil order itself;[9] for it is also a law of reason that of two evils the lesser should

---

[7] [See Tacitus, *Annals* I, xii, 4: "*Unum esse rei publicae corpus atque unius animo regendum.*" Spinoza adds "*tanquam*" (as if) to the characterization of the state guided by one mind.]

[8] [As found in Gebhardt (1925, 286, line 19). "(Section 5, Chapter 1)" should change places with "(Section 11, previous Chapter)."—S.S.]

[9] [Hobbes, *De cive* X, 1.]

be chosen. Therefore, we may conclude that nobody acts in a way contrary to what his own reason prescribes insofar as he does that which the law of the commonwealth requires to be done. And this everyone will more readily grant us when we have explained how far the commonwealth's power, and consequently its right, extends.

[7] The first thing to be considered is this, that just as in a state of Nature (Section 11, previous Chapter) the man who is guided by reason is most powerful and most in control of his own right; similarly the commonwealth that is based on reason and directed by reason is most powerful and most in control of its own right. For the right of a commonwealth is determined by the power of a people that is guided as though by a single mind. But this union of minds could in no way be conceived unless the chief aim of the commonwealth is identical with that which sound reason teaches us is for the good of all men.

[8] Secondly, we must also take into consideration that subjects are not in control of their own right and are subject to the commonwealth's right only to the extent that they fear its power or its threats, or to the extent that they are firmly attached to the civil order (Section 10 of previous Chapter). Hence it follows that all such things as no one can be induced to do by reward or threats do not fall within the rights of the commonwealth. For example, no one can surrender his faculty of judgment; for what rewards or threats can induce a man to believe that the whole is not greater than its parts, or that God does not exist, or that the body, which he sees to be finite is an infinite being,[10] in short, to believe something that is contrary to what he perceives or thinks? Likewise, what rewards or threats can induce a man to love one whom he hates, or to hate one whom he loves? And in this category must also be included those things so abhorrent to human nature that it regards them as the worst of all evils, such as that a man should bear witness against himself, should torture himself, should kill his own parents, should not endeavour to avoid death, and the like, to which no one can be induced by rewards or threats.[11] If we still persist in saying that the commonwealth has the right or power to command such things, we can conceive this only in the sense in which it might be said that a man has the right to be mad or to rave. For what else but lunacy would such a right be when no one can be bound by it? Here I am speaking expressly of those things which cannot be part of the commonwealth's right and from which human nature for the most part recoils. For despite the fact that a fool or a madman cannot be induced by any rewards or threats to carry out orders, and that a few men, devoted to some religious cult, regard the laws of the state as the worst of all evils,[12] yet the laws of the commonwealth are

---

[10] [This is perhaps a reference to the Incarnation, which Spinoza rejects: See Ep73.]

[11] [See Hobbes, *De cive* II, 18–19 and VI, 13. Hobbes argues, however, that the sovereign may legitimately command such actions, while the citizen may legitimately refuse obedience to them. "*Mortem, vel vulnera, vel aliud damnum corporis inferenti, nemo pactis suis quiuscunque obligatus non resistere. . . . Similiter neque tenetur quisquam, pactis ullis, ad se accusandum*" (*De cive* II, 18).]

[12] [Perhaps Spinoza is thinking of the Mennonites, who were conscientious objectors.]

not rendered void, since most of the citizens are restrained by them. Therefore, since those who fear nothing and hope for nothing are to that extent in control of their own right (Section 10 of the previous Chapter), they are therefore enemies of the state (Section 14 of the previous Chapter), and the state has the right to coerce them.

[9] The third and final point to be considered is this, that matters which arouse general indignation are not likely to fall within the right of the commonwealth. It is without doubt a natural thing for men to conspire together either by reason of a common fear or through desire to avenge a common injury. And since the right of the commonwealth is defined by the corporate power of the people,[13] undoubtedly the power of the commonwealth and its right is to that extent diminished, as it affords reasons for many citizens to join in a conspiracy. There are certainly some things to fear for a commonwealth, and just as every citizen, or every man in a state of nature, as he has more reason to fear, is the less in control of his own right, the same is true of a commonwealth. So much, then, for the right of the sovereign over his subjects. But before dealing with his right as against others, I think I ought to resolve a question that is wont to arise regarding religion.

[10] The following objection can be raised: Does not the civil order and the obedience of subjects such as we have shown to be requisite for a civil order do away with the religion whereby we are required to worship God? Still, if we consider the facts, we shall find nothing here to give us pause; for insofar as the mind uses reason, it is not subject to the rights of the sovereign but is in control of its own rights (Section 11 of the previous Chapter). So the true knowledge and love of God cannot be subject to anyone's jurisdiction, as is also the case with charity towards one's neighbour (Section 8, this Chapter). And if we further reflect that the highest form that charity can take is to safeguard peace and to promote harmony, we shall have no doubt that he truly does his duty who gives to each man such assistance is as consistent with the laws of the commonwealth, that is, with harmony and peace. As for external rites, it is certain that they can do nothing at all to help or hinder the true knowledge of God and the love that necessarily follows therefrom. So they are not to be regarded as of such importance that the peace and tranquillity of the state should be prejudiced on their account. Moreover, it is certain that I am not the champion of religion by right of Nature, that is (Section 3, previous Chapter), by divine decree. For I have no power, as Christ's disciples once had, to cast out unclean spirits and to perform miracles. And this power is so necessary for the propagation of religion in places where it is proscribed that without it not only does one lose one's labour, as the saying goes, but in addition one stirs up a host of troubles. All ages have beheld the most grievous examples of this. Therefore everyone, wherever he may be, can worship God with true piety and mind his own affairs, as is the duty of a private individual. But the burden of propagating religion should be left to God or to the sovereign, on whom alone devolves the care of public affairs. However, I return to my subject.

---

[13] [See Hobbes, *De cive* VI, 18.]

[11] Now that the right of the sovereign over citizens and also the duty of subjects has been explained, it remains for us to consider the sovereign's right as against the world at large. This is easily understood from what has already been said. For since (Section 2 of this Chapter) the sovereign's right is nothing other than the right of Nature itself, it follows that two states are in the same relation to one another as are two men in a state of Nature, but with this exception, that a commonwealth can take precautions against being subjugated by another commonwealth. This a man in a state of nature cannot do, seeing that he is every day overcome by sleep, frequently by sickness or mental infirmity, and eventually by old age. And besides these he is exposed to other troubles against which a commonwealth can render itself secure.

[12] A commonwealth, then, is in control of its own right to the extent that it can take steps to safeguard itself from being subjugated by another commonwealth (Sections 9 and 15 of previous Chapter); and (Sections 10 and 15 of previous Chapter) it is subject to another's right to the extent that it fears the power of another commonwealth, or is prevented by it from carrying out its own wishes, or, finally, it needs the other's help for its own preservation or prosperity. For there can be no doubt that if two commonwealths choose to afford each other mutual help, then both together are more powerful, and consequently have more right conjointly, than either by itself. See Section 13 of the previous Chapter.

[13] This can be more clearly understood if we bear in mind that two commonwealths are by nature enemies (Section 14 of previous Chapter), and so those who are outside a commonwealth and retain the right of Nature continue as enemies. Therefore if one commonwealth chooses to make war on another and to go to all lengths to render the other subject to its right, it may by right attempt to do so, since to wage war it is enough to have the will to do so. But it cannot come to any decision about peace without the willing cooperation of the other commonwealth. Hence it follows that the right to make war belongs to each separate commonwealth, whereas the right to peace belongs not to a single commonwealth but to at least two, which are therefore called "allies."[14]

[14] This treaty[15] of alliance remains effective[16] for as long as the motive for making the treaty—fear of loss or hope of gain—remains operative. But if the fear or the hope is lost to either of the two commonwealths, that commonwealth is left in control of its own right (Section 10, previous Chapter), and the tie by which the two commonwealths were bound together automatically disintegrates. Therefore every commonwealth has full right to break a treaty whenever it wishes, and it cannot be said to act treacherously or perfidiously in breaking faith as soon as the reason for fear or hope is removed.[17] For each of the con-

---

[14] [confoederatae.]
[15] [foedus.]
[16] [causa.]
[17] [Compare to Machiavelli, Prince, XVIII.]

tracting parties was on level terms in this respect, that whichever could first rid itself of fear would be in control of its own right, which it could use just is it pleased. Besides, no one makes a contract respecting the future except in the light of the circumstances of the time; when these change, the entire situation must be reconsidered. For this reason, each of the allied commonwealths retains the right to consult its own interests, and each therefore endeavours as far as it can to rid itself of fear and consequently to be in control of its own right and to prevent the other from becoming more powerful. If, then, a commonwealth complains that it has been deceived, it certainly cannot blame the bad faith of its ally but only its own folly in entrusting its security to another who is in control of his own right and for whom the safety of his own state is the supreme law.

[15] So to the commonwealths which have made a treaty of peace with each other there belongs the right to settle disputes that may arise concerning the terms or rules of the peace by which they have mutually bound themselves, because the terms of peace are a matter not just for the one commonwealth but for the contracting parties jointly (Section 13 this Chapter). If agreement cannot be reached, by that very fact they revert to a state of war.

[16] The greater the number of commonwealths that make a peace treaty with one another, the less is each to be feared by the others; that is, the less power does each of them have to make war. On the contrary, each is the more bound to observe the conditions of peace; that is (Section 13 of this Chapter), it is so much the less in control of its own right and must the more adapt itself to the common will of the allies.

[17] However, what we here say does not imply the annulment of that good faith which sound reason and religion bids us keep, for neither reason nor Scripture bids us keep every pledge we make. For example, if I have promised someone to keep safe some money which he has given me in secret to look after, I am not bound to keep my word from the time that I know, or believe I know, that the money given me to keep safe is stolen. I shall act more rightly if I see to it that the money is restored to its owners. So, too, if one sovereign has promised another to do something that time or reason have later shown, or appeared to show, to be prejudicial to the general welfare of his subjects, he is surely bound to break his word. Since Scripture, then, teaches us to keep faith only in the form of a general rule, leaving to each man to decide which special cases are to be excepted, it teaches nothing contrary to what we have just shown.

[18] But to avoid having to interrupt the thread of my argument repeatedly and to deal with similar objections hereafter, I should like to point out that all those things I have demonstrated follow from the most essential feature of human nature in whatever way it may be considered, namely, from the universal striving of all men to preserve themselves. This striving is inherent in all men, whether ignorant or wise; and therefore, in whatever way we consider men to be guided, whether by passion or by reason, the result is the same because the demonstration, as we have said, applies in all cases.

Chapter 4
[Rights of Sovereign Powers]

[1] The right of sovereigns, which is determined by their power, has been set forth in the previous Chapter, and we have seen that it consists primarily in this, that sovereigns are,[1] as it were, the mind of the state whereby all citizens must be guided. So they alone have the right to decide what is good, what is bad, what is fair, what is unfair—that is to say, what must be done and what must not be done by individual citizens or by all collectively. We see, therefore, that to the sovereign alone belongs the right to make laws, to interpret them in particular cases when there is any doubt, and to decide whether a given action is against or in conformity with the law (see Sections 3, 4, 5 of the previous Chapter). Again, the sovereign alone has the right to make war, to decide upon and to offer terms of peace, or to accept them when offered.[2] See Sections 12 and 13 of the previous Chapter.

[2] Since all these functions, and all the means required to execute them, are matters[3] that concern the state in its entirety, that is, are affairs of state, it follows that affairs of state depend on the guidance of him alone who holds the sovereignty.[4] It follows that it is within the sovereign's right alone to judge the actions of any man, to demand of anyone an account of his actions, to punish wrongdoers, to decide legal disputes between citizens, or to appoint experienced lawyers[5] to act in his place. Furthermore, it is his right alone to employ and to organise all the means to war and peace, namely, to found and fortify cities, to levy militia, to assign military duties, to issue commands as to what he wants done, to send out and to give audience to envoys for peaceful purposes, and, finally, to tax the people so as to meet all these expenses.

[3] Since the sovereign alone has the right to deal with public affairs or to appoint ministers for that purpose, it follows that a subject is committing treason if he engages in any public business on his own initiative without the knowledge of the supreme council, even though he believes that what he intended was in the best interests of the commonwealth.

[4] The question is often raised as to whether the sovereign is bound by the laws, and consequently whether he can do wrong. But since the words 'law' and 'wrongdoing' are quite often used with reference not only to the laws of a com-

---

[1] [I read *sint* for *sit* as found in Gebhardt (1925, 291, line 31).—S.S.]
[2] [See Hobbes, *De cive* VI, 18.]
[3] [I omit *omnia* found in Gebhardt (1925, 292, line 9).—S.S.]
[4] [*imperium*.]
[5] [*legum latarum peritos*, i.e., those experienced in the administration of the law(s). Spinoza's customary term for "lawyer" is *juris peritus*. Here it appears to be a matter of those to be appointed lawyers, rather than of appointing lawyers for some other task.]

monwealth but also to the universal rules governing natural things in general and reason in particular, we cannot without qualification assert that a commonwealth is not bound by laws, or that it cannot do wrong. For if a commonwealth were not bound by the laws or rules without which the commonwealth would not be a commonwealth, then it would have to be regarded not as a natural thing but as a chimera. So a commonwealth does wrong when it does, or suffers to be done, things that can cause its own downfall; and we then say that it does wrong in the sense in which philosophers or doctors say that Nature does wrong, and it is in this sense we can say that a commonwealth does wrong when it does something contrary to the dictates of reason. For it is when a commonwealth acts from the dictates of reason that it is most fully in control of its own right (Section 7 of the previous Chapter). Insofar, then, as it acts contrary to reason, it falls short of its own self, or does wrong. This can be more clearly understood if we reflect that when we say that every man has the power to do whatever he likes with an object over which he has right, this power has to be limited not only by the potency of the agent but also by the suitability of that which is the object of the action. If, for example, I say that I have the right to do whatever I like with this table, I am hardly likely to mean that I have the right to make this table eat grass. Similarly, although we say that men are not in control of their own right but are subject to the right of the commonwealth, we do not mean that men lose their human nature and assume another nature, with the result that the commonwealth has the right to make men fly, or—and this is just as impossible—to make men regard as honourable things that move them to ridicule or disgust. No, what we mean is this, that there are certain conditions that, if operative, entail that subjects will respect and fear their commonwealth, while the absence of these conditions entails the annulment of that fear and respect and together with this, the destruction of the commonwealth. Thus, in order that a commonwealth should be in control of its own right, it must preserve the causes that foster fear and respect; otherwise it ceases to be a commonwealth. For if the rulers or ruler of the state runs drunk or naked with harlots through the streets, acts on the stage,[6] openly violates or holds in contempt those laws that he himself has enacted, it is no more possible for him to preserve the dignity of sovereignty than for something to be and not be at the same time. Then again, to slaughter subjects, to despoil them, to ravish maidens and the like turns fear into indignation, and consequently the civil order into a condition of war.

[5] We see, then, in what sense it can be said that a commonwealth is bound by laws and can do wrong. But if by law we understand the civil law, which can be enforced by the civil law itself, and by wrongdoing that which is forbidden by civil law—that is to say, if these words are taken in their proper sense—then in no way can we say that a commonwealth is bound by laws and can do wrong. For the rules that govern and give rise to fear and respect, which the commonwealth is bound to preserve in its own interests, have regard not to civil law but to natural

---

[6] [Tacitus (*Annals* XVI, iv) accuses Nero of this practice.]

right, since (by the previous Section) they are enforceable not by civil law but by right of war. And a commonwealth is bound by them in just the same way as a man in a state of Nature who, so as to be in control of his own right or to avoid being his own enemy, is bound to take heed not to kill himself. And this taking heed is not a form of obedience; it is the exercising of human freedom. But civil laws depend solely on the commonwealth's decree, and the commonwealth, to maintain its freedom, does not have to please anyone but itself and to deem nothing as good or bad other than that which it itself decides is good or bad for itself. Therefore it has the right not only to be its own champion, to enact laws and interpret them, but also to repeal them and to pardon any offender from the fullness of its power.

[6] The contract[7] or laws whereby a people transfers its right to one council or one man should undoubtedly be broken when this is in the interests of the general welfare. But the right to judge whether or not it is in the interests of the general welfare to do so cannot rest with any private person but only with the ruler of the state (Section 3, this Chapter). So by civil right the ruler of the state remains the sole interpreter of these laws. Furthermore, no private person has the right to enforce these laws, and so in actual fact they are not binding on the ruler of the state. But if the laws are such that they cannot be broken without at the same time weakening the commonwealth—that is, without at the same time turning into indignation the common fear felt by the majority of the citizens—then by their violation the commonwealth is dissolved and the contract comes to an end. Thus the contract depends for its enforcement not on civil right but on right of war. So the ruler is bound to observe the terms of the contract for exactly the same reason as a man in the state of nature, in order not to be his own enemy, is bound to take care not to kill himself, as we said in the previous Section.

Chapter 5
[The Highest Aim of Society]

[1] In Section 11 of Chapter 2 we showed that a man is most completely in control of his own right when he is most guided by reason, and consequently (see Section 7, Chapter 3) that a commonwealth is most powerful and most completely in control of its own right if it is founded on and guided by reason. Now since the best method of ensuring that one preserves oneself as far as possible is to live in the way that reason prescribes, it follows that those actions are the best which are done by a man or commonwealth when it is most completely in control of its own right. We are not asserting that everything that is done by right is also done in the best way; it is one thing to till a field by right, another thing to till it in the best way. It is one thing, I say, to defend oneself, to preserve oneself, to give judgment,

---

[7] [See Gebhardt (1925, 294, line 13); I read *contractus* for *contractûs*. —S.S.]

etc., by right, another thing to defend and preserve oneself in the best way and to give the best judgment. Consequently, it is one thing to rule and to take charge of public affairs by right, another thing to rule in the best way and to direct public affairs in the best way. So now that we have discussed the right of every commonwealth in general terms, it is time for us to discuss the best way in which a state should be organised.

[2] The best way to organise a state is easily discovered by considering the purpose of civil order, which is nothing other than peace and security of life. Therefore the best state is one where men live together in harmony and where the laws are preserved unbroken. For it is certain that rebellions, wars, and contempt for or violation of the laws are to be attributed not so much to the wickedness of subjects as to the faulty organisation of the state.[1] Men are not born to be citizens, but are made so.[2] Furthermore, men's natural passions are everywhere the same; so if wickedness is more prevalent and wrongdoing more frequent in one commonwealth than in another, one can be sure that this is because the former has not done enough to promote harmony and has not framed its laws with sufficient forethought, and thus it has not attained the full right of a commonwealth. For a civil order that has not removed the causes of rebellion and where the threat of war is never absent and the laws are frequently broken is little different from a state of Nature, where every man lives as he pleases with his life at risk.

[3] But just as the vices of subjects and their excessive license and wilfulness are to be laid at the door of the commonwealth, so on the other hand their virtue and steadfast obedience to the laws must be attributed chiefly to the virtue and the absolute right of the commonwealth, as is evident from Section 15 of Chapter 2. Hence it is deservedly regarded as a remarkable virtue in Hannibal that there was never a mutiny in his army.[3]

[4] A commonwealth whose subjects are deterred from taking up arms only through fear should be said to be not at war rather than to be enjoying peace. For peace is not just the absence of war, but a virtue which comes from strength of mind; for obedience (Section 19, Chapter 2) is the steadfast will to carry out orders enjoined by the general decree of the commonwealth. Anyway, a commonwealth whose peace depends on the sluggish spirit of its subjects who are led like sheep to learn simply to be slaves can more properly be called a desert than a commonwealth.[4]

[5] So when we say that the best state is one where men pass their lives in harmony, I am speaking of human life, which is characterised not just by the circulation of the blood and other features common to all animals, but especially by reason, the true virtue and life of the mind.

[6] But be it noted that in speaking of the state as being established to this end, I meant one established by a free people, not dominion over a people acquired by

---

[1] [Machiavelli, *Discourses* III, 29.]
[2] [Hobbes, *De cive* I, 2, n. 1.]
[3] [Machiavelli, *Prince* XVII; *Discourses* III, 21.]
[4] [Tacitus, *Agricola* 30: "... *ubi solitudinem faciunt, pacem appellant.*"]

right of war. For a free people is led more by hope than by fear, while a subjugated people is led more by fear than by hope; the former seeks to engage in living, the latter simply to avoid death. The former, I say, seeks to live for itself, the latter is forced to belong to a conqueror; hence we say that the latter is a slave, the former is free. So the aim of a state that has been acquired by right of war is to dominate and to have slaves rather than subjects. And although, if we have regard to their right in a general way, there is no essential difference between a state created by a free people and one acquired by right of war, their aims, as we have just shown, are very different, and so too are the means by which each must be preserved.

[7] In the case of a prince whose sole motive is lust for power,[5] the means he must employ to strengthen and preserve his state have been described at some length by that keen observer, Machiavelli, but with what purpose appears uncertain. If he did have some good purpose in mind, as one should believe of so wise a man, it must have been to show how foolish are the attempts so often made to get rid of a tyrant while yet the causes that have made the prince a tyrant cannot be removed; on the contrary, they become more firmly established as the prince is given more grounds for fear.[6] This comes about when a people has made an example of its prince and glories in regicide as in a wonderful exploit.[7] Perhaps he also wished to show how wary a free people should be of entrusting its welfare absolutely to one man who, unless in his vanity he thinks he can enjoy universal popularity, must go in daily fear of plots. Thus he is compelled to look more to his own defence and in his turn to plot against the people rather than to look to their interests. I am the more inclined to take this view of that wise statesman because he is well known to be an advocate of freedom, and he has given some very sound advice as to how it should be safeguarded.[8]

Chapter 6
[Monarchy: Its Nature]

[1] Since men, as we have said, are led more by passion than by reason, it naturally follows that a people will unite and consent to be guided as if by one mind not at reason's prompting but through some common emotion, such as (as we said in Section 9, Chapter 3) a common hope, or common fear, or desire to avenge some common injury. Now since fear of isolation is innate in all men inasmuch as in isolation no one has the strength to defend himself and acquire the necessi-

---

[5] [*dominandi libidine*. The connotation is sexual (see the General Definitions of the Affects following E3Def48).]

[6] [Machiavelli, *Discourses* I, 55.]

[7] [No doubt a reference to the execution of England's Charles I in 1649. For Spinoza's more extended view on the subject, see TTP18/556.]

[8] [This last sentence is not included in the *Nagelate Schriften*.]

ties of life, it follows that men by nature strive for a civil order,[1] and it is impossible that men should ever utterly dissolve this order.

[2] Thus the quarrels and rebellions that are often stirred up in a commonwealth never lead to the dissolution of the commonwealth by its citizens (as is often the case with other associations) but to a change in its form—that is, if their disputes cannot be settled while still preserving the structure of the commonwealth. Therefore, by the means required to preserve a state I understand those that are necessary to preserve the form of the state without any notable change.

[3] Now if human nature were so constituted that men desired most of all what was most to their advantage, no special skill would be needed to secure harmony and trust. But since, admittedly, human nature is far otherwise constituted, the state must necessarily be so established that all men, both rulers and ruled, whether they will or no, will do what is in the interests of their common welfare; that is, either voluntarily or constrained by force or necessity, they will all live as reason prescribes. This comes about if the administration of the state is so ordered that nothing is entrusted absolutely to the good faith of any man. For no man is so vigilant that he does not sometimes nod, and no one has ever been so resolute and upright as not sometimes to break down and suffer himself to be overcome just when strength of mind is most needed. And it is surely folly to make demands on another that no one can himself satisfy, namely, that he should be more concerned for the interests of another than for his own, that he should avoid greed, envy, ambition, and so on, especially if he is one who is daily exposed to the strongest urges of every passion.

[4] Yet on the other hand experience seems to teach us that peace and harmony are best served if all power[2] is conferred on one man. For no state has stood so long without any notable change as that of the Turks, and, conversely, none have proved so short-lived as popular or democratic states, nor have any been so liable to frequent rebellion. But if slavery, barbarism, and desolation are to be called peace, there can be nothing more wretched for mankind than peace. Doubtless more frequent and more bitter quarrels are wont to arise between parents and children than between masters and slaves. Yet it is not to the advantage of household management to change paternal right into the right of ownership and to treat children as if they were slaves. It is slavery, then, not peace that is promoted by transferring all power[3] to one man; for peace, as we have already said, consists not in the absence of war but in the union or harmony of minds.

[5] And in fact, those who believe that one man by himself can hold the supreme right of the commonwealth are greatly mistaken. For right is determined by power alone, but the power of one man is far from being capable of sustaining so heavy a load. As a result, the man whom the people has chosen as king looks about him for generals or counsellors or friends to whom he entrusts his own se-

---

[1] [Hobbes, *De cive* I, 2, n. 1.]
[2] [*potestas.*]
[3] [*potestatem.*]

curity and the security of all citizens, so that the state, which is thought to be purely a monarchy, is in actual practice an aristocracy—not indeed overtly so, but a concealed one—and therefore of the worst kind. Furthermore, if the king is a boy, or a sick man, or burdened by old age, he is a king only on sufferance, and the sovereignty is really in the hands of those who administer the most important affairs of state, or of those who are nearest the king; not to mention that a king who is a slave to lust has all his governmental decisions controlled by the caprice of one or another concubine or sodomite.[4] "I had heard," says Orsines, "that women once used to rule in Asia: But for a eunuch to rule is really something new" (Curtius, Book X, Chapter 1).

[6] It is also beyond doubt that a commonwealth is always in greater danger from its citizens than from its enemies; for good men are but few. It therefore follows that he on whom the whole right of the state has been conferred will always be more afraid of citizens than of external enemies and will therefore endeavour to look to his own safety, not consulting the interests of his subjects but plotting against them, especially those who are renowned for their wisdom or whose wealth gives them too much power.

[7] There is this to be added, that kings fear their sons, too, more than they love them, and the more so as their sons are more skilled in the arts of peace and war and are more popular with the subjects because of their virtues. As a result, kings seek to bring up their sons in a way that removes cause for alarm. In this matter, his ministers are very zealous in obeying the king, and will make every effort to have as their next king one who is inexperienced and whom they can skilfully manipulate.

[8] From all this it follows that the more absolute the transfer of the commonwealth's right to a king, the less he is in control of his own right and the more wretched the condition of his subjects. Thus to establish a monarchy in proper order, it is necessary to lay firm foundations on which to build, from which would result security for the monarch and peace for his people, thus ensuring that the king is most fully in control of his own right when he is most concerned for the welfare of his people. I shall first briefly set forth what are these foundations for a monarchy, and then demonstrate them in an orderly way.

[9] One or more cities must be founded and fortified, all of whose citizens, whether dwelling within the walls or beyond them so as to farm the land, are to enjoy the same right of citizenship but on this condition: That each city must provide a fixed number of citizens for its own and the common defence. A city that cannot fulfil this requirement must be held in subjection on other terms.

[10] The military force must be recruited from citizens alone, with no exemptions and from no other sources.[5] So all men are required to possess arms, and no one is to be admitted to the roll of citizens until he has done his military training and has undertaken to practise these skills at appointed times of the year.

---

[4] [Possibly a reference to James I of England.]
[5] [See Machiavelli, *Prince* XII–XIII, and *Discourses* II, 20.]

Next, the military force from each clan[6] is to be divided into companies and regiments, and no one is to be chosen to command a company unless he is versed in military engineering.[7] Further, while the commanders of companies and regiments are to be appointed for life, the commander of the military force of one entire clan is to be appointed only in wartime, and hold his command for a year at most, and be debarred from extension of his command or from reelection. The latter commanders are to be appointed from the king's counsellors (of whom we are to speak in Section 15 and following), or from ex-counsellors.

[11] The townsmen and countrymen of all the cities,[8] that is, all the citizens, are to be divided into clans distinguished by some name and badge; and all who are born of any of these clans are to be received into the number of citizens and their names entered on the roll of their clans as soon as they reach an age when they can bear arms and know their duty. But an exception is to be made of those who are convicted criminals, or dumb, or mad, or menials gaining a livelihood by some servile occupation.

[12] The fields and the soil and, if possible, the houses as well should be public property,[9] that is, should belong to the sovereign, by whom they should be let at an annual rent to citizens, whether townsmen or country-dwellers. Apart from this, all citizens should be free or exempt from any form of taxation in time of peace. Of this rent, part should be allocated to the defence works of the commonwealth, part to the king's domestic needs. For in time of peace, it is still necessary to fortify cities as for war and to have in a state of readiness ships and other armaments.

[13] After a king has been chosen from one of the clans, none but his descendants are to be regarded as of noble rank, and they must therefore be distinguished by royal insignia from their own clan and the other clans.

[14] The male nobles related by blood to the reigning king and standing in the third or fourth degree of consanguinity to him should be forbidden to marry. Any children they may have should be accounted as illegitimate and unworthy of any office. They should not be acknowledged as heirs to their parents, whose estates should revert to the king.

[15] The number of king's counsellors who are nearest to him or second in rank should be considerable, and they should be chosen only from citizens: Three or four from each clan, or five if the clans number no more than six hundred. Together they will constitute one section of this council. They are elected not for life but for three, four, or five years, so that every year a third, fourth, or fifth part of their number must be appointed afresh. In making these appointments, how-

---

[6] [*familia.*]

[7] [In the seventeenth century, war was largely concerned with besieging or protecting fortresses or cities.]

[8] [In much of what follows in this chapter Spinoza follows Machiavelli closely, but modifies his principles to the Dutch situation. The importance that he accords to the cities is due in part to the fact that Holland was, in fact, a nation of cities, each a hub of commerce and industry.]

[9] [*publici juris.*]

ever, it is most important that from each clan at least one counsellor should be chosen who is a lawyer.[10]

[16] This selection of counsellors must be made by the king himself. At the time of the year appointed for the election of new counsellors, every clan must submit to the king the names of all its citizens who have attained their fiftieth year and have been duly proposed for this office. Of these, the king will choose whom he will.[11] But in the year when the lawyer of a clan is to be replaced by another, only the names of lawyers should be submitted to the king. Those who have served in this office of counsellor for the appointed time are not to continue in office nor to be entered on the list of candidates within a period of at least five years. The reason why it is necessary for one counsellor to be appointed from each clan every year is this: To avoid a situation where the council is composed alternately of inexperienced newcomers and experienced veterans, which is bound to happen if all the counsellors were to retire and be replaced together. But if one is appointed every year from each clan, then only a fifth, a fourth, or at the most a third of the council will consist of newcomers. Furthermore, if the king, through pressure of other business or for any other reason, is prevented for some time from attending to these appointments, then the counsellors themselves should make temporary appointments until the king appoints others or approves the council's choice.

[17] The primary duty of this council must be to uphold the fundamental laws of the state and to give advice on the conduct of affairs so that the king may know what measures to take for the public good, the king not being permitted to take any decision without first hearing the opinion of this council. But if, as will generally be the case, the council is not of one mind but continues to be divided even after discussing the same matter two or three times, there must be no further delay; the different opinions must be submitted to the king, as I shall explain in Section 25 of this Chapter.

[18] It should also be the duty of the council to publish the king's ordinances or decrees, to see that his decisions on matters of state are carried out, and to supervise the entire administration of the state as the king's deputies.

[19] Citizens should not be able to approach the king except through this council, to which all requests or written petitions should be given for presentation to the king. Likewise, ambassadors of other commonwealths may be granted permission to address the king only through this council. Letters, too, sent to the king from other kings must reach him through this council. To sum up, the king is to be regarded as the mind of the commonwealth, and this council as the mind's external senses or[12] body of the commonwealth, through which the mind[13] perceives the condition of the commonwealth and does what it decides is best for itself.

---

[10] [In addition to deputies, each of Holland's eighteen towns also sent a lawyer, the Pensionary, to the Provincial Estates.]

[11] [The stadtholders had the right to appoint the magistrates of a town from a list of candidates presented by the town.]

[12] [I read *seu* for *ceu* as found in Gebhardt (1925, 302, line 14).—S.S.]

[13] [I omit *per quod mens* as found in Gebhardt (1925, 302, line 15).—S.S.]

[20] Responsibility for bringing up the king's sons should also rest with this council, and likewise their guardianship if the king has died, leaving the succession to a child or young boy.[14] But in the meantime, to avoid leaving the council without a king, an elder from among the nobles of the commonwealth should be appointed to fill the king's place until the rightful heir reaches an age when he can sustain the burden of government.

[21] Candidates for election to this council must be such as are well acquainted with the nature of the government, the fundamental laws, and the state or condition of the commonwealth of which they are subjects. But he who seeks to fill the position of lawyer must know, in addition to the government and condition of his own commonwealth, that of other commonwealths with which it has any dealings. But only those who have reached their fiftieth year without any criminal conviction are to be entered on the list of candidates.

[22] In this council no decision is to be taken regarding affairs of state unless all members are present. If anyone is unable to attend through illness or for any other reason, he must send in his place someone from the same clan who is an ex-counsellor or who is entered on the list of candidates. If he fails to do this, and the council is forced to defer consideration of some business because of his absence, he should be fined a considerable sum. But the above should apply only when the issue to be debated affects the state as a whole, such as a question of war and peace, of repealing or enacting some law, of trade, etc. If the matter under discussion concerns just one or two cities, written petitions, etc., it will suffice if the greater part of the council is present.

[23] To preserve equality between the clans in all things and to establish a regular order in sitting, making proposals, and speaking, each clan is to have its turn for presiding at the sessions, that which is first at this session being last at the next. But among members of the same clan, precedence should go to the one who was first elected.

[24] This council should be summoned at least four times a year[15] to demand from ministers an account of their administration, to ascertain the state of affairs, and to consider whether further measures are called for. For it seems impossible that so great a number of citizens should be continuously available for public business. But since public business must nevertheless be carried on in the meantime, fifty or more members of the council should be appointed to stand in for the council when it is adjourned,[16] meeting every day in a chamber next to the king's apartment so as to exercise daily supervision over the treasury, the defences of the cities, the education of the king's son, and, to sum up, all the duties of the great council that we have just enumerated except that they should have no power to deal with fresh matters with regard to which no decision has been taken.[17]

---

[14] [So the education of the future William III was entrusted to loyal republicans by Jan de Witt.]

[15] [The Estates of Holland met with this frequency.]

[16] [In Holland the daily administration was the charge of the *Gecommitteerde Raden*, a representative of the Estates of the Province when they were not in session.]

[17] [These were also the functions of the *Gecommitteerde Raden*.]

[25] When the council meets, before any matter is brought forward, five or six or more lawyers from the clans that take precedence in that session should have audience with the king to present any written petitions or letters they may have received, inform him of the condition of affairs, and gather from him what business he requires them to bring forward in this council. When they have learnt this, they should return to the council, and the first in precedence should open the matter to be debated. If the matter is thought by some members to be important, voting must not proceed at once but must be deferred for such time as the urgency of the matter allows. The council therefore being adjourned to a fixed date, the counsellors from each clan will meanwhile be able to discuss the matter separately and, if they think it of sufficient importance, to consult ex-counsellors or candidates for the same council. If within the appointed time they can reach no agreement among themselves, that clan shall be deprived of its vote, for each clan can have but one vote.[18] Otherwise the lawyer of the clan, having received his instructions, should present before council the opinion they have judged best. The others should do likewise, and if, after hearing the grounds for each opinion, the majority of the council decide to consider the matter further, the council should again be adjourned to a date when each clan shall deliver its final opinion. Only then, before a full council, should voting proceed. Any opinion that is not supported by at least a hundred votes should be disregarded; the others should be submitted to the king by all the lawyers present at the council so that, after hearing each party's arguments, he may choose which he pleases. Then the lawyers should leave him and return to the council, where all should wait on the king at a time he has appointed to hear which opinion of those presented he considers should be adopted and what he decides should be done.

[26] For the administration of justice there must be another council composed only of lawyers whose duty should be to decide lawsuits and to punish offenders. But all the judgments they deliver must be confirmed by those acting in place of the Great Council, which will consider whether judgment has been pronounced in accord with proper judicial procedure and without partiality. But if the losing party can prove that one of the judges has been bribed by his adversary, or that he has some other general reason for friendship towards his adversary or hatred towards himself, or that the normal judicial procedure has not been observed, the judgment should be set aside. It may be that the above procedures could not be followed by those whose custom it is to use torture rather than arguments to convict the accused in criminal cases. However, I am not here concerned with any judicial procedure other than that which befits the good government of a commonwealth.[19]

[27] These judges, too, should be very many, and their number should be odd: E.g., sixty-one or fifty-one at least. No more than one judge should be appointed from each clan, and not for life. Here again some portion of them should retire

---

[18] [In the Estates of Holland each town had several deputies but only a single vote.]

[19] [These last two sentences are not included in the *Nagelate Schriften*.]

every year and an equal number of others be appointed. These should be from other clans and should be aged over forty.

[28] In this council no judgment is to be pronounced unless all the judges are present. If any judge is unable to attend the council for some considerable time, through illness or for any other reason, another judge should be appointed temporarily to take his place. In voting, each judge must give his verdict not openly but by secret ballot.[20]

[29] The remuneration of this council and of the deputies of the above-mentioned council should be as follows—first, the goods of those they have condemned to death and also of those who are fined; secondly, for every judgment delivered in civil suits, they should receive from the unsuccessful litigant a proportion of the total sum involved, and this should be for the benefit of both councils.

[30] Other councils subordinate to these should be appointed in every city. Here again their members should not be appointed for life, but every year a portion should be appointed only from those clans who dwell in that city. But there is no need to go further into these details.

[31] No payment for military service is to be made in time of peace. In time of war a daily payment should be made only to those who gain their livelihood by daily labour. But commanders and other company officers should expect no gain from war other than the spoil of the enemy.

[32] If an alien marries the daughter of a citizen, his children are to be regarded as citizens and enrolled in the mother's clan. Those of alien parentage who are born and brought up in the state should be allowed to acquire citizenship at a fixed price from the officers of some clan and to be enrolled in that clan. And even if the officers of the clan are bribed to admit some alien at less than the fixed price, the state cannot take any harm therefrom. On the contrary, means should be devised for facilitating an increase in the number of citizens and securing a great influx of population.[21] As for those who are not enrolled as citizens, it is reasonable that at least in wartime they should make up for their exemption from service by labour or some kind of tax.

[33] Ambassadors who have to be sent in time of peace to other commonwealths to make peace or to preserve it are to be appointed only from the nobles, and their expenses provided from the state treasury, not from the king's privy purse.[22]

[34] Those who attend at court and are the king's servants, being paid by the king from his own privy purse, are to be excluded from every administrative post

---

[20] [Secret balloting was the general procedural rule in Holland.]

[21] [Machiavelli, *Discourses* I, 6.]

[22] [The Dutch version of Spinoza's text, *De Nagelate Schriften*, adds here: "*Maar men noet zodanige bespieders verkiezen, die aan de Koning bequaam zullen schijnen.*" The Latin translation *not* appearing in the *Opera Posthuma*, "*Sed tales speculatores eligendi sunt qui regi periti videbuntur*," is rendered by Wernham (1958, 331) as "But secret agents must be chosen from such as seem suitable to the king."]

or office in the commonwealth. I say expressly, "being paid by the king from his own privy purse" so as to exclude the king's bodyguard. For there must be no other bodyguards but citizens of that same city, taking turns at keeping guard at court on the king's behalf before his doors.

[35] War is to be made only for the sake of peace, so that with the end of hostilities arms may be laid aside. Therefore when cities have been captured by right of war and the enemy defeated, the terms of peace must be such as not to entail the garrisoning of the captured cities. Either the enemy, on accepting the peace treaty, must be granted the opportunity of redeeming them at a price,[23] or else — if by reason of their menacing position this would result in an enduring threat from the rear — they must be utterly destroyed and their inhabitants resettled elsewhere.[24]

[36] The king should not be allowed to contract a foreign marriage; he should marry only a kinswoman or a fellow citizen.[25] But in the event of marriage to a citizen there must be this restriction, that her nearest kinsmen be debarred from holding any state office.

[37] The state must be indivisible. Therefore if the king has more than one child, the eldest should have the right of succession. By no means must it be permitted that the state be divided between them or be handed on undivided to all or to some of them, and still less is it permissible to give part of the state as a daughter's dowry. For it should in no way be permitted that daughters should inherit the throne.

[38] If the king dies without male issue, the nearest to him by blood must be regarded as heir to the throne, unless he should have married a foreign woman whom he refuses to divorce.

[39] As for the citizens, it is evident from Section 5 of Chapter 3 that each of them is bound to obey all the commands or edicts of the king published by the great council (for this condition see Sections 18 and 19 of this Chapter) even though he regards them as quite irrational; otherwise he may rightfully be compelled to do so. Such, then, are the foundations on which a monarchy should be built if it is to be stable, as we shall demonstrate in the next Chapter.

[40] As for religion, no churches whatsoever are to be built at the expense of the cities, nor should any laws be enacted concerning beliefs unless these are seditious and subversive of the commonwealth's foundations. So those who are granted permission to practise their religion publicly should build a church, if they wish, at their own expense. But the king may have a chapel of his own in the palace to practise the religion to which he adheres.

---

[23] [*potestas concedatur easdem pretio redimendi.*]

[24] [Again Spinoza follows Machiavelli closely. See *Prince* III; *Discourses* II, 23.]

[25] [Note also that though the Doges of Venice were subject to such a restriction, Spinoza is probably here thinking of the connection between the House of Orange and the British House of Stuart, which brought autocracy to Holland under William II (who married the daughter of Charles I), and which threatened to bring Catholicism under William III, who in 1676 sued for the hand of Mary (the daughter of the future James II).]

Chapter 7
[Monarchy: Its Organisation]

[1] Now that the foundations of monarchy have been described, it is here my task to give them a precise explanation in good order. To this end it must be especially noted that it is in no way contrary to practice for laws to be so firmly established that not even the king can repeal them. The Persians used to worship their kings as gods, yet even their kings did not have the power[1] to revoke laws once established, as is evident from Daniel, Chapter 6. And there are no cases, as far as I know, of a monarch's being chosen on absolute terms without any explicit conditions. Nor indeed is this in contradiction with reason or with the absolute obedience due to a king. For the fundamental laws[2] of the state should be regarded as the king's eternal decrees, so that his ministers are entirely obedient in refusing to execute his orders if he commands something that is opposed to the fundamental laws of the state. We may make this point clear with the example of Ulysses. His comrades were carrying out his own command in refusing to release him when he was bound to the ship's mast and bewitched by the Sirens' song,[3] although he ordered them to do so with all kinds of threats. And it is regarded as a mark of his good sense that he later thanked his comrades for rendering obedience to his first intention. Following this example of Ulysses, kings too are accustomed to instruct judges to have no regard for persons in administering justice, not even for the king himself if by some odd chance he issues a command that they know to be contrary to established law. For kings are not gods; they are but men, who are often enchanted by the Sirens' song. So if everything were to depend on the inconstant will of one man, there would be no stability. Thus, if a monarchy is to be stable, it must be so organized that everything is indeed done only by the king's decree—that is, that all law is the explicit will of the king—but not everything willed by the king is law. On this see Sections 3, 5, and 6 of the previous Chapter.

[2] Next it must be noted that in laying down the fundamental laws it is especially necessary to take account of human passions. It is not enough to have shown what ought to be done; the main task is to show how it can be brought about that men, whether led by passion or by reason, may still keep their laws firm and sure. If the right of the state, or public freedom, rests only on the feeble support of laws, not only can the citizens have no assurance of its maintenance, as we showed in Section 3 of the previous Chapter, but this will even prove their ruin. For it is certainly true that no condition of a commonwealth is more wretched than that of a good commonwealth that is beginning to totter—unless it collapses at one single

---

[1] [*potestatem.*]
[2] [fundamental laws = *fundamenta.*]
[3] [*Odyssey* XII, 156.]

blow and plunges into servitude, which seems highly unlikely.[4] So it would be far better for subjects to transfer their right unconditionally to one man than to covenant for guarantees of freedom that will prove untrustworthy and vain, or futile, and thus prepare a path to cruel servitude for later generations. But if I show that the foundations of monarchy as I have described them in the previous Chapter are strong and cannot be dismantled without arousing the indignation of the greater part of an armed people and that from them there follow peace and security for king and people, and if I deduce this from a general consideration of human nature, no one will be able to doubt that these foundations are good and true, as is evident from Section 9 of Chapter 3 and Sections 3 and 8 of the previous Chapter. That such is their nature I shall show as briefly as possible.

[3] That it is the duty of the sovereign[5] to be acquainted with the situation and condition of the state, to watch over the common welfare of all, and to bring about that which is to the benefit of the majority of his subjects, is universally acknowledged. But since one man alone cannot supervise everything and be always on the alert with a mind set for deliberation, and is often prevented by illness or old age or other causes from attending to public affairs, the monarch must have counsellors who would be acquainted with current issues and would assist the king with their advice and often act as his deputies, so that the state or commonwealth may continue in one and the same mind.

[4] But human nature is so constituted that each pursues his personal advantage with the utmost keenness, regarding as most equitable those laws which he thinks are necessary for the preservation and increase of his own fortune and upholding another's cause only so far as he believes his own position to be strengthened thereby. Hence it follows that counsellors must necessarily be appointed whose private fortune and advantage depend on the general welfare and the peace of all. So it is evident that if a certain number are appointed from every group or class of citizens, a proposal which receives the most votes in this council will be in the interests of a majority of subjects. And although this council, being composed of such a large number of citizens, must inevitably have among its members many of an uncultivated mind, it is nevertheless true that every man is reasonably competent and sagacious in matters in which he has been long and attentively engaged. Therefore if these appointments are restricted to those who up to their fiftieth year have been engaged in their own business without disgrace, they will be well-fitted to give advice relating to their own business, especially if in matters of greater importance they are granted time for reflection. Furthermore, it is far from true that a smaller council will not have among its members some men of this kind. On the contrary, it is largely composed of such men, since everyone there strives his best to have as colleagues dull-witted men who will look to him for guidance. In large councils there is no opportunity for this.[6]

---

[4] [Perhaps an ironic comment concerning the fall and murder of Jan de Witt in 1672.]

[5] [sovereign = *qui imperium tenet*, i.e., the sovereign in the modern sense.]

[6] [This is probably intended as a reply to Hobbes' criticism of large councils in *De cive* X, 10.]

[5] Furthermore, it is a fact that everyone would rather rule than be ruled, "for no one willingly yields sovereignty to another," as Sallust says in his first speech to Caesar.[7] It is therefore evident that an entire people will never transfer its right to a few men or to one man if they can reach agreement among themselves and if they do not allow the quarrels which are a common feature of large councils to reach the point of civil strife. So a people freely transfers to a king only that which is absolutely beyond its capacity[8] to possess, that is, a facility for settling disputes and for making rapid decisions. As for the not infrequent practice of appointing a king for the purpose of making war, on the grounds that kings are much more successful at waging war, it is downright folly for men, in order to wage war with greater success, to choose slavery in time of peace — if indeed there is really peace in the sort of state where, simply for the purpose of making war,[9] sovereignty has been conferred on one man, who is therefore best able in war to display his worth and his unique value to them all.[10] On the other hand, the outstanding feature of a democracy is that its excellence is much more manifest in peace than in war. But whatever be the reason for appointing a king, he cannot, as we have already said,[11] all alone know what is beneficial to the state; for this purpose he must have a number of citizens as counsellors, as we have shown in the previous Section. And as it is quite inconceivable that in a matter of policy there can be anything that has escaped the attention of such a large body of men, it follows that there can be no opinion conducive to the people's welfare that is not included among those submitted to the king by this council. Thus, since the people's welfare is the highest law, or the king's supreme right, it follows that the king's right is to choose one of the opinions advanced in council and not to make any decree or give any judgment contrary to the view of the entire council (see Section 25 of the previous Chapter). However, if all the opinions advanced in council had to be submitted to the king, it is possible that the king would always favour the small cities which have fewer votes.[12] For although the council's regulations should require that opinions be submitted to the king with no indication of their sponsors, it will never be possible to take such strict precautions that none will be divulged. Therefore there must necessarily be this provision, that an opinion supported by less than a hundred votes should be regarded as void; and this is a law which the larger cities will have to uphold with all their might.

[6] At this point, were it not my purpose to be brief, I might point out many other considerable advantages deriving from this council; but I shall mention just

---

[7] [Pseudo-Sallust, *Ad Caesarem Senem de Re Publica Oratio* I, 4: Again noted in TP8/12. The sentence ends with the word "ruled" in the *Nagelate Schriften*.]

[8] [*potestate*.]

[9] [This phrase is not found in the *Nagelate Schriften*.]

[10] [Spinoza is here rejecting Hobbes' argument (*De cive* X, 17) that, because kings make the best generals, monarchy is the best form of government.]

[11] [See TP7/3.]

[12] [In Holland the stadtholder could in effect neutralize the votes of larger cities by securing a plurality of votes from smaller ones.]

one that seems to me most important, namely, that there can be no greater incentive to virtue than the general hope of attaining this office. For it is by ambition that we are all chiefly led, as we have shown at some length in our *Ethics*.[13]

[7] That the greater part of this council will never be minded to wage war and will always be strongly attached and devoted to peace is beyond all doubt. For in addition to the constant fear of losing their property together with their freedom as a result of war, they will have to provide the extra financial resources required for war, and furthermore their children and relations, busy as they are with domestic concerns, will be forced to turn their energies to warfare and to go soldiering, whence they can never bring back home anything but unprofitable scars. Because, as we said in Section 31 of the previous Chapter, the military force must receive no pay, and, by Section 10 of the same Chapter, it must be recruited exclusively from citizens and no others.

[8] Another factor which is also of great importance in promoting peace and harmony is this, that no citizen may own real estate (see Section 12 of the previous Chapter). Hence the danger from war is practically the same for all; all will have to make a living by engaging in trade or by lending money to their fellow citizens—assuming that, as was once the case in Athens, a law is enacted forbidding the lending of money at interest to any but native inhabitants. So they will have to engage in commercial dealings that either make them mutually involved one with another or that require the same means for their furtherance.[14] Thus the greatest part of the council will generally have one and the same attitude of mind towards their common interests and peaceful activities; for, as we said in Section 4 of this Chapter, every man upholds another's cause only so far as he believes his own position to be strengthened thereby.

[9] It is beyond doubt that it will never occur to anyone to bribe this council. For if someone should win over one or two out of so considerable a number of men, he is hardly likely to gain anything from it; for, as we have said, an opinion supported by less than a hundred votes is void.

[10] Furthermore when this council is once established, it will not be possible to reduce the number of its members, as we shall see if we take into consideration the common passions of mankind. For all men are chiefly led by ambition, and there is no man of sound physical health who does not hope to live to a good old age. If, then, we calculate the number of those who actually attain their fiftieth or sixtieth year, and if we also take into account the large number of this council who are appointed every year, we shall see that there can hardly be anyone of those who bear arms who is not possessed of high hopes of rising to this lofty position. So all will uphold, to the best of their ability, this law concerning election to the council. For it should be noted that corruption, unless it creeps in unobtrusively, is easily prevented. However, a reduction in the number appointed from each single clan is more easily envisaged and would be less invidious than such a reduc-

---

[13] [See E3App44.]

[14] [The use by Spinoza of economic incentives to secure harmony prompted Vico's sneer in *Scienza Nuova* I, 335: "Benedict Spinoza speaks of the commonwealth as a society of shopkeepers."]

tion in the case of a few clans or the complete exclusion of one or two clans. Therefore (by Section 15 of the previous Chapter) the number of counsellors cannot be reduced unless a third, or fourth, or fifth part is removed simultaneously, which represents a considerable upheaval and is therefore altogether divorced from common practice. Nor is there any reason to fear delay or negligence in making appointments, since provision is made for this procedure by the council itself. See Section 16 of the previous Chapter.

[11] The king, then, whether motivated by fear of the people or by his desire to win over the greater part of an armed populace, or whether he is led by nobility of spirit to have regard to the public interest, will always ratify the opinion that is supported by most votes—i.e. (by Section 5 of this Chapter), that is of greater advantage to the greater part of the state; or else he will try, if possible, to reconcile the differing opinions submitted to him so as to gain popularity with all (wherein he will spare no effort)[15] and to show them what a prize they have in his single self, both in peace and in war. Thus he will be most fully in control of his own right and most fully sovereign when he has most regard for the general welfare of his people.

[12] For the king by himself cannot restrain all in fear; his power, as we have said, rests upon the number of his soldiers and especially on their valour and loyalty, which will always endure among men just so long as they are bound together by some need, be that need honourable or base. Hence it comes about that kings are more prone to urge on their soldiers than to keep them in check, to gloss over their vices rather than their virtues,[16] and generally, so as to exert pressure on the good, to seek out idlers and the debauched, giving them recognition, assisting them with money and influence, clasping their hands, throwing them kisses, and stooping to any form of servility as the price of despotism.[17] Therefore, to ensure that citizens should stand highest in the king's esteem and should be in control of their own right as far as the civil order or equity permits, it is necessary that the militia be composed solely of citizens and that citizens should be his counsellors; while on the other hand citizens become completely subjugated and are laying the foundations for perpetual warfare from the moment that they allow mercenary troops to be engaged,[18] men whose trade is war and who find their greatest power[19] amid discord and sedition.[20]

[13] That the king's counsellors should not be appointed for life, but for three, four, or five years at the most, is evident both from Section 10 and from what we have said in Section 9 of this Chapter. For if they were appointed for life, the greatest part of the citizens would have scarcely any hope of attaining this office, and this would result in great inequality among the citizens, leading to envy and in-

---

[15] [Terence, *Eunuchus* 312.]
[16] [Tacitus, *Histories* II, lxxxii, 1.]
[17] [Tacitus, *Histories* I, xxxvi, 2–3.]
[18] [I read *conduci* for *duci*. —S.S.]
[19] [*plurima vis*, which connotes force or physical power.]
[20] [Tacitus, *Histories* IV, i, 3.]

cessant murmurings and finally to outbreaks of sedition—which would no doubt be not unwelcome to kings who are eager to dominate. In addition, the counsellors, rid of all fear of their successors, would cast off all restraint with little opposition from the king. For the more they are hated by the citizens, the more they will cling to the king and the more ready they will be to fawn upon him. Indeed, even a five-year term of office still appears excessive, for in this space of time it seems not altogether impossible for a considerable part of the council, however large it may be, to be corrupted by bribes or favours. So it will be a much safer arrangement if every year, two out of each clan retire and are replaced by a like number (assuming that each clan is to have five counsellors) except in that year when the lawyer of a clan retires and another lawyer is appointed in his place.

[14] Moreover, no king can promise himself greater security than one who reigns in a commonwealth of this kind. For apart from the fact that he soon perishes whose safety is not desired by his own soldiers, it is quite certain that the greatest danger to kings is from those nearest them. So the fewer in number and consequently the more powerful the counsellors, the greater the danger to the king of their transferring the sovereignty to another. Indeed, nothing caused David more alarm than that his counsellor Achitophel had taken Absalom's side.[21] Then again, if all power[22] has been transferred absolutely to one man, it is[23] much simpler for it to be transferred from one man to another. Two common soldiers undertook to transfer the Roman Empire, and they succeeded (Tacitus, *Histories*, Book I).[24] I pass over the devices and cunning wiles which counsellors must employ to avoid falling victim to jealousy; for these are known only too well, and no reader of history can be unaware that the loyalty of counsellors has often proved their ruin. So for their own protection they have to be cunning, not loyal. But if counsellors are too many in number to unite in the same crime and are all equal with one another, and their term of office does not exceed four years, they cannot possibly be an object of fear to the king unless he attempts to deprive them of their freedom, whereby he will offend all citizens equally.[25] For (as Antonio Pérez well remarks) the exercise of absolute dominion is very dangerous to the ruler, very hateful to his subjects, and opposed to the established laws both divine and human, as is shown by countless examples.[26]

[15] Besides these laws, in the previous Chapter we have laid down other fundamental laws which are effective in securing for the king his sovereignty and for the citizens their freedom and peace. These we shall go into in due course, for it

---

[21] [See 2 Samuel 15:31.]

[22] [*potestas*.]

[23] [I read *quod* for *quae*.—S.S.]

[24] [Sovereignty was passed from Galba to Otho. See Tacitus, *Histories* I, xxv, 1.]

[25] [Spinoza may have in mind six members of the Estates of Holland, who were arrested by order of William II in 1650.]

[26] [See Pérez' *Relaciones de Rafael Peregrino* (Geneva, 1644). Pérez served as Secretary of State to Philip II of Spain, and wrote this work in order to justify his decision to expose the conduct of his (former) master.]

was my purpose first of all to explain those laws that concern the supreme council and which are of the greatest importance. I shall now go on to deal with the rest of them in the order in which I propounded them.

[16] There can be no doubt that citizens are that much more powerful and therefore more fully in control of their own right as their cities are larger and better fortified. For the safer their dwelling place, the more capable they are of safeguarding their freedom, that is, the less they need fear an enemy, without or within; and it is an assured fact that the wealthier men become, the more natural it is for them to take measures to protect themselves.[27] But those cities that stand in need of another's power for their preservation do not have equal right with that other; they are subject to another's right to the extent that they stand in need of the other's power. For we have shown in Chapter 2 that right is defined by power alone.

[17] It is also for this same purpose—viz. that citizens may keep control over their own right and may safeguard their freedom—that the military force should be composed only of citizens, with no exemptions. For an armed man is more fully in control of his own right than an unarmed man (see Section 12 of this Chapter), and in giving up their arms and entrusting their cities' defences to another, citizens are making an absolute transfer of their right to him, committing it entirely to his good faith. A further consideration is men's avarice, which is generally a prevailing motive; for it is impossible for mercenaries to be hired except at great expense, and citizens find very irksome the exactions needed to maintain soldiers in idleness. The fact that no one should be appointed to command the entire military force or a great part of it except under urgent necessity and then for a year at the most is familiar to all who have read history, sacred or profane. There is nothing that reason teaches more clearly than this; for it is obvious that the might of the state is then entrusted to one who will find opportunity enough to monopolise military glory and surpass the king in renown or to win the loyalty of the army by indulgence, generosity, and the other arts usually practised by generals whose aim is slavery for others and despotism for themselves. Finally, for the greater security of the state I have added this provision, that these army commanders are to be chosen from the king's counsellors or ex-counsellors, that is, from men who have reached an age when people choose the traditional and the safe in preference to the new and the perilous.[28]

[18] My purpose in saying that the citizens should be divided into clans and that an equal number of counsellors should be appointed from each clan was this, that the larger cities should have more counsellors proportionately to the number of their citizens and should have more voting power, as is fair. For the power of a state, and consequently its right, must be assessed from the number of its citizens; nor do I think that any more suitable means can be devised for maintaining this equality between citizens, because[29] all men are so constituted by nature that

---

[27] [Machiavelli, *Discourses* III, 24.]

[28] [The phrase is an adaptation from Tacitus, *Annals* I, ii, 1.]

[29] [I read *quia* for *qui*.—S.S.]

each wants to be identified with his own kind and to be distinguished by lineage from others.

[19] Furthermore, in a state of Nature the one thing a man cannot appropriate to himself and make his own is land[30] and whatever is so fixed to the land that he cannot conceal it anywhere or carry it away where he pleases.[31] Thus the land and whatever is fixed to it in the way we have described is especially the public property of the commonwealth, that is, of all those who by their united strength can claim it, or of him to whom all have delegated the power[32] to claim it.[33] Consequently, the land and whatever is fixed thereto must have, in the eyes of the citizens, a value as great as is their need to set their feet thereon and to be able to defend their common right or freedom. In Section 8 of this Chapter we have shown the advantages that must thereby accrue to the commonwealth.

[20] In order that the citizens should be, as far as possible, on terms of equality—a prime necessity in a commonwealth—none are to be regarded as noblemen except those of royal descent.[34] But if it were permissible for all of royal descent to marry or to have children, they would in time increase to a very large number and would become not only a burden to the king and all the citizens but very much an object of fear as well. For men who enjoy abundant leisure are prone to contemplate crime. Hence it is mainly on account of their nobles that kings are induced to go to war because, surrounded by nobles, they find more safety and security in war than in peace. But this being a well-known fact, I pass it by, as also my remarks in Sections 15 to 27 of the previous Chapter. For the main points have been established in this Chapter, and the rest are self-evident.

[21] The following points are also universally accepted: That the number of the judges should be too great to allow of a considerable part of them being bribed by a private individual; that they should not vote openly but by secret ballot; and that they deserve to be paid for their services. But it is the general custom to pay them an annual salary, with the result that they are in no great hurry to settle law suits and disputes frequently reach no end. Again, in cases where confiscated goods fall to the crown, it is not always justice or truth that are the main considerations, but the extent of a man's wealth. Informers are everywhere, and the wealthy are seized as prey. These evils, grievous and intolerable as they are, are excused on the grounds of the urgency of war but are continued even in time of

---

[30] [This passage summarizes nicely the distinction between Spinoza's 'state of Nature' (*status naturalis*) and Locke's 'natural state'. A central role of the social contract in Locke is the maintenance and preservation of property rights which preexist the contract. For Spinoza, property itself is a creation of civil society.]

[31] [I read *possit* for *potest*. — S.S.]

[32] [*potestatem.*]

[33] [Note that though Spinoza's monarch is to possess all land, his state lacks the hierarchical structure of a feudal system.]

[34] [Spinoza follows Machiavelli (*Discourses* I, 55) in regarding feudal nobles as enemies of civil order. Holland, in fact, had few such nobles.]

peace.[35] Still, the avarice of judges, those that are appointed for two or three years at the most, is kept in bounds by fear of their successors, not to mention again that the judges cannot own real estate; and to make a profit they must lend money to their fellow citizens. Thus they are compelled to have regard for the interests of their fellow citizens rather than to victimise them, particularly if there are a large number of judges, as we have said.

[22] But the military force, as we have said, is to be assigned no pay,[36] freedom being the supreme reward for military service. In a state of Nature it is simply for freedom's sake that each strives his best to defend himself, and he expects no other reward for his valour in war but his independence. Now in a civil order the citizens as a body are to be considered as a man in a state of Nature; so in fighting on behalf of that civil order they are all battling for themselves and serving themselves. But counsellors, judges, magistrates, etc. are serving others rather than themselves, and it is therefore right that they should be paid for their service. Moreover, in time of war there can be no nobler or more powerful incentive to victory than the idea of freedom. But if, on the other hand, only a portion of the citizens were to be detailed for military service—for which reason they must also be assigned some fixed pay—the king will necessarily distinguish these above the rest (as we have shown in Section 12 of this Chapter). Yet these are men skilled only in the arts of war, and in peace time, having too little to do, they become debauched and in the end are driven by poverty to think of nothing but rapine, civil discord, and war.[37] Thus we can assert that a monarchy of this kind is really a state of war; it is only the soldiers who enjoy freedom, the rest being slaves.

[23] Our remarks in Section 32 of the previous Chapter concerning the admission of foreigners I believe to be self-evident. Moreover, I think no one can doubt that those who are near kinsmen to the king should be at some distance from him and engaged in matters not of war but of peace, such as may bring honour to them and tranquillity to the state. Yet not even this has been deemed a sufficient precaution by Turkish despots who therefore regard it as an obligation to slaughter all their brothers. Nor is this surprising; for the more absolutely sovereignty has been transferred to one man, the more easily it can be transferred from one to another (as we have illustrated by an example in Section 14 of this Chapter). But in the case of a monarchy such as we are here describing—that is, one in which there is no mercenary soldiery—there can be no doubt that the measures we have proposed will be a sufficient provision for the king's safety.

[24] Nor can anyone call into question the measures we proposed in Sections 34 and 35 of the previous Chapter. And that the king should not marry a foreigner is easily proved. For apart from the fact that two commonwealths, even when united by treaty, remain in a state of hostility (Section 14, Chapter 3), it is of the

---

[35] [Tacitus, *Histories* II, lxxxiv, 1–2.]

[36] [See TP6/31. Spinoza appears to regard payments to rank and file in wartime as a subsistence allowance rather than a salary.]

[37] [This passage is an adaptation of Sallust, *Catiline* 5.]

utmost importance to see to it that the king's domestic concerns do not lead to war. And since quarrels and disputes are especially likely to arise from an alliance based on marriage, and since questions at issue between two commonwealths are generally decided by right of war, it follows that it is fatal for a state to enter into so close an alliance with another state. Of this we have a deadly example in Scripture. On the death of Solomon, who had married the daughter of the king of Egypt, his son Rehoboam waged a disastrous war against Shishak, king of Egypt, by whom he was utterly defeated.[38] Again, the marriage of Louis XIV, king of France, with the daughter of Philip IV sowed the seeds of another war.[39] And besides these, history provides numerous examples.

[25] The form of the state must be preserved unchanged; and so there must be but one king, a male, and the sovereignty must be indivisible. I have said that the king's eldest son should succeed his father by right; or else, if the king is without issue, his nearest kinsman. This is evident not only from Section 13 of the previous Chapter but also because the election of a king by the people should, if possible, be for all time; otherwise it will necessarily come about that the sovereignty of the state will frequently pass into the hands of the people, a drastic and therefore a very dangerous development. Those who maintain that the king, being master of the state and holding it by absolute right, can hand it on to whom he pleases[40] and choose whatever successor he pleases and that therefore the king's son is heir to the throne by right, are quite mistaken.[41] The king's will has the force of law just as long as he holds the sword of the commonwealth, for the right to rule is determined by power alone. Therefore a king can indeed abdicate, but he cannot hand over his sovereignty to another without the acquiescence of the people or its stronger part. To understand this more clearly, it should be noted that children are heirs to their parents not by natural right but by civil right, for it is only through the power of the commonwealth that one can be the owner of a particular property.[42] Therefore, by that same power or right whereby a man's will concerning his own property is held to be valid, that same will continues to be valid even after his death as long as the commonwealth endures. And it is for this reason that everyone in a civil order retains even after death the same right that he held when alive, because, as we have said, it is not so much by his own power as by the commonwealth's power, which is a continuing power, that a man can make decisions concerning his property. But with the king the case is quite different, for the king's will is the civil law itself, and the king is the commonwealth itself.[43] So there is a sense in which, with the death of the king, the common-

---

[38] [2 Chronicles 8:11; 12:2–9.]

[39] [The War of Succession for the possession of the Spanish Netherlands, 1667–1668.]

[40] [I read *velit* for *vellet*. —S.S.]

[41] [Hobbes argued in the *De cive* that it was best for subjects to be the inheritance of their king (X, 18), that the king was empowered to give or sell his sovereignty to another (IX, 13), and that he could bequeath it to anyone he pleased (VII, 15 and IX, 12).]

[42] [Again an anticipation and rejection of the Lockean account of property.]

[43] [See Hobbes' definition of a commonwealth in *De cive* V, 9.]

wealth dies, and civil order reverts to natural order; and thus sovereignty reverts naturally to the people, which therefore has the right to enact new laws and repeal the old.[44] So it is plain that no man succeeds the king by right except the one whom the people wills to be his successor, or, in the case of a theocracy like the ancient commonwealth of the Hebrews, one whom God has chosen through his prophet. We could also deduce this from the fact that the king's sword or right is in reality the will of the people or of its stronger part; or again from the fact that men, endowed with reason, can never give up their right so completely as to cease to be men and be accounted as sheep. But there is no need to pursue this further.

[26] Religious right, or the right to worship God, is something no one can transfer to another. However, we have discussed this at some length in the last two chapters of the *Tractatus theologico-politicus*, which it is unnecessary to repeat here. And now I think I have set forth briefly, but with sufficient clarity, the fundamental laws of a good monarchy. Their interconnection or conformity with the state will be readily apparent to anyone who will examine them all together with some attention. It remains only for me to remind the reader that the monarchy I here have in mind is one established by a free people, for whom alone these suggestions can be helpful; for a people accustomed to a different form of government will not be able to tear up the traditional foundations of their state, changing its entire structure, without great danger of overthrowing the entire state.[45]

[27] Yet perhaps our suggestions will be received with ridicule by those who restrict to the common people the faults that are inherent in all mankind, saying, "There is no moderation in the mob; they terrorise unless they are frightened,"[46] and, "The common people is either a humble servant or an arrogant master, there is no truth or judgment in it,"[47] and the like. But all men share in one and the same nature; it is power and culture that mislead us, with the result that when two men do the same thing we often say that it is permissible for the one to do it and not the other, not because of any difference in the thing done, but in the doer.[48] Pride is appropriate to rulers. Men are made proud by election to office for a year; so what about nobles who hold their distinction without end? But their arrogance is bedecked by an air of disdain, by magnificence, by lavishness, by a certain blending of vices and a kind of cultivated folly and a refined depravity, so that vices, each of which when taken separately and thus rendered conspicuous is seen as foul and base, appear to the naïve and the ignorant as honourable and becoming. Then again, "There is no moderation in the mob; they terrorise unless they are frightened." For freedom and slavery do not go well together. Finally, that "there is no truth or judgment in the common people" is not surprising, since the

---

[44] [So the "eternal election" of the king is fictitious. Spinoza's view here has more in common with Locke than with Hobbes.]

[45] [A not-so-veiled warning to his contemporaries who wanted to create a monarchy in the Dutch republic.]

[46] [Tacitus, *Annals* I, xxix, 3.]

[47] [Livy XXIV, xxv, 8; Tacitus, *Histories* I, xxxii, 1.]

[48] [Terence, *Adelphi* 823–825.]

important affairs of state are conducted without their knowledge, and from the little that cannot be concealed they can only make conjecture. For to suspend judgment is not a common virtue. So to seek to conduct all business without the knowledge of the citizens and then to expect them not to misjudge things and to put a bad interpretation on everything, this is the height of folly. For if the common people could practise restraint and suspend judgment on matters insufficiently known, or form correct judgment on the basis of scanty information, it would surely be more fit to rule than to be ruled. However, as we have said, all men have the same nature — all grow haughty with rule, terrorise unless they are frightened — and everywhere truth becomes a casualty through hostility or servility,[49] especially when despotic power is in the hands of one or a few[50] who in trials pay attention not to justice or truth but to the extent of a person's wealth.

[28] Again, mercenary troops, accustomed to military discipline and inured to cold and hunger, usually despise the mass of citizens as being by far their inferiors in the matter of storming cities or fighting pitched battles. But no one of sound mind will assert that for this reason a state will be less successful or less durable. On the contrary, no impartial observer will deny that a state is most durable of all if it just has enough power to protect its possessions without coveting what belongs to others and therefore strives by every means to avoid war and to preserve peace.

[29] The policies of this state, I admit, can hardly be concealed;[51] but everyone will also agree with me that it is far better for the honest policies of a state to be open to its enemies than for the guilty secrets of tyrants to be kept hidden from the citizens. Those who are able to shroud in secrecy their dealings with affairs of state have the state completely in their hands,[52] and their treatment of the citizens in peace is no less hostile than their attitude to the enemy in war. No one can deny that secrecy is often of service to a state, but no one can ever prove that the same state cannot subsist without it. But on the other hand, it is quite impossible to entrust absolute control of public affairs to any man while also maintaining one's freedom, and so it is folly to choose to avoid a small loss at the cost of a grave calamity. Naturally, it has always been the constant refrain of those who lust after dominion that, for a state, secrecy in the conduct of its affairs is of vital importance and they make other such assertions that, the more they are cloaked with a show of utility, the more they are likely to lead to oppressive slavery.[53]

[30] Finally, although no state, as far as I know, has included in its constitution all the features I have here described, we can nevertheless confirm from actual experience that this form of monarchy is the best, if we will but consider the reasons for the preservation of any civilised state and for its overthrow. But this is a task I

---

[49] [Tacitus, *Histories* I, i, 1.]
[50] [*praesertim ubi unus vel pauci dominantur.*]
[51] [Hobbes, *De cive* X, 14–15.]
[52] [*in potestate habent.*]
[53] [Tacitus, *Annals* I, lxxxi, 3.]

could not here undertake without wearying the reader. Nevertheless, I cannot pass over in silence one example which seems worthy of mention: I refer to the state of the Aragonese,[54] whose singular loyalty to their kings was matched by the steadfastness with which they preserved unbroken the constitution of their kingdom. As soon as they had rid themselves of the slavish yoke of the Moors they resolved to choose themselves a king. Being unable to agree among themselves as to the conditions for this election, they therefore decided to consult the Pope[55] on this matter. He, who in this affair conducted himself truly as the vicar of Christ, rebuked them because, not taking sufficient warning from the example of the Hebrews, they were so utterly set on seeking a king. But if they would not change their minds, he advised them to choose a king only after creating institutions that were equitable and suited to the character of the people; in particular, they should bring into being a supreme council, like the Ephors of the Spartans, which would provide a counterbalance to the kings and which would possess the absolute right to decide any disputes that might arise between king and citizens. Following this advice, then, they established laws that they considered to be the most equitable of which the supreme interpreter, and consequently the highest judge, should be not the king but a council called "The Seventeen," whose president is called "The Justice." So this Justice and the Seventeen, appointed for life not by vote but by lot, had absolute right to review and annul all judgments passed upon any citizen by other councils, whether political or ecclesiastical, or even by the king himself, so that any citizen had the right to summon the king himself before this tribunal. Furthermore, they at one time even had the right to elect and to depose the king.[56] But after the passage of many years, their king, Don Pedro, called "The Dagger,"[57] by means of canvassing, bribery, promises, and favours of every kind, finally secured the revocation of this right. (As soon as he had gained his point in the presence of all, he cut off— or, as I think more likely, wounded—his hand with a dagger,[58] declaring that the right of subjects to choose their king was bound to involve the shedding of royal blood.)[59] But he succeeded only on this condition, "that they have had, and continue to have, the right to take up arms against any violent action whereby anyone may seek to encroach on their dominion to their hurt, yea, even against the king himself and the prince, his heir, if he thus encroaches (on their

---

[54] [Spinoza's remarks on Aragon are probably derived from the *Relaciones de Rafael Peregrino* of Antonio Pérez (Geneva, 1644).]

[55] [Gregory VII.]

[56] [*habuerunt regem eligendi et potestate privandi.*]

[57] [Pedro IV (1336–1387).]

[58] [Spinoza reads Pérez' "*se cortó la mano*"as "he cut off his hand."]

[59] [Pérez wrote: "*Que tal fuero, y fuero de poder eligir Rey los vasallos, sangre de Rey avia de costar.*" The traditional interpretation, fostered by the anonymous English translation of Pérez published in 1715, interprets Pedro's shedding his blood in exchange for the abolition of such a privilege. Spinoza interprets Pérez as claiming instead that such a privilege (being able to elect or to depose the king) is dangerous to the king (see TP7/25), and this is probably the more correct reading.]

dominion)." It is obvious that by this condition they did not so much abolish as amend the above-mentioned right. For, as we have shown in Sections 5 and 6 of Chapter 4, it is not by civil right but by right of war that a king can be deprived of his power to rule; in other words, it is by violence alone that his subjects may resist his violence. Besides this condition they stipulated others,[60] which are irrelevant to our purpose. These usages, drawn up with universal consent, continued inviolate for an incredible space of time, kings and subjects behaving with equal loyalty to one another. But after Ferdinand, the first of them all to be styled "The Catholic," inherited the kingdom of Castile,[61] the Castilians, becoming envious of this privilege of the Aragonese, never ceased to urge Ferdinand to abolish those rights. But he, being not yet accustomed to absolute rule, did not venture to take action and replied to his counsellors as follows: "Apart from the fact that he had accepted the kingship of Aragon on terms with which they were acquainted, and had sworn faithfully to observe those terms and that to break one's faith is the act of a savage, he had come to the conclusion that his kingdom would be stable only as long as the king had no greater measure of security than that enjoyed by his subjects, so that neither would the king outweigh his subjects nor his subjects their king. For if either party were to become more powerful than the other, the weaker would attempt not only to recover its former equality but to retaliate upon the other through resentment at the injury it had suffered. This would result in the ruin of one or both." These are indeed wise words, which I could not sufficiently admire had they been uttered by a king accustomed to rule over slaves, not over free men. So the Aragonese retained their freedom after the time of Ferdinand—though no longer by right but by the favour of their kings, who exceeded them in power—right up to the time of Philip II, who oppressed them with more success but with no less cruelty than he oppressed the United Provinces. And although Philip III is supposed to have restored completely the original position, the Aragonese, of whom the majority were motivated by eagerness to flatter the powerful (for it is folly to kick against the pricks)[62] while the remainder were terrorised, have retained nothing but the plausible names and empty forms of freedom.[63]

[31] We conclude, therefore, that a people can preserve quite a considerable degree of freedom under a king, provided that it ensures that the king's power is determined only by the people's power and depends on the people for its maintenance. This has been the one and only guideline I have followed in laying down the foundations of monarchy.

---

[60] [The king in fact had to take an oath to maintain the rights, freedom, and customs of Aragon before being crowned.]

[61] [Ferdinand of Aragon (1476–1516) became regent of Castile through the testament of his wife Isabella.]

[62] [Terence, *Phormio* 77–78.]

[63] [Tacitus, *Annals* I, lxxxi, 3.]

Chapter 8
[Aristocracy: The First Model]

That an aristocracy should consist of a large number of patricians. Of its superiority, and that it comes closer than monarchy to an absolute form of government, and is therefore more suitable for the preservation of freedom.

[1] So far we have been dealing with monarchy. We shall now go on to explain the way in which an aristocracy should be established so as to be able to endure. We have defined aristocracy as a state where the government is in the hands of not one man but a certain number of men, whom we shall henceforth call patricians, chosen from the people. I say expressly, "in the hands of a certain number of chosen men," for the chief difference between this and a democracy is as follows, that in an aristocracy the right to govern depends solely on selection,[1] whereas in a democracy it depends mainly on a kind of innate right, or a right acquired by chance, as I shall explain in due course.[2] So even if the entire population of a state were to be enrolled as patricians, then provided that this right of enrolment is not hereditary and is not bequeathed to others in accordance with some general law, the government will still be entirely an aristocracy, since none but those expressly chosen are enrolled as patricians. Now if those chosen are only two in number, the one will endeavour to gain superiority over the other, and because of their excessive power the state is likely to split into two factions, or into three, four, or[3] five factions if the government is in the hands of three, four, or five men. But the more there are to share in the government, the weaker the factions will be. Hence it follows that for an aristocracy to be stable, the minimum number of patricians must be determined by consideration of the size of the state.

[2] Let us suppose, then, that for a state of medium size it suffices that there should be a hundred best men on whom the sovereign power of the state is conferred, and who therefore have the right to appoint their patrician colleagues when any one of their number dies. These men will naturally do their utmost to ensure that their children or their nearest kinsmen shall succeed them. Hence the sovereign power of the state[4] will always be vested in those whose fortune it is to be the children or kinsmen of patricians. And since out of a hundred men whom fortune raises to office hardly three are to be found who are singularly gifted with skill and understanding, it will come about that the sovereignty will be in the hands of, not a hundred, but no more than two or three men who excel in mental power and who

---
[1] [The town council of Amsterdam was recruited in this manner, often called "co-optation."]
[2] [See TP11/1–2.]
[3] [I read *aut* for *et.*—S.S.]
[4] [*summa imperii potestas.*]

will easily contrive to gather everything into their hands, each of them, ambitious as is the way of humans, preparing his path to monarchy. Thus, if our calculations are correct, in the case of a state which by reason of its size requires at least a hundred men of leading rank, the sovereign power[5] must be in the hands of at least five thousand patricians. For in this way there will never fail to be found a hundred men of outstanding mental gifts, it being assumed that out of fifty men who seek and attain office there will always be one not inferior to the best, as well as others who seek to emulate the qualities of the best and are therefore also worthy to govern.

[3] Patricians are most commonly the citizens of one city that is the capital of the entire state, so that the commonwealth or republic takes its name from that city, as was once the case with Rome, and is today with Venice, Genoa, etc. But the republic of Holland takes its name from a whole province, which is the reason why the subjects of this state enjoy greater freedom. Now before we can determine the foundations on which an aristocratic government must rest, we must note the difference there is between government in the hands of one man and government in the hands of a sufficiently large council, a difference which is indeed quite considerable. In the first place, as we remarked in Section 5, Chapter 6, the power of a single man is far from being equal to bearing the whole burden of government. Now this cannot be said of a sufficiently large council, for in asserting that a council is sufficiently large one is also denying that it is not equal to the burden of government. So whereas counsellors are quite indispensable to a king, this is certainly not the case with a council of this kind. Secondly, kings are mortal, whereas councils are everlasting, and so the sovereign power[6] that has once been conferred on a council never reverts to the people. This is not so with a monarchy, as we have shown in Section 25 of the previous Chapter. Thirdly, the rule of a king is often precarious by reason of his minority, sickness, old age, or for other causes, whereas the power of a council of this kind remains always one and the same. Fourthly, the will of one man is very changeable and inconstant, and it is for this reason that all law is indeed the king's declared will (as we said in Section 1 of the previous Chapter), but not everything the king wills must be law. This cannot be said of the will of a council which is sufficiently large. For since the council itself (as I have just shown) stands in no need of counsellors, all the declared will of the council must necessarily be law. We may therefore conclude that the sovereignty[7] conferred on a council of sufficient size is absolute, or comes closest to being absolute. For if there is such a thing as absolute sovereignty, it is really that which is held by the people as a whole.[8]

[4] Yet, insofar as this form of aristocratic sovereignty never reverts to the people (as has just been shown), and does not involve any consultation of the people, and

---

[5] [*imperii potestas.*]

[6] [*imperii potentia.*]

[7] [*imperium.*]

[8] [This is a veiled critique of Hobbes, who argued (*De cive* VI, 13) that sovereigns are equally absolute but not equally powerful. For Spinoza they are not absolute because they are not absolutely powerful.]

since everything willed by this same council is unconditionally law, it must be considered as quite absolute. Therefore its foundations ought to rest only on the will and judgment of that same council and not on the vigilance of the people, they being debarred both from offering advice and from voting. So the reason why in practice the government is not absolute can only be this, that the people is an object of fear to the rulers, thereby maintaining some degree of freedom for itself, which it asserts and preserves, if not by express law, by tacit understanding.

[5] It is therefore clear that this kind of state will be most efficient if it is so organised as to approach absolute sovereignty; that is, if the people are as little as possible an object of fear and if they retain no freedom except such as must necessarily be granted by the constitution of the state itself. This freedom is therefore a right belonging not so much to the people as to the state as a whole, a right which is upheld and preserved solely by the aristocrats as their own concern. For in this way practice will agree most closely with theory, as is clear from the previous Section and is also self-evident. For we cannot doubt that the more rights are asserted by the common people, the less sovereignty is in the hands of the patricians, as is the case in lower Germany,[9] where the corporations of artisans, commonly called Guilds,[10] possess such rights.

[6] The fact that sovereignty is conferred absolutely on the council need not give the common people any reason to fear oppressive slavery at its hands. For when a council is so large its will is determined by reason rather than mere caprice, because evil passions draw men asunder; and it is only when they have as their objective what is honourable, or at least appears so, that they can be guided as if by one mind.[11]

[7] So in determining the foundations for an aristocratic government one must ensure above all that they rest solely on the will and power of that same supreme council so that the council is as far as possible in control of its own right and in no danger from the people. To determine these foundations, resting as they do solely on the will and power of the supreme council, let us review those foundations for peace which, peculiar to a monarchy, are unsuited to this form of state. For if we replace these with other equally effective basic institutions suitable for an aristocracy, leaving the rest as already laid down, all causes of civil strife will undoubtedly be removed, or at least this government will be no less secure than a monarchy. On the contrary, it will be that much more secure and its condition that much superior as it comes closer than monarchy to absolute sovereignty, without endangering peace and freedom (see Sections 3 and 6 of this Chapter). For the greater the right of the sovereign the more does the form of the state agree with the dictates of reason (Section 5, Chapter 3), and therefore the fitter it is for the preservation of peace and freedom. Let us therefore run through what we said

---

[9] [A strip of territory on the left bank of the Rhine. It was at one time a Roman province including what are today parts of Belgium, Holland, and the German Rhineland.]

[10] [The Guilds had considerable influence in the town councils of the Netherlands.]

[11] [*nec una veluti mente duci possunt nisi quatenus honesta appetunt.* The qualifiers *veluti* and *quatenus* again indicate that the council has a mind only metaphorically.]

in Chapter 6 from[12] Section 9 on, so that we can reject what is unsuited to aristocratic government and see what is consistent with it.

[8] That it is necessary in the first place to found one or more cities, no one can doubt. But particular attention should be paid to the fortifications of that city that is the capital of the whole state, and also to those that are on the state's frontiers. For the city that is the capital of the whole state and holds the supreme right should be more powerful than all the others. However, in this kind of state it is quite unnecessary for all the inhabitants to be divided into clans.

[9] As for the armed forces, since in this kind of state equality is to be sought not between all citizens but only between patricians, and in particular the power of the patricians is greater than that of the common people, clearly the requirement that the armed forces should be formed only of subjects has no part to play in the laws or fundamental ordinances of this state. But it is of prime importance that no one should be enrolled as a patrician unless he is well trained in the art of war. Still, to exclude subjects from the armed forces, as some suggest, is surely foolish.[13] For military pay given to subjects remains within the realm, whereas that which is paid to foreign troops is a complete loss; and what is more, a most important bulwark of the state is weakened, since those who fight for hearth and home are sure to fight with especial valour. Hence it is also clear that those are no less mistaken who maintain that generals, colonels, captains, etc. should be appointed only from patricians. For what valour in battle is to be expected from soldiers who are deprived of all hope of winning glory and promotion? On the other hand, to establish a law forbidding the patricians to hire foreign troops when the situation requires it,[14] either for their protection and the suppression of civil strife or for any other reasons, is not only unwise but contrary to the supreme right of the patricians, concerning which see Sections 3, 4, and 5 of this Chapter. However, the commander of a single army or of the entire armed forces should be appointed only in time of war and only from the patricians; his command should last for a year at the most, with no possibility of extension of command or of later reappointment. Such a law, necessary in a monarchy, is even more so in an aristocracy. For although, as has already been said,[15] it can be much easier for sovereignty to be transferred from one man to another than from a free council to one man, yet it often happens that patricians are subjugated by their own commanders, to the much greater harm of the commonwealth. For when a monarch is removed, there is merely a change in tyrant, not a change in the form of the state; but in the case of aristocratic government this change cannot take place without

---

[12] [I read *ex* before *Art.*—S.S.]

[13] [Spinoza may be thinking of the Venetian aristocracy, which did not employ commoners in its armies. Machiavelli (*Discourses* I, 6) argues that this made it internally strong, but weak against external enemies.]

[14] [In times of crisis (e.g., 1617) the Dutch regents engaged professional troops, called *waardgelders* for protection despite the general Dutch abhorrence of mercenaries. Spinoza here allows this also as a last alternative.]

[15] [See TP7/14.]

the overthrow of the state and the destruction of the most prominent men. Of such an event Rome has offered the most grievous examples.[16] However, our reason for saying that in a monarchy the armed forces should serve without pay does not apply to a state of this kind. For since subjects are debarred both from counselling and from voting, they are to be regarded on the same footing as foreigners, and should therefore be engaged for military service on no less favourable terms than foreigners. Nor is there here any danger that these may be distinguished above the rest by the council. Rather, to avoid a situation where everyone, as is generally the case, sets an exaggerated value on his own deeds, it would be wiser for the patricians to assign a fixed payment to the soldiers for their service.

[10] Again, for this same reason, that all but patricians are foreigners, it cannot be without danger to the whole state that lands, houses, and all the soil should belong to the state and be let to the inhabitants at an annual rent. For subjects who have no stake in the state would all be likely to desert their cities in times of danger if they could carry wherever they pleased what goods they possessed. Therefore in this state lands and farms are to be sold, not let, to subjects, but on this condition, that they should also pay every year a certain proportion of their annual income and so on, as is done in Holland.

[11] Having considered these points, I now pass on to the basic institutions by which the supreme council should be supported and strengthened.[17] In Section 2 of this Chapter we have shown that in a state of medium size the members of this council should number about five thousand. So we must look for means to prevent the government from gradually falling into fewer hands, ensuring on the contrary that their number keeps pace with the growth of the state, that equality is maintained among the patricians as far as possible, and also that business is speedily dispatched in the councils, and finally, that while the power of the patricians or council should exceed that of the people, the people should suffer no harm thereby.

[12] Of these objectives, the main obstacle to attaining the first is jealousy. As we have said, men are by nature enemies, and even when they are joined and bound together by laws they still retain their nature. This, I believe, is why democracies turn into aristocracies, and these eventually into monarchies. I am quite convinced that most aristocracies were once democracies, for this reason, that a people in search of new territories, when it has found them and cultivated them, retains as a single body an equal right in government, because no one willingly grants sovereignty to another. But although each of them thinks it fair that he should have against another the same right as the other has against him, yet he thinks it unfair that foreigners who come to join them should have equal rights with them in a state which they have won for themselves by their toil and held at the cost of their blood. Nor do the foreigners themselves make any objection to this, having come to settle there not with view to being rulers but to promote their

---

[16] [Machiavelli, *Discourses* III, 24.]

[17] [Spinoza models these laws and the council in part on the Grand Council of Venice.]

private interests, and they are quite happy provided they are granted freedom to transact their own business in security.[18] But meanwhile the population increases through the influx of foreigners, who gradually adopt the national customs until finally they are not distinguishable by any difference but this, that they lack the right to hold office; and while their number increases day by day, that of the citizens for many reasons diminishes. Clans often die out, some men are disqualified by reason of their crimes, and many take no part in public affairs because of their straitened circumstances, while in the meantime the more powerful have this as their sole ambition, to rule alone. In this way government gradually falls into the hands of a few men, and at length by political manoeuvring into the hands of one man. And to these one could add other causes which destroy governments of this kind,[19] but since they are quite familiar I pass them by, and I shall now describe in an orderly way the laws by which the kind of state under discussion must be preserved.

[13] The principal law of this state must be that whereby the proportion of patricians to the population is determined. For (by Section 1 of this Chapter) a ratio should be maintained between the population and the patricians so that the number of patricians increases in proportion to the increase of the population. And this ratio (in accordance with what we said in Section 2 of this Chapter) should be about 1 to 50; that is to say, the number of patricians should never be less than this proportion. For (by Section 1 of this Chapter), the number of patricians may be much greater than that of the people with no change in the form of state. But it is only in their fewness that danger lies. As to how precautions may be taken against the violation of this law, I shall presently discuss this in its proper place.

[14] In some places patricians are chosen out of certain clans only;[20] but to lay this down as an explicit law is to invite disaster. For clans often die out, the exclusion of other clans can never be without disgrace, and, furthermore, it is contrary to this form of government for patrician status to be hereditary, by Section 1 of this Chapter. But this system would make the government seem[21] rather like a democracy, a democracy in the hands of very few citizens, such as we described in Section 12 of this Chapter. On the other hand, it is impossible—indeed absurd as I shall show in Section 39 of this Chapter—to try to prevent the patricians from appointing their own sons and kinsmen, thereby retaining the right to govern in the hands of certain clans. However, provided that they do not claim this privilege by express law and that the others are not excluded (I mean those who are born within the state, speak the mother tongue, have not married a foreign wife, are not of ill-fame or servants, and do not gain their livelihood by some menial occupation, among whom are also to be reckoned wine-shop keepers, tapsters, and

---

[18] [Machiavelli, *Discourses* I, 6.]
[19] [See Aristotle, *Politics* 1305b–1307b.]
[20] [Venice and Genoa are the two examples which Spinoza may have in mind. The clans of these two cities were called "families."]
[21] [I read *videretur* for *videtur*.—S.S.]

the like), the form of the state will nevertheless be preserved, and it will still be possible to maintain the ratio between patricians and the populace.

[15] Furthermore, if it be enacted by law that no young men can be appointed, it will never come about that a few clans could keep in their hands the right to govern. So a law should be enacted that no one under the age of thirty can be placed on the roll of candidates.[22]

[16] Thirdly, all patricians should be required by law to assemble at a particular location in the city at certain fixed times; and whoever fails to attend council, unless prevented by illness or some public business, should pay a heavy fine. Otherwise most patricians would neglect public affairs to attend to their private business.

[17] The duty of this council should be to enact and to repeal laws and to appoint their patrician colleagues and all ministers of state.[23] For one who holds the supreme right, which we have declared to belong to this council, cannot possibly grant to another the power[24] to enact and repeal laws without thereby ceding his own right and transferring it to him to whom he has granted that power. For he who even for a single day has the power to enact and repeal laws can change the entire form of the state. But one can, while retaining one's supreme right, delegate to others the task of dealing with the daily business of the state in accordance with the established laws. Moreover, if ministers of state were to be appointed by any other authority than this council, then the members of this council ought more rightly to be called minors than patricians.

[18] Some are wont to appoint a governor or leader over this council, either for life, as do the Venetians, or for a set period, as do the Genoese;[25] but they take such precautions as to make it clear that the state is much endangered by this practice.[26] And assuredly we cannot doubt that the state is thus brought close to monarchy. And as far as we can gather from history, the only reason for this practice is this, that before the establishment of these councils they had been subject to a governor or leader as if to a king. So while the appointment of a governor may meet the needs of a particular nation, this is not an essential requirement for aristocratic government considered simply as such.

[19] Nevertheless, since the sovereignty of this kind of state is vested in this council as a whole and not in each individual member (for otherwise it would be a gathering of an unorganised crowd); it is therefore necessary for the patricians to be so bound together by laws as to form, as it were, a single body directed by a single mind. But laws simply by themselves are weak and are easily broken when

---

[22] [In Venice a noble became a member of the Grand Council at the age of twenty-five.]

[23] [These were the functions also of the Grand Council of Venice, which conferred nobility only very sparingly.]

[24] [*potestatem.*]

[25] [In Venice the Doge received a lifetime appointment, whereas in Genoa it was only a two-year term.]

[26] [In Venice there were elaborate processes whose principal goal was that of making favoritism impossible.]

their guardians are the very persons who are in a position to transgress and the only persons who should take warning from the punishment of transgressors, and whose reason for punishing their colleagues is to curb their own desires through fear of the same punishment—which is quite absurd. So means must be sought to keep inviolate the orderly procedure of this supreme council and the laws of the state, yet ensuring the greatest possible equality among patricians.

[20] Now the appointment of a single governor or leader who also has the right to vote in council is bound to result in considerable inequality, especially in view of the power he must necessarily be granted so as to discharge his duty in comparative security. Therefore, taking everything into consideration, nothing can be devised more beneficial to the common welfare than to set up another council, subordinate to this supreme council, consisting of patricians whose sole duty would be to ensure that the laws of the state regarding assemblies and ministers of state are kept inviolate and who would accordingly have the power[27] to bring to judgment any minister of state guilty of transgressing the regulations pertaining to his office and to condemn him in accordance with established law. These we shall hereafter call syndics.[28]

[21] These syndics are to be appointed for life; for if they were appointed for a set period so as to be eligible later to fill other offices of state, we would fall into the absurdity which we have just indicated in Section 19 of this Chapter. But lest they should become too arrogant through a very long period of rule, none are to be elected to this office but those who are at least sixty years old and are ex-senators (see below).

[22] It will be easy for us to determine the number of these syndics, too, if we reflect that they stand to the patricians in the same relation as the entire body of patricians to the populace, which the patricians cannot govern if they fall below the right number. Therefore the number of syndics to patricians must be the same as that of patricians to the populace, that is, as 1 to 50 (Section 13 of this Chapter).

[23] Furthermore, to enable this council to discharge its duty in security, a part of the armed forces must be assigned to it, to which it may give whatever orders it pleases.[29]

[24] No salary is to be paid to syndics or to any minister of state, but they are to be assigned emoluments such that they cannot maladminister affairs of state without great loss to themselves. We cannot doubt that it is fair for the ministers of this state to be remunerated for their services, because the larger part of this state consists of the common people whose security is safeguarded by the patricians, while the commons themselves devote their time not to public affairs but

---

[27] [*potestatem.*]

[28] [The Areopagites of ancient Athens had supervisory and judicial powers similar to those which Spinoza will outline for the syndics, though he probably has in the mind the *Dieci* and *Avogadori di communi* of Venice, despite that these did not receive lifetime appointments. The syndics resemble the *Dieci* in possessing *dictatoria potestas*, but in other respects they resemble the *Avogadori*.]

[29] [The *Dieci* had a military guard.]

to their own private concerns. But on the other hand, since no one (as we said in Section 4, Chapter 7) upholds the cause of another except insofar as he believes his own interests to be served thereby, matters must be so arranged that ministers attending to public affairs serve their own interests best when they are most vigilant for the common good.

[25] Therefore the syndics, whose duty, as we have said, is to ensure that the laws of the state are kept inviolate, are to be assigned the following emoluments. Every householder who dwells anywhere within the state must pay to the syndics every year a coin of little value, say a quarter of an ounce of silver, so that the syndics may ascertain the number of inhabitants and may thus be informed what proportion of the number the patricians constitute. Next, every new patrician on his election must pay to the syndics a large sum, say twenty or twenty-five pounds of silver.[30] In addition, the fines imposed on absent patricians (those who have failed to attend a meeting of the council) must also be assigned to the syndics,[31] and when offending ministers have to submit to the syndics' jurisdiction and are fined a fixed sum or have their possessions confiscated, a portion of their goods must also be assigned to the syndics—not indeed to all of them, but only to those who are every day in session[32] and whose duty it is to summon the council of syndics, concerning which see Section 28 of this Chapter. To ensure that the council of syndics is always maintained at its proper number, when the supreme council is summoned at its customary time, priority must be given to an enquiry on this point. If this duty is neglected by the syndics, it should then be the task of the president of the senate (of whom we shall have occasion to speak presently) to bring this to the attention of the supreme council, to demand from the president of the syndics the reason for his silence, and to seek the opinion of the supreme council on this matter. If he too is silent, the question should be taken up by the president of the supreme court of justice, or if he too is silent, by any other patrician, who should demand a reason for their silence from the president of the syndics as well as from the presidents of the senate and of the court of law. To ensure in addition the strict observance of the law excluding younger men, there should be a requirement that all who have attained the age of thirty and are not excluded by express law from taking office should cause their names to be entered on a roll kept by the syndics, from whom they should receive at some set price a mark of honour conferred on them, this being permission to wear a particular ornament, granted only to them as a mark of distinction and prestige. And at the same time it should be laid down by law that no patrician may nominate for election anyone whose name is not entered on the general roll, under threat of a heavy penalty, and also that no one be permitted to refuse an office or duty that he has been elected to undertake.[33] Finally, to ensure the permanence of all the absolutely

---

[30] [The *Avogadori* of Venice had charge of the *Libro d'Oro*, the official rollbook of Venice's noble families.]

[31] [The *Avogadori* received a portion of the fines imposed on offenders.]

[32] [In Venice the three *Capi di Dieci* met daily at the ducal palace.]

[33] [In Venice refusal of such magistracies was punishable by fine.]

fundamental laws of the state, it must be ordained that if anyone in the supreme council calls into question any fundamental law such as that concerning the extension of command of any general or the reduction of the number of patricians and the like, he is guilty of treason, and not only must he be condemned to death with confiscation of his goods, but some sign of his punishment should be displayed in public as a permanent record of the event. But to give stability to the other general laws of the state, it is enough merely to ordain that no law can be repealed or new law enacted without the agreement first of the council of syndics and then of three-quarters or four-fifths of the supreme council.

[26] The right to summon the supreme council and to propose matters for its decision should rest with the syndics,[34] who should also be given first place in the council but without the right to vote. However, before they take their seats they must swear by the well-being of that supreme council and by the people's freedom that they will endeavour with the utmost zeal to preserve inviolate their traditional laws[35] and to act for the common good. Thereafter, through their secretary, they should disclose in due order the matters for discussion.

[27] To ensure that all patricians stand on equal terms[36] in making decisions and in electing ministers of state and that all business is speedily dispatched, the system observed by the Venetians deserves our full approval. To nominate ministers of state, they appoint some members of the council by lot,[37] and when these have nominated in due order the candidates for office, every patrician votes for or against the candidate by secret ballot, with the result that it is not known thereafter who voted one way or the other. Through this procedure not only do all patricians stand on equal terms in making decisions and business is speedily dispatched, but also each is absolutely free to cast his vote without incurring unpopularity, which is of first importance in councils.

[28] In the council of syndics, too, and in other councils the same procedure is to be followed; that is, voting must be by secret ballot. But the right to summon the council of syndics and to set its agenda ought to belong to their president, who should sit every day with ten or more other syndics to hear complaints and secret accusations[38] by the commons against ministers,[39] to take into custody the accused if circumstances so require, and to summon the council even before its appointed time if any one of them considers that there is danger in delay. This president and those who meet with him every day must be appointed by the supreme council and out of the number of syndics, not for life but for six months, and their term of

---

[34] [Meetings of the Grand Council of Venice were regularly summoned by the *Signoria* (the Doge, his six councillors, and the three *Capi Superiori*), but the *Avogadori* could summon extraordinary meetings of any council of the state.]

[35] [*jura patria.*]

[36] [*omnibus patriciis aequa sit potestas.*]

[37] [Thirty-six, divided into four groups of nine each.]

[38] [I read *accusatos* for *accusatores.* — S.S.]

[39] [In Venice anyone could denounce a citizen to the *Capi di Dieci* by placing a signed accusation in the mouth of the Lion of St. Mark.]

office is not to be renewed except after an interval of three or four years. And, as we have already said, confiscated goods and monetary fines, or some portion of these, are to be assigned to them. Other matters concerning the syndics we shall discuss in their proper place.

[29] The second council, to be subordinate to the supreme council, we shall call the senate.[40] Its duty should be to deal with public business, such as to promulgate the laws of the state, to organise the fortifications of cities in accordance with the laws, to give military commissions, to impose taxes on subjects and to arrange for the disbursement of the revenue, to reply to foreign envoys, and to decide where their own envoys are to be sent. But to appoint the envoys themselves should be the duty of the supreme council; for it is of the first importance to ensure that no patrician may be appointed to any office of state except by the supreme council, lest patricians themselves seek to curry favour with the senate. Next, all measures are to be referred to the supreme council if in any way they effect a change in the existing state of affairs, such as decisions on war and peace. Therefore the senate's decisions on war and peace, to be valid, must be confirmed by the authority of the supreme council. And for this reason I would hold that the imposition of new taxes is a question for the supreme council alone, not for the senate.[41]

[30] To determine the number of senators the following points should be taken into consideration. First, all patricians should have an equal hope of attaining senatorial rank; secondly, senators whose term of office has expired may nevertheless be eligible for reelection after no great interval, thus ensuring that the state may always be governed by men of skill and experience; and finally, among the senators there should be quite a number who have gained a reputation for wisdom and virtue. To secure all these objectives, no more effective means can be devised than this: It should be ordained by law that no one below the age of fifty may be admitted to senatorial rank and that four hundred—that is, about a twelfth part of the patricians—should be appointed for a year, and when this term has expired they should be eligible for reappointment after an interval of two years.[42] In this way there will always be about a quarter[43] of the patricians serving as senators, with only short intervals between their periods of service; and this number, together with the number of syndics, is unlikely to be much less than the number of patricians who have reached their fiftieth year. Thus for all patricians there will always be a good prospect of attaining the rank of senator or syndic, and yet these same patricians will always be holding senatorial rank with only brief intervals between, as we have said, and (by what was said in Section 2 of this Chapter) the senate will never lack men of outstanding wisdom and skill. And because this law cannot be broken without arousing the bitter jealousy of many patricians, no steps

---

[40] [Spinoza's senate seems to combine functions of the Council of the State of the Netherlands and the Venetian Senate.]

[41] [The Venetian Senate could only impose new taxes under authorization of the Grand Council.]

[42] [The term for Venetian senators was likewise one year, but they could be reappointed immediately.]

[43] [With Wernham, I read *quarta* for *duodecima*.—S.S.]

need to be taken to ensure its constant enforcement other than that every patrician who has reached the above-mentioned age should give proof thereof to the syndics. These will then enter his name on the roll of candidates for senatorial office and read it out in the supreme council, so that he may take a seat in the supreme council assigned to such persons, next to the seats of senators, along with others of the same status.

[31] The remuneration of senators must be of such a kind that they derive more advantage from peace than from war.[44] So they should be assigned a one or two percent duty on imports and exports; for we cannot doubt that they will then safeguard peace as vigorously as they can and will never seek to prolong a war. Nor should even senators, if some of them are merchants, be exempt from paying this duty; for such exemptions cannot be granted without great loss to commerce, as I think is generally realised. On the other hand, it should be ordained by law that no senator or ex-senator may fill any military post; and furthermore no one whose father or grandfather is a senator, or has held senatorial office within the previous two years, may be appointed commander in chief or colonel, officers who, as we said in Section 9 of this Chapter, are to be appointed only in time of war. We cannot doubt that those patricians who are not members of the senate will uphold these laws with all their might, with the result that senators will always have more to gain from peace than from war and will therefore never advocate war unless pressed to do so by the state's most urgent need. Now it may be objected to us that by this arrangement, i.e., the assigning of such considerable payments to syndics and senators, an aristocracy will be no less burdensome to subjects than any monarchy. But royal courts require greater expenditure, which does nothing, however, to safeguard peace, and peace cannot be purchased at too high a price; apart from which there are the following considerations. First, everything that in a monarchy is conferred on one man or a few men is here conferred on a great number. Next, kings and their ministers do not bear the burdens of the state in company with their subjects, whereas here the reverse is true; for the patricians, who are always chosen from the wealthier classes, make the greatest contribution to the commonwealth. Finally, the burdens of monarchy arise not so much from royal expenditure as from its secret policy. For however great may be the state burdens imposed on its citizens for the sake of safeguarding peace and freedom, yet they are borne and endured for the benefits of peace. What nation ever had to pay such heavy taxes as the Dutch? Yet[45] this nation, so far from being exhausted, has become so prosperous as to be the envy of all. So if the burdens of monarchy were imposed for the sake of peace, citizens would not find them oppressive. But, as I said, it is because of the secret policy of this kind of government that subjects sink beneath their burden; that is to say, it is because the worth of kings counts for more in war than in peace, and because those who wish to reign alone must do their

---

[44] [Members of the Netherlands Council of State were forbidden to engage in the provision of military stores, lest they should make profit from war.]

[45] [I read *Atqui* for *Atque*. — S.S.]

best to keep their subjects in a state of poverty.[46] I here omit other points noted some time ago by that wise Dutchman V. H.[47] because they are irrelevant to my purpose, which is merely to describe the optimum of each kind of state.

[32] Some of the syndics, appointed by the supreme council, are to sit on the senate but without the right to vote, to see whether the laws concerning that council are duly observed, and to take steps to summon the supreme council when any matter has to be referred from the senate to the supreme council. For the right to summon the supreme council and submit matters for its decision lies with the syndics, as we have already said. But before a vote is taken on matters like this, the president of the senate at that time will explain the state of affairs, giving the senate's view of the matter in question and the reasons for it. Thereafter the vote should be taken in the usual way.

[33] The entire senate should not meet every day, but, like all councils of considerable size, should assemble at certain fixed times.[48] However, since in the meantime state business has to be dealt with, a certain number of senators need to be chosen to act on behalf of the senate when it is not sitting. Their duties should be to summon the senate when there is need, to carry out its decisions on public business, to read letters addressed to the senate and the supreme council, and, finally, to discuss what matters are to be brought before the senate. But in order that all these things and the organisation of the council as a whole may be more easily grasped, I shall give a more detailed account of the entire matter.

[34] The senators, who, as we have said, must be appointed for a year, should be divided into four or six sections.[49] The first of these should preside over the senate for the first two or three months. When this time has expired, the second section should take the place of the first, and so on, each section taking first position in its turn at regular intervals, so that the section taking first position in the first period takes last position in the second period. Furthermore, for each section there should be appointed a president, together with a vice president to take his place when needed. That is to say, from each section two men are to be appointed, a president and a vice president, and the president of the first section should also preside over the senate during the first months, or in his absence his vice president should take his place, to be succeeded by the rest of the presidents in order as described above. Next, out of the first section a number should be chosen, by lot or vote, to deputise for the senate when it is not in session along with the president and the vice president, for such a period of time as their section holds first place in the senate. When this time has expired, a like number of men are again to be chosen, by lot or vote, from the second section to succeed the first section

---

[46] [Spinoza agrees with Hobbes (*De cive* X, 2) that such conduct is ultimately not in the ruler's interest; but, unlike Hobbes, he realizes that rulers often do not see where their interest lies.]

[47] [Most probably J. Van Hove (a.k.a. de la Court), whose *Consideratien can Staat ofte Polityke Weegschaal* (Amsterdam, 1661) was part of Spinoza's library.]

[48] [The Venetian Senate met twice weekly.]

[49] [Spinoza's explanation of the functions of these sections seems to rely upon the practices of the *prytaneis* of the ancient Athenian *boule*.]

together with their own president and vice president, to deputise for the senate; and so on with the rest. But it is not necessary that the election of these men—those who, as I said, should be chosen by lot or vote for periods of two or three months, and whom we shall hereafter call consuls—should be in the hands of the supreme council. For the reason we gave in Section 29 of this Chapter does not apply here, and much less so the reason stated in Section 17. It will therefore suffice if they are appointed by the senate and the syndics present at the meeting.

[35] As to their number, I cannot be quite precise, but they must certainly be sufficiently numerous as to make it difficult to corrupt them. For although they do not by themselves make any decisions on matters of state, yet they can defer the proceedings of the senate or, worst of all, lead the senate astray by bringing forward matters of no importance while holding back matters of greater importance; not to mention that if they were too few in number, the absence of one or two could bring public business to a halt. But since, on the other hand, these consuls are appointed for the very reason that large councils cannot attend every day to public business, a middle way must be sought, and the inadequacy of their number counterbalanced by the brevity of their term of office. Thus if only thirty or so are appointed for two or three months,[50] they will be too numerous to be corrupted in such a short period. And it is for this reason, too, I suggested that their successors should never be appointed until the very time when they take over the duties of their predecessors.

[36] Their duty, as we have said, is to summon the senate when any number of them, however few, think it necessary to put before it matters for its decision, to adjourn the senate, and to carry out its decisions on public business. How this is to be done in good order so as not to hold up business by useless discussions, I shall now briefly explain. The consuls should consider the matter to be put before the senate and the action that needs to be taken, and if they are all of one mind, they should summon the senate and, after duly explaining the point at issue, declare their own view and put it to the vote in the usual way without waiting for any other view. But if the consuls are divided in their opinions, the view taken by the majority must be put to the senate first, and if this is not approved by the majority of the senate and consuls and the total of doubtful and negative votes outnumber the affirmative—this being ascertained by secret ballot, as we have already mentioned—they should then bring forward the second opinion which had fewer votes from the consuls than the first opinion, and so on with the rest of the opinions. If none of these views is approved by a majority of the senate, there must be an adjournment to the next day or for a short period so that the consuls can meanwhile see whether they can find other measures which may give more satisfaction. If they can find no others, or if the majority of the senate does not approve those they have found, then the opinion of each senator is to be heard. If none of these, again, is supported by a majority of the senate, then each opinion is again to be put to the vote and a count be taken not only of affirmative votes, as

---

[50] [The Venetian *Collegio* consisted of twenty-six members, some holding office for a year, while the Doge was president for life.]

hitherto, but also of the doubtful and the negative votes. If the affirmative votes prove to be more numerous than either the doubtful or the negative votes, that opinion is to be regarded as carried, and on the contrary as lost if the negative votes prove more numerous than either the doubtful or the affirmative votes. But if in every case the doubtful votes are more numerous than the negative or affirmative votes, then the council of syndics should join with the senate, voting along with the senators, the votes being restricted to "for" and "against," ignoring votes that indicate indecision. In respect of matters referred by the senate to the supreme council, the same procedure should be followed. So much for the senate.

[37] As for the court of justice or tribunal, it cannot rest on the same foundations as the one under a monarchy, as described in Chapter 6, Sections 26 and following. For (Section 14 of this Chapter) it does not accord with the fundamental laws of this kind of state to take any account of families or clans. And there is this further consideration, that judges appointed solely by patricians might indeed be restrained by fear of their patrician successors from pronouncing an unjust verdict on one of their own class and perhaps might not even have the hardihood to punish him as he deserved; but, on the other hand, against the commons their audacity would know no bounds, and the rich would every day fall prey to their rapacity. I am aware that for this reason the policy of the Genoese, that of appointing judges not from patricians but from foreigners, is widely approved; but as a matter of principle it seems to me an absurd arrangement to call on foreigners rather than patricians to interpret the laws. For what are judges but interpreters of the laws? I am therefore convinced that here, too, the Genoese have had regard to their native character rather than to the real nature of this kind of state. So we, considering this question in principle, must devise means best suited to this form of government.

[38] With regard to the number of judges, however, a consideration of this kind of constitution does not demand any special figure; but, as in the case of monarchy, it is of prime importance to see that the judges are too numerous to be corrupted by a private person. For their duty is simply to ensure that no private person does wrong to another, and so to settle disputes between private persons, patricians as well as commoners, and to exact punishment from offenders, even from patricians, syndics, and senators insofar as these have offended against the laws by which all are bound. As for disputes which may arise between cities within the state, these are to be decided in the supreme council.

[39] Furthermore, the consideration that regulates the term of their appointment is the same in every state, as is also the requirement that a certain proportion should retire every year. Finally, although there is no need for each of them to come from a different clan, yet it is necessary that no two near kinsmen should sit on the bench together. This rule should apply to all other councils except for the supreme council, where it is enough if only it is provided by law that no one may nominate a kinsman at elections or vote in his case if he is nominated by another, and also that no two kinsmen may draw lots for any minister of state to be nominated.[51] This, I say, suffices in the case of a council composed of so large a

---

[51] [Similar regulations were enforced at elections in the Grand Council of Venice.]

number of men and for which no special emoluments are assigned. Thus no harm will accrue to the state from the above arrangements, so that it is absurd to pass a law excluding all kinsmen of patricians from the council, as we mentioned in Section 14 of this Chapter. Its absurdity is manifest, for the enactment of such a law by the patricians would be bound to entail an absolute surrender of their right by them all, and therefore the partisans of that same law would be not the patricians but the commons. This would be in flat contradiction with our conclusions in Sections 5 and 6 of this Chapter. But the constitutional law[52] requiring that a constant ratio be maintained between the number of patricians and people has for its main object to preserve the right and power of the patricians, ensuring that they are not too few to be capable of governing the people.

[40] However, judges are to be appointed by the supreme council from the patricians, that is (by Section 17 of this Chapter), from the lawmakers themselves. Their judgments in both civil and criminal cases shall be valid if pronounced in proper order and without partiality. On this subject the syndics shall be authorised by law to make enquiry, to judge, and to reach decisions.[53]

[41] The remuneration of judges should be the same as stated in Section 29, Chapter 6, namely, that for every judgment they make in civil cases they should receive from the losing party a certain proportion of the total sum involved. With regard to judgments made in criminal cases, the only difference here should be that goods confiscated and fines exacted for minor offences should be assigned to them alone. But there should be this condition, that they are never allowed to exact confession by torture. In this way they will be sufficiently deterred from treating the commons unfairly and from showing too much favour to patricians through fear. For avarice is quite enough to hold in check their fear, especially when avarice is cloaked under the specious title of justice. Furthermore, the judges are numerous and do not vote openly, but by secret ballot, so that if anyone is indignant at losing his case, he cannot put the blame on any one person. Again, respect for the syndics will restrain them from pronouncing an unjust, or at any rate an absurd, judgment and will prevent any single one of them from acting in bad faith; besides which, the judges being so numerous, there will always be one or two of whom the unscrupulous will stand in awe. Finally, as to the commons, they will also have a sufficient safeguard if they are allowed to appeal to the syndics,[54] who, as I have said, are authorised by law to make inquiry into judicial matters, to judge, and to make decisions. For no doubt the syndics will not be able to avoid the hatred of many of the patricians, whereas they will always be very popular with the commons, whose applause they will do all they can to win. To this end, when given the opportunity, they will never fail to reverse judgments which violate the rules of the court and to scrutinise the conduct of any judge, punishing those who are at fault; for nothing makes a greater impression on the people

---

[52] [*lex imperii*.]
[53] [Judges in Venice were appointed by the Grand Council.]
[54] [As the commoners' defenders, Spinoza's syndics resemble the *tribuni plebis* of ancient Rome, though the syndics' powers are greater.]

than this. Nor is it a drawback, but rather a great advantage, that such examples can rarely occur. For apart from the fact that a commonwealth must be ill-organised if it is continually making example of offenders (as we pointed out in Chapter 5, Section 2), it is of course the rarest events that achieve the widest publicity.

[42] Those who are sent as governors to cities or provinces should be of senatorial rank, because it is the duty of senators to exercise supervision over the fortification of cities, the treasury, the armed forces, etc. But those sent to govern regions at some distance would not be able to attend the senate. For this reason, only those appointed to cities on native soil should be chosen from the senate itself, while those to be sent to more distant places should be appointed from men of an age consistent with senatorial rank. Yet these measures, in my opinion, will not be enough to safeguard the peace of the entire state, that is, if neighbouring cities are altogether denied the right to vote, unless these are all so weak that they can be openly slighted—which is hardly likely. So it is necessary that the neighbouring cities be granted citizenship and that from each city twenty, thirty, or forty (the number would have to vary with the size of the city) chosen citizens be added to the roll of patricians. Of these, three, four, or five must be appointed every year to serve on the senate and one to serve as a syndic for life. And those who are senators are to be sent, together with the syndic, as governors of the city from which they were appointed.

[43] The judges to be appointed in each city should also be drawn from the patricians of the same city. But since these matters do not have reference to the fundamental laws of this state in particular, I do not think it necessary to discuss them at greater length.

[44] The secretaries and similar officials in any councils, since they do not have the right to vote, should be appointed from the commons. But since, through their long experience of handling affairs, these men are thoroughly conversant with the way business is transacted, it is often the case that more deference than is proper is shown to their advice and that the condition of the entire state depends largely on their guidance, which has been the ruin of the Dutch.[55] For this situation is bound to arouse much jealousy among many of the nobles. And we surely cannot doubt that a senate whose policy derives from the advice not of senators but of officials will be attended mostly by those who are lacking in energy, and the condition of such a state will be little better than that of a monarchy ruled by a few king's counsellors; for which see Chapter 6, Sections 5, 6, and 7. However, a state will be exposed to this evil to a greater or lesser degree according as it has been well- or ill-founded. For if the freedom of a state is not based on a sufficiently secure foundation, it is never defended without danger; and to avoid incurring this risk, patricians choose as ministers ambitious men from the commons who, when the situation later takes a different turn, are slaughtered like sacrificial animals to appease the wrath of those who are enemies to freedom.[56] But where free-

---

[55] [In 1672. Spinoza is thinking principally here of Oldenbarneveldt and de Witt.]
[56] [Oldenbarneveldt was executed by the stadtholder Maurice in 1619. De Witt was murdered by supporters of the Prince of Orange in the Hague in 1672.]

dom has a sufficiently secure foundation, patricians are eager to claim for themselves the glory of safeguarding it, and they are anxious to ensure that good policy in the conduct of affairs derives only from their advice. In laying the foundations of the state it is these two rules that we have particularly followed, namely, that the commons should be debarred both from giving advice and from voting (see Sections 3 and 4 of this Chapter); and so sovereignty should be vested in the whole body of patricians,[57] authority in the syndics and the senate, and the right to summon the senate, to bring forward, discuss, and deal with matters pertaining to the public welfare should lie with consuls appointed from the senate. And if it is also ordained that the secretary to the senate or to the other councils be appointed for four or five years at the most, with the addition of an assistant secretary appointed for the same period to lighten his load, or alternatively that there should be not one but several secretaries to the senate employed in different departments, it will never come about that the influence[58] of officials could be of any importance.

[45] Treasurers are likewise to be appointed from the commons, to be accountable not only to the senate but also to the syndics.

[46] With regard to religion, we have set forth our views at sufficient length in the *Tractatus theologico-politicus*. However, we omitted some points, the discussion of which was not there appropriate, to wit, that all patricians should be of the same religion, a very simple religion of a most universal nature as described in that treatise.[59] For it is of the first importance to guard against the patricians' being split into sects, showing favour some to this group, some to that, and furthermore against becoming victims to superstition, seeking to deprive their subjects of the freedom to say what they think. Secondly, although everyone should be granted freedom to say what he thinks,[60] large congregations should be forbidden, and so, while those who are attached to another religion are to be allowed to build as many churches as they wish, these are to be small, of some fixed dimensions, and some distance apart. But it is important that churches dedicated to the national religion should be large and costly, and that only patricians or senators should be permitted to administer its chief rites. Thus only patricians should be permitted to baptise, to solemnise marriages, to lay on hands; quite simply, they alone should be acknowledged as ministers of the churches and as guardians and interpreters of the national religion. But for preaching and for managing the church's finances and everyday business, some commoners should be appointed by the senate to act as the senate's deputies and therefore to be accountable to it for all their actions.

[47] Such are the measures that are relevant to the basic structure of this state,[61] to which I shall add a few others, less essential but still of considerable im-

---

[57] [I accept the bracketed Dutch.—S.S.]
[58] [*potentia*.]
[59] [See TTP14/517–519.]
[60] [Religious tolerance was a fundamental political belief in both Venice and the Netherlands.]
[61] [*imperii fundamenta*.]

portance. Patricians should appear in public distinguished by a particular style of clothing or dress and should be saluted by some special title, and all commoners should give way to them. If any patrician loses his possessions by some unavoidable misfortune and can prove this beyond any doubt, he should be reinstated in his former position from public funds. But if it is established that he has wasted his fortune through extravagance, luxurious living, gaming, debauchery, and so forth, or that he is hopelessly insolvent, he should lose his status and be regarded as unfit for any office or honour. For he who cannot manage himself and his private affairs will far less be capable of caring for the public interest.

[48] Those whom the law requires to take an oath will be much more concerned to avoid perjury if they are bidden to swear by the welfare and freedom of their native land and by its supreme council than if they are bidden to swear by God. For he who swears by God puts at stake a private good of which he alone knows the value,[62] but he who by his oath puts at stake the freedom and welfare of his country is swearing by the common good of all, the value of which is not set by him, and if he perjures himself, he thereby declares himself an enemy to his country.

[49] Academies founded at public expense are established not so much to encourage natural talents as to restrain them. But in a free commonwealth, arts and sciences will be best fostered if anyone who asks leave is allowed to teach publicly at his own expense and with his own reputation at risk.[63] But these and similar topics I reserve for another occasion, for my intention here has been to confine myself to matters relating only to aristocratic government.

Chapter 9
[Aristocracy: The Second Model]

[1] So far we have been considering an aristocracy that takes its name from just one city, the capital of the whole state. It is now time to deal with the kind where the sovereignty is held by several cities, a kind which I regard as preferable to the former.[1] To discover where lies the difference between them and the superiority of one to the other, we shall make a survey one-by-one of the fundamental laws of the former, rejecting those which are unsuited to the latter and replacing them with other laws to form the basis of the latter.

[2] Cities which enjoy the right of citizenship should be founded and fortified in such a way that whereas each of them cannot even subsist without the others, on the other hand one cannot secede from the others without causing consider-

---

[62] [For he may not believe in the God by whom he is required by law to swear: See Hobbes, *De cive* II, 21.]

[63] [See TTP20/569; see also the invitation to Spinoza to teach freely under the condition that he not "disturb the publicly established religion" and his reply, Ep47–48.]

[1] [Spinoza's primary model of this kind of aristocracy is the province of Holland.]

able damage to the whole state; for if such be the case they will always remain united. But cities that are so constituted that they can neither preserve themselves nor present a threat to the others are obviously not in control of their own right but completely subject to the others.

[3] The measures set out in Sections 9 and 10 of the previous Chapter result from a consideration of the general nature of aristocratic government, as is also the maintenance of a proportion between the number of patricians and the whole population, and the age and qualifications of candidates for the patriciate, so that on these points it can make no difference whether sovereignty is held by one city or by several. But with regard to the supreme council, another consideration must here arise. For if any city belonging to the state were chosen as a meeting-place for the supreme council, it would in fact be the capital of the state. So either there would have to be a system of rotation or else a place that does not possess the right of citizenship and that belongs equally to all must be chosen as this council's meeting-place.[2] But both these suggestions, easy as they are to state, are difficult in practice, with so many thousands of men having so frequently to quit their cities or to assemble in different places in turn.

[4] To enable us, taking account of the nature and constitution of this kind of state, to decide how to deal with this problem and how its councils should be organised, the following points should be considered. Each city has as much more right than a private person as it has more power than a private person (Section 4, Chapter 2), and consequently the right of each city of this state (see Section 2 of this Chapter) within its own walls or the bounds of its jurisdiction is to be measured by its power. Secondly, all the cities are bound together and united not as confederates but as constituting a single state with this reservation, that each city holds that much more right over government than others as it exceeds others in power; for to look for equality in unequals is to look for the absurd.[3] Citizens are indeed rightly regarded as equals, because the power of the individual compared with the power of the entire state is of no account. But the power of each city constitutes a great part of the power of the state, and the greater the city, the greater the power it contributes.[4] Therefore not all cities can be regarded as equals; just as the power of each, so the right of each should be assessed by its size. The ties by which they must be bound together so as to form a single state are primarily (Section 1, Chapter 4) the senate and the court of justice.[5] How they are to be

---

[2] [Prior to about 1593 the Estates of Holland met in different places at different times. In 1593 its meetings began to be held in the Hague, which prior to that year had lacked political rights.]

[3] [Each town represented in the Estates of Holland and each province represented in the States General had a single vote.]

[4] [This section and the next provide good examples of Spinoza's use of *potentia* and *potestas*. Throughout this section he uses the former, i.e., 'power' in the sense of the natural power or efficacy which a group has; and argues (in the next section) that its *potestas* (authority or constitutional power) should be proportionate to its natural power. Spinoza, however, is not always so consistent in his usage.]

[5] [Holland had only provincial courts and no supreme court.]

bound together by these ties in such a way that each of them still remains as far as possible in control of its own right, I shall now briefly explain.

[5] I assume that the patricians of each city, who (by Section 3 of this Chapter) are to vary in number in accordance with the size of the city, have the supreme right over their own city, and in that city's supreme council they have full power to fortify it, to enlarge its walls, to impose taxes, to enact and repeal laws, and, in general, to do everything they think necessary for the preservation and growth of their city.[6] But to deal with the common business of the state, a senate must be created on just the same lines as we described in the previous chapter, so that there will be no difference between this senate and the other except that this senate has, in addition, authority to decide any dispute arising between cities. For in a state which has no capital city this cannot be done by the supreme council, as was previously the case. See Section 38 of the previous Chapter.

[6] But in this state the supreme council[7] is not to be summoned unless the need arises to alter the form of the state itself, or in case of some difficulty to which the senators think themselves unequal; and so it will rarely happen that all the patricians are summoned to council. For, as we have said (Section 17, previous Chapter), the chief duty of the supreme council is to enact and and repeal laws, and secondly, to appoint ministers of state. Now the laws or general ordinances of the state are not to be altered as soon as they are instituted. However, if time and circumstances make it advisable to enact a new law or to change one already in force, the question can first be discussed in the senate. Once the senate has reached agreement, thereafter envoys should be sent by the senate to the cities to inform the patricians in each city of the senate's opinion, and if there is then a majority of cities in favour of the senate's opinion, it shall be valid, but otherwise void. This same procedure may be followed in appointing army commanders, in sending ambassadors abroad, and also in making decisions about waging war and accepting terms of peace. But in appointing the other ministers of state, since (as we have explained in Section 4 of this Chapter) each city should remain as far as possible in control of its own right and should hold as much more right in government as it exceeds other cities in power, it is necessary to observe the following procedure. Senators are to be chosen by the patricians of each city; that is, the patricians of any one city will appoint in their own council a certain number of senators from their citizen colleagues, a number that will be in the ratio of 1 to 12 to the number of patricians of that same city (see Section 30 of previous Chapter), and they will name those whom they wish to belong to each section, first, second, third and so on. In the same way the patricians of the other cities will appoint a number of senators varying in proportion to their own number and will distribute them between as many sections as we have said will constitute the senate (see Section 34, previous Chapter). As a result, in each section of the senate there will be a number of senators for every city proportionate to its size. But the presidents and

---

[6] [These powers were vested in the Council of State of the Netherlands beginning around 1588.]

[7] [Spinoza's supreme council closely resembles the full States General. The functions of the ordinary States General (which simply represented the full) are in turn performed by Spinoza's senate.]

vice presidents of the sections, being fewer in number than the cities, should be chosen by lot by the senate from those who have been appointed consuls. In appointing the supreme judges of the state, too, the same procedure should be followed, i.e., the patricians of each city should choose from their colleagues a number of judges in proportion to their own number. Thus it will come about that in appointing ministers every city will as far as possible be in control of its own right and that both in the senate and the court of law the right possessed by each city will be proportionate to its power; supposing, that is, that in deciding matters of state and in settling disputes the senate and the court of law follow the same procedure as we described in Sections 33 and 34 of the previous Chapter.

[7] Company commanders and colonels should also be appointed by the patricians.[8] For as it is fair that, for the common safety of the whole state, each city should be required to levy a a certain number of soldiers in proportion to its size, it is also fair that the patricians of each city, to match the number of regiments they are required to maintain, should be permitted to appoint as many colonels, commanders, ensigns, etc. as are needed to take charge of that part of the armed forces they provide for the state.

[8] No taxes are to be imposed by the senate on the subjects. To meet the expenditure required by decree of the senate for transacting public business, it is not the subjects but the cities that should be assessed by the senate, each city having to contribute a share of the expenditure proportionate to its size. This sum the patricians of the city will collect from their own townsfolk in whatever way they please, that is, either by direct assessment or, as is much fairer, by indirect taxation.

[9] Although the cities of this state are not all maritime and senators are not drawn exclusively from maritime cities, they can still be assigned the same remuneration that was laid down in Section 31 of the previous Chapter. For this purpose, means can be devised, in conformity with the state's constitution, whereby the cities may be more closely bound together. The other measures concerning the senate, the court of law, and, in general the entire state, indicated in the previous Chapter, are also to apply to this state. So we see that in a state where sovereignty is held by several cities it is not necessary to assign a fixed time or place for the meeting of the supreme council. However, for the senate and the court of law a place should be appointed in a country town or in a city that does not possess voting rights. But I return to matters that concern cities individually.

[10] The procedure to be followed by the supreme council of a single city in appointing city officials[9] and ministers of state and in making decisions should be the same as described in Sections 27 and 36 of the previous Chapter; for the considerations are the same in both cases. Next, there should be a council of syndics subordinate to the council, having the same relation to the city council as the council of syndics of the previous Chapter had to the council of the whole state. Its duties, within the bounds of the city's jurisdiction, should also be the same, and

---

[8] [I follow Wernham in preferring the *Nagelate Schriften* to the *Opera Posthuma*. — S.S. See Wernham (1958, 420).]

[9] [The *Nagelate Schriften* omits the words, *urbis et.*]

it should enjoy the same remuneration. But if the city, and consequently the number of patricians, is so small that it cannot have more than one or two syndics, these being insufficient to constitute a council, the supreme council of the city should assign judges to assist the syndics in their investigations as circumstances require, or else the issue must be referred to the supreme council of syndics. For every city should also send a number of their syndics to the place where the senate is in session, to see that the laws of the entire state are preserved inviolate and to sit on the senate without the right to vote.

[11] City consuls[10] are also to be appointed by the patricians of that city to form as it were the senate of that city. Their number I cannot determine, nor do I think it necessary, since matters of great weight concerning their city are dealt with by its supreme council, and those matters which concern the state as a whole, by the grand senate. However, if they are few in number, it will be necessary for them to vote openly in their council and not by secret ballot as in large councils. For in small councils where voting is in secret, he who is a little more cunning can easily detect the author of each vote and has many ways of outmanoeuvering members who are less sharp.

[12] In every city, too, judges are to be appointed by its supreme council; but their judgments should be subject to appeal to the supreme court of the state, except in a case of openly established guilt or a confessed debtor.[11] But these matters need not be pursued further.

[13] It remains, then, to discuss those cities that are not in control of their own right.[12] If these are situated on territory or land administered by the state and their inhabitants are of the same race and language, they ought to be regarded, just like villages, as parts of neighbouring cities, which means that each of them must be governed by some city or other that is in control of its own right. The reason for this is that patricians are not chosen by the supreme council of the state but by the supreme council of each city and will vary in number according to the number of inhabitants within the bounds of that city's jurisdiction (Section 5 of this Chapter). So it is necessary that the population of a city that is not in control of its own right should be included in the register of the population of another city that is in control of its own right, and should be under its guidance. But cities that have been captured by right of war and annexed to the state should be regarded as allied to the state, to be won over and bound by favour shown; or else colonies that would enjoy the right of citizenship should be sent there and the native population removed elsewhere; or else the city should be utterly destroyed.[13]

[14] These, then, are the measures which should form the basis of this kind of state. That it is better organised than the state which takes its name from one city only, I conclude from the following considerations. The patricians of each city, as

---

[10] [The city consuls are equivalent to the Burgomasters of Dutch towns.]
[11] [In Holland no appeal was permitted from town to provincial court in criminal cases.]
[12] [in control of their own right = *sui juris*. They are provided with specific constitutional rights because of their noninclusion in the larger cities.]
[13] [Machiavelli, *Prince* III and IV; *Discourses* II, 23.]

human ambition goes, will be anxious to maintain, and if possible extend, their right both in the city and the senate. They will therefore endeavour as best they can to win popularity with the people, governing by kindness rather than by fear and increasing their own numbers, since the more numerous they are, the more senators they will appoint from their own council (Section 6 of this Chapter) and consequently the more right they will have in the state (by the same section). Nor is it an objection to this view that, with each city intent on its own interests and jealous of the others, they will frequently be at odds with one another and waste time in disputes. For if "while the Romans debate, Saguntum is lost,"[14] on the other hand when all decisions are made by a few men who have only themselves to please, freedom and the common good are lost. The fact is that men's wits are too obtuse to get straight to the heart of every question, but by discussing, listening to others, and debating, their wits are sharpened, and by exploring every avenue they eventually discover what they are seeking, something that meets with general approval and that no one had previously thought of.[15] We have seen many examples of this in Holland.[16] Now if anyone retorts that the state of Holland has not long endured without a count or a deputy to take his place,[17] let him take this for a reply. The Dutch thought that to maintain their freedom it was enough for them to abandon their count and to cut off the head from the body of the state.[18] The thought of reorganising it in a different form has never entered their minds; they have left all its limbs as they had previously been, so that Holland has remained a county without a count, like a headless body, and the state without a name. So it is not surprising that most of its subjects have not known where its sovereignty lay. And even if this were not so, those who in fact held the sovereignty were far too few to be capable of governing the people and suppressing their powerful opponents.[19] As a result, the latter have often been able to plot against them with impunity and finally have succeeded in overthrowing them. Therefore the sudden[20] overthrow[21] of this same republic resulted not from waste of time in useless deliberations but from the defective constitution of that state and the fewness of its rulers.

[15] There is a further reason why this aristocracy, where the sovereignty is held by several cities, is to be preferred to the other. There is no need, as in the case of the first kind, to guard against the possibility of its entire supreme council's being overthrown by a sudden attack, because (by Section 9 of this Chapter) no time or

---

[14] [This proverb is based on Livy XXI, vii, 1.]
[15] [I accept the bracketed Dutch.—S.S.]
[16] [I read *Hollandia* for *Hollandice*.—S.S.]
[17] [This was the function of the stadtholders.]
[18] [Philip II of Spain.]
[19] [The Orangist party.]
[20] [I read *subita* for *subitâ*.—S.S.]
[21] [In 1672 with the murder of the de Witt brothers.]

place is appointed for its meetings. Moreover, powerful citizens are less to be feared in this type of state. For where freedom is enjoyed by a number of cities, it is not sufficient for someone's having designs on the sovereignty to seize just one city in order to hold dominion over the others. Finally, in this kind of state, freedom is shared by more of its members; for when one city has sole rule, regard is paid to the good of others only as far as it suits the ruling city.

CHAPTER 10
[Aristocracy: Its Organisation]

[1] Now that the fundamental laws of both kinds of aristocratic government have been explained in detail, it remains for us to enquire whether by reason of any discernible fault they are liable to disintegrate or change into a different form. The primary reason why states of this kind disintegrate is the one noted by that acute Florentine in his Book 3 on Livy, Discourse 1, where he says, "A state, like the human body, has every day something added to it which some time or another needs to be put right."[1] It is therefore necessary, he continues, that occasionally something should occur to bring the state back to the original principle on which it was first established. If this does not happen in due time, its defects will develop to such an extent that they cannot be removed without destroying the state itself. And this restoration, he tells us, can come about either by chance or through the wisdom and forethought of the laws or of a man of singular virtue. We cannot doubt that this is a matter of the greatest importance, and where no provision has been made against this danger, the state will not be able to endure by its own strength, but only by good fortune. On the other hand, where a proper remedy has been applied to counter this evil, the state cannot collapse through any defect of its own, but only through some mischance that could not have been avoided, as I shall go on to explain more clearly. The first remedy suggested to meet this evil was as follows: Every five years a dictator with supreme powers was appointed for one or two months, having the right to make enquiry, judge, and pronounce upon the conduct of senators and all ministers, and thus to restore the state to its original basis. But he who seeks to obviate the troubles to which a state is liable should apply remedies that are in conformity with the nature of the state and follow from its basic laws; otherwise in his efforts to avoid Charybdis he will fall upon Scylla. It is indeed true that all men, both rulers and ruled, have to be restrained by fear of punishment or loss, lest they be permitted to do wrong with impunity or with profit. But on the other hand it is also a fact that if this fear is shared by good and bad alike, the state will inevitably find itself in great peril. So since dic-

---

[1] [Machiavelli, *Discourses* III, 1.]

tatorial power[2] is absolute, it is bound to be a terror to all, especially if, as is here required, there is a fixed time for a dictator to be appointed. For then every ambitious man would canvass for this office, and it is certainly true that in time of peace, virtue is not so much regarded as wealth, so that the more arrogant the man, the more likely he is to gain office. Perhaps it is for this reason that the Romans used to appoint a dictator not at any fixed time but under pressure of some chance emergency.[3] Nevertheless, to quote Cicero's words, "The distended status of a dictator was displeasing to good citizens." And of course, since this dictatorial power is in essence regal, the state cannot occasionally turn into a monarchy, even for ever so short a time, without endangering its republican constitution. Furthermore, if no fixed time is assigned for the appointment of a dictator, no reckoning would be made of the time intervening between one dictator and another, though careful attention should be paid thereto, as we have said. Then again, the indefiniteness surrounding the whole business could easily result in its being overlooked. So unless this dictatorial power is permanent and firmly based, and thus of a kind that cannot be conferred on one man without destroying the form of the state, it will be very unsure, and consequently so will be the safety and preservation of the republic.

[2] But on the other hand we cannot possibly doubt (by Section 3, Chapter 6) that if it were feasible, while still preserving the form of the state, for the sword of the dictator to be permanent and fearsome only to the wicked, vices would never thrive to such a degree that they cannot be eradicated or corrected. So in order to secure all these conditions, we proposed the institution of a council of syndics subordinate to the supreme council with this in view, that the sword of the dictator should be permanently in the hands not of any natural person but of a civil body, whose members would be too many to make it possible to divide among themselves command of the state (Sections 1 and 2, Chapter 8) or to conspire together in any crime. In addition, they are debarred from undertaking any other offices of state, they are not the paymasters of the armed forces, and they are of such an age as to prefer present security to the dangers of innovation. Hence the state is in no danger from them, and consequently they cannot be a threat to the good but only to the wicked, and this in fact they will be. For as they are less in a position to commit crimes, so they are in a better position to suppress wickedness. For apart from the fact that they are well able to suppress its early manifestations[4] (since their council is a permanent institution), they are also sufficiently numerous to venture to accuse and condemn this or that powerful figure without fear of incurring unpopularity, especially since voting is by secret ballot and judgment is pronounced in the name of the whole council.

---

[2] [*Dictoria potestas* is the term Spinoza uses in this passage.]

[3] [The Roman dictator, appointed only in situations of emergency, held office for no more than six months. While Machiavelli (*Discourses* I, 34) held that this was highly beneficial to the state, Spinoza agrees with the contrary view of Cicero.]

[4] [*ita ad malitiam coercendam potentiores sunt*. The phrase comes from Ovid, *Remedia amoris*, 91.]

[3] Now at Rome the tribunes of the people were also in continuous office.[5] But they were not equal to the task of restraining the power of a Scipio; and furthermore, such measures as they thought salutary they were obliged to submit to the senate, who often frustrated their efforts by ensuring that the tribune from whom the senators had less to fear would be the one most in favour with the commons.[6] In addition, the authority of the tribunes as against the patricians depended on the support of the commons, and whenever the tribunes summoned a meeting of the commons they appeared to be raising a revolt rather than convoking a council. Troubles of this kind, naturally, have no place in the state we have described in the last two Chapters.

[4] However, the authority of the syndics can effect only this, that the form of the state is preserved, thus ensuring that the laws are not broken and that no one is permitted to profit from transgression. But it will certainly not be able to prevent the proliferation of vices that cannot be forbidden by law, such as those to which men are prone when they have too much leisure and which not infrequently lead to the collapse of the state.[7] For in time of peace men rid themselves of their fear, and from being fierce and savage they gradually become civilised or cultured, and from being cultured they become soft and sluggish, seeking to outdo one another not in virtue but in arrogance and extravagance. Hence they begin to despise the ways of their ancestors and to adopt foreign ways; that is, they begin to be slaves.[8]

[5] To prevent these evils, many attempts have been made to establish sumptuary laws, but in vain.[9] For all laws that can be broken without injury to another become a laughingstock, and far from restraining the desires and lusts of men, they even stimulate them, because "we are ever eager for what is forbidden and desire what is denied."[10] Nor do idle men lack cleverness to evade laws enacted to deal with things that cannot be absolutely forbidden, such things as banquets, gaming, personal adornment, and so forth, which are bad only when excessive and should be be judged in relation to the individual's fortune, and thus cannot be the subject of a general law.

[6] I therefore conclude that those vices that are prevalent in time of peace, and which we are now discussing, should never be directly prevented but only by indirect means, that is, by laying such a foundation to the state that most men — I won't say will be eager to live wisely, for that is impossible — will be guided by such feelings as will conduce to the greater good of the commonwealth. So our

---

[5] [See Machiavelli, *Discourses* I, 3. The *tribuni plebis* were appointed to protect the plebeians against the patricians.]

[6] [Machiavelli, *Discourses* III, 11.]

[7] [On sumptuary laws, see the following section.]

[8] [Machiavelli, *Discourses* I, 6.]

[9] [Sumptuary regulations had recently been introduced in Amsterdam. The modern equivalent would be laws to prevent victimless crime.]

[10] [Ovid, *Amores* III, iv, 17.]

chief objective should be this, that the wealthy, if they cannot be thrifty, should at any rate be eager for gain. For there is no doubt that if this love of gain, which is universal and constant, is nourished by desire for glory, most men will direct their main efforts to increasing their wealth by means that are not discreditable, so as to gain office and avoid utter disgrace.

[7][11] Now if we examine the fundamental laws of both kinds of aristocracy as I have explained them in the last two chapters, we shall see that this very result follows from them. For in both of them the number of rulers is so large that most of the wealthy have access to the governing body and to office of state. And if it is furthermore ordained that patricians who become insolvent should be degraded from patrician rank, and those who have lost their possessions through misfortune should be restored to their former status (as I suggested in Section 47, Chapter 8), no doubt all will do their best to preserve their property. Moreover, they will never covet foreign style of dress nor disdain their native style if it is ordained by law that patricians and candidates for office are to be distinguished by a particular form of dress. For this, see Sections 25 and 47 of Chapter 8. And in each state additional measures can be devised that conform with the nature of its territory and the character of the people, always having as their main concern that subjects should do their duty willingly rather than under constraint of the law.

[8] For a state that looks only to govern men by fear will be one free from vice rather than endowed with virtue. Men should be governed in such a way that they do not think of themselves as being governed but as living as they please and by their own free will, so that their only restraint is love of freedom, desire to increase their property, and hope of attaining offices of state. As for statues, triumphal processions, and other incentives to virtue, these are symbols of servitude rather than of freedom;[12] for it is slaves, not free men, who are assigned rewards for virtue. I do indeed admit that men are spurred on by such inducements, but whereas at first they were awarded to men of greatness, with the passage of time and the growth of jealousy they are granted to men of no account, exalted by their enormous wealth, to the great indignation of all good men. Then again, those who boast of their ancestors' triumphs and statues think they suffer injustice if they are not granted precedence over others. Finally, to omit other considerations, this much is certain, that equality, the abandonment of which must entail the loss of general freedom, cannot possibly be preserved if extraordinary honours are conferred by public decree on some man who is renowned for his virtue.

[9] With these proposals in mind, let us now see whether states of this kind can be destroyed by some cause that might have been avoided. Now if any state can be everlasting, it must be one whose constitution, being once correctly established, remains inviolate. For the constitution is the soul of the state; if this is preserved, the state is preserved. But a constitution cannot stay intact unless it is

---

[11] [The *Opera Posthuma* skips from Section 6 to Section 8 without a break for Section 7. It is included as a separate section in the *Nagelate Schriften*.]

[12] [Machiavelli (*Discourses* III, 28) approved of these positive reinforcers.]

upheld both by reason and by the common sentiment of the people; otherwise, if for instance laws are dependent solely on the support of reason, they are likely to be weak and easily overthrown.[13] So since we have shown that the fundamental laws of both kinds of aristocracy are in conformity with reason and with the common sentiments of men, we can therefore affirm that, if any states can be everlasting, these will necessarily be so; that is to say, they cannot be destroyed by any avoidable cause, but only by some unavoidable fatality.

[10] But an objection can still be raised as follows, that although the constitutions set forth above may have the support of reason and the common sentiment of men, there are times when they can nevertheless be overthrown, for there is no emotion that is not sometimes overpowered by a stronger contrary emotion. We often see the fear of death, for instance, overpowered by greed for another's property. Those who flee from the enemy in terror cannot be restrained by fear of some other danger; they hurl themselves into rivers or rush into flames to escape the enemy's sword. So however well a commonwealth is organised and however good its constitution,[14] yet when the state is in the grip of some crisis and everyone, as commonly happens, is seized with a kind of panic, they all pursue a course prompted only by their immediate fears with no regard for the future or the laws; all turn to the man who is renowned for his victories, they set him free from the laws,[15] they extend his command—a very bad precedent—and entrust the entire commonwealth to his good faith. This was indeed the cause of the fall of the Roman state.[16] But in reply to this objection I say, first, that in a properly organised commonwealth such a panic does not occur without good reason; and so this panic and the resulting confusion cannot be assigned to any cause that could have been avoided by human foresight. Next, it should be noted that in a commonwealth such as I have described above, it is impossible (Sections 9 and 25, Chapter 8) for any single man to attain such a high reputation as to become the centre of all eyes; he is bound to have several rivals who have strong support. So although widespread panic leads to some confusion in the commonwealth, no one will be able to evade the laws and appoint someone illegally to a military command without at once evoking the opposition of other[17] candidates. To settle such a dispute it will finally be found necessary to have recourse to the constitution that was once ordained and approved by all and to order the affairs of state in accordance with existing laws. I can therefore affirm absolutely that, while it is true that the state whose government is in the hands of one city only will be lasting, this is particularly true of the state whose government is in the hands of a number of

---

[13] [See TP7/2.]

[14] [constitution = *instituta jura* hereafter.]

[15] [Spinoza is probably thinking of the panic of 1672, during which William III was appointed stadtholder despite the Perpetual Edict of 1667.]

[16] [Machiavelli (*Discourses* III, 24) argues that the prolongation of military law caused Rome's loss of liberty.]

[17] [I read *aliorum* for *alios*. —S.S.]

cities; that is, it cannot disintegrate or be changed into any other form by any internal cause.

Chapter 11
[Democracy: Its Nature (unfinished)]

[1] I pass on at length to the third kind of state, the completely absolute state which we call democracy. The difference between this state and the aristocratic state consists mainly in this, that in an aristocracy it depends solely on the will and the free choice of the supreme council that any particular person be made a patrician. Thus no one has a hereditary right to vote and to undertake[1] offices of state, and no one can demand that right for himself by law, as is the case with the state now under discussion. For in this state all who are born of citizen parents, or on native soil, or have done service to the commonwealth,[2] or are qualified on any other grounds on which the right of citizenship is granted by law, all, I say, can lawfully demand for themselves the right to vote in the supreme council and to undertake offices of state; nor can they be refused except for crime or dishonour.

[2] So if it is ordained by law that the right to vote in the supreme council and to manage affairs of state should be restricted to older men who have reached a certain age, or to eldest sons as soon as they are of age, or to those who contribute a certain sum of money to the commonwealth, then although this could result in the supreme council's being composed of fewer citizens than that of the aristocracy which we have already discussed, yet states of this kind are still to be called democracies, because those of their citizens who are appointed to govern the commonwealth are appointed thereto not by the supreme council as being the best men, but by law. Now states of this kind, where it is not the best men who are appointed to govern but those who happen to be wealthy or to be eldest sons, may in this way appear as inferior to aristocracies. Yet if we reflect on what happens in practice, or on human nature in general,[3] the result will be the same in both cases, for patricians will always think those are the best men who are wealthy, or near akin to themselves, or close friends. It is true that, if patricians were of such a nature that in choosing their colleagues they could free them-

---

[1] [I read *subeundi* for *subeunda*. —S.S.]

[2] [In this chapter Spinoza follows the convention of his time in referring throughout to the commonwealth as *respublica*, since the seventeenth-century defenders of democracy were known as "republicans."]

[3] [*communem hominum conditionem*. Spinoza uses this phrase and *humana natura* coextensively in the *Ethica*, but there he has taken pains (E2P40Schol1) to explain that "human nature" does not refer to a unique "essence" (in the sense of the mediaeval realists), but rather to a general set of individual properties.]

selves from all bias and be guided only by zeal for the public good, there would be no state to compare with aristocracy. But experience has abundantly taught us that the very opposite is the case, especially with oligarchies where the will of the patricians, in the absence of rivals, is quite unrestrained by law. For in that situation the patricians take care to debar the best men from the council and to seek as colleagues men who are subservient to them, with the result that conditions in such states are far worse because election to the patriciate depends on the absolute free choice, unrestricted by any law, of a few men. But I return to my theme.

[3] From what has been said in the last Section it is evident that we can conceive different kinds of democracy. However, my purpose is not to discuss every one, but only that kind wherein all without exception who owe allegiance only to their country's laws and are in other respects in control of their own right and lead respectable lives have the right to vote in the supreme council and undertake offices of state. I say expressly, "who owe allegiance only to their country's laws" so as to exclude foreigners, who are deemed to be subject to another government. In addition to owing allegiance to the laws of the state, I added, "and are in other matters in control of their own right" so as to exclude women and servants who are under the control[4] of their husbands and masters, and also children and wards as long as they are under the control of parents and guardians. Lastly, I said, "who lead respectable lives" so as to exclude especially those who are in bad repute for their crimes or for a dishonourable way of life.

[4] Perhaps someone will ask whether it is by nature or by convention that women are subject to the authority of men.[5] For if this has come about simply by convention, there is no reason compelling us to exclude women from government. But if we look simply to experience, we shall see that this situation arises from their weakness. For nowhere is there an instance of men and women's ruling together; wherever in the world men and women are to be found, we find men ruling and women's being ruled and both sexes thus living in harmony. Against this, it is said of the Amazons who once held rule that they did not suffer men to stay in their native land, rearing females only and killing the males whom they had borne. Now if women were naturally the equal of men and were equally endowed with strength of mind and ability—qualities wherein human power and consequently human right consists—then surely so many and such a wide variety of nations would have yielded some instances where both sexes ruled on equal terms and other instances where men were ruled by women, being so brought up as to be inferior in ability. But as such instances are nowhere to be found, one is fully entitled to assert that women do not naturally possess equal right with men and that they necessarily give way to men. Thus it is not possible for both sexes to have equal rule, and far less so that men should be ruled by women. And if, fur-

---

[4] [Spinoza uses the Latin phrases *in potestate* and *sub potestate* for "under the control" here and in what follows.]

[5] [*sub potestate virorum*. Lipsius, *Monita et exempla politica*, II, ii.]

thermore, we consider human emotions, that men generally love women from mere lust, assessing their ability and their wisdom by their beauty and also resenting any favours which the women they love show to others and so on, soon we shall see that rule by men and women on equal terms is bound to involve much damage to peace. But I have said enough.

[The rest is lacking.]

The Letters

Correspondence to and from an author can be an invaluable aid to the reconstruction of his life and the understanding of his thought. So it is with Spinoza's letters. Although the political and ecclesiastical persecution of the time led the original editors of the Opera Posthuma—*his friends Lodewijk Meyer, Georg Hermann Schuller, and Johannes Bouwmeester—to delete personal matters and to disregard letters of a personal nature, the letters we have do help to understand Spinoza's biography. And many include important questions about issues of philosophical, theological, and scientific interest and Spinoza's responses to those questions. Without the correspondence, the depths of Spinoza's life and thought would be much more obscure indeed.*

The correspondence spans the years from 1661 to 1676 and includes letters to and from a variety of correspondents. The Opera Posthuma (O.P.) contained seventy-four letters in the Latin edition of 1677. The collected works published by J. Van Vloten and J. P. N. Land in 1882 added ten letters and ordered them chronologically; their numbering has become standard. The Gebhardt edition of 1925 added two letters, 30a and 67a, thus bringing the currently accepted total to eighty-six letters.

The period 1661–1665 includes an important correspondence between Spinoza and Henry Oldenburg, who became secretary of the Royal Society in London in 1662. Among the letters is Spinoza's lengthy discussion of Robert Boyle's treatise on nitre, which Oldenburg had sent to Spinoza (Ep6), and Spinoza's critique of the experimentalism that underlay Boyle's mechanical philosophy. Other letters deal with God, attributes, and additional metaphysical matters, as well as questions about knowledge. In 1665 Spinoza outlines to Oldenburg his reasons for writing a treatise on Scripture and what Oldenburg calls his views on "angels, prophecy and miracles." Later that fall, on 20 November 1665, Spinoza writes to Oldenburg about parts and wholes and, using the metaphor of a tiny worm living in the blood, he clarifies how and why he holds that both the human body and the human mind are parts of Nature. After a hiatus of about ten years, the correspondence with Oldenburg is revived in 1675 and 1676 and includes a heated discussion of the Theological-Political Treatise, *Spinoza's views expressed in it and in his* Ethics, *and the implications for moral and religious life.*

Oldenburg was a friend, though not as personal or close a one as men like Simon de Vries, Lodewijk Meyer, Pieter Balling, Johan Bouwmeester, and Jarig

Jelles. There are letters to and from these more intimate friends as well, dealing with a range of topics. Among them is the famous and important letter "on the infinite" (Ep12), written to Meyer on 20 April 1663. In later years Spinoza came to know Ehrenfried Walther von Tschirnhaus, a German aristocrat studying in Leiden and a person familiar with philosophers and scientists throughout Europe. Their correspondence of nine letters, between 1674 and 1676, discussed, among other topics, the important issue of free will and causal determinism, an issue also treated in the correspondence with Georg Hermann Schuller, the Amsterdam physician who may have introduced Spinoza to Tschirnhaus.

The letters not only cover a wide range of issues and engage a variety of correspondents, from close friends to acquaintances; they also differ in tone and detail. Often Spinoza is asked to clarify or defend himself. In his letters to John Hudde, an Amsterdam friend interested in optics and an elected political official, he discusses the proofs for God's necessary existence (Ep34–5). The correspondence with J. Louis Fabritius, professor of theology and philosophy at Heidelberg, concerns the offer to Spinoza to teach at that university and his refusal in 1673 (Ep47–8). These letters are respectful and businesslike. Different in tone are the letters from Alfred Burgh and Nicholas Steno, old friends, who wrote to Spinoza in 1675, seeking to convert him to Roman Catholicism, as they themselves had been converted. There is an aggressiveness and edge to these exchanges not present in the more collegial letters among other friends, a tension characteristic too of the earlier correspondence of 1664–1665 with the grain merchant Willem van Blyenbergh, about God, anthropomorphism, and human freedom (Ep18–24).

The technicality and abstractness of Spinoza's philosophical work have a crystalline power that keeps his personality at a distance. The letters give us access to Spinoza as a man and the concrete reality of his life and work. The Letters confirms what shows through his work only at moments—his personal character and his humanity.

M.L.M.

CONTENTS

[Dates in brackets are conjectural]

1. Oldenburg to Spinoza 16/26 August 1661
2. Spinoza to Oldenburg [September 1661]
3. Oldenburg to Spinoza 27 September 1661
4. Spinoza to Oldenburg [October 1661]
5. Oldenburg to Spinoza 11/21 October 1661
6. Spinoza to Oldenburg [Early 1662]
7. Oldenburg to Spinoza [July 1662]
8. de Vries to Spinoza 24 February 1663
9. Spinoza to de Vries [February 1663]
10. Spinoza to de Vries [March 1663]
11. Oldenburg to Spinoza 3 April 1663
12. Spinoza to Meyer 20 April 1663
12A. Spinoza to Meyer 26 July 1663
13. Spinoza to Oldenburg 17/27 July 1663
14. Oldenburg to Spinoza 31 July 1663
15. Spinoza to Meyer 3 August 1663
16. Oldenburg to Spinoza 4 August 1663
17. Spinoza to Balling 20 July 1664
18. Blyenbergh to Spinoza 12 December 1664
19. Spinoza to Blyenbergh 5 January 1665
20. Blyenbergh to Spinoza 16 January 1665
21. Spinoza to Blyenbergh 28 January 1665
22. Blyenbergh to Spinoza 19 February 1665
23. Spinoza to Blyenbergh 13 March 1665
24. Blyenbergh to Spinoza 27 March [1665]
25. Oldenburg to Spinoza 28 April 1665
26. Spinoza to Oldenburg May 1665
27. Spinoza to Blyenbergh 3 June 1665
28. Spinoza to Bouwmeester June 1665
29. Oldenburg to Spinoza [September 1665]
30. Spinoza to Oldenburg [Autumn 1665]
30A. Spinoza to Oldenburg 7 October 1665
31. Oldenburg to Spinoza 12 October 1665

32. Spinoza to Oldenburg 20 November 1665
33. Oldenburg to Spinoza 8 December 1665
34. Spinoza to Hudde 7 January 1666
35. Spinoza to Hudde 10 April 1666
36. Spinoza to Hudde [June 1666]
37. Spinoza to Bouwmeester 10 June 1666
38. Spinoza to Van der Meer 1 October 1666
39. Spinoza to Jelles 3 March 1667
40. Spinoza to Jelles 25 March 1667
41. Spinoza to Jelles 5 September 1669
42. Velthuysen to Ostens 24 January 1671
43. Spinoza to Ostens [February 1671]
44. Spinoza to Jelles 17 February 1671
45. Leibniz to Spinoza 5 October 1671
46. Spinoza to Leibniz 9 November 1671
47. Fabritius to Spinoza 16 February 1673
48. Spinoza to Fabritius 30 March 1673
48A. Jelles to Spinoza [April 1673]
48B. Spinoza to Jelles [19 April 1673]
49. Spinoza to Graevius 14 December 1673
50. Spinoza to Jelles 2 June 1674
51. Boxel to Spinoza 14 September 1674
52. Spinoza to Boxel [September 1674]
53. Boxel to Spinoza 21 September 1674
54. Spinoza to Boxel [September 1674]
55. Boxel to Spinoza [September 1674]
56. Spinoza to Boxel [September 1674]
57. Tschirnhaus to Spinoza 8 October 1674
58. Spinoza to Schuller [October 1674]
59. Tschirnhaus to Spinoza 5 January 1675
60. Spinoza to Tschirnhaus [January 1675]
61. Oldenburg to Spinoza 8 June 1675
62. Oldenburg to Spinoza 22 July 1675
63. Schuller to Spinoza 25 July 1675
64. Spinoza to Schuller 29 July 1675
65. Tschirnhaus to Spinoza 12 August 1675
66. Spinoza to Tschirnhaus 18 August 1675
67. Burgh to Spinoza 3 September 1675

67A. Steno to Spinoza [September 1675]
68. Spinoza to Oldenburg [September 1675]
69. Spinoza to Velthuysen [Autumn 1675]
70. Schuller to Spinoza [14 November 1675]
71. Oldenburg to Spinoza 15 November 1675
72. Spinoza to Schuller 18 November 1675
73. Spinoza to Oldenburg [November or December 1675]
74. Oldenburg to Spinoza 16 December 1675
75. Spinoza to Oldenburg [December 1675]
76. Spinoza to Burgh [December 1675]
77. Oldenburg to Spinoza 14 January 1676
78. Spinoza to Oldenburg 7 February 1676
79. Oldenburg to Spinoza 11 February 1676
80. Tschirnhaus to Spinoza 2 May 1676
81. Spinoza to Tschirnhaus 5 May 1676
82. Tschirnhaus to Spinoza 23 June 1676
83. Spinoza to Tschirnhaus 15 July 1676
84. Spinoza to a friend [1676]

THE LETTERS
OF CERTAIN LEARNED MEN
TO B.D.S.
AND THE AUTHOR'S REPLIES
CONTRIBUTING NOT A LITTLE TO THE
ELUCIDATION OF HIS OTHER WORKS

LETTER 1
To the most esteemed B.d.S., from Henry Oldenburg

[Known only from the O.P. The original is lost.]

Most illustrious Sir, esteemed friend,

With such reluctance did I recently tear myself away from your side when visiting you at your retreat in Rijnsburg, that no sooner am I back in England than I am endeavouring to join you again, as far as possible, at least by exchange of letters. Substantial learning, combined with humanity and courtesy—all of which nature and diligence have so amply bestowed on you—hold such an allurement as to gain the affection of any men of quality and of liberal education. Come then, most excellent Sir, let us join hands in unfeigned friendship, and let us assiduously cultivate that friendship with devotion and service of every kind. Whatever my poor resources can furnish, consider as yours. As to the gifts of mind that you possess, let me claim a share in them, as this cannot impoverish you.

At Rijnsburg we conversed about God, about infinite Extension and Thought, about the difference and agreement of these attributes, and about the nature of the union of the human soul with the body; and also about the principles of the Cartesian and Baconian philosophy. But since we then spoke about such important topics as through a lattice-window and only in a cursory way, and in the meantime all these things continue to torment me, let me now, by the right of the friendship entered upon between us, engage in a discussion with you and cordially beg you to set forth at somewhat greater length your views on the above-mentioned subjects. In particular, please be good enough to enlighten me on these two points: first, wherein you place the true distinction between Extension

---

Notes by Steven Barbone and Lee Rice (main annotators for this work), translator Samuel Shirley, and Michael L. Morgan appear in brackets. Unbracketed notes are Spinoza's.

and Thought, and second, what defects you find in the philosophy of Descartes and Bacon, and how you consider that these can be removed and replaced by sounder views. The more frankly you write to me on these and similar subjects, the more closely you will bind me to you and place me under a strong obligation to make an equal return, if only I can.

Here there are already in the press *Certain Physiological Essays*,[1] written by an English nobleman, a man of extraordinary learning. These treat of the nature of air and its elastic property, as proved by forty-three experiments; and also of fluidity and firmness and the like. As soon as they are printed, I shall see to it that they are delivered to you through a friend who happens to be crossing the sea. Meanwhile, farewell, and remember your friend, who is,

Yours in all affection and devotion,
Henry Oldenburg

London, 16/26 August 1661

LETTER 2
To the most noble and learned H. Oldenburg, from B.d.S.

[Known only from the O.P. The original is lost. No date is given, but a conjectural date is September 1661.]

Esteemed Sir,

You yourself will be able to judge what pleasure your friendship affords me, if only your modesty will allow you to consider the estimable qualities with which you are richly endowed. And although, with these qualities in mind, I feel myself not a little presumptuous in venturing upon this relationship, especially when I reflect that between friends all things, and particularly things of the spirit, should be shared, nevertheless this step is to be accredited not so much to me as to your courtesy, and also your kindness. From your great courtesy you have been pleased to belittle yourself, and from your abundant kindness so to enlarge me, that I do not hesitate to enter upon the friendship which you firmly extend to me and deign to ask of me in return, a friendship which it shall be my earnest endeavour diligently to foster.

As for my mental endowments, such as they are, I would most willingly have you make claim on them even if I knew that this would be greatly to my detri-

---

[1] [Robert Boyle's essays were published in 1661, with a Latin version published in London (1665) and Amsterdam (1667). The term 'physiological' is the same in sense as 'physical'—that which concerns nature. See *The Works of the Honourable Robert Boyle* (London, 1772, Vol. I, p. 359), *A physicochymical Essay, with some Considerations touching the differing parts and redintegration of Salt-Petre*. Sections 3–11 (pp. 377seq) deal with the experiments: *The history of fluidity and firmness*.]

ment. But lest I seem in this way to want to refuse you what you ask by right of friendship, I shall attempt to explain my views on the subjects we spoke of—although I do not think that this will be the means of binding you more closely to me unless I have your kind indulgence.

I shall begin therefore with a brief discussion of God, whom I define as a Being consisting of infinite attributes, each of which is infinite or supremely perfect in its own kind.[2] Here it should be observed that by attribute I mean every thing that is conceived in itself and through itself, so that its conception does not involve the conception of any other thing. For example, extension is conceived through itself and in itself, but not so motion; for the latter is conceived in something else, and its conception involves extension.[3]

That this is a true definition of God is evident from the fact that by God we understand a supremely perfect and absolutely infinite Being. The existence of such a Being is easily proved from this definition; but as this is not the place for such a proof,[4] I shall pass it over. The points I need to prove here in order to satisfy your first enquiry, esteemed Sir, are as follows: first, that in Nature there cannot exist two substances without their differing entirely in essence; secondly, that a substance cannot be produced, but that it is of its essence to exist; third, every substance must be infinite, or supremely perfect in its kind.[5]

With these points established, esteemed Sir, provided that at the same time you attend to the definition of God, you will readily perceive the direction of my thoughts, so that I need not be more explicit on this subject. However, in order to provide a clear and concise proof, I can think of no better expedient than to arrange them in geometrical style and to submit them to the bar of your judgment. I therefore enclose them separately herewith[6] and await your verdict on them.

Secondly, you ask me what errors I see in the philosophy of Descartes and Bacon. In this request, too, I shall try to oblige you, although it is not my custom to expose the errors of others. The first and most important error is this, that they have gone far astray from knowledge of the first cause and origin of all things. Secondly, they have failed to understand the true nature of the human mind. Thirdly, they have never grasped the true cause of error. Only those who are completely destitute of all learning and scholarship can fail to see the critical importance of true knowledge of these three points.

That they have gone far astray from true knowledge of the first cause and of the human mind can readily be gathered from the truth of the three propositions to which I have already referred; so I confine myself to point out the third error. Of Bacon I shall say little; he speaks very confusedly on this subject, and simply makes assertions while proving hardly anything. In the first place he takes for granted that the human intellect, besides the fallibility of the senses, is by its very

---

[2] [See E1Def6.]

[3] [These definitions are essentially the same as given in the *Ethics*: see E1Def3 and E1Def4.]

[4] [Spinoza in fact gives three proofs in E1P11.]

[5] [See E1P5, E1P6, E1P8.]

[6] [See *Ethics* Part 1, from the beginning to Prop. 4. (Footnote in the O.P.)]

nature liable to error, and fashions everything after the analogy of its own nature, and not after the analogy of the universe, so that it is like a mirror presenting an irregular surface to the rays it receives, mingling its own nature with the nature of reality, and so forth.[7] Secondly, he holds that the human intellect, by reason of its peculiar nature, is prone to abstractions,[8] and imagines as stable things that are in flux, and so on. Thirdly, he holds that the human intellect is in constant activity, and cannot come to a halt or rest.[9] Whatever other causes he assigns can all be readily reduced to the one Cartesian principle, that the human will is free and more extensive than the intellect, or, as Verulam more confusedly puts it, the intellect is not characterised as a dry light, but receives infusion from the will.[10] (We should here observe that Verulam often takes intellect for mind, therein differing from Descartes.) This cause, then, disregarding the others as being of little importance, I shall show to be false. Indeed, they would easily have seen this for themselves, had they but given consideration to the fact that the will differs from this or that volition in the same way as whiteness differs from this or that white object, or as humanity differs from this or that human being. So to conceive the will to be the cause of this or that volition is as impossible as to conceive humanity to be the cause of Peter and Paul.[11]

Since, then, the will is nothing more than a mental construction (*ens rationis*), it can in no way be said to be the cause of this or that volition. Particular volitions, since they need a cause to exist, cannot be said to be free; rather, they are necessarily determined to be such as they are by their own causes. Finally, according to Descartes, errors are themselves particular volitions, from which it necessarily follows that errors—that is, particular volitions—are not free, but are determined by external causes and in no way by the will. This is what I undertook to demonstrate. Etc.

LETTER 3
To the esteemed B.d.S., from Henry Oldenburg

[Known only from the O.P. The original is lost.]

Excellent Sir and dear friend,

Your very learned letter has been delivered to me and read with great pleasure. I warmly approve your geometrical style of proof, but at the same time I blame my

---

[7] [The reference is probably to *Novum Organum* I, 41, which deals with the "Idols of the Tribe."]
[8] [See *Novum Organum* I, 51.]
[9] [See *Novum Organum* I, 48.]
[10] [See Verulam's *Novum Organum*, Book 1, Aphorism 49. (Footnote in the O.P.)]
[11] [On the relation between 'humanity' and individual persons, see E1P8Schol2. Spinoza's claim that will is merely one mode of thought is developed in E1P32.]

obtuseness for not so readily grasping what you with such exactitude teach. So I beg you to allow me to present the evidence of this sluggishness of mine by putting the following questions and seeking from you their solutions.

The first is, do you understand clearly and indubitably that, solely from the definition of God which you give, it is demonstrated that such a Being exists? For my part, when I reflect that definitions contain no more than conceptions of our mind, and that our mind conceives many things that do not exist and is most prolific in multiplying and augmenting things once conceived, I do not yet see how I can infer the existence of God from the conception I have of him. Indeed, from a mental accumulation of all the perfections I discover in men, animals, vegetables, minerals and so on, I can conceive and form one single substance which possesses in full all those qualities; even more, my mind is capable of multiplying and augmenting them to infinity, and so of fashioning for itself a most perfect and excellent Being. Yet the existence of such a Being can by no means be inferred from this.

My second questions is, are you quite certain that Body is not limited by Thought, nor Thought by Body? For it is still a matter of controversy as to what Thought is, whether it is a corporeal motion or a spiritual activity quite distinct from what is corporeal.

My third question is, do you regard those axioms you have imparted to me as being indemonstrable principles, known by the light of Nature and standing in no need of proof? It may be that the first axiom is that of kind, but I do not see how the other three can be accounted as such. For the second axiom supposes that there exists in Nature nothing but substance and accidents, whereas many maintain that time and place are in neither category. Your third axiom, that 'things having different attributes have nothing in common' is so far from being clearly conceived by me that the entire Universe seems rather to prove the contrary. All things known to us both differ from one another in some respects and agree in other respects. Finally, your fourth axiom, namely, 'things which have nothing in common with one another cannot be the cause one of the other', is not so clear to my befogged intellect as not to require some light to be shed on it. For God has nothing formally in common with created things; yet we almost all hold him to be their cause.

Since, then, these axioms do not seem to me to be placed beyond all hazard of doubt, you may readily conjecture that your propositions based on them are bound to be shaky. And the more I consider them, the more I am overwhelmed with doubt concerning them. Against the first I hold that two men are two substances and of the same attribute, since they are both capable of reasoning; and thence I conclude that there are two substances of the same attribute. With regard to the second I consider that, since nothing can be the cause of itself, we can scarcely understand how it can be true that 'Substance cannot be produced, nor can it be produced by any other substance.' For this proposition asserts that all substances are causes of themselves, that they are each and all independent of one another, and it makes them so many Gods, in this way denying the first cause of all things.

This I willingly confess I cannot grasp, unless you do me the kindness of disclosing to me somewhat more simply and more fully your opinion regarding this high matter, explaining what is the origin and production of substances, the interdependence of things and their subordinate relationships. I entreat you, by the friendship on which we have embarked, to deal with me frankly and confidently in this, and I urge you most earnestly to be fully convinced that all these things which you see fit to impart to me will be inviolate and secure, and that I shall in no way permit any of them to become public to your detriment or injury.

In our Philosophical Society we are engaged in making experiments and observations as energetically as our abilities allow, and we are occupied in composing a History of the Mechanical Arts, being convinced that the forms and qualities of things can best be explained by the principles of mechanics, that all Nature's effects are produced by motion, figure, texture and their various combinations, and that there is no need to have recourse to inexplicable forms and occult qualities, the refuge of ignorance.

I shall send you the book I promised as soon as your Dutch ambassadors stationed here dispatch a messenger to the Hague (as they often do), or as soon as some other friend, to whom I can safely entrust it, goes your way.

Please excuse my prolixity and frankness, and I particularly urge you to take in good part, as friends do, what I have said frankly and without any disguise or courtly refinement, in replying to your letter. And believe me to be, sincerely and simply,

Your most devoted,
Henry Oldenburg

London, 27 September 1661

Letter 4
To the noble and learned Henry Oldenburg, from B.d.S.

[Known only from the O.P. The original is lost. No date is given, but a conjectural date is October 1661.]

Most esteemed Sir,

While preparing to go to Amsterdam to spend a week or two there, I received your very welcome letter and read your objections to the three propositions which I sent you. On these alone I shall try to satisfy you, omitting the other matters for want of time.

To your first objection, then, I say that it is not from the definition of any thing whatsoever that the existence of the defined thing follows, but only (as I demonstrated in the Scholium which I attached to the three propositions) from the definition or idea of some attribute; that is (as I explained clearly in the case of the definition of God), from the definition of a thing which is conceived through itself and in itself. The ground for this distinction I have also stated in the aforementioned Scholium with sufficient clarity, I think, especially for a philosopher. A philosopher is supposed to know what is the difference between fiction and a clear and distinct conception, and also to know the truth of this axiom, to wit, that every definition, or clear and distinct idea, is true. Once these points are noted, I do not see what more is required in answer to the first question.

I therefore pass on to the solution of the second question. Here you seem to grant that, if Thought does not pertain to the nature of Extension, then Extension will not be limited by Thought; for surely it is only the example which causes you some doubt. But I beg you to note, if someone says that Extension is not limited by Extension, but by Thought, will he not also be saying that Extension is not infinite in an absolute sense, but only insofar as it is Extension? That is, does he not grant me that Extension is infinite not in an absolute sense, but only insofar as it is Extension, that is, infinite in its own kind?[12]

But, you say, perhaps Thought is a corporeal activity. Let it be so, although I do not concede it; but this one thing you will not deny, that Extension, insofar as it is Extension, is not Thought; and this suffices to explain my definition and to demonstrate the third proposition.

The third objection which you proceed to raise against what I have set down is this, that the axioms should not be accounted as 'common notions' (*notiones communes*).[13] This is not the point I am urging; but you also doubt their truth, and you even appear to seek to prove that their contrary is more probable. But please attend to my definition of substance and accident,[14] from which all these conclusions follow. For by substance I understand that which is conceived through itself and in itself, that is, that whose conception does not involve the conception of another thing; and by modification or accident I understand that which is in something else and is conceived through that in which it is. Hence it is clearly established, first, that substance is prior in nature to its accidents; for without it these can neither exist nor be conceived. Secondly, besides substance and accidents nothing exists in reality, or externally to the intellect; for whatever there is, is conceived either through itself or through something else, and its conception either does or does not involve the conception of another thing. Thirdly,

---

[12] [The distinction between the two types of infinity is given in E1Def2. The proofs of the absolute infinity of extension and of thought are given in E2P1–P2.]

[13] [These are what Oldenburg had called 'indemonstrable principles' in the previous letter. Spinoza's casting of them as 'common notions' is in accordance with his discussion of them in E2P37–P40.]

[14] [Spinoza rarely uses the term 'accident', which is scholastic in origin. His preferred term is 'mode', which differs significantly in sense. He links the usage to 'modification or accident' in the next sentence.]

things which have different attributes have nothing in common with one another;[15] for I have explained an attribute as that whose conception does not involve the conception of another thing. Fourth and last, of things which have nothing in common with one another, one cannot be the cause of another; for since in the effect there would be nothing in common with the cause, all it would have, it would have from nothing.

As for your contention that God has nothing formally in common with created things, etc., I have maintained the exact opposite in my definition. For I said that God is a Being consisting of infinite attributes, each of which is infinite, or supremely perfect, in its kind.

As to your objection to my first proposition, I beg you, my friend, to consider that men are not created, but only begotten, and that their bodies already existed, but in a different form.[16] However, the conclusion is this, as I am quite willing to admit, that if one part of matter were to be annihilated, the whole of Extension would also vanish at the same time.

The second proposition does not make many gods, but one only, to wit, a God consisting of infinite attributes, etc.

LETTER 5
To the esteemed B.d.S., from Henry Oldenburg

[Known only from the O.P. The original is lost.]

My very dear friend,

Receive herewith the little book[17] I promised, and send me in return your opinion of it, especially with regard to the experiments he concludes concerning nitre, fluidity and solidity. I am most grateful to you for your learned second letter, which I received yesterday. Still, I very much regret that your journey to Amsterdam prevented you from answering all my doubts. I beg you to send me, as soon as your leisure permits, what was then omitted. Your last letter did indeed shed a great deal of light for me, but not so much as to dispel all the darkness. This will, I hope, be the happy outcome when you will have clearly and distinctly furnished me with your views on the true and primary origin of things. For as long as it is not quite clear to me from what cause and in what manner things began to be, and by what connection they depend on the first cause, if there be such a thing, then all that I hear and all that I read seems to me quite incoherent. I therefore

---

[15] [See E1P2–P3.]
[16] [See E1P8Schol2.]
[17] [This is Boyle's *Certain Physiological Essays* mentioned in Ep1.]

most earnestly beg you, most learned Sir, to light my way in this matter, and not to doubt my good faith and gratitude. I am,

Your very devoted,
Henry Oldenburg

London 11/21 October 1661

Letter 6
To the most noble and learned Henry Oldenburg, from B.d.S. containing comments on the book of the most noble Robert Boyle, on Nitre, Fluidity and Solidity

> [Printed in the O.P. The original is extant. The last two paragraphs of this translation appear only in the original. The letter is undated, but a conjectural date is early 1662.]

Esteemed Sir,

I have received the very talented Mr. Boyle's book, and read it through, as far as time permitted. I thank you very much for this gift. I see that I was not wrong in conjecturing, when you first promised me this book, that you would not concern yourself with anything less than a matter of great importance. Meanwhile, learned Sir, you wish me to send you my humble opinion on what he has written. This I shall do, as far as my slender ability allows, noting those points which seem to me obscure or insufficiently demonstrated; but I have not as yet been able to peruse it all, far less examine it, because of my other commitments. Here, then, is that I find worthy of comment regarding Nitre, etc.

Of Nitre

First, he gathers from his experiment on the redintegration of Nitre that Nitre is a heterogeneous thing, consisting of fixed and volatile parts. Its nature, however (at least as shown by its behaviour), is quite different from the nature of its component parts, although it arises from nothing but a mixture of these parts. For this conclusion to be regarded as valid, I suggest that a further experiment seems to be required to show that Spirit of Nitre is not really Nitre, and cannot be reduced to solid state or crystallised without the help of salt of lye. Or at least one ought to have enquired whether the quantity of fixed salt remaining in the crucible is always found to be the same from the same quantity of Nitre, and to vary proportionately with the quantity of Nitre. And as to what the esteemed author says (section 9) he discovered with the aid of scales, and the fact that the observed behaviour of Spirit of Nitre is so different from, and even sometimes contrary to, that of Nitre itself, in my view this does nothing to confirm his conclusion.

To make this clear, I shall briefly set forth what occurs to me as the simplest explanation of this redintegration of Nitre, and at the same time I shall add two or three quite easy experiments by which this explanation is to some extent confirmed. To explain what takes place as simply as possible, I shall posit no difference between Spirit of Nitre and Nitre itself other than that which is sufficiently obvious; to wit, that the particles of the latter are at rest whereas those of the former, when stirred, are in a state of considerable commotion. With regard to the fixed salt, I shall suppose that this in no way contributes to constituting the essence of Nitre. I shall consider it as the dregs of Nitre, from which the Spirit of Nitre (as I find) is itself not free; for they float in it in some abundance, although in a very powdery form. This salt, or these dregs, have pores or passages hollowed out to the size of the particles of Nitre. But when the Nitre particles were driven out of them by the action of fire, some of the passages became narrower and consequently others were forced to dilate, and the substance or walls of these passages became stiff and at the same time very brittle. So when Spirit of Nitre was dropped thereon, some of its particles began to force their way through those narrower passages; and since the particles are of unequal thickness (as Descartes has aptly demonstrated),[18] they first bent the rigid walls of the passages like a bow, and then broke them. When they broke them, they forced those fragments to recoil, and, retaining the motion they already had, they remained as equally incapable as before of solidifying and crystallising. The parts of Nitre which made their way through the wider passages, since they did not touch the walls of those passages, were necessarily surrounded by some very fine matter and by this were driven upwards, in the same way as bits of wood by flame or heat, and were given off as smoke. But if they were sufficiently numerous, or if they united with fragments of the walls and with particles making their way through the narrower passages, they formed droplets flying upwards. But if the fixed salt is loosened by means of water[19] or air and is rendered less active, then it becomes sufficiently capable of stemming the onrush of the particles of Nitre and of compelling them to lose the motion they possessed and to come again to a halt, just as does a cannonball when it strikes sand or mud. The redintegration of Nitre consists solely in this coagulation of the particles of Spirit of Nitre, and to bring this about the fixed salt acts as an instrument, as is clear from this explanation. So much for the redintegration.

Now, if you please, let us see first of all why Spirit of Nitre and Nitre itself differ so much in taste; secondly, why Nitre is inflammable, while spirit of Nitre is by no means so. To understand the first question, it should be noted that bodies in motion never come into contact with other bodies along their broadest surfaces, whereas bodies at rest lie on other bodies along their broadest surfaces. So parti-

---

[18] [See Descartes' *Principles of Philosophy* IV, 110.]

[19] If you ask why an effervescence takes place when Spirit of Nitre is poured onto the dissolved fixed salt, read the note on section 25.

cles of Nitre, if placed on the tongue while they are at rest, will lie on it along their broadest surfaces and will thus obstruct its pores, which is the cause of the cold sensation. Furthermore, the Nitre cannot be dissolved by saliva into such very minute particles. But if the particles are placed on the tongue while they are in active motion, they will come into contact with it by their more pointed surfaces and will make their way through its pores. And the more active their motion, the more sharply they will prick the tongue, just as a needle, as it either strikes the tongue with its point or lies lengthwise along the tongue, will cause different sensations to arise.

The reason why Nitre is inflammable and the Spirit of Nitre not so is this, that when particles of Nitre are at rest, they cannot so readily be borne upwards by fire as when they have their own motion in all directions. So when they are at rest, they resist the fire until such time as the fire separates them from one another and encompasses them from all sides. When it does encompass them, it carries them with it this way and that until they acquire a motion of their own and go up in smoke. But the particles of the Spirit of Nitre, being already in motion and separate from one another, are dilated in every direction in increased volume by a little heat of the fire; and thus some go up in smoke while others penetrate the matter supplying the fire before they can be completely encompassed by flame, and so they extinguish the fire rather than feed it.

I shall now pass on to experiments which seem to confirm this explanation. First, I found that the particles of Nitre which go up in smoke with a crackling noise are pure Nitre. For when I melted the Nitre again and again until the crucible became white-hot, and I kindled it with a live coal,[20] I collected its smoke in a cold glass flask until the flask was moistened thereby, and after that I moistened the flask yet further by breathing on it, and finally set it out to dry in the cold air.[21] Thereupon little icicles[22] of Nitre appeared here and there in the flask. Now it might be thought that this did not result solely from the volatile particles, but that the flame could be carrying with it whole particles of Nitre (to adopt the view of the esteemed author) and was driving out the fixed particles, along with the volatile, before they were dissolved. To remove such a possibility, I caused the smoke to ascend through a tube (A) over a foot long, as through a chimney, so that the heavier particles adhered to the tube, and I collected only the more volatile parts as they passed through the narrower aperture (B). The result was as I have said.

Even so, I did not stop at this point, but, as a further test, I took a larger quantity of Nitre, melted it, ignited it with a live coal and, as before, placed the tube (A) over the crucible; and as long as the flame lasted, I held a piece of mirror close to the aperture (B). To this some matter adhered which, on being ex-

---

[20] [Neither Spinoza nor Boyle appreciated the chemical contribution made by the coal to the reaction.]

[21] When I did this, the air was very clear.

[22] [The term *stiriolae* is here used in the sense of 'crystalline'.]

posed to air, became liquid. Although I waited some days, I could not observe any sign of Nitre; but when I added Spirit of Nitre to it, it turned into Nitre.

From this I think I can infer, first, that in the process of melting the fixed parts are separated from the volatile and that the flame drives them upwards separately from one another; secondly, that after the fixed parts are separated from the volatile with a crackling noise, they can never be reunited. From this we can infer, thirdly, that the parts which adhered to the flask and coalesced into little icicles were not the fixed parts, but only the volatile.

The second experiment, and one which seems to prove that the fixed parts are nothing but the dregs of Nitre, is as follows. I find that the more the Nitre is purified of its dregs, the more volatile it is, and the more apt to crystallise. For when I put crystals of purified or filtered Nitre in a glass goblet, such as A, and poured in a little cold water, it partly evaporated along with the cold water, and the particles escaping upwards stuck to the rim of the glass and coalesced into little icicles.

The third experiment, which seems to show that when the particles of Nitre lose their motion they become inflammable, is as follows. I trickled droplets of Spirit of Nitre into a damp paper bag and then added sand, between whose grains the Spirit of Nitre kept penetrating; and when the sand had absorbed all, or nearly all, the Spirit of Nitre, I dried it thoroughly in the same bag over a fire. Thereupon I removed the sand and set the paper against a live coal. As soon as it caught fire it gave off sparks, just as it usually does when it has absorbed Nitre itself.

If I had had time for further experimentation, I might have added other experiments which would perhaps make the matter quite clear. But as I am very much occupied with other matters, you will forgive me if I defer it for another time and proceed to other comments.

Section 5. When the esteemed author discusses incidentally the shape of particles of Nitre, he criticises modern writers as having wrongly represented it. I am not sure whether he includes Descartes; if so, he is perhaps criticising Descartes from what others have said. For Descartes is not speaking of particles visible to the eye. And I do not think that the esteemed author means that if icicles of Nitre were to be rubbed down until they became parallelepipeds or some other shape, they would cease to be Nitre. But perhaps he is referring to some chemists who admit nothing but what they can see with their eyes and touch with their hands.

Section 9. If this experiment could be carried out rigorously, it would completely confirm the conclusion I sought to draw from the first experiment mentioned above.

From section 13 to 18 the esteemed author tries to prove that all tangible qualities depend solely on motion, shape and other mechanical states. Since these demonstrations are not advanced by the esteemed author as being of a mathematical kind, there is no need to consider whether they carry complete conviction. Still, I do not know why the esteemed author strives so earnestly to draw this conclusion from this experiment of his, since it has already been abundantly proved by Verulam, and later by Descartes. Nor do I see that this experiment provides us with clearer evidence than other experiments readily available. For as far as heat is concerned, is not the same conclusion equally clear from the fact that if two pieces of wood, however cold they are, are rubbed against each other, they produce a flame simply as a result of that motion? Or that lime, sprinkled with water, becomes hot? As far as sound is concerned, I do not see what is to be found in this experiment more remarkable than is found in the boiling of ordinary water, and in many other instances. As to colour, to confine myself to the obvious, I need say no more than that we see green vegetation assuming so many and such varied colours. Again, bodies that give forth a foul smell emit even a fouler smell when agitated, and especially if they become somewhat warm. Finally sweet wine turns sour, and so with many other things. All these things, therefore, I would consider superfluous, if I may use the frankness of a philosopher. This I say because I fear that others, whose regard for the esteemed author is not as great as it should be, may misjudge him.[23]

Section 24. I have already spoken of the cause of this phenomenon. Here I will merely add that I, too, have found by experience that particles of the fixed salt float in those saline drops. For when they flew upwards, they met a plate of glass which I had ready for the purpose. This I warmed somewhat so that any volatile matter should fly off, whereupon I observed some thick whitish matter adhering to the glass in places.

Section 25. In this section the esteemed author seems to intend to prove that the alkaline parts are driven hither and thither by the impact of the salt particles, whereas the salt particles ascend into the air by their own force. In explaining the phenomenon I too have said that the particles of Spirit of Nitre acquire a more lively motion because, on entering the wider passages, they must necessarily be encompassed by some very fine matter, and are thereby driven upwards as are particles of wood by fire, whereas the alkaline particles received their motion from the impact of particles of Spirit of Nitre penetrating through the narrower passages. Here I would add that pure water cannot so readily dissolve and soften the fixed parts. So it is not surprising that when Spirit of Nitre is poured onto the solution of the said fixed salt dissolved in water, an effervescence should take place such as the esteemed author describes in section 24. Indeed, I think this effervescence will be more violent than if Spirit of Nitre were to be added to the fixed salt while it is still intact. For in water it is dissolved into very minute molecules which can be more readily separated and more freely moved than when all the parts of the salt lie on one another and are firmly attached.

Section 26. Of the taste of the acidic Spirit I have already spoken, and so it remains only to speak of the alkali. When I placed this on the tongue, I felt a sensation of heat, followed by a prickling. This indicates to me that it is some kind of lime; for in just the same way that lime becomes heated with the aid of water, so does this salt with the aid of saliva, perspiration, Spirit of Nitre, and perhaps even moist air.

---

[23] In the letter I sent I deliberately omitted these words.

Section 27. It does not immediately follow that a particle of matter acquires a new shape by being joined to another; it only follows that it becomes larger, and this suffices to bring about the effect which is the object of the esteemed author's inquiry in this section.

Section 33. What I think of the esteemed author's method of philosophising I shall say when I have seen the Dissertation which is mentioned here and in the Introductory Essay, page 33.[24]

On Fluidity

Section 1. "It is quite manifest that they are to be reckoned among the most general states . . . etc." In my view, notions which derive from popular usage, or which explicate Nature not as it is in itself but as it is related to human senses, should certainly not be regarded as concepts of the highest generality, nor should they be mixed (not to say confused) with notions that are pure and which explicate Nature as it is in itself. Of the latter kind are motion, rest, and their laws; of the former kind are visible, invisible, hot, cold, and, to say it at once, also fluid, solid, etc.

Section 5. "The first is the littleness of the bodies that compose it, for in the larger bodies . . . etc." Even though bodies are small, they have (or can have) surfaces that are uneven and rough. So if large bodies move in such a way that the ratio of their motion to their mass is that of minute bodies to their particular mass, then they too would have to be termed fluid, if the word 'fluid' did not signify something extrinsic and were not merely adapted from common usage to mean those moving bodies whose minuteness and intervening spaces escape detection by human senses. So to divide bodies into fluid and solid would be the same as to divide them into visible and invisible.

The same section. "If we were not able to confirm it by chemical experiments." One can never confirm it by chemical or any other experiments, but only by demonstration and by calculating. For it is by reason and calculation that we divide bodies to infinity, and consequently also the forces required to move them. We can never confirm this by experiments.

Section 6. ". . . great bodies are not well adapted to forming fluid bodies . . . etc." Whether or not one understands by 'fluid' what I have just said, the thing is self-evident. But I do not see how the esteemed author confirms this by the experiments quoted in this section. For (since we want to doubt what is certain)[25] although bones may be unsuitable for forming chyle and similar fluids, perhaps they will be quite well adapted for forming some new kind of fluid.

---

[24] [In the Latin edition Boyle had written: "We shall never be able to investigate so completely the subtle workings of nature that there would not remain many natural phenomena which cannot be explained by the principles of the atomical philosophy." The English version, which Spinoza did not see, was more cautious, claiming only that perhaps men would never be able to fully explain all things.]

[25] [Here we read 'certa' for Gebhardt's *incerta*.]

Section 10. "... and this by making them less pliant than formerly ... etc." They could have coagulated into another body more solid than oil without any change in the parts, but merely because the parts driven into the receiver were separated from the rest. For bodies are lighter or heavier according to the kinds of fluids in which they are immersed. Thus particles of butter, when floating in milk, form part of the liquid; but when the milk is stirred and so acquires a new motion to which all the parts composing the milk cannot equally accommodate themselves, this in itself brings it about that some parts become heavier and force the lighter parts to the surface. But because these lighter parts are heavier than air so that they cannot compose a liquid with it, they are forced downwards by it; and because they are ill adapted for motion, they also cannot compose a liquid by themselves, but lie on one another and stick together. Vapours, too, when they are separated from the air, turn into water, which, in relation to air, may be termed a solid.

Section 13. "And I take as an example a bladder distended with water rather than one full of air ... etc." Since particles of water are always moving ceaselessly in all directions, it is clear that, if they are not restrained by surrounding bodies, the water will spread in all directions. Moreover, I am as yet unable to see how the distention of a bladder full of water helps to confirm his view about the small spaces. The reason why the particles of water do not yield when the sides of the bladder are pressed with a finger—as they otherwise would do if they were free—is this, that there is no equilibrium or circulation as there is when some body, say our finger, is surrounded by a fluid or water. But however much the water is pressed by the bladder, yet its particles will yield to a stone also enclosed in the bladder, in the same way as they usually do outside the bladder.

Same section. "whether there is any portion of matter. ..." We must maintain the affirmative, unless we prefer to look for a progression to infinity, or to grant that there is a vacuum, than which nothing can be more absurd.

Section 19. "... that the particles of the liquid find admittance into those pores and are held there (by which means ... etc.)" This is not to be affirmed absolutely of all liquids which find admittance into the pores of other bodies. If the particles of Spirit of Nitre enter the pores of white paper, they make it stiff and friable. This may be seen if one pours a few drops into a small iron receptacle (A) which is at white heat and the smoke is channelled through a paper covering (B). Moreover, Spirit of Nitre softens leather, but does not make it moist; on the contrary, it shrinks it, as also does fire.

Same section. "Since Nature has designed them both for flying and for swimming. ..." He seeks the cause from purpose.

Section 23. "... though their motion is rarely perceived by us. Take then ... etc." Without this experiment and without going to any trouble, the thing is sufficiently evident from the fact that our breath, which in winter is obviously seen to be in motion, nevertheless cannot be seen so in summer, or in a heated room. Furthermore, if in summer the breeze suddenly cools, the vapours rising from water, since by reason of the change in the density of the air they cannot disperse through it as readily as they did before it cooled, gather again over the surface of the water in such quantity that they can easily be seen by us. Again, movement is often too gradual to be observed by us, as we can gather in the case of a sundial and the shadow cast by the sun; and it is frequently too swift to be observed by us, as can be seen in the case of an ignited piece of tinder when it is moved in a circle at some speed; for then we imagine the ignited part to be at rest at all points of the circle which it describes in its motion. I would here give the reasons for this, did I not judge it superfluous. Finally, let me say in passing that, to understand the nature of fluid in general, it is sufficient to know that we can move our hand in any direction without any resistance, the motion being proportionate to the fluid. This is quite obvious to those who give sufficient attention to those notions that explain Nature as it is in itself, not as it is related to human senses. Not that I therefore dismiss this piece of research as pointless. On the contrary, if in the case of every liquid such research were done with the greatest possible accuracy and reliability, I would consider it most useful for understanding their individual differences, a result much to be desired by all philosophers as being very necessary.

On Solidity

Section 7. "... (it seems consonant) to the universal laws of Nature...." This is Descartes' demonstration, and I do not see that the esteemed author produces any original demonstration deriving from his experiments or observations.

I had made many notes here and in what follows, but later I saw that the esteemed author had corrected himself.

Section 15. "... and once four hundred and thirty-two (ounces)..."[26] If one compares it with the weight of quicksilver enclosed in the tube, it comes very near to the true weight. But I would consider it worthwhile to examine this, so as to obtain, as far as possible, the ratio between the lateral or horizontal pressure of air and the perpendicular pressure. I think it can be done in this way:

Let CD in figure 1 be a flat mirror thoroughly smoothed, and AB two pieces of marble directly touching each other. Let the marble piece A be attached to a hook E, and B to a cord N. T is a pulley, and G a weight which will show the force required to pull marble B away from marble A in a horizontal direction.

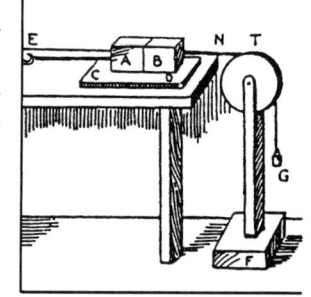

In figure 2, let F be a sufficiently strong silk thread by which marble B is attached to the floor, D a pulley, G a weight which will show the force required to pull mar-

---

[26] [This figure is in fact an error introduced by Boyle's Latin translator.]

ble A from marble B in a perpendicular direction.[27] It is not necessary to go into this at greater length.

Here you have, my good friend, what I have so far found worthy of note in regard to Mr. Boyle's experiments. As to your first queries, when I look through my replies to them I do not see that I have omitted anything. And if perchance I have put something obscurely (as I often do through lack of vocabulary), please be good enough to point it out to me. I shall take pains to explain it more clearly.

As to the new question you raise, to wit, how things began to be and by what bond they depend on the first cause, I have written a complete short work on this subject, and also on the emendation of the intellect,[28] and I am engaged in transcribing and correcting it. But sometimes I put the work aside, because I do not as yet have any definite plan for its publication. I am naturally afraid that the theologians of our time may take offence, and, with their customary spleen, may attack me, who utterly dread brawling. I shall look for your advice in this matter, and, to let you know the contents of this work of mine which may ruffle the preachers, I tell you that many attributes which are attributed to God by them and by all whom I know of, I regard as belonging to creation. Conversely, other attributes which they, because of their prejudices, consider to belong to creation, I contend are attributes of God which they have failed to understand. Again, I do not differentiate between God and Nature in the way all those known to me have done. I therefore look to your advice, for I regard you as a most loyal friend whose good faith it would be wrong to doubt. Meanwhile, farewell, and, as you have begun, so continue to love me, who am,

Yours entirely,
Benedict Spinoza

Letter 7
To the esteemed B.d.S., from Henry Oldenburg

[Known only from the O.P. The original is lost. The letter is undated, but a conjectural date is late in July 1662.]

It is many weeks ago, esteemed Sir, that I received your very welcome letter with its learned comments on Boyle's book. The author himself joins with me in thank-

---

[27] [At this point the *Opera Posthuma* letter breaks off with the remark, "The rest is lacking." The rest of the letter is translated from the original.]

[28] [This is the *Tractatus de intellectus emendation* (never completed).]

ing you most warmly for the thoughts you have shared with us, and would have indicated this more quickly had he not entertained the hope that he might soon be relieved of the quantity of business with which he is burdened so that he could have sent you his reply along with his thanks at the same time. However, so far he finds himself disappointed of this hope, being so pressed by both public and private business that at present he can do no more than convey his gratitude to you, and is compelled to defer to another time his opinion on your comments. Furthermore, two opponents have attacked him in print, and he thinks himself bound to reply to them at the first opportunity. These writings are directed not against his *Essay on Nitre* but against another book of his containing his Pneumatic Experiments,[29] proving the elasticity of air. As soon as he has extricated himself from these labours he will also disclose to you his thoughts on your objections. Meanwhile he asks you not to take amiss this delay.

The College of Philosophers of which I spoke to you has now, by our King's grace, been converted into a Royal Society and presented with the public charter[30] whereby it is granted special privileges, and there is a very good prospect that it will be endowed with the necessary funds.

I would by all means urge you not to begrudge scholars the learned fruits of your acute understanding both in philosophy and theology, but to let them be published despite the growlings of pseudo-theologians. Your republic is quite free, and in it philosophy should be pursued quite freely; but your own prudence will suggest to you that you express your ideas and opinions as moderately as you can, and for the rest leave the outcome to fate.

Come, then, excellent Sir, away with all fear of stirring up the pygmies of our time. Long enough have we propitiated ignorance and nonsense. Let us spread the sails of true knowledge and search more deeply than ever before into Nature's mysteries. Your reflections, I imagine, can be printed in your country with impunity, and there is no need to fear that they will give any offence to the wise. If you find such to be your patrons and supporters (as I am quite sure that you will find them), why should you dread an ignorant Momus? I will not let you go, honoured friend, until I have prevailed on you, and never will I permit, as far as in me lies, that your thoughts, which are of such importance, should be buried in eternal silence. I urgently request you to be good enough to let me know, as soon as you conveniently can, what are your intentions in this matter.

Perhaps things will be happening here not unworthy of your notice. The aforementioned Society will now more vigorously pursue its purpose, and maybe, pro-

---

[29] [Boyle's *New Experiments Physico-Mechanical touching the Spring of the Air and its Effects, made for the most part in a new Pneumatical Engine*. The air-pump was also called the *machina boyleana*, and was created by Robert Hooke and Boyle in 1659 after they read about the pump constructed by Guericke. This treatise contains an extended critique of Thomas Hobbes and of the Jesuit thinker Franciscus Linus, both of whom (like Spinoza) argued against the claim that there was any true vacuum in nature.]

[30] [The public charter for "The Royal Society" was granted on 15 July 1662.]

vided that peace lasts in these shores, it will grace the Republic of Letters with distinction. Farewell, distinguished Sir, and believe me to be,

Your very devoted and dear friend,
Henry Oldenburg

Letter 8
To the esteemed B.d.S., from Simon de Vries

[Printed in the O.P. The original is extant. There are certain omissions in the O.P. text.]

Most upright friend,

I have long wished to pay you a visit, but the weather and the hard winter have not favoured me. Sometimes I bewail my lot, in that the distance between us keeps us so far apart from one another. Fortunate, yes, most fortunate is your companion Casuarius[31] who dwells beneath the same roof, and can converse with you on the highest matters at breakfast, at dinner, and on your walks. But although we are physically so far apart, you have frequently been present in my thoughts, especially when I am immersed in your writings and hold them in my hand. But since not everything is quite clear to the members of our group (which is why we have resumed our meetings), and in order that you may not think that I have forgotten you, I have set myself to write this letter.

As for our group, our procedure is as follows. One member (each has his turn) does the reading, explains how he understands it, and goes on to a complete demonstration, following the sequence and order of your propositions. Then if it should happen that we cannot satisfy one another, we have deemed it worthwhile to make a note of it and to write to you so that, if possible, it should be made clearer to us and we may, under your guidance, uphold truth against those who are religious and Christian in a superstitious way, and may stand firm against the onslaught of the whole world.

So, when the definitions did not all seem clear to us on our first reading and explaining them, we were not in agreement as to the nature of definition. In this situation, in your absence, we consulted a certain author, a mathematician named Borelli.[32] In his discussion of the nature of definition, axiom and postulate, he

---

[31] [Johannes Caesarius, whose name is incorrectly spelled by de Vries, was probably born in Amsterdam in 1642 and is believed to have been a student of Franciscus Van den Enden through whom he may have become acquainted with Spinoza. Though the reasons as to why he may have been living with Spinoza are unclear, he is thought to have been part of a group of Collegiants who were known to frequent Rijnsburg while Spinoza resided there.]

[32] [Giovanni Alfonso Borelli (1608–1679) was a mathematician with many other interests: astronomy,

also cites the opinions of others on this subject. His own opinion goes as follows: "Definitions are employed in a proof as premisses. So they must be quite clearly known; otherwise knowledge that is scientific or absolutely certain cannot be acquired from them." In another place he writes: "In the case of any subject, the principle of its structure, or its prime and best known essential feature, must be chosen not at random but with the greatest care. For if the construction and feature named is impossible, then the result will not be a scientific definition. For instance, if one were to say, 'Let two straight lines enclosing a space be called figurals', the definitions would be of non-entities, and would be impossible. Therefore from these it is ignorance, not knowledge, that would be deduced. Again, if the construction or feature named is indeed possible and true, but unknown to us or doubtful, then the definition will not be sound. For conclusions that derive from what is unknown and doubtful are also uncertain and doubtful, and therefore afford us mere conjecture or opinion, and not sure knowledge."

Tacquet[33] seems to disagree with this view; he asserts, as you know, that it is possible to proceed directly from a false proposition to a true conclusion. Clavius,[34] whose view he (Borelli) also introduces, thinks as follows: "Definitions are arbitrary terms, and there is no need to give the grounds for choosing that a thing should be defined in this way or that. It is sufficient that the thing defined should never be asserted to agree with anything unless it is first proved that the given definition agrees with that same thing." So Borelli maintains that the definition of any subject must consist of a feature or structure which is prime, essential, best known to us, and true, whereas Clavius holds that it matters not whether it be prime, or best known, or true or not, as long as it is not asserted that the definition we have given agrees with some thing unless it is first provided that the given definition agrees with that same thing. We are inclined to favour Borelli's view, but we are not sure whether you, Sir, agree with either or neither. Therefore, with such various conflicting views being advanced on the nature of definition—which is accounted as one of the principles of demonstration—and since the mind, if not freed from difficulties surrounding definition, will be in like difficulty regarding deductions made from it, we would very much like you, Sir, to write to us (if we are not giving you too much trouble and your time allows) giving your opinion on the matter, and also on the difference between axioms and definitions. Borelli admits no real distinction other than the name; you, I believe, maintain that there is another difference.

Next, the third Definition[35] is not sufficiently clear to us. I brought forward as

---

physics, biology. As well as publishing an edition of Euclid (*Euclides restitutus*), he also published several other mathematical treatises. Like Descartes, he too finished his days under the protection of Queen Christiana of Sweden.]

[33] [Andreas Tacquet published *Elements of Plane and Solid Geometry* in 1654.]

[34] [Christopher Clavius (1537–1612) was another well known mathematician of the era. He helped to revise the Gregorian calendar, and in 1574 he published an edition of Euclid with commentary to which de Vries refers in this letter.]

[35] [Seee E1Def3–4.]

an example what you, Sir, said to me at the Hague, to wit, that a thing can be considered in two ways: either as it is in itself, or in relation to another thing. For instance, the intellect; for it can be considered either under Thought or as consisting of ideas. But we do not quite see what difference could be here. For we consider that, if we rightly conceive Thought, we ought to comprehend it under ideas, because with the removal of all ideas we would destroy Thought. So the example not being sufficiently clear to us, the matter still remains somewhat obscure, and we stand in need of further explanation.

Finally, at the beginning of the third Scholium to Proposition 8,[36] we read: "Hence it is clear that, although two attributes may be conceived as really distinct (that is, the one without the aid of the other), it does not follow that they constitute two entities or two different substances. The reason is that it is of the nature of substance that all its attributes—each one individually—are conceived through themselves, since they have been in it simultaneously." In this way you seem, Sir, to suppose that the nature of substance is so constituted that it can have several attributes, which you have not yet proved, unless you are referring to the fifth definition[37] of absolutely infinite substance or God. Otherwise, if I were to say that each substance has only one attribute, I could rightly conclude that where there are two different attributes there are two different substances. We would ask you for a clearer explanation of this.

Next, I am most grateful for your writings which were conveyed to me by P. Balling and gave me great pleasure, particularly the Scholium to Proposition 19.[38] If I can here serve you, too, in any way which is within my power, I am yours to command. You need only let me know. I have begun a course of anatomy, and am about half way through. When it is completed, I shall begin chemistry, and thus following your advice I shall go through the whole medical course. I must stop now, and await your reply. Accept my greetings, who am,

Your very devoted,
S. J. D'Vries

1663. Given at the Hague, 24 February
    To Mr. Benedict Spinoza, at Rijnsburg

---

[36] [Probably E1P10Schol in the finished version of the *Ethics*.]

[37] [See E1Def6.]

[38] [We are not able to determine about which proposition in the final version of the *Ethics* de Vries writes.]

Letter 9
To the learned young man Simon de Vries, from B.d.S.

[Printed in the O.P. The original is extant. The O.P. text is an abridged version of the original, and the last paragraph appears only in the Dutch edition of the O.P. The letter is undated. A conjectural date is February 1663.]

My worthy friend,

I have received your letter, long looked for, for which, and for your cordial feelings towards me, accept my warmest thanks. Your long absence has been no less regretted by me than by you, but at any rate I am glad that my late-night studies are of use to you and our friends, for in this way I talk with you while we are apart. There is no reason for you to envy Casearius. Indeed, there is no one who is more of a trouble to me, and no one with whom I have had to be more on my guard. So I should like you and all our acquaintances not to communicate my opinions to him until he will have reached a more mature age. As yet he is too boyish, unstable, and eager for novelty rather than for truth. Still, I am hopeful that he will correct these youthful faults in a few years time. Indeed, as far as I can judge from his character, I am reasonably sure of this; and so his nature wins my affection.

As to the questions raised in your group (which is sensibly organised), I see that your difficulties result from your failure to distinguish between the kinds of definition. There is the definition that serves to explicate a thing whose essence alone is in question and the subject of doubt, and there is the definition which is put forward simply for examination. The former, since it has a determinate object, must be a true definition, while this need not be so in the latter case. For example, if someone were to ask me for a description of Solomon's temple, I ought to give him a true description, unless I propose to talk nonsense with him. But if I have in my own mind formed the design of a temple that I want to build, and from its description I conclude that I will have to purchase such-and-such a site and so many thousands of stones and other materials, will any sane person tell me that I have reached a wrong conclusion because my definition may be incorrect? Or will anyone demand that I prove my definition? Such a person would simply be telling me that I had not conceived that which in fact I had conceived, or he would be requiring me to prove that I had conceived that which I had conceived, which is utter nonsense. Therefore a definition either explicates a thing as it exists outside the intellect—and then it should be a true definition, differing from a proposition or axiom only in that the former is concerned only with the essences of things or the essences of the affections of things, whereas the latter has a wider scope, extending also to eternal truths—or it explicates a thing as it is conceived by us, or can be conceived. And in that case it also differs from an axiom and proposition in requiring merely that it be conceived, not conceived as true, as in the case of an axiom. So then a bad definition is one which is not conceived.

To make this clearer, I shall take Borelli's example of a man who says that two straight lines enclosing an area are to be called figurals. If he means by a straight line what everybody else means by a curved line, his definition is quite sound (for the figure intended by the definition would be [as shown] or some such figure), provided that he does not at a later stage mean a square or any other such figure. But if by a straight line he means what we all mean, the thing is plainly inconceivable, and so there is no definition. All these considerations are confused by Borelli, whose view you are too much inclined to embrace.

Here is another example, the one which you adduce towards the end of your letter. If I say that each substance has only one attribute, this is mere assertion unsupported by proof. But if I say that by substance I mean that which consists of only one attribute, this is a sound definition, provided that entities consisting of more than one attribute are thereafter given a name other than substance.

In saying that I do not prove that a substance (or an entity) can have more than one attribute, it may be that you have not given sufficient attention to the proofs. I advanced two proofs, the first of which is as follows: It is clear beyond all doubt that every entity is conceived by us under some attribute, and the more reality or being an entity has, the more attributes are to be attributed to it. Hence an absolutely infinite entity must be defined . . . and so on. A second proof—and this proof I take to be decisive—states that the more attributes I attribute to any entity, the more existence I am bound to attribute to it; that is, the more I conceive it as truly existent. The exact contrary would be the case if I had imagined a chimera or something of the sort.

As to your saying that you do not conceive thought otherwise than under ideas because thought vanishes with the removal of ideas, I believe that you experience this because when you, as a thinking thing, do as you say, you are banishing all your thoughts and conceptions. So it is not surprising that when you have banished all your thoughts, there is nothing left for you to think. But as to the point at issue, I think I have demonstrated with sufficient clarity and certainty that the intellect, even though infinite, belongs to *Natura naturata*, not to *Natura naturans*.[39]

Furthermore, I fail to see what this has to do with understanding the Third Definition,[40] or why this definition causes you difficulty. The definition as I gave it to you runs, if I am not mistaken, "By substance I understand that which is in itself and is conceived through itself; that is, that whose conception does not involve the conception of another thing. I understand the same by attribute, except that attribute is so called in respect to the intellect, which attributes to substance a certain specific kind of nature." This definition, I repeat, explains clearly what

---

[39] [For the distinction, see E1P29Schol.]
[40] [E1Def3–4.]

I mean by substance or attribute. However, you want me to explain by example—though it is not at all necessary—how one and the same thing can be signified by two names. Not to appear ungenerous, I will give you two examples. First, by 'Israel' I mean the third patriarch: by 'Jacob' I mean that same person, the latter name being given to him because he seized his brother's heel.[41] Secondly, by a 'plane surface' I mean one that reflects all rays of light without any change. I mean the same by 'white surface', except that it is called white in respect of a man looking at it.

With this I think that I have fully answered your questions. Meanwhile I shall wait to hear your judgment. And if there is anything else which you consider to be not well or clearly enough explained, do not hesitate to point it out to me, etc.

Letter 10
To the learned young man Simon de Vries, from B.d.S.

[Known only from the O.P. The original is lost. Undated. A conjectural date is March 1663.]

My worthy friend,

You ask me whether we need experience to know whether the definition of some attribute be true. To this I reply that we need experience only in the case of those things that cannot be deduced from the definition of a thing, as, for instance, the existence of modes; for this cannot be deduced from a thing's definition. We do not need experience in the case of those things whose existence is not distinguished from their essence and is therefore deduced from their definition. Indeed, no experience will ever be able to tell us this, for experience does not teach us the essences of things. The most it can do is to determine our minds to think only about the certain essences of things. So since the existence of attributes does not differ from their essence, we shall not be able to apprehend it by any experience.

As to your further question as to whether things or the affections of things are also eternal truths, I say, most certainly. If you go on to ask why I do not call them eternal truths, I reply, in order to mark a distinction, universally accepted, between these and the truths which do not explicate a thing or the affection of a thing, as, for instance, 'nothing comes from nothing'. This and similar propositions, I say, are called eternal truths in an absolute sense, by which title is meant simply that they do not have any place outside the mind, etc.

---

[41] [See Genesis 25:26 for an account of Jacob's name and 35:10 for an account of the change of this name to Israel.]

Letter 11
To the esteemed B.d.S., from Henry Oldenburg

[Known only from the O.P. The original is lost.]

Excellent Sir and dear friend,

I could produce many excuses for my long silence, but I shall reduce my reasons to two: the illness of the illustrious Mr. Boyle and the pressures of my own business. The former has prevented Boyle from replying to your Observations on Nitre at an earlier date; the latter have kept me so busy over several months that I have scarcely been my own master, and so I have been unable to discharge the duty which I declare I owe you. I rejoice that, for the time at least, both obstacles are removed, so that I can resume my correspondence with so close a friend. This I now do with the greatest pleasure, and I am resolved, with Heaven's help, to do everything to ensure that our epistolary intercourse shall never in future suffer so long an interruption.

Before I deal with matters what concern just you and me alone, let me deliver what is due to you on Mr. Boyle's account. The observations which you composed on his short Chemical-Physical Treatise he has received with his customary good nature, and sends you his warmest thanks for your criticism. But first he wants you to know that it was not his intention to demonstrate that this is a truly philosophical and complete analysis of Nitre, but rather to make the point that the common doctrine of Substantial Forms and Qualities accepted in the Schools rests on a weak foundation, and that what they call the specific differences of things can be reduced to the magnitude, motion, rest and position of the parts.

With this preliminary remark, our Author goes on to say that his experiment with Nitre shows quite clearly that through chemical analysis the whole body of Nitre was resolved into parts which differed from one another and from the original whole, and that afterwards it was so reconstituted and redintegrated from these same parts that it lacked little of its original weight. He adds that he has shown this to be a fact, but he has not been concerned with the way in which it comes about, which seems to be the subject of your conjectures, and that he has reached no conclusion on that matter, since that went beyond his purpose. However, as to what you suppose to be the way in which it comes about, and your view that the fixed salt of Nitre is its dregs and other such theories, he considers that these are merely unproved speculations. And as to your idea that these dregs, or this fixed salt, has openings hollowed out to the size of the particles of Nitre, on this subject our Author points out that salt of potash combined with Spirit of Nitre constitutes Nitre just as well as Spirit of Nitre combined with its own fixed salt. Hence he thinks it clear that similar pores are to be found in bodies of that kind, from which nitrous spirits are not given off. Nor does the Author see that the necessity for the very fine matter, which you allege, is proved from any of the phenomena, but he says it is assumed simply from the hypothesis of the impossibility of a vacuum.

The Author says that your remarks on the causes of the difference of taste between Spirit of Nitre and Nitre do not affect him; and as to what you say about the inflammability of Nitre and the non-inflammability of Spirit of Nitre, he says that this presupposes Descartes' theory of fire,[42] with which he declares he is not yet satisfied.

With regard to the experiments which you think confirm your explanation of the phenomenon, the Author replies that (1) Spirit of Nitre is indeed Nitre in respect of its matter, but not in respect of its form, since they are vastly different in their qualities and properties, viz. in taste, smell, volatility, power of dissolving metals, changing the colours of vegetables, etc. (2) When you say that some particles carried upwards coalesce into crystals of Nitre, he maintains that this happens because the nitrous parts are driven off through the fire along with Spirit of Nitre, as is the case with soot. (3) As to your point about the effect of purification, the Author replies that through that purification the Nitre is for the most part freed from a certain salt which resembles common salt, and that its ascending to form icicles is something it has in common with other salts, and depends on air pressure and other causes which must be discussed elsewhere and have no bearing on the present question. (4) With regard to your remarks on your third experiment, the Author says that the same thing occurs with certain other salts. He asserts that when the paper is actually alight, it sets in motion the rigid and solid particles composing the salt and in this way causes them to sparkle.

Next, when you think that in the fifth section the noble Author is criticising Descartes, he believes that you yourself are here at fault. He says that he was in no way referring to Descartes, but to Gassendi and others who attribute to Nitre a cylindrical shape when it is in fact prismatic, and that he is speaking only of visible shapes.

To your comments on sections 13–18, he merely replies that he wrote these sections with this main object, to demonstrate and assert the usefulness of chemistry in confirming the mechanical principles of philosophy, and that he has not found these matters so clearly conveyed and treated by others. Our Boyle belongs to the class of those who do not have so much trust in their reason as not to want phenomena to agree with reason. Moreover, he says that there is a considerable difference between superficial experiments where we do not know what Nature contributes and what other factors intervene, and those experiments where it is established with certainty what are the factors concerned. Pieces of wood are much more composite bodies than the subject dealt with by the Author. And in the case of ordinary boiling water fire is an additional external factor, which is not so in the production of our sound. Again, the reason why green vegetation changes into so many different colours is still being sought, but that this is due to the change of the parts is established by this experiment, which shows that the

---

[42] [See Descartes, *Principles of Philosophy* IV, 80–119.]

change of colour was due to the addition of Spirit of Nitre. Finally, he says that Nitre has neither a foul nor a sweet smell; it acquires a foul smell simply as a result of its decomposition, and loses it when it is recompounded.

With regard to your comments on section 25 (the rest, he says, does not touch him) he replies that he has made use of the Epicurean principles which hold that there is an innate motion in particles; for he needed to make use of some hypothesis to explain the phenomenon. Still, he does not on that account adopt it as his own, but he uses it to support his view against the chemists and the Schools, demonstrating merely that the facts can be well explained on the basis of the said hypothesis. As to your additional remark at the same place on the inability of pure water to dissolve the fixed parts, our Boyle replies that it is the general opinion of chemists from their observations that pure water dissolves alkaline salts more rapidly than others.

The Author has not yet had time to consider your comments on fluidity and solidity. I am sending you what I here enclose so that I may not any longer be deprived of intercourse and correspondence with you. But I do most earnestly beg you to take in good part what I here pass on to you in such a disjointed and disconnected way, and to ascribe this to my haste rather than to the character of the illustrious Boyle. For I have assembled these comments as a result of informal talk with him on this subject rather than from any deliberate and methodical reply on his part. Consequently, many things which he said have doubtless escaped me, which were perhaps more substantial and better expressed than what I have here set down. All blame, therefore, I take on my own shoulders, and entirely absolve the Author.

Now I shall turn to matters that concern you and me, and here at the outset let me be permitted to ask whether you have completed that little work of such great importance, in which you treat of the origin of things and their dependence on a first cause, and also of the emendation of our intellect. Of a surety, my dear friend, I believe that nothing can be published more agreeable and more welcome to men who are truly learned and wise than a treatise of that kind. That is what a man of your talent and character should look to, rather than what pleases the theologians of our age and fashion. They look not so much to truth as to what suits them. So I urge you by our bond of friendship, by all the duties we have to promote and disseminate truth, not to begrudge or deny us your writings on these subjects. If, however, there is some consideration of greater weight than I can foresee which holds you back from publishing the work, I heartily beg you to be pleased to let me have by letter a summary of it, and for this service you will find me a grateful friend. There will soon be more publications[43] from the learned Boyle which I shall send you by way of requital, adding an account of the entire constitution of our Royal Society, of whose Council I am a member with twenty

---

[43] [These are the *Considerations touching the Usefulness of Experimental Natural Philosophy* and the *Experiments and Considerations touching Colours*, published respectively in 1663 and 1664, with Latin translations published at the same time.]

others, and joint secretary with one other. At present lack of time prevents me from going on to other matters. To you I pledge all the loyalty that can come from an honest heart, and an entire readiness to do you any service that lies within my slender powers, and I am, sincerely,

Excellent Sir, yours entirely,
Henry Oldenburg

London, 3 April 1663

LETTER 12
To the learned and wise Lodewijk Meyer, Doctor of Medicine and Philosophy, from B.d.S.

[Printed in the O.P. The original is lost, but a copy made by Leibniz has been preserved.]

Dearest friend,

I have received two letters from you, one dated January 11 and delivered to me by our friend N.N.,[44] the other dated March 26 and sent to me by an unknown friend from Leiden. They were both very welcome, especially as I gathered from them that all is well with you and that I am often in your thoughts. My most cordial thanks are due to you for the kindness and esteem you have always seen fit to show me. At the same time I beg you to believe that I am no less your devoted friend, and this I shall endeavour to prove whenever the occasion arises, as far as my slender abilities allow. As a first offering, I shall try to answer the request made to me in your letters, in which you ask me to let you have my considered views on the question of the infinite. I am glad to oblige.

The question of the infinite has universally been found to be very difficult, indeed, insoluble, through failure to distinguish between that which must be infinite by its very nature or by virtue of its definition, and that which is unlimited not by virtue of its essence but by virtue of its cause. Then again, there is the failure to distinguish between that which is called infinite because it is unlimited, and that whose parts cannot be equated with or explicated by any number, although we may know its maximum or minimum. Lastly, there is the failure to distinguish between that which we can apprehend only by the intellect and not by the imagination, and that which can also be apprehended by the imagination. I repeat, if men had paid

---

[44] [The friend "N.N." was quite possibly Pieter Balling, who was known to travel to and from Amsterdam and Rijnsburg and no doubt delivered letters for and from Spinoza. This letter was apparently circulated among many of Spinoza's friends, and came to be referenced as the 'Letter on the Infinite' or the 'Letter on Infinity'.]

careful attention to these distinctions, they would never have found themselves overwhelmed by such a throng of difficulties. They would clearly have understood what kind of infinite cannot be divided into, or possess any, parts, and what kind can be so divided without contradiction. Again, they would also have understood what kind of infinite can be conceived, without illogicality, as greater than another infinite, and what kind cannot be so conceived. This will become clear from what I am about to say. However, I shall first briefly explain these four terms: Substance, Mode, Eternity, Duration.

The points to be noted about Substance are as follows. First, existence pertains to its essence; that is, solely from its essence and definition it follows that Substance exists. This point, if my memory does not deceive me, I have proved to you in an earlier conversation without the help of any other propositions. Second, following from the first point, Substance is not manifold; rather there exists only one Substance of the same nature. Thirdly, no Substance can be conceived as other than infinite.[45]

The affections of Substance I call Modes. The definition of Modes, insofar as it is not itself a definition of Substance, cannot involve existence. Therefore, even when they exist, we can conceive them as not existing. From this it further follows that when we have regard only to the essence of Modes and not to the order of Nature as a whole, we cannot deduce from their present existence that they will or will not exist in the future or that they did or did not exist in the past. Hence it is clear that we conceive the existence of Substance as of an entirely different kind from the existence of Modes. This is the source of the difference between Eternity and Duration. It is to the existence of Modes alone that we can apply the term Duration; the corresponding term for the existence of Substance is Eternity, that is, the infinite enjoyment of existence or—pardon the Latin—of being (*essendi*).

What I have said makes it quite clear that when we have regard only to the essence of Modes and not to Nature's order, as is most often the case, we can arbitrarily delimit the existence and duration of Modes without thereby impairing to any extent our conception of them; and we can conceive this duration as greater or less, and divisible into parts. But Eternity and Substance, being conceivable only as infinite, cannot be thus treated without annulling our conception of them. So it is nonsense, bordering on madness, to hold that extended Substance is composed of parts or bodies really distinct from one another. It is as if, by simply adding circle to circle and piling one on top of another, one were to attempt to construct a square or a triangle or any other figure of a completely different nature. Therefore the whole conglomeration of arguments whereby philosophers commonly strive to prove that extended Substance is finite collapses of its own accord. All such arguments assume that corporeal Substance is made up of parts. A parallel case is presented by those who, having convinced themselves that a line is made up of points,[46] have devised many arguments to prove that a line is not infinitely divisible.

---

[45] [See E1P8.]

[46] [This argument, and its relation to the divisibility of extension, receives an extended treatment by Spinoza in E1P15Schol.]

However, if you ask why we have such a strong natural tendency to divide extended Substance, I answer that we conceive quantity in two ways: abstractly or superficially, as we have it in the imagination with the help of the senses, or as Substance, apprehended solely by means of the intellect. So if we have regard to quantity as it exists in the imagination (and this is what we most frequently and readily do), it will be found to be divisible, finite, composed of parts, and manifold. But if we have regard to it as it is in the intellect and we apprehend the thing as it is in itself (and this is very difficult), then it is found to be infinite, indivisible, and one alone, as I have already sufficiently proved.

Further, from the fact that we are able to delimit Duration and Quantity as we please, conceiving Quantity in abstraction from Substance and separating the efflux of Duration from things eternal, there arise Time and Measure: Time to delimit Duration and Measure to delimit Quantity in such wise as enables us to imagine them easily, as far as possible. Again, from the fact that we separate the affections of Substance from Substance itself, and arrange them in classes so that we can easily imagine them as far as possible, there arises Number, whereby we delimit them. Hence it can clearly be seen that Measure, Time and Number are nothing other than modes of thinking, or rather, modes of imagining. It is therefore not surprising that all who have attempted to understand the workings of Nature by such concepts, and furthermore without really understanding these concepts, have tied themselves into such extraordinary knots that in the end they have been unable to extricate themselves except by breaking through everything and perpetrating the grossest absurdities. For there are many things that can in no way be apprehended by the imagination but only by the intellect, such as Substance, Eternity, and other things. If anyone tries to explicate such things by notions of this kind which are nothing more than aids to the imagination, he will meet with no more success than if he were deliberately to encourage his imagination to run mad. Nor again can the Modes of Substance every be correctly understood if they are confused with such mental constructs (*entia rationis*) or aids to the imagination. For by so doing we are separating them from Substance and from the manner of their efflux from Eternity, and in such isolation they can never be correctly understood.

To make the matter still clearer, take the following example. If someone conceives Duration in this abstracted way and, confusing it with Time, begins dividing it into parts, he can never understand how an hour, for instance, can pass by. For in order that an hour should pass by, a half-hour must first pass by, and then half of the remainder, and the half of what is left; and if you go on thus subtracting half of the remainder to infinity, you can never reach the end of the hour. Therefore many who are not used to distinguishing mental constructs from real things have ventured to assert that Duration is composed of moments, thus falling into the clutches of Scylla in their eagerness to avoid Charybdis. For to say that Duration is made up of moments is the same as to say that Number is made up simply by adding noughts together.

Further, it is obvious from the above that neither Number, Measure, nor Time, being merely aids to the imagination, can be infinite, for in that case Number would not be number, nor Measure measure, nor Time time. Hence one can easily see why many people, confusing these three concepts with reality because of their ignorance of the true nature of reality, have denied the actual existence of the infinite. But let their deplorable reasoning be judged by mathematicians who, in matters that they clearly and distinctly perceive, are not to be put off by arguments of that sort. For not only have they come upon many things inexpressible by any number (which clearly reveals the inadequacy of number to determine all things) but they also have many instances which cannot be equated with any number, and exceed any possible number. Yet they do not draw the conclusion that it is because of the multitude of parts that such things exceed all number; rather, it is because the nature of the thing is such that number is inapplicable to it without manifest contradiction.

For example, all the inequalities of the space lying between the two circles ABCD in the diagram exceed any number, as do all the variations of the speed of matter moving through that area. Now this conclusion is not reached because of the excessive magnitude of the intervening space; for however small a portion of it we take, the inequalities of this small portion will still be beyond any numerical expression. Nor again is this conclusion reached, as happens in other cases, because we do not know the maximum and minimum; in our example we know them both, the maximum being AB and the minimum CD. Our conclusion is reached because number is not applicable to the nature of the space between two non-concentric circles. Therefore if anyone sought to express all those inequalities by a definite number, he would also have to bring it about that a circle should not be a circle.

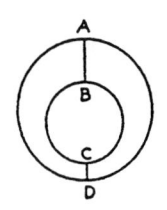

Similarly, to return to our theme, if anyone were to attempt to determine all the motions of matter that have ever been, reducing them and their duration to a definite number and time, he would surely be attempting to deprive corporeal Substance, which we cannot conceive as other than existing, of its affections, and to bring it about that Substance should not possess the nature which it does possess. I could here clearly demonstrate this and many other points touched on in this letter, did I not consider it unnecessary.

From all that I have said one can clearly see that certain things are infinite by their own nature and cannot in any way be conceived as finite, while other things are infinite by virtue of the cause in which they inhere; and when the latter are conceived in abstraction, they can be divided into parts and be regarded as finite. Finally, there are things that can be called infinite, or if you prefer, indefinite, because they cannot be accurately expressed by any number, while yet being conceivable as greater or less. For it does not follow that things which cannot be adequately expressed by any number must necessarily be equal, as is sufficiently evident from the given example and from many others.

To sum up, I have here briefly set before you the causes of the errors and confusion that have arisen regarding the question of the infinite, explaining them all, unless I am mistaken, in such a way that I do not believe there remains any question regarding the Infinite on which I have not touched, or which cannot be readily solved from what I have said. Therefore I do not think there is any point in detaining you longer on this matter.

However, in passing I should like it here to be observed that in my opinion our modern Peripatetics have quite misunderstood the demonstration whereby scholars of old sought to prove the existence of God. For, as I find it in a certain Jew named Rab Chasdai,[47] this proof runs as follows: "If there is granted an infinite series of causes, all things which are, are also caused. But nothing that is caused can exist necessarily by virtue of its own nature. Therefore there is nothing in Nature to whose essence existence necessarily pertains. But this latter is absurd; therefore also the former."[48] So the force of the argument lies not in the impossibility of an actual infinite or an infinite series of causes, but only in the assumption that things which by their own nature do not necessarily exist are not determined to exist by a thing which necessarily exists by its own nature.

I would now pass on—for I am pressed for time—to your second letter, but I shall be able more conveniently to reply to the points contained therein when you will kindly pay me a visit. So do please try to come as soon as you possibly can. For the time of my moving is rapidly approaching. Enough, farewell, and keep me ever in your thoughts, who am, etc.

Rijnsburg, 20 April 1663

Letter 12A
To Lodewijk Meyer, from B.d.S.

[Not in the O.P. nor in Gebhardt. Discovered by Offenberg and published in 1975.]

My very dear friend,

Yesterday I received your very welcome letter in which you ask, first, whether in Chapter 2 of Part I of the Appendix you have correctly indicated all propositions, etc., which are there cited from Part I of the Principia; secondly, whether my assertion in Part II that the Son of God is the Father himself should not be deleted; and finally, whether my statement that I do not know what theologians understand by the term 'personalitas' should not be changed. To this I reply,

---

[47] [Hasdai (or Ḥasdai, or Chasdai) Crescas was a celebrated Jewish theologian (1340?–1410). Crescas opposed the then-fashionable Aristotelian proof for the existence of God as first mover, made even more popular by Maimonides' and Thomas Aquinas' adaptations. Instead, Crescas suggested that it is not conceivable that the world should exist conditionally, and therefore it must be that there exist an uncaused cause which sustains all things.]

[48] [The argument to which Spinoza refers can be found in Bk. 1, Part 1, Ch. 3, and Bk. 1, Part 2, Ch. 3, of Crescas' major work, *Or Adonai*, also called *Or ha-Shem* (Ferrara: Abraham Usque, 1555).]

1. That everything you have indicated in Chapter 2 of the Appendix has been correctly indicated. But in Chapter 1 of the Appendix, page 1, you have indicated the Scholium to Proposition 4, whereas I would prefer you to have indicated the Scholium to Proposition 15, where my declared purpose is to discuss all modes of thinking. Again, on page 2 of the same chapter, you have written these words in the margin, 'Why negations are not *ideae*,' where the word 'negations' should be replaced by '*entia rationis*', for I am speaking of the '*ens rationis*' in general, and saying that it is not an 'idea.'

2. As to my saying that the Son of God is the Father himself, I think it follows clearly from this axiom, namely, that things which agree with a third thing agree with one another. However, since this is a matter of no importance to me, if you think that it may give offence to some theologians, do as seems best to you.

3. Finally, what theologians mean by the word '*personalitas*' is beyond me, though I know what philologists mean by it. Anyway, since the manuscript is in your hands, you can better decide these things yourself. If you think they ought to be changed, do as you please.

Farewell, my dear friend, and remember me who am,

Your most devoted,
B. de Spinoza

Voorburg, 26 July 1663

Letter 13
To the noble and learned Henry Oldenburg, from B.d.S.

[Known only from the O.P. The original is lost.]

Most noble Sir,

Your letter, which I have long looked for, I have at last received, and am also free to answer it. But before embarking on this task, I shall briefly relate the circumstances which have prevented an earlier reply.

When I moved my furniture here in April, I went to Amsterdam. There some of my friends requested me to provide them with a transcript of a certain treatise containing a short account of the Second Part of Descartes' *Principles* demonstrated in geometric style, and the main topics treated in metaphysics, which I had previously dictated to a young man[49] to whom I did not wish to teach my own opinions openly. Then they asked me to prepare the First Part too by the same method, as soon as I could. Not to disappoint my friends, I immediately set about

---

[49] [This was Caesarius: see Ep8.]

this work, completed it in two weeks and delivered it to my friends, who finally asked my permission to publish the whole thing. They readily obtained my consent, but on condition that one of them, in my presence, should give it a more elegant style and add a short preface warning readers that I do not acknowledge everything in the treatise as my own views, 'since I have written in quite a few things which are completely opposed to my own opinions', and should illustrate this fact by one or two examples. One of my friends who has undertaken the publication of this little book has promised to do all this,[50] and that is why I was delayed at Amsterdam for some time. And right from the time of my return to this village where I now live, I have scarcely been my own master because of friends who have been kind enough to call on me.

Now at last, my very dear friend, I have time enough to tell you this, and also to give you the reason why I am allowing this treatise to be published. Perhaps as a result there will be some men holding high positions in my country who will want to see other of my writing which I acknowledge as my own, and so will arrange that I can make them available to the public without risk of trouble. Should this come about, I have no doubt that I shall publish some things immediately; if not, I shall keep silent rather than thrust my opinions on men against my Country's wishes and incur their hostility. I therefore beg you, my honoured friend, to be patient until that time; for then you will either have the treatise in print or a summary of it, as you request. And if in the meantime you would like one or two copies of the work which is now in the press, when I am told so and I also find a convenient way of sending it, I shall comply with your wish.

I now turn to your letter. I thank you most warmly, as I should, and also the noble Boyle, for your outstanding kindness towards me and your goodwill. The many affairs in which you are engaged, of such weight and importance, have not made you unmindful of your friend, and indeed you generously promise that you will make every effort in future to avoid so long an interruption in our correspondence. The learned Mr. Boyle, too, I thank very much for being so good as to reply to my observations, in however cursory and preoccupied a way. I do indeed admit that they are not of such importance that the learned gentleman, in replying to them, should spend time which he can devote to reflections of a higher kind. For my part I did not imagine—indeed, I could never have been convinced—that the learned gentleman had no other object in view in his *Treatise on Nitre* than merely to demonstrate that the puerile and frivolous doctrine of Substantial Forms and Qualities rests on a weak foundation. But being convinced that it was the es-

---

[50] [This was Lodewijk Meyer. Meyer provided a brief introduction to the PPC, underlining the fact that Spinoza was axiomatizing Descartes' thought rather than his own. The present letter also indicates the order in which the PPC was written: first the second part, then the first, and presumably the third part added as an afterthought. It should also be noted that Balling's Dutch translation of the PPC appeared in 1664, the year following the Latin edition. It was more than a translation, but less than the new edition for which Meyer expressed hope in his preface. A number of new passages are added in the Dutch, and there is little reason to believe that these additions were not either made or approved by Spinoza himself.]

teemed Boyle's intention to explain to us the nature of Nitre, that it was a heterogeneous body consisting of fixed and volatile parts, I intended in my explanation to show (as I think I have more than adequately shown) that we can quite easily explain all the phenomena of Nitre, such as are known to me at least, while regarding Nitre as a homogeneous body, not heterogeneous. Therefore it was not for me to prove, but merely to hypothesize, that the fixed salt is the dregs of Nitre, so that I might see how the esteemed Mr. Boyle could prove to me that this salt is not the dregs but a very necessary constituent in the essence of Nitre without which it could not be conceived. For this, as I say, I thought to be the object of the esteemed Mr. Boyle's demonstration.

When I said that the fixed salt has passages hollowed out according to the dimensions of the particles of Nitre, I did not need this to explain the redintegration of Nitre. For from my assertion that its redintegration consists merely in the coagulation of the Spirit of Nitre, it is apparent that every calx whose passages are too narrow to contain the particles of Nitre and whose walls are weak is well fitted to halt the motion of the particles of Nitre, and therefore, by my hypothesis, to redintegrate the Nitre itself. So it is not surprising that there are other salts, such as tartar and potash, with whose aid Nitre can be redintegrated. My only purpose in saying that the fixed salt of Nitre has passages hollowed out in accord with the dimensions of the particles of Nitre was to assign a reason why the fixed salt of Nitre is more suited to redintegrate Nitre without much loss of its original weight. Indeed, from the fact that there are other salts from which Nitre can be redintegrated, I thought I might show that the calx of Nitre is not necessary for constituting the essence of Nitre, if the esteemed Mr. Boyle had not said that there is no salt more universal than Nitre; and so it might have lain concealed in tartar and potash.

When I further said that the particles of Nitre in the larger passages are encompassed by finer matter, I inferred this, as the esteemed Mr. Boyle says, from the impossibility of a vacuum. But I do not know why he calls the impossibility of a vacuum a hypothesis, since it clearly follows from the fact that nothing has no properties. And I am surprised that the esteemed Mr. Boyle doubts this, since he seems to hold that there are no real accidents. Would there not be a real accident, I ask, if Quantity were granted without Substance.

With regard to the causes of the difference of taste between Spirit of Nitre and Nitre itself, I had to suggest these so as to show how I could quite easily explain the phenomena of Nitre merely as a result of the difference I was willing to allow between Spirit of Nitre and Nitre itself, taking no account of the fixed salt.

My remarks as to the inflammability of Nitre and the noninflammability of Spirit of Nitre do not presuppose anything other than that for kindling of a flame in any body there needs be some matter that can separate and set in motion the parts of the body, both of which facts I think are sufficiently taught us by daily experience and reason.

I pass on to the experiments which I put forward so as to confirm my explanation not in any absolute sense but, as I expressly said, to some degree. Against the first experiment which I adduced, the esteemed Mr. Boyle advances nothing beyond what I myself have most expressly remarked. As for the others which I also attempted so as to free from suspicion that which the esteemed Mr. Boyle joins me in noting, he has nothing whatever to say. As to his remarks on the second experiment, to wit, that through purification Nitre is for the most part freed from a salt resembling common salt, this he only says but does not prove. For, as I have expressly said, I did not put forward these experiments to give complete confirmation to my assertions, but only because they seemed to offer some degree of confirmation to which I had said and had shown to be consistent with reason. As to his remark that rising to form little icicles is common to this and to other salts, I do not know how this is relevant; for I grant that other salts also have dregs and are rendered more volatile if they are freed from them. Against the third experiment, too, I see nothing advanced that touches me. In the fifth section I thought that our noble Author was criticising Descartes, which he has also done elsewhere by virtue of the freedom to philosophise granted to everyone without hurt to the reputation of either party. Others, too, who have read the writings of the esteemed Mr. Boyle and Descartes' Principles may well think like me unless they are expressly warned. And I still do not see that the esteemed Mr. Boyle makes his meaning quite clear; for he still does not say whether Nitre will cease to be Nitre if its visible icicles, of which alone he says he is speaking, were to be rubbed until they changed into parallelepipeds or some other shape.

But leaving these matters, I pass on to the esteemed Mr. Boyle's assertions in sections 13 . . . 18. I say that I willingly admit that this redintegration of Nitre is indeed an excellent experiment for investigating the nature of Nitre—that is, when we already know the mechanical principles of philosophy, and that all variations of bodies come about according to the laws of mechanics; but I deny that these things follow from the said experiment more clearly and evidently than from many other commonplace experiments, which do not, however, provide definite proof. As to the esteemed Mr. Boyle's remark that he has not found these views of his so clearly expounded and discussed by others, perhaps he has something I cannot see against the arguments of Verulam and Descartes whereby he considers he can refute them. I do not cite these arguments here, because I do not imagine that the esteemed Mr. Boyle is unaware of them. But this I will say, that these writers, too, wanted phenomena to accord with their reason; if they nevertheless were mistaken on certain points, they were but men, and I think that nothing human was alien to them.[51]

He says, too, that there is a considerable difference between those experiments (that is, the commonplace and doubtful experiments adduced by me) where we do not know what is contributed by Nature and what by other factors, and those where the contributing factors are clearly established. But I still do not see that the esteemed Mr. Boyle has explained to us the nature of the substances that are present in this affair, namely, the nature of the calx of Nitre and the Spirit of Nitre, so that these two seem no less obscure than those which I adduced, namely, common lime and water. As for wood, I grant that it is a more composite body

---

[51] [A reference to the familiar line from Terence: "*Homo sum, humani nihil a me alienumst.*"]

than Nitre; but as long as I do not know the nature of either, and the way in which heat is produced in either of them, what, I ask, does this matter? Again, I do not know by what reasoning the esteemed Mr. Boyle ventures to assert that he knows what Nature contributes in the matter under our consideration. By what reasoning, pray, can he demonstrate to us that the heat was not produced by some very fine matter? Perhaps because there was little lost from the original weight? Even if nothing had been lost, in my opinion no inference could be drawn; for we see how easily things can be dyed some colour as a result of a very small quantity of matter, without thereby becoming heavier or lighter to the senses. Therefore I am justified in entertaining some doubt as to whether there may not have been a concurrence of certain factors imperceptible to the senses, especially while it is not known how all those variations observed by the esteemed Mr. Boyle during the experiments could have arisen from the said bodies. Indeed, I am sure that the heat and the effervescence recounted by the esteemed Mr. Boyle arose from foreign matter.

Again, that disturbance of air is the cause from which sound originates can, I think, be more easily inferred from the boiling of water (I say nothing here of its agitation) than from this experiment where the nature of the concurrent factors is quite unknown, and where heat is also observed without our knowing in what way or from what causes it has originated. Finally, there are many things that emit no smell at all; yet if their parts are to some degree stirred up and become warm, they at once emit a smell; and if again they are cooled, they again have no smell (at least of human sense—perception)—such as amber, and other things which may also be more composite than Nitre.

My remarks on the twenty-fourth section show that Spirit of Nitre is not pure Spirit, but contains much calx of Nitre and other things. So I doubt whether the esteemed Mr. Boyle could have been sufficiently careful in observing what he says he has detected with the aid of scales, namely, that the weight of Spirit of Nitre which he added was roughly equal to the weight lost during detonation.

Finally, although to our eyes pure water can dissolve alkaline salts more rapidly, yet since it is a more homogeneous body than air, it cannot, like air, have so many kinds of corpuscles which can penetrate through the pores of every kind of calx. So since water is made up mostly of definite particles of a single kind which can dissolve calx up to a certain limit—which is not the case with air—it follows that water will dissolve calx up to that limit far more rapidly than air. But on the other hand, since air is made up of both grosser and far finer particles and all kinds of particles which can in many ways get through much narrower pores than can be penetrated by particles of water, it follows that air can dissolve calx of Nitre if not as rapidly as water (because it cannot be made up of so many particles of a particular kind) yet far more effectively and to a finer degree, and render it less active and so more apt to halt the motion of the particles of the Spirit of Nitre. For as yet the experiments do not make me acknowledge any difference between Spirit of Nitre and Nitre itself other than that the particles of the later are at rest, while those of the former are in very lively motion with one another. So the difference between Nitre and Spirit of Nitre is the same as that between ice and water.

But I do not venture to detain you any longer on these matters; I fear I have been too prolix, although I have sought to be as brief as possible. If I have nevertheless been boring, I beg you to forgive me, and at the same time to take in good part which is said frankly and sincerely by a friend. For I judged it wrong, in replying to you, to keep altogether silent on these matters. Yet to praise to you what I could not agree with would have been sheer flattery, than which I deem nothing to be more destructive and damaging in friendships. I therefore resolved to open my mind quite frankly, and in my opinion nothing is more welcome than this to philosophers. Meanwhile, if it seems more advisable to you to consign these thoughts to the fire than to pass them on the learned Mr. Boyle, they are in your hands. Do as you please, so long as you believe me to be a most devoted and loving friend to you and to the noble Mr. Boyle. I am sorry that my slender resources prevent me from showing this otherwise than in words. Still . . . etc.

17/27 July 1663

LETTER 14
Henry Oldenburg to the esteemed B.d.S.

[Known only from the O.P. The Latin original is lost. In the penultimate paragraph, the last sentence appears only in the Dutch edition of the O.P.]

Esteemed Sir, most honoured friend,

I find much happiness in the renewal of our correspondence. Know therefore how I rejoiced to receive your letter dated 17/27 July, and particularly on two accounts, that it gave evidence of your well-being and that it assured me of the constancy of your friendship. To crown it all, you tell me that you have committed to the press the first and second parts of Descartes' *Principia* demonstrated in the geometric style, while generously offering me one or two copies of it. Most gladly do I accept the gift, and I ask you please to send the treatise now in the press to Mr. Peter Serrarius[52] living at Amsterdam, for delivery to me. I have arranged with him to receive such a package and to send it on to me by a friend who is making the crossing.

But allow me to say that I am by no means content with your continued suppression of the writings which you acknowledge as your own, especially in a re-

---

[52] [Peter Serrarius was born in Belgium in 1663, lived in Amsterdam, and was a frequent visitor to London. Few details of his life are known. In 1667 he published, as a reply to Meyer's *Philosophy the Interpreter of Holy Scripture*, a treatise entitled *Responsio ad Exercitationem Paradoxam* (Amsterdam: Typis Cunradi, 1667).]

public so free that there you are permitted to think what you please and to say what you think. I wish you would break through those barriers, especially since you can conceal your name and thus place yourself beyond any risk of danger.

The noble Boyle has gone away: as soon as he returns to town, I shall communicate to him that part of your learned letter which concerns him, and as soon as I have obtained his opinion on your views, I shall write to you again. I think you have already seen his *Sceptical Chymist* which was published in Latin some time ago and is widely circulated abroad. It contains many Chemico-Physical paradoxes, and subjects the Hypostatical principles of the Spagyrists, as they are called, to a strict examination.[53]

He has recently published another little book which perhaps has not yet reached your booksellers. So I am sending it to you enclosed herewith, and I ask you as a friend to take in good part this little gift. The booklet, as you will see, contains a defence of the power of elasticity of air against a certain Francis Linus, who busies himself to explain the phenomena recounted in Mr. Boyle's *New Physico-Mechanical Experiments* by a thread of argument that eludes the intellect as well as all sense-perception.[54] Read it, weigh it, and let me know what you think of it.

Our Royal Society is earnestly and actively pursuing its purpose, confining itself within the limits of experiment and observation, avoiding all debatable digressions.

Recently an excellent experiment has been performed which greatly perplexes the upholders of a vacuum but is warmly welcomed by those who hold that space is a plenum. It is as follows. Let a glass flask A, filled to the brim with water, be inverted with its mouth in a glass jar B containing water, and let it be placed in the Receiver of Mr. Boyle's New Pneumatic Machine. Then let the air be pumped out of the Receiver. Bubbles will be seen to rise in great quantity from the water into the flask A and to force down all the water from these into the jar B below the surface of the water contained therein. Let the two vessels be left in this state for a day or two, the air being repeatedly evacuated from the said Receiver by frequent pumpings. Then let them be removed from the Receiver, and let the flask A be refilled with this water from which air has been removed and again inverted in the jar B, and let both vessels be once more enclosed in the Receiver. When the Receiver has again been emptied by the requisite amount of pumping, perhaps a little bubble will be seen to rise from the neck of the flask A, which, rising to the top and expanding with the continued pumping, will once again force out all the water from

---

[53] [The Spagyrists followed the views of Paracelsus (1490–1541) in rejecting the Aristotelian chemistry of the four elements (earth, fire, air, water) in favor of three ultimate principles: salt, sulphur and mercury. Like Boyle and most seventeenth-century chemists, they used 'principle' and 'element' interchangeably.]

[54] [The full title of Boyle's treatise was *Defensio doctrinae de elatere et gravitate aeris, adversus Franc. Lini objectiones*. It was published in 1663, and a copy was in the official inventory of Spinoza's library.]

the flask, as before. Then let the flask be again taken from the Receiver, filled to the top with water from which the air has been removed, inverted as before, and placed in the Receiver. Then let the Receiver be thoroughly evacuated of air, and when it has been well and truly evacuated, water will remain in the flask in such a state of suspension that it will not descend at all. In this experiment the cause which, according to Boyle, is believed to sustain the water in the Torricellian experiment (namely, the pressure of the air on the water in the vessel B)[55] seems completely removed, and yet the water in the flask does not descend.[56]

I had intended to add more, but friends and business call me away. I shall only add this: if you would like to send me the things you are having printed, please address your letter and packages in the following way . . . etc.

I cannot conclude this letter without urging you again and again to publish your own thoughts. I shall not cease to exhort you until you satisfy my request. In the meantime, if you should be willing to let me have some of the main points contained therein, oh! how I would love you and with how close a tie I would hold myself bound to you! May all go well with you, and continue to love me, as you do.

Your most devoted and dear friend,
Henry Oldenburg

London, 31 July 1663

Letter 15
Cordial greetings to Mr. Lodewijk Meyer, from B. de Spinoza

[Not in the O.P. This letter was discovered by Victor Cousin, and published in 1847.]

My dear friend,

The Preface which you sent me through our friend de Vries I now return to you through him. As you will see for yourself, I have made a few notes in the margin; but there still remain a few things which I have thought it better to let you have by letter.

---

[55] [Torricelli (1608–1647), once a collaborator with Galileo, created the barometer. His celebrated experiment (1643) showed that air pressure can support a column of water to a length inversely proportional to its specific gravity.]

[56] [We know now that it is the tensile strength of the water which must be taken into account to explain the null result of the experiment.]

First, where on page 4 you inform the reader of the occasion of my composing the First Part, I should like you also at the same time to point out, either there or wherever you please, that I composed it within two weeks. Thus forewarned, no one will imagine that what I present is so clear that it could not have been expounded more clearly, and so they will not be put out by a mere word or two which in some places they may find obscure.

Second, I should like you to mention that many of my demonstrations are arranged in a way different from that of Descartes, not to correct Descartes, but only the better to preserve my order of exposition and thus to avoid increasing the number of axioms. And it is also for the same reason that I have had to prove many things which Descartes merely asserts without proof, and to add other things which Descartes omitted.

Finally, my very dear friend, I beg you most earnestly to leave out what you wrote at the end against that petty man,[57] and to delete it entirely. And although I have many reasons for making this request of you, I shall mention only one. I should like everyone to be able readily to accept that this publication is meant for the benefit of all men, and that in publishing this book you are motivated only by a wish to spread the truth, and so you are chiefly concerned to make this little work welcome to all, that you are inviting men in a spirit of goodwill to take up the study of the true philosophy, and your aim is the good of all. This everyone will readily believe when he sees that no one is attacked, and that nothing is advanced which might be offensive to some person. If, however, in due course that person or some other chooses to display his malicious disposition, then you can portray his life and character, and not without approval. I therefore beg you to be good enough to wait until then, and to allow yourself to be persuaded, and to believe me to be your devoted and zealous friend,

B. de Spinoza

Voorburg, 3 August 1663

Our friend de Vries had promised to take this with him, but since he does not know when he is going back to you, I am sending it by someone else.

I am sending along with this a part of the Scholium to Proposition 27 of Part 2, as it begins on page 75, for you to give to the printer to be typeset again.

What I am here sending you will have to be printed again and 14 or 15 lines must be added, which can easily be inserted.[58]

---

[57] [We cannot determine the passage to which Spinoza refers, since it was apparently deleted as he requested.]

[58] [The first edition of the PPC (1663) shows clearly that eleven lines of small type had been interpolated on pages 76 and 77 after these pages had been typeset.]

Letter 16
Henry Oldenburg to the esteemed B.d.S.

[Known only from the O.P. The original is lost.]

Distinguished Sir and most honoured friend,

Scarcely three or four days have passed since I sent you a letter by the ordinary post. In that letter I made mention of a certain booklet written by Mr. Boyle, which has to be sent to you. At that time there appeared no hope of quickly finding a friend to deliver it. Since that time someone has come forward sooner than I expected. So receive now what could not then be sent, together with the dutiful greetings of Mr. Boyle who has now returned to town from the country.

He asks you to consult the preface which he wrote to his Experiments on Nitre, so as to understand the true aim which he set himself in that work: namely, to show that the doctrines of the more firmly grounded philosophy now being revived are elucidated by clear experiments, and that these experiments can very well be explained without the forms, qualities and the futile elements of the Schools.[59] In no way did he undertake to pronounce on the nature of Nitre, nor again to criticise opinions that may be expressed by anyone about the homogeneity of matter and the differences of bodies arising solely from motion, shape, and so on. He says that he meant only to show this, that the various textures of bodies produce their various differences, and that from these proceed very different effects, and that, as long as there has been no reduction to prime matter, some heterogeneity is properly inferred therefrom by philosophers and others. Nor would I think that there is disagreement between you and Mr. Boyle on the fundamental issue.

As to your saying that any calx, whose passages are too narrow to contain the particles of Nitre and whose walls are weak, is apt to halt the motion of the particles of Nitre and therefore to reconstitute the Nitre, Boyle replies that if Spirit of Nitre is mixed with other kinds of calx, it will not, however, combine with them to form true Nitre.

As to the argument you employ to deny the possibility of a vacuum, Boyle says that he knows it and has seen it before, but is not by any means satisfied with it. He says there will be an opportunity to discuss the matter on another occasion.

He has requested me to ask you whether you can provide him with an example where two odorous bodies, when combined into one, compose a body that is completely odourless, as Nitre is. Such, he says, are the parts composing Nitre; for Spirit of Nitre gives out a foul smell, while fixed Nitre is not without smell.

---

[59] [See the notes to Ep3, Ep6 and Ep14.]

He further asks you to consider well whether, in comparing ice and water with Nitre and Spirit of Nitre, you are making a proper comparison. For the whole of the ice is resolved only into water, and when the odourless ice turns again into water it remains odourless, whereas the Spirit of Nitre and its fixed salt are found to have different qualities, as the printed Treatise quite clearly tells us.

These and similar things I gathered from our illustrious author in conversation on this subject. I am sure that, through weakness of memory, my recollection does him grave injustice rather than credit. Since you are both in agreement on the main point, I am not inclined to enlarge any further on these matters. I would rather persuade you both to unite your abilities in striving to advance a genuine and firmly based philosophy. May I urge you especially, with your keen mathematical mind, to continue to establish basic principles, just as I ceaselessly try to entice my noble friend Boyle to confirm and elucidate them by experiments and observations repeatedly and accurately made.

You see, my dear friend, what I am striving for, what I am trying to attain. I know that our native philosophers in our kingdom will in no way fail in their duty to experiment, and I am no less convinced that you in your own land will actively do your part, whatever snarlings or accusations may come from the mob of philosophers or theologians. Having already exhorted you to this in numerous previous letters, I will restrain myself lest I weary you. I shall just make this one further request, that you will please send me with all speed by Mr. Serrarius whatever has already been committed to print, whether it be your commentary on Descartes or something drawn from your own intellectual stores. You will have me that much more closely bound to you, and will understand that, under any circumstance, I am,

Your most devoted,
Henry Oldenburg

London, 4 August 1663

Letter 17
To the learned and sagacious Pieter Balling, from B.d.S.

[Known only from the O.P. The original is lost. It was written in Dutch, and the Latin version which appears in the O.P. may have been made by Spinoza. The Dutch edition has what appears to be a re-translation from the Latin.]

Dear friend,

Your last letter, written, if I am not mistaken, on the 26th of last month, has reached me safely. It caused me no little sorrow and anxiety, though that has much diminished when I reflect on the good sense and strength of character which enable you to scorn the adversities of fortune, or what is thought of as such, at the very time when they are assailing you with their strongest weapons. Still, my anxiety increases day by day, and I therefore beg and beseech you not to regard it as burdensome to write to me without stint.

As for the omens which you mention, namely, that while your child was still well and strong you heard groans such as he uttered when he was ill and just before he died, I am inclined to think that these were not real groans but only your imagination; for you say that when you sat up and listened intently you did not hear them as clearly as before, or as later on when you had gone back to sleep. Surely this shows that these groans were no more than mere imagination which, when it was free and unfettered, could imagine definite groans more effectively and vividly than when you sat up to listen in a particular direction. I can confirm, and at the same time explain, what I am here saying by something that happened to me in Rijnsburg last winter.[60] When one morning just at dawn I awoke from a very deep dream, the images which had come to me in the dream were present before my eyes as vividly as if they had been real things, in particular the image of a black, scabby Brazilian whom I had never seen before. This image disappeared for the most part when, to make a diversion, I fixed my gaze on a book or some other object; but as soon as I again turned my eyes away from such an object while gazing at nothing in particular, the same image of the same Ethiopian kept appearing with the same vividness again and again until it gradually disappeared from sight.

I say that what happened to me in respect of my internal sense of sight happened to you in respect of hearing. But since the cause was quite different, your case was an omen, while mine was not. What I am now going to tell you will make the matter clearly intelligible.

The effects of the imagination arise from the constitution either of body or of mind. To avoid all prolixity, for the present I shall prove this simply from what we experience. We find by experience that fevers and other corporeal changes are the cause of delirium, and that those whose blood is thick imagine nothing but quarrels, troubles, murders and things of that sort. We also see that the imagination can be determined simply by the constitution of the soul, since, as we find, it follows in the wake of the intellect in all things, linking together and interconnecting its images and words just as the intellect does its demonstrations, so that there is almost nothing we can understand without the imagination instantly forming an image.

This being so, I say that none of the effects of the imagination which are due to corporeal causes can ever be omens of things to come, because their causes do not involve any future things. But the effects of imagination, or images, which have their origin in the constitution of the mind can be omens of some future event because the mind can have a confused awareness beforehand of something

---

[60] [Spinoza moved from Rijnsburg to Voorburg in 1663. Perhaps he visited Rijnsburg later, or perhaps he refers to the winter of 1662–1663.]

that is to come. So it can imagine it as firmly and vividly as if such a thing were present to it.

For instance (to take an example like your case), a father so loves his son that he and his beloved son are, as it were, one and the same. And since (as I have demonstrated on another occasion)[61] there must necessarily exist in Thought an idea of the affections of the essence of the son and what follows therefrom, and the father by reason of his union with his son is a part of the said son, the soul of the father must likewise participate in the ideal essence of his son, and in its affections and in what follows therefrom, as I have elsewhere demonstrated at some length. Further, since the soul of the father participates ideally in the things that follow from the essence of the son, he can, as I have said, sometimes imagine something from what follows on the essence of the son as vividly as if he had it in front of him—that is, if the following conditions are fulfilled: (1) If the event which is to happen in the course of the son's life is one of importance. (2) If it is such as we can quite easily imagine. (3) If the time at which this event will take place is not very remote. (4) Finally, if his body is in good order not only as regards health, but is also free and devoid of all the cares and worries that disturb the senses from without. It could also serve to promote this end if we are thinking of things which especially arouse ideas similar to these. For example, if while conversing with any person we hear groans, it will generally happen that when we again think of that same man, the groans which we heard while speaking to him are likely to come back to mind. This dear friend, is my opinion on the question that you raise. I have been very brief, I confess, but deliberately so, in order to give you material for writing to me at the first opportunity, etc.

Voorburg, 20 July 1664

Letter 18
To the esteemed B.d.S., from Willem van Blyenbergh

[Known only from the O.P. The original, which is lost, was written in Dutch, but may be what is in the Dutch edition of the O.P. The Latin is a translation from the Dutch.]

Sir and unknown friend,

I have now several times had the privilege of perusing your recently published *Treatise* with its Appendix,[62] giving it close attention. It would be more seemly to

---

[61] [This occasion is lost to us.]
[62] [This is the PPC with the *Cogitata Metaphysica* appended.]

tell others rather than yourself of the great solidity I found there, and the satisfaction it gave me. But I cannot refrain from saying this much, that the more frequently I peruse it with attention, the more it pleases me, and I am continually finding something that I had not noticed before. However, lest in this letter I appear a flatterer, I will not express too much admiration for the author; I know what price in toil the gods demand for all they give.

But not to keep you too long wondering who it is and how it happens that a stranger should assume the great liberty of writing to you, I will tell you that it is one who, impelled only by desire for pure truth, strives in this brief and transitory life to set his feet on the path to knowledge, so far as our human intelligence permits; one who in his search for truth has no other aim than truth itself; one who seeks to acquire for himself through science neither honours nor riches but truth alone, and the peace of mind that results from truth; one who among all truths and sciences takes pleasure in none more than metaphysical studies—if not in all of them, at least in some part of them—and finds all his pleasure in life in devoting thereto all the leisure hours that can be spared. But not everyone is as blessed as you, and not everyone applies himself as diligently as I imagine you have done, and therefore not everyone has attained the degree of perfection which I see from your work you have attained. In a word, it is one whom you would get to know more closely if you would graciously oblige him so very much as to help open a way and pierce through the tangle of his thoughts.

But to return to the Treatise. Just as I found therein many things which appealed very much to my taste, so I also encountered some things which I found difficult to digest. It would not be right for me, a stranger to you, to raise these matters, the more so because I do not know whether or not this would be acceptable to you. That is why I am sending this preliminary letter, with the request that, if in these winter evenings you have the time and the inclination to oblige me so much as to reply to the difficulties which I still find in your book, I may be permitted to send you some of them. But I adjure you not to be hindered thereby from any more necessary or more agreeable pursuit; for I desire nothing more eagerly than the fulfillment of the promise made in your book,[63] the fuller explication and publication of your views. What I am now at last entrusting to pen and paper I would rather have put to you in person on greeting you; but because first of all I did not know your address, and then the epidemic and finally my own duties prevented me, this was put off time after time.

But in order that this letter may not be entirely without content, and in the hope that you will not find this unwelcome, I shall raise only this one point. In several places both in the *Principia*[64] and in the *Cogitata Metaphysica*,[65] in explaining either your own opinion or Descartes', whose philosophy you were expounding, you maintain that to create and to preserve are one and the same thing

---

[63] [The promise for a fuller development was actually made by Meyer in his preface to the PPC.]
[64] [See PPC1P12.]
[65] [See CM2, Chapters 7, 10 and 11.]

(which is so self-evident to those who have turned their minds to it that it is a fundamental notion) and that God has created not only substances but the motions in substances; that is, that God not only preserves substances in their state by a continuous creation but also their motion and their striving. For instance, God, through his immediate will or action (whichever you like to call it), not only brings it about that the soul continues to exist and perseveres in its state, but is also related in the same way to the motion of the soul. That is, just as God's continuous creation brings it about that things go on existing, so also the striving and motion of things is due to the same cause, since outside God there is no cause of motion. Therefore it follows that God is not only the cause of the substance of the mind but also of every striving or motion of the mind, which we call the will, as you everywhere maintain. From this statement it also seems to follow necessarily either that there is no evil in the motion or will of the soul or that God himself is the immediate agent of that evil. For those things that we call evil also come about through the soul, and consequently through this kind of immediate influence and concurrence of God.

For example, the soul of Adam wants to eat of the forbidden fruit. According to the above statements, it is through God's influence that not only does Adam will, but also (as will immediately be shown) that he wills thus. So either Adam's forbidden act, insofar as God not only moved his will but also insofar as he moved it in a particular way, is not evil in itself, or else God himself seems to bring about what we call evil. And it seems to me that neither you nor Monsieur Descartes solve this difficulty by saying that evil is a non-being with which God does not concur.[66] For whence, then, did the will to eat come, or the Devil's will to pride? Since the will, as you rightly observe, is not anything different from the mind, but is this or that motion or striving of the mind, it has as much need of God's concurrence for the one motion as for the other. Now God's concurrence, as I understand from your writings, is nothing but the determining of a thing by his will in this or that manner. It therefore follows that God concurs with, that is, determines, the evil will insofar as it is evil no less than the good will. For the will of God, which is the absolute cause of all things that exist both in substance and in its strivings, seems to be the prime cause of the evil will insofar as it is evil.

Again, there occurs no determination of will in us without God's having known it from eternity; otherwise, if he did not know it, we are ascribing imperfection to God. But how could God have known it except through his decrees? So his decrees are the cause of our determinations, and thus it once again seems to follow that either the evil will is not anything evil or that God is the immediate cause of that evil.

And here the Theologians' distinction regarding the difference between the act and the evil adhering to the act has no validity. For God decreed not only the act but also the manner of the act; that is, God decreed not only that Adam should eat, but also that he necessarily ate contrary to command, so that it again seems

---

[66] [See CM2, Chapter 3; and CM3, Chapters 7, 10 and 11.]

to follow that either Adam's eating the apple contrary to command is no evil, or that God himself wrought that evil.

This much in your Treatise, esteemed Sir, is for the present incomprehensible to me; for the extremes on both sides are hard to maintain. But I expect from your penetrating judgment and diligence a reply that will satisfy me, and I hope to show you in the future how much I shall be obligated to you thereby.

Be assured, esteemed Sir, that my questions are prompted only by zeal for truth, and for no other personal interest. For I am a free person, not dependent on any profession, supporting myself by honest trading and devoting my spare time to these matters. I also humbly ask that my difficulties should not be unwelcome to you; and if you are minded to reply, as is my heartfelt desire, please write to W.v.B., etc.

Meanwhile, I shall be and remain,

Your devoted servant,
W.v.B.

Dordrecht, 12 December 1664

LETTER 19
To the learned and sagacious Willem van Blyenbergh, from B.d.S.

[Known only from the O.P. The original, which is lost, was written in Dutch, but may be printed in the Dutch edition of the O.P. The Latin is a translation from the Dutch, perhaps by Spinoza. The last paragraph appears only in the Dutch edition.]

My unknown friend,

Your letter of the 12th December, enclosed in another letter dated the 21st of the same month, I finally received on the 26th of that month while at Schiedam. I gathered from it that you are deeply devoted to truth, which you make the sole aim of all your endeavours. Since I have exactly the same objective, this has determined me not only to grant without stint your request to answer to the best of my ability the questions which you are now sending me and will send me in the future, but also to do everything in my power conducive to further acquaintance and sincere friendship. For my part, of all things that are not under my control, what I most value is to enter into a bond of friendship with sincere lovers of truth. For I believe that such a loving relationship affords us a serenity surpassing any other boon in the whole wide world. The love that such men bear to one another, grounded as it is in the love that each has for knowledge of truth, is as unshakable as is the acceptance of truth once it has been perceived. It is, moreover, the highest source of happiness to be found in things not under our command, for truth more than anything else has the power to effect a close union between different sentiments and dispositions. I say nothing of the considerable advantages that derive therefrom, not wishing to detain you any longer on a matter on which you need no instruction. This much I have said so that you may better understand how pleased I am, and shall continue to be, to have the opportunity of serving you.

To avail myself of the present opportunity, I shall now go on to answer your question. This seems to hinge on the following point, that it seems clearly to follow, both from God's providence, which is identical with his will, and from God's concurrence and the continuous creation of things, either that there is no such thing as sin or evil, or that God brings about that sin and that evil. But you do not explain what you mean by evil, and as far as one can gather from the example of Adam's determinate will, by evil you seem to mean the will itself insofar as it is conceived as determined in a particular way, or insofar as it is in opposition to God's command. So you say it is quite absurd (and I would agree, if the case were as you say) to maintain either of the following alternatives, that God himself brings to pass what is contrary to his will, or else that what is opposed to God's will can nevertheless be good. For my own part, I cannot concede that sin and evil are anything positive, much less than anything can be or come to pass against God's will. On the contrary, I not only assert that sin is not anything positive; I maintain that it is only by speaking improperly or in merely human fashion that we say that we sin against God, as in the expression that men make God angry.[67]

For as to the first point, we know that whatever is, when considered in itself without regard to anything else, possesses a perfection coextensive in every case with the thing's essence; for its essence is not the same thing. I take as an example Adam's resolve or determinate will to eat of the forbidden fruit. This resolve or determinate will, considered solely in itself, contains in itself perfection to the degree that it expresses reality. This can be inferred from the fact that we cannot conceive imperfection in things except by having regard to other things possessing more reality.[68] For this reason, when we consider Adam's decision in itself without comparing it with other things more perfect or displaying a more perfect state, we cannot find any imperfection in it. Indeed, we may compare it with innumerable other things much more lacking in perfection in comparison with it, such as stones, logs, and so forth. In actual practise, too, this is universally conceded. For everybody beholds with admiration in animals what he dislikes and regards with aversion in men, like the warring of bees, the jealousy of doves, and so on. In men such things are detested, yet we esteem animals as more perfect because of them. This being the case, it clearly follows that sin, since it indicates only imperfection, cannot consist in anything that expresses reality, such as Adam's decision and its execution.

---

[67] [The anthropomorphism of ordinary language in dealing with God is dealt with in the Appendix to the first part of the *Ethics*, as well as in TTP2 and TTP7.]

[68] [See the introduction to the fourth part of the *Ethics* for a more detailed exposition of the sense in which 'imperfection' is a creature of imagination.]

Letter 19   809

Furthermore, neither can we say that Adam's will was at variance with God's law, and was evil because it was displeasing to God. It would argue great imperfection in God if anything happened against his will, or if he wanted something he could not possess, or if his nature were determined in such a manner that, just like his creatures, he felt sympathy with some things and antipathy to others. Furthermore, this would be in complete contradiction to the nature of God's will; for since his will is identical with his intellect, it would be just as impossible for anything to take place in opposition to his will as in opposition to his intellect. That is to say, anything that would take place against his will would have to be of such a nature as likewise to be in opposition to his intellect, as, for example, a round square. Therefore since Adam's will or decision, regarded in itself, was neither evil nor yet, properly speaking, against God's will, it follows that God can be—or rather, according to the reasoning you refer to, must be—the cause of it. But not insofar as it was evil, for the evil that was in it was simply the privation of a more perfect state which Adam was bound to lose because of his action.

Now it is certain that privation is not something positive, and is so termed in respect of our intellect, not God's intellect. This is due to the fact that we express by one and the same definition all the individual instances of the same genus—for instance, all that have the outward appearance of men—and we therefore deem them all equally capable of the highest degree of perfection that can be inferred from that particular definition. Now when we find one thing whose actions are at variance with that perfection, we consider that it is deprived of that perfection and is astray from its own nature. This we would not do if we had not referred the individual to that particular definition and ascribed to it such a nature. Now God does not know things in abstraction, nor does he formulate general definitions of that sort, and things possess no more reality than that with which God's intellect and potency have endowed them, and which he has assigned to them in actual fact. From this it clearly follows that the privation in question is a term applicable in respect of our intellect only, and not of God's.

This, I believe, is a complete answer to the question. However, to make the path smoother and to remove every shadow of doubt, I think I ought still to answer the following two questions: First, why does Holy Scripture say that God requires the wicked to turn from their evil ways, and why, too, did he forbid Adam to eat of the fruit of the tree when he had ordained the contrary? Secondly, it seems to follow from what I have said that the wicked serve God by their pride, greed and desperate deeds no less than the good by their nobleness, patience, love, etc. For they, too, carry out God's will.

In reply to the first question, I say that Scripture, being particularly adapted to the needs of the common people, continually speaks in merely human fashion, for the common people are incapable of understanding higher things. That is why I think that all that God has revealed to the Prophets as necessary for salvation is set down in the form of law, and in this way the Prophets made up a whole parable depicting God as a king and lawgiver, because he had revealed the means that lead to salvation and perdition, and was the cause thereof. These means, which are simply causes, they called laws, and wrote them down in the form of laws; salvation and perdition, which are simply effects necessarily resulting from these means, they represented as reward and punishment. All their words were adjusted to the framework of this parable rather than to truth. They constantly depicted God in human form, sometimes angry, sometimes merciful, now looking to what is to come, now jealous and suspicious, and even deceived by the Devil. So philosophers and likewise all who have risen to a level beyond law, that is, all who pursue virtue not as a law but because they love it as something very precious, should not find such words a stumbling-block.

Therefore the command given to Adam consisted solely in this, that God revealed to Adam that eating of that tree brought about death, in the same way that he also reveals to us through our natural understanding that poison is deadly. If you ask to what end he made this revelation, I answer that his purpose was to make Adam that much more perfect in knowledge. So to ask God why he did not give Adam a more perfect will is no less absurd than to ask why he has not bestowed on a circle all the properties of a sphere, as clearly follows from what I have said above, and as I have demonstrated in the Scholium to Proposition 15 of my *Principles of Cartesian Philosophy Demonstrated in Geometrical Form*, Part 1.

As to the second difficulty, it is indeed true that the wicked express God's will in their own way, but they are not for that reason at all comparable with the good; for the more perfection a thing has, the more it participates in Deity, and the more it expresses God's perfection. Since, then, the good have incomparably more perfection than the wicked, their virtue cannot be compared with the virtue of the wicked, because the wicked lack the love of God that flows from the knowledge of God, and by which alone, within the limits of our human intellect, we are said to be servants of God. Indeed, not knowing God, the wicked are but an instrument in the hands of the Maker, serving unconsciously and being used up in that service, whereas the good serve consciously, and in serving become more perfect.

This, Sir, is all I can now put forward in answer to your question. I desire nothing more than that it may satisfy you. But if you still find any difficulty, I beg you to let me know, to see if I can remove it. You on your side need have no hesitation, but as long as you think you are not satisfied, I would like nothing better than to know the reasons for it, so that truth may finally come to light. I would have preferred to write in the language[69] in which I was brought up; I might perhaps express my thoughts better. But please excuse this, and correct the mistakes yourself, and consider me,

Your devoted friend and servant,
B. de Spinoza

The Long Orchard, 5 January 1665

I shall be staying at this Orchard for another three or four weeks, and then I intend to return to Voorburg. I believe I shall receive an answer from you before

---

[69] [Namely, Portuguese.]

then, but if your affairs do not permit it, please write to Voorburg with this address—to be delivered to Church Lane at the house of Mr. Daniel Tydeman, painter.

LETTER 20
To the esteemed B.d.S., from Willem van Blyenbergh

[This letter was written in Dutch. The original is extant. The Latin version in the O.P. is a translation from the Dutch.]

Sir, and esteemed friend,

When first I received your letter and read it through hastily, I intended not only to reply at once but also to make many criticisms. But the more I read it, the less matter I found to object to; and great as had been my longing to see it, so great was my pleasure in reading it.

But before I proceed to ask you to resolve certain further difficulties for me, you should first know that there are two general rules which always govern my endeavours to philosophise. One is the clear and distinct conception of my intellect, the other is the revealed Word, or will, of God. In accordance with the one, I try to be a lover of truth, while in accordance with both I try to be a Christian philosopher. And whenever it happens that after long consideration my natural knowledge seems either to be at variance with this Word or not very easily reconcilable with it, this Word has so much authority with me that I prefer to cast doubt on the conceptions I imagine to be clear rather than to set these above and in opposition to the truth which I believe I find prescribed for me in that book. And little wonder, since I wish to continue steadfast in the belief that that Word is the Word of God, that is, that it has proceeded from the highest and most perfect God who possesses far more perfection than I can conceive, and who has perhaps willed to predicate of himself and his works more perfection than I with my finite intellect can today perceive. I say 'can today perceive', because it is possible that by my own doing I have deprived myself of greater perfection, and so if perchance I were in possession of the perfection whereof I have been deprived by my own doing, I might realise that everything presented and taught to us in that Word is in agreement with the soundest conceptions of my mind. But since I now suspect myself of having by continual error deprived myself of a better state, and since you assert in *Principia*, Part 1, Proposition 15 that our knowledge, even when most clear, still contains imperfection, I prefer to turn to that Word even without reason, simply on the grounds that it has proceeded from the most perfect Being (I take this for granted at present, since its proof would here be inappropriate or would take too long) and therefore must be accepted by me.

If I were now to pass judgment on your letter solely under the guidance of my first rule, excluding the second rule as if I did not have it or as if it did not exist, I should have to agree with a great deal of it, as indeed I do, and admire your subtle conceptions; but my second rule causes me to differ more widely from you. However, within the limits of a letter, I shall examine them somewhat more extensively under the guidance of both the rules.

First of all, in accordance with the first stated rule, I asked whether, taking into account your assertions that creation and preservation are one and the same thing and that God causes not only things, but the motions and modes of things, to persist in their state (that is, concurs with them) it does not seem to follow that *there is no evil* or else that *God himself brings about that evil*. I was relying on the rule that nothing can come to pass against God's will, since otherwise it would involve an imperfection; or else the things that God brings about, among which seem to be included those we call evil, would also have to be evil. But since this too involves a contradiction, and however I turned it I could not avoid a contradiction, I therefore had recourse to you, who should be the best interpreter of your own conceptions.

In reply you say that you persist in your first presupposition, namely, that nothing happens or can happen against God's will. But when an answer was required to this problem, whether God then does not do evil, you say that sin is not anything positive, adding that only very improperly can we be said to sin against God. And in the Appendix, Part 1, Chapter 6 you say that *there is no absolute evil, as is self-evident*; for whatever exists, considered in itself without relation to anything else, possesses perfection, which in every case is co-extensive with the thing's essence. Therefore it clearly follows that sins, inasmuch as they denote nothing but imperfections, *cannot consist in anything that expresses essence*. If sin, evil, error, or whatever name one chooses to give it, is nothing else but the loss or deprivation of a more perfect state, then of course it seems to follow that to exist is indeed not an evil or imperfection, but that some evil can arise in an existing thing. For that which is perfect will not be deprived of a more perfect state through an equally perfect action, but through our inclination towards something imperfect because we misuse the powers granted us. This you seem to call not evil, but merely a lesser good, because things considered in themselves contain perfection, and secondly because, as you say, no more essence belongs to things than the divine intellect and power assigns to them and gives them in actual fact, and therefore they can display no more existence in their actions than they have received essence. For if the actions I produce can be no greater or lesser than the essence I have received, it cannot be imagined that there is a privation of a more perfect state. If nothing comes to pass contrary to God's will, and if what comes to pass is governed by the amount of essence granted, in what conceivable way can there be evil, which you call privation of a better state? How can anyone suffer the loss of a more perfect state through an act thus constituted and dependent? Thus it seems to me that you must maintain one of two alternatives: either that there is some evil, or, if not, that there can be no privation of a better state. For that there is no evil, and that there is privation of a better state, seem to be contradictory.

But you will say that, through privation of a more perfect state, we fall back into a lesser good, not into an absolute evil. But you have taught me (Appendix, Part 1, Chapter 3) that one must not quarrel over words. Therefore I am not now arguing as to whether or not it should be called an absolute evil, but whether the decline from a better to a worse state is not called by us, and ought rightly to be called, a worse state, or a state that is evil. But, you will reply, this evil state yet contains much good. Still, I ask whether that man who through his own folly has been the cause of his own deprivation of a more perfect state and is consequently now less than he was before, cannot be called evil.

To escape from the foregoing chain of reasoning since it still confronts you with some difficulties, you assert that *evil does indeed exist, and there was evil in Adam, but it is not something positive, and is called evil in relation to our intellect, not to God's intellect.* In relation to our intellect it is privation (but only insofar as we thereby deprive ourselves of the best freedom which belongs to our nature and is within our power), but in relation to God it is negation.

But let us here examine whether what you call evil, if it were evil only in relation to us, would be no evil; and next, whether evil, taken in the sense you maintain, ought to be called mere negation in relation to God.

The first question I think I have answered to some extent in what I have already said. And although I conceded that my being less perfect than another being cannot posit any evil in me because I cannot demand from my Creator a better state, and that it causes my state to differ only in degree, nevertheless I cannot on that account concede that, if I am now less perfect than I was before and have brought this imperfection on myself through my own fault, I am not to that extent the worse. If, I say, I consider myself as I was before ever I lapsed into imperfection and compare myself with others who possess a greater perfection than I, that lesser perfection is not an evil but a lower grade of good. But if, after falling from a more perfect state and being deprived thereof by my own folly, I compare myself with my original more perfect condition with which I issued from the hand of my Creator, I have to judge myself to be worse than before. For it is not my Creator, but I myself, who has brought me to this pass. I had power enough, as you yourself admit, to preserve myself from error.

To come to the second question, namely, whether the evil which you maintain consists in the privation of a better state—which not only Adam but all of us have lost through rash and ill-considered action—whether this evil, I say, is in relation to God a mere negation. Now to submit this to a thorough examination, we must see how you envisage man and his dependency on God prior to any error, and how you envisage the same man after error. Before error you depict him as possessing no more essence than the divine intellect and power has assigned to him and in actual fact bestows on him. That is, unless I mistake your meaning, man can possess no more and no less perfection than is the essence with which God has endowed him; that is to say, you make man dependent on God in the same way as elements, stones, plants, etc. But if that is your opinion, I fail to understand the meaning of *Principia*, Part 1, Proposition 15 where you say, "Since the will is free to determine itself, it follows that we have the power of restraining our faculty of assent within the limits of the intellect, and therefore of bringing it about that we do not fall into error." Does it not seem a contradiction to make the will so free that it can keep itself from error, and at the same time to make it so dependent on God that it cannot manifest either more or less perfection than God has given it essence?

As to the other question, namely, how you envisage man after error, you say that man deprives himself of a more perfect state by an over-hasty action, namely, by not restraining his will within the limits of his intellect. But it seems to me that both here and in the *Principia* you should have shown in more detail the two extremes of this privation, what he possessed before the privation and what he still retained after the loss of that perfect state, as you call it. There is indeed something said about what we have lost, but not about what we have retained, in *Principia*, Part 1, Proposition 15: *So the whole imperfection of error consists solely in the privation of the best freedom, which is called error.* Let us take a look at these two statements just as they are set out by you. You maintain not only that there are in us such very different modes of thinking, some of which we call willing and others understanding, but also that their proper ordering is such that we ought not to will things before we clearly understand them. You also assert that if we restrain our will within the limits of our intellect we shall never err, and, finally, that it is within our power to restrain the will within the limits of the intellect.

When I give earnest consideration to this, surely one of two things must be true: either all that has been asserted is mere fancy, or God has implanted in us this same order. If he has so implanted it, would it not be absurd to say that this has been done to no purpose, and that God does not require us to observe and follow this order? For that would posit a contradiction in God. And if we must observe the order implanted in us, how can we then be and remain thus dependent on God? For if no one shows either more or less perfection than he has received essence, and if this power must be known by its effects, he who lets his will extend beyond the limits of his intellect has not received sufficient power from God; otherwise he would also have put it into effect. Consequently, he who errs has not received from God the perfection of not erring; if he had, he would not have erred. For according to you there is always as much of essence given us as there is of perfection realised.

Secondly, if God has assigned us as much essence as enables us to observe that order, as you assert we are able to do, and if we always produce as much perfection as we possess essence, how comes it that we transgress that order? How comes it that we are able to transgress that order and that we do not always restrain the will within the limits of the intellect?

Thirdly, if, as I have already shown you to assert, I am so dependent on God that I cannot restrain my will either within or beyond the limits of my intellect unless God has previously given me so much essence and, by his will, has predetermined the one course or the other, how then, if the matter be deeply considered, can freedom of will be available to me? Does it not seem to argue a contradiction in God, to lay down an order for restraining our will within the limits of our intellect, and not to vouchsafe us as much essence or perfection as to enable us to observe that order? And if, in accordance with your opinion, he has granted us that much perfection, we surely could never have erred. For we must produce as much perfection as we possess essence, and always manifest in our actions the power granted us. But our errors are a proof that we do not possess a power of the kind that is thus dependent on God, as you hold. So one of these alternatives must be true: either we are not dependent on God in that way, or we do not have in ourselves the power of being able not to err. But on your view we do have the power not to err. Therefore we cannot be dependent on God in that way.

From what has been said I think it is now clear that it is impossible that evil, or being deprived of a better state, should be a negation in relation to God. For what is meant by privation, or the loss of a more perfect state? Is it not to pass from a greater to a lesser perfection, and consequently from a greater to a lesser essence, and to be placed by God in a certain degree of perfection and essence? Is that not to will that we can acquire no other state outside his perfect knowledge, unless he had decreed and willed otherwise? Is it possible that this creature, produced by that omniscient and perfect Being who willed that it should retain a certain state of essence—indeed, a creature with whom God continually concurs so as to maintain it in that state—that this creature should decline in essence, that is, should be diminished in perfection, without God's knowledge? This seems to involve an absurdity. Is it not absurd to say that Adam lost a more perfect state and was consequently incapable of practising the order which God had implanted in his soul, while God had no knowledge of that loss and of that imperfection? Is it conceivable that God should constitute a being so dependent that it would produce just such an action and then should lose a more perfect state because of that action (of which God, moreover, would be an absolute cause), and yet God would have no knowledge of it?

I grant that there is a difference between the act and the evil adhering to the act; but that 'evil in relation to God is negation' is beyond my comprehension. That God should know the act, determine it and concur with it, and yet have no knowledge of the evil that is in the act nor of its outcome—this seems to me impossible in God.

Consider with me that God concurs with my act of procreation with my wife; for that is something positive, and consequently God has clear knowledge of it. But insofar as I misuse this act with another woman contrary to my promise and vow, evil accompanies the act. What could be negative here in relation to God? Not the act of procreation; for insofar as that is positive, God concurs with it. Therefore the evil that accompanies the act must be only that, contrary to my own pledge or God's command, I do this with a woman with whom this is not permissible. Now is it conceivable that God should know our actions and concur with them, and yet not know with whom we engage in those actions—especially since God also concurs with the action of the woman with whom I transgressed? It seems hard to think this of God.

Consider the act of killing. Insofar as it is a positive act, God concurs with it. But the result of that action, namely, the destruction of a being and the dissolution of God's creature—would God be unaware of this, as if his own work could be unknown to him? (I fear that here I do not properly understand your meaning, for you seem to me too subtle a thinker to perpetrate so gross an error.) Perhaps you will reply that those actions, just as I present them, are all simply good, and that no evil accompanies them. But then I cannot understand what it is you call evil, which follows on the privation of a more perfect state; and furthermore the whole world would then be put in eternal and lasting confusion, and we men would become beasts. Consider, I pray, what profit this opinion would bring to the world.

You also reject the common description of man, and you attribute to each man as much perfection of action as God has in fact bestowed on him to exercise. But this way of thinking seems to me to imply that the wicked serve God by their works just as well as do the godly. Why? Because neither of them can perform actions more perfect than they have been given essence, and which they show in what they practise. Nor do I think that you give a satisfactory reply to my question in your second answer, where you say:—*The more perfection a thing has, the more it participates in Deity, and the more it expresses God's perfection. Therefore since the good have incalculably more perfection than the wicked, their virtue cannot be compared with that of the wicked. For the latter are but a tool in the hands of the master, which serves unconsciously and is consumed in serving. But the good serve consciously, and in serving become more perfect.* In both cases, however, this much is true—they can do no more; for the more perfection the one displays compared with the other, the more essence he has received compared with the other. Do not the godless with their small store of perfection serve God equally as well as the godly? For according to you God demands nothing more of the godless; otherwise he would have granted them more essence. But he has not given them more essence, as is evident from their works. Therefore he asks no more of them. And if it is the case that each of them after his kind does what God wills, neither more nor less, why should he whose achievement is slight, yet as much as God demands of him, not be equally acceptable to God as the godly?

Furthermore, as according to you we lose a more perfect state by our own folly through the evil that accompanies the act, so here too you appear to assert that by restraining the will within the limits of the intellect we not only preserve our present perfection but we even become more perfect by serving. I believe there is a contradiction here, if we are so dependent on God as to be unable to produce either more or less perfection than we have received essence—that is, than God has willed—and yet we should become worse through our folly, or better through our prudence. So if man is such as you describe him, you seem to be maintaining nothing other than this, that the ungodly serve God by their works just as much as the godly by their works, and in this way we are made as dependent on God as elements, plants, stones, etc. Then what purpose will our intellect serve? What purpose the power to restrain the will within the limits of the intellect? Why has that order been imprinted in us?

And see, on the other side, what we deprive ourselves of, namely, painstaking and earnest deliberation as to how we may render ourselves perfect in accordance with the rule of God's perfection and the order implanted in us. We deprive ourselves of the prayer and yearnings towards God wherefrom we perceive we have so often derived a wonderful strength. We deprive ourselves of all religion, and all the hope and comfort we expect from prayer and religion. For surely if God has no knowledge of evil, it is still less credible that he will punish evil. What reasons can I have, then, for not eagerly committing all sorts of villainy (provided I can escape the judge)? Why not enrich myself by abominable means? Why not indiscriminately do whatever I like, according to the promptings of the flesh? You will say, because virtue is to be loved for itself. But how can I love virtue? I have not been given that much essence and perfection. And if I can gain just as much contentment from the one course as the other, why force myself to restrain the will within the limits of the intellect? Why not do what my passions suggest? Why not secretly kill the man who gets in my way? See what an opportunity we give to all the ungodly, and to godlessness. We make ourselves just like logs, and all our actions like the movements of a clock.

From what has been said it seems to me very hard to maintain that only improperly can we be said to sin against God. For then what is the significance of the power granted to us to restrain the will within the limits of the intellect, by transgressing which we sin against that order? Perhaps you will reply, this is not a case of sinning against God, but against ourselves; for if it could properly be said that we sin against God, it must also be said that something happens against God's will, which according to you is an impossibility, and therefore so is sinning. Still, one of these alternatives must be true: either God wills it, or he does not. If God will its, how can it be evil in respect to us? If he does not will it, on your view it would not come to pass. But although this, on your view, would involve some absurdity, nevertheless it seems to me very dangerous to admit therefore all the absurdities already stated. Who knows whether, by careful thought, a remedy may not be found to effect some measure of reconciliation?

With this I bring to an end my examination of your letter in accordance with my first general rule. But before proceeding to examine it according to the second rule, I have yet two points to make which are relevant to the line of thought of your letter, both set forth in your *Principia*, Part 1, Proposition 15. First, you affirm that 'we can keep the power of willing and judging within the limits of the intellect'. To this I cannot give unqualified agreement. For if this were true, surely out of countless numbers at least one man would be found who would show by his actions that he had this power. Now everyone can discover in his own case that, however much strength he exerts, he cannot attain this goal. And if anyone has any doubt about this, let him examine himself and see how often, in despite of his intellect, his passions master his reason even when he strives with all his might.

But you will say that the reason we do not succeed is not because it is impossible, but because we do not apply enough diligence. I reply that if it were possible, then at least there would be one instance found out of so many thousands. But from all men there has not been, nor is there, one who would venture to boast that he has never fallen into error. What surer arguments than actual examples could be adduced to prove this point? Even if there were just a few, then there would be at least one to be found; but since there is not a single one, then likewise there is no proof.

But you will persist and say: if it is possible that, by suspending judgment and restraining the will within the bounds of the intellect, I can once bring it about that I do not err, why could I not always achieve this by applying the same diligence? I reply that I cannot see that we have this day as much strength as enables us to continue so always. On one occasion, by putting all my effort into it, I can cover two leagues in one hour; but I cannot always manage that. Similarly on one occasion I can by great exertion keep myself from error, but I do not always have the strength to accomplish this. It seems clear to me that the first man, coming forth from the hand of that perfect craftsman, did have that power; but (and in this I agree with you) either by not making sufficient use of that power or by misusing it, he lost his perfect state of being able to do what had previously been within his power. This I could confirm by many arguments, were it not too lengthy a business. And in this I think lies the whole essence of Holy Scripture, which we ought therefore to hold in high esteem, since it teaches us what is so clearly confirmed by our natural understanding, that our fall from our first perfection was due to our folly. What then is more essential than to recover from that fall as far as we can? And that is also the sole aim of Holy Scripture, to bring fallen man back to God.

The second point from the *Principia*, Part 1, Proposition 15 affirms that *to understand things clearly and distinctly is contrary to the nature of man*, from which you finally conclude that *it is far better to assent to things even though they are confused, and to exercise our freedom, than to remain for ever indifferent, that is, at the lowest degree of freedom*. I do not find this clear enough to win my assent. For suspension of judgment preserves us in the state in which we were created by our Creator, whereas to assent to what is confused is to assent to what we do not understand, and thus to give equally ready assent to the false as to the true. And if (as Monsieur Descartes somewhere teaches us)[70] we do not in assenting comply with that order which God has given us in respect of our intellect and will, namely, to withhold assent from what is not clearly perceived, then even though we may chance to hit upon truth, yet we are sinning in not embracing truth according to that order which God has willed. Consequently, just as the withholding of assent preserves us in the state in which we were placed by God, so assenting to things confused puts us in a worse position. For it lays the foundations of error whereby we thereafter lose our perfect state.

But I hear you say, is it not better to render ourselves more perfect by assenting to things even though confused than, by not assenting, to remain always at the lowest degree of perfection and freedom? But apart from the fact that we have denied this and in some measure have shown that we have rendered ourselves not better but worse, it also seems to us an impossibility and practically a contradiction that God should make the knowledge of things determined by himself extend

---

[70] [See Descartes' *Principles of Philosophy* I, XXXI; and also Spinoza's scholium to PPC1P15.]

beyond the knowledge that he has given us. Indeed, God would thus contain within himself the absolute cause of our errors. And it is not inconsistent with this that we cannot complain of God that he did not bestow on us more than he has bestowed, since he was not bound so to do. It is indeed true that God was not bound to give us more than he has given us; but God's supreme perfection also implies that a creature proceeding from him should involve no contradiction, as would then appear to follow. For nowhere in created Nature do we find knowledge other than in our own intellect. To what end could this have been granted us other than that we might contemplate and know God's works? And what seems to be a more certain conclusion than that there must be agreement between things to be known and our intellect?

But if I were to examine your letter under the guidance of my second general rule, our differences would be greater than under the first rule. For I think (correct me if I am wrong) that you do not ascribe to Holy Scripture that infallible truth and divinity which I believe lies therein. It is indeed true that you declare your belief that God has revealed the things of Holy Scripture to the prophets, but in such an imperfect manner that, if it were as you say, it would imply a contradiction in God. For if God has revealed his Word and his will to men, then he has done so for a definite purpose, and clearly. Now if the prophets have composed a parable out of the Word which they received, then God must either have willed this, or not willed it. If God willed that they should compose a parable out of his Word, that is, that they should depart from his meaning, God would be the cause of that error and would have willed something self-contradictory. If God did not will it, it would have been impossible for the prophets to compose a parable therefrom. Moreover, it seems likely, on the supposition that God gave his Word to the prophets, that he gave it in such a way that they did not err in receiving it. For God must have had a definite purpose in revealing his Word; but his purpose could not have been to lead men into error, thereby, for that would be a contradiction in God. Again, man could not have erred against God's will, for that is impossible according to you. In addition to all this, it cannot be believed of the most perfect God that he should permit his Word, given to the prophets to communicate to the people, to have a meaning given it by the prophets other than what God willed. For if we maintain that God communicated his Word to the prophets, we thereby maintain that God appeared to the prophets, or spoke with them, in a miraculous way. If now the prophets composed a parable from the communicated Word,— that is, gave it a meaning different from that which God intended them to give— God must have so instructed them. Again, it is as impossible in respect of the prophets as it is contradictory in respect of God, that the prophets could have understood a meaning different from that which God intended.

You also seem to provide scant proof that God revealed his Word in the manner you indicate, namely, that he revealed only salvation and perdition, decreeing the means that would be certain to bring this about, and that salvation and perdition are no more than the effects of the means decreed by him. For surely if the prophets had understood God's word in that sense, what reasons could they have had for giving it another meaning? But I do not see you produce a single proof to persuade us that we should prefer your view to that of the prophets. If you think your proof to consist in this, that otherwise the Word would include many imperfections and contradictions, I say that this is mere assertion, not proof. And if both meanings were squarely before us, who knows which would contain fewer imperfections? And finally, the supremely perfect Being knew full well what the people could understand, and therefore what must be the best method of instructing them.

As to the second part of your first question, you ask yourself why God forbade Adam to eat of the fruit of the tree when he had nevertheless decreed the contrary; and you answer that the prohibition to Adam consisted only in this, that God revealed to Adam that the eating of the fruit of the tree caused death just as he reveals to us through our natural intellect that poison is deadly for us. If it is established that God forbade something to Adam, what reasons are there why I should give more credence to your account of the manner of the prohibition than to that given by the prophets to whom God himself revealed the manner of the prohibition? You will say that your account of the prohibition is more natural, and therefore more in agreement with truth and more befitting God. But I deny all this. Nor can I conceive that God has revealed to us through our natural understanding that poison is deadly; and I do not see why I would ever know that something is poisonous if I had not seen and heard of the evil effects of poison in others. Daily experience teaches us how many men, not recognising poison, unwittingly eat it and die. You will say that if people knew it was poison, they would realise that it is evil. But I reply that no one knows poison, or can know it, unless he has seen or heard that someone has come to harm by using it. And if we suppose that up to this day we had never heard or seen that someone had done himself harm by using this kind of thing, not only would we be unaware of it now but we would not be afraid to use it, to our detriment. We learn truths of this kind every day.

What in this life can give greater delight to a well-formed intellect than the contemplation of that perfect Deity? For being concerned with that which is most perfect, such contemplation must also involve in itself the highest perfection that can come within the scope of our finite intellect. Indeed, there is nothing in my life for which I would exchange this pleasure. In this I can pass much time in heavenly joy, though at the same time being much distressed when I realise that my finite intellect is so wanting. Still, I soothe this sadness with the hope I have — a hope that is dearer to me than life — that I shall exist hereafter and continue to exist, and shall contemplate that Deity more perfectly than I do today. When I consider this brief and fleeting life in which I look to my death at any moment, if I had to believe that there would be an end of me and I should be cut off from that holy and glorious contemplation, then surely I would be more wretched than all creatures who have no knowledge of their end. For before my death, fear of death would make me wretched, and after my death I would be nothing, and therefore wretched in being deprived of that divine contemplation.

Now it is to this that your opinions seem to lead, that when I cease to be here, I shall for ever cease to be. Against this the Word and will of God, by their inner testimony in my soul, give me assurance that after this life I shall eventually in a more perfect state rejoice in contemplation of the most perfect Deity. Surely, even if that hope should turn out to be false, yet it makes me happy as long as I hope. This is the only thing I ask of God, and shall continue to ask, with prayers, sighs and earnest supplication (would that I could do more to this end!) that as long as there is breath in my body, it may please him of his goodness to make me so fortunate that, when this body is dissolved, I may still remain an intellectual being able to contemplate that most perfect Deity. And if only I obtain that, it matters not to me what men here believe, and what convictions they urge on one another, and whether or not there is something founded on our natural intellect and can be grasped by it. This, and this alone, is my wish, my desire, and my constant prayer, that God should establish this certainty in my soul. And if I have this (and oh! if I have it not, how wretched am I!), then let my soul cry out, "As the hart panteth after the water-brook, so longeth my soul for thee, O living God. O when will come the day when I shall be with thee and behold thee?"[71] If only I attain to that, then have I all the aspiration and desire of my soul. But in your view such hopes are not for me, since our service is not pleasing to God. Nor can I understand why God (if I may speak of him in so human a fashion) should have brought us forth and sustained us, if he takes no pleasure in our service and our praise. But if I have misunderstood your views, I should like to have your clarification.

But I have detained myself, and perhaps you as well, far too long; and seeing that my time and paper are running out, I shall end. These are the points in your letter I would still like to have resolved. Perhaps here and there I have drawn from your letter a conclusion which may chance not to be your own view; but I should like to hear your explanation regarding this.

I have recently occupied myself in reflecting on certain attributes of God, in which your appendix has given me no little help. I have in effect merely paraphrased your views, which seem to me little short of demonstrations. I am therefore very much surprised that L. Meyer says in his Preface that this does not represent your opinions, that you were under an obligation thus to instruct your pupil in Descartes' philosophy, as you had promised, but that you held very different views both of God and the soul, and in particular the will of the soul. I also see stated in that Preface that you will shortly publish the *Cogitata Metaphysica* in an expanded form. I very much look forward to both of these, for I have great expectations of them. But it is not my custom to praise someone to his face.

This is written in sincere friendship, as requested in your letter, and to the end that truth may be discovered. Forgive me for having written at greater length than I had intended. If I should receive a reply from you, I should be much obliged to you. As to writing in the language in which you were brought up, I can have no objection, if at least it is Latin or French. But I beg you to let me have your answer in this same language, for I have understood your meaning in it quite well,

---

[71] [Compare Psalms 42:1–2. The quotation is not exact.]

and perhaps in Latin I should not understand it so clearly. By so doing you will oblige me, so that I shall be, and remain,

Your most devoted and dutiful,
Willem van Blyenbergh

Dordrecht, 16 January 1665

In your reply I should like to be informed more fully what you really mean by negation in God.

LETTER 21
To the learned and accomplished Willem van Blyenbergh, from B.d.S.

[Known only from the O.P. The original, which is lost, was written in Dutch, and translated into Latin, perhaps by Spinoza. The version in the Dutch edition appears to be a re-translation from the Latin.]

Sir, and friend,

When I read your first letter, I had the impression that our views were nearly in agreement. From your second letter, however, which I received on the 21st of this month, I realise that this is far from being so, and I see that we disagree not only in the conclusions to be drawn by a chain of reasoning from first principles, but in those very same first principles, so that I hardly believe that our correspondence can be for our mutual instruction. For I see that no proof, however firmly established according to the rules of logic, has any validity with you unless it agrees with the explanation which you, or other theologians of your acquaintance, assign to Holy Scripture. However, if it is your conviction that God speaks more clearly and effectually through Holy Scripture than through the light of the natural understanding which he has also granted us and maintains strong and uncorrupted through his divine wisdom, you have good reason to adapt your understanding to the opinions which you ascribe to Holy Scripture. Indeed, I myself could do no other. For my part, I plainly and unambiguously avow that I do not understand Holy Scripture, although I have devoted quite a number of years to its study. And since I am conscious that when an indisputable proof is presented to me, I find it impossible to entertain thoughts that cast doubt upon it, I entirely acquiesce in what my intellect shows me without any suspicion that I am deceived therein, or that Holy Scripture, without my even examining it, can contradict it. For truth is not at odds with truth, as I have made clear in my Appendix (I cannot indicate the chapter, for I do not have the book here with me in the country).⁷² And even if I were once to find untrue the fruits which I have gathered from my natural understanding, they would still make me happy; for I enjoy them, and seek to pass my life not in sorrowing and sighing, but in peace, joy and cheerfulness, and so I ascend a step higher. Meanwhile I realise (and this gives me the greatest satisfaction and peace of mind) that all things come to pass as they do through the power of a most perfect Being and his immutable decree.

To return to your letter, I owe you many and sincere thanks for having confided in me in time your method of philosophising, but I do not thank you for attributing to me the sort of opinions you want to read into my letter. What grounds did my letter give you for attributing to me these opinions: that men are like beasts, that men die and perish after the manner of beasts, that our works are displeasing to God, and so forth? (It is in this last point that our disagreement is most striking, for I take your meaning to be that God is pleased with our works just like someone who has attained his end when things fall out as he wished.) For my part, surely I have clearly stated that the good worship God, and by their constancy in worship they become more perfect, and that they love God. Is this to liken them to beasts, or to say that they perish in the manner of beasts, or that their works are not pleasing to God?

If you had read my letter with more care, it would have been obvious to you that our point of disagreement lies in this alone: are the perfections received by the good imparted to them by God in his capacity as God, that is, by God taken absolutely without ascribing any human attributes to him—this is the view I hold—or by God in his capacity of judge? The latter is what you maintain, and for this reason you take the line that the wicked, because they do whatever they can in accordance with God's decree, serve God no less than the good serve him. But this in no way follows from what I say. I do not bring in the notion of God as judge, and so my evaluation of works turns on the quality of the works, not on the potency of the doer, and the reward that follows from the action does so by the same necessity as it follows from the nature of a triangle that its three angles have to be equal to two right angles. This will be obvious to everyone who attends simply to the following point, that our supreme blessedness consists in love towards God, and that this love flows necessarily from the knowledge of God that is so heartily urged on us. This can be readily demonstrated in a general way if only one has regard to the nature of God's decree, as I have explained in my Appendix.⁷³ I admit, however, that all those who confuse God's nature with the nature of man are quite unqualified to understand this.

I had intended to end this letter here, so as not to bore you any further with matters which (as is evident from the very devout addition at the end of your letter) serve for jest and derision, and are of no value. But not to reject your request

---

⁷² [Spinoza is probably referring to CM2, Chapter 8.]
⁷³ [See CM1, Chapter 3 and CM2, Chapter 11. For the intellectual love of God, see also E5P30–P36.]

entirely, I shall proceed further to explain the terms 'negation' and 'privation', and attempt briefly to throw more light on any obscurities in my previous letter.

First, then, I say that privation is not an act of depriving; it is nothing more than simply a state of want, which in itself is nothing. It is only a construct of the mind (*ens rationis*) or a mode of thinking which we form from comparing things with one another. For instance, we say that a blind man is deprived of sight because we readily imagine him as seeing. This imagining may arise from comparing him with those who can see, or from comparing his present state with a past state when he could see. When we consider the man from this perspective, comparing his nature with that of others or with his own past nature, we assert that sight pertains to his nature, and so we say that he is deprived of it. But when we consider God's decree and God's nature, we can no more assert of that man that he is deprived of sight than we can assert it of a stone. For to say that sight belongs to that man at that time is quite as illogical as to say that it belongs to a stone, since nothing more pertains to that man, and is his, than that which God's intellect and will has assigned to him. Therefore God is no more the cause of his not seeing than of a stone's not seeing, this latter being pure negation. So, too, when we consider the nature of a man who is governed by a lustful desire and we compare his present desire with the desire of a good man, or with the desire he himself once had, we assert that this man is deprived of the better desire, judging that a virtuous desire belonged to him at that point of time. This we cannot do if we have regard to the nature of the decree and intellect of God. For from that perspective the better desire pertains to that man's nature at that point of time no more than to the nature of the Devil or a stone. Therefore from that perspective the better desire is not a privation but a negation. So privation is simply to deny of a thing something that we judge pertains to its nature, and negation is to deny something of a thing because it does not pertain to its nature.

From this it is clear why Adam's desire for earthly things was evil only in respect to our intellect, not God's intellect. For granted that God knew the past and present state of Adam, this does not mean that he understood Adam as deprived of a past state, that is, that the past state pertained to his nature. If that were so, God would be understanding something that was contrary to his will, that is, he would be understanding something that was contrary to his own understanding. Had you grasped this point, and also that I do not concede the sort of freedom that Descartes ascribes to the mind—as L. Meyer testified on my behalf in his Preface—you would have found no trace of contradiction in what I have said. But I see now that it would have been far better if in my first letter I had adhered to Descartes' line, that we cannot know in what way our freedom, and whatever stems from it, can be reconciled with the providence and freedom of God (see my Appendix, various passages). Consequently, we cannot find any contradiction between God's creation and our freedom because it is beyond us to understand how God created the world and—which is the same thing—how he preserves it. I thought you had read the Preface, and that I would be failing in the duty of friendship, which I sincerely offered, if I did not give you my genuine opinion. But no matter.

However, as I see that you have not yet thoroughly understood Descartes' meaning, I ask you to give careful consideration to the following two points. First, neither Descartes nor I have ever said that it pertains to our nature to restrain our will within the limits of the intellect, but only that God has given us a determinate intellect and an indeterminate will, yet in such a way that we know not to what end he has created us. Further, an indeterminate or perfect will of that kind not only renders us more perfect but is also very necessary for us, as I shall point out in due course.

Secondly, our freedom lies not in a kind of contingency nor in a kind of indifference, but in the mode of affirmation and denial, so that the less indifference there is in our affirmation or denial, the more we are free. For instance, if God's nature is known to us, the affirmation of God's existence follows from our nature with the same necessity as it results from the nature of a triangle that its three angles are equal to two right angles. Yet we are never so free as when we make an affirmation in this way. Now since this necessity is nothing other than God's decree, as I have clearly shown in my Appendix, hence we may understand after a fashion how we act freely and are the cause of our action notwithstanding that we act necessarily and from God's decree. This, I repeat, we can understand in a way when we affirm something that we clearly and distinctly perceive. But when we assert something that we do not clearly and distinctly grasp—that is, when we suffer our will to go beyond the bounds of our intellect—then we are not thus able to perceive that necessity and God's decrees; however, we do perceive the freedom of ours that is always involved in the will (in which respect alone our actions are termed good or bad). If we then attempt to reconcile our freedom with God's decree and his continuous creation, we confuse that which we clearly and distinctly understand with that which we do not comprehend, and so our effort is in vain. It is therefore sufficient to us to know that we are free, and that we can be so notwithstanding God's decree, and that we are the cause of evil; for no action can be called evil except in respect of our freedom. So much I have said concerning Descartes in order to show that in this matter his position is perfectly consistent.

Turning now to my own position, I shall first briefly draw attention to an advantage that accrues from my view, an advantage that lies chiefly in this, that by this view of things our intellect places our mind and body in God's hands free from all superstition. Nor do I deny the utility for us of prayer, for my intellect does not extend so far as to embrace all the means that God possesses for bringing men to the love of himself, that is, to salvation. My opinion is so far from being pernicious that, on the contrary, for those who are not hampered by prejudices and childish superstition it is the one means of obtaining the highest degree of blessedness.

When you say that by making men so dependent on God I reduce them to the level of elements, plants and stones, this is enough to show that you have completely misunderstood my views and are confusing the field of intellect with that of the imagination. If you had apprehended by pure intellect the meaning of dependence on God, you would certainly not think that things, insofar as they depend on God, are dead, corporeal and imperfect. (Who has ever dared to speak so basely of the supremely perfect Being?) On the contrary, you would realise that it is for this reason, and insofar as they depend on God, that they are perfect. So this dependence on God and necessity of action through God's decree can be best understood when we have regard, not to logs and plants, but to created things of the highest degree of intelligibility and perfection. This is quite clear from my second observation on the meaning of Descartes, which you should have noted.

I am bound to express astonishment at your saying that if God does not punish wrongdoing (that is, in the way that a judge inflicts a punishment which is not entailed by the wrongdoing itself, for this alone is the point at issue), what consideration hinders me from plunging headlong into all sorts of crime? Surely, he who refrains from so doing by fear of punishment—which I do not impute to you—in no way acts from love and by no means embraces virtue. For my own part I refrain, or try to refrain, from such behaviour because it is directly opposed to my particular nature, and would cause me to stray from the love and knowledge of God.

Again, if you had given a little thought to the nature of man and had understood the nature of God's decree as explained in my Appendix,[74] and had finally known how inference should be made before a conclusion is reached, you would not have so rashly asserted that my view puts us on a level with logs and the like, nor would you have saddled me with all the absurdities you imagine.

With regard to the two points which, before proceeding to your second rule, you say you fail to understand, I reply first that Descartes suffices for arriving at your conclusion, namely, that if only you pay attention to your nature, you experience the ability to suspend judgment. But if you are saying that you do not find in your own experience that our power over reason today is great enough to enable us always to do the same in the future, to Descartes this would be the same as to say that we cannot see today that as long as we exist we shall always be thinking things, or retain the nature of a thinking thing—which surely involves a contradiction.

To your second point I say, with Descartes, that if we could not extend our will beyond the bounds of our very limited intellect, we should be in a most wretched plight. It would not be in our power even to eat a piece of bread, or to move a step, or to halt. For all things are uncertain, and fraught with peril.

I pass on now to your second rule, and I assert that for my part, while I do not ascribe to Scripture the sort of truth that you believe to be contained in it, yet I think that I ascribe to it as much authority, if not more, and that I am far more cautious than others in not assigning to it certain childish and absurd doctrines, for which one must needs be supported either by a thorough knowledge of philosophy or by divine revelation. So I am quite unmoved by the explanations of Scripture advanced by the common run of theologians, especially if they are of the kind that always take Scripture literally by its outward meaning. Apart from the Socinians, I have never found any theologian so stupid as not to see that Holy Scripture very often speaks of God in merely human style and expresses its meaning in parables.

---

[74] [See CM2, Chapters 7–9.]

As for the contradiction which you vainly, in my opinion, try to show, I think that by parable you understand something quite different from what is generally accepted. Who has ever heard that a man who expresses his concepts in parables goes astray from his intended meaning? When Micaiah told King Ahab that he had seen God sitting on his throne and the celestial hosts standing on his right hand and on his left, and that God asked them who would deceive Ahab,[75] that was surely a parable wherein the Prophet on that occasion (which was not one for teaching the high doctrines of theology) sufficiently expressed the main purport of the message he was charged to deliver in God's name. So in no way did he stray from his intended meaning. Likewise the other prophets by God's command made manifest to the people the Word of God in this way, as being the best means—though not means enjoined by God—of leading people to the primary objective of Scripture, which according to Christ himself[76] consists of loving God above all things, and your neighbour as yourself. High speculative thought, in my view, has nothing to do with Scripture. For my part I have never learned, nor could I have learned, any of God's eternal attributes from Holy Scripture.

As to your fifth argument (namely, that the prophets made manifest the Word of God in that way), since truth is not contrary to truth it only remains for me to prove (as anyone will agree who understands the methodology of proof) that Scripture, as it stands, is the true revealed Word of God. A mathematically exact proof of this proposition can be attained only by divine revelation. I therefore said, 'I believe, but do not know in a mathematical way, that all things revealed by God to the prophets . . .' etc. For I firmly believe, but do not know in a mathematical way, that the prophets were the trusted counsellors and faithful messengers of God. So there is no contradiction whatsoever in what I have affirmed, whereas many contradictions can be found on the other side.

The rest of your letter, namely, where you say, 'Finally, the supremely perfect being knew . . .' etc., and thereafter what you adduce against the example of poison, and lastly, what concerns the Appendix, and what follows on that,—none of this, I say, is relevant to the question at issue. With regard to Meyer's Preface, it is certainly also shown therein what Descartes had yet to prove in order to construct a solid demonstration concerning free will, and it adds that I favour a contrary opinion, and how so. This I shall perhaps explain in due course, but at present this is not my intention.

I have not thought about the work on Descartes[77] nor have I given it any further consideration since it was published in Dutch. I have good reason for this, which it would take too long to discuss here. So there remains nothing more to say than that I am, etc.

[Schiedam, 28 January 1665]

---

[75] [See I Kings 22:19 and II Chronicles 18:18.]
[76] [See Matthew 22:37.]
[77] [The reference is to the Dutch translation by P. Balling (1664) of the PPC.]

Letter 22

To the highly esteemed B.d.S., from Willem van Blyenbergh

[The original, which is extant, was written in Dutch and was printed in the Dutch edition of the O.P. The Latin version is a translation from the Dutch.]

Sir, and worthy friend,

I received your letter of 28 January in good time, but affairs other than my studies have prevented me from replying sooner. And since your letter was liberally besprinkled with sharp reproofs, I scarce knew what to make of it. For in your first letter of 5 January you very generously offered me your sincere friendship, assuring me that not only was my letter of that time very welcome, but also any subsequent letters. Indeed, I was urged in a friendly way to put before you freely any further difficulties I might wish to raise. This I did at some greater length in my letter of 16 January. To this I expected a friendly and instructive reply, in accordance with your own request and promise. But on the contrary I received one that does not savour overmuch of friendship, stating that no demonstrations, however clear, avail with me, that I do not understand Descartes' meaning, that I am too much inclined to confuse corporeal with spiritual things, etc., so that our correspondence can no longer serve for our mutual instruction.

To this I reply in a friendly way that I certainly believe that you understand the above-mentioned things better than I, and that you are more accustomed to distinguish corporeal from spiritual things. For in metaphysics, where I am a beginner, you have already ascended to a high level, and that is why I sought the favour of your instruction. But never did I imagine that I would give offence by my frank objections. I heartily thank you for the trouble you have taken with both your letters, especially the second, from which I grasped your meaning more clearly than from the first. Nevertheless, I still cannot assent to it unless the difficulties I yet find in it are removed. This neither should nor can give you cause for offence, for it is a grave fault in our intellect to assent to a truth without having the necessary grounds for such assent. Although your conceptions may be true, I ought not to give assent to them as long as there remain with me reasons for obscurity or doubt, even if those doubts arise not from the matter as presented, but from the imperfection of my understanding. And since you are very well aware of this, you should not take it amiss if I again raise some objections, as I am bound to do as long as I cannot clearly grasp the matter. For this I do to no other end than to discover truth, and not to distort your meaning contrary to your intention. I therefore ask for a friendly reply to these few observations.

You say that no more pertains to the essence of a thing than that which the divine will and power allows it and in actual fact gives to it, and when we consider the nature of a man who is governed by desire for sensual pleasure, comparing his present desires with those of the pious or with those which he himself had at another time, we then assert that that man is deprived of a better desire, because we judge that at that time the virtuous desire pertains to him. This we cannot do if we have regard to the nature of the divine decree and intellect. For in this respect the better desire no more pertains to that man at that time than to the nature of the Devil, or a stone, etc. For although God knew the past and present state of Adam, he did not on that account understand Adam as deprived of a past state, that is, that the past state pertained to his present nature, etc. From these words it seems to me clearly to follow, subject to correction, that nothing else pertains to an essence than that which it possesses at the moment it is perceived. That is, if I have a desire for pleasure, that desire pertains to my essence at that time, and if I do not have that desire, that non-desiring pertains to my essence at the time when I do not desire. Consequently, it must also infallibly follow that in relation to God I include as much perfection (differing only in degree) in my actions when I have a desire for pleasure as when I have no such desire, when I engage in all kinds of villainy as when I practise virtue and justice. For at that time there pertains to my essence only as much as is expressed in action, for, on your view, I can do neither more nor less than what results from the degree of essence I have in actual fact received. For since the desire for pleasure and villainy pertains to my essence at the time of my action, and at that time I receive that essence, and no more, from the divine power, it is only those actions that the divine power demands of me. Thus is seems to follow clearly from your position that God desires villainy in exactly the same way as he desires those actions you term virtuous.

Let us now take for granted that God, as God and not as judge, bestows on the godly and the ungodly such and so much essence as he wills that they should exercise. What reasons can there be why God does not desire the actions of the one in the same way as the actions of the other? For since God gives to each one the quality for his action, it surely follows that from those to whom he has given less he desires only proportionately the same as from those to whom he has given more. Consequently God, regarded only in himself, wills the greater and the lesser perfection in our actions, wills the desires for pleasure and the virtuous desires, all alike. So those who engage in villainy must of necessity engage in villainy because nothing else pertains to their essence at that time, just as he who practises virtue does so because the divine power has willed that this should pertain to his essence at that time. So again I cannot but think that God wills equally and in the same way both villainy and virtue, and insofar as he wills both, he is the cause of both, and to that extent they must both be pleasing to him. It is too hard for me to conceive this of God.

I see indeed that you say that the pious serve God. But from your writings I can only understand that serving God is merely to carry out such actions as God has willed us to do, and this is what you also ascribe to the impious and the licentious. So what difference is there in relation to God between the service of the pious and the impious? You say too that the pious serve God, and by their service continually become more perfect. But I cannot see what you understand by 'becoming more perfect', nor what is meant by 'continually becoming more perfect'. For the impious and the pious both receive their essence, and likewise their preservation or continual creation of their essence, from God as God, not as judge, and both fulfil God's will in the same way, that is, in accordance with God's decree. So what difference can there be between the two in relation to God? For the 'continually becoming more perfect' derives not from their actions but from the will of God. So if the impious through their actions become more imperfect, this derives not from their actions but only from the will of God; and both only carry out God's will. So there can be no difference between the two in relation to God. What reasons are there, then, why these should become continually more perfect through their actions, and the others be consumed in serving?

But you seem to locate the difference between the actions of the one and the other in this point, that the one includes more perfection than the other. I am quite sure that herein lies my error, or yours, for I cannot find in your writings any rule whereby a thing is called more or less perfect except as it has more or less essence. Now if this is the standard of perfection, then surely in relation to God's will villainy is equally as acceptable to him as the actions of the pious. For God as God, that is, in regard only to himself, wills them in the same way, since in both cases they derive form his decree. If this is the only standard of perfection, errors can only improperly be so called. In reality there are no errors, in reality there are no crimes; everything contains only that essence, and that kind of essence, which God has given it; and this essence, be it as it may, always involves perfection. I confess I cannot clearly comprehend this. You must forgive me if I ask whether murder is equally as pleasing to God as almsgiving, and whether, in relation to God, stealing is as good as righteousness. If not, what are the reasons? If you say yes, what reasons can I have which should induce me to perform one action which you call virtuous rather than another? What law or rule forbids me the one more than the other? If you say it is the law of virtue itself, I must certainly confess that by your account I can find no law whereby virtue is to be delineated or recognised. For everything depends inseparably on God's will, and consequently the one action is equally as virtuous as the other. Therefore I do not understand your saying that one must act from love of virtue, for I cannot comprehend what, according to you, is virtue, or the law of virtue. You do indeed say that you shun vice or villainy because they are opposed to your own particular nature and would lead you astray from the knowledge and love of God. But in all your writings I find no rule or proof for this. Indeed, forgive me for having to say that the contrary seems to follow from your writings. You shun the things I call wicked because they are opposed to your particular nature, not because they contain vice in themselves. You avoid them just as we avoid food that we find disgusting. Surely he who avoids evil things just because they are repugnant to his nature can take little pride in his virtue.

Here again a question can be raised; if there were a mind to whose particular nature the pursuit of pleasure or villainy was not repugnant but agreeable, could he have any virtuous motive that must move him to do good and avoid evil? But how is it possible that one should be able to relinquish the desire for pleasure when this desire at that time pertains to his essence, and he has in actual fact received it from God and cannot free himself from it?

Again, I cannot see in your writings that it follows that the actions which I call wicked should lead you astray from the knowledge and love of God. For you have only done what God willed, and could not have done more, because at that time no more was assigned to your essence by the divine power and will. How can an action so determined and dependent make you stray from the love of God? To go astray is to be confused, to be non-dependent, and this according to you is impossible. For whether we do this or that, manifest more or less perfection, that is what we receive for our essence at that point of time immediately from God. How, then, can we go astray? Or else I do not understand what is meant by going astray. However, it is here, and here alone, that must lurk the cause of either my or your misapprehension.

At this point there are still many other things I should like to say and ask.

1. Do intelligent substances depend on God in a way different from lifeless substances? For although intelligent beings contain more essence than the lifeless, do they not both stand in need of God and God's decrees for their motion in general and for their particular motions? Consequently, insofar as they are dependent, are they not dependent in one and the same way?

2. Since you do not allow to the soul the freedom that Descartes ascribed to it, what difference is there between the dependence of intelligent substances and that of soulless substances? And if they have no freedom of will, in what way do you conceive dependence on God, and in what way is the soul dependent on God?

3. If our soul does not have that freedom, is not our action properly God's action, and our will God's will?

There are many other questions I should like to raise, but I dare not ask so much of you. I simply look forward to receiving first of all your answer to the foregoing pages. Perhaps thereby I shall better be able to understand your views, and then we could discuss these matters rather more fully in person. For when I have received your answer, I shall have to go to Leiden in a few weeks, and shall give myself the honour of greeting you in passing, if that is acceptable to you. Relying on this, with warm salutations I say that I remain,

Your devoted servant,
W. v. Blyenbergh

Dordrecht, 19 February 1665

If you do not write to me under cover, please write to Willem van Blyenbergh, Grainbroker, near the great Church.

P.S. In my great haste I have forgotten to include this question, whether we cannot by our prudence prevent what would otherwise happen to us.

Letter 23

To the learned and accomplished Willem van Blyenbergh, from B.d.S.

[Reply to the preceding.]

Sir and friend,

This week I have received two letters from you; one of 9 March, which served only to inform me of the other of 19 February, sent to me from Schiedam. In the latter I see that you complain of my having said that 'no demonstration can avail with you', etc., as if I had said that with regard to my reasoning because it did not immediately satisfy you. That is far from my meaning. What I had in mind were your own words, 'And if ever after long consideration it should come about that my natural knowledge should appear to be either at variance with that Word or not easily . . . etc., that Word has so much authority with me that I prefer to cast doubt on the conceptions I imagine to be clear rather than . . . etc.' So I only repeated briefly your own words. Therefore I do not believe that I have given the slightest reason for offence, the more so because I adduced these words as an indication of the great difference between us.

Moreover, since you said at the end of your second letter that your only wish is to persevere in your belief and hope, and that other matters which we discuss with one another concerning our natural understanding are indifferent to you, I thought, as I still think, that no advantage could come of my writings, and it would therefore be more sensible for me not to neglect my studies (which I must otherwise relinquish for so long) for things which cannot yield any profit. And this does not contradict my first letter, for then I regarded you as a pure philosopher who (as is granted by many who consider themselves Christians) has no other touchstone for truth than our natural understanding, not theology. But you have taught me otherwise, showing me that the foundation on which I intended to build our friendship was not laid as I thought. Lastly, with regard to the other remarks, this happens quite commonly in the course of disputation without on that account exceeding the bounds of courtesy, and I have therefore ignored such things in your second letter and shall also do likewise with this one. So much regarding your displeasure, so as to show that I have given no reason for it, and far less for thinking that I cannot brook any contradiction. Now I shall turn again to answering your objections.

First, then, I assert that God is absolutely and effectively the cause of everything that has essence, be it what it may. If now you can demonstrate that evil, error, villainy and so on are something that expresses essence, I will entirely agree with you that God is the cause of villainy, evil, error, etc. I think I have sufficiently shown that that which constitutes the specific reality of evil, error and villainy does not consist in anything that expresses essence, and therefore it cannot be said that God is its cause. For example, Nero's matricide, insofar as it contained something positive, was not a crime; for Orestes too performed the same outward act and had the same intention of killing his mother, and yet he is not blamed, or at least not as Nero. What then was Nero's crime? Nothing else than that by that deed he showed that he was ungrateful, devoid of compassion and obedience. Now it is certain that none of these things express any essence. Therefore neither was God the cause of any of them, but only of Nero's action and intention.

Furthermore, I should like it here to be noted that while we are speaking philosophically, we ought not to use the language of theology. For since theology has usually, and with good reason, represented God as a perfect man, it is therefore natural for theology to say that God desires something, that God is displeased with the deeds of the impious and pleased with those of the pious. But in philosophy, where we clearly understand that to ascribe to God those attributes which make a man perfect would be as wrong as to ascribe to a man the attributes that make perfect an elephant or an ass, these and similar words have no place, and we cannot use them without utterly confusing our concepts. So, speaking philosophically, we cannot say that God wants something from somebody, or that something is displeasing or pleasing to him. For these are all human attributes, which have no place in God.

Finally, I should like it to be noted that although the actions of the pious (that is, those who have a clear idea of God in accordance with which all their actions and thoughts are determined) and of the impious (that is, those who have no idea of God but only confused ideas of earthly things, in accordance with which all their actions and thoughts are determined), and, in short, the actions of everything that exists, follow necessarily from God's eternal laws and decrees and constantly depend on God, they nevertheless differ from one another not only in degree but in essence. For although a mouse is as dependent on God as an angel, and sorrow as much as joy, yet a mouse cannot on that account be a kind of angel, nor sorrow a kind of joy.

Herewith I think I have answered your objections (if I have rightly understood them, for I am sometimes in some doubt as to whether the conclusion you reach does not differ from the proposition you seek to prove). But that will be more clearly evident if, from this basis, I reply to the questions you propose:

1. Is murder as pleasing to God as almsgiving?
2. Is stealing, in relation to God, as good as righteousness?
3. If there were a mind to whose particular nature the pursuit of pleasure and villainy was not repugnant, but agreeable, could it have any virtuous motive that must move it to do good and avoid evil?

To the first I reply that (speaking philosophically) I do not know what you mean by 'pleasing to God'. If the question is whether God does not hate the one and love the other, or whether the one has not done God an injury and the other a favour, then I answer No. If the question is whether men who murder and men who give alms are equally good and perfect, again I answer No.

As to the second question, I say that if 'good in relation to God' means that the righteous man does God some good and the thief some evil, I reply that neither the righteous man nor the thief can cause God pleasure or displeasure. But if the question is whether both actions, insofar as they are something real and caused by God, are not equally perfect, then I say that if we attend only to the actions and the way they are done, it may well be that they are both equally perfect. If you then ask whether the thief and the righteous man are not equally perfect and blessed, I answer No. For by a righteous man I understand one who has a steadfast desire that each should possess his own, which desire I show in my *Ethics*[78] (which I have not yet published) arises necessarily in the pious from the clear knowledge they have of themselves and of God. And since the thief has no such desire, he necessarily lacks the knowledge of God and of himself; that is, he lacks the principal thing that makes us men.

If, however, you still ask what can move you to perform the action which I call virtuous rather than the other, I reply that I cannot know which way, out of the infinite ways there are, God uses to determine you to such actions. It may be that God has clearly imprinted in you the clear idea of himself, and through love of himself makes you forget the world and love the rest of mankind as yourself; and it is clear that such a constitution of mind is opposed to all else that men call evil, and so they cannot subsist in the same subject.

But this is not the place to explain the fundamentals of Ethics, or to prove everything I say; for I am concerned simply to answer your objections and defend my position.

Finally, as to your third question, it presupposes a contradiction. It is just as if someone were to ask me whether, if it accorded better with a man's nature that he should hang himself, there would be any reason why he should not hang himself. However, suppose it possible that there could be such a nature. Then I say (whether I grant free will or not) that if anyone sees that he can live better on the gallows than at his own table, he would be very foolish not to go and hang himself. And he who saw clearly that he would in fact enjoy a more perfect and better life or essence by engaging in villainy than by pursuing virtue would also be a fool if he did not do just that. For in relation to such a perverted human nature, villainy would be virtue.

As to your other question which you added at the end of your letter, since one could ask a hundred such questions an hour without arriving at the conclusion of any one of them, and since you yourself do not press for an answer, I shall leave it unanswered.

For the present I shall only say that I shall expect you at about the time as arranged, and that you will be very welcome. But I should like it to be soon, for I

---

[78] [The version of the *Ethics* which we possess has nothing which states this in the manner Spinoza does here. But see E4P37Schol2 and E4P72.]

am already planning to go to Amsterdam for a week or two. Meanwhile I remain, with cordial greetings,

Your friend and servant,
B. de Spinoza

Voorburg, 13 March 1665

LETTER 24
To the esteemed B.d.S., from Willem van Blyenbergh

[The original, which was written in Dutch, is extant, and is printed in the Dutch edition of the O.P. The Latin is a translation.]

Sir and friend,

When I had the honour of visiting you, time did not allow me to stay longer with you. And far less did my memory permit me to retain all that we discussed, even though on parting from you I immediately gathered all my thoughts so as to be able to remember what I had heard. So on reaching the next stopping-place I attempted on my own to commit your views to paper, but I found that in fact I had not retained even a quarter of what was discussed. So please forgive me if once again I trouble you by raising questions regarding matters where I did not clearly understand your views, or did not well remember them. (I wish I could do you some service in return for your trouble). These questions are:

First, when I read your *Principia* and *Cogitata Metaphysica*, how can I distinguish between what is stated as Descartes' opinions and what is stated as your own?

Second, is there in reality such a thing as error, and wherein does it consist?

Third, in what way do you maintain that the will is not free?

Fourth, what do you mean by having Meyer say in the Preface "that you do indeed agree that there is a thinking substance in Nature, but you nevertheless deny that this constitutes the essence of the human mind. You hold that just as Extension is infinite, so Thought is not limited, and therefore just as the human body is not Extension absolutely but only Extension determined in a definite way according to the laws of extended Nature through motion and rest, so too the human mind is not Thought absolutely but only Thought determined in a definite way according to the laws of thinking Nature through ideas; and this mind is necessarily inferred to exist when the human body comes into being"?

From this I think it seems to follow that just as the human body is composed of thousands of small bodies, so too the human mind is composed of thousands of thoughts; and just as the human body on its disintegration is resolved into the thousands of bodies of which it was composed, so too our mind, when it leaves the body, is resolved again into the multitude of thoughts of which it was composed. And just as the separated bodies of our human body no longer remain united with one another and other bodies come between them, so it also seems to follow that when our mind is disintegrated, the innumerable thoughts of which it was composed are no longer united, but separated. And just as our bodies, on disintegrating, do indeed remain bodies but not human bodies, so too after death our thinking substance is dissolved in such a way that our thoughts or thinking substances remain, but their essence is not what it was when it was called a human mind. So it still appears to me as if you maintained that man's thinking substance is changed and dissolved like corporeal substances, and indeed in some cases, as you (if my memory serves me) maintained of the wicked, they are even entirely annihilated and retain no thought whatever. And just as Descartes, according to Meyer, merely assumes that the mind is an absolutely thinking substance, so it seems to me that both you and Meyer in these statements are also for the most part merely making assumptions. Therefore I do not here clearly understand your meaning.

Fifth, you maintained both in our conversation and in your last letter of 13 March that from the clear knowledge that we have of God and of ourselves there arises our steadfast desire that each should possess his own. But here you have still to explain how the knowledge of God and of ourselves produces in us the steadfast desire that each should possess his own; that is, in what way it proceeds from the knowledge of God, or lays us under the obligation, that we should love virtue and abstain from those actions we call wicked. How does it come about (since in your view killing and stealing, no less than almsgiving, contain within them something positive) that killing does not involve as much perfection, blessedness and contentment as does almsgiving?

Perhaps you will say, as you do in your last letter of 13 March, that this question belongs to Ethics, and is there discussed by you. Buy since without an explanation of this question and the preceding questions I am unable to grasp your meaning so clearly that there still do not remain absurdities which I cannot reconcile, I would ask you kindly to give me a fuller answer, and particularly to set out some of your principal definitions, postulates and axioms on which your *Ethics*, and this question in particular, is based. Perhaps you will be deterred by the amount of trouble and will excuse yourself, but I beseech you to grant my request just this once, because without the solution of this last question I shall never be able to understand what you really mean. I wish I could offer you some recompense in exchange. I do not venture to limit you to one or two weeks, I only beg you to let me have your answer here before your departure to Amsterdam. By so doing you will lay me under the greatest obligation, and I shall show you that I am, and remain, Sir,

Your most devoted servant,
Willem van Blyenbergh

Dordrecht, 27 March

To Mr. Benedictus de Spinoza, staying at Voorburg. *Per couverto.*

LETTER 25
To the esteemed B.d.S., from Henry Oldenburg

[Known only from the O.P. The original is lost.]

Esteemed Sir, and very dear friend,

It gave me great pleasure to learn from a recent letter from Mr. Serrarius that you are alive and well and remember your Oldenburg. But at the same time I bitterly blamed my fortune (if it is right to use such a word) for my having been deprived over so many months of that most welcome correspondence which I previously enjoyed with you. The fault is to be assigned partly to the accumulation of business, partly to some dreadful domestic misfortunes, for my abundant devotion to you and my faithful friendship will always stand on a firm footing and continue unshaken. Mr. Boyle and I often talk about you, your learning and your profound reflections. We should like to see the offspring of your talent brought to birth and entrusted to the warm embrace of the learned, and we are confident that you will not disappoint us in this.

There is no reason why Mr. Boyle's essay on Nitre, on Solidity and Fluidity should be printed in Holland, for it has already been published here in Latin, and there only lacks opportunity for sending you copies. I therefore ask you not to let any of your printers attempt such a thing. Boyle has also published a notable Treatise on Colours,[79] both in English and Latin, and at the same time Experimental Observations on Cold, Thermometers, etc.,[80] which contains many excellent things, and much that is new. Nothing but this unfortunate war[81] prevents my sending you these books. There has also appeared a notable treatise on sixty Microscopic observations,[82] where there are many bold but philosophical assertions, that is, in accordance with mechanical principles. I hope that our booksellers will find a way of sending copies of all these to your country.

I long to receive from you yourself what you have been doing or have in hand. I am,

Your devoted and affectionate,
Henry Oldenburg

London, 28 April 1665

---

[79] [The exact title was *Experiments and Considerations touching Colours* (1664).]
[80] [*New Experiments and Observations upon Cold* (1665).]
[81] [England declared war against the Netherlands in January of 1665.]
[82] [Robert Hooke's *Micrographia* (1665). Hooke (1635–1703) was a collaborator with Boyle in the construction of the air-pump, and when Oldenburg died in 1677, Hooke succeeded him as Secretary of the Royal Society.]

Letter 26
To the noble and learned Henry Oldenburg, from B.d.S.

[Known only from the O.P. The original is lost. The letter is undated, but the opening sentence indicates that it must be May 1665.]

Most honourable friend,

A few days ago a friend of mine said he had been given your letter of 28 April by an Amsterdam bookseller, who had doubtless received it from Mr. Serrarius. I was very glad to be able to hear at last from you yourself that you are well, and that you are as kindly disposed to me as ever. For my part, whenever opportunity arose, I never failed to ask after you and your health from Mr. Serrarius and Christiaan Huygens, Z.D.,[83] who had also told me that he knows you. From the same Mr. Huygens I also gathered that the learned Mr. Boyle is alive and has published in English that notable Treatise on Colours, which he would lend me if I understood English. So I am pleased to know from you that this Treatise, together with the other on Cold and Thermometers (of which I had not yet heard) have been granted Latin citizenship and common rights. The book on microscopic observations is also in Mr. Huygens' possession, but, unless I am mistaken, it is in English.

He has told me some wonderful things about these microscopes, and also about certain telescopes made in Italy,[84] with which they have been able to observe eclipses of Jupiter caused by the interposition of satellites,[85] and also a kind of shadow on Saturn as if made by a ring.[86] These events cause me to wonder not a little at the rashness of Descartes,[87] who says that the reason why the planets next to Saturn (for he thought that its projections were planets, perhaps because he never saw them touch Saturn) do not move may be because Saturn does not rotate on its own axis. For this is not in agreement with his own principles, and he could very easily have explained the cause of the projections from his own principles had he not been labouring under a false preconception, etc.

(Voorburg, May 1665)

---

[83] ['Z.D.' stands for *Zeelhemi Dominum* (Squire of Züylichem), where Huygens' father had an estate.]

[84] [These were constructed by Giuseppe Compani in Rome. Huygens tried and failed to learn how they were made. Huygens was himself quite secretive about his own work on lenses and warned his brother not to impart any information about them to either John Hudde or Spinoza.]

[85] [Jupiter's satellites were first discovered by Galileo, who observed only four of them. The shadow cast on Jupiter by its satellites, which were also called the Medicean stars, was first announced by Dominico Cassini in Rome (1665).]

[86] [Galileo had mistaken Saturn's rings for projections or satellites. They were first clearly observed by Huygens in 1656.]

[87] [See Descartes' *Principles of Philosophy*, III, 154.]

Letter 27

To the courteous and accomplished Willem van Blyenbergh, from B.d.S.

[The original, written in Dutch, is extant. The Latin translation in the O.P. was perhaps made by Spinoza. The text of the Dutch edition appears to be a re-translation from the Latin.]

Sir and friend,

When I received your letter of 27 March, I was about to leave for Amsterdam, and so I left it at home only half-read, intending to answer it on my return and thinking that it contained only matters relating to the first question. But later on reading it through, I found that its contents were quite different. Not only did it ask for proof of those things I had caused to be included in the Preface—intending only to indicate to everyone my thoughts and opinions, but not to prove or explain them—but also proof of a large part of the *Ethics*, which as everyone knows must be based on metaphysics and physics. I therefore could not make up my mind to satisfy you on this matter, but looked for an opportunity of asking you in person in a friendly way to desist from your request, while at the same time giving you reason for my refusal and finally pointing out that these matters do not contribute to the solution of your first question, but on the contrary for the most part depend on that question. So it is by no means the case that my opinion regarding the necessity of things cannot be understood without the solution to these new questions; for the solution of the latter and of what pertains to them cannot be grasped without first understanding the necessity of things. For, as you know, the necessity of things touches metaphysics, and knowledge of this must always come first.

However, before I could obtain the desired opportunity, I received another letter this week under cover from my landlord. This seems to indicate some displeasure at the delay, and has therefore compelled me to write these few lines informing you briefly of my decision and intention. This I have now done. I hope that when you have thought the matter over you will willingly desist from your request, while nevertheless retaining your goodwill towards me. For my part, I shall show in every way I can or may, that I am,

Your well disposed friend and servant,
B. de Spinoza

To Mr. Willem van Blyenbergh, Grainbroker, at Dordrecht, near the great church

Voorburg, 3 June 1665

LETTER 28
To the learned and experienced Johan Bouwmeester, from B.d.S.

[This letter is extant, but does not appear in the O.P. It was first published by Van Vloten in 1860. On the back of the letter is a note, presumably by one of the editors of the O.P., to the effect that the letter was 'of no value'. Hence its omission. It is undated but can be assigned to June 1665.]

My very special friend,

I don't know whether you have completely forgotten me, but there are many circumstances which make me think so. First, when I was about to set out on my journey and wanted to bid you good-bye, and felt sure, being invited by you yourself, that I would find you at home, I was told that you had gone to the Hague. I returned to Voorburg, confident that you would at least call on me in passing; but you, if it pleases the gods, have returned home without greeting your friend. Finally, I have waited three weeks, and in all that time I have seen no letter from you. So if you want to banish this opinion of mine, you will easily do so by a letter, in which you can also indicate some way of arranging our correspondence, of which we once talked in your house.

Meanwhile I should like to ask you in all earnestness, indeed, to beseech and urge you by our friendship, to apply yourself with real energy to serious work, and to prevail on yourself to devote the better part of your life to the cultivation of your intellect and your soul. Now, I say, while there is yet time, and before you complain that time, and indeed you yourself, have slipped by.

Next, to say something about our proposed correspondence so as to encourage you to write more freely, you should know that I have previously suspected and am practically certain that you have rather less confidence in your abilities than is right, and that you are afraid that you may ask or propose something unbefitting a man of learning. But is it not unseemly for me to praise you to your face and recount your gifts? Still, if you fear that I may communicate your letters to others to whom you would then become a laughing-stock, on this matter I give you my word that I shall henceforth regard them as sacred and shall not communicate them to any mortal without your leave. On these terms you can begin our correspondence, unless perchance you doubt my good faith, which I don't believe. However, I look to hear your views on this from your first letter.

At the same time I also expect some of the conserve of red roses[88] which you promised, although I have now for a long time felt better. On leaving there, I

---

[88] [Bouwmeester was a physician, and, as it was held that a conserve of red roses is remedial for dis-

opened a vein once, but the fever did not abate (although I was somewhat more active even before the bloodletting because of the change of air, I think). But I have suffered two or three times with tertian fever, though by good diet I have at last rid myself of it and sent it packing. Where it went I know not, but I don't want it back.

With regard to the third part of my Philosophy, I shall soon be sending some of it to you, if you wish to be its translator, or to our friend de Vries. Although I had decided to send none of it until I had finished it, yet since it is turning out to be longer than expected, I don't want to keep you waiting too long. I shall send it up to about the eightieth proposition.[89]

I hear much about English affairs,[90] but nothing certain. The people do not stop suspecting all kinds of evil, and no one can find any reason why the fleet does not set sail. And indeed the situation does not yet seem secure. I fear that our side want to be too wise and far-sighted. Still, the event will show in due course what they have in mind and what they are after — may the gods prosper it. I should like to know what our people there are thinking, and what they know for certain, but more than that, and above all else, that you consider me . . . etc.

(Voorburg, June 1665)

LETTER 29
To the esteemed B.d.S., from Henry Oldenburg

[Not in the O.P. First published in 1860 by Van Vloten.]

Excellent Sir, and honoured friend,

From your last letter, written to me on 4 September,[91] it is clear that your devotion to our affairs goes very deep indeed. You have laid under an obligation not only me but the most noble Boyle, who joins me in sending you the warmest thanks on this account, and will repay your courtesy and kindness with whatever service he can render when opportunity arises. You can rest assured that this ap-

---

eases of the lungs, he probably prescribed this remedy to Spinoza. Note that this letter is the earliest indication we have of the tuberculosis which eventually killed Spinoza.]

[89] [The third part of the *Ethics* has only 59 propositions, not 80. We believe that Spinoza had originally thought that this work would include only three parts and that he decided to divide it into five parts.]

[90] [At the time, the Dutch were at war with the English, and the Dutch navy remained in the harbors instead of engaging the English. Spinoza's worries turned out to be reasonable since when the Dutch did finally attack on June 13, 1665, it was a disastrous defeat for them.]

[91] [We do not possess this letter by Spinoza, but it is clear from Oldenburg's remarks that it dealt in part with Spinoza's intentions for the TTP.]

plies to me as well. As regards that over-officious man who, in spite of the translation of the *Treatise on Colours* which has already been prepared here, has nevertheless determined to provide another, he will perhaps realise that he has done himself no good by his absurd over-eagerness. For what will happen to his translation if our Author enlarges the Latin version, prepared here in England, with a considerable number of experiments that are not to be found in the English version? It is inevitable that our version, soon to be distributed, will then have complete preference over his, and be held in much higher esteem by all men of good sense. But let him please himself, if he so wishes; we shall look to our own affairs in the way we think best.

Kircher's *Subterranean World*[92] has not yet appeared in our English world because of the plague, which hinders almost all communication. Then there is also this terrible war, which brings with it a veritable Iliad of woes, and very nearly eliminates all culture from the world.

Meanwhile, however, although our Philosophical Society holds no public meetings in these dangerous times, yet there are some of its Fellows who do not forget that they are such. So some are privately engaged in experiments on Hydrostatics, some on Anatomy, some on Mechanics, some in other experiments. Mr. Boyle has conducted an investigation into the origin of Forms and Qualities as it has hitherto been treated in the Schools and by teachers, and he has composed a treatise on this subject,[93] no doubt a notable one, which will shortly go to press.

I see that you are not so much philosophising as theologising, if one may use that term, for you are recording your thoughts about angels, prophecy and miracles. But perhaps you are doing this in a philosophic way. Of whatever kind it be, I am sure that the work is worthy of you and will fulfil my most eager expectations. Since these difficult times are a bar to freedom of intercourse, I do at least ask you please to indicate in your next letter your plan and object in this writing of yours.

Here we are daily expecting news of a second naval battle,[94] unless perchance your fleet has again retired into harbour. The courage which you hint is the subject of debate among you is of a bestial kind, not human. For if men acted under the guidance of reason, they would not so tear one another to pieces, as anyone can see. But why do I complain? There will be wickedness as long as there are men: but even so, wickedness is not without pause, and is occasionally counterbalanced by better things.

While I was writing this, a letter was delivered to me from that distinguished astronomer of Danzig, Mr. John Hevel.[95] In this he tells me among other things

---

[92] [Athanasius Kircher (1601–1680) was born in Germany and educated by the Jesuits at Fulda, joined the Jesuit Order in Mainz, and later became Professor of Philosophy, Mathematics, and Oriental Languages at Würzburg. Because of the Thirty Years' War, he fled to Avignon in 1631 and settled in Rome four years later. This work, published in 1665, deals with forces and processes inside the earth.]

[93] [Published in 1666.]

[94] [The Dutch fleet set out on 14 August 1665 to engage the English fleet, but due to poor weather no battle occurred.]

[95] [Johann Hevelius (or Hevel, or Höwelcke), 1661–1687. He studied jurisprudence at Leiden and

that his *Cometography*, consisting of twelve books, has already been in the press for a whole year, and that four hundred pages, or the first nine books, are completed. He also tells me that he has sent me some copies of his *Prodromus Cometicus*, in which he gives a full description of the first of the two recent comets; but these have not yet come to hand. He has decided, moreover, to publish another book concerning the second comet also, and to submit it to the judgment of the learned. What, I pray you, do your people think of the pendulums of Huygens,[96] and particularly of those that are said to show the measure of time so exactly that they can serve to find the longitude at sea?[97] And also what is happening about his *Dioptrics* and his *Treatise on Motion*, both of which we have been long awaiting? I am sure he is not idle; I would only like to know what he is about.

Keep well, and continue to love,

Your most devoted,
H.O.

To Mr. Benedictus Spinosa,
In the Baggyne Street,
At the house of Mr. Daniel, painter, in Adam and Eve

Letter 30
To the noble and learned Henry Oldenburg, from B.d.S.

> [Not in the O.P. This is part of a letter which survives in a letter from Oldenburg to Boyle (published in The Works of Robert Boyle, 1772). In his letter Oldenburg quotes from a letter he had written to Sir Robert Moray, wherein is quoted a long extract from a letter which Spinoza had written to Oldenburg (in Latin). Spinoza's letter is clearly a reply to Letter 29. A conjectural date is autumn 1665.]

... I rejoice that your philosophers are alive, and are mindful of themselves and their republic. I shall expect news of what they have recently done, when the war-

---

lived in Danzig. In 1641 he built a private observatory, equipped with a large telescope, and published many observations. He discovered four comets and suggested that they had a parabolic orbit. His *Prodromus Cometicus* (1668) dealt with a comet observed in 1664. In 1668 he published *Cometographia*, which dealt with comets generally.]

[96] [Huygens' *Horologium* (1658) described the pendulum clock which he invented in 1656. The *Dioptrics* was begun in 1654, the *De Motu Corporum* in 1663, and both were published posthumously in 1700.]

[97] [The method which Huygens proposed for measuring longitudes at sea by means of pendulum clocks was described in detail in his *Brevis Institutio de usu Horologiorum ad Inveniendas Longitudines*, which is summarized in the *Philosophical Transactions of the Royal Society* 47, 10 May 1669.]

riors are sated with blood and are resting so as to renew their strength somewhat. If that famous scoffer[98] were alive today, he would surely be dying of laughter. For my part, these troubles move me neither to laughter nor again to tears, but rather to philosophising, and to a closer observation of human nature. For I do not think it right to laugh at nature, and far less to grieve over it, reflecting that men, like all else, are only a part of nature, and that I do not know how each part of nature harmonises with the whole, and how it coheres with other parts. And I realise that it is merely through such lack of understanding that certain features of nature — which I thus perceived only partly and in a fragmentary way, and which are not in keeping with our philosophical attitude of mind — once seemed to me vain, disordered and absurd. But now I let everyone go his own way. Those who wish can by all means die for their own good, as long as I am allowed to live for truth.

I am now writing a treatise on my views regarding Scripture.[99] The reasons that move me to do so are these:

1. The prejudices of theologians. For I know that these are the main obstacles which prevent men from giving their minds to philosophy. So I apply myself to exposing such prejudices and removing them from the minds of sensible people.
2. The opinion of me held by the common people, who constantly accuse me of atheism. I am driven to avert this accusation, too, as far as I can.
3. The freedom to philosophise and to say what we think. This I want to vindicate completely, for here it is in every way suppressed by the excessive authority and egotism of preachers.[100]

I have not yet heard that any Cartesian explains the phenomena of the recent comets on Descartes' hypothesis,[101] and I doubt whether they can thus be properly explained. . . .

---

[98] [Democritus (460–370 B.C.) was alleged to have spent much of his time deriding human stupidity and vanity.]

[99] [Namely, the *Tractatus Theologico-Politicus*.]

[100] [The clergy of the Calvinist Church exploited the war between Holland and England in order to overthrow the de Witts and their party, which defended religious liberty.]

[101] [The reference is to Descartes' account of vortices, by which he tried to account for planetary revolution and also the motion of comets. Spinoza's inability to see how the account could explain planetary motion probably explains why the PPC remained unfinished (the third part, of which only several pages were written, was to deal with vortices).]

LETTER 30A
To Henry Oldenburg, from B.d.S.

[Not in the O.P. nor in Gebhardt. The letter from Oldenburg to Sir Robert Moray mentioned in the preamble to Letter 30 has been recovered, and was printed by Wolf in 1935. In this letter, dated 7 October 1665, another extract from Spinoza's letter is quoted. This does not appear in Gebhardt.]

... I have seen Kircher's *Subterranean* World with Mr. Huygens, who has a higher regard for his piety than for his abilities. This may be because Kircher discusses pendulums and concludes that they can be of no use to determine longitude, an opinion quite opposed to that of Huygens. You want to know what our people here think of Huygens' pendulums. As yet I cannot give you any definite information on this subject, but this much I know, that the craftsman who has the sole right to manufacture them has stopped work altogether because he cannot sell them. I don't know whether this is due to the interruption of commerce or to the excessively high price he is demanding, for he values them at three hundred Caroline florins each. When I asked Huygens about his *Dioptrics* and about another treatise dealing with Parhelia, he replied that he was still seeking the answer to a problem in *Dioptrics*, and that as soon as he found the solution he would set that book in print together with his treatise on Parhelia. However, for my part I believe he is more concerned with his journey to France (he is getting ready to go to live in France as soon as his father has returned) than with anything else. The problem which he says he is trying to solve in *Dioptrics* is as follows: Is it possible to arrange the lenses in telescopes in such a way that the deficiency in the one will correct the deficiency in the other, and thus bring it about that all parallel rays passing through the objective lens will reach the eye as if they converged on a mathematical point? As yet this seems to me impossible. Further, throughout his *Dioptrics*, as I have both seen and gathered from him (unless I am mistaken), he treats only of spherical figures. As for the *Treatise on Motion* about which you also ask, I think you may look for it in vain. It is quite a long time since he began to boast that his calculations had shown that the rules of motion and the laws of nature are very different from those given by Descartes, and that those of Descartes are almost all wrong. Yet up to now he has produced no evidence on this subject. I know that about a year ago he told me that all his discoveries made by calculation regarding motion he had since found verified by experiment in England. This I can hardly believe, and I think that regarding the sixth rule of Motion in Descartes,[102] both he and Descartes are quite in error. ...

---

[102] [See *Principia* II, 50.]

Letter 31
To the esteemed B.d.S., from Henry Oldenburg

[Known only from the O.P. The original is lost.]

Most excellent Sir, and valued friend,

In loving good men you are doing what beseems a wise man and a philosopher, and you have no reason to doubt that they love you in return and value your merits as they should. Mr. Boyle joins with me in sending cordial greetings, and urges you to pursue your philosophising with energy and rigour. Above all, if you have any light to cast on the difficult question as to how each part of Nature accords with its whole, and the manner of its coherence with other parts, please do us the favour of letting us know your views.

The reasons which you mention as having induced you to compose a treatise on Scripture have my entire approval, and I am desperately eager to see with my own eyes your thoughts on that subject. Mr. Serrarius will perhaps soon be sending me a little parcel. If you think it proper, you may safely entrust to him what you have already written on this matter, and you can be assured of our readiness to render services in return.

I have read some of Kircher's *Subterranean World*, and although his arguments and theories do not indicate great talent, the observations and experiments we find therein are a credit to the author's diligence and his will to deserve well of the republic of philosophers. So you see that I attribute to him something more than piety, and you can easily discern the intention of those who besprinkle him with this Holy Water.

When you speak of Huygens' *Treatise on Motion*, you imply that Descartes' Rules of motion are nearly all wrong. I do not have to hand the little book which you published some time ago on 'Descartes' *Principia* demonstrated in geometric fashion'. I cannot remember whether you there point out that error, or whether you followed Descartes closely so as to gratify others. Would that you may at last bring to birth the offspring of your own mind and entrust it to the world of philosophers to cherish and foster! I recall that you somewhere indicated that many of those matters of which Descartes himself affirmed that they surpass human comprehension—indeed, even other matters more sublime and subtle—can be plainly understood by men and clearly explained.[103] Why do you hesitate, my friend, what do you fear? Make the attempt, go to it, bring to completion a task of such high importance, and you will see the entire company of genuine philosophers supporting you. I venture to pledge my word, which I would not do if I doubted my ability to redeem it. In no way could I believe that you have in mind

---

[103] [Spinoza states this in the Preface to PPC1.]

to contrive something against the existence and providence of God, and with these crucial supports intact religion stands on a firm footing, and any reflections of a philosophical nature can either be readily defended or excused. So away with delays, and suffer nothing to divert you.

I think it likely you will soon hear what is to be said about the new comets. Hevel of Danzig and the Frenchman Auzout,[104] both learned men and mathematicians, are at odds regarding the observations that were made. At present the controversy is under examination, and when the dispute is decided the entire affair, I imagine, will be communicated to me, and by me to you. This much I can already assert, that all astronomers — or at any rate those known to me — are of the opinion that there were not one but two comets, and I have not yet met anyone who has tried to explain their phenomena according to the Cartesian hypothesis.

If you receive any more news regarding the studies and work of Mr. Huygens and of the success of his pendulums in the matter of ascertaining longitude, and of his removing to France,[105] I beg you please to let me know as soon as possible. To this add also, I pray you, what is perhaps being said in your country about a peace treaty, about the intentions of the Swedish army[106] which has been sent to Germany, and about the progress of the Bishop of Munster.[107] I believe that the whole of Europe will be involved in war next summer, and everything seems to be tending towards a strange transformation. As for us, let us serve the supreme Deity with a pure mind, and cultivate a philosophy that is true, sound and profitable. Some of our philosophers who followed the King to Oxford hold frequent meetings there, and are concerned to promote the study of physics. Among other things, they have recently begun to investigate the nature of sounds. They will be making experiments, I believe, to find out in what proportion weights must be increased, without any other force, to stretch a string so that its tension may produce a higher note of a kind that has a set consonance with the previous sound. More about this another time. Farewell, and remember your most devoted

Henry Oldenburg
London, 12 October 1665

---

[104] [Adrien Auzout (d. 1691) was a member of the Paris Academy. Hevelius claimed that the comet observed in 1664 had appeared near the first star of the constellation Aries, and Auzout argued that it appeared near the bright start in the left horn of that constellation. The Royal Academy took up the matter in *Philosophical Transactions of the Royal Society* 9, 12 February 1666, and decided in favor of Auzout.]

[105] [When Jean Baptiste Colbert became Controller-General of France in 1665, he made an effort to bring to Paris many foreign scholars and scientists. Huygens was invited there in 1665 and moved to Paris in 1666.]

[106] [During the war with Holland, the British attempted to persuade the Swedish government to send an army to attack the Dutch, but no army was ever sent.]

[107] [Christoph Bernhard von Galen (1606–1678), the Bishop of Munster, invaded Holland in 1665 at the encouragement of his British allies.]

Letter 32
To the most noble and learned Henry Oldenburg, from B.d.S.

[The original of this letter is extant, and held by the Royal Society, London. Spinoza retained a slightly different version of it, and it is from this that the text of the O.P. is printed. The differences are unimportant.]

Most noble Sir,

Please accept my most grateful thanks for the kind encouragement which you and the most noble Mr. Boyle have given me in the pursuit of philosophy. As far as my poor abilities will allow, I shall continue in this way, with the assurance meanwhile of your assistance and goodwill.

When you ask for my views on 'how we know the way in which each part of Nature accords with the whole, and the manner of its coherence with other parts', I presume that you are asking for the grounds of our belief that each part of Nature accords with the whole and coheres with other parts. As to knowing the actual manner of this coherence and the agreement of each part with the whole, I made it clear in my previous letter that this is beyond my knowledge. To know this it would be necessary to know the whole of Nature and all its parts. So I shall attempt to give the reasoning that compels me to this belief. But I would first ask you to note that I do not attribute to Nature beauty, ugliness, order or confusion. It is only with respect to our imagination that things can be said to be beautiful, ugly, well-ordered or confused.[108]

By coherence of parts I mean simply this, that the laws or nature of one part adapts itself to the laws or nature of another part in such wise that there is the least possible opposition between them. On the question of whole and parts, I consider things as parts of a whole to the extent that their natures adapt themselves to one another so that they are in the closest possible agreement. Insofar as they are different from one another, to that extent each one forms in our mind a separate idea and is therefore considered as a whole, not a part. For example, when the motions of particles of lymph, chyle, etc., adapt themselves to one another in accordance with size and shape so as to be fully in agreement with one another and to form all together one single fluid, to that extent only are the chyle, lymph, etc., regarded as parts of the blood. But insofar as we conceive the particles of lymph as differ-

---

[108] [See E4Pref for a more expanded statement of the themes contained in this paragraph. Oldenburg refers to this letter as being 'on the unity of nature' in a letter to Boyle dated 21 November 1665.]

ent from the particles of chyle in respect of shape and motion, to that extent we regard them each as a whole, not a part.

Now let us imagine, if you please, a tiny worm living in the blood, capable of distinguishing by sight the particles of the blood—lymph, etc.—and of intelligently observing how each particle, on colliding with another, either rebounds or communicates some degree of its motion, and so forth. That worm would be living in the blood as we are living in our part of the universe, and it would regard each individual particle of the blood as a whole, not a part, and it could have no idea as to how all the parts are controlled by the overall nature of the blood and compelled to mutual adaptation as the overall nature of the blood requires, so as to agree with one another in a definite way. For if we imagine that there are no causes external to the blood which would communicate new motions to the blood, nor any space external to the blood, nor any other bodies to which the parts of the blood could transfer their motions, it is beyond doubt that the blood would remain indefinitely in its present state and that its particles would undergo no changes other than those which can be conceived as resulting from the existing relation between the motion of the blood and of the lymph, chyle, etc. Thus the blood would always have to be regarded as a whole, not a part. But since there are many other causes which do in a definite way modify the laws of the nature of the blood and are reciprocally modified by the blood, it follows that there occur in the blood other motions and other changes, resulting not solely from the reciprocal relation of its particles but from the relation between the motion of the blood on the one hand and external causes on the other. From this perspective the blood is accounted as a part, not as a whole. So much, then, for the question of whole and part.

Now all the bodies in Nature can and should be conceived in the same way as we have here conceived the blood; for all bodies are surrounded by others and are reciprocally determined to exist and to act in a fixed and determinate way, the same ratio of motion to rest being preserved in them taken all together, that is, in the universe as a whole. Hence it follows that every body, insofar as it exists as modified in a definite way, must be considered as a part of the whole universe, and as agreeing with the whole and cohering with the other parts. Now since the nature of the universe, unlike the nature of the blood, is not limited, but is absolutely infinite, its parts are controlled by the nature of this infinite potency in infinite ways, and are compelled to undergo infinite variations. However, I conceive that in respect to substance each individual part has a more intimate union with its whole. For, as I endeavoured to show in my first letter written some time ago when I was living at Rijnsburg, since it is of the nature of substance to be infinite, it follows that each part pertains to the nature of corporeal substance, and can neither be nor be conceived without it.

So you see in what way and why I hold that the human body is a part of Nature. As regards the human mind, I maintain that it, too, is a part of Nature; for I hold that in Nature there also exists an infinite power of thinking which, insofar as it is infinite, contains within itself the whole of Nature ideally, and whose thoughts proceed in the same manner as does Nature, which is in fact the object of its thought.

Further, I maintain that the human mind is that same power of thinking, not insofar as that power is infinite and apprehends the whole of Nature, but insofar as it is finite, apprehending the human body only. The human mind, I maintain, is in this way part of an infinite intellect.

However, to provide here an explanation and rigorous proof of all these things and of other things closely connected with this subject would take far too long, and I do not imagine that you expect this of me at this moment. Indeed, I am not sure that I have rightly understood your meaning, and my reply may not be an answer to your question. This I should like you to let me know.

As to what you say about my hinting that the Cartesian Rules of motion are nearly all wrong, if I remember correctly I said that Mr. Huygens thinks so, and I did not assert that any of the Rules were wrong except for the sixth,[109] regarding which I said I thought that Mr. Huygens too was in error. At that point I asked you to tell me about the experiment which you have conducted in your Royal Society according to this hypothesis. But I gather that you are not permitted to do so, since you have made no reply on this matter.

The said Huygens has been, and still is, fully occupied in polishing dioptrical glasses. For this purpose he has devised a machine in which he can turn plates, and a very neat affair it is. I don't yet know what success he has had with it, and, to tell the truth, I don't particularly want to know. For experience has taught me that in polishing spherical plates a free hand yields safer and better results than any machine. Of the success of his pendulums and the time of his moving to France I have no definite news as yet.

The Bishop of Munster, having made an ill-advised incursion into Frisia like Aesop's goat into the well, has met with no success.[110] Indeed, unless winter begins very early, he will not leave Frisia without great loss. There is no doubt that he embarked on this audacious venture through the persuasion of some traitor or other. But all this is too stale to be written as news, and for the last week or two there has been no new development worth mentioning. There appears to be no hope of peace with the English. But a rumour has recently been spread because of conjectures concerning the sending of a Dutch ambassador to France, and also because the people of Overijsel, who are making every effort to bring in the Prince of Orange—in order, as many think, to annoy the Dutch rather than to benefit themselves—have thought up a certain scheme, namely, to send the said Prince to England as mediator. But the facts are quite otherwise. The Dutch at present have no thoughts of peace, unless matters should reach such a point that they would buy peace. There is as yet some doubt as to the plans of the Swede. Many think that he is making for Metz, others for Holland. But these are simply guesses.

---

109 [The sixth law states: "If a body C was at rest and exactly equal in size to a body B which moves towards it, then it must in part be pushed by B and in part cause B to rebound; so that if B approaches C with four degrees of velocity, it must transfer one degree to it and return in the direction from which it had come through the other three degrees" (*Principia* II, 50).]

110 [The unsuccessful invasion of Holland took place on 23 September 1665. After several failed efforts, the Bishop made peace with the Dutch on 18 April 1666.]

I wrote this letter last week, but I could not send it because the wind prevented my going to the Hague. This is the disadvantage of living in the country. Rarely do I receive a letter at the proper time, for unless an opportunity should chance to arise for sending it in good time, one or two weeks go by before I receive it. Then there is frequently a difficulty preventing me from sending a reply at the proper time. So when you see that I do not reply to you as promptly as I should, you must not think that this is because I forget you. Meanwhile, time presses me to close this letter; of the rest on another occasion. Now I can say no more than to ask you to give my warm greetings to the most noble Mr. Boyle, and to keep me in mind, who am,

In all affection yours,
B. de Spinoza

Voorburg, 20 November 1665

I should like to know whether the belief that there were two comets is held by all astronomers as a result of their motion, or in order to preserve Kepler's hypothesis.[111]

To Mr. Henry Oldenburg,
Secretary of the Royal Society,
In the Pall Mall,
in St. James' Fields,
London

LETTER 33
To the highly esteemed B.d.S., from Henry Oldenburg

[Known only from the O.P. The original is lost.]

Excellent Sir, much cherished friend,

Your philosophical thoughts on the agreement of the parts of Nature with the whole and on their interconnection are much to my liking, although I do not quite follow how we can banish order and symmetry from Nature, as you seem to do, especially since you yourself admit that all its bodies are surrounded by others and

---

[111] [Despite his revolutionary three laws of motion, Kepler (1571–1630) remained something of a 'closet Aristotelian' in holding that the fixed stars were parts of a solid sphere with the sun as its center. The interior of this sphere was filled with the ether. He attempted to account for the origin of comets as the condensates of the ether at random points, which were eventually destroyed by the light of the sun.]

are reciprocally determined both to exist and to act in a definite and regular manner, while at the same time the same proportion of motion to rest is preserved in them all. This itself seems to me good grounds for true order. But perhaps I do not here understand you sufficiently, any more than in your previous writing regarding Descartes' laws. I wish you would undertake the task of making clear to me wherein you consider that both Descartes and Huygens went wrong in regard to the laws of motion. By rendering this service you would do me a great favour, which I would strive with all my might to deserve.

I was not present when Mr. Huygens here in London carried out the experiments confirming his hypothesis.[112] I have since learned that, among other experiments, someone suspended a ball of one pound weight in the manner of a pendulum, and, on being released, it struck another ball similarly suspended but weighing only half a pound, at an angle of forty degrees, and that Huygens, making a brief algebraic calculation, had predicted the result, which answered exactly to his prediction. A certain distinguished person, who had proposed many such experiments which Huygens is said to have solved, is away.[113] As soon as I can meet this absent person, I shall perhaps give you a fuller and clearer account of this affair. Meanwhile I do most earnestly beseech you not to refuse the above-mentioned request of mine, and also to be kind enough to let me know whatever else you have discovered about Huygens' success in polishing telescopic glasses. Now that by the grace of God the plague is markedly less violent, I hope that our Royal Society will soon return to London and resume its weekly meetings. You can rest assured that I shall communicate to you whatever of its proceedings is worth knowing.

I have previously made mention of anatomical observations. No so long ago Mr. Boyle (who sends you his very kind greetings) wrote to me that some distinguished anatomists of Oxford had informed him that they had found the windpipe of certain sheep and also oxen crammed with grass,[114] and that a few weeks ago the said anatomists[115] were invited to view an ox which for almost two or three days on end had held its neck rigid and upright, and had died of a disease quite unknown to its owners. When the parts relating to the neck and throat were dissected, they were surprised to find that the windpipe deep inside the very trunk was stuffed with grass, as if someone had forcibly rammed it in. This provided just cause for an enquiry as to how such a great quantity of grass could have got there, and also, when it had got there, how such an animal could have survived so long.

Moreover, the same friend told me that a certain doctor of an enquiring nature, likewise of Oxford, has found milk in human blood. He relates how a girl, having eaten an ample breakfast at seven in the morning, was bled in the foot at eleven on the same day. The first blood was collected in a dish, and after a short

---

112 [These experiments are summarized in the *Philosophical Transactions*, 46 (12 April 1669), p. 100.]
113 [The reference may be to Lord Brouncker (1620–1684).]
114 [Reported in the *Philosophical Transactions*, 6 (6 November 1665).]
115 [These were Josiah Clark (1639–1714) and Richard Lower (1631–1691).]

space of time assumed a white colour; some later blood was gathered in a smaller vessel which, unless I am mistaken, they call an 'acetabulum' (in English, saucer), and immediately assumed the form of a milky cake. Five or six hours later the doctor returned and examined both lots of blood. That which was in the dish was half blood and half chyliform, and this chyle floated in the blood like whey in milk, whereas that which was in the 'saucer' was entirely chyle, without any appearance of blood. When he heated each of the two separately over a fire, both liquids solidified. The girl was quite well, and was bled only because she had never menstruated, although she had a good colour.

But I turn to politics. Here there is a wide-spread rumour that the Israelites, who have been dispersed for more than two thousand years, are to return to their homeland.[116] Few hereabouts believe it, but many wish it. Do let your friend know what you hear about this matter, and what you think. For my part, I cannot put any faith in this news as long as it is not reported by trustworthy men from the city of Constantinople, which is most of all concerned in this matter. I am anxious to know what the Jews of Amsterdam have heard about it, and how they are affected by so momentous an announcement, which, if true, is likely to bring about a world crisis.

There seems as yet no hope of peace between England and the Netherlands.

Tell me, if you can, what the Swede and the Brandenburger are about,[117] and believe me to be

Your most devoted,
Henry Oldenburg

London, 8 December 1665[118]

P.S. I shall shortly let you have news, God willing, as to what our philosophers think about the recent comets.

---

[116] [The reference is to a movement led by Sabbatai Zevi (1626–1676), who was a false messiah rather than a proto-Zionist. Spinoza's reply to this letter, unfortunately, is lost. Peter Serrarius was no doubt Oldenburg's main source of information regarding Zevi. He was known to have been in contact with Oldenburg.]

[117] [The reference is to strained relations between Sweden and Brandenburg concerning the possession of Hither Pomerania.]

[118] [Following this letter there is a gap of approximately ten years in the correspondence between Spinoza and Oldenburg. This gap is partly explained by the war between England and Holland (1665–1667), the Great Fire (1666), and the imprisonment of Oldenburg in the Tower of London (30 June until 26 August 1667).]

Letter 34

To the highly esteemed and sagacious John Hudde, from B.d.S.

[The original of this letter is extant, and held by the Royal Society, London. Spinoza retained a slightly different version of it, and it is from this that the text of the O.P. is printed. The differences are unimportant.]

Most esteemed Sir,

The proof of the unity of God on the ground that his nature involves necessary existence, which you asked for and I undertook to provide, I have hitherto been unable to send you because of other demands on my time. To engage upon it now, I shall make the following assumptions:[119]

1. The true definition of each single thing includes nothing other than the simple nature of the thing defined. Hence it follows that:

2. No definition involves or expresses a plurality, or a fixed number of individuals, since it involves and expresses only the nature of the thing as it is in itself. For example, the definition of a triangle includes nothing but the simple nature of a triangle, and not a fixed number of triangles, just as the definition of mind as a thinking thing or the definition of God as a perfect Being includes nothing other than the nature of mind and of God, and not a fixed number of minds or Gods.

3. There must necessarily be a positive cause of each thing, through which it exists.

4. This cause must either be placed in the nature and definition of the thing itself (because in effect existence belongs to its nature or is necessarily included in it) or outside the thing.

From these assumptions it follows that if in Nature there exists a fixed number of individuals, there must be one or more causes which could have produced exactly that number of individuals, no more and no less. For example, if there should exist in Nature twenty men (whom, to avoid confusion, I shall suppose to exist all at the same time and to be the first men in Nature), to account for the existence of these twenty it would not be enough to conduct an investigation into the cause of human nature in general. A reason must also be sought as to why twenty men, not more and not less, exist; for (in accordance with the third hypothesis) a reason and cause must be assigned for the existence of every man. But this cause (in accordance with the second and third hypothesis) cannot be contained in the na-

---

[119] [The numbered assumptions and immediate consequences which Spinoza draws from them are further expanded in E1P8Schol2.]

ture of man himself, for the true definition of man does not involve the number of twenty men. So (in accordance with the fourth hypothesis) the cause of the existence of these twenty men, and consequently of each single man individually, must lie outside them. Therefore we must conclude absolutely that all things which are conceived to exist as a plurality are necessarily produced by external causes, and not by virtue of their own nature. Now since (according to our hypothesis) necessary existence pertains to God's nature, it must be that his true definition should also include necessary existence, and therefore his necessary existence must be concluded from his true definition. But from his true definition (as I have already proved from the second and third hypothesis) the necessary existence of many Gods cannot be concluded. Therefore there follows the existence of one God only. Q.E.D.

This, esteemed Sir, seems to me at present the best way of proving the proposition. On a previous occasion[120] I have proved this same proposition in a different way, making use of the distinction between essence and existence; but having regard to the consideration which you pointed out to me, I have preferred to send you this proof. I hope it will satisfy you, and, awaiting your judgment on it, I remain meanwhile, etc.

Voorburg, 7 January 1666

LETTER 35
To the highly esteemed and sagacious John Hudde, from B.d.S.

[The original, written in Dutch, is lost. The Latin version in the O.P. was probably made by Spinoza. The Dutch edition of the O.P. prints a text that appears to be a re-translation from the Latin.]

Most esteemed Sir,

In your last letter dated 30 March[121] you have made perfectly clear what I found rather obscure in the letter you wrote me on 10 February. So since I now know what is your real line of thought, I shall frame the question in the form in which it presents itself to you, namely, whether there is only one Being which subsists through its own sufficiency or force. This I not only affirm, but undertake to prove from this basis, that its nature involves necessary existence. This may be most eas-

---

[120] [The proof to which Spinoza alludes is probably like that given as E1P7Dem.]

[121] [No such letter from Hudde to Spinoza is extant. It was probably destroyed by the editors of the O.P.]

ily proved from God's understanding (as I did in Proposition 11 of my Geometrical Proofs of Descartes' *Principia*), or from others of God's attributes. To embark upon this task, I shall first of all briefly show what properties must be possessed by a Being that includes necessary existence. These are:

1. It is eternal. For if a determinate duration were ascribed to it, beyond the bounds of its determinate duration this Being would be conceived as not existing, or as not involving necessary existence, and this would be in contradiction with its definition.[122]

2. It is simple, and not composed of parts. For in respect of their nature and our knowledge of them component parts would have to be prior to that which they compose. In the case of that which is eternal by its own nature, this cannot be so.[123]

3. It cannot be conceived as determinate, but only as infinite. For if the nature of that Being were determinate, and were also conceived as determinate, that nature would be conceived as not existing beyond those limits. This again is in contradiction with its definition.[124]

4. It is indivisible.[125] For if it were divisible, it would be divided into parts either of the same or of a different nature. In the latter case it could be destroyed, and thus not exist, which is contrary to the definition. In the former case, every part would include necessary existence through itself, and in this way one could exist, and consequently be conceived, without another. Therefore that nature could be understood as finite, which, by the foregoing, is contrary to the definition. Hence it can be seen that if we were to ascribe any imperfection to such a Being, we would at once fall into a contradiction. For whether the imperfection we would ascribe to such a nature lay in some defect, or in some limitations which such a nature would possess, or in some change which it might undergo from external causes through its lack of force, we are always reduced to saying that this nature which involves necessary existence does not exist, or does not exist necessarily.[126] Therefore I conclude that—

5. Everything that includes necessary existence can have in itself no imperfection, but must express pure perfection.[127]

6. Again, since it can only be the result of its perfection that a Being should exist by its own sufficiency and force, it follows that if we suppose that a Being which does not express all the perfections exists by its own nature, we must also suppose that a Being which comprehends in itself all the perfections exists as well.

---

[122] [See E1P19.]

[123] [See E1P15.]

[124] [See E1P20–P21.]

[125] [See E1P15.]

[126] [The account of the indivisibility of substance (and of *res extensa*) is further amplified in E1P15Schol. The existence proof is given in E1P7. The fact that Spinoza has here reversed the order indicates that he did not regard the order or status (as axioms or theorems) of the propositions in the *Ethics* to be invariant.]

[127] [This claim is expanded in E1P17 Schol.]

For if that which is endowed with less power exists by its own sufficiency, how much more does that exist which is endowed with greater power.[128]

To come now to the point at issue, I assert that there can only be one Being whose existence pertains to its own nature, namely, that Being which possesses in itself all perfections, and which I shall call God. For if there be posited a Being to whose nature existence pertains, that Being must contain in itself no imperfection, but must express every perfection (Note 5). And therefore the nature of that Being must pertain to God (whom, by Note 6, we must also claim to exist), since he possesses in himself all perfections and no imperfections. Nor can it exist outside God; for if it were to exist outside God, one and the same nature involving necessary existence would exist in double form, and this, according to our previous demonstration, is absurd. Therefore nothing outside God, but only God alone, involves necessary existence. This is what was to be proved.

These, esteemed Sir, are at present the points I can put before you to prove what I have undertaken. I should like occasion to prove to you that I am, etc.

Voorburg, 10 April 1666

LETTER 36
To the highly esteemed and sagacious John Hudde, from B.d.S.

[The original, written in Dutch, is lost. The Latin version in the O.P. was perhaps made by Spinoza. The text of the Dutch edition of the O.P. appears to be a re-translation from the Latin.]

Most esteemed Sir,

Something has prevented me from replying any sooner to your letter dated 19 May. As I understand that for the most part you suspend judgment about the proof which I sent you (because of the obscurity, I imagine, which you find in it), I shall here endeavour to explain its meaning more clearly.

First, then, I enumerated four properties which must be possessed by a Being existing through its own sufficiency or force. These four properties and the other properties similar to them I reduced to one in the fifth note. Then, in order to deduce from a single assumption everything necessary for the proof, in the sixth note I endeavoured to prove the existence of God from the given hypothesis; and then,

---

[128] [See E1P17Schol, and also the third of the three versions of the ontological proof which Spinoza gives in E1P11.]

taking nothing more as known except the bare meaning of words, I reached the conclusion which was sought.

This in short was my intention, this my aim. I shall now clarify the meaning of each link individually, and first I shall begin with the assumed properties.

In the first you find no difficulty; it is nothing but an axiom, as is the second. For by simple I mean only that which is not composite or composed of parts that are different in nature, or of other parts that agree in nature. The proof is certainly of universal application.[129]

The meaning of the third note you have understood very well, insofar as it makes the point that, if the Being is Thought, it cannot be conceived as determined in Thought, but only as undetermined, and if the Being is Extension it cannot be conceived as determined in Extension, but only as undetermined. And yet you deny that you understand the conclusion, which is simply based on this, that it is a contradiction to conceive under the negation of existence something whose definition includes existence, or (which is the same thing) affirms existence. And since 'determinate' denotes nothing positive, but only the privation of existence of that same nature which is conceived as determinate, it follows that that whose definition affirms existence cannot be conceived as determinate. For example, if the term 'extension' includes necessary existence, it is just as impossible to conceive extension without existence as extension without extension. If this is granted, it will also be impossible to conceive determinate extension. For if it were conceived as determinate, it would have to be determined by its own nature, that is, by extension, and this extension by which it would be determined would have to be conceived under the negation of existence. This, according to the hypothesis, is a manifest contradiction.

In the fourth note I intended only to show that such a Being cannot be divided into parts of the same nature or into parts of a different nature, whether or not those parts of a different nature involve necessary existence. For in the latter case, I said, it could be destroyed, since to destroy a thing is to resolve it into such parts that none of them express the nature of the whole, while the former case would be inconsistent with the three properties already established.

In the fifth note I have only assumed that perfection consists in being, and imperfection in the privation of being. I say 'privation'; for although Extension, for instance, denies of itself Thought, this is not an imperfection in it. But if it were deprived of extension, this would indeed argue imperfection in it, as would be the case if it were determinate. And the same would apply if it were to lack duration, position, etc.

You grant the sixth note absolutely, and yet you say that your difficulty remains quite unresolved, namely, as to why there could not be several beings existing through themselves but of different natures, just as Thought and Extension are

---

[129] [Individuation on the basis of parts of *different* natures is the basis of the physical account of material bodies following E2P13Schol. The social account of the origin of the civil community given beginning at E4P37Schol2 is based on parts (i.e., citizens) of *similar* natures.]

different and perhaps can subsist through their own sufficiency. From this I cannot but believe that you understand this in a sense far different from mine. I think I can see in what sense you understand it; but in order not to waste time, I shall only make clear my own meaning. I say, then, with regard to the sixth note, that if we suppose that something which is indeterminate and perfect only in its own kind exists by its own sufficiency, then we must also grant the existence of a being which is absolutely indeterminate and perfect.[130] This Being I shall call God. For example, if we are willing to maintain that Extension or Thought (which can each be perfect in its own kind, that is, in a definite kind of being) exist by their own sufficiency, we shall also have to admit the existence of God who is absolutely perfect, that is, the existence of a being who is absolutely indeterminate.

At this point I would have you note what I recently said regarding the word 'imperfection'; namely, that it signifies that a thing lacks something which nevertheless pertains to its nature. For example, extension can be said to be imperfect only in respect of duration, position, or magnitude; that is to say, because it does not last longer, because it does not retain its position, or because it is not greater. But it will never be said to be imperfect because it does not think, for nothing like this is demanded of its nature which consists solely in extension, that is, in a definite kind of being, in which respect alone it can be said to be determinate or indeterminate, imperfect or perfect. And since God's nature does not consist in one definite kind of being, but in being which is absolutely indeterminate, his nature also demands all that which perfectly expresses being; otherwise his nature would be determinate and deficient. This being so, it follows that there can be only one Being, God, which exists by its own force. For if, let us say, we suppose that Extension involves existence, it must needs be eternal and indeterminate, and express absolutely no imperfection, but only perfection. And so Extension will pertain to God, or will be something that expresses God's nature in some way; for God is a Being which is indeterminate in essence and omnipotent absolutely, and not merely in a particular respect. And thus what is said of Extension (arbitrarily chosen) must also be affirmed of everything which we shall take to be of a similar kind. I therefore conclude, as in my former letter, that nothing outside God, but God alone, subsists by its own sufficiency. I trust that this is enough to clarify the meaning of my former letter; but you will be the better judge of that.

I might have ended here, but since I am minded to get new plates made for me for polishing glasses, I should very much like to have your advice in this matter. I cannot see what we gain by polishing convex-concave glasses. On the contrary, if I have done my calculations correctly, convex-plane glasses are bound to be more useful. For if, for convenience, we take the ratio of refraction[131] as 3 to 2, and in the accompanying diagram we insert letters according to your arrangement in your little *Dioptrics*, it will be found on setting out the equation that NI

---

[130] [This claim is the converse of E1P9.]

[131] [This ratio has the sine of the angle of incidence as numerator, and the sine of the angle of refraction as denominator.]

or, as it is called $z = \sqrt{[(9/4)zz - xx]} - \sqrt{[1 - xx]}$.[132] Hence it follows that if x = 0, z = 2, which then is also the longest. And if x = 3/5, z will be 43/25, or a little more; that is, if we suppose that the ray BI does not undergo a second refraction when it is directed from the glass towards I. But let us now suppose that this ray issuing from the glass is refracted at the plane surface BF, and is directed not towards I but towards R. If therefore the lines BI and BR are in the same ratio as is the refraction—that is, as is here supposed, a ratio of 3 to 2—and if we then follow out the working of the equation, we get $NR = \sqrt{(zz - xx)} - \sqrt{(1 - xx)}$. And if again, as before, we take x = 0, then NR = 1, that is, equal to half the diameter. But if x = 3/5, NR will be 20/25 + 1/50, which shows that this focal length is less than the other, although the optic tube is less by a whole semi-diameter. So if we were to make a telescope as long as DI by making the semi-diameter = 1½ while the aperture BF remained the same, the focal length would be much less. A further reason why convex-concave glasses are less satisfactory, apart from the fact that they require twice the labour and expense, is that the rays, being not all directed to one and the same point, never fall perpendicularly on the concave surface. However, as I have no doubt that you have long since considered these points and have made more rigorous calculations about them, and have reached a decision on this question, I seek your opinion and advice regarding it, etc.

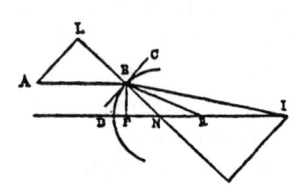

[Date probably June 1666]

LETTER 37
To the learned and experienced Johan Bouwmeester, from B.d.S.

[The original is lost, but an old copy is extant, differing in a few details from the O.P. text. The last sentence appears only in the old copy.]

Most learned Sir, and very special friend,[133]

I have been unable to reply any sooner to your last letter which reached me quite some time ago. Various concerns and troubles have kept me so occupied that it is

---

[132] [Spinoza uses 'xx' where we would use an exponential for squaring. The exponential notation had been introduced by Descartes, but was not widely adopted until after the seventeenth century.]

[133] [Johan Bouwmeester (1630–1680) was a medical doctor and a member of the discussion group formed at Franciscus Van den Enden's school.—M.L.M.]

only with difficulty that I have at last managed to extricate myself. However, since I have now obtained some degree of respite, I will not fail in my duty, but I want first of all to express my very warm thanks for your love and devotion towards me which you have abundantly shown so often by deeds, and now by letter, etc.

I pass on to your question, which is as follows: whether there is or can be a method such that thereby we can make sure and unwearied progress in the study of things of the highest importance; or whether our minds, like our bodies, are at the mercy of chance, and our thoughts are governed more by fortune than by skill. I think I shall give a satisfactory answer if I show that there must necessarily be a method whereby we can direct and interconnect our clear and distinct perceptions, and that the intellect is not, like the body, at the mercy of chance. This is established simply from the following consideration, that one clear and distinct perception, or several taken together, can be absolutely the cause of another clear and distinct perception. Indeed, all the clear and distinct perceptions that we form can arise only from other clear and distinct perceptions which are in us, and they acknowledge no other cause outside us. Hence it follows that the clear and distinct perceptions that we form depend only on our nature and its definite and fixed laws, that is, on our power itself alone, and not on chance, that is, on causes which, although acting likewise by definite and fixed laws, are yet unknown to us and foreign to our nature and power. As for the other perceptions, I do admit that they depend in the highest degree on chance. From this it is quite clear what a true method must be and in which it should especially consist, namely, solely in the knowledge of pure intellect and its nature and laws.[134] To acquire this, we must first of all distinguish between intellect and imagination,[135] that is, between true ideas and the others—fictitious, false, doubtful, and, in sum, all ideas which depend only on memory. To understand these things, at least as far as the method requires, there is no need to get to know the nature of mind through its first cause; it is enough to formulate a brief account of the mind or its perceptions in the manner expounded by Verulam.[136]

I think that in these few words I have explained and demonstrated the true method, and at the same time shown the way to attain it. It remains, however, for me to advise you that for all this there is needed constant meditation and a most steadfast mind and purpose, to acquire which it is most important to establish a fixed way and manner of life, and to have a definite aim in view. But enough of this for the present.

Farewell, and love him who has for you a sincere affection.

Bened. de Spinoza
Voorburg, 10 June 1666

---

[134] [The brief summary of his method given here is further developed in the unfinished *Tractatus de intellectus emendatione* (TIE).]

[135] [See E2P40Schol, where Spinoza develops the distinction among three kinds of knowledge (imagination, reason, intuition). The term *imaginatio* in Spinoza refers most generally to sensory perception.]

[136] [I.e., Francis Bacon, in the *Organon*.]

LETTER 38

To the accomplished John Van der Meer, from B.d.S.

[The original, written in Dutch, is lost. The Latin is a translation.]

Sir,[137]

While living in solitude here in the country, I reflected on the problem you once put to me, and found that it was very simple. The proof, universally stated, is based on this, that the fair gambler[138] is one who makes his chance of winning or losing equal to that of his opponent. This equality is to be measured by the chances of winning and the money which the opponents stake and risk; that is, if the chances are the same for both sides, each should stake and risk the same sum of money, but if the chances are unequal, one must stake and lay down as much more money as his chances are greater. Thus the prospects on both sides are equal, and consequently the game will be fair. If, for example, A playing against B has two chances of winning and only one of losing, and B on the other hand has only one chance of winning and two of losing, it seems clear that A should risk as much for each chance of winning as B for his; that is, A must wager twice as much as B.

In order to show this more clearly, let us suppose that three persons, A, B and C, are playing together with equal chances and each lays down an equal sum of money. It is clear that, since each lays an equal stake, each also risks only one third in order to gain two thirds, and that, since each is playing against two, each has only one chance of winning against two or losing. If we suppose that one of the three, say C, withdraws before the beginning of play, it is clear that he should take back only what he has staked, that is, a third part, and that B, if he wants to buy C's chance and take his place, must put down as much as C withdraws. To this A cannot object, for it makes no difference to him whether he must play with his one chance against the two chances of two different men or against two chances of one man alone. If this is the case, it follows that if one person holds out his hand for another to guess one out of two numbers, winning a certain sum of money if he guesses right or losing a like sum if he is wrong, the chances on both sides are equal, as well for him who invites the guess as for him who is to make the guess. Again, if he holds out his hand for the other to guess at the first attempt one out of three numbers and to win a certain sum of money if he guesses right or to lose half that sum if he guesses wrong, the chances will be equal on both sides, just as

---

[137] [Nothing whatever is known about John Van der Meer, to whom this letter is addressed.]

[138] [The history of the calculus of probability began with reflections on betting odds of the sort which Spinoza here offers. Huygens and many others of Spinoza's contemporaries dealt with the subject.]

both sides have an equal chance if he who holds out his hand allows the other two guesses on condition that, if he guesses right, he wins a certain sum of money, or if he is wrong, he loses twice that amount.

The chances are also equal if he allows him three guesses at one of four numbers so as to win a certain sum of money if he is right or to lose three times as much if he is wrong; or to have four guesses at one of five numbers so as to win one amount if he is right or lose four times that amount if he is wrong, and so on. From all this it follows that for him who holds out his hand it is all the same if the other has as many guesses as he likes at one out of many numbers provided that, in return for the number of times he proposes to guess, he also stakes and risks an amount which is equivalent to the number of tries divided by the sum of the numbers. If, for instance there are five numbers and the guesser is allowed only one guess, he must stake $1/5$ against the other's $4/5$; if he is to make two guesses, he must stake $2/5$ against the other's $3/5$; if three guesses, then $3/5$ against $2/5$, and, by continuation, $4/5$ against $1/5$ and $5/5$ against 0.[139] Consequently, for him who invites the guess, if, for example, he risks only $1/6$ of the stake to win $5/6$, it will be just the same whether one man guesses five times or five men each guess once, which is the point at issue in your problem.

1 October 1666

Letter 39
To the worthy and sagacious Jarig Jelles, from B.d.S.

[The original, written in Dutch, is lost. It may be the text reproduced in the Dutch edition of the O.P. The Latin is a translation.]

Worthy Sir,[140]

Various obstacles have hindered me from replying any sooner to your letter. I have checked the points you made regarding Descartes' *Dioptrics*. On the question as to why the images at the back of the eye become larger or smaller, he takes account of no other cause than the crossing of the rays proceeding from the different points of the object, according as they begin to cross one another nearer to or further from the eye, and so he does not consider the size of the angle which the rays make when they cross one another at the surface of the eye. And although this last cause is the most important to be considered in the case of telescopes, yet he seems deliber-

---

[139] [Within the context of the Bayesian calculus of probability, the property to which Spinoza is appealing is the 'value of a wager', defined as the product of the probability of winning and the payoff.]

[140] [Jarig Jelles (1619/20?–1683) was one of the editors of the O.P.]

ately to have passed it over in silence because, I imagine, he knew of no means of gathering rays proceeding in parallel from different points onto as many other points, and therefore he could not determine this angle mathematically.

Perhaps he was silent so as not to give any preference to the circle above other figures which he introduced; for there is no doubt that in this matter the circle surpasses all other figures that can be discovered. For the circle, being everywhere the same, has everywhere the same properties. For example, the circle ABCD has the property that all the rays coming from the direction A and parallel to the axis AB are refracted at its surface in such a manner that they all thereafter come together at point B. Likewise, all rays coming from the direction C and parallel to the axis CD are refracted at the surface in such a way that they all come together at point D. This can be said of no other figure, although hyperbolae and ellipses have infinite diameters. So the case is as you describe; that is, if no account is taken of anything except the length of the eye or of the telescope, we should be obliged to manufacture very long telescopes before we could see objects on the moon as distinctly as those on earth. But, as I have said, the chief consideration is the size of the angle made by the rays issuing from different points when they cross one another at the surface of the eye. And this angle also becomes greater or less as the foci of the glasses fitted in the telescope differ to a greater or lesser degree. If you desire to see the proof of this I am ready to send it to you whenever you wish.

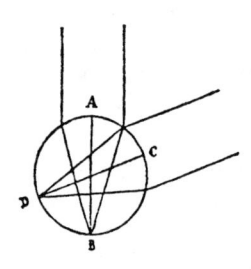

Voorburg, 3 March 1667

Letter 40
To the worthy and sagacious Jarig Jelles, from B.d.S.

[The original, written in Dutch, is lost. It may be the text reproduced in the Dutch edition of the O.P. The Latin is a translation.]

Worthy friend,

I have duly received your last letter dated the 14th of this month, but various obstacles have prevented me from replying sooner.

With regard to the Helvetius affair,[141] I have spoken about it with Mr. Vossius,[142] who (not to recount in a letter all that passed between us) laughed heartily

---

[141] [Johannes Fridericus Helvetius was physician to the Prince of Orange.]

[142] [Isaac Vossius (1618–1689). He wrote on the Septuagint and on poetry, and was made Canon of Windsor in 1673.]

at it, and even expressed surprise that I should question him about such a silly thing. However, disregarding this, I went to the silversmith named Brechtelt, who had tested the gold. Taking quite a different view from Vossius, he said that between the melting and the separation the gold had increased in weight, and had become that much heavier as was the weight of the silver he had introduced into the crucible to effect the separation. So he firmly believed that the gold which had transmuted his silver into gold contained something singular. He was not the only one of this opinion; various other persons present at the time also found that this was so. Thereupon I went to Helvetius himself, who showed me the gold and the crucible with its interior still covered with a film of gold, and told me that he had introduced into the molten lead scarcely more than a quarter of a grain of barley or of mustard-seed. He added that he would shortly publish an account of the whole affair, and went on to say that in Amsterdam a certain man (he thought it was the same man who had visited him) had performed the same operation, of which you have no doubt heard. This is all I have been able to learn about this matter.

The writer of the book you mention (in which he presumes to show that Descartes' arguments in the Third and Fourth Meditation proving the existence of God are false) is assuredly fighting his own shadow, and will do more harm to himself than to others. Descartes' axiom is, I admit somewhat obscure and confused as you have also remarked, and he might have expressed it more clearly and truthfully thus: 'The power of thought to think or to comprehend things is no greater than the power of Nature to be and to act'.[143] This is a clear and true axiom, whence the existence of God follows most clearly and forcefully from the idea of him. The argument of the said author as related by you shows quite clearly that he does not yet understand the matter. It is indeed true that we could go on to infinity if the question could thus be resolved in all its parts, but otherwise it is sheer folly. For example, if someone were to ask through what cause a certain determinate body is set in motion, we could answer that it is determined to such motion by another body, and this again by another, and so on to infinity. We could reply in this way, I say, because the question is only about motion, and by continuing to posit another body we assign a sufficient and eternal cause of this motion. But if I see a book containing excellent thoughts and beautifully written in the hands of a common man and I ask him whence he has such a book, and he replies that he has copied it from another book belonging to another common man who could also write beautifully, and so on to infinity, he does not satisfy me.[144] For I am asking him not only about the form and arrangement of the letters, with which alone his answer is concerned, but also about the thoughts and

---

[143] [What is at issue here is Descartes' use of the notion of 'difficulty' in describing acts of comprehension (as well as divine conservation).]

[144] [The argument refers to the explanation of the representational content of a cognition or idea, which Spinoza—following Descartes—calls its 'objective reality'. The objective reality of a representation cannot be explained by an infinite series of causes, although just such a series does explain its formal reality.]

meaning expressed in their arrangement, and this he does not answer by his progression to infinity. How this can be applied to ideas can easily be understood from what I have made clear in the ninth axiom of my Geometrical Proofs of Descartes' *Principles of Philosophy*.

I now proceed to answer your other letter, dated 9 March, in which you ask for a further explanation of what I wrote in my previous letter concerning the figure of a circle. This you will easily be able to understand if you will please note that all the rays that are supposed to fall in parallel on the anterior glass of the telescope are not really parallel because they all come from one and the same point. But they are considered to be so because the object is so far from us that the aperture of the telescope, in comparison with its distance, can be considered as no more than a point. Moreover, it is certain that, in order to see an entire object, we need not only rays coming from a single point but also all the other cones of rays that come from all the other points. And therefore it is also necessary that, on passing through the glass, they should come together in as many other foci. And although the eye is not so exactly constructed that all the rays coming from different points of an object come together in just so many foci at the back of the eye, yet it is certain that the figures that can bring this about are to be preferred above all others. Now since a definite segment of a circle can bring it about that all the rays coming from one point are (using the language of Mechanics) brought together at another point on its diameter, it will also bring together all the other rays which come from other points of the object, at so many other points. For from any point on an object a line can be drawn passing through the centre of the circle, although for that purpose the aperture of the telescope must be made much smaller than it would otherwise be made if there were no need of more than one focus, as you may easily see.

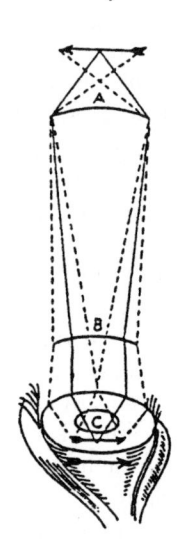

What I here say of the circle cannot be said of the ellipse or the hyperbola, and far less of other more complex figures, since from one single point of the object only one line can be drawn passing through both the foci. This is what I intended to say in my first letter regarding this matter.

From the attached diagram you will be able to see the proof that the angle formed at the surface of the eye by rays coming from different points becomes greater or less according as the difference of the foci is greater or less. So, after sending you my cordial greetings, it remains only for me to say that I am, etc.

Voorburg, 25 March 1667

LETTER 41

To the worthy and sagacious Jarig Jelles, from B.d.S.

[The original, written in Dutch, is lost. The Dutch edition of the O.P. probably reproduces the original text, and the Latin version is a translation from this.]

Most worthy Sir,

I shall here relate in brief what I have discovered by experiment regarding the question which you first put to me in person, and later in writing; and to this I shall add my present opinion on this subject.[145]

I had a wooden tube made for me, 10 feet long with a bore of $1\tfrac{2}{3}$ inches, to which I affixed three perpendicular tubes, as in the accompanying figure. In order first to find out whether the pressure of the water in the tube B was as great as in E, I closed the tube at A with a piece of wood made for the purpose. Then I made the mouth of B so narrow that it could hold a small glass tube, like C. Then, having filled the tube with water by means of the vessel F, I noted the height to which the water rose through the narrow tube C. Then I closed the tube B, and, removing the stopper at A, I allowed the water to flow into the tube E which I had fitted up in the same way as B, and when I refilled the whole tube with water, I found that it rose to the same height in D as it had done in C. This led me to believe that the length of the tube was no hindrance, or very little.

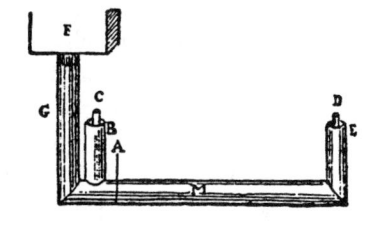

But to make a more rigorous investigation, I also sought to find out whether the tube E could fill a vessel of a cubic foot, which I had made for the purpose, in as short a time as tube B. In order to measure the time, not having a pendulum clock to hand, I made do with a bent glass tube, like H, whose shorter part was immersed in water while the longer was suspended in open air. When I had made these preparations, I first let the water flow through the tube B in a stream equal to the bore of the tube until the vessel of a cubic foot was full. Then with accurate scales I weighed the amount of water that had meanwhile flowed into the

---

[145] [This is the sole letter surviving from the period 1668–1670. Adriaan Koerbagh, a friend of Spinoza, was imprisoned in Amsterdam in 1668, and died there under extreme conditions in 1669. It was one of the several periods of religious repression in Holland, and people were cautious of corresponding with one another on any subject which might draw the attention of the religious authorities. Spinoza was also busy with the writing of the *Tractatus Theologico-Politicus*, which was to reflect much of the religious dissension of the period.]

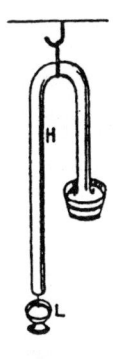

868 The Letters

bowl L, and found that it weighed about four ounces. Then I closed the tube B, and let the water flow through the tube E, in an equally dense stream, into the cubic foot vessel. When this was full, I weighed again, as before, the water which had meanwhile flowed into the small basin, and I found that it did not weigh even half an ounce more. But since the steams from both B and E had not constantly flowed with the same force, I repeated the operation, and first brought as much water as we had found from our first experiment we needed to have at hand. There were three of us as busy as could be, performing the aforementioned experiment more accurately than before, but not as accurately as I could wish. Still, I obtained sufficient information to reach a fairly sure conclusion, for I found practically the same difference on the second occasion as on the first.

On consideration of this matter and these experiments, I find myself forced to the conclusion that the difference that can be produced by the length of the tube has an effect only at the beginning, that is, when the water begins its flow; but when it has been flowing for a short while, it will flow with as much force through a very long tube as through a short tube. The reason for this is that the pressure of the higher water always retains the same force, and that all the motion which it communicates it continually regains through the action of gravity; and so it will also continually communicate this motion to the water in the tube until the latter, being forced forward, has gained as much speed as is equivalent to the force of gravity which the higher water can impart to it. For it is certain that, if the water in the tube G in the first moment imparts to the water in the long tube M one degree of speed, then in the second moment, if it retains its original force as it is presumed to do, it will communicate four degrees of speed to the same water, and so on until the water in the longer tube M has acquired exactly the degree of speed that the gravitational force of the higher water in tube G can give it. Therefore the water flowing through a tube forty thousand feet long, after a short space of time and solely through the pressure of the higher water, would acquire as much speed as if the tube M were only one foot long. If I had been able to get more exact instruments, I could have determined the time needed for the water in the longer tube to acquire so much speed. However, I do not think this is necessary, since the main point is adequately determined, etc.

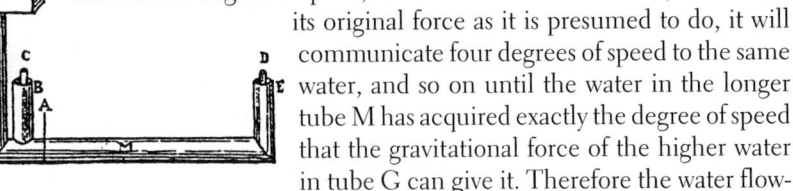

Voorburg, 5 September 1669

Letter 42

To the learned and accomplished Jacob Ostens, from Lambert de Velthuysen, M.Dr.

[Known only from the O.P. The original is lost.]

Most learned Sir,

Having at last obtained some free time, I at once turned my attention to satisfying your wishes and requests.[146] You ask me to let you know my opinion and the verdict I pronounce on the book entitled *Discursus Theologico-Politicus*[147] and this I am now resolved to do as far as my time and my ability permit. I shall not go into every detail, but I shall give a summarised account of the author's thinking and his attitude to religion.

I do not know of what nationality he is or what manner of life he pursues, and this is not of any importance. The methodical reasoning of the book itself is evidence enough that he is not unintelligent, and that his discussion and close examination of the controversies among Christians in Europe is not careless and superficial. The writer of this book is convinced that, in making assessment of the opinions which cause men to break forth into factions and divide into parties, he will achieve greater success if he puts aside and renounces prejudice. Therefore he has energetically striven to rid his mind of all superstition. But in seeking to show himself free from superstition, he has gone too far in the opposite direction, and, to avoid the accusation of superstition, I think he has renounced all religion. At any rate, he does not rise above the religion of the Deists, of whom there are considerable numbers everywhere (so deplorable is the morality of our age), and especially in France. Mersenne[148] has published a treatise against them, which I remember once reading. But I think that scarcely anyone of the Deists has written on behalf of that evil cause so maliciously, so cleverly and cunningly as the author of this dissertation. Furthermore, unless I am mistaken, this man does not rank himself among the Deists, and does not suffer men to retain the slightest portions of religious worship.

He acknowledges God and declares him to be the maker and founder of the universe. But he asserts that the form, appearance and order of the world are wholly necessary, equally with God's nature and the eternal truths, which he holds

---

[146] [Lambert van Velthuysen (1622–1685) studied philosophy, theology and medicine at the University of Utrecht. While his liberal views brought him into conflict with the Calvinists, he regarded the TTP as both atheistic and fatalistic.]

[147] [*Discursus* should of course be *Tractatus*.]

[148] [Marin Mersenne (1588–1648) was educated at a Jesuit college and wrote various theological treatises. He was a friend of Descartes and defended him against charges of unorthodoxy.]

to be established independently of God's control. And so he also explicitly declares that all things come to pass by an invincible necessity and ineluctable fate. And he asserts that for those who think aright no room is left for precepts and commandments, but men's want of understanding has brought such expressions into use, just as the ignorance of the multitude has given rise to modes of speech whereby emotions are ascribed to God. And so God likewise adapts himself to men's understanding when he exhibits to men in the form of command those eternal truths and the other things that must necessarily come to pass. He tells us that the necessity of the occurrence of those things that are governed by laws and are thought to be not amenable to the will of men is the same as the necessity of the nature of a triangle. And so what is embodied in the precepts does not depend on man's will, nor will any good or evil befall men as they neglect or heed them, any more than God's will can be influenced by prayer or his eternal and absolute decrees be mutable. So precepts are in like case with decrees and have this in common, that men's ignorance and lack of understanding has moved God to allow them to be of some use to those who cannot form more perfect thoughts about God and need wretched aids of this kind to excite in them a love of virtue and a hatred of vice. And so we can see that the author makes no mention in his writing of the use of prayer, just as he makes no mention of life or death or of any reward or punishment which must be allotted to men by the judge of the universe.

And this he does in accordance with his principles. For what place can there by for the last judgment? Or what expectation of reward or punishment, when all is attributed to fate, and when it is asserted that all things emanate from God by an ineluctable necessity, or rather, when he asserts that this universe in its entirety is God? For I fear that our author is not very far removed from that opinion; at any rate there is not much difference between asserting that all things necessarily emanate from God's nature and that the universe itself is God.

However, he locates man's highest pleasure in the cultivation of virtue, which he says is its own reward and the stage for the display of all that is finest. And so he holds that the man who understands things aright ought to devote himself to virtue not because of God's precepts and law, nor through hope of reward or fear of punishment, but because he is enticed by the beauty of virtue and the joy which a man feels in the practise of virtue.

He therefore asserts that it is only to outward appearance that God, through the prophets and through revelation, exhorts men to virtue by the hope of reward and the fear of punishment, two things that are always conjoined in law. For in the case of men of the common sort their minds are so constituted and so ill-trained that they can be urged to the practise of virtue only by arguments deriving from the nature of law, and from fear of punishment and hope of reward. But men of true judgment understand that there is no truth or force underlying such arguments.

Nor does he think it of any importance even if it correctly follows from this axiom of his that the prophets and the holy teachers—and so God himself, who spoke to men through their mouths—employed arguments which, if their nature be considered, are in themselves false. For quite openly and in many places, when occasion offers, he proclaims and emphasizes that Holy Scripture is not intended to teach truth and the natures of things which are mentioned therein, and which it uses for its own purpose to train men to virtue. And he denies that the prophets were so learned as to be quite free from the errors of the common people when they constructed arguments and devised reasons whereby they exhorted men to virtue, although the nature of moral virtues and vices was clearly discerned by them.

So the author furthermore tells us that even when the prophets were admonishing of their duty those to whom they were sent, they were not free from mistakes of judgment. Yet this did not detract from their holiness and credibility, although they employed speech and arguments that were not true, but were adapted to the preconceived beliefs of those whom they were addressing, thereby urging men to those virtues which no one ever doubts and are not the subject of any controversy among mankind. For the purpose of the prophet's mission was to promote the cultivation of virtue among men, and not to teach any truth. So he considers that such error and ignorance on the part of the prophet was not injurious to his hearers whom he was inspiring to virtue, for he thinks it matters little what arguments incite us to virtue provided that they are not subversive of moral virtue, for the encouragement of which they were devised and promulgated by the prophet. For he thinks that the grasping of truth in regard to other matters makes no contribution to piety, since moral holiness is not in fact to be found in such truth, and he holds that knowledge of truth, and also of mysteries, is necessary only to the extent that it promotes piety.

I think the author has in mind the axiom of those theologians who make a distinction between the words of the prophet when he is proclaiming doctrine and his words when he is merely narrating something. This distinction, if I am not mistaken, is accepted by all theologians, and he quite wrongly believes that his own doctrine is in agreement with this.

He therefore considers that all those who deny that reason and philosophy are the interpreters of Scripture will be on his side. For it is generally agreed that in Scripture there are predicated of God a great many things which are not applicable to God, but are adapted to human understanding in such a way that men may be moved by them and be awakened to the love of virtue. This being so, he thinks it must be accepted that the holy teacher intended by these untrue arguments to educate men to virtue, or else anyone who reads Holy Scripture is entitled to judge the intended meaning of the holy teacher according to the principles of his own reason. This latter view the author utterly condemns and rejects, and along with it the view of those who agree with the paradoxical theologian[149] that reason is the interpreter of Scripture. For he considers that Scripture must be understood literally, and that men must not be granted freedom to interpret as they please in a rationalistic way what is to be understood by the words of the prophet, so as to decide in the light of their own reasoning and acquired knowledge when it is that

---

[149] [The 'paradoxical theologian' is Lodewijk Meyer, whose *Philosophia Sanctae Scripturae Interpres* appeared in 1666.]

the prophets spoke literally and when figuratively. But there will be opportunity to discuss this later.

To return to the theme from which I have digressed somewhat, the author, adhering to his principles of the fatalistic necessity of all things, denies that any miracles occur contrary to the laws of Nature.[150] For, as I have already remarked above, he asserts that the natures of things and their order are something no less necessary than the nature of God and the eternal truths. So he teaches that for something to depart from the laws of Nature is just as impossible as that the three angles of a triangle should not be equal to two right angles, that God cannot bring it about that a lighter weight should raise a heavier weight, or that a body moving with two degrees of motion can overtake a body moving with four degrees of motion. Therefore he asserts that miracles are subject to the universal laws of Nature, which he says are just as immutable as the very natures of things, these natures being contained within the laws of Nature. He does not admit any other power of God than the regular one which is displayed in accordance with Nature's laws, and he thinks that no other can be imagined, because it would destroy the natures of things and would be self-contradictory.

In the author's view, then, 'a miracle is an unexpected occurrence whose cause is unknown to the common people'.[151] Thus, when it appears that after prayers have been offered in due form an imminent disaster has been averted or a much desired good has been obtained, this same common people attributes it to the power of prayer and God's special dispensation, whereas, according to the author, God has already decreed absolutely from eternity that those things should come to pass which the common people attribute to his special intervention and display of power. For the prayers are not the cause of the decree: the decree is the cause of the prayers.

All this doctrine of fate and the invincible necessity of things, both in respect to the natures of things and also their occurrence in our daily lives, he bases on the nature of God, or to speak more clearly, on the nature of God's will and intellect which, while nominally different, are in reality identical in God. So he asserts that God has willed this universe and all that successively happens in it with the same necessity as that by which he knows this same universe. Now if God necessarily knows this universe and its laws, as also the eternal truths contained in those laws, he concludes that God could no more have created a different universe than he could overturn the natures of things and make twice three equal to seven. And therefore, just as we could not conceive anything different from this universe and the laws that govern the coming into being and the perishing of things, and anything of this kind imaginable by us would be self-defeating, so he tells us that the nature of the divine intellect, of the entire uni-

---

[150] [Spinoza's note at this point: "He is unjust in so saying, for I have expressly proved that miracles afford no knowledge of God. God is far better comprehended from the constant order of Nature."]

[151] [The references in this and the discussion following are to TTP6, which is devoted to miracles. The author misinterprets Spinoza at many points, but Spinoza himself (see Ep43) corrects the majority of these misunderstandings.]

verse, and of those laws which Nature obeys is so constituted that God could no more have understood by his intellect any things different from those that now exist than it is possible for things now to be different from themselves. He therefore concludes that, just as God cannot now bring about things that are self-destructive, so God can neither invent nor know natures different from those that now exist. For the comprehension and understanding of such natures is just as impossible (since in the author's view it posits a contradiction) as the production of things different from those which now exist is impossible now. For all such natures, if conceived as different from those which now exist, would necessarily be opposed to those which now exist, because the natures of things contained in this universe being in the author's view necessary, they cannot possess that necessity from themselves but only from God's nature, from which they necessarily emanate. For he does not follow the line of Descartes—whose doctrine he nevertheless wants to appear to have accepted—that just as the natures of all things are different from the nature and essence of God, so their ideas are freely in the divine mind.

By these arguments, which I have now recounted, the author has paved the way to what he has to tell us in the final section of the book, towards which all the teachings of the preceding chapters are directed. There it is his aim to convince the magistrate and all mankind of this axiom, that to the magistrate belongs the right of establishing the divine worship which must be publicly observed in the state. Further, it is right for the magistrate to permit citizens to think and to speak of religion as their mind and feelings bid them, and this freedom should also be granted to subjects in the matter of external acts of worship, to the extent that this does not detract from their devotion to moral virtue or piety. For since there can be no controversy about these virtues, and the knowledge and practise of other things do not hold any moral virtue, he concludes that God cannot be displeased at whatever religious rites men additionally adopt. Here the author is speaking of those religious rites that do not constitute moral virtue and are not relevant to it, and which are not opposed to virtue or alien to it, but which men adopt and profess as aids to true virtue so that they may thus become acceptable and pleasing to God through their devotion to these virtues. For God is not offended by devotion to and practise of rites which, while they are indifferent and have no bearing on virtue or vice, men nevertheless associate with the practise of piety, and employ as a help towards the cultivation of virtue.

To prepare men's minds for the acceptance of these paradoxical views, the author first asserts that the entire form of worship established by God and delivered to the Jews—that is, to the citizens of the Israelite commonwealth—was designed only that they might live happily in their commonwealth, but that for the rest the Jews were not dear and pleasing to God above other nations. God, he says, has frequently made this known to the Jews through the prophets, rebuking them for their ignorance and error in identifying holiness and piety with the form of worship established and prescribed for them by God, whereas the former should have been located only in devotion to the moral virtues, that is, in the love of God and regard for one's neighbour.

And since God has instilled into the minds of all nations the principles and, as it were, the seeds of virtue so that, of their own accord and almost without any instruction, they may judge of the difference between good and evil, from this he concludes that God has not left other nations destitute of the means of gaining true blessedness, but has shown himself equally beneficent to all men.

Indeed, to affirm the equality of Gentiles with Jews in all matters which can in any way be of assistance and use in the pursuit of true happiness, he declares that the Gentiles have not been without prophets, and this he proceeds to prove by examples. He goes so far as to intimate that God exercised his sovereignty over other nations through the medium of good angels whom, following the usage of the Old Testament, he calls Gods. So the religious rites of other nations, he says, were not displeasing to God as long as they were not so corrupted by human superstition as to estrange men from true holiness, and did not incite men to engage in such acts in their worship as were inconsistent with virtue. But for special reasons peculiar to that people, God forbade the Jews to worship the Gods of the Gentiles who, under God's ordinance and superintendence, were worshipped by the Gentiles with the same right as those angels, appointed as guardians of the Jewish commonwealth, were accounted as Gods by the Jews in their own way, and were afforded divine honours.

And since the author thinks it commonly accepted that external forms of worship are not in themselves pleasing to God, he dismisses as unimportant what rites are involved in this external form of worship, provided that it is of a kind so conformable with God as to arouse reverence for God in men's minds and to incite them to the love of virtue.

Again, since he thinks that the whole substance of religion is contained in the cultivation of virtue, and regards as pointless all knowledge of mysteries that is not inherently adapted to promote virtue, and holds as more important and essential the sort of knowledge that is more effective in teaching men virtue and inspiring them thereto, he concludes that we should approve, or at least not reject, all those opinions touching God, his worship, and all matters concerning religion which are held to be true by those who cherish them, and whose purpose is that uprightness may thrive and flourish. In support of this doctrine he cites the prophets themselves as authors and supporters of his view. Being instructed that God does not regard as important what kind of thoughts men entertain about religion, but that he finds acceptable that form of worship and all these opinions which proceed from love of virtue and reverence for the divine, the prophets have even gone so far as to advance arguments for promoting virtue which are not in themselves true, but were considered to be so by those they were addressing, and which were intrinsically of a kind to spur men on to a more eager devotion to virtue. He therefore assumes that God left the choice of arguments to the prophets, who would employ those suited to the times and to the modes of thought of their particular audiences who, in accordance with their understanding, would regard such arguments as good and effective.

This he thinks to be the reason why different divine teachers employed different and often mutually conflicting arguments, why Paul taught that man was not justified by works whereas James urged the opposite. For James, so the author thinks, saw that Christians were distorting the doctrine of justification by faith, and he therefore insisted that man is justified by faith and by works. For he realised that it was not in the interests of Christians of his time to stress and to expound, as Paul had done, the doctrine of faith whereby men calmly rested on God's mercy and paid little attention to good works. Paul had to deal with the Jews, who erroneously placed their justification in the works of the Law especially delivered to them by Moses. Thinking that they were thus raised above the Gentiles and that they had a way of blessedness prepared for them alone, they rejected the method of salvation by faith whereby they were put on a level with the Gentiles and stripped bare of all special status. Since therefore, taking into account the difference of the times and audiences and other factors, both these teachings, that of Paul and James, met with great success in turning men to piety, the author thinks that it was part of apostolic wisdom to employ now the one, now the other.

And this is one of the reasons why the author thinks it quite inconsistent with truth to try to explain the sacred text by means of reason and to make reason the interpreter of Scripture, or to interpret one holy teacher with the aid of another; for they are of equal authority, and the words they employed are to be explained by the mode of speech and peculiarity of expression which came naturally to those teachers. In investigating the true meaning of Scripture we must pay heed not to the nature of the case, but only to the literal meaning.

Therefore, since Christ himself and the other divinely sent teachers[152] instructed us and showed by their own example and way of life that only by love of virtue do men attain happiness, and that other things should be regarded as of little account, the author proposes that the sole concern of the magistrate should be that justice and uprightness should flourish in the commonwealth. The magistrate should not regard it as any part of his duty to deliberate as to what form of worship and what doctrines are most in accord with truth, but should ensure that such are not adopted as place an obstacle in the way of virtue, even though they are favoured by those who profess them. Thus, without any offence to the Deity, the magistrate has no difficulty in allowing different religious rites in his commonwealth. In order to make his point, the author takes the following line. He holds that the character of those moral virtues whose practise has social implications and which are concerned with external actions is such that their exercise should not fall within the scope of anyone's private judgment and decision; the cultivation, exercise and practical application of these virtues should depend on the sovereign power of the magistrate. For this there are two reasons: externally directed acts of virtue derive their nature from the circumstances of their performance, and secondly, a man's duty to perform such external actions is measured by

---

[152] [The suggestion here that Christ's role for Spinoza is little more than that of teacher is also not a correct reading of Spinoza, for whom Christ occupies a unique position not equivalent to that of prophet or apostle. See TTP4. This is not to suggest, however, that Spinoza countenances the inconsistent notion of a 'god-man': see Ep73 to Oldenburg. Deciphering Spinoza's precise position on Christ's nature is problematic partly due to the absence of a prolonged discussion on his part.]

the good or harm arising therefrom, with the result that those externally directed actions, if not performed at the appropriate time, lose the character of virtuous action and their opposites must be reckoned as virtues. The author thinks that there are other kinds of virtue whose existence is confined to the mind; these always preserve their character, and do not depend on the changing state of external circumstance.

A disposition to cruelty and harshness, a failure in love of one's neighbour and of truth, is never to be countenanced. But occasions may arise when it is permissible, not indeed to abandon this attitude of mind and love of the said virtues, but either to restrict their application in regard to external actions or even to engage in actions which, to outward appearance, are thought to be inconsistent with these virtues. And so it may come about that it is not then the duty of an upright man to set truth in the public domain, and in speech or writing to let citizens share in that truth and to communicate it to them, if we think that more harm than good will ensue for the citizens from that promulgation. And although individuals have the duty to embrace all men in love and never to be divorced from that sentiment, it frequently happens that we may be justified in dealing severely with some men when it is established that we would suffer great harm from a display of clemency. In the same way it is universally agreed that it is not at all times opportune to proclaim all truths, whether they pertain to religion or to civil life. And he who teaches that roses should not be cast before swine if there is any danger that the swine will savage those offering the roses, likewise considers that it is not the duty of a good man to instruct the common people on certain religious questions which, published and spread abroad among the populace, could well cause such disturbance in the commonwealth or Church as to bring more injury than benefit on the citizens and the godly.

Now civil societies, from whom sovereign power and authority to pass laws cannot be disjoined, among other things have established that it must not be left to individuals to decide what is for the good of men who are united in a civic body, but that this must be entrusted to the rulers. The author therefore argues that it is the right of the magistrate to decide which and what kind of doctrines should be publicly taught in the commonwealth, and that it is the duty of subjects, so far as concerns public pronouncement, to refrain from teaching and professing doctrines which the magistrate has by law forbidden to be publicly professed. For God has no more entrusted this to the judgment of private individuals than he has allowed them, contrary to the views and decrees of the magistrate or the opinion of judges, to engage in actions which render ineffective the force of law, and frustrate the intention of magistrates. For the author considers that, in such matters as concern external forms of worship and public pronouncements thereon, there can be general agreement, and that the question of external forms of divine worship is entrusted to the magistrate's judgment with as much confidence as there is granted him the right and power to evaluate injury done to the state and to punish it by force. For just as a person of private station is not bound to adjust to the magistrate's judgment his own judgment as to injury done to the state, but can entertain his own opinion, while yet being bound in some circumstances to lend assistance in carrying out the magistrate's sentence, in the same way, so the author thinks, it is the prerogative of those of private station in the commonwealth to judge as to the truth and falsity, as also of the necessity, of any doctrine. And a private person cannot be bound by the laws of the state to hold the same views on religion, although the magistrate must judge what doctrines are to be publicly proclaimed, and it is the duty of private persons not to voice their own views on religion when these differ from those of the magistrate, and to do nothing whereby the laws concerning worship enacted by the magistrate may lose their effectiveness.

But since it may happen that the magistrate, differing from many of the populace on points of religion, decides that certain doctrines should be publicly taught which are not favoured by the populace, and the magistrate nevertheless believes that respect for the Deity demands the public profession of those doctrines in his commonwealth, the author has seen that there remains the problem that citizens may suffer considerable harm because of the differing judgments of magistrate and populace. Therefore to the preceding proposals the author adds another which may satisfy magistrate and subjects and also preserve religious freedom intact, namely, that the magistrate need not fear God's wrath even if he allows in his commonwealth the practise of sacred rites which in his judgment are wrong— provided that they are not opposed to the moral virtues and do not subvert them. The grounds for this view cannot escape you, since I have already recounted them at some length. For the author asserts that God is indifferent and unconcerned as to what religious beliefs men cherish, favour and defend, or what religious rites they publicly practise. All such things are to be accounted as having no affinity with virtue and vice, although it is everyone's duty to make his own dispositions with view to choosing those doctrines and that form of worship which will enable him to make the greatest progress in the love of virtue.

Here, most accomplished Sir, you have in brief space a summary of the doctrine of the political-theologian, which in my judgment banishes and thoroughly subverts all worship and religion, prompts atheism by stealth, or envisages such a God as can not move men to reverence for his divinity, since he himself is subject to fate; no room is left for divine governance and providence, and the assignment of punishment and reward is entirely abolished. This, at the very least, is evident from the author's writing, that by his reasoning and arguments the authority of all Holy Scripture is impaired, and is mentioned by the author only for form's sake; and it similarly follows from the position he adopts that the Koran, too, is to be put on a level with the Word of God. And the author has not left himself a single argument to prove that Mahomet was not a true prophet. For the Turks, too, in obedience to the command of their prophet, cultivate those moral virtues about which there is no disagreement among nations, and, according to the author's teaching, it is not uncommon for God, in the case of other nations to whom he has not imparted the oracles given to the Jews and Christians, to lead them by other revelations to the path of reason and obedience.

So I think I have not strayed far from the truth, nor am I unfair to the author, if I denounce him as teaching sheer atheism with furtive and disguised arguments.

L.v.V.
Utrecht, 24 January 1671 (Old Style)

LETTER 43
To the learned and accomplished Jacob Ostens, from B.d.S.

[The original is extant, and differs in unimportant details from the Latin text of the O.P. The date is uncertain, but is probably 1671.][153]

Most learned Sir,

You are doubtless surprised that I have kept you waiting so long, but I can hardly bring myself to answer that man's letter, which you kindly sent me. Nor do I do so now for any other reason than to keep my promise. But to satisfy myself, too, as far as that can be, I shall discharge my debt in as few words as possible, and briefly show how perversely he has misinterpreted my meaning—whether from malice or ignorance, I cannot say. But to the matter in hand.

First, he says 'it is of no importance to know of what nationality I am, or what manner of life I pursue'. But surely if he had known this, he would not have been so readily convinced that I teach atheism. For atheists are usually inordinately fond of honours and riches, which I have always despised, as is known to all who are acquainted with me. Then, to pave the way to the end he has in view, he says that I am not unintelligent, doubtless so that he may more easily establish that I have argued cleverly, cunningly, and with evil intent on behalf of the evil cause of the Deists. This is a clear indication that he has not understood my line of reasoning. For who can be so clever and so astute as to pretend to present so many powerful arguments in support of something he deems false? Whom, I say, will he hereafter believe to have written in all sincerity, if he thinks that the fictitious can be proved as soundly as the true? But this does not now surprise me, for thus was Descartes once maligned by Voetius,[154] and this is what often happens to all good men.

---

[153] [The original draft of the letter is in the Orphanage of the Baptist Collegiants in Amsterdam. A facsimile was printed in W. Meyer's edition of 1903, and also in Van Vloten's *Ad Benedicti de Spinoza Opera Supplementum* (1860).]

[154] [Gysbertus Voetius (1588–1676), a Dutch theologian who studied in Leiden. In 1634 he became Professor of Theology and Oriental Studies at the University of Utrecht and three years later became Vicar of Utrecht. An extreme Calvinist, he succeeded in persuading the University of Utrecht to condemn the philosophy of Descartes in 1642. The following year there appeared a

He then continues, 'to avoid the accusation of superstition, I think he has renounced all religion'. What he understands by religion and what by superstition, I do not know. Does that man, pray, renounce all religion, who declares that God must be acknowledged as the highest good, and that he must be loved as such in a free spirit? And that in this alone does our supreme happiness and our highest freedom consist? And further, that the reward of virtue is virtue itself,[155] while the punishment of folly and weakness is folly itself? And lastly, that everyone is in duty bound to love his neighbour and obey the commands of the sovereign power? I not only said this explicitly, but also proved it with the strongest arguments. But I think I see in what mire this man is stuck. He finds nothing to please him in virtue itself and in intellect, and would choose to live under the impulsion of his passions but for one obstacle, his fear of punishment. So he abstains from evil deeds and obeys the divine commandments like a slave, reluctantly and waveringly, and in return for this servitude he expects to reap rewards from God far sweeter to him than the divine love itself, and the more so as he dislikes the good that he does, and does it unwillingly.[156] Consequently, he believes that all who are not restrained by this fear lead unbridled lives and renounce all religion. But I let this pass, and turn to his conclusion, where he seeks to prove that I teach atheism by clandestine and disguised arguments.

The basis of his reasoning is this, that he thinks that I do away with God's freedom and subject him to fate. This is completely false. For I have asserted that everything follows by an inevitable necessity from God's nature in just the same way that all assert that it follows from God's nature that he understands himself. Surely no one denies that this necessarily follows from the divine nature, and yet no one conceives that God, in understanding himself, is under the compulsion of some fate; it is conceived that he does so altogether freely, although necessarily. Here I find nothing that is beyond anyone's perception. And if he still believes that these assertions are made with evil intent, what does he think of his own Descartes,[157] who declared that nothing is done by us that is not pre-ordained by God; nay, that we are at every single moment created by God anew, as it were, and that nevertheless we act from freedom of our own will.[158] This is surely something, as Descartes himself admits, that no one can understand.

Furthermore, this inevitable necessity of things does not do away with either divine or human laws. For moral precepts, whether or not they receive the form of law from God himself, are still divine and salutary. And whether the good that

---

pamphlet, of his authorship or inspiration, attacking the Cartesian philosophy as the root of atheism. Descartes replied to the pamphlet in his *Epistola ad celeberrimum virum D. Gisbertim Voetium.*]

[155] [See E5P41–P42.]

[156] [This theme, the attitude of the *vulgus* to the practice of religion based on fear and expectancy of reward, is developed in E5P41Schol.]

[157] [See Descartes' *Principia* I, 39.]

[158] [Divine conservation in Descartes is further discussed by Spinoza in PPC1P12, and pre-ordination in PPC1P19.]

follows from virtue and love of God is bestowed on us by God as judge, or whether it emanates from the necessity of the divine nature, it will not on that account be more or less desirable, just as on the other hand the evils that follow from evil deeds are not less to be feared because they necessarily follow from them. And finally, whether we do what we do necessarily or freely, we are still led by hope or by fear. Therefore he is wrong in saying that 'I assert that no room is left for precepts and commandments', or, as he goes on to say, 'there is no expectation of reward or punishment when all is attributed to fate, or when it is asserted that all things emanate from God by an inevitable necessity'.

I do not here inquire why it is the same, or not very different, to assert that all things emanate necessarily from God's nature and that the universe is God, but I should like you to note that which he adds in no less malignant vein, 'that I hold that a man ought to devote himself to virtue not because of God's commandment and law, nor through hope of reward or fear of punishment, but . . . etc.' This you will certainly find nowhere in my Treatise; on the contrary, in Chapter 4 I expressly said that the substance of the divine law (which is divinely inscribed in our minds, as I said in Chapter 12) and its supreme commandment is to love God as the highest good; that is, not from fear of some punishment (for love cannot spring from fear) nor from love of something else from which we hope to derive pleasure—for then we should be loving the object of our desire rather than God himself. And in the same chapter I showed that God has revealed this very law to his prophets, and whether I maintain that this law of God received its authoritative form from God himself or whether I conceive it to be like the rest of God's decrees which involve eternal necessity and truth, it will nevertheless remain God's decree and a teaching for salvation. And whether I love God freely or through the necessity of God's decree, I shall still love God, and I shall be saved. Therefore I can now say that this man is to be classed with those of whom I said at the end of my Preface[159] that I would prefer them to leave my book entirely alone rather than make themselves a nuisance by misinterpreting it, as is their wont in all cases, and hinder others without any benefit to themselves. Although I think that this suffices to show what I intended, I consider it worthwhile to add some brief observations. He is wrong in thinking that I am referring to that axiom of the theologians who make a distinction between the words of a prophet when he is proclaiming dogma and his words when he is merely narrating something. If by this axiom he means the one which I attributed in Chapter 15 to a certain Rabbi Judah Alpakhar,[160] how could I have thought that my view agrees with this when in the same chapter[161] I rejected it as false? But if he is thinking of some other ax-

---

[159] [In the penultimate paragraph of the Preface to the TTP, Spinoza admonishes the reader that the work is not intended for the common public or for the superstitious.]

[160] [Alpakhar (sometimes also found in its Arabic form, 'Alfakhar') was a distinguished rabbi of Toledo, and physician to King Ferdinand III. An opponent of Maimonides' Aristotelianism, he died in 1235. The opening pages of TTP15 offer a summary of his position as Spinoza understood it.]

[161] [Maimonides is also criticized in TTP15. The general claim that philosophy is the proper inter-

iom, I confess that I still do not know of it, and so I could hardly have been referring to it.

Furthermore, I do not see why he says that I think that all those will agree with me who deny that reason and philosophy are the interpreters of Scripture. For I have refuted the views both of these and of Maimonides.

It would take too long to review all his remarks which indicate that it is in no equable spirit that he has passed judgment on me. So I move on to his conclusion where he says that 'I have left myself with no argument to prove that Mahomet was not a true prophet', which he tries to prove from the views I have expressed. Yet from these it clearly follows that Mahomet was an impostor, since he completely abolishes the freedom which is granted by that universal religion revealed by the natural and prophetic light, and which I have shown ought to be fully granted. And even if this were not so, am I bound, pray, to show that some prophet is false? On the contrary, the prophets were bound to show that they were true prophets. And if he replies that Mahomet, too, taught the divine law and gave sure signs of his mission as did the other prophets, there is certainly no reason for him to deny that Mahomet was a true prophet.

As for the Turks and the other Gentiles, if they worship God by the exercise of justice and by love of their neighbour, I believe that they possess the spirit of Christ and are saved, whatever convictions they may hold in their ignorance regarding Mahomet and the oracles.

So you see, my friend, that this man has strayed far from the truth. Yet I grant that he does me no injury, but much to himself, when he is not ashamed to proclaim that I teach atheism with clandestine and disguised arguments.

In general, I do not think that you will here find any expression which you might consider over-harsh against this man. However, if you come across anything of that sort, please either delete it or amend it as you think fit. It is not my intention to provoke him, whoever he may be, and to get for myself enemies of my own making. It is because this is often the result of disputes of this kind that I could scarcely prevail on myself to reply, and I would not have done so had I not promised.

Farewell. To your prudence I entrust this letter, and myself, who am . . . etc.

---

preter of Scripture was defended by Lodewijk Meyer in his *Philosophia Sanctae Scripturae Interpres* (Amsterdam, 1666).]

Letter 44

To the most worthy and judicious Jarig Jelles, from B.d.S.

[The original, written in Dutch, is lost. The Dutch edition of the O.P. probably reproduces the original text, and the Latin version is a translation from this.]

Worthy friend,

When Professor N.N.[162] recently paid me a visit, he told me, among other things, that he had heard that my *Tractatus Theologico-Politicus* had been translated into Dutch, and that somebody, he did not know who, proposed to get it printed. I therefore beg you most earnestly please to look into this, and, if possible, to stop the printing. This is not only my request but that of many of my good friends who would not wish to see the book banned, as will undoubtedly happen if it is published in Dutch. I have every confidence that you will do me and our cause this service.

Some time ago one of my friends sent me a little book entitled *Homo Politicus*, or *Political Man*,[163] of which I had already heard a great deal. I have read it through, and found it the most pernicious book that can be devised by man. The highest good of the man who wrote it is wealth and honours. To this he shapes his doctrine, and shows the way to attain them, and that is, by inwardly rejecting all religion and outwardly assuming such as will best serve his advancement, and furthermore by keeping faith with no one except insofar as it conduces to his advantage. For the rest, his highest praise is reserved for dissembling, breaking promises he has made, lying, perjuring, and many other such things. When I read this, I had some thought of writing a short book indirectly criticising it, in which I would treat of the highest good, and then indicate the restless and pitiable condition of those who are greedy for money and covet honours, and finally, prove by clear reasoning and abundant examples that through insatiable desire for honours and greed for riches commonwealths must necessarily perish, and have perished.

How far superior, indeed, and excellent were the reflections of Thales of Miletus[164] compared with this writer is shown by the following account. All things, he

---

[162] [A. Wolf (1928, 438–439) conjectures that this may have been Professor Theodorus Kraanen (also spelled 'Craanen'), a Cartesian at the University of Leiden.]

[163] [Believed to have been written by Christophorus Rapp, this book appeared in 1644 and was published anonymously.]

[164] [Thales of Miletus (circa 600 B.C.) was as much an astronomer as he was a philosopher, and he is given credit for writing an almanac and for introducing the Phoenician practice of navigation using the Little Dipper. The story repeated here by Spinoza is found in Diogenes Laertius' *Lives of the Philosophers*, I, 26.]

said, are in common among friends. The wise are the friends of the Gods, and all things belong to the Gods; therefore all things belong to the wise. In this way this wise man makes himself the richest, by nobly despising riches instead of greedily pursuing them. But on another occasion he proved that it is not out of necessity but by choice that the wise possess no riches. When his friends reproached him for his poverty, he answered them, "Do you want me to show you that I can acquire that which I consider unworthy of my effort, and which you so eagerly seek?" And when they assented to this, he hired all the presses throughout Greece; for being well versed in the courses of the stars, he had seen that in the current year there would be a great abundance of olives, which had been very scarce in the preceding years. Then he let out at a high price the presses which he had hired cheaply, for people needed them to press the oil out of the olives. In this way in one year he acquired great wealth, which he then distributed with a liberality equal to the shrewdness by which he had acquired it.

I conclude by assuring you that I am, etc.

The Hague
17 February 1671

LETTER 45
To the illustrious and esteemed B.d.S., from Gottfried Leibniz

[The original is extant. The Latin text of the O.P. differs from it only slightly, omitting Hudde's name and the postscript.]

Illustrious and most honoured Sir,

Among your other achievements which fame has spread abroad I understand is your remarkable skill in optics. For this reason I venture to send this essay, such as it is, to you, than whom I am not likely to find a better critic in this field of study. This paper which I send you, and which I have entitled *A Note on Advanced Optics*,[165] I have published in order to communicate more conveniently with friends or interested parties. I hear that the highly accomplished Hudde, too, is eminent in this field, and he is doubtless well known to you. So if you can also obtain for me his judgment and approval, you will add immensely to your kindness.

The paper itself explains very well what it is about, ...

I believe you have received the *Prodromus* of Francis Lana, S.J.,[166] written in

---

[165] [Leibniz's *Notitia opticae promotae* was published in 1671.]

[166] [Franciscus Lana (1631–1687) was Professor of Philosophy and of Mathematics in Rome. The *Prodromo, overo Saggio di alcune inventioni nuove premesse all'Arte maestra* was published in Brescia in 1677.]

Italian, which also contains some notable suggestions on Dioptrics. But John Oltius,[167] too, a young Swiss, who is very learned in these matters, has published his *Physical-Mechanical Reflections on Vision,* in which he promises a certain machine for polishing all kinds of glasses, which is very simple and of general application. He also says that he has discovered a method for gathering *all* the rays coming from all the points of an object into as many other corresponding points. But this applies only to an object at a certain distance and of a certain shape.

However, the point of my proposal is this, not that all the rays from *all* the points should be gathered again—for this is impossible, as far as our present knowledge goes, in the case of objects at every distance and of every shape—but that the rays should be gathered equally from points outside the optic axis as from on the optic axis, and therefore the apertures of the glasses can be of any size without impairing distinctness of vision. But this will await your expert judgment.

Farewell, honoured Sir, and favour

Your faithful admirer,
Gottfried William Leibniz,
Doctor of Laws and Councillor of Mainz
Frankfurt, 5 October 1671 (New Style)

P.S. If you will favour me with an answer, the most noble Diemerbroek,[168] Lawyer, will, I hope, be willing to take charge of it. I think you have seen my new *Physical Hypothesis*; if not, I will send it.

To Mr. Spinosa, celebrated doctor and profound philosopher
At Amsterdam
Per couverto

Letter 46

To the most learned and noble Gottfried Leibniz, Doctor of Laws and Councillor of Mainz, from B.d.S.

[The original is extant. The O.P. Latin text seems to have been composed from Spinoza's own copy. There are some slight differences.]

Most learned and noble Sir,

I have read the paper which you kindly sent me, and I am very grateful to you for letting me have it. I regret that I have not been able fully to grasp your meaning, though I believe you have explained it clearly enough. I therefore beg you to answer these few queries. Do you believe that there is a reason for restricting the size of the

---

[167] [This person is unknown.]
[168] [J. de Diemerbroek was a lawyer in Utrecht.]

aperture of the glasses other than that the rays coming from a single point are not collected precisely at another point but over a small space (which we usually call a mechanical point), whose size varies with that of the aperture? Secondly, do those lenses which you call 'pandochal'[169] correct this fault? That is, does the mechanical point, or the small space at which the rays coming from the same point are gathered after refraction, remain the same size whether the aperture is great or small? For if the lenses achieve this, one may enlarge their aperture as much as one likes, and they will therefore be far superior to lenses of any other shape known to me; otherwise I do not know why you so warmly commend them above ordinary lenses. For circular lenses have everywhere the same axis, and so when we employ them, all the points of an object must be considered as if placed in the optic axis. And although all the points of an object are not equidistant, the resulting difference cannot be perceptible in the case of far distant objects, because then the rays coming from a single point would be regarded as entering the glass in parallel. However, in cases where we wish to apprehend several objects at one glance (as happens when we employ very large circular convex lenses), I believe your lenses can be effective in representing the entire field more distinctly. But I shall suspend judgment on all these points until you explain your meaning more clearly, as I earnestly beg you to do.

I sent the other copy to Mr. Hudde, as you requested. He has replied that he does not have time at present to examine it, but hopes to be free to do so in a week or two.

The *Prodromus* of Francis Lana has not yet come into my hands, nor the *Physico-Mechanical Reflections* of John Oltius; and, which is more to be regretted, neither have I been able to see your *Physical Hypothesis*. At any rate, it is not on sale here at the Hague. I shall be most grateful if you send it to me, and if I can be of service to you in any other way, you will always find that I am,

Most honourable Sir,
Yours entirely,
B. de Spinoza

The Hague, 9 November 1671

Mr. Dimerbruck[170] does not live here, so I am forced to give this to the ordinary letter-carrier. I have no doubt that you know somebody here at the Hague who would be willing to take charge of our correspondence. I should like to know who it is, so that our letters can be dispatched more conveniently and safely. If the *Tractatus Theologico-Politicus* has not yet reached you, I shall send you a copy if you care to have it. Farewell.

To the most noble and eminent Mr. Gottfried William Leibniz
Doctor of Laws and Councillor of Mainz

Dispatched on 8 December 1671

---

[169] [The term 'pandochal' means 'all-receptive' (for rays of light).]

[170] [This is the same 'Diemerbroek' of the previous letter, but Spinoza has altered the spelling.]

Letter 47
To the acute and renowned philosopher, B.d.S. from J. Louis Fabritius

[Known only from the O.P. The original is lost.]

Renowned Sir,

His Serene Highness the Elector Palatine,[171] my most gracious lord, has commanded me to write to you who, while as yet unknown to me, are strongly recommended to his Serene Highness, and to ask you whether you would be willing to accept a regular Professorship of Philosophy in his illustrious University. The annual salary will be that currently paid to regular Professors. You will not find elsewhere a Prince more favourably disposed to men of exceptional genius, among whom he ranks you. You will have the most extensive freedom in philosophising, which he believes you will not misuse to disturb the publicly established religion. I have pleasure in complying with the request of the most wise Prince. Therefore I do most earnestly beg you to let me have your answer as soon as possible, and to entrust your answer to the care of Mr. Grotius, His Serene Highness the Elector's resident at the Hague, or to Mr. Gilles Van der Mek, to be forwarded to me in the packet of letters regularly sent to the Court, or else to avail yourself of any other convenient means you deem most suitable. I will add only this, that if you come here, you will have the pleasure of living a life worthy of a philosopher, unless everything turns out contrary to our hope and expectation.

And so farewell, with my greetings, most honoured Sir,

From your most devoted,
J. Louis Fabritius
Professor at the University of Heidelberg
and Councillor to the Elector Palatine

Heidelberg, 16 February 1673

---

[171] [This was Karl Ludwig, the brother of Queen Christina of Sweden, who was Descartes' patroness.]

LETTER 48

To the most honourable and noble Mr. J. Louis Fabritius, Professor in the University of Heidelberg and Councillor to the Elector Palatine, from B.d.S.

[Known only from the O.P. The original is lost.]

Most honourable Sir,

If I had ever had any desire to undertake a professorship in any faculty, I could have wished for none other than that which is offered me through you by His Serene Highness the Elector Palatine, especially on account of the freedom to philosophise which this most gracious Prince is pleased to grant, not to mention my long-felt wish to live under the rule of a Prince whose wisdom is universally admired. But since I have never intended to engage in public teaching, I cannot induce myself to embrace this excellent opportunity, although I have given long consideration to the matter.[172] For, first, I reflect that if I am to find time to instruct young students, I must give up my further progress in philosophy. Secondly, I do not know within what limits the freedom to philosophise must be confined if I am to avoid appearing to disturb the publicly established religion. For divisions arise not so much from an ardent devotion to religion as from the different dispositions of men, or through their love of contradiction which leads them to distort or to condemn all things, even those that are stated aright. Now since I have already experienced this while leading a private and solitary life, it would be much more to be feared after I have risen to this position of eminence. So you see, most Honourable Sir, that my reluctance is not due to the hope of some better fortune, but to my love of peace, which I believe I can enjoy in some measure if I refrain from lecturing in public. Therefore I most earnestly beg you to pray His Serene Highness the Elector to grant me more time to deliberate on this matter. And please continue to commend to the favour of the most gracious Prince his most devoted admirer, whereby you will oblige even more,

Most honourable and noble Sir,

Yours entirely,
B.d.S.

The Hague, 30 March 1673

---

[172] [Spinoza's caution was in fact validated by subsequent events. The year after this letter was written the French seized Heidelberg and closed the university there.]

Letter 48A
Confession of the Universal and Christian Faith, contained in a letter to N.N. from Jarig Jelles

[Not in the O.P. Published by Jan Rieuwertsz.][173]

Worthy friend,

(1) I have complied with your earnest request desiring me to let you know by letter[174] my sentiments regarding my faith or religion, and all the more readily since you declare that your motive for so asking is that some persons are trying to persuade you that the Cartesian philosophers (among whom you are pleased to number me) entertain a strange opinion, lapsing into the ancient heathendom, and that their propositions and basic principles are opposed to the basic principles of the Christian Religion and of Piety, etc. In my own defence, then, I shall first of all say that the Cartesian philosophy touches religion so little that Descartes' propositions find followers not only among various religious persuasions but also among Roman Catholics, so that what I shall say about religion should be taken as my own particular view, not that of the Cartesians. And although I do not seek to engage in controversy with others and to stop the mouths of calumniators, I shall however be pleased to satisfy you and others like you. And while it is not my intention to prescribe a universal creed, or again to determine the essential, fundamental and necessary doctrinal tenets, but only to acquaint you with my views, I shall still endeavour, as well as I can, to comply with the terms which, according to Jacobus Acontius, are required for a universal Confession acceptable to all Christians, namely, that it should contain only that which must necessarily be known, that which is quite true and certain, that which is attested and confirmed by testimonies, and, finally, that which is expressed as far as possible in the same words and phrases as were used by the Holy Spirit. Here, then, is a Confession which I think to be of this kind. Read it attentively, judge it not lightly, and be as-

---

[173] [Ep48a and the first fragment of Ep48b were published by Rieuwertsz, a significant fact inasmuch as he had physical possession of the Spinoza correspondence. The reliability of these passages is thus as high as those published in the O.P. Things stand differently with respect to the second fragment of Ep48b, since our text is based on Hallmann's notes and partial transcription. The two fragments of Ep48b differ so remarkably in content that we suspect that they may actually be drawn from two different letters, one referring to an early version of Jelles' *Confession*, and the other to a later and revised text.]

[174] [The letter is mentioned in Bayle's Dictionary (see Wolf 1928, 442–443), from which Wolf drew a summary of it.]

sured that, just as I have taken my stand on truth, so shall I seek to impart it to you in this letter.

[The body of the *Confession* follows here, concluding with these words:]

(2) I trust that herewith I shall have accomplished even more than you yourself had expected, and that you will therefore deem that I have fulfilled that which you asked of me.

(3) In return I ask of you only that you will please consider carefully and prudently what I have said, and then judge of the reports you have received concerning my religious opinion.

(4) If you find anything here that may seem to you false or in opposition to Holy Scripture, I beg you to let me know this, and also the reason why it seems so to you, so that I can look into it. Those who hold as opposed to Holy Scripture and false whatever does not accord with their Formulations[175] or Confessions of faith will doubtless judge that much contained in my letter is of this kind. But I am confident that those who test it against truth (which I have shown above to be the only unerring measure and touchstone for truth and falsity, for honesty and dishonesty, etc.) will judge differently, which I also expect of you.

(5) Here you have my view as far as concerns the Christian religion, and also the proofs and reasoning on which it rests. It is now for you to judge whether those who build on such a groundwork and try to live in accordance with such understanding are Christians or not, and whether there is any truth in the reports which some people have made to you regarding my opinions.

(6) Finally, for my part I ask you to examine all this carefully and dispassionately. I wish you enlightenment of understanding, and conclude by testifying that I am, etc.,

Your devoted friend,
Jarig Jelles

[Amsterdam 1673]

---

[175] [The *Formulieren* was often a formal summary of beliefs published as a pamphlet. (The information in this note was provided by Francis Pastijn, Milwaukee.)]

Letter 48B

To the most courteous and learned Jarig Jelles, from B.d.S.

[Not in the O.P. These are fragments of a letter written in Dutch by Spinoza to Jarig Jelles, in response to Jelles' request for his opinion of Jelles' book Confession of Faith.*]*[176]

(1) Sir and most illustrious friend,

It is with pleasure that I have read through the writings that you sent me, and found them such that I can suggest no alterations in them.[177]

(2) The date of the letter was 19 April 1673, dispatched from the Hague and addressed to Jarig Jelles, who had sent him his *Confession of the Universal Christian Faith*, and had asked him his opinion. In this reply Spinoza gave him no praise nor many indications of approval, but merely stated that "it is open to some criticism. On page 5 of the manuscript you assert that man is inclined by nature to evil, but through the Grace of God and the Spirit of Christ he becomes indifferent to good and evil. This, however, is contradictory, because he who has the Spirit of Christ is necessarily impelled only to good." In this letter Spinoza also makes reference to Mr. Kerckring,[178] a doctor, whom he had consulted on some anatomical questions. Near the end of the letter to Jelles he wrote, "I will send you the *Known Truth*[179] as soon as Mr. Vallon[180] returns my copy. But if he takes too long over it, I will make arrangements through Mr. Bronckhorst[181] for you to get it." The ending was, "I remain, with cordial greetings,

Your devoted servant,
B. Spinoza."

---

[176] [The fragments here translated were reported by (1) Bayle, in his *Historical and Critical Dictionary*, 1702, and by (2) Dr. Hallmann, who found the letter in the possession of Rieuwertsz junior in 1703.]

[177] [The first fragment of this letter leaves it rather ambiguous whether Spinoza actually agrees with Jelles' *Confession* or whether he merely suggests no changes. Rieuwertsz's postscript includes a short statement which appears to support the first interpretation, and which is followed by the first of the two fragments of this letter.]

[178] [Dirck Kerckring (1639–1693) was a physician who had studied Latin at Van den Enden's school at about the same time Spinoza was there.]

[179] [There are no extant copies of this book or manuscript.]

[180] [We are not sure who this man was. Conjectures are that he may have been a professor friend of Spinoza's at the University of Leiden or that 'Vallon' is a corruption of 'De Vallan' who was a professor at the University of Utrecht, or of 'De Volder' who taught at the University of Leiden. Other possibilities have also been suggested, but who exactly this man was remains still a mystery.]

[181] [Probably this was Hendrick Van Bronckhurst. He wrote the poem which introduced the Dutch translation of the PPC.]

Letter 49
To the esteemed John George Graevius, from B.d.S.

[Not in the O.P. The original is extant.]

Most esteemed Sir,

Please send me as soon as you can the letter concerning the death of Descartes, of which I think you have long ago made a copy; for Mr. de V. has several times asked me to return it. If it were my own, I should not be in any hurry. Farewell, honoured Sir, and remember me, your friend, who am,

Yours in all love and devotion,
Benedictus de Spinoza

The Hague, 14 December 1673

Mr. John George Graevius,[182]
Regular Professor of Rhetoric, at Utrecht

Letter 50
To the most worthy and judicious Jarig Jelles, from B.d.S.

[The original, written in Dutch, is lost. The O.P. gives a Latin translation. The text of the Dutch edition of the O.P. appears to be a re-translation from the Latin.]

Most worthy Sir,

With regard to political theory, the difference between Hobbes[183] and myself, which is the subject of your inquiry, consists in this, that I always preserve the natural right in its entirety, and I hold that the sovereign power in a State has right

---

[182] [John Graevius was professor of rhetoric at the University of Utrecht.—M.L.M.]
[183] [Thomas Hobbes (1588–1679) was a celebrated political philosopher whose works include *Leviathan, Behemoth, De corpore, De homine* and *De cive* (Spinoza had a copy of the last-mentioned book in his library). While there are many similarities between Spinoza and Hobbes, the two are very different. Spinoza holds that a person *never* loses his or her rights, whether in the state of nature (Hobbes' war-like state) or in community.]

over a subject only in proportion to the excess of its power over that of a subject. This is always the case in a state of nature.[184]

Further, with regard to the demonstration that I establish in the Appendix to my Geometrical Proof of Descartes' Principles, namely, that God can only improperly be called one or single, I reply that a thing can be called one or single only in respect of its existence, not of its essence. For we do not conceive things under the category of numbers unless they are included in a common class. For example, he who holds in his hand a penny and a dollar will not think of the number two unless he can apply a common name to this penny and dollar, that is, pieces of money or coins. For then he can say that he has two pieces of money or two coins, because he calls both the penny and the dollar a piece of money or a coin. Hence it is clear that a thing can not be called one or single unless another thing has been conceived which, as I have said, agrees with it. Now since the existence of God is his very essence, and since we can form no universal idea of his essence, it is certain that he who calls God one or single has no true idea of God, or is speaking of him very improperly.

With regard to the statement that figure is a negation and not anything positive, it is obvious that matter in its totality, considered without limitation, can have no figure, and that figure applies only to finite and determinate bodies. For he who says that he apprehends a figure, thereby means to indicate simply this, that he apprehends a determinate thing and the manner of its determination. This determination therefore does not pertain to the thing in regard to its being; on the contrary, it is its non-being. So since figure is nothing but determination, and determination is negation, figure can be nothing other than negation, as has been said.

The book which the Utrecht Professor[185] wrote against mine and has been published after his death, I have seen in a bookseller's window. From the little that I then read of it, I judged it not worth reading through, and far less answering. So I left the book lying there, and its author to remain such as he was. I smiled as I reflected that the ignorant are usually the most venturesome and most ready to write. It seemed to me that the . . . . set out their wares for sale in the same way as do shopkeepers, who always display the worse first. They say the devil is a crafty fellow, but in my opinion these people's resourcefulness far surpasses him in cunning. Farewell.

The Hague, 2 June 1674

---

[184] [The psychological concept of the state of nature is introduced in E4P37Schol, and further developed in TTP16, but is notably absent in the unfinished TP.]

[185] [This was Regner Van Mansvelt, who published *Adversus Anonymum Theologico-Politicum, Liber Singularis* (One Book against the the Anonymous *Theological-Political* [*Tractate*]) in 1674.]

LETTER 51
To the most acute philosopher B.d.S., from Hugo Boxel

[The original, written in Dutch, is lost. The O.P. gives a Latin translation. The text of the Dutch edition of the O.P. appears to be a re-translation from the Latin.]

Most esteemed Sir,

My reason for writing to you is that I should like to know your opinion of apparitions and spectres, or ghosts; and if they exist, what you think regarding them, and how long they live; for some think that they are immortal, while others think they are mortal. In view of my doubt as to whether you admit their existence, I shall proceed no further. However, it is certain that the ancients believed in their existence. Theologians and philosophers of our times still believe in the existence of creatures of this kind, although they do not agree as to the nature of their essence. Some assert that they are composed of very delicate and fine matter, while others think that they are spiritual beings. But, as I began by saying, we are much at variance on this subject, for I am doubtful as to whether you grant their existence; yet it cannot escape you that there are to be found throughout antiquity so many instances and stories of them that it would indeed be difficult either to deny them or to call them into doubt. This much is certain, that if you admit their existence, you still do not believe that some of them are the souls of the dead, as the upholders of the Roman faith will have it.

Here I will end, and await your reply. I will say nothing about the war,[186] nothing about rumours, for it is our lot to live in such times . . . etc. Farewell.

14 September 1674

---

[186] [This is the continuing war between Holland and France.]

Letter 52

To the highly esteemed and judicious Hugo Boxel, from B.d.S.

[The original, written in Dutch, is lost, but is probably reproduced in the Dutch edition of the O.P. The Latin is a translation.]

My dear Sir,

Your letter, which I received yesterday, was most welcome, both because I wanted to have news of you and because it assures me that you have not entirely forgotten me. And although some might think it a bad omen that ghosts or spectres should have been the occasion of your writing to me, I, on the contrary, discern in this something of greater significance; for I reflect that not only real things but trifles and fancies can turn to my advantage.

But let us set aside the question as to whether ghosts are delusions and fancies, since it seems to you strange not only to deny such things but even to cast doubt on them, being convinced as you are by the numerous stories related by ancients and moderns. The great respect in which I have always held you, and still hold you, does not permit me to contradict you, still less to humour you. The middle course which I shall take between the two is to ask you please to select, from the numerous ghost stories you have read, one or two that are least open to doubt and which prove most clearly the existence of ghosts. For, to tell the truth, I have never read a trustworthy author who showed clearly that they exist. I still do not know what they are, and no one has ever been able to inform me. Yet it is certain that in the case of a thing so clearly demonstrated by experience we ought to know what it is; otherwise we can hardly conclude from a story that ghosts exist, but only that there is something, but no one knows what it is. If philosophers want to call these things we do not know 'ghosts', I shall not be able to refute them, for there are an infinite number of things of which I have no knowledge.

Finally, my dear Sir, before I go further into this matter, I beg you to tell me what kind of things are these ghosts or spirits. Are they children, fools or madmen? For what I have heard of them seems to suggest silly people rather than intelligent beings, or, at best childish games or the pastime of fools. Before concluding, I shall put before you one further consideration, namely, that the desire men commonly have to narrate things not as they are but as they would like them to be can nowhere be better exemplified than in stories about spirits and ghosts. The main reason for this is, I believe, that since stories of this kind have no other witnesses than the narrators, the author of such stories can add or suppress circumstantial details as he pleases without having to fear that anyone will contradict him. In particular, he makes things up to justify the fear that has seized him regarding his dreams and fancied apparitions, or also to confirm his courage, his credibility and his esteem. Besides this I have found other reasons that move me to doubt, if not the stories themselves, at least the details included therein, which serve most of all to support the conclusion meant to be drawn from these stories. Here I shall stop, until I hear from you what are the stories which have so convinced you that you think it absurd even to doubt them.

[The Hague, September 1674]

Letter 53
To the very sagacious philosopher B.d.S., from Hugo Boxel

[The original, written in Dutch, is extant. The Latin version in the O.P. may have been made by Spinoza.]

Most sagacious Sir,

The reply you have sent me is just what I expected from a friend, and one who holds an opinion at variance with mine. This latter point is of no importance, for friends may well disagree on indifferent matters without ever impairing their friendship.

Before you give your own opinion, you ask me to say what sort of things ghosts are, whether they are children, fools or madmen, and so forth, and you add that all that you have heard of them seems to proceed from lunatics rather than from intelligent beings. The old proverb is true, that a preconceived opinion hinders the search for truth.

I say that I believe that there are ghosts. My reasons are, first, that it contributes to the beauty and perfection of the universe that they should exist. Second, it is probable that the Creator has created them because they resemble him more closely than do corporeal creatures. Third, just as there is a body without soul, so there is a soul without body. Fourth and last, I believe that there is no dark body in the upper air, region or space that is without its inhabitants, and therefore the immeasurable space extending between us and the stars is not empty but filled with inhabitants that are spirits. The highest and uppermost are true spirits, while the lowest in the nethermost region of air are possibly creatures of very delicate and fine substance, and also invisible. So I think that there are spirits of all kinds, except perhaps of the female sex.

This reasoning will not convince those who perversely believe that the world was made by chance. Besides these arguments, our daily experience shows that there are ghosts, of whom there are many stories, old and modern, and even present-day. They are related in Plutarch's treatise *On Famous Men* and in other of his works, by Suetonius in his *Lives of the Caesars*, by Wierus in his books on ghosts[187] and also by Lavater,[188] who deal with this subject at length, drawing on other writers. Cardanus, too,[189] celebrated for his learning, speaks of them in his books *De Subtilitate* and *De Varietate* and in his autobiography, where he recounts the appearances of ghosts in his own case and in that of his relations and friends. Melanthon,[190] a lover of truth and a man of understanding, and many others bear witness as to their own experiences. A certain burgomaster of Sc., a learned and wise man who is still alive, once told me that work was heard going on at night in his mother's brewery in the same way as it was heard by day when brewing was taking place, and swore to me that this occurred on several occasions. The same sort of thing has happened to me more than once, which I shall never forget. These experiences and the afore-mentioned reasons have convinced me that there are ghosts.

As regards devils who torment poor people in this life and the next, that is another question, as also is the practise of magic. I consider that stories told on these matters are fables. Sir, in treatises concerning ghosts you will find an abundance of details. Besides those I have mentioned, you can look up, if you please, the younger Pliny, Book 7, his letter to Sura, Suetonius' *Life of Caesar*, chapter 32, Valerius Maximus, Book 1, chapter 8, sections 7 and 8, and also the *Dies Geniales* of Alexander ab Alexandro.[191] No doubt you have access to these books. I make no mention of monks and clerics, who report so many apparitions and sightings of spirits, ghosts and devils, and so many stories, or rather, fables of spectres that people are bored by them and sick of reading them. These things are also dealt with by the Jesuit Thyraeus in his book which he entitles *Apparitiones Spirituum*.[192] But these people expound such subjects merely for their own gain, and to prove that there is a purgatory, which is for them a mine from which they extract so much silver and gold. This, however, is not true of the above-mentioned writers and other writers of our times, who deserve more credibility for being without any such motivation.

You say at the end of your letter that to commend me to God is something you cannot do without smiling.[193] But if you are still mindful of the conversation we

---

[187] [Johannes Wierus (b. 1515 or 1516) was a physician in Düsseldorf. He published *De praestigiis Daemonum* in 1563 as a protest against the prosecution of witches. The book was followed on *De lamiis* (*On Ghosts*) and *Pseudomonarchia daemonum* (*On the Hierarchy of Hell*). The original text of this letter has 'Wierius', which is corrected to 'Wierus' in the O.P.]

[188] [Ludwig Lavater (1527–1586), a Protestant Minister in Zurich, wrote a treatise on ghosts, *Tractatus de Spectris, Lemuribus, Fragoribus, Variisque Praesagiis* (Geneva, 1580).]

[189] [Girolamo Cardanus (1501–1576) became Professor of Medicine in Pavia in 1547. His *De Subtilitate Rerum* appeared in 1551, and *De Rerum Varietate* in 1557. Although he insisted on the inviolability of laws of nature, he claimed that he had the assistance of a guardian daemon.]

[190] [This is probably the German Reformer Philipp Melanchton (1497–1560).]

[191] [Alexander ab Alexandro (1461–1523) was an Italian lawyer. His *Genialium Dierum, Libri Sex*, dealing mostly with antiquities, was published in 1522.]

[192] [Petrus Thyraeus (1546–1601), professor at Würzburg, published the *De Apparitionibus Spirituum* in 1600 at Cologne.]

[193] [The last two paragraphs of this letter are in the original but not in the O.P. The reference to Spinoza's letter is obscure.]

had some time ago, you will realise that there is no need for alarm over the conclusion I reached at the time in my letter, etc.

In answer to the passage in your letter where you speak of fools and lunatics, I will state the conclusion of the learned Lavater with which he ends his first book on *Night Ghosts*. It goes as follows. "He who ventures to repudiate so many unanimous witnesses, both ancient and modern, seems to me undeserving of belief in anything he asserts. For just as it is a mark of rashness to give unquestioning belief to all those who assert that they have seen ghosts, so on the other hand it would be sheer effrontery to contradict, rashly and shamelessly, so many historians, Fathers, and others of great authority."

21 September 1674

LETTER 54
To the highly esteemed and judicious Hugo Boxel, from B.d.S.

[The original, written in Dutch, is lost. The O.P. gives a Latin version, perhaps by Spinoza, and this has been re-translated into Dutch in the Dutch edition. Conjectural date, September 1674.]

Most esteemed Sir,

Relying on what you say in your letter of the 21st of last month, that friends may disagree on an indifferent matter without impairing their friendship, I will clearly state what I think of the arguments and stories from which you conclude that 'there are ghosts of all kinds, but perhaps not of the female sex'. The reason for my not having replied sooner is that the books you quoted are not to hand, and I have found none but Pliny[194] and Suetonius. But these two will save me the trouble of consulting the others, for I am sure that they all talk the same sort of nonsense, and love tales of extraordinary events which astonish men and compel their wonder. I confess that I was not a little amazed, not at the stories that are narrated, but at those who write them. I am surprised that men of ability and judgment should squander their gift of eloquence and misuse it to persuade us of such rubbish.

Still, let us dismiss the authors and turn to the issue itself, and I shall first devote a little time to a discussion of your conclusion. Let us see whether I, who deny that there are ghosts or spirits, am thereby failing to understand those writers who have written on this subject, or whether you, who hold that such things exist, are not giving the writers more credibility than they deserve. On the one

---

[194] [A copy of Pliny's *Letters* is listed in the inventory of Spinoza's library compiled after his death.]

hand you do not doubt the existence of spirits of the male sex, while on the other hand you doubt the existence of any of the female sex. This seems to me more like caprice than genuine doubt, for if this were really your opinion, it would be more in keeping with the popular imagination which makes God masculine rather than feminine. I am surprised that those who have seen naked spirits have not cast their eyes on the genital parts; perhaps they were too afraid, or ignorant of the difference.

You will retort that this is to resort to ridicule, not to argue the case; and so I see that your reasons appear to you so strong and so well-founded that no one, at least in your judgment, can contradict them unless there is someone who perversely thinks that the world was made by chance. This impels me, before I deal with your preceding arguments, to give a brief account of my view on the question as to whether the world was made by chance. My answer is that, as it is certain that chance and necessity are two contrary terms, so it is also clear that he who affirms that the world is the necessary effect of the divine nature is also denying absolutely that the world was made by chance, whereas he who affirms that God could have refrained from creating the world is declaring in an indirect way that it was made by chance, since it proceeded from an act of will which might not have been.[195] Since this belief and this view is quite absurd, it is commonly and unanimously admitted that God's will is eternal and has never been indifferent, and therefore they must also necessarily grant (note this well) that the world is the necessary effect of the divine nature. Let them call it will, intellect, or any name they please, they will still in the end come to realise that they are expressing one and the same thing by different names. For if you ask them whether the divine will does not differ from the human will, they will reply that the former has nothing in common with the latter but the name; and furthermore they will mostly admit that God's will, intellect, and essence or nature are one and the same thing.[196] And I, too, to avoid confusing the divine nature with human nature, do not ascribe to God human attributes—will, intellect, attention, hearing, etc. I therefore say, as I have already said, that the world is the necessary effect of the divine nature, and was not made by chance.

This, I think, is enough to convince you that the opinion of those (if indeed such there be) who say that the world was made by chance is entirely opposed to my opinion, and on this basis I proceed to examine the arguments from which you infer that there exist ghosts of all kinds. As a general remark, I would say of them that they seem to be conjectures rather than reasons, and I find it very difficult to believe that you take them to be conclusive arguments. However, whether they be conjectures or reasons, let us see whether they can be accepted as well-founded.

---

[195] [The position described and criticized here is in fact the one espoused by Leibniz in the *Theodicy*. It is criticized further in E1P33Schol2.]

[196] [That intellect and will are predicated equivocally of God and of finite things is argued in E1P17Schol, where Spinoza makes the claim that, "They could be no more alike than the celestial constellation of the Dog and the dog that barks."]

Your first reason is that it pertains to the beauty and perfection of the universe that ghosts should exist. Beauty, most esteemed Sir, is not so much a quality in the perceived object as an effect in him who perceives. If we were more long-sighted or more short-sighted, or if we were differently constituted, the things which we now think beautiful would appear ugly, and the ugly, beautiful. The most beautiful hand, seen through a microscope, would appear repulsive. Some things seen at a distance are beautiful, but when viewed at close range, ugly. So things regarded in themselves, or as related to God, are neither beautiful nor ugly. Therefore he who says that God has created the world so as to be beautiful must necessarily affirm one of two alternatives: either that God made the world so as to suit the desire and the eyes of men, or the desire and the eyes of men to suit the world. Now whichever of these alternative views we adopt, I do not see why God had to create ghosts and spirits in either case. Perfection and imperfection are designations not much different from beauty and ugliness. Therefore, not to be tedious, I merely ask which would contribute more to the adornment and perfection of the world—that there should be ghosts, or that there should be a multiplicity of monsters, such as Centaurs, Hydras, Harpies, Griffins, Arguses and other such absurdities? Truly, the world would have been handsomely embellished if God, to suit our fancy, had adorned and furnished it with things which anyone can easily imagine and dream of, but no one can ever understand!

Your second reason is that, since spirits express God's image more than do other corporeal creatures, it is also likely that God has created them. I frankly confess that I still do not understand in what respect spirits express God more than do other creatures. This I do know, that between the finite and the infinite there is no relation, so that the difference between God and the greatest and most excellent created thing is no other than that between God and the least created thing. This argument, therefore, is wide of the mark. If I had as clear an idea of ghosts as of a triangle or a circle, I should not hesitate to affirm that they have been created by God. However, since the idea I have of them is just like the ideas of Harpies, Griffins, Hydras, etc., which I form in my imagination, I cannot consider them as anything other than dreams, which are as different from God as being from non-being.

Your third reason (that just as a body can exist without soul, so a soul must exist without body) seems to me equally absurd. Tell me, pray, whether it is not also probable that memory, hearing, sight, etc., can exist without bodies, since some bodies are found to be without memory, hearing, sight, etc.? Or a sphere exist without a circle, because a circle exists without a sphere?

Your fourth and last reason is the same as the first, and I refer you to my answer. Here I shall merely observe that I do not know which are those highest and lowest regions which you conceive in infinite matter, unless you take the Earth to be the centre of the universe. For if the Sun or Saturn is the centre of the universe, then the Sun or Saturn, not the Earth, will be the lowest. Therefore, leaving aside this and any remaining consideration, I conclude that these and similar arguments will not convince anyone that ghosts and spectres of all kinds exist, except those who, shutting their ears to the voice of reason, suffer themselves to be led astray by superstition, which is so hostile to right reason that, so as to lower the prestige of philosophers, it prefers to believe old wives' tales.

As regards the stories, I have already said in my first letter that I do not altogether deny them, but only the conclusion drawn from them. I may add that I do not consider them so trustworthy as not to doubt many of the circumstantial details, which are often added for adornment rather than to render more plausible the truth of the story or the inference to be drawn therefrom. I had hoped that from so many stories you would have produced one or two which are least open to doubt, and which would have clearly proved the existence of ghosts or spectres. The case of the burgomaster, who was ready to conclude that they exist because he heard them working by night in his mother's brewery just as he was wont to hear work going on by day, seems to me ridiculous. Similarly, it would also be too tedious to examine here all the stories that have been written about these silly incidents. So, to be brief, I refer to Julius Caesar who, as Suetonius tells us, laughed at such things, and yet was favoured by fortune, according to what Suetonius relates of that Prince in his biography, chapter 59. In the same way, all who reflect on the effects of mortal imaginings and emotions must laugh at such things, whatever may be adduced to the contrary by Lavater and others who share his delusions on this subject.

Letter 55

To the most sagacious philosopher, B.d.S., from Hugo Boxel

[The original, written in Dutch, is lost. The O.P. gives a Latin version, perhaps by Spinoza, and this has been re-translated into Dutch in the Dutch edition. Conjectural date, September 1674.]

Most sagacious Sir,

I am later than expected in replying to your letter because a slight illness has deprived me of the pleasure of study and meditation, and has prevented me from writing to you. Now, thanks be to God, I have recovered my health. In this reply I shall follow your letter step by step, passing over your outcry against those who have written about ghosts.

I say, then, that I think there are no ghosts of the female sex because I deny that they give birth. As to their shape and constitution I say nothing, because this does not concern me. A thing is said to happen fortuitously when it comes about regardless of the doer's intention. When we dig the ground to plant a vine or to make a pit or a grave, and find a treasure of which we have never had a thought, this is said to happen by chance. He who acts of his own free will in such a way that he can either act or not act can never be said to act by chance if he chooses to act;

for in that case all human actions would be by chance, which would be absurd. 'Necessary' and 'free', not 'necessary' and 'fortuitous', are contrary terms. Granted that God's will is eternal, it still does not follow that the world is eternal, for God could have determined from eternity to create the world at a set time.

You go on to deny that God's will has ever been indifferent, which I dispute; nor is it as necessary as you think to pay such strict attention to this point. Neither does everyone agree that God's will is necessary, for this involves the concept of necessity. Now he who attributes will to someone means thereby that he can either act or not, according to his will; but if we ascribe necessity to him, he must act of necessity.

Finally, you say that you avoid granting any human attributes in God lest you should confuse the divine nature with human nature. Thus far I agree, for we do not apprehend in what way God acts, or in what way he wills, understands, thinks, sees, hears, etc. However, if you completely deny of God these activities and our most sublime conceptions of him, and you assert that these are not in God eminently and in a metaphysical sense, then I do not understand your God, or what you mean by the word 'God'. What we fail to apprehend ought not to be denied. Mind, which is spirit and incorporeal, can act only along with the most subtle bodies, namely, the humours. And what is the relation between body and mind? In what way does mind act along with bodies? For without these the mind is at rest, and when these are in a disordered state the mind does what it should not have done. Show me how this comes about. You cannot, and neither can I. Yet we see and sense that the mind does act, and this remains true in spite of our failure to perceive how this acting comes about. In the same way, although we do not understand how God acts and we refrain from ascribing to him human activities, yet we ought not to deny of him that, in an eminent way and beyond our comprehension, these activities are in accord with our own, such as willing, understanding, seeing and hearing with the intellect, though not with eyes or ears. Similarly, wind and air can destroy, and even overthrow, lands and mountains without the use of hands or other tools; yet this is impossible for men without the use of hands and machines. If you attribute necessity to God and deprive him of will and free choice, this raises some doubt as to whether you are not depicting and representing as a monster him who is an infinitely perfect being. To attain your purpose you will need other arguments to form a basis, for in my opinion those you have advanced have no solidity. And even if you can prove them, there are perhaps other arguments to counterbalance yours. But setting this aside, let us proceed.

To establish the existence of spirits in the world, you demand conclusive proofs. There are few of these in the world, and, apart from mathematics, none of these are as certain as we would wish. Indeed, we are satisfied with probable conjectures which are likely to be true. If the arguments by which things were proved were quite conclusive, only the foolish and the obstinate would be found to contradict them. But, my dear friend, we are not as fortunate as that. In this world we are less demanding; to some extent we rely on conjecture, and in our reasoning we accept the probable in default of demonstrative proof. This is evident from all the sciences, both human and divine, which abound in controversies and disputes whose prevalence is the reason why so many different opinions are everywhere to be found. That is why, as you know, there were once philosophers called Sceptics who doubted everything. They used to debate the case for and against so as to arrive at the merely probable in default of true reasons, and each of them believed what he thought more probable. The moon is situated directly below the sun, and therefore the sun will be obscured in some region of the earth, and if the sun is not obscured in daytime, then the moon is not situated directly below it. This is conclusive proof, reasoning from cause to effect and from effect to cause. There are some proofs of this sort, but very few, which cannot be contradicted by anyone if only he grasps them.

With regard to beauty, there are some things whose parts are in proportion with one another, and are better composed than others. God has bestowed on man's understanding and judgment a sense of agreeableness and harmony with that which is well-proportioned, and not with that which lacks proportion. This is the case with harmonious and discordant sounds, where our hearing can well distinguish between harmony and discord because the former brings pleasure and the latter annoyance. A thing's perfection is also beautiful, insofar as it lacks nothing. Of this there are many examples, which I omit to avoid prolixity. Let us only consider the world, to which we apply the term Whole or Universe. If this is true, as indeed is the case, the existence of incorporeal things does not spoil it or degrade it. Your remarks as to Centaurs, Hydras, Harpies, etc., are quite misplaced, for we are speaking of the most universal genera, of the prime grades of things, which comprehend under them various and innumerable species: we are speaking of the eternal and the temporal, cause and effect, finite and infinite, animate and inanimate, substance and accident or mode, the corporeal and the spiritual, and so on.

I say that spirits are like God because he also is spirit. You demand as clear an idea of spirits as of a triangle, which is impossible. Tell me, I beg you, what idea you have of God, and whether it is as clear to your intellect as is the idea of a triangle. I know that you have none such, and I have said that we are not so fortunate as to be able to apprehend things by means of conclusive proofs, and that, for the most part, the probable holds sway in this world. Nevertheless, I affirm that just as body can exist without memory, etc., so can memory, etc., exist without body, and that just as a circle can exist without a sphere, so too can a sphere exist without a circle. But this is to descend from the most universal genera to particular species, which are not the object of this discussion.

I say that the Sun is the centre of the world, that the fixed stars are more distant from the earth than is Saturn, and Saturn than Jupiter, and Jupiter than Mars. So in the limitless air some bodies are more distant from us and some nearer to us, and these we term higher and lower.

It is not the upholders of the existence of spirits who discredit philosophers, but those who deny it; for all philosophers, both of ancient and modern times, think themselves convinced of the existence of spirits. Plutarch bears witness to this in his treatises on the opinions of philosophers and on the daemon of Socrates, and so do all the Stoics, Pythagoreans, Platonists, Peripatetics, Empedocles, Maximus Tyrius, Apuleius and others. Of modern philosophers not one denies spectres. Reject, then, the testimony of so many wise men who had eyes and ears, reject the narratives of so many philosophers, so many historians. Assert that they are all foolish and crazy like the common herd—and yet your answers are unconvincing, even absurd, and generally irrelevant to the main point at issue, and you fail to produce any proof to confirm your view. Caesar, along with Cicero and Cato, does not laugh at spectres, but at omens and presentiments. And yet, if he had not mocked at Spurina[197] on the day he was to die, he would not have suffered all those stab-wounds from his enemies. But let this suffice for the time, etc.

Letter 56
To the highly esteemed and judicious Hugo Boxel, from B.d.S.

[The original, written in Dutch, is lost. The O.P. gives a Latin version, perhaps by Spinoza, and this has been re-translated into Dutch in the Dutch edition. Conjectural date, September 1674.]

Most esteemed Sir,

I hasten to reply to your letter received yesterday, for if I delay any further I shall have to postpone my reply longer than I could wish. I should have been anxious about your health, had I not learned that you are better. I hope that you are by now completely recovered. When two people follow different first principles, the difficulty they experience in coming together and reaching agreement in a matter involving many other questions might be shown simply from this discussion of ours, even if it were not confirmed by rational considerations. Tell me, pray, whether you have seen or read any philosophers who have maintained that the world was made by chance, taking chance in the sense you give it, that God had a set aim in creating the world and yet departed from his resolve. I am unaware that any such idea has ever entered the thoughts of any man. I am similarly at a loss to understand the reasoning whereby you try to convince me that chance and necessity are not contraries. As soon as I perceive that the three angles of a triangle are necessarily equal to two right angles, I also deny that this comes about by chance; likewise, as soon as I perceive that heat is the necessary effect of fire, I also deny that this happens by chance. That 'necessary' and 'free' are contraries seems no less absurd and opposed to reason. Nobody can deny that God freely knows himself and all other things, and yet all are unanimous in granting that God knows himself necessarily. Thus you fail, I think, to make any distinction between constraint (*coac-*

---

[197] [The story is related in Suetonius' *Caesar*, chapter 81.]

tio) or force, and necessity.[198] That a man wills to live, to love, etc., does not proceed from constraint, but is nevertheless necessary, and far more so is God's will to be, to know and to act. If, in addition to these points, you reflect that a state of indifference is nothing but ignorance or a condition of doubt, and that a will that is always constant and determined in all things is a virtue and a necessary property of the intellect, you will see that my view is in complete accord with the truth. If we maintain that God was able not to will what he willed, but that he was not able not to understand what he willed, we are attributing to God two different kinds of freedom, the freedom of necessity, and the freedom of indifference. Consequently, we shall conceive God's will as different from his essence and his intellect, and in this way we shall fall into one absurdity after another.

The attention which I requested in my former letter you have not deemed necessary, and if is for this reason that you have failed to direct your thoughts to the main point at issue, and have disregarded what was most relevant.

Further, when you say that you do not see what sort of God I have if I deny in him the actions of seeing, hearing, attending, willing, etc., and that he possesses those faculties in an eminent degree, I suspect that you believe there is no greater perfection than can be explicated by the afore-mentioned attributes. I am not surprised, for I believe that a triangle, if it could speak, would likewise say that God is eminently triangular, and a circle that God's nature is eminently circular. In this way each would ascribe to God its own attributes, assuming itself to be like God and regarding all else as ill-formed.

The briefness of a letter and the pressure of time do not permit me to deal with my view of the divine nature and with the questions you have propounded; anyway, to bring up difficulties is not to advance rational arguments. It is true that in this world we often act from conjecture, but it is not true that philosophical thinking proceeds from conjecture. In the common round of life we have to follow what is probable, but in speculative thought we have to follow what is true. A man would perish of hunger and thirst if he refused to eat and drink until he had obtained perfect proof that food and drink would be good for him, but this does not hold in the field of contemplation. On the contrary, we should take care not to admit as true anything that is merely probable. When one false proposition is allowed entry, innumerable others follow.

Again, because the sciences of things divine and human abound with quarrels and controversies, it cannot be concluded therefrom that the whole of the subject-matter with which they deal is uncertain. There have been many whose zeal for controversy was such that they even scoffed at geometrical proof. Sextus Empiricus and other Sceptics whom you quote say that it is false that the whole is greater than its part, and they pass similar judgment on other axioms.

However, leaving aside and granting the fact that in default of proof we must be content with the probable, I say that a probable proof must be such that, al-

---

[198] [Spinoza constantly inveighs against the confusion between external coercion and internal necessity. The libertarian notion of a freedom of indifference makes freedom into random activity or caprice.]

though open to doubt, it cannot be contradicted; for that which can be contradicted is akin, not to truth, but to falsehood. If, for example, I say that Peter is alive because I saw him yesterday in good health, this is indeed probable insofar as nobody is able to contradict me. But if somebody else says that yesterday he saw Peter unconscious, and that he believes that since then Peter has died, he makes my statement seem false. That your conjecture regarding spectres and ghosts seems false and has not even a show of truth, I have demonstrated so clearly that I find nothing in your reply worthy of consideration.

To your question as to whether I have as clear an idea of God as of a triangle, I reply in the affirmative. But if you ask me whether I have as clear a mental image of God as of a triangle, I reply in the negative. We cannot imagine God, but we can apprehend him by the intellect.[199] Here it should also be observed that I do not claim to have complete knowledge of God, but that I do understand some of his attributes—not indeed all of them, or the greater part—and it is certain that my ignorance of very many attributes does not prevent me from having knowledge of some of them. When I was studying Euclid's Elements, I understood early on that the three angles of a triangle are equal to two right angles, and I clearly perceived this property of a triangle although I was ignorant of many others.

As regards spectres or ghosts, I have not as yet heard of any intelligible property of theirs; I have heard only of fantasies beyond anyone's understanding. In saying that spectres or ghosts here below (I follow your usage of words, though I do not know why matter here below should be inferior to matter above) are made of very tenuous, rarefied and subtle substance, you seem to be speaking of spiders' webs, air or mist. To say that they are invisible is, in my view, tantamount to saying not what they are, but what they are not. But perhaps you wish to indicate that they render themselves visible or invisible as and when they please, and that our imagination will find no more difficulty in this than in other impossibilities.

The authority of Plato, Aristotle and Socrates[200] carries little weight with me. I should have been surprised if you had produced Epicurus, Democritus, Lucretius or one of the Atomists or defenders of the atoms.[201] It is not surprising that those who have thought up occult qualities, intentional species, substantial forms and a thousand more bits of nonsense[202] should have devised spectres and ghosts, and given credence to old wives' tales with view to disparaging the authority of Democritus, whose high reputation they so envied that they burned all the books

---

[199] [See E2P47: "The human mind has an adequate knowledge of the eternal and infinite essence of God."]

[200] [The inventory of Spinoza's library contains a Latin translation of the complete works of Aristotle, but nothing whatever by Plato.]

[201] [Epicurus (341–271 B.C.), Democritus (460–370 B.C.) and Lucretius (99–55 B.C.) all supported the atomic theory, and were accordingly held in favor by seventeenth-century scientists.]

[202] [The terms 'intentional species' and 'substantial forms' are mediaeval. They were widely criticized in the seventeenth century as involving an appeal to unknown and unknowable ("occult") qualities of things which explain nothing. This is the same accusation which the Cartesians (and Leibniz) were to make against Newton's theory of gravitation as a *vis insita*.]

which he had published amidst so much acclaim.[203] If you are minded to put your trust in such people, what reason have you to deny the miracles of the Holy Virgin and all the saints? These have been reported by so many renowned philosophers, theologians and historians that I could produce a hundred of these latter to scarcely one of the former.

In conclusions, most esteemed Sir, I find that I have gone further than I intended, and I will trouble you no longer with matters which I know you will not concede, your first principles being far different from my own, etc.

Letter 57
To the most distinguished and acute philosopher, B.d.S., from Ehrenfried Walther von Tschirnhaus

[Known only from the O.P. The original is lost. The letter was addressed to Schuller, who transmitted to Spinoza the part that concerned him.]

Distinguished Sir,

It surprises me, to say the least, that when philosophers demonstrate that something is false, at the same time they are showing its truth. For Descartes, at the beginning of his Method,[204] thinks that the certainty of the intellect is equal for all, and in the *Meditations* he proves it. The same line is taken by those who think that they can prove something to be certain on the grounds that it is accepted by separate individuals as being beyond doubt.

But setting this aside, I appeal to experience, and I humbly request you to give careful consideration to the following. For thus it will be found that if of two men one affirms something and the other denies it, and they are fully conscious of what it is they are saying, although they appear verbally to contradict each other, yet when we consider what is in their minds they are both speaking the truth, each according to his own thinking. I bring up this point because it is of immeasurable value in our common dealings, and if this single fact were taken into account, innumerable controversies and the ensuing disputes would be averted, even though this truth in conception is not always true in an absolute sense, but is taken as true only on the basis of what is assumed to be in a man's understanding. This rule is of such general application that it holds good in the case of all men, even those

---

[203] [The story comes from Diogenes Laertius, *Lives of the Philosophers*.]

[204] [The Dutch version has 'in the same paragraph' instead of 'at the beginning of his Method'. The opening paragraphs of this letter have been obviously omitted, and probably referred to specific passages in Descartes. The Dutch editors probably made the change in the light of the omission.]

who are mad or are asleep. For whatever they say they see (although it may not appear so to us) or have seen, it is quite certain that this is really so.

This is also seen very clearly in the case under consideration, that of Free Will. For both he who argues for and he who argues against seem to me to speak the truth, according to how one conceives freedom. Descartes says that that is free which is not compelled by any cause, whereas you say that it is that which is not determined to something by any cause. I agree with you that in all things we are determined to something by a definite cause, and that thus we have no free will. But on the other hand I also agree with Descartes that in certain matters (as I shall soon make clear) we are not in any way compelled, and so have free will. The present question will furnish me with an example.

The problem is of a threefold nature. First, do we have in an absolute sense a power over things which are external to us? This is denied. For example, that I am at this moment writing a letter is not something that is absolutely within my power, since I would certainly have written sooner had I not been prevented either by my being away or by the company of friends. Secondly, do we have in an absolute sense power over the movements of our bodies which follow when the will determines them thereto? I reply affirmatively with this reservation—if we are in good health; for if I am well, I can always set myself to write, or not. Thirdly, when I am in a position to exercise my reason, can I do so quite freely, that is, absolutely? I reply in the affirmative. For who would tell me, without gainsaying his own consciousness, that I can not in my thoughts think that I want to write or not to write? And with regard to the act of writing, too, since external causes permit (and this concerns the second question) that I should possess the capacity both to write and not to write, I agree with you that there are causes which determine me to write just now—that you wrote to me in the first place and in that letter requested me to reply as soon as I could, and, with the present opportunity arising, I would not willingly let it pass. I also agree with Descartes, on the testimony of my consciousness, that things of that kind do not on that account constrain me, and that I can still (as seems impossible to deny) really refrain from writing, in spite of those considerations. And, again, if we were under the compulsion of external circumstances, who could possibly acquire the habit of virtue? Indeed, if this point were granted, all wickedness would be excusable. But does it not frequently come about that, being determined to something by external things, we still resist this with a firm and steady mind?

To give a clearer explanation of the above rule, you are both telling the truth according to your own conception, but if we look to absolute truth, this belongs only to Descartes' view. For in your mind you are assuming as certain that the essence of freedom consists in our not being determined by any thing. On this assumption both sides are in the right. However, the essence of any thing consists in that without which it cannot even be conceived, and freedom can surely be clearly conceived, even though in our actions we are determined to something by external causes, or even though there are always causes which incite us to act in a certain way, but without being completely dominant. But freedom cannot be conceived at all on the assumption that we are under compulsion. See, in addition, Descartes, Volume 1, letters 8 and 9, and also Volume 2, page 4. But let this suffice. I beg you to reply to the difficulties here raised, and you will find me not only grateful, but also, health permitting,[205]

Your most devoted,
N.N.

8 October 1674

Letter 58
To the most learned and wise G. H. Schuller, from B.d.S.

[Known only from the O.P. The original is lost.]

Most wise Sir,

Our friend J.R.[206] has sent me the letter which you were kind enough to write to me, together with your friend's judgment of the views expressed by Descartes and myself on the question of free will, for which I am most grateful. Although I am at present fully occupied with other matters and my health is also causing me some concern, I feel impelled both by your exceptional courtesy and by your devotion to truth, which I particularly value, to satisfy your wish as far as my slender abilities allow. Indeed, I do not know what your friend means in the section preceding his appeal to experience and his request for careful attention. As to what he goes on to say, 'if one of two men affirms something of a thing and the other denies it' etc., this is true if he means that the two men, while using the same words, nevertheless have different things in mind. I once sent some examples of this to our friend J.R., and I am now writing to him to let you have them.

So I now pass on to that definition of freedom which he ascribes to me, but I do not know whence he has taken it, I say that that thing is free which exists and acts solely from the necessity of its own nature,[207] and I say that that thing is constrained (*coactus*) which is determined by something else to exist and to act in a fixed and determinate way. For example, although God exists necessarily, he nevertheless exists freely because he exists solely from the necessity of his own nature. Similarly,

---

[205] [The last phrase, beginning 'and you will find me . . .', is found only in the Dutch edition.]

[206] [Most likely this is Jan Rieuwertsz of Amsterdam, who was a bookseller and a publisher. His bookstore was a center for liberal thinkers, and he published all Spinoza's works (though in secret except for the PPC).]

[207] [The definition of 'freedom' is given in E1Def7, and E1P17 states that "God acts solely from the laws of his own nature, constrained by none."]

too, God freely understands himself and all things absolutely, because it follows solely from the necessity of his own nature that he should understand all things. So you see that I place freedom, not in free decision, but in free necessity.

However, let us move down to created things, which are all determined by external causes to exist and to act in a fixed and determinate way. To understand this clearly, let us take a very simple example. A stone receives from the impulsion of an external cause a fixed quantity of motion whereby it will necessarily continue to move when the impulsion of the external cause has ceased. The stone's continuance in motion is constrained, not because it is necessary, but because it must be defined by the impulsion received from the external cause. What here applies to the stone must be understood of every individual thing, however complex its structure and various its functions. For every single thing is necessarily determined by an external cause to exist and to act in a fixed and determinate way.[208]

Furthermore, conceive, if you please, that while continuing in motion the stone thinks, and knows that it is endeavouring, as far as in it lies, to continue in motion. Now this stone, since it is conscious only of its endeavour[209] and is not at all indifferent, will surely think it is completely free, and that it continues in motion for no other reason than that it so wishes. This, then, is that human freedom which all men boast of possessing, and which consists solely in this, that men are conscious of their desire and unaware of the causes by which they are determined. In the same way a baby thinks that it freely desires milk, an angry child revenge, and a coward flight. Again, a drunken man believes that it is from his free decision that he says what he later, when sober, would wish to be left unsaid. So, too, the delirious, the loquacious, and many others of this kind believe that they act from their free decision, and not that they are carried away by impulse. Since this preconception is innate in all men, they cannot so easily be rid of it. For although experience teaches us again and again that nothing is less within men's power than to control their appetites, and that frequently, when subject to conflicting emotions, they see the better course and pursue the worse,[210] they nevertheless believe themselves to be free, a belief that stems from the fact that in some cases our desire has no great force and can easily be checked by the recurrence to mind of some other thing which is frequently in our thoughts.

I have now, if I am not mistaken, sufficiently set forth my views on free and constrained necessity and on imaginary human freedom, and with this your friend's objections are readily answered. For when he says, along with Descartes,[211] that the free man is he who is not constrained by any external cause, if by con-

---

[208] [See E1P28, which asserts that the chain of causes is infinite.]

[209] [Here 'endeavour' is *conatus*, which is introduced beginning at E3P6 and plays a major role not just in Spinoza's psychology but also in the account of virtue central to his moral philosophy.]

[210] [Viz., "*meliora videant et deteriora sequantur.*" Spinoza uses this expression elsewhere; see E3P2Schol. It is original to Spinoza in this form, but is found in Ovid (*Metamorphoses*, VII, 20), in another form: "*Video meliora proboque, deteriora sequor*" (I see and approve the better, but I follow the worse). Cf. Paul's Epistle to the Romans, 7:15–19.]

[211] [A more extended critique of Descartes' account of freedom is given in E1P33Schol2.]

strained he means acting against one's will, I agree that in some cases we are in no way constrained and that in this sense we have free will. But if by constrained he means acting necessarily, though not against one's will, I deny that in any instance we are free, as I have explained above.

But your friend, on the contrary asserts that 'we can employ our rational faculty in complete freedom, that is, absolutely', in which assertion he is somewhat overconfident. 'For who', he says, 'would deny, without gainsaying his own consciousness, that with my thoughts I can think that I want to write, or do not want to write?' I should very much like to know what consciousness he is talking about, apart from that which I illustrated above with the example of the stone. For my part, not to gainsay my own consciousness—that is, reason and experience—and not to cherish prejudice and ignorance, I deny that, by any absolute power of thought, I can think that I want, or do not want, to write. But I appeal to the consciousness of the man himself, who has doubtless experienced in dreams that he has not the power to think that he wants, or does not want, to write, and that, when he dreams that he wants to write, he does not have the power not to dream that he wants to write. I think that he must likewise have experienced that the mind is not at all times equally fitted to thinking of the same object, but that just as the body is more fitted to have the image of this or that object aroused in it, so the mind is more apt to regard this or that object.

When he further adds that the causes of his resolving to write have indeed urged him to write, but have not constrained him, if you will weigh the matter impartially he means no more than this, that his mind was at the time in such a state that causes which might not have swayed him at other times—as when he is assailed by some strong emotion—were at this time easily able to sway him. That is, causes which might not have constrained him at other times did in fact constrain him then, not to write against his will, but necessarily to want to write.

When he goes on to say that 'if we were constrained by external causes, nobody could acquire the habit of virtue', I do not know who has told him that we cannot be of strong and constant mind from the necessity of fate, but only from free will.

As to his final remark, that 'on this basis all wickedness would be excusable', what of it? Wicked men are no less to be feared and no less dangerous when they are necessarily wicked. But on this point please see my Appendix to Books 1 and 2 of *Principia Cartesiana* demonstrated in geometric form, Part II, Chapter 8.[212]

Lastly, I should like your friend who raises these objections to tell me how he reconciles the human virtue that springs from free decision with God's preordainment. If he admits with Descartes that he does not know how to effect this reconciliation, then he is trying to hurl against me the weapon by which he himself is already transfixed. But to no purpose. If you will examine my view attentively, you will see that it is quite consistent.

The Hague
[October 1674]

---

[212] [The appendix to the PPC is entitled *Cogitata Metaphysica* (CM). CM2.8 is entitled, "Of the Will of God."]

LETTER 59

To the most distinguished and acute philosopher, B.d.S., from Ehrenfried Walther von Tschirnhaus

[Known only from the O.P. The original is lost.]

Most distinguished Sir,

When shall we have your Method of rightly directing the reason in acquiring knowledge of unknown truths, and also your General Treatise on Physics? I know that you have but recently made great advances in these subjects. I have already been made aware of the former, and the latter is known to me from the lemmata attached to the second part of your *Ethics*,[213] which provide a ready solution to many problems in physics. If time and opportunity permit, I humbly beg you to let me have the true definition of motion, together with its explanation. And since extension when conceived through itself is indivisible, immutable, etc., how can we deduce a priori the many and various forms that it can assume, and consequently the existence of figure in the particles of a body, which yet are various in any body and are different from the figures of the parts which constitute the form of another body?

In our conversation you pointed out to me the method you adopt in seeking out truths as yet unknown. I find this method to be of surpassing excellence, and yet quite simple, as far as I understand it; and I can say that by following this single procedure I have made considerable advances in mathematics. I would therefore like to have from you the true definition of an adequate, a true, a false, a fictitious and a doubtful idea. I have sought the difference between a true and an adequate idea, but as yet I have not been able to discover anything but this: on investigating a thing and a definite concept or idea, then (in order further to discover whether this true idea was also the adequate idea of some thing) I asked myself what was the cause of this idea or concept. On discovering this, I again asked what was the cause of this further concept, and thus I continued enquiring into the causes of the causes of ideas until I could come upon a cause for which I could not again see any other cause than this, that out of all possible ideas which I had at my command, this one alone also positively existed. If, for example, we ask wherein consists the true source of our errors, Descartes will reply that it consists in our giving assent to things not yet clearly perceived. But although this be a true idea of the matter in question, I shall still be unable to determine all that it is necessary to know on this subject unless I also possess an adequate idea of this mat-

---

[213] [These are the axioms, lemmata and definitions following E2P13, which deal with the principle of individuation as Spinoza conceives it and also offer a basic outline of Spinoza's physics.]

ter. To acquire this I again ask what is the cause of this concept—that is, why we give assent to things not clearly understood, and I reply that this comes about through our lack of knowledge. But at this point we cannot raise the further question as to what is the cause of our not knowing some things, and therefore I realise that I have discovered the adequate idea of our errors.

Here, incidentally, let me put this question to you. Since it is established that many things expressed in an infinite number of ways have an adequate idea of themselves, and that from any adequate idea all that can possibly be known of the thing can be inferred, though they can be more easily elicited from one idea than from another, is there any means of knowing which idea should be utilised in preference to another? For example, an adequate idea of a circle consists in the quality of its radii, but it also consists in the equality with one another of an infinite number of rectangles constructed from the segments of intersecting chords. One could go on and say that the adequate idea of a circle can be expressed in an infinite number of ways, each of which explicates the adequate nature of a circle. And although from each of these everything else knowable about a circle can be deduced, this comes about more easily from one idea than from another. So, too, one who considers the applicates of curves[214] will make many inferences concerning the measurements of curves, but this will be done more effectively if we consider tangents, etc.

In this way I have tried to give some indication of the progress I have made in this study. I await its completion, or if I am anywhere in error, its correction, and also the definition I have asked for. Farewell.

5 January 1675

Letter 60
To the noble and learned Ehrenfried Walther von Tschirnhaus, from B.d.S.

[Known only from the O.P. The original is lost.]

Most noble Sir,

Between a true and an adequate idea I recognise no difference but this, that the word 'true' has regard only to the agreement of the idea with its object (*ideatum*),

---

[214] [The method of exhaustion was the oldest method for measuring the area under a curve by evaluating the perimeter of polygons tangential to the curve as their sides increased until a limit was reached. The method of applicates (or ordinates) involved drawing lines at right angles across the curves so as to be bisected by their diameters. The method of exhaustion led to the integral calculus (developed by Leibniz and Newton), whereas that of applicates developed into co-ordinate geometry.]

whereas the word 'adequate' has regard to the nature of the idea in itself.[215] Thus there is no real difference between a true and an adequate idea except for this extrinsic relation.

Next, in order that I may know which out of many ideas of a thing will enable all the properties of the object to be deduced, I follow this one rule, that the idea or definition of the thing should express its efficient cause.[216] For example, in order to investigate the properties of a circle, I ask whether from the following idea of a circle, namely, that it consists in an infinite number of rectangles, I can deduce all its properties; that is to say, I ask whether this idea involves the efficient cause of a circle. Since this is not so, I look for another cause, namely, that a circle is the space described by a line of which one point is fixed and the other moveable. Since this definition now expresses the efficient cause, I know that I can deduce from it all the properties of a circle, etc. So, too, when I define God as a supremely perfect Being,[217] since this definition does not express the efficient cause (for I take it that an efficient cause can be internal as well as external), I shall not be able to extract therefrom all the properties of God, as I can do when I define God as a Being, etc. (see *Ethics*, Part 1, Definition 6).[218]

As for your other questions, namely, concerning motion, and those which concern method, since my views on these are not yet written out in due order, I reserve them for another occasion.

As to your remarks that he who considers the applicates of curves will make many deductions regarding the measurement of curves, but will find this easier by considering tangents, etc., I think, on the contrary, that the consideration of tangents will make it more difficult to deduce the many other properties than the consideration of a succession of applicates; and I assert absolutely that from certain properties of a thing (whatever be the given idea) some things can be discovered more easily and others with greater difficulty—though they all concern the nature of that thing. But this one point I consider should be kept in mind, that one must seek such an idea that everything can be elicited therefrom, as I have said above. For if one is to deduce from some thing all that is possible, it necessarily follows that the last will prove more difficult than the earlier, etc.

The Hague
[January 1675]

---

[215] [See E2Def4.]

[216] [From an axiomatic perspective, this claim amounts to the requirement that all definitions be constructive. Spinoza's understanding of geometrical construction follows closely that of Thomas Hobbes.]

[217] [Spinoza here gives his own reasons for rejecting this definition, used by Descartes (see the third Meditation). For Spinoza, the definition of a thing is that from which all the properties of that thing can be deduced. Cf. E1P8Schol2.]

[218] [E1Def6: "By God I mean an absolutely infinite being; that is, substance consisting of infinite attributes, each of which expresses eternal and infinite essence."]

LETTER 61
To the esteemed B.d.S., from Henry Oldenburg

[Known only from the O.P. The original is lost. The date, wrongly given in the Latin, is correctly given in the Dutch edition.]

With hearty greetings.

As the learned Mr. Bourgeois, Doctor of Medicine of Caen and an adherent of the reformed religion, is about to leave for Holland, I cannot let pass this convenient opportunity of letting you know that some weeks ago I expressed my gratitude to you for the Treatise you sent me (though it was never delivered), but that I have some doubt as to whether my letter duly reached you.[219] In that letter I indicated my opinion of the Treatise. This opinion, anyway, now that I have given more proper attention and thought to the matter, I have come to consider far too premature. At the time some things seemed to me to tend to the endangerment of religion, when I was assessing it by the standard set by the common run of theologians and the accepted formulae of the Creeds (which seem to me far too influenced by partisan bias). But on reconsidering the whole matter more closely, I find much that convinces me that, so far from intending any harm to true religion and sound philosophy, on the contrary you are endeavouring to commend and establish the true purpose of the Christian religion, together with the divine sublimity and excellence of a fruitful philosophy. So since I now believe this to be your set intention, I most earnestly beg you to be good enough to explain what you are now preparing and have in mind to this end, writing regularly to your old and sincere friend who wholeheartedly longs for a most successful outcome for such a divine undertaking. I promise on my sacred oath that I will divulge nothing of this to any mortal, if you enjoin silence on me, and that I will strive only for this, gradually to prepare the minds of good and wise men to embrace those truths which you will one day bring forth into the broader light of day, and to dispel the prejudices which have been conceived against your thoughts.

If I am not mistaken, I think you have a very profound insight into the nature and powers of the human mind, and its union with the body. I earnestly beg you to let me have your thoughts on this subject. Farewell, distinguished Sir, and continue to think well of the most devoted admirer of your teaching and your virtue, Henry Oldenburg.

London, 8 June 1675

---

[219] [There is no trace of this letter, presumably written in 1670 following the publication of the TTP.]

Letter 62
To the esteemed B.d.S., from Henry Oldenburg

[Known only from the O.P. The original is lost.]

Now that our epistolary intercourse has been so happily resumed, most esteemed Sir, I would not want to fail in the duty of a friend by any interruption in our correspondence. Since I understand from your reply dated 5 July[220] that it is your intention to publish the five-part Treatise of yours,[221] please allow me, out of your genuine affection for me, to advise you not to include in it anything that may seem in any way to undermine the practise of religious virtue. This I strongly urge because there is nothing our degenerate and wicked age looks for more eagerly than the kind of doctrines whose conclusions may appear to give encouragement to prevalent vices.

For the rest, I shall not decline to receive some copies of the said Treatise. I would only ask this of you, that in due course they should be addressed to a certain Dutch merchant staying in London, who will then have them sent to me. There would be no need to mention the fact that the particular books have been forwarded to me; for, provided that they reach me safely, I have no doubt that I shall easily arrange to distribute them among my various friends, and to obtain a fair price for them. Farewell, and when you have time, write back to,

Your most devoted,
Henry Oldenburg

London, 22 July 1675

---

[220] [This letter is unknown.]

[221] [In Ep28 (1665, to Bouwmeester), Spinoza's plans appear to have been to divide the *Ethics* into three parts. By 1675 its division was the fivefold one in which it was finally published after his death.]

Letter 63

To the distinguished and acute philosopher B.d.S., from G. H. Schuller

[The original is extant. The O.P. text is somewhat abridged. The translation is taken from the original.]

Most noble and distinguished Sir,

I should blush for my long spell of silence which has exposed me to the charge of ingratitude for the favour which, of your kindness, you have extended to my undeserving self, if I did not reflect that your generous courtesy inclines to excuse rather than accuse, and if I did not know that, for the common good of your friends, you are engaged in important studies such that it would be culpable and wrong to disturb without good cause. For this reason I have kept silent, being content meanwhile to learn from friends of your good health. But the purpose of this letter is to inform you that our noble friend Mr. von Tschirnhausen,[222] who is in England and still, like us, enjoying good health, has three times in his letters to me bidden me to convey to you, Sir, his dutiful regards and respectful greetings. He repeatedly asks me to put before you the following difficulties, and at the same time to ask for the reply he seeks from you.

Would you, Sir, please convince him by a positive proof,[223] and not by *reductio ad absurdum*, that we can not know any more attributes of God than thought and extension? Further, does it follow from this that creatures constituted by other attributes can not on their side have any idea of extension? If so, it would seem that there must be constituted as many worlds as there are attributes of God.[224] For example, our world of extension, to call it so, is of a certain size; there would exist worlds of that same size constituted by different attributes. And just as we perceive, apart from thought, only extension, so the creatures of those worlds must perceive nothing but their own world's attribute, and thought.

---

[222] [Ehrenfried Walther von Tschirnhaus (1651–1708) was a German count and a brilliant thinker. —M.L.M.]

[223] [Note printed in the O.P.: "I earnestly beg you please to solve the problems here raised, and to send me your reply."]

[224] [A common misinterpretation of Spinoza is to see each attribute as constituting a distinct world or substance, and this view has its historic roots in these remarks by Tschirnhaus. Part of the difficulty, however, lies in the incompleteness of Spinoza's own explanation of the nature of the attributes, and perhaps more has been written on this aspect of his metaphysics than on any other. It is common to distinguish a 'subjective' from an 'objective' interpretation of the attributes.]

Secondly, since God's intellect differs from our intellect both in essence and existence, it will therefore have nothing in common with our intellect, and therefore (Book 1, Proposition 3)[225] God's intellect cannot be the cause of our intellect.

Thirdly, in the Scholium to Proposition 10[226] you say that nothing in Nature is clearer than that each entity must be conceived under some attribute (which I understand very well), and that the more reality or being it has, the more attributes appertain to it. It would seem to follow from this that there are entities which have three, four, or more attributes, whereas from what has been demonstrated it could be inferred that each entity consists of only two attributes, namely, a certain attribute of God and the idea of that attribute.

Fourthly, I should like to have examples of those things immediately produced by God, and of those things produced by the mediation of some infinite modification. It seems to me that thought and extension are of the first kind, and of the latter kind, intellect in thought and motion in extension, etc.[227]

These are the questions, distinguished Sir, which our afore-mentioned Tschirnhausen joins with me in asking you to elucidate, if it should be that you have time to spare. He further relates that Mr. Boyle and Oldenburg had formed a very strange idea of your character. He has not only dispelled this, but has furthermore given them reasons that have induced them to return to a most worthy and favourable opinion of you, and also to hold in high esteem the *Tractatus Theologico-Politicus*. In view of your directions,[228] I did not venture to inform you of this.

Be assured that I am in all things at your service, and that I am, most noble Sir,

Your most devoted servant,
G. H. Schuller

Amsterdam, 25 July 1675

Mr. A. Gent[229] and J. Rieuw[230] send their dutiful greetings.

---

[225] [In its final form E1P3 says only that two substances having different attributes have nothing in common. E1P17Schol deals with the predication of 'intellect' to both finite modes and to God.]

[226] [E1P10Schol. The proposition asserts that each attribute must be conceived through itself.]

[227] [Note printed in the O.P.: "The face of the whole of Nature, which, although varying in infinite ways, always remains the same. See Part 2, Proposition 13, Scholium."]

[228] [Had Spinoza requested that Schuller and Tschirnhaus not speak about him or his works? This is also suggested in Ep70 and Ep72.]

[229] [We are unable to identify this man.]

[230] [Jan Rieuwertsz.]

Letter 64
To the learned and experienced G. H. Schuller, from B.d.S.

[Known only from the O.P. The original is lost.]

Most experienced Sir,

I am glad that you have at last found opportunity to favour me with one of your letters, always most welcome to me. I earnestly beg you to do so regularly..., etc.

And now to the questions you raise. To the first I say that the human mind can acquire knowledge only of those things which the idea of an actually existing body involves, or what can be inferred from this idea. For the power of any thing is defined solely by its essence (Prop. 7, Part III, *Ethics*),[231] and the essence of mind consists (Prop. 13, II)[232] solely in its being the idea of an actually existing body. Therefore the mind's power of understanding extends only as far as that which this idea of the body contains within itself, or which follows therefrom. Now this idea of the body involves and expresses no other attributes of God than extension and thought. For its ideate (*ideatum*), to wit, the body (Prop. 6, II) has God for its cause insofar as he is considered under the attribute of extension, and not under any other attribute. So (Ax. 6, I)[233] this idea of the body involves knowledge of God only insofar as he is considered under the attribute of extension. Again, this idea, insofar as it is a mode of thinking, also has God for its cause (same Prop.) insofar as he is a thinking thing, and not insofar as he is considered under any other attribute. Therefore (same Axiom) the idea of this idea involves knowledge of God insofar as he is considered under the attribute of thought, and not under any other attribute. It is thus clear that the human mind—i.e., the idea of the human body—involves and expresses no other attributes of God except these two. Now (by Prop. 10, II),[234] no other attribute[235] of God can be inferred or conceived from these two attributes, or from their affections. So I conclude that the human mind can

---

[231] [E3P7: "The conatus with which each thing endeavours to persist in its own being is nothing but the actual essence of the thing itself."]

[232] [E2P13: "The object of the idea constituting the human mind is the body—i.e., a definite mode of extension actually existing, and nothing else."]

[233] [E1Ax6: "A true idea must agree with its ideate."]

[234] [E2P10: "The being of substance does not pertain to the essence of man; i.e., substance does not constitute the form of man."]

[235] [Spinoza speaks in the opening definitions and propositions of E1 of an "infinity of infinite attributes." Though he cannot speak of the *number* of attributes as infinite, this is because his concept of number is finitary. E1P9 clearly requires that the attributes be infinite in number in the modern (transfinite) sense of this term.]

attain knowledge of no other attribute of God than these two, which was the point at issue. With regard to your further question as to whether there must therefore be constituted as many worlds as there are attributes, I refer you to the Scholium on Prop. 7, II of the *Ethics*.[236]

Moreover, this proposition could be more easily demonstrated by *reductio ad absurdum*, a style of proof I usually prefer to the other in the case of a negative proposition, as being more appropriate to the character of such propositions. But you ask for a positive proof only, and so I pass on to the second question, which asks whether, when both their essence and existence are different, one thing can be produced from another, seeing that things that differ thus from one another appear to have nothing in common. I reply that since all particular things, except those that are produced by like things, differ from their causes both in essence and existence, I see no difficulty here. As to the sense in which I understand God to be the efficient cause of both the essence and existence of things, I think I have made this quite clear in the Scholium and Corollary to Prop. 25, I of the *Ethics*.[237]

The axiom in the Scholium to Prop. 10, I, as I have indicated towards the end of the said Scholium, derives from the idea we have of an absolutely infinite Entity, and not from the fact that there are, or may be, entities having three, four, or more attributes.[238]

Lastly, the examples you ask for of the first kind are: in the case of thought, absolutely infinite intellect; in the case of extension, motion and rest. An example of the second kind is the face of the whole universe, which, although varying in infinite ways, yet remains always the same. See Scholium to Lemma 7 preceding Prop. 14, II.[239]

Thus, most excellent Sir, I think I have answered your objections and those of our friend. If you think there still remains any difficulty, I hope you will not hesitate to tell me, so that I may remove it if I can. Farewell, etc.

The Hague, 29 July 1675

---

[236] [E2P7 is the famous proposition expressing the parallelism: "The order and connection of ideas is the same as the order and connection of things."]

[237] [E1P25 states that God is efficient cause both of the existence and the essence of things.]

[238] [E1P10Schol in fact denies Tschirnhaus' interpretation of an infinity of attributes as constitutive of an infinity of entities.]

[239] [E2P13Schol, Spinoza does not use the expression, 'face of the entire universe', but speaks of conceiving the whole of nature as one infinite individual whose parts vary in infinite ways without any change in nature itself. Motion-and-rest and infinite intellect are called immediate infinite modes (of extension and thought respectively), but it is curious that Spinoza gives an example only for extension of an infinite mediate mode.]

Letter 65
To the acute and learned philosopher B.d.S., from Ehrenfried Walther von Tschirnhaus

[Known only from the O.P. The original is lost.]

Most esteemed Sir,

Will you please let me have a proof of your assertion that the soul can not perceive any more attributes of God than extension and thought. Although I can understand this quite clearly, yet I think that the contrary can be deduced from the Scholium to Prop. 7, Part II of the *Ethics*, perhaps only because I do not sufficiently perceive the correct meaning of this Scholium. I have therefore resolved to explain how I come to this conclusion, earnestly begging you, esteemed Sir, to come to my aid with your customary courtesy wherever I do not rightly follow your meaning.

My position is as follows. Although I do indeed gather from your text that the world is one, it is also no less clear therefrom that the world is expressed in infinite modes, and that therefore each single thing is expressed in infinite modes. Hence it seems to follow that, although the particular modification which constitutes my mind and the particular modification which expresses my body are one and the same modification, this is expressed in infinite modes—in one mode through thought, in another through extension, in a third through some attribute of God unknown to me, and so on to infinity. For there are infinite attributes of God, and the order and connection of their modifications seems to be the same in all cases. Hence there now arises the question as to why the mind, which represents a particular modification—which same modification is expressed not only by extension but by infinite other modes—why, I ask, does the mind perceive only the particular modification expressed through extension, that is, the human body, and not any other expression through other attributes?

But time does not permit me to pursue this subject any further. Perhaps these difficulties will all be removed by continued reflection.

London, 12 August 1675

Letter 66
To the noble and learned Ehrenfried Walther von Tschirnhaus, from B.d.S.

[Known only from the O.P. The original is lost.]

Most noble Sir,

... However, in reply to your objection, I say that although each thing is expressed in infinite modes in the infinite intellect of God, the infinite ideas in which it is expressed cannot constitute one and the same mind of a particular thing, but an infinity of minds. For each of these infinite ideas has no connection with the others, as I have explained in that same Scholium to Proposition 7, Part II of the *Ethics*,[240] and as is evident from Prop. 10, Part I.[241] If you will give a little attention to these, you will see that no difficulty remains, etc.

The Hague, 18 August 1675

Letter 67
To the learned and acute B.d.S., from Alfred Burgh

[Known only from the O.P. The original is lost.]

Many greetings.

On leaving my country I promised to write to you, should anything worthy of note occur during my journey. Since such an occasion has now arisen, and one of the greatest importance, I am discharging my debt. I have to tell you that, through God's infinite mercy, I have been brought back to the Catholic Church and have been made a member thereof. As to how this came about, you will be able to learn in more detail from the letter I have sent to the illustrious and wise Mr. Craenen, Professor at Leiden. I will here add these few remarks which have regard to your own good.

The more I have admired you in the past for the penetration and acuity of your mind, the more do I now moan and lament for you. For although you are a man

---

[240] [The brevity of Spinoza's answer to Tschirnhaus ignores the fact that Spinoza himself writes, at the end of E2P7Schol, "For the present, I cannot give a clearer explanation."]

[241] [E1P10: "Each attribute of substance must be conceived through itself."]

of outstanding talent, with a mind on which God has bestowed splendid gifts, a lover of truth and indeed a most eager one, yet you allow yourself to be entrapped and deceived by that most wretched and arrogant Prince of evil spirits. For what does all your philosophy amount to, except sheer illusion and chimera? Yet you entrust to it not only your peace of mind in this life, but the eternal salvation of your soul. See on what a poor foundation is grounded all that is yours. You claim to have finally discovered the true philosophy. How do you know that your philosophy is the best out of all those that have ever been taught in this world, are at present being taught, or will ever be taught in the future? To say nothing of possible future philosophies, have you examined all those philosophies, throughout the entire world? And even if you have examined them properly, how do you know that you have chosen the best? You will say, my philosophy is in agreement with right reason, while the rest are opposed to it. But all other philosophers except for your followers disagree with you, and with the same right they claim for themselves and their philosophy exactly what you claim for yours, and accuse you of falsity and error just as you do them. It is therefore clear that, to make manifest the truth of your philosophy, you have to propound arguments which are not shared by other philosophies but are peculiar to your own; otherwise it must be admitted that your philosophy is as unsure and as futile as all the others.

However, I shall now confine myself to your book, to which you have given that impious title, and in this I shall make no distinction between your philosophy and your theology since you yourself do in fact confuse one with the other, though with diabolical cunning you pretend to claim that they are distinct from one another and that they have different principles. I proceed as follows.

Perhaps you will say, others have not read Holy Scripture as many times as I, and it is from Holy Scripture itself, the recognition of whose authority constitutes the difference between Christians and other peoples of the whole world, that I prove my case. But how? I explain Holy Scripture, you say, by placing the clear passages side by side with the more obscure, and by this method of interpretation I reach my conclusions, or confirm those that are already formed in my brain. I beseech you to think carefully what you are saying. For how do you know that you are making correct use of that comparison, and again, that the comparison even when properly made suffices to interpret Holy Scripture and thus allows you to make a correct interpretation of Holy Scripture? Especially since Catholics say—and this is very true—that the entire Word of God was not committed to writing, and thus Holy Scripture cannot be explained through Holy Scripture alone, I will not say by one man, but even by the Church itself, which is the sole interpreter of Holy Scripture. For the Apostolic traditions, too, must be taken into account, as is proved from Holy Scripture itself and the testimony of the Holy Fathers, and as is also in accord both with right reason and with experience. Now since the principle you adopt is utterly false, leading to perdition, where stands all your teaching, based and built as it is on this false foundation?

So then, if you believe in Christ crucified, acknowledge your most evil heresy, regain your senses after this distortion of your true nature, and be reconciled with the Church.

In what way does the method you use to prove your teachings differ from that which all heretics who have ever left the Church of God, are now leaving it, or will ever leave it, have used, are using, or will use? For, like you, they all adopt the same principle, that is, they rely on Holy Scripture alone to form and lend weight to their doctrines.

Do not be beguiled because maybe the Calvinists or so-called Reformers, or the Lutherans or the Mennonites or the Socinians, etc., cannot refute your doctrine. For these, as I have said, are in the same hapless plight as you, and sit under the shadow of death.

But if you do not believe in Christ, you are more wretched than I can say. Yet there is an easy remedy; turn away from your sins, try to realise the deadly arrogance of your wretched, insane way of reasoning. You do not believe in Christ; why is this? You will say, because the teaching and life of Christ does not agree with my principles, and the teaching of Christians about Christ does not agree with my teaching. But again I say, do you then dare to think yourself greater than all those who have ever arisen in the State or the Church of God, the patriarchs, prophets, apostles, martyrs, doctors, confessors and virgins, the countless saints, and even, blasphemously, our Lord Jesus Christ himself? Do you alone surpass then in doctrine, in manner of life, and in all else? Will you, a sorry little creature, a vile little worm of the earth, nay, mere ashes and food for worms, in your unspeakable blasphemy claim pre-eminence over the Incarnate Infinite Wisdom of the Eternal Father? Will you alone think yourself wiser and greater than all who have ever been in the Church of God from the beginning of the world, and have believed, or even now believe, in the Christ to come, or in the Christ who has already come? On what foundation rests this arrogance of yours, so rash, so mad, to be deplored and execrated?

You deny that Christ is the son of the living God, the Word of the Father's eternal wisdom, made manifest in the flesh, and that he suffered and was crucified for mankind. Why? Because all this is not in harmony with your principles. But apart from the fact that it is now proved that your principles are not true, but false, rash, and absurd, I now say further that even if you relied on true principles and built all your philosophy on them, you could not any the more explain through them all those things that are in the world, have happened or are happening, nor could you brazenly assert, when something appears to be in contradiction with those principles, that this is therefore impossible in actuality, or false. For there are very many things, innumerable things, which, even if there is some degree of certainty in our knowledge of natural things, you will never be able to explain, nor even to remove the obvious contradiction there is between such phenomena and your explanations of the rest, explanations which you regard as most certain. From your principles you will never give a satisfactory explanation of the things done in witchcraft, and in spells simply by the utterance of certain words, or by merely carrying on one's person those words or inscriptions marked out on some material, or of the amazing behaviours shown by those possessed by demons. Of all these I have seen various examples, and I am well acquainted with the indubitable testimony of many trustworthy persons in countless such cases, who speak with one voice.

How can you reach conclusions regarding the essences of all things, granted that some ideas in your mind do adequately agree with the essences of those things of which they are the ideas? For you can never be sure whether ideas of all created things are there in the human mind naturally, or whether many of them, if not all, can be produced in the mind, and are in fact produced, by external objects, and even through the agency of good or evil spirits, and through clear divine revelation. How, then, while disregarding the testimony and experience of other men, to say nothing about submitting your judgment to the divine omnipotence—can you from your principles define precisely and establish with certainty the actual existence or non-existence, the possibility or impossibility of existence, of the following things (that is, that they actually exist or not, or that they may exist or not, in Nature)—a divining rod for detecting metals and underground waters, the stone sought by the alchemists, the power of words and inscriptions, apparitions of various spirits, both good and evil, and their power, skill, and ability to possess people, the restoration of plants and flowers in a glass jar after they have been burned, sirens, the frequent appearance of little men in mines, as is reported, the antipathies and sympathies of so many things, the impenetrability of a human body, and so on? No, my philosopher, even if you were gifted above others with a mind a thousand times more subtle and acute than that which you possess, you would not be able to account for any of these things. And if in passing judgment on these and like matters you are relying solely on your intellect, then assuredly you are now adopting the same attitude to those matters which are beyond your knowledge and understanding, and which you therefore regard as impossible, and which in truth you ought to regard as unsubstantiated only until you are convinced by the testimony of numerous trustworthy witnesses. Yours is the way, I imagine, that Julius Caesar would have thought if someone had told him that a powder can be manufactured, and would become common in future ages, whose power could be so effective that it would blow up castles, entire cities, even the very mountains, and which, being confined in any place, when ignited would expand in an extraordinary way, shattering everything that might impede its action. Julius Caesar would never have believed this; he would have laughed this man to scorn, as one seeking to convince him of something contrary to his own judgment, his experience, and his supreme military knowledge.

But let us return to our theme. If you have no understanding of the things aforementioned and cannot judge of them, why will you, wretched man swollen with diabolical pride, rashly judge of the awesome mysteries of the life and passion of Christ, which Catholic teachers themselves declare to be beyond our understanding? Why will you keep on raving, with your idle and futile chatter on the subject of the countless miracles and signs which, after Christ, his apostles and disciples and thereafter many thousands of saints have performed through the omnipotent power of God in witness to and confirmation of the truth of the Catholic Faith, and which, through that same omnipotent mercy and goodness of God, occur even in our day in countless numbers throughout the whole world? And if you cannot contradict these, as you certainly cannot, why do you keep on with your clamour? Surrender, turn away from your errors and sins; put on humility, and be born again.

But furthermore, let us come down to the question of factual truth, which is the real foundation of the Christian religion. How will you dare deny, if you give it proper attention, the import of the consensus of so many myriads of men, some thousands of whom have vastly surpassed you, and do now surpass you, in doctrine, in learning, in solidity that is truly subtle, and in the perfection of their lives? Unanimously, with a single voice, they all affirm that Christ, the incarnate Son of the living God, suffered, was crucified, and died for the sins of mankind, rose again, was transfigured, and reigns in heaven as God along with the eternal Father in unison with the Holy Spirit. And other things relating to this they also affirm, that by the same Lord Jesus, and later in his name by the Apostles and the rest of the saints, through the omnipotent power of God countless miracles have been wrought in the Church of God, and are still being wrought, which not only exceed human understanding but are opposed to ordinary sense. (Even to this day there remain innumerable material indications of them and visible signs scattered far and wide throughout the world.) Taking your line, might I not deny that there ever were ancient Romans in the world, and that the Emperor Julius Caesar suppressed their free republic and changed their government to monarchy? Of course, I would be taking no account of the many monuments that meet our eyes, which time has bequeathed us in witness of Roman power, or again of the testimony of all those weighty authors who have written histories of the Roman republic and monarchy, and in particular those that relate the many deeds of Julius Caesar. I would be taking no account of the judgment of so many thousands of men who have either seen for themselves the said monuments, or have believed, and still believe, in their existence (this being vouched for by countless witnesses) just as much as in the said histories. And on what grounds? That last night I had dreamed that the monuments surviving from the time of the Romans are not real things but mere illusions, and likewise that the stories told of the Romans are just like those childish stories told in books called romances about Amadis de Galliis and heroes of that sort; and also that Julius Caesar either never existed in the world or, if he existed, was a man of melancholic temperament who did not really crush the freedom of the Romans and raise himself to the throne of imperial majesty, but was led to believe that he had accomplished these mighty deeds by his own foolish imagination or by the persuasion of flattering friends. Again, might I not in like manner deny that the kingdom of China was occupied by the Tartars, that Constantinople is the seat of the Turkish Empire, and any number of such things? If I were to deny these things, would anyone think me in control of my senses, or regard me as other than a pitiable case of madness? For all these matters are based on the consensus of belief of several thousands of men, and therefore their certainty is indubitable, since it is impossible that all who make these assertions, and indeed many more assertions, have deceived themselves, or have deliberately deceived others for so many centuries in succession—indeed, for the many centuries that stretch from the world's earliest years right up to the present day.

Consider, secondly, that the Church of God, continuing an uninterrupted existence from the beginning of the world right up to this day, persists unmoved and stable, whereas all other religions, pagan or heretical, have had at least a later beginning, if not already an end, and the same must be said of royal dynasties and the opinions of all philosophers whatever.

Consider, thirdly, that through the advent of Christ in the flesh the Church of God was advanced from the religion of the Old Testament to that of the New Testament, and was founded by Christ himself, Son of the living God, and thereafter was continued by the apostles and their disciples and successors. These were men regarded by the world as untaught, who yet confounded all philosophers, although they taught a Christian doctrine opposed to ordinary sense, exceeding and transcending all human reasoning. They were regarded by the world as abject, lowly, of humble birth, unassisted by the power of early kings or princes; on the contrary, they endured from them every form of persecution, and suffered all other worldly adversities. The more the most powerful Roman Emperors exerted themselves to hinder and indeed to suppress their work, putting to death with every form of martyrdom as many Christians as they could, the more that work flourished. Thus in a short space of time the Church of Christ spread throughout the world, and finally, with the conversion to the Christian faith of the Roman Emperor himself and the Kings and Princes of Europe, the Ecclesiastical Hierarchy attained to that vastness of power such as we may admire today. All this was done through charity, gentleness, patience, trust in God, and the other Christian virtues (and not by the clash of arms, the violence of mighty armies, and the devastation of territories, which is the way that worldly Princes extend their boundaries), and, according to Christ's promise, the gates of Hell did not prevail against the Church. Here, too, ponder over the frightful and unspeakably stern punishment which has reduced the Jews to the ultimate degree of wretchedness and disaster because they were responsible for the crucifixion of Christ. Read through, consider again and again the histories of all the ages, and you will not find there the faintest suggestion of anything like this occurring in the case of any other association.

Observe, in the fourth place, that there are included in the nature of the Catholic church, and in fact inseparable from that church, the following characteristics; its antiquity, whereby, succeeding to the Jewish religion, which was at that time the true religion, it reckons its beginning from Christ sixteen and a half centuries ago, throughout which time it traces an uninterrupted line of succession of Pastors, so that as a result this Church alone possesses sacred and divine books, pure and uncorrupted, along with the equally sure and immaculate tradition of the unwritten Word of God. Next, its immutability, whereby its teaching, and the ministering of the Sacraments just as was ordained by Christ himself and the Apostles, is preserved inviolate and, as is agreed, in full vigour. Next, its infallibility, whereby it determines and decides all things pertaining to the Faith with supreme authority, sureness and truth, in accordance with the power bestowed on it to this end by Christ himself, and the guidance of the Holy Spirit, whose bride the Church is. Next, its status as above reform, for since it cannot be corrupted or be deceived or deceive others, it obviously can never stand in need of reform. Next, its unity, whereby all its members hold the same beliefs, teach the same faith, have one and the same altar and all the Sacraments in common, and finally, are united by mutual obedience to pursue one and the same end. Next, the inseparability of any soul from the Church, on any pretext whatsoever, without its immediately incurring eternal damnation, unless it be re-united to the Church before death by repentance. This makes it clear that all heresies are a deviation from the Church, whereas the Church remains ever consistent with itself and firmly based, in as much as it is built on a Rock. Next, its vast extension, whereby it is spread throughout the world, and visibly so. This cannot be affirmed of any other association, schismatic, heretical or pagan, or of any political government or philosophical doctrine, just as neither is it true that any of the said characteristics of the Catholic Church belong to, or can belong to, any other association. And finally, its continued duration to the end of the world, which was assured for it by the Way, the Truth and the Life,[242] and which is also clearly demonstrated by recognition of all the said characteristics, likewise promised to it and granted by the same Christ through the Holy Spirit.

In the fifth place, reflect that the admirable order by which the Church, a body of such immensity, is guided and governed, clearly shows that it has a very special dependence on God's Providence, and that its administration is wonderfully arranged, protected and guided by the Holy Spirit, in the same way that the harmony discerned in all the arrangements of this universe points to the Omnipotence, Wisdom and Infinite Providence which created all things, and still preserves them. In the case of no other association is there preserved such an order, so beautiful, so close-knit and uninterrupted.

In the sixth place, consider that apart from the fact that innumerable Catholics of both sexes (of whom there are still many about today, some of whom I myself have seen and know) have lived admirable and holy lives, and through the omnipotent power of God have wrought many miracles in the worshipful name of Jesus Christ, and also that every day there still take place instantaneous conversions of very many people from a wicked life to a better, truly Christian and holy life—consider, I say, that Catholics as a class are the more humble as they are more holy and perfect, and think themselves less worthy, and assign to others the praise for a more holy life. Even the greatest sinners still constantly retain a proper respect for sacred things, confess their own wickedness, rebuke their own vices and imperfections, and desire to be freed from these and to correct themselves. So it can be said that the most perfect heretic or philosopher that ever was can scarcely deserve to rank with the least perfect Catholics. Hence it is also clear, and most evidently follows, that the Catholic teaching is the wisest, and admirable in its profundity—in a word, it is superior to all the other teachings of this world, in that it makes men to be better than all others belonging to any association whatsoever, and teaches and communicates to them the sure way to peace of mind in this life, and to the attainment of eternal salvation of the soul thereafter.

In the seventh place, give earnest heed to the public confessions of the many heretics hardened by their obstinacy, and of philosophers of the greatest weight.

---

[242] [See John 14:6.]

These, on receiving the Catholic faith, have at last seen and realised that beforehand they were wretched, blind and ignorant—nay, foolish and mad—when, swollen with pride and inflated with their windy arrogance, they wrongly convinced themselves that they far surpassed others in the perfection of their doctrine, their learning, and their lives. Of these some thereafter lived most holy lives and left behind them the record of countless miracles, while others went to their martyrdom eagerly and with the utmost joy. Some, among whom was the Divine Augustine, even became the most discerning, profound, wise, and therefore most valuable teachers of the Church—indeed, its very pillars.

And finally, in the seventh place, reflect on the wretched and uneasy lives of atheists, though they may sometimes put on a very cheerful appearance and try to present themselves as living a joyful life, completely at peace in their hearts. Have regard especially to their most unhappy and horrifying death, of which I myself have seen many instances and am equally certain of many others—innumerable others—from other men's accounts and from history. Learn from their example to be wise in time.

Thus you see, or at least I hope you see, how rash you are to put your trust in the opinions formed by your brain. (For if Christ is the true God and at the same time man, as is most certain, see to what you are reduced. By persisting in your abominable errors and in your grievous sins, what else do you expect but eternal damnation? Reflect for yourself how horrifying this is.) Think how little reason you have to scoff at the whole world except your wretched adorers, how foolishly proud and puffed up you have become by the thought of the superiority of your talent and by men's admiration of your vain—indeed, utterly false and impious—doctrine, how basely you make yourself more wretched than the very beasts by doing away with your own freedom of will. And even if you really did not experience and acknowledge your freedom of will, yet how could you have deluded yourself into thinking that your opinions deserve the highest praise, and even rigorous imitation?

If you do not wish (banish the thought) that God or your neighbour should have pity on you, do you yourself at least have pity on your own plight, whereby you are endeavouring to make yourself more wretched than you now are, or even more wretched in the future if you continue in this way.

Come to your senses, philosopher, acknowledge the folly of your wisdom, and that your wisdom is madness. Practise humility instead of pride, and you will be healed. Pray to Christ in the Most Holy Trinity, that he may see fit to take pity on your plight and receive you. Read the Holy Fathers and the Doctors of the Church, and they will instruct you as to what to do so as not to perish, but to have eternal life. Consult Catholics who are deeply learned in their faith and of good life, and they will tell you many things that you have never known, and that will amaze you.

I have written you this letter with a truly Christian purpose, firstly, that you may know the love I bear you, Gentile though you be; and secondly, to ask you not to persist in ruining others as well as yourself.

I will therefore conclude thus: God wishes to snatch your soul from eternal damnation, if only you wish it. Do not hesitate to obey the Lord who, having called you so many times through others, is now calling you perhaps for the last time through me, one who, having achieved this grace from the ineffable mercy of God himself, wholeheartedly prays for the same for you. Do not refuse it; for if you will not hearken now to God when he calls you, the wrath of our Lord will be kindled against you, and you risk being abandoned by his Infinite Mercy to become the hapless victim of the Divine Justice that is all-consuming in its wrath. May Almighty God avert this to the greater glory of his Name and the salvation of your soul, and also as a salutary example to be imitated by your many most unhappy followers, through our Lord and Saviour Jesus Christ, who with the Eternal Father lives and reigns in unison with the Holy Spirit, God for ages without end. Amen.

Florence, 3 September 1675

Letter 67A
A letter from Nicholas Steno to the Reformer of the New Philosophy, concerning the true philosophy

> [This letter was printed in Florence in 1675. The original is not extant. There is no doubt that it was intended for Spinoza, referred to as the 'Reformer of the New Philosophy'. The book referred to is clearly the Tractatus Theologico-Politicus.]

I observe that in your book[243] (of which others have told me you are the author, and this I also suspect for various reasons) your overriding concern is with public security, or rather, with your own security, which according to you is the aim of public security; and yet you have advocated measures that are opposed to this desired security, while altogether neglecting that part of yourself whose security should have been your prime objective. That you have chosen measures opposed to the security you seek is apparent from this, that while public peace is what you seek, you are creating complete confusion, and while aiming to free yourself from all danger, you are exposing yourself quite unnecessarily to the gravest danger. That you have entirely disregarded that part of yourself which should have been your chief concern is clear from this, that you concede to all men the right to think and say about God whatever they please, provided it is not such as to destroy the obedience due, according to you, not so much to God as to man. This is the same as to confine the entire good of man within the bounds of the goods of civil government, that is, the goods of the body. And to say that you reserve the care of the soul for philosophy does nothing to advance your case, for two reasons; your phi-

---

[243] [Clearly the TTP is intended.]

losophy treats of the soul through a system framed from suppositions, and furthermore you abandon those unfit for your philosophy to a way of life just like that of automata destitute of soul, born with a body only.

Since I see shrouded in such darkness a man who was once my good friend, and even now, I hope, not unfriendly to me (for I am persuaded that the memory of our former close relationship still preserves a mutual love) and since I remember how I too was once entangled, if not in exactly the same errors, yet errors of a most serious kind, the more the gravity of the dangers from which I escaped makes evident God's mercy towards me, the more I am moved by compassion for you to pray for the same heavenly grace for you which was vouchsafed me, not through my own deserts but solely through Christ's goodness. And, to add deeds to prayers, I offer myself as most ready to examine along with you all those arguments which you may be pleased to examine as to how one may discover and hold fast the true way to true security. And although your writings show you to be far removed from the truth, yet the love of peace and truth which I once perceived in you and is not yet extinguished in your darkness affords me some hope that you will give a ready hearing to our Church, provided that you are given a sufficient explanation as to what she promises to all, and what she provides for those who are willing to come to her.

As to the first, the Church promises to all a true security, an eternal security, or the abiding peace which is the accompaniment of infallible truth, and at the same time offers the means necessary for the attainment of so great a good—first, sure forgiveness for ill deeds; second, a most perfect standard for right action; third, a true practical perfection of all occupations in accordance with this standard. And this it offers not only to the learned or those endowed with subtle intellect and who are free from the distractions of business, but to all without distinction, of every age, sex and condition. Lest this should move you to wonder, know that while there is indeed required of the convert active cooperation as well as non-resistance, yet these things come to pass through the inward working of him who pronounces the outward word through visible members of the Church. And although he tells the convert that he must grieve for his sins in the eyes of God and must display before the eyes of men works that sufficiently mark this repentance, and that he must believe certain things about God, body and soul, etc., his intended meaning is not that the penitent has only his own strength in essaying these tasks. For nothing else is required of the penitent but that he should not refuse his assent and co-operation in doing and believing these things, which alone is within his power, since to will these things, and having willed them to do them, depends on the Spirit of Christ which anticipates, accompanies and perfects your co-operation. If you have not yet understood this, I am not surprised, and it is not my present objective—indeed, it is not within my capacity—to get you to understand these things. However, lest these things should appear to you entirely divorced from reason, I shall give you a brief outline of the form of Christian government, as far as this can be done by a new dweller in that state, or rather by a stranger who still tarries on the lowest benches.

The aim of this government is that man should direct not only his outward actions but also his most secret thoughts according to the order established by the author of our universe; or, what amounts to the same thing, that the soul in its every action should look to God as its author and judge. In this regard the life of every man who is tainted by sin can be divided into four stages. The first stage is one in which a man performs all his actions as if his thoughts were not subject to any judge, and this is the condition of men who are either not yet cleansed by baptism or are hardened in sin after baptism. This stage is sometimes called blindness, because the soul takes no account of God who beholds it, as when it is said in Wisdom 2, "Their wickedness blinded them";[244] sometimes it is called death, because the soul lies hidden as if buried within the pleasures that pass away, and it is in this sense that Christ said, "Let the dead bury their dead,"[245] and many other things of that sort. Nor is it inconsistent with this condition to discourse at length, and often truly, of God and the soul; but since he treats of these subjects as of things remote or external to him, this results in perpetual doubts concerning them, many contradictory ideas, and frequently occurring lapses if not in external works, at any rate in thought; and this because his soul, deprived of the spirit that lends life to action, is moved like a dead thing by every breeze of desire. The second stage is when a man, ceasing to resist the word of God, either external or internal, begins to heed his call. Recognising by the beam of this supernatural light that in his opinions there is much that is false, in his actions much that is wrong, he gives himself wholly to God who, administering to him his Sacraments through his servants, bestows on him under visible signs an invisible grace. This stage of those who are born again is called infancy and childhood, and the word of God preached to them is compared with milk. The third grade is when, through the continual exercise of virtue by mastering its desires, the mind is made ready for a proper understanding of the mysteries concealed in the sacred letters. These are not grasped by the soul until with a heart now clean it reaches the fourth stage, when it begins to see God and attains the wisdom of the perfect. And here there is the perpetual uniting of the will, sometimes of a mystical kind, of which there exist many examples among us even today.

So the entire established order of Christianity is directed to this end, that the soul may be taken from a state of death to a state of life, that is, that the soul which beforehand had its mind's eyes turned away from God and fixed on error should now turn its eyes away from all error and fix them steadfastly on God in all its actions of body and mind, willing and not willing whatever its author, the author of the entire order, wills and does not will. So if you will make a thorough investigation of all the facts, you will find in Christianity alone a true philosophy, teaching of God what is worthy of God, and of man what is proper to man, and guiding its adherents to true perfection in all their actions.

As for the second point, only the Catholic Church fulfils all its promises to whose who do not fight against it, for only the Catholic Church has produced perfect examples of virtue in every age, and still today, in persons of every age, sex and condition, it is preparing what posterity must venerate. And one may not

---

[244] [See Wisdom 2:21.]

[245] [See Matthew 8:22; cf. also Luke 9:60.]

doubt its good faith in promising eternal security, seeing that it is furnishing means ancillary to this end in a miraculous way, all with the utmost fidelity. I have not yet completed my fourth year in the Church, and yet I have already seen such examples of sanctity that I must truly exclaim with David, "Thy testimonies are very sure."[246] I say nothing of bishops, I say nothing of priests, whose words heard by me in friendly intercourse, as I would testify with my own blood, were human symbols of the divine spirit, such a blameless life do they evince, such forceful eloquence. Nor shall I name the many who have embraced a way of life under the strictest rules, of whom the same could be said. I shall merely adduce examples of two kinds, one of persons converted from a most evil to a most holy way of life, the other of simple folk, as you would call them, who nevertheless without any studying have acquired the highest conceptions of God at the feet of the crucified one. Of this kind I am acquainted with some whose occupation is with the mechanical arts, bound to servile tasks, both men and women, who through the practise of the godly virtues have been raised to an understanding of the wondrous nature of God and the soul, whose life is holy, their words divine, and their deeds not infrequently miraculous, such as foretelling the future and other things which I omit for brevity's sake.

I know what objections you can raise to miracles, nor do we put our trust solely in miracles; but when we see the result of a miracle to be the perfect conversion of a soul from vice to virtue, we rightly ascribe this to the author of all virtues. For I regard as the greatest of all miracles that those who have spent thirty, forty years or more in the full gratification of their desires should in a moment of time turn away from all wickedness and become the most holy examples of virtue, such as I have seen with my own eyes and embraced with my own hands as they often moved me and others to tears of joy. There is no God like our God. Surely, if you study past history, if you study the present state of the Church, not in the books of our adversaries nor from those who are either dead among us or at any rate have not yet matured beyond childhood, but, as you would do in studying any other doctrine, from those whom your own people avow to be true Catholics, you will see that the Church has always stood by its promises and continues to do so to this day, and you will find there such proof of credibility as will satisfy you, especially since your sentiments concerning the Pope of Rome are much milder than those of our other adversaries, and you admit the necessity of good works. But do please examine our case from our own writings, as your own teachings regarding the strength of prejudice will readily persuade you to do.

I would gladly have instanced the passages of Scripture which assign authority to the Pope, which you deny for no other reason than that you do not find it so stated in the Scriptures, nor do you grant that the Christian commonwealth is like that of the Jews. But because your view on the interpretation of Scripture differs from our teaching which assigns this solely to the Church, I pass over this argument on this occasion, and I say, in the second place, that Christian government, whose one aim is the unity of the Faith, the Sacraments and Charity, admits only

---

[246] [See Psalms 93:5.]

of one head, whose authority consist not in making arbitrary innovations—which our adversaries falsely allege—but in ensuring that matters belonging to the divine right, or necessary matters, remain always unchanged, while matters belonging to human right, or indifferent matters, may be changed as the Church shall judge with good cause to be expedient—for example, if it should see that the wicked are misusing different things for the subversion of the necessary. Hence, in interpreting Holy Scripture and in determining the dogmas of the Faith, its object is the preservation of the dogmas and interpretations handed down by God through the Apostles, and the proscription of innovative and merely human dogmas. I shall not speak of other matters subject to its authority, since the uniformity of belief and action so often taught by Christ is enough to show you the point of monarchic rule.

So if you are guided by true love of virtue, if you delight in the perfection of actions, make a thorough search of all the societies there are in the world, and nowhere else will you find that the pursuit of perfection is undertaken with such zeal, crowned with such success, as with us; and this argument by itself can serve you as a demonstration that truly "this is the finger of God."[247]

But to recognise this more readily, probe into your own self and scrutinise your soul; for a thorough investigation will show you that it is dead. You concern yourself with matter in motion as if the moving cause were absent or non-existent. For it is a religion of bodies, not of souls, that you are advocating, and in the love of one's neighbour you discern actions necessary for the preservation of the individual and the propagation of the species, whereas you pay very little or no regard to those actions whereby we acquire knowledge and love of our author. You believe that all others, too, are dead like you, you who deny to all the light of grace because you have not experienced it yourself, and you think there is no certainty except of a demonstrative kind, unaware as you are of the certainty of faith which surpasses all demonstrations. As for that demonstrative certainty of yours, within what narrow bounds is it enclosed! Scrutinise, I pray, all those demonstrations of yours and bring me just one which shows how the thinking thing and the extended thing are united, how the moving principle is united with the body that is moved. But why do I ask for demonstrations of these matters from you who cannot even give me a likely explanation of their modes, so that without the help of suppositions you cannot explain the sensation of pleasure or pain, nor the emotion of love and hatred. So the entire philosophy of Descartes, however diligently examined and reformed by you, cannot explain to me in demonstrative form even this single phenomenon, how the impact of matter on matter is perceived by a soul united to matter. But with regard to matter itself, I ask, what knowledge do you give us except for a mathematical assessment of quantity in respect of figures which are not yet proved to consist of any kind of particles, except hypothetically? What is more divorced from reason than to deny the divine words of one whose divine works are obvious to the senses, on the grounds that they are inconsistent with merely human proofs based on hypotheses? And again, though you do not even

---

[247] [See Exodus 8:19.]

understand the physical structure of the body which enables the mind to perceive corporeal objects, yet to pronounce an opinion on this physical structure which, when glorified by change from corruptible to incorruptible, is once more to be united with the soul?

I am indeed fully convinced that to invent new principles explaining the nature of God, the soul, and the body, is just the same as to invent fictitious principles. Even reason tells us that it is inconsistent with divine providence that, while the holiest of men have failed to discover the true principles of these things for so many thousands of years, in our age they are to be disclosed for the first time by men who have not even attained to the perfection of moral virtues. Indeed, I am inclined to believe as true only those principles concerning God, the soul and the body which have been preserved from the beginning of created things until this day constantly in one and the same society, the City of God. Among the first teachers of these principles, that old man[248] who was responsible for St. Justin's move from a worldly philosophy to a Christian philosophy said, "There have been philosophers in the ancient times, blessed, just, dear to God, who spoke with the inspiration of the Holy Spirit, and prophesied that these things would be which are now coming to pass." It is principles propounded by such philosophers and transmitted to us through successors like them in an uninterrupted chain, and through philosophers of the same kind made available even today to him who seeks them in the spirit of right reason — it is such principles alone I would believe to be true, when sanctity of life proves the truth of doctrine. Examine thoroughly both the principles and the doctrines of this philosophy, not in the writings of its enemies nor in those of its parasites, who for their wickedness are rated with the dead, or for their ignorance with children, but in the writings of its masters, perfected in all wisdom, dear to God and probably even now sharing in life eternal, and you will acknowledge that the perfect Christian is the perfect philosopher, even if it were merely an old woman, or a maidservant busied with menial tasks, or one seeking a living by washing rags, in the world's judgment an ignorant person. And then you will cry out with St. Justin, "I find this to be the one philosophy, safe and good."[249]

If you should wish, I will gladly take upon myself the task of showing you how your doctrine is inferior to ours, sometimes through its contradiction, sometimes through its uncertainty. Yet I would prefer that, recognising in your doctrine a few errors as compared with the assured credibility that is a feature of ours, you would become a disciple of the said teachers and, as first-fruits of your repentance, offer to God a refutation of your errors which you yourself recognise through the illumination of the divine light, so that if your first writings have turned aside a thou-

---

[248] [The quotation following is a loose version of a passage in Justin, *Dialogue with Trypho*, VIII, 1. Justin had two teachers, the first having introduced him to Stoic, Peripatetic and Pythagorean philosophy, and another who taught him Platonism. The reference to the 'old man', otherwise unidentified, is probably to the second.]

[249] [See Justin, *Dialogue with Trypho*, VIII.]

sand minds from the true knowledge of God, their recantation, corroborated by your own example, may bring back to him, accompanied by you like a second Augustine, a thousand thousand. This grace I pray for you with all my heart. Farewell.

[September 1675]

LETTER 68
To the most noble and learned Henry Oldenburg, from B.d.S.

[Reply to Letter 62. Known only from the O.P. The original is lost.]

Most noble and esteemed Sir,

At the time when I received your letter of 22 July, I was setting out for Amsterdam, intending to put into print the book of which I had written to you.[250] While I was engaged in this business, a rumour became wide-spread that a certain book of mine about God was in the press, and in it I endeavour to show that there is no God. This rumour found credence with many. So certain theologians, who may have started this rumour, seized the opportunity to complain of me before the Prince[251] and the Magistrates. Moreover, the stupid Cartesians, in order to remove this suspicion from themselves because they are thought to be on my side, ceased not to denounce everywhere my opinions and my writings, and still continue to do so.[252] Having gathered this from certain trustworthy men who also declared that the theologians were everywhere plotting against me, I decided to postpone the publication I had in hand until I should see how matters would turn out, intending to let you know what course I would then pursue. But the situation seems to worsen day by day, and I am not sure what to do about it.

Meanwhile I do not want to delay any longer my reply to your letter. First, I thank you most warmly for your friendly warning, of which, however, I should like a fuller explanation so that I may know what you believed to be the doctrines which seemed to undermine the practise of religious virtue. For the things that seem to me to be in accord with reason I believe to be most beneficial to virtue. Secondly, if it is not burdensome to you, I should like you to point out to me the passages in the *Tractatus Theologico-Politicus* which have proved a stumbling-block to learned

---

[250] [This was the *Ethics*.]

[251] [The Prince of Orange owed a considerable debt to the Calvinist clergy who helped bring about the downfall of democracy in Holland.]

[252] [By attacking Spinoza politically the Cartesians sought to reinforce their own orthodoxy in the public eye.]

men. For I want to clarify this Treatise with some additional notes,[253] and, if possible, remove prejudices which have been conceived against it. Farewell.

[September 1675]

LETTER 69
To the most learned Lambert van Velthuysen, from B.d.S.

[Not in the O.P. The original came into the possession of a Professor Tydeman of Leiden, who published it in 1824. It is now lost.]

Most distinguished and esteemed Sir,

I am surprised that our friend Nieuwstad[254] has said that I am considering a refutation of those writings which for some time have been published against my treatise, and that among them I propose to refute your manuscript.[255] For I know that I have never had in mind to rebut any of my adversaries, so undeserving of reply did they all seem to me. Nor do I remember having said to Mr. Nieuwstad anything other than that I proposed to clarify some more obscure passages of the said treatise with some notes,[256] and to add to them your manuscript together with my reply, if you would kindly grant permission. This I asked him to seek from you, adding that if perhaps you are reluctant to grant this permission on the grounds that my reply contains some rather harsh observations, you would have complete authority to correct or delete them. But meanwhile I am not at all annoyed with Mr. Nieuwstad: I merely want to let you know how the matter stands so that, if I cannot obtain the permission I seek, I may at least make it clear that I never had any intention of publishing your manuscript against your will. And although I believe that this can be done without in any way endangering your reputation provided that your name does not appear in it, I shall do nothing unless you grant me permission to publish it. However, to confess the truth, I would be much more obliged to you if you would put in writing the arguments which you believe you can bring against my treatise and append them to your manuscript. This I most earnestly beg you to do, for there is no one whose arguments I would more gladly

---

[253] [Notes to the TTP were inserted by Spinoza by his own hand in some versions of this letter. These notes were published in a French translation of the TTP (1678), and the original Latin notes were published in 1802 by C. T. de Murr (*Benedict de Spinoza Adnotationes ad Tractatum Theologico-Politicum*). This 1802 edition contained a facsimile of the notes in Spinoza's own writing.]

[254] [Joachim Nieuwstad was Secretary of the city of Utrecht from 1662 until 1674.]

[255] [The manuscript to which Spinoza refers is Velthuysen's letter to Ostens, Ep42.]

[256] [See notes to the preceding letter.]

consider. I know that you are devoted solely to the pursuit of truth, and that you are a man of exceptional sincerity of mind.[257] For this reason I urgently beg you not to be unwilling to undertake this labour, and believe me to be,

With great respect,
B. de Spinoza

Mr. Lambert Velthuysen, Doctor of Medicine
De Nieuwe Gracht, Utrecht
The Hague
[Autumn 1675]

LETTER 70
To the most illustrious and acute philosopher, B.d.S., from G. H. Schuller, Doctor of Medicine

[Not in the O.P. The original is extant, and was first published by Van Vloten in 1860.]

Most learned and illustrious Sir, my most venerable patron,

I hope that you have duly received my last letter, together with the *Processus* of an anonymous writer,[258] and that you still enjoy good health, as I do.

I had had no letter for three months from our friend Tschirnhaus, whence I had entertained the gloomy conjecture that he had met with misfortune in journeying from England to France. But now, having received a letter, I am overjoyed and, in obedience to his request, it is my duty to convey its contents to you, and to let you know, with his most dutiful greetings, that he has arrived safely in Paris, that he has there met Mr. Huygens as we had advised him to do, and has therefore made every effort to win his favour, so that he is highly regarded by him. He mentioned that you, Sir, had recommended him to seek an introduction to Huygens, for whom you have the highest regard. This pleased him very much, so that he replied that he likewise had a high regard for you, and had lately received from

---

[257] [Spinoza's attitude toward Velthuysen is far more positive than that which he displayed in Ep43. In the Preface to his own works, published in 1680, Velthuysen notes that he had many conversations with Spinoza during their joint stay in Utrecht (1673). It is not known whether Velthuysen gave to Spinoza the requested permission; but, in any case, Spinoza never had the opportunity to prepare an enlarged edition of the TTP.]

[258] [This was the *Processus anonymi*, which judging from Spinoza's response in Ep72, was not written so anonymously, but by a relative of Schuller. Also judging from Spinoza's remarks, it seems that it was a book on alchemy, a discipline for which Spinoza had little interest.]

you the *Tractatus Theologico-Politicus*, which is esteemed by many there, and there are eager inquiries as where any more writings of the same author are published. To this Mr. Tschirnhaus has replied that he knows of none except for the 'Proofs of the First and Second Parts of Descartes' Principia'. Otherwise he said nothing about you except for the above, and hopes that this will not displease you.

Huygens has recently sent for our Tschirnhaus and informed him that Mr. Colbert[259] is looking for someone to instruct his son in mathematics, and if a situation of this kind was acceptable to him, he would arrange it. To this our friend replied by asking for some time to think it over, and eventually declared himself willing to accept. So Huygens came back with the answer that Mr. Colbert was very happy with this proposal, especially as his ignorance of the French language would compel him to speak to his son in Latin.

As to the objection he recently advanced, he replies that the few words I wrote at your instruction have given him a deeper understanding of your meaning, and that he has already entertained the same thoughts (since they particularly admit of explanation in these two ways), but that he had taken the line set out in his objection for the following two reasons. First, because otherwise Propositions 5 and 7 of Book II would seem to be in contradiction.[260] 'In the first of these it is maintained that ideata are the efficient cause of ideas, whereas in the proof of the latter this seems to be refuted by reason of the citing of Axiom 4, Part I.[261] Or else, as I am inclined to think, I am not correctly applying the axiom in accordance with the author's intention, and this I would very much like to learn from him, if his leisure permits. The second cause which has prevented me from following his explanation as set out is this, that in this way the attribute of Thought is given a much wider scope than the other attributes.[262] Now since each of the attributes constitutes the essence of God, I fail to see how the one thing does not contradict the other. I will add only this, that if I may judge other minds by my own, there will be considerable difficulty in understanding Propositions 7 and 8 of Book II,[263]

---

[259] [Jean Baptiste Colbert (1619–1683) was the Chancellor of the Exchequer under the reign of Louis XIV. He attempted to draw several of the day's leading scientists and scholars to Paris.]

[260] [As Spinoza notes in his reply (Ep72), Tschirnhaus is apparently confused. E2P5 states: "The formal being of ideas recognises God as its cause only insofar as he is considered as a thinking thing, and not insofar as he is explicated by any other attribute; that is, the ideas both of God's attributes and of individual things recognise as their efficient cause not the things of which they are ideas — that is, the things perceived — but God himself insofar as he is a thinking thing." E2P7 is the celebrated statement of parallelism: "The order and connection of ideas is the same as the order and connection of things."]

[261] [E1Ax4: "The knowledge of the effect depends on, and involves, the knowledge of the cause."]

[262] [Tschirnhaus' claim that, in allowing both ideas of things (bodies) and ideas of ideas, Spinoza had violated the parallelism by making thought more extensive than extension, has been echoed by many commentators to the present day.]

[263] [For E2P7 see above. E2P8: "The ideas of non-existing individual things must be comprehended in the infinite idea of God in the same way as the formal essences of individual things or modes are contained in the attributes of God." In his reply (Ep72), Spinoza ignores this question; but, in the scholium to E2P8, he notes, "Should anyone want an example for a clearer understanding of

and this simply because the author has been pleased (doubtless because they seemed so plain to him) to explain the demonstrations attached to them so briefly and sparingly'

He further relates that in Paris he has met a man named Leibniz[264] of remarkable learning, most skilled in the various sciences and free from the common theological prejudices. He has established a close friendship with him, based on the fact that like him he is working at the problem of the perfecting of the intellect, and indeed he considers there is nothing better or more important than this. In Ethics, he says, Leibniz is most practised, and speaks solely from the dictates of reason uninfluenced by emotion. He adds that in physics and especially in metaphysical studies of God and the Soul he is most skilled, and he finally concludes that he is a person most worthy of having your writings communicated to him, if consent is first given; for he thinks that the Author will derive considerable advantage therefrom, as he undertakes to show at some length, if this should please you. But if not, have no doubt that he will honourably keep them secret in accordance with his promise, just as in fact he has made not the slightest mention of them. This same Leibniz thinks highly of the *Tractatus Theologico-Politicus*,[265] on which subject he once wrote you a letter, if you remember. I would therefore ask you out of your gracious kindliness, unless there is strong reason against it, not to refuse your permission, but if you can, to let me know your decision as soon as possible. For when I have received your reply, I can send our Tschirnhaus an answer, which I am anxious to do Tuesday evening, unless you are delayed by more important business.

Mr. Bresser[266] has returned from Cleves, and has sent here a considerable quantity of the native beer. I have asked him to send you half a tun, which he has promised to do with his most friendly greetings.

Finally, I beg you to excuse the clumsiness of my style and the haste of my pen, and to command me in any service, so that I may have a real occasion of proving that I am,

Most illustrious Sir,
Your most ready servant,
G. H. Schuller

---

this matter, I can think of none at all that would adequately explicate the point with which I am here dealing." Perhaps this scholium resulted from Tschirnhaus' puzzlement.]

[264] [Leibniz stayed in Paris from 1672 until 1676 trying to persuade Louis XIV to direct his attentions to Egypt and to leave Europe in peace.]

[265] [As a diplomat, Leibniz acquired the habit of professing whatever views were most likely to please his audience. In his own writings he described the TTP as "intolerably impudent" and "monstrous."]

[266] [Possibly Jan Bresser who is incorrectly believed by some to have written the poem which precedes the PPC. Whether he is originally from the Cleves district or was simply visiting there is also not known, but it is coincidental that Schuller is from that area while Tschirnhaus served time in the army there.]

Letter 71

To the esteemed B.d.S., from Henry Oldenburg, with many greetings

[Known only from the O.P. The original is lost.]

As far as I can gather from your last letter, the issuing of the book intended by you for the general public is in danger.[267] I cannot but approve your purpose in signifying your willingness to elucidate and moderate those passages in the *Tractatus Theologico-Politicus* which have proved a stumbling-block to readers. I refer in particular to those which appear to treat in an ambiguous way of God and Nature, which many people consider you have confused with each other. In addition, many are of the opinion that you take away the authority and validity of miracles, which almost all Christians are convinced form the sole basis on which the certainty of Divine Revelation can rest. Furthermore, they say that you are concealing your opinion with regard to Jesus Christ, Redeemer of the World, sole Mediator for mankind, and of his Incarnation and Atonement, and they request you to disclose your attitude clearly on these three heads. If you do so, and in this matter satisfy reasonable and intelligent Christians, I think your position will be secure. This is what I, who am devoted to you, wish you to know in brief. Farewell.

15 November 1675

P.S. Please let me know soon that these few lines have duly reached you.

Letter 72

To the most learned and experienced G. H. Schuller, from B.d.S.

[Not in the O.P. The original, in private hands, was first published in 1860 by Van Vloten.]

Most experienced Sir, and honoured friend,

I am very pleased to learn from your letter, received today, that you are well and that our friend Tschirnhaus has happily accomplished his journey to France. In

---

[267] [Oldenburg's naïveté is apparent here, since Spinoza never intended any of his writings after the PPC for the general public, one reason why he was opposed to the effort to publish the Dutch translation of the TTP.]

his conversations with Mr. Huygens he has, in my opinion, conducted himself with discretion, and furthermore I am very glad that he found so convenient an opportunity for that which he had intended.

I do not see what he finds in Axiom 4, Part I to contradict Proposition 5, Part 2. For in this proposition it is asserted that the essence of any idea has God for its cause insofar as he is considered as a thinking thing, while that axiom says that the knowledge or idea of an effect depends on the knowledge or idea of the cause. But to tell the truth, I do not quite follow the meaning of your letter in this matter, and I believe that either in your letter or in his copy there is a slip of the pen. For you write that in Proposition 5 it is asserted that *ideata* are the efficient cause of ideas, whereas this very point is expressly denied in that same proposition. I now think that the whole confusion arises from this, and so at present it would be pointless for me to try to write at greater length on this matter. I must wait until you explain his meaning to me more clearly, and until I know whether he has a sufficiently correct copy.[268]

I believe I know Leibniz, of whom he writes, through correspondence, but I do not understand why he, a councillor of Frankfurt, has gone to France. As far as I can judge from his letter, he seemed to me a person of liberal mind and well versed in every science. Still, I think it imprudent to entrust my writings to him so hastily. I should first like to know what he is doing in France, and to hear our friend Tschirnhaus' opinion of him after a longer acquaintance and a closer knowledge of his character. However, greet that friend of ours in my name with all my duty, and if I can serve him in any way, let him command what he will, and he will find me most ready to comply in all things.

I congratulate our most worthy friend Mr. Bresser on his arrival or his return. I thank him very much for the beer that is promised, and shall repay him in whatever way I can. Finally, I have not yet made trial of the *Process* of your kinsman, nor do I think that I can turn my mind to essay it. For the more I think about it, the more I am convinced that you have not made gold, but have insufficiently separated out what was hidden in the antimony. But more of this on another occasion; at the moment I am pressed for time. Meanwhile, if I can be of service to you in any matter, here I am, whom you will always find,

Most distinguished Sir,
Your very good friend and ready servant,
B. de Spinoza

The Hague, 18 November 1675
Mr. G. H. Schuller, Doctor of Medicine,
de Kortsteegh in de gestofeerde hoet, Amsterdam

---

[268] [These propositions are printed as notes to Ep70. Spinoza's assumption that Tschirnhaus may have received a corrupted text of them is plausible in the light of Tschirnhaus' strange reading in Ep70.]

Letter 73
To the most noble and learned Henry Oldenburg, from B.d.S.

[Printed in the O.P. The original is lost, but a copy made by Leibniz is extant.]

Most noble Sir,

I received your very short letter, dated 15 November, last Saturday. In it you merely indicate those passages of the *Tractatus Theologico-Politicus* which have proved a stumbling-block to readers, whereas I had also hoped to learn from it what were those passages which appeared to undermine the practise of religious virtue, of which you had previously made mention.[269] However, in order to disclose to you my attitude concerning the three heads which you single out, I say in the first place that I entertain an opinion on God and Nature far different from that which modern Christians are wont to uphold. For I maintain that God is the immanent cause, as the phrase is, of all things, and not the transitive cause. All things, I say, are in God and move in God, and this I affirm together with Paul and perhaps together with all ancient philosophers, though expressed in a different way, and I would even venture to say, together with all the ancient Hebrews, as far as may be conjectured from certain traditions, though these have suffered much corruption. However, as to the view of certain people that the *Tractatus Theologico-Politicus* rests on the identification of God with Nature (by the latter of which they understand a kind of mass or corporeal matter) they are quite mistaken.

Next, as to miracles, I am on the contrary convinced that the certainty of divine revelation can be based solely on the wisdom of doctrine, and not on miracles, that is, on ignorance, as I have shown at some length in Chapter 6, 'On Miracles'. Here I will add only this, that the chief distinction I make between religion and superstition is that the latter is founded on ignorance, the former on wisdom. And this I believe is the reason why Christians are distinguished from other people not by faith, nor charity, nor the other fruits of the Holy Spirit, but solely by an opinion they hold, namely, because, as they all do, they rest their case simply on miracles, that is, on ignorance, which is the source of all wickedness, and thus

---

[269] [Spinoza is being a consistent Spinozist here, without realizing that neither Oldenburg nor the many critics of the TTP accept the divorce between obedience (which is the goal of faith) and truth (which is the goal of philosophy) whose demonstration is one of the central theses of the TTP. Oldenburg has in fact given Spinoza a list of objectionable philosophical claims, whereas what Spinoza had sought was an indication of how, in the eyes of his critics, the TTP undermined the *practice* of obedience and virtue.]

they turn their faith, true as it may be, into superstition. But I doubt very much whether rulers will ever allow the application of a remedy for this evil.[270]

Finally, to disclose my meaning more clearly on the third head, I say that for salvation it is not altogether necessary to know Christ according to the flesh; but with regard to the eternal son of God, that is, God's eternal wisdom, which has manifested itself in all things and chiefly in the human mind, and most of all in Christ Jesus, a very different view must be taken. For without this no one can attain to a state of blessedness, since this alone teaches what is true and false, good and evil. And since, as I have said, this wisdom has been manifested most of all through Jesus Christ, his disciples have preached it as far as he revealed it to them, and have shown themselves able to glory above all others in that spirit of Christ. As to the additional teaching of certain Churches, that God took upon himself human nature, I have expressly indicated that I do not understand what they say. Indeed, to tell the truth, they seem to me to speak no less absurdly than one who might tell me that a circle has taken on the nature of a square.[271]

This, I think, suffices to explain what is my opinion on those three heads. As to whether it is likely to please the Christians of your acquaintance, you will know better than I. Farewell.

[Conjectural date, November or December 1675]

LETTER 74
To the most esteemed and learned B.d.S., from Henry Oldenburg

[Known only from the O.P. The original is lost.]

Many greetings.

As you seem to accuse me of excessive brevity, I shall clear myself of that charge on this occasion by excessive prolixity. You expected, I see, an account of those opinions in your writings which seem to your readers to do away with the practise of religious virtue. I will tell you what it is that particularly pains them. You appear to postulate a fatalistic necessity in all things and actions. If this is conceded

---

[270] [As a good republican, Spinoza is here claiming that it is only in a democracy that government can afford to permit free access to information and universal education. His experience with the Calvinist clergy's effort to restore the monarchy certainly provided ample support for this claim in his own time.]

[271] [While Spinoza's denial of the godhood of Christ is quite unambiguous in the TTP, Oldenburg was probably correct in claiming that the account of Christ given in the TTP is, if not ambiguous, at least not clear.]

and affirmed, they say, the sinews of all law, all virtue and religion are severed, and all rewards and punishments are pointless. They consider that whatever compels or brings necessity to bear, excuses; and they hold that no one will thus be without excuse in the sight of God. If we are driven by fate,[272] and if all things, unrolled by its unrelenting hand, follow a fixed and inevitable course, they do not see what place there is for blame and punishment. What wedge can be applied to this knot, it is very difficult to say. I would be glad to know and to learn from you what help you can give in this matter.

As to your views on the three heads I mentioned, which you were kind enough to disclose to me, the following questions arise. First, in what sense do you take miracles and ignorance to be synonymous and equivalent terms, as you appear to do in your last letter? For the raising of Lazarus from the dead and the resurrection of Jesus Christ from death seem to surpass all the force of created Nature and to belong only to the divine power; nor does it argue a culpable ignorance that this must necessarily exceed the bounds of an intelligence that is finite and confined within definite limits. Or do you not deem it proper for the created mind and science to acknowledge in the uncreated mind and supreme Deity such science and power that it can see deeply into and bring to pass things, the reason and manner of which are beyond understanding and explanation by us petty men? We are men; we should regard as foreign to us nothing that is human.

Again, since you admit that you cannot grasp the idea that God did indeed assume human nature, may one ask in what way you understand those texts of our Gospel and the passages in the Epistle to the Hebrews, of which the former declares 'the Word was made flesh',[273] and the latter 'the Son of God took not on him the nature of angels, but he took on him the seed of Abraham'.[274] And the whole trend of the Gospel, I should think, implies that the only-begotten Son of God, the Word (who was both God and with God), manifested himself in human nature, and by his passion and death paid the ransom on behalf of us sinners, the price of redemption.[275] I would much like to learn what you have to say regarding these and similar matters that would be consistent with the truth of the Gospel and the Christian religion, to which I believe you are well disposed.

I had intended to write more fully, but I am interrupted by the visit of friends, to whom I think it wrong to refuse the duties of courtesy. But what I have already committed to paper will suffice, and will perhaps prove irksome to you as a philosopher. So farewell, and believe me to be ever an admirer of your learning and knowledge.

London, 16 December 1675

---

[272] [Oldenburg is interpreting Spinoza as a fatalist rather than as a determinist.]

[273] [See John 1:14.]

[274] [See Hebrews 2:16.]

[275] [See I Timothy 2:5–6 and Matthew 20:27.]

Letter 75
To the most noble and learned Henry Oldenburg, from B.d.S.

[Printed in the O.P. The original is lost, but a copy made by Leibniz is extant.]

Most noble Sir,

I see at last what it was that you urged me not to publish. However, since this is the principal basis of all the contents of the treatise which I had intended to issue, I should here like to explain briefly in what way I maintain the fatalistic necessity of all things and actions.

In no way do I subject God to fate, but I conceive that all things follow with inevitable necessity from God's nature in the same way that everyone conceives that it follows from God's nature that God understands himself. Surely no one denies that this follows necessarily from God's nature, and yet no one conceives that God is forced by some fate to understand himself; it is conceived that God understands himself altogether freely, though necessarily.

Next, this inevitable necessity of things does not do away with either divine or human laws. For moral precepts, whether or not they receive from God himself the form of command or law, are nonetheless divine and salutary, and whether the good that follows from virtue and the divine love is bestowed on us by God as judge, or whether it emanates from the necessity of the divine nature, it will not on that account be more or less desirable, just as on the other hand the evils that follow from wicked deeds and passions are not less to be feared because they necessarily follow from them. And finally, whether we do what we do necessarily or contingently, we are still led by hope and fear.

Furthermore, men are without excuse before God for no other reason than that they are in God's hands as clay in the hands of the potter,[276] who from the same lump makes vessels, some to honour and some to dishonour. If you would give just a little attention to these few points, I doubt not that you will find it easy to reply to all objections that are usually raised against this view, as many have already discovered along with me.

I have taken miracles and ignorance as equivalents because those who endeavour to establish the existence of God and religion from miracles are seeking to prove the obscure through the more obscure, of which they are quite ignorant; and in this way they are introducing a new style of argumentation, reduction not

---

[276] [See Romans 9:20–21.]

to the impossible, as the phrase is, but to ignorance.[277] However, I have sufficiently expressed my view on miracles, if I am not mistaken, in the *Tractatus Theologico-Politicus*. Here I will add only this, that if you will consider the following points, that Christ did not appear to the Senate, nor to Pilate, nor to any of the unbelievers, but only to the Saints, that God has neither right nor left and is not in any one place but is everywhere in accordance with his essence, that matter is everywhere the same, that God does not manifest himself in some imaginary space beyond the world, and that the frame of the human body is restrained within its proper limits only by the weight of the air, you will easily see that this appearance of Christ is not unlike that whereby God appeared to Abraham when he saw the three men whom he invited to eat with him.[278] But, you will say, all the Apostles were fully convinced that Christ rose again after death and that he really did ascend to heaven; and this I do not deny. For Abraham, too, believed that God partook of a meal with him, and all the Israelites believed that God descended from heaven to Mount Sinai in the midst of fire, and spoke to them directly. Yet these and many other events of this kind were appearances or revelations adapted to the understanding and beliefs of those men to whom God wished to reveal his mind by these means. I therefore conclude that Christ's resurrection from the dead was in fact of a spiritual kind and was revealed only to the faithful according to their understanding, indicating that Christ was endowed with eternity and rose from the dead (I here understand 'the dead' in the sense in which Christ said 'Let the dead bury their dead'),[279] and also by his life and death he provided an example of surpassing holiness, and that he raises his disciples from the dead insofar as they follow the example of his own life and death.

It would not be difficult to explain the entire teaching of the Gospel in accordance with this hypothesis. Indeed, it is only on this hypothesis that Chapter 15 of the First Epistle to the Corinthians can be explained and Paul's arguments understood, which otherwise, according to the usually accepted hypothesis, appear weak and easily to be refuted, to say nothing of the fact that Christians have interpreted in a spiritual way all that the Jews have interpreted according to the flesh.

I agree with you as to human weakness. But permit me to ask you in turn, do we petty men have such an understanding of Nature that we can determine how far its force and power extend, and what is beyond its power? Since nobody can make such a claim without arrogance, one may therefore without presumption explain miracles through natural causes as far as possible; and as to those which because of their absurdity we can neither explain nor prove, it will be better to suspend judgment, and to base religion, as I have said, solely on the wisdom of doctrine.

Finally, the reason why you believe that the passages in the Gospel of John and in the Epistle to the Hebrews are opposed to the views I have expressed in this, that you interpret the phraseology of Oriental languages according to the norm

---

[277] [The thrust of Spinoza's argument in the TTP is that belief in miracles in fact inevitably leads to disbelief in the existence of God.]

[278] [See Genesis 18:1–2.]

[279] [See Matthew 8:22 and Luke 9:60.]

of European speech; and although John wrote his Gospel in Greek, his idiom was Hebraic.[280]

Be that as it may, do you believe that when Scripture says that God manifested himself in a cloud, or that he dwelt in a tabernacle and a temple, that God assumed the nature of a cloud, a tabernacle and a temple? But the most that Christ said about himself was this, that he was the temple of God, because undoubtedly, as I have said in my previous letter, God manifested himself most of all in Christ; and John, to express this more effectually, said that the Word was made flesh. But enough for now.

[December 1675]

Letter 76
Greetings to the noble young man, Alfred Burgh, from B.d.S.

[Reply to Letter 67]
[Printed in the O.P. The original is lost, but a copy made by Leibniz is extant.]

What I could scarcely believe when it was told me by others, I now at last learn from your letter; not only have you become a member of the Roman Church, as you say, but you are also its very keen champion, and have already learned to curse and rage without restraint against your opponents. I had intended to make no reply to your letter, being convinced that time rather than argument was what you needed so as to be restored to yourself and your family, not to mention other reasons to which you once gave your approval when we were discussing the case of Steno[281] (in whose footsteps you now follow). But some of my friends, who with me had formed great hopes for you from your excellent natural abilities, have strenuously urged me not to fail in the duties of a friend, and to reflect on what you lately were rather than what you now are, and so on. These representations have at last induced me to write you these few words, which I earnestly beg you please to read with patience.

I shall not here recount the vices of priests and popes, as opponents of the Roman Church are wont to do, so as to discredit them with you. Such accusations are often advanced from unworthy motives, and are intended to annoy rather than

---

[280] [This theme is echoed also in the TTP, since Spinoza there claims that understanding the text of Scripture requires a knowledge of the linguistic and cultural connotations which underlie it. This is one reason why he avoids a detailed interpretation of the New Testament, for want of a knowledge of Greek.]

[281] [See Ep67A.]

to instruct. Indeed, I will concede that in the Roman Church there are to be found more instances of men of great learning and upright life than in any other Christian Church; for since this Church has more members, there will also be found in it more men of every character. Still, unless perchance you have lost your memory together with your reason, you will not be able to deny that in every Church there are very many honourable men who worship God with justice and charity. For we have known many such among the Lutherans, the Reformed Church, the Mennonites and the Enthusiasts, and, to say nothing of others, you know of your own relations who, in the time of the Duke of Alva, suffered every kind of torture steadfastly and freely for the sake of their religion. You must therefore grant that holiness of life is not peculiar to the Roman Church, but is common to all.

Since we know by this (to quote from the Apostle John, First Epistle, Chapter 4 verse 13) that we dwell in God and God dwells in us,[282] it follows that whatever distinguishes the Roman Church from others is of no real significance, and consequently is constructed merely from superstition. For, as I have said with John,[283] justice and charity are the one sure sign of the true catholic faith, the true fruits of the Holy Spirit, and wherever these are found, there Christ really is, and where they are not, Christ is not. For only by the Spirit of Christ can we be led to the love of justice and charity. Had you been willing to meditate aright on these things, you would not have ruined yourself nor would you have brought bitter grief on your kinsfolk who now sorrowfully bewail your plight.

But I return to your letter, in which first of all you lament that I allow myself to be ensnared by the prince of evil spirits. But please be of good cheer and come to yourself again. When you were in your senses, if I am not mistaken, you used to worship an infinite God by whose efficacy all things absolutely come into being and are preserved; but now you dream of a Prince, God's enemy, who against God's will ensnares most men (for the good are few) and deceives them, whom God therefore delivers over to this master of wickedness for everlasting torture. So divine justice permits the Devil to deceive men with impunity, but does not permit men, haplessly deceived and ensnared by the Devil, to go unpunished.

Now these absurdities might so far be tolerated if you worshipped a God infinite and eternal, not one whom Chastillon, in a town which the Dutch call Tienen, gave to horses to eat, and was not punished.[284] And do you bewail me, wretched man? And do you call my philosophy, which you have never beheld, a chimera? O youth deprived of understanding, who has bewitched you into believing that you eat, and hold in your intestines, that which is supreme and eternal?

Still, you appear to be willing to resort to reason, and you ask me 'how I know that my philosophy is the best of all those that have ever been taught in this world,

---

[282] [Spinoza inserted this verse from I John on the title page of the TTP.]

[283] [See TTP, Chapter 16. The reference is to I John 4:7–8.]

[284] [This probably refers to an incident in May of 1635 when a Franco-Dutch army attacked the Spanish army in Belgium. The French general Gaspard de Coligny was a Huguenot, and after sacking the town he ordered the eucharistic hosts to be thrown to the horses as an expression of his disgust with Catholic idolatry.]

are now being taught, or will ever be taught in the future'. But surely I have far better right to put that question to you. For I do not presume that I have found the best philosophy, but I know that what I understand is the true one.[285] If you ask me how I know this, I reply that I know it in the same way that you know that the three angles of a triangle are equal to two right angles. That this suffices no one will deny who has a sound brain and does not dream of unclean spirits who inspire us with false ideas as if they were true. For truth reveals both itself and the false.[286]

But you, who presume that you have at last found the best religion, or rather, the best men to whom you have pledged your credulity, how do you know that they are the best out of all those who have taught other religions, are teaching them now, or will teach them in the future? Have you examined all those religions, both ancient and modern, which are taught here and in India and throughout the whole world? And even if you have duly examined them, how do you know that you have chosen the best? For you can give no grounds for your faith. You will say that you give acceptance to the inward testimony of the Spirit of God, whereas others are ensnared and deceived by the Prince of wicked spirits. But all who are outside the Roman Church claim with the same right for their church what you claim for yours.

As to what you add about the common consent of myriads of men and the uninterrupted ecclesiastical succession and so on, this is the same old song of the Pharisees.[287] Just as confidently as the adherents of the Roman Church, they produce their myriads of witnesses who, with just as much pertinacity as the Roman witnesses, recount what they have merely heard just as if they had experienced it themselves. Again, they trace their lineage as far back as Adam. With like arrogance they boast that their Church, continuing to this day, endures unmoved and unshaken in spite of the bitter hatred of heathens and Christians. More than any other people they rely on their antiquity. With one voice they cry that their traditions were given them by God himself, that they alone preserve the Word of God, written and unwritten. No one can deny that all other sects have issued from them, while they have remained steadfast over some thousands of years with no government to constrain them, solely through the efficacy of superstition. The miracles they tell of are enough to weary a thousand tongues. But their chief source of pride is that they count far more martyrs than any other nation, a number that is daily increased by those who have suffered for the faith they profess with amazing stead-

---

[285] [Spinoza is using 'best' here in the sense of 'complete'. In fact, no philosophy (his or any other) can claim completeness on Spinoza's own count; since philosophy by its very nature is a finitary activity and deals at most with a finite number of the divine attributes. No matter how adequate or true a philosophy should be, infinite orders of nature will lie beyond its range of understanding.]

[286] [This is a major theme of the unfinished *Tractatus de intellectus emendatione*. An idea is said to be false only in relation to a given true idea which lies at the base of human understanding.]

[287] [Spinoza uses the term 'Pharisee' to refer to and condemn the adherents of rabbinic Judaism, which is based on the Talmud and the belief in the so-called Oral Torah (or "Law"). Central to the belief is the claim (made also by Roman Catholicism) of an unbroken chain of succession. The term is also used in this sense in the work of Gabriel da Costa (known more commonly as Uriel da Costa) (1585–1640), who certainly did not originate the sense.]

fastness. I myself know among others of a certain Judah called 'the faithful' who, in the midst of flames when he was already believed dead, started to sing the hymn which begins 'To Thee, O God, I commit my soul', and so singing, died.[288]

The organisation of the Roman Church, which you so warmly praise, I admit is politic and a source of gain to many, nor would I believe there is any better arranged for deceiving the people and controlling men's minds if it were not for the organisation of the Mahomedan Church, which far surpasses it. For ever since this superstition originated, no schisms have arisen in their Church.[289]

If, therefore, you reckon up your accounts aright, you will see that it is only your third point that is in favour of Christians, namely, that men who were unlearned and of humble condition were able to convert practically the whole world to the Christian faith. But this point militates in favour not of the Roman Church, but of all Churches that profess the name of Christ.

But suppose that all the arguments that you offer tell in favour only of the Roman Church. Do you think that by these arguments you can prove with mathematical certainty the authority of that same Church? Since this is far from being so, why do you want me to believe that my demonstrations are inspired by the Prince of wicked spirits, and yours by God? Especially as I see, and your letter clearly shows, that you have become the slave of this Church not so much through love of God as fear of Hell, which is the single cause of superstition.[290] Is this your humility, to put no trust in yourself but in others, who are condemned by a great number of people? Do you take it for arrogance and pride that I resort to reason, and that I give my acceptance to this, the true Word of God, which is in the mind and can never be distorted or corrupted? Away with this destructive superstition, and acknowledge the faculty of reason which God gave you, and cultivate it, unless you would be counted among the beasts. Cease, I say, to give the title of mysteries to your absurd errors, and do not shamefully confuse those things which are unknown to us or not yet discovered with things that are shown to be absurd, as are the fearsome secrets of this church, which you believe to transcend the understanding the more so as they are opposed to right reason.

However, the fundamental principle of the *Tractatus Theologico-Politicus* that Scripture must be explained only through Scripture, which you so wantonly and unreasonably proclaim to be false, is not mere supposition but is categorically proved to be true or sound, particularly in Chapter 7 which also refutes the opinions of its adversaries. See also what is proved towards the end of Chapter 15. If you will pay attention to these things and also examine the histories of the Church (of which I see that you are quite ignorant) so as to realise how false are many Papal traditions, and through what turn of events and with what craft the Pope of

---

[288] [Don Lope de Vera y Alarcon ('Judah the Faithful') was, like Uriel da Costa, a convert (or 'revert', since he was born into a crypto-Jewish family) to Judaism. He was burned at the stake on 25 July 1644. An account of his martyrdom is given by Manasseh ben Israel in his *Esperança de Israel* (Amsterdam, 1652).]

[289] [Spinoza is, of course, completely ignorant of the history of Islamic religion.]

[290] [This theme is echoed in E5P42Schol.]

Rome finally gained supremacy over the Church six hundred years after the birth of Christ, I have no doubt that you will at last recover your senses. That this may come about is my sincere wish for you. Farewell, etc.

[December 1675]

LETTER 77
To the esteemed B.d.S., from Henry Oldenburg, with greetings

[Reply to Letter 75]
[Known only from the O.P. The original is lost.]

You hit the mark exactly when you perceive that the reason why I advised against the publication of the doctrine of the fatalistic necessity of all things is my fear lest the practise of virtue may thereby be impeded, and rewards and punishments be made of little account. The points made by you on this subject in your last letter do not as yet appear to solve this problem or to set the human mind at rest. For if in all our actions, both moral and natural, we human beings are in God's power just as clay in the hands of the potter, on what grounds, pray, can any one of us be blamed for acting in this or that way, when it was quite impossible for him to act otherwise? Can we not, each one of us, reply to God, 'Your unbending fate and your irresistible power has compelled us to act in this way, nor could we have acted otherwise. Why, then, and with what right will you deliver us up to such dreadful punishments which could in no way have been avoided, inasmuch as you control and direct all things through a supreme necessity in accordance with your will and pleasure?' When you say that men are without excuse in the eyes of God for no other reason than that they are in the power of God, I would turn that argument the other way round and would say, I think with more reason, that it is just because they are in the power of God that men are excusable. For everyone has this excuse to hand, 'Ineluctable is your power, O God, and therefore I think I deserve to be excused for not acting otherwise'.

Again, in insisting that miracles and ignorance are equivalents, you seem to confine the power of God and the knowledge of men, even the most intelligent of men, within the same bounds, as if God cannot do or effect anything of which men cannot give an account if they exert their faculties to the full. Furthermore, the history of Christ's passion, death, burial and resurrection seems to be depicted in such vivid and natural colours that I even venture to appeal to your conscience; do you, provided that you are convinced of the truth of the narrative, believe that these things should be taken allegorically rather than literally? The details of this event so lucidly recorded by the Evangelists seem to urge strongly that the narrative should be taken literally.

These are the brief observations I want in turn to make regarding your argument, and I earnestly beg you to forgive them and to answer them with your customary candour of a friend. Mr. Boyle sends his kind regards. The present proceedings of the Royal Society I shall explain on another occasion. Farewell, and keep me in your affection.

Henry Oldenburg

London, 14 January 1676

LETTER 78
To the noble and learned Henry Oldenburg, from B.d.S.

> [Printed in the O.P. The original is lost, but a copy made by Leibniz is extant.]

Most noble Sir,

When I said in my previous letter[291] that the reason why we are without excuse is that we are in God's power as clay in the hands of the potter, I meant to be understood in this sense, that no one can accuse God for having given him a weak nature or a feeble character. For just as it would be absurd for a circle to complain that God has not given it the properties of a sphere, or a child suffering from kidney-stone that God has not given it a healthy body, it would be equally absurd for a man of feeble character to complain that God has denied him strength of spirit and true knowledge and love of God, and has given him so weak a nature that he cannot contain or control his desires. In the case of each thing, it is only that which follows necessarily from its given cause that is within its competence. That it is not within the competence of every man's nature that he should be of strong character, and that it is no more within our power to have a healthy body than to have a healthy mind, nobody can deny without flying in the face of both experience and reason.

"But," you urge, "if men sin from the necessity of their nature, they are therefore excusable." You do not explain what conclusion you wish to draw from this. Is it that God cannot be angry with them, or is it that they are worthy of blessedness, that is, the knowledge and love of God? If the former, I entirely agree that God is not angry, and that all things happen in accordance with his will. But I deny that on that account all men ought to be blessed; for men may be excusable, but nevertheless be without blessedness and afflicted in many ways. A horse is excusable for being a horse, and not a man; nevertheless, he needs must be a horse, and not a man. He who goes mad from the bite of a dog is indeed to be excused; still, it is right that he should die of suffocation. Finally, he who cannot

---

[291] [See Ep75.]

control his desires and keep them in check through fear of the law, although he also is to be excused for his weakness, nevertheless cannot enjoy tranquillity of mind and the knowledge and love of God, but of necessity he is lost. I do not think I need here remind you that Scripture, when it says that God is angry with sinners, that he is a judge who takes cognizance of the actions of men, decides, and passes sentence, is speaking in merely human terms according to the accepted beliefs of the multitude; for its aim is not to teach philosophy, nor to make men learned, but to make them obedient.

Again, I fail to see how you come to think that, by equating miracles with ignorance, I am confining God's power and man's knowledge within the same bounds.

The passion, death and burial of Christ I accept literally, but his resurrection I understand in an allegorical sense. I do indeed admit that this is related by the Evangelists with such detail that we cannot deny that the Evangelists themselves believed that the body of Christ rose again and ascended to heaven to sit at God's right hand, and that this could also have been seen by unbelievers if they had been present at the places where Christ appeared to the disciples. Nevertheless, without injury to the teaching of the Gospel, they could have been deceived, as was the case with other prophets, examples of which I gave in my last letter. But Paul, to whom Christ also appeared later, rejoices that he knows Christ not after the flesh, but after the spirit.

I am most grateful to you for the catalogue of the books of the distinguished Mr. Boyle.[292] Lastly, I wait to hear from you, when you have an opportunity, about the present proceedings of the Royal Society. Farewell, most honoured Sir, and believe me yours in all zeal and affection.

The Hague, 7 February 1676

Letter 79
To the esteemed Mr. Benedict de Spinoza, from Henry Oldenburg

[Not in the O.P. The original is lost, but a copy, perhaps intended for the printers of the O.P., has been preserved.]

Many greetings.

In your last letter written to me on 7 February, there seem still some points open to criticism. You say that man cannot complain that God has denied him true knowledge of Himself and strength sufficient to avoid sin, because there belongs to the nature of each thing nothing other than what necessarily follows from its

---

[292] [Oldenburg published in 1677 a catalogue of Boyle's works in the *Philosophical Transactions* of the Royal Society, vol. 130. He apparently sent Spinoza an advance copy of the catalogue.]

cause. But I say that inasmuch as God, the creator of men, has formed them in his own image, which seems to include in its concept wisdom, goodness and power, it seems bound to follow that it is more within man's power to have a healthy mind than a healthy body, seeing that the physical health of the body depends on mechanical principles, whereas the health of the mind depends on deliberate choice and purpose. You also say that men can be excusable, and yet suffer many afflictions. This seems harsh at first sight, and what you add by way of proof, that a dog who goes mad from a bite[293] is indeed excusable but is nevertheless rightly killed, does not appear to settle the matter. For the killing of such a dog would argue cruelty, were it not necessary for the protection of other dogs or other animals, or even men, from a maddening bite of that kind. But if God had endowed men with a healthy mind, as he can do, no contagion of vices would need to be feared. And indeed it seems very cruel that God should deliver men up to eternal, or at least dreadful temporary, torments because of sins which they could in no way have avoided. Moreover, the whole tenor of Holy Scripture seems to suppose and imply that men can refrain from sin. For it is full of denunciations and promises, proclamations of rewards and punishments, all of which seem to argue against the necessity of sinning and to imply the possibility of avoiding punishment. To deny this would be to say that the human mind operates no less mechanically than the human body.

Furthermore, your continual assumption that miracles and ignorance are equivalent appears to rest on this foundation, that a creature can and should have complete insight into the Creator's infinite power and wisdom. I am still firmly convinced that this is quite otherwise.

Finally, your assertion that Christ's passion, death and burial is to be taken literally, but his resurrection allegorically, is not supported by any argument that I can see. In the gospels, Christ's resurrection seems to be narrated as literally as the rest. And on this article of the resurrection stands the whole Christian religion and its truth, and with its removal the mission of Christ Jesus and his heavenly teaching collapse. You cannot be unaware how urgently, when he was raised from the dead, Christ laboured to convince his disciples of the truth of the resurrection properly so called. To seek to turn all this into allegory is the same as if one were to set about destroying the entire truth of Gospel history.

These are the few observations which I again wish to bring to your attention, in accordance with my freedom to philosophise. I earnestly beg you to take them in good part.

London, 11 February 1676

I shall give you a full account of the present studies and investigations of the Royal Society, if God grants me life and health.[294]

---

[293] [In this letter, Oldenburg has misunderstood Spinoza's Latin regarding the mad dog, and takes 'canis' as nominative rather than genitive. Spinoza has the dog biting, rather than being bitten.]

[294] [This is in fact the last letter in the extant correspondence between the two men. Oldenburg wrote

LETTER 80
To the acute and learned philosopher, B.d.S., from Ehrenfried Walther von Tschirnhaus

[Known only from the O.P. The original is lost. The last paragraph appears only in the Dutch edition of the O.P.]

Esteemed Sir,

First, I find it very difficult to understand how the existence of bodies having motion and figure can be demonstrated a priori, since there is nothing of this kind to be found in Extension, taken in the absolute sense. Secondly, I should like you to inform me in what way one is to understand the following passage in your letter[295] on the Infinite: 'Yet they do not draw the conclusion that it is because of the multitude of parts that such things exceed all number'. For, in fact, in the case of such infinites all mathematicians always seem to demonstrate that the number of parts is so great as to exceed any assignable number; and in the example of the two circles which you adduce you do not seem to clear up this point, as you had undertaken to do. For there you merely show that they do not reach this conclusion from the excessive magnitude of the intervening space and 'because we do not know its maximum and minimum', but you do not demonstrate, as you intended, that they do not reach this conclusion from the multitude of parts.

Further, I have learned from Mr. Leibniz that the tutor of the Dauphin of France, by name Huet,[296] a man of outstanding learning, is going to write about the truth of human religion, and to refute your *Tractatus Theologico-Politicus*. Farewell.

2 May 1676

---

again to Spinoza in October 1676 and entrusted the letter to Leibniz for transmission; but the latter never delivered it. In a letter written the day following Spinoza's death, Oldenburg complains of its non-delivery.]

[295] [This is Ep12.]

[296] [Pierre Daniel Huet (1630–1721) was appointed as assistant tutor to the Dauphin in 1670. In 1676 he became a priest and was later made bishop (1685). The book probably intended is the *Demonstratio evangelica* (1679). Another attack on the TTP, *Quaestiones aletnanae de concordia rationis et fidei*, was published in 1690.]

Letter 81

To the most noble and learned Mr. Ehrenfried Walther von Tschirnhaus, from B.d.S.

[Known only from the O.P. The original is lost.]

Most noble Sir,

My statement in my letter concerning the Infinite,[297] that it is not from the multitude of parts that an infinity of parts is inferred, is clear from this consideration: if it were inferred from the multitude of parts, we would not be able to conceive a greater multitude of parts, but their multitude would have to be greater than any given number. This is not true, because in the entire space between the two nonconcentric circles we conceive there to be twice the number of parts as in half that space, and yet the number of parts both in the half as well as the whole of this space is greater than any assignable number.[298]

Further, from Extension as conceived by Descartes, to wit, an inert mass, it is not only difficult, as you say, but quite impossible to demonstrate the existence of bodies. For matter at rest, as far as in it lies, will continue to be at rest, and will not be set in motion except by a more powerful external cause.[299] For this reason I have not hesitated on a previous occasion to affirm that Descartes' principles of natural things are of no service, not to say quite wrong.

The Hague, 5 May 1676

Letter 82

To the acute and learned philosopher B.d.S., from Ehrenfried Walther von Tschirnhaus

[Known only from the O.P. The original is lost.]

Most learned Sir,

I should like you to do me the kindness of showing how, from Extension as conceived in your philosophy, the variety of things can be demonstrated a priori. For

---

[297] [Ep12.]

[298] [This is another indication of Spinoza's reserving the term 'number' for finite magnitudes: he will speak of 'infinity' but not of an 'infinite number'. The false assumption that multiplying an infinite number by a finite number (here, two) produces an infinity with 'twice the number of parts' was common to seventeenth-century thinkers, and appears also in Newton.]

[299] [Spinoza's conception of extension or matter is, unlike that of Descartes, essentially dynamic. Mo-

you mention Descartes' view, by which he maintains that he cannot deduce this variety from Extension in any other way than by supposing that this was an effect produced in Extension by motion started by God. Therefore, in my opinion, it is not from inert matter that he deduces the existence of bodies, unless you discount the supposition of God as mover. For you have not shown how this must necessarily follow a priori from the essence of God, a point whose demonstration Descartes believed to surpass human understanding. Therefore, knowing well that you entertain a different view, I seek from you an answer to this question, unless there is some weighty reason why you have hitherto refrained from making this public. If there had been no need for this—which I do not doubt—you would have given some kind of indication of your meaning. But be quite assured that, whether you speak to me frankly or with reserve, my regard for you will remain unchanged.

However, my particular reasons for making this request are as follows. In mathematics I have always observed that from any thing considered in itself—that is, from the definition of any thing—we are able to deduce at least one property; but if we wish to deduce more properties, we have to relate the thing defined to other things. It is only then, from the combination of the definitions of these things, that new properties emerge. For example, if I consider the circumference of a circle in isolation, I can infer nothing other than that it is everywhere alike or uniform, in respect of which property it differs essentially from all other curves; nor shall I ever be able to deduce any other properties. But if I relate it to other things, such as the radii drawn from the centre, or two intersecting chords, or many other things, I shall in some way be able to deduce more properties. This seems to be at variance to some extent with Proposition 16 of the *Ethics*,[300] almost the most important proposition of the first book of your Treatise. In this proposition it is taken for granted that several properties can be deduced from the given definition of any thing, which seems to me impossible if we do not relate the thing defined to other things. In consequence, I fail to see how from an Attribute considered only by itself, for example, Extension, an infinite variety of bodies can arise. Or if you think that, while this cannot be inferred from a single Attribute considered by itself, it can so be from all taken together, I should like you to instruct me on this point, and how this should be conceived. Farewell, etc.

Paris, 23 June 1676

---

tion must be imposed on the material universe in Descartes' view by divine 'thrust'. This is because there is no concept of force within Cartesian physics and it must be imported by God. This feature figures heavily in Descartes' explanation of divine concurrence.]

[300] [E1P16: "From the necessity of the divine nature there must follow infinite things in infinite ways, that is, everything that can come within the scope of infinite intellect."]

Letter 83
To the most noble and learned Mr. Ehrenfried Walther von Tschirnhaus, from B.d.S.

[Known only from the O.P. The original is lost. The signature appears only in the Dutch edition of the O.P.]

Most noble Sir,

With regard to your question as to whether the variety of things can be demonstrated a priori solely from the conception of Extension, I think I have already made it quite clear that this is impossible. That is why Descartes is wrong in defining matter through Extension; it must necessarily be explicated through an attribute which expresses eternal and infinite essence. But perhaps, if I live long enough,[301] I shall some time discuss this with you more clearly; for as yet I have not had the opportunity to arrange in due order anything on this subject.

As to what you add, that from the definition of any thing, considered in itself, we can deduce only one property, this may hold good in the case of the most simple things, or in the case of mental constructs (*entia rationis*), in which I include figures, but not in the case of real things.[302] Simply from the fact that I define God as an Entity to whose essence existence belongs, I infer several properties of him, such as that he necessarily exists, that he is one alone, immutable, infinite, etc. I could adduce several examples of this kind, which I omit for the present.

Finally, I beg you to enquire whether Mr. Huet's Treatise (the one against the *Tractatus Theologico-Politicus*), of which you previously wrote, has yet been published, and whether you will be able to send me a copy. Also, do you yet know what are the recent discoveries about refraction?[303]

And so farewell, most noble Sir, and continue to hold in your affection,

Yours,
B.d.S.

The Hague, 15 July 1676

---

[301] [Spinoza died only seven months after writing this letter.]

[302] [Spinoza was partly indebted to Hobbes in his account of constructive definition.]

[303] [This could refer to Newton's discovery in 1670 that a prism refracts white light into colored beams which have various capacities for further refraction; this was communicated in 1672 and discussed for several more years. It could also refer to Erasmus Bartholinus' 1669 publication *Experimenta crystalli islandici disdiaclastici*, which reported on the double refraction achieved by passing light through a piece of Iceland spar.]

Letter 84
To a friend, concerning the *Tractatus Politicus*

[Printed in the O.P., but not in the correspondence. It appears as a Preface to the Tractatus Politicus. *The original is lost, and it is not known to whom it was addressed.]*

Dear friend,

Your welcome letter was delivered to me yesterday. I thank you most sincerely for the considerable trouble you take on my behalf. I should not let pass this opportunity, etc., if I were not engaged in a certain matter which I believe to be more important, and which I think will be more to your liking, namely, in composing a Political Treatise, which I began some time ago at your suggestion. Of this Treatise six chapters are already completed. The first is a kind of Introduction to the work itself; the second deals with natural right; the third with the right of Sovereign Powers; the fourth with the question of what political matters are under the control of Sovereign Powers; the fifth with what is the ultimate and highest aim a Society can contemplate; and the sixth with the way a monarchy should be organised so as not to degenerate into tyranny. At present I am engaged on the seventh chapter, in which I justify methodically all those sections of the preceding sixth chapter that concern the constitution of a well organised monarchy. Then I shall pass on to Aristocracy and Democracy, and finally to Laws and other particular questions concerning Politics.[304]

And so, farewell, etc.

[The Hague, 1676]

---

[304] [The TP ends with an incomplete Chapter 11, which was to have begun the extended discussion of democracy.]

INDEX

This index is selective. For terms with very frequent occurrence, only principal passages have been referenced. Readers who seek more complete indexical references (passages and terms) should consult the Hackett editions of the individual works. Note also that a complete lexicon of Spinoza's writings is also available: Emilia Giancotti, *Lexicon Spinozanum* (The Hague: Martinus Nijhoff, 1970).

Abraham: 397, 411, 574, 575, 946
abstraction: 241, 763
Acontius, Jacobus: 888
action: 245, 276, 281, 333, 351, 428, 832–3
active: 278, 282, 333, 366–7, 380
activity: 100, 278–9, 284–6, 380, 763
Adam: 15, 55, 190, 430, 432, 806–7, 808–10, 820, 824, 829
adequate: *see* ideas
affect(s): *see* emotion
affection: 182–3, 186, 217–8, 233–4, 259–62, 278–9, 311, 351, 371; *see also* perception
affirmation: 272, 274–6
Alexander the Great: 388, 455, 538
allies: 532, 694
Alpakhar, Jehuda (Alfakhar): 520–3, 880
ambiguity: 463–5
ambition: 293, 295, 298, 308, 318, 366, 369, 370
Ambrose: 558
Amsterdam: 31, 723, 765, 767, 787, 792–3, 797, 835, 836, 838, 839, 853, 865, 935
angels: 203
anger: 300, 317, 369, 345, 686
angles: 48, 176, 177, 253, 272–3, 276
anthropocentrism: 242
Apostles, the: 398, 498–503, 504, 508, 922
appetite: 210, 284, 311, 323, 366, 533, 909–10

Aquinas: 40, 58, 791
aristocracy: 677, 680, 687, 702, 723–52
Aristotle: 1, 55, 64, 83, 196–7, 210, 443, 510, 728, 905
Ark of the Covenant: 505–6
army: *see* military
astronomers, astronomy: 847
atheism: 405, 844, 877, 878–9, 928
attribute: xiii, 45, 50, 56–7, 61, 102, 104, 137, 182–3, 217–9, 221–2, 245, 330–1, 760, 762, 766–7, 776, 780, 782, 916–7, 918–9, 920
authority, political: 534–5, 558–65, 571; religious: 471, 558–65
axiom(s): 220, 266, 441, 457, 524; *see also* method

Bacon, Francis: 760, 761, 762–3, 771, 795, 861
Balling, Pieter: 2, 108, 676, 755, 780, 787, 802
belief: 62, 63, 66, 67, 441, 514
Bible: 384, 391, 396, 398, 435, 456, 458–9, 466, 467, 484–509, 524, 525, 584–675, 811–23, 826–7, 844, 846, 869–78, 950; *see also* Scripture
blessedness: xi, 214, 276, 358, 363, 378, 382, 428, 442, 443, 467, 470, 523, 524–5, 580, 823, 825
blood: 848–9, 852–3

961

Blyenbergh (Blijenbergh), Willem van: 756, 804, 807, 811, 822, 828, 831, 832, 835–6, 839

body: 7, 21, 60, 87–90, 94, 104, 106, 107, 128, 129, 139, 149, 150, 151, 152, 156, 172, 173, 212, 217, 244, 252–6, 260–3, 278–9, 729, 764, 768–76, 801, 911, 918–9, 955, 956, 957

bondage (slavery): 276, 320, 334–5; *see also* freedom

Borelli (Borellus), Giovanni: 778–9, 782

Bouwmeester, Johan: 108, 584, 755, 840, 860, 915

Boxel, Hugo: 893, 894, 895, 897, 900, 903

Boyle, Robert: 31, 755, 761, 767, 768–76, 777, 784–6, 793–7, 798–9, 801–2, 837, 838, 841–2, 843, 846, 848, 851, 852, 917, 952, 953

Burgh, Albert (Augustus): 756, 921, 947

Buxtorf, J.: 584, 590

Cabbalists: 486

Caesarius (Casearius), Johannes: 108–9, 778, 781, 792, 900, 903

Calvinists: 923

Cardanus, Girolamo: 896

Cartesian(ism): *see* Descartes, René

Catholicism: 425, 708, 756, 888, 893, 921–9, 930–5, 947–51

causality: 48, 49, 50–1, 54, 55, 81–2, 84, 100, 103, 131–3, 141, 158, 159, 174, 220–1, 246–8, 278, 368, 426, 428, 444, 446–7, 762–3, 764, 908–10; *see also* God

certainty: 10–11, 116, 124, 125, 128, 129, 187, 268–9; *see also* doubt

cheerfulness: 285, 343

chimera: 15, 178, 183, 697

chosen people: *see* Israel

Christ: 398, 399, 415, 431–2, 436, 460–1, 501, 509, 555, 561, 881, 922–9, 940, 943, 944, 946–7, 953, 954

Christian(ity): 390, 440, 462, 562, 564, 811, 869, 874–5, 889, 914, 921–9, 930–5

Cicero, M.: 748, 903

citizens and citizenship: 277, 341, 532, 561, 568, 690–1, 699, 702, 703, 705, 708, 713, 715, 724, 752

civil law: *see* law
civil right: *see* right
Clavius, Christopher: 779
clear and distinct: 17, 22, 37, 62, 121, 124, 125, 126–7, 139, 141–2, 143, 144, 220, 262, 264, 269, 366, 369, 370–1, 766, 818, 825, 861, 905
cognition: 249–50
Colbert, Jean Baptiste: 938
command(s): 430, 432, 450, 557, 558, 560, 581, 692
common notions: 220, 266–7, 766
commonwealth: 277, 439, 461, 531, 558, 560, 566–72, 689, 690–3, 694–5, 697–8, 699, 704, 751; *see also* the state
comprehension: 574–5
conatus: 188, 283–6, 289–90, 297, 309, 332–4, 375; *see also* human nature
conceive (conception): 15, 26, 138, 218, 244, 249–50, 683
confusion: 48, 113, 261–4, 319, 372, 457
conjecture: 901–2, 904–5
contingency: 54, 184, 236, 245, 263, 269, 322
contract: 552, 694–5, 698, 710
Covenant, the: 418, 540; *see also* contract
creation: 42, 43, 59, 105, 136, 138, 141, 188–9, 203–6, 240–1, 767, 776
creature: 26, 180–1, 183, 204, 208
Crescas, Hasdai: 791

death: 342, 355, 379–81
Decalogue: 396, 430
deception: 22, 63, 124, 125, 141, 142, 274–5, 323–4, 357, 569, 580, 686, 695; *see also* doubt
deduction: 7, 26, 441, 469, 957
definition: 25, 26, 56, 67–8, 220–1, 236, 426, 766, 778–9, 781–2, 783, 854–5, 913, 957, 958
Deists: 869, 878
democracy: 530–1, 677, 687, 711, 723, 727, 728, 752
Democritus: 844, 905
Descartes, René and Cartesianism: xii, 1, 31, 108–9, 110–7, 117–20, 121–7, 128, 132, 133, 134, 135, 137, 139, 147, 153, 156, 174, 182, 195, 210, 277, 363–5, 760, 761, 762–3, 769, 771, 775, 785,

792, 793, 795, 797, 800, 802, 805, 818, 821, 824–7, 828, 831, 835–6, 838, 844, 845, 846, 847, 850, 852, 863, 865–6, 873, 878–9, 888, 891, 892, 906, 907, 908–10, 911, 913, 933, 935, 938, 956, 957, 958
desire (*cupiditas*): 46–7, 63, 65–6, 68–70, 71–2, 80–1, 83–4, 284–6, 311, 329–32, 351–2, 358, 366, 417, 527, 684; see also emotion
determinism: see necessity
devil: 85–6, 98–9, 684, 896
doubt: 13, 21–2, 121–4, 130, 187–8, 257, 269, 275, 764, 904–5
dream: 122, 275, 282, 396, 398, 803
dualism: 247, 251, 255, 258–9, 271–82; see also attribute
duration: 185–6, 190–1, 204, 205, 206, 244, 262–3, 270, 320, 374, 380, 788–90

East India Company: 440
Egypt: 413, 439, 539, 576
emotion(s): 63, 64–6, 68–70, 70–1, 71–2, 72–3, 73–5, 75–6, 76–7, 78–9, 107, 277–8, 284–9, 307–9, 324–31, 339–40, 346, 366, 389, 681, 686, 693, 702, 727, 751; see also affect; affection; desire
enemy: 533, 561, 686, 694, 715
England: 556–7, 841, 842, 850, 853
envy: 71, 291, 296, 298–9, 307, 314, 359, 372, 727
Epicureans: 786
Epicurus: 905
error: 142–5, 257, 264, 269, 271–3, 274–6, 762–3, 812–9, 835, 911–2
essence: 8, 9, 15–6, 25, 26, 27, 48, 59, 91, 100, 181, 183, 221, 244, 283, 683, 812, 828, 830; see also conatus
esteem: 72, 298; as honor (*gloria*): 294, 300, 316, 350
eternal, eternity: 29, 146, 185–6, 189–91, 205, 217, 270–1, 374, 376–7, 380–1, 783, 788–90
Ethics: 2, 31, 213–382, 395, 403, 405, 414, 416, 417, 418, 426, 427, 428, 430, 431, 432, 527, 531, 676, 680, 689, 712, 752
Euclid: 117, 368, 466, 779, 905
evil: 3, 55–6, 59–60, 67, 70, 78, 92–3, 188–9, 198–9, 242, 298, 322, 326, 334–6, 351, 354, 358–9, 372, 432, 685, 692, 806–7, 808–10, 812–8, 832–3
Exodus: 396
experience: 274, 280, 783, 803, 906–7
experiment: 755, 768–76, 784–6, 793–7, 801–2, 842, 847, 867–8
extension: xiii, 147, 149, 150, 151, 181, 245, 247, 251, 274, 279, 760, 766, 956–7
Ezra: 478–80, 579

Fabritius, J. Louis: 756, 886, 887
faith: 514, 515, 516–7, 518, 519, 524–5, 562, 888–9
falsity: 264, 268, 273, 323; see also ideas (true and false)
fear: 73, 74, 288–9, 313, 345–6, 352–3, 355, 369, 388, 438, 686, 692, 693, 694, 695, 699, 700, 750, 879
fluidity: 149, 157–8, 173, 761, 773–5
force: 150, 167, 170, 171, 172–3, 324–5, 352, 358
freedom: 52, 55, 84, 85, 86, 100– 2, 143, 181, 185, 207, 210, 217, 236, 271, 281, 355, 357–8, 363, 378, 390, 393, 438, 526, 531, 566–72, 580–1, 684–5, 698, 715, 717, 756, 763, 824–5, 831, 835, 844, 879, 887, 904, 907, 908–10, 945, 951, 952–3, 953–4
friendship: 296, 337–8, 339–40, 356, 359–60, 760, 761, 807–8

Galileo, G.: 838
Gassendi, P.: 785
generosity: 360
gentiles: 445, 452
geometry: 230, 248, 253, 267–8, 278
ghosts: 893, 894–5, 895–7, 897–900, 900–3, 905
God: 14, 22, 37–40, 40–1, 47, 48–50, 50–3, 53–8, 61, 69–70, 79, 80, 85, 86, 89, 94, 97–8, 99, 101, 102, 124, 126–7, 128, 133, 147, 151, 152, 158, 159, 175, 181–2, 183, 185, 186–9, 189–208, 217, 222–9, 230, 232–5, 238, 245, 249–50, 270–2, 371–82, 395, 397, 400–1, 411, 419, 420, 427, 428, 429, 444–8, 450, 460, 504, 507, 511–3, 514, 516, 517–8, 521, 534, 558, 573, 581, 684, 760, 762,

God (*continued*)
  764, 767, 776, 780, 806–7, 808–10, 811–22, 822–7, 829–31, 832–7, 847, 854–5, 856–7, 857–9, 865–6, 869–78, 879–80, 892, 901, 903–5, 913, 916–7, 918–9, 935, 940, 942; *see also* knowledge; intellectual love of God
good: 3–4, 6, 64, 67, 69, 78, 92–3, 242, 298, 320–2, 326, 335–6, 338–9, 343, 351, 358–9, 362, 428; *see also* evil
Graevius, John: 891

happiness: 5, 86–90, 99–100, 276, 322, 330–2, 415–6, 428, 434
harmony: 242, 330–1, 342–3, 359–62, 699
hatred: 46, 65, 70–1, 85, 286–303, 344–5, 391, 686
Hebrew (language): 394, 403, 433, 434, 436, 458, 462, 463, 464, 465, 466, 573, 578, 579, 580, 584–675, 946–7
Hebrew(s): *see* Israel; Jews
Heidelberg: 886, 887
Helvetius, Johannes: 864–5
Hevelius (Hervelius, Hevel, Höwelcke), Johann: 842–3, 847
history: 457, 459, 462, 465, 467, 471, 477–8, 485, 496
Hobbes, Thomas: 526, 580, 677, 683, 686, 689, 691, 692, 696, 699, 701, 710, 711, 718, 720, 724, 735, 741, 777, 891, 913, 958
Holland: 557, 703, 704, 705, 706, 707, 708, 711, 714, 716, 741, 742, 745
honesty: 470, 720
Hooke, Robert: 837
Hudde, John: 756, 838, 854, 855, 857, 883, 885
Huet, Pierre Daniel: 955, 958
human nature: 5–6, 60, 62, 67, 239, 279, 295, 438, 536, 569, 573–4, 681, 682, 684, 692, 695, 697, 701, 710, 752; vis-à-vis emotions: 287–309, 324–5, 331, 335–8, 340, 358–9, 362
Huygens, Christiaan: 838, 843, 845, 846, 847, 850, 852, 937–8, 941

Ibn Ezra, Abraham: 412, 493, 494, 573, 576, 604

ideas: 22, 23, 29, 38, 59, 62, 67, 79–80, 84, 91, 94, 105, 106, 121–2, 127, 178–9, 218, 234, 244, 257, 263–71, 273, 309, 323, 911, 912–3, 918–9, 941; true and false: 11, 12, 17–21, 24, 28, 29, 38, 74, 141–2, 187
ignorance: 239, 363, 382, 685
imagination: 21, 24–5, 38–9, 226, 256–7, 269–70, 273, 373, 378, 399, 403–5, 407, 412, 451, 510, 524, 787, 789, 803–4, 848, 861, 899
imperfect(ion): 45, 237, 320–1, 859; *see also* perfection
impiety: 506, 514, 517, 201
individuals: 244, 250, 267, 308–9
infinity: 29, 38, 40, 44, 103, 131, 192, 762, 766, 787–91, 955, 956
intellect: 6, 10, 22, 23, 24, 25, 27, 28–9, 143, 184, 202, 234–5, 246, 273–4, 510, 813–8, 850, 861
intellectual love of God: 69–70, 86, 94, 214, 334, 358, 371–3, 377–9, 428, 429, 823
intuitive science (*scientia intuitiva*): *see* knowledge; intellectual love of God
Israel: 392, 393, 400, 413, 415–26, 430–1, 437, 439, 445, 450, 452, 458, 463, 470, 471, 477, 504, 505, 519, 539–2, 552–5, 559, 560, 561, 562, 563, 564–5, 577, 583, 853

Jelles, Jarig: 2, 108, 384, 755–6, 863, 864, 867, 882, 888, 889, 890, 891
Jews: 390, 395–6, 422–6, 440, 443, 514, 873–4
Job: 492
John (Apostle): 516
Josephus: 456, 489, 535, 553
Joshua: 398, 409, 422, 452, 476, 581–2
joy: 5, 71–2; as pleasure: 284–96, 300–2, 311, 326, 345–6
Judah: 481
judges: 706–7, 737–9, 745
judgment: 273–6, 686, 691, 692; *see also* error; falsity
justice: 340–1, 344, 360, 532, 558–9, 568, 689, 948

kings: 245–6; *see also* monarchy
Kings: 477

Kircher, Athanasius: 842, 845, 846
knowledge: 10–11, 27, 28, 38, 60, 62–3, 66, 67, 78, 94, 98, 128, 129, 131, 267–8, 271, 326, 334, 395, 428, 513, 514, 685; of God: 374–7
Koerbagh, Adriann: 2, 31, 383, 384, 676, 867

Lana, Franciscus: 883, 885
language: 458, 462, 463–5, 469, 488, 580
Lavater, Ludwig: 896, 897, 900
law(s): 96–7, 209, 341, 357, 361, 426–34, 435–44, 446, 526, 529–34, 545, 557–61, 580, 581, 680, 681, 683, 688, 690–2, 696, 697–8, 699, 709, 718, 725, 729–30, 743, 751, 809–10, 879–80
Leibniz, Gottfried: 883, 884, 885, 939, 941, 955
Leviathan: see Hobbes, Thomas
Levites: 545, 549, 551
liberty: *see* freedom
life: 196–7, 345, 355; rules for: 369
Locke, John: 716, 719
love: 5, 46–7, 63, 64–5, 68–70, 78, 79, 85, 96, 286–303, 309–10, 312, 343–5, 880; *see also* intellectual love of God
Lucretius: 905

Machiavelli, Niccolò: 542, 681, 694, 699, 700, 702, 703, 707, 708, 715, 716, 726, 727, 728, 747, 748, 749, 750, 751
madness: 18, 344, 360
Maimonides, Moses: 394, 397, 399, 400, 407, 408, 421, 443, 468–70, 493, 520, 523, 578, 791, 880–1
masses: 239, 322, 381
matter: 149, 151, 153, 176, 177
Matthew (Apostle): 466
meaning: 468
mechanics (mechanical): 755
Melanchton (Melanthon), Philipp: 896
memory: 16–23, 178, 257–8, 281–2, 373, 378
Mersenne, Marin: 869
metaphor: 520–1, 523
method, philosophical or axiomatic-deductive: 6, 9–13, 14, 22, 25, 28, 118–9; for interpreting Scripture: 457, 463, 467, 468, 861

Meyer (Meijer), Lodewijk: 2, 108, 109, 116, 120, 128, 383, 573, 584, 755, 756, 787, 791, 793, 797, 799, 821, 824, 827, 835–6, 871, 881
military: 702–3, 707, 712, 715, 717, 720, 726–7, 744
mind: 11, 17, 20, 27, 28, 29, 128, 139, 208–9, 211, 212, 244, 250–2, 255–6, 258–61, 271–2, 279, 284–6, 374, 684, 686, 687, 729, 762–3, 849–50
miracles: 98, 203, 384, 444–56, 457, 462, 872, 932, 940, 942–3, 944, 945–6, 951, 953, 954
modes: 44–5, 60, 61, 62, 67, 104, 105, 130, 180, 204, 217, 220, 224, 227, 231, 233–5, 244–8, 788, 917, 919, 921
monarchy: 555–6, 677, 680, 687, 700–8, 709–22, 726, 727, 748
monism: *see* substance
Moses: 396, 397, 398, 399, 411, 413, 416, 422, 431, 436, 439, 449, 451, 459, 468, 472–6, 499–500, 504, 506, 510, 511–2, 537, 539–44, 550, 552, 562, 564–5, 566, 581–2, 946
motion: 44, 50, 59, 87, 88, 89, 90, 91, 106, 147–9, 153–9, 173, 242, 252–5, 279–80, 281, 342, 768–76, 848–9, 911

Nature, naturalism: 11–2, 20, 26, 27, 43–5, 47, 53, 58–9, 85, 87, 92, 94, 103, 104, 105, 106, 209, 234–5, 247, 320–5, 358–9, 379, 417, 426, 428, 444–8, 450, 452, 454, 457, 460, 506, 526–8, 683, 684, 685, 688, 776, 942
necessity: 14, 21, 51–3, 133, 138, 183, 206, 217, 220–1, 231–4, 269–70, 430, 432, 445–6, 684, 839, 856–7, 898, 903–4, 943–4, 945
Nero: 697, 833
nobility: *see* aristocracy; monarchy

obedience: 392, 510, 511, 513, 515, 516–8, 519, 523, 534, 537, 548, 581, 689, 691, 693, 699
obscurity: 463
Oldenburg, Henry: 31, 62, 63, 64–6, 67, 70, 75, 76, 93, 755, 760, 761, 763, 765, 767, 768, 776, 784, 792, 797, 799, 801, 802, 837, 838, 841, 843, 845, 846, 847,

Oldenburg, Henry (*continued*)
848, 851, 853, 914, 915, 917, 935, 940, 942, 943, 945, 951, 952, 953, 954–5
optics: 863–4, 866, 883–4, 884–5, 958
order: 11, 12, 27, 186, 235–6, 239, 247, 365, 688, 709
Ostens, Jacob: 869, 878
Ovid: 466, 748, 749

pain: *see* sadness
particles: 166, 175, 786
passions: 63, 64–6, 68–78, 85, 86, 90, 284–6, 278, 307, 319, 351, 364, 366, 681, 682, 709; *see also* emotion
patriotism: 560
Paul (Apostle): 423, 432, 434, 500, 502, 503, 511, 527
peace: 390, 434, 554, 691, 693, 695, 696, 699, 701, 711, 712, 717, 734
Pentateuch: 416, 472–6, 499–500
perception, sense: 7–9, 14, 29, 122, 244, 250, 255–7, 259, 441
perfect(ion): 29, 39–40, 43, 46, 51–3, 67, 85, 99, 103, 131, 138, 140, 189, 192, 223–6, 244, 275, 284–5, 311–2, 320–2, 380–1, 428, 764, 812, 823, 830
Pharisees: 415, 422, 436, 462, 470, 472, 486–8, 490, 494, 495, 497, 507, 508, 520, 535, 555, 579, 949
physics: 339, 381, 911
piety: 390, 514, 517, 518, 520, 521, 533, 555, 560, 561, 563, 572, 688
Plato: 55, 179, 510, 905
pleasure: *see* joy
Pliny: 896, 897
Plutarch: 902
Popes, the: 470
potency: 206
power: 131, 151, 193, 201–3, 245, 278–87, 320, 323–4, 363, 366–7, 368, 372–3, 403, 439, 444, 527, 530, 536, 544, 567, 683, 685–6, 687, 692, 694, 700, 701, 713, 718, 742
preservation: 137, 138, 140, 141, 151, 207, 283–4, 311, 324–6, 332–3, 342, 683, 684, 694, 695
pride: 85, 315–6, 346, 348–50, 366
privation: 144–5, 263, 323, 809, 824

prophecy (prophets): 248, 384, 392, 394–6, 403–4, 404–15, 421, 431, 454, 462, 466, 469, 491, 498–502, 506–7, 508, 510, 513, 514, 524, 525, 553–4, 559, 573, 809, 819, 827, 870–2
providence: 53, 55
punishment: 96, 201, 440, 810

Rapp, Christophorus: 882
reason: 46–7, 59, 66, 78, 92–3, 180, 196, 267, 269–70, 330–1, 333–4, 337–9, 351–5, 357, 363, 389, 394, 443–4, 452, 457, 467, 468, 520–4, 528, 530, 581, 684, 685, 686, 688, 691, 692, 695, 697, 719, 751
religion: 315, 339, 381, 390, 456, 506, 510, 521, 535, 555, 558, 559, 562–4, 689, 693, 708, 740, 879, 887, 888–9, 914, 915, 942
repentance: 75
revelation: 392, 394–7, 405–14, 462, 498, 502, 524, 534, 573, 589
Rieuwertsz, Jan: 908, 917
right(s): 340–1, 359, 393, 526, 532, 536–9, 552, 559, 562, 566, 583, 681, 682, 683, 685–6, 687, 690–2, 697
Royal Society: 777, 786, 798, 850, 852, 952–3
rule: 439–40
rulers: 536–9, 544; *see also* sovereignty and the sovereign
rest: 44, 87, 89, 91, 106, 159, 167, 169; *see also* motion

sadness: 78–9, 285–9, 297–8, 300–2, 311, 326, 345–6
salvation: 378, 382, 467, 580
Schuller, Georg: 755, 756, 908, 916, 917, 918, 937, 929, 940, 941
Scripture: 391–2, 395, 401–7, 409, 416, 418, 419, 434, 438, 441–3, 445, 449, 455, 456–71, 485–8, 495, 497, 504–9, 510–3, 514, 519, 520–6, 578, 755, 809–10, 822–3, 826–7, 844, 846, 869–78, 922–9, 950; *see also* Bible; method (for interpreting Scripture)
security: 682, 691, 699, 929
self-interest: 239, 330–2, 333, 381
Seneca: 438

Serrarius, Peter: 797, 802, 837, 838, 846
Sextus Empiricus: 904
Shlomo ben Yitzchak, Rabbi (Rashi): 496–7, 604
sin: 682, 688, 689, 812–8; *see also* evil
slavery: 85, 531, 700
social contract: 438; *see also* contract
Socrates: 902–5
Solomon: 433, 437, 449
soul: 16, 60, 88–90, 90–2, 95, 104–7, 128, 208, 821
sovereignty and the sovereign: 530–2, 534–5, 536–9, 544–52, 554, 557–65, 566–7, 568, 572, 573, 581, 687, 690–3, 694, 696, 698, 702, 710, 725, 729
space: 147, 149, 150, 151, 176; *see also* extension
state, the: 340, 342–3, 439, 471, 526, 529–35, 536, 552–5, 558, 567, 572, 580, 682, 684, 688, 689, 690, 691, 693, 696, 699, 701, 708, 710, 747, 750, 751
state of nature, the: 340–1, 533, 558, 580, 676, 687, 692, 694, 696, 698, 699, 716, 892
Steno, Nicholas: 756, 929, 947
Stoicism: xi, 31, 363
substance: 40–5, 46, 60, 102, 103, 127, 128, 131, 137, 139, 146–7, 150, 180, 189, 196, 217–24, 247, 762, 764–5, 766, 782–3, 788–9
Suetonius: 895, 896, 897, 900, 903
superstition: 353, 362, 388–9, 457, 487, 942, 949–50

Tacitus: 538, 547, 549, 566, 581, 680, 691, 697, 699, 713, 714, 717, 719, 720, 722
Tacquet, Andreas: 779
Talmud: 413, 422
Terence: 719, 722, 795
Thales: 882
theologians: 240, 456, 457, 510, 513, 684, 792, 844
theology: 57, 394, 472, 519, 520, 523–5, 842
thought: 30, 45, 46, 58, 67, 88, 102, 104, 105, 127, 204, 217, 230–1, 234–5,
244–5, 248, 259, 760, 761, 764, 766, 780, 782, 804, 938–9; *see also* attribute
Thyraeus, Petrus: 896
time: 185–6, 204; *see also* duration
Torricelli, E.: 799
treason: 533
truth: *see* ideas (true and false)
Tschirnhaus, Ehrenfried Walther von: 756, 906, 911, 912, 916, 917, 920, 921, 937–8, 939, 940, 941, 955, 956, 958
Turks: 390, 701, 717
tyranny (tyrants): 555, 556–7

universal religion: 506, 517–8
universe: 218
utility: 529

vacuum: 147, 152, 785, 794, 798–9, 801
Valerius Maximus: 896
Van der Meer, John: 862
Van Mansvelt, Regner: 892
Velthuysen, Lambert van: 869, 936, 937
Verulam: *see* Bacon, Francis
vice: 681, 749, 750
virtue: 99, 276, 323, 331–3, 345–51, 355–8, 382, 403, 434, 699, 750, 830, 834, 870
Voetius, Gybertus: 878–9
Vossius, Isaac: 864–5
Vries, Simon de: 2, 676, 755, 778, 780, 781, 783, 799, 800, 841, 891

war: 694, 695, 696, 699, 700, 708, 711, 712
weight: 151
wickedness: 426, 124–5, 143, 180, 181, 209–11, 212, 910
Wierus, Johannes: 895–6
will: 63, 80–3, 83–5, 235, 272–6, 284, 363–5, 684, 763, 806
Witt, Jan de: 676, 705, 739
words: 23, 24, 97, 98, 179, 183, 403, 487, 488, 505, 506, 580

Zeno: 153–6
Zevi, Sabbatai: 853